D0024638

BUSINESS POLICY

TEXT AND CASES

BUSINESS POLICY

TEXT AND CASES

JOSEPH L. BOWER
Donald Kirk David Professor of
Business Administration

CHRISTOPHER A. BARTLETT
Professor of Business Administration

C. ROLAND CHRISTENSEN
Robert Walmsley University Professor

ANDRALL E. PEARSON
Class of 1958 Professor of
Business Administration

KENNETH R. ANDREWS
Donald Kirk David Professor of
Business Administration Emeritus

All of the Graduate School of
Business Administration
Harvard University

SEVENTH EDITION

Homewood, IL 60430
Boston, MA 02116

Case material of the Harvard Graduate School of Business Administration is made possible by the cooperation of business firms, who may wish to remain anonymous by having names, quantities, and other identifying details disguised while basic relationships are maintained. Cases are prepared as the basis for class discussion rather than to illustrate either effective or ineffective handling of administrative situations.

Associate publisher: Martin F. Hanifin
Project editor: Paula M. Buschman
Production manager: Carma W. Fazio
Compositor: Graphic World Inc.
Typeface: 10/12 Melior
Printer: R. R. Donnelley & Sons Company

Library of Congress Cataloging-in-Publication Data

Business policy : text and cases / Joseph L. Bower . . . [et al.].—
7th ed.
p. cm.
Includes index.
ISBN 0-256-08602-8
1. Corporations—United States—Case studies. 2. Industrial management—United States—Case studies. I. Bower, Joseph L.
HD2785.B78 1991
658.4′012—dc20 90-42473
CIP

Printed in the United States of America

1 2 3 4 5 6 7 8 9 0 DOC 7 6 5 4 3 2 1 0

To
Edmund P. Learned
For reasons he knows well

PREFACE

The seventh edition of *Business Policy: Text and Cases* provides concepts, text, and cases for a course in Business Policy. Building on previous editions, the authors have again incorporated changes in both text and case material that we hope will increase the usefulness of this edition.

In the development of this edition we have retained those cases which our users have found most helpful in accomplishing the objectives of their course. Fourteen of the holdover cases are listed as all-time best sellers by the Harvard Business School Publishing Division. They provide challenging and fun discussion vehicles for education in the policy process as well as apt illustration that there is a timeless quality to fundamental administrative tasks of general management.

In the seventh edition, as in preceding efforts, we have emphasized four basic educational themes. First, the material focuses on the tasks of general management in leading the overall enterprise, in contrast to the tasks of a specialist manager whose responsibilities are limited to a subdepartment of the total organization. Second, our text and cases highlight strategic management as a key function and responsibility of the line general manager, not as a staff planning activity. Third, critical to the success of any firm is the general manager's ability to manage the process by which an organization both formulates and implements its strategy. These case histories encourage apprentice managers to practice vicariously the organizational process of goal definition and accomplishment. Finally, a study of this material emphasizes the importance of general management practice as a professional activity. The general manager is responsible to multiple constituencies with conflicting needs and goals. He or she must manage that organization so as to achieve both economic and social-ethical goals.

The text and cases in this edition expand the attention given to the interdependence of strategy formulation and implementation. We have always viewed achieving commitment to purpose as essential to superior accomplishment, but now participation in the process of setting and amending goals is more explicitly emphasized as essential to commitment. The kind of corporation implied by our approach is now more clearly than ever the responsive, innovative, informal, and flexible corporation that builds on the strengths and traditions of its past while adapting to, and bringing about, changes in the marketplace. In an increasingly egalitarian world, the general manager who leads a traditional pyramidal organization faces a major question as to his or her authority and administrative practices. We believe that leadership of the kind of corporation most likely to thrive in the early 21st century makes itself influential in stimulating continuous consideration of strategic alternatives by everyone whose cooperation is essential to the success of the chosen purpose.

The evolution of this book has been encouraged by many individuals—both business managers and academic instructors and students—who have taken the time and effort to send us suggestions for improvements. We are in their debt. Their continuing interest has helped us to develop a Policy course which can be taught effectively at the undergraduate, graduate, and executive seminar levels.

All students of Business Policy participate in a long-term, evolving intellectual adventure. The basic administrative processes and problems with which Business Policy is concerned have been part of organizational life for centuries, but the history of Business Policy as an academic field dates back less than seven decades.

This edition builds on substantial contributions made by former and present Policy colleagues; it carries their efforts further along the way to better understanding and greater applicability. In particular, this edition includes more material with an international outlook, especially the intensity and turbulence of the contemporary global economic battle, and new cases dealing with the problems of transforming U.S. companies so that they are competitive.

The specific core ideas—the concept of corporate strategy and the organization plan for this book—were developed at the Harvard Business School in the early 1960s under the leadership of three now emeriti professors—Kenneth R. Andrews, C. Roland Christensen, and Edmund P. Learned. While course concepts and materials continue to undergo steady modification, course objectives have been maintained. In the hands of many colleagues developing cases, doing research in general management, and teaching in both years of the MBA Program and executive programs, the emphasis on elements of corporate strategy has changed. The material in the first half of this book dealing with the formulation of corporate purpose is now often taught as a separate course in competitive strategy with truncated focus on the economic aspects of a company competing in its industrial environment. That is the case at Harvard Business School.

Book One of this text addresses corporate strategy as a combination of market opportunity, company resources, and individual and social values that gives direction to the company in its industry and society. Book Two with its emphasis on implementation and the *process* by which ideas are translated into action through organization and administrative activity illustrates the extent to which the development of economic strategy is virtually an outcome of a continuing effort by general management to maintain and enhance the prosperity of the enterprise.

The concept of corporate strategy articulated in this textbook has been derived from the careful study in hundreds of company situations of the uniformities that constitute the way decisions about corporate strategy are made and carried out. Distinguishing more from less successful experience has led to a theory about how the formulation and execution of corporate purpose can be more effective against all the economic, organizational, and social tests that are properly applied to it. The idea of corporate strategy is a simple practitioner's theory. It is a kind of Everyman's conceptual scheme made for use in real life in unstructured, complex, and unique situations. Brought to its full power in intelligent use, it is capable of including the most extensive combination of interrelated variables involved in the most important of all business decisions.

The first function of the general manager, as we say again later, is leadership of the continuous process of determining the nature of the enterprise and setting, revising, and attempting to achieve its goals. Corporate strategy, as a concept, defines the manager's central function, whether he or she is a staff specialist contributing in depth and detail to the identification of alternatives or the senior executive who must finally sign off on the decision and submit it to the board of directors.

Our modest characterization of this conceptual scheme as finding its power only in its application to the unique situation (that is, history, organization, present strengths, and future opportunity) of a particular company should not mislead you. It has been derived, not from theoretical modeling or laboratory inquiries and simulations of management science, but from experience. The authors, besides being familiar with the literature of strategic management and organizational behavior, have been teaching and doing research in Business Policy for a combined total of 175 years. They have written or supervised the preparation of more than 400 case studies of domestic, foreign, and multinational companies. They each have prepared or studied for class from 200 to 400 cases written by others. They have served as consultants to about 200 companies on strategy problems. They either now serve or have served on 390 different corporate boards of directors. Apart from case collections, they have authored 15 books, mostly research based.

We conclude from this varied experience that no more comprehensive or useful theory of general management is currently possible. The combination of objective and subjective elements, of economic and personal purposes, and of complex ethical and social responsibilities makes automatic outcomes impossible. Close competitive analysis may point to a generic economic or business strategy. A unique corporate strategy, however, will reflect judgment, aspiration, desire, and determination in ways which no theoretical model can prescribe. All-purpose management formulas are transparent fantasies. We cannot tell you from our conceptual scheme what the strategy should be in any one company we do not know; this book will help you find out, in a company you do know, how to approach your own conclusion.

How is this conceptual scheme translated into effective management practice? What is the relationship of strategy to the education of general managers? We would summarize our answers to these problems as follows:

> The uniqueness of a good general manager lies in one's ability to lead effectively organizations whose complexities he or she can never fully understand, where a capacity to control directly the human and physical forces comprising that organization is severely limited, and where he or she must make or review and assume ultimate responsibility for present decisions which commit concretely major resources for a fluid and unknown future.
>
> These circumstances—lack of knowledge, lack of an ability to control directly, and a mixture of past, present, and future time dimensions in every decision—make the concept of strategy so important for the generalist, senior manager. For strategy gives a manager reasonably clear indications of what one should try to know and understand in order to direct an organization's efforts. It counsels on what to decide, what to review, and what to ignore. It gives guidelines as to which critical, central activities and processes one should attempt to influence or, on rare occasions, attempt to control. It encourages a general manager to view every event and question from multiple time dimensions.
>
> Chester Barnard said that the highest managerial traits are essentially intuitive, "being so complex and so rapid, often approaching the instantaneous, that they could not be analyzed by the person within whose brain they take place." If Barnard is correct, and we think that he is, how do those of us interested in management education strive to contribute to the development of future general managers? We do this first by disciplined classroom drill with the concept of strategy. Drill in the formal and analytic sense—what is the current strategy of the firm? What are its strengths and weaknesses? Where, in the firm's perceived industry, are profit and service opportunities? And how can those corporate capacities and industry opportunities be effectively related? This framework of questions helps to give order to the familiar chaos of complex organizations. It provides the manager with a map relating past, present, and future, industry and company, and specific decisions to wider corporate strategy.
>
> Moreover, this analytic classroom process focuses attention on a key administrative skill—the process of selecting and ordering data so that management asks the critical questions appropriate to a particular situation. Here the choice of abstraction level is key, for the question has to be stated in a way that avoids the specific that has no meaning and the general that has no content.

> We seek also, via the classroom case discussion process, to educate in the nonlogical—that mixture of feeling and sentiment, comment and commitment, certainty and uncertainty—which goes into every decision and judgment. Such directed group discussions force attention to the human dimensions through which the analytic framework is filtered in real life. It serves further to emphasize the ongoing or process nature of the general manager's world.
>
> It is a combination of these two forces—the analytic framework of strategic planning and the process framework emphasizing human interaction, the complexities of persons, and the difficulty of communication and persuasion—that make up our Business Policy educational fare. It is the discipline of practicing these two processes via a case discussion countless times that helps us to contribute to education for the future generalist.

The Business Policy subject area continues to evolve and develop. The need for professionally trained generalists—the men and women who make our organized society's critical decisions—is great. We continue to believe that this challenge will be met, at least in part, by all of us who work in the Policy area, both in academic and practical pursuits, throughout this country and the world. And we hope this book will be of some help in meeting that challenge.

Joseph L. Bower

ACKNOWLEDGMENTS

The history of the Business Policy course at the Harvard Business School began in 1911, when a small group of instructors first developed a course outline and materials for a pioneering venture in education for general management. Those of us who currently teach and do research in the Business Policy area are in debt to those pioneers who provided the academic platform on which current efforts rest. We wish to especially recognize and thank the pioneering efforts of A. W. Shaw, the first Policy professor at the Harvard Business School, and M. T. Copeland, George Albert Smith, Jr., and Edmund P. Learned, who provided almost 60 years of dedicated leadership to course ideals and development. We are in their debt, as we are to those colleagues who worked under the leadership and who assisted in past course development.

Many members of the Harvard Business School faculty have contributed to the constant development of our field. We appreciate the help of present members of the teaching group. Francis J. Aguilar, Joseph L. Badarraco, Christopher A. Bartlett, Norman A. Berg, J. Ronald Fox, James L. Heskett, John B. Matthews, Cynthia Montgomery, Michael E. Porter, Malcolm S. Salter, Howard H. Stevenson, David B. Yoffie, and Michael Y. Yoshino.

Our sincere appreciation goes to the supervisors and authors of the cases included in this edition. To the following our thanks: Joseph L. Badaracco for Allied Chemical (A); Norman A. Berg for The Lincoln Electric Company; E. Tatum Christiansen* for Schlumberger Ltd.: Jean Riboud Excerpts from "A Certain Poetry"; Nass Dassabhoy for Note on the Major Home Appliance Industry—1984 (Condensed), and the Competitive Positioning in the Dishwasher Industry Series; Hideo Ishida, Susan Ehrlich, and Richard Pascale for Honda Motor Company and Honda of America; Richard Hamermesh with Francis J. Aguilar for General Electric: Strategic Position

* Using material with the permission of The Putnam Publishing Group.

1981 and General Electric 1984, with Nass Dassabhoy for Cleveland Twist Drill (A), with E. Tatum Christiansen for PC&D, and with Karen D. Gordon and John P. Reed for Crown Cork & Seal Company, Inc., a revised case based on an earlier document written by James Garrison and William D. Guth; Christine Harris and Mark Fuller for Marks and Spencer, Ltd.; Rosabeth Kanter and Paul S. Myers for Banc One Corporation (1989); Adam Klein, David C. Rikert, and Michael Roberts for Phil Knight: CEO at NIKE; and Paul Lawrence and Shirley Spence for Millipore Corporation (A).

We are also indebted to Edmund P. Learned for his development of The Rose Company case; Laura Nash for Peter Green's First Day; Richard T. Pascale and Leonard A. Schlesinger for Transformation at Ford; John W. Rosenblum for the Basic Industries and Industrial Products, Inc. cases; Howard Stevenson for Head Ski Company, Inc.; Martha Weinberg for Continental Airlines (A).

We owe continued thanks to Kenneth R. Andrews for the text material found in this book. His capacity to articulate course concepts and principles for the practitioner is demonstrated not only in this book but also in his pioneering volume, *The Concept of Corporate Strategy*.

Edmund P. Learned, a "great" in the development of the Business Policy field of study, continues to enjoy his well-deserved retirement. We rededicate this book to him. All who have been touched by his teaching and research efforts realize his major contributions to private and public administration. He was our teacher, counselor, and friend.

Dean John H. McArthur and Professor Jay W. Lorsch, director of the Division of Research, provided us with intellectual support and practical administrative assistance. We are in their debt.

Marguerite Dole took on the management task of producing this edition of *Business Policy: Text and Cases* and carried out this assignment with her usual blend of efficiency and good humor.

We hope this book, within which the efforts of so many good people are compressed, will contribute to constructive concern for corporate purpose and accomplishments and to the continuing and effective study and practice of Business Policy in private, semiprivate, and public organizations.

J.L.B.
C.A.B.
C.R.C.
A.E.P.
K.R.A.

CONTENTS

INTRODUCTION

Cases

Cases

Cases

Cases

CONCLUSION

Cases

INTRODUCTION

Introduction

BUSINESS POLICY AS A FIELD OF STUDY

This book is an instrument for the study of Business Policy. As a field in business administration, Policy is *the study of the functions and responsibilities of senior management, the crucial problems* that affect success in the total enterprise, and *the decisions* that determine the direction of the organization, shape its future, and when well implemented secure its achievement. The problems of policy in business, like those of policy in public affairs, have to do with the choice of purposes, the development and recognition of organizational identity and character, the continuous definition of what needs to be done, the mobilization of resources for the attainment of goals in the face of competition or adverse circumstance, and the definition of standards for the enforcement of responsible and ethical behavior. The accomplishment of predetermined or evolving corporate purposes of high quality is usually the outcome of sophisticated and detailed attention to policy.

The Policy Point of View

In Business Policy, the problems considered and the point of view assumed in analyzing and dealing with them are those of the chief executive, chairman, or president, whose primary responsibility is the enterprise as a whole. But while the study of Business Policy (under whatever name it may be called) is considered the capstone of professional business education, its usefulness goes far beyond the direct preparation of future general managers and chief executives for the responsibilities of office. In an age of increasing complexity and advancing specialization, and in companies where no person knows how to do what every other person does, it becomes important that the functional specialists—controller, computer scientist, financial analyst, market researcher, purchasing agent—acquire a unique nontechnical capacity. This essential qualification is the ability to recognize corporate purpose; to recommend its clarification, development, or change; and to shape their own contributions, not by the canons of specializations but by their perception of what a cost-effective purposeful organization requires of them. The special needs of individuals and the technical requirements of specialized groups and disciplines inevitably exhibit expensive points of view that ultimately come into conflict with one another and with the central purposes of the organization they serve. The specialists who are able to exercise control over this tendency in organizations and keep their loyalty to the conventions of their own specialty subordinate to the needs of their company become free to make creative contributions to its progress and growth. To be thus effective in their organization, they must have a sense of its mission, of its character, and of its importance. If they do not know the purposes they serve, they can hardly serve them well. Most users of this book will neither be nor become corporate chief executive officers. But virtually all can benefit from the detachment implicit in the impartial, functionally unbiased, results-oriented attitude we will call the chief executive's point of view.

Relevance of Policy to All Organization Members

The purposes of organized effort in business as elsewhere are usually somewhat unclear, apparently contradictory, and constantly changing. Except in abstract language they cannot be communicated once and for all to the variety of persons whose effort and commitment are demanded. It is not enough, therefore, for senior executives to issue statements of policy and for junior managers to salute and go about their business. In each subunit of an organization and in each individual, corporate purpose must become meaningful in ways that announcement and repetition cannot accomplish. It must be brought into balance with individual and departmental needs, satisfactions, and noneconomic aspirations. But if corporate purpose is to be reconciled with (rather than subordinated to) individual and departmental purposes, then there must be widespread knowledge of the considerations on which corporate policy is based and understanding of the risks by which it is threatened. In addition, the adaptation of corporate purpose to changing circumstances, to tactical countermoves by competitors, or to newly identified opportunities is assisted if there can be *informed* participation in policy thinking by subordinate managers from different ranks and groups. This advantage, however, can be realized only if these subordinates are capable of looking beyond the narrow limits of their own professionalization. Thus the study of Policy is not as remote from the immediate concern of apprentice managers or students of business as it first appears. In fact whenever people are challenged—in business or out—by the problem of establishing goals for *themselves* that will shape productive and satisfying lives, they will find the study of the process of determining institutional purpose of central relevance. It is helpful to personal as well as to corporate decision. It permits discovery of the individual's own powers and the purposes to which they might well be devoted.

The study of Business Policy provides, therefore, a direct if distant preparation for performance as a general manager and a less direct but more immediate broadening of the perspective of the technician. In addition, it may be viewed as resulting in certain *knowledge, attitudes,* and *skills*. Some of these are unique to Policy studies. Others may have germinated in other activities in learning. But the latter are brought to fruition by examination of the most fundamental issues and problems that confront the professional manager in the course of a business career. It may prove useful to characterize briefly the expected outcomes.

OBJECTIVES IN KNOWLEDGE

The choice of objectives and the *formulation* of policy to guide action in the *attainment* of objectives depend upon many variables unique to a given organization and situation. It is not possible to make useful generalizations about the nature of these variables or to classify their possible combinations in all situations. Knowledge of what, *in general,* Policy is and should be is incomplete and inconclusive. The knowledge to be gained from Policy studies is, therefore, primarily a familiarity with an approach to the policy problems of business and public affairs which makes it possible, in conjunction with attitudes and skills to be discussed later, to combine these variables into a pattern *valid for one organization*. This pattern may then be examined against accepted criteria and tested for its quality. Policy must first be a study of situations.

Knowledge of Concepts

The basic concept that students of Policy will in time come to understand is the concept of *strategy,* since the design and implementation of strategy provide the intellectual substance of this study. What is meant by *strategy* and, more important, how this concept may be usefully employed in the choice and accomplishment of purpose is the subject of the rest of this book. Strategy will be the idea unifying the discussions in which students will engage. These discussions will involve cerebral activities more important than simply acquiring information.

Knowledge of Situations

An abundance of information about business practice is, nonetheless, a by-product of the study of Business Policy and other cases. In their deliberately planned variety, the cases in this book encompass many industries, companies, and business situations. Although the information contained in these cases is provided mainly to permit consideration of policy issues, the importance of this incidental knowledge should not be underestimated. Breadth of exposure to the conventions, points of view, and practices of many industries is inoculation against the assumption that all industries are basically the same or that all men and women in business share the same values and beliefs. Thus consideration of the policy problems of a number of different industries guards against distraction by the particular in seeking out the nature of the universal.

For this reason it is hoped that students—although they may be, or plan to be, engineers in a utility or vice presidents of a railroad—will not resent learning about retailing in England or earthmoving in Japan. Knowledge of the environment and problems of other industries and companies is something that students may never consciously use. It will nevertheless widen the perspective they bring to their own problems. It may stimulate the imagination they put to work in introducing innovation into the obsolescent practices of their own industry. It should provide a broader base for their powers of generalization.

The study of strategy as a concept will be relatively systematic. The acquisition of information about the management problems of the many firms and industries whose strategic problems are presented in this book will be less orderly. Both are important. In particular the time spent in mastering the detail of the cases will ultimately seem to be of greater value than at first appears. Graduates of a demanding Policy course feel at home in any management situation and know at once how to begin to understand it.

The Literature of Policy

A considerable body of literature purporting to make general statements about policymaking and strategic management is in existence. It generally reflects either the unsystematically reported evidence of individuals or the logical projection to general management of concepts taken from engineering, economics, psychology, sociology, or mathematics. Neither suffices. What people wise in practice have to say is often instructive, but intuitive skill cannot be changed into conscious skill by exposition alone. The disciplines cited have much to do with business, but their purposes are not ours. Knowledge generated for one set of ends is not readily applicable to another. Besides reported experience and borrowed concepts, the literature of the field also includes independent research in Business Policy, guided by designs derived from the idea of strategy. Such research has been for some time under way and begins to make a claim on our attention. We shall often allude to the expository literature of Business Policy. The most useful literature for our purposes, however, is not that of general statements, but case studies.[1] These present not illustrations of principle but data from which generalizations may to a limited degree be derived and to which the idea of strategy may be usefully applied. The footnotes of the text portions of this book constitute a useful bibliography for further reading. The books referred to comprise a relevant but incidental source of knowledge. Look to these books in order to learn not information or theory but skills in using both.

OBJECTIVES IN ATTITUDES

Knowledge of either concepts or cases is less the objective of the study of Policy than certain attitudes and skills. What managers know by way of verifiable fact about management appears to us less important than the attitudes, aspirations, and values they bring to their tasks. Instructors in Policy do not have a dogma which they force upon their students, but most of them, like their students, appear to be influenced in their analysis and conclusions by characteristic assumptions. Thus indoctrination is implicit in the study of ideas and cases included in this book. This indoctrination—tempered by the authors' exhortation to students to think for themselves—is comprised of some important beliefs of which you should be aware.

The Generalist Orientation

The attitudes appropriate to the resolution of policy problems are several. First, the frame of mind which you will be encouraged to adopt and which will influence the outcome of your thinking is that of the *generalist* rather than the specialist. Breadth, it follows, takes precedence over depth. Since attitudes appropriate for the generalist are not always appropriate for the specialist, the two will sometimes come into conflict. Efforts to resolve this conflict in practice should help to prove that breadth which is shallow is no more satisfactory than depth which is narrow.

The Practitioner Orientation

A second outlook encountered in the study of Business Policy is the point of view of the *practitioner* as opposed to that of the researcher or scientist. A willingness to act in the face of incomplete information and to run the risk of being proved wrong by subsequent events will be developed in the

[1] In addition to the cases in this book, the reader is referred to such volumes as C. Roland Christensen, Norman A. Berg, Malcolm S. Salter, and Howard H. Stevenson, *Policy Formulation and Administration*, 9th ed. (Homewood, Ill.: Richard D. Irwin, 1985); Michael E. Porter, *Cases in Competitive Strategy* (New York: Free Press, 1983); J. Ronald Fox, *Managing Business-Government Relations* (Homewood, Ill.: Richard D. Irwin, 1982); and John B. Matthews, Kenneth E. Goodpaster, and Laura L. Nash, *Policies and Persons* (New York: McGraw-Hill, 1985). Many other cases from a variety of sources are listed in the bibliographies of HBS Case Services, Soldiers Field, Boston, MA 02163.

classroom as pressure is brought to bear on students to make decisions on the problems before them and to determine what they, as the managers responsible, would do about them. Despite the explosion of knowledge and the advance of electronic data processing, it is still true that decisions affecting the business firm as a whole must almost always be made in the face of incomplete information. Uncertainty is the lot of all thoughtful leaders who must act, whether they are in government, education, or business. Acceptance of the priority of risk taking and problem resolution over completeness of information is sometimes hard for students of science and engineering to achieve. Though natural and understandable, hesitation in the face of the managerial imperative to make decisions will impede the study of Policy. At the same time, rashness, overconfidence, and the impulse to act without analysis will be discouraged.

The Professional Orientation

The third set of attitudes to be developed is the orientation of the professional manager as distinct from the self-seeking contriver of deals and of the honest person rather than the artist in deception. The energetic opportunist sometimes has motives inconsistent with the approach to policy embodied in this book. This is not to say that quick response to opportunity and entrepreneurial energy are not qualities to be admired. Our assumption will be that the role of the business manager *includes but goes beyond* the entrepreneurial function. We shall examine what we acknowledge to be the obligations of the business community to the rest of society. We shall be concerned with the *quality* as well as the *clarity* of the alternative purposes we consider and of the values that govern our final choice. Maximum short-run profit is *not* what we mean when we consider the purpose of business enterprise. At the same time it is assumed that profit is indispensable. It is one of the necessary *results* of business activity.

The Innovative Manager

A fourth set of attitudes to be evoked is one that attaches more value to creativity and innovation than to maintenance of the status quo. We have grown accustomed to innovation stemming from new inventions and advancing technology. But suiting policy to changing circumstances includes also the application of a firm's long-established strengths to unexplored segments of the market via innovations in price, service, distribution, or merchandising.

In any course of study that has as its object enabling practitioners to learn more from subsequent experience than they otherwise might, the attitudes appropriate to the professional activity being taught are as important as knowledge. It is therefore expected that students will take time to determine for themselves the particular point of view, the values, and the morality they feel are appropriate to the effective exercise of general management skills. Much more could be said about the frame of mind and qualities of temperament that are most appropriate to business leadership, but we will expect these to exhibit themselves in the discussion of case problems.

OBJECTIVES IN SKILLS

Extensive knowledge and positive attitudes, desirable as both are, come to nothing if not applied. The skills that a course in Business Policy seeks to develop and mature are at once analytical and administrative. Since even with a variety of stimulation and the use of case situations drawn from life, the reality of responsibility can only be approximated in a professional school, we may look to make most progress now in analytical power and to use it later in actual experience to develop executive ability.

Analytical Ability

The study of Policy cases, unlike, for example, the effort to comprehend these expository notes, requires students to develop and broaden the analytical ability brought to the task from other studies. The policy problems of the total enterprise are not labeled as accounting, finance, marketing, production, or human problems. Students are not forewarned of the kind of problem they can expect and of which tool kit they should have with them. They must now consider problems in relation to one another, distinguish the more from the less important, and consider the impact of their approach to one problem upon all the others. They will bring to the cases their knowledge and abilities in special fields, but they will be asked to diagnose first the total situation and to persist in seeking out central problems through all the distraction offered by manifest symptoms.

The study of Policy, besides having its own jurisdiction, has an integrative function. It asks the analyst to view a company as an organic entity comprising a system in itself, but one related also to the larger systems of its environment. In each diagnostic situation, you are asked to pull together the separate concepts learned in functional and basic discipline courses and adapt them to a less structured set of problems. The strategic analyst must be able to see and to devise patterns of information, activities, and relationships. The facts given or the problems observed, if dealt with one at a time, soon overwhelm the mind.

Strategic Analysis

Besides extending to the company as a multifaceted whole the knowledge and analytic skills developed in less comprehensive studies, students of Policy must acquire some additional abilities. These are particularly needed to deal with the concept of strategy. Under the heading of thinking about strategy, you will be asked to examine the economic environment of the company, to determine the essential characteristics of the industry, to note its development and trends, and to estimate future opportunity and risks for firms of varying resources and competence. You will appraise the strengths and weaknesses of the particular firm you are studying when viewed against the background of its competition and its environment. You will be asked to estimate its capacity to *alter* as well as to *adapt* to the forces affecting it. Finally you will be expected to make a decision putting market opportunity and corporate capability together into a suitable entrepreneurial combination.

As you think about this decision you will encounter many feasible alternatives. Your own preferences for kind of product and the level of quality for price to be offered the consumer will influence your choice of product and market. Your values will influence your judgment and the reactions of your associates to your recommendations or decisions.

At this point you will realize the full measure of the new skill required. The strategic decision is the one that helps determine the nature of the business in which a company is to engage and the kind of company it is to be. It is effective for a long time. It has wide ramifications. It is the most important kind of decision to be made for the company. It requires the best judgment and analysis that can be brought to it. Practice in making this decision while still safe from most of the consequences of error is one of the most important advantages offered by an education for business.

Making Analysis Effective

But the analysis is not the whole of the task implied by the concept of strategy. Once the entrepreneurial decision has been determined, the resources of the organization must be mobilized to make it effective. Devising organizational relationships appropriate to the tasks to be performed, determining the specialized talents required, and assisting and providing for the development of individuals and subgroups are essential tasks of strategic management and policy implementation. These tasks, together with prescribing a system of incentives and controls appropriate to the performance required and determining the impetus that can be given to achievement by the general manager's personal style of leadership, demand that you bring to the discussion of Policy everything previously learned about administrative processes.

Administrative skills can be approached, though not captured, in the classroom. Patterns of action will be judged as consistent or inconsistent with the strategy selected according to criteria which must be developed. Students approach the study of Business Policy with skills nurtured in studies like accounting and control, personnel and human relations, financial management, manufacturing, and marketing. The balanced application of these skills to the accomplishment of chosen purpose in a unique organizational situation is the best test of their power. Any failure to see the impact on the total company of a decision based on the tenets of a special discipline will be sharply called to its proponent's attention by the defenders of other points of view. Conflicts of functional bias, which often lead to political stalemate, must yield at last to an integration dictated by corporate purpose.

General Management Skills

General management skills center intellectually upon relating the firm to its environment and administratively upon coordinating departmental specialties and points of view. Some students of business and even some students of Policy believe that these skills cannot be taught. General management is indeed an art to be learned only through years of responsible experience. And even through experience it can be learned only by those with the necessary native qualities: intelligence, a sense of responsibility, and administrative ability.

But if education means anything at all, students with the requisite native qualities can learn more readily and more certainly from experience and can more readily identify the kinds of experience to seek if they have at their disposal a conceptual framework with which to comprehend the analytical and administrative skills they will require and the nature of the situations in which they will find themselves. If, in addition, they have had practice in making and debating the merits of policy decisions, they will be more likely to grow in qualifications for senior management responsibility than if they are submerged in operational detail and preoccupied by intricacies of technique.

This book is not a manual for policymakers or a how-to-do-it checklist for corporate planners. In fact it virtually ignores the mechanisms of planning on the grounds that, detached from strategy, they miss their mark. Our book is unaffected by the current backlash against a new kind of strategic planning we have never had in mind. We emphasize the long-term future, the development of superior competence, the recognition and encouragement of noneconomic values and ethical standards, and the need to measure the quality of performance other than by short-term profits and current share price. Our message is a strong challenge to the students of business who will seek wealth in the financial community rather than in building a business providing quality products important to customers or offering services that elevate the comfort, convenience, or quality of everyday life.

The central idea described here will indeed be useful for those more interested in capital markets than in providing goods and services or more interested in extracting personal wealth than increasing corporate wealth. But it is not designed for them. Nor do we think that even for the managers of productive business can the conceptual framework described here take the place of informed judgment. All the knowledge, professional attitudes, and analytical and administrative skills in the world cannot fully replace the intuitive genius of some of the natural entrepreneurs you will encounter in this book. Native powers cannot be counterfeited by reading books.

We do not propose the acquisition of knowledge in the usual sense. We plan instead to give men and women with latent imagination the opportunity to exercise it in a disciplined way under critical observation. We expect to prepare people for the assumption of responsibility by exposing them, for example, to the temptation of expediency. We plan to press for clarification of personal purposes and to challenge shoddy or ill-considered values. We expect to affect permanently analytical habits of mind in a way that will permit assimilation of all, rather than part, of experience. The ideas, attitudes, and skills here discussed are adequate for a lifetime of study of one of the most vitally important of all human activities—leadership in organizations. Education is the prelude to true learning.

Universal Need for Policy Skills

The need for general management ability is far too acute to be left to uninstructed development. The ideas, attitudes, and skills that comprise this study are much in demand not only throughout our own economy but also—in this age of rapid economic development abroad—throughout the world. The alleged failure of American management to adapt to new requirements for success in international competition can be traced to various kinds of counter-strategic shortsightedness. Leadership in industries no longer automatically dominated by American technology requires now, in companies large and small, a world perspective on opportunity. A changing society also requires new imagination in achieving productivity in organizations committed to energetic achievement.

In addition to their utility, these ideas are their own reward. For those who wish to lead an active life, or to provide for themselves and their families the material comfort and education that make culture possible, or to make substantial contributions to human welfare, the acquisition of policy skills is essential. Not all who turn to business are called to leadership, to be sure, but all are affected by it. No one suffers from study of its place in business.

THE NATURE OF THE TEXT AND CASES

The vehicles here provided for making progress toward these objectives are the text and cases that follow. All the cases are drawn from real life; none is selected to prove a point or draw a moral. Accuracy has been attested to by the sources from which information was taken; disguise has not been allowed to alter essential issues.

The text is designed to assist in the development of an effective approach to the cases. Its content is important only if it helps students make their analyses, choose and defend their conclusions, and decide what ought to be done and how it can be accomplished.

The text is dispersed throughout the book so as to permit a step-by-step consideration of what is involved in corporate strategy and in the subactivities required for its formulation and implementation. The order of cases is only partially determined by the sequence of ideas in the text. Each case should be approached without preconceptions as to what is to come. To make conceptual progress without predetermining the students' analysis of the problem or the nature of their recommendations, the cases focus initially on problems in strategy formulation and later on problems of building the organization and leading it to the accomplishment of the tasks assigned. As the course unfolds, considerations pertinent to previous cases are included in new cases. Students should not feel constrained in their analysis by the position of the case in the book; they are free to decide that an apparent problem of strategy implementation is actually a problem of strategy choice. However, the increasing complexity of the material provided will enable most students to feel a natural and organic evolution of subject matter in keeping with their own evolving understanding, perspective, and skill.

The text suggests only that order is possible in approaching the enormous purview of Policy. The concept of strategy is an idea that experience has shown to be useful to researchers and practitioners alike in developing a comprehension of policy problems and a pragmatic approach to them. It is not a "theory" attended in the traditional sense by elegance and rigor. It is not really a "model," for the relationships designated by the concept are not quantifiable. But in lieu of a better theory or a more precise model, it will serve as an informing idea to which we can return again and again with increasing understanding after dealing with one unique case situation after another. The idea is intended to sharpen the analytical skills developed in the process of case discussion and to serve as the basis for identifying uniformities and generalizations that will be useful later on in practice. Our energies should be spent not so much on perfecting the definition of the concept as on using it in preparing to discuss the cases and in coming to conclusions about their issues. Students will not really learn how to distinguish effective from ineffective recommendations and good from bad judgment by study of these words or any others, but rather by active argument with their classmates under challenge by their instructors. Such discussion should always end in the clarification of standards and criteria. The cases, we know from experience, provide stimulating opportunity for productive differences of opinion.

To see how the complexity of choice among all the possibilities confronting a person or a company can be understood and managed by application of the idea of corporate strategy is an exciting illumination. Such insight banishes irresolution, empowers leadership, and unleashes the suppressed capability of organizations.

The Chief Executive's Job: Roles and Responsibilities

WHAT GENERAL MANAGEMENT IS

We pointed out in the introduction to this book that Business Policy is essentially the study of the knowledge, skills, and attitudes constituting general management. *Management* we regard as leadership in the informed, planned, purposeful conduct of complex organized activity. *General* management is, in its simplest form, the management of a total enterprise or of an autonomous subunit. Before we examine some cases presenting the range of decision issues we will consider more thoroughly later on, we should look at the position of the general manager. The senior general manager in any organization is its chief executive officer, who for the purposes of simplicity we will often call the *president*. As we said earlier, the role of the chief executive in examining the situation of a company may be initially an uncomfortable assignment for students of some modesty who think themselves insufficiently prepared for such high responsibility. It is nonetheless the best vantage point from which to view the processes involved in (1) the conception of organization purpose, (2) the commitment of an organization to evolving but deliberately chosen purposes, and (3) the integrated effort appropriate to achieving purpose and sustaining adaptability.

ROLES OF THE CHIEF EXECUTIVE OFFICER

We will therefore begin by considering the *roles* that presidents must play. We will examine the *functions* or characteristic and natural actions that they perform in the roles they assume. We will try to identify *skills* or abilities that put one's perceptions, judgment, and knowledge to effective use in executive performance. As we look at executive *roles, functions,* and *skills,* we may be able to define more clearly aspects of the *point of view* that provide the most suitable perspective for high-level executive judgment.

Many attempts to characterize executive roles and functions come to very little. Henri Fayol, originator of the classical school of management theory, identified the roles of planner, organizer, coordinator, and controller, initiating the construction by others of a later vocabulary of remarkable variety. Present-day students reject these categories as vague or abstract and indicative only of the objectives of some executive activity. Henry Mintzberg, who among other researchers has observed managers at work, identifies three sets of behavior—interpersonal, informational, and decisional. The interpersonal roles he designates as *figurehead* (for ceremonial duties), *leader* (of the work of his organization or unit), and *liaison* agent (for contacts outside his unit). Information roles can be designated as *monitor* (of information), *disseminator* (internally), and *spokesman* (externally). Decisional roles are called *entrepreneur, disturbance handler, resource allocator,* and *negotiator.*[1]

Empirical studies of what managers do are corrective of theory but not necessarily instructive in educating good managers. That most unprepared managers act intuitively rather than systematically in response to unanticipated pressures does not mean that the most effective do so to the same extent. If in fact the harried, improvisatory, overworked performers of 10 roles do not really know *what* they are doing or have any priorities besides degree of urgency, then we are not likely to find out what more effective management is from categorizing their activities. On the other hand it is futile to offer unrealistic exhortations about long-range planning and organizing to real-life victims of forced expediency.

The simplification which will serve our approach to Policy best will leave aside important but easily understood activities. The executive may make speeches, pick the silver pattern for the executive lunchroom, negotiate personally with important customers, and do many things human beings have to do for many reasons. Roles we may study in order to do a better job of general management can be viewed as those of *organization leader, personal leader,* and *chief architect of organization purpose.* As leader of persons grouped in a hierarchy of suborganizations, the president must be taskmaster, mediator, motivator, and organization designer. Since these roles do not have useful job descriptions saying what to do, one might better estimate the nature of the overlapping responsibility of the head of an organization than to draw theoretical distinctions between categories. The personal influence of leaders becomes evident as they play the roles of communicator or exemplar and attract respect or affection. When we

---

[1] See Henry Mintzberg, *The Nature of Managerial Work* (New York: Harper & Row, 1973), and for a different pattern of roles, John P. Kotter, *The General Managers* (New York: Free Press, 1982).

examine finally the president's role as architect of organization purpose, we may see entrepreneurial or improvisatory behavior if the organization is just being born. If the company is long since established, the part played may be more accurately designated as manager of the purpose-determining process or chief strategist.

COMPLEXITY OF GENERAL MANAGEMENT TASKS

The point of this nontechnical classification of role is not its universality, exactness of definition, or inclusiveness. We seek only to establish that general managers face such an array of functions and must exercise so various a set of skills as to require a protean versatility as performing executives. When you see Howard Head invent and perfect the metal ski, set up his company, devise a merchandising and distribution program of a very special kind, you see him in a role different from his arranging for the future of his business, his maintaining year-round production in a cyclical industry in order to meet the needs of his work force, his withdrawal from supervision of the company, and his selection of a successor. We make no claim to definitiveness in distinguishing executive roles as just attempted. It is essential to note, however, that the job of the general manager demands successful action in a *variety* of roles that differ according to the nature of the problem observed or decision pending, the needs of the organization, or the personality and style of the president. The simpleminded adherence to one role—one personality determined, for example—will leave presidents miscast much of the time as the human drama they preside over unfolds.

We are in great need of a simple way to comprehend the total responsibility of chief executives. To multiply the list of tasks they must perform and the personal qualities they would do well to have would put general management capability beyond that of reasonably well-endowed human beings. Corporate chief executives are accountable for everything that goes on in their organizations. They must preside over a total enterprise made up often of the technical specialties in which they cannot possibly have personal expertness. They must know their company's markets and the ways in which they are changing. They must lead private lives as citizens in their communities and as family members, as individuals with their own needs and aspirations. Except for rare earlier experience, perhaps as general managers of a profit center in their own organizations, they have found no opportunity to practice being president before undertaking the office. Only the brief study of Policy, for which this book is intended to be the basis, has been available as the academic preparation for general management. New presidents are obliged to put behind them the specialized apparatus their education and functional experience have provided them. Engineers, for example, who continue to run their companies strictly as engineers will soon encounter financial and marketing problems, among others, that may force their removal.

This book, together with the directed series of case discussions which will bring its substance alive, is intended to provide a way for the observer to comprehend the complexity of the president's job and for the president to put past experience in a new perspective and comprehend the world of which he or she has been put in charge. We will elaborate briefly the functions, skills, and points of view which give force and substance to the major roles we have just designated. This may lay a foundation for later discussion of the performance of chief executives in the cases that follow. In due course we will have an organizing perspective to reduce to practicable order the otherwise impossible agenda of the president.

THE CEO AS ORGANIZATION LEADER

Chief executives are first and probably least popular persons who are responsible for results attained in the present as designated by plans made previously. Nothing that we will say shortly about their concern for the people in their organizations or later about their responsibility to society can gainsay this immediate truth. Achieving acceptable results against expectations of increased earnings per share and return on the stockholder's investment requires the CEO or president to be continually informed and ready to intervene when results fall below what had been expected. Changing circumstances and competition produce emergencies upsetting well-laid plans. Resourcefulness in responding to crisis is a skill which most successful executives develop early.

But the organizational consequences of the critical taskmaster role require presidents to go beyond insistence upon achievement of planned results. They must see as their second principal function the creative maintenance and development of the organized capability that makes achievement possible. This activity leads to a third principle—the integration of the specialist functions which enable their organizations to perform the technical tasks in marketing, research and development, manufacturing, finance, control, and personnel, which proliferate as technology develops and tend to lead the company in all directions.[2] If this coordination is successful in harmonizing special staff activities, presidents will probably have performed the task of getting organizations to accept and order priorities in accordance with the companies' objectives. Securing commitment to purpose is a central function of the president as organization leader.

The skills required by these functions reveal presidents not solely as taskmasters but as mediators and motivators as well. They need ability in

[2] See P. R. Lawrence and J. W. Lorsch, *Organization and Environment: Managing Differentiation and Integration* (Boston: Harvard University Graduate School of Business Administration, 1967), for a study of the process of specialization and coordination.

the education and motivation of people and the evaluation of their performance, two functions which tend to work against one another. The former requires understanding of individual needs, which persist no matter what the economic purpose of the organization may be. The latter requires objective assessment of the technical requirements of the task assigned. The capability required here is also that required in the integration of functions and the mediation of the conflict bound to arise out of technical specialism. The integrating capacity of the chief executive extends to meshing the economic, technical, human, and moral dimensions of corporate activity and to relating the company to its immediate and more distant communities. It will show itself in the formal organization designs which are put into effect as the blueprint of the required structured cooperation. The perspective demanded of successful organization leaders embraces both the primacy of organization goals and the validity of individual goals. Besides this dual appreciation, they exhibit an impartiality toward the specialized functions and have criteria enabling them to allocate organization resources against documented needs. The point of view of the leader of an organization almost by definition requires an overview of its relations not only to its internal constituencies but to the relevant institutions and forces of its external environment. We will come soon to a conceptual solution of the problems encountered in the role of organizational leader.

THE CEO AS PERSONAL LEADER

The functions, skills, and appropriate point of view of chief executives hold true no matter who they are or who make up their organizations. The functions that accompany presidential performance of their role as communicator of purpose and policy, as exemplar, and as the focal point for the respect or affection of subordinates vary much more according to personal energy, style, character, and integrity. Presidents contribute as persons to the quality of life and performance in their organizations. This is true whether they are dynamic or colorless. By example they educate junior executives to seek to emulate them or simply to learn from their behavior what they really expect. They have the opportunity to infuse organized effort with flair or distinction if they have the skill to dramatize the relationship between their own activities and the goals of corporate effort.

All persons in leadership positions have or attain power which in sophisticated organizations they invoke as humanely and reasonably as possible in order to avoid the stultifying effects of dictatorship, dominance, or even markedly superior capacity. Formally announced policy, backed by the authority of the chief executive, can be made effective to some degree by clarity of direction, intensity of supervision, and the exercise of sanctions in enforcement. But in areas of judgment where policy cannot be specified without becoming absurdly overdetailed, chief executives establish in their own demeanor even more than in policy statements the moral and ethical level of performance expected. At the national level of executive behavior, even presidents reveal in their deportment their real regard for the highest levels of ethical conduct. The results are traceable in the administrations of Presidents Kennedy, Johnson, Nixon, and Carter. Failure of personal leadership in the White House leads to demoralization different only in scale and influence from corporate analogies. The behavior of President Reagan strikingly illustrates the influence of personal style—one which outshines doubts about the wisdom of his foreign policy or his command of economic issues. As Reagan's charisma fades, President Bush juxtaposes caution and respect for results.

Formal correctness of structure and policy is not enough to inspire an organization. Enthusiasm for meeting ethical problems head on and avoiding shoddy solutions comes not so much from a system of rewards and punishments as from the sentiments of loyalty or courage stimulated by the personal deportment of the chief executive. By the persons they are, as much as by what they say and do, presidents and CEOs influence their organizations, affect the development of individuals, and set the level of organized performance. At this moment in the history of American business enterprise, conscious attention to the essential integrity of the chief executive becomes an important requirement if confidence in the corporate institutions of a democratic society is to be restored.

The skills of the effective personal leader are those of persuasion and articulation made possible by saying something worth saying and by understanding the sentiments and points of view being addressed. Leaders cultivate and embody relationships between themselves and their subordinates appropriate to the style of leadership they have chosen or fallen into. Some of the qualities lending distinction to this leadership cannot be deliberately contrived, even by an artful schemer. The maintenance of personal poise in adversity or emergency and the capacity for development as an emotionally mature person are essentially innate and developed capabilities. It is probably true that some personal preeminence in technical or social functions is either helpful or essential in demonstrating leadership related to the president's personal contribution. Credibility and cooperation depend upon demonstrated capacity of a kind more tangible and attractive than, for example, the noiseless coordination of staff activity.[3]

The relevant aspects of the executive point of view brought to mind by activities in the role of personal leader are probably acknowledgment of one's personal needs and integrity as a person and acceptance of the importance to others of their own points of view, behavior, and feelings.

---

[3] See Abraham Zaleznik, *The Managerial Mystique: Restoring Leadership in Business* (New York: Harper & Row, 1989).

Self-awareness will acquaint leaders with their own personal strengths and weaknesses and keep them mindful of the inevitable unevenness of their own preparation for the functions of general management. These qualities may be more important in the selection of a general manager than in the study of general management. But students of the cases that follow will quickly see the personal contributions of John Welch in General Electric and the values of John Connelly in Crown Cork & Seal.

Michael Maccoby, author of *The Gamesman,*[4] once conducted a provocative inquiry into executive character types. Using some terms of dubious usefulness, he designates these as the craftsman, the jungle fighter, the company man, and the gamesman. The craftsman is dedicated to quality but unable to lead changing organizations. The jungle fighter is the antihero who after rising rapidly is destroyed by those he has used. The company man is committed to corporate integrity and success but is said to lack the daring required to lead innovative organizations. The gamesman is the dominant type—able and enthusiastic, a team leader whose main goal is the exhilaration of victory. His main defect is said to be that his work has developed his intellectual but not his emotional gifts. Despite the disclaimer that each person is a combination of types, these attention-getting labels produce caricature in the effort to distinguish overlapping or coexisting traits. Similarly, labels applied to roles suggest distance between them.

Despite the shortcomings of such classification, the work of psychoanalysts like Maccoby brings support to the thesis developed here that such qualities as generosity, idealism, and courage should accompany the gifts of persons devoted to their company and its objectives. If Maccoby is right in saying that the gamesman (by which he seems to mean quarterback or captain) is the representative type in leading American corporations today, then we have come a long way from the Carnegies, Rockefellers, and Astors of the 19th century. We would still have a long way to go. The route passes directly through the pages that follow.

The prototype of the chief executives we are developing is, in short, the able victory-seeking organizational leader who is making sure in what is done and in the changes pioneered in purpose and practice that the game is worth playing, the victory worth seeking, and life and career worth living. If the stature of corporation presidents as professional persons is not manifest in their concern for their organizations, they will not perform effectively over time either in the role of organization or personal leader. If we concede that the gamesman should be concerned with what the game is for, we are ready to consider the role of the president in the choice of corporate objectives. That choice determines what the contest is about.

[4] Michael Maccoby, *The Gamesman* (New York: Simon & Schuster, 1976).

THE CEO AS ARCHITECT OF ORGANIZATION PURPOSE

To go beyond the organizational and personal roles of leadership, we enter the sphere of organization purpose, where we may find the atmosphere somewhat rare and the going less easy. We think students of the companies described in these cases will note, as they see president after president cope or fail to cope with problems of various economic, political, social, or technical elements, that the contribution presidents make to their companies goes far beyond the apparently superficial activities that clutter their days.

The attention of presidents to organization needs must extend beyond answering letters of complaint from spouses of aggrieved employees to appraisal (for example) of the impact of their companies' information, incentive, and control systems upon individual behavior. Their personal contribution to their company goes far beyond easily understood attention to key customers and speeches to the Economic Club to the more subtle influence their own probity and character have on subordinates. We must turn now to activities even further out—away from immediate everyday decisions and emergencies. Some part of what a president does is oriented toward maintaining the development of a company over time and preparing for a future more distant than the time horizon appropriate to the roles and functions identified thus far.

The most difficult role—and the one we will concentrate on henceforth—of the chief executive of any organization is the one in which he serves as custodian of corporate objectives. The entrepreneurs who create a company know at the outset what they are up to. Their objectives are intensely personal, if not exclusively economic, and their passions may be patent protection and finance. If they succeed, like Howard Head, in passing successfully through the phase of personal entrepreneurship, where they or their bankers or families are likely to be the only members of the organization concerned with purpose, they find themselves in the role of planner, managing the process by which ideas for the future course of the company are conceived, evaluated, fought over, and accepted or rejected.

The presidential functions involved include establishing or presiding over the goal-setting and resource-allocation processes of the company, making or ratifying choice among strategic alternatives, and clarifying and defending the goals of the company against external attack or internal erosion. The installation of purpose in place of improvisation and the substitution of planned progress in place of drifting are probably the most demanding functions of the chief executive. Successful organization leadership requires great human skill, sensitivity, and administrative ability. Personal leadership is built upon personality and character. The capacity for determining and monitoring the adequacy of the organization's continuing purposes implies as well analytic intelligence of a high order.

The president we are talking about is not a two-dimensional poster or television portrait.

The crucial skill of the president concerned with corporate purpose includes the creative generation or recognition of strategic alternatives made valid by developments in the marketplace and the capability and resources of the company. Along with this, in a combination not easily come by, runs the critical capacity to analyze the strengths and weaknesses of documented proposals. The ability to perceive with some objectivity corporate strengths and weaknesses is essential to sensible choice of goals, for the most attractive goal is not attainable without the strength to open the way to it through inertia and intense opposition, with all else that lies between.

Probably the skill most nearly unique to general management, as opposed to the management of functional or technical specialties, is the intellectual capacity to conceptualize corporate purpose and the dramatic skill to invest it with some degree of magnetism. As we will see, the skill can be exercised in industries less romantic than space, electronics, or environmental reclamation. John Connelly did it with tin cans. No sooner is a distinctive set of corporate objectives vividly delineated than the temptation to go beyond it sets in. Under some circumstances it is the president's function to defend properly focused purpose against superficially attractive diversification or corporate growth that glitters like fool's gold. Because defense of proper strategy can be interpreted as mindless conservatism, wholly appropriate defense of a still valid strategy requires courage, supported by detailed documentation.

Continuous monitoring, in any event, of the quality and continued suitability of corporate purpose is over time the most sophisticated and essential of all the functions of general management alluded to here. Because of its difficulty and vulnerability to current emergency, this function may not be present in some of the companies the student will encounter in the pages that follow. Because of its low visibility, this activity may not be noticed at first in cases where it is properly present. The perspective which sustains this function is the kind of creative discontent which prevents complacency even in good times and seeks continuous advancement of corporate and individual capacity and performance. It requires also constant attention to the future, as if the present did not offer problems and opportunities enough.

ENORMITY OF THE TASK

Even so sketchy a record of what a president is called upon to do is likely to seem an academic idealization, given the disparity between the complexity of role and function and the modest qualifications of those pressed into office. Like the Molière character who discovered that for 40 years he had been speaking prose without knowing it, many managers have been programmed by instinct and experience to the kind of performance that we have attempted to decipher here. For the inexperienced, the catalog may seem impossibly long.

Essentially, however, we have looked at only three major roles and four sets of responsibilities. The roles deal with the requirements for organizational and personal leadership and for conscious attention to the formulation and promulgation of purpose. The four groups of functions encompass (1) securing the attainment of planned results in the present, (2) developing an organization capable of producing both technical achievement and human satisfactions, (3) making a distinctive personal contribution, and (4) planning and executing policy decisions affecting future results.

Even thus simplified, how to apply this identification of executive role and function to the incomparably detailed confusion of a national or international company situation cannot possibly be made clear in the process of generalization. Students using this text will wish to develop their own overview of the general manager's task, stressing those aspects most compatible with their own insight and sense of what to do. No modifications of the deliberately nontechnical language of this summary should slight the central importance of purpose. The theory presented here begins with the assumption that the life of every organization (corporate or otherwise), every subunit of organization, and every human group and individual should be guided by an evolving set of purposes or goals which permits forward movement in a chosen direction and prevents drifting in undesired directions.

NEED FOR A CONCEPT

The complexity of the president's job and the desirability of raising intuitive competence to the level of verifiable, conscious, and systematic analysis suggest the need, as indicated earlier, for a unitary concept as useful to the generalist as the canons of technical functions are to the specialist. We will propose shortly a simple practitioner's theory which we hope will reduce the four-faceted responsibility of the company president to more reasonable proportions, make it susceptible to objective research and systematic evaluation, and bring to more well-qualified people the skills it requires. The central concept we call "corporate strategy." It will be required to embrace the entire corporation, to take shape in the terms and conditions in which its business is conducted. It will be constructed from the points of view described so far. Central to this Olympian vantage point is impartiality with respect to the value of individual specialties, including the one through which the CEO rose to generalist responsibilities. It will insist upon the values of the special functions in proportion to their contribution to corporate purpose and ruthlessly dispense with those not crucially related to the objectives sought. It necessarily will define the president's role in such a way as to allow delegation of much of the general management responsibility described here without loss of clarity. After students have examined and discussed the roles, functions, and skills evident or missing from the cases that immediately follow these comments, we will present the concept of corporate strategy itself. Our hope will be to make challenging but practicable the connection between the highest priority for goal setting and a durable but flexible definition of a company's goals and major company-determining policies. How to define, decide, put into effect, and defend a conscious strategy appropriate to emerging market opportunity and company capability will then take precedence over, and lend order to, the fourfold functions of general management here presented.

Despite a shift in emphasis toward the anatomy of a concept and the development of an analytical approach to the achievement of valid corporate strategy, we will not forget the chief executive's special role in contributing quality to purpose through standards exercised in the choice of what to do and the way in which it is to be done and through the projection of *quality* as a person. It will remain true, after we have taken apart analytically the process by which strategy is conceived, that executing it at a high professional level will depend upon the depth and durability of the president's personal values, standards of quality, and clarity of character. We will return in a final comment on the management of the strategic process to the truth that the president's function above all is to be the exemplar of a permanent human aspiration—the determination to devote one's powers to jobs worth doing. Conscious attention to corporate strategy will be wasted if it does not elevate the quality of corporate purpose and achievement.

Head Ski Company, Inc.

In 1967 the Head Ski Company, Inc., seemed to be at a turning point. In its 17 years of existence, the company had enjoyed great success as a specialized manufacturer of high-quality skis, under the entrepreneurial leadership of its founder, Howard Head. Recently, however, the company had moved to a more structured management organization and had embarked on several diversification ventures.

Head Ski had been formed in 1950 to sell metal skis designed by its founder. In the company's first year, six employees turned out 300 pairs of skis. By the 1954–1955 skiing season, output reached 8,000 pairs, and by 1965 it passed 133,000. Growth in dollar sales and profits was equally spectacular. When Head went public in 1960, sales were just over $2 million and profits just under $59,000. By 1965 sales were up to $8.6 million and profits had reached $393,713. In the next two years, volume continued to rise, although less dramatically. In the 53-week period ended April 30, 1966, sales were $9.1 million and profits $264,389. In the year ended April 29, 1967, sales were $11.0 million and profits $401,482. (For financial data, see Exhibit 1.)

THE INDUSTRY

Skiing was one of the most dynamic segments of the growing market generated by leisure-time activities. The industry association, Ski Industries America (SIA), estimated that skiing expenditures—including clothing, equipment, footwear, accessories, lift tickets, travel, entertainment, food, and lodging—had risen from $280 million in 1960 to $750 million in 1967, and were projected to reach $1.14 billion by 1970, reflecting both an increasing number of skiers and greater per capita expenditures. In 1947, the number of active skiers in the United States was estimated at less than 10,000. SIA believed there were 1.6 million in 1960 and 3.5 million in the 1966–1967 ski season, and predicted 5 million for 1970. Another industry source estimated that the number of skiers was increasing by 20 percent a year.

Of the $750 million total skiing expenditures in the 1966–1967 season, an estimated $200 million was spent at retail for

Harvard Business School case 313–120.

ski equipment and skiwear. A wide variety of skis was available in several price ranges, as shown in Table 1. Although many manufacturers made all three types of skis and some had multiple brands, the industry was highly fragmented. Ninety-eight manufacturers belonged to the SIA.

Observers noted that the ski industry was changing rapidly. *Ski Business* summed up an analysis of recent trends as follows:

- Imports of low-priced adult wood skis into the U.S. are skidding sharply.
- U.S. metal skis are gaining faster than any other category.
- The ski equipment and apparel market is experiencing an unusually broad and pronounced price and quality uptrend.
- Ski specialty shop business appears to be gaining faster than that of the much publicized department stores and general sporting goods outlets.
- The growth in the national skier population is probably decelerating and may already have reached a plateau.[1]

As the *Ski Business* article emphasized, the market was growing even faster in dollar value than in physical volume:

> Foreign skis clearly lost in 1966 at the gain of domestic manufacturers. (The total of imported and domestic skis sold in the United States is believed to be running at over 900,000 pairs annually.) By conservative estimate, U.S. metal-ski production in 1966 (for shipment to retail shops for the 1966–1967 selling season) was up by at least 40,000 pairs from 1965. . . .
>
> But far more important than the domestic American ski gain (which will continue now that American fiberglass ski makers are entering the market) is the remarkable upward price shift. Thus while 10 percent fewer foreign skis entered the United States in 1966, the dollar value of all the skis imported actually rose by more than 10 percent or $700,000. . . . Here was the real measure of growth of the ski market; it was not in numbers, but in dollars. The principal beneficiary of this remarkable upward shift in consumer preference for higher product quality is, of course, the ski specialty shop. The skier bent on purchasing $140 skis and $80 boots will tend to put his confidence in the experienced specialist retailer. The ski specialist shops, themselves, are almost overwhelmed by what is happening. Here's one retailer's comment: "Just two or three years ago, we were selling a complete binding for $15. Now skiers come into our shop and think nothing of spending $40 for a binding."
>
> Most of the department store chains and sporting goods shops contacted by *Ski Business* were also able to report increased business in 1966–1967, but somehow the exuberant, expansionist talk seems to have evaporated among nonspecialty ski dealers. Montgomery Ward, for instance, says that ski equipment sales have not come up to company expectations. Ward's has specialized in low-end merchandise for beginning and intermediate skiers. . . . Significantly, department stores or sporting goods shops

TABLE 1
NUMBER OF SKI BRANDS (AND MODELS) BY PRICE RANGE

Price Range	*Wood*	*Metal*	*Fiberglass*
< $50	69	0	0
$50 – 100	27	22 (28 models)	24 (35 models)
< $100	3	28 (73 models)	39 (81 models)
All price ranges	85	49	53

Source: *Skiing International Yearbook*, 1967.

[1] John Fry, *Ski Business*, May–June 1967, p. 25.

> which reported the largest sales increases tended to be those which strive hardest to cast their image in the ski specialist mold. . . .[2]

Ski imports served both the low-priced and the high-priced market, as shown in Exhibit 2. Most of the decline in import volume is due to a sharp reduction in the number of Japanese skis; most other countries actually increased their ski exports to the United States. More than half the 530,000 pairs of skis imported from Japan were thought to be children's skis, which helped explain the low average valuation of the Japanese product ($6.84 a pair f.o.b.).[3]

The market for skis retailing at $100 or more was estimated at approximately 250,000 pairs a year. Sales of the leading competitors in this high-priced segment are shown in Table 2. Fischer was believed to have worldwide sales of $15–$18 million. Kniessl was thought to be about the same size as Head worldwide, but only about one-tenth Head's size in the United States. Another large company, AMF Inc., was entering the market with a fiberglass ski offered by its Voit recreational products division. Voit also manufactured water skis, a wide variety of aquatic equipment, and rubber products. AMF's 1966 sales were $357 million, with bowling equipment representing 22 percent of the total and other recreational equipment approximately 20 percent.

A skier's choice of equipment was determined in part by his skill level. (Appendix A outlines the differences in construction and performance among skis of various types.) Of the 3.5 million skiers active in 1966–1967, 17,000 were regarded as racers; 75,000 were considered experts; and another 100,000 were sufficiently skillful to be classed as strong recreational skiers.

TABLE 2
HIGH-PRICED SKIS

Brand	*Type*	*Estimated Sales (000 pairs)*	*Price Range*
Head (U.S.)	Metal	125	$115–175
Hart (U.S.)	Metal	44	100–175
Kniessl (Austria)	Epoxy	20	150–200
Yamaha (Japan)	Epoxy	13	79–169
Fischer (Austria)	Wood, metal, epoxy	13	112–189

Source: *Skiing International Yearbook*, 1967

THE MARKET

Skiing was considered to be a sport that attracted the moderately well-to-do and those on the way up. A 1965 *New York Times* article outlined the costs of participation:

> A statistical study released early this year by the Department of Commerce disclosed that the American skier has a median age of 26.2 and a median annual income of $11,115. Moreover, it showed that about two thirds of all skiers are college graduates.
>
> How do these young, affluent and intelligent men and women spend their skiing dollars? At a typical resort, a person might spend each day $10 for accommodations, $10 for food, $5 for a lift ticket and $10 for renting everything needed to attack the slopes from pants and parka to skis, boots, poles and bindings. . . .
>
> The initial purchases of a person determined to have his or her own good equipment and to look well while skiing could easily be about $200. For this amount, a skier could buy everything from winter underwear to goggles and

[2] Ibid.
[3] Ibid.

perhaps even have a bit left over for a rum toddy in the ski lodge the first night of his trip.

For instance, ski boots cost from $20 to $150 and average $50 a pair. Skis range from $30 to $200 and poles from $5 to $35.

When it comes to apparel, costs vary considerably. Snow jackets or parkas might cost as little as $20 or as much as $1,000 for those made with fur. Many jackets are available, though, at about $30.

Stretch pants have an average price of about $20. Other apparel requirements for skiing include sweaters which retail from $10 to $50; winter underwear, which costs about $5; and ski hats and caps, which sell for $3 and up.[4]

Fashion consciousness was apparent in the design of ski equipment and skiwear, and in the advent of a new type of skier. *The Wall Street Journal* reported on this phenomenon under the headline, "The Nonskiers: They Flock to Ski Resorts for the Indoor Sports."

> Want to take up a rugged, outdoor sport? Cross skiing off your list.
>
> The sport has gone soft. Ski resorts now have all the comforts of home—if your home happens to have a plush bar, a heated swimming pool, a padded chairlift, boutiques and a built-in baby sitter. . . . Skiing, in fact, has become almost an incidental activity at some ski resorts; indeed, some of the most enthusiastic patrons here at Squaw Valley and other resorts don't even know how to ski. They rarely venture outdoors.
>
> So why do they come here? "Men, M-E-N. They're here in bunches, and so am I, baby," answers slinky, sloe-eyed Betty Reames as she selects a couch strategically placed midway between the fireplace and the bar. . . .
>
> Squaw Valley houses half a dozen bars and restaurants and often has three different bands and a folksinger entertaining at the same time. Aspen, in Colorado, throws a mid-winter Mardi Gras. Sun Valley, in Idaho, has a shopping village that includes a two-floor bookstore and boutique selling mini-skirts.
>
> Life has also been made softer for those skiers who ski. . . . Also some resorts are making their chair lifts more comfortable by adding foam padding. But even that isn't enough for some softies. "What? Me ride the chairlift? Are you crazy? I'd freeze to death out in the open like that," says blonde Wanda Peterson as she waits to ride up the mountain in an enclosed gondola car. She doesn't stand alone. The line for the gondola is 200 strong; the nearby chairlift, meanwhile, is all but empty. . . .
>
> For beginning skiers most resorts offer gentle, meticulously groomed inclines that make it almost impossible to fall. "We try to make it so that the person who has no muscle tone and little experience can't be fooled, can't make a mistake," says one resort operator. "Then we've got him. He's a new customer as well as a happy man."
>
> Once he gets the hang of it—whether he's any good or not—the happy man starts spending lots of money, and that's what the resorts love.[5]

Capitalizing on the concern for style, some manufacturers of skiwear and ski equipment developed new colors and annual model changes to inspire a sense of product obsolescence and fad purchases.

HEAD COMPANY HISTORY

The first successful metal ski was developed by Howard Head, chairman and founder of the company bearing his name. Combining the experience of an aircraft

[4] *New York Times*, December 12, 1965.

[5] *The Wall Street Journal*, February 1967.

designer with dedication to a sport he enjoyed, he spent more than three years developing a ski that did not break, turned easily, and tracked correctly without shimmying and chattering. Others had tried to produce metal skis, but Head succeeded almost five years before the introduction of the next competitive product, the Hart metal ski. *Ski Magazine* described the factors underlying Howard Head's success:

> He was obsessed, to be sure, and being relatively unencumbered by stockholders, high overhead and strong yearnings for luxurious living, he was well braced for the long haul. . . .
>
> "I made changes only where I had to make them," he has said of the days when his skis were undergoing trial by fire.
>
> "When they broke, I made them stronger only where they broke. . . ."[6]

In 1960 Howard Head described the early years of his enterprise and the trials that surrounded it:

> Twelve years ago I took six pairs of handmade metal skis to Stowe, Vermont, and asked the pros there to try them out. It had taken about a year to make those six pairs of skis. The design, based on engineering principles of aircraft construction, was radically different from any ever tried before. I thought it was sound but the pros weren't a bit surprised when all six pairs promptly broke to pieces. After all, others before me had tried to make metal skis and all they had proved was what everyone knew anyway—a ski had to be made of wood.
>
> That was in January 1948. Today about 60 percent of all high-grade skis sold in the United States are metal skis. The reasons for this revolution in the ski manufacturing industry are simple. People like the way metal skis ski, they like their durability, and they like their easy maintenance. . . .
>
> Many small refinements and changes in design have been introduced through the years because of our continued testing and development program and to meet the advances in technique and changes in skiing conditions. But the basic structural design hasn't changed, which speaks well for the original concept.[7]

Howard Head traced his involvement in the ski business to his personal interest in technical problems:

> When I started out, I was a mechanical design engineer—the whole origin of the business was the feeling that it should be possible to build a better ski. What started as an engineering puzzle ended as a business.
>
> I distinctly remember wondering at that time whether we would ever grow to the point where we would be making 5,000 pairs of skis a year.

Price–volume considerations had little influence on Head's initial marketing policy. Although most skiers were then using war surplus skis that cost $20, including bindings, the first Head metal skis were priced at $75. As Howard Head described it, quality was the overriding consideration:

> The great disadvantage of all metal skis is simply their high price. This became apparent to us when we were pioneering the original metal ski and found it was going to cost a good bit more than a wood ski. We didn't let that stop us because we believed the striking advantages of a metal ski more than compensated for its high price. As it turned out, even with a higher

[6] *Ski Magazine*, January 1964.

[7] "On Metal Skis," manuscript by Howard Head, 1960.

initial price, Head Skis proved to cost less in the long run because they are so durable. . . .

> In the early days people had no way of knowing the skis would last so long that they actually ended up costing less than cheaper skis. They simply liked them enough to go ahead and buy them in spite of the price.[8]

The Head skis found a market that was quite unexpected. Despite their high price, they appealed more to relatively inexperienced skiers than to racers. Among skiers, Heads became known as "cheaters" because they could make almost anyone look good. "They practically turn themselves," it was said. Soon the black plastic top of the Head ski became a ubiquitous status symbol on the slopes.

PRODUCT POLICY

The keynote of Howard Head's product policy was quality. His fundamental belief was that the consumer should get all he pays for and pay for all he gets. Over the years, the product line was considerably upgraded. Several times the company recalled particular models or production runs of skis that had been found defective. One executive commented that recalls had been made without hesitation, even when the company was in a precarious financial condition.

Asked what distinguished his company from its competition, Howard Head replied:

> I believe it is a tradition of attention to detail which grew out of its entrepreneurial history. In every aspect we attempt to follow through. Service, dealer relations, product quality, style, advertising, are all important and must be done in the best way we know how.
>
> We stress continued emphasis on quality of product and quality of operating philosophy. We pay meticulous attention to the individual relationships with dealers and the public.
>
> I have attempted to make creativity, imagination, and standards of perfection apply across the board. This was always our desire, and we only failed to live up to it when the business got too big for the existing staff. The philosophy remained constant, and now we have the people to live up to it.
>
> We get a return on this attention to detail. The feedback from success allows us to maintain the necessary staff to insure continuation of this philosophy. We allow no sloppiness.

Head skis came in one color—black. Different models were indicated only by the color (blue, red, yellow, or black) of the base and of the name "Head" embossed on the top of the ski. The use of a chrome top was once considered, but rejected because it would be difficult to see against the snow, and would create glare. Moreover, black was preferred as a conservative color that would go with anything. Howard Head explained that he "did not want to complicate the consumer's choice."

> I deeply believe in sticking to function and letting style take care of itself. We have stuck so rigorously to our black color because it is honest and functional that it has become almost a trademark. While we constantly make minor improvements, we never make an important model change unless there is a performance reason for it. In other words, we skipped the principle of forced obsolescence, and we will continue to skip it.

This consciously chosen policy was staunchly maintained, while competitors introduced six or eight different colors and

[8] Ibid.

CRITICAL FEATURES OF A SKI'S DESIGN

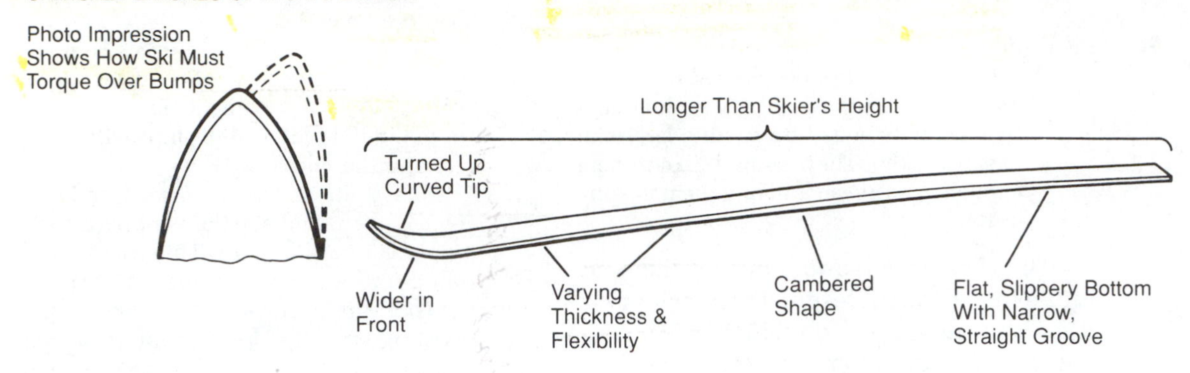

yearly color changes to keep up with fashion.

Apart from color and style, skis had to be designed to perform well on the slopes. Specifically, the three critical functions were tracking, traversing, and turning.[9] Producing a ski that would perform well in all three respects required a delicate balancing of design considerations.

Ski distributors and retailers interviewed described some critical features of a ski's design. As shown above, the ski had to be flexible, designed with a cambered or arched shape to distribute the skier's weight over the entire ski, and manufactured so as to be straight, without warp or twist. The tip of the ski had to be pointed and turned up to permit the skier to navigate difficult terrain and soft snow without changing direction. The bottom of the ski was also critical: it had to provide a slippery surface for ease of travel, and had to be perfectly flat except for a center groove which helped the skier to achieve tracking stability. The edges of the ski had to be sharp for holding and turning purposes. All of those interviewed stressed that for maximum performance, the skier had to select skis of the proper length.

Howard Head found a proper combination of these elements for the recreational skier in his earliest metal ski. This Standard model underwent substantial improvement in the following years. Until 1960, however, the goal of providing the best ski for experts eluded Head and other metal ski makers. As Head put it, "During the early years at Head Ski, we were too busy making the best ski we could for the general public to spend much time developing a competition ski."

Experts complained that metal skis were too "soft" and tended to vibrate badly at racing speeds. This problem was substantially solved in 1960, when Head introduced its Vector model. The

[9] *Tracking:* A ski pointed down a slope and allowed to run freely should hold a straight course—over bumps and through hollows and on every type of snow surface. *Traversing:* A ski should be able to hold a straight line while moving diagonally across a slope over obstacles and various snow conditions. *Turning:* When a skier releases the edges of his skis, the skis must be capable of slipping sideways, and when edged, they must bite into the snow evenly. (A skiing turn is nothing more than a sideslip carved into an arc by the controlled bite of the edges.)

HEAD'S COMPETITION SKI

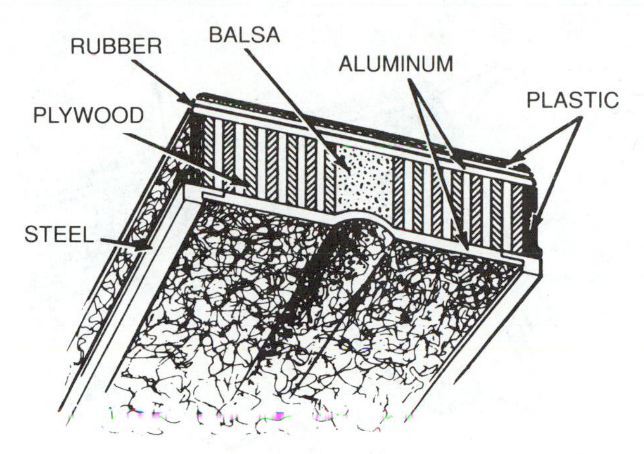

Competition followed in 1962 and later entirely replaced the Vector. In these skis, an imbedded layer of neoprene dampened vibrations and considerably improved performance. Whereas most competitors in the 1960 Squaw Valley Olympics had stuck to their wooden skis, by the end of 1962 Head skis were in wide use. Of 141 racers who finished among the top six in races conducted by the International Professional Ski Race Association in Canada and the United States, 77 had used Head skis. About half the skis used in the U.S. National Junior and Senior Championships that year were also Heads.

By 1966 Head had established itself as an important factor in the ski racing world. An American had set the world speed record—106.527 mph—on Head skis. In major international competitions in 1966, one third of all finishers in the top 10 places at all events were on Head skis, and Head was the outstanding single manufacturer on the circuit, with 18 gold medals, 15 silver medals, and 15 bronze medals.

The 1968 Head line included a ski for every type of skier, from the unskilled beginner to the top professional racer, as described in Appendix B.

Head experimented constantly with new designs and frequently introduced minor modifications to improve the performance and durability of its product. A major change in product construction, such as a move to the fiber-reinforced plastic ski, was thought unlikely, however. Howard Head commented:

> We think that the metal sandwich construction is the best material. We do not see this situation changing in the foreseeable future. Certainly now, the other exotic materials are not gaining ground. They lack the versatility of application of the metal sandwich ski. The epoxy or fiber-reinforced plastic skis have low durability and don't have the wide performance range of our skis.
>
> We believe that the advantage of the metal ski is that you can build in any performance characteristic you desire. Naturally, we have a research department investigating other materials,

A FIBER-REINFORCED PLASTIC SKI

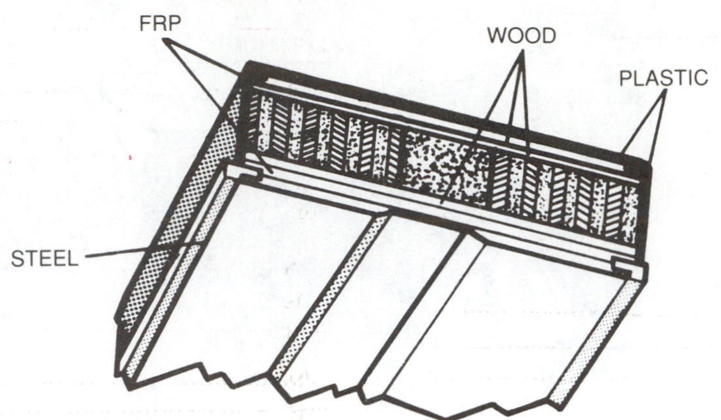

but until a major improvement is found we should stick to our basic material. We can always build the best ski for beginners, and we can adapt that ski to get the performance required by experts.

MARKETING POLICIES

Head's emphasis on quality extended beyond the product to the dealer and service network. The company sold only through a limited number of franchised dealers who had satisfied management that they knew something about skis and skiing. Ten district sales managers were employed; they sold to about 900 dealers throughout the United States. Of these, about 85 percent were ski specialty shops, 12 percent were large full-line sporting goods stores, and the remainder were full-line department stores (see Exhibit 3). Head skis were distributed in Europe through an exclusive distributor, Walter Haensli of Klosters, Switzerland, who had sold 19 percent of Head's 1964 output. His share of sales appeared to be declining gradually.

The company believed that a Head franchise was valuable to a dealer. Many large stores that wanted to sell Heads were turned down, and Saks Fifth Avenue waited eight years before it was given a franchise. As Howard Head described it, the dealer played a critical role in Head sales:

> Getting Saks Fifth Avenue as a dealer is consistent with our operating philosophy of expecting the same quality from our dealers as from ourselves.
>
> Once they become a dealer, however, we get to know the people involved and work closely with them. Increasingly, we are recognizing the business value of providing more assistance and leadership to our dealers in helping them to do a better job for their customers.
>
> Even a large, well-managed department store or sporting goods store may need help in the specialized area of skis. They may need help in display stock selection, or even personnel selection. We are increasingly concerned about the type of personnel who sell skis. There is a high degree of dependence on the salesman. He must be a good skier himself.

> We have seen instances of two department stores of essentially identical quality in the same area, where one store could sell 8 pairs of skis a year and the other 300, simply because of a different degree of commitment to getting the right man to sell. Skis can only be sold by a floor salesman who can ski and who can sell from personal experience.

The company was convinced that selling skis was an exacting business. The ski size had to be matched to the individual's height and body weight; flexibility had to be chosen correctly depending on use, and bindings had to be mounted properly.

Head offered extensive after-sale service. Dealers were expected to maintain service facilities for minor repairs, and skis were sent back to the factory for sharpening edges, rebuilding the plastic portion of the ski, or matching a single ski if the mate had been broken beyond repair. Even in the busiest part of the season, service time was kept under three weeks.

In March 1967, Harold Seigle, the newly appointed president and chief operating officer of Head, issued a "management news bulletin" outlining the company's marketing philosophy:

> **1.** Our current selective dealer organization is one of Head Ski Company's most valuable assets, next to the product itself.
>
> **2.** Our continued sales growth will be based on a market-by-market approach aimed at increasing the effectiveness of our present dealers and by the very selective addition of new dealers wherever present dealers prove to be inadequate rather than by mass distribution and merchandising techniques.
>
> **3.** Our future marketing efforts, particularly personal selling, advertising, merchandising, and sales promotion, will be geared to the specific needs of our dealers to sell all Head Ski products.
>
> **4.** We want and will have the finest sales forces in the industry . . . who rely upon personal integrity, service, and hard work to do a professional selling job rather than inside deals and short cuts.
>
> **5.** We feel that, next to quality products, strong personal selling at the manufacturer's level and the retail level is paramount to our continued success and tends to transcend other facets of marketing that contribute to the sale of merchandise.

Advertising was done on a selective basis. A marketing journal reported:

> The company invests about 2 percent of gross sales in advertising, split between the skiing magazines (50 percent) and *Sports Illustrated, The New Yorker,* and *Yachting*—"the same kind of people like to sail."
>
> The most effective promotion, however, is probably the ski itself. Head is delighted at the growing demand for his skis in the rental market. "We sold 10,000 pairs—almost 10 percent of our business—for rental last year.," he points out, "and everyone who rents those skis becomes a prospect."[10]

Ski rental was seen as the best way to introduce a customer to the ease of skiing on Heads. Accordingly, Head gave dealers an additional 12–15 percent discount on skis purchased for rental.

In general, the Head Ski Company took a soft-sell approach. Unlike many sporting goods companies, Head did not rely on personal endorsements of famous skiers. According to one executive, it was impossible under American amateur rules even to feature an amateur skier on a poster.

[10] *Sales Management/The Magazine of Marketing,* February 5, 1965.

Professional endorsements were probably ineffective anyway, since so many other sporting goods companies used them, and most people knew that such testimony could be bought. In an effort to get actual news pictures of famous skiers or racers using Head skis, the company did lend skis to racers for one year. Even this practice was expensive and had to be tightly controlled. A good skier might need upwards of nine pairs of skis a year, which would represent an expenditure of nearly $1,000. On the other hand, Head felt this type of promotion yielded a significant secondary benefit of product development information.

Head also collaborated with United Airlines in making a promotional film showing famous ski slopes. Head was mentioned in the title, at the end, and occasionally in the body of the show. The film was popular with ski clubs and other organizations that wished to promote interest in the sport.

Head skis received additional publicity through skiwear and resort advertisements. As *Sales Management* put it:

> So great is the world-wide prestige of Head skis that although Howard Head claims he makes no promotional tie-in deals, the ski buff can hardly miss seeing the familiar black skis in ads for anything from parkas to ski resorts. They're status symbols.[11]

PRODUCTION

Head skis were produced in three steps. The Detail Department made up the various components parts, including the core, the nose piece, the tail piece, the top plastic, the top and bottom skins, the running surface, and the edges. The separate pieces were then assembled in the Cavity Department. Here, too, the various layers were laid into a mold and heated and bonded under controlled temperature and pressure. The skis were then roughed out on a band saw. From this point on, all work was done on the skis as a pair. In the Finishing Department, the skis were ground to final form, buffed, polished, and engraved.

Manufacture involved a great deal of handwork, of which 70 percent required a high degree of skill. Because of the basic nature of the assembly process, operations did not lend themselves to mass production techniques.

Howard Head commented on the difficulty of the manufacturing process and on the relationship between costs and price:

> [There are] approximately 250 different operations, involving a great number of specially developed machines, tools, and processes. None of the processes is standard. It all had to be developed more or less from scratch.
>
> Some of the special-purpose machines involved are those for routing the groove in the bottom aluminum, for attaching the steel edges, and for profiling the ski after it comes out of the presses. Also there are the bonding procedures that require an unusual degree of control of heat and pressure cycles.
>
> Supplementing all the special-purpose machines, we have learned to make rather unusual use of band saws. A good example of a demanding band-saw operation is the profiling of the plywood and plastic core elements. Since the stiffness of a ski at any point goes up as the square of the spacing between the top and bottom sheets, i.e., the core thickness, a normal band-saw tolerance of about .010″ would grossly affect our flexibility pattern and would be out of the question. However, by special adaptors and guides, we are actu-

[11] Ibid.

> ally able to band saw these parts in high production at about 10 seconds apiece to a tolerance of plus or minus .002′′ over the entire contour.
>
> An example of effective but low cost equipment in our factory is the press used to laminate 3′ × 10′ sheets of plywood core material to their corresponding sheets of sidewall plastic. This operation requires a total load of some 90,000 pounds. By using a roof beam as the reaction point, the floor for a base, and three screw jacks for pressure, we are able to produce enough material for 600 pairs of skis at one shot with equipment costing a total of about $250.
>
> It's been our policy from the start to put absolute emphasis on quality of product. We never compromise on old material, nor reject a new one on the basis of cost. In principle, if better skis could be made out of sheet platinum, I suspect we would wind up with it. In other words, it is our policy to make the best product we can regardless of cost and then price it accordingly to the trade.

At the beginning of 1967, Head's 105,668-square-foot plant in Timonium, Maryland, was divided between manufacturing and warehouse facilities (93,040 square feet) and office space (12,628 square feet). The plant included a cafeteria, locker rooms, and shower areas for the workers. In May, Head completed the fifth addition to the plant since its construction in 1959.

Production at Head was on a three-shift basis throughout the year, with skis being made for inventory during the slow months. There were over 600 employees.

Six attempts had been made to unionize the plant, but all had been rejected, several times by three-to-one majorities. One warehouse employee with 12 years' seniority said, "It's a nice place to work. We don't need a union. If you have a problem, Mr. Head will listen to you."

All employees received automatic step raises based on seniority, as well as merit reviews and raises. In addition a profit-sharing trust plan had generally added 6–7 percent to the employees' salaries. These funds became fully vested after three years.

Another important benefit for exempt salaried employees was the year-end bonus plan. The amount of the bonus depended on the employee's salary class and the company's profitability. For the lowest-paid group, the bonus was 3 percent if pretax profits on sales were under 2 percent, but 10–11 percent if profits were 8–12 percent. For the middle group, no bonus was paid if profits were 2 percent or below, but the rate was 20–22 percent if profits ranged between 8 and 12 percent. Rates for the top group were not disclosed, but it was indicated that their bonus plan was even more steeply skewed. For most of the past several years, the payoffs had been at or near the upper range.

FINANCE

The initial financing of Head Ski Company was $6,000 from Howard Head's personal funds. In 1953, Howard Head sold 40 percent of the stock in the company for $60,000. This, together with retained earnings and normal bank debt, financed expansion until 1960, when common stock was issued. Additional financing was required to continue the rapid expansion, and in January 1965 a $3,527,500 package was sold, made up of 5½ percent convertible subordinated debentures in the face amount of $2,125,000, and 42,500 shares of common stock. Until the stock issue of 1965, Howard Head had owned 42.4 percent of the common stock, and the other directors and officers had owned 46.1 percent. Full conversion of the new issue would represent 17.1 percent ownership.

At no time had there been any question about Howard Head's commanding role in any important decisions. Expansion was viewed by many in the company as a defensive tactic. They reasoned, "If you do not grow as fast as the market will allow you to, you are taking a substantial risk that someone else will come in and take that market away from you." In addition, the new funds provided capital for two diversifications started in 1966: The Head Ski and Sportswear Co., and the Head plastics division.

Although Head's earnings growth had slowed (see Exhibit 1), the stock market continued to evaluate its prospects at 29 to 60 times previous years' earnings. During the period January 1966 to July 1967, the company's stock price ranged from 9⅜ to 17¾. As recently as January 1965, the stock had sold at 22¾.

ORGANIZATION

Before the appointment of Harold Seigle as chief operating officer in January 1967, Howard Head presided directly over the various departments and marketing functions. There was no overall marketing director. Even in the 1960–1966 period, when the company had an executive vice president, Mr. Head indicated that he had concerned himself with the operating details of the business.

Harold Seigle reorganized the company along functional lines. Reporting to the president were the vice president for operations, the treasurer, and the directors of marketing, quality control, and personnel. Of the 26 managers appearing on the organization chart (Exhibit 4), 12 had been with Head one year or less. Asked about the potential difficulties of that situation, Head responded: "I would only say that if you are to have a lot of new people, you must have one man in command who is an experienced and gifted professional at utilizing people. My job is to support and use that man."

Howard Head reviewed the steps through which the organization had reached its current structure:

> I think that this is typical of the kind of business that starts solely from an entrepreneurial product basis, with no interest or skills in management or business in the original package. Such a business never stops to plan. The consuming interest is to build something new and to get acceptance. The entrepreneur has to pick up the rudiments of finance and organizational practices as he goes along. Any thought of planning comes later. Initially he is solely concerned with the problems of surviving and building. Also, if the business is at all successful, it is so successful that there is no real motivation to stop and obtain the sophisticated planning and people-management techniques. Such a business is fantastically efficient as long as it can survive. One man can make all of the important decisions. There is no pyramidal team structure.
>
> In our case this approach worked quite successfully until about 1955, when we sold 10,000 pairs of skis and reached the $500,000 sales level. The next five years from 1955 to 1960 saw a number of disorganized attempts to acquire and use a more conventional pyramidal organizational system. To put it succinctly, what was efficient at the $500,000 level was increasingly inefficient as we reached $1 million, then $2 million in sales. One man just couldn't handle it. I made too many mistakes. It was like trying to run an army with only a general and some sergeants. There were just no officers, to say nothing of an orderly chain of command.
>
> 
>
> In 1960 came the first successful breakthrough, where I finally developed the ability to take on a general manager who

later became an executive vice president. It was hard for me to learn to operate under this framework. The most striking thing missing from this period was a concept of people-management. I spent five years gradually learning not to either over- or under-delegate.

Let me interject that the final motivation necessary to make a complete transition to an orderly company came because the company got into trouble in 1965–1966. Even five years after the beginning of a team system, the company got into trouble, and this was the final prod which pushed me to go all the way. It is interesting that it took 12 years. Up until 1960 the company was totally under my direction. From 1960 to 1965 we stuttered between too much of my direction and not enough.

The chief difficulty for me was to learn to lay down a statement of the results required and then stay out of details. The weakness was in finding a formula of specifying objectives, then giving freedom as long as the objectives were met.

The appointment of Hal Seigle as president brought us a thoroughly sophisticated individual who can bring us the beginning of big business methods. On my part, this change has involved two things: first, my finally recognizing that I wanted this kind of organization; second, the selection of a man with proven professional management skills.

Unfortunately, with an entrepreneur there are only two courses which can be taken if the company is to grow beyond a certain size. He can get the hell out, or he can really change his method of operation. I am pleased that this company has made the transition.

Now more than ever the company is using my special skills and abilities, but I am no longer interfering with an orderly and sophisticated management and planning system. We have given the company new tools to operate with, and I have not pulled the rug out from under them.

I am reserving my energies for two things. First, there is a continuation of my creative input—almost like a consultant to the company. Second, I have taken the more conventional role of chairman and chief executive officer. In this role I devote my efforts to planning and longer-range strategy.

I feel that I can serve in both capacities. I can only be successful in the role of creative input if I can be solely a consultant without authority. It has to be made clear in this role that anything said is for consideration only. It has been demonstrated that this role is consultative, since some of my suggestions have been rejected. I like this role because I like the freedom. I can think freer, knowing that my suggestions will be carefully reviewed.

Of course, in areas of real importance like new product lines such as binding or boots, adding new models to the ski line, or acquisitions, etc., I must exert authority, channeled through the president.

Before joining Head, Harold Seigle had been vice president and general manager of a $50 million consumer electronics division of a $150 million dollar company. His appointment was viewed as "contributing to a more professional company-operating philosophy." He hoped to introduce more formalized methods of budget control and to "preside over the transition from a 'one man' organization to a traditionally conceived functional pattern."

Seigle introduced a budgeting system broken down into 13 periods each year. Reports were to be prepared every four weeks comparing target with actual for each of the revenue or expense centers, such as marketing, operations, the staff functions, and the subsidiaries. The hope was eventually to tie the bonus to performance against budget. Previously statements had been prepared every four weeks, but only to compare actual results against the previous year's results.

Being new to the company, Seigle found he was spending much of his time on operating problems. He believed, however, that as the budget system became completely accepted and operational, he would be able to devote more of his time to looking ahead and worrying about longer-term projects. He said: "Ideally, I like to be working 6 to 18 months ahead of the organization. As a project gets within 6 months of actual operation, I will turn it over to the operating managers." He had hired a manager for corporate planning with whom he worked closely.

A VIEW TOWARD THE FUTURE

Head's first diversification was to ski poles, which were relatively simple to manufacture and could be sold through existing channels. As with the skis, Head maintained the highest standards of quality and style. The poles were distinguished from the competition by their black color and their tapered shape and extra-light weight, which were then unavailable on other high-priced, quality ski poles. At $24.50, Head's prices were well toward the upper end of a spectrum that ranged as low as $5 for some brands. Success in selling poles encouraged the company to look at other products it might add.

Two further steps were taken toward diversification in late 1966, when Head formed a plastics division and established a subsidiary, Head Ski and Sportswear, Inc.

The plastics division's activity centered on high molecular weight plastics. A March 1967 press release described this activity:

> Head Ski Co., Inc. has signed a license agreement with Phillips Petroleum Company . . . to use a new method developed by Phillips for extruding ultra-high molecular weight high-density polyethylene into finished products. . . .
>
> Developmental equipment has been installed at the Head plant here and limited quantities of sheet have been extruded and tested in the running surface of Head skis with excellent results. . . . Production of ski base material is scheduled for this Spring. . . .
>
> In addition to its own running surface material, the Head plastics division has been developing special ultra-high molecular weight high density polyethylene compounds to serve a variety of industrial applications. . . .
>
> Ultra-high molecular weight high density polyethylene is an extremely tough abrasion-resistant thermoplastic capable of replacing metal and metal alloys in many industrial areas. Compared with regular high density resins, the ultra-high molecular weight material has better stress-cracking resistance, better long-term stress life and less notch sensitivity.

Company executives considered the diversification into skiwear the more important move. Howard Head described the logic of this new venture:

> Skiwear is "equipment" first and fashion second. We are satisfied that our line of skiwear is better than anything done before. It represents the same degree of attention to detail which has characterized our hardware line.

The president of the new subsidiary, Alex Schuster, said:

> Many people thought that Head should stay in hardware such as poles, bindings, and wax. As I see it, however, by going into skiwear we are taking advantage of ready-made distribution and reputation. There is no reason why the good will

SAMPLES OF THE NEW HEAD SKIWEAR

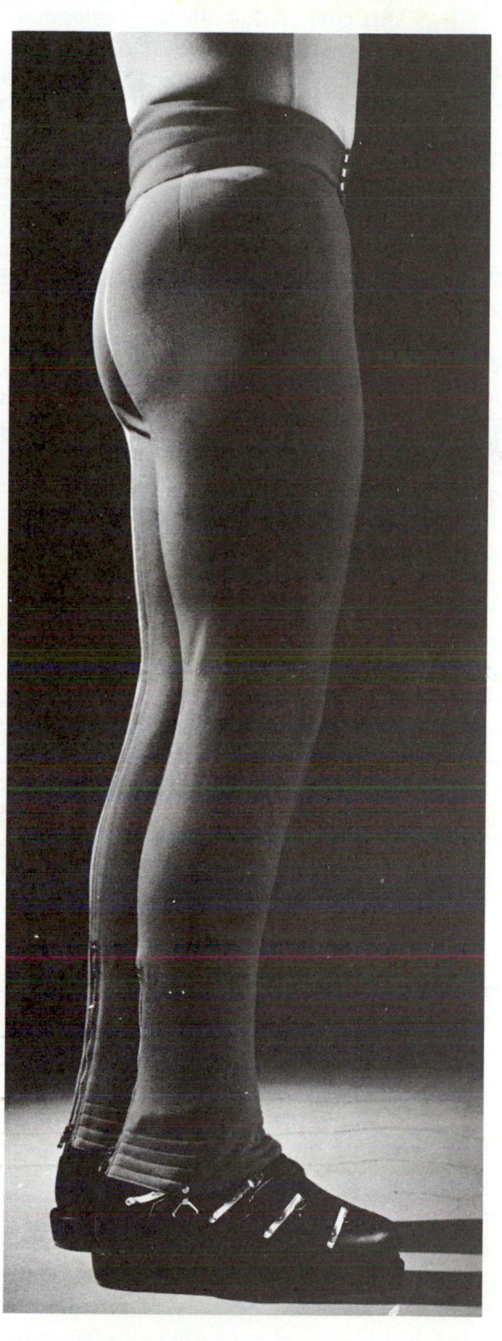

developed through the years can't be related to our endeavor.

This new market offers a greater potential and reward than the more hardware-oriented areas. Any entry into a new market has difficulties. These can only be solved by doing things right and by measuring up to the Head standards. Having a Head label commits us to a standard of excellence.

Assuming that we live up to those standards, we shall be able to develop into a supplier in a small market, but with formidable potential. We are creating a skill base for further diversification.

Our products are engineered, not designed. We are concerned with the engineered relationship among fabric, function, and fit. The engineering details are not always obvious, but they are related to functional demands. Emphasis is placed on function over fashion, yet there is definite beauty created out of concern for function. We are definitely in tune with fashion trends.

We will provide a complete skiing outfit—pants, parkas, sweaters, accessories, socks, and gloves. We will offer a total coordinated look.

Along with the design innovations, we shall offer innovations in packaging, display and promotion. We have to go beyond simply preparing the proper apparel.

Head Ski and Sportswear did both manufacturing and subcontracting. The products that had the highest engineering content were made in the Head plant. Sweaters were contract-made to Head specifications by one of Europe's leading sweater manufacturers.

The collection was first shown to dealers in April 1967, and was scheduled for public release for the 1967–1968 skiing season. The initial response of dealers and the fashion press was extremely encouraging. *Ski Business* reported:

Head's Up.

. . . way up, in fact 194 percent ahead of planned volume on its premier line of skiwear.

Anyone who expected Howard Head's entry into the world of fashion to be presented in basic black was in for a surprise. Ironically the skiwear collection that blasted off with the hottest colors in the market is offered by a man who is totally color blind. . . .

On pants: The $55 pant was the big surprise. It was our top seller—way beyond expectations—and the basic $45 pant came in second in sales. Another surprise was the $70 foam waisted pant for which we only projected limited sales—it's a winner. . . .

On orders: "Way beyond expectations. Ninety percent of the orders are with ski shops and 10 percent with the department stores. Naturally we are committed to selling to Head Ski dealers but it definitely is not obligatory."[12]

The sportswear subsidiary had been set up in a separate plant five miles from Head's Timonium headquarters. It was an autonomous operation with a separate sales force and profit responsibility. The initial premise was that the sportswear would be distributed through current Head dealers, but Harold Seigle indicated the marketing decisions of the sportswear division would be made independently of decisions in the ski division. Although Head dealers were offered the Head sportswear line, it was not sold on an exclusive basis. Distribution would be directly from factory salesmen to the dealer. Within the company, the need for a separate and different type of sales force was acknowledged. As one executive phrased it, "I can't imagine our ski salesmen trying to push

[12] John Fry, *Ski Business*, May–June 1967, p. 46.

soft goods. Our salesmen got into the business first and foremost because they were excellent skiers." As with skis and poles, the product line was to be maintained at the high end of the spectrum in both quality and price.

Harold Seigle believed Head would continue to grow rapidly in the future. He saw the potential of doubling the ski business in the next five years. Although he characterized the sportswear business as a "good calculated risk," he thought it offered the potential of expanding to annual sales of $5–$8 million. Beyond that, he felt that Head might go in three possible directions. First, he believed that Head should once again explore the opportunities and risks of moving into the other price segments of the ski market, either under another brand or with a nonmetallic ski. Although he estimated Head could sell 50,000 or more pairs of skis in a lower price range, the risks were high. Seigle also felt Head should explore the opportunity in other related ski products, such as boots or bindings. Finally, he believed Head should eventually expand into other specialty sporting goods, preferably of a counter-seasonal nature.

In looking to these new areas, Harold Seigle believed Head should adhere to a two-part product philosophy:

> Any new product which Head will consider should: (1) be consistent with the quality and prestige image of Head Ski; (2) entail one or more of the following characteristics:
>
> a. High innovative content.
> b. High engineering content.
> c. High style appeal.
> d. Be patentable.
>
> We will consider getting into new products through any of the normal methods such as internal product development, product acquisition, or corporate acquisition. If we are to move into a new area we definitely want to have a product edge. For example, if we were to manufacture a boot, we would want to be different. We would only seriously consider it if we had a definite product advantage, such as if we were to develop a high-quality plastic boot.

Howard Head, in speaking of the future, voiced the following hopes:

> I would like to see Head grow in an orderly fashion sufficient to maintain its present youth and resiliency. That would mean at least 20–25 percent per year. This statement does not preclude the possibility that we might grow faster. We believe the ski business alone will grow 20–25 percent per year. As our staff capabilities grow, we will probably branch out into other areas.
>
> As to our objectives for the next five years, I would say that the first corporate objective is to maintain healthy growth in the basic ski business. It is the taproot of  all that is good in Head. Second, we must be certain that any new activity is carefully selected for a reasonable probability of developing a good profit and an image platform consistent with the past activity of Head.

APPENDIX A

TYPES OF SKIS

Wood Skis

If you are on a tight budget, well-designed wood skis at low prices are available from domestic and foreign manufacturers. Wood is a bundle of tubular cellulose cells bound together in an elastic medium called lignin. The internal slippage of wood skis not only lets them torque over the bumps in traverse, but damps any tendency to vibrate or chatter on hard rough surfaces.

There are wood skis for any snow, any speed, and they are fun to ski on. Their only problem is a lack of durability. Wood skis are fragile. Besides, as wood skis are used, the internal slippage of the fibers increases, and they lose their life.

In choosing a wood ski, it is probably wise to pay more than the minimum price. Multiple laminations of hickory or ash, a soft flex pattern, interlocking edges, polyethylene base, plastic top and sidewalls, tip and tail protectors are some of the features a beginner or intermediate should look for in a better wood ski. When you get past the $40 to $70 range, your own dealer's recommendations will be your best guarantee of value.

CROSS-SECTION OF A WOOD SKI

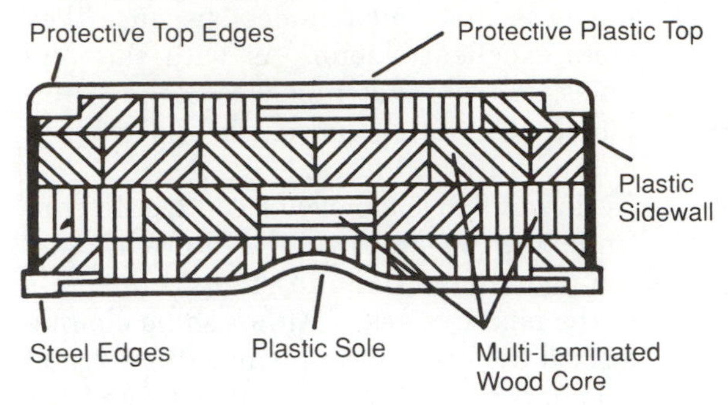

FRP Skis

A few years ago there were only a handful of "epoxy" skis on the market, and skiers were eyeing them with mixed interest and distrust. Now the available models have multiplied almost unbelievably. New companies have been formed and many of the established manufacturers have now brought out versions of their own. The plastic skis are still new enough for most skiers to be confused about their true nature—and with good reason, since there are so many types.

The word *epoxy* is part of the confusion. The true family resemblance of all the skis that are currently being lumped under that designation is the use of glass fibers locked into a plastic medium to create layers of great strength. The plastics engineers use the term *fiber-reinforced plastic* (FRP) to designate this type of structural solution. It is very strong.

There are three basic elements of FRP construction: the plastic material or resin; the glass fibers themselves; and the method of combining, curing, and shaping the composite reinforcing layer. Variation of any of these three elements affects the characteristics of the end product.

The reinforcing layers used in these new designs derive their strength from the combined strength of millions of fine glass fibers or threads locked in the plastic layer. The potential strengths of materials in this family of structural plastics can exceed those of aluminum or steel. Unfortunately, there is no simple way to evaluate them or describe the materials actually in use. The wide variety of glass fibers, resins, and systems of molding and curing the fiber-reinforced layer produces a wide range of results. These can be evaluated only by laboratory tests or, finally, by actual in-service results.

FRP materials are being used for all sorts of sporting goods, industrial, and space-age applications. The strength-to-weight ratio is attractively high, and the possibility of creating new reinforced shapes by means of molding operations has proved to be attractive enough to encourage a great deal of experimentation. Skis seem to adapt to this structural technique.

Metal Skis

In the search for more durable skis, the metal skis took over the quality market about a decade ago, and are widely accepted as ideal for both recreational skier and expert. Except for specialized racing uses, the wooden skis have been largely outmoded in the better ski market. Today, the fiber-reinforced plastic designs are the only challengers to the primacy of the metals.

Metal skis obtain their strength from aluminum sheets that are light in weight but very strong. The structure of a metal ski is somewhat like an "I" beam; when the ski is bent, the bottom sheet is stretched and the top sheet is compressed. The core material serves as the web—the vertical portion of the "I"—and must be attached to the top and bottom metal sheets securely enough to resist the shearing stress that occurs when the ski is bent.

Service Potential of Metal Skis

The possibility of rebuilding and refinishing metal skis has been one of the key sales attractions of the metal ski in this country. So long as bonding remains intact, only the effects of wear and tear—rocks, skis banging together, rough treatment in transportation, etc.—limit the life of the skis. The possibility of having the plastic surfaces and edges, or even the structural members themselves, replaced has strong appeal for the skier investing well over $100 in his skis. The rebuilding potential also tends to keep the trade-in and used resale value of the skis higher, making it less expensive for the skier to move to higher performance or more recent models as his skiing ability—or his desire for something new—dictates. The American companies were the first to develop rebuilding techniques, but more recently European factories have been establishing service centers in the United States.

Service Potential of FRP Skis

One of the problems facing the manufacturers of fiber-reinforced plastic skis has been how to service and rebuild them—once the normal wear and tear of skiing has taken its toll. Only the metal skis, it has seemed, could be refinished and rebuilt.

Though it is true that you cannot heat up an FRP ski, melt the glue, resand, recoat, and reconstruct it quite as easily as you can a metal ski, progress has been made in this direction during the past season. Several manufacturers have set up regional service centers.

What these various service centers can accomplish is considerable. They are replacing bases and edges. They are renewing and refinishing top surfaces. In some cases, the structural fiberglass members can be separated from the wood core and replaced, producing in effect a brand new ski. The sum of all this is real benefit to the average skier, who is unwilling to discard a pair of skis every season or so. The gap between metal and FRP skis, as far as service potential is concerned, is being narrowed. You will find that the costs range over approximately the same spread as metal skis and that guarantee provisions are similar.

Source: *Skiing International Yearbook 1967,* pp. 63–68. Copyright by Ziff-Davis Publishing Co. Reprinted with permission.

APPENDIX B

THE HEAD PRODUCT LINE, 1968

The most important design consideration is you—the type of skier you are and where you ski. That's why your dealer was able to offer you nine different models of Head Skis to choose from. You can be sure the model he helped you select was the optimum—for you.

Standard—The Most Forgiving Ski. For beginners of average size and athletic ability up to intermediates learning stem christies. Also for the better, occasional skier who prefers an easy-going, lively light-weight ski that practically turns for him.

The *Standard* is medium soft in flex overall for easy turning and responsiveness. Engineered side camber and relative overall width contribute to ease and slow-speed stability. Its light weight and torsional rigidity make traversing and other basic maneuvers simple. Thin taper in the tip allows the Standard to cut easily through the heaviest snow, instead of ploughing.

Standard. $115. Thirteen sizes from 140 to 215 cm. Black top, sidewalls and bottom; white engraving.

Master—More of a Challenge. For the skier who has mastered the basic techniques and wants to begin driving the skis and attacking the slope. As lively as the Standard, this is also the ski for the heavier, more athletic beginner who wants more "beef" underfoot.

The *Master* is like the Standard in basic shape but thicker and heavier. The tip radius is longer for extra shock absorption. Slightly stiffer flex overall acts as a heavy-duty shock absorber over bumps.

Master. $135. Nine sizes from 175 to 215 cm. Black top and sidewalls; blue base and engraving.

The Fabulous 360—The Most Versatile Ski. Finest all-around ski ever made—for the skier beginning stem christies on through the expert class. Remarkable for its ease of turning as well as its steadiness and precision, the *360* is the serious skier's ski for attack or enjoyment on the slope, under any condition of snow or terrain.

With its smooth-arcing flex pattern, the 360 has the supple forebody of the other recreational skis, but is slightly stiffer at the tail. Its side camber is similar to that of the *Giant Slalom*. Narrower overall than the Standard or Master. Rubber damping in the lightweight topskin unit makes the 360 a very responsive ski, allowing the expert to control his turns beautifully and set his edges precisely. Tip splay is designed to give easiest entrance through snow and to provide excellent shock absorption, particularly in heavily moguled areas.

The Fabulous 360. $115. Eleven sizes from 170 to 220 cm. Black top and sidewalls; yellow base and engraving.

Slalom—The Hot Dog. For the expert skier who likes to stay in the fall-line, slashing through quick short-radius turns on the steepest, iciest, slopes. The *Slalom* has been totally redesigned this year to fit the special needs of the expert recreational skier, who wants the lightest, fastest-reacting, and best ice-holding ski possible.

Slalom is Head's narrowest ski overall. And, thanks to the lightweight topskin unit and core, it is also one of Head's lightest skis. Lightness and narrowness allow for carved or pivoted turns, reflex-fast changes in direction. Special engineered side camber and relative softness at the thin waist give the ultimate in "feel" and control on ice. Neoprene rubber gives the damping and torque necessary for a top-performance ice ski.

Slalom. $160. Five sizes from 190 to 210 cm. Black top and sidewalls. Racing red base and engraving.

Downhill—Bomb! Widest and heaviest Head ski, the *Downhill* is for the advanced skier—recreational or competitor—who wants to blast straight down the slope. It offers the ultimate in high-speed performance, tracking ability, and stability over bumps and moguls.

The long tip splay and supple forebody is the secret of the Downhill's exceptional speed advantage. It virtually planes over the surface of the slope. With its firm mid-section and tail acting like the rudder of a hydroplane, the Downhill affords the skier utmost control coupled with great turning ability at slower speeds. Heavy duty topskin unit and added rubber damping contribute to the stability and high-speed "quietness" of the Downhill. This is the elite international-class racing ski, and experts have found it an excellent powder ski as well.

Downhill. $175. Seven sizes from 195 to 225 cm. Black top and sidewalls. Yellow base and engraving.

Giant Slalom—Grace Plus Speed. The *"GS"* incorporates the best features of the Downhill and Slalom models. It offers the expert skier—recreational and/or competitor—the optimum in stable all-out speed skiing, combined with precise carving and holding ability in high-speed turns. It is another favorite on the international racing circuit.

The *Giant Slalom's* ability and precision come from a unique combination of sidecut and relatively stiff flex. The GS is similar to the 360 in overall dimensions, but has a stiffer flex pattern than the 360, particularly underfoot. This gives the GS the versatility of the 360 but with greater control at high speeds. Tip splay is designed for maximum shock absorption and easy riding.

Giant Slalom. $165. Nine sizes from 175 to 215 cm. Black top and sidewalls. Yellow base and engraving.

Youngster's Competition—Junior Hot Dog. Carrying the Giant Slalom engraving, this ski is designed for expert youngsters who want, and can handle, a faster, more demanding ski than the small size Standard. Similar in cut and performance characteristics to the Giant Slalom, but without the GS's neoprene damping, to provide the junior racer with easier turning ability.

Youngster's Competition. $120. Two sizes, 160 and 170 cm. Black top and sidewalls; yellow bottom and engraving.

Shortski—Fun without Effort. Not just a sawed-off Standard, but a totally different ski with totally different proportions. Very wide for its length, quite stiff overall, the *Shortski* is the only ski of its kind with an engineered side camber. Ideal for quick learning of the fundamentals of skiing. Also for the older or more casual skier who enjoys being on the slopes and wants the easiest-possible tracking and turning ski every built.

Shortski. $115. Four sizes from 150 to 190 cm. Black top, sidewalls and bottom. White engraving.

Deep Powder—Sheer Buoyancy on the Slopes. Super soft flexibility and buggy-whip suppleness allow this specialized ski to float in powder, while maintaining easy turning plus full control and tracking ability on packed slopes.

The *Deep Powder* is very wide and soft overall, with a "hinge-like" effect in the forebody that enables it to glide through the deepest powder.

Deep Powder. $115. Five sizes from 195 to 215 cm. Black top, sidewalls and bottom. White engraving.

Source: Head's *Ski Handbook,* 1968.

EXHIBIT 1

A. Consolidated Balance Sheet

	As of April 29, 1967	*As of April 30, 1966*	*As of April 24, 1965*
Assets			
Current assets			
Cash	$ 263,896	$ 233,330	$ 162,646
Short-term commercial paper receivable	1,200,000	800,000	1,200,000
Notes and accounts receivable—less reserve	242,632	174,127	334,503
Inventories—valued at lower of cost or market	3,102,069	3,522,235	2,815,042
Prepayment and miscellaneous receivables	402,879	223,864	207,279
Total current assets	5,211,476	4,953,556	4,719,470
Fixed assets, at cost			
Buildings—pledged under mortgage	1,010,149	1,012,085	1,014,738
Machinery and equipment	1,540,707	1,059,274	847,974
Other	715,809	213,692	147,336
	3,265,945	2,285,051	2,010,048
Less accumulated depreciation	1,123,203	892,153	822,255
Total fixed assets	2,142,742	1,392,898	1,187,793
Other assets			
Unamortized bond discount and expenses	252,004	263,564	277,636
Cash surrender value of life insurance	133,568	120,589	103,117
Other	70,194	22,364	28,583
Total other assets	455,766	406,517	409,336
Total assets	$7,809,984	$6,752,971	$6,316,599
Liabilities and Stockholders' Equity			
Current liabilities			
Accounts payable	$ 829,826	$ 299,040	$ 521,031
Current portion of long-term debt	23,100	21,000	20,600
Accrued expenses	549,720	413,865	451,062
Income taxes payable	333,514	299,452	39,102
Other	51,120	91,271	94,899
Total current liabilities	1,787,280	1,124,628	1,126,694
Long-term debt			
Mortgage on building (5¾) payable to 1978	331,115	376,036	396,646
Convertible subordinated debentures	2,125,000	2,125,000	2,125,000
		2,501,036	2,521,646
Less current portion		21,000	20,600
Total long-term debt	2,456,115	2,480,036	2,501,046
Commitments and Contingent Liabilities/ Stockholders' Equity			
Common stock—par value 50¢ per share (authorized 2,000,000 shares; outstanding 1966, 915,202 shares; 1965, 882,840 shares adjusted for 2-for-1 stock split-up effective September 15, 1965)	459,401	457,601	220,710
Paid-in capital	1,679,700	1,679,700	1,820,323
Retained earnings	1,412,488	1,011,006	647,826
Total stockholders' equity	3,566,589	3,148,307	2,688,859
Total liabilities and stockholders' equity	$7,809,984	$6,752,971	$6,316,599

EXHIBIT 1 *(concluded)*

B. Consolidated Statement of Earnings

	52 Weeks Ended April 29, 1967	*53 Weeks Ended* April 30, 1966*	*52 Weeks Ended* April 24, 1965*	*52 Weeks Ended* April 25, 1964*
Net sales	$11,048,072	$9,080,223	$8,600,392	$6,018,779
Cost of sales	7,213,188	6,357,169	5,799,868	4,033,576
Gross profit	3,834,884	2,723,054	2,800,524	1,985,203
Expenses				
Selling, administrative, and general	2,756,939	2,029,531	1,697,659	1,169,392
Research and engineering	327,857	239,851	303,884	102,358
Total expenses	3,084,796	2,269,382	2,001,543	1,271,750
Income before income taxes and nonrecurring charges	750,088	453,672	798,981	713,453
Federal and state income taxes	348,606	221,034	392,515	367,542
Income before nonrecurring charges	401,482	232,638	406,466	345,911
Nonrecurring debt expense—after giving effect to income taxes			63,678	
Net earnings	401,482	232,638	342,788	345,911
Net earnings as restated	401,482	264,389	393,713	376,788
Earnings per share before nonrecurring charges	.44	.26	.51	.40
Earnings per share after nonrecurring charges	.44	.26	.43	.40
Earnings per share as restated		.29	.49	.48

Note: Earnings per share are based on average shares outstanding of 904,237 in 1966 and 801,196 in 1965 after giving effect to the 2-for-1 stock split-up effective September 15, 1965, and the 3-for-1 stock split on July 7, 1964.

*Earnings restated April 29, 1967 to give effect to an adjustment in the lives of depreciable assets for federal income tax purposes.

C. Summary of Financial Data

	52 Weeks Ended April 29, 1967	*53 Weeks Ended April 30, 1966*	*52 Weeks Ended April 24, 1965*	*52 Weeks Ended April 25, 1964*	*52 Weeks Ended April 27, 1963*
Net sales	$11,048,072	$90,080,223	$8,600,392	$6,018,779	$4,124,445
Net earnings	401,482	264,389	393,713	376,788	191,511
Expenditures for plant and equipment	1,027,854	304,102	558,865	513,130	272,154
Depreciation	249,961	238,161	211,683	132,497	79,719
Working capital	3,424,196	3,828,928	3,542,857	1,525,015	654,676
Plant and equipment and other assets, net	2,598,508	1,799,415	1,745,839	1,187,246	701,875
Long-term debt	2,456,115	2,480,036	2,501,046	1,176,647	287,245
Shareholders' equity	3,566,589	3,148,307	2,787,650	1,535,614	1,069,306
Earnings per share	.44	.29	.49	.48	.25
Average shares outstanding	916,542	904,237	801,196	777,600	777,600

Note: Average shares outstanding reflect the 2-for-1 stock split-up effective September 15, 1965, and 3-for-1 stock split on July 7, 1964. Statistical data for the years 1963 to 1966, inclusive, have been adjusted to reflect retroactive adjustments.

Source: Company records

EXHIBIT 2
1966 SKI IMPORTS BY COUNTRY OF ORIGIN

	Number of Pairs	Increase (Decrease) from 1965	Value ($000s)	Average Value per Pair ($)* 1966	1965
Japan†	529,732	(89,632)	$3,626	7	6
Austria	72,536	(20,872)	1,512	21	21
West Germany	44,736	9,959	1,010	23	18
Yugoslavia	22,540	5,122	255	11	11
Finland	10,184	5,411	98	10	9
Italy	7,494	351	196	26	14
Canada	7,091	6,350	150	21	23
France	5,257	2,828	265	50	49
Switzerland	2,835	1,155	124	44	39
Sweden	2,767	1,131	22	8	9
Australia	2,307	2,307	114	49	
Norway	1,125	(698)	18	16	6
Belgium	129	129	6	49	

*F.o.b. plant price: does not include charges for shipping, handling, tariff (16⅔%), excise tax, or profit for trading company or wholesaler.

†More than half the Japanese imports were thought to be children's skis, which helps explain the low average pair value.

Source: *Ski Business*, May-June 1967, p. 31.

EXHIBIT 3
NUMBER OF HEAD DEALERS

	On January 1	Newly Franchised	Terminated or Not Renewed	At Year End
1967	900*	30	n.a.	—
1966	727*	n.a.	n.a.	900
1965	670	96	39	727
1964	560	167	57	670
1963	454	136	30	560
1962	390	105	41	454

Note: In addition the franchised dealers had approximately 300 branches that are not included in the above figures.

*Estimated

Source: Company records

EXHIBIT 4
HEAD ORGANIZATION CHART, JUNE 1967

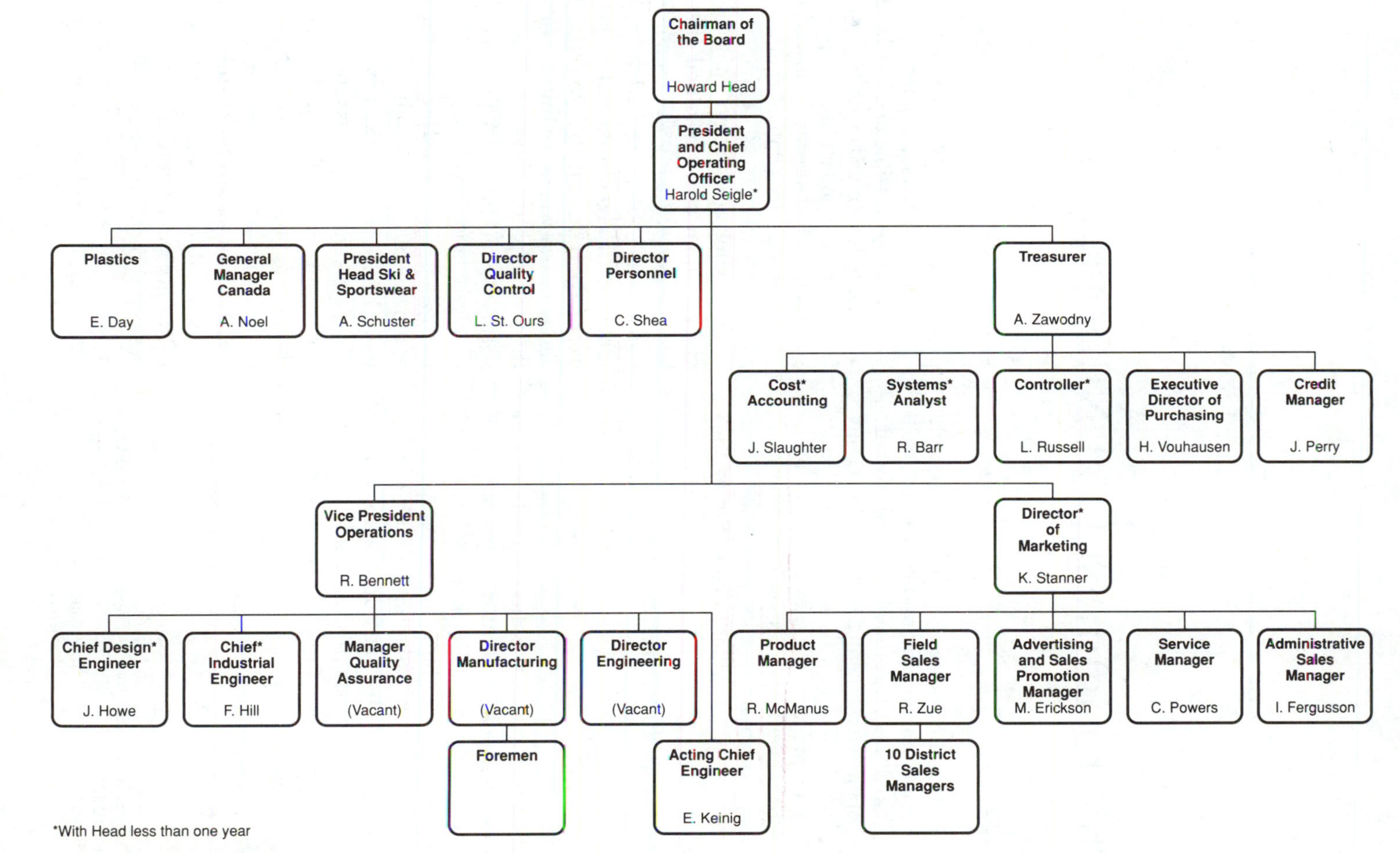

*With Head less than one year

Source: Company records.

Phil Knight: CEO at NIKE (1983)

> I have always felt that if we had the right product at the most economical cost, we'll figure out a way to sell it. Everybody talks about our marketing, and it has been good. But it's been good because we've had a good product with enough margin for the right marketing expense. And it's all worked because of the people we've had.
>
> Phil Knight—Spring 1983

THE FIRST 20 YEARS

Introduction

In 1962, during his final semester at Stanford Business School, Phil Knight wrote a term paper about a business opportunity to create a better track shoe. Knight had been a track star himself as an undergraduate at the University of Oregon in Eugene, where he had run a 4:13 mile on coach Bill Bowerman's track team.

In spring 1983 he reflected on the term paper and the origins of his business idea:

> Adidas shoes were beginning to dominate the U.S. market, and it didn't make any sense, because West Germany was not the place to put shoe machinery. I thought it might be possible to take over the market with low-priced, but high-quality and smartly merchandised imports from Japan, as had already happened with cameras and other optical equipment.

Following graduation in 1962, Knight visited Japan and presented himself as a shoe importer, using the name "Blue Ribbon Sports" (BRS), to Onitsuka, the manufacturer of Tiger brand shoes. He received exclusive rights for BRS to distribute Tiger shoes in the western United States. When the first 50 pairs arrived in 1964 Knight and coach Bowerman each invested $500 and officially launched BRS.

In its early years, BRS was primarily a company of athletes selling to other athletes. Phil Knight worked as a CPA, later as a business school professor, not turning his full attention to BRS until 1969. By then, the product had improved, thanks to Bowerman's design changes, and the company was building a strong brand name among serious athletes. According to Knight, BRS's growing popularity resulted in "reverse leverage": order-rich and cash-poor!

By 1972 sales were $2 million, and Onitsuka decided it wanted to do its own

Harvard Business School case 390–038.

U.S. distribution. Onitsuka offered to buy 51 percent of BRS and threatened to end all supplies if the company refused.

Knight and his colleagues scrambled for alternatives. Armed with their own design, they persuaded Japan's sixth largest trading company, Nissho Iwai, to find the manufacturing sources *and* to provide financing and export/import services to BRS. The new shoes were called NIKE (a name Jeff Johnson, NIKE's first full-time employee said, appeared to him in a dream) and bore the "swoosh" logo (created by a now-famous graduate design student for $35). Knight recalled:

> There have been some real triumphs along the way. I can remember in 1976. . .we'd never had a guy make the Olympic team in NIKE shoes and thought we had a good chance in the Olympics trials down in Eugene. In the first event, we were 1, 2, 3, and I just went berserk!! While you can feel good about the financial performance and things like that, moments of elation like the race in Eugene are real treasures.

Knight felt that NIKE morale was aided by the product. "There's a feeling of 'We did it!' when you see the product on the feet of someone crossing the finish line on TV." That tie to the values and ideals of sports was fundamental at NIKE.

Despite the focus on product excellence, the company remained aware it was a business. Knight remarked:

> Profit is like the score in a dual track meet. It's the way you decide if you've won or lost. But how you get there—that is through your values, the training, the trying to take every step better than anybody else. We'd like to be the biggest and best in our business in the world. And we're a growth company, not 15 percent but 30 percent or more. Sure, we could slow down our growth, tighten up, and pay some dividends—but that's not who we are, not who we intend to become.

Bob Woodell, who had joined Knight in 1967, added:

> It's easy to get caught up in getting shoes on eight zillion athletes in the next Olympics or whatever. But profit is how this game is scored. We play this game in good part for the competition of it, not just to have more money or so the stock will be worth more. We'd really like to believe that the young whippersnappers from Oregon, who everybody thinks are country bumpkins, can be best in the world.

NIKE went public in late 1980. By 1982 every world record in men's track from the 800 meters to the marathon had been set by athletes wearing NIKE shoes. The product line now included shoes for the not-so-serious athlete and athletic clothes. Sales had risen to $694 million by year-end 1982, from $2 million 10 years before, and net earnings had grown from $60,000 to $49 million over the same period (see Exhibit 1 for financial details). NIKE had displaced Adidas as the dominant force in the United States.

The Athletic Footwear and Apparel Industry

Until the late 1960s, the U.S. athletic footwear market was divided between the ubiquitous canvas sneaker and a small market (approximately 10 percent) of specialized performance shoes for sports such as football, soccer, and track. These latter shoes were primarily imported. Athletic clothes were dominated by generic grey "sweats" used by all except more serious sportspeople.

In the 1970s came the revolution: America discovered jogging, and health and fitness in general became national obsessions, particularly for the younger and more affluent. By 1982, according to industry experts, nearly 35 million people ran frequently, and half the population was doing some form of exercise—most wearing a new generation of sports shoes and clothing designed to aid performance and prevent injury. A lighter running shoe or a sleeker speed-skating suit could cut important 10ths of a second from the time of a world-class competitive athlete. For the average runner, a shoe's proper cushioning and support were important to reducing injury to feet, shins, and knees.

Two other factors fueled the dramatic change in this industry: comfort and style. One industry observer commented:

> Running was never the lifeblood of running shoe sales. Comfort was. And anyone who tried on a running shoe was reluctant to step back into a less comfortable conventional shoe. No wonder women want to walk to work with high heels under their arms and running shoes on their feet.

The athletic look soon became socially acceptable, indeed fashionable, for a wide range of activities. Many "followers" began to purchase particular brands in imitation of star athletes or movie stars—or high school opinion leaders.

Comfort and appearance formed the basis for the "ath-leisure" segment of the market, thought to be many times larger than the authentic, participation-based segment. Products sold to "ath-leisure" consumers were designed with color, styling, and general comfort as the primary criteria. Although they resembled "authentic" products, they were not necessarily for actual participation in many sports.

The overall branded athletic footwear market in the United States grew from about $800 million in 1978 to about $1.9 billion in 1982. This represented about half of the total athletic shoe dollar volume (the other half consisted of cheap, unbranded shoes from dozens of sources) and 15 percent of all footwear sales. Similarly, the active-wear apparel market grew from around $3 billion in 1977 to $6 billion in 1982, which represented less than 10 percent of the total apparel market.

As the market took off in the mid-1970s, performance shoe companies, rather than the sneaker makers, met demand. Rapid innovation flourished as the companies sought to develop shoes that the top athletes would wear and that influential trade sources, such as *Runner's World*, would rate highly. As one observer explained: "In the emerging market for an unfamiliar product, consumers relied on a brand name, established by the implicit or explicit endorsement of an athlete or by the ratings. And later, as the shoes became fashionable, that brand name again sold the shoes." Athletes and sporting event organizers discovered that the shoe companies were willing to pay for visibility, and "promotion" (as it was called) became a lucrative—or expensive, depending upon your side of the fence—proposition.

Competitors differed most strikingly in their product lines. One issue was products to be offered in a market consisting of sport-based submarkets, including running, basketball, racquet (tennis and squash), and field (such as baseball, football, and soccer); as well as children's and "leisure." A second issue was price, with a range from the $20 to $30 ath-leisure shoe to the $60 to $100 sport-specific competitive shoe. Along these dimensions, some competitors offered a full line, while others were more specialized. Competitors also made different sourcing decisions—from self-manufacture in domestic plants to purchase from contract factories in the Far East. (For more detail, see Exhibit 2.)

The Competition

In 1982 NIKE dominated the branded athletic shoe market with an estimated 30 percent market share; Adidas followed with 19 percent, Converse (9 percent), Puma (7 percent), and Keds (7 percent). Adidas and Puma were West German companies focusing on more technically sophisticated shoes for specialty sports and performance-conscious athletes. Adidas was the worldwide leader in athletic footwear and apparel with $2 billion in sales in 1982—40 percent came from apparel.

A growing number of *specialty companies* also were targeting specific market segments. New Balance, originally aimed at runners, grew from $1.6 million in 1976 to $50 million in 1982 as it broadened its line to include basketball, tennis, and leisure shoes, as well as athletic apparel. The company manufactured in the United States and initially sold to specialty running stores, later expanding to top department stores. Other specialty names were Brooks ($16 million) for running shoes, and Etonic ($37 million) for golf and tennis shoes (acquired by Colgate-Palmolive in 1976).

Finally, several older *sneaker companies* moved to participate in the running/exercise boom. Converse was acquired by Allied Chemical in 1976 and was again sold to managers and investors in 1982 (sales reached $200 million). Another was Keds ($83 million), which Stride Rite acquired from Uniroyal in 1979.

The Active-Wear Apparel Business.

In the late 1960s Adidas became the first athletic footwear company to exploit its brand name by introducing sports clothing for athletes. By 1982 almost every major competitor had followed suit. Observers agreed that a strong brand awareness was a necessity for a footwear company as it took the plunge into apparel. "Fundamentally," one explained, "the brand name conjured up an authentic, athletic image that appeals to the athlete, for on- and off-track wear, and to the consumer who doesn't actively participate but who identifies with athletes and the active lifestyle."

Apparel, however, was clearly different from shoes: "The apparel world is driven by fashion, not technical performance. It is fast-paced, products die quickly, and there is any army of copiers waiting in the wings to knock off whatever design is hot."

Several footwear companies, New Balance and Etonic among them, supplied only "authentic, performance" clothing. Others, including NIKE and Adidas, sold both performance and ath-leisure items. At the authentic end of the active-wear spectrum, the footwear companies competed with a number of small specialty outfits that focused on high-performance clothing for athletes. At the ath-leisure end of the active-wear spectrum, they competed with the major sportwear houses, including Levi Strauss, Izod La Coste, and Merona, as well as the hundreds of smaller sportswear firms that were aggressively developing active-wear lines.

NIKE Strategy

Although NIKE continued to compete primarily in the branded athletic footwear business, by 1982 sales of other items had risen to 16 percent, from 3 percent in 1978.

The footwear product line strategy accommodated expanding athletic sports and ath-leisure sales. Based on the original racing shoe, NIKE exploited its design capabilities, marketing channels, and its name recognition in four directions:

1. To other *sports:* soccer, football, tennis, etc.
2. To other *users:* joggers, nonathletes, children.
3. To other *features:* greater specialization of sole, lacing, and external materials for different individuals' comfort.
4. To other *products:* leisure shoes, apparel.

From 1972 to 1982, NIKE's product line grew from 13 to 156 basic models or, with color and material variations, to 270 separate products (see Exhibit 3 for figures from 1978 on). NIKE shoes were offered in a standard array of sizes (each in one width) at suggested retail prices from $15 to $90. About 100 models registered sales of over $1 milliion each in 1982. (Exhibit 4 shows growth in revenues by product grouping.)

NIKE managers viewed the footwear market as a pyramid (Figure 1), with a small peak (serious athletes) and a broad base (the millions of Americans who wore athletic footwear in a casual or "street" way). During the 1970s, the company maintained its strong position at the top of this pyramid. In addition, its presence extended downward to much larger segments—although it continued throughout most of the decade to avoid the low-end mass merchandiser base. Achieving this expansion, managers believed, was due to the strength of the NIKE brand name. And this, they insisted, was based on the company's reputation at the top.

NIKE's marketing activities, therefore, consistently focused on the top of this pyramid. Most, falling under the rubric of "promotion," involved getting NIKE shoes on the feet of visible athletes and NIKE's name associated with sports—Knight's "world-of-foot" policy. NIKE spent about $20 million in 1982 on promotion.

At the same time, NIKE remained active at the grassroots level, sponsoring local

FIGURE 1
THE MARKET PYRAMID

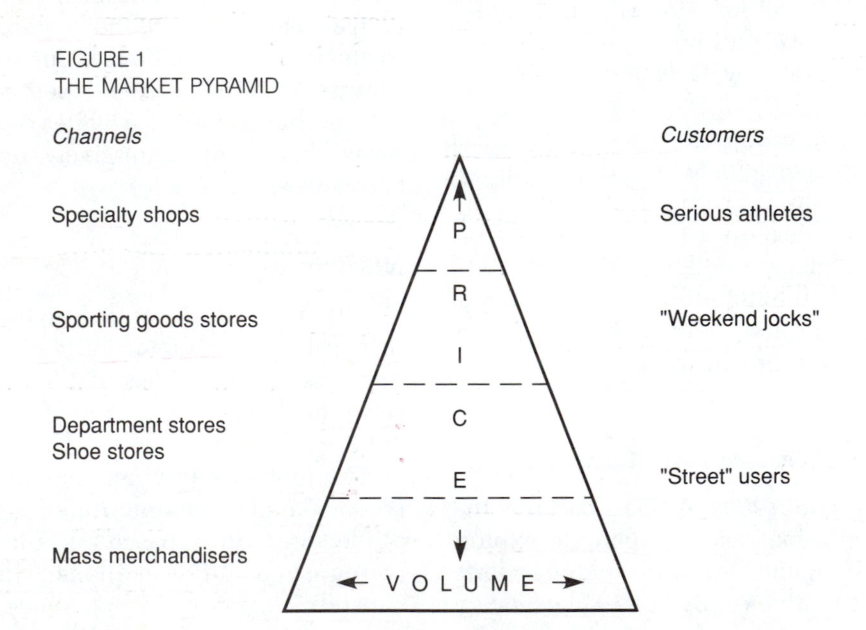

races, presenting clinics for area high school coaches and trainers, and donating shoes to promising local athletes. NIKE employees themselves, typically athletes or former athletes, added credibility to these business efforts.

The company's advertising budget (about $6 million in 1982, with 60% earmarked for co-op programs with dealers) targeted serious participants through specific sports media such as *The Runner* magazine. Ad messages ranged from quite technical to more mood-oriented. Signaling a gradual start to broader advertising, the company sponsored a national TV ad during the New York Marathon in October 1982.

R&D

Bill Bowerman instilled a development ethic from the outset. In 1978 the company outgrew Bowerman's kitchen and opened its R&D center in Exeter, New Hampshire. An early innovation was the patented "Air Sole" (gas under pressure encapsulated within the midsole material to provide superior cushioning).

Exeter had four departments. The *Advanced Concept* department studied NIKE's potential use of new and advanced materials resulting from both in-house research and ideas submitted by inventors, designers, and medical professionals. The *Chemistry and Materials Research* department tested the characteristics and durability of materials used in NIKE footwear. At the *Sport Research Laboratory*, scientists analyzed performance athletic shoe characteristics such as flexibility, cushioning, rearfoot and forefoot control, and energy economy. The lab also analyzed feedback from athletes who participated in extensive field tests of NIKE prototypes. The *Product Development* department used the data, information, and testing results received from the other departments to design and develop new NIKE shoes.

In 1982 NIKE spent $5.7 million (approximately 1 percent of sales) on R&D, which placed it ahead of almost all competitors. One industry observer commented:

> While all the companies are doing some research, NIKE will tend to produce the more revolutionary advances and the others the more evolutionary ones.

Sourcing. Although NIKE established its own manufacturing facilities in Exeter, New Hampshire, in 1974 and in Saco, Maine, in 1978, sourcing shoes in the low-cost Far East was a cornerstone of Knight's original concept. (See Figure 2.) It remained the dominant practice as the company grew through the 1970s (see Exhibit 5), although handling the intricacies of growing trade protectionism and import quotas required ingenuity. What made the approach work, executives believed, was the company's ability to find and develop contract factories, closely monitor them for quality, and forecast production needs effectively.

Once a source was developed, NIKE expatriate technicians continued to work closely with it. "This has been the real key," production executive Ron Nelson explained. "Our people are living there and working with the factories as the product is going down the lines. This is a lot different from accepting or rejecting the product at the end of the line—especially at the end of a three-month pipeline to the United States!"

The heart of NIKE's production scheduling system was the Futures sales program. Started in the early 1970s, it eventually accounted for about 65 percent of

FIGURE 2
NIKE SHOE SOURCES BY COUNTRY, FISCAL 1982
Forty Million Pairs

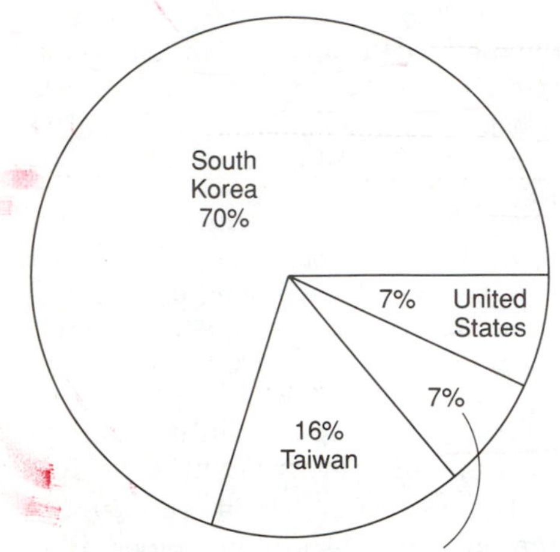

Source: Company records.

footwear sales. Under the program, a retailer ordered five or six months in advance of delivery. In return, the retailer received a 5–7 percent discount and guaranteed delivery during a two-week window around the target date. This was valuable to retailers, who competed in a rapidly growing business notorious for unreliable suppliers. As one said, "You can count on three things in this world—death, taxes, and Futures." And it was valuable for NIKE: retailer shelf space was committed to NIKE, the company received reliable, early information on trends, and most important, 65 percent of production was presold goods.

Sales and Distribution. The basic pattern for NIKE's sales and distribution was also set in the early years. The company used independent sales representatives, paid entirely on commission, to reach an expanding base of accounts. The reps were largely order takers, and NIKE itself performed all order processing, credit, and physical distribution work from three increasingly automated regional warehouses/offices in Oregon, New Hampshire, and Tennessee. The Futures program was the key sales program.

By year-end 1982, the account base had expanded to 9,500 accounts (operating 13,000 outlets) in the four retail channels. (See Exhibit 6.)

Leisure Shoes

In 1980 NIKE made an unsuccessful foray into the nonathletic shoe with the "Air Casual." Even further away from the "real athlete" or "ath-leisure" markets, this strictly casual shoe made no pretense at any possible athletic use and was purely fashion-oriented. This first failure slowed the initial development of this segment, which reached $14 million in sales by 1982.

Apparel

NIKE T-shirts were introduced at the 1972 Olympic trials, but the company did not seriously enter the business until 1978. Its first steps were faltering. As *Fortune* reported, "The company made an almost fatal first step when it aimed the introductory line at lower-middle class consumers instead of its usual, richer buyers." Bob Woodell was assigned to the division in early 1980. With a strong brand name, NIKE's apparel line grew quickly. Sales rose from $2 million in 1979 to an estimated $100 million for 1983, while the number of styles increased from 45 (in 1980) to 270. Observing this growth, one specialty store owner commented, "NIKE apparel is nothing special in and of itself. But it has the NIKE name on it." (For sales and style increases see Exhibit 7.)

NIKE used the same independent rep agencies to sell the line, although the agencies usually hired salespeople who handled only apparel. Sales were concentrated in department and specialty stores, and limited advertising appeared in magazines such as *Seventeen* and *Rolling Stone.*

International

By the early 1980s NIKE was committed to growing internationally. By 1982 international sales, primarily from footwear, were $43 million: Europe—$27 million; Japan—$12 million; Latin America—$3 million; all others—$1 million. These figures were projected to double in 1983.

International sales were made through a local distribution network built in the late 1970s and supported by regional NIKE offices for marketing, and from Asia for sourcing. While sales grew quickly, so did the complexity of managing this global trend and competing in a series of fundamentally different markets.

Financing the Growth

Cash and credit were always problems in the early years of NIKE, when it operated on a nine-month business cycle with only six months financing. To raise the necessary cash, NIKE depended on the goodwill of local bankers. Later, NIKE negotiated interest-bearing payables with its new Japanese "partner," Nissho Iwai. In 1980 NIKE went public with an offering of $11 per share (see Exhibits 8A and 8B).

NIKE Management

The source of NIKE's leadership and spirit was Phil Knight, considered a man with strong passions and an overriding commitment to excellent products. A person unafraid of making decisions when necessary, he also strongly believed in teamwork and maintaining an informal, open atmosphere across the organization. A major strength was his ability to gain commitment at the highest practical level. Remarked a senior manager:

> His style is to give some general directions, not a lot of specifics. You get a general feeling and that's what you go out and try to do. For example, I've been working on a contract with an athlete. Knight told me, "Don't spend much money, but don't let anybody else sign her." What the hell does he mean by that? It may be impossible, but I'll try to do something of that nature.

Another added:

> One thing Knight has taught us is that you can always do something better. He's not a stroker, doesn't let you gloat on a success. "Not bad!" is a supreme accolade. Perhaps that's where we avoid some of the phoniness found in so many places.

Of his role in the organization, Knight said:

> When I'm at what I consider my best, I am thinking in conceptual terms—where we want to be, how we are going to get there. Then I'll go out and spend some time in the area I've been thinking about and really probe in depth. Actually, this is what I ought to be doing. It's a constant fight to avoid getting overwhelmed by daily operating issues and ceremonial duties.

The values of competition, excellence, individual effort, team commitment, and a never-ending pursuit of improvement could be traced to Knight and his core management's participation in Bill Bowerman's track team at the University of Oregon. (Knight's celebration of Bowerman's contribution to the spirit of NIKE was demonstrated in a company advertisement. See Exhibit 9.)

Knight often recalled Bowerman's influence in "tattooing" values into his track team:

> You can't make a silk purse out of a sow's ear. But take an athlete with some talent, and with motivation and desire, he can do much more than a super talent who sits on his ass.

In the early years at NIKE, Knight hired "simply good people," who were expected to do everything and moved rapidly from one position to another to bring their individual skills to a particular problem. This eventually became basic management philosophy. According to Knight:

> The idea that the brains are all at the top of an organization is really kind of silly. And nobody at the top ever does anything—it's the folk down the line that make it work. I learned that early. I had a great concept about bringing in shoes from Japan to compete with the German shoes, but I wouldn't have gotten far with it if I hadn't bumped into Jeff Johnson. He really made it work. And Jeff in turn had to rely on other people. I have a lot of respect for how we did that, and I guess that's the way this company has always worked.

In the early 1980s the company modified its functional organization with a product-line unit. Apparel and International were assigned to separate units, and the U.S. domestic footwear marketing operation was split into four product lines (see Exhibit 10). The organization remained fluid enough, however, to respond to significant market changes or special events; for example, a "marketing group" was set up to prepare for the 1984 Los Angeles Olympics.

A shortage of talented managers led to further periodic organizational changes. The promotions function, for example, was decentralized to product lines in early 1982, only to be recentralized nine months later. Knight explained: "In an organization our size, the structure we choose clearly depends on the people we have to work with. . . . But after a while we began to see certain benefits in the very fact of moving. People developed a broader understanding, and that's helpful."

As the company grew and jobs were divided into smaller, more manageable, and increasingly more specialized chunks, NIKE developed several mechanisms to pull its business tasks together into a reasonably coherent whole.

Meetings, NIKE's principal communication and problem-solving mechanism, occurred at all organizational levels and ranged from informal conversations to formal product-line reviews. Most meetings were scheduled in response to needs rather than according to preset cycles; these sessions were open, sprinkled with humor, yet reflected an underlying seriousness of purpose. Managers appeared able to discuss issues along multiple dimensions, and several often took the lead in moving a session forward. "We don't invite the organization chart to a meeting," Bob Woodell said. "We invite people who can contribute to the issue."

For executive decision making three "concentric" circles radiated from Knight. Knight had worked a long time and formed very close relationships with several of his managers—Woodell, Strasser, and Hayes, in particular (the group was known as the "Gang of Four") (see Exhibit 11). Knight typically talked with his closest associates every couple of days. As Woodell described it:

> We go back a ways, and he is comfortable with us. We're real different, but have worked together long enough that

> we understand each other's strengths, can communicate reasonably quickly, have all done a lot of the jobs in the company.
>
> Knight's a difficult person to get to know, and few are close to him. With most people he avoids conflict and confrontation. But with Strasser, Hayes, and me, he'll absolutely seek it out.
>
> One day, Phil called me up and was just whaling on me for something in distribution—a small part of my job. Finally, I said, "Knight, so and so are integrally involved in this problem, they're the ones who can do something about it. Why the hell are you calling and beating on me?"
>
> He said, "Because they're no fun to give s--- to and you are." He didn't want to talk to those other guys then, he wanted to get it off his chest so he called me and yelled at me about it.

Knight relied on the 11-person executive group (see Exhibit 12), known as "The Friday Club" (due to their regular biweekly Friday meetings), to provide companywide coordination. Twice a year, the group went off-site for a week. "This is about the most enjoyable part of the business for me," Knight reported. Discussions were frank, and executives considered them critical opportunities to get back in touch with what everyone was doing and where the company was headed. Representative issues discussed during one meeting included:

- Production and R&D: ways to improve the new product transition from design to production; R&D priorities; factory capacities and capabilities.
- Control: the excess inventory situation; the growing space requirements in the Beaverton area.
- Marketing: the appropriate advertising/promotion balance (currently 1 to 3 in dollars); the Los Angeles Olympics; the overall marketing focus; the defective product return policy; broadening the sales pyramid (Should retailers such as Sears be added?).
- People: Are the right people in the right slots?

A third "circle" included a larger group of managers involved in more impromptu meetings to respond to issues of the day. Kirk Richardson, who was in charge of the product lines at the time, described a meeting of this group:

> Several of us got real concerned that we were sapping our brand strength with some bonehead decisions and poor control in the sales area. We'd hammer away at this in staff meetings, and finally Woodell and Strasser said, "S———, let's get together and hash this thing out." So we got the relevant people from across the country together off-site for several days. Bob and Rob gave us a little direction, and we helped fill them in on what the problem seemed to be from our perspective. We then worked on it for a couple of days and identified a series of concrete steps we thought we should take. We got back together with Woodell and Strasser, and they poked at us pretty hard and then said, "Let's do it."

Although various individuals, particularly the senior managers, served informally in coordinating roles over the years, the company recently began to define this job formally. For example, a major responsibility of a product-line manager was to coordinate all activities relating to that line—R&D, advertising, promotion, selling, and so forth. "We were tired," one noted, "of screw-ups like the sales reps pushing a shoe that we were phasing out."

Traditionally, NIKE had used formal management reports and systems relatively little, although top management did consider two reports of particular importance.

A daily summary of orders and shipments (in effect, Futures and sales) indicated whether things were going as expected; a comprehensive monthly accounting report detailed the whole operation, enabling trouble spots to be identified.

As the company grew, more and varied management systems were established, typically in response to specific needs. For example, middle managers in the production scheduling, product-line management, product development, and sales areas designed a formal planning tool to help coordinate their increasingly interdependent work.

It was easier to install these systems than to gain full acceptance of, and adherence to, the discipline they imposed. Treasurer Gary Kurtz commented on the introduction of an annual budgeting process in 1978:

> Budgets are part of the evolution of any company, and we're moving toward more bottom-line accountability by product area. There's been a reluctance to get involved initially, but we find it's a matter of education, of trying to get people to the point at which they understand the process and don't just treat it as a bureaucratic procedure. As I try to explain, running a business without good numbers would be like trying to manage a baseball team without the statistics.

While Knight approved the department budgets,[1] formal reviews with the department managers were seldom conducted. Woodell saw the budget as a "scorecard" rather than a planning tool:

> It's a kind of a financial plan with checkpoints so we can look at our results during the year and ask, how are we coming, are we ahead or behind, what's happening? It's not an authorization in advance to go spend money. As each decision comes along, you have to rethink it. We'll either decide to do it or we won't, and that process doesn't have a whole lot to do with budgets.

On the other hand, R&D Director Ned Frederick felt the budget system had brought a greater emphasis in product-line accountability:

> We are more oriented toward managing profits today. We see this mostly from the product-line folks, in a decision not to go with a particular product or to change a product in some way so as to improve the gross profit margin. We've always had a lively dialogue with those folks, but the dialogue didn't used to be about gross profit margins.

Providing Rewards

Most people considered NIKE an exciting place to work, for the company, in effect, asked them to join a team. As Woodell expressed it, "What we like is for people to come in and say, 'I want to contribute.' " In return, management "took care of people," in part with pay, but more with opportunities for growth, responsibility, and contribution. As Knight explained, "It's really not so much salary as it is job responsibility, or the perception of it."

Wages and salaries were considered roughly comparable to those of other local companies. Each employee (including all managers) was reviewed once a year; annual raises were awarded at this time, with managers asked to tie the increase to individual performance. There was no organized incentive compensation program. Inevitably, how such procedures were administered varied, yet there was a general

---

[1] The budgets were prepared by the department managers on the basis of the sales forecast developed by Nelson and Knight.

sense within NIKE that the company was "fair."

Nonetheless, managers who joined NIKE in later years often had to prove themselves before becoming accepted as team members. David Chang, a former architect, joined in 1982 and commented on his settling-in experiences.

> Despite all the seemingly jocular, fraternity house sort of things, there is a great deal of pressure on new people. It's not the pressure of an IBM or ITT, but the pressure of lack of direction, of not having the familiar accoutrements of job descriptions, performance goals, and organization charts to tell you what you're supposed to do. After being at NIKE a couple of weeks, for example, I went into Del's office and said, "Could you give me a little direction as to what I'm supposed to do?" Strasser was there, and he broke into peals of laughter. For months, he would poke his head into my office and ask, "Have you gotten any direction yet?" as if that was the most absurd thing in the world to ask for.
>
> A new person needs to have a strong sense of self, yet not be defensive. You can't be afraid to say "I don't know" or to ask for help. There's a feeling here that nobody knows it all; this is a business where we're writing the book from scratch.

THE THIRD DECADE BEGINS

As the company entered its third decade in 1983, both accolades and caution seemed appropriate. In March the *New York Times* reported:

> In recent months, the cooling of NIKE's domestic shoe sales has pinched profits. On February 24, 1983, NIKE announced that earnings for the third quarter ended February 28 would show the first quarterly decline in the company's history—largely because of "lower than anticipated shoe sales," Gary Kurtz, NIKE's treasurer, said. The surprise statement, which prompted NIKE's over-the-counter per-share bid to drop to $16 from $23 a share in one week, followed a second quarter in which earnings were flat despite a 30 percent increase in revenue.

The sales shortfall sparked debate within NIKE. Some felt that it was a short-term response to the current recession. Others believed it reflected more fundamental issues. Overall, three factors were apparent, however: growth in the core domestic athletic footwear market was slowing; NIKE's rapid growth during the previous decade had stretched systems and people; NIKE, as a publicly traded company, presented the original tightly-knit entrepreneurial group with new challenges.

The following comments typify concerns expressed in spring 1983 and describe some of management's actions in response to the concerns.

Phil Knight

> In January (1983), it became clear that shipments and bookings weren't tracking the way we expected. As we dug into that situation, we realized that we weren't going to get the growth we had expected, and it became clear that over the next few years, the company is going to be a little different animal to manage. For example, as demand slows, we're going to have to manage the operating expenses more tightly.
>
> I met with Woodell, Strasser, and Hayes in February and we realized that the process we had to go through—taking a good, hard look at the whole company and sort of confirming or realigning the directions in which we were headed as a company—would just be more efficient with 4 than with 11.

Starting in March, we went around the company on a series of department audits, which is something we don't do in a normal year. We wanted to review what was going on, trying to check that people were working on the right things, to ask if we were getting the most benefit from major costs such as promo and advertising, to help people focus on some of the immediate problems. For example, in the production area, we realized we had too much capacity and that we had to decide which factories to cut. There were some heated arguments about this, because the issues went beyond dollars and cents. [Ultimately, NIKE's Exeter, New Hampshire, plant was closed and five (of 30) Far Eastern factories were cut.]

Bob Woodell

We dug back into operations. The third-quarter earnings figure was really the first sign that everything we touched didn't turn to gold. Futures were down, and the product line seemed to be getting a bit stale. At the same time, there was a subtle shift in our marketplace. The athletic look wasn't the number one "in" thing anymore; people were starting to dress up a bit more.

We also started to see some cracks in the organization. It seemed to take forever to get a shoe to market, with so much coordination required between product management in Beaverton and development in Exeter. And when a product did come through, it sometimes wasn't the right one.

An example is the bicycling shoe. In general we think in terms of a market pyramid; our approach has to start with the best shoe at the top of the pyramid, and have that drive the sale of less technical shoes lower in the pyramid. Someone decided that we needed to develop the absolute top-of-the-line bicycling shoe, and we spent over a year doing so. But they didn't develop any basic, simple shoes; nor is it clear that the pyramid concept works in the bicycle shoe market. I don't think bicyclists "look up the pyramid" to see what the pros were wearing.

Yet it would be unfair to say that these things caught us completely by surprise. We knew that growth was covering up a multitude of sins. We made a conscious decision not to try to clean most of them up while we were still riding the rocket straight up; but to wait until things started to slow down a bit. And now that's happening.

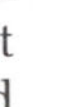

Del Hayes

Our early years were characterized by no structure—period. This was an incredibly effective approach for awhile. Then things changed. The business got so large and so complex that it was impossible for Phil, or any of us, to play the same role. We started to lose our hands-on feel for the business.

A middle manager elaborated on the themes reflected in the foregoing comments:

There was a real dilemma here. Growth had led us to compartmentalize, to define jobs more narrowly. And this had created a kind of tunnel vision.

For instance, about this time, orders came in from our sales force for the summer/fall season. Typically, we try to ship these out by June 1. Well, it turns out one particular shoe was still in Korea and wasn't going to be in the States until June 10, which means it wouldn't have gotten to the stores until the third week in June. This shoe is a basketball shoe, which dealers usually don't place on the shelves until July 1, anyway.

But because it said "ship June 1" on the order, a clerk decided to have the shoes air-freighted from Korea, which cost us an additional $50,000.

The clerk did check with a supervisor, who was busy and who didn't really know what was going on either. This is what happens when people don't see the big picture. Yet, it is this very sense of freedom and autonomy that has made this company what it is. How do we preserve *it* while instituting the structure and systems we need?

While Knight saw considerable agreement about the nature of NIKE's challenges in 1983, he remained uncertain about how those issues should be addressed.

EXHIBIT 1
RECENT NIKE FINANCIAL STATEMENTS
1976–1982 Income Statement and Selected Financial Data, in Thousands of Dollars Except per Share Data

	Fiscal Year Ending May 31							
	1983	*1982*	*1981*	*1980*	*1979*	*1978*	*1977*	*1976*
Net sales	$867,212	$693,582	$457,742	$269,775	$149,830	$71,001	$28,711	$14,100
Cost of sales	589,986	437,885	328,133	196,683	103,466	50,560	20,004	10,036
Selling, general, and administrative	132,400	95,354	61,045	39,917	22,372	11,000	4,963	2,526
Interest expense	28,646	24,538	17,859	9,144	4,569	1,598	637	348
Net income	$ 57,201	$ 49,036	$ 25,955	$ 12,505	$ 9,723	$ 3,856	$ 1,522	$ 600
Average number of common shares	37,158	35,708	34,031	16,140	16,828	17,135	16,843	16,192
Net income per share	$ 1.53	$ 1.37	$ .76	$ .77	$ .58	$ .22	$ .09	$ .04
Return on equity	23%	37%	31%	45%	60%	59%	n.a.	n.a.
Employees at year end		3,600	2,700	2,300	1,600	720	n.a.	n.a.

Note: No dividends have been paid on common shares.
n.a. = not available.
Source: Company annual reports, 10-Ks, and prospectus.

EXHIBIT 1 *(concluded)*
RECENT NIKE FINANCIAL STATEMENTS
Balance Sheet in Millions of Dollars

	As of May 31			
	1983	*1982*	*1981*	*1980*
Assets				
Cash	$ 13	$ 5	$ 2	$ 2
Accounts receivable	151	130	87	64
Inventory	283	203	120	56
Other	0	7	4	2
Current assets	447	345	213	124
Property, plant, and equipment	61	41	24	14
Less accumulated depreciation	(21)	(12)	(8)	(4)
Other	0	1	1	1
Total assets	$487	$375	$230	$135
Liabilities and Stockholders' Equity				
Current portion of long-term debt	$ 2	$ 4	$ 7	$ 4
Notes payable to banks	132	113	61	37
Accounts payable	91	74	42	37
Other	30	42	28	17
Current liabilities	255	233	138	95
Long-term debt	11	9	9	11
Other	1	1	0	0
Total liabilities	267	243	147	106
Common stock at stated value	3	2	2	0
Capital in excess of stated value	77	27	27	0
Retained earnings	161	103	54	29
Stockholders' equity	241	132	83	29
Total liabilities and stockholders' equity	$508	$375	$230	$135

*Includes NIAC—Nissho Iwai American Corp.
Source: Company annual reports and 10-Ks.

EXHIBIT 2
BRANDED ATHLETIC FOOTWEAR SUBMARKETS—1982

	Racquet		*Running*		*Basketball*		*Field*		*Other*
Percent of total	35%		30%		15%		15%		5%
Leading competitors (market share)	NIKE	40%	NIKE	50%	Converse	35%	Puma	30%	Hiking and Walking: small but growing as older people discover walking.
	Adidas	20	New Balance	15	Puma	30	Adidas	20	
	Tretorn	6	Adidas	10	NIKE	20	Hyde	10	
Comments	Common for street use; tennis has not been growing but may in coming years.		Growth of 6 to 8% expected, depending on how long people continue to run, and how many are diverted to home exercise.		Beginning to decline: fewer teens; Title IX* bulge over.		Team sports depend on increase in industrial leagues; soccer will grow but at expense of football.		Leisure: Moderate growth, unless a model captures imagination of young people.

Note: Data based on sales in athletic specialty and sporting goods channels only.
*Title IX, a federal statute, required that educational institutions provide athletic programs and facilities for women similar to those traditionally provided for men.

EXHIBIT 3
NIKE FOOTWEAR PRODUCT LINE

Fiscal Year	*Basic Models*	*Total Products, with Variations*
1978	63	81
1979	90	136
1980	99	150
1981	139	225
1982	156	270
1983 (est.)	185	340

Source: Company records.

EXHIBIT 4
SALES SUMMARY BY PRODUCT LINE
Fiscal Year Ending May 31 – In Millions of Dollars

	1982		*1981*		*1980*		*1979*		*1978*	
	Dollars	*Percent*	*Dollars*	*Percent*	*Dollars*	*Percent*	*Dollars*	*Percent*	*Dollars*	*Percent*
Revenues										
Footwear:										
Running*	$236	34%	$149	33%	$108	40%	$ 80	54%	$39	56%
Court:										
Basketball	144	21	105	23	62	23	28	18	14	20
Racquet sports	59	9	61	13	47	17	26	17	12	17
Cleated (field sports)	14	2	9	2	4	2	2	1	1	1
Emerging:										
Children's	106	15	64	14	21	8	6	4	2	2
Leisure	14	2	8	2	2	1	1	1	1	1
Total footwear	581	84	399	87	245	91	144	96	70	97
Apparel	70	10	33	7	8	3	2	1	1	2
International	43	6	26	6	17	6	4	3	1	1
Total revenues	$694	100%	$458	100%	$270	100%	$150	100%	$71	100%

*About 17 percent of the "Running" category were high-end shoes specifically designed for serious athletic use.
Source: Company annual reports and 10-Ks.

EXHIBIT 5
TYPICAL COST BUILDUP, MODERATE-PRICED NIKE SHOE

Labor	$ 1.10	10%
Materials	5.20	48
Overhead and profit	2.70	25
Factory cost	9.00	83
Shipping and duty	1.50	14
NIAC commission*	.36	3
NIKE cost	10.86	100
NIKE margin	5.87	56
Retailer cost	16.73	
Retailer margin	12.22	58
Retail price	$28.95	

*NIAC—Nissho Iwai American Corp.
Source: Company records.

EXHIBIT 6
SUMMARY OF ACCOUNTS

Type	*Percent of Accounts*	*Percent of Sales*
National accounts*	—	15%
Specialty shops	15%	14
Department stores	27	19
Sporting goods stores	29	26
Shoe stores	29	26
	100%	100%

*Major customers such as J.C. Penney and Footlocker.
Source: Company records.

EXHIBIT 7
NIKE APPAREL DIVISION

Fiscal Year	*Sales $ millions*	*Styles*	*SKUs**
1979	$ 2	n.a.	n.a.
1980	8	45	480
1981	33	115	1,464
1982	70	215	3,272
1983 (est.)	100	270	4,774

*A stockkeeping unit measures the total number of product variations, not only style but color and size.
Source: Company records.

EXHIBIT 8A
NIKE PUBLIC EQUITY OFFERINGS AND MARKET PERFORMANCE

NIKE went public on December 2, 1980, at $11 per share.* In anticipation of a public offering, the company had created two classes of stock: A-voting and B-nonvoting.

Management maintained control of the voting shares, while the class B shares were sold to the public. The class B shareholders did, however, retain the limited right to elect one of the seven members of the board.

The company offered its B shares to the public for a second time on October 14, 1982, at a price of $24.31 per share.

A summary of the equity offerings, and the stock's performance is offered below.

NIKE; Public Offering Summary (Thousands of Shares)
Number of shares outstanding prior to offering: 32,352

	1st Offering	*2nd Offering*
Shares outstanding after offering	35,072	37,272
Class A	30,318	22,532†
Class B	4,754	14,740
Share price at offering	$11.00	$24.31
Shares sold (all Class B)	4,754	3,000
Primary	2,720	2,200
Secondary	2,034	800‡
Funds raised ($ millions)	52.3	72.9
Primary	29.9	53.5
Secondary	22.4	19.4
Company valuation ($ millions)	385.7	906.1
Directors' and officers' percent of shares		
Total	57%	50%
Class A	65%	83%
P.H. Knight's percent of shares		
Total	46%	42%
Class A	53%	69%§

*All data adjusted for 2:1 split January 1983.

†The total number of Class A shares is decreasing as these shares are converted to Class B shares and sold to the public.

‡The sale of secondary shares does not represent a net increase in shares outstanding as existing A shares are converted to B shares and then sold by these shareholders to the public.

§Both the directors'/officers' and Knight's percentage share of the Class A stock is increasing over this period as other (nondirector and nonofficer) Class A shareholders sell their Class A shares.

Source: NIKE prospectus and annual report.

EXHIBIT 8B
NIKE STOCK MARKET PERFORMANCE SUMMARY

	*Price per Share**		*Earnings per Share*†	
Quarter Ending	*High*	*Low*	*High*	*Low*
12/80 offering	$11		13.75	
2/28/81	11.62	8.75	18.6	14.2
5/31/81	11.50	8.50	14.0	10.4
8/31/81	15.50	9.25	7.8	5.8
11/30/81	13.88	8.88	10.8	6.9
2/28/82	15.36	13.50	12.4	10.9
5/31/82	15.25	12.36	11.2	9.1
8/31/82	20.12	14.75	8.7	6.4
11/30/82	27.12	20.00	20.5	15.1
2/28/83	28.00	15.75	28.0	15.8
5/31/83	21.37	15.12	13.7	9.7

*Reflects 2:1 split in January 1983.
†Based on annualized earnings per share for quarterly period stated.

EXHIBIT 9
THE SPIRIT THAT MOVES US

For 24 years at the University of Oregon, he never recruited. And when athletes came to him, he put them to work in sawmills. Cut anyone who couldn't keep up the grades. He knew more people succeed because of mental toughness than physical ability.

He took the U.S. Track and Field team to Munich in '72. And came back complaining the Olympic games aren't conducted for athletes. But for aristocrats and pseudo-aristocrats.

To the A.A.U. and now the Athletics Congress, he remains a thorn in the side. Fighting in the courts for what he calls the emancipation of the athlete.

His literary career has been sporadic at best. But for thousands of Americans he is the writer who convinced them to take to the streets. And pound it out, year after year.

At NIKE, we know him as the renegade inventor. Who made an excuse to his wife so he could skip church and fool around with a waffle iron.

He's the guy on our board of directors who comes prepared to raise hell. Share a laugh. And to never let us forget the real point of the whole thing—to help athletes perform.

Bill Bowerman. Stubborn, demanding. Given to sudden outbursts and moments of magical insight.

We wouldn't be the same without him.

Source: Company records.

EXHIBIT 10
SKETCH OF THE NIKE ORGANIZATION

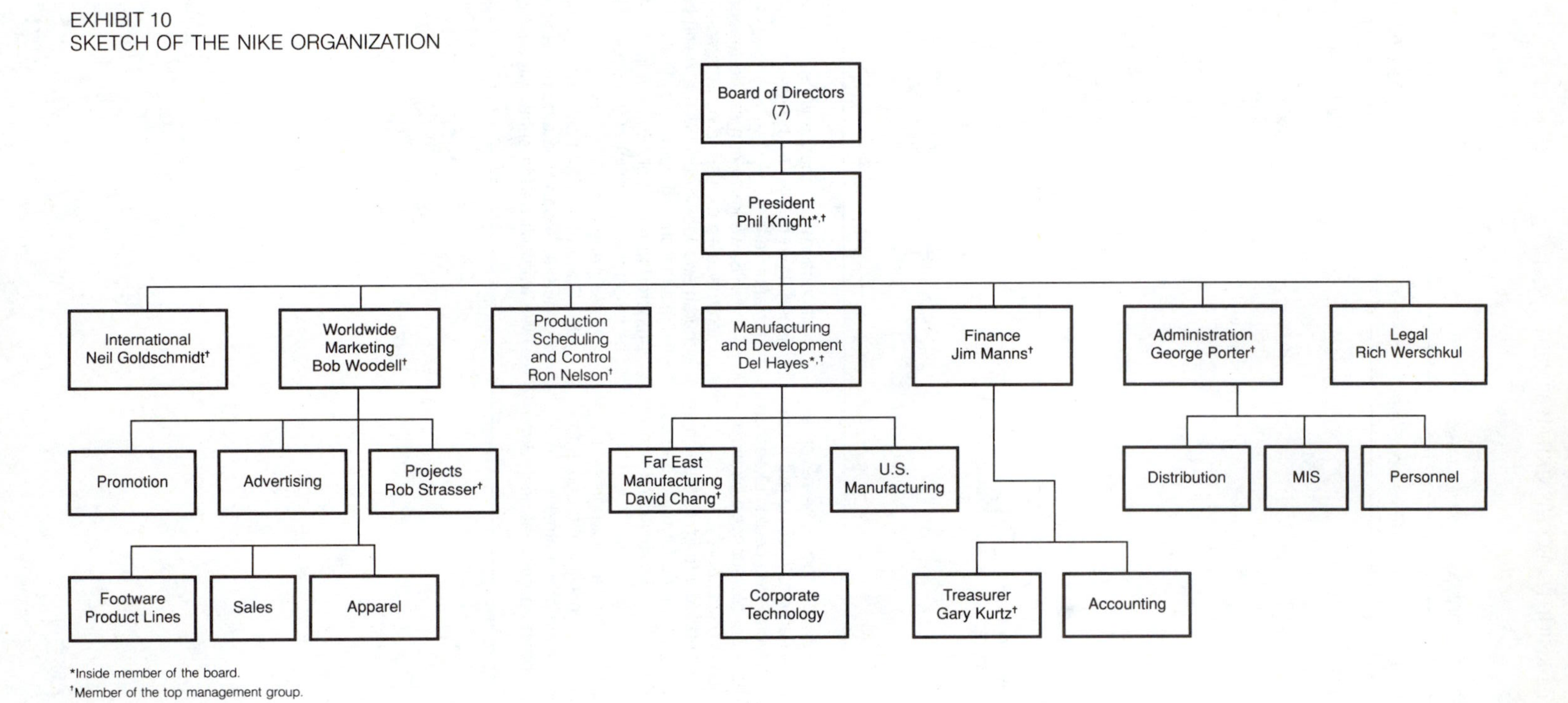

*Inside member of the board.
†Member of the top management group.

Source: Researchers' interpretation.

EXHIBIT 11
THE "GANG OF FOUR"

Phil Knight, 44, was a native of Portland. He believed his greatest strength was as a long-term thinker and planner. He was very competitive. Reflecting on the company's success he said, "Hell, there is no secret. There is just the basic attention to details and doing all the parts of the business right."

Bob Woodell, 38, was a son of Portland too, and attended the Eugene campus where he was a champion long jumper. In a sports accident he broke his back and was permanently paralyzed in his legs. He held every post at NIKE, except legal and accounting. He was a fiercely no-nonsense person and loved to quote another manager: "We like people who ain't afraid to strap on a tin bill and pick s——— with the chickens."

Del Hayes, 47, was a CPA at *Price Waterhouse* where he was previously Knight's boss. He provided the "numbers power" and a detailed appreciation of the manufacturing process.

Rob Strasser, 38, had been a new member of a Portland law firm in 1972 when he was placed on the Blue Ribbon Sports account in their dispute with Tiger Shoes. He joined NIKE in 1976. He described NIKE:

> It's the best American capitalism has to offer, a "no bull———, let's get out and solve the problem" frame of mind.

EXHIBIT 12
NIKE SENIOR MANAGEMENT, 1983

Executive	*Age*	*Joined Company*	*Background*	*Current Responsibilities*
Phil Knight	44	Founder, 1964	MBA, CPA	President and chairman
Bob Woodell	38	1967	College	Vice president and worldwide marketing
Del Hayes	47	1975 (part time from 1971)	CPA	Executive vice president, manufacturing and development
Rob Strasser	38	1976 (association from 1972)	Lawyer	Vice president, marketing projects
Ron Nelson	40	1976	CPA	Production
Rich Werschkul	36	1977	Lawyer	Corporate counsel
Jim Manns	44	1979	CPA, Business	Vice president, finance
Gary Kurtz	36	1979	Banker	Treasurer
David P. C. Chang	52	1981	Architect	Vice president, Far East manufacturing
Neil Goldschmidt	41	1981	Public management	Vice president, international
George Porter	51	1982	CPA, Business	Vice president, administration

Continental Airlines (A)

Shortly after 7 A.M. in January 1984 Frank Lorenzo, chairman of Continental Airlines (CAL), opened a meeting of CAL's top decision makers. The only adornments in the austere Houston conference room were paper cups of lukewarm coffee and the suitcases of the three CAL managers who had arrived on early morning flights from Los Angeles and Honolulu. Indeed, the entire group of six men gathered for the meeting more closely resembled a weary but exhilarated athletic team returning from an out-of-town trip than the prototype top management of a firm with $1 billion in revenues whose tactics and progress were being monitored daily by the national and international media.

Lorenzo launched immediately into the subject of the meeting:

> Even though I was skeptical of the profit potential and strategic value of our South Pacific operations before I was involved with this company, George's proposal to expand our service to the Honolulu-Guam market looks good.
>
> We would need some additional aircraft to do this, and we are stretched a little thin at the moment. But we've done before most of the things we'd have to do to make it successful: I think that we can raise the money, find the right planes and put them in the air. The one new wrinkle is that when we've done this before, we haven't been bankrupt. That fact imposes some constraints, and probably allows for some opportunities that we've got to look at carefully.
>
> I'm particularly concerned that we think about the implications of this proposal for our overall positioning as a business. Will the bankruptcy judge allow us to do it, and how would the proposal affect our ongoing strategy for dealing with the creditors' committees in court? Would it affect what the unions do, both in the courtroom and as they make their case to the public? Is there anything about this kind of move that could be damaging to an increasingly favorable public sentiment about Continental?

HISTORY AND BACKGROUND OF CONTINENTAL AIRLINES

The Continental Airlines of which Frank Lorenzo was chairman was the product of a 1982 merger of Texas International Airlines and "old" Continental, two airlines

Harvard Business School case 385–006.

with different traditions, styles, and positions in the industry. (See Exhibit 1 for a map of the merged routes.)

The "old" Continental was founded in 1934 as Varney Speed Lines. In 1936, Robert Six became the fledgling airline's general manager. Working with a limited route structure and a roster of only 16 employees, Six moved the airline to Denver in 1937 and renamed it Continental, a name that reflected his aspirations for the company. By the mid-1970s, under Six's leadership, Continental had become a medium-sized national carrier with revenues of more than $900 million and a reputation for impeccable service, generous compensation and benefits packages for employees, and high morale.

Throughout the 1970s the "Proud Bird with the Golden Tail" had modest profits. With the passage by Congress of the Airline Deregulation Act in 1978, however, Continental, like many other airlines, found itself floundering in an environment in which all the rules had been rewritten. Before deregulation, the federal government through the Civil Aeronautics Board (CAB) had retained jurisdiction over both airline rates and routes and had generally sought to avoid price competition and entry of new competitors. Airlines had competed not on price but on service and frequency of flights. While not immune to the boom and bust cycle of the industry, Continental had relied on its image as an airline that had focused successfully on providing frequent, full-service cross-country flights. But the company was not prepared to compete on price to attract customers, and with the passage of deregulation was hard pressed to adapt quickly to market demands. Continental's post-deregulation difficulties were increased because it had a linear route system. Delta and many of the new entrants had in place, or were able to create, "hub and spoke" systems in which short-hop flights could feed passengers to a central base for profitable long-haul flights. Continental had neither the equipment nor the experience to adapt its system quickly enough to find a niche in this market. Neither did it have the marketing mass, traffic strength, and resources that helped insulate the large carriers such as American and United against low-cost competition.

In addition, Continental had internal problems. In 1978 Six announced his wish to retire as CEO and his intention to select his successor from among the current top management of the company. This announcement set off fierce competition and feuding among several of the leading candidates for the job. In an attempt to stabilize the organization, Six changed his mind about his decision to name someone inside the company to be CEO and in 1980 named Alvin Feldman, CEO of Frontier Airlines, to the job. Six's decision precipitated a mass exodus of top management at the same time that Continental was beginning to face serious financial stress because of the deregulated environment.

Unlike Continental, Texas International Airlines (TXI) had begun as a regional airline. It functioned in the prederegulation era using "hand-me-down" routes and equipment to feed local traffic into the trunk system dominated by the major national carriers. In 1972 when it was taken over by Frank Lorenzo and Robert Carney, Houston-based TXI was plagued by many of the problems faced by local service carriers: small markets, short hauls, and an uneconomic mix of aircraft had led to the demise of a number of small regional airlines. While TXI, with its outdated fleet, $7 million negative net worth, $20 million working capital deficit, and nickname of "Tree Top Airlines," might not have appeared to be a particularly attractive takeover candidate, it represented for Carney and Lorenzo a good opportunity to build on their experience.

After graduating from Harvard Business School in 1963, both men had taken jobs in New York, Carney in investment banking and Lorenzo at TWA. In 1970 they raised $1.5 million in a small public offering to form Jet Capital, a firm that initially specialized in providing advice and arranging equipment leases for small, regional airlines. Later, they began looking for an airline to buy, an unusual goal in what was then an industry characterized by long-term stability in ownership and management. They first set their sights on troubled, on-strike Mohawk Airlines. When the attempt to take over Mohawk failed, they turned in 1971 to TXI and worked out a plan for Jet Capital to acquire 25 percent of TXI's equity and the majority of the voting rights for $1.15 million. Even after they had arranged the financial transaction to acquire the airline, however, CAB approval of their purchase was delayed because of opposition by Howard Hughes, who hoped to combine TXI with Hughes Air West to form a southern-tier carrier. It was not until September 1972 that Lorenzo as president and Carney as executive vice president gained control of the airline.

The new management immediately began to recruit new personnel and to focus on controlling costs, redeploying aircraft to serve the denser route segments, and petitioning the CAB to be allowed to drop unprofitable service. In 1973 TXI earned $258,000 and in 1974, $317,000. The airline's rebuilding seemed to be successfully underway as they modernized their fleet and began to deliver frequent, reliable service. In 1975, the new management suffered a setback: rather than budge from their position that labor costs had to be lowered and productivity increased in order to improve their competitive position, they took a strike and finished the year with a $4.37 million loss. In 1976, they rebounded and persuaded the CAB to allow TXI to offer off-peak discount "peanuts fares," the first discount fares allowed an interstate carrier in the industry, and an early signal of the change in climate that would ultimately accommodate deregulation.

In 1978 TXI earned $13 million and TXI officials began to look at possibilities for expansion. As Douglas Tansill, a charter director of Jet Capital, and at that time an employee of White Weld, described it:

> Frank was always creative about understanding the financial markets and how to use them. In early 1978 we did a unit offering of subordinated debentures and common stock, a new kind of deal for an airline. This increased Frank's awareness that there was money out there, money that could be used, if he chose, to acquire the undervalued assets that he also saw. He wanted to expand in a way that made sense. This included the possibility of looking for an airline to buy, an option that would allow him to expand his business in a quantum leap by purchasing equipment at a discount and increasing the network of routes that fed into his Houston hub.
>
> National Airlines became the target. At this time there hadn't been a takeover, much less a hostile takeover, in the industry in years. But what Frank proposed made sense, and throughout 1978 and 1979 we did a series of creative financings that allowed TXI to build the war chest.

The TXI attempt to take over National turned into a three-way battle with Eastern and Pan American, a battle Pan Am ultimately won. TXI, however, came away from the takeover attempt $47 million richer as a result of its sale of National stock.[1] The cash generated by the run at National gave Lorenzo and Carney an opportunity to expand and restructure. In the period following the takeover attempt they took three significant initiatives.

In 1980 Lorenzo and Carney established Texas Air Corporation (TAC), a publicly traded holding company with majority ownership held by Jet Capital, to serve as a parent not only of TXI but also of the other enterprises they were considering. Also, in 1980, they founded New York Air, a non-union carrier designed to challenge Eastern on its highly profitable Boston–New York–Washington route. In 1981 they took New York Air public, retaining control by Texas Air of a majority of New York Air's stock. Finally, when it became clear that they were not going to win control of National, they began to search for another airline to provide them with longer routes and larger equipment that would complement TXI's short-hop routes and small planes. By 1981 their leading candidate was Continental, and they began to acquire stock.

Though the logic of merging the two airlines into a hub-and-spoke system with focused strength in Houston and Denver may have been compelling, the battle that ensued was one of the most bitter in the history of the airline industry. Continental employees, many of whom had long tenure with the company, proposed and fought for an employee stock purchase plan that, had it been implemented, would have prevented the TXI takeover. The acrimony generated by the battle was further aggravated when Continental's president, Alvin Feldman, desolate because of the recent death of his wife and because of his inability to stop TXI, committed suicide.

On October 31, 1982, Continental and Texas International consolidated operations, becoming the nation's eighth largest airline and a wholly owned subsidiary of TAC, with Frank Lorenzo as chairman and Robert Carney as chairman of the executive committee (see Exhibit 2).

THE START-UP OF THE "NEW" CONTINENTAL

The new Continental was a financially troubled company from its inception. The combined companies had a long-term debt of $642 million and equity of $142 million. During the year of the CAL–TXI battle, the management of the old Continental had focused on fighting the takeover rather than responding to the company's mounting losses. The new CAL finished 1982 with net losses of $41.8 million and during the first nine months of 1983 lost $161 million. (Exhibit 3 is a summary of selected financial data for CAL. Exhibit 4 is a summary of selected data for TAC.)

In part, Continental's difficulties reflected those of the industry as a whole during this period. Between 1979 and June 30, 1983, the industry had lost $2.2 billion. Several factors had precipitated these losses. Fuel prices had escalated. The downturn in the economy had put a damper on passenger traffic, and rising interest rates had limited airlines' access to the capital markets. The grounding of DC-10 aircraft and the strike and subsequent dismissal of air traffic controllers had limited the flexibility of many airlines to fly the equipment they had to destina-

[1] In 1981, National Airlines took TXI to court, arguing that TXI was liable under Section 16 (b) of the Securities and Exchange Act of 1934 for "short swing profits." The U.S. District Court determined TXI's liability to be $1,149,195 plus interest and cost, a judgment that was upheld on appeal. Texas Air Corporation assume the liability in 1982 and paid it in 1984.

tions they chose on schedules that made sense. Finally, many established carriers were being pushed hard by the new low-cost, low-priced competitors spawned by deregulation. The new competitors, most of which were non-union carriers, enjoyed a significant advantage in labor costs: in the first quarter of 1983 the average annual salary paid to an employee of the major national carriers was $42,000, while the average for an employee of a post-deregulated, start-up domestic carrier was $22,000.

In addition to having to operate in a difficult industry climate, Continental faced a number of problems stemming from its history and place in the industry. One of the reasons the old Continental was a desirable acquisition for TXI was that it allowed TXI access to a second hub, in Denver, with cross-country feeder routes. But CAL's route structure was also an extremely competitive one, in which it was forced to go head-to-head both with major carriers such as American and United and with the new, low-cost carriers. In addition, 60 percent of Continental's traffic was generated by travel agents using computerized reservations systems controlled by American and United and biased in favor of bookings on the owner airline. Finally, the old Continental was constrained by union contracts mandating some of the highest labor costs in the industry.

The issue of labor costs was particularly pressing, and even before TXI's takeover, George Warde, Alvin Feldman's successor, had begun to call for work force concessions. But even before the merger was consummated, Warde, a former president of American Airlines who had been brought in by Six to shore up the company, found the labor issue intractable:

> Sure, everyone could see the principle, the macro need to cut back on costs. But nobody was willing to say, "For the good of the whole, I'll cut my own salary," especially in light of the fact that the old CAL was dead, filled with the superannuated or people waiting to bail out with their golden parachutes. There was no way we were going to be able to get people to agree readily to take cuts for the good of the company. "What company?" and "Why should I?" were the implicit responses.

The new Continental management continued to focus on decreasing labor costs. In 1982, Continental won nearly $100 million in concessions over two years from its pilots, although neither the unionized machinists nor the flight attendants followed suit. In March 1983, 15 percent of the airline's personnel were laid off. During the summer, the headquarters staff was moved from Los Angeles to Houston, which had become the dominant hub of the company. The move, another effort to reduce costs, caused discontent among many of the "old Cal" employees and became a sym-bol of what some labeled the "callous" attitude toward employees of the new management.

Despite this effort to cut labor costs, the airline continued to lose money at an increasingly rapid rate. In July 1983, the company lost $8 million. In August, $17 million. On August 12 the machinists, represented by the International Association of Machinists and Aerospace Workers (IAM) went on strike after Continental refused to agree to a union proposal for a 36 percent wage increase with no work-rule concessions. On the first day of the strike, Continental operated at 85 percent of capacity, and, as the month progressed, returned to full capacity. In the process, CAL management eliminated 800 machinist union jobs by hiring outside contractors, primarily in its flight kitchens and cabin cleaning areas.

During August and September, Continental officials unsuccessfully sought $100 million in contract concessions from the Airline Pilots Association (ALPA) and the Union of Flight Attendants (UFA). On September 14 CAL management announced its intention to implement a new economic plan to restructure labor cost permanently. The $150 million annual cost-reduction plan included requests for cost savings of $30 million from agent, clerical, reservations, and management groups, $20 million from the mechanics, $40 million from the flight attendants, and $60 million from pilots. In return, CAL management proposed that four million shares of CAL stock held by Texas Air be donated to an employee stock ownership plan and that a permanent profit-sharing plan be established. The proposal was turned down by all union representatives, except the TWU (representing several dozen flight dispatchers), which agreed to the plan. In addition, the company's nonunion personnel, the largest employee group, voted overwhelmingly for the plan.

On September 21 Continental president Stephen Wolf resigned. On September 22 the Continental board of directors met to consider the position of the company and reached the conclusion that if CAL were to pay salaries, debt service, pension contributions, and some back payments to vendors, the company would run out of working capital by September 30. (See the Appendix for an example of CAL management's analysis of the situation.)

THE BANKRUPTCY AND ITS AFTERMATH

> There is no halfway procedure. There is no Chapter 5½.
>
> Frank Lorenzo, chairman
> Continental Airlines
> *Business Week*, November 7, 1983

On Saturday, September 24, Continental Airlines filed a petition for reorganization under Chapter 11 of the United States Bankruptcy Code. Citing as the precipitating factors in reaching the decision the deteriorating financial position of the airline and inability to reach agreements with union groups on pay and benefit concessions and work-rule changes, Continental ceased all domestic service. At the same time, TAC issued a statement saying its management was confident that CAL's filing for reorganization would not cause financial difficulties or problems with creditors for TAC or its other subsidiaries. TAC Senior Vice President Robert Snedeker assured the press and financial community that "Texas Air continues to maintain substantial liquidity and significant asset value. The company has always operated and will continue to operate its subsidiaries independently from one another, and, as such, the profitable operations of New York Air, Texas Air's other principal subsidiary, will not be affected."

Throughout the weekend immediately following the bankruptcy filing, CAL's top management cleared the payroll of 8,000 jobs, laying off 65 percent of the work force. At the same time, they unilaterally implemented new wage and work rules for all employees: pilots' salaries were cut from an average of $78,000 to $43,000 for captain and $28,000 for flight officers. All employees, including top management, took at least a 15 percent pay cut and Chairman

Lorenzo decreased his own salary from $257,000 to the $43,000 salary of a senior captain. "It all sounds very neat and tidy," recalled Bruce Hicks, the airline's chief spokesman,

> but it was like a very bad version of *War and Peace*. On Monday morning, there were several dozen employees milling in the lobby of the building waiting to find out if they still had a job and, therefore, would be allowed upstairs to their offices. Because the job cutting was not completed until the wee hours of the morning, a number of people were not notified and only those whose names were on a master list were being allowed past Security into the corporate offices. And even then there were some people inadvertently left off the working list, and that caused some confusion and obviously very tense moments for those people.
>
> It was a very sad time for everybody. It was sad for those who could not come to work and it was sad for those who did when their friends could not.
>
> It was a surrealistic world. We had no carefully thought-out plan for how you run an airline in bankruptcy—no one had ever done it before. How many people and which ones do you need in a marketing department that has to shrink 65 percent? It wasn't a question of did we make mistakes: it was a question of trying to control the magnitude of the mistakes as we wrote and executed the plan simultaneously. We were dealing with a world turned upside down.

Two days after the announcement of the Chapter 11 filing, Continental resumed 27 percent of its flights. Before filing for reorganization CAL had flown to 78 cities in the continental United States, as well as providing service between the United States and Mexico, Venezuela, Hawaii, Australia, New Zealand, and the Far East and Micronesia. In addition to continuing international service throughout the filing process, by September 27 Continental had launched limited service to 25 of the 78 cities previously served. Customers stood in long lines to take advantage of Continental's $49 "welcome back fares," good through September 30. "We knew that to keep the airline going we *had* to get people on our planes," recalled Doug Birdsall, vice president of market planning. "That meant we had to price it just right. How did we do it during that hectic time? Not scientifically, I can tell you that: rather, by excellent instinct informed by good experience."

On October 1, four days after Continental resumed flying, the unionized pilots and flight attendants went on strike over the wage cuts and work rules. Both management and union employees recognized that wage reductions and labor cost constituted the most critical issue facing the new Continental. Previously, labor costs accounted for 35 percent of Continental's operating expenses; they fell to 20 percent after the bankruptcy filing and promulgation of new work rules. Recognizing that the early days of resumed service would be crucial ones, the pilots' and flight attendants' unions picketed Continental's gates in most major airports. In addition, the ALPA approved an assessment of its members to cover extraordinary benefits for striking CAL pilots for an unlimited period: a striking captain received $45,000 a year, $2,000 more than a working CAL captain. Continental's management filled its employee ranks by attracting many of the union members who were willing to work on the new wage scale and began to hire flight attendants, many of whom had been laid off by other airlines in the troubled industry.

Following the filing, Continental gradually restored service. During October and November, the CAL system expanded to 50 percent of prepetition capacity. By mid-January 1984, the airline was operating at 56 percent, and management was projecting 75 percent by March 1 and 90 percent by mid-summer (see Exhibit 5 for the 1984 CAL route system). During the rebuilding phase, Continental officials staked out the airline's niche as a carrier with strong presence in the Houston and Denver hubs, providing low-cost, high-frequency, full-service flights.

The airline's special promotional fares continued through mid-October. Continental next offered simplified peak and off-peak coach fares that ranged from 30 to 70 percent less than the standard coach fares of other airlines. To be able to hold this position, Continental had not only to lower labor costs, but to meet a break-even load factor of 65 percent. From November 1983 through January 1984, Continental had the highest monthly load factors of any of the major airlines, with 63.1 percent in November, 66.8 percent in December, and 65.1 percent in January.

In addition to operating and expanding the new Continental, management was heavily involved in legal proceedings. Shortly after filing the reorganization petitions, Continental officials sought the Bankruptcy Court's approval to reject its union and other employee-related executory contracts. The ALPA, UFA, and IAM, representing the three largest groups of Continental's unionized employees, filed a motion to dismiss the company's bankruptcy petition. During December, U.S. bankruptcy Judge R. F. Wheless conducted hearings that included eight days of testimony by company and union officials. Characterizing Continental's Chapter 11 petition as the "fruit of the poisonous tree," union lawyers argued that the airline, with more than $200 million in total current assets, had been solvent at the time of the petition and that Continental had filed solely and calculatedly to get rid of its collective bargaining agreements. Continental's lawyers argued, on the other hand, that Continental, with a negative net worth of $51.4 million when it filed, was obviously insolvent and that, should the court rule that it had to honor its labor contracts, Continental would be forced to liquidate. Testifying before the judge, Lorenzo described the bankruptcy proceedings as "an admission of failure, an admission that we had not been able to turn this company around. . . . Continental filed for Chapter 11 because we had reached the end of the line, the last resort."

The court hearings concluded on January 3. On January 17 Judge Wheless denied the union's motion to dismiss Continental's Chapter 11 petition. Explicitly dismissing the union's argument that Continental's filing was engineered over time by management as the means by which it could reject union contracts, Wheless concluded that "neither the sole nor the primary purpose of filing was to reject these executory contracts." Instead, he suggested, Continental filed for reorganization under Chapter 11 "for the purpose of attempting to keep the company alive and functioning. . . . The primary purpose in filing these proceedings was to keep the airline operating so as to best utilize its going-concern value. The management of the company owed this obligation to its shareholders and to its creditors." In the opinion, Judge Wheless also agreed to begin hearing the airline's motion to be allowed to dissolve its union contracts.

THE MANAGEMENT OF CONTINENTAL AIRLINES

The bankruptcy and subsequent reemergence of Continental during the fall and winter of 1983 were subjects of widespread interest and controversy. At the center of much of the media and public attention was Continental's chairman, Frank Lorenzo, who seemed to have become a lightning rod for many of the most intense feelings and beliefs evoked by Continental's actions. Continental's pilots picketed at airports and carried posters depicting Lorenzo with a Hitler mustache or behind bars, with a caption that read "Wanted: For the Murder of Continental Airlines." In describing and analyzing events at Continental, the press also often focused on Lorenzo. "Why is Lee Iacocca the most popular business man in America and Frank Lorenzo the most reviled?" asked an editorial writer for the *Denver Post:*

> When Chrysler got into trouble, Iacocca saved it the old-fashioned way, by begging for a government handout. . . . Lorenzo, in contrast, knew Continental lacked the political muscle to rescue itself on the backs of American taxpayers. . . . Instead of joining Iacocca at the corporate entrance to the U.S. Treasury Department's soup kitchen, Lorenzo decided to try capitalism. . . .
>
> Free enterprise isn't supposed to be a popularity contest. We'd rather have rough, abrasive Frank Lorenzo playing the game by the rules and saving consumers money in the process than watch smooth, charming Lee Iacocca rewrite them at public expense.

The son of a hairdresser, Frank Lorenzo grew up in New York. He graduated from Columbia University in 1961 and entered Harvard Business School in the same year. "From the time I first knew him, when he was 19 or so, Lorenzo always wanted to run an airline," recalled one of his HBS classmates. "And you have to remember that that was before airlines were interesting, like *real* businesses: they were regulated, they'd been dominated by the old pilots-turned-executives for years. But that's what Lorenzo wanted to do. It was tolerated: you know, there have to be some outliers in every class."

Lorenzo's philosophy about the airline business was shaped by his experience in running Texas International. He spoke of two factors as being especially significant in influencing his view of the business:

> First, we "grew up" next to Southwest, an airline that, because it was based in a state large enough to generate substantial intrastate business, understood the power of the marketplace early. Those guys were scrappers. Instead of telling customers how they had to behave because they were so big and powerful, they were out aggressively trying to understand their markets. They pioneered the masterful use of the fare structure. And, to this day, they know how to think about their customers.
>
> The second experience I'll never forget was going to Washington in the middle of the '70s to testify against deregulation. Here I was, the president of a little airline in the middle of Texas with a fleet of old planes. We had a pig in a poke; there was no way that we didn't want the government to continue regulating what we did. But as I talked to the smart staff people who were working on the legislation, I saw several things clearly. First, deregulation was probably going to happen. Second, it would come with the force of a tidal wave and turn the airline business upside down, putting power into the hands of consumers. And third, I thought that it was a wave that could be ridden.

Although Lorenzo had made his career working for airlines and since 1972 had been a chief executive officer, he never was an integral part of, or blended in easily with, the industry leadership. As one industry analyst and long-time observer of the industry explained:

> He's never been a member of the club. They don't trust him. His style is so different; he crashes in and takes on the big ones. He took over TXI when you didn't *buy* an airline, pushed for off-peak fares when it was clear that that would add turbulence to the environment—and he took a strike at TXI. . . .
>
> The airline world doesn't (or *didn't* until deregulation) allow for Lorenzo's style. I've been in and watched this business for 30 years. The two cardinal rules have always been: (1) if you can do anything to avoid a strike, do it, but whatever you do, don't try to fly; and (2) when you're in financial difficulties, near bankruptcy, don't fly. The safety of the passengers may be endangered.
>
> Lorenzo just rolls over these canons. Also, his attempt to take over National reinforced his image as a renegade. The other guys in the industry regarded him as a pirate, more as a speculator than as someone who wants to operate an airline.

This perception of Lorenzo as not a typical old-boy airline executive was widely shared on Wall Street, and was reinforced by his active and innovative involvement in raising money for his companies. Even before taking Jet Capital public in 1970, Lorenzo had been intimately involved in financing new equipment purchases and expansion of his base. Rather than relying on any single investment banking firm, Lorenzo had maintained a close relationship with long-time associate Douglas Tansill, a Harvard Business School classmate, who described their relationship:

> unusual, largely because Frank is unique. Through the years, we've done some totally innovative deals with Frank—the first unit offering of subordinated debentures and common stock for an airline, the first Eurodollar convert in the industry, a very creative Eurodollar floating rate note issue. In each case, then and in the future, Frank either readily and quickly embraced an idea presented to him by us, even if it hadn't been done before, or brought the idea to us for execution. He understands finance as well as the best in the business and has a great sense of timing.

But according to another long-time associate, Texas Air's senior vice president Robert Snedeker, Lorenzo's facility and talent with finance occasionally proved to be a mixed blessing, especially in dealing with certain elements of the financial community and the media:

> The Street at times seems to view negatively those who it perceives to be financially oriented. Perhaps it's a competitive thing. Frank and the senior management have never been viewed as "airline people" by the Street, even though many have spent their whole careers around airlines.
>
> Unfortunately, this can lead to some simplistic stereotyping of the company when they analyze its operations. We're never quite sure whether or not the people on the Street have done a full financial analysis, or, instead, are just relying on these stereotypes.
>
> These labels often lead them to some conclusions that don't necessarily follow. For example, we sometimes hear, "You must be lousy managers because you're good finance people." Or, based on a quick look at the turnover of presidents of our airlines, they seem ultimately to come around to the much-repeated refrain of "even if those guys are right about where the business is going, they'll never get anyone to run their airlines. . . ."

The lack of continuity since 1980 among top management of airlines in which he was involved was consistently raised as an indication of what many saw as Lorenzo's weakness as a manager. Certainly the list of former TXI, New York Air, and Continental officials is a distinguished one, and includes those who became competitors, such as Don Burr, the founder of People Express, and Steve Wolf, the president of Republic Airlines. One insider explains the turnover as being caused by "the clash of bright, sometimes brilliant, guys with big egos."

Lorenzo gave his own assessment:

> The turnover in our organizations has to be viewed in the context of the environment at our company at the particular time. Burr was with us for seven years—not exactly a short stint—before leaving to take advantage of the newly passed deregulation laws. While Wolf left after a short 10 months, the instability of that relationship is better understood, I believe, when one realizes that the company lost over $100 million during that period—in increasing amounts. While personalities play a role, they don't play nearly the role that some of our critics and ex-managers would have you believe.
>
> In addition, we've always tended to hire bright, ambitious guys, guys who you know won't stay forever. We take risks with people. Burr was a money manager from Wall Street. Mike Levine (former president of New York Air) was a law professor. Phil Bakes was a government lawyer, and he'll be great at Continental.
>
> In building our companies and our boards, we've always tried to look at what skills we need and at who can give us good direction. Our boards have always consisted of people who can help us understand a piece of the world, not like some other airline boards of civic do-gooders whose only concern is what constituencies they might offend by doing something controversial. For example, Bob Sakowitz (Continental board member and president of Sakowitz, Inc.) is one of the more brilliant marketing people around. It doesn't matter that he runs retail stores and we run an airline. He can give us good advice on marketing.
>
> We've always selected the people in our organization the same way—for their particular skills and to give us a blend.

THE CAL MANAGEMENT TEAM

The top management of Continental Airlines did indeed encompass an eclectic mix of backgrounds. The major holdovers from the old Continental were several senior operating managers. Of this group, among the most prominent and active in the major decision making of the new Continental were Richard Adams, senior vice president for operations and a 22-year Continental employee, and George Warde, manager of the Far East region. The younger officers came from more disparate backgrounds. Although the new Continental had no known organizational chart, prominent among this group were Phil Bakes, executive vice president, Barry Simon, legal counsel, Douglas Birdsall, vice president for market operations and Mickey Foret, treasurer. Of this group Birdsall, 40 years old, was the only career airline employee, having been recruited to the old Continental from Eastern Airlines shortly before the TXI takeover.

Perhaps prototypical of the new-style manager in the TAC companies was Phil Bakes. Bakes, a 39-year-old Harvard-trained lawyer, had worked for the Civil Aeronautics Board and as the chief of staff for Senator Edward Kennedy's Judiciary Subcommittee's hearings on airline deregulation. It was in this context that he first met Lorenzo, who had come to testify against deregulation. Bakes described it:

> Working on airline deregulation in the Senate, I'd met just about every airline CEO. Lorenzo was just different: he had a vision. I remember having a conversation with him about deregulation. Unlike many of the other guys, he caught onto it, including its risks and opportunities, right away. It was the most intellectually challenging encounter I had with any of the airline chiefs.
>
> When, years later, he proposed that I join him, I jumped. I'm not in this for security: I've never looked ahead more than two or three years in my own career. I always knew that I eventually wanted to get out of law and into business, especially an entrepreneurial business. Here I saw an opportunity to learn 30 years of business in 30 months, with a group of very smart people who were not afraid to take risks. I won't ever regret having jumped at that.

Also present at many of the meetings involving long-range commitments of CAL resources were Robert Snedeker and Charles Goolsbee, both senior officers of Texas Air. Snedeker, a 41-year-old graduate of Harvard Business School, had been associated with Lorenzo since 1968 and had been a chief strategist in most of TXI's and TAC's capital and financial negotiations. Goolsbee, a lawyer and TAC general counsel and at 49 one of the senior members of the Lorenzo team, provided legal advice for the parent company. Although TAC had distanced itself from Continental, Goolsbee and Snedeker were involved in many key decisions involving equipment purchases and in other resource allocation decisions with long-range implications.

The environment in which the top managers of Continental plied their trade was anything but formal. Housed in a stark new building perched on the edge of one of Houston's major roadways, Continental's headquarters had a lived-in feeling: at six o'clock in the evening the faint aroma of coffee brewing mingled with that of pizza being reheated in a microwave oven. The building bustled with activity at all hours, although much of the activity seemed governed by few formal rules or procedures. This lack of formality and of rigid adherence to calendars or schedules was notable at the highest level of the organization. According to Birdsall:

> Our meetings are hard to characterize. We schedule arrival times, no departure times. We finish when everyone gets tired and hungry.
>
> Our meetings go from free-form to rigid-form to no-form, depending on the week. Nobody's much of a stickler for procedures for the sake of procedures. We don't care much about whether the budget information presented in the meetings does or does not conform to damn accounting standards or a rigid format, just so long as you convey what you need to convey.
>
> And we certainly don't waste our time writing everything down and then Xeroxing copies to send to everybody. We write down the material on things that involve capital commitments, irreversible decisions. But we have no time for tracking the "no-brainers," the decisions that require no tracks, like the latest personnel procedure or the addition or deletion of 10 computer mnemonics from our system. American would have not one, but two memos on these subjects. But that's just not the way we operate.

The assignment and delegation of responsibility among top management were handled informally and were characterized by one observer as operating "like a good zone defense in football, where players converge on problems in their territory."

Bakes's characterization of the organization's methods of operation dovetailed with this description:

> We're stretched very thin around here. We have about 20 people responsible for running a large airline. People work together without turf battles because we don't have time for them. Each person knows what he's responsible for. We have no notes and no committees. Committees body-check everything useful that might get done. I learned in government that if you organize a task force or a committee you'll get a report in which you *will* find out all the problems. But you'll also become paralyzed. You can't possibly do that with an organization in flux.

Goolsbee described the TAC enterprises as

> the least institutionalized organizations I've worked for. It's a hard environment to get used to, both because you have to work so hard and because you have to reorient your thinking to the risk-taking aspect. I had to convince myself that security isn't important: what's fun, what's important, is trying something new and challenging.
>
> Frank wants the organization to be able to turn on a dime. As a result, people here sometimes lay back and wait to see what he's going to do, or do something only to have to redo it. This can be costly in extra legal and accounting costs. And one problem with having the organization turn on a dime is that you have to deal with that half of the organization that's still going in the other direction.

Although decisions at Continental were made in a flexible, informal manner, management had a clear view of Continental's corporate objectives. According to Bakes, these included:

1. Achieving profitability.
2. Improving the climate for participatory management by employees.
3. Becoming a low-cost producer.
4. Removing Continental from bankruptcy.
5. Solidifying Continental's position in its defined market niche as a low-cost, full-service airline providing a quality product with a simplified pricing structure.

Both Lorenzo and Bakes emphasized that to solidify Continental's position the airline would have to improve the quality of its product distribution network, particularly its methods of ticketing, and to"put meat on the bones of the company"by expanding it to a size that would strengthen its hubs in Denver and Houston and ensure its position as number one or a solid number two in each of the markets it served.

As for Lorenzo's own goals, a long-term observer speculated:

> I believe that what Frank wants Continental to be is a great big survivor, of a size somewhere between Northwest and American. And Frank wants to control it.
>
> Frank started deregulation with an unplayable hand and he played it as well as he could. He's amassed a large amount of capital and assets in a very short time. Now he really wants a viable airline.
>
> He hasn't made money yet because he hasn't had a chance to. Throughout this enterprise he's emphasized a kind of value added that doesn't produce returns quickly. But, ultimately, he has to produce—and he knows it.

RUNNING A BANKRUPT COMPANY

> Chapter 11 is not pleasant. It's sort of like going through open-heart surgery and brain surgery at the same time.
>
> A Continental Airlines lawyer
> *The Wall Street Journal,*
> February 24, 1984

> The thing that's so difficult about the bankruptcy setting is that there are so many people involved, all posturing. Everybody's got turf to defend. It's like having several more boards of directors.
> Charles Goolsbee

In addition to facing the financial problems associated with bankruptcy, the most pressing of which was the need for sources of cash to continue the company's operations, the CAL management also was confronted with a legal and political context in which very little was predictable. The environment in which Continental was attempting to carry out its goals had been turbulent even before the company's Chapter 11 filing; its uncertainty increased dramatically after the filing, for the rules and guidelines for management of companies in bankruptcy were in flux.

The 1978 Bankruptcy Code and its predecessor, the 1898 Bankruptcy Act, provide for two kinds of bankruptcy. The first, which can be either involuntary or voluntary, requires liquidation of the property of the debtor; the second, specified in Chapters 11 and 13, provides for debtor rehabilitation. The purpose of such a reorganization is to allow management to restructure the finances and operations of the firm so it can once again become a functioning economic unit and continue to provide jobs, pay off creditors, and give shareholders a return on their investment.

In April 1983, Wilson Foods Corporation, the nation's largest pork butcher, had filed for protection under Chapter 11, announcing that the primary purpose of its filing was to enable the company to reject costly existing collective bargaining agreements. Continental in its filing had picked up on the logic of the Wilson case, arguing that rehabilitation was preferable to liquidation, and that the only conceivable way the company could continue to function was to abrogate its employment agreements. At the time of the Continental filing, however, cases based on the Wilson logic were working their way through the court system on appeal; how the court would decide the question of whether companies could use Chapter 11 to terminate employee contracts was unclear.

There was a second source of uncertainty about the broad rules that would govern Continental's bankruptcy proceeding. In the 1978 Bankruptcy Reform Act, Congress had established a special set of bankruptcy courts designed to take pressure off the U.S. District Court system. The legislation created positions for special bankruptcy judges, with 14-year terms and jurisdiction only over bankruptcy issues, to replace the bankruptcy "referees" responsible to district court judges in the old system. In 1982, in *Northern Pipeline Construction* v. *Marathon Construction,* the Supreme Court had ruled in favor of a plaintiff who had filed a suit arguing that the bankruptcy judges were not legitimate members of the federal judiciary because they were not appointed for life, as specified in Article III of the Constitution. Because this ruling called into question the legitimacy of the whole bankruptcy court system, the Supreme Court had given Congress a deadline of April 1, 1984, to rewrite the bankruptcy code to address the issue of jurisdiction. As early as the fall of 1983 it was clear that the impending Congressional rewrite would provide an opportunity for special interests to insert provisions and would also serve as a forum for debate about the desirability and legitimacy of using Chapter 11 to abrogate employment contracts.

In addition to the uncertainty about the broad legal parameters that would govern the bankruptcy, Continental's management faced all of the difficulties of running a company governed by the constraints of the bankruptcy court. As a Chapter 11 debtor, Continental was required to file a reorganization plan that satisfied both the judge and a committee or set of committees of creditors. The judge could determine the makeup of the committees, and, in Continental's case, the committees consisted of separate groups of bank creditors, secured institutional creditors, unsecured creditors, unionized employees, and nonunionized employees.

In addition to being charged with the authority to approve any final proposal for reorganization, the judge and the committees were allowed to become involved with the ongoing business of rehabilitation in a number of ways. They had the right to consult with management, monitor all proceedings in the court, and assess the company's acts, conduct, and financial status. To facilitate this, the creditors' committees were permitted to hire staff to be paid for by the debtor. The judge, with the advice of the creditors, was required to monitor monthly financial transactions by the company and to approve any new lending agreements or major commitments of resources. In short, Continental had to be prepared to transact much of its business in public, in writing, and under the microscope of the bankruptcy court.

Barry Simon, Continental's counsel, described the situation:

> We had some things going for us. The goal of the bankruptcy statutes is to permit rehabilitation of debtors, so we began with a favorable basis in law. Because of this, a "success" for the judge would be a revitalized company.
>
> But we had to file a plea in court to do *anything* we wanted to do. And we were faced with the fundamental difference between the Continental management, which wanted to build a successful company and make a profit, and the creditors, who wanted to pull out their money and satisfy their more short-term objectives.

THE ISSUE AT HAND: FLYING THE NEW PACIFIC ROUTES

It was against this backdrop that the meeting was held to consider the proposal to expand Continental's service to the South Pacific.

The old Continental had flown routes in the South Pacific for many years. At the time it was taken over by Texas International, Continental had authority, granted by the Civil Aeronautics Board and foreign governments, to fly a series of routes to Australia, New Zealand, Japan, the Philippines, Taiwan, Hong Kong, Fiji, and a number of islands in Micronesia. Continental had continued to fly its international routes throughout the bankruptcy, and its operations in both the South Pacific and mid-Pacific had been financially successful.

After the Chapter 11 filing and its attendant cut in labor costs, the routes began to look even more attractive, for, unlike CAL's domestic routes, the international routes were highly regulated and much of CAL's competition came from foreign carriers with high labor costs. In addition, in late November 1983, Pan American had announced its intention to cease its Honolulu-Guam nonstop flights on April 1, 1984.

Following Pan Am's announcement, Warde had suggested to Lorenzo and Bakes that an expansion of service be considered, and with their preliminary approval, he and his staff had developed a proposal to expand Continental's routes and establish a Honolulu hub. Having worked with CAL equipment experts, Warde argued that he could add profitable capacity with the addition to the Continental fleet of two DC-10-30s, small, longer-range versions of DC-10-10s that could fly nonstop from Honolulu to Sydney and to Guam without refueling. Specifically, Warde proposed: (1) introduction of nonstop service to Guam from San Francisco and Honolulu; (2) increased nonstop service, with additional nonstop flights to Sydney and introduction of new nonstop flights to Auckland; and (3) direct Honolulu-Guam service.

Warde's forecasts for 1984 showed that even without the new aircraft the Pacific route system could generate $10.7 million, a figure that would account for 36 percent of CAL's projected profits. He projected in pro formas that the addition of the 10-30s flying the new South Pacific routes could generate an additional profit of $3.38 million in 1984. (For a summary of management's analysis of important considerations, see Exhibit 6.)

CAL and TAC management had been aware since November that McDonnell-Douglas was willing to sell two used DC 10-30s and also knew that the aircraft might be attractive on the Pacific routes. During preliminary negotiations with McDonnell-Douglas, the price on the aircraft had been established at $15.5 million each. In addition, the two aircraft would require an overhaul costing approximately $7 million, bringing the total projected cost to almost $40 million.

It was clear that Continental was in no position to purchase the aircraft. Therefore, Snedeker proposed that it lease the planes through a transaction to be arranged by E. F. Hutton, and that the underlying debt be secured by a lien on the aircraft, further supported by a limited "first loss deficiency guarantee" from McDonnell-Douglas and by recourse to Texas Air. (See Exhibit 7 for a summary of the lease proposal.)

Snedeker, in viewing the transaction as one that would require the financial support of TAC, assessed the proposal this way:

> The right aircraft available at the right time. The 10-30s suit Continental's needs, and the opportunity exists to buy them at attractive prices. Also, I'm convinced that the aircraft themselves are a good investment. The market seems to have turned around. I'm convinced that the 10-30s have good collateral value.
>
> TAC's involvement is critical. Douglas will only help us finance with the credit of TAC. But it seems like a good venture for TAC because of the aircraft value, and, in addition, TAC owns 90 percent of Continental, so we have a strong stake in helping them succeed.
>
> Of course there are certain risks. The time frames for arranging the deal and financing are tight: both planes are supposed to be in service by July 1984. TAC could go ahead with the agreement and the bankruptcy court could disallow it. Also, in the process of negotiating the agreement, we could set a precedent for there being a tangible linkage between CAL and TAC that creditors might jump on. And of course, we have to anticipate that the decision to acquire the aircraft might create a certain amount of animosity among lower levels of Continental; you can imagine them saying, "Here we are starving, and they're off buying planes."
>
> The piece of this that we haven't really done before is buy equipment in a bankruptcy setting. But the skin gets thick, and overall it doesn't seem too risky.

Vice President for Market Planning Birdsall had mixed reactions to the proposal:

> Certainly in terms of a business proposition the numbers seem to make sense. I've been convinced for a long time that the Pacific routes with the right configuration can make money. In fact, several years ago we put together a plan to fly Honolulu–

> Guam in competition with Pan Am, but given all of the difficulties the company was facing, decided not to do it at that time. It just so happened that Pan Am decided to stop serving the route at what was an inopportune moment for Continental.
>
> But I must confess to having the reaction of "I'm busy." I have a bankrupt airline that's growing at a rate of 20 percent a month to run. You can't always follow the Lorenzo rule to "defy all the laws of gravity and do what makes good economic sense."
>
> I'm concerned about controlling risk. For me, some of the risk in this comes from flying the routes in that part of the world. I don't know their market, have no intimate understanding of what's going on in Guam and Fiji. In the United States I can put 10 planes in the air in an hour and feel comfortable, but there—I don't know the territory as well. Maybe we should just go for one plane and between the Mid Pacific and South Pacific opportunities, one would be relatively certain that one of the two is going to work very well. Of course, that isn't in keeping with what seems to be our motto around here: "If I'm going to die, I'd just as soon not spend 20 years doing it."

Continental's legal counsel, Barry Simon, focused his assessment of the proposal on how it would affect the company's position in court:

> There is something a little incongruous about having teams of lawyers fighting in court for every penny and then laying on top of that a proposal to find $40 million to buy new planes.
>
> There seem to me to be several risks associated with this particular proposal. Several of the creditors are pushing us to sell off our assets and become a nice little airline. In light of this, even if we were to get approval from the judge, the unions and some of the creditors are likely to appeal, especially since we're footing the bill for their legal costs. This could cause significant delay and the delay could make it impossible to get financing and could kill the whole deal.
>
> On the other hand, there are business reasons for the proposal and the judge has so far been receptive to the arguments we have made. [At this point, Continental had won most of its pleas before the court.] I think we could convince him on this matter, too. Also, the expansion would create jobs and the unions would be hard pressed to oppose that.

Executive Vice President Phil Bakes was the last to speak:

> My first strong reaction is to jump on the opportunity. It's the first time since I've joined the company that we can do something other than keep the blood from flowing. I think a positive decision would provide a very loud answer to the question, "What is your mindset about the future?"
>
> There's compelling logic to it as a business decision, in spite of the risk. I'm very leery of falling victim to the logic of the school of thought that says here are all of the ways that things might go wrong. I'd rather commit to the thing in a wholehearted way, as an opportunity, not as a risk. The more committed we are—to McDonnell-Douglas, the judge, E. F. Hutton, and the rest—the more difficult it will be to stop us. It's for this reason that if we decide to fly the routes, I want to go for both planes, not just one: we don't want the judge to feel that he's being nibbled to death. We should put our cards on the table. We have a growth strategy for the Pacific because of our marketing strength there and our low costs. We already have a significant investment out there. Pan Am's departure and the state of the current used aircraft market present opportunities.

This isn't to say that I don't see some risk in the proposal. If we can't get the aircraft and get them refurbished in the time we could use up a lot of cash, and although we're improving, we're not exactly flush with money. In addition, I think that trying to figure out what our numbers are for places like Hong Kong and Taipei is risky: we don't have years and years of traffic data and history as we do in this country. Also, at Continental we haven't really acquired any assets for a long time and $40 million is a big commitment.

Finally, I see as a major aspect of the risk the possible fallout from the symbolic aspects of this proposal for Continental to expand. In this sense, the 10-30s are stalking horses. If we can handle this, it may help us to expand our other parts of the business. But if we can't do it, when the summer comes and we try to put on additional flights and build the airline, we'll have everybody breathing down our necks. If we go with the proposal, one thing is clear to me, and that's that our credibility will be on the line.

APPENDIX

FRANK LORENZO'S PRESENTATION TO CONTINENTAL AIRLINES' PILOTS, SEPTEMBER 20, 1983

The company's financial position is most serious. The massive losses that are continuing at the company will very shortly erode our current cash and liquid resources. That liquidity is largely the product of investments made by American General, the public, and Texas Air Corporation. We will not allow this company to deplete its resources. We, therefore, have some immediate choices: implement a new operating plan including dramatic relief from our current cost structure, or take steps that protect our cash and other assets while we still have substantial cash resources.

We truly regret that these stark alternatives fall so squarely on the pilot group at Continental. The pilots are the group which approximately one year ago voluntarily revised its contract in hope of reducing expenses and saving the company. Little did we then realize how swiftly the marketplace would be upon us and how harshly it would treat Continental's cost and revenues. The pilots of Continental also continued to fly during our continued efforts to resist IAM strike-backed demands that would result in absorbing cost increases. We appreciate both of these efforts in our common interest.

Though we regret the circumstances we now find ourselves in and the role the pilots will play—one way or another—we believe there is no responsible alternative left open to us.

The reasons we have reached this conclusion are basically four.

First, the company is losing money at an alarming rate—$84 million in the first six months and another $7.4 million loss in July. July had originally been projected to bring a $25.5 million profit and just a few months ago we lowered that to an $8.4 million profit. The economic warfare being waged by the IAM is taking its toll. The company's shareholders' equity or net worth is close to zero, and our cash resources are diminishing rapidly.

Second, our operating costs are too high to ever allow the company to be profitable or to bring a significant return to shareholders. This is true even with the new IAM wages and work rules we implemented. Therefore, unless we can reduce our operating costs very significantly and promptly, it makes no business sense to continue as we have been doing. As a result of the new wages and work rules due to the IAM strike, we will be able to reduce our IAM costs by about $20 million annually. Our goal is an overall annual cost reduction of $150 million; we believe that this requires a $60 million reduction from the pilots, $40 million from the flight attendants, and a $30 million reduction in other costs, including other employee groups.

Third, pilot expenses at Continental are a large portion of total labor expenses. Pilots' expenses are about $130 million per year, or over 25 percent of the total annual costs of $520 million, based on the May 1983 cost levels. Pilot wages, benefits, and work rules at Continental create significantly higher costs than we can afford. For example, if the Continental pilots worked under the same contract as the "new" Braniff, our pilot costs would be reduced by $90 million per year, or about 70 percent. Completely new-entrant airline pilot cost structures would save even more than that. These are the cost structures we compete against. Other nonpilot cost reduction programs, such as IAM flight attendants, corporate overhead, and so on, although necessary, are not sufficient unless pilot costs are reduced significantly and permanently.

Fourth, if our costs cannot be reduced significantly and immediately it is not an acceptable business risk to go into the off-peak season without a credible plan to preserve our cash resources. We are not going to go out of business as Braniff did, that is, with no cash. Rather, we are firmly committed to take other steps to protect our remaining liquidity and our assets.

The more basic reason we face these stark choices is because of the new world out there today. Only the efficient airlines with marketplace cost structures will survive. This is certainly true of Continental, and carriers like Republic, Western, and Pan Am. And, it is also true of carriers even like American and United. The giants realize this fact and are following a strategy unique to themselves in order to survive. They have stockpiled truly awesome financial resources to provide the strength and time to grow. This growth is nourished under new labor contracts that have very low new-hire rates, thus building lower unit cost structures into their entire company. In the meantime, the giants are benefiting from biased travel agent computer reservation systems that distort traffic patterns and competitive market shares. Before that distortion is fully redressed, the giants may or may not be sufficiently prepared for the cost pressures of the marketplace. Delta's recent massive losses show how fickle the marketplace is to even the apparent giants.

No matter how intelligently we manage our business, we cannot have labor costs that are dramatically higher than our competitors and survive. Although it is perfectly clear that reducing costs *alone* will not solve the company's problems and that much remains to be done on the revenue side, nevertheless it is also true that a precondition to success is a dramatic reduction in our cost structure. Unless we do this, we will run out of the time it takes to improve revenues.

So while we continue to work on revenue improvements and acknowledge that there is much to do, we have concluded that reducing costs dramatically is a necessary first step to survival.

You have often heard me say that I did not author "deregulation." In fact, at first I opposed it in the U.S. Congress because I thought it would harm Texas International.

Today, I philosophically believe in deregulation. Although it is tough on all of us and on the company we work for—and Continental could perish because of it—I much prefer over the long-term to be subject to the rule of the marketplace, rather than the bureaucrat.

But, we must heed the rule of the marketplace. The latest example of how harsh but inevitable that marketplace is came last week when People Express announced plans to commence Newark–Houston service five times per day at unrestricted fares, a fraction of some of our recent discount fares, to say nothing of our regular fares.

The People Expresses, the Southwests, the American Wests, the Frontier Horizons are drastically altering Continental's marketplace. Unless we change with the marketplace, we will perish.

Other courses of action that are evolutionary, not revolutionary, do not work for Continental.

EXHIBIT 1
MERGED AIRLINE ROUTES

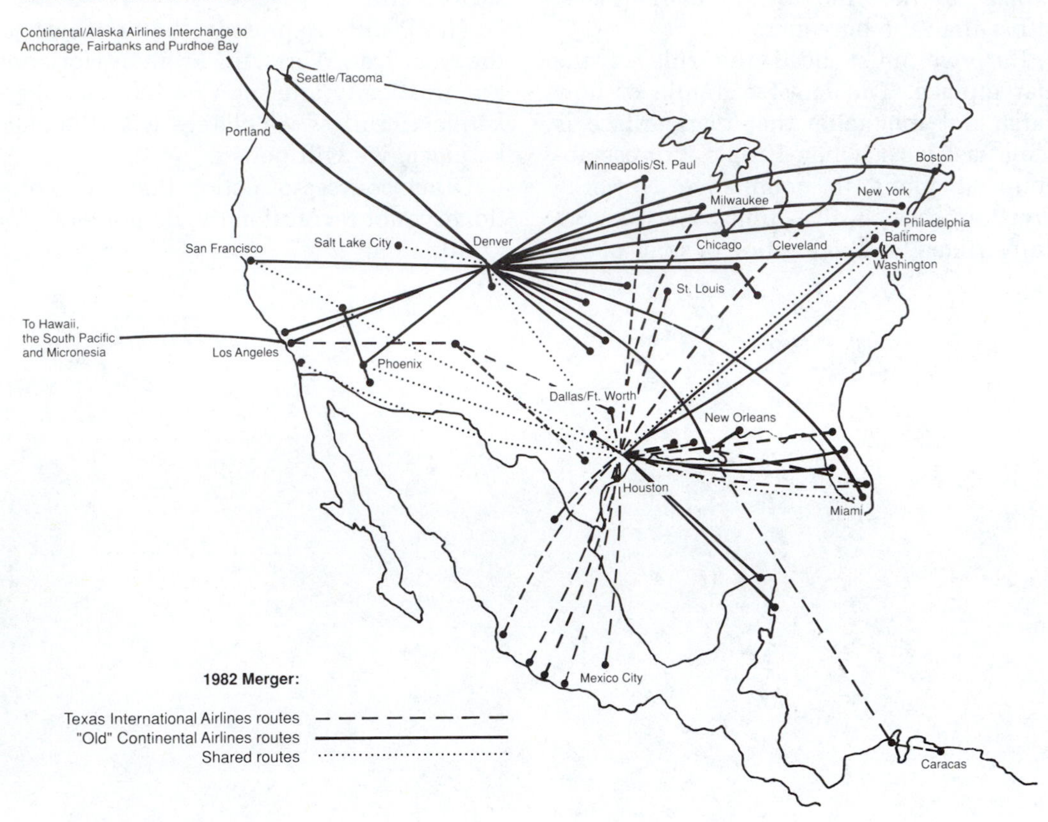

Source: Company documents.

EXHIBIT 2
STOCK OWNERSHIP

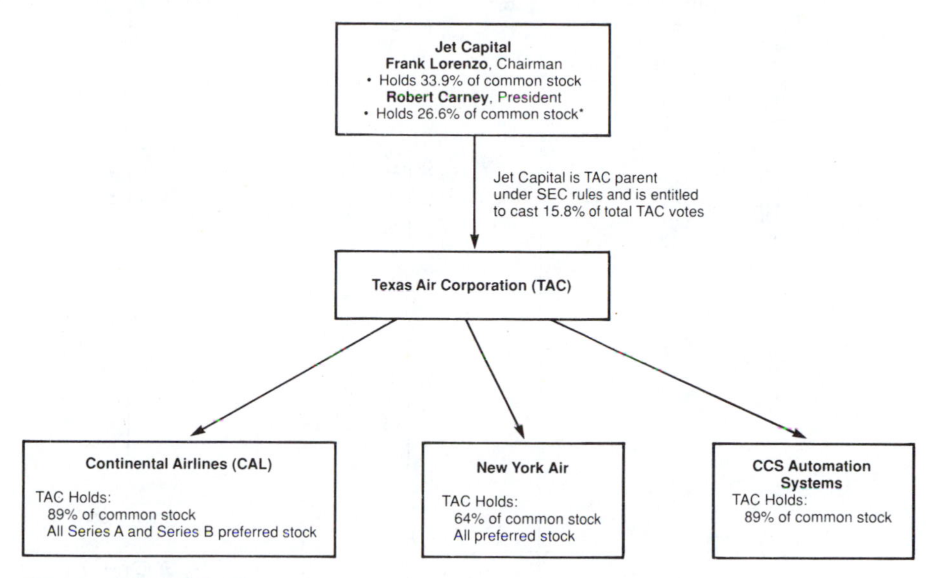

*Remainder of stock held in small lots.

Source: 1983 TAC annual report and 1981 TAC proxy.

EXHIBIT 3
CAL SELECTED FINANCIAL AND STATISTICAL DATA, 1979–1983
Dollars in Thousands

Dollars in Thousands	*1983*	*1982*	*1981*	*1980*	*1979*
Operating revenues					
Passenger	$ 995,994	$1,261,642	$1,245,215	$ 879,593	$807,694
Other	116,991	165,373	154,435	112,426	120,288
Total operating revenues	1,112,985	1,427,015	1,399,650	992,019	927,982
Operating expenses					
Wages, salaries, and related costs	420,600	492,053	532,866	401,481	380,089
Aircraft fuel	321,509	437,560	432,425	295,255	227,614
Depreciation and amortization	75,991	86,950	84,002	59,262	56,353
Other	445,206	445,045	398,823	282,229	271,847
Total operating expenses	1,263,306	1,461,608	1,448,116	1,038,227	935,903
Nonoperating expenses (income)					
Interest expense	69,304	89,152	100,526	42,099	30,182
Capital interest	(181)	(1,348)	(4,521)	(4,974)	(1,673)
Other	(996)	(77,460)	(60,724)	(47,500)	(4,645)
Total nonoperating expenses, net	68,127	10,344	35,291	(10,375)	23,864
Earnings (loss) before income taxes	(218,448)	(44,937)	(83,757)	(35,833)	(31,785)
Income taxes (credits)	—	(3,133)	(3,859)	(15,129)	(18,600)
Net earnings (loss)	$ (218,448)	$ (41,804)	$ (79,898)	$ (20,704)	$ (13,185)
Assets, Liabilities, and Stockholders' Equity					
Current assets:					
Cash and temporary investments	$ 64,686	$ 37,123	$ 76,082	$ 31,717	$ 34,670
Accounts receivable, net	84,449	152,495	155,306	106,381	118,629

Spare parts and supplies, net	27,728	33,422	42,729	36,938	23,497
Prepayment and other	21,946	26,828	15,661	5,816	5,007
Total current assets	198,809	249,868	289,778	180,852	181,803
Property and equipment:					
Owned property and equipment (net)	546,040	619,758	706,847	482,715	545,590
Capital leases	124,958	134,868	145,365	115,544	—
Total property and equipment	670,998	754,626	852,212	598,259	545,590
Total other assets	38,336	48,575	41,051	5,038	11,314
Total assets	$ 908,143	$1,053,069	$1,183,041	$784,149	$738,707
Current liabilities:					
Current portion of long-term debt	17,087	68,780	66,943	38,305	53,484
Current portion of capital leases	3,452	5,116	4,169	1,631	—
Accounts payable	16,812	119,314	111,595	64,549	82,131
Other	63,387	198,857	205,641	141,950	116,061
Total current liabilities	100,738	392,067	388,348	246,435	251,676
Estimated liabilities subject to Chapter 11 reorganization proceedings	737,610	—	—	—	—
Long-term obligations	172,178	583,948	679,629	328,797	243,979
Other (deferred credits)	6,812	27,185	23,391	18,043	30,195
Stockholders' equity:					
Stock and paid-in capital	182,420	121,704	121,704	88,953	88,698
Retained (deficit) earnings	(291,615)	(71,835)	(30,031)	101,921	124,159
Total stockholders' equity	(109,195)	49,869	91,673	190,874	212,857
Total liabilities and stockholders' equity	$ 908,143	$1,053,069	$1,183,041	$784,149	$738,707

Note: 1979–1980 Continental Airlines only; 1981—pro forma CAL and TXI combined; 1982–1983—CAC.
Source: Continental Airlines company records.

EXHIBIT 4
TAC SELECTED FINANCIAL AND STATISTICAL DATA, 1979–1983
Dollars in Thousands Except per Share Data

	1983	1982	1981	1980	1979
Summary of operations					
Operating revenues					
Passenger	$1,124,189	$1,356,122	$ 649,491	$ 266,837	$213,218
Other	122,026	160,198	69,909	24,659	20,943
Total operating revenues	1,246,215	1,516,320	719,400	291,496	234,161
Operating expenses	1,382,087	1,562,289	760,246	284,949	218,825
Operating income (loss)	(135,872)	(45,969)	(40,846)	6,547	15,336
Other income (expense)					
Interest and debt expenses, net	(67,785)	(87,107)	(40,964)	(4,238)	(11,067)
Minority interest in subsidiaries	—	20,861	12,077	27	—
Other, net	25,793	60,107	17,755	4,284	44,026
Total other income (expense)	(41,992)	(6,139)	(11,132)	73	32,959
Income (loss) before income taxes	(177,864)	(52,108)	(51,978)	6,620	48,295
Income tax (credit) provision	2,076	(3,133)	(4,793)	2,630	6,900
Extraordinary items	—	—	—	—	—
Net income (loss)	$ (177,864)	$ (48,975)	$ (47,185)	$ 3,990	$ 41,395
Net income (loss) per share					
Primary	$ (14,58)	$ (7.27)	$ (8.11)	$ 0.55	$ 5.88
Fully diluted	$ (14.58)	$ (7.27)	$ (8.11)	$ 0.55	$ 4.84
Financial Summary					
Current assets	$ 304,455	$ 326,391	$ 352,549	$ 195,490	$156,927
Current liabilities	134,547	415,956	405,002	82,871	68,452
Property and equipment, net	839,525	839,332	928,358	177,988	158,507
Total assets	1,177,959	1,191,976	1,301,316	385,749	319,201
Long-term debt, net	259,212	515,948	605,001	196,236	154,491
Obligations under capital leases, net	55,656	144,808	156,213	11,347	13,940
Redeemable preferred stock	23,219	24,464	4,400	4,899	5,548
Stockholders' equity	(49,649)	63,477	40,453	84,325	75,670
Common stock price range	11¾–4¾	13⅞–4	15⅛–5⅛	14¾–6⅜	13⅝–7½

Statistical Summary

*Continental Airlines**					
Available seat miles (000)	15,396,477	19,270,121	17,474,238	17,865,646	19,175,563
Revenue passenger miles (000)	9,274,257	11,157,365	10,069,734	10,359,077	11,674,282
Load factor	60.2%	57.9%	57.6%	58.0%	60.9%
Revenue passengers	10,236,004	11,335,711	10,285,713	11,404,046	13,192,855
Average fare per passenger	$97.30	$111.30	$121.06	$100.49	$77.38
Average yield per revenue passenger mile	10.74¢	11.31¢	12.37¢	11.06¢	8.74¢
Average length of passenger trip (miles)	906	872	850	828	885
Revenue aircraft miles (000)	110,703	137,678	127,393	135,480	146,097
Average length of aircraft flight (miles)	662	638	620	585	590
Average daily utilization of aircraft (block hours)	7:19	9:02	9:08	9:51	10:46
New York Air†					
Available seat miles (000)	1,146,584	1,110,478	735,494		
Revenue passenger miles (000)	656,601	606,654	460,832		
Load factor	57.3%	54.6%	67.2%		
Revenue passengers	2,103,681	1,738,095	1,562,017		
Average fare per passenger	$60.94	$54.36	$40.89		
Average yield per revenue passenger mile	19.5¢	15.57¢	13.86¢		
Average length of passenger trip (miles)	312	349	295		
Revenue aircraft miles (000)	10,307	9,878	6,238		
Average length of aircraft flight (miles)	300	330	287		
Average daily utilization of aircraft (block hours)	8:08	8:45	8:90		

*Reflects the combined operations of Continental and Texas International.

†New York Air began service in December 1980.

Source: Texas Air Corporation 1982, 1983 annual report.

EXHIBIT 5
CAL ROUTE SYSTEM, 1984

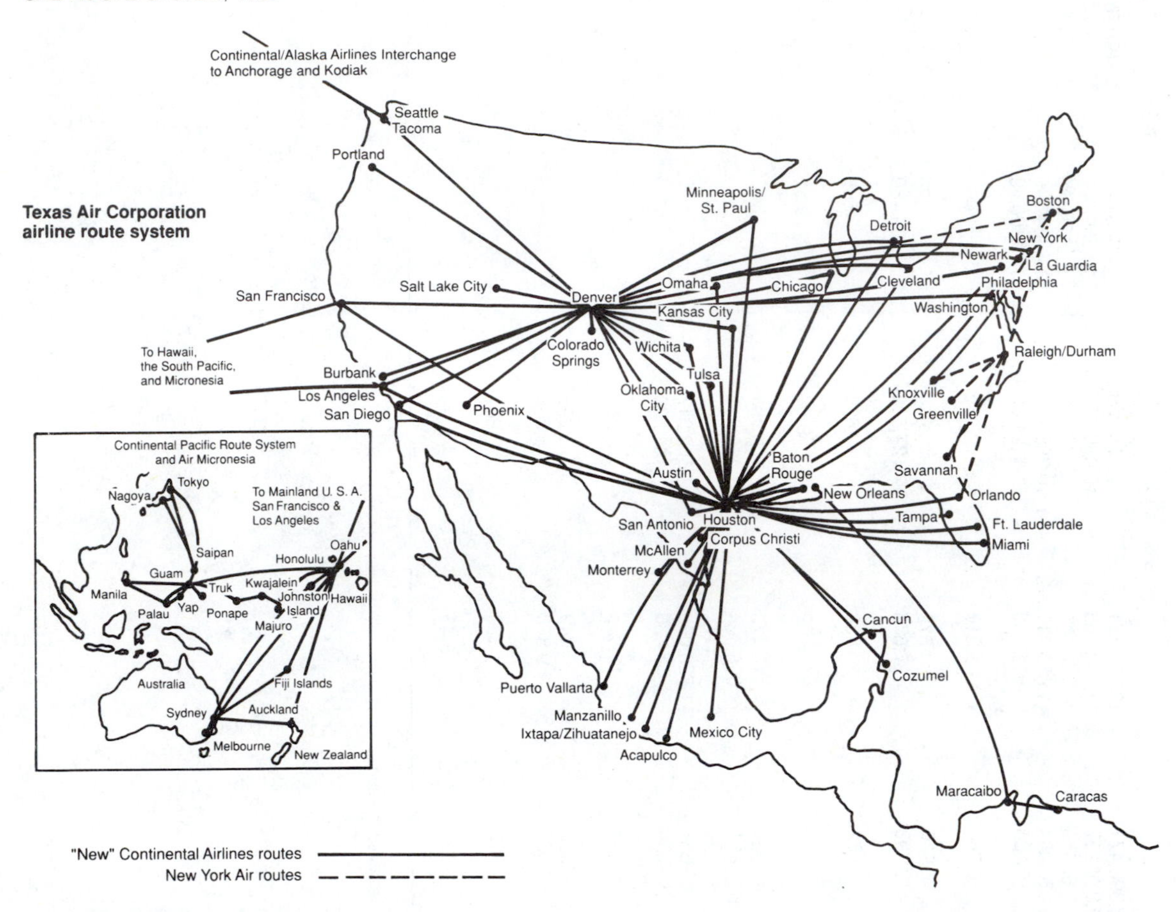

Source: Company documents.

EXHIBIT 6
ANALYSIS OF SOUTH PACIFIC ROUTE DECISION

I. Mid-Pacific Strategic Factors
Profitable franchise $9.1 million in 1983*
Pan Am withdrawing April 1
Preempt competitive incursions:
- SPIA
- Aloha
- Hawaiian

Build natural traffic flows between points with strong current Continental indentity:
- HNL–West Coast
- Guam–Micronesia, Japan, and Philippines

Enhances value of Continental's limited entry routes
Capitalize on Continental's Pacific market identity
Efficient utilization of resources—no new stations
Continues the planned development of the Mid-Pacific
Nagoya —Summer 1983
Guam-Tokyo —March 1984
Guam-Honolulu —April 1984

II. South Pacific Strategic Factors
Profitable franchise $5.3 million in 1983*
Respond to competitive changes:
- Additional nonstops to Sydney
- Introduction nonstop service to Auckland

Build natural traffic flow between U.S.–South Pacific and Mid-Pacific
Efficient utilization of existing resources; no new stations
Fill Honolulu void
Why now?
Synergistic with Honolulu–Guam
Competitors are strategically redeploying in April
Market conditions are correct
Implements deferred 1983 expansion

III. Potential Risks of Action Considered
Mid-Pacific:
Deterioration of Guam market
Price competition
Essential air service requirements
Air Micronesia dispute
South Pacific:
Foreign currency devaluations
Nonstops obtain disproportionate share of traffic
Negative publicity
Reversal of traffic growth trends

IV. Potential Risks of Nonaction Considered
Mid-Pacific;
Deterioration of profitable franchise
Loss of the major trade link
Forgone profitable opportunity
South Pacific
$15.6 million of revenue diversion
Encourage further expansion of competitor's service
Only significant window for expansion
Loss of market position
Threatens position within the higher quality market

*Eleven months ended November 30, 1983.
Source: Continental Airlines company records.

EXHIBIT 7
SUMMARY OF *PROPOSED* PRINCIPAL TERMS: TWO USED DC-10-30 AIRCRAFT
Continental Airlines Corporation–Texas Air Corporation

Aircraft: Two used DC-10-30s with CF6-50C2 engines installed; engines and airframes to be overhauled and modified as required for CAC operation.

Price (each aircraft): To be mutually agreed upon including $15.5 million base cost of "as is"–"where is" aircraft delivered from MDC, plus completed overhauls and certain modifications (all at a cost of approximately $3.5 million) necessary to meet lessee cockpit, cabin, and other operating standards.

Delivery: On or about 6/1/84 and 7/1/84 with engine/airframe overhauls to be accomplished prior to delivery.

Lessee: Continental Airlines Corporation (CAC).

Owner-lessor: Texas Air Corporation (TAC) or its assigns.

Base lease term: Ten (10) years beginning upon delivery.

Lease payments: Approximately $300,000 per month, paid quarterly in advance.

Renewal options: Lessee shall have the right to renew the lease for an additional five-year term at the same lease rate.

Net lease: The lease will be "net" to the owner-lessor, with the lessee responsible for maintenance, insurance, registration, and compliance with applicable laws and taxes.

Fees and expenses: All costs of outside counsel, documentation, and out-of-pocket expenses will be shared equally by lessor and lessee. Both parties agree to use in-house capabilities to the maximum extent possible to minimize such costs.

CAC option to buy: CAC will have the option to buy the aircraft for its market value at the end of the base lease term or the renewal period.

Maintenance reserves: Will be required only if TAC is unable to obtain long-term debt without maintenance reserve requirements.

Source: Continental Airlines company records.

BOOK ONE

DETERMINING CORPORATE STRATEGY

The Concept of Corporate Strategy

When we were looking at the chief executive's job, we promised that a simple central concept called *corporate strategy* would be developed here. It would be offered, we said, as a means to reduce the general management function to manageable proportions and enable technical specialists to understand the proper relationship between their departmental objectives and the goals of their companies. We come now to the central idea of this course and this book. We will look at what strategy is, what form it takes in different kinds of companies, what tests of validity may be applied to it, and what it is good for. If you think back to your discussion of Head Ski, NIKE, or Continental Airlines, you may already be able to see or imagine what does or can happen to this idea in living organizations and sense both its inherent difficulties and its power.

WHAT STRATEGY IS

As the outcome of the decision process we will later analyze in detail, corporate strategy is the pattern of decisions in a company that (1) determines, shapes, and reveals its objectives, purposes, or goals; (2) produces the principal policies and plans for achieving these goals; and (3) defines the business the company intends to be in, the kind of economic and human organization it intends to be, and the nature of the economic and noneconomic contribution it intends to make to its shareholders, employees, customers, and communities. In an organization of any size or diversity, corporate strategy usually applies to the whole enterprise, while business strategy, less comprehensive, defines the choice of product or service and market or individual businesses within the firm. *Business strategy*, that is, determines how a company will compete in a given business and position itself among its competitors. *Corporate strategy* defines the businesses in which a company will compete, preferably in a way that focuses resources to convert distinctive competence into competitive advantage. Both are outcomes of a continuous process of *strategic management* that we will later examine at length.

The strategic decision contributing to this pattern is one that is effective over long periods of time, affects the company in many different ways, and focuses and commits a significant portion of its resources to expected outcomes. The pattern resulting from a series of such decisions will probably define the central character and image of a company, the individuality it has for its members and various publics, and the position it will occupy in its industry and markets. It will permit the specification of particular objectives to be attained through a timed sequence of investment and implementation decisions and will govern directly the deployment or redeployment of resources to make these decisions effective.

Some aspects of such a pattern of decision may be in an established corporation unchanging over long periods of time, like a commitment to quality, or high technology, or certain raw materials, or good labor relations. Other aspects of a strategy must change as or before the world changes, such as product line, manufacturing process, or merchandising and styling practices. The basic determinants of company character, if purposefully institutionalized, are likely to persist through and shape the nature of substantial changes in the allocation of resources and of product policy.

It would be possible to extend the definition of strategy for a given company to separate a central character and the core of its special accomplishment from the manifestations of such characteristics in changing product lines, markets, and policies designed to make activities profitable from year to year. *The New York Times*, for example, after many years of being shaped by the values of its owners and staff, is now so self-conscious and respected an institution that its nature is likely to remain unchanged, even if the services it offers are altered drastically in the direction of other outlets for its news-processing capacity.

It is important not to take the idea of strategy apart—to separate goals from the policies designed to achieve those goals or even to overdo the difference between the formulation of strategy and its implementation. The interdependence of purposes, policies, and organized action is crucial to the particularity of an individual strategy. It is the unity, coherence, and internal consistency of a company's strategic decisions that give the firm its identity and individuality, its power to mobilize its strengths, and its likelihood of success in the marketplace. It is the interrelationship of a set of goals and policies that crystallizes from the formless reality of a company's environment a set of problems an organization can seize upon and solve.

We mean the term *strategy*, therefore, to suggest that *pattern* among goals is more important than any array of separate purposes. The variety of valid and attractive objectives is nearly infinite. Impressionistic selection results in uncoordinated and inefficient pursuit. Superficially attractive financial goals like high return on equity and high profit margins, for example, are in practice or at any one time incompatible with high rates of growth in sales or market share. As we will see, different kinds of objectives limit other kinds. Financial goals may impose constraints on organization development and social goals. An organization objective of maximum decentralization will put limits on short-term attainment of cost control. The objective of continuous employment subordinates at once responsiveness to peaks of demand.

The interrelation among objectives is the key to coherence and consistency. The pattern of goals and policies, rather than their separate substance, is the source of the uniqueness which ideally should distinguish every company from its competitors. Especially when values visibly affect economic choices, the special character of a company becomes apparent to its employees and customers. Breaking up the system of corporate goals and the character-determining major policies for attainment leads to narrow and mechanical conceptions of strategic management and endless logic chopping.

Many popular terms and current buzzwords allude to various aspects of goal setting. Whether you wish to refer to a view of the total corporation as its *vision* or a statement of purpose as its *mission statement,* for example, is up to you. Language has many ways of describing so central an activity as choice of purpose. We should get on to understanding the need for strategic decision and for determining the most satisfactory pattern of goals in concrete instances. Refinement of definition can wait, for you will wish to develop definition in practice in directions useful to you. In the meantime, remember that what you are doing has no meaning for yourself or others unless you can sense and say or imply to others what you are doing it for. The quality of all administrative action and the motives lending it power cannot be understood without knowing their relationship to purpose.

SUMMARY STATEMENTS OF STRATEGY

Before we proceed to clarification of the strategy concept by application, we should specify the terms in which strategy is usually expressed. A summary statement of strategy will characterize the product line and services offered or planned by the company, the markets and market segments for which products and services are now or will be designed, and the channels through which these markets will be reached. The means by which the operation is to be financed will be specified, as will the profit objectives and the emphasis to be placed on the safety of capital versus level of return. Major policy in central functions, such as marketing, manufacturing, procurement, research and development, labor relations, and personnel, will be stated where they distinguish the company from others;

and usually the intended size, form, and character of the organization would be included.

In a statement of Howard Head's intuitive or consciously designed strategy for Head Ski, some of these categories would be missing (profit objectives, for example) but others stressed (such as quality of product). Each company, if it were to construct a summary strategy from what it understands itself to be aiming at, would have a different statement with different categories of decision emphasized to indicate what it wanted to be or do.

To indicate the nature of such a statement, a student of Heublein, a famous old Policy case, deduced this statement from the account of the company before it was acquired by R. J. Reynolds and when it was about to acquire Hamm's Brewery:[1]

> Heublein aims to market in the United States and via franchise overseas a wide variety of high-margin, high-quality consumer products concentrated in the liquor and food business, especially bottled cocktails, vodka, and other special-use and distinctive beverages and specialty convenience foods, addressed to a relatively prosperous, young-adult market and returning over 15 percent of equity after taxes. With emphasis on the techniques of consumer goods marketing [brand promotion, wide distribution, product representation in more than one price segment, and very substantial offbeat advertising directed closely to its growing audience], Heublein intends to make Smirnoff the number one liquor brand worldwide via internal growth [and franchise] or acquisitions or both. Its manufacturing policy rather than full integration is in liquor to redistill only to bring purchased spirits up to high-quality standards. It aims to finance its internal growth through the use of debt and its considerable cash flow and to use its favorable price earnings ratio for acquisitions. Both its liquor and food distribution are intended to secure distributor support through advertising and concern for the distributor's profit.

Although it might be argued that the statement was not clearly in the chief executive's mind when he contemplated purchasing Hamm's Brewery and therefore did not help him refrain from that unfortunate decision, it was in his experience and in the pattern of the company's past strategic decisions—at least as reported in the case. Note also that this statement must be regarded as only a partial summary, for it omits reference to the kind of human organization Heublein means to be for its members and the responsibility its leaders feel for such strategy-related social problems as alcoholism. But even without mention of organization or social responsibility substrategies, this statement raises a multimillion dollar

[1] The Heublein case may be found in earlier editions of this book or obtained from HBS Case Services.

question about the beer business as a compatible element in the company's marketing mix.

REASONS FOR NOT ARTICULATING STRATEGY

For a number of reasons companies seldom formulate and publish as complete a statement as we have just illustrated. Conscious planning of the long-term development of companies has been until recently less common than individual executive responses to environmental pressure, competitive threat, or entrepreneurial opportunity. In the latter mode of development, the unity or coherence of corporate effort is unplanned, natural, intuitive, or even nonexistent. Incrementalism in practice sometimes gives the appearance of consciously formulated strategy, but it may be the natural result of compromise among coalitions backing contrary policy proposals or skillful improvisatory adaptation to external forces.[2] Practicing managers who prefer muddling through to the strategic process at the heart of Business Policy would never commit themselves to an articulate strategy.

Other reasons for the scarcity of concrete statements of strategy include the desirability of keeping strategic plans confidential for security reasons and ambiguous to avoid internal conflict or even final decision. Skillful incrementalists may have plans in their heads which they do not reveal to avoid resistance and other trouble in their own organization. A company with a large division in an obsolescent business which it intends to drain of cash until operations are discontinued could not expect high morale and cooperation to follow publication of this intent. Since in any dynamic company, strategy is continually evolving, the official statement of strategy, unless it were couched in very general terms, would be as hard to keep up to date as an organization chart. Finally, a firm that has internalized its strategy does not feel the need to keep saying what it is, valuable as that information might be to new members.

DEDUCING STRATEGY FROM BEHAVIOR

The cases in this book enable students of Policy to do what the managements of the companies usually have not done. In the absence of explicit statements, we may deduce from decisions observed what the pattern is and what the company's goals and policies are, on the assumption

[2] For an extended account of incrementalism, see David Braybrooke and Charles E. Lindblom, *A Strategy of Decision* (New York: Free Press, 1963), and James Brian Quinn, *Strategies for Change: Logical Incrementalism* (Homewood, Ill.: Richard D. Irwin, 1980). H. Edward Wrapp's "Good Managers Don't Make Policy Decisions," *Harvard Business Review*, July–August 1984, pp. 8 ff., is a widely read analysis of purposeful incrementalism. See also James Brian Quinn, Henry Mintzberg, and Robert M. James, *The Strategy Process* (Englewood Cliffs, N.J.: Prentice-Hall, 1988).

that some perhaps unspoken consensus lies behind them. Careful examination of the behavior described in the cases will reveal what the strategy must be. At the same time we should not mistake apparent strategy visible in a pattern of past incremental decisions for conscious planning for the future. What will pass as the current strategy of a company may almost always be deduced from its behavior, but a strategy for a future of changed circumstance may not always be distinguishable from performance in the present. For all of Howard Head's skill in integrating a series of product development, distribution, merchandising, service, manufacturing, and research and development decisions around the metal ski, was he as well prepared as he might have been for the advent of the fiberglass ski? The essence of strategic decision is its reach into the future.

FORMULATION OF STRATEGY

Corporate strategy is an organization process, in many ways inseparable from the structure, behavior, and culture of the company in which it takes place. Nevertheless, we may abstract from the process two important aspects, interrelated in real life but separable for the purposes of analysis. The first of these we may call *formulation;* the second, *implementation.* Deciding what strategy should be may be approached as a rational undertaking, even if in real life emotional attachments (as to metal skis or investigative reporting) may complicate choice among future alternatives (for ski manufacturers or alternative newspapers). The principal subactivities of strategy formulation as a logical activity include identifying opportunities and threats in the company's environment and attaching some estimate or risk to the discernible alternatives. Before a choice can be made, the company's strengths and weaknesses should be appraised together with the resources on hand and available. Its actual or potential capacity to take advantage of perceived market needs or to cope with attendant risks should be estimated as objectively as possible. The strategic alternative which results from matching opportunity and corporate capability at an acceptable level of risk is what we may call an *economic strategy.*

The process described thus far assumes that strategists are analytically objective in estimating the relative capacity of their company and the opportunity they see or anticipate in developing markets. The extent to which they wish to undertake low or high risk presumably depends on their profit objectives. The higher they set the latter, the more willing they must be to assume a correspondingly high risk that the market opportunity they see will not develop or that the corporate competence required to excel competition will not be forthcoming.

So far we have described the intellectual processes of ascertaining what a company *might do* in terms of environmental opportunity, of deciding what it *can do* in terms of ability and power, and of bringing these two considerations together in optimal equilibrium. The determination of strategy also requires consideration of what alternatives are preferred, quite apart from economic considerations, by the chief executive and by his or her immediate associates as well. The acquiescence or, better, the enthusiastic engagement of all whose productivity and creativity are important in achieving superior performance grows out of participation in the process of strategic decision. Personal values, aspirations, and ideals do, and in our judgment quite properly should, influence the final choice of purposes. Thus what the people in a company *want to do* must be brought into the strategic decision.

Finally, strategic choice has an ethical aspect—a fact much more dramatically illustrated in some industries (chemicals and nuclear power, for example) than in others. Just as alternatives may be ordered in terms of the degree of risk that they entail, so may they be examined against the standards of responsiveness to the expectations of society that the strategist elects. Some alternatives may seem to the executive considering them more attractive than the others when the public good or service to society is considered. What a company *should do* thus appears as a fourth element of the strategic decision.

The ability to identify the four components of strategy—(1) market opportunity, (2) corporate competence and resources, (3) personal values and aspirations, and (4) acknowledged obligations to segments of society other than stockholders—is nothing compared to the art of reconciling their implications in a final pattern of purpose. Taken by itself, each consideration might lead in a different direction.

If you put the various aspirations of individuals in any organization you know against this statement, you will see what we mean. Even in a single mind contradictory aspirations can survive a long time before the need to calculate trade-offs and integrate divergent inclinations becomes clear. Growth opportunity attracted many companies to the computer business after World War II. The decision to diversify out of typewriters and calculators was encouraged by growth opportunity and excitement. But the financial, technical, and marketing requirements of this business exceeded the capacity of most of the competitors of IBM. The magnet of opportunity and the incentive of desire obscured the calculations of what resources and competence were required to succeed. Most crucially, where corporate capability leads, executives do not always want to go. Of all the components of strategic choice, the combination of resources and competence is most crucial to success.

THE IMPLEMENTATION OF STRATEGY

Since effective implementation can make a sound strategic decision ineffective or a debatable choice successful, it is as important to examine the processes of implementation as to weigh the advantages of available strategic alternatives. The implementation of strategy is composed of a series of subactivities which are primarily administrative. If purpose is determined, then the resources of a company can be mobilized to accomplish it. An organizational structure appropriate for the efficient performance of the required tasks must be made effective by information systems and relationships permitting coordination of subdivided activities. The organizational processes of performance measurement, compensation, and management development—all of them enmeshed in systems of incentives and controls—must be directed toward the kind of behavior required by organizational purpose. The role of personal leadership is important and sometimes decisive in the accomplishment of strategy. Although we know that organization structure and processes of compensation, incentives, control, and management development influence and constrain the formulation of strategy, we should look first at the logical proposition that structure should follow strategy in order to cope with the organizational reality that strategy also follows structure. When we have examined both tendencies, we will understand and to some extent be prepared to deal with the interdependence of the formulation and implementation of corporate purpose. Figure 1 may be useful in understanding the analysis of strategy as a pattern of interrelated decisions.

FIGURE 1

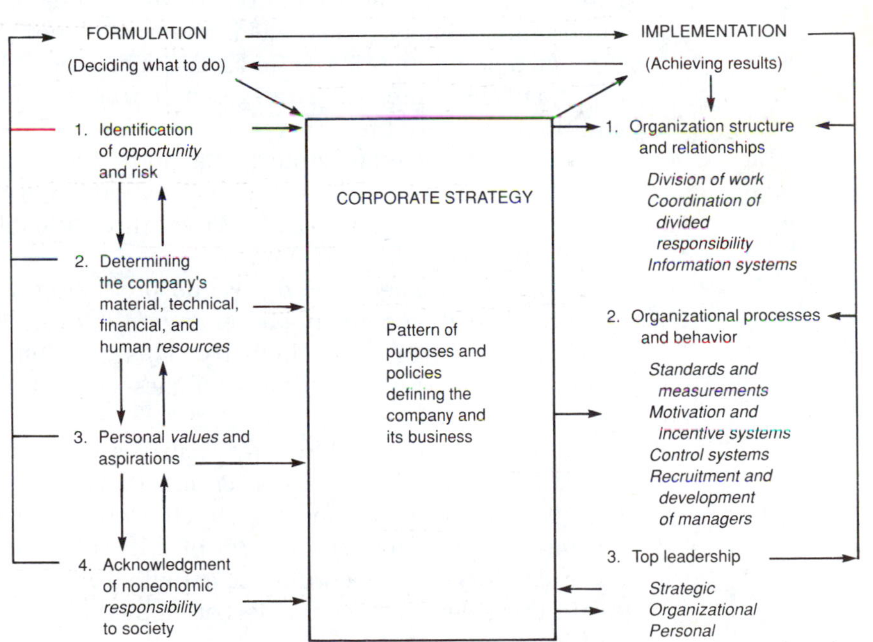

KINDS OF STRATEGIES

The most important characteristic of a corporate pattern of decision that may properly be called strategic is its uniqueness. A creative reconciliation of alternatives for future development is made unique by the special characteristics of an organization, its central competence, history, financial and technical resources, and the aspirations and sense of responsibility of its leaders. The environment—market opportunity and risk—is more nearly the same for major companies operating in the same geographical regions than are the resources, values, and responsibility components of strategy. For the company unequipped to dominate the full range of opportunity, the quest for a profitable segment of, or niche in, a market is, if successful, also likely to distinguish one company from another. In fact in an industry where all companies seem to have the same strategy, we will find trouble for all but the leaders—as at various times American Motors, Chrysler, and Ford have had different degrees of difficulty following General Motors, which got where it is by *not* following the previous industry leader, Henry Ford.

In seeking its position of uniqueness, there are two fundamental types of competitive advantage that a company can possess: *lower cost* and/or *differentiation.* A lower cost position can potentially come from many sources that reflect the firm's strategy, among them larger scale, favorable raw material supplies, or proximate location. A lower cost position yields the firm higher profitability than rivals at whatever the industry price. Differentiation, or the superiority of the company in meeting special or important customer needs, yields the firm higher profitability than rivals through a premium price. Differentiation may potentially result from many aspects of the company's strategy, including its product quality, servicing ability, or delivery time.

Every truly successful strategy that outperforms competitors exploits one or both of these two sources of competitive advantage, achieved in a manner that is sustainable against rivals. We see three possible generic strategies for sustaining competitive advantage:

1. *Overall cost leadership.* While producing a product or service of good quality, the company strives to be the overall cost leader across its entire product line in the industry. This position is achieved through a range of supporting functional policies compatible with industry economics.

2. *Differentiation.* The company strives to be distinctive in an important aspect of most of its products or services that the customer values. Costs are kept close to those of competitors, but the strategic emphasis is on achieving and maintaining the chosen form of differentiation, quality, or style, for example, through the coordinated activities of each functional department. Again this selective superiority is attempted across the entire product line and in all its markets.

3. *Focus.* Unable to be the low-cost producer industrywide or to achieve comprehensive differentiation, the firm selects a narrower strategic target and concentrates its entire efforts at serving a distinctively defined market segment. In so doing, the firm is able to achieve lower costs, differentiation, or both in serving the chosen market even though it cannot achieve these competitive advantages industrywide or across the broadest possible product line. Possible strategic targets may include portions of the product line, particular customer segments, limited geographic areas, particular distribution channels, or some combination of these. The essential logic of the focused strategy is that the firm competing in this way can serve its target better than the competitor with the divided loyalties of serving a special target along with others in a more broadly based strategy.

Usually, the firm must make a choice among these three fundamentally different approaches to achieving a competitive advantage because the functional requirements and organizational needs of each are different. Generally, for example, the firm achieving differentiation does so at the price of higher costs. In a few industries where the economics allow it, however, a firm can be both cost leader and differentiated at the same time. The enviable position is nirvana, remote from the pain and turmoil of competition.

On the way to this happy state, companies encounter other generic strategies, less universal than low-cost differentiation and focus but more common. The generation of strategic alternatives is sometimes approached with growth the dominant consideration.

Low-Growth Strategies

1. *No change.* The strategy properly identified and checked out against the tests of validity outlined below can be closely monitored, fine tuned for minor defects, and managed for maximum cash flows, with low investment in forced growth. Defensive contingencies will be designed for unexpected change, and efficient implementation will be the focus of top-management attention. During recessions and after the onset of conservation and environmental protection, this strategy is more attractive than it was in the heyday of "more is better." The profit to be made from doing better what a company already knows how to do rather than investing heavily in growth is the attraction of this strategy, which can be protected by achievement of low costs. Its disadvantage is the possiblity of being overtaken or displaced by new developments and the restriction of opportunity for organization members. Positions in cost advantage and differentiation may be less vulnerable if growth goals are modest.

2. *Retreat.* The possibility of liquidation is not to be sought out but may be for companies in deep trouble a better choice than continuing the struggle. Less drastic alternatives than complete liquidation include discontinuance or divestment of marginal operations or merging with another company, ceding control. This alternative may come to mind as you look at one or two of the cases in this book. It would have come up more often in earlier editions around cases from the farm equipment, typewriter, and sewing machine businesses. Consolidation may protect a market niche.

3. *Focus on limited special opportunity.* A more constructive course of contraction is concentration on a profitable specialty product or a limited but significant market niche, as if Head had elected to concentrate on high-priced, high-quality skis without diversification into ski wear and other equipment. Success in a narrow line almost always tempts a company to broaden its line, but the McIlhenny strategy (Tabasco sauce only) may not be totally obsolete. If the proper focus is chosen, the limits may relax and growth may come in any case. Once the risk of limited life is accepted, the advantages of the no-change strategy can be sought.

Forced-Growth Strategies

1. *Acquisition of competitors.* In the early stages of its development, a company with a successful strategy and proven record of successful execution can acquire small competitors in the same business to expand its market. Eventually antitrust regulation will put an end to this practice, unless the prospective acquisition is very small or on the edge of bankruptcy. Such acquisitions are usually followed by an adaptation of strategy either by the parent or acquired company to keep the total company a single business or one dominated by its original product-market specialization. Lower costs do not follow automatically from growth by acquisition.

2. *Vertical integration.* A conservative growth strategy, keeping a company close to its core competence and experience in its industry, consists of moving backward via acquisition or internal development to sources of supply and forward toward the ultimate customer. When a newspaper buys a pulp and paper mill and forest lands or news agencies for distribution, it is extending its strategy but not changing materially the nature of its business. Increasing the stages of integration provides a greater number of options to be developed or closed out as, for example, the making of fine paper and the distribution of magazines. Vertical integration serves lower costs better than it serves product differentiation.

3. *Geographical expansion.* Enlargement of territory can be accomplished by building new plants and enlarging marketing organizations or by acquisition of competitors. For a sizable company the opportunity to enlarge international operations, by export and establishment of plants and marketing activities overseas, with or without foreign partners, may protect against contraction forced by domestic competition. You could have considered the possibility of Head Ski's seeking growth overseas, where 19 percent of its sales were accomplished by a single agent about whom almost nothing is said in the case.

4. *Diversification.* The avenue to growth which presents the most difficult strategic choices is diversification. Diversification can range from minor additions to basic product line to completely unrelated businesses. It can be sought through internal research and development, the purchase of new product ideas or technology, and the acquisition of companies. It may have nothing to do with either lower costs or differentiation of product or service and detract seriously from both.

KINDS OF COMPANIES

The process of strategic decision differs in complexity depending upon the diversity of the company in question. Just as having the range of strategy from liquidation to multinational diversification in mind will stimulate the generation of strategic alternatives, so a simple way of differentiating kinds of companies will help us see why different kinds of companies have different kinds of problems in making their activities coherent and effective and in setting a course for the future.

Bruce Scott has developed a model of stages of corporate development in which each stage is characterized by the way a firm is managed and the scope of strategic choice available to it.[3] *Stage I* is a single-product (or line of products) company with little or no formal structure run by the owner who personally performs most of the managerial functions and uses subjective and unsystematic measures of performance and reward and control systems. The strategy of this firm is what the owner-manager wants it to be.

Stage II is the single-product firm grown so large that functional specialization has become imperative. A degree of integration has developed between raw materials, production processes, distribution, and sales. The search for product or process improvement is institutionalized in research and development, and performance management and control and compensation systems become systematic with the formulation of policy to guide delegation of operating decisions. The strategic choice is still under top control and centers upon the degree of integration, size of market share, and breadth of product line.

Stage III is a company with multiple-product lines and channels of distribution with an organization based on product-market relationships rather than function. Its businesses are not to a significant degree integrated; they have their own markets. Its research and development are oriented to new products rather than improvements, and its measurement and control systems are increasingly systematic and oriented to results. Strategic alternatives are phrased in terms of entry into, and exit from, industries and allocation of resources by industry and rate of growth.

[3] See Bruce R. Scott, "Can Industry Survive the Welfare State?" *Harvard Business Review*, September–October 1982, pp. 70–84.

If a company grows, it may pass from stage I to stage III, although it can become very large while still in stage II. Its strategic decisions will grow in complexity. The stages of development model has proved productive in relating different kinds of strategies to kinds of companies and has led other researchers into productive classification. Leonard Wrigley and Richard P. Rumelt have carried Scott's work forward to develop suggestive ways of categorizing companies and comparing their strategies.[4]

First, of course, is the *single-business* firm (stages I and II firms) with 95 percent or more of its revenues arising from a single business—an oil company or flour-milling company, for example, or as you will see, Crown Cork & Seal.

Second is the *dominant business* consisting of firms diversified to some extent but still obtaining most of their revenues from a single business. The diversification may arise from end products of integration, with products stemming from strengths of the firm or minor unrelated activities. A large oil company in the petrochemical and fertilizer business would fall in this category.

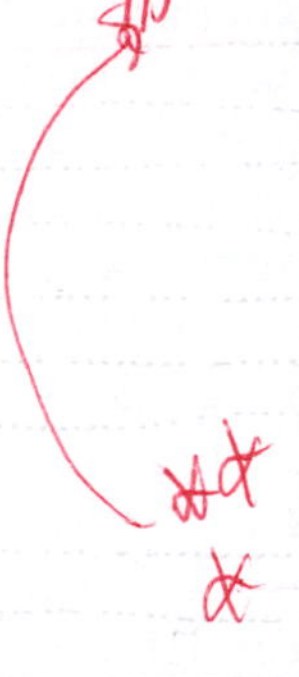

Third is the *related business* comprising diversified firms in which the diversification has been principally accomplished by relating new activities to old—General Electric and Westinghouse, for example.

Fourth is the *unrelated business.* These firms have diversified primarily without regard to relationships between new businesses and current activities. The conglomerate companies fall in this category.

Each of these categories has subdivisions devised by Rumelt which you may wish to examine at a more advanced stage of Policy studies. In the meantime it is interesting to note that Rumelt has found significantly superior performance in the related businesses, suggesting that the strategy of diversifying from the original business to a significant degree has been the most successful strategic pattern among the Fortune 500 under conditions prevailing in recent years.

The range of strategy and the kind of company which different growth strategies have produced suggest, in short, that the process of defining the business of a company will vary greatly depending on the degree of diversification under way in the company. The product-market choices are crystal clear in Crown Cork & Seal and a single-business oil company; they could not be exhaustively listed for General Electric. That top management decides product-market questions in such a company, except in such instances as entry into nuclear energy, is conceivable only as an oversimplification.

---

[4] Leonard Wrigley, "Division Autonomy and Diversification" (Ph.D. dissertation, Harvard Business School, 1970); and Richard P. Rumelt, *Strategy Structure and Economic Performance* (Boston: Division of Research, Harvard Business School, 1974). Malcolm Salter has added a refinement to stage III in "Stages of Corporate Development," *Journal of Business Policy* 1, no. 1 (1970), pp. 40–51.

As diversification increases, the definition of the total business turns away from literal description of products and markets (which become the business of the separate product divisions) toward general statements of financial results expected and corporate policy in other areas. A conglomerate firm made up of many different businesses will have many different strategies, related or not, depending upon the desire for synergy in the strategic direction of the total enterprise. The overall strategy of a highly diversified firm may be only the total of its divisional strategies. That it should be more than that is a matter for argument. To make it so puts heavy demands on the ability to conceptualize corporate purpose.

The task of identifying the coherence and unity of a conglomerate is, of course, much greater than that of even a multidivision-related business. Students should be prepared, then, to adapt the beginning definition offered here to the complexity of the business they are examining. Since the trend over time is product diversity in growing firms and evolution from stage I to stage III, it is well to have this complication in mind now.

For as Norman Berg makes clear in "Strategic Planning in Conglomerate Companies," strategic choice is not merely the function of the chief executive office.[5] It is of necessity a multilevel activity, with each unit concerned with its own environment and its own objectives. The process will reflect the noneconomic goals of people at the level at which proposals are made. In a conglomerate of unrelated businesses the corporate staff is small, the divisions are relatively autonomous, and the locus of strategic planning is in the divisions. This makes supervision of the strategic planning process and allocation of resources, depending upon the evaluation of strategies submitted, the strategic role of the corporate senior managers.

The differences in the application of a concept of strategy to a modest single business on the one hand and to a multinational conglomerate on the other – although important – mean that the ability to conceive of a business in strategic terms must be distributed throughout the organization in a complex company. The problems of choosing among strategic alternatives and making the choice effective over time, together with the problems of ensuring that such organization processes as performance measurement do not impede the choice, must be part of the management ability of many people besides the general managers. All those involved in the strategic process, it follows, are vitally concerned with how a strategy can be evaluated so that it may be continued, amended, or abandoned as appropriate. Operating level managers who make a strategic proposal

---

[5] Norman A Berg, "Strategic Planning in Conglomerate Companies," *Harvard Business Review*, May–June 1965, pp. 79–92. See also his "What's Different about Conglomerate Management?" *Harvard Business Review*, November–December 1969, and "Corporate Strategy in the Diversified Firm," Chapter 12 in his *General Management: An Analytical Approach* (Homewood, Ill.: Richard D. Irwin, 1984).

should be able to test its validity against corporate norms if for no other reason than their own survival. Those who must approve and allocate funds to such proposals should have a criterion to evaluate their worth going beyond a general confidence (or lack of it) in the ability of the proponents.

CRITERIA FOR EVALUATION

How is the actual or proposed strategy to be judged? How are we to know that one strategy is better than another? A number of important questions can regularly be asked. As is already evident, no infallible indicators are available. With practice they will lead to reliable intuitive discriminations.

1. *Is the strategy identifiable and has it been made clear either in words or practice?*

The degree to which attention has been given to the strategic alternatives available to a company is likely to be basic to the soundness of its strategic decision. To cover in empty phrases ("Our policy is planned profitable growth in any market we can serve well") an absence of analysis of opportunity or actual determination of corporate strength is worse than to remain silent, for it conveys the illusion of a commitment when none has been made. The unstated strategy cannot be tested or contested and is likely therefore to be weak. If it is implicit in the intuition of a strong leader, the organization is likely to be weak and the demands the strategy makes upon it are likely to remain unmet. A strategy must be explicit to be effective and specific enough to require some action and exclude others.

2. *Is the strategy in some way unique?*

As we have already said, a fully developed strategy will visibly differentiate any company from its competitors. For producers of commodities, like chlorine or cement, the difference will not be found in the product itself but in the way it is marketed, delivered, produced, or priced. For manufacturers of proprietary products, the problem of differentation lies in substitute products or in future direct competition when patents expire. The sameness that afflicts companies not strategically managed usually arises from industry structure, from similarities in the technology of production, and from conventions developed to limit competition, regulate market share, and educate newcomers in how things are done. Uniqueness is more the product of imagination than experience.

3. *Does the strategy exploit fully domestic and international environmental opportunity?*

An unqualified yes answer is likely to be rare even in the instance of global giants such as General Motors. But the present and future dimensions of markets can be analyzed without forgetting the limited resources of the planning company in order to outline the requirements of balanced growth and the need for environmental information. The relation between market opportunity and organizational development is a critical one in the design of future plans. Unless growth is incompatible with the resources of an organization or the aspirations of its management, it is likely that a strategy that does not purport to make full use of market opportunity will be weak also in other aspects. Vulnerability to competition is increased by lack of interest in market share.

4. *Is the strategy consistent with corporate competence and resources, both present and projected?*

Although additional resources, both financial and managerial, are available to companies with genuine opportunity, the availability of each must be finally determined and programmed along a practicable time scale. This may be the most difficult question in this series. The key factor which is usually left out is the availability of management for effective implementation or the opportunity cost implicit in the assignment of management to any task.

5. *Are the major provisions of the strategy and the program of major policies of which it is comprised internally consistent?*

A foolish consistency, Emerson said, is the hobgoblin of little minds, and consistency of any kind is certainly not the first qualification of successful corporate CEOs. Nonetheless, one advantage of making as specific a statement of strategy as is practicable is the resultant availability of a careful check on fit, unity, coherence, compatibility, and synergy—the state in which the whole of anything can be viewed as greater than the sum of its parts. For example, a manufacturer of chocolate candy who depends for two thirds of his business upon wholesalers should not follow a policy of ignoring them or of dropping all support of their activities and all attention to their complaints. Similarly, two engineers who found a new firm expressly to do development work should not follow a policy of accepting orders that, though highly profitable, in effect turn their company into a large job shop, with the result that unanticipated financial and production problems take all the time that might have gone into development. An examination of any substantial firm will reveal at least some details in which policies pursued by different departments tend to go in different directions. Where inconsistency threatens concerted effort to achieve budgeted results within a planned time period, consistency becomes a vital rather than merely an esthetic problem.

6. *Is the chosen level of risk feasible in economic and personal terms?*

Strategies vary in the degree of risk willingly undertaken by their designers. For example, a small food company in pursuit of its marketing strategy once deliberately courted disaster in production slowdowns and in erratic behavior of cocoa futures. But the choice was made knowingly and the return was likely to be correspondingly great. The president was temperamentally able to live under this pressure and presumably had recourse if disaster struck. At the other extreme, another company had such modest growth aspirations that the junior members of its management were unhappy. They would have preferred a more aggressive and ambitious company. Although risk cannot always be known for sure, the level at which it is estimated is, within limits, optional. The riskiness of any future plan should be compatible with the economic resources of the organization and the temperament of the managers concerned.

7. *Is the strategy appropriate to the personal values and aspirations of the key managers?*

Until we consider the relationship of personal values to the choice of strategy, it is not useful to dwell long upon this criterion. But to cite an extreme case, the deliberate falsification of warehouse receipts to conceal the absence of soybean oil from tanks which are supposed to contain it would not be an element of competitive strategy to which most of us would like to be committed. A strong personal attraction of leisure, to cite a less extreme example, is inconsistent with a strategy requiring all-out effort from the senior members of a company. Or if, for example, a new president abhors conflict and competition, then it can be predicted that the hard-driven firm of an earlier day will have to change its strategy. Conflict between personal preferences, aspirations, and goals of the key members of an organization and the plan for its future is a sign of danger and a harbinger of mediocre performance or failure.

8. *Is the strategy appropriate to the desired level of contribution to society?*

Closely allied to the value is the ethical criterion. As the professional obligations of business are acknowledged by an increasing number of senior managers, it grows more and more appropriate to ask whether the current strategy of a firm is as socially responsible as it might be. Although it can be argued that filling any economic need contributes to the social good, it is clear that manufacturers of cigarettes might well consider diversification on grounds other than their fear of future legislation. That the strategy should not require violations of law or ethical practice to be effective became abundantly clear with the revelation in the mid-70s of widespread bribery and questionable payments, particularly in overseas activities. Honesty and integrity may seem exclusively questions of implementation, but if the strategy is not distinctive, making it effective in competition may tempt managers to unethical practice. Thus a drug manufacturer who emphasizes the production of amphetamines at a level beyond total established medical need is inevitably compelling corruption. The meeting of sales quotas at the distribution level necessitates distribution of the drug as "speed" with or without the cooperation of prescribing physicians. To the extent that the chosen economic opportunity of the firm has social costs, such as air or water pollution, a statement of intention to deal with these is desirable and prudent. Ways to ask and answer this question will be considered in the section on the company and its responsibilities to society.

9. *Does the strategy constitute a clear stimulus to organizational effort and commitment?*

For organizations which aspire not merely to survive but to lead and to generate productive performance in a climate that will encourage the development of competence and the satisfaction of individual needs, the strategy selected should be examined for its inherent attractiveness to the organization. Some undertakings are inherently more likely to gain the commitment of able men of goodwill than others. Given the variety of human preferences, it is risky to illustrate this difference briefly. But currently a company that is vigorously expanding its overseas operations finds that several of its socially conscious young people exhibit more zeal in connection with its work in developing countries than in Europe. Generally speaking, the bolder the choice of goals and the wider range of human needs they reflect, the more successfully they will appeal to the capable membership of a healthy and energetic organization.

10. *Are there early indications of the responsiveness of markets and market segments to the strategy?*

Results, no matter how long postponed by necessary preparations, are, of course, the most telling indicators of soundness, so long as they are read correctly at the proper time. A strategy may pass with flying colors all the tests so far proposed and may be in internal consistency and uniqueness an admirable work of art. But if within a time period made reasonable by the company's resources and the original plan the strategy does not work, then it must be weak in some way that has escaped attention. Bad luck, faulty implementation, and competitive countermoves may be more to blame for unsatisfactory results than flaws in design, but the possibility of the latter should not be unduly discounted. Conceiving a strategy that will win the company a unique place in the business community, that will give it an enduring concept of itself, that will harmonize its diverse activities, and that will provide a fit between environmental opportunity and present or potential company strength is an extremely complicated task.

We cannot expect single tests of soundness to deliver a complete evaluation. But an analytical examination of any company's strategy against the several criteria here suggested will nonetheless give anyone concerned with making, proving, or contributing to corporate planning more than enough to think about.

PROBLEMS IN EVALUATION

The evaluation of strategy is as much an act of judgment as is the original conception, and it may be as subject to error. The most common source of difficulty is the misevaluation of current results. When results are unsatisfactory, as we have just pointed out, a reexamination of strategy is called for. At the same time, outstandingly good current results are not necessarily evidence that the strategy is sound. Abnormal upward surges in demand may deceive marginal producers that all is well within their current strategy, until expansion of more efficient competitors wipes out their market share. Extrapolation of present performance into the future, overoptimism and complacence, and underestimation of competitive response and of the time required to accommodate to changes in demand are often by-products of success. Unusually high profits may blind unwary managers to impending environmental change. Their concern for the future can under no circumstances be safely suspended. Conversely, a high-risk strategy that has failed was not necessarily a mistake, so long as the risk was anticipated and the consequences of failure carefully calculated. In fact, a planning problem confronting a number of diversified companies today is how to encourage their divisions to undertake projects where failure can be afforded but where success, if it comes, will be attended by high profits not available in run-of-the-mill, low-risk activities.

Although the possibility of misinterpreting results is by far the commonest obstacle to accurate evaluation of strategy, the criteria previously outlined suggest immediately some additional difficulties. It is as easy to misevaluate corporate resources and the financial requirements of a new move as to misread the environment for future opportunities. To be overresponsive to industry trends may be as dangerous as to ignore them. The correspondence of the company's strategy with current environmental developments and an overreadiness to adapt may obscure the opportunity for a larger share of a declining market or for growth in profits without a parallel growth in total sales.

The intrinsic difficulty of determining and choosing among strategic alternatives leads many companies to do what the rest of the industry is doing rather than to make an independent determination of opportunity and resources. Sometimes the companies of an industry run like sheep all in one direction. The similarity among the strategies, at least in some periods of history, of insurance companies, banks, railroads, and airplane manufacturers may lead one to conclude these strategic decisions were based on industry convention more than on independent analysis.

A strategy may manifest an all-too-clear correspondence with the personal values of the founder, owner, or chief executive. Like a correspondence with dominant trends and the strategic decisions of competitors, this one may also be deceptive and unproductive. For example, a personal preference for growth beyond all reasonable expectations may be given undue weight. It should be only one factor among several in any balanced consideration of what is involved in designing strategy. Too little attention to a corporation's actual competence for growth or diversification is the commonest error of all.

It is entirely possible that a strategy may reflect in an exaggerated fashion the values rather than the reasoned decisions of the responsible manager or managers. That imbalance may go undetected. The entire business community may be dominated by certain beliefs of which one should be wary. A critic of strategy must be at heart enough of a nonconformist to raise questions about generally accepted modes of thought and conventional thinking that substitute for original analysis.

The timid may not find it prudent to challenge publicly some of the ritual of policy formulation. But even for them it will serve the purposes of criticism to inquire privately into such sacred propositions as the one proclaiming that a company must grow or die or that national planning for energy needs is anathema.

Another canon of management that may engender questionable strategies is the idea that cash funds in excess of reasonable dividend requirements should be reinvested whether in revitalization of a company's traditional activities or in mergers and acquisitions that will diversify products and services. Successful operations, a heretic might observe, sometimes bring riches to a company that lacks the capacity to reemploy them. Yet a decision to return to the owners substantial amounts of capital which the company does not have the competence or desire to put to work is an almost unheard-of development. It is therefore appropriate, particularly in the instance of very successful companies in older and stable industries, to inquire how far strategy reflects a simple desire to put all resources to work rather than a more valid appraisal of investment opportunity in relation to unique corporate strengths. We should not forget to consider an unfashionable alternative—namely, that to keep an already large worldwide corporation within reasonable bounds, a portion of the assets might well be returned to stockholders for investment in other enterprises.

Much more serious misevaluation of strategy stems from a pervasive conflict between the academic interests of financial economics and the practitioner orientation of the concept of corporate strategy. The use of simple ratios, like the relation of debt to equity, or simple measures, like return on an investment, return on equity, or earnings per share, as determinants of decision often leads to shortsighted moves to satisfy a measure rather than to make a strategic investment. (The related misuse of portfolio analysis leads similarly to mechanical appraisal of separate businesses rather than relating the separate businesses to the future of the company as a whole.) Capital budgeting that applies discounted cash flow analysis and hurdle rates to separate projects often bypasses strategic consideration of the project. Improper use of discounted cash flow analysis ignores the difficulties of estimating discount rates, future cash flows, and the project's impact on the company's cash flow from other assets and on the firm's future investment opportunities.

The distortion in evaluating and shaping strategy by overuse of financial formulas and rules of thumb is unwittingly perpetrated by financial analysts, financial economists, and students of financial theory who appear unaware of the need to make financial policy serve rather than dominate corporate strategy. Parochial use of financial expertise, in short, can pervert the strategic process by appearing to justify project-by-project rather than strategy-dominated decisions. It originates in the simplistic assumption

(with implicit emphasis on the short term) that the single purpose of corporate enterpise is the enhancement of shareholder wealth.[6]

The identification of opportunity and choice of purpose are such challenging intellectual activities that we should not be surprised to find that persistent problems attend the proper evaluation of strategy. But just as the criteria for evaluation are useful, even if not precise, so the dangers of misevaluation are less menacing if they are recognized. We have noted some inexactness in the concept of strategy, the problems of making resolute determinations in the face of uncertainty, the necessity for judgment in the evaluation of soundness of strategy, and the misevaluation into which human error may lead us. None of these alters the commonsense conclusion that a business enterprise guided by a clear sense of purpose rationally arrived at and emotionally ratified by commitment is more likely to have a successful outcome, in terms of profit and social good, than a company whose future is left to guesswork and chance. Conscious strategy does not preclude brilliance of improvisation or the welcome consequences of good fortune. Its cost is principally thought and work for which it is hard but not impossible to find time.

APPLICATION TO CASES

As you attempt to apply the concept of strategy to the analysis of Crown Cork & Seal, Caterpillar Tractor, Komatsu Limited, and later cases, try to keep in mind three questions:

1. What is the strategy of the company?
2. In the light of *(a)* the characteristics of its industry and developments in its environment, *(b)* its own strengths and weaknesses, and *(c)* the personal values influencing decision, is the strategy sound?
3. What recommendations for changed strategy might advantageously be made to the CEO?

Whatever other questions you may be asked or may ask yourself, you will wish constantly to order your study and structure your analysis of case information according to the need to *identify, evaluate,* and *recommend.*

---

[6] Students interested in pursuing the relation of financial policy to corporate strategy should read Stewart C. Myers, "Finance Theory and Financial Strategy," in Arnoldo Hax, *Readings on Strategic Management* (Cambridge, Mass.: Ballinger Publishing Co., 1984), pp. 177–88; Richard R. Ellsworth, "Subordinate Financial Policy to Corporate Strategy," *Harvard Business Review,* November–December 1983, pp. 119 ff.; and "Capital Markets and Competitive Decline," *Harvard Business Review,* September–October 1985, pp. 177 ff. For the route to reconciliation, see Gordon Donaldson's important book: *Managing Corporate Wealth: The Operation of a Comprehensive Financial Goals System* (New York: Praeger Publishers, 1984).

By now you have an idea of strategy, which discussion of the cases will greatly clarify. You know how it is derived and some of its uses and limitations. You have been given some criteria for evaluating the strategies you identify and those you propose. And you have been properly warned about errors of judgment which await the unwary.

The cases which immediately follow will permit you to consider what contributions if any the concept of strategy (if mostly missing as a conscious formulation) would have made to these companies. What strategic alternatives can be detected in the changing circumstances affecting their fortunes? Which ones would you choose if you were responsible or asked to advise? By the time these cases have been examined, you will be ready to turn from the nature and uses of strategy to a study in sequence of its principal components—environmental opportunity, corporate capability, personal aspirations, and moral responsibility.

Crown Cork and Seal Company, Inc.

In 1977, Crown Cork and Seal Company was the fourth largest producer of metal cans and crowns[1] in the United States. Under John Connelly, chairman and CEO, Crown had raised itself up from near bankruptcy in 1957. After 20 years of consistent growth, the company had emerged as a major force in both the domestic and international metal container markets (see Exhibit 1).

During those 20 years, Crown Cork and Seal had concentrated its manufacturing efforts on tin-plated cans for holding beer, soft drinks, and aerosol products. By 1977, however, the ozone controversy and the trend toward legislative regulation of non-returnable containers was threatening Crown's domestic business. Was it time for a change in Crown's formula for success or merely time for a reaffirmation of Connelly's basic strategic choices?

To explore these questions, this case looks at the metal container industry, Crown's strategy and position within that industry, and the nature of the problems facing the company during mid-1977.

THE METAL CONTAINER INDUSTRY IN 1977

The metal container industry included 100 firms and a vast number of product lines. This section describes the product segments in which Crown competed, examines the industry's competitive structure, and looks at three industrywide trends: (1) increasing self-manufacture, (2) new material introductions, and (3) the effect of the "packaging revolution" on the competitive atmosphere.

The Products

Metal containers made up almost a third of all packaging products used in the United States in 1976. Metal containers included traditional steel and aluminum cans, foil containers, and metal drums and pails of all shapes and sizes. Of these, metal cans were the largest segment, reaching a value of $7.1 billion in 1976. Cans were being used in more than three fourths of all metal-container shipments.

Harvard Business School case 378–024.

[1] Crowns are flanged bottle caps, originally made with an insert of natural cork—hence the name Crown Cork and Seal.

Cans were composed of two basic raw materials: aluminum and tin-plated steel. Originally, they were formed by rolling a sheet of metal, soldering it, cutting it to the right size, and attaching two ends, thereby forming a three-piece, seamed can. In the late 1960s, a new process introduced by the aluminum industry made possible a two-piece can. The new can was formed by pushing a flat blank of metal into the deep cup, which eliminated the need for a separate bottom. The product makers adopted the term "drawn and ironed" from the molding procedure.

The aluminum companies that developed the process, Alcoa and Reynolds, had done so with the intention of turning the process over to can manufacturers and subsequently increasing raw material sales. However, when the manufacturers were reluctant to incur the large costs involved in line changeovers, the two aluminum companies began building their own two-piece lines and competing directly in the end market.

The new can had advantages in weight, labor, and materials costs and was recommended by the Food and Drug Administration, which was worried about lead from soldered three-piece cans migrating into the can's contents. Tin-plated can producers soon acknowledged the new process as the wave of the future. They quickly began to explore the possibilities for drawing and ironing steel sheets. By 1972 the technique was perfected, and investment dollars had begun to pour into line changeovers and new equipment purchases. Exhibit 2 illustrates the rapid switch to the two-piece can in the beverage industry. In the beer segment alone, almost half of the total cans used in 1974 were made by the new process.

Growth

Between 1967 and 1976 the number of metal cans shipped from the manufacturers grew at an average of 3.4 percent annually. As shown in Table 1, the greatest

TABLE 1
METAL CAN SHIPMENTS 1967–1976
In Thousands of Base Boxes

	1967	*1972*	*1973*	*1974*	*1975*	*1976*
Total metal cans	133,980	168,868	180,482	188,383	177,063	179,449
By product						
Food cans	67,283	64,773	68,770	73,104	68,127	64,984
Beverage cans	42,117	75,916	84,617	89,435	85,877	90,084
Soft drinks	14,580	31,660	35,631	36,499	33,284	39,488
Beer	27,537	44,256	48,986	52,936	52,593	50,596
Pet foods	5,797	6,694	7,121	7,083	6,057	6,121
General packaging cans	18,783	21,485	19,974	18,761	17,002	18,391
Motor oil	n.a.	3,095	2,756	2,533	n.a.	n.a.
Paints	n.a.	6,086	5,562	5,202	n.a.	n.a.
Aerosols	n.a.	5,877	6,103	5,765	4,808	5,097
All other	n.a.	6,427	5,553	5,261	n.a.	n.a.

Note: A base box contains 31,360 square inches.
n.a. = not available.
Source: Standard and Poor's Industry Survey, *Containers, Basic Analysis,* March 24, 1977, p. C123; *Metal Can Shipments Report 1974,* p. 6.

gains were in the beverage segment, while shipments of motor oil, paints, and other general packaging cans actually declined. A 6 percent decline in total shipments in 1975 turned around as the economy picked up in all areas except basic food cans. For the future, soft drink and beer cans were expected to continue to be the growth leaders.

Industry Structure

In 1977 the U.S. metal can industry was dominated by four major manufacturers. Two giants, American Can and the Continental Can Division of the Continental Group, together made up 35 percent of all domestic production. National Can and Crown Cork and Seal were also major forces with market shares of 8.7 and 8.3 percent, respectively (see Exhibit 3).

Equipment. A typical three-piece can line cost $750,000 to $1 million. In addition, expensive seaming, end-making, and finishing equipment was required. Since each finishing line could handle the output of 3 or 4 can-forming lines, the minimum efficient plant required at least $3.5 million in basic equipment. Most plants had 12 to 15 lines for the increased flexibility of handling more than one type of can at once. However, any more than 15 lines became unwieldy because of the need for duplication of setup crews, maintenance, and supervision.

The new two-piece can lines were even more expensive. Equipment for the line itself cost approximately $8.5 million, and the investment in peripheral equipment raised the per-line cost to $10-$15 million. Unlike three-piece lines, minimum efficient plant size was one line and installations ranged from one line to five lines.

Conversion to these two-piece lines virtually eliminated the market for new three-piece lines. No firms were installing new three-piece lines and the major manufacturers were selling complete, fully operational three-piece lines "as is" for $175,000 to $200,000. Many firms were shipping their old lines overseas to their foreign operations where growth potential was great. There were few entrenched firms, and canning technology was not well known or understood.

Pricing. The can industry was very competitive. The need for high capacity utilization and the desire to avoid costly line changeovers made long runs of standard items the most desirable business. As a result, most companies offered volume discounts to encourage large orders. From 1968 to 1975, industrywide profit margins declined 44 percent, reflecting sluggish sales and increased price competition. This trend hurt the small company, which was less able to spread its fixed costs. Raising prices above industry-set norms, however, was dangerous. Continental tried this in the fall of 1963 with the announcement of a 2 percent price hike. Other manufacturers refused to follow its lead, and by mid-1964 Continental was back to industry price levels with a considerably reduced market share.

Distribution. Because of the product's bulk and weight, transportation was a major factor in a can maker's cost structure. (One estimate put transportation at 7.6 percent of the price of a metal can, with raw materials playing the largest part at 64 percent and labor following at 14.4 percent.) A manufacturer's choice of lighter raw materials and plant location could have a large impact on total costs. Most estimates put the radius of economical distribution for a plant at between 150 and 300 miles.

TABLE 2
METAL CAN PRODUCTION BY MARKET

	1970	1971	1972	1973	1974	1975	1976
For sale	81.8%	80.9%	80.8%	78.2%	76.7%	73.7%	74.2%
For own use	18.2	19.1	19.2	21.8	23.3	26.3	25.8

Suppliers and Customers

At one time the big U.S. steel companies were the sole suppliers of metallic raw material used by the metal container industry. Can companies, in turn, were the fourth largest consumers of steel products. During the 1960s and 1970s, aluminum—and to a lesser extent, fiber-foil and plastic—suppliers increasingly entered traditional tinplate markets.

On the customer side, over 80 percent of the metal can output was purchased by the major food and beer companies. Since the can constituted about 45 percent of the total costs of beverage companies, most had at least two sources of supply. Poor service and uncompetitive prices could be punished by cuts in order size. Because can plants were often set up to supply a particular customer, the loss of a large order from that customer could greatly cut into manufacturing efficiency and company profits. As one can executive caught in the margin squeeze commented, "Sometimes I think the only way out of this is to sell out to U.S. Steel or to buy General Foods."[2]

INDUSTRY TRENDS

Three major trends had plagued the metal container manufacturers since the early 1960s: (1) the continuing threat of self-manufacture; (2) the increasing acceptance of other materials such as aluminum, fiber-foil, or plastic for standard tinplate packaging needs; and (3) the "packaging revolution" leading to new uses and thus new characteristics for containers.

Self-Manufacture

In the years 1971 to 1977, there had been a growing trend toward self-manufacture by large can customers, particularly of the low-technology standard items. As shown in Table 2, the proportion of "captive" production increased from 18.2 to 25.8 percent between 1970 and 1976. These increases seemed to come from companies gradually adding their own lines at specific canning locations rather than from full-scale changeovers. However, the temptation for major can users such as food and beer producers to begin making their own cans was high. As a result of such backward integration, Campbell Soup Company had actually become one of the largest producers of cans in the United States. The introduction of the two-piece can was expected to dampen the trend toward self-manufacture, since the end users did not possess the technical skills to develop their own two-piece lines.

New Packaging Materials

Aluminum. The greatest threat to the traditional, tin-plated can was the growing popularity of the new, lighter-weight aluminum can. The major producers of this

[2] "Crown Cork and Seal Company and the Metal Container Industry," HBS Case Services no. 6-373-077, Harvard Business School.

TABLE 3
METAL CAN PRODUCTION BY MATERIAL

	1970	1971	1972	1973	1974	1975	1976
Steel	88.4%	86.9%	82.6%	81.4%	79.0%	74.7%	72.5%
Aluminum	11.6	13.1	17.4	18.6	21.0	25.3	27.5

can were the large aluminum companies, led by Reynolds Metals and Aluminum Company of America (Alcoa). Some traditional tin-plated can producers, such as Continental and American, also produced a small proportion of aluminum cans.

From 1970 to 1976 aluminum usage for cans increased, moving up from 11.6 to 27.5 percent of the total metal can market. It was expected to reach a 29 percent share in 1977 (see Table 3). In absolute numbers, steel use remained fairly level while aluminum use tripled in those years (see Exhibit 4). Most of the inroads were made in the beer and soft drink markets, where aluminum held 65 percent and 31 percent shares respectively in 1976. Additional gains were expected, as aluminum was known to reduce the problems of flavoring, a major concern of both the brewing and soft drink industries.

Aluminum had several other important advantages over tinplate. First, its lighter weight could help reduce transportation costs. In addition, aluminum was easier to lithograph, producing a better reproduction at a lower cost. Finally, aluminum was favored over steel as a recycling material, because the lighter aluminum could be transported to recycling sites more easily, and recycled aluminum was far more valuable.

Aluminum's major disadvantage was its initial cost. In 1976 the stock to manufacture 1,000 12-ounce beverage cans cost $17.13 using steel and $20.81 using aluminum. Moreover, "in early 1977, steel producers raised the price of tinplate by only 4.8 percent, in contrast to an increase for aluminum can stock of about 9.7 percent. [They did this] in an effort to enhance the competitiveness of steel vis-à-vis aluminum."[3] Some industry observers also expected the gap to widen as the auto companies increased their usage of aluminum and thus drove up aluminum prices. The two-piece tin-plated cans were also considerably stronger than their aluminum counterparts.

Other Materials. Two other raw materials threatened tinplate as the primary product in making containers: the new paper-and-metal composite called fiber-foil and the growing varieties of plastics. *Fiber-foil* cans were jointly developed by the R. C. Can Company and Anaconda Aluminum in 1962 for the motor oil market. They caught on immediately, and by 1977 this composite material was the primary factor in the frozen juice concentrate market as well. *Plastics* represented the fastest growing sector of the packaging industry and the principal force in packaging change. The plastic bottle offered an enticing variety of advantages over glass bottles, including weight savings, resistance to breakage, design versatility and thus lower shelf-space requirements. While can makers felt little initial effects from the introduction of plastics, they too

[3] Standard and Poor's Industry Survey, *Containers, Basic Analysis,* March 24, 1977, p. C123.

could suffer if plastic bottles began to replace the cans being used as packaging for carbonated soft drinks.

The Packaging Revolution

Not only was the traditional package being reshaped and its materials reformulated, but by the 1970s containers also served a new purpose. Starting in the late 1950s the package itself became increasingly important in the marketing of the product it contained. The container was an advertising vehicle, and its features were expected to contribute to total product sales. This had serious implications for the metal can industry. Although the tin can was functional, aluminum was easier to lithograph and plastic enabled more versatile shapes and designs. Pressure for continuing innovation to enhance marketing meant that companies had to make greater R&D expenditures in order to explore new materials, different shapes, more convenient tops, and other imaginative ideas with potential consumer appeal.

Increasingly, metal can companies would have to contend with the research and marketing strengths of such giant integrated companies as Du Pont, Dow Chemical, Weyerhaeuser, Reynolds, and Alcoa. In response to the integration of packaging by these major material suppliers, some metal can manufacturers began to invest in their own basic research. In 1963, American announced the start of construction on a research center where investigations in such areas as solid-state physics and electrochemistry might reveal potential sources of new products.[4]

[4] "Crown Cork and Seal Company and the Metal Container Industry," p. 14.

THE COMPETITION

By the late 1960s all three of Crown Cork and Seal's major competitors had diversified into areas outside the metal container industry. However, in 1977 all three still remained major producers of metal cans (see Exhibit 3).

Continental Group

Because of the extent of its diversification, Continental changed its name in 1976, making Continental Can only one division of the large conglomerate. Although only 38 percent of the total company's sales were in cans, it still held the dominant market share (18.4 percent) of the U.S. metal can market. The remainder of Continental's domestic sales were in forest products (20 percent) and other plastic and paper packaging materials (9 percent).

In 1969 Continental began focusing its investment spending on foreign and diversified operations. In 1972 the company took a $120 million after-tax extraordinary loss to cover the closing, realignment, and modernization of its domestic can-making facilities over a three-year period. Of the $120 million loss, close to 70 percent resulted from fixed asset disposals, pension fund obligations, and severance pay. By 1976 almost one third of the company's revenues came from its overseas operations, which covered 133 foreign countries. Domestic investment went primarily to paper products and the plastic bottle lines. Very little was allocated for the changeover to new two-piece cans.

American Can

American also reduced its dependence on domestic can manufacture and, even more than Continental, emphasized unrelated product diversification. American competed in the entire packaging area—metal and composite containers, paper, plastic, and laminated products. In 1972 American "decided to shut down, consolidate, or sell operations that had either become obsolete or marginal [which] resulted in an after-tax extraordinary loss of $106 million."[5]

By 1976 20 percent of the company's sales came from consumer products such as household tissues, Dixie paper cups, and Butterick dress patterns. American's large chemical subsidiary brought in 15 percent of sales and another 15 percent came from international sales. Return on sales for the domestic container segment of American's business had remained stable at about 5 percent for the last five years. For this period American's average return on equity (7.1 percent) was the lowest of the four major can manufacturers, a result of relatively poor performance in its diversified areas (see Exhibit 3).

National Can

National's attempt to join the trend toward diversification achieved somewhat mixed results. Until 1967 National was almost solely a can producer. After that, through acquisitions the company moved into glass containers, food canning, pet foods, bottle closures, and plastic containers. However, instead of generating future growth opportunities, the expansion into food products proved a drag on company earnings. Pet foods and vegetable canning fared poorly in the 1974-1975 recession years, and the grocery division as a whole suffered a loss in 1976. As a result, National began a stronger overseas program to boost its earnings and investment.

Crown Cork and Seal

While its three major competitors turned to diversification, Crown Cork and Seal continued to manufacture primarily metal cans and closures. In 1976 the company derived almost 65 percent of its sales from tin-plated cans; crowns accounted for 29 percent of total sales and 35 percent of profits. The remaining sales were in bottling and canning machinery. In fact, Crown was one of the largest manufacturers of filling equipment in the world. Foreign sales—of crowns primarily—accounted for an increasingly large percentage of total sales (Exhibit 5). In 1976 Crown's return on sales was almost twice that of its three larger competitors. Over the previous 10 years Crown's sales growth was second only to National Can, and Crown was first in profit growth. The following sections describe Crown's history and strategy.

CROWN CORK AND SEAL COMPANY

Company History

In August 1891 a foreman in a Baltimore machine shop hit upon an idea for a better bottle cap—a round piece of tin-coated steel with a flanged edge and an insert of natural cork. This crown-cork top became the main product of a highly successful small venture, the Crown Cork and Seal Company. When the patents ran out, however, competition became severe. The faltering Crown Cork was bought out in 1927 by a competitor, Charles McManus, who then shook the company back to life, bursting upon the "starchy" firm, as one

[5] Crown Cork and Seal, Annual Report, 1972, p. 3.

old-timer recalled, "like a heathen in the temple." *Fortune,* in 1962, described the turnaround:

> Under the hunch-playing, paternalistic McManus touch, Crown prospered in the 30s, selling better than half the U.S. and world supply of bottle caps. Even in bleak 1935 the company earned better than 13 percent on sales of $14 million.
>
> The overconfidence led to McManus's first big mistake. He extended Crown's realm into canmaking. Reasoning soundly that the beer can would catch on, he bought a small Philadelphia can company. But reasoning poorly, he plunged into building one of the world's largest can plants on Philadelphia's Erie Avenue. It grew to a million square feet and ran as many as 52 lines simultaneously. A nightmare of inefficiency, the plant suffered deepened losses because of the McManus mania for volume. He lured customers by assuming their debts to suppliers and sometimes even cutting prices below costs. The Philadelphia blunder was to haunt Crown for many years.[6]

With all his projects and passion for leadership, McManus had no time or concern for building an organization that could run without him.

> Neither of his two sons, Charles Jr. and Walter, was suited to command a one-man company, although both had been installed in vice presidents' offices. Crown's board was composed of company officers, some of whom were relatives of the boss. The combination of benevolent despotism and nepotism had prevented the rise of promising men in the middle ranks. When McManus died in 1946, the chairmanship and presidency passed to his private secretary, a lawyer named John J. Nagle.
>
> In a fashion peculiar to Baltimore's family-dominated commerce, the inbred company acquired the settled air of a bank, only too willing to forget it lived by banging out bottle caps. In the muted, elegant offices on Eastern Avenue, relatives and hangers-on assumed that the remote machines would perpetually grind out handsome profits and dividends. In the postwar rush of business, the assumption seemed valid. The family left well enough alone, except to improve upon the late paternalist's largess. As a starter, Nagle's salary was raised from $35,000 to $100,000.
>
> Officers arrived and departed in a fleet of chauffeured limousines. Some found novel ways to fill their days. A brother-in-law of the late McManus fell into the habit of making a day-long tour of the junior executives' offices, appearing at each doorway, whistling softly, and wordlessly moving on. After hours, the corporate good life continued. More than 400 dining and country club memberships were spread through the upper echelons. A would-be visitor to the St. Louis plant recalls being met at the airport, whisked to a country club for drinks, lunch, cocktails, and dinner, and then being returned to the airport with apologies and promises of a look at the plant "next time."[7]

Up to the early 1950s, Crown ran on a combination of McManus momentum and the last vestiges of pride of increasingly demoralized middle managers, who were both powerless to decide and unable to force decisions from above.

> Dividends were maintained at the expense of investment in new plant; what investment there was, was mostly uninspired. From a lordly 50 percent in 1940, Crown's share of U.S. bottle cap sales [in the early 1950s] slipped to under 33

[6] The Unoriginal Ideas that Rebuilt Crown Cork," *Fortune,* October 1962, pp. 118–64.

[7] Ibid.

> percent. In 1952 the chaotic can division had such substantial losses that the company was finally moved to act. The board omitted a quarterly dividend. That brought the widow McManus, alarmed, to the president's office. President Nagle counseled her to be patient and leave matters to him.[8]

Matters soon grew worse. A disastrous attempt at expansion into plastics followed a ludicrous diversification into metal bird cages. Then in 1954 a reorganization, billed to solve all problems, was begun. The plan was modeled after Continental's decentralized line and staff. The additional personnel and expense were staggering and Crown's margins continued to dip. One observer noted, "The new suit of clothes, cut for a giant, hung on Crown like an outsized shroud." The end seemed near.

John Connelly Arrives

John Connelly was the son of a Philadelphia blacksmith who, after working his way up as a container salesman, formed his own company to produce paper boxes. His interest in Crown began when he was rebuffed by the post-McManus management, which "refused to take a chance" on a small supplier like Connelly. *Fortune* described Connelly's takeover:

> By 1955, when Crown's distress had become evident to Connelly, he asked a Wall Street friend, Robert Drummond, what he thought could be done with the company. "I wrote him a three-page letter," Drummond recalls, "and John telephoned to say he'd thrown it into the wastebasket, which I doubted. He said, 'If you can't put it into one sentence you don't understand the situation.'" Drummond tried again and boiled it down to this formula: "If you can get sales to $150 million and earn 4% net after taxes and all charges, meanwhile reducing the common to one million shares, you'll earn $6 a share and the stock will be worth $90."[9]

That was good enough for Connelly. He began buying stock and in November 1956 was asked to be an outside director—a desperate move for the ailing company.

> The stranger found the parlour stuffy. "Those first few meetings," says Connelly, "were like something out of *Executive Suite*. I'd ask a question. There would be dead silence. I'd make a motion to discuss something. Nobody would second it, and the motion would die." It dawned on Connelly that the insiders knew even less about Crown than he did.
>
> He toured the plants—something no major executive had done in years. At one plant a foreman was his guide. His rich bass graced the company glee club, and he insisted on singing as they walked. Connelly finally told him to shut up and sit down. The warning system silenced, Connelly went on alone and found workers playing cards and sleeping. Some were building a bar for an executive.
>
> At another plant he sat in on a meeting of a dozen managers and executives, ostensibly called to discuss the problem posed by customers' complaints about poor quality and delivery. The fault, it seemed, lay with the customers themselves—how unreasonable they were to dispute Crown's traditional tolerance of a "fair" number of defective crowns in every shipment; how carping they were to complain about delays arising from production foul-ups, union troubles, flat tires, and other acts of God. Connelly kept

[8] Ibid.

[9] Ibid.

silent until a pause signaled the consensus, then he confessed himself utterly amazed. He hadn't quite known what to make of Crown, he said, but now he knew it was something truly unique in his business life—a company where the customer was always wrong. "This attitude," he told the startled executives, "is the worst thing I've ever seen. No one here seems to realize this company is in business to make money."[10]

The Crisis

In April 1957 Crown Cork and Seal was on the verge of bankruptcy. The 1956 loss was $241,000 after preferred dividends, and 1957's promised to be worse. Bankers Trust Company had called from New York to announce the withdrawal of their $2.5 million line of credit. It seemed that all that was left was to write the company's obituary when John Connelly took over the presidency. His rescue plan was simple—as he called it, "just common sense."

Connelly's first move was to pare down the organization. Paternalism ended in a blizzard of pink slips. The headquarters staff was cut from 160 to 80. Included in the departures were 11 vice presidents. The company returned to a simple functional organization and in 20 months Crown had eliminated 1,647 jobs or 24 percent of the payroll. As part of the company's reorganization, Connelly discarded divisional accounting practices; at the same time he eliminated the divisional line and staff concept. Except for one accountant maintained at each plant location, all accounting and cost control was performed at the corporate level; the corporate accounting staff occupied half the space used by the headquarters group. In addition, the central research and development facility was disbanded.

The second step was to make each plant manager totally responsible for plant profitability, including any allocated costs. (All company overhead, estimated at 5 percent of sales, was allocated to the plant level.) Previously, plant managers had been responsible only for controllable expenses at the plant level. Under the new system, the plant manager was responsible even for the profits on each product manufactured in the plant. Although the plant manager's compensation was not tied directly to profit performance, one senior executive pointed out that the manager was "certainly rewarded on the basis of that figure."

The next step was to slow production to a halt and liquidate $7 million in inventory. By mid-July Crown paid off the banks. Planning for the future, Connelly developed control systems. He introduced sales forecasting, dovetailed with new production and inventory controls. This move took control away from the plant managers, who were no longer able to avoid layoffs by dumping excess products into inventory.

By the end of 1957 Crown had, in one observer's words, "climbed out of the coffin and was sprinting." Between 1956 and 1961 sales increased from $115 million to $176 million, and profits soared. After 1961 the company showed a 15.45 percent increase in sales and 14 percent in profits on the average every year. However, Connelly was not satisfied simply with short-term reorganizations of the existing company. By 1960, Crown Cork and Seal had adopted strategy that it would follow for at least the next 15 years.

[10] Ibid.

CROWN'S STRATEGY

Products and Markets

Recognizing Crown's position as a smaller producer in an industry dominated by giants,[11] Connelly sought to develop a product line built around Crown's traditional strengths in metal forming and fabrication. He chose to return to the area he knew best—tin-plated cans and crowns—and to concentrate on specialized uses and international markets.

A dramatic illustration of Connelly's commitment to this strategy occurred in the early 1960s. In 1960 Crown held over 50 percent of the market for motor oil cans. In 1962 R. C. Can and Anaconda Aluminum jointly developed fiber-foil cans for motor oil, which were approximately 20 percent lighter and 15 percent cheaper than the metal cans then in use. Crown's management decided not to continue to compete in this market and soon lost its entire market share.

In the early 1960s Connelly singled out two specific applications in the domestic market: beverage cans, and the growing aerosol market. These applications were called "hard to hold," because the cans required special characteristics either to contain the product under pressure or to avoid affecting taste. The cans had to be filled in high-speed lines. In the mid-1960s, growth in demand for soft drink and beer cans was more than triple that for traditional food cans.

Crown had an early advantage in aerosols. In 1938 McManus had tooled up for a strong-walled, seamless beer can, which was rejected by brewers as too expensive. In 1946 it was dusted off and equipped with a valve to make the industry's first aerosol container. However, little emphasis was put on the line until Connelly spotted high growth potential in the mid-1960s.

In addition to the specialized product line, Connelly's strategy was based on two geographic thrusts: expand to national distribution in the United States and invest heavily abroad. The domestic expansion was linked to Crown's manufacturing reorganization; plants were spread out across the country to reduce transportation costs and to be nearer customers. Crown was unusual in that it set up no plants to service a single customer. Instead, Crown concentrated on providing products for a number of customers near their plants. Also, Crown developed its lines totally for the production of tin-plated cans, not for aluminum. In international markets Crown invested heavily in undeveloped nations, first with crowns and then with cans as packaged foods became more widely accepted.

Manufacturing

When Connelly took over in 1957, Crown had perhaps the most outmoded and inefficient production facilitites in the industry. In the post-McManus regime, dividends had taken precedence over new investment, and old machinery combined with the cumbersome Philadelphia plant had given Crown very high production and transportation costs. Soon after he gained control, Connelly took drastic action, closing down the Philadelphia facility and investing heavily in new and geographically dispersed plants. From 1958 to 1963, the company spent almost $82 million on relocation and new facilities. By 1976, Crown had 26 domestic plant locations versus 9 in 1955. The plants were small (usually under 10 lines versus 50 in the old Philadelphia

[11] In 1956 Crown's sales were $115 million compared with $772 million for American and $1 billion for Continental.

complex) and were located close to the customer rather than the raw material source.

Crown emphasized flexibility and quick response to customer needs. One officer claimed that the key to the can industry was "the fact that nobody stores cans" and when customers need them, "they want them in a hurry and on time. . . . Fast answers get customers."[12] To deal with rush orders and special requests, Crown made a heavy investment in additional lines, which were maintained in setup condition.

Marketing/Service

Crown's sales force, although smaller than American's or Continental's, kept close ties with customers and emphasized Crown's ability to provide technical assistance and specific problem solving at the customer's plant. This was backed by quick manufacturing responses and Connelly's policy that, from the top down, the customer was always right. As *Fortune* described it:

> At Crown, all customers' gripes go to John Connelly, who is still the company's best salesman. A visitor recalls being in his office when a complaint came through from the manager of a Florida citrus-packing plant. Connelly assured him the problem would be taken care of immediately, then casually remarked that he planned to be in Florida the next day. Would the plant manager join him for dinner? He would indeed. As Crown's president put the telephone down, his visitor said that he hadn't realized Connelly was planning to go to Florida. "Neither did I," confessed Connelly, "until I began talking."[13]

Research and Development

Crown's R&D focused on enhancing the existing product line. According to Connelly, "We are not truly pioneers. Our philosophy is not to spend a great deal of money for basic research. However, we do have tremendous skills in die forming and metal fabrication, and we can move to adapt to the customer's needs faster than anyone else in the industry."[14] Research teams worked closely with the sales force, often on specific customer requests. For example, a study of the most efficient plant layout for a food packer or the redesign of a dust cap for the aerosol packager were not unusual projects.

Crown tried to stay away from the basic research and "all the frills of an R&D section of high-class, ivory-towered scientists." Explained John Luviano, the company's new president:

> There is a tremendous asset inherent in being second, especially in the face of the everchanging state of flux you find in this industry. You try to let others take the risks and make the mistakes as the big discoveries often flop initially due to something unforeseen in the original analysis. But somebody else, learning from the innovator's heartaches, prospers by the refinement.[15]

This sequence was precisely what happened with the two-piece drawn and ironed can. The original concept was developed in the aluminum industry by Reynolds and Alcoa in the late 1960s. Realizing the can's potential, Crown, in connection with a major steel producer,

---

[12] "Crown Cork and Seal Company and the Metal Container Industry," p. 28.

[13] "The Unoriginal Ideas," p. 164.

[14] "Crown Cork and Seal Company and the Metal Container Industry," p. 30.

[15] Ibid., p. 29. Mr. Luviano became president in 1976, while Connelly remained chairman and chief operating officer.

refined the concept for use with tinplate. Because of Crown's small plant manufacturing structure and Connelly's willingness to move fast, Crown was able to beat its competitors into two-piece can production. Almost $120 million in new equipment was invested from 1972 through 1975, and by 1976 Crown had 22 two-piece lines in production—far more than any competitor.[16]

Crown was also credited with some important innovations. The company initiated the use of plastic as a substitute for cork as a crown liner, and in 1962 it introduced the first beverage-filling machine that could handle both bottles and cans.

Financing the Company

After Connelly took over, he used the first receipt from the inventory liquidation to get out from under the short-term bank obligations. He then steadily reduced the debt-equity ratio, from 42 percent in 1956 to 18.2 percent in 1976. In 1970 the last of the preferred stock was bought back, eliminating preferred dividends as a cash drain. From 1970 on, the emphasis was on repurchasing the common stock (see Exhibit 1). Each year Connelly set ambitious earnings goals and most years he achieved them, reaching $2.84 per share in 1976. That year marked a critical time for Connelly's financial ambitions. As he said in the 1976 annual report:

> A long time ago we made a prediction that some day our sales would exceed $1 billion and profits of $60 per share. Since then the stock has been split 20-for-1 so this means $3 per share. These two goals are still our ambition and will remain until both have been accomplished. I am sure that one, and I hope both, will be attained this year [1977].

International Expansion

Another aspect of Crown's efforts was its continuing emphasis on international growth, particularly in developing nations (Exhibit 6). With sales of $343 million and 60 foreign plant locations, Crown was, by 1977, the largest producer of metal cans and crowns overseas. In the early 1960s, when Crown began to expand internationally, the strategy was unique. In many cases the company received 10-year tax shelters as initial investment incentives. At that time Connelly commented:

> Right now we are premature but this has been necessary in order for Crown to become established in these areas. . . . If we can get 20 percent to 40 percent of all new geographic areas we enter, we have a great growth potential in contrast to American and Continental. . . . In 20 years I hope whoever is running this company will look back and comment on the vision of an early decision to introduce canmaking in underdeveloped countries.[17]

John Connelly's Contribution to Success

Many claimed that John Connelly himself was the driving force behind Crown's dramatic turnaround and that it was his ambition and determination that kept the company on the road to success. Connelly has been described as a strong-willed individual whose energetic leadership convinced and inspired his organization to meet his goals.

---

[16] In 1976, there were 47 two-piece tinplate and 130 two-piece aluminum lines in the United States.

[17] "Crown Cork and Seal Company and the Metal Container Industry," p. 33.

Yet Connelly was no easy man to please. He demanded from his employees the same dedication and energy that he himself threw into his work. As one observer wrote in 1962:

> At 57 Connelly is a trim, dark-haired doer. The 7-day, 80-hour weeks of the frenetic early days are only slightly reduced now. The Saturday morning meeting is standard operating procedure. Crown's executives travel and confer only at night and on weekends. William D. Wallace, vice president for operations, travels 100,000 miles a year, often in the company plane. But Connelly sets the pace. An associate recalls driving to his home in the predawn blackness to pick him up for a flight to a distant plant. The Connelly house was dark, but he spotted a figure sitting on the curb under a street light engrossed in a looseleaf book. Connelly's greeting, as he jumped into the car: "I want to talk to you about last month's variances."[18]

In 1977 at age 72, Connelly still firmly held the reins of his company.[19] "He'll never retire. He'll die with his boots on,"[20] noted one company official. Despite comments such as these, Connelly had raised John Luviano—age 54 and a 25-year veteran at Crown—to the presidency of the company.

OUTLOOK FOR THE FUTURE

In 1977 observers of Crown Cork and Seal had a favorable question: how long can this spectacular performance last? Until then, Crown's sales and profit growth had continued despite recession, devaluation, and stiff competition from the giants of the industry. However, in 1977 the ozone scare and the potential legislation on nonreturnable containers threatened the company's beverage and aerosol business.

The Ozone Controversy

In 1973 two University of California chemists advanced the initial theory that fluorocarbons—gases used in refrigerators, air conditioners, and as a propellant in aerosols—were damaging the earth's ozone shield. (Ozone forms an atmospheric layer that prevents much of the sun's ultraviolet radiation from reaching the earth's surface.) Their theory was that the fluorocarbons floated up into the stratosphere where they broke up, releasing chlorine atoms. These atoms then reacted with the ozone molecules, causing their destruction. The problem was compounded because after the reaction the chlorine atom was free to attack other ozone molecules, causing accelerated break-up of the ozone layer. Proponents of the theory asserted that "fluorocarbons have already depleted ozone by 1 percent and will eventually deplete it by 7 to 13 percent, perhaps within 50 to 80 years, if the use of fluorocarbons continues at recent levels."[21]

Proponents of the theory argued that there was real danger in allowing the destruction of the ozone shield. As this shield was depleted and more radiation passed through, they predicted, the number of cases of skin cancer would rise alarmingly. Dr. Sherwood Rowland, one of the original proponents of the theory, explained:

> If aerosol use were to grow at 10 percent annually (half the growth rate of the 1960s), stratospheric ozone content would fall by 10 percent by 1994. Scientists figure this would mean a 20 percent

---

[18] "The Unoriginal Ideas," p. 163.

[19] Connelly reportedly owned or controlled about 18 percent of Crown's outstanding common stock.

[20] *Financial World*, November 26, 1975, p. 12.

[21] *The Wall Street Journal*, December 3, 1975, p. 27.

> increase in ultraviolet radiation reaching the earth and cause by itself at least 60,000 new cases of skin cancer annually in the United States, roughly a 20 percent increase.[22]

They also cited the possibility of crop damage, genetic mutation, and climate change.

Although many studies were in progress, by the end of 1976 the theory had not yet been conclusively proven. There were still some major questions about the types and amounts of reactions that would take place in the stratosphere. Nonetheless, most tests supported the basic thesis that fluorocarbons were in some way damaging the ozone layer.

After the ozone theory was publicized, the reaction against aerosols was severe. Aerosols provided about 60 percent of the fluorocarbons released into the air annually. In 1974 aerosol production declined almost 7 percent in reaction to the recession and the fluorocarbon problem. Only 2.6 billion aerosol containers were used, down from 2.9 billion in 1973. Action began immediately—on the scientific front to test the ozone theory and on the legislative front to restrict the use of fluorocarbons.

Soon a bitter battle broke out between industry spokespeople and those advocating an immediate ban: One industry spokesperson, who requested anonymity, said, "All the scientific theories against fluorocarbons are just that—theories, not facts. What we need is more research before there are any more bans or badmouthing. We don't want another false scare."[23] A member of the Natural Resource Defense Council looked harshly upon the aerosol industry's position. "It's like Watergate," he said. "They want to see a smoking gun. We'll have to wait 25 years for that, and by then irreparable damage will have been done."[24]

Despite industry protests and with the support of some additional studies, state legislators began to introduce antifluorocarbon bills. Georgia led the way in June 1975 by passing a bill banning fluorocarbon aerosols effective March 1, 1977. Successful industry lobbying kept other actions to a minimum until May 1977, when federal agencies proposed a nationwide ban. Calling fluorocarbons an "unacceptable risk to individual health and to the earth's atmosphere,"[25] the commissioner of the Food and Drug Administration outlined a three-step phaseout of fluorocarbon manufacture and use. The first step in the ban would be a halt to all manufacture of chlorofluorocarbon propellants for nonessential uses. This ban would take effect October 15, 1978. In the second step, on December 15, 1978, all companies would have to stop using existing supplies of the chemicals in making nonessential aerosol products. The third step would be a halt to all interstate shipment of nonessential products containing the propellant gases. This part of the ban would go into effect April 15, 1979.[26]

The Future for Aerosols. Opinions differed widely as to the extent of the problems the ozone issue would cause the industry. By 1977 the latest estimates were that the fluorocarbon ban would cost container manufacturers over $132 million in lost sales from 1977 to 1980. This was much less than most of the original esti-

---

[22] Ibid.
[23] *New York Times,* June 22, 1975, p. F3.
[24] Ibid.
[25] *New York Times,* May 12, 1977, p. 1.
[26] Ibid.

mates due to the success of efforts in the previous two years in finding fluorocarbon substitutes. Most of the solutions involved finding substitute propellants or changing the aerosol valve.

A propellant is the pressurized gas used to hold the suspended molecules of aerosol products as they are sprayed out. Until the early 1970s the most common propellant material was fluorocarbon, which was used in about half of the aerosol cans sold. By 1977 the possibility of substituting hydrocarbons was being explored for many applications. However, although they were less expensive, hydrocarbons were known to be more flammable and thus more dangerous to mix with the many personal-care products that include alcohol as an ingredient. Other proposed alternatives included using carbon dioxide or special pressurized cans that did not release propellants at all.

In May 1977 the new Aquasol valve promised to be one of the most promising ways of eliminating fluorocarbons. Developed by Robert Abplanalp, the inventor of the original aerosol valve, the Aquasol used a dual-duct system (rather than the traditional one-duct) that kept the product separate from the propellant. Abplanalp claimed that fillers could get twice as much product into a can with the new valve because the product did not have to be mixed with the propellant. Also, hydrocarbons could be used more safely for many applications.

Industry Recovery. By 1977 recovery in the aerosol market had already begun, with shipments for 1976 up 6 percent. It seemed likely that this trend would continue because of the strong appeal aerosols had for the consumer. In a 1974 study over 59 percent of the population had heard of the ozone problem, yet about 25 percent said they would be "very disturbed to do without" aerosol products. Industry optimism was moderated, however, by the growing popularity of pump sprays and other nonaerosol products, and by the tendency of the consumer not to differentiate between fluorocarbons and aerosols using other propellants.

Regulating Nonreturnable Containers

Crown's future was also threatened by moves to legislate restriction on the use of nonreturnable containers. By 1976 Oregon, Vermont, and South Dakota already regulated the use of disposable containers. Laws requiring mandatory deposits for most beverage containers were approved in November 1976 by voter referendums in Maine and Michigan, while they were turned down by narrow margins in Massachusetts and Colorado. The existing laws required a 5-cent deposit on all bottles and cans, refundable when the empties were brought back for recycling or reuse. Nationally, the Environmental Protection Agency banned throwaways from federal property—parks, federal buildings, and military posts—starting in October 1977.

The main problem was litter. Although it was estimated that only 1 percent of the American population were litterers, the extent of the damage was staggering. Unfortunately, disposable cans contributed significantly to the problem. While containers made up only 8 percent of the solid waste in the United States, they made up 54 to 70 percent of highway litter by volume. A second issue was the potential savings of raw materials and energy that could be obtained from reusing containers.

Economic Impact. Part of the controversy involved the potential economic impact of legislative bans on nonreturnables. Industry sources agreed that the laws would bring an increase in beer and soft drink prices and eliminate thousands of jobs. The environmentalists countered that consumers paid 30 to 40 percent more for beverages in throwaway containers. "Any increased cost due to retooling would be offset by savings in the use of returnable bottles or recycled cans," claimed a spokesperson for the Michigan United Conservation Clubs. He added that "any jobs lost in the canning or bottling industries would be offset by additional jobs in transportation and handling."[27]

Prospects for the Future. Despite a powerful industry lobby, the fight against nonreturnables gained momentum. In July 1977 legislation was being considered by the Congressional Committee on Energy and National Resources to require deposits on throwaways nationwide. Although the Senate had once rejected a ban on pull tops, some states, including Massachusetts, had passed such bills effective in 1978. Returnable bottles, which could be used by more than one manufacturer, were being encouraged under the new laws, but it seemed unlikely that cans would be totally banned. Instead, various schemes for deposits and recycling were emphasized. Proposals were made that metal cans can be collected, crushed, melted, and reused to make new cans. Under the new system it was uncertain who would pay the extra transportation costs and whether lower raw material prices to the can maker would result. Unfortunately for tinplate users like Crown, the new system favored aluminum cans because of the higher value of the reclaimed metal and the recycling network that already existed for aluminum products.

CROWN'S FUTURE GROWTH

Crown's usual optimistic forecasts continued into 1977. The 1976 annual report all but ignored the aerosol and bottle bill issues. The strategy stayed the same: no major basic R&D efforts, but quick attention to meeting customer needs and leadership in new applications that involved the traditional metal can. Thus, despite current problems in its markets, some industry observers saw no reason why the company's good record wouldn't continue:

> Even with Connelly's eventual retirement, his Number 2 man seems certain to keep Crown on its upward profits growth trend. While others—like National Can—have ventured into uncharted and at times unprofitable waters, Crown has prospered by doing what it knows best. Under that strategy, prosperity is likely to continue reigning for Crown.[28]

---

[27] *New York Times,* October 30, 1976, p. F1.

[28] *Financial World,* November 26, 1975, p. 12.

EXHIBIT 1

FINANCIAL STATEMENTS, 1956–1976

Dollars in Thousands except Where Indicated Otherwise

	1976	*1975*	*1974*	*1973*	*1972*	*1971*	*1966*	*1961*	*1956*
Net sales	$909,937	$825,007	$766,158	$571,762	$488,880	$448,446	$279,830	$176,992	$115,098
Cost of products sold (excluding depreciation)	$757,866	$683,691	$628,865	$459,183	$387,768	$350,867	$217,236	$139,071	$ 95,803
Selling and administrative expense	$ 39,910	$ 30,102	$ 28,649	$ 23,409	$ 20,883	$ 21,090	$ 18,355	$ 15,311	$ 13,506
Percent of net sales	3.5%	3.6%	3.7%	4.1%	4.3%	4.7%	6.6%	8.7%	11.7%
Interest expense	$ 3,885	$ 7,374	$ 6,973	$ 4,407	$ 4,222	$ 5,121	$ 4,551	$ 1,252	$ 1,150
Depreciation expense	$ 26,486	$ 25,402	$ 25,525	$ 20,930	$ 18,654	$ 16,981	$ 9,381	$ 4,627	$ 2,577
Taxes on income	$ 43,500	$ 34,925	$ 33,298	$ 26,725	$ 24,900	$ 24,560	$ 12,680	$ 7,625	$ 105
Net income	$ 46,183	$ 41,611	$ 39,663	$ 34,288	$ 31,193	$ 28,474	$ 16,749	$ 6,653	$ 277
Percent of net sales	5.1%	5.0%	5.2%	6.0%	6.4%	6.3%	6.0%	3.8%	.2%
Earnings per common share	$ 2.84	$ 2.43	$ 2.20	$ 1.81	$ 1.58	$ 1.41	$ .80	$ .28	$ (.01)
Plant and equipment									
Expenditures	$ 21,568	$ 47,047	$ 52,517	$ 40,392	$ 28,261	$ 33,099	$ 32,729	$ 11,819	$ 1,931
Accumulated investment	$398,377	$401,657	$371,297	$335,047	$316,266	$313,214	$223,153	$107,258	$ 65,196
Accumulated depreciation	$149,306	$143,406	$129,924	$116,191	$105,377	$101,314	$ 68,359	$ 45,004	$ 31,167
Current asset/liability ratio	1.8	1.6	1.4	1.6	1.7	1.6	1.5	2.7	3.2
Long-term debt	$ 25,886	$ 29,679	$ 34,413	$ 37,922	$ 31,234	$ 41,680	$ 57,890	$ 17,654	$ 21,400
Short-term debt	$ 2,984	$ 30,419	$ 45,043	$ 28,504	$ 17,221	$ 31,381	$ 44,784	$ 5,190	$ 6,500
Shareholders' investment	$316,684	$292,681	$262,650	$243,916	$230,366	$211,847	$110,841	$ 77,540	$ 50,299
Number of									
Preferred shares	0	0	0	0	0	0	79,370	139,540	275,000
Common shares, average	16,235,040	17,137,030	18,000,792	18,894,105	19,726,799	20,211,810	20,606,835	21,594,720	24,155,800

Source: Crown Cork and Seal Company, Inc., 1976 Annual Report, pp. 4, 5.

EXHIBIT 2
BEVERAGE CAN SHIPMENTS
In Billions of Cans

	1972	1973	Change 1972–1973	1974	Change 1973–1974
Soft drink cans:					
Total	15,596	17,552	+12.5%	17,980	+2.4%
Three-piece	14,217	15,779	+11.0%	15,589	−1.2%
Percent of total	91.2%	89.9%		86.7%	
Two-piece	1,379	1,773	+28.6%	2,391	+34.9%
Percent of total	8.8%	10.1%		13.3%	
Beer cans:					
Total	21,801	24,131	+10.7%	26,077	+8.1%
Three-piece	14,746	14,363	−2.6%	13,237	−7.8%
Percent of total	67.6%	59.5%		50.8%	
Two-piece	7,055	9,768	+38.5%	12,840	+31.4%
Percent of total	32.4%	40.5%		49.2%	

Source: *Metal Cans Shipments Report 1974*, Can Manufacturers Institute, p. 6.

EXHIBIT 3
COMPARISON OF 1976 PERFORMANCE OF MAJOR METAL CAN MANUFACTURERS
Dollars in Millions

	Continental Group	American Can	National Can	Crown Cork and Seal
Total company performance				
Sales	$3,458.0	$3,143.0	$917.0	$910.0
Net income	$ 118.3	$ 100.9	$ 20.7	$ 46.2
Sales growth, 1967–76	147%	107%	317%	202%
Profit growth, 1967–76	51%	33%	160%	145%
Return on equity, 5-year average	10.3%	7.1%	11.9%	15.8%
Debt ratio	34%	35%	46%	23%
Metal can segments (domestic)				
Sales	$1,307.8	$1,177.6	$616.0	$575.0
Pretax income	$ 73.0	$ 64.9	$ 36.4	$ 49.0
As a percent of sales	5.6%	5.4%	5.0%	8.5%
Market share	18.4%	16.6%	8.7%	8.3%
Number of can plants	70	48	41	26
International (sales of all products)				
Sales	$1,147.2	$ 475.1	n.a.	$343.0
Net income (before taxes)	$ 63.4	$ 41.5	small loss	$ 39.4

n.a. = not available
Source: *Wall Street Transcript*, November 3, 1975, pp. 41, 864, and company 10-K reports.

EXHIBIT 4
METAL CAN SHIPMENTS
In Millions of Base Boxes

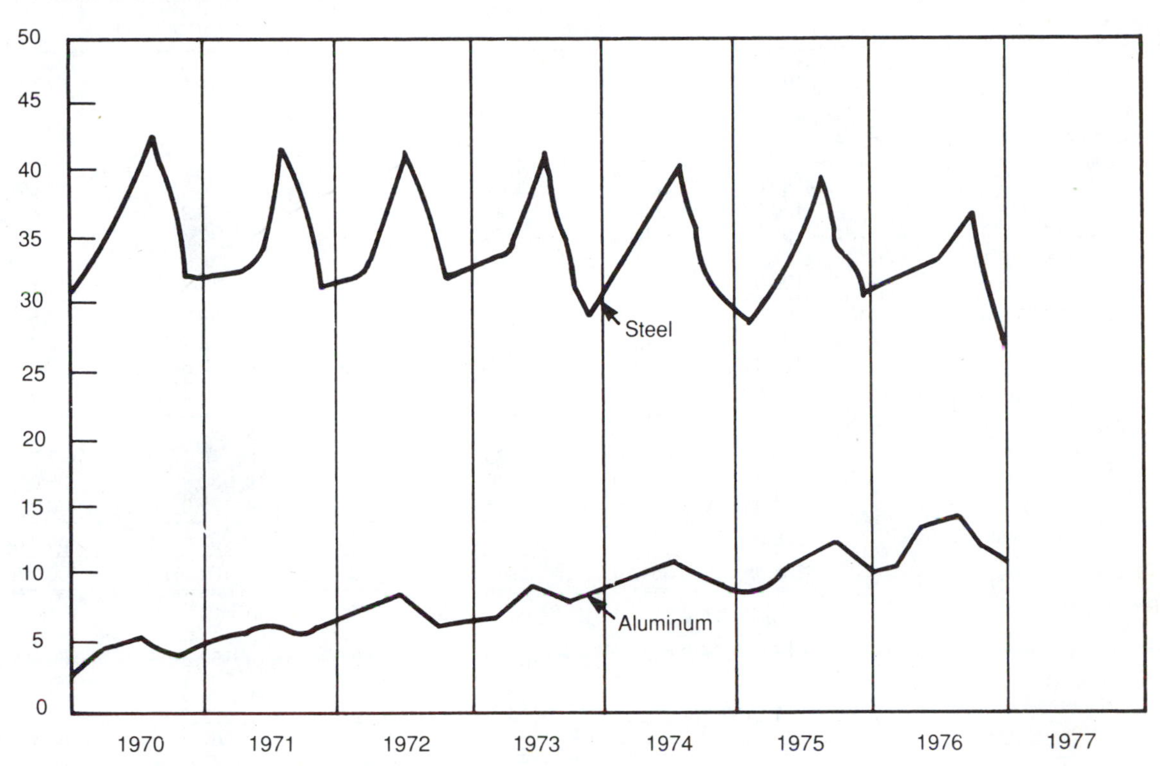

Source: Standard and Poor's Industry Survey, *Containers, Basic Analysis,* March 24, 1977, p. C123.

EXHIBIT 5
ESTIMATED BREAKDOWN OF CROWN CORK AND SEAL'S SALES AND PRETAX INCOME

	Dollars in Millions			*Percentages*		
	1974	*1975*	*1976**	*1974*	*1975*	*1976**
Sales						
Domestic:						
Cans						
Beer	$180.0	$209.0	$232.0	23.5%	24.7%	24.6%
Soft drinks	120.0	128.0	140.0	15.7	15.2	14.8
Food	55.0	65.0	70.0	7.2	7.7	7.4
Other (mainly aerosols)	100.0	91.0	101.0	13.0	10.7	10.7
Total cans	455.0	493.0	543.0	59.4	58.3	57.5
Crowns	25.0	29.0	32.0	3.3	3.4	3.4
Machinery	20.0	24.0	27.0	2.6	2.8	2.8
Total domestic	500.0	546.0	602.0	65.3	64.5	63.7
International:						
Cans	46.0	57.0	73.0	6.0	6.7	7.7
Crowns	200.0	220.0	242.0	26.1	30.0	25.6
Machinery	20.0	24.0	28.0	2.6	2.8	3.0
Total international	266.0	301.0	343.0	34.7	35.5	36.3
Total sales	$766.0	$847.0	$945.0	100.0%	100.0%	100.0%
Pretax income						
Domestic:						
Cans	$41.0	$ 43.0	$ 46.0	53.9%	52.2%	50.9%
Crowns	2.0	2.0	3.0	2.6	2.4	3.3
Machinery	1.5	2.0	2.0	2.0	2.4	2.2
Total domestic	45.5	47.0	51.0	58.5	57.0	56.4
International:						
Cans	4.0	6.0	8.0	5.3	7.3	8.9
Crowns	25.6	26.4	28.4	33.6	32.1	31.4
Machinery	2.0	3.0	3.0	2.6	3.6	3.3
Total international	31.6	35.4	39.4	41.5	43.0	43.6
Total pretax income	$76.1	$ 82.4	$ 90.4	100.0%	100.0%	100.0%
Pretax margins						
Domestic:						
Cans				9.0%	8.7%	8.5%
Crowns				8.0	6.9	9.4
Machinery				7.5	8.3	7.4
Total domestic				8.9	8.6	8.5
International:						
Cans				8.6	12.5	11.0
Crowns				13.0	12.3	11.6
Machinery				10.0	12.5	10.7
Total international				11.9	11.8	11.5
Total pretax margins				9.9%	9.7%	9.6%

*1976 figures are estimated and thus do not match actual numbers on other exhibits.
Source: *Wall Street Transcript,* November 3, 1975, pp. 41, 865.

EXHIBIT 6 CROWN CORK AND SEAL'S FACILITIES

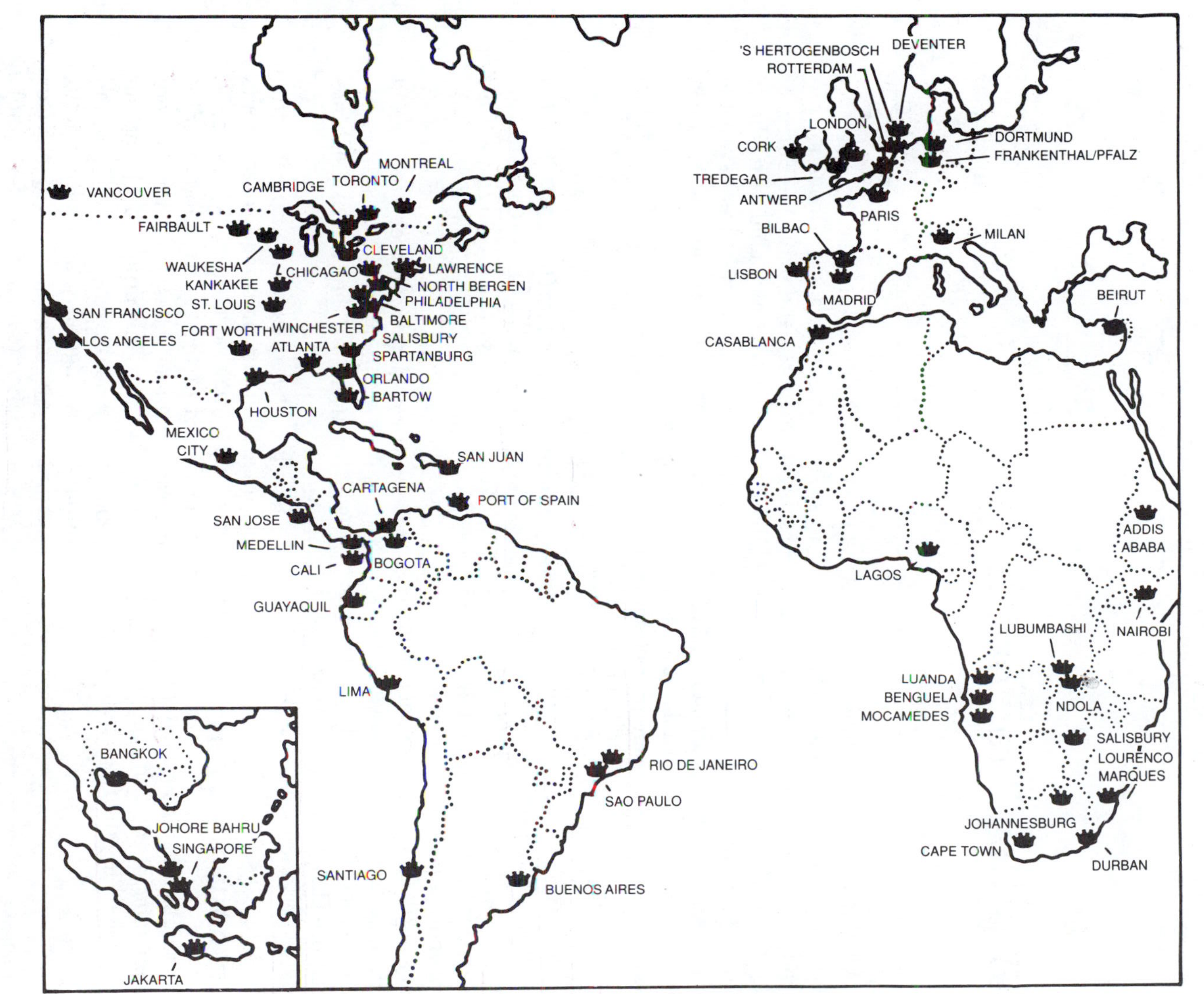

Source: Crown Cork and Seal Company, Inc., 1972 Annual Report.

Caterpillar Tractor Co.

It was late afternoon on October 20, 1981, and a positive mood pervaded the corporate headquarters of Caterpillar Tractor Co. (Cat) in Peoria, Illinois. Preliminary reports showed that Cat, the world's largest manufacturer of earthmoving equipment (EME), was headed for the best financial results in its history. Sales in 1981 were projected to reach $9.2 billion, exceeding the previous high of $8.6 billion achieved in 1980, and profits were expected to jump from the previous year's $565 million to about $580 million. A top management meeting had been called by Lee Morgan, chairman and chief executive officer, to review the preliminary results and appraise Cat's competitive strategy for the next several years. Morgan wanted to know what measures were required to ensure that the company's impressive performance continued.

WORLD EME INDUSTRY, 1981

EME represented about 70 percent of the dollar sales of the construction equipment industry in 1981, encompassing a diverse range of machines such as excavators, bulldozers, graders, loaders, off-highway tractors, and haulers. Some of these machines were available with wheels or crawler tracks, and most were available in a wide range of sizes and horsepower (hp) ratings.

The Market

Worldwide demand for EME doubled between 1973 and 1980. Overall, the United States exported roughly one third of its production. (See Exhibit 1 for shipments by year, including exports.) Estimates of worldwide market size varied between $14 billion and $15 billion for 1981, depending on the type of machines included.

Besides the original equipment, the world market for parts and attachments was substantial, accounting for as much as one third of the construction machinery sales volume. Most attachments were sold along with the prime mover at the time of sale and were included in the initial sales figures. Generally, profit margins were substantially higher for parts and attachments than for whole machines.

Harvard Business School case 385–276.

The Users

The construction and mining industries were the key users of EME, the former representing over 60 percent of the market and the latter almost 30 percent. Forestry represented the balance.

The term *construction industry* usually included work relating to buildings, dams, airports, roads, waste disposal, and so forth. The United States accounted for roughly 50 percent of world new-construction expenditures, or an estimated $230 billion in 1980. Repairs and maintenance expenditures were believed to be another $75 billion worldwide.

Since 1979 the construction industry in the United States had faced a major downturn. The Commerce Department considered the industry depressed, with a 12 percent drop in aggregate hours worked by construction workers and a seasonally adjusted unemployment rate of 16 percent in late 1981. (See Exhibit 2 for some data relating to the industry.) The end of the interstate highways program in the late 1960s had shrunk the road construction market considerably.

The EME demand depended largely on the pace at which machines were substituting for labor. Thus, demand had traditionally been higher in developed countries than in developing ones. Recent trends, however, were changing the overall demand pattern (see Table 1). Since the mid-1970s, the oil-rich Middle Eastern countries had witnessed a massive rise in construction activity. Among the less developed countries (LDCs) in general, considerable potential existed, since they required extensive infrastructure. Many, however, faced financing problems.

TABLE 1
WORLDWIDE CONSTRUCTION EXPENDITURE, 1981

Region	*Expenditure Percent*	*Projected Real Annual Growth Rates, 1982–1986*
United States	50.0%	1%
Canada	3.5	2
Latin America	7.5	4
Europe	5.0	2
Middle East	7.5	5
Asia and Australia	26.5	6%
Total	100.0%	6%

Source: Compiled data from various 1981 issues of *Engineering News Record* and *First Boston Research.*

The construction industry was highly concentrated and U.S. dominated—although both these characteristics were changing. All of the industrial nations had indigenous construction capabilities, and many had successfully expanded their operations overseas. Several of the "advanced developing countries" were also upgrading their construction services and entering the international market. Until recently, the U.S. contractors, who had a large domestic base and assured U.S. government-sponsored construction work abroad, had also won a large portion of the overseas construction contracts. A survey indicated that 29 companies accounted for 94 percent of non-U.S. construction and 54 percent of U.S. construction in 1980. These firms were facing increasing competition, however, from Third World construction firms, which tended to use their low-cost labor as their main competitive weapon, shifting work crews to construction sites worldwide. Many observers felt that non-U.S. companies were better placed to bid for and perform contracts in developing countries since they did not face curbs similar to the U.S. Foreign Corrupt Practices Act (FCPA) of 1977, which forbids U.S. companies from indulging in unethical activities such as bribery and kickbacks in overseas dealings.

Third World contractors also benefited by being more flexible. A vice president of the leading Filipino construction firm was quoted as saying that his company looked for joint ventures with local firms in developing countries, since these arrangements enabled his company "to enjoy government treatment normally reserved for indigenous contractors." Many U.S. companies also noted that foreign companies received financial and diplomatic support from their home governments when bidding and favorable tax treatment on earnings outside their own countries. The South Korean government established an overseas construction fund of about $500 million "to help finance development of new markets and technology." Similarly, India coordinated the efforts of the Indian companies in pooling information on working conditions abroad and in pooling resources for joint ventures. (See Table 2 for Asian success in Middle Eastern contracts in recent years. For purposes of comparison, it should be noted that as late as 1975, U.S. companies claimed more than one third of Middle Eastern construction contracts in dollar terms.)

TABLE 2
MIDDLE EASTERN CONSTRUCTION CONTRACTS AWARDED TO COMPANIES OF DIFFERENT NATIONALITIES

Country or Region of Origin	*1979*	*1980*
Middle East	16.52%	27.38%
United States	16.86	6.88
Japan	17.32	9.89
France	14.84	19.67
West Germany	12.69	8.94
South Korea	9.45	12.82
United Kingdom	6.87	7.16
Eastern Europe	4.52	5.07
Philippines	0.93	2.19
	100.00%	100.00%
Amount ($ millions)	$39,429	$33,967

Source: *Constructor*, January 1982.

Usually, in overseas projects, the machinery was brought in by the sole contractor or by one of the partners in a consortium, who also took responsibility for disposing of the machines when the contract ended. Frequently the heavy equipment was sold locally or shipped to nearby markets; sometimes it was moved to another site where the operating company or members of a consortium were working. This "overhang" of used equipment was large in the Middle East. The equipment's value was written off over varying periods, ranging from one to five years.

Construction companies all over the world operated under severe cost and time constraints. Scheduling machine use efficiently and minimizing downtime were considered vital for success, and some companies used computerized systems to schedule parts changes. In the United States, high capital and energy costs had led some construction companies to use their equipment longer and to rent, rather than buy, additional equipment.

Equipment purchase decisions were generally made by committees of high-level management and technical personnel in large construction companies and by a few top executives in smaller ones. A survey conducted in the late 1970s indicated that the manufacturer's reputation, machine performance, and dealer capability were the most important criteria for decision making, followed closely by price and parts availability.

Governments were generally more price sensitive than contractors and relied more on the manufacturer's ability to deal directly with them to provide maintenance and repair facilities. In many developing countries, particularly in the Far East, the major buyers were a few large, state-owned enterprises. Their bids for machines specifically sought quotations that included prices for parts needed over the next two years.

The mining industry was another important user of EME. All types of open-pit mining used these machines, and new markets appeared as the search for energy alternatives to oil intensified with coal, oil from shale sands, and nuclear power. Four countries—the United States, the USSR, China, and Australia—possessed 60 percent of the world's reserves and current production of coal. Much of the coal production was by open-pit surface mining that was less costly but also more capital intensive and demanded more skilled labor. The U.S. coal industry, the world's largest and most export oriented, was operating at 77 percent of installed capacity in 1981. Surface mining, however, faced many environmental constraints, as did other fuel minerals, such as oil-shale-sands development and uranium mining.

Six nonfuel minerals—iron, copper, aluminum, zinc, nickel, and lead—represented roughly three-quarters of the total value of world mineral production in 1976. Since the late 1960s mining of these minerals in almost all the developing countries had come under state control. The related expropriations of foreign mining companies' assets had led to the development of new mines in politically safe countries such as Canada and Australia. The state-owned mining enterprises, lured by very high mineral prices in the early 1970s, also undertook large expansion and new capacity-creation projects.

One UN study on new mine-opening expenditures concluded that between 1978 and 1990 about $12 billion (1977 dollars) would be spent annually in the developed and developing countries, and the latter's share would be $4 billion.

Distribution

Internationally, EME manufacturers sold through dealers, who provided direct support and after-sales service. The rule of thumb was that a crawler tractor, over its six-year economic life, would require service and parts equal to its initial cost.

Normal industry practice had been to create dealerships with exclusive geographic territories but separate sales agreements for each product line handled. Many manufacturers believed that a full-line franchise not only hindered dealer specialization but also limited the manufacturer's ability to get maximum market coverage for all its products.

Because most dealers carried their inventories on their own accounts, they were characterized by high capitalization and required relatively high dollar sales volume. Individual sales had high per unit value and generally demanded greater service than, for example, agricultural equipment. Customers stressed dealer relationships and/or dealer reputation as an important factor in their purchasing decisions.

The Suppliers

The EME industry began in the late 1800s with the development of steam-powered equipment, developing as a derivative of the agricultural tractor. Except for Cat, most of the world's major EME manufacturers were also leaders in the agricultural equipment market.

Rather than high-technology breakthroughs, the industry had focused more on constant improvement of existing products to make them more energy efficient, comfortable, or suitable for specific kinds of jobs. In 1981 U.S. construction equipment manufacturers spent $432 million on R&D, on sales of about $17 billion. In comparison, the automobile industry spent 4.9 percent of sales on R&D, and heavy machinery manufacturers spent 2.3 percent.

About two thirds of the total product cost of construction equipment was in heavy components—engines, axles, transmissions, and hydraulics—whose manufacturing was capital intensive and highly sensitive to economies of scale. Because of the secrecy surrounding the operations of EME manufacturers, it was difficult to quantify scale effects. Some industry observers tended to compare the EME industry with the agricultural tractor industry, however, where it was estimated that the optimum scale of operation was about 90,000 units a year and the costs fell by 11 percent between 60,000 and 90,000 units. Although others questioned the validity of the comparison, there appeared to be general agreement that economies of scale did exist up to a level of 90,000 units, but there was considerable disagreement over the extent of cost disadvantage resulting from lower levels of output.

The cost structure of a typical large bulldozer appears in Table 3. Except for some highly specialized products, the basis for profitable operation was believed to be volume production. Many manufacturers had also sought economies by integrating backward into components such as engines and axles. Steel purchases were particularly important to a company's economics since they represented approximately 15 percent of the product cost. Steel prices varied widely, with Japanese steel costing on average about 30 percent less than U.S.-made steel.

Several large developing countries, such as Mexico, Brazil, Argentina, and India, had demanded at least partial local manufacture of EME sold in their markets. Other countries erected nontariff barriers, such as specification requirements that also pressured EME companies to build offshore plants.

TABLE 3
COST STRUCTURE OF A LARGE BULLDOZER
Equivalent to CAT D–6

		Percent of Cost
Labor		35.0%
Components and subassemblies	12.4	
Overhead	18.0	
Assembly	4.6	
Purchased materials and components		49.6
Overhead		15.4
		100.0%

Source: Boston Consulting Group.

Competition

In 1981 there were seven major contenders in the EME industry and a myriad of smaller local specialists. The majors—Caterpillar (Cat), J.I. Case (a division of Tenneco), John Deere, Clark Equipment, Fiat-Allis, International Harvester (IH), and Komatsu (of Japan)—accounted for more than 90 percent of dollar sales worldwide. Their market shares through the 1970s are shown in Exhibit 3.

All companies had to contend with Cat's dominance in almost all market segments. This had encouraged the smaller firms to approach these markets indirectly. As one industry participant put it, their strategy was to "nibble away, moving in as Cat moved up to bigger equipment, forcing Cat to protect its heels here and head there." Some manufacturers chose to offer a full line of only one type of product, such as loaders or scrapers, while others chose to offer one product of each type. Often competitors brought out either a larger or a smaller version of a Cat product. (The major competitors' positions in various product segments appear in Exhibit 4.)

International Harvester (IH). IH was a large U.S. firm with basic products in three industries: heavy-duty trucks, agricultural equipment, and construction equipment. In the heavy-duty truck sector (45 percent of sales in 1980), it faced tough competitors such as GM and Ford, which were low-cost producers in an industry where competition was often on price. In the mature and cyclical agricultural equipment sector, competition centered on having a strong dealer network. IH was second to John Deere in market share in the United States, with 30 percent compared with Deere's 36 percent. In 1980, 40 percent of IH's sales came from the farm sector. In construction equipment it competed head-on with Cat. IH had a strong distribution system, with 70 dealers and 200 outlets worldwide, but particularly strong in Asia and Eastern bloc countries. After Cat, IH had the second-broadcast product line. It produced some components, such as engines, castings, fasteners, and bearings, and purchased 50 percent to 70 percent of its parts requirements. In 1980 IH's sales in EME were $750 million (12 percent of sales). IH's results in recent years had been poor, and the company was reportedly in financial difficulty.

J.I. Case. Case was an independent farm equipment company before being purchased by Tenneco in 1970. It had since diversified away from the very competitive, highly cyclical farm equipment industry. By 1981 construction equipment represented 67 percent of Case's sales. Many of the company's 11 plants in the United States produced components and finished products for both agricultural and construction equipment, and the same distribution channels were used to distribute both. Case's network of 1,200 independent dealers and 219 company-owned retail outlets was almost all in the United States and Canada. Its product strategy focused on a few products and offered a wide array of machines in each category. For instance, in the hydraulic excavator segment Case offered 13 models, with horsepowers ranging from 120 to 445. This compared with Cat's offering of five models between 85 and 325 hp and John Deere's two models within the same range. Acquiring a 40 percent interest in Poclain of France in 1977, Case gained access to the technology of a leading hydraulic excavator producer. Poclain's European marketing subsidiaries and its Brazilian excavator assembly operation came with the acquisition.

John Deere. Deere led the world in farm equipment manufacture, offering a full line with a concentration on large horsepower tractors. More than 85 percent of Deere's sales of $5,450 million in 1981 came from farm equipment and the balance from construction equipment. In the latter category, the company offered a full line but only one or two models for each product. Deere reportedly had over 25 percent of the U.S. crawler market. The company's loyal 2,300-dealer network was a major asset, and according to one report, Deere was rapidly expanding its small base of overseas distributors. The same report said that Deere aimed to be number two in the United States in construction equipment and number four worldwide. In the farm sector, the company was reputedly a low-cost producer. Although Deere depended heavily on outside sourcing for components, there was extensive integration of manufacturing, especially in engines, transmissions, and components linked to Deere designs and specifications. Deere had manufacturing and/or assembly operations in several countries, including France, Germany, Brazil, South Africa, Australia, and Spain, although only the

French operation was related to construction equipment. Deere spent heavily on R&D, devoting 4.4 percent of sales to it in 1981. The company had industry production "firsts," such as the dual-path hydrostatic drive for tracked equipment and microcomputers to control some transmission functions. It was implementing CAD/CAM programs to lower its manufacturing costs further.

Komatsu. This company dominated the Japanese construction equipment industry and was the second-largest EME company worldwide. It held a 60 percent market share within Japan but was a distant second to Cat worldwide. Until the late 1960s Komatsu had been a small Japanese EME producer with a limited line of inferior-quality products. In the mid-1960s, when Cat announced a joint venture with Mitsubishi, Komatsu's management was motivated to revitalize the company. Through licensing agreements with Cummins for diesel engines, IH for large wheel loaders, and Bucyrus-Erie for excavator designs, the company developed its technology. With the benefit of a labor cost advantage relative to U.S. and European competitors and the postwar Japanese construction boom, Komatsu not only survived but also prospered over the next decade. When domestic demand slowed in the mid-1970s, the company looked to export markets. Komatsu exported mainly whole machines although, responding to government requests, it had set up assembly plants in Mexico and Brazil in the 1970s. It cultivated cordial relationships with governments in communist and Third World countries.

Outside Japan, Komatsu lacked an effective dealer network. In the large U.S. market, for instance, it relied on nonexclusive dealerships that usually catered to small contractors. Komatsu's machines were often cheaper than Cat's. Said Lee Morgan, Cat's CEO, "Generally speaking, Komatsu's products are priced at least 10 to 15 percent below Caterpillar's. That says clearly what they believe our value is versus theirs."

Other Competitors. Among other major manufacturers, Clark Equipment focused on one type of product, the loader. The company faced severe competition from low-cost producers, and the recession had not helped. Fiat-Allis competed with a full line, emphasizing heavier models. The company tended to compete on price but was not considered a serious competitive threat due to its poor reputation for quality and reliability.

Since 1975 a new German-based company, IBH Holding Company (IBH), had burgeoned. It had been put together through the acquisition of a handful of money-losing French, German, and American operations by a 37-year-old entrepreneur and Harvard MBA, Dieter Esch. He planned to make the company a full-line competitor and felt it would be "the number two company in the industry after Caterpillar." In early 1981 IBH acquired Terex Corporation, a GM subsidiary that specialized in making a wide range of EME, giving IBH a much-needed U.S. manufacturing and marketing base. Only six months after the acquisition, IBH had already turned Terex around. IBH had integrated several sets of distributors (some 600 worldwide) and found it difficult to manage spare parts inventories and to keep service levels high. Moreover, IBH did not make most parts itself, and it had an equity base of only $70 million.

Besides these larger companies, smaller national competitors were particularly strong in some countries. J.C. Bamford, for instance, held a 40 percent share of the

U.K. market. The company planned to increase its overseas sales, taking advantage of the falling pound sterling.

CAT'S BACKGROUND

Headquartered in Peoria, Illinois, Cat was a multinational company that designed, manufactured, and marketed products in two principal categories: (1) earthmoving, construction, and materials-handling machinery and equipment and related parts; and (2) engines for earthmoving and construction machines, for on-highway trucks, and for marine, agricultural, industrial, and other applications, as well as electric power generation systems. Cat was the world's largest manufacturer of EME. Of the company's expected $9.2 billion in sales in 1981, 57 percent would be overseas (see Exhibits 5, 6, and 7). Products and components manufactured in the United States accounted for 68 percent of these non-U.S. sales. Cat's large geographic base and its broad product line were intended to protect it from a dependence on the domestic business cycle. Estimated parts sales represented about 35 percent to 45 percent of total revenue, although their exact contribution was never revealed by the company.

Cat's rise to global dominance stemmed from a mixture of good luck, shrewd judgment, and world history. The company was fortunate to be based in the United States, where the proliferation of highways that followed the development of the auto industry led to strong demand for EME. In the late 1920s Raymond Force, a farsighted chief executive, pulled Cat out of the overcrowded farm equipment business to concentrate on this growing EME segment. World War II created tremendous demand for EME, and the U.S. Army decided to make Cat's bulldozers its standard equipment. From 1941 to 1944 Cat's sales tripled. When the U.S. Army withdrew from Europe and Asia after the war, it left behind the bulky machines for local use. Foreign users became familiar with Cat machines, and local mechanics learned to service Cat equipment, thereby laying the foundation for the emergence of a formidable worldwide EME producer.

The company's management engaged in careful strategic analysis and tried to take a long-term view of its business. In more than half a century, Cat had suffered only one year of loss; that was in 1932 at the height of the Great Depression. The strength of the company's classic strategic posture of high-quality products backed by effective service was well understood throughout the company, and management was committed to its maintenance and defense. A senior executive said in an interview: "Our competitive position and our management strengths are a hell of a hurdle for competitors to overcome. We not only have a strong defensible strategic position, we just know our business better than anyone else, and we work harder at it."

Marketing

Cat seized the postwar opportunity with both hands, establishing independent dealerships to service the machines left in Europe and Asia. These dealers quickly became self-sustaining, and along with the strong U.S. dealership network, they became the core of Cat's marketing strategy. In 1981 the company had 129 full-time independent dealers overseas, operating 605 branches worldwide, each branch capable of providing service and spare parts backup. In the United States the corresponding figures were 87 dealers and 284 branches. These dealers' combined net worth nearly equaled that of Cat itself (see Exhibit 8).

Cat tied the dealers close to it by enhancing the dealers' positions as entrepreneurs. When one of the U.S. dealers established a production line to rebuild Cat engines and a shop that refurbished track shoes and other tractor parts, Cat management supported the efforts despite the fact that customers could buy rebuilt parts that lasted about 80 percent as long as new ones at only half the cost.

Cat helped the dealers maintain appropriate inventory levels. The company established a national computer network that enabled its U.S. dealers to order any part from the central distribution depot in Illinois for delivery the next day. Cat offered to repurchase parts or equipment that the dealers could not sell. When introducing new products, the company first built up a two-month supply of spare parts. Cat guaranteed that if parts were not delivered within 48 hours anywhere in the world, the customer got them free.

The company conducted regular training programs for dealers and product demonstrations for their customers. It even offered a course in Peoria for dealers' children, encouraging them to remain in the family business. Cat's chairman summed up his company's attitude, "We approach our dealers as partners in the enterprise, not as agents or middlemen. We worry as much about their performance as they do themselves."

An average Cat dealer had a net worth of $4 million and annual sales of $100 million in the United States. The field population of Cat machines approached 20 times that of the nearest competitor. Because of its financial strength, an average dealership could expand its selling and servicing capabilities at the same pace that Cat expanded its product line. In 1980 Cat dealers spent more than $200 million on new buildings and equipment. No Cat dealer had failed in recent years. In fact some of the larger dealerships abroad were held by other multinationals, such as General Electric (in Colombia and Venezuela) and Unilever (in Africa). Although no reliable figures were available, it was believed that dealers received a margin of 25 percent on list (retail) prices of Cat machines and considerably higher margins on parts.

Cat advertised its products heavily in specialist magazines like the *Engineering News Record*. Mostly its advertisements focused on a single product, often a new introduction.

Manufacturing

The second leg of Cat's strategy was to concentrate on manufacturing excellence. All Cat products were substantially the same, wherever made. Cat invested heavily in a few large-scale, state-of-the-art component manufacturing facilities—many of them near Peoria—to meet worldwide demand. The company then used these centralized facilities to supply overseas assembly plants that also added local features. Local plants not only avoided the high transportation cost of end products but also helped the company respond to the demands of local governments for manufacturing investment.

The company manufactured in 22 plants in the United States, three in the United Kingdom, two in Brazil, Canada, and France, and one each in Australia and Belgium. It also manufactured through 50 percent-owned ventures in Japan and India and a 49 percent-owned company in Mexico. Another 50/50 joint venture was being

TABLE 4
CAT'S CAPITAL EXPENDITURE PROGRAM
Dollar Amounts in Millions

Year	*Capital Expenditures*	*Gross Plant*	*Cap. Exp. as Percent Gross Plant (at previous year-end)*
1981*	$713.2	$5,454.3	15.0%
1980	749.2	4,750.8	17.8
1979	675.9	4,209.7	18.6
1978	543.4	3,637.0	17.2
1977	516.5	3,165.6	18.9
1976	495.0	2,734.5	21.8
1975	446.0	2,266.9	24.0
1974	349.7	1,856.4	22.6
1973	263.7	1,543.2	20.2
1972	132.8	1,303.5	9.8
1971	123.6	1,361.1	9.9
1970	$113.2	$1,251.5	9.7%

*Estimated.
Source: First Boston.

negotiated in Indonesia. Five of the U.S. plants produced mainly engines, both for incorporation into Cat's machines and for sale to other equipment manufacturers and dealers. Five U.S. plants made only turbine-engine and related system components for Solar Turbines Incorporated, a wholly owned subsidiary. All other U.S. plants produced various EME machines.

Throughout the 1970s Cat continued to expand its plants although it typically operated at less than 75 percent capacity. In 1981 Cat had an estimated $12 billion of sales capacity (both machines and engines). To achieve break-even, the company had to sell about $6.8 billion each year. According to senior management, it was better to shave profit margins in times of soft demand than to risk losing customers because shipments were late or products were poorly made. The company was highly integrated backward with nearly 90 percent of its components and parts made in-house.

Cat's commitment to manufacturing excellence showed in its capital-spending program. (See Table 4 for recent trends in capital expenditure programs.) Much of the capital spending was motivated by an internal Cat study in the late 1970s that concluded there was enormous growth potential in the earth-moving industry. Another aspect of this ambitious capital-spending program was Cat's commitment to flexible manufacturing systems. Obsolete equipment was being replaced by more up-to-date, electronically controlled equipment.

Quality control also attracted management's attention. In 1980 Cat started experimenting with quality circles, an approach that encouraged assembly-line workers to form problem-solving groups to identify and analyze problems and recommend solutions. The company also used employee newsletters to emphasize the importance of increasing productivity to meet foreign competition, especially from Japan.

Cat's use of automation to achieve productivity gains was not well received by its workers. In 1979 the company and the United Auto Workers union (UAW) went through an unusually bitter strike that led to an 11-week walkout by 40,000 workers in Peoria and a 7-week stoppage at other U.S. plants. In 1980 the company laid off 5,600 workers, further souring management-labor relations. Many observers felt that labor relations was Cat's Achilles' heel. In press releases, Cat contended that its workers were paid an average of $20 per hour, compared with $11 Komatsu paid its workers. Since labor costs represented nearly two thirds of the value added at Cat, management felt that it was imperative for costs to be contained. (See Table 5 for a comparison of the value-added structures.)

TABLE 5
VALUE-ADDED STRUCTURE AT CAT AND KOMATSU

	Cat	*Komatsu**
Labor costs	66.4%	50.2%
Depreciation	10.2	10.4
Interest expenses	5.1	−4.8
Net income	13.2	17.1
Taxes	5.1	25.2
Other	—	1.9
Total	100.0%	100.0%

*About half of the total domestic sales of Komatsu were derived from direct sales to end-users who usually purchased machines under installment credit. This enabled Komatsu to earn interest at a rate higher than its borrowings. Further, Komatsu had substantial marketable securities as liquid assets.
Source: Nomura Securities.

Cat's manufacturing system was not without its critics. One industry observer remarked:

> Cat's engineers are terrific in engineering but not in organizing. They know that if they let production go overseas, the U.S. operations will have to act as a buffer, causing production to yo-yo. They would prefer to use exports from the United States to keep production levels constant. Their approach is to keep volume concentrated so that they can automate and cut labor.

The observer also criticized Cat's production system, saying it was "five years behind the production systems used in Japan," resulting in "high overheads and setup costs."

Overseas Expansion

Cat's top management had developed a worldview of its business. Initially, overseas dealers depended primarily on the parts business of U.S. construction companies, shuttling machines around the world from job to job. Through its long-term commitment to international markets, however, Cat cemented its relationship with its dealers and encouraged them to devote primary attention to Cat products. The typical overseas dealership did more than half of its business in Cat's products. In the United States and Canada, the proportion was 80 percent.

During the 1950s and 1960s Cat opened offices in the United Kingdom, Europe, Brazil, Canada, Mexico, and Australia. It built manufacturing facilities in the United Kingdom, France, and Canada in the mid-1950s, and in Brazil, Belgium, and Australia in the early 1960s. The late 1960s saw the establishment of the Mexican joint venture. Although some of this foreign expansion was motivated by the fear of being locked out of markets through protectionist measures, most moves were the result of a management belief that wherever a market existed in an industrially advanced country, a local competitor would eventually emerge to serve it and later move abroad. Thus, unless Cat itself was on the scene, it would not be able to compete effectively.

In the early 1960s the company tried to enter the Japanese market. First it attempted to link up with Komatsu, but Komatsu wanted only a licensing agreement. Cat then began talking to Mitsubishi. Immediately, Komatsu went to the Ministry of International Trade and Industry (MITI), asking it to block the new venture until Komatsu upgraded its product line. MITI obliged. After Komatsu had concluded a deal with Cummins Engine for the manufacture of engines under license, MITI authorized the Cat-Mitsubishi joint venture.

Because it saw its domestic and international operations as being closely linked, Cat preferred to maintain complete managerial control over all subsidiaries through 100 percent ownership. It agreed to joint ventures only when required by host government policies, and until 1981, had not set up a minority-owned subsidiary abroad. Furthermore, Cat ensured strategy unity in the worldwide operations by sending some of its best senior managers abroad to manage the operations of its subsidiaries. When they returned to Peoria, these managers took more of a world view of the company's operations. The executive compensation system for expatriates stressed their contribution to Cat's worldwide performance.

Cat's international marketing operations viewed the world in three parts. North and South America were served by the U.S. operation as well as by the Brazilian, Mexican, and Canadian facilities. Europe, the Middle East, and Africa were served by the European facilities. The Far East received its products from Japan, Australia, and India although the large Australian market was served mostly from the United States. Despite these regional options, many of the large machines and several key components, such as transmissions, were sourced only from the United States.

This division of the world led to friction between Mitsubishi and Cat. For instance, in the 1970s an independent dealer in British Columbia imported Mitsubishi-Cat machines and started selling them at a lower price and yet making profits. The regular Cat dealer for the region complained to Peoria, and Cat management directed the Japanese venture to refrain from selling direct in North America. In Australia, a similar situation prevailed.

The company's international sales efforts were coordinated by the sales managers based in Peoria, directing Cat's field representatives, who, in turn, communicated with the dealers. The sales managers tried to maintain consistent worldwide pricing and dealer policies, but industry observers felt that Cat's prices in the United States were consistently higher than in overseas markets. "They have never known an acceptable return on European production – even in the best years," said one analyst. In 1981 according to the same analyst, Cat's operating margin abroad was about 7 percent compared with 20 percent in the United States.

Product Development

Research and development expenditures at Cat were substantial – $363 million in 1981. Most research was targeted directly toward product development, product improvement, and applied research. Cat undertook basic research when it needed materials or components that its suppliers could not provide. For instance, Cat developed a beadless tire for its big loaders and then licensed the technology to Goodyear.

A senior executive summed up the company's approach to product development: "Unless a product is highly capital intensive, will benefit from high technology, and is marketable through our current distribution system, it will not fit our product development strategy." Cat was rarely the first with a new offering, preferring to let other companies go through the trial-and-error stage, then following quickly with the most trouble-free product in the market. One of the company's vice presidents said, "Market share for us is not an objective. Building sophisticated, durable, reliable products and providing good support is." By constant adaptation, Cat engineers had created 120 different machines, serving almost as many market segments.

Pricing

Cat's products were usually priced at a premium of 10 to 20 percent over the nearest competitive model, but management felt that its product quality and service excellence merited such a premium. It tried to avoid overpricing and did not factor in some costs, such as new plant start-up costs, into its pricing calculations. This had meant lower profit margins during the years of major capacity expansion. Because of Cat's uniform pricing policy, dealers all over the world were billed in dollars, irrespective of the origin of the machines. The prices were generally based on the U.S. manufacturing cost, but when the dollar was strong, Cat had to be flexible.

In the EME industry, a large part of the profit was in spare parts. A large crawler tractor cutting into rocks in an iron ore mine will use up parts worth as much as the original equipment within two years or so. Although Cat never revealed the data, one industry estimate was that Cat's profit margin on parts was at least twice that on original equipment.

Diversification

Cat's stated objective was to grow 6 to 7 percent a year in real terms throughout the 1980s. Because its domestic construction business was becoming increasingly mature, the company decided to achieve this through related diversification. In mid-1981 the company purchased the Solar Turbines Division from financially troubled IH for $505 million. Solar made turbine engines, natural gas compressors, generators, and power drives; 80 percent of its sales went to the oil and natural gas industry with more than 50 percent outside the United States.

Cat's competitive strategy in engines was built on a huge captive base; the company was the world's largest consumer of engines over 400 hp. In addition, since the late 1960s, it had developed and supplied engines for Ford trucks, and by 1981 supplied over a third of Ford's truck engine needs. It aimed to become the low-cost producer by using up-to-date technologies and factories. The capital expenditure record of the engine division detailed in Exhibit 9 shows the company's commitment.

Cat's purchase of Solar Turbines came 16 years after its previous acquisition (in 1965, the company had acquired Towmotor to gain a foothold in the lift-truck business). Lee Morgan explained why his company had not followed the acquisition route of competitors like Clark Equipment and Massey-Ferguson:

> Most companies look at diversification as a proliferation of products in many different lines, but that misses the point. A tractor does not really care whether it works in agriculture, oil exploration, or road building, and that is the essence of

diversification—being involved in many sectors of the economy.

Financial Policies

Cat was a financially conservative company with a low dependence on debt. It traditionally offered low dividend payout ratios, using retained earnings for financing. The company used the last-in, first-out (LIFO) method of inventory valuation and treated its R&D costs as expenses in the years incurred.

Cat's balance sheet was not as tight as some competitors' due to the company's manufacturing policies. One supplier estimated that half of his and Cat's work-in-progress inventory maintained by Cat and its suppliers resulted from a safety stock to guard against quality problems. In early 1981 Morgan singled out the Japanese inventory control system as one of the keys to Japanese success in manufacturing. He stated, "What the factory needs today should be either made today or delivered today."

Personnel and External Relations Policies

Cat hired only individuals who expressed a willingness to work their way up from a factory and dedicate their entire careers to the company. It hired management recruits directly from college, often people with technical degrees. As a rule, the company did not hire MBAs. Over two thirds of Cat's top executives were born in Illinois or neighboring states. Morgan joined the company in 1946, after graduating from the University of Illinois, and spent most of his career in sales. The company president, Robert Gilmore, was a 44-year company veteran who rose through the ranks via an apprenticeship in manufacturing after graduating from high school. The company conducted its own in-house management development programs.

This approach to recruitment and training had led to a close-knit management group (inbred in the view of critics) who worked, lived, and socialized together. They were so dedicated to their work that they were sometimes described as having "yellow paint in their veins," a reference to the ubiquitous yellow of Cat's machines. This approach was carried abroad as well. Most employees in the company's sales subsidiary in Geneva lived in one suburb referred to locally as "Caterpillar Village." In Japan, all of the company's American employees were housed in one Tokyo apartment complex and traveled to work together in one bus. This clubbiness was reinforced by the company's closemouthed conduct of its business. It routinely refused to provide information to the press unless it thought it absolutely necessary. The same treatment was meted out to security analysts and even the industry association, the Construction Industry Manufacturers Association (CIMA). The company also discouraged its dealers from joining the Association of Equipment Distributors.

An important feature of Cat's operations was the extent to which the company dominated the economy of Illinois in general and Peoria in particular. Cat's high wages provided the region with Illinois' third-highest per capita income. Cat was proud of its contribution to the local community, and its senior managers often reiterated the company's commitment to Peoria. In 1981 the company was in the midst of constructing a training center in downtown Peoria as well as a huge addition to its Morton worldwide parts distribution center nearby. With considerable reluctance, Cat reduced its local work force from a peak of 36,000 in 1979 to its 1981 level of 33,500. This represented over 20 percent of the area's work force, and was more than 15 times the payroll of Peoria's second-largest employer.

Management Systems and Style

One key element in Cat's management systems was what the company called being "severally responsible." Under this value system, all staff and operating people in a department felt responsible for obtaining results. The company believed this promoted a cooperative, team-building approach. "This is no place for individual star performers," said Morgan. "We encourage an uncommon amount of subordination of personal wishes to the good of the company." In keeping with that tradition of excising the cult of personality, the public relations department put out no personal profile of Morgan or any other top manager.

Cat was one of the first companies to respond constructively to emerging criticisms of multinational corporations. Morgan said, "At Caterpillar, we seek friendly, cooperative relationships with governments. To that end, we are willing to make some substantial commitments—not only in terms of capital but also in terms of operating principles." Those operating principles were spelled out in the *Caterpillar Code of Worldwide Business Conduct*, first published in 1974, two years before the OECD guidelines on multinational enterprise came into being. The code set a high standard of behavior for its managers and set forth the company's expectations of fair treatment by host governments.

Another aspect of Cat's management style had been its consistent willingness to take a long-term view of the company's fortunes and spend today for tomorrow's growth. Morgan again: "In our business, the lead times are long. It takes 10 years or more to develop and introduce a new product. To us, short-term planning means the next 5 years." To further the long-term approach, the company strove toward a simple management structure that encouraged easy and informal communication. Said Morgan, "The root of our organizational process is the ability of anyone to walk into my office. . . . We try to see to it that the rate of bureaucracy does not get out of hand here."

Cat had long resisted the idea of a separate corporate planning office, believing that its line managers throughout the organization understood the company's well-established strategic principles and functional policies. At the core of its strategy was a defense of its dominant competitive position through continuous product development and long-term investment in its production facilities and marketing channels.

Typically, top management decisions were arrived at by consensus. For instance, product development was monitored through a product control department comprising representatives from manufacturing, marketing, and engineering that assessed potential competition and forecast sales volumes for five years. The final decision rested with a committee composed of the chairman, some executives from his office, and several key vice presidents. "People begin bouncing ideas off one another in a series of meetings," said Morgan. "I am presumably the guy who makes a decision, but I am greatly influenced by the consensus."

There was no question, however, that Peoria dominated the entire company. Besides maintaining strong central financial and production controls, headquarters kept constant tabs on the company's operation worldwide, and no problem was considered undeserving of its attention. In fact, no management promotion above the level of department head was authorized without the chairman's personal approval.

SITUATION IN OCTOBER 1981

In late 1981 Cat faced an unsettled economic environment. Since 1979 the U.S. economy had been in a downturn. The Federal Reserve's anti-inflationary tight money policy, which had raised interest rates, had severely affected the construction industry. The 1982 consensus forecast among economists predicted a deeper recession and gradually declining interest rates. Having benefited from the depreciation of the dollar in the late 1970s, Cat management was also concerned about forecasts of a continued strengthening of the U.S. currency.

The 1979 oil shock had stimulated construction in some of the oil-rich countries. By late 1981, however, the oil price rise had forced a recession on non-oil-developing countries. Meanwhile, demand for crude had softened, and some economists predicted an oil glut in the 1980s. This threatened to upset the massive development plans of countries such as Nigeria and Mexico.

In late 1981 much talk also circulated in the world financial press about the global debt crisis. Many large developing countries, such as Mexico, Brazil, Argentina, Nigeria, and South Korea, were facing a severe liquidity crunch, and international banks were reportedly reluctant to increase their already large exposure to LDCs. Simultaneously, developed countries were proposing reductions in foreign aid, and commodity prices were also registering deep declines.

The Far East and Australia was the only region showing hopeful signs. The ASEAN countries—Singapore, Malaysia, Indonesia, the Philippines, and Thailand—had been growing impressively over the last five years, and this trend was expected to continue. South Korea, Taiwan, and Japan were also prospering. Australia's minerals-led boom, temporarily dampened by the world recession, was expected to reassert itself through the 1980s.

In 1981 the U.S. EME industry was operating at about 60 percent of capacity. Capacity utilization rates for the last few years had been around 65 percent. In 1980 the industry had employed about 190,000 people; it was estimated that by the end of 1981, the number would have fallen to about 152,000.

FUTURE STRATEGY

Morgan opened his management meeting with the news that the UAW delegates had given advance notice that in light of Cat's outstanding financial results, the union would be asking for substantial increases at next year's triennial contract negotiation. It also expected to recoup the benefits lost after the bitter 1979 strike.

As well as beginning to think about the company's approach to these demands, Morgan also wanted to engage his managers in a discussion of how Cat might respond to the changing industry and emerging competitive environment.

EXHIBIT 1
U.S. INDUSTRY SHIPMENTS, INCLUDING EXPORTS
Number of Units

	Total Shipments					Exports				
	1977	*1978*	*1979*	*1980*	*1981**	*1977*	*1978*	*1979*	*1980*	*1981**
Tractors										
Crawler	19,847	22,058	19,468	16,446	15,785	n.a.	8,850	6,902	7,063	7,466
Wheel	2,798	6,013	4,962	6,895	4,254	1,591	2,285	2,289	1,381	1,733
Loaders										
Crawler	6,146	7,040	6,321	4,455	3,286	n.a.	1,270	1,117	1,211	1,422
Wheel	14,331	18,214	21,628	17,103	13,168	3,626	3,352	3,213	5,710	4,645
Track Shovel	21,011	23,401	29,409	23,837	16,915	3,431	3,645	5,364	6,633	4,678
Hauler										
Rear Dump	2,816	2,330	2,486	1,877	1,930	1,007	816	1,051	1,163	1,190
Bottom Dump	60	2,775	n.a.	3,187	2,855	n.a.	388	n.a.	n.a.	n.a.
Scrapers	4,898	5,012	4,075	2,571	2,403	1,211	1,187	1,253	1,156	1,317
Graders	6,117	7,372	7,257	7,165	5,947	2,606	2,537	2,183	3,074	3,062
Excavators										
Crawlers	4,207	5,007	5,084	3,562	2,338	783	790	1,167	857	722
Wheel	855	995	645	410	460	145	150	n.a.	66	69
Cable	214	127	165	82	60	46	46	31	62	30

*Estimated.
n.a. = not available.
Source: Bureau of the Census; CIMA, *Outlook 1984.*

EXHIBIT 2
NEW CONSTRUCTION OUTPUT INDICATORS FOR THE UNITED STATES

	Total Value		*As Percentage of GNP*			
Year	*Current $ ($ bil.)*	*Constant $ ($ bil.)*	*Current $ (%)*	*Constant $ (%)*	*Value per Capita Constant 1972 $*	*Construction Index 1972 = 100*
1970	94.9	107.0	9.7	9.9	522	88.6
1971	110.0	116.0	10.3	10.3	560	94.8
1972	124.1	123.9	10.6	10.4	593	100.0
1973	137.9	126.9	10.6	10.1	603	108.7
1974	138.5	109.1	9.8	8.7	515	126.9
1975	134.5	97.2	8.8	7.9	455	138.4
1976	151.1	105.0	8.9	8.1	488	143.9
1977	174.0	111.3	10.9	8.3	513	156.3
1978	205.5	116.9	9.7	8.1	535	175.7
1979	229.0	114.7	9.5	7.7	520	199.0
1980	228.7	103.5	8.7	6.9	465	221.7

Source: *Construction Review,* June 1981.

EXHIBIT 3 MARKET SHARE POSITIONS OF MAJOR EME PRODUCERS

	1971	*1972*	*1973*	*1974*	*1975*	*1976*	*1977*	*1978*	*1979*	*1980*
Caterpillar[a]	56.0%	56.0%	53.0%	53.0%	54.4%	56.1%	53.6%	51.9%	50.0%	53.3%
Komatsu	10.3	10.9	11.6	9.0	9.2	11.3	11.8	14.3	14.8	15.2
J.I. Case	6.7	6.9	8.9	8.3	7.2	7.4	8.5	9.4	10.5	10.3
Fiat-Allis[b]	4.3	4.0	3.8	7.3	7.7	6.3	6.5	6.1	5.8	5.7
Deere	5.8	6.2	6.3	6.1	4.7	5.2	6.6	6.7	7.1	6.6
International Harvester	11.0	10.0	10.1	9.7	10.0	7.6	7.2	6.6	7.1	5.1
Clark	5.9	6.0	6.3	6.6	6.8	6.1	5.8	5.0	4.7	3.8
Total	100.0%	100.0%	100.0%	100.0%	100.0%	100.0%	100.0%	100.0%	100.0%	100.0%
IBH[c]	—	—	—	—	0.5	0.5	0.6	0.7	1.4	4.2
Total sales ($ millions)[d]	$4,063	$4,954	$6,190	$7,651	$8,840	$8,773	$10,130	$12,841	$14,027	$14,916
Year-to-year change	—	21.3%	24.9%	23.6%	15.5%	−0.8%	15.5%	26.8%	9.2%	6.3%
Price increase[e]	4%	5%	12%	10%	18%	6%	8%	9%	11%	12%
Real growth[e]	—	16%	13%	13%	(3%)	(7%)	7%	18%	(2%)	(6%)

Note: The figures relating to Massey-Ferguson Limited have not been included in this table. MF held less than 2 percent of the market in 1980, and in the previous years, it seldom held more than 3.5 percent.

[a]Includes sales from Caterpillar-Mitsubishi joint venture net of sales to and from Caterpillar.

[b]Allis-Chalmers only before 1974.

[c]IBH Holding, AG—founded in 1975 with growth through acquisitions of 10 European equipment manufacturers through 1980. In 1980 IBH acquired Hymac (U.K.) and Hanomag (Germany). In 1982 IBH acquired Terex from General Motors.

[d]Excludes IBH.

[e]Wertheim & Co., Inc., estimates.

Source: Wertheim & Co., Inc.

EXHIBIT 4 COMPETITORS' POSITIONS IN PRODUCT SEGMENTS

	Cat	*Komatsu*	*J.I. Case*[a]	*Int'l. Harv.*	*Deere*	*IBH*[b]	*Fiat-Allis*	*Clark*
Backhoes[c]			XXX	X	XX	XX	X	
Excavators[d]	XXX	XX	XX		XX			
Tractors								
Crawler over 90 hp	XXX	XX	X	XX	X	X	XX	
Crawler under 90 hp	XX	XX	XX	XX	XXX	X	X	
Wheel[e]	XXX	X	X	XX	X	X	X	XX
Graders	XXX	X			XX		X	X
Loaders								
Crawler	XXX	XX	X	X	XX	X	X	
Wheel	XXX	XX	X	XX	XX	X	X	XX
Off-highway trucks[f]	XX	X	X	XX	X	XX	X	XX
Scrapers	XXX	X		X	X	X	X	X
Other[g]	XXX	XX	X	XX	X	X	X	XX

Note: XXX denotes leading position; XX denotes major participation; X denotes minor participation.

[a]A subsidiary of Tenneco, Inc.

[b]IBH Holding, A.G.—founded in 1975 with growth through acquisitions of 10 European equipment manufacturers through 1980.

[c]Other participants include J.C. Bamford in the United Kingdom, Ford Motor, and Volvo in Sweden.

[d]Other participants include Koehring Co. and Poclain (40% owned by J.I. Case) in France, Hitachi and Mitsubishi in Japan, Orenstein & Koppel (O&K) and Liebherr in Germany, and J.C. Bamford and Priestman (Acrow) in the United Kingdom.

[e]Other participants include Ford Motor, Volvo, O&K, J.C. Bamford, and Leyland.

[f]Other participants include Unit Rig & Equipment Co. (private), Volvo, Euclid (Daimler-Benz), and Leyland.

[g]Includes skidders, compactors, and attachments.

Source: Wertheim & Co., Inc.

EXHIBIT 5
CATERPILLAR'S INCOME STATEMENT
Dollars in Millions, Except per Share Amounts

Fiscal year	*1976*		*1977*		*1978*		*1979*		*1980*		*1981**	
	$	%	$	%	$	%	$	%	$	%	$	%
Net sales	*$5,042.30*	*(100.0)*	*$5,848.90*	*(100.0)*	*$7,219.20*	*(100.0)*	*$7,613.20*	*(100.0)*	*$8,597.80*	*(100.0)*	*$9,154.50*	*(100.0)*
Cost of goods sold	3,720.20	(73.8)	4,312.00	(73.7)	5,349.30	(74.1)	5,888.50	(77.3)	6,627.10	(77.1)	6,933.30	(75.7)
Selling, general, and administrative expenses	453.20	(9.0)	489.20	(8.4)	586.00	(8.1)	662.00	(9.7)	769.50	(8.9)	868.70	(9.5)
Depreciation and amortization	184.10	(3.7)	210.50	(3.6)	257.10	(3.6)	311.80	(4.1)	370.20	(4.3)	448.40	(4.9)
Net operating income	684.80	(13.6)	837.20	(14.3)	1,026.80	(14.2)	750.90	(9.9)	831.00	(9.7)	904.1	(9.9)
Nonoperating income (expense)	0.00		0.00		48.00		80.00		112.60		107.30	
Interest expense	42.50	(0.8)	60.10	(1.0)	111.90	(1.6)	139.10	(1.8)	173.20	(2.0)	224.80	(2.5)
Pretax income	643.30	(12.8)	779.20	(13.3)	963.20	(13.3)	725.50	(9.5)	796.70	(9.3)	802.80	(8.8)
Income taxes	260.10	(5.2)	334.10	(5.7)	396.90	(5.5)	233.90	(3.1)	231.90	(2.7)	223.90	(2.4)
Current taxes	271.60		308.30		395.90		271.60		243.50		240.30	
Deferred income taxes	(11.50)		25.80		1.00		(37.70)		(11.60)		(16.40)	
Profit after tax	383.20	(7.6)	445.10	(7.6)	566.30	(7.8)	491.60	(6.5)	564.80	(6.6)	578.90	(6.3)
Common dividends per share	$1.46		$1.58		$1.88		$2.10		$1.33		n.a.	

*Estimated.
n.a. = not available.
Source: Annual reports.

Ind. Avg.

EXHIBIT 5 *(concluded)*
CATERPILLAR'S BALANCE SHEET
Dollars in Millions

At December 31	*1976*	*1977*	*1978*	*1979*	*1980*	*1981**
Assets						
Current assets	$2,096.90	$2,252.30	$2,628.30	$2,606.90	$2,932.90	$3,544.40
Cash and equivalents	88.10	209.40	244.50	147.20	104.00	81.00
Receivables	604.60	648.10	767.80	692.70	912.40	994.30
Inventories	1,244.90	1,288.60	1,522.30	1,670.20	1,749.60	2,213.80
Other current assets	159.30	106.20	93.70	96.80	166.90	255.30
Fixed assets	1,797.00	2,093.30	2,402.80	2,796.40	3,165.30	3,740.50
Long-term investments	78.30	72.50	58.80	35.30	103.50	120.00
Net plant	1,698.60	1,999.10	2,281.40	2,687.80	3,008.50	3,396.20
Accumulated depreciation	1,082.60	1,222.10	1,418.50	1,638.00	1,822.90	2,154.60
Deferred charges	0.00	0.00	0.00	23.50	0.00	0.00
Intangibles	0.00	0.00	0.00	0.00	0.00	146.40
Other assets	20.10	21.70	62.60	49.80	53.30	77.90
Total assets	$3,893.90	$4,345.60	$5,031.10	$5,403.30	$6,098.20	$7,284.90
Liabilities and stockholders' equity						
Current liabilities	$ 821.20	$ 955.80	$1,237.10	$1,386.10	$1,711.50	$2,369.50
Short-term debt	59.90	99.90	146.90	463.20	446.60	847.60
Notes payable	30.90	87.30	112.60	404.20	430.30	747.00
Current long-term debt	29.00	12.60	34.30	59.00	16.30	100.60
Accounts payable	622.70	677.70	724.00	645.00	890.00	1,120.90
Income taxes payable	138.60	178.20	236.70	133.40	198.10	189.40
Other current liabilities	0.00	0.00	129.50	144.50	176.80	211.60
Deferred taxes	11.30	36.00	23.90	0.00	23.10	97.70
Long-term debt	1,034.10	1,011.00	1,018.00	951.90	931.60	960.90
Total liabilities	1,866.60	2,002.80	2,279.00	2,338.00	2,666.20	3,428.10
Stockholders' equity	2,027.30	2,342.80	2,752.10	3,065.30	3,432.00	3,856.80
Total liabilities and net worth	$3,893.90	$4,345.60	$5,031.10	$5,403.30	$6,098.20	$7,284.90

*Estimated.
Source: Annual reports.

EXHIBIT 6
DISTRIBUTION OF CATERPILLAR'S OVERSEAS SALES

	1973	1977	1978	1979	1980	1981
Africa and Middle East	14%	30%	25%	23%	26%	36%
Asia/Pacific	12	14	17	20	19	19
Europe	50	25	27	28	26	19
Latin America	13	20	19	17	18	17
Canada	11	11	12	12	11	9
Total	100%	100%	100%	100%	100%	100%
Overseas sales as percent of Cat's total sales	49.1%	50.7%	48.1%	53.8%	57.1%	56.6%

Source: Form 10-K reports.

EXHIBIT 7
MIX OF CATERPILLAR SALES BY THIRD WORLD REGION
Dollars in Millions

	1977	1978	1979	1980	1981
Latin America					
Exports from United States	$ 438	$ 506	$ 476	$ 617	$ 654
Sales of foreign manufactured products	162	168	240	262	249
Total sales	600	674	716	879	903
Exports percent of total sales	73%	75%	66%	70%	72%
Africa/Middle East					
Exports from United States	$ 509	$ 497	$ 580	$ 765	$1,236
Sales of foreign manufactured products	376	370	380	517	650
Total sales	885	867	960	1,282	1,886
Exports percent of total sales	58%	57%	60%	60%	66%
Asia/Pacific*					
Exports from United States	$ 291	$ 398	$ 528	$ 641	$ 687
Sales of foreign manufactured products	119	168	236	280	239
Total sales	410	566	764	921	926
Exports percent of total sales	71%	70%	69%	70%	74%
Third World total					
Exports from United States	$1,238	$1,401	$1,584	$2,023	$2,577
Sales of foreign manufactured products	557	706	856	1,059	1,138
Total sales	1,795	2,107	2,440	3,082	3,715
Exports percent of total sales	65%	66%	65%	66%	69%
Caterpillar worldwide sales	$5,848	$7,219	$7,613	$8,598	$9,154
Exports to Third World percent of Cat	21%	19%	21%	24%	28%
Third World sales percent of Cat	30%	29%	32%	36%	40%

*Includes Australia and New Zealand.
Source: Form 10-K reports.

EXHIBIT 8
DATA ON CATERPILLAR DEALERS, 1981

Cat Dealers	*Inside U.S.*	*Outside U.S.*	*Worldwide*
Full-line dealers	87	129	216
Lift-truck dealers exclusively	12	4	16
Branch stores	284	605	889
Employees	24,913	53,657	78,570
Service bays	4,708	5,117	9,825
Investment in new facilities and equipment in last five years ($ millions)	$375	$515	$890
Floor space added for sales, service, and parts in last five years (square feet in millions)	7.4	5.2	12.6
Total dealer floor space (square feet in millions)	16.4	16.9	33.3
Combined net worth ($ millions)	$1,400	$2,197	$3,597

Source: Annual report.

EXHIBIT 9
CATERPILLAR ENGINE DIVISION'S OPERATING RECORD
Dollars in Millions

Year Ends December 31	*Net Sales*	*Operating Profit*	*Operating Margin (%)*	*Total Engine Sales*[a]	*Engine Division Capital Spending*	*Outside Sales As % Cat's Sales*
1981[b]	2,049	364	17.8	2,983[c]	410	22/24[c]
1981[d]	1,805	389[e]	21.6	2,492	n.a.	20
1980	1,400	218	15.6	2,156	214	16
1979	1,138	124	10.9	1,680	183	15
1978	1,057	234	22.1	1,644	146	15
1977	771	156	20.1	1,259	168	17
1975	482	n.a.	n.a.	n.a.	n.a.	10
1970	174	n.a.	n.a.	n.a.	n.a.	8

[a] Including internal usage at transfer price.
[b] Including Solar, estimated.
[c] As if Solar, purchased in July 1981, had been present for a full year.
[d] Excluding Solar, estimated.
[e] Estimated; reflects absence of $25 million write-down at Solar after acquisition.
n.a. = not available
Source: First Boston.

Komatsu Limited

In late January 1985 Chairman Ryoichi Kawai of Komatsu Limited, the world's second-largest earthmoving equipment (EME) company, saw the quarterly financial results of Caterpillar Tractor Co. (Cat), its archrival. With his understanding of the industry and of his competitor's problems, he was not surprised to see Cat's losses continuing but was not expecting the figure to be so high. The $251 million fourth-quarter loss brought the company's full-year loss to $428 million, closing out Cat's third straight unprofitable year. Although it meant that Komatsu appeared to be closing in on a competitor that had dominated the industry for so long, Kawai knew his competitor well enough to understand that Cat would fight hard to regain its preeminent position.

The realizaton that the industry structure was changing led Kawai to reflect on Komatsu's position. Since his company had become a major player in the industry, it might be necessary to reappraise its competitive strategy. "After all," mused Kawai, "one important lesson to be drawn from Cat's decline is that success today does not necessarily imply success tomorrow."

WORLD EME INDUSTRY

The demand for EME depended mainly on the general level of construction and mining activities, and both industries had undergone considerable change during the 1970s.[1] In the construction industry, for example, it became increasingly clear that in most developed countries the major nonrecurring construction expenditures such as highway programs, water management programs, land clearing, and housing had been largely completed. In the last quarter of the century, developing countries would probably provide most of the large remaining infrastructure projects.

Among developing countries, financing considerations played a significant part in buying decisions for all capital equipment. Further, the state sector was often a signif-

Harvard Business School case 385–277.

[1] A detailed industry review is contained in the companion case, "Caterpillar Tractor Co.," HBS case 385–276, and only a brief summary of the key issues is presented here.

icant buyer, and for EME, the buying behavior typically stressed up-front bidding procedures that regularly included not only machines but also spare parts for a period of two years or more.

The mining industry had also undergone considerable change during the 1970s. In many less developed countries (LDCs) mining belonged to the state sector. This contributed to the surplus production and widely gyrating prices of many minerals. The economic uncertainty and political instability in several of the traditional source countries caused mining companies to explore mineral development in developed countries such as Australia. In the energy sector, the oil crises of 1973 and 1979 triggered a construction boom in the Middle East, and major developments elsewhere as other sources of energy were tapped.

The worldwide EME industry had traditionally been dominated by a handful of firms, almost all of them North American. The industry giant was Cat, based in Peoria, Illinois. Throughout the 1960s and the 1970s the company held a market share of over 50 percent. (Exhibit 1 shows the market share trend from 1971 to 1984.) The company built an unmatched reputation for quality and service in construction equipment. Its dealer network in North America and abroad, particularly in Europe and Latin America, had been an important source of its strength. The company's carefully planned competitive strategy emphasized the building of advanced, enduring machines using components made in specialized plants (mostly in the United States), selling them at premium prices, and offering fast, high-quality field service. Cat's high point came in 1981, when the sales and profits hit record levels of $9.2 billion and $580 million, respectively.

Industry Developments Since 1981

As the U.S. recession deepened in the early 1980s, the value of contracts signed by the top 400 U.S. construction companies fell by a third from $170 billion in 1981 to $115 billion in 1983. Much of Europe and Latin America was also in the throes of a recession, and the overseas portion of U.S. construction companies' contracts fell by 45 percent from 1981 to 1983.

During the same period many LDCs, particularly in Latin America and Africa, faced uncertain economic environments with low commodity prices, problems associated with debt servicing and new borrowing, and recession in their principal export markets such as the United States and Western Europe. Furthermore, the softening of oil prices meant that the Middle East no longer remained the center of activity for large construction contracts as it had been in the 1970s. The only economies with much economic resilience were in the Far East.

The competition in the EME industry had intensified during this period. The substantial capacity built during the more prosperous years of the late 1970s far exceeded industry demand. IBH, a German firm formed through the acquisition of many smaller European companies, registered extraordinary growth for several years. By 1983, however, this major European competitor faced bankruptcy proceedings. International Harvester (IH), an industry veteran, was forced to sell its EME business to Dresser in 1983. Almost all the companies had suffered losses since 1981, with U.S. exporters particularly hurt by a dollar that appreciated 40 percent between 1981 and 1984 in trade-weighted terms.

Cat's performance, however, held the attention of most industry observers.

Although it had been known to pay generous hourly rates to its workers, Cat's labor relations had deteriorated. In the October 1982 wage negotiations, the company, citing the labor cost differential of more than 45 percent compared with its Japanese rival, sought to contain costs. Cat's treasurer was quoted as saying, "We can handle a 10 to 15 percent differential but not 45 percent."

The United Auto Workers union (UAW) would have none of it. Citing Cat's extraordinarily good performances in prior years, the UAW demanded a share in the prosperity. However, considering the company's worries about future prospects, the UAW made what in other days would have been a generous offer: to continue the old contract for three years with cost-of-living allowances (COLA) continued as before plus 3 percent raises annually, but no new add-ons. The company turned down the union proposal and stuck to its offer: no basic pay increases for three years; COLA for two of the three years but at a trimmed-down rate. Further, Cat wanted reductions in paid time off and more management flexibility in work scheduling between areas without having to consider workers' seniority.

A bitter 204-day strike (one of the largest on record against a major U.S. company) was finally broken in May 1983. Facing inventory shortages and the prospect of its dealer network not being able to meet customer demand, Cat conceded to almost all the union's demands except the additional 3 percent annual increase in COLA. Said one industry analyst, "The settlement will do little to ameliorate what has become a hostile relationship between Cat and the UAW."

With the strike behind it, the company was optimistic that it would post a profit in 1984. Indeed, a robust U.S. economic recovery lifted Cat's domestic sales 30 percent above 1983 levels. Foreign sales also increased 11 percent in 1984, with strong gains in Canada, Australia, Japan, and Europe offsetting overall declines in developing countries. Although total physical volume increased 26 percent over 1983 levels, sales revenue rose by only 21 percent due to "intense price competition." Cat managers blamed excess industry capacity and the strength of the U.S. dollar for this situation.

In response to continuing losses, Cat initiated a cost-reduction program in 1982, and management claimed that its 1984 costs were 14 percent below 1981 levels adjusted for inflation and volume. Furthermore, the company consolidated the operations of five U.S. plants and halted the construction of a national parts warehouse, resulting in 1984 write-offs of $226 million. In late 1984 management decided to close five other facilities. The full benefits of the consolidations and closings were not reflected in 1984's results, but management indicated that its efforts "could permit the company to be moderately profitable in 1985," acknowledging that this implied gaining sales at the expense of competitors. (Selected financial data for the period from 1979 to 1984 appear in Exhibit 2.)

KOMATSU LIMITED

In 1983 Komatsu Limited, the Osaka-based Japanese company with its headquarters in Tokyo, had consolidated net sales of $3.2 billion, with 81 percent of the sales emanating from the EME sector and the balance from a diversified base of manufactures, such as diesel engines, presses, machine tools, industrial robots, solar batteries, and steel castings. Yet, only two decades earlier, Komatsu had been just one of many small local equipment manufacturers living in the shadow of Cat.

Background

Komatsu was established in 1921 as a specialized producer of mining equipment. The company's basic philosophy since its earliest days emphasized the need to export. The founder of the company, Mr. Takeuchi, had stressed in his management goals statement as early as 1921 the requirement for management to have two important perspectives—an "overseas orientation" and a "user orientation." A year later Komatsu acquired an electric furnace and started producing steel castings. In 1931 the company successfully produced a two-ton crawler type of agricultural tractor, the first in Japan. During the Second World War Komatsu became an important producer of bulldozers, tanks, howitzers, and so forth.

In the postwar years the company reoriented itself toward industrial EME. The company's bulldozer was much in demand in the late 1950s as Japan's postwar reconstruction started in earnest. There was little competitive pressure on Komatsu either to augment its product line or to improve the quality of products. The company president acknowledged, "The quality of our products in terms of durability during that period was only half that of the international standards." Unable to persuade dealers to sell its equipment, the company set up its own branch sales office and authorized small local repair shops to be Komatsu service agents. Given the poor quality of the machines, it is not surprising that customers complained of the company's poor service capability. Thus, despite the booming demand and the tariff-sheltered market, by 1963, Komatsu remained a puny, $168 million manufacturer of a limited line of EME, lacking technical know-how to produce sophisticated machines.

The turning point came in 1963, when the Japanese Ministry of International Trade and Investment (MITI) decided to open the EME industry to foreign capital investment. MITI felt it was necessary to continue to protect the emerging Japanese auto and electronics industries. As a quid pro quo, the EME industry was to be opened up since MITI officials believed that Japan did not possess a long-run competitive advantage in this industry. Cat decided to take advantage of the opportunity, and Komatsu was suddenly faced with a formidable competitor in its own backyard. Komatsu opposed the proposed Mitsubishi-Cat joint venture, but MITI was only willing to delay the project for two years. Yashinari Kawai, Komatsu's president, decided he must immediately take advantage of the Japanese government's policies, which demanded that foreign companies help the Japanese companies in return for access to Japan's markets. He planned to make his company a competitor of world standards.

The 1960s

In his single-minded drive for survival, Kawai set two goals: the acquisition of the necessary advanced technology from abroad and the improvement of product quality within the company. A manager who had been at Komatsu during this time recalled:

> Our mission was made very clear by the president. There was no question that the rapid upgrading of quality standards was the priority task that had to be promoted. It was the only way Komatsu could survive the crisis.

The company entered licensing arrangements with two major EME manufacturers in the United States—International

Harvester and Bucyrus-Erie. The former was well known for its wheel-loader technology, and the latter was a world leader in excavator technology. Komatsu also concluded a licensing and technology collaboration agreement with Cummins Engine in the United States, which led the world in diesel engine development. Komatsu paid a substantial price for this technological access, not only in financial payments but also in restrictions on exports that it had to agree to as part of the arrangements. Recognizing that its dependence on these licensees left it vulnerable, the company established its first R&D laboratory in 1966 to focus on the application of electrical engineering developments.

Komatsu also launched a quality upgrading program in its factories. The program, one of the first to reflect the Total Quality Control (TQC) concept, was an adaptation and extension of the well-known Japanese quality-control-circles system in manufacturing operations. The objective of TQC was to ensure the highest quality in every aspect of Komatsu's operations. A company spokesperson explained, "The TQC umbrella spreads over all our activities. Virtually everything necessary to develop, to produce, and to service our products—and to keep customers around the world satisfied with those products' high performance, reliability, and durability—is incorporated into our scheme of Total Quality Control." All personnel—from top management to every worker on the assembly line—was expected to strive for TQC. Komatsu management was proud of receiving the highly coveted 1964 Deming Prize for quality control within three years of launching TQC.

In 1964 the company also began Project A. The project aimed to upgrade the quality of the small and medium-sized bulldozers, Komatsu's primary domestic market product. A top manager recalled, "The president commanded the staff to ignore the costs and produce world-standard products. He told us to disregard the Japanese Industrial Standards [JIS]." The first batch of upgraded products reached the market in 1966. The project produced spectacular results. The durability of the new products was twice that of the old ones, and despite the fact that Komatsu doubled the length of its warranty period, the number of warranty claims actually decreased by 67 percent from the previous level.

At this stage the company launched the second phase of Project A as cost reductions took precedence. Every aspect of design, production facilities, parts assembly, assembly-line systems, and the operation processes was subjected to thorough scrutiny, and costs were pared down. Between 1965 and 1970 the company increased its domestic market share from 50 to 65 percent despite the advent of the Mitsubishi-Caterpillar joint venture in Japan.

The company also benefited in other ways as reflected by the company president's comments:

> The product quality improvement activities greatly improved the quality of work within the company. A crisis atmosphere prevailed in the company when the project was being implemented, resulting in a spirit of unity between the management and staff. This was perhaps the most valuable achievement of the project.

The Early 1970s

By the early 1970s Komatsu's management sensed the need for aggressive expansion abroad. The company had achieved dominance within Japan. With domestic construction activity leveling off, however, it appeared as if the EME market was reaching maturity with little prospect of substantial growth. Meanwhile, management was aware of the rise of natural resources activities throughout the world, and particularly the construction boom in the Middle East in the post-1974 period.

Up until the 1960s the company's exports were largely based on inquiries received from abroad. The first large export order came from Argentina in 1955. During the early 1960s the company began opening a market in Eastern bloc countries. Yashinari Kawai was committed to promoting Japan's trade relations with the USSR and China. He and his son Ryoichi, a promising young Komatsu manager, conducted extensive negotiations in both countries and developed excellent relations with many high-level officials.

In the mid-1960s the company turned its attention to Western Europe. Large-scale shipments to Italy were followed by exports to other countries. In 1967 Komatsu Europe was established as a European marketing subsidiary, to better coordinate the delivery of parts and the provision of field service. In the same year the first Komatsu machines were exported to the United States. In 1970 Komatsu America was established to develop business in the huge North American market. In most of these markets Komatsu concentrated on selling a limited product line, typically crawler-tractors and crawler-loaders, which were the most common equipment on construction sites. By pricing 30 to 40 percent below similar Cat equipment, the company soon established a foothold in most target markets.

Unlike Cat, whose servicing dealer network covered the globe, Komatsu had no such sales and service system. Even in Japan the company was trying to supplement its company-owned branches and small repair shops with an independent dealer structure. Overseas, Komatsu found it even more difficult to establish strong sales and service capabilities. Companies with the resources and skills to be strong dealers were already locked into one of the competitive EME distribution networks. To ensure good service by those dealers it had signed up, Komatsu maintained extensive parts inventories in each country—"a deliberate overkill," according to one dealer. When it could not get dealers, however, Komatsu handled the sales function directly, at least initially. Its links with Japanese trading companies helped to locate important projects, and the company's overseas subsidiaries would often follow these up to sell directly to government agencies or large companies.

In 1972 Komatsu launched a new project called Project B. This time the focus was on the exports. The large bulldozer, the company's main export item, was chosen for improvement. The aim was similar to Project A's: to upgrade the quality and reliability of its large bulldozer models and bring them up to world standards, then work on cost reductions. Once these aims were realized, the company planned to launch similar efforts for the other lines of export products such as power shovels. Although Project B's main objective was to develop the company's overseas markets, the new machines were also offered in Japan and further reinforced Komatsu's domestic position.

The mid-1970s also saw the beginnings of efforts to penetrate the markets of LDCs, and in particular the fast-growing industrializing countries in Asia and Latin America. In 1974 the company established a new presale service department that provided assistance from the earliest stage of planned development projects in LDCs. The services that the department made available to LDCs free of cost included advice on issues such as site investigation, feasibility studies, planning of projects, selections of machines, training of operators, and so on. Komatsu also started developing its own exclusive dealer network in some of the large LDCs. In Southeast Asia and Africa, where payment terms for imported machines often involved some form of countertrade, the company also used the services of Japanese trading companies. With all these efforts, Komatsu's ratio of exports to total sales grew from 20 percent in 1973 to 41 percent in 1974 and to 55 percent in 1975.

During the early 1970s the company's R&D efforts continued apace with some attention to basic research as well as product development. Much of the effort, however, focused on the needs of the domestic market since the licensing arrangements constrained export efforts in some important new product areas. New excavator models were brought onto the market in this period, as were completely new products such as pipe layers, large dump trucks, and hydroshift vehicles.

The Late 1970s

By 1976 the Japanese market was highly concentrated, with Komatsu taking a 60 percent share and the Mitsubishi-Cat joint venture left with slightly over 30 percent. However, there was no indication of much market growth in the near future, since worldwide demand for construction equipment was slowing. Komatsu management decided to focus on improving the competitiveness of its products.

A four-part cost-reduction plan was initiated, the first part being dubbed the "V-10 campaign." The V-10 goal was to reduce the cost by 10 percent while maintaining or improving product quality. The second part of the overall plan called for reducing the number of parts by over 20 percent. The third part aimed at value engineering, specifically focusing on redesigning the products to gain economies in materials or manufacturing. The fourth part was a rationalization of the manufacturing system. By the end of the decade the company was well on its way to achieving all these goals.

As Komatsu planned this ambitious cost-reduction plan, an unexpected development occurred that required immediate management attention. In the fall of 1977 the Japanese yen began appreciating rapidly against most major currencies. For example, the yen/dollar exchange rate went from 293 at the end of 1976 to 240 a year later. Management responded by adopting a policy of using a pessimistic internal yen/dollar exchange rate of 180 for planning purposes. Manufacturing was responsible for achieving a cost structure that could be profitable even at this "worst-scenario" rate. After trading at a high of ¥179 to the dollar in mid-1978, the yen weakened considerably against the dollar and most other currencies in 1979 (see Exhibit 3.)

During the late 1970s Komatsu also accelerated its product development program. Between 1976 and 1981 the number of models offered in the five basic categories of EME (bulldozers, excavators, dump trucks, loaders, and graders) increased from 46 to 77. When Komatsu introduced its off-highway dump trucks and hydraulic excavators earlier than Cat, management proudly hailed the company's new leadership in technical development and innovation. "We are not content to produce the same type of equipment year after year," said one technical manager, "but are always looking at the latest technical developments and are trying to see how we can adapt them to our products." An example of this approach was the application of electronic technology to all types of machinery. Komatsu had the distinction of introducing the world's first radio-controlled bulldozer, amphibious bulldozer, and remote-controlled underwater bulldozer. These unique products were aimed at special uses such as toxic dump sites and underwater mining.

The 1980s

Until 1980 Komatsu was impeded by the narrow product line it offered abroad. According to a senior manager, the market for EME could be divided into the bidding market (dominant in most developing countries) and the commercial market (dominant in most developed countries). Although Komatsu's bulldozers and loaders were generally adequate to meet the needs of the former, demand in such markets was highly erratic. Any company that aspired to become a global competitor needed to gain a strong foothold in the commercial market, and to do so, it was almost a competitive necessity to be a full-line manufacturer with an extensive sales and service network.

The decision to become a full-line supplier, however, meant that Komatsu had to reevaluate its licensing relationships with technology suppliers. In exchange for help in obtaining essential know-how from Bucyrus-Erie and International Harvester for the manufacture of excavators and loaders, Komatsu signed agreements giving American licensers a tight grip over Komatsu's exports of its products and a veto over the introduction of competing products in Japan. In 1980 Komatsu objected to Bucyrus-Erie's terms restricting the export of two new products using the latter's technology. When Bucyrus demurred, Komatsu appealed to Japan's fair trade commission. After appropriate deliberations, the government agency agreed with Komatsu that it was a restrictive business practice that impaired competition. This finding allowed Komatsu to buy its way out of the contract, paying Bucyrus $13.6 million to get the data it wanted and another $6 million for royalties on the balance of the contract in May 1981. In early 1982 Komatsu had an opportunity to buy out of its obligations to International Harvester. When financially strapped Harvester was looking for cash, Komatsu bought back IH's half interest in its loader business for $52 million.

One senior manager of Komatsu summed up the approach very matter-of-factly, "Komatsu had digested its licensed technology and had established its own technology. Therefore, we just got out of the various licensing agreements." Freed of the constraints of the licensing agreements, Komatsu could sell hydraulic excavators and wheel loaders to world markets. The company emerged as a full-line competitor.

In the early 1970s Komatsu started to reorganize its distributor network worldwide, aiming to supplement the direct sales offices with more servicing dealers similar to Cat's. In 1983 the company had 8 marketing subsidiaries abroad, more than 20 overseas offices, and some 160 distributors in foreign countries. It maintained liaison offices in Havana, Warsaw, Moscow, and Peking (Beijing). In the United States, it established five regional centers for parts distribution and service. At each of these centers Japanese engineers were available to help dealers' repair departments with significant problems.

Komatsu management recognized that its 56 dealers in the United States were no match for the Cat distribution system. On average, only 30 percent of a Komatsu-America dealer's sales were of the company's products. Without exception, they all carried other lines as well, such as Clark and Fiat-Allis. Dealers were reluctant to become exclusive, often citing the small field population of Komatsu machines and its narrow product line. As the company broadened its product range, it began a heavy advertising campaign in specialist trade magazines, stressing its full-line capability and its product reliability.

Komatsu celebrated its 60th anniversary in 1981. That year it launched a new product called "EPOCHS," which stood for "Efficient Production-Oriented Choice Specifications." The project's theme was reconciliation of two contradictory demands. The aim was to "improve production efficiency without reducing the number of product specifications required by the market." The overseas expansion in the 1970s taught management that customer requirements varied widely by market and by application. For example, in Australia prospects were excellent in coal and iron-ore mining, but the tough operating requirements surpassed the capabilities of machines designed for Japanese construction applications. Komatsu responded by designing bulldozers, power shovels, and dump trucks adapted to mining conditions in Australia. To better its competition, it sent field engineers to survey Australian miners and elicited their comments and complaints about the equipment. The company then incorporated the needed improvements into its products.

As its export market increased, the company faced demands to adapt its products to suit the user requirements in different countries and diverse applications. These requirements varied with each country's environmental conditions and legal requirements. Such adaptations, however, were costly in terms of production efficiency, parts inventory, and field service management. The purpose of the EPOCHS project was to allow the company to respond to the diverse market needs without compromising its cost position.

The project focused attention on the linkages between production and marketing requirements, thereby reinforcing the spirit of TQC, which emphasized the connection between user needs and product development. The EPOCHS project led to the development of a standardized core module for major products and the required number of parts to create the market-determined variety of finished models. This approach was expected to reconcile the contradictory needs of the production and marketing departments.

By the end of 1983 the company's manufacturing had become fully integrated, producing almost all of its components and parts in-house (it was the largest producer of steel castings in Japan, for example). Komatsu prided itself on what it called the *integrated* and *concentrated* production system. From the selection of raw materials to the production and assembly of finished products, it was all part of a single, coordinated system. Further, main components of Komatsu products, regardless of size, were manufactured exclusively in individual plants.

Komatsu products were manufactured in 14 separate plants, 13 of them in Japan. The fully owned Brazilian subsidiary produced medium-sized bulldozers for Brazil and other countries in the region. In 1975 the company established a 49 percent-owned Mexican joint venture for the production of large-scale bulldozers for Mexico and neighboring countries.

Komatsu continued to emphasize its commitment to R&D. By 1982 four separate research labs specialized in production engineering, design engineering, electrical applications, and electronic applications.

Product development centers were located in four major plants. A new research laboratory integrating the engineering and electrical labs was in the offing in 1982. The R&D expenditures as a percentage of sales increased from 4.3 percent in 1981 to 5.3 percent in 1982 and to 5.8 percent in 1983. In comparison, the average for the Japanese mechanical equipment industry was 1.7 percent in 1982.

The R&D staff was elated when the company decided in 1981 that it was ready to participate in the International Construction Equipment Exposition (Conexpo) in Houston. Komatsu displayed some machines not previously seen—prototypes of products that would be marketed in 1982 or later. One of the main attractions at Conexpo was Komatsu's 1,000 hp bulldozer, bigger than Cat's top-of-the-line 700 hp machine. Officially, Cat's response was cool, saying that it had no plans to follow suit. But according to Komatsu managers, the most interested observers at their exhibit were Cat technicians. One Komatsu manager reportedly photographed four Cat managers examining and measuring the company's equipment at the exposition. "Ten years ago," he smiled, "we would have been the ones caught doing that."

Nonetheless, concern persisted about the depressed state of the construction industry worldwide, and Komatsu managers began talking increasingly about other business opportunities. In 1979 top management launched a companywide project called "F and F." The abbreviation stood for "Future and Frontiers," and its objective was to develop new products and new businesses. The project encouraged suggestions from all employees, asking them to consider both the needs of society and the technical know-how of the company. Management followed up on many of the 3,500 suggestions submitted, eventually leading to the development of such diverse new products as arc-welding robots, heat pumps, an excavating system for deep-sea sand, and amorphous silicon materials for efficient exploitation of solar energy.

Komatsu's R&D laboratories played an important role in this new diversification thrust, and the company planned to quadruple the number of research professionals within five years. Further, a joint research agreement with Cummins Engine provided for the sharing of information on diesel equipment improvements, including a heat pump Komatsu had developed that reportedly cut fuel costs by about 40 percent. The company also announced a breakthrough in developing a cast-iron alloy that was superior to the conventional aluminum alloy in heat resistance, noise generation, and fuel economy for use in high-speed diesel engines.

In the early 1980s Japanese-made industrial robots accounted for 80 percent of the world market, and Komatsu was already one of the top manufacturers focusing on arc-welding and material-handling robots, which it also put to use in its own factories.

Komatsu in 1984

By 1984 Komatsu managers had good reason to be proud of their company's record of the previous two decades. (See Exhibit 4 for a summary of the financial results of the company.) It still held a 60 percent market share in Japan, helped in part by sales to its fully owned construction and real estate subsidiaries. The company's domestic sales and service network was acknowledged to be the most extensive and efficient in Japan. Sales activities were conducted by 10 regional offices, 50 branch offices, and over 100 other sales offices. In addition, 100 independent dealers handled Komatsu products and were backed by the company's computerized parts supply system, which guaranteed a replacement part within 48 hours anywhere in the world.

Exports expanded so that they represented well over half of Komatsu's total sales in 1983. The company continued to strengthen its relationships with the Eastern bloc and had a backlog of orders for equipment for the Siberian natural resource project. The Reagan administration's embargo in December 1981 on the sale of Cat pipe-laying equipment to Russia handed the total business to the Japanese company. Komatsu also signed a contract with the Soviets to develop a scraper based on a Russian design, using Japanese components, and was collaborating with the Russians on a big crawler-dozer and dump truck. Komatsu's sales to the Soviet Union were soon expected to overtake Cat's.

Worldwide, the company's marketing efforts gathered momentum. In Australia, its products were well received in mining circles. Referring to his company's decision to buy Komatsu's machines, the managing director of one of the largest mining companies in Australia said:

> Having come to consider the market its monopoly, Caterpillar became very offhand with its customer relations. Our analysis suggested that the Komatsu machines offered significant dollar savings and outperformed the equivalent Caterpillar equipment. Komatsu's spares backup should be rated good. The operators also seemed to like the machines.

Despite competitors' suggestions to the contrary, Komatsu dealers generally denied that they were still competing mainly on price. A U.S. dealer commented:

> When you're selling against number one, you need some price advantage. But we tell contractors you can give them 10 percent more machine for 10 percent less money. That's not selling price in my book.

Although Komatsu had undoubtedly been highly successful over the previous two decades, the company's senior management felt that stagnant world demand would lead to fierce competition in the EME industry and could threaten Komatsu's growth. The internal consensus was that the existing distribution network represented a point of vulnerability. Almost inevitably, a senior Komatsu marketing executive compared his company with Cat:

> We have some gaps in our overseas sales network. Caterpillar's distribution network surpasses that of Komatsu in terms of capital, assets, number of employees, and experience. Caterpillar has greater strength in user financing and sales promotion. Indeed, some of our major dealers went bankrupt in the 1980 recession, and that taught us a major lesson about the need for financially strong dealers.

Managers hoped that Komatsu's continued efforts to produce new and differentiated products would help it to build a network of exclusive distributors overseas. Although the company could point to some progress on this objective in Europe, Asia, and Australia, it faced a much tougher task in the United States, where its market share was only 5 percent in 1983 (see Exhibit 5).

Responding to the demands of local governments, the company had commenced assembly operations in Brazil and Mexico. It was also working on a joint-venture proposal with its local dealer in Indonesia, where it held a 70 percent market share in the EME business. But Komatsu's preference had consistently been to design, manufacture, and export machines from Japan, despite the potential problems related to such a highly centralized production system. The rise of trade frictions between the European Community and the United States on the one hand and Japan on the other represented the most obvious risk in the early 1980s. A dumping complaint had been filed against Komatsu in Europe, and the EEC Commission was considering the imposition of countervailing duties. Another risk for a centrally sourced company was the possible loss of competitive position due to adverse exchange-rate movements. And finally, the logistical economics of shipping heavy equipment around the world could become a burden. According to the president of Komatsu-America Corporation, freight for bulldozers and loaders amounted to 6 to 7 percent of Komatsu's landed cost in the United States. For other machines it could be 10 percent or more.

Again, Komatsu managers compared their company with Cat:

> Caterpillar has production throughout the world. It is easier for them to shift production in response to protectionism, exchange-rate fluctuations, and changes in other competitive factors. Komatsu has production plants only in a few developing countries, where it had to establish them [due to local pressures]. Consequently, Komatsu has less flexibility in the face of changes in competitive factors.

Komatsu's market approach continued to emphasize the twin orientations toward overseas markets and consumer satisfaction laid down 60 years earlier by the founder. During the 1970s two additional themes had emerged. A senior manager described them succinctly. "'The first is vertical integration based on the philosophy that you must start with good raw materials if you want to manufacture good machines. The second is the Total Quality Control (TQC) practices that pervade all our actions."

At Komatsu TQC went beyond just management practice. It epitomized management philosophy, representing the value system of the workers and managers alike. According to one top manager:

> It is the spirit of Komatsu. For every issue or problem, we are encouraged to go back to the root cause and make the necessary decisions. Not only does TQC help us resolve short-run management problems, but it also lays the foundation for future growth. Thus, it is a key to management innovation.

Komatsu extended its quality commitment to its dealers and suppliers. Working closely with suppliers, the company trained them in adopting its TQC system. The dealers were also encouraged to take advantage of its offer of free services to help implement such a system in their companies. In 1981 Komatsu achieved the distinction of being awarded the Japan Quality Control Prize, considered by many to be the world's supreme quality-control honor. Furthermore, its quality-control circle at the Osaka plant had twice won gold medals from the Union of Japanese Scientists and Engineers, topping the 178,000 quality-control circles of all companies in Japan.

The management practice of relying on the TQC system was supplemented by another system called the "PDCA" management cycle. The initials stood for Plan, Do, Check, and Act. The starting point for the PDCA cycle was the long-term plan announced by the top management team, and the company president's policy statement issued at the beginning of the year. Company president Ryoichi Kawai referred to this as "management by policy." He said:

> Personally, I believe that a company must always be innovative. To this end, the basic policy and value of the target must be clarified so that all the staff members

> can fully understand what the company is aiming for in a specific time period. This is the purpose of the management by policy system.

The policy statements became the basis for management focus and follow-up action. As one of the managers described the PDCA system:

> A plan is made, it is executed, its results are checked, and then new actions are planned. Every activity is based on this cycle, including companywide management control systems, production, marketing, and R&D. Because of this, the corporate ability to achieve the targets set improves. These steps also improve the workers' morale and management's leadership.

The management team at Komatsu believed that the intertwined system of TQC, PDCA, and management by policy contributed to company performance and employee development. In the words of one senior manager:

> Tangible results from these systems have been twofold—increasing market share through quality improvement and productivity improvement leading to cost reduction. But equally important is the achievement of the intangibles such as improved communications among departments and setting up of clear common goals.

Ryoichi Kawai again:

> A human being donates his energy to work in order to enjoy and lead an enriched and satisfying life. . . . We think that it is necessary to satisfy the workers' monetary as well as other needs simultaneously. First of all, there is the satisfaction of achievement in work. Second, there is the satisfaction of cooperating with a colleague and receiving the approval of others. Third, there is the satisfaction of witnessing an institution grow and achieve maturity. It is satisfaction, pride, and consciousness toward participation that make workers feel that they are contributing to a great objective and are doing important work in the company.

As a result, Komatsu had a long history of good labor relations, and the company believed this had been important in its ability to improve productivity and achieve cost competitiveness. Statistics compiled by Nomura Securities showed that between 1976 and 1981 labor productivity rose at an annual compound rate of 15.2 percent at Komatsu compared with the 10.6 percent annual rate at Cat. Both companies were investing heavily in plant capital expenditure during the period.

Despite the high productivity of its workers, the average Komatsu employee earned only 55 percent of the wages paid to Cat employees. Together with lower raw material costs (particularly steel), this low-cost, high-productivity labor force was clearly one of Komatsu's basic assets (see Tables 1 and 2).

Pondering the Future

It was quite in character for Ryoichi Kawai, the chairman of Komatsu, to ponder the future direction for the company that he had headed since 1964, succeeding his father, Yashinari Kawai. Like his father, he had graduated from the elite Tokyo University and had served in the government bureaucracy. He became the youngest department head in MITI's history before joining Komatsu in 1954. Like every other company executive, he had spent time with workers on the factory floor and was familiar with the company's products and production processes.

TABLE 1
COST STRUCTURE OF A LARGE BULLDOZER
(Equivalent to CAT D-6)

		Percent of Cost
Labor		35.0%
Components and subassemblies	12.4	
Overhead	18.0	
Assembly	4.6	
Purchased materials and components		49.6
Overhead		15.4
		100.0%

Source: Boston Consulting Group.

TABLE 2
STEEL PRICE COMPARISON: U.S./JAPAN
Dollars per Ton

	U.S.	Japan*	Japan/U.S.
Hot-rolled mill coil	494	359	73%
Hot-rolled steel plate	635	445	70%

Note: Assumed yen-dollar rate is $1 = ¥220.
* Contracted price. Actual prices are often lower due to negotiations between suppliers and the users.
Source: Boston Consulting Group.

Kawai had been described in the press as a "workaholic," who often spent his lunch time at his desk partaking of the $3 box lunch from the company cafeteria. He traveled abroad frequently to pursue business deals. Although considered a mild and gentle person, he reportedly had a tight grip on the company. In an interview with *Fortune* magazine, he hinted at his philosophy of life. "In the government you are only requested to do your best. In a company, it is one's duty to earn money and pay your workers. You can't get there by just doing your best."

Kawai greatly admired Cat and often spoke of modeling his company after it. Despite his generous praise of his American competitor, however, he seemed to cherish the idea of beating Cat some day. He likened the competition to a tennis match. "As you know, in a tennis tournament, you can be losing in the middle of the game but win at the late stage." This spirit of competition with Cat pervaded the entire company. Komatsu's in-house slogan was "Maru-C," which roughly translated meant "Encircle Caterpillar." Reportedly, the company continuously monitored events in Peoria, and one of the main jobs of Komatsu's executives in the United States was to keep tabs on any and all relevant press reports. Cat's monthly in-house letter to its employees, which featured new product introductions and other company-related news, was required reading for all Komatsu executives, and copies were sent by express mail to Tokyo for analysis at the corporate headquarters.

As Kawai continued to think about the possible changes in Komatsu's competitive strategy, he kept reminding himself that complacency is one vice his company had to guard against. "Eternal vigilance is not the price of liberty alone. It is also the price of prosperity."

EXHIBIT 1
MARKET SHARES OF MAJOR EME PRODUCERS

	1971	*1972*	*1973*	*1974*	*1975*	*1976*	*1977*
Cat*	56.0%	55.0%	53.0%	53.0%	54.4%	56.1%	53.6%
Komatsu	10.3	10.9	11.6	9.0	9.2	11.3	11.8
J.I. Case	6.7	6.9	8.9	8.3	7.2	7.4	8.5
Fiat-Allis†	4.3	4.0	3.8	7.3	7.7	6.3	6.5
Deere	5.8	6.2	6.3	6.1	4.7	5.2	6.6
International Harvester	11.0	10.0	10.1	9.7	10.0	7.6	7.2
Clark	5.9	6.0	6.3	6.6	6.8	6.1	5.8
Total	100.0%	100.0%	100.0%	100.0%	100.0%	100.0%	100.0%
IBH‡	—	—	—	—	0.5	0.5	0.6
Total industry sales (mil.)§	$4,063	$4,954	$6,190	$7,651	$8,840	$8,773	$10,130
Year-to-year change	—	21.3%	24.9%	23.6%	15.5%	−0.8%	15.5%
Price increase‖	4%	5%	12%	10%	18%	6%	8%
Real growth‖	—	16%	13%	13%	(3%)	(7%)	7%

* Includes sales from Mitsubishi-Cat joint venture net of sales to and from Cat.
† Allis-Chalmers only before 1974.
‡ IBH Holding, AG—founded in 1975 with growth through acquisitions of 10 European equipment manufacturers through 1980. In 1980 IBH acquired Hymac (U.K.) and Hanomag (Germany). In 1981 IBH acquired Terex from General Motors.
§ Excludes IBH up to 1980 but includes it thereafter.
‖ Wertheim & Co. estimates.
Source: Wertheim & Co., Inc.

1978	*1979*	*1980*	*1981*	*1982*	*1983*	*1984‖*
51.9%	50.0%	53.3%	50.8%	45.7%	43.9%	43.0%
14.3	14.8	15.2	16.1	19.6	23.6	25.0
9.4	10.5	10.3	9.7	9.9	9.6	10.0
6.1	5.8	5.7	5.3	5.8	4.8	4.3
6.7	7.1	6.6	5.0	4.8	5.9	6.5
6.6	7.1	5.1	4.7	3.5	3.3	3.0
5.0	4.7	3.8	3.2	2.9	3.1	3.5
100.0%	100.0%	100.0%				
0.7	1.4	4.2	5.3	7.8	5.8	4.7
$12,841	$14,027	$14,916	$14,788	$12,098	$10,956	$13,956
26.8%	9.2%	6.3%	−0.9%	−23.35	−9.4%	27.3%
9%	11%	12%	9%	5%	3%	0%
18%	(2%)	(6%)	(10%)	(28%)	(12%)	27%

EXHIBIT 2
SELECTED FINANCIAL DATA ON CATERPILLAR
Dollars in Millions, Except per Share Amounts

	1984	*1983*	*1982*	*1981*	*1980*	*1979*
Sales	$6,576	$5,424	$6,469	$9,154	$8,598	$7,613
Profit (loss) for year—consolidated	$(428)	$(345)	$(180)	$579	$565	$492
Profit (loss) per share of common stock	$(4.47)	$(3.74)	$(2.04)	$6.64	$6.53	$4.92
Return on average common stock equity	(13.8)%	(10.0)%	(4.9)%	15.9%	17.4%	16.9%
Dividends paid per share of common stock	$1.25	$1.50	$2.40	$2.40	$2.325	$2.10
Current ratio at year-end	1.5:1	2.5:1	2.87:1	1.50:1	1.71:1	1.88:1
Total assets at year-end	$6,223	$6,968	$7,201	$7,285	$6,098	$5,403
Long-term debt due after one year at year-end	$1,384	$1,894	$2,389	$961	$932	$952
Capital expenditures for land, buildings, machinery, and equipment	$234	$324	$534	$836	$749	$676
Depreciation and amortization	$492	$506	$505	$448	$370	$312
Research and engineering costs	$345	$340	$376	$363	$326	$283
Average number of employees	59,776	58,402	73,249	83,455	86,350	89,266
Average number of shares of common stock outstanding	95,919,938	92,378,405	87,999,086	87,178,522	86,458,748	86,406,162

Source: Annual reports.

EXHIBIT 3
CURRENCY MOVEMENTS: EFFECTIVE EXCHANGE RATES
1975 average = 100

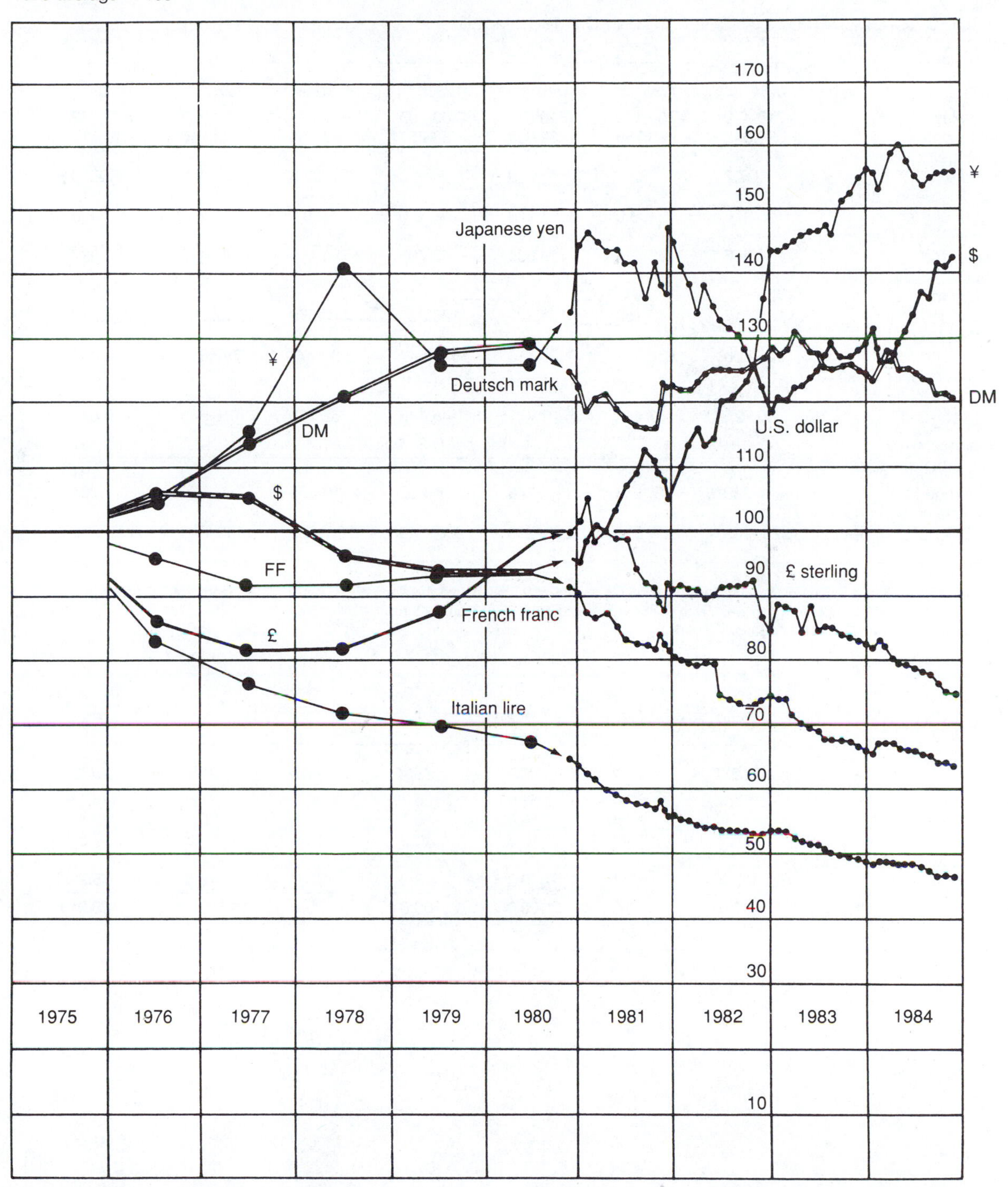

Source: *Multinational Business*, no. 4, 1984.

EXHIBIT 4
SELECTED CONSOLIDATED FINANCIAL DATA ON KOMATSU LIMITED
Millions of Yen

	1984	*1983*	*1982*	*1981*	*1980*	*1979*	*1978*
Net sales	¥713,472	¥750,530	¥810,379	¥703,705	¥647,773	¥558,229	¥479,732
Net income	22,642	26,265	32,639	33,257	27,766	23,746	19,617
Earnings per common share	27.2	32.6	41.9	44.0	37.8	32.8	27.6
Cash dividends per common share	8.0	8.0	8.0	8.0	8.0	8.0	8.5
Working capital at year-end	154,466	120,829	119,695	63,705	58,469	43,496	26,927
Property, plant, and equipment at year-end	157,617	143,182	134,223	120,225	110,579	107,767	110,459
Total assets at year-end	943,806	888,324	930,685	877,544	830,773	792,847	739,031
Long-term debt—less current maturities at year-end	80,722	57,442	67,731	48,443	62,755	76,925	70,871
Exchange rates	*Yen per U.S. Dollar*						
Rate at year-end	252	232	234	220	203	239	191
Average rate	239	238	248	222	225	220	204
Range of high and low rate	223–252	227–247	230–278	206–240	203–251	200–249	179–240

Note: Komatsu had a number of subsidiaries involved in construction, real estate development, overseas sales, and other activities in addition to the parent company, which was involved in earthmoving equipment manufacture.
Source: Annual reports and Form 20F reports.

EXHIBIT 5
KOMATSU'S SALES BY GEOGRAPHIC REGION

	1977	*1978*	*1979*	*1980*	*1981*	*1982*	*1983*
Japan	57.7%	62.4%	62.6%	56.7%	50.7%	41.8%	46.1%
Asia and Oceania	11.2	11.6	15.8	18.3	22.5	30.6	30.5
America (North and South)	18.7	15.7	12.3	11.8	11.8	7.8	7.5
Europe, Middle East, and Africa	12.4	10.3	9.3	13.2	15.0	19.8	15.9
Total	100.0	100.0	100.0	100.0	100.0	100.0	100.0

Source: Form 20F reports.

The Company and Its Environment: Relating Opportunities to Resources

Determination of a suitable strategy for a company begins in identifying the opportunities and risks in its environment. This chapter is concerned with the identification of a range of strategic alternatives, the narrowing of this range by recognizing the constraints imposed by corporate capability, and the determination of one or more economic strategies at acceptable levels of risk. We shall examine the complexity and variety of the environmental forces which must be considered and the problems in accurately assessing company strengths and weaknesses. Economic strategy will be seen as *the match between qualification and opportunity that positions a firm in its environment.* We shall attempt in passing to categorize the kinds of economic strategies that can result from the combination of internal capability and external market needs and to relate these categories to the normal course of corporate development.

THE NATURE OF THE COMPANY'S ENVIRONMENT

The environment of an organization in business, like that of any other organic entity, is the pattern of all the external conditions and influences that affect its life and development. The environmental influences relevant to strategic decision operate in a company's industry, the total business community, its city, its country, and the world. They are technological, economic, social, and political in kind. The corporate strategist is usually at least intuitively aware of these features of the current environment. But in all these categories change is taking place at varying rates—fastest in technology, less rapidly in politics. Change in the environment of business necessitates continuous monitoring of a company's definition of its business lest it falter, blur, or become obsolete. Since by definition the formulation of strategy is performed with the future in mind, executives who take part in the strategic planning process must be aware of those aspects of their company's environment especially susceptible to the kind of change that will affect their company's future.

Technology. From the point of view of the corporate strategist, technological developments are not only the fastest unfolding but the most far-reaching in extending or contracting opportunity for an established company. They include the discoveries of science, the impact of related product development, the less dramatic machinery and process improvements, and the progress of automation and data processing. We see in technical advance an accelerating rate of change—with new developments arriving before the implications of yesterday's changes can be assimilated. Industries hitherto protected from obsolescence by stable technologies or by the need for huge initial capital investment become more vulnerable more quickly than before to new processes or to cross-industry competition. Science gives the impetus to change not only in technology but also in all the other aspects of business activity.

Major areas of technical advance foreseen by students of the management of technology include increased mastery of energy, its conservation and more efficient use; the reorganization of transportation; technical solutions to problems of product life, safety, and serviceability; the further mechanization of logistical functions and the processing of information; alteration in the characteristics of physical and biological materials; and radical developments in controlling air, water, and noise pollution. The primary impact upon established strategies will be increased competition and more rapid obsolescence. The risks dramatized by these technical trends are offset by new business opportunities opened up for companies that are aggressive innovators or adept at technical hitchhiking. The need intensifies for any company either to engage in technical development or to maintain a technical intelligence capability enabling it to follow quickly new developments pioneered by others.

Ecology. It used to be possible to take for granted the environment's physical characteristics and find them favorable to industrial development. Plant sites were chosen using criteria like availability of process and cooling water, accessibility to various forms of transportation, and stability of soil conditions. With the increase in sensitivity to the impact on the physical environment of all industrial activity, it becomes essential, both to comply with law and behave responsibly, to consider how planned expansion and even continued operation under changing standards will affect and be perceived to affect the air, water, traffic density, and quality of life of any area that a company would like to enter. The trade-off between economic production and preservation or improvement of the ecological status quo has been dramatically revealed in the use of plentiful high-sulfur coal in the generation of electric power. Predictions involving high risk must be made about how such trade-offs will be resolved in the ebb and flow of public opinion.

Economics. Because business is more accustomed to monitoring economic trends than those in other spheres, it is less likely to be taken by surprise by such massive developments as the internationalization of competition, the return of Eastern Europe to trade with the West, the slower than projected development of the Third World countries and the resulting backlash of poverty and starvation, the increased importance of the large multinational corporations and the consequences of host country hostility, recurrence of recession, and inflation. The consequences of world economic trends need to be monitored in the detail relevant to an industry or company.

Society. Social developments of which strategists keep aware include such influential forces as the quest for equality for minority groups; the demand of women for opportunity and recognition; the changing patterns of work and leisure; the effects of urbanization upon the individual, family, and neighborhood; the rise of crime; the decline of conventional morality; the changing composition of world population; and the role of the professions in society.

Politics. The political forces important to the business firm are similarly extensive and complex—the changing relations between once and now communist and noncommunist countries (East and West) and between the prosperous and poor countries (North and South); the relation between private enterprise and government, between workers and management; the impact of national planning on corporate planning; and the redefinition of conservative and liberal ideology.

Although it is not possible to know or spell out here the significance of such technical, economic, social, and political trends and possibilities for the strategist of a given business or company, some simple things are clear. Changing values will lead to different expectations of the role business should perform. Business will be expected to execute its mission not only with economy in the use of energy but with sensitivity to the ecological environment. Organizations in all walks of life will be called upon to be more explicit about their goals and to meet the needs and aspirations (for example, for education) of their membership.

In any case, change threatens all established strategies. We know that a thriving company—itself a living system—is bound up in a variety of interrelationships with larger systems comprising its technological, economic, social, and political environment. If environmental developments are destroying and creating business opportunities, advance notice of specific instances relevant to a single company is essential to intelligent planning. Risk and opportunity in the last decade of the 20th century require of executives a keen interest in what is going on outside their companies. More than that, a practical means of tracking developments promising good or ill, and profit or loss, needs to be devised.

Industry. Although the industry environment is the one most company strategists believe they know most about, the opportunities and risks that reside there are often blurred by familiarity and the uncritical acceptance of the established relative position of competitors. Michael Porter, in an effort to develop strategically useful analysis of the structure of industries, has decided the nature of competition in an industry and its profit potential are affected by certain structural determinants—the threat of entry by new firms, the relative power of suppliers and customers, and the development of substitute products by other industries. Whether an industry is fragmented, emerging, maturing, or declining affects strategic opportunity as much as whether it produces basic commodities or products reflecting rapid technological change.[1]

A close look at any industry will reveal its strategic dimensions and the strategic groups consisting of companies that have made similar decisions about these dimensions. Strategy formulation in this view becomes a decision of which strategic group to compete in, without precluding the preservation of competitive advantage within the group. Reading market signals consciously or unconsciously offered by competitors gives clues to competitors' motives, goals, internal situations, and intentions. The strategic significance of changes in industry structure as it evolves around competitors' jockeying for position should be determined in the firm's search for opportunity in the total environment.

TRACKING THE CHANGING ENVIRONMENT

Unfortunately the development of knowledge in a flourishing business civilization has produced no easy methodology for continuous surveillance of the trends in the environment of central importance to a firm of ordinary capabilities. Predictive theories of special disciplines such as economics, sociology, psychology, and anthropology do not produce comprehensive appraisal readily applicable to long-range corporate strategic decision. At the same time many techniques do exist to deal with parts of the problem—economic and technological forecasting, detailed demographic projections, geological estimates of raw material reserves, national and international statistics in which trends may be discerned. More information about the environment is available than is commonly used.

The underuse of technical information appears in Frank Aguilar's research in how managers in the chemical industry obtained strategic

[1] See Michael E. Porter's *Competitive Strategy: Techniques for Analyzing Industries* (New York: Free Press, 1980).

information about environmental change.[2] Aguilar found that even in this technically sensitive industry, few firms attempted any systematic means for gathering and evaluating such information. Publications provided only about 20 percent of the information from all sources, with current market and competitive information from personal sources dominating the total input of information. Internally generated information comprised only 9 percent of the total, and more information received was unsolicited than solicited. (Interestingly enough, very few people in subordinate positions felt they were getting useful strategic information from their superiors.)

Aguilar's findings were corroborated by studies of other industries. The obvious moral of these studies is that the process of obtaining strategic information is far from being systematic, complete, or even really informative about anything except current developments, at least in these industries. This research shows that it is possible to organize better the gathering and integrating of environmental data through such means as bringing miscellaneous scanning activities together and communicating available information internally.

Certain large companies organize this function. General Electric once maintained a Business Environment Section at its corporate headquarters. It prepared reports on predicted changes for use by GE divisions. Consulting firms, future-oriented research organizations, and associations of planners provide guidance for looking ahead. Databases (electronically accessible) have proliferated beyond the ability to make use of them. The sense of futility experienced by executives in the face of overabundant information is reduced when they begin the task by defining their strategy and the most likely strategic alternatives they will be debating in the foreseeable future. Decision on direction spotlights the relevant environment. You cannot know everything, but if you are thinking of going into the furniture business in Nebraska, you will not be concerned about the rate of family formation in Japan. Clarification of present strategy and the few new alternatives it suggests narrows sharply the range of necessary information and destroys the excuse that there is too much to know.

IDENTIFICATION OF OPPORTUNITIES AND RISKS

For the firm that has not determined what its strategy dictates it needs to know or has not embarked upon the systematic surveillance of environmental change, a few simple questions kept constantly in mind will highlight changing opportunity and risk. In examining your own company or one you are interested in, these questions should lead to an estimate of opportunity and danger in the present and predicted company setting.

---

[2] Frank J. Aguilar, *Scanning the Business Environment* (New York: Macmillan, 1967).

1. *What are the essential economic, technical, and structural characteristics of the industry in which the company participates?*

Whether these are in flux or not, such characteristics may define the restrictions and opportunities confronting the individual company and will certainly suggest strategy. For example, knowledge that the cement industry requires high investment in plant, proximity to certain raw materials, a relatively small labor force, and enormous fuel and transportation costs suggests where to look for new plant sites and what will constitute competitive advantage and disadvantage. The nature of its product may suggest for a given company the wisdom of developing efficient pipeline and truck transportation and cheaper energy sources rather than engaging in extensive research to achieve product differentiation or aggressive price competition to increase its market share.

2. *What industry trends are apparent that might change this underlying structure?*

Changes in substitute products occurring as a result of research and development, for example, affect the substitution threat facing the industry. For example, the glass container industry's development years ago of strong, light, disposable bottles and, more recently, combinations of glass and plastic recouped part of the market lost by glass to the metal container. The need for the glass industry to engage in this development effort was made apparent by the observable success of the metal beer can. Similarly, the easy-opening metal container suggested the need for an easily removable bottle cap in order to cope with the substitution threat. Increased sophistication of buyers of contract aerosol packaging, coupled with increasing ease of their vertical integration into the business themselves, made buyers increasingly powerful and price sensitive and had a strong depressing effect on industry profits.

3. *How might foreseeable changes in the social, political, and macroeconomic context affect the industry or the firm?*

Broad changes in society, government policy, or macroeconomic conditions can have a dramatic impact on the industry or on the company's position in its industry. Deregulation has thrown the domestic U.S. airline and trucking industries into bitter price wars and a scramble for consolidation. Both the glass bottle and the metal container face increasingly effective attack by environmentalists, who constitute a noneconomic and nontechnical force to be reckoned with. Container industries should have begun long since, for example, to develop logistical solutions to the legislatively mandated returnable bottle and can.

4. *What are the goals, assumptions, strategies, and capabilities of the important existing and potential competitors in the industry and their likely future behavior?*

A realistic assessment of competitors must guide the goals a company sets for itself. A small rubber company, in an industry led by Uniroyal,

Goodyear, Goodrich, and Firestone, will not, under the economic condition of overcapacity, elect to provide the automobile business with original tires for new cars. The capabilities of competitors, quite apart from the resources of the firm, may suggest that a relatively small firm should seek out a niche of relatively small attraction to the majors and concentrate its powers on that limited segment of the market.

5. *What are the critical requirements for future success for the company?* Industry structure, the capabilities of competitors and their expected behavior, and broader social, political, and macroeconomic trends all define the critical tasks the company must perform to ensure its strategic health and survival. In the ladies' belt and handbag business, style and design are critical, but so (less obviously) are relationships with department store buyers. In the computer business, a sales force able to diagnose customer requirements for information systems, to design a suitable system, and to equip a customer to use it is more important than the circuitry of hardware given the positions of the various competitors.

Although the question of what tasks are most critical for the company may be chiefly useful as a means of identifying risks or possible causes of failure, it may also suggest opportunity. Imagination in perceiving new requirements for success under changing conditions, when production-oriented competitors have not done so, can give a company leadership position. For example, opportunity for a local radio station and the strategy it needed to follow changed sharply with the rise of television, and those who first diagnosed the new requirements paid much less for stations than was later necessary.

6. *Given the analysis of the industry, competitors, and broader context, what range of strategic alternatives is available to companies in this industry?* The force of this question is obvious in the drug industry. The speed and direction of pharmaceutical research, the structure of the industry, the behavior of competitors, the characteristics of worldwide demand, the different and changing ideas about how adequate medical care should be made available to the world's population, the concern about price, and the nature of government regulation suggest constraints within which a range of opportunity is still vividly clear. Similarly, in a more stable industry, there is always a choice. To determine its limits, an examination of environmental characteristics and developments is essential.

OPPORTUNITY AS A DETERMINANT OF STRATEGY

Awareness of the environment and analysis of the behavior of competitors is not a special project to be undertaken only when warning of change becomes deafening; it is a continuing requirement for informed choice of purpose. Planned exploitation of changing opportunity ordinarily follows a predictable course which provides increasing awareness of areas to which a company's capabilities may be profitably extended. A useful way to perceive the normal course of development is to use Bruce Scott's stages referred to briefly in a previous discussion.

The manufacturer of a single product (stage I) sold within a clearly defined geographical area to meet a known demand finds it relatively easy to identify opportunity and risk. As an enterprise develops a degree of complexity requiring functional division of management decision, it encounters as an integrated stage II company a number of strategic alternatives in its market environments which the stage I proprietor is too hard pressed to notice and almost too overcommitted to consider. Finally, stage III companies, deployed along the full range of diversification, find even a greater number of possibilities for serving a market profitably than the resources they possess or have in sight will support. The more one finds out what might be done, the harder it is to make the final choice.

The diversified stage III company has another problem different from that of trying to make the best choice among many. If it has divisionalized its operations and strategies, as sooner or later in the course of diversification it must, then divisional opportunities come into competition with each other.

The corporate management will wish to invest profits not distributed to stockholders in those opportunities that will produce the greatest return to the corporation. If need be, corporate management will be willing to let an individual division decline if its future looks less attractive than that of others. The division on the other hand will wish to protect its own market position, ward off adverse developments, prolong its own existence, and provide for its growth. The division manager, who is not rewarded for failures, may program projects of safe but usually not dramatic prospects. The claims regarding projected return on investment, which are submitted in all honesty as the divisional estimate of future opportunity, can be assumed to be biased by the division's regard for its own interest and the manager's awareness of measurement.

The corporate management cannot be expected to be able to make independent judgments about all the proposals for growth which are submitted by all the divisions. On the other hand, all divisions cannot be given their heads, if the corporation's needs for present profit are to be met and if funds for reinvestment are limited. In any case, the greatest knowledge about the opportunities for a given technology and set of markets should be found at the divisional level.[3]

---

[3] See Christopher A. Bartlett and Sumantra Ghoshal, *Managing across Borders: The Transnational Solution* (Boston: Harvard Business School Press, 1989).

The strategic dilemma of a conglomerate world enterprise is the most complex in the full range of policy decisions.[4] When the variety of what must be known cannot be reduced by a sharply focused strategy to the capacity of a single mind and when the range of a company's activities spans many industries and technologies, the problems of formulating a coherent strategy begin to get out of hand. Here strategy must become a managed process rather than the decision of the chief executive officer and his immediate associates. Bower and Prahalad have shown in important research how the context of decision can be controlled by the top-management group and how power can be distributed through a hierarchy to influence the kind of strategic decision that will survive in the system. The process of strategic decision can, like complex operations, be organized in such a way as to provide appropriate complementary roles for decentralization and control.

To conceive of a new development in response to market information, analysis of competitive strategy, and prediction of the future is a creative act. To commit resources to it only on the basis of projected return and the estimate of probability constituting risk of failure is foolhardy. More than economic analysis of potential return is required for decision, for economic opportunity abounds far beyond the ability to capture it. That much money might be made in a new field or growth industry does not mean that a company with abilities developed in a different field is going to make it. We turn now to the critical factors that for an individual company make one opportunity better than another.

IDENTIFYING CORPORATE COMPETENCE AND RESOURCES

The first step in validating a tentative choice among several opportunities is to determine whether the organization has the capacity to prosecute it successfully. The capability of an organization is its demonstrated and potential ability to accomplish, against the opposition of circumstance or competition, whatever it sets out to do. Every organization has actual and potential strengths and weaknesses. Since it is prudent in formulating strategy to extend or maximize the one and contain or minimize the other, it is important to try to determine what they are and to distinguish one from the other.

It is just as possible, though if anything more difficult, for a company to know its own strengths and limitations if it is to maintain a workable

---

[4] Joseph L. Bower, *Managing the Resource Allocation Process* (Boston: Division of Research, Harvard Business School, 1970); and C. K. Prahalad, "The Strategic Process in a Multinational Corporation" (doctoral thesis, Harvard Business School, 1975), partially summarized in "Strategic Choices in Diversified MNCs," *Harvard Business Review*, July–August 1976, pp. 67–78.

surveillance of its changing environment. Subjectivity, lack of confidence, and unwillingness to face reality may make it hard for organizations as well as for individuals to know themselves. But just as it is essential, though difficult, that a maturing person achieve reasonable self-awareness, so an organization can identify approximately its central strength and critical vulnerability.

Howard H. Stevenson made the first formal study of management practice in defining corporate strengths and weaknesses as part of the strategic planning process.[5] He looked at five aspects of the process: (1) the attributes of the company which its managers examined, (2) the organizational scope of the strengths and weaknesses identified, (3) the measurement employed in the process of definition, (4) the criteria for telling a strength from a weakness, and (5) the sources of relevant information. As might be expected, the process Stevenson was looking at was imperfectly and variously practiced in the half dozen companies he studied. He found that the problems of definition of corporate strengths and weaknesses, very different from those of other planning processes, center mostly upon a general lack of agreement on suitable definition, criteria, and information. For an art that had hardly made a beginning, Stevenson offered a prescriptive model for integrating the considerations affecting definition of strength or weakness. Indicative of the primitive stage of some of our concepts for general management, Stevenson's most important conclusion is that the attempt to define strengths and weaknesses is more useful than the usual final product of the process.

Stevenson's exploratory study in no way diminishes the importance of appraising organization capability. It protects us against oversimplification. The absence of criteria and measures, the disinclination for appraising competence except in relation to specific problems, the uncertainty about what is meant by "strength" and "weakness," and the reluctance to imply criticism of individuals or organizational subunits—all these hampered his study but illuminated the problem. Much of what is intuitive in this process is yet to be identified. Both for a competitor and for one's own company, one can inquire into strengths and weaknesses in functional components like marketing, manufacturing, research and development, finance, or control; and the impact that growth may have on functional capability and on the quality of management; and the capacity to respond quickly to competitive moods and to adapt to the changing environment. Raising questions like these quickens the power of self-awareness, even if definitive judgments are hard to come by.

To make an effective contribution to strategic planning, the key attributes to be appraised should be identified and consistent criteria established for

[5] Howard H. Stevenson, "Defining Corporate Strengths and Weaknesses: An Exploratory Study" (doctoral thesis deposited in Baker Library, Harvard Business School, 1969). For a published summary article of the same title, see *Sloan Management Review*, Spring 1976.

judging them. If attention is directed to strategies, policy commitments, and past practices in the context of discrepancy between organization goals and attainment, an outcome useful to an individual manager's strategic planning is possible. The assessment of strengths and weaknesses associated with the attainment of specific objectives becomes in Stevenson's words a "key link in a feedback loop" which allows managers to learn from the success or failures of the policies they institute.

Although this study does not find or establish a systematic way of developing or using such knowledge, members of organizations develop judgments about what the company can do particularly well—its core of competence. If consensus can be reached about this capability, no matter how subjectively arrived at, its application to identified opportunity can be estimated. Surely as much success can be achieved in developing analysis of one's own company as in examining the strategy of competitors.[6]

Sources of Capabilities. The powers of a company constituting a resource for growth and diversification accrue primarily from experience in making and marketing a product line. They inhere as well in (1) the developing strengths and weaknesses of the individuals comprising the organization, (2) the degree to which individual capability is effectively applied to the common task, and (3) the quality of coordination of individual and group effort.

The experience gained through successful execution of a strategy centered upon one goal may unexpectedly develop capabilities which could be applied to different ends. Whether they should be so applied is another question. For example, a manufacturer of salt can strengthen his competitive position by offering his customers salt-dispensing equipment. If in the course of making engineering improvements in this equipment a new solenoid principle is perfected that has application to many industrial switching problems, should this patentable and marketable innovation be exploited? The answer would turn not only on whether economic analysis of the opportunity shows this to be a durable and profitable possibility but also on whether the organization can muster the financial, manufacturing, and marketing strength to exploit the discovery. The former question is likely to have a more positive answer than the latter. In this connection, it seems important to remember that individual and unsupported flashes of strength are not as dependable as the gradually accumulated product- and market-related fruits of experience.

Even where competence to exploit an opportunity is nurtured by experience in related fields, the level of that competence may be too low for any great reliance to be placed upon it. Thus a chain of children's clothing stores might well acquire the administrative, merchandising, buying, and

[6] See Hiroyuki Itami, *Mobilizing Invisible Assets* (Cambridge: Harvard University Press, 1987) for an important concept of "Strategic Dynamics."

selling skills that would permit it to add departments in women's wear. Similarly, a sales force effective in distributing typewriters may gain proficiency in selling office machinery and supplies. But even here it would be well to ask what distinctive ability these companies could bring to the retailing of soft goods or office equipment to attract customers away from a plethora of competitors.

Identifying Strengths. The distinctive competence of an organization is more than what it can do; it is what it can do particularly well. To identify the less obvious or by-product strengths of an organization that may well be transferable to some more profitable new opportunity, one might well begin by examining the organization's current product line and by defining the functions it serves in its markets. Almost any important consumer product has functions which are related to others into which a qualified company might move. The typewriter, for example, is more than the simple machine for mechanizing handwriting that it once appeared to be when looked at only from the point of view of its designer and manufacturer. Closely analyzed from the point of view of the potential user, the typewriter is found to contribute to a broad range of information processing functions. Any one of these might have suggested an area to be exploited by a typewriter manufacturer. Tacitly defining a typewriter as a replacement for a fountain pen as a writing instrument rather than as an input-output device for word processing is the explanation provided by hindsight for the failure of the old-line typewriter companies to develop the electric typewriter and the computer-related input-output devices it made possible before IBM did. The definition of product which would lead to identification of transferable skills must be expressed in terms of the market needs it may fill rather than the engineering specifications to which it conforms.

Besides looking at the uses or functions to which present products contribute, the would-be diversifier might profitably identify the skills that underlie whatever success has been achieved. The qualifications of an organization efficient at performing its long-accustomed tasks come to be taken for granted and considered humdrum, like the steady provision of first-class service. The insight required to identify the essential strength justifying new ventures does not come naturally. Its cultivation can probably be helped by recognition of the need for analysis. In any case, we should look beyond the company's capacity to invent new products. Product leadership is not possible for a majority of companies, so it is fortunate that patentable new products are not the only major highway to new opportunities. Other avenues include new marketing services, new methods of distribution, new values in quality-price combinations, and creative merchandising. The effort to find or to create a competence that is truly distinctive may hold the real key to a company's success or even to its future development. For example, the ability of a cement manufacturer to run a truck fleet more effectively than its competitors may

FIGURE 1
SCHEMATIC DEVELOPMENT OF ECONOMIC STRATEGY

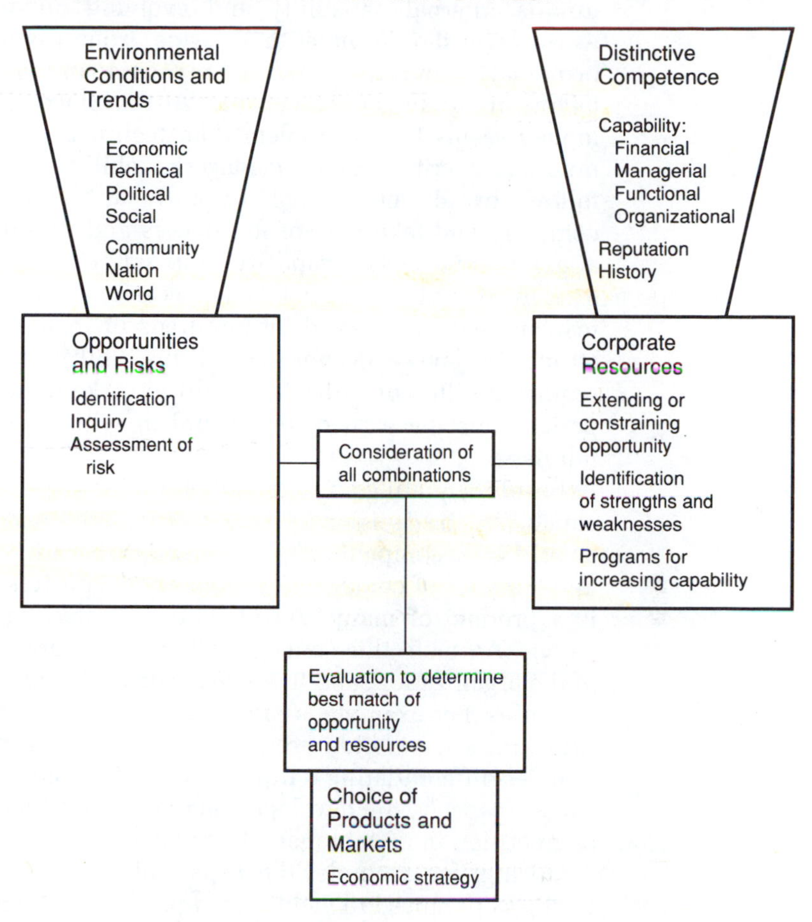

constitute one of its principal competitive strengths in selling an undifferentiated product.

Matching Opportunity and Competence. The way to narrow the range of alternatives, made extensive by imaginative identification of new possibilities, is to match opportunity to competence, once each has been accurately identified and its future significance estimated. It is this combination which establishes a company's economic mission and its position in its environment. The combination is designed to minimize organizational weakness and to maximize strength. In every case, risk attends it. And when opportunity seems to outrun present distinctive competence, the willingness to gamble that the latter can be built up to the required level is almost indispensable to a strategy that challenges the organization and the people in it. Figure 1 diagrams the matching of opportunity and resources that results in an economic strategy.

Before we leave the creative act of putting together a company's unique internal capability and evolving opportunity in the external world, we should note that—aside from distinctive competence—the principal resources found in any company are money and people—technical and managerial people. At this stage of economic development, money seems less a problem than technical competence, and the latter much less critical than managerial ability. In reading the cases that follow, by all means look carefully at the financial records of each company and take note of its success and its problems. Look also at the apparent managerial capacity and, without underestimating it, do not assume that it can rise to any occasion. The diversification of American industry is marked by hundreds of instances in which a company strong in one endeavor lacked the ability to manage an enterprise requiring different skills. The right to make handsome profits over a long period must be earned. Opportunism without competence is a path to fairyland.

Besides equating an appraisal of market opportunity and organizational capability, the decision to make and market a particular product or service should be accompanied by an identification of the nature of the business and the kind of company its management desires. Such a guiding concept is a product of many considerations, including the managers' personal values. As such, this concept will change more slowly than other aspects of the organization, and it will give coherence to all the variety of company activities. For example, a president who is determined to make his or her firm into a worldwide producer and fabricator of a basic metal, through policies differentiating it from the industry leader, will not be distracted by excess capacity in developed markets, low metal prices, and cutthroat competition in certain markets. Such a firm would not be sidetracked into acquiring, for example, the Pepsi-Cola franchise in Africa, even if this business promised to yield a good profit. (That such a firm should have an experimental division exploring offshoot technology is, however, entirely appropriate.)

Uniqueness of Strategy. In each company, the way in which distinctive competence, organizational resources, and organizational values are combined is or should be unique. Differences among companies are as numerous as differences among individuals. The combinations of opportunity to which distinctive competence, resources, and values may be applied are equally extensive. Generalizing about how to make an effective match is less rewarding than working at it. The effort is a highly stimulating and challenging exercise. The outcome will be unique for each case and each situation, but each achievement of a viable economic strategy will leave the student of strategy better prepared to take part in real-life strategic decisions.

APPLICATION TO CASES

Students could profitably bring to the cases they study not only the questions suggested earlier but the following as well:

- What really is our product? What functions does it serve? To what additional functions might it be extended or adapted?
- What is happening to the market for our products? Is it expanding or contracting? Why?
- What are our company's major strengths and weaknesses? From what sources do these arise?
- Do we have a distinctive or core competence? If so, to what new activities can it be applied?
- What are our principal competitors' major strengths and weaknesses? Are they imitating us or we them? What comparative advantage over our competitors can we exploit?
- What is our strategy? Is the combination of product and market an optimum economic strategy? Is the central nature of our business clear enough to provide us with a criterion for product diversification?
- What, if any, better combinations of market opportunities and distinctive competence can our company effect, within a range of reasonable risk?

These questions will prove helpful throughout the course in the task of designing or validating an economic strategy. However, they are never wholly sufficient, for the strategic decision is never wholly economic in character. Corporate strategy is much more than a series of product-market decisions.

Wal-Mart Stores' Discount Operations

In October 1985 *Forbes* declared Sam Walton the richest person in the United States. With his four children, he owned stock worth $2.8 billion. That put him $1 billion ahead of the next person on the list, H. Ross Perot. By the end of April 1986, Walton's net worth had swelled by another $1.6 billion.

Walton's fortune consisted of a 39 percent stake in Wal-Mart Stores, a retailer that had focused historically on the Southwest. Although Wal-Mart had begun to diversify into other areas, discounting still accounted for 91 percent of the company's sales in 1985 and 96 percent of its pretax profits. Wal-Mart had consistently led other discounters in both profitability and growth. Exhibit 1 summarizes Wal-Mart's history over the past decade; Exhibit 2 compares its performance with that of its competitors. As a result of such comparisons, Wal-Mart's market value in early 1986 was twice K mart's, even though it was only a third as large. Analysts thought that Wal-Mart would overtake K mart as the largest discounter by the turn of the century, but they were divided over whether Wal-Mart stock remained a good buy at a price-earnings multiple of 26.

This case describes discount retailing and the distinctive features of Wal-Mart's discount operations. It also sketches the areas into which Wal-Mart was diversifying in the mid-1980s.

DISCOUNT RETAILING

Discount stores emerged in the United States in the mid-1950s. They followed on the heels of supermarkets, which sold food at unprecedentedly low margins. Discount stores extended this approach to general merchandise by charging gross margins that were 10–15 percent lower than those of conventional department stores. To compensate, discount stores cut costs to the bone: fixtures were distinctly unluxurious, in-store selling was limited, and ancillary services, such as tailoring, delivery, and credit, were scarce.

The discounters' timing was just right. Consumers had become increasingly better

Harvard Business School case 387–018.

informed since World War II. Supermarkets had educated them about self-service, many categories of general merchandise had matured, and TV had intensified advertising by manufacturers. Government standards also bolstered consumers' self-confidence. Many were ready to try cheaper, self-service retailers except for products that were big-ticket items, technologically complex, or "psychologically significant."

Discount retailing burgeoned as a result. Discounters' sales grew from $2 billion in 1960 to $68 billion in 1985. Penetration continued: by the year 2000, discounters' sales were expected to climb to $98 billion (in 1985 dollars).[1]

But too many players had gotten into discounting at the local, regional, or national level. Industry growth peaked in the 1970s: during that decade, the number of stores increased by 64 percent and (undeflated) sales by 144 percent. Over the 1980–1985 period, the number of discount stores increased by only 8 percent. Several large chains—including King's, Korvette's, Mammoth Mart, W.T. Grant, Two Guys, and Woolco—failed in the late 1970s and early 1980s; many of the padlocked stores were acquired and recycled by survivors. (Exhibit 3 depicts the average economics of discounting in 1984.)

WAL-MART'S DISCOUNT STORES

History

Although Wal-Mart Stores was incorporated in 1969, it was rooted in the variety store—franchised by Ben Franklin—that Sam Walton had opened in Newport, Arkansas, in 1945. Through 1962, Sam Walton and his brother, Bud, built up a chain of 16 variety stores in rural Arkansas that was considered Ben Franklin's most successful franchisee. But regional entry by discount stores increasingly worried Sam Walton; competitive pressure eventually led him to travel the country, scouting retailing alternatives. Despite the conventional wisdom that a full-line discount store needed a population base of at least 100,000, Walton became convinced that discounting could work in small Southwestern towns. In his words, "If we offered prices as good or better than stores in cities that were four hours away by car, people would shop at home."[2] Since Ben Franklin was unresponsive, Walton set out to build his own discount chain.

By 1970, Walton had steadily expanded his chain to 30 discount stores in rural Arkansas, Missouri, and Oklahoma. But the cost of goods sold—almost three quarters of discounting revenues—rankled. As Walton put it:

> Here we were in the boondocks, so we didn't have distributors falling over themselves to serve us like competitors in larger towns. Our only alternative was to build our own warehouse so we could buy in volume at attractive prices and store the merchandise.[3]

Since warehouses, at $5 million or more apiece, were rather capital-intensive, Walton took the company public and raised $3.3 million.

After 1970, Wal-Mart's discount operations mushroomed. At the end of 1985, Wal-Mart operated 859 "Discount City"

---

[1] E. G. May, C. W. Ress, and W. J. Salmon, *Future Trends in Retailing* (Marketing Science Institute, February 1985).

[2] *Business Week,* November 5, 1979, p. 145.

[3] *Forbes,* August 16, 1982, p. 43.

stores, with distribution centers in five locations. (Exhibit 4 traces the pattern of store expansions, and Exhibit 5 maps Wal-Mart's discounting network at the end of 1985.) In describing the pattern of expansion, David Glass (later Wal-Mart's president and chief operating officer) said, "We are always pushing from the inside out. We never jump and then backfill."[4] During 1986, Wal-Mart planned to add another 115 discount stores to its network.

Well over half of Wal-Mart's stores were still located in towns with populations between 5,000 and 25,000, a higher proportion than the rest of the industry. About one third of Wal-Mart's stores were located in metropolitan areas or counties that were not served by any of Wal-Mart's competitors. The comparable figure for other discounters in the states in which Wal-Mart operated was 12 percent. In locations where it was alone, Wal-Mart often commanded an unmatched 10–20 percent of total retail sales.

Increasingly, however, Wal-Mart had turned to more densely populated areas for growth. The average size of a Wal-Mart store had increased from 42,000 square feet in 1975 to 47,000 square feet by 1980 and 57,000 square feet by 1985. In 1985, new Wal-Mart stores averaged 63,000 square feet—about the same size as the other discount stores being opened in the same regions. Increases in average size reflected, in part, Wal-Mart's development of 85,000- to 100,000-square-foot stores in order to penetrate midsized cities and encircle larger ones. Wal-Mart expected that eventually a quarter of its stores would exceed 85,000 square feet.[5]

[4] *Business Week,* November 5, 1979, p. 146.
[5] *Discount Store News,* December 9, 1985, p. 62.

Wal-Mart's competitors had come to notice that over the 1975–1985 period, population had grown faster in the Sunbelt than in the rest of the United States, and in nonmetropolitan areas than in metropolitan ones. As a result, they had begun to encroach on Wal-Mart's sales territories; K mart, for example, competed in over half of them by 1985. In an attempt to mitigate competition, Wal-Mart was testing 30,000-square-foot stores for towns with populations between 1,000 and 5,000. Company spokespeople claimed that stores of this size would open up 1,000 locations in areas previously considered saturated.

Purchasing and Distribution

Wal-Mart, like other discount chains, had centralized purchasing. Unlike some of its competitors, however, Wal-Mart did not base orders for most stockkeeping units (SKUs) on centralized sales forecasts. Instead, it used in-store terminals to wire merchandise requests to a central computer. The central computer would either transmit the requests to the Wal-Mart distribution center that supplied the store, or, if stocking levels there were low, reorder the merchandise. Wal-Mart never filled out-of-stock areas with different merchandise.

To expedite deliveries, Wal-Mart's central computer was linked directly to several hundred of its 3,000 vendors. Wal-Mart had developed a reputation for bargaining very hard with them. Unlike some other discounters, Wal-Mart took no more than a fifth of its volume from any one vendor. In 1985, no vendor accounted for more than 2.8 percent of the company's total purchases.

Only 20 percent of the inbound merchandise—a smaller proportion than at either Sears or K mart—was shipped directly from the vendors to the stores. The rest passed through Wal-Mart's two-step hub-and-spoke distribution network. One of Wal-Mart's 400-plus truck-tractors would bring the merchandise into a distribution center, where it would be sorted automatically onto another truck and delivered to the store—usually within 48 hours of the original request. Each store received at least three full or partial truckloads a week. Because Wal-Mart stores were packed together, one truck could resupply two or three on a single trip. Any merchandise that had to be returned was carried back to the distribution center for consolidation. Since many vendors operated warehouses or factories within Wal-Mart's territory, trucks also picked up new shipments on the return trip. In the early 1980s, Wal-Mart's trucks were running 60 percent full on backhauls.

Wal-Mart opened its first distribution center—a 72,000-square-foot facility—at its headquarters in Bentonville, Arkansas, in 1970. The initial cost of that distribution center was $5 million; it was meant to serve 80 to 100 Wal-Mart stores within a 250-mile radius, and it was enlarged as Wal-Mart's store network grew. By 1978 the company's radius of operations had widened to 400 miles. In that year, Wal-Mart opened a distribution center at Searcy, Arkansas, to serve eastern Arkansas and the growing store networks in Louisiana, Missisissippi, and Tennessee. Distribution centers were inaugurated in three other locations in the next seven years: Palestine, Texas (1979), to serve the southeastern part of that state; Cullman, Alabama (1983), to serve Tennessee, Alabama, Kentucky, Georgia, and the Carolinas; and Mt. Pleasant, Iowa (1985), to serve Illinois, Iowa, and Indiana. By the end of 1985, Wal-Mart operated 3.9 million square feet of distribution space in five locations. It was scrambling to add another 2.6 million square feet in 1986, primarily in three new distribution centers: Douglas, Georgia; Plainview, Texas; and Brookhaven, Mississippi. Rapid store expansion was the reason: the new distribution centers were needed to contain delivery times and transportation costs and to cope with regional differences in consumer preferences. Ultimately each center was meant to serve up to 175 stores within a 150- to 300-mile radius.

This was the same distance that Wal-Mart stores were from their distribution centers in the early 1980s. Wal-Mart's cost of inbound logistics, which it had to shoulder, had then averaged 2 percent of sales—about half the figure for the industry as a whole. The savings fed directly into gross margins. However, rapid expansion had nudged these costs upward: in 1984, they accounted for 2.8 percent of sales and in 1985, 4 percent. They were expected to drop back to 3 percent of sales once the new distribution centers were completed in 1986.

Store Operations

Wal-Mart leased all but 47 of the 859 stores it operated at the end of 1985. Stores were constructed or redeveloped to its specifications by independent contractors. Almost all the store leases could be renewed for 5 to 15 years at the end of their terms. Some of the leases provided for contingent additional rentals based on sales levels. Since 1979, the company had decided to stay out of locations that could not be expanded.

Building rentals accounted for 1.8 percent of sales in the late 1970s—the lowest level for any major discounter. Two factors had since contained them: (1) an increase in sales per average square foot from $110 in 1979 to $171 by 1985 and (2) the bargain-basement acquisition in the 1980s, of the leases for 120 Kuhn's Big-K and Woolco stores. Despite these factors, average building rentals had probably edged upward by 0.1 percent as Wal-Mart moved into larger, more contested towns.

Store hours ran from 9 A.M. to 9 P.M.; most Wal-Mart stores were open seven days a week. (Exhibit 6 sketches the layout of a relatively large Wal-Mart store.) Each store had 36 merchandise departments. Store managers were allowed considerable autonomy in allocating space among them, ordering stock, and setting up displays. The ambiance of Wal-Mart stores resembled K mart's: since the mid-1970s, both had launched expensive store-improvement programs to move slightly upscale, although they remained less luxurious than higher-priced discounters such as Caldor, Target, and Venture. More of a Wal-Mart store's gross area was available for selling space because the company's distribution network reduced back-room storage requirements. Inventory turns exceeded 4.5 in 1985—well above the levels posted by other discounters.

On average, 29 percent of a Wal-Mart store's sales were accounted for by soft goods (apparel, linen, and fabrics), compared with roughly 35 percent for the industry as a whole. Wal-Mart placed more emphasis on hard goods (hardware, housewares, automobile supplies, and small appliances): these constituted 28 percent of Wal-Mart's sales but only 22 percent of the industry's. Hard goods generated more sales per square foot than soft goods (for the industry as a whole, about $150 versus about $125), built up more traffic, and required fewer markdowns. The gross margins on them, however, tended to be lower (about 29 percent versus 35 percent for soft goods).

The other important product categories at Wal-Mart were stationery and candy (11 percent of sales), sporting goods and toys (10 percent), health and beauty aids (9 percent), gifts, records, and electronics (5 percent), shoes (3 percent), pharmaceuticals (3 percent), and jewelry (2 percent). Most discounters had traditionally farmed out the last three categories, in at least some locations, to in-store licensees for fees ranging from 5 to 14 percent of the licensees' sales. Wal-Mart was no exception: in 1975, nearly all of its shoe, pharmaceutical, and jewelry departments were handled by licensees. Over the next decade, it took over many of these specialty departments—by all accounts, quite successfully—after they failed to match sales gains in other parts of its stores. By 1985, it ran over two thirds of these specialty departments, and licensee fees accounted for only 0.2 percent of Wal-Mart's discount sales. Fees from licensing averaged 0.4 percent of sales for the industry as a whole.

The Wal-Mart system included over 70,000 SKUs—a larger number than most other chains, because Wal-Mart was the primary source of merchandise in many of the rural communities that it served. The average store probably stocked 35,000 SKUs; that number increased with store size. Wal-Mart had led the industry in 1971 by installing a computerized system to track inventory. In 1985 each Wal-Mart store had a computer that tracked sales and performed accounting functions. Full inventories of all stores were kept in the central computer at headquarters; they were updated weekly. A $20 million satellite network was to be inaugurated in 1986 to ease real-time communications between all stores and headquarters and to cap telephone costs, which had spiraled to $10 million. Industry observers already considered Wal-Mart's reaction time in adjusting inventory to be superior to that of its competitors.

In a major drive to improve productivity, Wal-Mart, like other large discounters, was switched to electronic scanning of the Uniform Product Code (UPC) at the point of sale. This would speed checkouts, bypass paperwork, and simplify inventory management, reorders, and postaudits of merchandising programs. UPC scanning was expensive, however: equipping one store with the capability might cost up to $500,000. Wal-Mart had equipped 25 of its stores in 1983, 66 more in 1984, and another 144 in 1985. In 1986 it planned to install UPC scanning in every new store and in 200 existing ones. The goal, which it shared with major competitors such as K mart, was full conversion by 1988 or early 1989.

Marketing

Branded merchandise, most of it nationally advertised, accounted for a majority—one source said 95 percent—of Wal-Mart's nonclothing sales. Most of the clothing sold, in contrast, was private label. Approximately 70 percent of all Wal-Mart merchandise was common to all its stores; the rest was tailored to local needs.

Wal-Mart's marketing theme was emblazoned on the facade of every Discount City: "We Sell for Less." Consumers clearly agreed. According to a survey conducted in 1985 by *Discount Store News* and Leo J. Shapiro Associates, consumers shopped Wal-Mart primarily for the price-sensitive categories of health and beauty aids, housewares, and appliances. They were not as influenced by it in apparel, hardware, and consumer electronics.

Wal-Mart was very competitive in terms of prices. Its store managers had more latitude in setting prices than did their counterparts in "centrally priced" chains such as Caldor and Venture. Goldman, Sachs had compared Wal-Mart's everyday shelf prices with its competitors' in three markets in late 1983 and early 1984.[6] The most competitive market covered the eastern suburbs of St Louis: in one of the suburbs—called Belleville—a Wal-Mart and a K mart were located right next to each other. Wal-Mart's prices there were 1.3 percent lower than K mart's. K mart priced 9 percent lower in Belleville than in Fairview, eight miles away, where it competed—at a greater distance—with Venture and Target. The second market, between Dallas and Fort Worth, was somewhat less competitive: Wal-Mart, K mart, and Target were each separated by four to six miles. There, Wal-Mart's prices were 7.6 percent lower than Target's, and 10.4 percent lower than K mart's. The final market studied—Franklin, Tennessee, 18 miles south of Nashville—was one in which Wal-Mart had no local competition. Wal-Mart's prices in Franklin were 6 percent above those in its urban location in Nashville, where it was located right next to K mart.

Wal-Mart's promotional strategy was governed by its philosophy of "everyday low prices." Many discounters, such as Caldor, Target, and K mart, cut prices 20–30 percent on selected items nearly

[6] Joseph H. Ellis, "Wal-Mart Stores, Inc.," Goldman, Sachs, May 9, 1984.

every week in order to build traffic, highlight seasonal trends, and control their sales mix. There were numerous costs, though: advertising in local newspapers or catalog mailings to prospective customers, anticipatory buildup of inventories, scheduling snarl-ups, extra payroll costs, and additional markdowns on residual merchandise. To measure the success of a promotion, items had to be counted before and afterward;[7] even this measure was imperfect because many customers deferred purchases at higher everyday prices in anticipation of sales. As a result, a few discounters, such as Hills Department Stores, ran no promotions at all. Wal-Mart fell between these extremes by running 13 promotions a year: one each month except in December, when it ran two. Promotional prices were 10–20 percent below everyday ones. By one account, Wal-Mart's sales tables—jammed between regular store fixtures—generated twice as many sales dollars per square foot as those of its competitors.

Wal-Mart's advertising expenditures had averaged 1.1 percent of sales in the second half of the 1970s. Circulars and newspaper advertisements accounted for the bulk of this figure. Spot TV was the primary nonprint medium used. Television advertising had increased from $1.0 million (14 percent of the total) in 1977 to $3.7 million (29 percent of the total) in 1979. Wal-Mart had subsequently stopped disclosing aggregate advertising figures. In 1985, however, it spent $16.3 million on spot TV, almost entirely in major metropolitan markets. It typically advertised heavily when it entered such a market; for instance, in entering Nashville, it outspent other discounters in the area and then dropped back after it established a presence.

Wal-Mart's terms of sale, like other discounters', were primarily cash-and-carry. Although Wal-Mart did accept MasterCard and VISA, credit transactions accounted for less than 5 percent of its total sales in 1982. Wal-Mart had a "no questions asked" policy on returns.

In 1985, Wal-Mart was using computer-aided design to develop a program that would suggest a merchandise mix for each store, based on more than 100 factors—including climate, customers' recreational preferences, their ethnic mix, and other demographic factors. Management thought that the increasing diversity of the communities Wal-Mart served made such a program essential.

Human Resources Management

At the end of 1985, Wal-Mart employed over 100,000 full-time and part-time employees. None of them were unionized. Company spokesmen invariably emphasized their importance to the company. The annual report for the fiscal year ending January 31, 1986, was typical. Its cover highlighted the word *people;* the report went on to add, "Wal-Mart's 'Our People Make the Difference' explanation for past success is more than a slogan or a philosophy—it's the very heart of Wal-Mart." Almost all Wal-Mart managers wore buttons that said, "We Care About Our People."

Wall Street analysts agreed that there *was* something different about Wal-Mart's human resource management policies. Top management spent the bulk of the week within Wal-Mart's stores. Employees (officially called associates) were polled for

[7] UPC scanning was alleviating this particular problem, because it allowed automatic tracking of sales.

their views on what merchandise to include and how to display it. Several incentives had been installed, including profit sharing and encouragement of employee stock purchases. Store managers' base salaries were supplemented by a percentage of their unit's pretax profits if they exceeded corporate targets. But the program with the most tangible impact on the bottom line dealt with "shrinkage"—a euphemism for pilferage or shoplifting. Shrinkage, which was embedded in the cost of goods sold, dissipated over 2 percent of most retailers' sales revenues. In the mid-1970s shrinkage ran at 2.2 percent in Wal-Mart stores as well. Wal-Mart then began passing on half of any reductions in shrinkage in a particular store to the employees there. By the mid-1980s, this program and tight inventory control had reduced shrinkage to 1.3 percent of sales.

Wal-Mart had been named one of the 100 best companies to work for in the United States. This was in spite of rather than because of its pay scales, which were considered tightfisted. Salary and wage expenses accounted for roughly 11.5 percent of sales in the late 1970s. This figure had declined to 10.1 percent of sales by 1985. Capital investments to improve labor productivity—such as UPC scanning—were one of the major reasons for the drop.

Administration

Wal-Mart's administrative style emphasized frugality. Corporate offices were cramped and, according to *Business Week* (October 14, 1985, p. 142), "Visitors to Bentonville often mistake Wal-Mart's office building, with its lobby decorated in Early Bus Station, for a warehouse." The administrative style also differed from competitors' in its very heavy emphasis on communication within the company.

Wal-Mart's 12 regional vice presidents were the cornerstones of this communication network; each of them lived in or around Bentonville. Those at K mart or Target, in contrast, would have overseen geographic areas three to four times as large, lived in the field, and, with their regional offices, cost perhaps an extra 2 percent of sales. Every Monday, each of Wal-Mart's regional vice presidents was flown out to the region in which the 75-odd stores each supervised were located. Through Thursday, these vice presidents visited their stores to gather feedback from store management, employees, and customers. They were flown back to Bentonville for a day-long merchandising meeting on Friday in which they reviewed the week's performance.

On Saturday, the regional vice presidents and 250 other employees, including the chairman or vice chairman, met at 7:30 A.M. to discuss the previous week's results and settle on directions for the coming weeks. One observer described this meeting as "an amalgam of nuts-and-bolts merchandising set against a backdrop of almost religious fervor."[8] The meeting usually wound up by 11 A.M.; each vice president then got on the phone with seven or eight district managers to relay plans for advertising and merchandising and other pertinent information. District managers, in turn, held a conference call with all their store managers. Before the end of the day, each store manager would have apprised his or her department managers of the latest programs. Once the satellite network was installed, the Saturday morning meeting would be beamed directly to all stores.

As chairman and chief executive officer, Sam Walton continued to play a very active

[8] *Discount Store News*, December 9, 1985, p. 44.

role, at the age of 68, in running Wal-Mart. His days typically began at 6 A.M. and stretched into the evening, although he had been known to drop into a distribution center at 4 A.M. for coffee and doughnuts with his employees. He still spent three or four days a week on the road visiting stores, and he also met with each new supplier. Sam Walton doubled as chief cheerleader: at store openings, he delivered pep talks from atop a table, and in 1984 he kept a pledge to put on a grass skirt and dance a hula on Wall Street to celebrate the achievement of 1983's profit targets. In April 1986 *Financial World* named him its CEO of the year.

DIVERSIFICATION

Before the 1980s, Wal-Mart had made only one attempt at diversification: it opened two do-it-yourself hardware and lumber stores in the mid-1970s, then quickly closed them. But in 1983 and 1984, it started three new ventures: dot Discount Drug, Helen's Arts and Crafts, and Sam's Wholesale Clubs. By the end of 1985, two dots and three Helen's had been opened. Helen's appeared to be on hold. Although Wal-Mart officials announced that dot had made the transition from an experimental chain into a full-fledged venture, analysts did not think it would contribute significantly to investment, sales, or earnings in the coming decade.

The venture that the analysts *were* excited about was Sam's—a warehouse club. Warehouse clubs had been in existence only a decade but were being hailed as the most exciting retail format since discounting. Warehouse clubs limited their gross margins to 9–10 percent, implying prices 20 percent below those of conventional discounters and supermarkets. Clubs stocked only 3,500 items and tried to unload their merchandise before the payment for it was due—usually within 30 days of receipt. To generate such high turnovers, they located in areas with populations of 400,000 to 500,000, stocked only top-selling items (including food), packaged items in large quantities, and targeted the owners of small businesses and prescreened, low-risk groups of individual customers. Business customers typically had to pay a $25 annual membership fee; individual customers could either pay a $25–$50 annual fee and receive the same prices, or forgo the fee and be charged 5 percent higher prices. The stores themselves were large warehouses—often the size of two football fields—with rudimentary fixtures, limited signage and marking of merchandise, and no salesclerk service, credit, or delivery.

In 1985 warehouse club sales had reached $4.4 billion. They were expected to exceed $20 billion by the early 1990s. Over a dozen companies had jumped into the business; in total, they operated over 100 warehouses at the end of 1985, compared with 43 at the end of 1984. Each warehouse cost between $5 million and $10 million to start. Only two companies had yet seen any return on their investment: (1) Price Company, which had pioneered the concept in 1975, turned its inventory 20 times a year and held a 40 percent market share, and (2) Wal-Mart's Sam's Wholesale Clubs, which turned inventory about 12 times a year and held a market share slightly under 20 percent. The other large competitors included affiliates of Kroger, Zayre, and W. R. Grace, and three "independents": Costco, Pace Membership Warehouse, and Wholesale Club. All of them had started by focusing on different geographic areas; none yet matched Sam's warehouse volumes or inventory turnovers, let alone Price's.

In 1985 companies for the first time began to compete in the same locations for warehouse business. This trend was expected to intensify because there were only about 100 metropolitan areas in the United States with populations of half a million or larger. The impact of competition was still a matter for conjecture. As one analyst put it:

> It is not yet clear whether two or more competitors can exist profitably in a single market, or how severely profitability is affected. Because warehouse clubs, as currently structured, depend on memberships—solicited directly to wholesale customers and to "group" members through savings and loan clubs, credit unions and employee organizations—being the first warehouse club to solicit and introduce the concept in a market can be a major competitive advantage.[9]

Wal-Mart had opened its first Sam's Wholesale Club in April 1983 in Oklahoma City. It added 2 more that year, 8 in 1984, and 12 in 1985. (Exhibit 7 lists the locations in which Sam's Wholesale Clubs operated by the end of 1985.) Although Wal-Mart did not disaggregate its financial data, one analyst pegged Sam's sales at $43 million in 1983, $222 million in 1984, and $777 million in 1985; the corresponding estimates of pretax income were $0.3 million, $5.7 million, and $26.0 million.[10] In 1985, Sam's had lowered Wal-Mart's gross margin by 1.0 percent of sales and its selling, general, and administrative expenses by 0.6 percent. In 1986 Wal-Mart expected to add another 18 warehouses to Sam's network.

Sam's mix differed from the mix in Wal-Mart's discount stores, and it bought its merchandise independently of them. Wal-Mart spokespeople acknowledged that they had built up Sam's in the image of the Price Company. They were quick to point out, however, that Sam's did have several distinctive features. It leased its warehouses, trimming the initial investment in each by about $4 million, emphasized soft goods, had begun to promote itself by mailing seasonal flyers to members, and was broadening its base by offering memberships to all Wal-Mart stockholders. Wal-Mart also claimed that because of the company's discounting experience, Sam's was more viable in smaller areas than competing warehouse clubs: as evidence, it cited 1986 openings in Greenville, South Carolina (with a population of 125,000), and Jackson, Mississippi (with a population of 175,000). In mid-1986 management reported that in the three markets in which Sam's operated side-by-side with Wal-Mart discount stores, operating results had been above average because of greater customer traffic.

By 1985 Sam's had built up a broader national presence than any of its competitors, including the Price Company—which was still concentrated in California and Arizona. Analysts projected that Sam's locations would expand to 100 by 1990, its revenues to $6.5 billion, and its pretax income to $260 million.

---

[9] Joseph H. Ellis, "The Warehouse Club Industry: An Update, " Goldman, Sachs, January 17, 1985.

[10] Joseph H. Ellis, "Wal-Mart: Updated Statistics and Projections," Goldman, Sachs, March 21, 1986.

EXHIBIT 1
CORPORATE HISTORY
Dollars in Millions

	1976	1977	1978	1979	1980	1981	1982	1983	1984	1985
Operating flows:										
Net sales	$479	$678	$900	$1,248	$1,643	$2,445	$3,376	$4,667	$6,401	$8,451
License fees and other income	5	8	10	10	12	18	22	36	52	55
Cost of goods sold	353	504	661	919	1,208	1,787	2,458	3,418	4,722	6,361
Operating, selling, general, and administrative expenses	95	135	182	252	332	495	677	893	1,181	1,485
Interest cost	5	7	10	13	17	31	39	35	48	57
Taxes	15	20	27	33	44	66	100	161	231	276
Net income	16	21	29	41	56	83	124	196	271	327
Balances:										
Current assets	99	151	192	267	345	589	721	1,006	1,303	1,784
Property, plant, equipment, and capital leases	68	101	131	191	246	333	458	628	870	1,303
Current liabilities	43	75	99	170	178	340	347	503	689	993
Long-term debt	19	21	26	25	30	105	106	41	41	181
Long-term obligations under capital leases	41	59	72	97	135	154	223	340	450	595
Common shareholders' equity	$ 64	$ 96	$127	$ 165	$ 248	$ 324	$ 488	$ 738	$ 985	$1,278
Number of stores at end of period:										
Discount stores	153	195	229	275	330	491	551	642	745	859
Sam's Wholesale Clubs	0	0	0	0	0	0	0	3	11	23

Note: Numbers may not add due to rounding, deferred income taxes, etc.
Source: Annual reports.

EXHIBIT 2
FINANCIAL PERFORMANCE OF SELECTED DISCOUNTERS, 1974–1984 (%)

	Return on Equity	*Sales Growth*	*Earnings-per-Share Growth*
Dayton-Hudson	20.6%	17.0%	18.8%
Heck's	14.1	11.7	NM*
K mart	15.9	14.3	13.9
Rose's Stores	14.1	11.2	22.5
Wal-Mart	33.0	40.3	38.8
Zayre	13.1%	11.5%	21.2%

*NM indicates *not meaningful.*
Source: *Forbes.*

EXHIBIT 3
THE INDUSTRYWIDE ECONOMICS OF DISCOUNTING IN 1984
Percent of Net Sales

Net sales	100.0%
License fees and other income	1.1
Cost of goods sold	71.9
Payroll expense	11.2
Advertising expense	2.3
Rental expense	2.2
Miscellaneous expense	7.6
Operating income	5.9
Net income	2.7%

Source: *Operating Results of Self-Service Discount Department Stores* (National Mass Retailing Institute, August 1985).

EXHIBIT 4
GEOGRAPHIC DISTRIBUTION OF WAL-MART'S DISCOUNT STORES AT YEAR-END, 1976–1985

State	*1976*	*1977*	*1978*	*1979*	*1980*	*1981*	*1982*	*1983*	*1984*	*1985*	*Percent of Total Discount Stores (1985)*
Alabama	0	0	0	1	9	37	40	42	47	51	23%
Arkansas	47	50	54	57	64	69	70	71	70	71	45
Colorado	0	0	0	0	0	0	0	0	0	2	2
Florida	0	0	0	0	0	0	1	8	23	37	9
Georgia	0	0	0	0	0	6	7	16	28	39	17
Illinois	0	6	11	16	20	24	30	33	37	47	12
Indiana	0	0	0	0	0	0	0	1	2	6	2
Iowa	0	0	0	0	0	0	0	2	6	13	8
Kansas	7	8	9	10	16	19	20	24	28	31	21
Kentucky	2	2	3	4	7	28	28	35	40	43	22
Louisiana	4	6	6	7	12	20	26	43	44	49	22
Mississippi	7	12	13	18	20	25	27	28	28	34	27
Missouri	44	57	61	64	71	76	78	79	82	90	40
Nebraska	0	0	0	0	0	0	1	1	4	8	9
New Mexico	0	0	0	0	0	0	0	1	2	11	17
North Carolina	0	0	0	0	0	0	0	1	1	1	0
Oklahoma	29	34	42	46	48	56	59	66	69	71	36
South Carolina	0	0	0	0	0	18	18	18	23	25	19
Tennessee	7	10	10	17	18	54	56	59	67	67	30
Texas	6	10	20	36	45	59	90	114	143	160	27
Virginia	0	0	0	0	0	0	0	0	1	1	1
Wisconsin	0	0	0	0	0	0	0	0	0	2	2
Total	153	195	229	276	330	491	551	642	745	859	18%

Source: Annual reports.

EXHIBIT 5
WAL-MART'S DISCOUNTING NETWORK AT END OF 1985

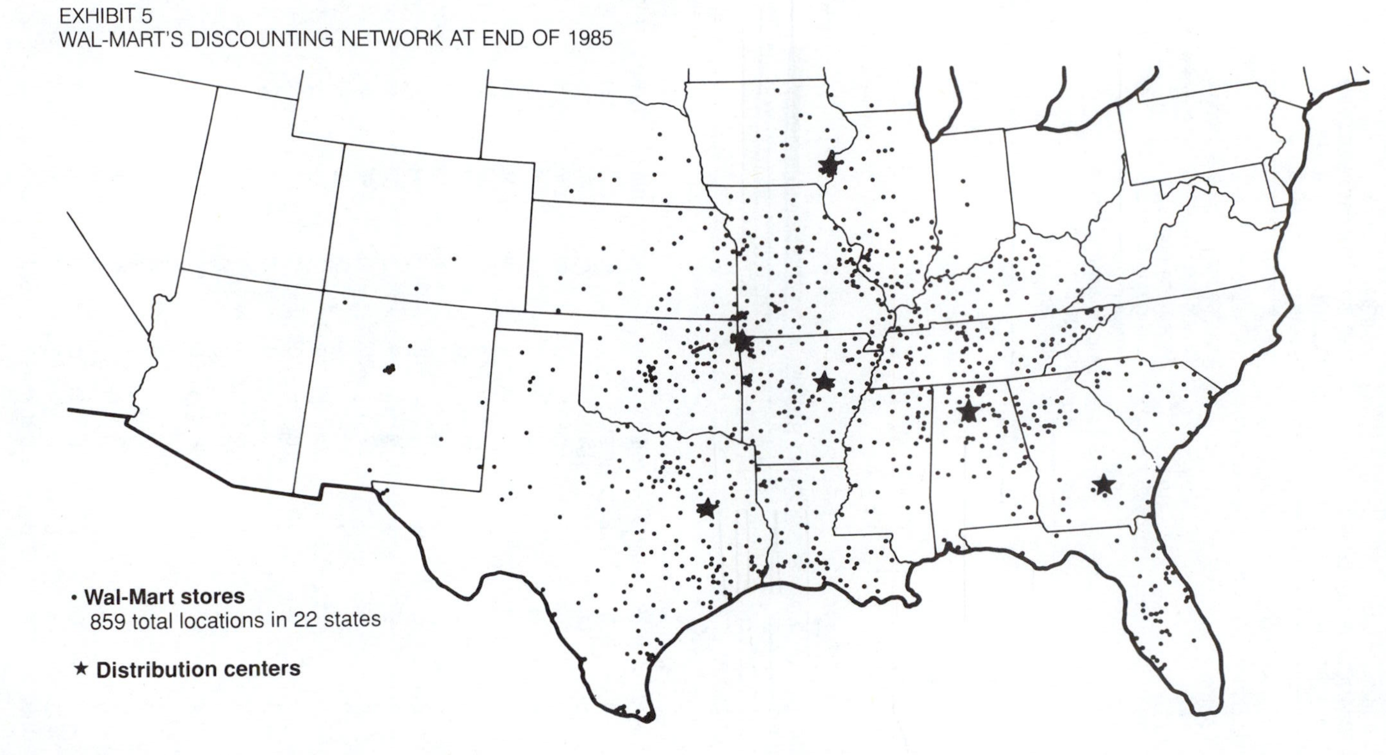

Source: Annual reports.

EXHIBIT 6
LAYOUT OF A LARGE WAL-MART STORE IN FESTUS, MISSOURI

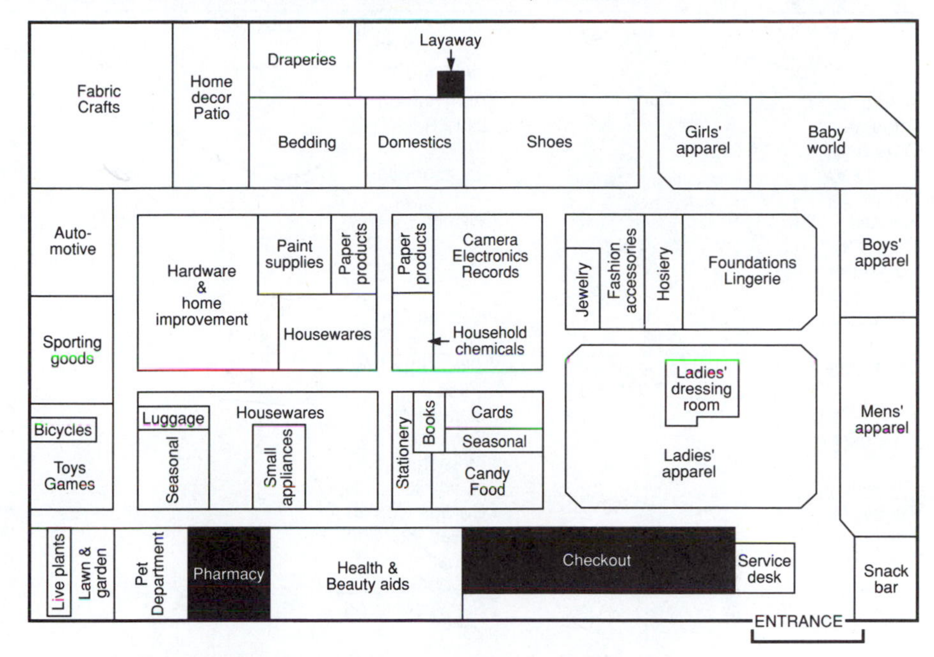

Note: Size of store is 85,000 square feet.
Source: *Discount Store News,* December 9, 1985.

EXHIBIT 7
LOCATIONS OF SAM'S WHOLESALE CLUBS

	Locations in December 1985	*Additional Leases for 1986*
Alabama	Birmingham	–
Arkansas	Little Rock	–
Colorado	–	Colorado Springs
Florida	Jacksonville	Orlando
Illinois	–	East St. Louis
Kansas	Wichita	–
Kentucky	–	Louisville
Louisiana	–	New Orleans (2)
Mississippi	–	Jackson
Missouri	Kansas City	–
	St. Louis	–
Oklahoma	Oklahoma City	Oklahoma City
	Tulsa	–
South Carolina	Charleston	Greenville
Tennessee	Knoxville	Memphis
	Memphis	Nashville
	Nashville	–
Texas	Corpus Christi	Amarillo
	Dallas–Ft. Worth (4)	Dallas
	Houston (3)	El Paso
	Lubbock	Houston (2)
	San Antonio (2)	Waco
Total	23	17

Source: Annual reports.

Note on the Paper Machinery Industry

The 1970s was a decade of unusually traumatic change for companies engaged in building the large and expensive machines used to make paper and board. Along with their customers, the paper manufacturers, these companies had been severely affected by three important changes that had occurred in the global economic, political, and social environment during the decade—the dramatic oil price increases of 1973 and 1979, the widely fluctuating but generally increasing interest rates, and the tightening regulations on industrial pollution.

Partly as a result of these environmental discontinuities, and partly because of other unrelated developments, the structure of the paper machinery industry worldwide and the nature of competitive interaction changed quite dramatically in the 1970s. By 1980 companies in this industry were faced with quite a different set of opportunities and threats than existed a decade previously.

Harvard Business School case 383–185.

To provide some understanding of the important issues facing paper machine manufacturers, this note first provides background information on the market they served, the paper industry, particularly focusing on factors affecting the capital investment decisions critical to machine manufacturers. The note, then, describes the major competitors vying for this business, and outlines their recent strategy.

In a companion case, Dominion Engineering Works (383–184), the strategic choices facing one company are examined in detail.

PAPER MANUFACTURING

The fate of paper machine builders was inextricably linked to the health of their customers, the paper manufacturers. By 1980 most developed and developing countries had established national paper industries, but the largest and most efficient by far was the North American industry, which accounted for more than 40 percent of the total global production of 190 million tons. (See Exhibit 1.) The

U.S. industry had, to its advantage, that country's large, well-managed forest reserves as well as a per capita consumption rate (274 kgs.), twice that of Japan (140 kgs.), two and a half times that of Western Europe (110 kgs.), and over 10 times that of most developing countries. And Canada's vast spruce forests and lower cost energy sources resulted in cost advantages that enabled it to supply even the competitive U.S. market with two thirds of its newsprint needs.

The paper industry on the whole was quite mature at this time, though growth spurts were experienced now and then in various parts of the world, often in response to government-initiated policies aimed at developing a domestic industry to reduce dependence on paper imports. In the late 1960s, for example, Japan's paper industry was expanding, with government support, at an annual rate of 8 to 10 percent. By 1974, however, rising oil prices had put a lid on further expansion in that country. In the mid- and late 1970s the major growth areas were Latin America and Asia, where government sponsorship and the use of new pulping materials such as bamboo and sugarcane encouraged important new development. Worldwide, though, the annual growth rate of the industry had decreased from 5.8 percent in the late 1960s to 2.6 percent in the late 1970s. In large part this was due to the negligible growth taking place in the large industrial markets of Europe and North America.

If growth was slow, it was also highly cyclical. In the recession of the mid-1970s, for example, paper consumption in most developed countries dropped dramatically. Papermaking is an energy-intensive industry, and the oil price increases of 1973 encouraged extensive stockpiling by customers hoping to beat the expected rise in the cost of paper. Following 1974's sharp increases, demand dropped precipitously in 1975. The deepening recession encouraged users to reduce bloated inventories, cut waste, and find substitutes for increasingly expensive paper products. In Western Europe, total consumption dropped from 40 million tons in 1974 to 29.8 million tons in 1975. In the United States consumption fell from 65 million tons in 1974 to 56 million tons in 1975.

Such sudden and extreme drops could be devastating in an industry such as papermaking. With an average of 5.6 percent of current U.S. sales revenues going into new investment (a rate second only to that of the large chemical companies), papermaking was a highly capital-intensive business. One industry expert claimed that a drop in operating rates below 91 percent of capacity could cause prices to go "soft"; only at 94 percent of capacity would price increases hold. The U.S. paper industry had sunk below the soft level in 1967, 1971–72, and 1975–77, although by 1978 and 1979 it was again operating at 91–92 percent of capacity. The Western European industry, however, was down to 82 percent of capacity by the end of the 70s, and industry spokesmen claimed there was surplus capacity sufficient to meet demand forecasts through 1990.

In addition to their surplus capacity, most of the non-Scandinavian countries of Western Europe faced another problem. Although scale economies had become increasingly important in the paper industry, Italy, Spain, Portugal, and France still operated a large number of small machines. While machine size varies with product (newsprint machines, for example, are typically larger than tissue machines), the smallness of the European machine population is striking (see Exhibit 2).

In the industry downturn of the mid-1970s, as in previous downturns, capacity shutdowns and consolidations were widespread, especially in North America. In Europe many of the smaller machines were shut down, though others were kept operative through government intervention. In the late 1970s six European governments came to the aid of faltering companies in their countries, providing financing and other means of support. The usual reason given was job protection and reduction of dependence on imports.

While the paper industry was dealing with the problems of slow growth and cyclical demand, it also had to contend with rapid increases in operating costs. Pulp prices in the United States doubled between 1973 and 1978; rapidly rising labor rates reached 20 percent above the average for all manufacturing; and energy costs were soaring. Manufacturers, with their excess capacity, often found it difficult to pass these increases on to customers and, as a consequence, profit margins narrowed substantially in the mid-1970s. The cyclical demand and low margins resulted in industrywide ROI levels that not only fluctuated widely, but were also well below the average for all manufacturers (see Exhibit 3).

One result of these difficult economic conditions was a slight decrease, through exit and consolidation, in the number of companies competing in the industry. By most measures, however, the industry was far from concentrated. More than 500 paper manufacturers competed for a share of the U.S. market, and the top 15 accounted for less than 50 percent of the total capacity. European firms were generally smaller and the industry even less concentrated. Only 3 of the world's 20 largest paper companies were European.

PAPER MACHINE INVESTMENT

Papermaking is a continuous production process which forms and presses pulp fibers into thin sheets. The paper machine is a series of discrete units designed to form a mixture of pulp and water in flat sheets, press out the moisture, dry the sheets, and, in a sense, iron them smooth (see schematic and description of process in the appendix).

The first commercial paper machine was built in England in 1804 by the Fourdrinier brothers, and no fundamental change was made in the technology until the 1960s. At that time, Dominion Engineering Works, in cooperation with the industry-sponsored Pulp and Paper Research Institute of Canada (PPRIC), developed the new twin-wire former, which was faster, more energy efficient, and smaller than the fourdrinier. The twin-wire forming concept represented a fundamental process change which revolutionized the initial part of papermaking by forming the pulp mixture between two wire-mesh screens, which allowed for rapid, controlled drainage. The twin-wire method contributed to better sheet formation, increased uniformity, and improved physical properties.

The various grades of paper on the market in the late 1970s (see Exhibit 4) were produced by the same basic method, but the machines differed in design. A machine designed to produce newsprint could not also produce kraft paper or tissue. Twin-wire machines had been found most suitable for newsprint and tissue production, although a newsprint twin-wire machine was substantially larger than a tissue machine, and had quite different headbox design.

Compounding the paper industry's profit problems of the 1970s was the sudden and dramatic increase in the cost of this machinery. The higher costs largely reflected the need for new, more sophisticated designs, and more expensive materials in response to the industry's changing environment. First, as previously noted, papermaking was a highly energy-intensive process, particularly in the pressing and drying operations (it took six to eight barrels of oil to produce each ton of paper). As a result, when oil prices skyrocketed in 1973, paper machines had to be drastically redesigned to improve their energy efficiency.

Second, due to the large amount of chemical waste produced by the pulping process, paper manufacturers had become a major target of the environmental movement, and 10 to 16 percent of the industry's capital investment in the years 1973 to 1980 went into improvements aimed at protecting the environment. New machines had to be designed as closed systems that recycled polluting chemicals. Not only did this require new basic designs, but also the use of more expensive corrosion-resistant materials, particularly stainless steel.

By 1979 a paper machine like the one illustrated in the appendix might cost between $15 and $20 million—three times the cost of a similar capacity machine in 1973. A greenfield investment in a fully integrated, large-scale paper mill as of 1979 would cost over $250 million.

In response to these and other cost increases in the late 1970s, more and more companies began rebuilding their existing machines instead of purchasing new ones. Since a complete rebuild might cost less than half the price of a new machine, machines 50 and 60 years old were being rebuilt rather than scrapped.[1] In 1966–70 rebuilding accounted for 10 percent of the increases in worldwide capacity; in 1971–75, for more than 20 percent; in 1976–78, for almost 25 percent.

Paper machines had much longer useful life than most industrial machinery. They were installed in excavated beds, and paper mills were literally built around them. The permanence of the investment decision tended to make the industry very conservative, wary of change, and slow to accept new technologies. In 1979 the average age of the paper machines operating in the United States was 25 years; in Canada, 34 years; in Scandinavia, 22 years, and in the EEC, 23 years. The trend toward rebuilding, combined with the environment-related investment of the 1970s and the continuing economic difficulties of the period, had contributed to a decisive drop in the demand for paper machines by the end of the decade. Fewer new machines had been installed, and total new capacity additions decreased substantially. (See Exhibit 5.)

The industry optimistically predicted a reversal of this trend, and in early 1979 announcements of capacity expansion

[1] A typical newsprint machine built in 1930 might have a width of 176 inches and an operating speed of 1,000 feet per minute. By 1980, widths in excess of 300 inches and speeds in excess of 3,000 feet per minute gave the new machines a considerable efficiency advantage. While a rebuild could not change the width, it could increase machine speed and efficiency. Typically (but not always), the rebuild contract was given to the machine's original manufacturer, particularly when good relations had been maintained over the years. Although a rebuild contract generated less revenue than selling a new machine, some suppliers saw it as a way of protecting their installed base of machines, maintaining customer loyalty, and ensuring future parts and service revenues. If a contract went out for a new machine, there was a greater risk that a competitive supplier might be successful.

plans for the 1980s lent some credence to these forecasts. (See Exhibit 6.)

A more detailed forecast of the demand for new machines by country and by product appears as Exhibit 7.

Paper Machine Purchase Decision

Traditionally, a salesman's personal relationship with a purchasing agent, or a paper company's old ties with a particular machine builder, or even the supplier's general industry reputation were of central importance to the paper machine purchase decision. Since there were no great differences between machines in this mature industry, paper companies bought the security of the supplier's continued service and support over the machine's life.

However, in the late 1970s the pressures of increased machinery cost, lowered profitability, and excess capacity in the paper industry soon brought about changes. The decisions began to be made at a higher organization level, the evaluation process was becoming more sophisticated, and the decision criteria were tightening. In all, the process was becoming far more technical, and financial analysis was being accepted as having a more central role in the formal evaluation process.

Typically, the paper company established a purchasing committee of technical and management personnel and, often, of outside experts. This committee then gathered information on all potential suppliers and their machines. Special attention went to the following factors:

Supplier	*Machine*
Reliability in meeting deadlines	Quality of output
Engineering and technical assistance	Machine reliability
After-sales service	Efficiency
Finance terms (interest rate, progress payments)	Price

The weighting of these criteria varied by the type of machine purchased. The decision on a wide-width, high-speed machine using a new type of stock might give more weight to the supplier's ability to provide engineering assistance and after-sales service, while the choice of a low-speed machine to produce a standard product might be made largely on the price of the machine and its efficiency.

The committee went to a variety of sources for its information on potential suppliers. If one of the company's own plants owned a machine of the grade in which they were interested, the committee members would visit the plant to discuss the machine's operating characteristics and talk about the quality of the supplier's service. If the company did not own such a machine, the committee would visit the plant of another manufacturer to gather data. A great deal of information was exchanged within the paper industry, and it was common practice to allow committees from competitive companies to view and discuss machinery. Suppliers, in fact, went to considerable lengths to install good reference machines, knowing that product reputations both good and bad were transmitted rapidly throughout the industry.

COMPETITION

In the 1970s more than 50 companies around the world were manufacturing paper machines. The industry's stable technology had made it possible for any good general engineering shop to build a basic machine. As the technology began to change, however, some shakeout was expected.

Exhibit 8 details the shifting global market shares of the major paper machine manufacturers during the 1960s and the

1970s. Exhibit 9 outlines by country the market share of key companies and includes data on orders in hand at the end of 1979.

A more detailed description of the major players in the worldwide paper machine industry follows.

Beloit

By the 1960s it was clear that Beloit was a leader in the paper machine business. The privately held, family-managed company had been founded in Beloit, Wisconsin, in 1858. In addition to its principal product of paper machines, the company also manufactured pulp-mill and stock-preparation equipment, paper-handling and converting equipment, and processing machinery for food, chemicals, and plastics. In the 1960s the company began to spread its operations abroad, and by 1977 Beloit's worldwide sales were $350 million, its net income was $20 million, and its net worth was $120 million. The company's cash position was very strong indeed.

In 1980 Beloit's worldwide operations included five plants in the United States, manufacturing facilities in the United Kingdom, Brazil, Canada, Spain, and Italy, and licensees in Japan, India, and Poland. The company had done well abroad, managing, for example, to dominate the Canadian market for tissue, fine-paper, and linerboard machines within five years of its entry into that country in 1965. In subsequent years, Beloit also achieved a substantial share of Canada's newsprint machine market and by 1978 was thought to have captured more than 50 percent of that country's total paper machinery market.

The company's president, Harry Moore, was proud of Beloit's worldwide facilities:

> Our round-the-world strength lies in the fact that we now have plants in various places to take advantage of financing and tariff situations in different countries to suit the needs of our customers and of Beloit at the time of an order. The overseas part of our business is growing faster than the domestic and each year we find there is more and more interchange between our various plants, companies, and licensees.

Beloit's leadership position in the world paper machinery industry had been threatened in the 1970s, when the U.S. market slowed down and competition from abroad increased. Between 1970 and 1974, Beloit's share of world capacity installation dropped dramatically. The company reacted by aggressively expanding its facilities. It doubled its capacity in Spain, launched a $20 million expansion of its U.S. facilities, and began studying construction of a plant in Brazil. It maintained its commitment to research and development, adding to its 62,000-square-foot research center at Rockton, Illinois, which included a pilot plant to experiment with a new second generation twin-wire former. Mr. Moore commented on the company's R&D priorities:

> We're getting into more sophisticated forming for secondary fibers and recycled paper. We want our new twin-wire former to be able to make many grades, not just the big bulk grades. We are also working to improve size and width limits.

Beloit's strong technical reputation was reinforced by its commitment to customer service. It had the largest sales force in the industry, with a staff of over 50 in the field and 20 inside to serve the U.S. market. Sales coverage in foreign locations was also strong. In Canada, for example, the company maintained a six-person field sales force. Beloit's sales personnel were regarded as aggressive and competent, and they were well supported by technical backup, financing packages, advertising programs, and a broad line of products.

Voith

Also a force in the industry was another old, established company, J.M. Voith of Heidenheim, Germany. Aftertax profits in a bad year (1977) had been $9.2 million (DM19 million). The family-owned engineering firm had gradually diversified its original paper machine line, which in 1979 accounted for 33 percent of sales, to include driving technology (12 percent), hydropower plants (12 percent), ship's propulsion, machine tools, and plastic processing machines (25 percent).

In the late 1960s Voith realized that relying solely on its German plants was placing the company at a competitive disadvantage, and that the time had come to look abroad. In the mid-1970s, responding to a national effort to build an efficient paper industry, Voith built a plant in Brazil that was generally regarded as the world's most modern and efficient. The Brazilian government responded by closing its borders to competitive imported equipment for five years and providing the company with access to its generous export financing. Soon after, Voith began shipping machines from Brazil to other Latin American countries and the United States.

In 1974 Voith acquired Morden Machines, an Oregon company selling paper-stock-preparation equipment, and also set up a 50 percent joint venture with another American firm, Allis-Chalmers. Within four years Voith had bought out its partner and constructed a new manufacturing plant in Appleton, Wisconsin. By 1978 the company had established subsidiary operations in four European countries, the United States, India, Japan, and Brazil. Of its 1977 sales of $485 million (DM1 billion), two thirds were for markets outside of Germany.

The company's commitment to research and development was strong, and the research center at Heidenheim was large and well equipped. Of special interest was the field of nonwood fibers, which were gaining in importance as the paper industry spread into new countries. "We now have twin-wire machines," the company's R&D director said, "that can make various grades of paper from bagasse (sugarcane pulp), eucalyptus, grass, reed, and straw pulp. This technology has enabled us to provide turnkey paper mills in Sri Lanka, China, India, and Iran." The company's technology gave it a broad product line of machines catering to all segments of the industry.

The company maintained joint projects with three major paper mills and cooperative research efforts at universities in Germany, France, Brazil, and Sweden. About 5 percent of the sales revenues on their paper machines was going into R&D. The research staff numbered 75, of whom 25 were engineers and scientists.

Voith's sales force was generally well regarded, although some U.S. customers had complained of the German company's reluctance to adapt to the method of local industry. Nevertheless, the company won three major machine orders after its break with Allis-Chalmers, two in 1977 and another in 1978, which gave Voith an estimated 10 percent share of the U.S. market. The machines were sourced from Germany, Brazil, and the new Wisconsin plant, respectively.

TVW (The Finnish Consortium)

With encouragement from their government, the three Finnish companies of Tampella, Valmet, and Wartsila combined their overseas paper machinery operations in 1976. They continued to operate independently on the domestic scene but overseas were jointly represented in manufacturing subsidiaries, sales companies, agents, and licensees.

Tampella, one of Finland's largest fully integrated forest products companies, was particularly well known in the paper machinery industry for its board and heavy-grade paper machines and its stock preparation equipment. Tampella's total sales in 1979 were $330 million, with aftertax profits at $1.4 million. Paper machinery accounted for about 17 percent of total sales.

Valmet was a diversified engineering and machinery company established by the Finnish government in the 1920s. Its current shareholders were the Finnish State, the Bank of Finland, and the Social Insurance Institution. Consolidated sales for 1979 were $1.1 billion of which $250 million was for paper machinery. Total aftertax profits were $8 million. The paper machine group was known for its medium- and fine-grade paper machines and driers, and was believed to be operating at full capacity in 1980. Its paper machine order book reportedly had $500 million in outstanding orders.

Wartsila was another diversified engineering company with a specialty in paper finishing machines such as winders, coaters, and roll wrappers. Wartsila had been taking some heavy losses in its Shipbuilding Division, and in 1979 reported a $12 million loss on total sales of $480 million. Paper machinery accounted for about 15 percent of sales and was thought to be quite profitable.

All three companies were aggressive competitors. Faced with slowing domestic demand in the late 60s, they began separately to expand their sales bases and soon garnered 30 percent of the Western European market and 20 percent of the Eastern bloc. They then turned toward the United States and by the mid-70s had placed 13 machines in that country. Breaking with industry tradition, they guaranteed not only their machines' technical specifications, but also performance capabilities such as daily tonnage. Other companies were forced to follow suit. Even the fact that their machines were all built in Finland, with its higher labor costs, did not seem to place these companies at a disadvantage. In fact, they often quoted prices 10 to 20 percent below their U.S. counterparts, a practice that led to speculation by some U.S. competitors that their government was supporting them. At one point, a dumping case was brought against Valmet by the American company, Beloit.

When they combined their foreign efforts, the three Finnish companies improved sales remarkably. After selling only 31 machines in the previous five years, the 1976–80 period saw sales of 52 machines around the world. The complementary product lines of the three companies made it possible for TVW to offer turnkey projects and a very broad product line backed by cooperative technology. And the Finnish Export Credit Association made it possible for TVW to provide attractive financing. In 1980 they offered 9 percent loans for seven years, with the first repayment due six months after order rather than immediately, as was customary in the industry.

Through most of the 1970s the Finns seemed more interested in setting up sales companies in the United States than in building manufacturing plants in foreign countries. (In the United States TVW acquired the Madden Machine Co.) Toward the end of the decade, however, this situation was beginning to change. In a 1978 interview for a trade magazine, Valmet's president noted:

> Local manufacturing facilities are an obvious need today in most marketing areas, and we are studying the possibility of starting manufacturing in several countries, including Brazil. . . . As machine rebuilds become more important, customers will demand shorter delivery times than for new machines. We are investigating manufacturing facilities in the United States or Canada to meet that need.

TVW's cooperative approach to R&D also gave them a major advantage. They had a broad, well-engineered product line including a twin-wire machine developed in the early 1970s. A twin-wire pilot machine (located in one of TVW's four pilot plants) was rebuilt in late 1977 to allow it to run with a wide range of pulp furnishes including Argentine willow, Turkish pine, rice straw, and waste paper.

Black Clawson

Black Clawson was one of the two dominant full-line paper machine companies in the United States in the 1960s, with an estimated 25 percent of the domestic market and 15 percent of the installed capacity worldwide. By the late 1970s, however, the company's paper machine business appeared to have lost much of its drive and focus, and its global market share dropped to 2 percent. Sales in 1978 were at $85 million and profits $3 million.

This was a private company, with subsidiaries in Canada, Europe, and South America. In addition to paper machines the company produced pulping equipment, paper coaters and converters, and lumber machinery. Manufacturing plants were located in the United States as well as in Canada, the United Kingdom, France, and Brazil.

The company's principal customer was Parson and Whitmore, another company held by Black Clawson's owners. Parson and Whitmore, whose annual sales were in excess of $250 million, owned and operated paper mills and also built them on a turnkey basis.

While Black Clawson, like other industry leaders, had developed a twin-wire former, the company's R&D had been cut back in the 1970s and concentrated more on technology related to pulp and stock preparation. In 1979, however, the company's labs announced that they were turning their attention to a "fourth generation twin-wire former rated at production speeds of up to 4,000 fpm that would be suitable for making quality printing paper."

KMW (Swedish Company)

The Swedish company, Karlstads Mekaniska Werkstad (KMW), had been a major supplier to its nation's pulp and paper manufacturers since the late 19th century. The company also built water turbines and marine propellers, but two thirds of its $100 million sales in 1978 involved paper machines.

In the late 60s the company had received a major boost when, because of some patents it held, it was able to extract from the Canadian Pulp and Paper Research Institute a license to manufacture the twin-wire former PPRIC had designed for newsprint production. KMW then adapted the twin-wire technology for tissue. The company entered the U.S. market in the late 1960s and, although its aggressive pricing resulted in a dumping suit in 1972, it had received orders for 11 of its twin-wire machines by 1976.

However, KMW had continued to generate losses for two reasons. First, the company's manufacturing plants were confined to Sweden, and second, the company was putting as much as 5 percent of sales into R&D. With its U.S. success, KMW decided to go abroad with a complete sales, servicing, and manufacturing company. In 1976 an American subsidiary was established with senior managers lured from the industry's top companies, including Beloit and Dominion, and a 12-person sales force.

By 1977 KMW had completed a manufacturing facility in North Carolina, but most of the company's research was still carried out in Sweden. Tissue machines were KMW's specialty, and by the late 70s the company had established itself as a dominant supplier of this product segment.

Dominion Engineering Works

Blessed with vast forests, cheap hydropower, and the huge U.S. market at its doorstep, the Canadian paper industry boomed in postwar years. Since 1920, this industry's main machine supplier had been Dominion Engineering Works (DEW), one of Canada's largest industrial equipment builders. DEW built paper machines along with mining equipment, hydroturbines, and rolling mills in its large, general-purpose engineering shop near Montreal.

A few years after its acquisition by General Electric's Canadian subsidiary in 1962, DEW began to experience stiff competition on paper machine bids from Beloit, and later from other non-Canadian machine companies. Fortunately, DEW had cooperated on the development of the twin-wire former, a breakthrough technology sponsored by the government- and industry-sponsored research group, PPRIC. By the early 1970s, this innovation was helping DEW to win back market share lost to the foreign competition.

However, a severe downturn hit the Canadian paper industry in the mid-70s and forced the company to cut back its operations severely. Being part of GE's Canadian subsidiary, DEW's attention had been devoted almost entirely to developing the Canadian market, and even the sales of its two overseas licensees did little to offset the loss of volume in the Canadian market.

With investment incentives from the government, the Canadian paper industry began its recovery in 1978. However, DEW faced a major organization and market rebuilding job if it was to regain its previous 50 percent share of the Canadian market.

Japanese Manufacturers

When, with government encouragement, the Japanese paper industry began to boom in the late 1960s, Western manufacturers rushed to participate in the expansion, appointing local heavy engineering companies as their licensees. The access to technology provided by this arrangement allowed these licensees to dominate the booming Japanese market in the early 1970s.

Beloit's licensee captured almost 40 percent of the market, followed by Black Clawson's licensee and that of Ahlstrom, a Finnish manufacturer. Dominion's and TVW's licensees took smaller shares. Voith, which had sold four machines into Japan in the 70s, was building its own plant there. Twenty other unaffiliated Japanese companies also competed in this industry.

Most Japanese manufacturers were adversely affected when expansion of the paper industry in Japan abruptly slowed down with the double impact of oil price increases and changing government priorities. Capacity installed in the last half of the decade was less than a third of that brought onstream in the boom years 1970–75. As a result, the splintered Japanese companies seemed to be fading from the competitive scene, at least temporarily.

FUTURE INDUSTRY OUTLOOK

Although industry forecasts in 1980 indicated that the recent increase in new machine orders would continue well into the new decade, some experienced managers were skeptical. But regardless of their views of the strength and duration of the recovery, most observers recognized that the basic industry structure and the nature of competition had been permanently changed by the events of the 1970s, and that many of the old industry assumptions and previous strategic approaches would have to change in the 1980s.

EXHIBIT 1
WORLD PAPER CAPACITY, 1979

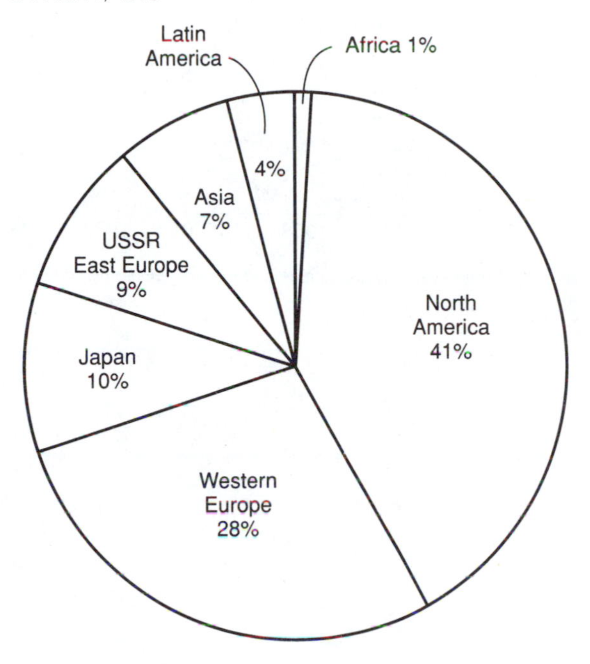

EXHIBIT 2
PAPER MACHINE POPULATION, 1979

	Number of Paper Machines	Average Size (Tons p.a.)	Over 100,000 Tons p.a.
United States	1,800 (combined)	41,000	40%
Canada		52,000	30
Scandinavian countries	400	40,000	50
EEC	2,260	13,000	10

EXHIBIT 3
RETURN ON INVESTMENT IN U.S. PAPER INDUSTRY, 1960–1976

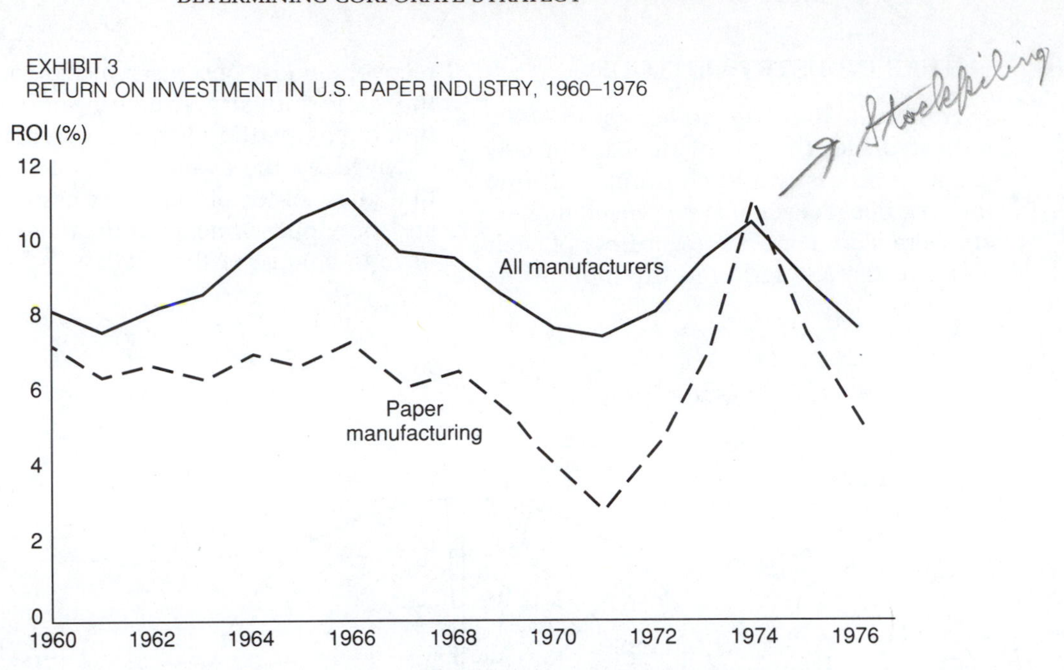

Source: Federal Trade Commission and Securities and Exchange Commission data.

EXHIBIT 4
WORLD PAPER CAPACITY, 1979 PRODUCT SEGMENTS

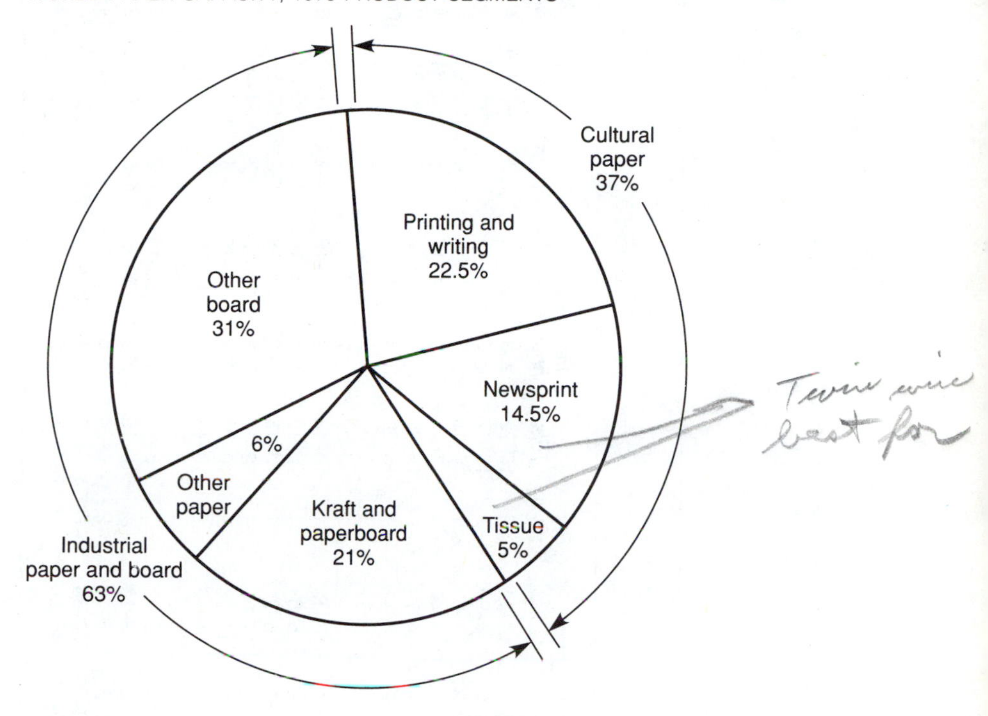

EXHIBIT 5
EXPANSION OF GLOBAL CAPACITY, 1965–1978

	Number of New Machines		*New Capacity Installed (million tons)*	
Period	*Total*	*Per Annum*	*Total*	*Per Annum*
1965–69	800	160	27.3	5.5
1970–74	588	117	23.4	4.7
1975–78	307	77	14.5	3.6

EXHIBIT 6
FORECASTS OF EXPANSION IN CAPACITY, 1979–1990

			New Capacity (million tons)		
Period	*Total Capacity to Be Built (million tons)*	*Rebuilds*	*Total*	*Per Annum*	*Announced Expansion (1979)*
1979–85	50.8	16.0	34.8	5.0	27.0
1986–90	38.6	11.5	27.1	5.4	10.8

EXHIBIT 7
DEMAND FORECASTS FOR NEW PAPER MACHINES, 1979–1985 AND 1986–1990

		Newsprint		Printing and Writing		Tissue		Kraft Paper and Paperboard		Other Paper		Other Board		Total	
		Total	Per Annum	Total	Per Annum	Total	Per Annum	Total	Per Annum	Total	Per Annum	Total	Per Annum	Total	Per Annum
North	1979–85	8–9	1	15–17	2	22–25	3–4	12–14	2	18–22	2–3	21–23	3	96–110	14–16
America	1986–90	4–5	1	10–11	2	10–11	2	8–9	1–2	13–17	2–3	12–15	2–3	57–68	11–14
Western	1979–85	6–7	1	20–21	3	15–18	2–3	4–6	<1	10–15	1–2	25–30	3–4	80–97	11–14
Europe	1986–90	2–3	<1	15–18	3	12–13	2	3–4	<1	7–9	1–2	14–17	3	53–64	11–13
Japan	1979–85	4–5	<1	14–15	2	14–17	2–3	4–7	0–1	15–20	2–3	15–17	2	66–81	9–12
	1986–90	1–2	<1	10–14	2–3	9–10	2	3–4	<1	15–20	3–4	10–11	2	48–61	10–12
Oceania	1979–85	1–2	<1	1–2	1	0–1	1	0–1	<1	1–3	1	0–2	<1	3–11	0–2
	1986–90	1	<1	2–3	<1	0–1	<1	0–1	<1	0–2	<1	1–2	<1	4–10	1–2
Soviet	1979–85	2–3	<1	6–7	1	5–9	1	7–10	1	10–14	1–2	11–16	1–2	41–59	6–8
Union	1986–90	2–3	<1	5–6	1	10–12	2	5–6	1	6–10	1–2	8–10	1–2	36–47	7–9
Eastern	1979–85	1–2	<1	3–4	1	5–7	1	5–9	1	10–15	1–2	14–18	2	38–55	5–8
Europe	1986–90	1–2	<1	3–4	<1	4–6	1	4–6	1	12–17	2–3	10–13	3	34–48	7–10
Asia	1979–85	9–11	1–2	38–39	5	13–15	2	16–20	2–3	16–20	2–3	30–36	4–5	122–141	17–20
	1986–90	5–6	1	22–24	4–5	6–8	1	11–12	2	10–13	2–3	16–20	3–4	70–83	14–17
Africa	1979–85	4–5	<1	4–5	<1	3–4	1	5–6	<1	5–7	<1	8–12	1–2	29–39	4–6
	1986–90	2–3	<1	4–5	1	2–3	<1	3–4	1	5–8	1–2	7–10	1–2	23–33	4–7
Latin	1979–85	7–8	1	17–18	2	15–17	2	9–13	1–2	10–15	1–2	28–32	4–5	86–103	12–15
America	1986–90	4–5	1	17–18	3	9–10	2	9–10	2	16–24	3–5	16–19	3–4	71–86	14–17
Total	1979–85	42–52	6–7	118–128	16–18	92–113	13–16	62–86	9–12	95–131	14–19	152–186	21–26	561–696	78–101
Total	1986–90	22–30	4–6	88–103	18–21	62–74	12–15	46–56	9–11	84–120	17–24	94–117	19–23	396–500	79–101

Source: Jaakko Poyry (forecasting and consulting firm specializing in the paper industry).

EXHIBIT 8
MARKET SHARES OF MAJOR PAPER MACHINE SUPPLIERS IN THE WORLD, 1965–1978

	1965–1969		*1970–1974*		*1975–1978*	
Supplier	*Capacity (% total tonnage)*	*Numbers (% total machines)*	*Capacity (% total tonnage)*	*Numbers (% total machines)*	*Capacity (% total tonnage)*	*Numbers (% total machines)*
Beloit group	30%	16%	16.1%	10.9%	25.2%	14.7%
Japanese manufacturers	7	6	19.3	15.0	11.5	10.4
TVW group	11	3	15.5	5.6	11.6	4.6
Voith group	5	6	9.08	8.0	12.6	13.0
Black Clawson	12	7	6.3	3.7	2.4	2.3
KMW	2	1	4.6	1.5	2.5	1.0
Escher-Wyss	2	3	2.8	3.7	4.1	4.2
Soviet manufacturers	—	—	3.0	3.1	2.5	3.3
Dominion	3	1	2.1	0.9	2.6	1.0
Over Meccanica (DEW licensee)	1	2	0.8	3.2	2.7	4.2
Fampa	1	1	1.6	1.7	1.6	2.3
Er-We-Pa	1	2	1.5	1.5	0.8	1.0
Allis-Chalmers	2	1	—	—	2.3	0.7
Carcano	1	3	—	0.2	2.3	2.3
Manchester Machine	—	—	0.5	0.7	1.6	1.0
Bruderhaus	—	1	0.9	1.5	0.8	1.6
Subtotal	78	53	84.0	61.2	87.1	67.6
Others	22	47	5.7	12.9	5.2	14.5
Not known			10.3	25.9	7.7	17.9
Total	100%	100%	100.0%	100.0%	100.0%	100.0%
	27.3 million tons	800 machines	23.4 million tons	588 machines	14.5 million tons	307 machines

Ranked according to the capacity installed in 1970–1978.

EXHIBIT 9
WORLD MARKET SHARE (%) BASED ON INSTALLED CAPACITY (HISTORICAL) AND ORDERED CAPACITY AS OF END 1979

	Beloit			*Voith*			*TVW*			*KMW*		
	1970–74	*1975–78*	*Orders**	*1970–74*	*1975–78*	*Orders**	*1970–74*	*1975–78*	*Orders**	*1970–74*	*1975–78*	*Orders**
North America	28.3	45.6	49.2	—	4.3	7.0	20.8	11.7	38.0	12.0	5.9	1.0
Europe	19.2	15.9	11.2	17.6	16.1	32.3	27.0	25.7	42.0	5.0	2.9	9.6
Japan	—	—	—	4.1	16.3	—	1.5	—	—	1.5	—	—
Oceania	38.5	63.6	—	—	22.7	—	—	—	100.0	—	—	—
Comecon	13.4	20.8	19.1	5.7	8.6	13.0	17.5	6.1	5.7	4.2	—	—
Asia	8.0	7.5	8.5	1.8	4.5	18.9	—	—	15.7	—	—	2.7
Africa	40.5	60.4	21.7	—	—	—	—	—	—	—	—	—
Latin America	11.6	17.4	17.0	30.7	33.0	46.8	3.6	7.0	10.0	—	—	—

	DEW			*Black Clawson*			*Japanese*		
	1970–74	*1975–78*	*Orders**	*1970–74*	*1975–78*	*Orders**	*1970–74*	*1975–78*	*Orders**
North America	5.9	6.5	2.9	16.8	1.9	—	2.7	1.4	—
Europe	2.3	2.7	—	.6	1.0	—	—	—	—
Japan	0.5	—	—	2.2	—	—	77.9	75.9	63.3
Oceania	—	—	—	45.6	—	—	15.9	13.6	—
Comecon	—	—	—	—	—	—	—	15.4	—
Asia	—	—	—	—	14.1	4.2	34.3	13.9	6.4
Africa	—	—	—	11.1	14.9	20.5	—	—	24.5
Latin America	—	—	—	21.3	5.2	4.8	3.7	0.27	—

*Orders on hand (end 1979) for period 1980+.

APPENDIX

PAPERMAKING

Papermaking is a continuous production process which forms and presses wood and other pulps into thin sheets. First the pulp is prepared in large tubs where the fibers are cut, beaten, and refined. Various chemicals are then added to impart specific characteristics to the end product, and the prepared stock—about .5 percent fiber and 99.5 percent water—flows into the paper machine.

Forming

The forming section is the first in the series of discrete units that make up the paper machine. Here the pulp mixture is spread into an even sheet of desired thickness and some of the water is removed.

In the late 1970s the three basic types of forming units in use differed from one another in the methods employed to form the fiber web and to drain off the water:

In the *fourdrinier,* the most common type of former, the pulp mixture was pumped into a headbox and then out through a narrow opening (the "slice") onto a wide, flat belt of fine mesh screen. As the wire carried the stock along, water was removed by spinning rolls which created a vacuum under the screen, by a series of flat suction boxes also located under the screen, and by a perforated suction roll called the "couch" roll.

The *cylinder* former differed from the fourdrinier primarily in that the headbox, wire, and underlying forming table were replaced by a wire-covered cylinder partially immersed in prepared stock. A vacuum was maintained from inside the cylinder, and as the cylinder revolved the sheet was formed on the screen and the water was drained off. The cylinder was particularly useful in producing multilayered products, as a number of cylinders could be employed simultaneously, using different stock for each.

The *twin-wire* former, pictured below, produced a sheet between two wire-screen belts, with the advantage of rapid, controlled drainage. This contributed to better sheet formation, greater uniformity, and improved physical properties. The twin-wire former was capable of higher speeds, was more energy efficient, and was smaller by half than the fourdrinier.

Pressing

After leaving the last roller of the forming section, the sheet, still very wet and easily damaged, left the wire and was transferred to the press section. Here the moisture content was further reduced, to about 65 percent, while the sheet of paper was cushioned and protected by felts of high-quality wool. The sheet then passed into the drying section.

Drying

In the drying section, steam heat reduced the remaining moisture content to 4–7 percent of the final product. To strengthen the paper, starch might be added as the sheet passed through the dryer.

Calendering

The sheet then passed through a series of cast-iron calender rolls to improve smoothness and gloss. The calendered paper was then slit, reeled to desired widths, trimmed, inspected, and packaged.

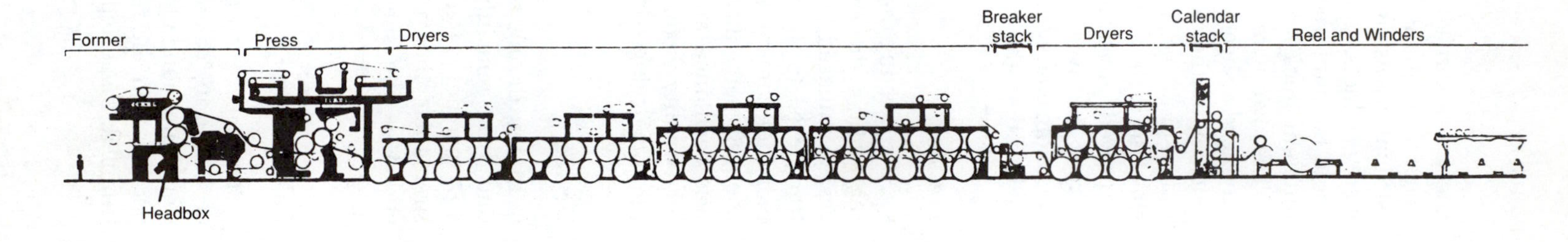

TYPICAL COST: PAPRIFORMER NEWSPRINT MACHINE
In Millions of Dollars

Headbox	$1.3	Calender	1.8
Twin-wire former	3.2	Reel	0.6
Press	3.2	Winder	1.0
Dryer	6.3	Controls	0.6
		Total	$18.0

Dominion Engineering Works

During the summer of 1980 Walter Fell, newly appointed general manager of the Canadian firm, Dominion Engineering Works (DEW), considered the prospects of his company's paper machine operation. Accounting for 16 percent of DEW's sales, paper machinery was one of DEW's major businesses. Although he was impressed by the revival of DEW's paper machine business over the last couple of years, Mr. Fell was aware that DEW faced some serious competition from a number of larger firms that were expanding rapidly worldwide.

Historically, the company's paper machinery efforts had been limited to the Canadian market, but DEW's parent company, Canadian General Electric, was now pressuring DEW to reevaluate its international competitiveness. Canadian General Electric was no longer content to be a "mini GE" serving only the Canadian market, and unless a business within the corporation could demonstrate its international competitive ability, it could cease to expect long-term support. For the managers at DEW, and for Walter Fell in particular, the task was to determine whether DEW's paper machinery business could establish itself and hold its own against worldwide competitors.

DEW COMPANY BACKGROUND

During World War I, when European manufacturers were unable to provide service or parts to Canada's paper mills and power companies, Dominion Bridge Company was urged to set up a paper machinery operation on Canadian soil. The company established Dominion Engineering Works as a new subsidiary, and in its first decade of operation DEW built 43 paper machines and established itself as the major supplier to the Canadian paper industry. As the new company grew, it added mining equipment and steel rolling mills to its original product line of hydroturbines and paper machines, in each case becoming the first Canadian manufacturer of such equipment.

In 1962 DEW was acquired by Canadian General Electric (CGE), the rationale for acquisition being that DEW and CGE had several complementary businesses with numerous customers in common. Combining

Harvard Business School case 383–184.

the companies would serve these customers better. It would also provide CGE and its parent company, the U.S. giant, General Electric, with entry into some completely new areas, including paper machinery.

In 1979 CGE was GE's largest foreign affiliate, with sales in excess of $1.3 billion (see Exhibit 1). Organizationally, DEW was part of CGE's Apparatus and Heavy Machinery Division (see Exhibit 2). The plant was a 1.2 million-square-foot general engineering shop occupying 85 acres outside Montreal and employing almost 2,000 people. It boasted some of the largest capacity equipment in the country and was able to handle everything from gigantic turbines to small machine parts.

Although paper machinery had been one of DEW's more profitable product lines in earlier decades, and again as late as the mid-1970s, in recent years return on sales for the pulp and paper section had been well below DEW's average. (For a comparison of DEW's paper machinery with other lines see Exhibit 3.)

GE is a results-oriented company and below-budget performance was not taken lightly. As one manager in the DEW operation explained:

> GE has been running at around 6 percent return on sales while CGE has been struggling to stay at half that level. That means they have been taking a lot of heat in Toronto (CGE headquarters) and we feel it here in DEW. Dominion is running under budget again this year and even though paper machinery is doing OK, it will be tough for all of us. Strategic plans and long-term investments are still important in GE, but you have to live in the real world of current results as well.

Canadian General Electric, in 1980, was placing a good deal of pressure on its businesses to improve their short-term operating performance through various cost control and productivity programs. More important, the company was urging its subsidiaries to broaden their horizons, to look beyond Canada and recognize the global dimensions of their industry structure. CGE was determined to change its original mission and become an internationally focused company with a growing range of products unique in the GE system. "World-class technical and cost competitiveness" was the goal.

It was against this background that Walter Fell was assessing DEW's paper machinery business. Before outlining DEW's position, however, it is important to take a look at the industry served by DEW's paper machinery and to examine in brief the strategies of DEW's competitors in the field.

THE PAPER MACHINE INDUSTRY

A detailed industry review is contained in the companion case, Note on the Paper Machine Industry 383–185, and only a brief summary of the key issues is presented here.

The fate of the paper machine manufacturers was inextricably linked to the health of their customers, the paper manufacturers. Unfortunately, the 1970s had been a difficult decade in the paper industry. Demand growth was not only slowing, but was also becoming increasingly cyclical. Papermaking capacity, which was expanded in good times, lay idle during downturns in the demand cycle such as the period from the mid- to late 1970s. In such times, prices weakened and profitability fell.

These problems were exacerbated by three important economic and political developments of the 70s. Increasing oil prices, soaring interest rates, and tightening environmental regulations all had direct and severe impacts on the paper industry, and led to rapidly escalating operating costs. In this environment, it was not surprising that the global demand for new paper machines dropped from an annual average of 160 machines in the late 1960s to less than half that level a decade later.

To add to the turbulence, some well-entrenched papermaking practices were being challenged. Technologically, the newly developed "twin-wire" machines began to replace the traditional fourdinier equipment, based on technology 150 years old. Furthermore, a trend to using different raw materials in paper manufacture was also affecting machine builders. In developing countries, nonwood fibers were becoming increasingly important, while in the industrial world, recycled paper was seen as a defense against escalating pulp costs.

Faced with declining demand for new machines in their home markets, several of the major paper machine builders began to expand abroad in the late 1960s. In particular, the U.S. company Beloit, German-based Voith, and the Finnish consortium TVW established sales offices and manufacturing operations in industrialized and developing countries worldwide. Their objectives were not only to tap these additional markets, but also to gain access to various incentive programs offered by host country governments, to achieve sourcing flexibility and perhaps lower labor costs, and to develop their technology in response to the new materials being used as papermaking stock.

The shares of the paper machinery market accounted for by these three large companies increased substantially. By 1974, they had already captured a combined worldwide market share of 40 percent on a tonnage installed basis, and by 1979, that figure had increased to 52 percent. As of the end of 1979, the "Big Three" held a 68 percent share of all new orders placed for the period 1980 and beyond. It seemed as if small- and medium-sized companies like DEW risked being trampled as the three dominant companies jostled for position as the leading global paper machine company.

DEW'S POSITION AND STRATEGY

Changing conditions in the world paper industry during the late 60s represented an obvious challenge to DEW's traditional strategy. Protected by a tariff on machinery imports, Dominion had successfully pursued its "national champion" role from the 1920s, when the company was founded, until the 1960s. In 1964, however, the major U.S. company, Beloit, established a Canadian subsidiary; before the decade was out, Beloit dominated the national market in tissue, linerboard, and fine-paper machines. Dominion retained its preeminence in the newsprint machine market, but it was clear to the company that Beloit was a force to be reckoned with.

Dominion reacted to the new competitive challenge in two ways. First, like its competitors, DEW looked abroad for other market opportunities and soon established licensees in Italy and Japan. Second, the company innovated technologically. DEW's research engineers had cooperated with the Pulp and Paper Research Institute of Canada (a body organized by the Canadian paper industry and financed to a large extent by government research grants) in the development of the first twin-wire former. The invention was quickly recognized as a major advance in papermaking technology, the first in over 150 years. It seemed particularly suited to the newsprint segment, but subsequently was adapted for tissue and printing and writing paper manufacture.

DEW hoped that the Papriformer, (PPRIC's trade name for its twin-wire machine) would give the company a significant edge on its competitors and, indeed, for some time it did. Armed with its new product, DEW moved into the U.S. market and won a major contract in 1972. DEW now employed a U.S. salesman and based him in Texas to take advantage of the rapid expansion of the paper industry in the American South. In five years, DEW had taken orders for seven machines—an impressive performance with a new invention in a conservative industry.

To keep up with the new surge in demand, DEW decided to restrict design changes and customization of the Papriformer to a minimum. The idea was to standardize the machine as much as possible. Unfortunately, however, a number of DEW's customers were experimenting at this time with new materials like deinked, recycled newsprint and thermomechanical pulp. When the companies called on DEW for help, some felt that the response was disappointing. The product engineering manager who joined Dominion during this period recalled:

> We were convinced that the problems we were experiencing were due to the various elements being changed by the customer. However, in retrospect, I would have to say that DEW did not follow up quickly enough with sufficient engineering capability to help the customer correct some of the problems which emerged. We simply did not have the available personnel resources. The reaction of the customer was to blame the Papriformer rather than the changes in process they were trying to make. Our reputation suffered a little.

The lack of personnel resources was tied to the economic downturn of 1975 and to DEW's parent company's response to that situation. When DEW's major businesses reported a decline in orders during the recession, Canadian GE pressured operating management to cut costs in order to protect profits. The paper machinery section of DEW cut its sales force from 25 to 9, its advance design staff from 8 to 3, and its product engineers and draftsmen from 35 to 14.

Following the company's initial success with the Papriformer, not a single paper machine was sold in the four years from 1975 to 1979. The only business booked by the Pulp and Paper Section was for spare parts, components, and small or partial rebuilds. DEW's paper machinery business was operating around breakeven, with no relief in sight.

At the end of 1977, DEW recruited Tom McGarrell, an engineer and manager who had spent eight years with Beloit, the world's largest paper machine manufacturer, and seven years with Abitibi-Price, the world's largest newsprint manufacturer. When McGarrell became manager of the Pulp and Paper Section, sales were running at 40 percent of their 1974 peak, and new orders booked over the previous three years were less than half that of the three years prior to that.

With no new machine order received in two and a half years, McGarrell knew that morale in the Pulp and Paper Section was low and that support by senior DEW management was, at best, tentative. There was talk of acquiring a manufacturing and marketing base in the United States, but McGarrell felt that the company's priorities lay elsewhere:

> I felt we had an urgent task to face in rebuilding our internal pulp and paper organization. Furthermore, we had done

> little to improve our technology in seven or eight years while competitors like Beloit, Voith and TVW had used the mid-70s as a time to upgrade their products. We suddenly woke up when the market picked up in 1978–79 and we found we were losing orders. Our machine technology was out of date and our market share was slipping.

McGarrell acknowledged the seriousness of the threat from abroad, with Beloit, Black Clawson, Voith, and particularly TVW making themselves felt in Canada. The foreign onslaught, he believed, had reduced DEW's share of the large and attractive Canadian market from 50 percent in 1972–74 to 10–12 percent in 1977–79. DEW's defense of the Canadian newsprint market segment on which it had focused was slipping.

However, the battle McGarrell faced within the company was almost as challenging as the one taking place externally. As he put it:

> Within the company there was a strong belief that nothing had changed apart from a cyclical downturn. People had a hard time accepting the fact that DEW did not have a 50 percent market share and that we were not the technological leaders. They had assumed that when the cycle turned up we would be carried with it. That wasn't the case. We were being left behind.

McGarrell spent his first three years with DEW rebuilding his organization and improving performance of the existing product lines. The following paragraphs detail the situation in each of DEW's major functional areas.

Manufacturing

DEW's 1.2 million-square-foot plant, though large, was a general engineering shop and, as such, it suffered certain cost disadvantages in comparison with plants specializing in paper machine production. Management believed, however, that the differential was no more than 5 or 10 percent and that the disadvantage was more than compensated for when downturns in the very cyclical paper industry left specialist plants idle. (See Exhibit 3 for an illustration of the high variability in DEW's order patterns and an indication of the time lag between receiving and shipping an order.) But the general shop had its problems, especially in hard times, as a DEW manufacturing manager explained:

> First, because we run a general engineering shop we tend to have general-purpose tools rather than specialized equipment. Tools have been grouped by function, and the production flow for a particular machine may be somewhat inefficient.
>
> Second, in competition for capacity with our other product lines, paper machinery orders may suffer. In general, the equipment necessary for making paper machines is smaller and more common than that required, say, for a turbine. In a crunch the paper machinery work is most easily subcontracted, and that raises costs.
>
> Finally, there is a more subtle problem that paper machines face in a plant such as ours. The manufacturing area is evaluated on its dollar volume. If it is near the end of a period and there is a need to try to meet budget, the larger, more expensive units are pushed through the system. It is easier to get a turbine through the plant than a lot of small components for a paper machine.

DEW's manufacturing suffered, of course, from the threefold increase in the cost of materials that afflicted the industry in the 1970s. Environmental problems with the traditional equipment, as mentioned earlier, forced up the costs of materials—and materials accounted for almost half of machine cost—as stainless steel replaced the less expensive materials used formerly.

At the same time, labor costs rose to a point where they were accounting for 30 to 40 percent of the cost of a new machine. Companies such as Voith and Beloit were quick to take advantage of cheaper labor costs in Spain, Brazil, and other countries, but DEW was reluctant to use foreign sources. Despite savings it could obtain by sourcing from its Italian licensee, Over Meccanica, DEW felt that customers were displeased to learn of the foreign manufacture of their multimillion-dollar machines. Then, too, DEW was pressing the Canadian government to support local manufactures and could hardly supply its home market with foreign-made machines. DEW felt it was able, nonetheless, to quote prices in the United States comparable with Beloit's, although, as one manager pointed out, the slightest strengthening of the Canadian dollar would make this difficult to continue.

DEW's manufacturing manager believed, in any case, that internal problems were the key to DEW's high labor costs. Uneven work flow and the loss of experienced personnel had cut into the company's efficiency.

> When the market fell away in the mid-1970s, we had to cut back people at all levels. In the plant that meant the loss of critical skills and expertise that had been developed over the years. Without building a complete machine in four years, we lost the ability to manage the product flow through the plant, and we lost efficiency in our operations. For example, to machine a dryer head used to take us six or seven hours in 73 and 74. But in 1979, after the personnel cutbacks and the new order drought, the same operation was taking over 35 hours. We're now down to 20 hours, but we're still trying to relearn our old efficient methods, and it's really costing us.

With the market upturn of the late 1970s, the Pulp and Paper Section was able to convince management to expand and upgrade its paper machine manufacturing capability. By 1980 more than $3 million worth of new plant and equipment was being installed, and overall capacity was expected to increase from one and a half to two and a half complete paper machines a year.

Marketing

The Canadian market for paper machinery took off in 1978 and 1979 following an upturn in the economy and the announcement of a new five-year government program to finance up to 11 percent of the cost of upgrading plant and equipment. DEW saw in this program not only a capital investment stimulus "that should help us get through the next valley in the investment cycle," but also a barrier to foreign competitors. As one senior manager explained, "When, for example, TVW won a contract that was 11 percent funded by the Canadian government, we were able to raise a hell of a fuss. Essentially, these projects have to be supplied by Canadian manufacturers now."

The government also offered an export financing program that provided 10- to 15-year loans to overseas buyers at 9½ percent interest in an era when the prime rate was approaching 20 percent. Despite this assistance from the government, DEW's sales force continued to face tough competition both at home and abroad. The Finnish consortium TVW, in particular, was pricing aggressively to gain a share of the Canadian market. And to make matters worse, recent tariff reductions on paper machinery from 15 to 13¼ percent were only the beginning of a series of reductions agreed to under GATT (General Agreement on Tariffs and Trade) negotiations.

One of Tom McGarrell's first moves when he took over DEW's Pulp and Paper Section was to appoint Roman Caspar, then manager of the company's Advanced Design Engineering, as marketing manager. Caspar, in turn, set about rebuilding the company's depleted sales force, which had gone from 25 to 9 in the cutbacks of the mid-1970s. By 1980 he had the staff back up to 23, with 9 field personnel: 7 covering Canada, 1 responsible for the United States, and 1 for export markets.

Caspar felt that DEW had concentrated too heavily on the newsprint segment of the Canadian market, turning overseas only in slack times. He pointed to the success of DEW's Italian licensee, Over Meccanica, in selling five Papriformers during the company's last slack period, 1974–78. Some of these had been for fine-paper and tissue applications. And he noted, too, that DEW's Japanese licensee had entirely missed the Japanese boom of 1968–74, largely because DEW had not made an aggressive effort to adapt its headbox design to local needs. Caspar commented:

> These are the kinds of problems and opportunities I feel I should be working on now, but there seems to be an internal resistance to letting me do so. The message seems to be to focus on the Canadian market.

Research and Development

When he took over DEW's Pulp and Paper Section, Tom McGarrell found three groups of engineers, scientists, and technologists under his control. Research Services did basic research relating to any of DEW's businesses, and was funded to a large extent by federal research grants. One of McGarrell's early efforts was to focus their efforts on issues that were less abstract and more directly related to the company's products and markets.

Advanced Design Engineering was responsible for basic paper machine design. In Tom McGarrell's view, they had been too focused on internal experiments that interested them, and not at all aware of the design breakthroughs being made on competitive machines. His objective was to shift their attention outward to respond more to changing market and competitive realities.

Product Engineering was responsible for drawing specifications and adapting basic machine designs to specific customer needs. However, when McGarrell inherited the group it was so understaffed it was unable to handle major design changes. Even operating manuals could not be prepared, with the result that customers were calling for assistance more frequently.

In keeping with his stated policy of rebuilding the organization, Tom McGarrell brought in new managers from other top companies and pushed to expand each group while narrowing its focus to meet the immediate needs of the company. His greatest frustration was that DEW had no pilot plant of its own and had to rely on the facilities of Over Meccanica, PPRIC, or even customers' plants to do its testing. By 1979, however, McGarrell felt that DEW had caught up with most of the technological advances made by its competitors in the mid-70s. He explained:

> The work we've done over the last few years should help us broaden our product line from our present newsprint dominance. We have a new former in development that should give us the uniform fiber distribution needed to sell machines for

> printing and writing paper. Over Meccanica's experience with tissue machines should help us make the changes needed in headbox and drainage configuration to get into that segment. It won't be easy to break into these markets, but now that we have the basis right, at least we can begin to work on it.
>
> Technological changes come in waves which correspond to new industry priorities. Several years ago, when the major concern was pollution control, the forming process became critical. When energy costs rose, pressing and drying technology was key. We've been catching up in these areas, but I believe we can now begin work in the critical concern of the future—productivity. We are working on a major project jointly with a customer and the Pulp and Paper Institute that I'm very excited about.

Tom McGarrell was very optimistic about DEW's ability to regain the technological leadership it had lost in the early 1970s.

> I think we have learned a great deal in the last few years. Even though DEW is under budget pressure this year, we are not being forced to cut key personnel as we were in the past. In fact, we will add two or three people to our Advanced Engineering Group next year, and our overall R&D budget should exceed $1 million compared to less than $100,000 when I first arrived. In my view that should give us the chance to regain our leadership position.

As of mid-1980, DEW had added a second new machine order to the one received in 1979, breaking the order drought that had continued since 1974 (see Exhibit 5). McGarrell felt he had the momentum to launch a major new offensive in the paper machine business. The only cloud on the horizon was his belief that the paper industry was headed into a cyclical downturn in 1981.

SENIOR MANAGEMENT'S DECISION

As Dominion Engineering's new general manager, Walter Fell knew that his evaluation of the paper machine business would be critical. He also realized that he had to take into account not only the external competitive situation but also Canadian GE's goal of shedding its mini GE image and achieving international competitiveness.

Walter Fell saw some clear advantages for DEW's paper machine business. The company had certainly been a world technological leader with the twin-wire Papriformer; and CGE was the only part of the GE system that had paper machine technology and manufacturing capability. He commented:

> There is a lot about this business that makes sense for us strategically. The critical question is whether we can become a world-scale competitor. Now, you can't make a business world class in two weeks, or even in a year. We need to think about what we can do by 1985. For the paper machine business the question is what route to follow. Is an acquisition more feasible than an internal growth program? Do we have to become a full-line company or can we stay with our specialized newsprint line? Do we have to conquer the world in one fell swoop or can we take a more focused and gradual approach?
>
> These are the questions I'm looking to Tom McGarrell, Roman Caspar, and the others to answer. I've told them they have an AAA credit rating and that we're not stopped from doing anything. In fact, the chairman has been floating ideas about acquisitions for awhile. But before we do anything, we have to know what it is we're trying to become and justify the way to get there.

What to do with the paper machinery business had become a hot topic at DEW in the summer of 1980. Not only was Walter Fell eager to have the topic analyzed by the time he sent DEW's strategic plan to CGE in Toronto, but there was a competitive development that concerned Tom McGarrell. Rumors were circulating in the industry that the industry leader, Beloit, had been showing an interest in KMW, the Swedish manufacturer that dominated the tissue machine market. Apparently, KMW's financial performance had been poor in recent years, and some industry observers were convinced that its parent company was willing to discuss the sale of the business.

EXHIBIT 1
GENERAL ELECTRIC COMPANY
Dollar Amounts in Millions; per Share Amounts in Dollars

	1979	1978	1977	1976
Summary of operations				
Sales of products and services to customers	$22,460.6	$19,653.8	$17,518.6	$15,697.3
Net earnings	$ 1,408.8	$ 1,229.7	$ 1,088.2	$ 930.6
Earnings per common share	$6.20	$5.39	$4.79	$4.12
Dividends declared per common share	$2.75	$2.50	$2.10	$1.70
Earnings as a percentage of sales	6.3%	6.3%	6.2%	5.9%
Earned on average share owners' equity	20.2%	19.6%	19.4%	18.9%
Current assets	$ 9,384.5	$ 8,755.0	$ 7,865.2	$ 6,685.0
Current liabilities	6,871.8	6,175.2	5,417.0	4,604.9
Working capital	$ 2,512.7	$ 2,579.8	$ 2,448.2	$ 2,080.1
Short-term borrowings	$ 871.0	$ 960.3	$ 772.1	$ 611.1
Long-term borrowings	946.8	993.8	1,284.3	1,322.3
Minority interest in equity of consolidated affiliates	151.7	150.8	131.4	119.0
Share owners' equity	7,362.3	6,586.7	5,942.9	5,252.9
Total capital invested	$ 9,331.8	$ 8,691.6	$ 8,130.7	$ 7,305.3
Earned on average total capital invested	17.6%	16.3%	15.8%	15.1%

CANADIAN GENERAL ELECTRIC COMPANY LTD.
Dollar Amounts in Thousands, Except per Share Amounts

	1979	1978	1977	1976
Sales of products and services	$1,338,730	$1,103,965	$1,079,727	$879,427
Net earnings (before extraordinary items)	$38,330	$33,612	$30,534	$32,699
Net earnings per share	$4.69	$4.11	$3.73	$4.00
Earnings as a percentage of sales	3.0%	3.2%	2.9%	3.7%
Current assets	$ 681,216	$ 532,129	$ 496,860	$406,778
Current liabilities	432,993	310,076	312,651	239,219
Total assets	$ 904,148	$ 730,274	$ 666,024	$571,187
Average number of employees	19,767	18,662	18,823	17,512

1975	1974	1973	1972	1971	1970
$14,105.1	$13,918.2	$11,944.6	$10,473.7	$9,556.7	$8,833.8
$ 688.5	$ 705.3	$ 661.4	$ 572.6	$ 509.5	$ 363.0
$3.07	$3.16	$2.97	$2.57	$2.30	$1.66
$1.60	$1.60	$1.50	$1.40	$1.38	$1.30
4.9%	5.1%	5.5%	5.5%	5.3%	4.1%
15.7%	17.8%	18.4%	17.5%	17.2%	13.4%
$ 5,750.4	$ 5,334.4	$ 4,597.4	$ 4,056.8	$3,700.0	$3,383.1
4,163.0	4,032.4	3,588.2	2,920.8	2,893.8	2,689.4
$ 1,587.4	$ 1,302.0	$ 1,009.2	$ 1,136.0	$ 806.2	$ 693.7
$ 667.2	$ 655.9	$ 675.6	$ 453.3	$ 581.7	$ 670.2
1,239.5	1,402.9	1,166.2	1,191.2	1,016.2	691.3
104.6	86.4	62.4	53.4	50.4	45.0
4,617.0	4,172.2	3,774.3	3,420.2	3,105.4	2,819.1
$ 6,628.3	$ 6,317.4	$ 5,678.5	$ 5,118.1	$4,753.7	$4,225.6
12.5%	13.4%	13.7%	12.7%	12.3%	10.2%

1975	1974	1973	1972	1971	1970
$822,134	$709,913	$583,414	$530,174	$495,755	$489,992
36,075	23,893	18,680	16,504	13,212	11,359
$4.41	$2.92	$2.28	$2.02	$1.62	$1.39
4.4%	3.4%	3.2%	3.1%	2.7%	2.3%
$441,296	$382,615	$256,300	$233,667	$240,943	$253,379
288,830	246,996	131,572	126,543	141,864	149,819
$602,435	$563,754	$429,720	$409,951	$412,918	$409,922
18,789	19,193	17,890	17,583	17,950	19,789

EXHIBIT 2
PARTIAL ORGANIZATION CHART

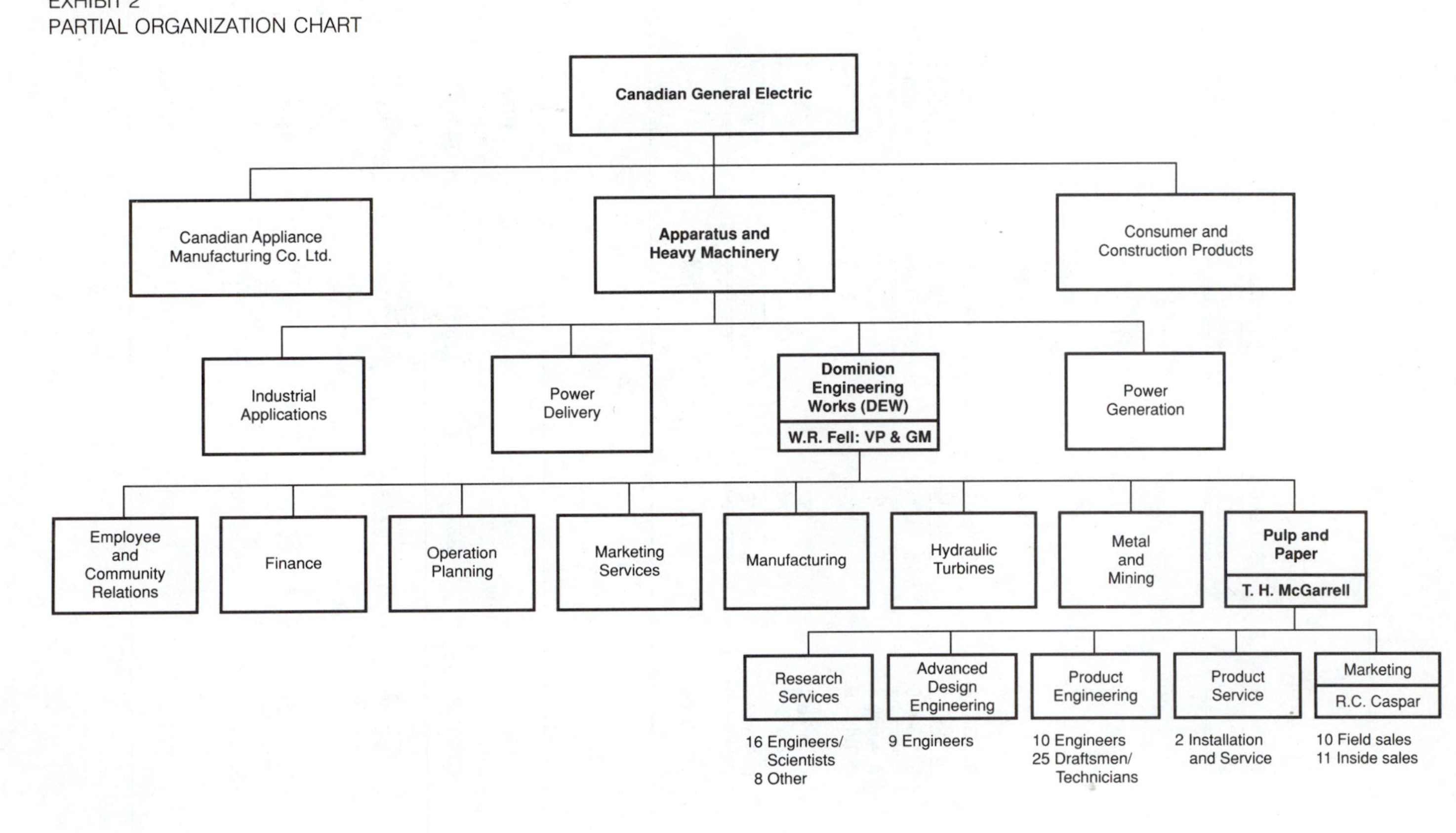

EXHIBIT 3
SUMMARY OF OPERATIONS BY PRODUCT, 1979

	Pulp and Paper	*Hydraulic*	*Metal and Mining*	*Manufacturing*	*Field Installations*	*Adjustments/ Eliminations*	*Total*
Orders received	27,391	22,788	100,771	723	3,253	(788)	154,138
Unfilled orders (at end of period)	24,188	117,604	97,358	664	27,074	(727)	266,161
Sales	11,202	35,887	16,728	719	5,455	(823)	69,168
Inventory costs							
Material	$5,158	$ 9,432	$ 6,258	$ 36	$3,620	(1,110)	$23,394
Conversion cost	3,121	15,516	7,931	633	745	8	27,954
Cont. engineering	679	1,170	596	—	—	—	2,445
Total inventory costs	$8,958	$26,118	$14,785	$669	$4,365	(1,102)	$53,793
Inventory margin	2,244	9,769	1,943	50	1,090	279	15,375
Period costs							
Manufacturing:							
(Over)/under-absorbed expenses	$ 467	$ 817	$ 692	$178	—	—	$ 2,154
Depreciation	341	1,206	647	55	—	—	2,249
Engineering and marketing							
Direct expense	$ 782	$ 1,645	$ 1,879	—	—	—	$ 4,306
Allocated expenses (research, marketing service)	$ 138	$ 265	$ 142	$ 3	$ 39	—	$ 509
Warranty expense	$ 116	$ 267	$ 265	$ 18	—	—	$ 666
Finance and administration:							
Allocated finance and corporate charges	811	2,249	1,633	70	266	(200)	4,829
Other	—	—	—	—	—	690	690
Total period cost	$2,655	$ 6,449	$ 5,258	$324	$ 227	$490	$15,403
Income from sales	$ (411)	$ 3,320	(3,315)	(274)	863	(211)	(28)
Other income	244	220	(28)	—	15	(7)	444
Total income	$ (167)	$ 3,540	(3,343)	(274)	878	(218)	416
Income tax	(97)	1,402	(1,517)	(123)	381	(474)	(428)
Net operating income	(70)	2,138	(1,826)	(151)	497	256	844
Net interest (on progress payments)	277	495	433	43	12	—	1,174
Net Income	$ 207	2,633	(1,393)	(194)	509	256	2,018
Inventory margins	20.0%	27.2%	11.6%	7.0%	20.0%	#	22.2%
Net income to sales	1.8%	7.3%	(8.3)%	(27.0)%	9.3%	#	2.9%

EXHIBIT 4
ORDERS RECEIVED AND SALES BILLED
Dollars in Thousands

	1967	1968	1969	1970	1971	1972	1973	1974	1975	1976	1977	1978
Paper section												
Orders	11,025	12,300	10,100	7,144	7,600	13,046	14,623	20,022	5,919	9,310	9,056	11,092
Sales	17,984	13,967	12,795	11,223	5,951	5,885	8,274	19,960	16,804	11,982	8,751	8,588
Hydraulic section												
Orders	30,136	12,603	4,215	13,997	15,965	11,105	30,129	42,133	15,083	6,464	67,586	36,378
Sales	8,630	7,669	9,286	12,052	15,460	13,287	16,871	18,084	19,571	23,599	19,215	30,319
Metal and mining section												
Orders	20,253	14,464	20,332	17,439	24,249	17,196	35,704	72,344	38,761	14,086	15,424	19,350
Sales	20,529	22,319	18,826	23,960	19,567	21,973	15,446	19,276	45,351	53,185	24,630	14,562
Total DEW												
Orders	61,414	39,367	34,647	38,580	47,814	41,347	80,456	134,499	59,763	29,860	92,066	66,820
Sales	47,143	43,955	30,907	47,235	40,978	41,145	40,591	57,320	81,726	88,766	52,596	53,469

EXHIBIT 5
PAPER MACHINES BY DOMINION ENGINEERING WORKS LIMITED, MONTREAL, CANADA

Year	*Purchaser*	*Location*	*New or Rebuild*	*Wire Width*	*Product*	*Design Speed (F.P.M.)*
1968	Facelle Company	USA	New (2)	214″	Tissue	4,000
1968	MacMillan Bloedel Ltd.	Canada	New	238″	Newsprint	2,500
1969	M.P. Industrial Mills (Man. Forestry Resources, Ltd.)	Canada	New	280″	Pulp & Bag	2,500
1970	B.C. Forest Products Ltd.	Canada	New	178″	Pulp	500
1972	St. Regis Paper (Southland)	USA	New (Papriformer*)	326″	Newsprint	3,500
1972	Kruger Inc.	Canada	Rebuild (Papriformer*)	174″	Newsprint	2,500
1973	Kruger Inc.	Canada	New (Papriformer*)	261″	Newsprint	3,000
1973	Consolidated-Bathurst	Canada	Rebuild (Papriformer*)	238″	Newsprint	2,500
1974	F.F. Soucy Inc.	Canada	New (Papriformer*)	261″	Newsprint	3,000
1974	Garden State Paper Co.	USA	Rebuild (Papriformer*)	261″	Newsprint	3,000
1974	Consolidated-Bathurst	Canada	Rebuild (2 Papriformers*)	238″	Newsprint	3,000
1979	Kruger Inc.	Canada	Rebuild	160″	Newsprint	3,000
1979	MacMillan Bloedel	Canada	Rebuild	186″	Linerboard	2,300
1979	Midtec Paper Corp.	USA	New	249″	Newsprint	3,000
1980	Quebec North Shore	Canada	Rebuild	262″	Newsprint	3,000
1980	Consolidated-Bathurst	Canada	Rebuild (Papriformer*)	238″	Newsprint	3,000
1980	Donohue-Normick Inc.	Canada	New (Papriformer*)	326″	Newsprint	4,000

*Papriformer is DEW's trade name for its twin-wire former.

Note on the Major Home Appliance Industry in 1984 (Condensed)

Major home appliances had sales in excess of $12 billion in 1984 in the United States, and represented one of the largest consumer goods industries. At one time many of the major automotive and consumer electronics manufacturers had participated in the business, but all of them (except General Electric) had withdrawn. By early 1983 with the Japanese gaining a foothold in the United States in the microwave oven market and most of the domestic manufacturers operating at 50 to 60 percent of their overall capacity, the future of the industry seemed uncertain.

PRODUCTS

The products of the appliance industry could be classified in terms of customer use and technology. Based on customer use, appliances were sold for the kitchen (refrigerators, freezers, ranges, dishwashers, and disposals); for the home laundry (washers and dryers); and for room air conditioning. Technologically, appliances fell into three categories: water bearing (dishwashers, disposals, clothes washers, and some dryers); refrigerating (refrigerators, freezers, and room air conditioners); and cooking (ranges).

Refrigerators. Refrigerators had historically been the largest-selling appliance (see Exhibits 1 and 2). Since the product's average life expectancy was 15 years, manufacturers expected that replacement sales alone would come to about 5.5 million units a year during the 1980s. But with sales of only about 4.3 million, 1982 turned out to be the worst year since 1963. Refrigerators were the only appliance product whose saturation exceeded 100 percent. Some households had two or more units, and many nonhousehold entities like offices and dorm rooms also had a refrigerator.

Manufacturers seemed to disagree as to likely future trends in refrigerators. In the regular-size segment, which represented about 90 percent of the market, a key issue was whether customers would shift future purchases toward smaller sizes. Until 1981 customers making replacement purchases

---

Harvard Business School case 385–211.

TABLE 1
PERCENT OF REFRIGERATOR SHIPMENTS BY SIZE

Size (cubic feet)	*1982*	*1981*	*1980*	*1979*	*1978*
6.5–11	4.0%	3.7%	5%	6%	8%
12–13	7.8	7.8	9	9	10
14–15	25.7	24.7	23	22	21
16–17	24.7	24.0	23	22	21
18–19	18.8	19.2	19	18	19
20–21	10.8	11.4	11	12	12
22 and over	8.2	9.2	10	10	10

Source: *Merchandising* magazine, November issues, 1978–82.

had tended to upgrade to slightly larger models (see Table 1). But in 1982 there was a definite shift downwards in the three largest size categories.

The argument for downsizing was based on three trends. First, the average size of the household was declining as the number of divorces, childless couples, and single-person households increased. In addition, the prices of refrigerators had risen considerably, and consumers with a limited budget might prefer to give up size rather than features or quality. Finally, rising energy costs had created an incentive to use appliances with lower operating costs. On the other hand, despite trends in household size, kitchens were not getting any smaller. People were doing more entertaining at home, and kitchens were increasingly becoming the focal point of the home. As Charles Dowd, vice president, sales and marketing, for Admiral (Magic Chef), remarked, "I have yet to meet a consumer who said her refrigerator was too large."[1]

Compact units of less than 6.5 cubic feet had been gaining share of the overall refrigerator market since 1978. Though sales of the 2-cubic-foot models were declining, the 3- to 5-cubic-foot models had been growing consistently. These small undercounter refrigerators were characteristically used in four situations: (1) by students, retirees, and single people living in dorms, retirement homes, and even studio apartments; (2) in professional and business offices; (3) as a second home unit outside the kitchen; and (4) in boats, recreational vehicles, motel rooms, etc.

Imports had gained a strong position in the compact segment, representing 40–48 percent of the market of the previous five years. Imports also played a small but growing role in the standard-size segment, though most of these units were refrigerator-freezer combinations, which have traditionally been more popular abroad than in the United States.

Three companies—Whirlpool, GE, and White—together represented 80 percent of the market and had traditionally controlled it. The top five—including Admiral and Amana—made up 95 percent of the market (Exhibit 3).

Freezers. Freezer sales had been in the doldrums since the recession of 1975 (Exhibit 1). Until then, freezer sales had maintained momentum even when the overall industry was depressed. In difficult times, people tended to economize by buying food in larger quantities during

[1] "Mart Money Maker," *Mart*, January 1982.

special sales and in larger packages with lower unit costs; thus they needed more freezer space. In the late 1970s, one of the worst inflationary-recessionary periods, freezer sales languished. After continued gains since 1961, saturation leveled off at around 45 percent. Freezers had the longest life expectancy of any appliance, and the product features had not changed in decades. Sales of compact freezers had also remained constant over the last 10 years.

Whirlpool was the clear leader in freezers, followed by White, with Admiral (Magic Chef) a distant number 3 (Exhibit 3). These three companies controlled 80 percent of the market. In 1981 Magic Chef had acquired Revco, but had not been able to hold on to all of Revco's market share.

Air Conditioners. Air conditioner sales were more volatile than those of any other appliance since demand was seasonal and dependent on the weather. The 1970s had illustrated this pattern. In 1974, retailers got caught with excess inventory which was reflected in their orders for 1975 and 1976.

The energy crisis had hurt air conditioner sales after the all-time high of 5.9 million sold units in 1970. As an industry analyst noted:

> Air conditioners were the first to feel the brunt of the energy issue . . . utilities not only virtually discontinued their promotional support, but even in many areas, seemed to discourage air conditioner purchases by harping on the theme of using them as little as possible. . . . Whirlpool officials also make the point that room air conditioners use something less than 1 percent of residential energy yet are "drawing about 90 percent of the fire."[2]

Despite the volatility of the business, competitors' market share positions had remained remarkably stable. The three full-line appliance manufacturers—GE, Whirlpool, and White—together had just over 50 percent of the market; the three specialists—Fedders, Friedrich, and Addison—together had slightly under 40 percent (Exhibit 3).

Cooking Appliances. The introduction of microwave ovens represented the most radical technological change in the appliance industry. Traditionally, the choice had been between gas and electric ranges, each with its own merits and limitations with regard to cost, cleanliness, efficiency, safety, and so on. Until the late 1960s, gas ranges had had a slight edge over electric ranges in the number of units sold. Recently, however, the trend had moved toward electric ranges and ovens.

During the early 1970s microwave ovens were introduced by electronics companies outside the traditional appliance industry. At first, the microwave was seen primarily as a novelty or luxury item rather than a basic cooking medium, and its use was limited to the quick reheating and defrosting of foods. From the mid-1970s on, however, microwave oven sales took off. Despite stagnation of the overall appliance industry, microwave oven sales continued to grow steadily until 1982 when microwaves became the single largest-selling appliance product. The growth would not have been possible without significant technological improvements, including improved electronic controls, and the overcoming of a major safety scare; although all manufacturers complied with stringent government safety tests, some concerns about microwave radiation still lingered.

[2] "Air Treatment," *Merchandising,* November 1982.

TABLE 2
PERCENT OF U.S. HOUSEHOLDS OWNING A MICROWAVE OVEN

1972	*1973*	*1974*	*1975*	*1976*	*1977*	*1978*	*1979*	*1980*	*1981*
0.4%	1.1%	2.1%	3.5%	5.9%	8.7%	11.7%	15.2%	19.4%	24.4%

Source: Home Furnishing: Standard & Poor's Industry Surveys.

Microwave ovens represented one of the only two real growth markets for appliance manufacturers, as shown in Table 2.

In 1977 the two leaders were Litton, with a 25 percent market share, and Amana, with 20 percent (Exhibit 4). Litton, a conglomerate, offered no home appliance other than cooking products in its entire product line. Amana, owned by Raytheon, had a larger stake in the home appliance business. Of the dedicated major appliance manufacturers, GE and Tappan each had only 10 percent of the microwave market.

In 1979 GE introduced the "Spacemaker," which could be installed on the wall over a range. This product, the only microwave oven that did not require counterspace, enabled GE to move into first place, while Litton and Amana, despite heavy advertising, dropped back to second place. The other significant competition came from Japanese manufacturers (Sharp, Sanyo, Panasonic, and others).

Laundry. The market for laundry products, though less saturated than those for some other appliance products, seemed to be growing more slowly than most. Industry observers felt that washer saturation of a little over 70 percent and dryer saturation of about 65 percent would not be surpassed in the foreseeable future (Exhibit 2). Those who currently did not own laundry appliances (mainly apartment dwellers) had access to coin-operated machines. Even if they wanted to buy washers and dryers for their exclusive use, few apartments had the necessary space and plumbing facilities.

Since laundry equipment constituted more than 25 percent of total major appliance unit sales, manufacturers were continually striving to introduce innovations that would boost sales. Some new products reduced water and energy consumption, others improved dependability and performance. Manufacturers had also developed more compact, stackable appliances. The expanding use of microelectronics, though not a major feature, allowed elaborate cycle control options on the higher-priced models.

Market share had remained remarkably stable in laundry products in the past six years (Exhibit 5). Almost 90 percent of the market was controlled by the Big Four—Whirlpool with 40 percent and GE with 20 percent, followed by White and Maytag with 15 percent each.

Dishwashers. With a saturation level of under 45 percent and the best-selling models retailing between $400 to $500 (with the top of the line being between $700 and $800), dishwashers appeared to offer true growth potential that seemed to be on the decline. Dishwashers were one of the most complicated of all appliances to manufacture, because they involved a combination of electrical, mechanical, and hydraulic (plus electronic in some models) technology.

The dishwasher market had been dominated by Design and Manufacturing

(D&M). A privately held firm specializing in dishwashers, D&M had consistently maintained a market share of 45 percent for the past decade. GE had been a steady number 2 with 25 percent market share, while Hobart-KitchenAid followed with 15 percent. (See Exhibit 6.)

Because of the product's high price and low saturation level, GE had targeted the dishwasher for future investments. In 1982 it was in the process of improving its technology by switching from a porcelain tub to a plastic tub, based on earlier successes on high end models. It also seemed possible that Whirlpool, who previously had not been a major participant, could make a strong bid for some of the Sears business, which was presently sourced entirely from D&M.

Disposals. In contrast to all other appliances, disposals were sold primarily through plumbing contractors. Until 1980, GE was the leader in this market, followed by In-Sink-Erator, a wholly owned subsidiary of Emerson Electric. Disposals were Emerson's only home appliance product. When GE decided to exit disposals, In-Sink-Erator became the leader, with a 60 percent market share, followed by Anaheim Manufacturing with a 25 percent share. Anaheim was acquired by Tappan in 1965.

Compactors. The trash compactor market was dominated by Whirlpool and GE, with a combined market share of 75 percent. Although saturation is less than 5 percent, potential growth seemed limited, and manufacturers did not attach much importance to this product.

PRODUCT DESIGN AND INNOVATION

Innovations in product design took three forms: (1) customer-oriented features, (2) reducing manufacturing costs through process improvements, and (3) new products that expanded the market.

Feature innovations had been plentiful. Because many appliance markets were highly saturated, features were a useful way of speeding up replacement demand and differentiating products from those of competitors. Examples include the self-cleaning oven, pilotless gas ranges, side-by-side refrigerators, "Servador" refrigerators, and so on. In recent years there had been an emphasis in almost all appliances on electronic timers and controls, and on energy efficiencies. Most often features were introduced at the top of the line and made available on lower-priced models within a few years. Generally the manufacturers' brands had the newest and most elaborate features, followed by the national retailers, who usually copied the previous year's successful top-of-the-line features.

In the area of process innovations, a trend toward the use of plastic rather than metal, foam rather than fiberglass insulation, coiled rather than flat steel, prepainted rather than in-house-painted cases, and so forth, had helped reduce manufacturing costs. Occasionally these changes had made the product intrinsically better as well (e.g., lighter, slimmer, or more spacious).

The only true new product innovation that had been successful, the microwave oven, was developed outside the appliance industry. The combination washer-dryer was an innovation that had not proved popular in the United States, though it had sold well in Europe. In 1982, the market verdict was not yet in for the compact and mini models of refrigerators, freezers, washers, dryers, and so on. Innovations of a sort, these products had been introduced chiefly by the foreign manufacturers.

MARKETS

There were two major end-use markets for appliances in the United States: retail and contract. A wide variety of retail outlets sold to the consumer. A significant share of appliances moved from manufacturer to consumer through the private brand market, which consisted of mass merchandisers and other manufacturers that needed certain products to make up a full line. In the contract market, construction firms, builders, contractors, mobile home manufacturers, or kitchen remodelers made the purchase decision.

The Contract Market.[3] Contract sales were directly related to new housing starts. Since World War II, this segment had grown to a peak in 1973 when it represented 33 percent of total appliance shipments. With the collapse of new housing construction during 1973–1975, contract sales dwindled, and in 1976 accounted for about 25 percent of shipments where they had remained through 1982.

Manufacturers sold appliances to the contract segment both directly to the large builders and indirectly through local builder suppliers. Direct sales to construction firms and mobile home manufacturers were made by corporate salesmen for most of the full-line companies and to a limited extent by independent distributors for the smaller manufacturers. Direct sales accounted for 80 percent of contract sales, and it was thought that the trend toward apartment living could increase their importance.

Appliances were crucial in selling homes even though they represented no more than 10 percent of total home costs. In the industry it was generally believed that consumers did not have the knowledge to evaluate objectively the quality of the dwelling units; on the other hand, they had opinions as to the quality of various brands of appliances and associated this judgment with the quality of the dwelling unit. Because of the perceived importance of appliance brand image, builders seldom bought private brands.

Builders, however, were very cost conscious. They typically bought the middle and lower end of the product line. By buying all the appliances from one manufacturer they could save on transportaton costs and also establish the leverage to command a lower price. When a dwelling unit was ready for the appliance, it was crucial that the appliance be there. By maintaining a relationship with one manufacturer, the builder could apply pressure for timely delivery.

All the major companies active in the contract market sold full product lines. Some manufacturers also provided kitchen designing services to large builders, and all were able to advise builders how to match the quality of the appliance to the dwelling unit. Highly trained salesmen attempted to convince the builders of the merits of a particular brand.

Not all appliances were of equal importance to the housing market. Builders typically concentrated on three products: standard range/oven, dishwashers, and disposers. Of buyers surveyed, 53.1 percent felt a refrigerator should also be a standard feature, and another 34 percent were willing to pay for it as an option. Microwave ovens also seemed to be of some importance, as more than half of buyers felt they should be either standard or optional. A survey by the National Association of Home Builders also

[3] Parts of this section are taken from M.S. Hunt, "Note on the Major Home Appliance Industry," 1972.

suggested that the builders and manufacturers might not be fully tapping the home buyer's willingness to pay extra for optional products such as refrigerators, washers, and dryers.

The Retail Market. A study of the major home appliance and TV set market concluded that the purchase decision was precipitated by four major events (household move, family change, product failure, and wealth increase) and three catalysts (initial homemaking, seasonal gift-giving, and promotional offer).[4] The precipitating event was ordinarily preceded by an extended period of low-level involvement in information gathering (from parents, relatives, friends, media, etc.). For a short time after the stimulus event, purchasers sought information more intensively (visiting stores, looking in catalogs, calling up family and friends, etc.), trying to learn about available brands, price, performance (features), credit, and so on. Sales skills at the retail level were found to have a considerable influence on the purchase decision.

The study also shed light on several other aspects of appliance purchasing behavior. First, although people who had moved recently accounted for only 21 percent of the population, they purchased 60 percent of all the ranges, 53 percent of the refrigerators, 49 percent of the dryers, 47 percent of the dishwashers, and 43 percent of the washing machines. They were only slightly more likely than others to purchase air conditioners (25 percent) and freezers (22 percent). Second, while most appliance decisions were made jointly by the husband and wife, it was the wife who played the major role in the early stages: initiation, search, and determination of style and size. The husband became more involved in choosing a brand and determining how much to spend. Third, family, friends, and neighbors exercised considerable influence on the decision makers, since their advice was considered trustworthy, and they had a knowledge of the prospective buyers' needs and lifestyles. Neighbors also exerted a subtle pressure to "keep up with the Joneses." Fourth, most appliance purchasers visited only one store, which indicated a significant level of store and brand loyalty. The growth in the market share of private brands also reflected this tendency.[5] Fifth, appliances had a good performance record in use. In 1976, appliances accounted for just 4 percent of consumer grievances as measured by the Office of Consumer Affairs, compared with 19 percent for automobiles. Finally, appliances, like old soldiers, seldom died, they just faded away. A survey of refrigerator disposition found that 25 percent were sold, 19 percent given away, 20 percent traded, 8 percent converted, 4 percent rented or loaned, and only 23 percent thrown away.

Appliances were sold under the brand names of both retailers and manufacturers (either the original manufacturer or one that had sourced it from the original maker). National retail chains like Sears and Penney carried the Kenmore, Coldspot, and Penncrest lines as their only brands. Especially in the case of Sears,

[4] Peter Dickson and William Wilkie, "The Consumption of Household Durables: A Behavioral Review."

[5] From 1966 to 1970, a survey found that private brands grew from 36 to 43 percent of the total for freezers, 38 to 42 percent for washing machines, 35 to 40 percent for dryers, 14 to 24 percent for refrigerators, 12 to 13 percent for ranges, and 10 to 14 percent for dishwashers.

these national retail brands were designed by the retailer, manufactured according to its specifications, and heavily advertised. Sears accounted for more than half of the sales for Whirlpool, Roper, Sanyo, and D&M, and had recently started sourcing particular appliance types from more than one manufacturer. Some retailers, primarily large department stores, which sourced private-label products to be used as a bottom-of-the-line brand and sold primarily on price, discontinued this practice in the 1980s.

Appliances were sold through four major kinds of retail outlets: appliance dealers, national chain stores/mass merchandisers, discount stores, and department stores. Since the mid-1970s, the national chain stores had gained share in almost all product lines (Exhibit 7), primarily because of deeper penetration by Sears, which accounted for 50 percent of the sales in this category. Appliance stores also gained share, to a lesser extent, because of the emergence of large regional chain stores specializing in appliances (e.g., Lechmere, Polk Brothers, Trader Horn). Small independent appliance dealers held their own by providing personalized, special service which the large retailers could not offer. The biggest losers were the traditional department stores, many of which had gradually phased out their major home appliance departments. After significant gains in the 1960s and early 1970s, the discount stores (Kmart, Korvette's, Caldor's) had started to slip in the standard-size appliances, but had maintained or improved their position in compact appliances, microwave ovens, and room air conditioners.

Consumers showed considerable brand loyalty in their appliance purchases. Asked whether they would buy the same brand again when purchasing a new appliance, 70.1 percent of a survey sample said they would, 13.6 percent would not, while 16.3 percent did not know.[6] These figures represent an average for 10 different appliance products, with dishwashers at the very top with 81.3 percent. Interestingly enough, dishwashers were one of the products most likely to have been sourced externally by the manufacturer or retailer. A mid-1970s survey found that the most important factor in the purchase of cooking appliances was "reputation of brand."[7] Other significant factors included "special features," "overall appearance/styling," "good value for money/price," and so on. Less often cited factors were "manufacturer/store reputation for service" and "past experience with brand."

Companies exploited the importance of brand names in several ways. Maytag, GE, and other top-of-the-line firms used a "pull" strategy to get the customer committed to the brand before entering the store, thus making switching difficult. The "push" strategy, in contrast, encouraged switching in the store, by offering some unique product attribute and most often a lower price to clinch the sale. Manufacturers at the middle or lower end of the line, like White and Magic Chef, gave the retailer higher margins and advertising allowances to encourage them to push their products. Finally, the "sell-up" strategy used heavy advertising of low-priced models to pull customers into the store, where the salesmen were trained and financially motivated to push them into the higher-priced models. This combination strategy was characteristically practiced by the national retailers like Sears.

---

[6] *Look*, National Appliance Survey, 1963.

[7] "Cooking Appliance Survey," *Newsweek*, 1975.

DISTRIBUTION AND SERVICE

Manufacturers, retailers, and independents all had a stake in appliance distribution. GE was the only manufacturer that owned its entire distribution network. Some large manufacturers owned their distribution networks only in high-volume areas and used independent distributors elsewhere. Whirlpool, for example, owned 50 percent of its distribution, mainly in the Sunbelt states, and otherwise worked through independents. Most of the other manufacturers and retailers relied heavily on independent distributors. Sears, though, was the exception in having a 100 percent retailer-owned distribution.

Even the very largest manufacturer could not match the costs of an independent distributor that represented several noncompeting manufacturers, since the distributor could spread its warehousing, transportation, sales, and collections costs across its entire product mix. On the other hand, whoever owned the distribution had substantial influence over the retailers in areas such as inventory, pricing, selection of dealers, and advertising. Certain smaller manufacturers, like Maytag and Hobart-KitchenAid, bypassed the independent distributor as they concentrated on the high-price, high-quality image with top-of-the-line products. They sold and shipped directly to carefully selected, exclusively franchised dealers with whom they had a very close working relationship.

Two recent developments were complicating the wholesale and distribution side of the appliance industry. The first was a trend toward more drop shipments direct from the factory to the dealer, bypassing the distributor's warehouse. One large Whirlpool distributor estimated that in 1982, 60 percent of the units sold in his region did not pass through his warehouse. These direct dealer shipments cut costs about $18 per unit. The second trend was the emergence of buying groups. Sometimes dealers grouped their purchases and pressed the distributor for volume discounts. Similarly, large chains could shop for prices across several distributors' territories to get the best possible deal. Finally, some individual entrepreneurs had begun to act as subwholesalers, spotting imperfections in the marketplace and making deals wherever the opportunity arose.

GE was the only manufacturer and Sears and Penney's were the only retailers with their own appliance service networks. Other firms relied on franchised or freelance independent service agents. These service agents had no connection with independent distributors.

THE APPLIANCE VALUE CHAIN

The appliance business could be broken down into six major activities: product design; purchase or manufacture of components; manufacturing, final assembly, and testing; distribution and warehousing; sales and advertising; and after-sales service. For a typical appliance product, costs broke down as follows:

Sales	100%
Manufacturing cost	65–75
(a) Fully integrated	
–Raw materials	30–40
–Labor	6–10
–Plant and equipment	12–20
–General administration	12–20
(b) Not integrated	
–Components	35–45
–Labor and overhead	30–40
Transportation and warehousing	5–7
Advertising	1–2
Sales and other marketing	4–8
Service	2–5
Product R&D	2–5
Overhead	3–10

The optimum size of a finished goods plant was thought to be an annual capacity of 500,000 units for refrigerators, ranges, dishwashers, and washer/dryers; and 100,000 units for air conditioners. Though at one time production costs were estimated to be 10 to 40 percent higher in plants one-half to one-fifth the optimal size, the advent of robotics had led to current thinking that the optimum plant size could be much smaller than what it used to be. Plants were dedicated facilities, since each product category required its own specialized equipment on the assembly line. Even within a plant, different model configurations (e.g., top-mounted versus side-by-side) required their own dedicated lines, and some large manufacturers found it more efficient to manufacture them in separate plants. Vertically integrated manufacturers produced their own compressors, plastic molding, wiring harnesses, electronic controls, and so on. Even the most integrated manufacturer bought many components outside, however, since there were many efficient and competitive suppliers.

Full-line manufacturers that had concentrated their production and/or distribution facilities in one location were able to achieve economies (approximately 8–10 percent of transportation costs) by shipping full carloads loaded with different kinds of appliances. On the other hand, those whose production facilities were geographically dispersed had the advantage of shipping shorter distances to reach their markets. Producers of more than one line tended to use shared sales forces and brand names.

Economies were achieved in installation and after-sales service by companies that had sufficient volume to justify providing their own service rather than relying on independent service agents. Having its own service facility could also enhance the appliance maker's brand image. Although economies of scale were theoretically possible in product design, they had the least impact on overall cost position.

Most appliance companies offered a full range of products even if they did not produce all items themselves. A firm would fill the gaps in its line by putting its own brand name on products it purchased from another manufacturer. This practice was not confined to partial-line producers: everybody in the industry bought some product from someone else (see Exhibit 8).

INDUSTRY HISTORY

Prior to World War II, most appliance manufacturers produced a limited line of appliances developed from the original products of their companies.[8] General Electric started a refrigerator business, Maytag made washers, and Hotpoint produced electric ranges. The lines broadened but not until after World War II did manufacturers begin to offer full lines of products. Expansion continued in the following decade.

After 1955, however, the industry experienced overcapacity, leading to concentration through mergers and acquisitions among the manufacturers, and a proliferation of brands, both national and private. By the mid-1970s there was some feeling that home appliances were destined to become commodities, allowing the Japanese to become a dominant industry force. Others thought that certain peculiar industry forces, such as the giant vertically integrated retailers (e.g., Sears Roebuck), would lead to the development of a unique structure. Finally, some believed that

[8] This section has been compiled from: "Note on the Major Home Appliance Industry," prepared in 1972 by Michael S. Hunt, under the supervision of Professor Joseph L. Bower.

entirely new products and revolutionary changes in existing products would drastically alter the industry.

The industry almost doubled in size as several products grew very rapidly during the 1960s. (See Exhibit 1.) Room air conditioner and dishwasher unit sales almost quadrupled, and clothes dryers almost tripled. Even products in highly saturated markets—like refrigerators and ranges, which were already present in 99 percent of wired homes—experienced an increase of roughly 50 percent in unit sales over the decade. At the same time, the individual products themselves were changing. New features were added and the capacity of home appliances increased (witness the trend toward larger refrigerators and air conditioners). Product reliability also improved, and real prices declined about 10 percent. Interestingly, these advances came during the period of mounting public criticism of the automobile industry's failure to produce a better and less expensive product.

The major home appliance industry in 1970 shipped 28.2 million units with a retail value slightly over $6 billion. This represented an 82 percent increase in units and a 62 percent increase in dollar sales since 1961. It was believed that the coming decade promised even greater growth. In the next three years the industry achieved real growth of almost 30 percent. In 1973 some 39 million units were shipped, and the average price level was less than in 1961. Consumers seemed to sense the great value, as even appliances with a high saturation rate continued to score steady gains, buoyed by a robust economy.

As 1973 ended, economists began to project a slowdown in the economy, and consumer confidence surveys suggested a restraint in future spending. The Arab oil embargo had created considerable uncertainty about energy supply, and it was feared that fuel shortages might lead to material shortages as well. On the bright side, however, the market for dishwashers, air conditioners, and freezers was far from saturated, and new appliance products like microwave ovens and trash compactors seemed well positioned to take off.

By the close of 1974 the economy was in a recession, and consumers were not buying. The only bright spot seemed to be freezer sales, which were helped by the high price of food, along with the impact of the oil embargo on shopping trips. As real disposable incomes continued to decline, buyers deferred hard goods purchases as long as possible and simply did not replace their older appliances.

In 1975, as new housing starts fell to their lowest level in more than a decade, appliance shipments were lower than in any of the past seven years. Sales were down almost 30 percent from 1973 levels. Recognizing its vulnerability to downturns in housing construction, which accounted for an estimated 20 to 30 percent of appliance sales, the industry began paying greater attention to the replacement market in 1976 and 1977. However, the housing market rebounded in 1977 and 1978. Concurrently, consumers' disposable income was rising and credit was becoming more readily available, together with increased consumer confidence due to a robust economy. As a result of these trends, 1978 and 1979 were two of the three best years the industry had seen (1973 remained the all-time high).

Inflation put an end to the long period of stable retail price levels after 1975, however. Manufacturers found their profit margins squeezed by rising operating costs. Compounding the problem of rising costs, growth slowed in 1980. Housing starts were lower than in any year since 1975, and in 1981 declined further, to the lowest level in more than 20 years. The industry also seemed to be a victim of its own sturdy quality. The average life expectancy of an appliance was 10–15 years, and many functioned adequately for quite a bit longer. During tough economic times, consumers tended to invest in repair jobs to prolong their appliances' lives a few more years. It was estimated that about 40 percent of these repairs were of the do-it-yourself variety.

1983 began on a more positive note, and as the economy recovered, all signs seemed to be pointing to a significant upturn in housing and a surge in appliance sales. The domestic appliance manufacturers were ready for the long-awaited turnaround. And according to some, so too were the Japanese.

COMPETITORS

All the major automobile manufacturers except Chrysler had appliance divisions at one time: Frigidaire of General Motors, Philco of Ford, Kelvinator of American Motors, Franklin of Studebaker. The other two major automotive-related companies in the appliance business were Bendix and International Harvester. All of these firms had divested their appliance business units, most of which had been acquired by White Consolidated.

The giants in the electric/electronics industry—GE, RCA, Westinghouse, McGraw Edison, Emerson Electric—had also been involved in the appliance business. Only GE remained as a major force, while Emerson Electric, through its subsidiary, In-Sink-Erator, manufactured only disposals. Diversified companies in the appliance business included Rockwell, United Technologies, Borg-Warner, Litton, Raytheon, and Dart & Kraft. Still participating in 1982 were Litton, Raytheon (Caloric, Amana, Speed Queen, and Modern Maid), and Dart & Kraft (Hobart-KitchenAid).

According to a long-time industry observer, there had been approximately 300 specialist appliance manufacturers in the United States at the end of World War II. Almost all were quite small, regional, and focused on a single product area. Only about 15 remained active in 1982, most notably Whirlpool, Magic Chef, Maytag, Tappan (acquired by Electrolux of Sweden in 1979), D&M (Design and Manufacturing), and Roper (41 percent owned by Sears).

Current appliance industry participants fell into three broad categories: *(a)* those that manufactured a full range of appliance product groups (General Electric, Whirlpool, White Consolidated, and Magic Chef); *(b)* those that manufactured a partial line, one or two groups of appliances (Raytheon, Maytag, Tappan, Hobart-KitchenAid, and Thermador-Waste King); and *(c)* specialists that concentrated on only one product (In-Sink-Erator for disposals; D&M for dishwashers; Litton, Sharp, Sanyo, and Panasonic for microwave ovens; Fedders, Friedrich, Addison, and Emerson for room air conditioners).

GE and Whirlpool, with sales of over $2 billion each, had traditionally led the industry. As an analyst put it, "To gain market share, you need a pricing edge and no one can have a lower price structure than GE and Whirlpool."[9] GE had a powerful name and brand image and was the most vertically integrated of all the appliance companies. It manufactured some of its components and was the only appliance manufacturer that owned its entire

[9] James Majid of Shearson Loeb Rhodes Inc., quoted in *Industry Week*, January 21, 1980.

distribution and service facilities. Whirlpool owed its leadership position to its unique 50-year relationship with Sears, which accounted for just over half of Whirlpool's sales at the factory level. At retail, Sears was the leader in most product categories. Since Whirlpool was the prime manufacturer for most Sears products, it had the economies of scale needed to compete head-to-head with GE.

The third-ranked position belonged to White Consolidated, with approximately $1.5 billion in sales. White had built its position exclusively through acquisitions. While antitrust considerations prevented GE and Whirlpool from acquiring other appliance businesses, White was able to take over the troubled appliance divisions of all the automobile manufacturers and of Westinghouse in rapid succession as they were put up for sale. However, White had not yet integrated the acquired companies into a single organization. The company's brand names included Frigidaire, White-Westinghouse, Gibson, Kelvinator, and Philco. Traditionally, dealers have been reluctant to carry many lines, which may become a problem for White.

Less than half the size of White were Raytheon, Magic Chef, and Maytag (numbers 4, 5, and 6 in the industry). Raytheon had entered the business only in 1965, and had grown mainly by acquisition, its distinctive advantage being high technology. Magic Chef and Maytag, two long-established names in the industry, had historically stayed away from any acquisitions and concentrated on their special markets: ranges and laundry products, respectively. With recent acquisitions, however, both firms had become almost full-line manufacturers. Maytag had acquired Jenn-Air and Hardwick, both range manufacturers. Magic Chef acquired Admiral and Renco-Rheem. Both Maytag and Magic Chef shared with White and Raytheon the problems of having diverse locations and brand names. As a top executive of Whirlpool put it: "It'll take those people five years to digest those purchases, to find the right kind of distribution . . . but when they do—with the volumes they can get—it'll give them a better cost structure and make it tougher for specialist companies."[10] Tappan by itself ranked number 7, but its acquisition by Electrolux made it a strong potential competitor. A leading appliance manufacturer in Europe, Electrolux had been rapidly expanding through acquisition and had strong product lines precisely where Tappan had a gap—in the refrigerator business.

The remainder of the industry consisted of a few specialists focused on microwave ovens and dishwashers, the least saturated markets, which offered the greatest potential for further growth. Litton and three Japanese firms—Sharp, Sanyo, and Panasonic—had a considerable stake in the microwave market. The dishwasher specialist was the last of the true independents—privately held D&M (1982 sales, $170 million), which over the last decade had been the unchallenged leader in this segment.

One observer summed up the competitive rivalry and industry consolidation aptly:

> You can't see the change on the showroom floor, but the appliance industry has been through a turbulent period of mergers and purchases. Many of those familiar brands

[10] *Industry Week*, January 21, 1980.

> now belong to a new owner. The industry's leaders, GE and Whirlpool, are being pursued by a crowd of competitors. Every firm is trying to emphasize its lineup's strengths and shore up its weak points. Not everyone will succeed.[11]

INTERNATIONAL COMPETITION

Unlike the other major consumer durable products—especially automobiles and consumer electronics—major home appliances had resisted becoming vulnerable to imports and had not globalized in spite of many formidable manufacturers in the United States, Europe, and Japan.

Europe

The European market though in a state of flux was very much dominated by the Europeans. The six major markets were Italy, West Germany, the United Kingdom, France, Sweden, and Holland:[12]

Italy produced more appliances than any other European nation, 42 percent of total unit output. Efficient mass production techniques and design quality had allowed Italian manufacturers to take over the middle and low end of the European market. Zanussi was by far the largest manufacturer in Europe. The other major Italian appliance producers were Indesit, Merloni, Candy, and Philips (a subsidiary of the Dutch Philips).

Germany was a large, rich market with high-quality products. Its industry was the second largest in Europe, accounting for 21 percent of all units produced. The two full-line producers, Siemens Bosch and AEG Telefunken, dominated their home market and used this base to export aggressively in high-quality product segments.

Though the United Kingdom was the third largest European appliance producer, a large part of its domestic market went to imports. More than three quarters (78 percent) of domestic refrigerator and freezer sales in 1979 were imports, primarily from Italy. The two largest full-line producers, Hoover and General Electric, were not among the top 10 in Europe (Exhibit 9A). Both were in the process of closing some plants, as the U.K. producers were squeezed between low-cost imports at the bottom end of the market, and high-quality German products at the top.

France was a large and fairly rich market, with significant imports from Italy and Germany. Recently nationalized, Thomson-Brandt was the sole French appliance manufacturer, covering the entire product spectrum. It used product differentiation to protect its position from low-priced imports, and had a 40 percent market share in refrigerators and washing machines. (Philips claimed to be a close second in France.) Increasingly, Thomson-Brandt was looking toward export markets.

There were two other countries of significance, each dominated by a major domestic producer. One was Sweden, a large, developed market with very demanding consumers, where Electrolux had nationalized the industry. The second was Holland, a small though rich market, with Philips being the sole Dutch manufacturer. Philips also had extensive multinational operations. While the U.S. industry had seen a steady trend toward consolidation and nationalization, the European market

---

[11] Michael A. Verespej, "Appliances' New Lineups for the '80s," *Industry Week*, January 21, 1980.

[12] The description of each of the countries is based on Catherine Barr's "Merloni Group," HBS case, 1982.

was quite fragmented. According to an industry observer:

> [This is] not just the end of one upheaval but the opening of another that could last for the rest of the decade. . . . The European market is now similar in size and maturity to that of the United States. But there are at least 400 companies involved in the manufacture of white goods. The industry is still painfully out of gear with its marketplace. . . . The pressures on Europe's industry are mainly internal. For this is one sector which cannot blame the Americans or the Japanese for its misfortunes.[13]

In Germany, AEG had bought up about 50 companies in an attempt to become the market leader. In 1982, however, it was close to financial collapse and was being dismembered, with Zanussi, Philips, Electrolux, and Siemens Bosch negotiating to purchase various parts. The third largest German company, Bauknecht, was in the bankruptcy courts, and Philips had acquired a minority share in the firm with the option of buying future control. In response to the increasing success of low-cost Italian imports in the Scandinavian market, Electrolux had nationalized the industry by buying up many smaller manufacturers and consolidating their operations. It hoped to challenge Zanussi's leadership in Europe, and through its acquisition of Tappan had gained a foothold in the United States (the only European appliance manufacturer to do so). In 1984 Electrolux was attempting to buy Zanussi. Since certain creditors objected it was not certain whether it would succeed. Thomson-Brandt, the recently nationalized French producer, also had ambitious plans for exports outside Europe. The company's director of exports commented:

> Our domestic market is Europe, and it is saturated; demand is on the decline. . . . Therefore, it is only logical that any company that can afford to invest in other markets should do so. . . . I believe the United States, Canada, and Japan all offer an opportunity for our products. But at this stage, we are only evaluating the feasibility.[14]

The success of European appliances in the U.S. market seemed likely to depend on whether a trend toward downsizing developed. European manufacturers had considerable experience in producing versatile, well-designed compact appliances with the latest in electronic features. As in the United States, the fastest-growing appliances in Europe were microwave ovens and dishwashers. (See Exhibit 9B for saturation levels in European countries.) For example, in Germany, fewer than 1 percent of households reportedly had microwave ovens.

Japan

There were at least six major Japanese companies that manufactured appliances: Hitachi, Mitsubishi, Panasonic, Sanyo, Sharp, and Toshiba. Considering the success of Japanese consumer durable goods, in the U.S. market,[15] appliance executives were cautiously looking over their shoulders in 1982.

The Japanese had about 30 percent of the microwave oven market and 40 percent

[13] Christian Tyler, *The Financial Times*.

[14] Jules Arbose, *International Management*, December 1979. *Appliance Management*, April 1983.

[15] The Japanese made 93 percent of all motorcycles sold in the United States, 21 percent of automobiles (40 percent in California; 50 percent in subcompacts), 34 percent of color TVs. *Merchandising*, May 1982.

of the compact refrigerator market, and had just introduced a miniwasher. While the compact refrigerator market had remained steady at less than 1 million units for the past five years, the market for microwave ovens had been growing consistently, becoming the second largest-selling appliance product in the United States in 1981.

The Japanese strategy for the U.S. appliance market seemed to be two-pronged: exports and setting up manufacturing plants in the United States. As reported by an industry analyst:

> Matsushita, Sharp, and Sanyo will soon be making about 50,000 ovens a month in the United States—20 percent of total annual sales. Toshiba America Inc. may join them later this year. And Sanyo's San Diego plant is making 1,000 compact refrigerators a day, approximately 40 percent of the U.S. market. The Japanese appear to be picking their targets carefully, avoiding head-to-head competition with major U.S. manufacturers in mature product lines. . . . However, Sanyo does have plans to add a full-size refrigerator. . . .[16]

U.S. RESPONSE

Daniel Krum, CEO of Maytag, assessed the impact of changing demographics in the 80s, and summed up the challenge facing the appliance industry:

> Our historic customer is changing. Families consisting of both parents plus children are now a minority in the United States. They have been outnumbered by the combined total of one-parent families, childless married couples, persons living alone, and groups of unrelated people living together. . . . This means that the appliances we designed for families in the 1960s and 1970s may not do for the 1980s and 1990s. Living in smaller housing with fewer children suggests a need for appliances that are different. Perhaps stackable, and storable, and smaller, but still offering all the features and amenities that go with today's sophisticated appliances.
>
> Up until now many of the products we make have not been seriously challenged from abroad. Foreign makers have not been inclined to produce and export the full-size major appliances that the American market requires, without a viable domestic market of their own. But as we in the United States edge closer to what is being manufactured abroad, to perhaps produce a "world appliance"—one that can be sold throughout the United States, Europe, and Japan—the possibility of greater competition may grow. The potential would grow for vast new markets for U.S. manufacturers, but it also may well invite increased foreign competition within the United States.[17]

PROSPECTS FOR THE FUTURE

Future growth prospects for appliances are shown in Exhibit 10. Halfway through 1983, it appeared that the appliance industry may just turn out to be the unlikely leader of a renaissance in U.S. manufacturing. According to a major business publication:

> America's appliance industry is headed for sparkling good times. After a long brutal shakeout in which even such heavyweights as General Motors finally called it quits, a handful of survivors are

[16] "An Appliance Boom that May Not Last," *Business Week,* March 10, 1980.

[17] "AHAM: Execs Wrestle with Tough Problems," *Mart,* June 1982.

poised to reap the benefits of a boom fueled by a burst of housing starts and a long-awaited resurgence of replacement demand. Sales have already turned up, and the appliance makers, long renowned for high levels of productivity, are beginning a ferocious battle for market share.

The major appliance industry is stronger than ever. The struggle that winnowed out inefficient producers left a group of bigger and better-capitalized companies. There may be a lesson here for the increasing number of politicians and business leaders who espouse the notion that government should assume a larger role in protecting and reviving American industries. Left to its own devices, at least one mature industry has managed to revitalize itself.[18]

[18] Lisa Miller Mesdag, *Fortune*, July 25, 1983.

EXHIBIT 1
SUMMARY OF TOTAL SHIPMENTS (DOMESTIC AND EXPORTS) IN MILLIONS OF UNITS, AND THEIR RETAIL VALUE IN MILLIONS OF DOLLARS

	1961	*1966*	*1971*	*1972*	*1973*	*1974*
Refrigerators	3.48	4.98	5.69	6.32	7.01	6.27
	$1,027	$1,328	$1,542	$1,706	$1,936	$1,819
Freezers	1.05	1.10	1.44	1.58	2.70	3.52
	$ 293	$ 256	$ 311	$ 342	$ 580	$ 804
Air conditioners	1.50	3.35	5.44	4.51	5.35	4.56
	$ 389	$ 699	$1,147	$ 911	$1,069	$ 931
Gas ranges	1.81	2.18	2.55	2.66	2.48	1.95
	$ 272	$ 421	$ 517	$ 565	$ 544	$ 447
Electric ranges	1.55	2.01	2.71	3.12	3.64	3.23
	$ 411	$ 447	$ 601	$ 707	$1,016	$ 844
Microwave ovens	—	—	.10	.33	.44	.64
	—	—	$ 45	$ 130	$ 167	$ 217
Dishwashers	.62	1.53	2.48	3.20	3.70	3.32
	$ 155	$ 330	$ 542	$ 676	$ 800	$ 759
Disposals	.80	1.41	2.29	2.77	2.97	2.55
	$ 64	$ 85	$ 138	$ 172	$ 193	$ 194
Compactors	—	—	.10	.21	.32	.32
	—	—	$ 26	$ 48	$ 70	$ 66
Washers	3.44	4.45	4.61	5.11	5.98	5.34
	$ 882	$1,018	$1,077	$1,212	$1,434	$1,349
Dryers	1.24	2.36	3.38	3.93	4.55	3.89
	$ 245	$ 422	$ 583	$ 689	$ 821	$ 741
Total	15.49	23.37	30.79	33.85	39.04	35.59
	$3,738	$5,006	$6,529	$7,158	$8,630	$8,171
Average price	$ 241	$ 214	$ 212	$ 212	$ 221	$ 230

Source: *Merchandising* magazine.

1975	*1976*	*1977*	*1978*	*1979*	*1980*	*1981*	*1982*
4.90	5.37	6.39	6.81	6.54	6.05	5.87	5.10
$ 1,474	$1,748	$ 2,585	$ 3,461	$ 3,413	$ 3,359	$ 3,510	$ 3,161
2.74	1.79	1.98	1.83	2.19	2.08	1.93	1.54
$ 653	$ 469	$ 549	$ 566	$ 786	$ 840	$ 836	$ 706
2.67	2.96	4.15	4.93	4.39	3.79	4.14	3.12
$ 641	$ 741	$ 1,166	$ 1,563	$ 1,527	$ 1,393	$ 1,654	$ 1,312
1.62	1.83	1.75	1.80	1.79	1.53	1.50	1.38
$ 383	$ 484	$ 537	$ 619	$ 643	$ 583	$ 619	$ 585
1.36	2.73	3.35	3.60	3.29	2.81	2.63	2.12
$ 657	$ 817	$ 1,078	$ 1,293	$ 1,309	$ 1,170	$ 1,134	$ 932
.84	1.49	2.25	2.55	2.92	3.69	4.53	4.27
$ 337	$ 626	$ 995	$ 1,171	$ 1,338	$ 1639	$ 2140	$ 1999
2.70	3.14	3.36	3.56	3.50	2.72	2.57	2.23
$ 697	$ 855	$ 994	$ 1,082	$ 1,138	$ 960	$ 952	$ 858
2.08	2.52	2.94	3.31	3.32	2.89	3.07	2.69
$ 187	$ 252	$ 324	$ 285	$ 295	$ 277	$ 321	$ 293
.23	.25	.28	.30	.29	.23	.21	.18
$ 52	$ 57	$ 66	$ 72	$ 74	$ 62	$ 60	$ 52
4.48	4.75	5.12	5.28	5.18	4.71	4.67	4.18
$ 1,399	$1,621	$ 1,830	$ 1,831	$ 1,832	$ 1,765	$ 1,812	$ 1,757
3.06	3.37	3.62	3.68	3.60	3.19	3.16	2.82
$ 762	$ 887	$ 1,000	$ 938	$ 980	$ 935	$ 2,003	$ 964
27.68	30.20	35.10	37.65	37.01	33.69	34.28	29.04
$ 7,242	$8,552	$11,124	$12,881	$13,335	$12,983	$14,044	$12,139
$ 262	$ 283	$ 317	$ 342	$ 360	$ 385	$ 410	$ 418

EXHIBIT 2 PRODUCT LINE DATA—1982

	Total Units (millions)	Retail Value (millions of dollars)	Import Units (millions)	Import Value (millions of dollars)	Saturation (percent)	Average Life Expectancy (years)	Expected Replacement Demand 1984
Refrigerators							
Standard	4.37	$2,937	.16	$19	99.9%	13	5.46
Compact	.49	100	.41	29			
Freezers							
Standard	1.29	621	.10	16	42.8	15	1.19
Compact	.23	70					
Room air conditioners	2.75	1,173	—	—	27.0	11	3.20
Gas ranges	1.38	585	—	—	42.7	16	3.67
Electric ranges	2.04	902	—	—	58.2		
Microwave ovens	4.20	1,979	1.15	204	25.6	12	.44
Smooth-top ranges	.10	64	—	—	2.0	—	
Washers							
Standard	3.79	1,641	—	—	73.6	12	4.49
Compact	.25	74	—				
Dryers							
Standard	2.61	898	—	—	65.3	13	2.70
Compact	.17	56	—	—			
Dishwashers	2.18	846	—	—	44.5	11	3.00
Disposals	2.69	293	—	—	49.7	10	2.78
Compactors	.18	52	—	—	3.1	10	.10

Source: For "Units Shipped," "Retail Value," and "Saturation (Percent)" (1961–1978): *Merchandising* magazine. For "Saturation (Percent)" (1979 and 1982), "Life Expectancy," and "Units to be Replaced": *Appliance* magazine.

EXHIBIT 3 ANALYSIS OF COMPANY MARKET SHARE, REFRIGERATION
Percentage

		1982	*1981*	*1980*	*1979*	*1978*	*1977*	*1969*	*1964*	*1954*
Whirlpool	Refrigerator	30%	31%	31%	27%	27%	25%	27%	24%	8%
	Freezer	36	36	30	30	30	30	*	31	13
	Air conditioner	17	17	17	17	17	15	*	25	10
GE/	Refrigerator	25	28	26	30	30	30	21	21	26
Hotpoint	Freezer	*	*	*	*	*	*	*	6	7
	Air conditioner	20	20	20	20	20	20	*	12	8
White	Refrigerator	21	21	21	25	25	30	27	18	19
	Freezer	34	34	25	25	25	25	*	5	5
	Air conditioner	15	15	15	15	15	15	*	4	10
Magic Chef	Refrigerator	14	11	11	12	12	10	7	6	*
(Admiral)	Freezer	13	13	9	9	9	15	*	*	*
Revco	Freezer	—	—	15	15	15	15	*	*	*
Raytheon	Refrigerator	5	5	5	*	*	*	*	*	*
(Amana)	Freezer	7	7	*	*	*	*	*	*	*
Fedders	Air conditioner	14	15	15	15	15	15	*	11	4
Friedrich	Air conditioner	12	12	12	12	12	10	*	*	*
Addison	Air conditioner	10	10	10	10	10	10	*	*	*
Others	Refrigerator	5	4	6	6	6	5	20	37	47
	Freezer	10	10	21	21	21	15	*	51	75
	Air conditioner	12	11	11	11	11	15	*	48	68

*Could mean either does not manufacture, or insignificant market share, or figures not available and hence included in "Others"
Sources: For years 1977 to 1982: *Appliance magazine*. For years 1954, 1964, and 1969: "Note on the Major Home Appliance Industry."

EXHIBIT 4
ANALYSIS OF COMPANY MARKET SHARE, RANGES AND OVENS
Percentage

	Ranges/ Ovens	*1982*	*1981*	*1980*	*1979*	*1978*	*1977*	*1969*	*1964*	*1954*
Whirlpool	Electric	9%	9%	9%	9%	*	*	19%	20%	9%
	Microwave	5	4	*	*	*	*	*	*	*
GE/Hotpoint	Electric	33	35	35	35	35%	35%	15	13	12
	Microwave	16	19	21	13	13	10	*	*	*
White (including	Gas	6	*	*	*	*	*	*	*	*
Frigidaire)	Electric	18	18	18	18	18	20	11	9	7
Magic Chef	Gas	20	20	20	20	20	25 >	13	6	5
(Admiral)	Electric	5	5	5	5	13	10 >			
	Microwave	4	4	*	*	*	*			
Maytag (Jenn-	Gas	11	10	10	10	10	10			
Air and Hard-	Electric	7	5	5	5	*	*			
wick)	Microwave	1	1	*	*	*	*			
Raytheon	Gas	18	15	12	12	12	10			
(Amana and	Electric	8	*	*	*	*	*			
Caloric)	Microwave	10	14	13	20	20	20			
Electrolux	Gas	20	20	20	20	20	20 >	12	6	7
(Tappan)	Electric	6	6	6	6	10	10 >			
	Microwave	12	8	8	13	13	10			
Roper (41 per-	Gas	15	15	15	15	15	15 >	2	*	*
cent owned	Electric	7	8	8	8	10	10 >			
by Sears)	Microwave	1	*	*	*	*	*			
Litton	Microwave	11	14	14	23	20	25			
Sharp	Microwave	10	11	8	13	13	15			
Sanyo	Microwave	15	9	*	*	*	*			
Matsushita	Microwave	5	4	*	*	*	*			
Others	Gas	10	20	23	23	23	20 >	25	46	60
	Electric	7	14	14	14	14	15 >			
	Microwave	10	10	36	18	21	20			

*Could mean either does not manufacture, or insignificant market share, or figures not available and hence included in "Others."

Sources: For years 1977 to 1982: *Appliance* magazine. For years 1954, 1964, and 1969: "Note on the Major Home Appliance Industry," 1972.

EXHIBIT 5
ANALYSIS OF COMPANY MARKET SHARE, WASHERS AND DRYERS
Percentage

		1982	*1981*	*1980*	*1979*	*1978*	*1977*	*1969*	*1964*	*1954*
Whirlpool	Washers	41%	40%	40%	40%	40%	45%	46%	27%	18%
	Dryers (E)	40	40	40	40	40	40 >	45	43	26
	Dryers (G)	40	40	40	40	40	40			
GE/Hotpoint	Washers	20	20	20	20	20	20	16	11	8
	Dryers (E)	20	20	20	20	20	20 >	14	8	6
	Dryers (G)	15	15	15	15	15	15			
White	Washers	14	14	14	14	14	*	12	8	8
	Dryers (E)	15	15	15	15	15	10 >	9	8	9
	Dryers (G)	15	15	14	14	14	10			
Magic Chef	Washers	5	5	5	5	5	*			
(Norge)	Dryers (E)	5	5	5	5	5	*			
	Dryers (G)	5	5	5	5	5	*			
Maytag	Washers	15	15	15	15	15	15	10	11	8
	Dryers (E)	15	15	15	15	15	15 >	9	9	2
	Dryers (G)	15	15	15	15	15	15			
Others	Washers	5	6	6	6	6	20	16	43	58
	Dryers (E)	5	5	5	5	5	15 >	23	32	57
	Dryers (G)	10	10	11	11	11	20			

*Could mean either does not manufacture, or insignificant market share, or figures not available and hence included in "Others."

Sources: For years 1977 to 1982: *Appliance* magazine. For years 1954, 1964 and 1969: "Note on the Major Home Appliance Industry," 1972.

EXHIBIT 6
ANALYSIS OF COMPANY MARKET SHARE, CLEAN-UP PRODUCTS

		1982	*1981*	*1980*	*1979*	*1978*	*1977*	*1969*	*1964*	*1954*
Whirlpool	Dishwashers	7%	6%	*	*	*	*	5%	10%	*
	Compactors	45	45	45%	45%	45%	45%	*	*	*
GE/Hotpoint	Dishwashers	22	20	25	25	25	25	29	30	38%
	Disposals	—	—	35	35	35	40	*	*	*
	Compactors	30	30	30	30	30	30	*	*	*
White	Dishwashers	4	4	*	*	*	*	15	7	12
Maytag	Dishwashers	6	6	6	6	*	*	*	*	*
	Disposals	2	2	*	*	*	*	*	*	*
Hobart	Dishwashers	15	15	15	15	15	15	20	10	11
(KitchenAid)	Disposals	4	3	10	10	10	10	*	*	*
	Compactors	10	10	*	*	*	*	*	*	*
Thermador	Dishwashers	2	2	*	*	*	*	*	*	*
(Waste King)	Disposals	7	6	*	*	*	*	*	*	*
	Compactors	1	1	*	*	*	*	*	*	*
Design and Manufacturing	Dishwashers	42	45	45	45	45	45	25	18	*
In-Sink-Erator (Emerson Electric)	Disposals	60	60	25	25	25	18	*	*	*
Tappan	Disposals	20	25	20	20	10	15	*	*	*
(Anaheim)	Compactors	7	7	*	*	*	*	*	*	*
Others	Dishwashers	2	2	9	9	15	15	6	25	31
	Disposals	7	4	10	10	20	17	*	*	*
	Compactors	7	7	20	20	20	20	*	*	*

*Could mean either does not manufacture, or insignificant market share, or figures not available and hence included in "Others."
Sources: For years 1977 to 1982: *Appliance* magazine. For years 1954, 1964, and 1969: "Note on the Major Home Appliance Industry."

EXHIBIT 7
PERCENT OF APPLIANCE SALES BY TYPE OF OUTLET, 1982

	Standard Refrigerator	*Standard Freezer*	*Air Conditioner*	*Compact Refrigerator*	*Compact Freezer*	*Gas Range*
Appliance stores	33	15	28	25	18	42
Catalog/chain stores (Sears, Penney, etc.)	29	47	22	38	41	31
Department stores	8	14	13	9	12	3
Discount stores	5	13	25	18	16	5
Furniture stores	5	4	2	2	5	6
Catalog showroom	—	—	3	7	4	1
Builder/contractor	12	1	4	1	—	7
Kitchen remodeler	2	—	1	1	—	5
Plumbing contractor	—	—	—	—	—	—
Home improvement centers	—	—	—	—	—	—
Other	7	6	2	5	4	1

Source: *Merchandising.*

Electric Range	*Microwave*	*Standard Washer/ Dryer*	*Compact Washer/ Dryer*	*Dishwasher*	*Disposal*	*Compactor*
40	36	34	49	26	9	26
22	27	39	14	25	17	28
5	8	8	11	3	2	11
3	11	8	12	7	—	2
4	4	4	10	2	—	—
1	4	3	5	—	—	1
10	2	4	1	28	28	21
9	4	—	—	6	11	9
—	—	—	—	1	23	1
—	—	—	—	2	10	3
5	4	—	—	—	—	—

EXHIBIT 8
THE PRIVATE BRAND PICTURE: MANUFACTURERS WHO PRODUCE FOR THE VARIOUS PRIVATE BRANDERS

1. Refrigerators
   Admiral (Magic Chef)
   - Crossley Group
   - Magic Chef
   - Montgomery Ward
   - O'Keefe & Merritt
   - Tappan
   - Western Auto

   General Electric
   - Firestone Tire & Rubber Co.
   - J.C. Penney [out of business]*

   Whirlpool
   - Sears [also from White]

   White Consolidated
   - Gamble Skogmo
   - Marquette

2. Freezers
   Admiral (Magic Chef)
   - Crossley Group
   - Montgomery Ward
   - O'Keefe & Merritt
   - Tappan
   - Western Auto

   General Electric
   - Firestone Tire & Rubber Co.
   - J.C. Penney [out of business]*

   Whirlpool
   - Sears

   White Consolidated
   - Gamble Skogmo
   - Marquette

3. Dishwashers
   Design & Manufacturing
   - Admiral [from GE]*
   - Caloric
   - Chambers [from KitchenAid]*
   - Gaffers & Sattler
   - Magic Chef [from GE]*
   - O'Keefe & Merritt
   - Roper
   - Sears
   - Tappan

   General Electric
   - J.C. Penney [out of business]*

4. Disposals
   Anaheim Manufacturing (Tappan)
   - Admiral
   - Caloric
   - Earl's Plumbing
   - Gaffers & Sattler
   - GE/Hotpoint
   - Magic Chef
   - Modern Maid
   - O'Keefe & Merritt
   - Tappan

   In-Sink-Erator
   - Elkay [from Kelvinator]*
   - Frigidaire
   - Granger (Dayton)
   - Kelvinator
   - Roper
   - Sears
   - Tru-Value
   - Wards [from Waste-King]*
   - White-Westinghouse

5. Compactors
   General Electric
   - J.C. Penney

   Tappan
   - Caloric
   - Modern Maid

   Whirlpool
   - Modern Maid
   - Sears

6. Ranges (electric)
   Litton
   - J.C. Penney (microwave combinations)

   Magic Chef
   - Crossley Group
   - Gamble Skogmo
   - Sears
   - Montgomery Ward

   White Consolidated
   - J.C. Penney

7. Ranges (gas)
   Magic Chef
   - Crossley Group
   - Gamble Skogmo
   - Sears

   Roper
   - Jenn-Air

   Tappan
   - Montgomery Ward

   White Consolidated
   - J.C. Penney [out of business]*

8. Microwave Ovens
   Litton
   - North American
   - Phillips (Norelco)

   Magic Chef
   - Crossley Group
   - Gamble Skogmo

   Sanyo
   - Sears

   Sharp
   - Montgomery Ward

9. Washers
   General Electric
   - J.C. Penney [out of business]*

   Norge (Magic Chef)
   - Admiral
   - Crossley Group
   - Magic Chef
   - Marquette
   - Montgomery Ward
   - Western Auto

   Whirlpool
   - Sears

10. Dryers
    General Electric
    - J.C.Penney [out of business]*

    Norge (Magic Chef)
    - Admiral
    - Crossley Group
    - Magic Chef
    - Marquette
    - Montgomery Ward
    - Western Auto

    Whirlpool
    - Sears [also stackable from White]

*Telephone conversation with publisher of *Appliance* magazine on 2/21/84 for [changes].
Source: *Appliance*, September 1982.

EXHIBIT 9A
TOP 10 APPLIANCE MANUFACTURERS IN EUROPE

	Country	Appliance Sales (000 units)	
		1977	*1981*
1. Zanussi	Italy	3,872	4,000
2. Philips	Holland	2,583	2,800
3. Siemens-Bosch	Germany	2,200	2,300
4. AEG Telefunken	Germany	2,050	2,200
5. Electrolux	Sweden	1,540	2,000
6. Thomson-Brandt	France	1,950	1,600
7. Indesit	Italy	2,120	1,300
8. Merloni	Italy	773	1,200
9. Bauknecht	Germany	1,430	1,200
10. Candy	Italy	805	900

EXHIBIT 9B
SATURATION LEVELS FOR SELECTED APPLIANCES IN EUROPE, 1978–1979

	Washers	*Dishwashers*	*Refrigerators*	*Freezers*	*Electric Ranges*
Germany	88%	20%	95%	47%	70%
Italy	88	16	89	28	3
U.K.	77	3	91	44	41
France	72	13	83	23	10
Sweden	65	21	94	66	89
Holland	87	11	98	44	8

EXHIBIT 10
SIX-YEAR FORECAST BY APPLIANCE MANUFACTURERS

	1982 Projected	*1983*	*1984*	*1985*	*1986*	*1987*	*1988*
Refrigerators							
—Standard	4,418	4,640	4,965	5,288	5,432	5,586	5,806
—Compact	540	560	570	580	590	600	610
Freezers							
—Standard	1,423	1,487	1,591	1,627	1,691	1,753	1,805
—Compact	270	280	295	305	310	315	320
Air conditioners	2,850	2,978	3,267	3,270	3,435	3,500	3,633
Ranges/ovens							
—Gas	1,387	1,445	1,529	1,580	1,620	1,672	1,752
—Electric	2,061	2,213	2,343	2,458	2,551	2,634	2,710
—Microwave	3,864	4,485	4,892	5,188	5,150	5,300	5,446
Dishwashers	2,066	2,226	2,464	2,699	2,798	2,875	2,989
Disposals	2,600	2,856	3,055	3,236	3,113	3,197	3,260
Compactors	151	165	193	205	216	230	250
Washers							
—Standard	4,083	4,183	4,348	4,494	4,477	4,547	4,693
—Compact	269	282	295	307	312	320	330
Dryers							
—Standard (electric)	2,167	2,245	2,349	2,441	2,428	2,483	2,578
(gas)	574	498	626	649	646	653	679
—Compact	176	194	204	210	215	220	225

Source: *Appliance* magazine, January 1983.

Competitive Positioning in the Dishwasher Industry (A)

THE DISHWASHER MARKET

> Dishwasher sales rose dramatically—up to 40 percent—during the first quarter of this year [1983] compared with the same period in 1982, merchants told *Merchandising*. . . . Most said they have done little to spark the upturn in sales . . . when homes and apartments are built, they said dishwashers are bought. Also making purchases, merchants added, are consumers who can't afford to move. Instead they are remodeling their kitchens and putting in new dishwashers.[1]

As the economy recovered in 1983, increases in dishwasher sales led the appliance industry to a long-awaited turnaround. With a saturation level of under 45 percent, and the best-selling models retailing between $400 to $500 (with the top of the line being between $700 and $800), dishwashers appeared to be a true growth opportunity for an otherwise mature industry that seemed to be on the decline.

The manufacture of dishwashers is one of the most complicated of all appliances because it involves the combining of electrical, mechanical, and hydraulic (plus electronic in some models) technology. Ironically, the clear market share leader for dishwasher manufacturing was neither GE nor Whirlpool, who between them were either number 1 or number 2 in almost all appliance categories (Exhibit 1). Nor was it any of the top seven appliance manufacturers, who between them controlled anywhere from 80 percent to 90 percent of the appliance industry, but instead a small privately held company called D&M (Design and Manufacturing).

D&M got its start in the 1950s, because GE, who was the leader then, and Hobart and Frigidaire, who were far behind tied for the number 2 position, were all pursuing similar strategies of higher price and brand image in the dishwasher market. None of them was willing to serve the needs of retailers like Sears, whom they saw as their direct competition.

[1] Liz Leshin, "Dishwasher Sales Soar 40% Thanks to Construction Surge," *Merchandising*, May 1983.

Harvard Business School case 385–045.

This series of cases is designed so that discussion can focus on the major decision facing Sears in 1983 concerning its source for dishwashers. The (B) case describes the basic operation of its historical supplier, D&M. The (C) case introduces Sears in 1983. The (D) case describes GE, Sears's major competitor in home appliances. And the (E) case describes the alternatives under consideration at Sears in 1983.

EXHIBIT 1

	G.E.	*Whirlpool*
Refrigerators	#2	#1
Freezers	—	#1
Air conditioners	#1	#2
Gas ranges	—	—
Electric ranges	#1	#3
Microwave ovens	#1	#6 or 7
Washers	#2	#1
Dryers (E)	#2	#1
Dryers (G)	#2 (3-way tie)	#1
Dishwashers	#2	#4 (2-way tie)
Disposals	— (#1 until 1980)	—
Compactors	#2	#1

Competitive Positioning in the Dishwasher Industry (B)

DESIGN AND MANUFACTURING CO. (D&M)[1]

In 1959 Samuel Regenstrief left Philco to purchase the appliance division of Avco. Like so many of the other major manufacturers after World War II, Avco had gotten into the appliance business. And like many of these same manufacturers, Avco's appliance division started incurring substantial losses for want of effective distribution, and so Avco decided to sell out.

A D&M executive described the purchase of the Avco Division as follows:

> The Avco Division had a good production facility and a good dishwasher. What it lacked was a viable approach to the market. In simple terms, it lacked management. The Avco Division was precisely what Sam was looking for. Its book value was low because the plant was almost fully written off. It was also incurring heavy losses. Hence, Sam could afford to buy it and Avco could afford to sell it. Sam had the management capability to turn it around and turn it around he did.

Regenstrief described why he decided to go into the dishwasher business:

> It was clear to me that the dishwasher market was going to take off. The dishwasher accomplished a chore most families disliked and gave the housewife more free time. It also was beneficial from a health standpoint since very hot water could be used.
>
> I also felt that the national retailers offered a very attractive market. Originally manufacturers were creating the need for a specific brand of appliance. The "Frigidaire refrigerator" and "GE range" were examples of this. But as consumers came into closer contact with a wider range of appliances and appliances became more uniform in quality, the need that was being created was the need for the appliance. Value became key. National retailers gave the most value per dollar. In my opinion their success will continue because they are catering to the needs of today's consumers – the need for value.

---

[1] This case is excerpted from HBS case "Design & Manufacturing" (D&M) (372–343).

Harvard Business School case 385–046.

> There was another more philosophical reason for my interest in dishwashers. Home appliances like dishwashers improve the quality of life. I feel that the social problems that face this country arise from the great divergence in the quality of life. In the late 1950s dishwashers were too expensive to be purchased by any but the rich. This in my opinion contributed to the divergence in the quality of life.
>
> Yet the only measure of performance available to a businessman is profits. The dishwasher business offered a unique opportunity. By going into it with the intention of mass producing appliances and selling to national retailers and other manufacturers, I would make a profit only by continually lowering my production costs. Dishwasher prices would fall and dishwashers would quickly become available to any consumer that wanted one. Hence, by concentrating on profits I could make a positive contribution to society.

In commenting on D&M's strategy, Mr. Regenstrief stated:

> Our basic approach hasn't really changed over the last 12 years. We are in business to make as high profits as possible by fashioning and manufacturing a quality dishwasher and selling it to national retailers and other manufacturers. To succeed we have to have a product of competitive quality and a low-cost position in the industry.
>
> The reason that the low-cost position is crucial is that we can succeed only if we can sell a product for less than our customer can make it or buy it elsewhere. Our maximum margin is determined entirely by our production efficiency relative to our customers, our present competitors, and our future competitors.
>
> Given the importance of cost to this approach, I have been concerned with getting volume up and costs down since day one. We needed volume to have the operating efficiencies necessary for low cost. But we also need the most efficient product facility possible. As a result, we often scrap a piece of machinery a year or two after we buy it, if we can replace it with a better machine.
>
> The whole reason for starting D&M was that I felt that we could get the volume to make the strategy work. GE was skimming the cream off the market and no one was around to do what I wanted to do. The market had obvious growth potential. By getting in first and getting the volume we could have a natural advantage.
>
> Things have changed in the last 12 years. GE, for example, is now willing to slug it out on a cost basis where volume is involved. But we have the volume and the efficiency now to play this game profitably. No one can match our production costs today.

To achieve this strategy D&M had a very lean, informal, and flexible organization structure, where communication and responsibility cut across functional and hierarchical lines. This resulted in a strong commitment throughout the company to getting costs down and volume up by whatever means were necessary. As Regenstrief commented:

> I could draw you an organization chart, but it would be meaningless. . . . If I see that production costs are out of line for a given day, I don't call up Bud Kaufman, my production vice president. I call the foreman responsible and find out why. If his explanation doesn't suit me, or it happens again, then I talk to Bud. . . . This goes all the way down to the worker. If he is going to run out of parts it is his responsibility to get them—not just tell his foreman.

To ensure that he got the best out of his people, Mr. Regenstrief used bonuses and profit sharing (97 percent of the stock was owned by company employees, with the vast majority owned by Sam Regenstrief). As he put it:

> Our executives are rewarded heavily on the basis of corporate performance. Bonuses in a good year may be greater than salary. We carry this philosophy down to the worker level. A worker may earn 25 percent of his salary in bonus during a good year. Since our basic wage is competitive with other manufacturers, this means that we are among the highest paying firms in the industry. We do this not out of a sense of altruism but rather to guarantee that we get maximum effort out of everyone.
>
> My general approach is to keep the corporate overhead as low as possible. I want the best possible managers, but as few as possible. The same is true with our data collection. I want to know exactly what is going on in as few numbers as possible.

All of D&M's functional policies reflected the personal philosophy of Sam Regenstrief:

> Our approach to production is based on two concepts—simplicity and standardization. We want to produce the least complicated product and get as much standardization as possible in the parts. This allows us longer production runs and lower costs.
>
> We are continually installing new, more efficient equipment. The age of the equipment we replace is not important. We scrap equipment and take a capital loss whenever we find a better way to make the product. When we wanted to speed up the production flow by combining several of our operations which were in outlying buildings, we could not afford to build a new plant. So we figured out an ingenious way of building the new plant over the existing ones (which were later torn down), without slowing up production.
>
> I handle sales. The crucial three factors in each contract are price, volume, and design specification. In setting the price I start with a margin I am trying to achieve for our total sales. But with regards to each of 13 companies I set the price based on what they could produce it for and/or what it will take to keep them in business. Hence, I have to consider the companies' volume and their marketing and distribution costs. I want to supply as many companies as possible but only if each of them can give me the volume I need. With regards to design I give more leeway to the companies with higher volume. I occasionally will give a new company more leeway than their volume deserves to get them established in the market. But if the volume doesn't come I won't carry them.

It was generally agreed at D&M that the chief thrust of their product development was defensive. However, having a good defense resulted in occasional innovations. They only introduced a new feature or product (e.g., the countertop dishwasher) where they felt that there could be considerable demand and being first would be a strong advantage.

"Our basic philosophy in this area is to maintain D&M's position in the industry by helping our customers maintain theirs," stated Dr. Harold DeGroff, vice president of New Product Development and professor of business policy at Purdue University. He continued:

> We basically work in three areas—new features, environmental acceptance (e.g., noise and safety), and new processes. The first area is handled by our engineering staff at Connersville while the second two areas are handled at a facility we built in Lafayette, Indiana, near Purdue University, because they draw heavily on Purdue for part-time consultants.
>
> To understand our approach you have to understand the needs of our customers. The large national retailer we sell to needs a product of competitive quality that he can sell at a low price. He is particularly concerned with having unique features,

and he also needs to have those successful features that his competitors have. With the rest of our customers, dishwashers serve the purpose of broadening their product line. They need the dishwasher especially for the builder market, and this market is highly competitive.

In areas like noise and safety we are continually faced with the threat of new standards or tightening of old standards. We have to be ready to respond. In the area of new processes, we are faced with the threat of a whole new way to clean dishes. We are periodically working on ultrasonics and other approaches to protect ourselves from being out of business should one of these new technologies come to market.

Since D&M was responsible for repairs incurred during warranty, they had a rigid quality control inspection system and they also engaged in training their customers' service personnel. This enabled them to minimize the service expense for any given breakdown.

D&M had no substantial long-term debt. The rapid expansion in output and hence plant and equipment throughout the 1960s was financed almost entirely out of current profits. As one D&M executive described it, "After the first couple of years, the capital needed for expansion didn't really make much of a dent in current profits."

In commenting on the first 12 years of D&M, Mr. Regenstrief stated:

When I acquired the Avco Division it had a core of good engineering and production talent as well as the physical plant. With this as a base, we got rid of everything but the dishwasher, sink, and cabinet business. The latter two we kept until the mid-60s before dropping them because of their contribution to overhead. This contribution helped in the early days.

Starting with less than 100 employees and 60,000 units we have grown to a position of being the largest producer of dishwashers in the world with over 25 percent of the U.S. market. Our sales go to a leading national retailer and to 12 manufacturers. We now have in excess of 1,600 employees.

Prices have fallen over the last 12 years. We have, however, at the same time reduced costs considerably, but our margin has also decreased. Total profits have definitely increased.

Between 1961 to 1971, D&M's unit volume grew by 800 percent, while its revenues grew by 730 percent. As 1971 ended, Samuel Regenstrief, who by then was in his early 60s, commented on the future of D&M:

The future looks good. Only 25 percent of the U.S. homes have dishwashers. This means that there is considerable growth potential for the product. If anything, the market share of national retailers will expand because they offer the greatest value. Hence, I see no reason to expect our growth to slow.

Of course I am concerned about competition. A lot of companies would like to take our business away from us. To do that they would need our volume. The only way they could get it is if they introduced a significantly better product and could match our costs. Since we are continually improving our product I doubt if anyone could do this. But it is certainly something we are always looking at. It is one reason we stay lean and flexible. We must be able to move quickly to match any major changes in the product.

My biggest problem is to develop the management capability of D&M so that we can continue to fashion a better product at a lower cost. Our success over the last 12 years has been based on accomplishing these two tasks, and I see no reason for any change in the future.

Competitive Positioning in the Dishwasher Industry (C)

SEARS, ROEBUCK AND CO.

Though Sears does not manufacture a single appliance product, it is the largest seller of major home appliances, with a reported market share of approximately 35 percent. For Sears the problem has always been how to compete with the branded manufacturers, on both cost and features, when some leading manufacturers have been unwilling to sell to Sears on terms that can allow it to compete.

This case begins with Sears's early history, and its strategic uncertainty in the early 1970s. Then it examines some of the forces that lie behind Sears's success in the major home appliance business, the most important of which is its sourcing strategy.

EARLY HISTORY[1]

In 1895 Richard Sears in partnership with Alvah Roebuck began the profitable exploitation of the rural American market. "In his semiannual catalogue, Sears offered the American farmer a wide variety of goods and, because he purchased in large quantities and often directly from the manufacturer, offered them at a lower price than did the local merchants and storekeepers."[2]

In 1925 Sears initiated under General Wood a strategy of entry into direct retail selling based on store location, concentration on hard goods, mass purchasing, and limited backward integration into the production of these goods. To guarantee supply and eliminate the middlemen, Sears also purchased common shares (often a controlling interest) of its suppliers of "big ticket items."

Sears's growth placed increasing pressure on its highly centralized, functional organization. In the 1920s and 1930s a new form of organization developed. The merchandising functions (e.g., purchasing, designing, and advertising) were controlled at the corporate level, while the retail

[1] This section is excerpted from the HBS case "Sears, Roebuck and Company" (373–010).

Harvard Business School case 385–047.

[2] Chandler, *Strategy and Structure,* p. 226.

operations were each organized into profit-center territories with each store manager having considerable autonomy as to his actions.

A second major change after World War II was the move away from factory ownership. With the increasing complexity of the product and production process, and Sears's rapidly increasing retail volume, backward integration became less attractive. Furthermore, it was to Sears's advantage to have its suppliers sell their own national brand because it forced the manufacturer to keep up on new product development and achieve economies from higher volume. Since Sears needed products with competitive features, it required its suppliers to have strong product development capability.

Sears also began to adopt distinctive brand names (e.g., Coldspot and Kenmore) under which to sell its appliances nationally—thereby creating the concept of a retail national brand. One observer commented that "the mutual dependency between these suppliers and Sears allows Sears to buy at a low price while allowing the suppliers a fair profit, especially when the cost savings on their other sales are considered. And then," he said, "the organization takes over."

Appliance Organization

Two segments of the Sears organization were of crucial importance to its appliance business—the buying department at the corporate level and the department managers' offices at the store level. The merchandising department was responsible for the development, procurement, and promotion of all merchandise sold in Sears stores or catalogs. Reporting to each merchandising vice president were national merchandising managers, each with responsibility for a given group of products—for example, home laundry, freezers, air conditioners, and dehumidifiers, refrigerators, and kitchens (including ranges, disposals, and dishwashers).

The two key positions under the national merchandising manager were the buyer and retail sales manager. The buyer was responsible for everything having to do with his product. He determined the source of the product, the purchase price, product design, product research and development, retail pricing, service, and most important of all, sales and profit. The retail merchandising office was responsible for advertising, promotion, placement within the store, and so forth. Though the merchandising manager and his staff had no power to compel the retail stores to use their services or products, the stores typically followed the appliance policies set by the buyers.

At the retail end of the chain, each retail store was also a profit center. Reporting to the store manager were department heads responsible for various product groups within the store. These department heads, with the store manager's approval, and within the corporate policy guidelines, had the power to set product policy for that store, but they usually followed the buyers' guidelines. A bonus based on profits was a large part of total compensation for the store managers, which many believed was crucial to Sears's success in the appliance field.

Appliance Strategy

Sears's appliance strategy was characterized as a focused approach to retailing through merchandising. In order to get the sales and profit growth expected from appliances, Sears concentrated on heavy advertising to generate traffic, maintaining consistent quality and providing good service, and taking advantage of the natural traffic a Sears store generates. The product line design was based on the top-of-the-line product having the most advanced features, while the lowest-priced product, though of the same quality, had the least features. In between would be carefully spaced pricing points, each associated with a separate feature. Sears believed this gave their customers the opportunity to get the best buy at whatever level they could afford. It also contributed to Sears's financial success.

A second part of Sears's strategy also was based on volume. The higher the volume, the lower the cost to the manufacturers in selling to Sears, and the lower would be Sears's distribution costs. The latter cost reduction was based on the savings achieved from shipping full carloads to both regional warehouses and the larger Sears stores. This savings could be as much as 8 to 10 percent of the freight cost.

In describing Sears's pricing policy, the national merchandising manager for Home Laundry stated:

> After we have established the top-of-the-line and the bottom-of-the-line (our opening price point) we ask, "How many models do we need to fill the gap?" On the one hand, each price point must give the consumer real benefits as compared to the price point below it. On the other hand, the jump between price points must not be so great that the consumer will not be willing to move up. And we do not want to have too many price points, since every increase in stockkeeping units increases inventories. On automatic washing machines we have six basic retail price points.[3]

There were two key aspects to the pricing policy: the bottom-of-the-line price was set to be as low or lower than any of Sears's competitors, and there were a limited number of carefully spaced "pricing points"—each point associated with a separate feature.

Prior to the late 1960s, service represented Sears's clearest competitive advantage. Only Sears offered a service contract backed up by its own servicemen, while other manufacturers were forced to rely on franchised service operations. Just as important, the ability to locate service facilities in or near its stores allowed Sears store managers to supervise the service operation. Sears suppliers, however, were responsible for breakdowns during the warranty periods, which motivated them to design as reliable a product as possible as well as one that was easily serviceable. This competitive advantage for Sears began to erode by 1970, as GE started developing factory service outlets in most metropolitan areas with a population over 100,000.

Competitive Environment in the 1960s and 1970s

While in the past Montgomery Ward had been thought of as Sears's closest retail competition, by 1970 J.C. Penney had become the second largest retailer in the United States. Penney had been growing more rapidly than Sears in both sales and profits during the 60s and early 70s.

Penney was tied in with GE, Sears's largest competitor in the appliance market. GE had contracted to sell appliances to Penney for resale under the Penncrest name. This alliance between the largest national full-line appliance manufacturer and the second largest retailer was expected to be a source of trouble for Sears's appliance business in the future. At the

[3] Ibid., p. 302.

least, such an arrangement would help both GE and Penney make inroads on Sears's current volume advantage.

This threat was especially great if Sears suppliers were unable to attack the builder market successfully. If the suppliers' volume would drop, with this decline would come loss of scale economies. On the other hand, if Sears suppliers did penetrate this market segment successfully, Sears's business would not be as important to them. Hence, Sears was in danger of losing its buying power.

Despite these changes in the environment, Sears management did not appear to be directing a large part of its attention to the appliance business. Indications were that the primary changes in Sears's strategy went in the opposite direction—placing heavier relative emphasis on soft goods. A *Business Week* article suggested that Sears's new strategy was to maintain growth despite bigness, by broadening their market and diversifying.[4] To accomplish this, as the company approached saturation of its traditional middle-class market, Sears planned to aim for the low- and high-income segments of the market which it had previously eschewed. Soft goods, especially clothing, were expected to lead the way.

STRATEGIC REVERSAL—1970–1980[5]

By 1975, Sears was reporting sudden reverses in its sales and earning trends, while its competitors were having rising earnings. The business press attributed this to Sears's awesome size, the apparent drift in its strategic thrust, and the resulting image confusion it created among its customers. Some speculated that the 1960s' move into higher-priced merchandise and toward soft goods had hurt the company. The higher prices were eroding Sears's solid base of "needs" shoppers, but failing to attract upper income buyers. Sears for too long had been identified not with leather jackets and cocktail dresses but with pliers, refrigerators, and linens. Between 1967 and 1974, Sears's overall market share relative to its competitors' had decreased from 35 to 30 percent, while Penney's went from 14 to 16 percent, Kresge's 7 to 13 percent, and Woolworth's 8 to 10 percent.

Along with the setback in market share and earnings, there were changes in management and strong internal dissension about Sears's new strategic directions. This led to McKinsey & Co. being called in as consultants, as Sears felt that among other things "we needed an independent referee." McKinsey spent three months trying to convince Arthur Wood (CEO of Sears) and Charlie Meyer (VP Planning) to first focus on strategy. At the end of that time, McKinsey realized that they could not have been more wrong. "If we had worked on strategy first, it would have taken until 1983 to get any action," the McKinsey partner in charge admitted. He added: "The *impact of structure* and process at Sears was greater than any other situation I have seen in shaping the strategy and in inhibiting the consideration of new strategic directions."

McKinsey made two major recommendations. The first was that the 51 buying departments be organized into nine merchandising groups, each headed by a vice president. In addition, the territory managers were to significantly reduce their role in

[4] "How Giant Sears Grows and Grows," *Business Week*, December 16, 1972.

[5] This section is excerpted from HBS cases "Sears, Roebuck and Co. (B) and (C)" (580–131 and 132) written by Professor E. Raymond Corey.

merchandising decision making, which put the group and zone managers, who were closer to the marketplace, in more direct communication with headquarters buyers.

In 1977 a new strategy was launched to regain market share, to reestablish the Sears value image, and to build store traffic. The strategy was to use price promotions frequently and in depth. In retrospect, the emphasis on promotions and the severity of the price cuts exceeded prudent norms and led to a profit collapse. "But," according to one Sears executive, "1977 proved that the system worked. The field delivered what was asked of it." The 1978 goals, however, gave high priority to regaining margin percentage points as opposed to increasing market share.

On February 1, 1978, Edward Telling was named by Arthur Wood as his successor, becoming the 10th chairman in Sears history. Telling, who had worked his way up from the selling floor, described Sears's retail strategy for the 1980s:

> Sears strategy? First, you have to recognize that this is an exceedingly difficult retail climate. The expansion in square footage of retail store space in the last decade is unbelievable. It's very important for us to know exactly where we fit.
>
> To the customer, Sears is a state of mind: we serve the middle 60 percent on the economic scale. We offer quality at a reasonable price; we build goods to last. We offer fashion but not high style.
>
> We compete against Kmart, Penney, Wards, a lot of specialty shops (but not fashion shops), and in many towns, the local department store.

Thus Sears returned to its identity of 15 years earlier: a store for middle-class, home-owning America, offering quality at low prices.

APPLIANCE STRATEGY FOR THE 1980s

By 1983, of the nine Sears merchandising groups, the Home Appliance group was the second largest, contributing 19 percent of the total sales. The Home Appliance group consisted of four major product categories: (1) ranges and cooking equipment, (2) laundry, refrigeration, and air conditioning, (3) home entertainment (brown goods), and (4) vacuum cleaners and sewing machines. Dishwashers, disposals, and compactors were not part of the Home Appliance group, but instead, were part of the Kitchen Improvement section, which was part of the Building Materials group.

At the retail level, the appliance products took up 5 percent of the store space, while generating 20 percent of its volume, and contributing even greater to its profitability. The major home appliance strategy was based on "having a captive product, a captive sales organization, and a captive service network."

Product Planning

Sourcing Relationships. The foundation of Sears's appliance strategy was its strong relationship with its suppliers. And of all its suppliers, none has been more important than Whirlpool. Sears in 1982 accounted for just over 50 percent of Whirlpool's sales. Whirlpool supplied 100 percent of Sears's laundry products, 70 percent of the air conditioners, and 65 percent of the refrigerator and freezer products—the other 35 percent of refrigerators and freezers and 30 percent of the air conditioners being supplied by White. Since Whirlpool in the 1950s did not manufacture either ranges or dishwashers, Roper supplied most of Sears's electric and gas ranges and sales to Sears accounted for

78 percent of its total. D&M (Design and Manufacturing) supplied all their dishwasher requirements.

A senior executive recalled the Whirlpool-Sears partnership as it has evolved over time:

> It is an interesting paradox that when Sears started in the retail business, the big companies were not interested in supplying to us, so we had no choice but to deal with the little guys. We started buying from a lot of small companies, and one such company was the 1900 Corporation, which made a tub with a hand device for washing clothes. That was Sears's first entry into selling laundry appliances.
>
> During this time Bendix was the first to come out with an automatic washer. But it had a lot of problems. At that time there were no detergents, and the housewives used soap instead. The soap in those days contained quite a bit of grease, and grease was not compatible with the mechanical parts of the washing machines.
>
> The 1900 Corporation invented an automatic machine that would solve the problem that the Bendix machine was having, but they needed $1 million to gear up for production. This they did not have, nor could they raise. General Wood, the head of Sears at that time, decided to give them $1 million in return for an equity position, and thus began a long-lasting relationship. Soon was born the first of many millions of "Kenmore" machines. In its early days, the Kenmore washing machine was called a "jeep," because when it went into its spin cycle, it moved around like a jeep. The Bendix machine was a front load, while the Kenmore was a vertical access top load, and though Kenmore had fewer mechanical difficulties, it did have the problem of moving around during the spin cycle, which became obvious if the clothes were not evenly distributed. This problem was solved not in the factory, but in the customer's home, by the Sears salesmen. The salesmen would go into each customer's home, see where the machine was to be placed, and bolt the machine firmly to the floor. In homes where the machine could not be bolted to the floor, they would bolt it to a concrete base and then place it in position.
>
> Just as it was buying laundry machines from the 1900 Corporation, Sears bought refrigerators from the Seeger Corporation. Since Seeger wanted to become more of a full-line company, Sears arranged for the merger of the two companies, which was called Whirlpool. However, neither of the companies had any distribution or sales network to market their products to the general public. At that time RCA, which was heavily into brown goods, had no white goods (unlike GE, which had both white and brown goods), but they had the distribution expertise, so these two companies were put together. Thus, in the early 1950s, Sears was instrumental in the creation of RCA/Whirlpool, which enabled Whirlpool to get launched under its own brand into the marketplace, using RCA's distribution and sales network. In the 1970s RCA decided to concentrate on the brown goods, and cashed in its RCA/Whirlpool equity, leaving Whirlpool to manage on its own. However, to this day, Whirlpool and RCA share many of the same distributors.
>
> Though Sears no longer has any equity in Whirlpool either, its relationship has grown stronger over the years and exemplifies Sears's philosophy of wanting its suppliers to grow with it. This bond is further cemented by the management relationships between the companies. When Whirlpool needed someone to head up its marketing for outside sales, they took John Hurley from Sears for the job. Hurley then brought some other Sears people. The ex-CEO of Whirlpool, Bud Gray, was a store manager for Sears in New York at one time. His successor, John Platt, was responsible for the Sears account at Whirlpool.

Roper, too, in which Sears had a 41 percent equity, was a Sears creation.

> We were buying electric ranges from Newark Manufacturing, and we were buying farm equipment from David Bradley, and some other products from a third company, so we put the three companies together to form the Roper Corporation.

When relationships with domestic suppliers have not worked out, Sears has turned to Japanese manufacturers. Unable to devise a satisfactory supply arrangement with a major U.S. television manufacturer, Sears invested in Warwick for its TV sets. But Warwick was unable to produce to Sears's satisfaction. So Sears arranged for Whirlpool to acquire Warwick. However, Whirlpool's strength was in metal bending, and they could not make Warwick successful, either. So Sears assisted Whirlpool in finding Sanyo to buy Warwick, and took equity in the Sanyo Manufacturing Co. of USA, which has a plant in Arkansas.

Sears did not seem to feel that its equity positions in its suppliers created any conflict of priorities:

> Our buyers have the independence to make their decisions based on their criteria. We have only taken equity positions when that was the only way to make sure that the supplier provided us with what we needed. White goods are highly capital- intensive, and so we would much rather invest $10 million to open a new store than take an equity position in a supplier.

In keeping with its sourcing philosophy, Sears generally preferred to work with one, rather than multiple suppliers:

> If we are going to penetrate an industry, we must get the economies of scale. So we want to simplify. Why should we be buying from different manufacturers; because at the servicing level this would complicate the process!

When a Sears supplier does not offer a specific type of appliance, Sears may source it elsewhere, especially if it feels the product represents a limited market. While Whirlpool made the icemaker refrigerator, it did not sell well in the East because it required special piping and water connections that were not feasible or permitted in many apartment buildings. Hence Sears went to White for its purchases of these models. But when Sears perceives a major trend in the market not currently met by its supplier, it will try to induce its primary supplier to begin manufacturing the product. Thus, when Sears wanted to carry side-by-side refrigerators, it persuaded Whirlpool to make them. Sometimes the decision to go to another manufacturer comes down to costs:

> If we want a 28-inch refrigerator, and Whirlpool says it would cost $350,000 to tool up for it, and if Gibson [part of White Consolidated] already has an acceptable product, then we buy it from Gibson.

Product Design. Features are what distinguishes Sears products from their competitors' at the consumer level. They facilitate full-line selling, allowing the Sears sales force to demonstrate different features available at different price points. At the design stage, Sears tries to structure its product line so that the value of the features to the customer at the higher-priced models will outweigh the increases in sales price.

Even in product design, Sears maintains its partnership relationship with its suppliers who can also be its competitors:

> We take a major share of Whirlpool's products, so we get top choice of their

> latest designs. Sunburg and Farrar are the designers who do design work for both Whirlpool and Sears. The critical evaluation of their design work is that an objective group of persons can look at the two designs, and say they are quite different, though designed by the same firm. We also have our in-house designers who make sure that when the Sears identity comes on, there is no similarity in our product as compared to anyone else's.

However, Sears's approach to product planning is quite conservative:

> In product planning we use a lot of field input on what's selling, what the customers want, and what the competitors are selling. But overall we don't stray too far from our successful products. We would much rather stay with the tried and true products than be on the cutting edge.

Cost Leverages. A key element of Sears's sourcing strategy is its price negotiations with its suppliers. Sears buys most of its appliance products on a negotiated cost plus basis. It constantly works with its suppliers to make them the most cost-efficient producers. Hence, Sears knows generally what its suppliers' costs are for material, labor, and burden (overhead) for each product. To obtain economies of scale, Sears encourages its suppliers to sell a distinctly different line of merchandise to others, and so Sears competes with its suppliers downstream on the value chain where its real strengths lie. The point at which Sears stops being its supplier's partner, and instead becomes its competitor, is when the product acquires the Sears identity on the production line.

Sears's goal is to share as much of the production and assembly process with the suppliers' products as possible, as all costs are shared in cost plus contracts until the point at which the Sears product is differentiated from the manufacturer's product. From this point on, Sears starts to absorb all the costs for its product line.

Most Sears products have a 15 to 20 percent cost advantage over the manufacturer's product, because it costs the manufacturer at least that much more than Sears to distribute, market, sell, and service their product. While Sears can spread its distribution, warehousing, advertising, and selling costs across its entire retail product offerings, the manufacturer has far more limited economies of scale, and perhaps more important, has less expertise in retailing.

> We use this cost advantage to either put some of it back into product design or we use it to be more price competitive. For example, we recently made some design improvements in our washing machines by putting in an access panel on top of the machine. Now, for most repairs, the serviceman only has to open the panel instead of having to turn the machine around. This saves eight minutes of a service call, and we have about a thousand servicemen working an average of eight calls a day. We are continuously trying to take the costs out of this business. We want to be the residual legatee of the appliance business.

Marketing and Sales

Sears looks upon the major home appliance marketplace as "a bell-shaped curve," according to one of the national merchandising managers:

> Ten percent of each end is not our market, it's the remaining 80 percent that we consider our major marketplace. We are number 3 in brown goods, but number 1 in white goods. (The number 1 and number 2 in brown goods—RCA and Zenith—were not willing to sell to Sears, "the way we like to buy".)

At the retail level, 85 percent of the appliance sales are made directly at the stores, and 15 percent are through catalog sales. However, these catalog sales are made through small outlets where the models are displayed, so the customer can look at both the catalog and the merchandise before ordering.

There are two forces that are critical to their market share leadership.

> Our drawing power and selling power. Drawing power is the percent of people who shop our brand. Selling power is the percent of people who buy our brand, as a percent of those who were drawn to our brand. The key to achieving significant drawing power is advertising and price, while the key to selling power is the ability of the sales force to sell.
>
> This is a very advertising-sensitive market, and we have found in market after market that the biggest advertiser is often the market share leader. There is a direct correlation between advertising spending and market share vis-à-vis each of the competitors.
>
> But Sears's main advantage is that we have a highly trained sales force of product specialists who know their products and have a strong incentive to sell. Moreover, we had a wide range of well-organized and orderly price point increases.

For contract sales, Sears has a separate marketing effort concentrating on the builder market. The importance of this market to Sears is the volume, which contributes to higher economies of scale (e.g., it was estimated that in 1981, contract sales volume lowered the overall cost of manufacturing and as a result the cost of all refrigerators was reduced $3.75 per unit). Though it is not a leader in the contract market, Sears had two things going for them. One, the Sears name and service capabilities, and two, the ability to provide the builder with a total package that nobody else could: appliances, sinks, tubs, carpets, other home improvements, and furnishings.

Service Network

The capability of providing service and repair for the appliances sold is a key factor in developing consumer loyalty. Sears is the only retailer and one of the only three appliance sellers to own its service network (the other two being GE and Whirlpool). This control over one's own service network contributed a great deal to Sears's leadership position, and also has discouraged other retailers from getting into appliances.

> The greater advantage of having your own service network is that every time a serviceman enters your home, he is a silent salesman. In the eyes of the housewife, he is a very credible source and thus can greatly influence future buying decisions while repairing or servicing the appliance. This makes him quite an important cog in the wheel of building the replacement market for Sears.

Prospects for the Future

With J.C. Penney's recent decision to leave the major home appliance marketplace, Sears occupies a unique position as the only retailer with such tremendous influence in the industry. Surveying Sears's position as the residual legatee, a senior executive explained:

> What is meant by being the residual legatee? Sears is committed to the appliance business like no other national retailer. Penney's could no longer afford to remain in appliances. In a major strategic move, they decided to concentrate on soft goods and get out of products that are

Sears's strengths—Automotive, Home Improvement, and Major Home Appliances. Ward's are deflating their thrust in home appliances.

Sears, on the other hand, features home appliances very strongly. If you will go into any of our "stores of the future," you will find the finest presentation of home appliance products anywhere. For us, there is no national competition, there is only local competition like Lechmere in Boston or Polk Brothers in Chicago or local dealers, many of whom have a high turnover.

GE has always thought of Sears as their major competition, but their real competitor is going to be Whirlpool. Besides, GE is at the mercy of its local dealers, and the local dealers sell a mix of products. Nobody controls its sales like Sears does.

Montgomery Ward has recently started buying from Maytag. But it is not using Maytag as a private brand. Instead it is using the Maytag brand to draw people into the stores, so that it can then sell them Wards' own lower-priced private brand products, as frequently its Maytag prices are not locally competitive.

This is a mature business, and the industry in 1983 was functioning between 65 and 70 percent capacity. If there is any market share change it will be the big guys who will take away from the smaller ones. After Sears, GE, and Whirlpool, there really is no full-line name of any significance.

White does not make a single product under its own name, and that is their major problem. Presently McKinsey & Co. are doing a major strategy study for them. Magic Chef meanwhile faces financial problems.

Maytag, though quite profitable so far, is now attempting to become full line. They have gone into dishwashers and ranges, but they are going to have problems finding distributors, because their present distributors and dealers are already handling KitchenAid or Amana or some other line.

Raytheon still is not full line, and could be a candidate to purchase KitchenAid but will still have problems at the service end because they provide service through independent contractors.

So there still is more settling in the industry to happen. It probably will be like the automobile industry with the "Big Three" remaining, while the other small companies like American Motors and others are just struggling to get along.

Competitive Positioning in the Dishwasher Industry (D)

GENERAL ELECTRIC (GE)

> General Electric, which neglected its major-appliance business from 1978 to 1981 while it debated about whether to be in appliances at all, is gunning to reassert itself. . . . Now that it has decided to stay in the appliance business, GE strikes terror in the hearts of smaller players. Its dishwashers and microwave ovens are nudging their way to big market shares in the two fastest-growing segments of the industry. (*Fortune,* July 25, 1983.)

EARLY BACKGROUND[1]

GE entered the appliance field in 1918 with the acquisition of Hotpoint. Hotpoint, which produced and marketed irons and ranges, operated as a separate division and constituted GE's sole effort to that time in the appliance field. Hotpoint's business grew rapidly through the 20s. In the 1930s, with the advent of the electric refrigerator, GE introduced its own appliance brand. Gradually during the 1930s and after the war, the GE and Hotpoint lines expanded independently and began to compete with one another. Independent development continued through the 1950s under GE's decentralized organization structure, although the two appliance divisions were formally merged in 1952.

In the 1950s GE adopted a policy of building capacity ahead of demand. Construction of the vast Louisville manufacturing facility was the result. The goal seemed to be to achieve high market share and attendant scale manufacturing economies. Low unit production costs thus attained later gave GE a distinct competitive advantage in the increasingly price-sensitive appliance industry. This advantage was not shared as fully by the Hotpoint line, which maintained separate and more modest production facilities into the 1960s.

In the 1960s development of the appliance business took a back seat at GE to three new capital-intensive businesses: computers, breeder reactors, and heavy jet

[1] This section is from HBS cases, "Note on the Major Home Appliance Industry" (372–349) and "Associated Electrical Manufacturers" (372–344).

Harvard Business School case 385–048.

aircraft engines. The 1960s did, however, see the merger of Hotpoint and GE production facilities in 1965.

As GE entered the 1970s the appliance business again moved to the forefront as a potential money-maker in the wake of disappointments and even some outright failures in three glamour businesses in the 1960s. Organizationally, GE integrated Hotpoint and GE appliance lines into one centrally coordinated appliance group. This merely gave official recognition to the informal working arrangements followed since the merger of production facilities in 1965.

In the 1970s GE strove for maximum coverage in the marketplace with three product brands—GE, Hotpoint, and Penncrest (made for J.C. Penney). With these three brands, they believed they could cover the major market segments. In the retail market GE was able to get its products into more stores with three brands than they could with one. The GE brand had a larger number of models, which were higher featured—higher priced than the Hotpoint brand models. The Penncrest brand was the private label brand for Penney's. As one Hotpoint executive explained: "We needed volume and Sears's success suggested that this area would give us volume. We could go after the Penney's account without substantial risk to our brand image."

GE believed its biggest competitor was not any of the other appliance manufacturers, but Sears. According to a senior GE executive:

> Sears has the advantage of directly controlling retail price and advertising as well as their salesmen. This allows Sears to advertise low-feature/low-price products and then sell the customer up to more expensive items. Along with the traffic a Sears store generates, Sears will get a chance to sell to most classes of purchasers. We want to maximize coverage so that we get a shot at them also. By being in most of the important retail appliance stores and by selling through Penney's we feel we will get a chance to sell our products.

The other major thrust of GE's appliance strategy was in the contract (new construction) segment of the appliance market. Here the GE brand and reputation for innovation were a tremendous asset in competing for the business of home builders. Manufacturing and distribution muscle also helped in fighting for share in this highly price-sensitive market. With Sears absent, both the GE and Hotpoint brands had achieved important market positions. As one of the executives described GE's strength in 1971:

> We have now and have had since the very beginning good relations with the big builders. This not only has educated us to their needs, but also guarantees us a good chance to sell to the largest part of the market. We have a strong brand image which is very important for the builders. We have a very fine logistic system and can provide reliable service. Finally, we are the volume producer—an important advantage in a highly competitive industry.
>
> In this market Sears is not an important threat as of now, and because of its poor brand image we do not anticipate it becoming one in the near future. In this market segment we feel confident that we can grow and grow profitably.

To this the group executive added:

> If the growth over the next decade in the appliance industry is going to come up from the contract market segment, then our success as a group is highly dependent on our success in this market.

Summarizing what most executives felt to be GE's prime weakness—lack of control over retail salesmen, advertising, and price—one GE executive commented:

> The main area where we are at a disadvantage is in direct control over retail strategy. We just can't do what Sears can do. Even if we wanted to forward integrate we wouldn't have the talent to make the move successfully. We just don't have retail skills.

In the early 1970s the strategic planning system at GE had been completely revised and the strategic planners for the appliance group had, after careful consideration, prepared two growth strategies for the next decade. The first was the conservative position, where the goal was to grow by 75 percent in terms of unit volume over the next decade. This was the rate at which they expected the industry to grow, and hence in this scenario GE would maintain its market share. The second strategy was more ambitious, as its goal was to grow faster than the industry and increase market share in several product categories.

Either alternative entailed a significant increase in manufacturing capacity, with a capital investment of several hundred million dollars. So the only real choice was whether to continue this expansion on a normal or an accelerated basis, as the commitment to expansion had already been made. This was to be a repeat of the successful strategy followed by GE after World War II, when they had decided to build capacity ahead of demand. Their goal was to achieve high market share by becoming the most efficient producer. This meant achieving economies of scale in manufacturing. Hence, GE decided to build another huge appliance manufacturing complex similar to the one in Louisville, this time in Columbia, Maryland. It was to be called "Appliance Park East"; however, it never became fully operational.

MANUFACTURING BASE

The Louisville appliance park when built was considered by GE to be the largest, most efficient appliance facility in the world. In contrast, their major manufacturing competitors—Whirlpool and White—had acquired their plants which were geographically scattered. Moreover, GE was the most vertically integrated. It had integrated backwards into various components—compressors, plastic moulding, wiring harnesses, electronic controls, and so forth, and had integrated forward into distribution, sales, and service. However, the twin strategies of "economies of scale" and "vertical integration" seemed to require a high capacity utilization to result in least-cost production. But instead, according to an industry executive well versed in plant functions, the Louisville complex was suffering from "diseconomies of scale." He believed that the difference between an 85 percent capacity operation and a 50 percent capacity operation would amount to a 20 percent increase in labor and overhead costs on a per unit basis. The next thing he felt one had to recognize is that there are almost no economies of scale in purchasing that would not be available to most of the appliance manufacturers.

He added that, even at the theoretically optimum utilization, there were trade-offs between large plants and smaller plants that were often not recognized. In coming down to half the plant size from the minimum efficient scale (see Industry Note), one would not incur that big a penalty—a 5–10 percent theoretical cost efficiency—but this would be more than compensated for in having a more manageable plant, less chances of unionization, more flexible work practices, higher productivity of all workers, and even better quality control. A GE executive admitted: "We would not build another Louisville-size plant."

As for multiplant locations he said:

> There are relatively negligible economies of scale, once you are past full carload shipments. Ideally there would be separate plants located centrally around the country, specializing in one product type.

As for the threat from Japanese manufacturers, one of the GE executives who had just returned from a trip to Japan commented:

> There is no secret to having a world class manufacturing plant. It's just that the United States made a big mistake of letting their plants get 30 years old. Japanese plants are now state-of-the-art. They have power and free system on their lines, all foot pedals instead of hand controls, automatic screwdrivers, etc., and moreover they devote 25 percent of their assembly line for testing.

He felt that the reason the Japanese had made an entry into small refrigerators is because "the domestic manufacturers have left a window open in the small-size, high-feature niche of the market." He felt that they had a much easier entry in microwave ovens than they would have in larger appliances because "in major appliances one winds up paying shipping costs for transporting cubic feet of air." He believed that their main thrust would be in the area of electronic components. "The Japanese content of U.S. appliances will grow as components can be shipped efficiently. Also, Korean manufacturers [of components] will become important."

Under this backdrop GE in the early 1980s moved towards a strategy of more outside sourcing and away from vertical integration, especially for the electronic components in microwave ovens. GE had divested itself of the "disposals" business and would be sourcing them from outside in order to maintain its full-line posture. They had also divested themselves of the central air-conditioning business, in order to focus on their other major home appliances. Their investment priorities were to be in dishwashers and microwave ovens, with dishwashers being the area of major focus. The thrust in dishwashers was twofold: "First, to achieve the highest level of automation in the factory; and second to make a major switch to a plastic tub." According to a GE executive:

> In the dishwasher market, the key requirements are: reliability, cost, noise, wash performance, and energy use. Since dishwashers are a water-bearing product, plastics are definitely superior from a corrosion, cost, and noise viewpoint. The major hurdle for every manufacturer has been to make the plastic more durable. This is where we made the R&D investment. Our biggest competitor, D&M, is making a major investment in the powder porcelain process and is staying with porcelain tubs. Whirlpool, on the other hand, is going partially plastic with their doors.

STRUCTURE AND STRATEGY

To implement their strategy of growth and in keeping with GE's philosophy of decentralization, the Appliance Group was reorganized in 1970. The most important change then was the elimination of separate sales divisions for GE and Hotpoint, and instead, the setting up of separate sales divisions for retail and contract, to emphasize the importance of the latter. Also a staff function for strategic planning was added. The four major product divisions—Air Conditioning, Refrigerators, Home Laundry, and Kitchen Appliances—continued as profit centers.

Ten years later, in what industry observers considered a major revamping, GE decided to centralize and cut back its organization structure. The individual profit centers which by 1981 had grown to six (Kitchen Appliances was split into Ranges and Dishwashers, and Compressors was added) ceased to exist. Instead, all manufacturing, marketing, sales, and technology were centralized by function. Paul Van Orden, the executive vice president in charge of the Consumer Products Sector and to whom the Home Appliance Group reported, put it this way:

> What we have encountered has been three tough years. . . . In response we have restructured several of our businesses internally. . . . As the consumer business went through its growth phase, there was a tendency to keep adding structure. We did it, and we weren't the only ones. . . .
>
> We were structured by product category. We've now recognized that major appliances are essentially one business . . . and we've reorganized along functional lines. . . . Our major appliance group has gone through some organizational turmoil . . . but Roger Schipke has a strong group of people.[2]

This organization turmoil Van Orden referred to was most likely the matrix organization structure that preceded the centralization structure. One veteran GE executive commenting on the matrix organization felt that "it was a disastrous experiment. It was the worst possible form of organization. It had great problems." This was also the period when GE was totally enamored by strategic planning and developed the Strategic Business Unit (SBU) concept. As reported in the *New York Times* Reginald Jones, then GE's chairman, explained:[3]

> We couldn't plan for refrigerators independently of ranges. So we superimposed over the organizational structure a strategic planning structure of SBUs—single departments or several as long as they were unique from a planning point of view. . . . That's what strategic planning is all about: How you allocate resources for optimum growth.

The *New York Times* went on to note:

> The GE way is to assign different priorities to different SBUs forming a matrix of enterprises, some of which are always weaning, and some of which are always nurturing. The budget reflects these priorities. The result, theoretically at least, is continued growth with steady profits.
>
> GE categorizes all its SBUs into one of four classifications, which the SBUs, in turn, use to categorize each of their individual product lines. First come "invest/grow" businesses. . . . Then there are "selectivity/grow" and "selectivity/earnings" businesses. . . . Finally there are "harvest/divest" businesses. . . .
>
> To all this Mr. Jones has now added yet another layer of strategic planning. He has grouped the SBUs with five broad "sectors" that amount to super SBUs.

The Major Appliance SBU was a part of the Consumer Products Sector. (The other SBUs in the sector were lighting products, houseware and audio products, room air

---

[2] "GE: Tough Times, Tough Decisions," *HFD Retail Home Furnishings*, February 14, 1983.

[3] Anthony J. Parisi, "Management: GE's Search for Synergy," *New York Times*, April 16, 1978.

conditioners, television receivers, and broadcasting and cablevision. Heading up the Major Appliance SBU was Roger Schipke who formerly was the general manager of the laundry and dishwasher product division.

With the major home appliance plants operating at 50 percent capacity, the future outlook of the industry a little uncertain, and Jack Welch's well-publicized management philosophy—of not wanting to remain in a business where GE is not, nor has prospects of becoming, number 1 or number 2—looming in the background, the centralized organization structure reflected the appliance division's new priorities. As Paul Van Orden, executive vice president Consumer Products Sector put it:

> If you are going to be a significant factor, you are going to have to cut costs and take away business from the others. . . . In the hard goods business, you have to be careful that you don't get too wrapped up in the product engineering and manufacturing processes and neglect the consumer. . . . We also want to pay more attention to the retail structure and product positioning.[4]

COMEBACK IN THE MARKETPLACE

The major challenge facing GE in 1982, as stated by a product management executive, is "how to achieve better capacity utilization." The way they hoped to achieve this was through a two-pronged approach: "First, increase volume. Second, rationalize the factories."

In the late 1970s and early 1980s, the housing market took a real downturn and GE's strength became its vulnerability. Historically the appliance market had been retail 70 percent and contract 30 percent, with GE's mix being retail 60 percent and contract 40 percent. By 1981 the contract market was down to 20 percent of the total and GE was hurting badly. An industry publication reported:

> General Electric's major-appliance sales were the "biggest difficulty" in the firm's consumer products sector last year, according to GE chairman John Welch. "We were hit perhaps harder than anyone else in the industry as a result of our strong contract position and the downturn in housing completion," Welch said recently. "It was a tough year for GE in the appliance business, and we lost a point or two of market share as a result of the relative weakness in the contract vs. retail segments."[5]

On the retail side, too, there were troubles, as Penney's, which was GE's largest customer, decided in 1982 to get out of selling major appliances, as a result of a strategic shift in their merchandising policy. In November 1982, looking back on what went wrong over the past decade, one of the general managers for product management at GE appliance division said:

> During the peak years of the mid-1970s, some significant errors were made in projecting the growth of the industry. First, the projections on housing starts were way too high. Second, too much importance was put on the "keeping-up-with-the-Joneses" factor; instead the replacement cycles have stretched out significantly further than projected with a 40 percent rate of do-it-yourself repairs. While the corrosion factor in dishwashers and laundry washers reduced their life, there is very little that breaks down in

[4] "GE: Tough Times, Tough Decisions."

[5] "Newswatch," *Mart*, February 1982.

> refrigerators and ranges, so there is no definite "have to replace in" number of years. Third, the projections were made on a straight line trend of the past basis rather than on a saturation basis.

One of the general managers for the plants commented:

> Having a correct perception of the market is of great significance. The market has contracted, and the critical issue is how grossly people misforecasted the market. There is a dramatic difference between where people perceived the market would be and where it finally ended up. We were late in lacing up to the realities of the situation.

According to *Business Week*[6] it was more than just poor forecasting:

> Far more pervasive, however, has been the effect of bottom-line pressure on the quality of many of its consumer products. GE spending decisions for several years have clearly underlined the cash-cow status of that sector. In 1976, for example, consumer products contributed 22 percent of GE's net income while receiving only 12 percent of the company's $740.4 million capital budget for new plant and equipment.
>
> Keeping margins up on decreased investments is obviously desirable, but not at the cost of quality. And Welch concedes that GE's product quality in consumer goods has dropped in its customers' estimation.
>
> Welch has wrestled with this problem since 1977, when he first took over management of consumer products. His most ambitious program to date is under way right now at a dishwasher manufacturing plant in Louisville. There, GE is investing $38.6 million to create a new showcase factory for use as a model for other GE appliance operations. The object is to build the premier quality dishwasher in the United States at a reasonable price—not only by giving workers the latest tools and technology but also by allowing workers to stop the line at key points to prevent defects from being built in. "That means even if production numbers are not met," adds Welch.
>
> The new plan envisions making GE's Building 3, already the largest dishwasher plant in the world, the most modern facility as well by 1983. About 60 percent of the current equipment will be replaced with more sophisticated machines and automated assembly systems.
>
> Richard O. Donegan, senior vice president and group executive of GE's major appliance business, hints that the dishwasher plant is only the beginning. Depending on the nature of the competition and the success of this effort in improving GE's market share and sales, he suggests possible investment of as much as $1 billion in his group over the next five years. Through the investments already made, he notes, GE's appliance production lines now employ 50 percent of the industrial robots used throughout the company.
>
> Because so many manufacturers have sold their major appliance businesses in the last six years (the list includes Westinghouse, General Motors, and Rockwell International), GE has gained market share in refrigerators, color TVs, and central air conditioners since 1974, according to *Appliance Manufacturer* estimates. But GE's dishwasher line dropped to 18 percent in 1980 from its 26 percent share in 1974, and its washing machines dropped to 16 percent of the market from their 18 percent share. "A consumer punch in the eye," Welch notes, "does not go away for maybe a decade." Moreover, he adds, if quality is not improved, "we will not be a major factor in the appliance business in the mid-1980s."

[6] "Corporate Strategies: General Electric—The Financial Wizards Switch Back to Technology," *Business Week*, March 16, 1981.

By early 1983 GE appeared to be on the brink of a comeback as it heralded its modernized dishwasher plant as the most technologically advanced dishwasher manufacturing system in the world. In rebuilding this plant it may have signaled a new trend for U.S. manufacturing. As an industry publication reported:[7]

> It all began about 4 years ago—the work culminated in Project C, the remodernization of General Electric's dishwasher plant in Louisville, Kentucky. "We had two objectives," says Raymond L. Rissler, manager, Project C programs operation. "Our first was to build a better product—one that could be produced with consistent high quality, hour after hour, day after day. And second, to build the product better—to provide a method of manufacture that would enable it to be built at a high rate of productivity with a substantial gain over traditional approaches. The concepts we applied to meet these objectives began with a focused factory—focused on the manufacture of Perma-Tuf built-in dishwashers." . . .
>
> "The first thing we did was change our organization," said Schipke, "we made our structure leaner, more agile. Not the usual pruning, but a complete turnaround. Then we turned to technology. Instead of applying technology for technology's sake, we went after low cost and high quality with products that were right for today's consumer. Then we rebuilt the manufacturing system while production continued. Last year we produced over 600,000 dishwashers while the plant was being remodernized." . . .
>
> In 1977–78 management began to become more aware of automation, particularly in Japan. "A number of us visited leading companies in Japan and began to give more thought to the need for concurrent product and process design so we could come out winning on all objectives," said Rissler. "We began some information exchange with some Japanese firms, taking a priority view of it. . . . We borrowed films from Japanese firms; one showed a line that makes washer motors. Only two people work on the line—one a step-up man and the other a quality auditor." . . .
>
> "When I returned from Japan in 1981," says Moeller, "I was convinced that we had to make major changes in the way we assemble products if we were going to be a world class competitor. This modernized plant was to be a role model. We set our sights very high and were willing to take risks! We had very high expectations for the people, the product, and the process . . . and, believe me, we achieved them."

To make sure that it would not lose in the marketplace the gains it was making at the plant, GE demonstrated that it was just as willing to learn from its competitors as it was willing to learn from the Japanese. A major business publication reported:[8]

> General Electric, which has not been particularly responsive to dealers, is now following Whirlpool's lead and beefing up its dealer support systems. Says one security analyst, "GE made a study of everything Whirlpool was doing right and copied it."
>
> This year GE will give up its single-brand status, having won contracts to make dishwashers for Magic Chef and Tappan under their brand names. GE has stopped Maytag's growth in dishwashers and is even threatening KitchenAid: the last rating of dishwashers by *Consumer Reports* back in 1980 gave the GE model

---

[7] James Stevens, "Forging the Focused Factory," *Appliance*, June 1983.

[8] Lisa Miller Mesdag, "The Appliance Boom Begins," *Fortune*, July 25, 1983.

> higher marks, and GE has been feasting on that rave review ever since.

However important these gains were for GE, the bigger opportunity was to get some of Sears's business, which in the past might have been unthinkable. Sears was currently in the process of evaluating all the dishwasher manufacturers and had even approached GE. Roger Schipke believed GE not only had the most advanced product, but a new philosophy to go with it:

> The GE challenge is to enter the private label arena more strongly than in the past. This objective combined with a philosophic change that recognized Sears as a *customer,* and not as a competitor, led to the opening of discussion with them on several products.

Competitive Positioning in the Dishwasher Industry (E)

SEARS'S DISHWASHER DILEMMA

By mid-1983, though Sears was in a commanding position in its home appliance business, there was one area where they felt they might be vulnerable. It was the dishwasher product line. As part of a major companywide reorganization, Sears's top management had decided to move dishwashers and compactors from the Building Materials group to the Home Appliance group. Though the formal organization change was to be effective January 1, 1984, to all intents and purposes the shift in responsibility had already occurred.

Sears bought 100 percent of its dishwasher products from Design and Manufacturing (D&M), which was still privately owned, and had done so ever since Sam Regenstrief founded D&M. However, for the past 10 years there had been a steadily increasing concern at Sears on what would happen to D&M after Sam Regenstrief. Thus Sears found itself in a dilemma. One important component of Sears's sourcing strategy was to ensure that its suppliers have stable top management over a long term, and one-man shows were always a big concern. On the other hand, the success of Sears's merchandising strategy was based on buying from the lowest-cost producer, who would meet acceptable quality standards and specifications.

> Over the years we had many discussions at Sears to consider whether we should have other sources, but it always comes down to the fact that because of D&M's cost position, it does not make economic sense to go anywhere else. Sam was one of the outstanding small entrepreneurs in this country. He was extremely innovative and cost conscious, and he had one thought in mind—to make a very good dishwasher at low cost.

In the past five years the leadership situation at D&M had become Sears's primary concern, especially after Sam Regenstrief began to suffer health problems around 1978. This meant he had to turn the reins over to someone else, though he retained ownership control of the com-

Harvard Business School case 385–049.

pany. He chose as his successor his nephew-in-law, Marvin Silberman, who had worked at D&M. When Silberman left the company he was replaced by Lee Burke, 67, who was one of Sam's long-time trusted lieutenants. The day-to-day operations were managed by Lee Burke.

Eighty to 85 percent of D&M stock is owned by the Regenstrief Foundation, whose board consists of Sam, his wife, and some of Sam's friends. (The Regenstriefs have no children.) The foundation is engaged primarily in medical research in conjunction with Indiana University.

Another concern that Sears had from time to time about D&M was in the area of product quality. As D&M's volume with Sears and its overall market share grew over the years, they seemed to have a constant problem of monitoring their quality. In the mid-1970s, Sears had to have an extensive product recall of its dishwashers because of a wiring defect. According to a Sears executive:

> D&M, through Lee Burke, seems to have rededicated itself to quality in the last few years, and as a result their quality has vastly improved. But this has also increased their costs.

Because of Sears's lead position in the dishwasher consumer market, a third area of concern for Sears was GE's significant investment in the dishwasher product and manufacturing process. GE was the only manufacturer to come out with a plastic tub and had invested $38 million in modernizing their dishwasher plant with robotics and other state-of-the-art technology. Historically, dishwashers were loaded from the top into a porcelain tub inside. D&M was the first to come out with a front-loading dishwasher which the other manufacturers soon followed. Just prior to the oil crunch of 1974–75, GE started experimenting with the plastic tub which tested out successfully and so they began phasing out of porcelain and into plastics for their tubs and door liners on all their models. D&M remained with porcelain, though it improved its technology to go to a powder-coated porcelain product (Exhibit 1). Whirlpool, too, remained with porcelain for its tub, but went with plastics for its door liner.

In the plastics versus porcelain debate, both materials had their pros and cons though it seemed porcelain was quite meaningful to the consumer. According to an industry expert:

> From the customer's viewpoint, our research shows that white porcelain has always represented high quality and comes out ahead of plastic, especially for the tub; for the door liner, the plastic is fine and well accepted. Not only does the porcelain tub have a higher aesthetic value in appearance, it can also last longer. However, it has one major problem: unlike plastic, it is prone to developing nicks (due to contact with dropped metal utensils) which then start to rust. So, with plastics, even though it stains over the years, you can put a 10-year guarantee, which you cannot put on porcelain. GE has a unique advantage, and today it would be rather prohibitive for any other manufacturer to convert totally to plastics.

By the beginning of 1981 Sears decided that no longer could it jeopardize Sears's future in the dishwasher product line with a business-as-usual approach:

> For the first time, we decided that we better go out and look over the entire dishwasher industry with a fresh perspective, and so we decided to visit the various manufacturers: KitchenAid, Maytag, White Consolidated, Whirlpool, and GE. After some initial discussions the first

> three companies were out of the running. And so it came down to Whirlpool and GE, both being acceptable manufacturers. Now it was up to Sears decision makers to decide whether we should be taking on a secondary supplier to D&M, or even making one of them our primary supplier. Because of unusual circumstances this decision has taken a long time.

One member of the decision-making group who would be responsible for this decision described his dilemma:

> You have to really understand our history of relationships with these three companies (D&M, Whirlpool, and GE) to appreciate how tough this decision is.
>
> GE had always looked at Sears as an intense competitor. To them, selling to Sears was just not compatible. The policy at GE was that the GE product would only carry the GE name, and so even what they made for Penney's was made by Hotpoint.
>
> GE today has a different attitude in doing business with Sears than they had even a few years ago. Now they are looking at us as a customer, and for the past six months have been bidding for our business with an eagerness that we never expected. Our buyers have made several trips to the GE plant and they are really impressed with their modernized plant which is by far the most advanced of any. More important, they found the people at GE much more open to satisfying our needs, and their costing is in line too. Additionally, at our testing laboratory, where our engineers test models that they randomly buy from retail outlets, they approved the GE model, so now they even have a very satisfactory, quality product, which was not true for their older products. What has happened almost overnight is the beginning of a new relationship between GE and Sears. The folks in Louisville [GE's appliance division headquarters] are going to be disappointed if they don't get at least some of Sears's business.
>
> Now Whirlpool, as you know, has been doing business with us—the Sears way—for decades, so the working bond between the two organizations is very strong, which is an important factor. For many years Whirlpool has been interested in Sears's dishwasher business and presented various models, though none of them was good enough for us. It was not until Sears started to look at GE and others that Whirlpool realized that Sears would be amenable, so they became conscious of a better featured, lower-cost private brand for Sears. They have put emphasis on quality, and as for their costing, it is comparable to GE. You really don't know the true costs anyway, for the first couple of years of doing business together, until things settle down. So a lot depends on the product. Whirlpool has been working on a product with the self-cleaning filtering system which they claim is superior.[1]
>
> There is no question it would be very hard for Sears to pull back from D&M after all these years. As you know, Sears is very loyal to its suppliers, and we have all the confidence in D&M. But who is there after Lee Burke? More important, is D&M going to be able to match Whirlpool and GE in R&D investments? Though D&M hesitated at first, when they fully grasped that we were seriously looking around, they put in an extra effort on quality and material cost-effectiveness. But they are still behind on development of product innovation, features, and so on. I am told our people have been telling

[1] Both Whirlpool and GE have a filtering system that reuses the water, while D&M has a direct flush-out system. In the past, dishwashers used up to eight water changes; however, with the emphasis on energy conservation, many manufacturers have got it down to four water changes. The main advantage of a reusable water system is not in the saving of water, but in the saving of energy that goes to heat the water.

D&M for many years to invest in improving product quality and features, and we have even gone so far as to offer to pay more for a higher-caliber product. But Sam had his philosophy, which was: "I pay my people top money to make a quality product. I don't need to build up my overhead." There is no question that D&M is still the lowest-cost producer, and that their quality is not only acceptable but has improved recently.

Our marketing people tell us that in the 1980s, dishwasher sales will grow faster than any other appliance, and they want something with a little more pizzazz and quality, especially at the top of the line.[2]

In the effort to evaluate all possibilities, the Sears buyers even looked beyond the United States. One of them commented:

> We feel that some day, someone is going to come up with a totally new system to clean dishes. We went to Switzerland to look at the "Ultrasonic" system, which cleans dishes with high-speed sound waves. But at this point it is too expensive and not feasible for us.

Since both GE and Whirlpool had made it a high priority to win some of Sears's dishwasher business, top management from both the companies were involved in pitching for the account. Recognizing the high sensitivity of their decision, the Sears buyers reiterated what they have always expected from their suppliers:

> We have to be very conscious of our customers' desire for top quality, but at an affordable price. The price-value trade-off is still the number 1 motivation. In the final analysis, who gets how much of our business depends a great deal on who earns it in this arena.

---

[2] The Sears dishwasher line consisted of 15 models as follows:
- –Six 24" under-the-counter models
- –Three 18" under-the-counter models
- –Three 24" portable models
- –Three 18" portable models

The very top of the line would be the most feature-laden, 24" under-the-counter model, followed by the 18" under-the-counter model.

EXHIBIT 1

	1970	1976	1982
Kitchenaid		Redesigned tub and door	
Maytag	Introduced first dishwasher	Redesigned Cost reduced	
D & M	18" dishwashers	Electronics Powdered porcelain	
Whirlpool	Silverware on door	Plastic door	Electronics
WCI	Purchased Westinghouse design		Electronics
General Electric	P/T 'A'	P/T 'B'	Electronic GSD2500

Uniroyal-Goodrich Tire Company

The April 1989 Uniroyal-Goodrich Operations Review meeting was drawing to a close, and Chuck Ames, chairman and CEO of Uniroyal-Goodrich, felt optimistic. Looking back at his first year as the head of Clayton & Dubilier's largest LBO, he could point to numerous milestones. Profits had increased dramatically, and the company was meeting its financial obligations. The organization was taking decisive action in setting a new strategy. Key personnel additions had strengthened senior management, and the management team was pulling together much more effectively. Nevertheless, some serious questions remained. Competition was increasing in the North American tire business, as newly consolidated global players sought to increase their share of the market. Decisions had to be made about how to rationalize production and marketing of the company's two main brands. Above all, a high degree of financial leverage limited the range of options. The company had made impressive progress, but it was not out of the woods yet.

HISTORY OF UNIROYAL-GOODRICH

The Uniroyal LBO

On April 10, 1985, a corporation controlled by investor Carl Icahn launched a tender offer to acquire a controlling interest in Uniroyal at $18 per share; the total value of the offer was approximately $311 million. Upon completion of the offer, remaining shareholders would receive undetermined debt securities valued at $18 per share. Subsequent filings with the SEC revealed that Icahn controlled 3,165,000 Uniroyal shares, or 9.29 percent of the company. Uniroyal stock led the New York Stock Exchange most active list, advancing $.875 per share to $18.75. As recently as the fall of 1984 the stock had been trading at $11 per share. The fact that the stock closed higher than the Icahn offer indicated that the market anticipated a higher offer, possibly from a leveraged buyout or a foreign buyer. Some analysts, however,

Harvard Business School case 390–005. Revised January 1990.

were skeptical. One was quoted by the *New York Times:*

> I don't think the company has enough intrinsic earning power to justify a higher price and I don't see anything in the asset base to suggest it has a high liquidation value.[1]

At the time of the offer Uniroyal consisted of three main business units, outlined in Exhibit 1. The Tire and Related Products segment manufactured tires in North America for cars, trucks, and off-the-road and recreational vehicles. The company was the number one supplier of original equipment tires to General Motors and also sold replacement tires through independent distributors and dealers. The Chemical, Rubber, and Plastic Materials segment developed, manufactured, and marketed a range of products including specialty chemicals, plastic additives, and natural and synthetic rubbers. Management believed this segment had the most promising future growth potential. Engineered Products and Services produced power transmission and timing belts, plastics, coated fabrics, adhesives, and sealants.

Uniroyal management immediately began studying a range of alternatives to maximize shareholder value. These included various forms of recapitalization transactions (in which shareholders would receive cash or securities), mergers with other corporations, or a leveraged buyout. A potential $21 per share bid from Ethyl Corporation, a chemicals concern, broke down, apparently because Ethyl became concerned that it would be unable to sell Uniroyal's tire business to a third party. Management entered into substantive negotiations with Clayton and Dubilier (C&D) during the week of April 29 concerning an LBO at $22 per share. This transaction was subject to C&D's ability to secure financing, and Icahn's willingness to withdraw his offer. C&D retained the investment banking firm of Drexel Burnham Lambert to arrange financing.

On May 6, 1985, the Uniroyal board of directors unanimously approved the $22 per share C&D buyout proposal; the total transaction was valued at approximately $900 million. The acquisition was financed from borrowings of $300 million under a $350 million credit agreement with a group of banks, issuance of $560 million of senior and subordinated debt securities to a group of institutional investors, $26 million from the issuance of Redeemable Second Preferred stock, and $15 million from the sale of common stock in the newly formed CDU Holding Company. After the acquisition, members of the Uniroyal management team owned 22.5 percent of this common stock. Uniroyal also entered into an agreement in which it paid $5.9 million to Icahn, who in turn agreed to support the buyout.

Uniroyal was an unusual acquisition for C&D. Martin Dubilier, one of the firm's founders, recalled:

> From what we saw it was apparent that you couldn't finance it in the historical sense. You couldn't expect to build the business and sell it off later and make any money because of the heavy capital spending needs of the tire business over the next five years. We felt that you would have to either sell the tire business or you had to sell the chemical business. From very early in the game we decided that we wanted to create an incentive to make sure that everybody would focus on the same issue, of selling one of the main businesses.

The acquisition financing package contained substantial penalties if Uniroyal had not retired $750 million of debt by the end

[1] *New York Times,* April 11, 1985, page D1.

of 1987. Since this was far more than the company could generate from operations, C&D immediately began negotiating the sale of operating divisions. It soon became apparent that the sale of the tire business would not raise enough cash to make the required debt reduction. Dubilier decided that the best option would be to harvest cash from the tire business through a joint venture.

> We went to Goodrich and started negotiating with them, and they obviously hated their tire business much more than Uniroyal hated their tire business. It made a lot of sense to us to try to put those two together, and to incur debt that we could pay to each party. We really got as much out of it by restructuring it as we would have got out if we sold it, and we still owned half of it. We felt there was a lot of synergism.

B.F. Goodrich proved more than willing to participate in the venture. The company had been diversifying into vinyl resin production, specialty chemicals, and aerospace products, and it was not enthusiastic about the prospects of the tire business. Their 1984 annual report contained this evaluation, "The tire industry represents a textbook example of an industry selling a commodity product in a cyclical market."

In January 1986, Uniroyal and Goodrich announced the formation of the Uniroyal-Goodrich Tire Company (UGTC), a 50–50 joint venture which combined the tire operations of the two companies. The new venture took out bank loans of $450 million and paid an initial distribution of $225 million to each of its parents.

C&D proceeded to sell off Uniroyal's other operations. The Engineered Products segment was sold in two parts: Uniroyal Plastics was acquired by Polycast Technology Corp. for $100 million, and Gates Rubber paid $125 million for the Power Transmission belt business. Avery Inc. acquired the chemicals division for $710 million in an LBO financed by Drexel. These transactions effectively completed the liquidation of Uniroyal.

The Uniroyal-Goodrich Joint Venture

At first glance the Uniroyal-Goodrich merger seemed to offer outstanding opportunities. During the early 1980s, top managers at both Uniroyal and B.F. Goodrich viewed tires as an unattractive, mature business; they looked at their tire operations as "cash cows." However, on a stand-alone basis, neither company had the resources to meet increasingly powerful global competitors such as Goodyear and Michelin. Exhibit 2 shows financials for major industry competitors. Combining the two companies offered opportunities to improve profitability by gaining scale and rationalizing overheads. The two companies also had complementary strengths in market position. David Schaub, president, Company Brand Division, spoke of the initial enthusiasm:

> On Day 1 we ran a new flag up the pole and people were excited. Everybody felt that there was a great fit between the two companies. One was strong in OE, one was strong in the replacement market. The original impact was that the joint venture strengthened us in the great North American tire market.

TIRE INDUSTRY CHARACTERISTICS

Manufacturing

Although substantial investments have been made to increase the level of automation in the tire building process, tire production still requires a high level of skilled labor. In the first step of tire manufacturing, plies of rubberized fabric are wrapped around a wide drum. The tire builder controls the rotation of the drum as a number of successive layers are added. A reinforcing wire bead is placed at the edges of the drum, and additional strips of rubber are added over the bead. Next, the sidewall rubber and tread are wrapped around and the layers are pressed together with rollers. A belted radial tire may consist of over 20 separate layers. At this point, the "green tire," which resembles a barrel with both ends open, is removed from the tire building machine and moves on to vulcanizing. In the vulcanizing step, the tire is placed in a heated pressurized mold. Besides molding in the tread design, vulcanizing toughens the rubber compounds and bonds the parts of the tire into an integral unit.

Exhibit 3 shows the cost breakdown for a typical tire manufacturer. High rates of capacity utilization are considered critical to labor efficiency and overhead absorption. Most tire makers are backward integrated into the manufacture of synthetic rubber and tire reinforcing fabric, the main materials of tire building. Labor relations have historically been characterized by industry-wide contracts with the United Rubber Workers Union, although some recently constructed plants were nonunion.

Markets

Tires are purchased as original equipment for new cars, or by consumers to replace worn tires. Exhibit 4 shows sales trends for original equipment and replacement tires. Major manufacturers control the original equipment market, while shares of the replacement market are much more fragmented. Exhibit 5 shows 1987 original equipment and replacement shares. In addition to a "flag" brand such as Goodrich, tire producers also produced private label brands for retailers such as Sears or Western Auto. Although these tires typically had lower profit margins for the manufacturer, private label production helped fill up production capacity.

Original equipment demand obviously depended on new car production, and was thus tied to the health of the domestic auto industry and the overall health of the economy. Replacement demand was most directly affected by the number of miles driven by motorists, and also by the durability of tires.

Replacement tires reach the consumer through a number of different channels. Firestone and Goodyear sell largely through a nationwide chain of company-owned stores, but the majority of replacement tire sales are through independent tire dealers. Exhibit 6 shows trends in market share for the different tire retail channels.

Recent Trends in the North American Tire Market

On August 4, 1986, hundreds of red, white, and blue balloons were sent aloft at the new Uniroyal-Goodrich headquarters in Akron, Ohio, to commemorate the Uniroyal-Goodrich joint venture. Over the previous decade, there had been little cause for celebration in the U.S. tire industry. A number of trends had combined to force substantial restructurings, plant closings, and declines in employment. One of these was technological. Exhibit 7 shows the growing penetration of radial tires in the overall automotive market. By 1981 essentially all new cars were equipped with radials, and bias and bias-belted construction were rapidly losing share in the replacement market. Although radials cost more initially, they offered better handling and gas mileage, and they tended to last twice as long as bias tires. Also, as competition increased among radial tire suppliers, the price premium eroded substantially. The shift to radials caused two types of problems for tire makers. First, plants that produced bias tires could not be easily converted to produce radials. Second, longer radial tire life dramatically reduced the demand for replacement tires. With tires lasting 45,000 to 60,000 miles, an average car needed only three sets of tires during its usable life of around 160,000 miles, down from eight sets of 20,000 mile bias tires.

The industry was also hurt in a number of ways by the oil shocks of the 70s. Higher oil prices caused people to curtail recreational driving, which reduced demand for replacement tires. Since petroleum is the major raw material for synthetic rubber, higher oil prices drove costs up. Also, the trend towards smaller cars put pressure on sales, since smaller tires are priced lower and generally have lower margins.

As the dollar appreciated in the early 1980s, the industry came under severe import competition. See Exhibit 8.

These factors combined to cause a wave of plant closings. In the decade before the Uniroyal-Goodrich joint venture, 27 plants, mostly bias-ply facilities, were closed, and industry employment fell by 50 percent to 90,000 workers by 1986. Many industry executives had concluded that the tire business did not offer attractive long-term opportunities, and most tire producers diversified into both related and unrelated industries in search of growth. Before the joint venture, there was speculation that both Uniroyal and Goodrich were looking for ways to exit the tire business entirely.

UGTC: The Joint Venture

The combined Uniroyal-Goodrich operations spanned the range of the automotive tire industry. Uniroyal was the leading supplier of original equipment tires to General Motors, providing almost 40 percent of their tires. This was considered to be a secure relationship, but it made UGTC sensitive to changes in GM's market share. Goodrich had exited the original equipment market in 1981, but remained strong in replacement markets with its T/A brand of performance tires.

The two organizations took differing approaches to replacement tire distribution. Uniroyal sold through 56 distributors with exclusive rights to assigned geographic territories, while Goodrich sold directly to dealers. In addition to the Uniroyal and Goodrich "flag" brands, the company had a number of private brand accounts, including K mart. Exhibit 9 shows the approximate breakdown of sales by category.

The combined company operated five tire plants in the United States and two in Canada. All plants were unionized except the Ardmore, Oklahoma, facility. Exhibit 10 lists these plants and their capacities.

Results of the Joint Venture

Early results from the Uniroyal-Goodrich Tire Company (UGTC) were not encouraging. As Martin Dubilier recalled, "It turned out that in the first month we made our forecast. It was also the last month we made it." Problems became clear in several areas. First, differences in the cultures of the two organizations prevented smooth coordination. Patrick Ross from Goodrich became chairman and CEO, with Sheldon Salzman from Uniroyal serving as vice chairman and COO. Both companies had equal representation on the board of directors. David Schaub, president, Company Brand Division, described the conflict:

> At B.F. Goodrich, a few people at the top made decisions behind closed doors. After the decisions were made, everybody executed on the plan. That type of a style can be fast as hell when it works. Uniroyal was very much an open-door, people-oriented style. Human resource development was a very heavy element in their strategy. The joint venture became discernably a "we-they" situation, and the interplays interfered with the process and progress. People were counting noses, trying to see which side was on top.
>
> With the board split 50–50, decisions just didn't get made. We'd send decisions upstairs for resolution, and you'd think that gravity would bring them down. Newton was wrong: we'd flip a coin, and it stood on its edge every time.

The combined operation failed to meet its profit projections. Jim Mehta, vice president–strategic planning, outlines some of the difficulties:

> Various projects began to exploit synergies in distribution, especially purchasing synergies, and to restructure logistics. These yielded results, but the market collapsed on the OE side. GM lost market share, and the total new car market contracted. The plants had to deal with shorter production runs, coupled with different management styles, and really no sense of strategic direction.

Factory costs increased with the start-up costs of moving certain Goodrich tires to former Uniroyal factories. Manufacturing staffs had to revise operating procedures to make tires in the new facilities, since the two companies had significantly different production technologies. These changes were complicated by friction over management styles. Lloyd Spalter, executive vice president–operations, recalls:

> There were basic philosophical differences between Uniroyal and Goodrich in operations. Goodrich was highly centralized, with a big corporate engineering department. A few people made the decisions, and the plants implemented them. At Uniroyal, the attitude was, hey, the guys in the plant have to live with these decisions. We want their designs and input. We ended up with a kind of middle-of-the-road solution, more centralized than at Uniroyal, and people have struggled with it.

UGTC was unable to meet the minimum fixed charge covenants of its debt agreements for the quarter ending November 30, 1986. The company was able to negotiate a waiver of this covenant along with a reduction of the ratio through March 30, 1987. Management believed that the new ratio requirements would be achievable, but the company was again unable to meet the coverage requirement on November 30, 1987. While the company was able to meet its interest payments during 1986 and 1987, bank borrowings had increased from $356.6 million in November of 1986 to $439.7 million, and available lines of credit had declined to $102.8 million. There was some question whether the organization could meet future debt obligations without reorganization and financial restructuring.

For C&D, these financial shortfalls created critical short-term issues. Uniroyal Holdings, which controlled Uniroyal's half of the joint venture, was counting on distributions from the joint venture to pay pension and medical benefits for Uniroyal retirees. Without these payments, the company faced an immediate financial crisis. Martin Dubilier recalled the sense of urgency:

> A year after we closed the deal there were two general ledgers, two cost systems, two sets of green tires. Everything was being run as if there were two independent companies, only it was worse because there was no leadership. It got to the point where margins began to deteriorate rather rapidly, their share of market was going down, quality was poor. It was just awful, it was a disaster, it was a business going out of business. And the sad part about it was that nobody would buy it if it went out of business. Nobody would buy it out of bankruptcy because they would have to take on the liabilities for a large number of retired workers. You couldn't sell it by plant because nobody wanted to buy those antiquated plants. The business would have gone to importers. Nineteen thousand people would have been out of work, and we would have had another 45 million tires coming in from overseas.

The Uniroyal-Goodrich LBO

In November 1987, C&D initiated a buyout of B.F. Goodrich's 50 percent interest in the business. Both C&D and John Ong, chairman of B.F. Goodrich, agreed that current organization was not working, and that the tension between Ross and Salzman was paralyzing the organization. To resolve this conflict, C&D brought in Chuck Ames to replace Ross as CEO and to begin turning the company around. Ames, a 1954 graduate of Harvard Business School, spent his early career at McKinsey before moving to Reliance Electric as president and chief operating officer in 1972. He became CEO in 1976, and continued in that role until 1980, one year after Reliance had been acquired by Exxon. During his tenure, Reliance's sales climbed from $339 million in 1972 to $1.34 billion in 1979, net income rose from $13.6 million to $67.9 million, and ROE increased from 11 to 22 percent. He was CEO of Acme Cleveland from 1981 to 1987, guiding the company through a period of significant restructuring and intense foreign competition for the company's machine tool and drill bit businesses.

Ames saw his role as different from the previous CEO assignments he had held.

> When I came into UGTC, I didn't see my role as one of getting involved in the day-to-day operations of the business. We named Sheldon Salzman president, and it was clear from day one that he would run the business. I set out to accomplish three objectives: Selecting a strong management team and getting it to function as a team; putting a manufacturing strategy in place; and pulling a marketing strategy together.
>
> My long term objective is to return to Clayton and Dubilier and focus my efforts on my partnership duties there. Right now, I'm not so much making decisions as getting things done through our management team. I needed the CEO authority, but I didn't want to use it, and never had to. Sheldon picked up quickly on what needed to be accomplished and he's proven to be an outstanding manager and team leader.

Cost Reductions

Ames and Salzman took immediate moves to cut costs. They began with aggressive steps to reduce personnel expenses. Ames assumed that salaried payroll could be reduced by 500–600 people by completing the staff rationalizations that hadn't taken place during the joint venture and by streamlining the organization. Salaried headcount was cut by 330 in March 1988, a reduction of approximately 7 percent. This yielded $4 million savings (net of termination costs) in 1988, and an expected $15 million annually beginning in 1989. Ames believed that further reductions could be made, but realized that work methods would have to change first because many parts of the organization were overburdened.

Further savings came from union concessions. A new three-year agreement with the United Rubber Workers union called for a base-wage freeze for the term of the contract, and a one-year freeze on cost-of-living adjustments. In return, the company agreed to keep all five U.S. plants open through 1991, and granted the union stock appreciation rights, which reward the employees for the increase in value of UGTC stock in the event the company was sold. The new contract reduced costs by $19 million in 1988, with projected savings of $28 million in 1989 and $30 million in 1990.

Ames and Salzman also launched a profit improvement program to reduce manufacturing costs. For example, they budgeted $26 million in savings in 1988 from productivity and manufacturing efficiency improvement. Steps in this area included standardization of green tires to reduce scrap and set-up times associated with changing over to different tire specifications. Other savings occurred from scaling back expense levels for travel, contract employment, risk insurance, worker's compensation, and the like.

Budget Review Process

To make sure that these potential savings were actually realized, Ames and Salzman instituted extensive monthly budget review meetings, in which variances from plan were examined in detail. Jim Mehta described the process:

> When someone misses their budget target, they have to explain what happened, and what they are going to do to make sure that it doesn't happen again. This involves some firefighting as people are forced into action. The process communicates the urgency of the budget down to line managers, who send cost reduction ideas back up. There is some serendipity involved in finding the numbers.

Annual budgets were prepared using both a bottom-up and a top-down process. Plant managers were given mix and volume estimates, and set manning levels accordingly. After building up their cost estimates, they budgeted cost improvements based on new productivity-improving capital projects, other planned improvements, and an estimate of further gains that they would uncover during the year. These plant budgets and budgets from other functional areas were combined and compared to the company's cash requirements for investment and debt service. In many cases, top managers had to ask for revisions of the original budgets to meet overall corporate needs.

Establishing Multiple Profit Centers

Ames believed the impact of the budgeting process could be sharpened by breaking the organization up into multiple profit centers along market lines, including OEM, private label, and flag brands. Previously, UGTC had been a functional organization with Ross and Salzman sharing P&L responsibility. Ames admits to being a fanatic about profit centers:

> When you break into profit centers you get more strategic options for growth, because more people are focused on building profits. It's also the best way to focus on costs. Of course, you have to be smart enough to work around the problems: people may try to game the financials to make their operation look good at the expense of another group. They may also

> try to maximize short-term profits at the expense of the long term by cutting R&D and quality. There's always a risk, and you need to manage around it.

Problems with financial systems made the initial cost allocations to the profit centers somewhat imperfect, but the impact on management was significant. James Pursley, president, International and Private Brand Division, noted:

> As a result of the profit center concept, more people are looking at profit orientation. At the same time, more decision rights have been given to the profit centers. It used to be that people thought, "R&D's business is R&D's business." Now people are saying "Hey, what they do impacts us. They're doing things in support of *our* business." You didn't get in and challenge some of the things that you do today. I think the profit center concept is the best thing to happen since the buyout.

This impact was also felt at the tire plants. Lloyd Spalter noted:

> We turned the plant managers into businessmen. We made them much more responsible for the financial performance of their operations, and not just for producing a certain volume. We now have higher expectations from them in the areas of financial analysis of the business, and for conformance to budgets.

BUILDING THE MANAGEMENT TEAM

The management team was strengthened by bringing in additional team members from outside the tire industry. Rich Barbieri was brought in as vice president–finance. After 17 years in line management at American Cyanamid, Barbieri joined the Parallel Group, an operations-oriented consulting firm. Parallel worked closely with Salzman while he was turning around Uniroyal tire operations in 1979. Barbieri went on to run two successful leveraged buyouts of manufacturing firms. Max Enoch, brought in as vice president–marketing and sales development, also had LBO experience. Enoch was previously vice president–marketing at Arnold Foods, an extraordinarily successful C&D LBO. Jim Mehta, vice president–strategic planning, was recruited from McKinsey, where he had been managing consulting assignments at UGTC. The new organization brought the team together in frequent interfunctional problem-solving meetings. Before, there had been little interfunctional coordination. Recently, management had become a more effective team. Barbieri commented:

> When I started here, we had very nice meetings. Nobody ever openly disagreed or raised their voice. I told Shel, "You're not getting enough conflict here! Problems are not getting raised." Now lately we've been having some healthy conflict.

Top managers were also trying to improve their communication with the rest of the organization. Once per month, each senior manager met with a group of six to eight employees selected at random for an off-the-record discussion of current issues in the company. They found a continuing level of concern about layoffs. Schaub described the situation:

> During the cost-cutting moves of early 1988, with salary freezes and people leaving, the level of tension among the staff was very high: you could see it in their faces. After that, people were waiting for another shoe to drop. Now (March 1989) people are finally starting to believe that the layoffs are done for now. They're putting more effort into work and less into worrying.

Impact of the LBO on Management

C&D allowed the UGTC management team an unusual degree of flexibility in deciding whom to allow to invest in the LBO. In a typical LBO, fewer than 10 top managers are allowed to invest, but at UGTC a total of 114 managers put money into the deal. In many cases, managers took out substantial loans to buy stock. Opinions were divided on the effect this had on management. Ames believes that the opportunity to invest played a role in attracting several members of the management team. He also feels that by having a substantial portion of their net worth at risk, managers were more focused on delivering results. David Schaub felt that the process hadn't gone far enough. He believed everyone at the company, including hourly employees, should have been given a chance to invest to promote greater employee involvement. Rich Barbieri was more skeptical:

> Basically, you have 114 people waiting to see what the top six guys are going to do. I have not seen a change in attitude. They're waiting for the top guys to make a killing, then, well, ride on their coat tails. They said attitudes would change at Eastern Airlines when the employees owned 30 percent of the company. They didn't change.

Top managers agree that the substantial debt load the company carried has had an impact on the overall sense of urgency. In completing the LBO, UGTC borrowed $360 million from banks and issued $398 million of high-yield securities. Barbieri noted that the pressure to make the budget in order to meet debt covenants is felt by the entire top management group. Schaub commented:

> Every day when I turn the key I know that I have money to make. We have $10 million of interest a month, divided by 30 days. I can do the calculation.

This pressure to make debt service payments had a substantial impact on options for manufacturing strategy.

MANUFACTURING STRATEGY

After factoring in aggressive cost reduction targets, volume increases, and margin improvement, C&D budgeted $500 million dollars for capital spending from 1988–92. All other cash from operations would be used to service debt. Ames felt that these amounts were adequate:

> I think that by spending 1.5 times depreciation we should be able to get higher quality *and* improved productivity. This has been the source of a big running argument with managers at UGTC; they want to spend $850 million over the next five years. I've learned over the years that big capital expenditure budgets are usually too high. The best thing is to say no to requests for more capital. It's easy to spend capital when it's not your money.

Initially, there were substantial disagreements over how this budget should be spent. Quality was definitely a high priority, but debt service requirements created pressure to invest for productivity improvement. There was also disagreement about whether OE or replacement should receive the bulk of investment dollars.

In the OE market, Uniroyal was a recognized leader, but this was a difficult position to maintain. Lloyd Spalter explained the situation:

> Original equipment drives quality of manufacturing in this business. GM makes stringent demands on suppliers, and these demands are tightened every year. Every time one supplier comes up with an

> improvement it becomes the standard that all other suppliers have to meet. Since GM is such an important customer, Uniroyal has always made the necessary investments to maintain quality. After Goodrich decided to exit the original equipment business, their quality levels fell way behind.

General Motors had rated the Ardmore, Oklahoma, plant the best in the country, but other product lines were slipping. In the private label category, a 1985 dealer survey rated Uniroyal number one in quality among domestic producers. By late 1987, a similar survey showed that the company had slipped to number three. Other companies had been more effective in their investments to improve quality.

Pressure to maintain and upgrade quality levels eventually dominated discretionary capital spending allocations, but substantial investments in other areas could not be avoided. Lloyd Spalter, executive vice president–operations, outlined priorities:

> Our top priority is the basic maintenance that we need to do to keep the plants running. Number two is required investment for environmental compliance and safety. These two areas will take up about 30 percent of our budget over the next few years. The next priority is tire molds; new molds are a must when you bring out a new tread design. Molds have been running around $15-$18 million per year. Our fourth priority is quality, and we need to continue substantial upgrading of our OE quality for GM. In recent years we have had to spend as much as $40-$50 million in this area. Our fifth priority is quality improvement for the T/A, which is becoming the bread and butter of the company. We expect to spend about 40 percent of our total capital spending dollars on quality, with approximately an even split between OE and replacement. Finally, whatever is left over will be spent on productivity improvement.
>
> We will probably spend 10 percent of our budget on cost reduction projects. We will also make some investments in our synthetic rubber and textile plants, but this will be less than 10 percent of total spending.

The manufacturing managers were frustrated by the lack of capital for productivity improvements, but they were compensating by relying on employee-involvement programs to generate cost reduction ideas. Spalter explained:

> When you get the brains of 1,500 to 2,000 people at each plant working on the issues, you come up with some very clever ideas. The programs are highly structured team efforts; employees have been trained in statistical evaluation techniques. They get together one hour per week on company time for brainstorming sessions to come up with quality improvement and cost reduction ideas. In two plants, these programs have been supported with pay-for-productivity programs that allow tire builders to benefit directly from their improved productivity.
>
> These programs have grown out of 10 years of experience with employee involvement at the Uniroyal Ardmore plant, and 5 years of experience at Opelika. We believe that we are at the forefront of companies using employee involvement.

The manufacturing staff was also actively evaluating the possibility of reducing fixed costs by reconfiguring production into fewer plants. Although the union contract prevented plant closings through 1991, some managers contended that by increasing productivity and moving production, the company could potentially close one facility. This could reduce manufacturing overhead by $20 million per year.

Setting Marketing Strategy

Marketing strategy included a range of complex and interrelated issues. UGTC needed to decide the roles of its two flag brands, Uniroyal and Goodrich. Uniroyal had a very strong position in original equipment as the number one supplier to GM, but it lacked strong replacement sales. Uniroyal managers felt that there were great opportunities to gain share in the replacement market, if only to reflect Uniroyal's share in OE. Additional dealer support and advertising programs would be needed to capitalize on this opportunity.

Goodrich had a reputation as an outstanding producer of high performance tires, the fastest-growing segment of the tire market. Auto manufacturers were increasingly including performance tires as part of a "sport option" package for their new car models. Performance tires offered higher margins to manufacturers, and they tended to wear out faster, spurring higher replacement sales. Exhibit 12 shows the rising market share of performance tires. Some managers believed that Goodrich's reputation could be used to gain sales to auto makers. However, the company had chosen to exit the OE business in 1981, and other manufacturers, including Michelin, were aggressively trying to gain share in OE.

Disagreements about the right marketing strategy came up during the joint venture. James Pursley, president, International and Private Brand Division, recalled:

> Where the first problem came up was in early 1987 during our long-term strategic planning. I recommended that we emphasize Goodrich replacement brands and take resources away from Uniroyal. In my mind it was pretty simple: there weren't enough resources to develop two major brands. The T/A (B.F. Goodrich's high-performance brand) was the best opportunity. In the early days people thought, "Hell, Uniroyal has the franchise with GM," so the majority of resources went to OE. From my perspective, we wasted two years. It was just a matter of resources.

In early 1989 there was a growing consensus that high performance represented the best opportunity for UGTC. The company decided to invest $10 million in a television ad campaign aimed at increasing brand awareness of Goodrich performance tires. The ads touted Goodrich T/A tires as "athletic shoes for your car." The ads were well received by test audiences, and dealer reaction was very enthusiastic. Goodrich also increased its presence in the OE market, with commitments for approximately 1 million tires from GM over the 1989 model year. It was hoped that customers would also buy Goodrich replacement tires for these cars when the time came.

Other managers felt that the company should try to capitalize on Uniroyal's strength in OE by bringing out a line of high performance tires under the Uniroyal brand. Another more radical option was to systematically phase out one of the two flag brands. Although this would be a difficult option, it made sense to consider it before devoting resources to building two separate brands. There were also immediate issues about distribution channels. Uniroyal had granted exclusive territorial distributorship in 1984 in hopes that this would encourage more aggressive retail sales efforts. The new channel organization had not caused any increase in Uniroyal's share of the replacement market.

Margin Improvement: Mix Issues

Extensive investment in improved accounting information allowed accurate comparison of the profitability of different segments of the business. In 1988 the finance staff produced the following comparative estimates:

Product	Relative Margin*
Flag replacement	100
Private label replacement	75
Original equipment	100
Flag high performance	150

*Disguised data.

The new information systems also allowed computation of the profitability of individual tire sizes and grades and customer account profitability. This new data allowed Ames to change sales-force compensation from volume-driven to margin-driven performance plans. The new focus caused a shift of mix away from private label towards flag replacement and high performance, reversing the trend of the previous five years.

MARKET TRENDS: GLOBAL MERGERS

Uniroyal-Goodrich was not the only U.S. tire company dealing with integration issues. As Ames began to deal with the problems of the new LBO, the industry had gone through an unprecedented period of rationalization. In 1987 GenCorp Inc. sold its General Tire business to Continental AG of West Germany. In 1988 Bridgestone Corp. of Japan won a bidding war with Pirelli Group of Italy to Firestone. Later in the year, Pirelli acquired Armstrong Tire Company. These acquisitions left the United States with only two publicly held competitors in the global tire industry, Cooper Tire and Goodyear, which remained public only after an expensive take-over defense against Anglo-French financier Sir James Goldsmith.

In early 1989, this left UGTC facing a number of large, well-financed global competitors, who were announcing substantial commitments to building their share of the North American tire market. Goodyear, with 20 percent of the 1987 worldwide tire market, had announced 1989 capital spending plans of $760 million, up sharply from $492 million in 1988. Michelin, which controlled 18 percent of world production, planned to expand its North American capacity 30 percent by 1992, spending over $700 million. Bridgestone, with 16 percent world market share, planned to spend $1 billion through 1992 to expand Firestone's auto service center and tire retailing network, and to upgrade plant capacity to produce high performance tires. Continental/General, with 8 percent share, had a $670 million program to upgrade all of its North American plants over four years. Pirelli, rising to 7 percent world share, earmarked $100 million to increase Armstrong's high performance OE capacity.

Many UGTC managers were concerned at the willingness of international competitors to invest and potentially earn poor short-term returns in a drive for increased market share. Michelin, Continental/General, and Pirelli were all bidding aggressively to increase their share of the OE market. In 1988 they were given an opportunity to divide up Firestone's 18.5 percent share of General Motors business over the next two years. GM decided to eliminate Firestone as an OE supplier after the Bridgestone acquisition.

Financial Issues

Bank covenants from the LBO financing gave Ames little room for error. In addition to substantial interest on bank borrowings and subordinated debt, preferred dividend payments to Uniroyal could not be omitted unless UGTC stood in default of debt covenants. Since Uniroyal needed these payments to meet pension and medical benefit obligations, shortfalls were unacceptable. The company also had scheduled principal payments of $30 million per year to contend with.

The management team felt that there might be some opportunities for inventory reductions as part of manufacturing improvements, but these would be fairly minor. There were no substantial opportunities for sales of unrelated assets. UGTC had more reinforcing fabric production capacity than it needed, and it also operated the largest SBR facility in the world, but manufacturing personnel were wary of losing control of these key raw materials.

The only viable option for meeting the financial commitments was the old-fashioned way: operating earnings. To achieve these earnings, the company would have to continue to cut costs and improve margins through increased sales of high performance tires and flag brands. Operating earnings were projected to rise from $107 million in 1988, $159 million in 1989, $190 million in 1990, and $220 million in 1991.

Reviewing his progress to date, Ames felt the right direction had been set:

> We didn't have a lot of time to do things by the book. You need to make up your mind, based on experience, that certain things can be done. You don't have time to wait for McKinsey to present its plans or to sit in a room and do extensive analysis. Yes, we may have ruffled some feathers and damaged morale, but there was no alternative. We had to improve profit performance now!

EXHIBIT 1
UNIROYAL BUSINESS SEGMENT INFORMATION
Year Ending December 31, 1984, in Millions of Dollars

	Tires and Related Products	*Chemical, Rubber, Plastic Materials*	*Engineered Products*	*Corporate and Other*	*Total*
Sales	1,018.4	671.9	431.4		2,121.7
Operating earnings	85.3	110.2	36.5		232.0
Depreciation	26.7	18.5	9.9	6.1	61.2
Capital expenditures	42.9	35.6	17.1	2.7	98.3
Assets	502.6	443.2	189.8	317.8	1,453.4

EXHIBIT 2
TIRE COMPANY FINANCIAL INFORMATION
In Millions of Dollars

	1978	1979	1980	1981	1982	1983	1984	1985	1986	1987
Sales										
Armstrong	377.0	393.3	401.3	560.5	575.9	594.7	665.6	767.8	800.1	1,196.4
Cooper Tire	260.7	283.2	324.0	393.9	430.4	457.8	555.4	522.6	577.5	665.8
Firestone Tire	4,878.1	5,284.2	4,850.5	4,361.0	3,869.0	3,866.0	4,001.0	3,836.0	3,501.0	3,867.0
GenCorp	2,199.2	2,294.9	2,215.2	2,175.2	2,061.7	2,184.4	2,727.1	3,020.8	3,099.0	1,619.0
Goodrich	2,593.5	2,988.1	3,079.6	3,184.6	3,005.3	3,191.7	3,437.9	3,200.5	2,553.2	2,168.0
Goodyear Tire	7,489.1	8,238.7	8,444.0	9,152.9	8,688.7	9,735.8	10,241.0	9,585.1	9,103.1	9,905.2
Uniroyal	2,735.9	2,574.6	2,299.5	2,260.1	1,967.2	2,040.3	2,121.7			
Net income										
Armstrong	9.6	8.5	(16.4)	16.6	15.6	18.0	25.4	10.0	7.7	20.5
Cooper Tire	5.6	5.2	12.8	17.3	19.0	21.4	23.9	18.5	23.0	30.7
Firestone Tire	(148.3)	77.7	(122.0)	129.0	73.0	100.0	63.0	51.0	68.0	112.8
GenCorp	115.5	81.7	40.8	110.9	61.7	74.6	61.5	121.6	130.0	66.0
Goodrich	70.1	82.6	61.7	91.5	(32.8)	10.3	66.9	4.3	12.9	83.9
Goodyear Tire	226.1	146.2	206.7	243.9	216.6	357.5	391.7	301.3	276.1	440.1
Uniroyal	5.9	(120.5)	(7.8)	45.3	25.6	55.5	100.2			
Return on sales										
Armstrong	2.5%	2.2%	−4.1%	3.0%	2.7%	3.0%	3.8%	1.3%	1.0%	1.7%
Cooper Tire	2.1%	1.8%	4.0%	4.4%	4.4%	4.7%	4.3%	3.5%	4.0%	4.6%
Firestone Tire	−3.0%	1.5%	−2.5%	3.0%	1.9%	2.6%	1.6%	1.3%	1.9%	2.9%
GenCorp	5.3%	3.6%	1.8%	5.1%	3.0%	3.4%	2.3%	4.0%	4.2%	4.1%
Goodrich	2.7%	2.8%	2.0%	2.9%	−1.1%	0.3%	1.9%	0.1%	0.5%	3.9%
Goodyear Tire	3.0%	1.8%	2.4%	2.7%	2.5%	3.7%	3.8%	3.1%	3.0%	4.4%
Uniroyal	0.2%	−4.7%	−0.3%	2.0%	1.3%	2.7%	4.7%			
Return on equity										
Armstrong	7.5%	6.4%	−14.7%	13.3%	11.4%	9.6%	12.2%	4.2%	4.2%	10.1%
Cooper Tire	10.0%	9.5%	19.5%	21.1%	15.7%	15.3%	14.9%	10.5%	11.8%	13.9%
Firestone Tire	−10.5%	5.3%	−9.1%	8.9%	5.6%	7.8%	5.1%	4.4%	5.8%	9.6%
GenCorp	12.1%	8.2%	4.1%	10.7%	6.1%	7.9%	6.7%	12.8%	12.4%	*
Goodrich	8.1%	8.9%	6.4%	8.2%	−3.2%	0.9%	6.1%	0.6%	1.6%	8.5%
Goodyear Tire	10.7%	6.8%	9.0%	10.3%	8.8%	11.9%	12.4%	8.6%	9.2%	24.0%
Uniroyal	0.9%	−19.0%	−1.6%	8.7%	4.8%	8.3%	13.8%			

*General Tire operations sold in October 1987; following 1987 restructuring, GenCorp has negative net worth.

EXHIBIT 3
TIRE MANUFACTURING COST BREAKDOWN

Materials	52%
Other variable costs	3
Labor and benefits	24
Depreciation	3
Manufacturing overhead	18

EXHIBIT 4
OEM AND REPLACEMENT SALES TRENDS
In Millions of Units

	1979	*1980*	*1981*	*1982*	*1983*
Replacement	135	120	123	130	134
Original equipment	51	37	37	33	44
Total	186	157	160	163	178

EXHIBIT 5
1987 U.S. PASSENGER TIRE MARKET SHARE

	Original Equipment	*Replacement*
Goodyear	33.4%	16.0%
Firestone	21.9	9.0
Uniroyal-Goodrich	18.5	6.5
Goodrich	—	4.0
Uniroyal	18.5	2.5
Michelin	12.9	8.5
General	12.7	3.0
Continental	.4	
Pirelli	.1	1.5
Dunlop	.1	2.5
Sears		7.5
Multi-Mile		3.0
Kelly-Springfield		2.5
Cooper		2.5
Armstrong		2.5
Cordovan		2.0
Dayton		2.0
Bridgestone		2.0
Remington		2.0

EXHIBIT 6
REPLACEMENT TIRE SALES BY CHANNEL
Percent of Total Units

	1979	*1980*	*1981*	*1982*	*1983*	*1984*	*1985*	*1986*	*1987*	*1988*
Tire dealerships	45%	47%	51%	53%	54%	55%	55%	56%	56%	56%
Service stations	13	12	11	10	9	9	9	8	8	7
Tire company stores	10	9	9	9	10	10	10	11	11	12
Miscellaneous outlets	2	3	3	3	3	3	3	3	2	2
Auto dealerships	2	2	2	2	2	2	2	2	2	2
Chain stores	28	27	24	23	22	21	21	20	21	21

EXHIBIT 7
SHARE OF TIRE UNIT SALES BY CONSTRUCTION TYPE

	1980	*1981*	*1982*	*1983*	*1984*	*1985*	*1986*	*1987*	*1988*
Total									
Radial	57.7%	60.4%	63.0%	73.0%	79.0%	81.0%	82.7%	87.4%	91.6%
Bias belted	11.2	14.0	17.0	12.0	5.0	4.0	9.6	7.8	4.4
Bias	31.1	25.6	20.0	15.0	16.0	15.0	7.7	4.8	4.0
Replacement									
Radial		59	64	70	75	81	86	91	93
Bias belted		16	15	13	13	11	10	6	4
Bias		25	21	17	12	8	4	3	3
Retail prices									
Radial	$72.71	$72.13	$65.00	$60.00	$55.50	$54.80	$53.80	$51.80	$52.85
Bias belted	49.90	44.41	44.00	43.66	39.00	39.95	38.00	37.90	38.40
Bias	41.98	37.95	39.00	39.95	37.15	36.63	35.00	35.50	38.00

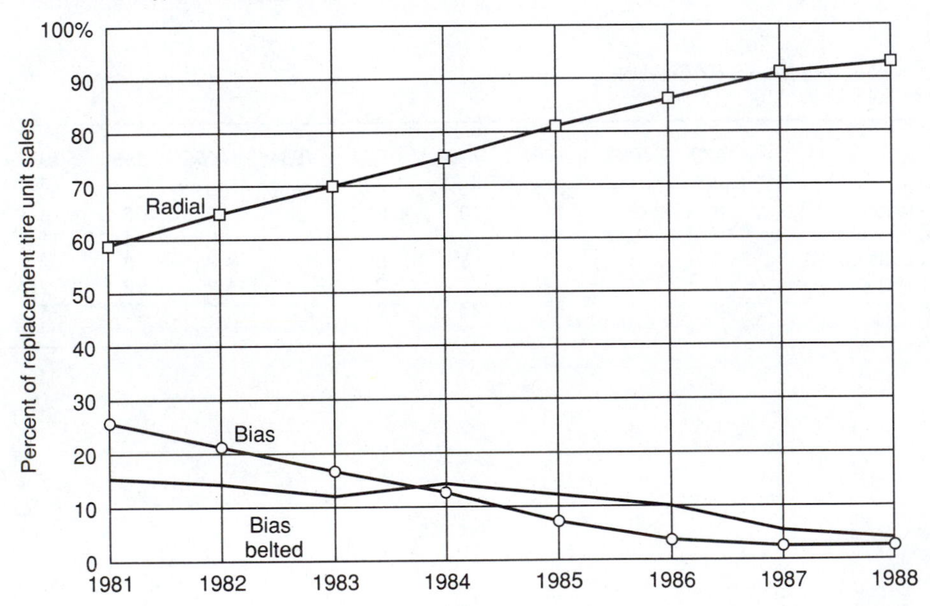

EXHIBIT 7 (*concluded*)
U.S. TIRE MARKET
Median Retail Tire Prices

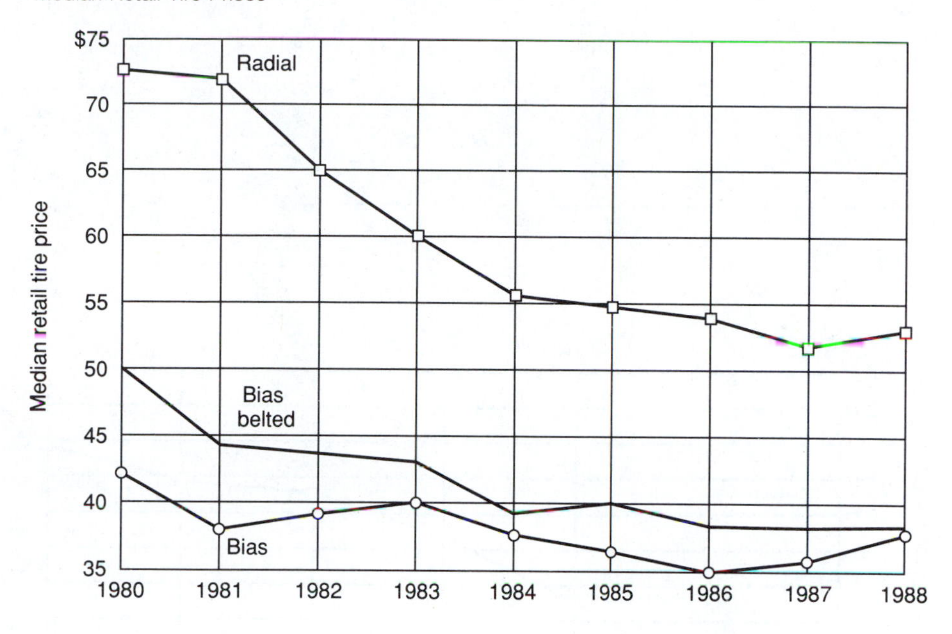

EXHIBIT 8
IMPORT SHARE OF U.S. AUTOMOBILE REPLACEMENT TIRE MARKET

1975	7.6%
1982	12.8
1983	17.0
1984	20.8
1985	23.2
1986	23.8
1987	25.7

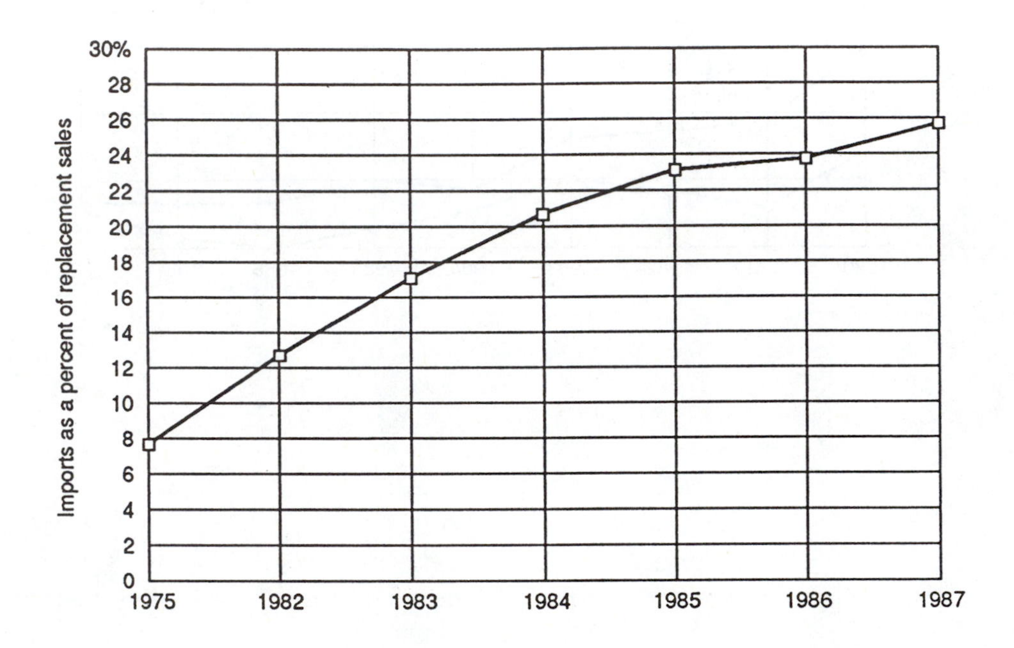

EXHIBIT 9
UGTC TIRE SALES BY MARKET SEGMENT
Year Ending November 30, 1987

	Units (thousands)	*Sales (millions)*
Replacement		
Uniroyal and Goodrich brands	15,336	$ 731.7
Private label	18,157	485.4
Total replacement	33,493	1,217.1
Original equipment	11,454	414.7
Export (primarily Goodrich replacement)	1,463	57.1
Total	46,410	$1,688.9

EXHIBIT 10

Location	*Former Parent*	*Daily Capacity*
Ardmore, OK	Uniroyal	31,500
Eau Claire, WI	Uniroyal	29,300
Opelika, AL	Uniroyal	26,500
Tuscaloosa, AL	Goodrich	32,300
Ft. Wayne, IN	Goodrich	28,800
Kitchener, Ontario	Uniroyal	19,600
Kitchener, Ontario	Goodrich	12,000
Total		180,000

EXHIBIT 11
GENERAL MOTORS SHARE OF TOTAL U.S. NEW CAR REGISTRATIONS

1982	43.9
1983	43.9
1984	44.4
1985	42.1
1986	39.6
1987	34.7
1988	34.4

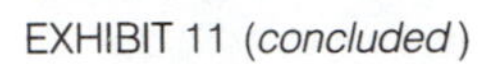

EXHIBIT 11 (*concluded*)

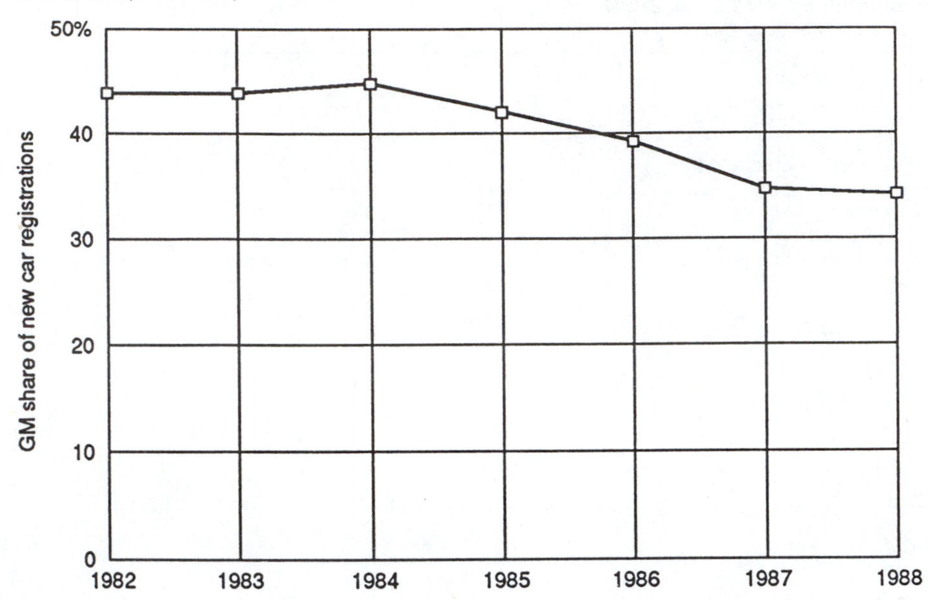

EXHIBIT 12
PERFORMANCE TIRE SHARE OF U.S. TIRE MARKET
Percent of Total Units

	1985	*1986*	*1987*	*1988*	*1989*
Original equipment	13.0%	15.0%	21.0%	25.0%	32.0%
Replacement	14.0	17.0	22.0	25.0	30.0

EXHIBIT 13
UGTC INCOME STATEMENTS

			Budget		
	1985	*1986*	*1987*	*1988*	*1989*
Sales	2,495.0	2,140.6	2,047.0	2,177.5	2,343.8
Cost of sales	1,925.1	1,658.8	1,605.2	1,723.4	1,812.7
Gross margin	569.9	481.8	441.8	454.1	531.1
	22.8%	22.5%	21.6%	20.9%	22.7%
SG&A	479.4	395.1	362.3	347.3	371.7
Restructuring charges	93.5				
Formation costs		19.6	3.0		
Operating income	(3.0)	67.1	76.5	106.8	159.4
		3.1%	3.7%	4.9%	6.8%
Interest expense	58.5	55.4	53.9	80.6	104.0
Other income	11.1	0.7	10.2	18.5	8.5
Income before taxes	(50.4)	12.4	32.8	44.7	63.9
Net income	(65.7)	6.6	22.1	33.7	37.7
Dividend requirements	(9.3)	(8.5)	(8.4)	(7.3)	(14.5)
Net of dividends	(75.0)	(1.9)	13.7	26.4	23.2

Note: 1985 and 1986 financials adjusted to reflect UGTC bank borrowings of $450 million.

EXHIBIT 14
UGTC BALANCE SHEET DATA

	11/30/86	*11/30/87*	*12/31/88*
Current assets			
Cash	16.1	29.9	17.6
Accounts receivable	390.8	383.1	370.7
Inventories	309.8	367.1	370.6
Other current assets	8.3	6.5	6.8
Total current assets	725.0	786.6	765.7
Investments	23.6	26.0	32.9
Net property, plant, and equipment	710.1	761.9	798.8
Other assets	22.9	31.4	58.0
Total assets	1,481.6	1,605.9	1,655.4
Current liabilities			
Accounts payable	147.6	192.8	200.3
Short-term bank borrowings	31.8	19.9	
Current portion of long-term debt	0.7	0.2	30.0
Accrued expenses	174.9	175.9	188.8
Other current liabilities	15.6	7.2	
Total current liabilities	370.6	396.0	419.1
Long-term liabilities			
Accrued pension liability	182.4	176.4	175.3
Long-term bank debt	204.7	209.2	298.3
Subordinated debt			415.0
Short-term obligations expected to be refinanced	125.0	220.0	
Other long-term liabilities	97.4	104.4	70.3
Total long-term liabilities	609.5	710.0	958.9
Net worth	501.5	499.9	277.4
Total liabilities and net worth	1,481.6	1,605.9	1,655.4

EXHIBIT 15
UGTC CONSOLIDATED STATEMENT OF CHANGES IN FINANCIAL POSITION

	Four Months Ending 11/30/86	Year Ending		Budget 12/31/89
		11/30/87	12/31/88	
Funds provided from operations				
Net income	16.8	22.1	33.7	37.7
Expenses not involving the use of funds:				
Depreciation	23.1	51.4	58.1	59.3
Other	12.5	(6.4)		
	52.4	67.1	91.8	97.0
Changes in working capital items				
Accounts receivable	(36.0)	7.7	(14.9)	(20.8)
Inventories	27.1	(57.3)	8.8	13.5
Accounts payable	38.2	45.2	18.8	6.3
	29.3	(4.4)	12.7	(1.0)
Other-net	58.6	7.4	(2.0)	9.4
Funds provided from operation	140.3	70.1	102.5	105.4
Borrowings at formation	450.0			
Dividends and distributions	(450.0)	(29.5)	(7.3)	(14.5)
Capital expenditures	(35.3)	(107.7)	(80.7)	(100.0)
Financing activity				
Financing costs			(16.3)	
Change in bank borrowings	(118.5)	80.9	11.7	8.8
Increase in cash	(13.5)	13.8	9.9	(0.3)

The Company and Its Strategists: Relating Corporate Strategy to Personal Values

Up to this point we have argued that an awareness of purpose and a sense of direction strengthen a company's ability to survive in changing circumstances. We have seen, to be sure, the difficulties of understanding clearly both a company's circumstances and its strengths and weaknesses. The action implied by these difficulties is an objective and alert surveillance of the environment for threats and opportunities and a detached appraisal of organizational characteristics in order to identify distinctive competence. We have considered the suitable combination of a company's strengths and its opportunities to be a logical exercise characterized by perhaps not precise but reasoned, well-informed choices of alternatives assuring the highest possible profit. We have been examining the changing relationship of company and environment almost as if a purely economic strategy, uncontaminated by the personality or goals of the decision maker, were possible.

STRATEGY AS PROJECTION OF PREFERENCE

We must acknowledge at this point that there is no way to divorce the decision determining the most sensible economic strategy for a company from the personal values of those who make the choice. Executives in charge of company destinies do not look exclusively at what a company might do and can do. In apparent disregard of the second of these considerations, they sometimes seem heavily influenced by what they personally *want* to do.

We are ourselves not aware of how much desire affects our own choice of alternatives, but we can see it in others. In the 1950s George Romney, then president of American Motors, began a dramatic promotion of economic sensible transportation which might have early developed the market for small cars later successfully exploited by the Japanese. After the solvency of his company was assured he preferred to repay every dollar of debt to investing in research and development of variations in the small car that might have retained leadership in even then a growing segment of the market. Almost certainly we see reflected here the higher value Romney placed on economy than on consumer preferences, on liquidity over debt, and other values derived more from his character and religious upbringing than from an objective monitoring of the best course for American Motors to follow. Romney's successors, with less distinctive personal values, reverted to the General Motors big-car strategy.[1]

Frank Farwell came from IBM to the presidency of Underwood in 1955, it has been reported, saying that he would be damned if he would spend his life peddling adding machines and typewriters. This aversion may explain why Underwood plunged into the computer business without the technical, financial, or marketing resources necessary to succeed in it. Similarly, when Adriano Olivetti purchased control of Underwood after three days of hurried negotiations, he may well have been moved by his childhood memory of visiting Hartford and by the respect for the world's once leading manufacturer of typewriters that led his father to erect in Ivrea a replica of the red-brick, five-story Hartford plant.[2] That he wanted to purchase Underwood so badly may explain why he and his associates did not find out how dangerously it had decayed and how near bankruptcy it had been brought.

The three presidents of J. I. Case in the years 1953 and 1963 seem to have been displaying their own temperaments as they wracked the company with alternating expansionism and contraction far beyond the need to respond to a cyclical industry environment.[3] In all these cases the actions taken can be rationalized so as not to seem quite so personal as we have suggested they are.

THE INEVITABILITY OF VALUES

We will be able to understand the strategic decision better if we admit rather than resist the dimension of preference. If we think back over the discussions of earlier cases in this book, the strategies we recommended for the companies probably reflected what *we* would have wanted to do had we been in charge of those companies. We told ourselves or assumed that our

[1] See "American Motors," in Edmund P. Learned, C. Roland Christensen, Kenneth R. Andrews, and William D. Guth, *Business Policy: Text and Cases* (Homewood, Ill.: Richard D. Irwin, 1965), p. 103. This classic case is also available from Harvard Business School Case Services.

[2] See "Underwood-Olivetti (AR)," in Learned et al., *Business Policy: Text and Cases,* p. 212, and HBS Case Services, case 312–017.

[3] "J. I. Case Company," in Learned et al., *Business Policy,* pp. 82–102, and HBS Case Services, case 309–270.

personal inclinations harmonized with the optimum combination of economic opportunity and company capability. The professional manager in a large company, drilled in analytical technique and the use of staff trained to subordinate value-laden assumptions to tables of numbers, may often prefer the optimal economic strategy because of its very suitability. Certain entrepreneurs, whose energy and personal drives far outweigh their formal training and self-awareness, set their course in directions not necessarily supported by logical appraisal. Such disparity appears most frequently in small privately held concerns or in companies built by successful and self-confident owner-managers. The phenomenon we are discussing, however, may appear in any company, especially (if it is large) in its divisions.

Our problem now can be very simply stated. In examining the alternatives available to a company, we must henceforth take into consideration the preferences of the chief executive. Furthermore, we must also be concerned with the values of other key managers who must either contribute to or assent to the strategy if it is to be effective. Finally, at a higher level of sophistication, the strategy should appeal to all employees. Their detailed exposure to opportunity for superior implementation can contribute, under receptive leadership, to improved productivity and continuous adaptation to customer needs. Bureaucratic constraints and autocratic multilayered supervision often choke off the constructive by-products of the kind of enthusiastic cooperation that convergence of individual and corporate goals produces.

We therefore have three levels of reconciliation to consider—first, the divergence between the chief executive's preference and the strategic choice which seems most economically defensible; second, the conflict among several sets of managerial personal values which must be reconciled not only with an economic strategy but with each other; and third, the difference in motivation of management and the work force that must be transcended by participation in, and acceptance of, at least the organization components of the strategy.

Thus when Mr. Edgar Villchur, inventor of the acoustic suspension loudspeaker, founded Acoustic Research, Inc.,[4] in 1954, he institutionalized a desire to bring high-fidelity sound to the mass market at the lowest possible cost. He licensed his competitors freely and finally gave up his original patent rights altogether. He kept not only his prices but his dealer margins low, maintained for a considerable time a primitive production facility and an organization of friends rather than managers, and went to great lengths to make the company a good place to work, sharing with employees the company's success. The company was dominated by Mr. Villchur's desire to have a small organization characterized by academic,

[4] "Acoustic Research, Inc.," in Learned et al., *Business Policy*, pp. 466–519, and HBS Case Services case 312–020.

scientific, and intellectual rather than "commercial" values. Product development was driven by some of these values away from the acoustical technology which Mr. Villchur's personal competence would have suggested into development of record players, amplifiers, and tuners which were to offer less in superiority over competitive products than did his speakers. Again these were priced far below what might have been possible.

Mr. Abraham Hoffman, for years vice president and treasurer, had the task of trying to overcome his superior's reluctance to advertise, to admit the validity of the marketing function, and of maintaining the business as a profitable enterprise. That the company had succeeded in at long last developing and producing a music system of great value in relation to its cost and in winning the respect of the high-fidelity listener market does not alter the fact that the first determination of strategy came more from Mr. Villchur's antibusiness values than from an analytical balancing of opportunity and distinctive competence. The latter would have led, with perhaps much greater growth and profitability, into acoustical systems, public-address equipment, long-distance communications, hearing aids, noise suppression, and the like—all areas in which technical improvement in the quality of available sound is much needed.

We must remember, however, that it is out of Mr. Villchur's determination and goals that his company came into being in the first place. The extraordinary accomplishments of an antimarketing company in the marketplace are directly traceable to the determination to innovate in quality and price. The reconciliation between Mr. Villchur's values and Mr. Hoffman's more business-oriented determination to manage the company's growth more objectively occurred only when the company was sold to Teledyne, Mr. Villchur retired to his laboratory, and Mr. Hoffman became president. The quality achievements of this firm have been rewarded, but the economic potential of its strategy was for years unrealized.

We should in all realism admit that the personal desires, aspirations, and needs of the senior managers of a company actually *do* play an influential role in the determination of strategy. Against those who are offended by this idea either for its departure from the stereotype of single-minded economic man or for its implicit violation of responsibilities to the shareholder, we would argue that we must accept not only the inevitability but the desirability of this intervention. If we begin by saying that all strategic decisions must fall within the very broad limits of the manager's fiduciary responsibility to the owners of the business and perhaps to others in the management group, then we may proceed legitimately to the idea that what a manager wants to do is not out of order. The conflict which often arises between what general managers want to do and what the dictates of economic strategy suggest they ought to do is best not denied or condemned. It should be accepted as a matter of course. In the study of organization behavior, we have long since concluded that the personal needs of the hourly worker must be taken seriously and at least partially satisfied as a means of securing the productive effort for which wages are paid. It should, then, come as no surprise to us that the CEOs of corporations also arrive at their work with their own needs and values, to say nothing of their relatively greater power to see that they are taken into account.

RECONCILING DIVERGENT VALUES

If we accept the inevitability of personal values in the strategic decision governing the character and course of a corporation, then we must turn to the skills required to reconcile the optimal economic strategy with the personal preferences of the executives of the company. There is no reason why a better balance could not have been struck in Acoustic Research without sacrifice to the genius of the founder or the quality of life in his company. It is first necessary to penetrate conventional rationalization and reticence to determine what these preferences are. For without this revelation, strategic proposals stemming from different unstated values come into conflict. This conflict cannot be reconciled by talking in terms of environmental data and corporate resources. The hidden agenda of corporate policy debates makes them endless and explains why so many companies do not have explicit, forthright, and usefully focused strategies.

To many caught up in the unresolved strategic questions in their own organizations, it seems futile even to attempt to reconcile a strategic alternative dictated by personal preference with other alternatives oriented toward capitalizing on opportunity to the greatest possible extent. In actuality, however, this additional complication poses fewer difficulties than at first appear. The analysis of opportunity and the appraisal of resources themselves often lead in different directions. To compose three, rather than two, divergent sets of considerations into a single pattern may increase the complexity of the task, but the integrating process is still the same. We can look for the dominant consideration and treat the others as constraints; we can probe the elements in conflict for the possibilities of reinterpretation or adjustment. We are not building a wall of irregular stone so much as balancing a mobile of elements, the motion of which is adjustable to the motion of the entire mobile.

As we have seen, external developments can be affected by company action and company resources, and internal competence can be developed. If worse comes to worst, it is better for a person to separate from a management whose values he or she does not share than to pretend agreement or to wonder why others think as they do. Howard Head, whose passionate dedication to the metal ski not only produced a most successful business but delayed unnecessarily its entry into plastic skis, realistically retired from his diversified business and sold his holdings. It is not necessary, however, for all members of management to think alike or to have the same personal values, so long as strategic decision is not delayed or rendered ineffective by these known and accepted differences. Large gains are possible simply by raising the strategic issues for discussion by top management, by admitting the legitimacy of different preferences, and by explaining how superficial or fundamental the differences are.

Collision between a management-determined change in strategy and the organization that is charged with carrying it out is not a feasible subject for one-on-one discussion with everyone. We must deal now not with the personal preferences of individuals but with the culture that develops in organizations to establish certain values as dominant with unimportant variations left untouched. *Culture* has become a buzzword among consulting firms, especially as the importance of implementation has been recognized by those previously concerned with portfolio analysis, competitive strategy, and other logical or analytical approaches to strategy formulation.

Every organization develops an informal pattern of relationships in which authority is recognized and traditional ways of doing things evolve. Some organizations like Lincoln Electric, which prizes individual achievement and rewards it handsomely, are spare, no-nonsense, highly productive organizations more than holding their own against competition. Others, like Du Pont, become institutions in which research and development, safety, and corporate uniformity tend to homogenize scores of divisions in dozens of industries. This process makes them more culturally Du Pont than ready to succeed in the stringent rough and tumble of their own competitive environments. In many such instances an admirable history has produced a dominant culture that displaces the succession of strategic decisions that changes in the marketplace require. Rather than attempt a classification of cultures, we ask you to look at Head Ski and Crown Cork & Seal reflecting now on those elements of their culture which would be difficult to change, should your recommendations require such change. A searching inquiry into the interconnection of strategy and institutionalized values is one key to successful implementation.

MODIFICATION OF VALUES

The question whether individual values can actually be changed or corporate culture modified during the reconciliation process is somewhat less clear. A value is a view of life and a judgment of what is desirable that is very much a part of a person's personality and a group's morale. From parents, teachers, and peers (we are told by psychologists), we acquire basic values, which change somewhat with acquired knowledge, analytical ability, and self-awareness but remain a stable feature of personality. Nonetheless the preference attached to goals in concrete circumstances is not beyond influence. The physicist who leaves the university to work in a profit-making company because of a combined fondness for his work and material comfort, may ask to continue to do pure rather than applied research, but he presumably does not want his company to go bankrupt. The conflict in values is to some degree negotiable, once the reluctance to expose hidden agendas is overcome. Retaining the value orientation of the scientist, the ambivalent physicist might assent to a strategic alternative stressing product development rather than original investigation, at least for a specified time until the attainment of adequate profit made longer range research feasible.

The recent restructuring of American industry has forced drastic changes in the culture of organizations. Foreign competition has revealed that American wage rates are often uncompetitive in relation to productivity. The architects of hostile takeovers, looking to sell assets of target companies, identify and dispense with what they consider to be unproductive assets, divisions, jobs, and people. The staff sections of corporate headquarters, grown large in the attempt to give expert attention to everything that might well rather than must be done, have been slashed. Downsizing and consequent layoffs, painful as they are to contemplate, attract attention to the problem being addressed. Survivors, however demoralized, are energized by the struggle to survive and become aware of the need to develop new ways to get done what must be done. It is unfortunate in such instances that less drastic measures were not undertaken earlier. Strategic innovation is a practical alternative to violent restructuring.

Even so large a company as General Motors, in trouble surprisingly deep, is with difficulty restructuring itself for leadership in an industry changing in ways that make its previous organization structure, procurement, labor relations, and production methods obsolete. Whether it will win this battle is unclear. Du Pont continues to attempt to define its mission, adapt its culture-shaping policies to the conditions of the industries in which it participates, and differentiate its management style to suit the needs of subsidiaries. The merger of a large international oil company with its oil-field and market cultural characteristics has dramatized the decorum and stability of Du Pont and called it into question. General Electric radically reduced its corporate staff and assigned responsibility to its divisions to succeed on their own against their competitors rather than to view themselves as under the protection of the corporate monogram. A new kind of giant corporation is in the making.

That under adversity the culture of an organization and the values of its leaders can change has been recently established beyond doubt. Units divested dramatically from their corporate parents have often become more profitable and pleasant to work in as the burden of corporate allocations and compliance with corporate policy has been lifted. The opportunity wasted by our basic industries is that presented by this book. The conditions confronting the automobile, steel, chemical, textile, and footwear industries have been visible for years. The failure to adapt to change that had become clearly inevitable reflects the triumph of habit and short-term measurement of results over strategic assessment of company position in a changing world. The faltering of American industry, affected to be sure by forces other than managerial ineptness, is a dramatic background to the need to devise a strategy proof against a conservative culture suppressing innovation and adaptation.

AWARENESS OF VALUES

Our interest in the role of personal values in strategic formulations should not be confined to assessing the influence of other people's values. Despite the well-known problems of introspection, we can probably do more to understand the relation of our own values to our choice of purpose than we can to change the values of others. Awareness that our own preference for an alternative opposed by another stems from values as much as from rational estimates of economic opportunity may have important consequences. First, it may make us more tolerant and less indignant when we perceive this relationship between recommendations and values in the formulations of others. Second, it will force us to consider how important it really is to us to maintain a particular value in making a particular decision. Third, it may give us insight with which to identify our biases and thus pave the way for a more objective assessment of all the strategic alternatives that are available. These consequences of self-examination will not end conflict, but they will at least prevent its unnecessary prolongation.

The object of this self-examination is not necessarily to endow us with the ability to persuade others to accept the strategic recommendations we consider best; it is to acquire insight into the problems of determining purpose and skill in the process of resolving them. Individuals inquiring into their own values for the purpose of understanding their own positions in policy debates can continue to assess their own personal opportunities, strengths and weaknesses, and basic values by means of the procedures outlined here. For a personal strategy, analytically considered and consciously developed, may be as useful to an individual as a corporate strategy is to a business institution. The effort, conducted by each individual, to formulate personal purpose might well accompany his or her contributions to organizational purpose. If the encounter leads to a clarification of the purposes one seeks, the values one holds, and the alternatives available, the attempt to make personal use of the concept of strategy will prove extremely worthwhile.

Introducing personal preference forces us to deal with the possibility that the strategic decision we prefer (identified after the most nearly objective analysis of opportunity and resources we are capable of) is not acceptable to other executives with different values. Their acceptance of the strategy is necessary to its successful implementation. In diagnosing this conflict, we try to identify the values implicit in our own choice. As we look at the gap between the strategy which follows from our own values and that which would be appropriate to the values of our associates, we look to see whether the difference is fundamental or superficial. Then we look to see how the strategy we believe best matches opportunity and resources can be adapted to accommodate the values of those who will implement it. Reconciliation of the three principal determinants of strategy which we have so far considered is often made possible by adjustment of any or all of the determinants.

The role of self-examination in coming to terms with a conflict in values over an important strategic determination is not to turn all strategic decisions into outcomes of consensus. Some organizations—you can see them in this book—are run by persons who are leaders in the sense that they have power and are not afraid to use it. It is true that business leaders, in Zaleznik's words, "commit themselves to a career in which they have to work on themselves as a condition for effective working with other people."[5] At the same time a leader must recognize that "the essence of leadership is choice, a singularly individualistic act in which a [person] assumes responsibility for a commitment to direct an organization along a particular path. . . . As much as a leader wishes to trust others, he has to judge the soundness and validity of his subordinates' positions. Otherwise, the leader may become a prisoner of the emotional commitments of his subordinates, frequently at the expense of making correct judgments about policies and strategies."[6]

When a management group is locked in disagreement the presence of power and the need for its exercise conditions the dialogue. There are circumstances when leadership must transcend disagreement that cannot be resolved by discussion. Subordinates, making the best of the inevitable, must accept a follower role. When leadership becomes irresponsible and dominates subordinate participation without reason, it is usually ineffective or is deposed. Participants in strategic disagreements must know not only their own needs and power but those of the chief executive. Strategic planning, in the sense that power attached to values plays a role in it, is a political process.

You should not warp your recommended strategy to the detriment of the company's future in order to adjust it to the personal values you hold or observe. On the other hand you should not expect to be able to impose without risk and without expectation of eventual vindication and agreement an unwelcome pattern of purposes and policies on the people in charge of a corporation or responsible for achieving results. Strategy is a human construction; it must in the long run be responsive to human needs. It must ultimately inspire commitment. It must stir an organization to successful striving against competition. People have to have their hearts in it.

[5] Abraham Zaleznik and Manfred F. R. Kets de Vries, *Power and the Corporate Mind* (Boston: Houghton Mifflin, 1975), p. 207.

[6] Ibid., p. 209.

Marks and Spencer, Ltd.

The principles on which the business was founded do not change. The original ideas have been expanded to conform to the changing requirements of a more knowledgeable and discerning public—a public that has broadened to include wider strata of the community.

In the course of the years, we have built up three great assets:

1. The goodwill and confidence of the public.
2. The loyalty and devotion of management and staff throughout the system.
3. The confidence and cooperation of our suppliers.

The principles upon which the business is built are:

1. To offer our customers a selective range of high-quality, well-designed, and attractive merchandise at reasonable prices.
2. To encourage our suppliers to use the most modern and efficient techniques of production and quality control dictated by the latest discoveries in science and technology.
3. With the cooperation of our suppliers, to enforce the highest standard of quality control.
4. To plan the expansion of our stores for the better display of a widening range of goods and for the convenience of our customers.
5. To foster good human relations with customers, suppliers, and staff.

These five tenets constituted the fundamental operating principles of Marks and Spencer (M&S), according to Lord Marks of Broughton, chairman of the firm from 1916 to 1964. Through application of these principles, M&S had achieved outstanding success. By 1974 M&S was the largest retail organization in the United Kingdom. Each week more than 13 million customers made purchases at the firm's 251 stores, which offered some 700 food and 3,000 nonfood (primarily textile) items. Textiles supplied 71 percent of M&S sales in 1974, food 27 percent, and exports 2 percent. The company accounted for 12 percent of British consumer expenditures for clothing and footwear and held over one third of the

Harvard Business School case 375–358.

market in women's lingerie and men's underwear.

Despite the disappointing British economic situation, M&S prospered in 1974. While national income declined 2 percent and inflation rose 15–18 percent, M&S posted record sales, with pretax profit climbing 10 percent (see Exhibit 1). While sales per square foot for Britain's top retailers averaged $180 per year, M&S's reached $260. The company's Marble Arch outlet in London achieved sales per square foot of $1,000, earning it a listing in *The Guinness Book of World Records* as the most profitable store in the world.

A board of 22 executives managed M&S from the firm's offices in Baker Street, London, where buying, merchandising, distribution, quality control, and finance were centralized. M&S sold all of its merchandise under the exclusive St. Michael brand name. The company owned no production facilities, relying instead on a broad network of suppliers from whom it ordered some $25 million worth of goods each week.

M&S's major competitors included a supermarket chain with food sales nearly twice M&S's; two retailing firms that imitated M&S but sold cheaper, lower-quality goods; and an American-style department store that emphasized more fashion-oriented goods at lower prices and quality.

THE EARLY YEARS

The business principles enunciated by Lord Marks originated in the experiences of his father, Michael Marks, the founder of M&S. In 1884 the elder Marks, a Polish Jew, began visiting the town markets of northern England, setting up stalls that featured the sign, "Don't Ask the Price—It's a Penny." The slogan proved so popular that Marks adopted the penny price in all his stalls. The simplicity of the single fixed price allowed Marks to give up keeping accounts and inspired him to search continually for goods as varied and excellent as could be sold for a penny. High turnover counterbalanced the low profit margins.

Marks's business flourished, and in 1894 he took Thomas Spencer into partnership. By 1903, when Spencer retired, the company boasted 40 branches. In that year Marks and Spencer, Ltd., was formed, with control entirely in Marks and Spencer family hands, and the headquarters was moved to Manchester. Spencer died in 1905, Marks in 1908. After Marks's death, control of M&S temporarily passed out of family hands.

1914–1939

When the founder's son, Simon Marks (later Lord Marks) regained control of the firm in 1914, it was a national chain with 140 branches. Although only 10 percent were in market halls, M&S maintained its traditional policies of open display, easy accessibility to goods, and self-selection. Management also strove to make M&S a place where employees were happy and proud to work. Each store had a manageress (term used by M&S management) in charge of training. A heated room was provided for the staff as a place to eat and relax.

With the accession of Simon Marks, a strong family influence returned to M&S. Simon exercised overall direction while his brother-in-law, Israel Sieff (later Lord Sieff), took charge of buying and merchandising. After their deaths, their descendants continued to dominate M&S into the 1970s. (In 1975 M&S had no outside directors.) Two outside influences also had profound impact on M&S in the decade after 1914: first, Chaim Weizmann, the brilliant chemist and famous Zionist leader, encouraged Marks and Sieff in commitments that became cornerstones of the modern M&S. Weizmann interested them in the applications and benefits of new technologies and inspired them to regard their business as a social service to both customers and employees. Second, a 1924 visit to the United States allowed Simon Marks to study American chain stores. He returned to England determined to transform M&S into a chain of "super stores" featuring continuous merchandise flow and a central organization acutely sensitive to consumer needs.

M&S went public in 1926 and within 10 years had a branch in every major town. Enhanced staff amenities accompanied this rapid growth. The welfare department, founded in 1933, supervised a variety of employee facilities and expanded medical and dental services that included chiropody (especially significant to people who spend hours on their feet). A pension plan was initiated in 1936.

Changes also occurred in M&S's relations with its suppliers. In 1928 M&S registered the St. Michael brand name (honoring M&S's founder) and became the first department store in the United Kingdom to set the goal of selling only "own-brand" merchandise. To assure the highest product quality, M&S insisted on close cooperation with suppliers and stressed the use of technological advances in materials and production processes. In 1928 M&S's large orders enabled the company to overcome traditional wholesale opposition and place orders directly with producers. Food purchases, upon which management imposed extremely strict standards, followed a similar pattern.

1945–1955

In the decade following the war, M&S's sales rose 450 percent, and pretax profits 351 percent. The St. Michael brand gradually emerged on all products and became increasingly identified in consumers' minds with quality and value. Concentrating on a limited product range, M&S developed a dominant position in many textile lines.

Sales growth led to store modernization and expansion. After postwar controls were abolished in the 1950s, growth accelerated rapidly (see accompanying table).

OPERATION SIMPLIFICATION, 1956

On February 16, 1956, Lord Marks, chairman of M&S, was presented with a budget that exceeded the previous year's by millions of pounds. He reacted strongly to the increases and launched a companywide campaign to eliminate the burgeoning

COMPANY GROWTH, 1946–1974

	Sales (£000)*	*Profits (£000)*	*Number of Stores*	*Total Store Space (000/sq. ft.)*
1946	£ 19,693	£ 2,027	224	1,407
1955	108,375	9,168	234	2,461
1968	282,308	33,871	241	3,939
1974	571,650	76,825	251	5,489

*Including exports. Food sales ranged from 14 percent of total sales (1957) to 27 percent (1974).

load of paperwork, which appeared to be chiefly responsible for rising overhead. As Lord Marks remarked to Israel Sieff, "It's not a law of business growth that administrative costs continue to increase." The campaign, known as Operation Simplification, aimed at liberating staff, management, and supporting services from paperwork so that they could focus on one task: increasing sales in pounds sterling.

The general principles of Operation Simplification were:

1. Sensible approximation: The price of perfection is prohibitive; approximation often suffices and costs less.
2. Exception reporting: Events generally occur as arranged, and only exceptions need be reported.
3. Never legislate for exceptions: Detailed manuals are unnecessary (M&S went from 13 manuals to 2), and local decision making enhances willingness to assume responsibility.
4. Decategorization: Those below management and supervisory levels are more useful in a "general staff" category than as specialists.
5. People can be and need to be trusted: Eliminating checks and controls saves time and money, while improving staff self-confidence and sense of responsibility. Management control is more effectively exercised by selective spot checks.

Lord Marks set a goal of allowing store staff, management, and support services to focus on one task—increasing sales in pounds sterling. The new system made senior executives responsible for profitability. They determined one markup target for food and another for textiles. With margins thus standardized, the selectors focused on finding goods of acceptable quality that would turn over rapidly. Stores then worked to use space and to serve customers in ways that would achieve maximum sales.

To insure the effectiveness of the system, Lord Marks enlisted the personal support of head office managers, who then assumed responsibility for improving efficiency in their areas. The campaign, which culminated in a symbolic bonfire of old records, eliminated 26 million pieces of paper—120 tons—per year and reduced the staff from 32,000 to 22,000. The abolition of countless forms and routines freed senior managers to get personally involved in their departments.

On the drive for simplicity, Lord Sieff wrote: "Both the executives and the merchandisers of the department should *probe* into the goods in the stores *with seeing eyes and a critical mind.* The department supervisor and the salesgirl are his best sources of information. To depend on statistics is to asphyxiate the dynamic spirit of the business."

Lord Sieff described the process as "the method whereby the interested and inquiring mind of the executive and his colleagues penetrates beneath the surface of things and discovers the facts."

The emphasis on probing became an integral part of the M&S management philosophy. Brian Howard, director of foods, illustrated the merits of probing,

> We get concerned when statistics get on paper, because they hide things. For example, suppose I had a report on sales at a store that showed for a day

	Beginning Stock	*Sales*	*Ending Stock, End of Day*
Item A	100	100	0
Item B	50	20	30

> I might conclude on the basis of a day's sales that sales of A to B were 5:1 and act accordingly. But if I looked after lunch, I might find that the sales for the morning showed

	Beginning Stock	*Sales*	*Ending Stock, End of Morning*
Item A	100	100	0
Item B	50	10	40

> I have to ask the store manager to learn that the proper order is more like 10:1. That's why we distrust statistics and value probing.

Simplicity remained a touchstone for M&S management in the 1970s. In 1974 M&S inaugurated a "Good Housekeeping" campaign to limit paperwork, with probing still occupying an important place. It was conducted not only at the head office but also, and especially, in the stores. All senior executives frequented stores, many stopping on their way home from work. In 1974 only 10 of M&S's 251 stores failed to receive a visit from a senior board member.

Each director was expected to wear M&S clothes and every weekend received a hamper of M&S food. Both policies allowed executives to monitor product quality personally. On Saturdays each board member and senior executive toured two or three stores. Managers frequently encountered other executives in stores while probing. For example, a researcher accompanied Howard on a Saturday tour of the Uxbridge store. Over coffee Howard assembled a textile sales manager, junior executives in food and textiles, a food technologist, and the store manager. All were headed for other stores. As a head office employee remarked about the directors, "They work 60 hours during the week, they visit stores on Saturday, and they talk about it on Sunday. They live, eat, and breathe M&S."

During the Saturday visits, executives spent a great deal of time talking with employees. The following describes incidents during a 1974 store tour conducted for the casewriter by the chairman, Sir Marcus Sieff, and Brian Howard:

> Staines was a small store but did £40,000 per week. We arrived around 9:15 and were greeted by one of the supervisors. The store traffic seemed brisk but the staff manageress thought it a little below normal.
>
> A very young food department supervisor was asked to take us around. She was flustered but did her best to answer questions. It was easy to see what was meant by the necessity at M&S of being able to give straight, clear answers. Brian Howard expected her to know her numbers and her situation. There were problems of short produce deliveries, and he wanted them described. He also offered comments on store layout.
>
> Later the staff manageress took us around upstairs. The warehouse space floor was spotless. The atmosphere was one of easy-going efficiency and competence.

Leaving Staines, Howard drove on to the Reading store to meet Sir Marcus Sieff. Sir Marcus led his party around the store. All that he was wearing that day, except his shoes—slacks, shirt, sweater, and jacket—were available on the racks in the store. His questions dealt entirely with merchandise and people. What was moving? The store manager offered from memory current sales numbers representing percentage comparison with previous weeks and years. Department managers added comments.

Of a shirt, Sir Marcus Sieff commented, "Here's one of our mistakes. Have you reduced this?"

"Yes, but it still isn't moving. We'll have to take it down another pound."

"Why isn't there a price notice?" Sir Marcus asked a young sales supervisor.

"We just got these this morning, chairman, and the sign is being made. We buy this from Burlington. We've ordered 2 million yards of this fabric so far. It's moving very well."

Looking at a child's snowsuit jacket at £6.25 (approximately $15), Sir Marcus said, "Is that our price? We've *got* to get a less expensive range. Our customers can't afford that."

Everyone had a pad, from the chairman down, and all took their own notes.

"Did your boss come in to work today?" he asked a warehouse foreman whose wife worked as a sales clerk. "Yes, chairman."

"How is Mary?"

"She's well, thank you."

On a tour of the lunchroom and offices, Sir Marcus asked for the hairdresser by name ("She's the queen of Reading"), and gave numerous directives.

"I want 'switch the lights out please' signs near the doors whenever the switches aren't near the door. They have to learn we have a balance of payments problem. When do our window lights go off?"

"6:30."

"When do we close?"

"6:00."

"I want them off at 6:00."

Driving to his home for lunch, Sir Marcus commented on what he had learned. "Some lines we like don't move—like this jacket. We have to find out why. We have a problem on having enough stock for the period after New Year's without carrying too much inventory. And that store has some good people. They're doing a good job."

OTHER DEVELOPMENTS

Personnel

The fifth point of the general principles of Operation Simplification reemphasized M&S's traditional commitment to the well-being of its employees. M&S implemented this commitment by establishing company-financed social and recreational clubs at Baker Street and in each store and by upgrading medical and pension benefits. When Lord Sieff succeeded to the chairmanship in 1964, he reiterated the company's concern: "M&S started with people. We—Lord Marks and I—both felt that making people happy was the great thing in life. So, when we got into the stores, we automatically thought in these lines. For instance, we found that the girls were going without lunch when they were broke or busy. So we put in lunchrooms and saw to it that they got time to eat their meals."

A 1969 speech by Managing Director (later Chairman) Sir Marcus Sieff reflected similar sentiments:

> The guiding light of business enterprise is attention to human relations within the business. Firms, like our own, that study human relations—in some places they are called labor relations or industrial relations—are often asked to supply people to lecture on the subject. It is very difficult. How can you tell people to do things that you know they are not doing because they are the way they are? You cannot get the goodwill of the people who work for you by changing words such as *canteen* into *dining room*, *navvy* to *worker*, *office boy* to *junior clerk*, and so on, or even just by paying higher wages. In the last analysis, good labor relations come from workers approving of the kind of people they believe their employers to be.
>
> Good human relations can only develop if top management believes in its

> importance and then sees that such a philosophy is dynamically implemented. They must come in a sensible way, which we have found brings in response, with few exceptions, from all grades of staff. This response expresses itself in loyalty to the firm's cooperation with management, greater labor stability, and a willing acceptance of new and more modern methods. The majority of workers under such conditions take pride in doing a good job. All this results in greater productivity and higher profits. This enables management to provide all those facilities that make for contented and hard-working staff and to pay better wages based on genuinely increased productivity.

Management designed the M&S personnel organization to implement their philosophy of concern (see Exhibit 2). In each outlet, a store personnel executive oversaw the training, movement, and welfare of the store's staff. The job of the head office personnel executive was similar but somewhat less structured due to the close relationships between headquarters' top executives and staff. Of particular importance was the post of pension and welfare executive, who not only ran M&S's pension plan but also looked after retired M&S employees. Retired employees remained attached to a particular store from which the company provided various services, including a free medical plan and periodic lunches. The pension plan itself—long noncontributory—provided well above average benefits.

Concerning these policies Sir Marcus commented, "The word *welfare* has an old-fashioned sound reminiscent of the Victorian era, but I do not know a better one to replace it. People do have troubles, and it is a fundamental part of a good staff policy to be able unobtrusively and, above all, speedily to give help and advice when needed."

M&S also offered current employees a rich and varied program of free activities including riverboat trips, table tennis, and bowling and concert tickets. Of these amenities Sir Marcus said, "They should be of such a nature that executives are pleased to take advantage of them. . . . If the facilities are not good enough for top management, then they are not good enough for staff whatever the grade." By 1972 annual welfare costs at M&S exceeded £4.5 million.

Ultimate responsibility for the company's personnel and welfare policies rested with a welfare committee of nine senior managers. The committee, which met weekly, handled those cases that exceeded local store authority or that required a "common handwriting." The committee's decisions were never questioned.

M&S's emphasis on family atmosphere and employee welfare resulted in a distinctive work environment. An employee described M&S's "house rules":

1. The first thing to remember is that it is a *family* business. Because we're a family business, we care for people. It's a paternal business. How does that affect the professional? You have to receive your inoculation. If you get a violent reaction, you'd better go. And then you grow with the business. It comes back to a recruitment policy. We have to get them young and train them ourselves.
2. You can't be a loner. You have to be part of the team.
3. You have to spread your decisions around. Some in-house decisions are "I don't like it." You learn to accept a decision and wait your time to come back with it.
4. You have to learn how to handle people in an ordinary, decent way.

5. Nobody succeeds who can't talk clearly and simply to the management.

Marketing

M&S's marketing philosophy, like its personnel policy, developed from traditional antecedents. The late Lord Israel Sieff summarized it thus:

> The future of the business depends on quick imaginative study of what the people need–not of what the public can be persuaded to buy. Only in supplying real needs will a business flourish in the long term. Only by giving the people what on reflection they continue to want will a business earn the respect of the customer, which is essential to anything more durable than a cheapjack's overnight success. So long as Marks and Spencer continues to study what the people need, and efficiently produces it by means of a staff humanely organized, we can meet any economic trend and challenge.

M&S believed in offering the customer a selective and streamlined range of products aimed at rapid turnover. In Lord Sieff's words, "In each section there are a few lines which do a large percentage of the business and, generally speaking, it is these items whose development merits our first consideration. It is no use wasting time on articles that can have no future." The 3,000-item range of textile products included women's clothing and lingerie, men's clothing and underwear, children's clothing, footwear, domestic furnishings, floor coverings, accessories, and toiletries. Among the 700 food offerings were bakery goods, confectionaries, produce, poultry and meat, dairy products, beverages, and frozen foods. The articles selected typically offered the consumer very high quality at moderate—rather than low—prices. This combination of quality and price encouraged customers to associate M&S with "value for money."

Though M&S had always attempted to maintain a policy of one markup percentage for all merchandise, the range of markups had been expanding. Markups for food ranged from 18 to 24 percent with a target of 23 percent; textiles, from 26 to 33 percent with a target of 30 percent. In 1974 the annual report announced that margins had been "deliberately and substantially" cut, with "attendant loss of profit" to counteract rising prices and costs.

M&S never held sales, and it reduced merchandise for clearance purposes only. It did little advertising (0.3 percent of sales versus 2–3 percent in the United States), which was limited to information (i.e., new product line). Executives believed that the products sold themselves and so relied largely on word of mouth.

Sales within the store were for cash only, as executives believed that credit only increased costs. The company provided no fitting rooms but did maintain a liberal refund policy. M&S accepted virtually all returns on face value, thus eliminating customers' anxieties.

President J. Edward Sieff summarized M&S's basic marketing principles, "We do what's best for our suppliers, staff, and customers, and we get better at it all the time."

Production and Product Line Organization

In 1960 Lord Marks stated, "It is easy enough to test goods when they are made. What is more important is to be sure they will be well made from the start. What we want to have is process control and testing at the point of production."

Although M&S did not manufacture the goods it sold, it was often responsible for

75–90 percent of a supplier's output. The company worked closely with the approximately 175 food and 400 nonfood independents providing St. Michael merchandise to M&S specifications. Indeed, according to Brian Howard, "Management at M&S is concerned with a flow that begins with the manufacture of synthetic fibers or the import of raw goods and ends with what we hope is a steady movement of merchandise across store counters."

Supplier relationships often stretched back 30 years or more, allowing many suppliers to share in M&S's growth. In 1975 the company employed over 250 scientists, engineers, and support staff, working in teams with merchandising departments and suppliers to develop product specifications and monitor product quality. Suppliers manufactured goods according to an M&S-planned schedule and held them until the company requested delivery to specific stores, at which time M&S accepted title.

Responsibility for handling the flow from suppliers to M&S rested with the merchandise teams (see Exhibit 3). Within the textiles division two subdivisions existed, each headed by a managing director. One director supervised men's and boys' wear, home furnishings, footwear, accessories, and new products; the other, women's and girls' wear. Reporting to the managing director of each subdivision were one or more senior executives, each of whom had charge of one or more product lines handled by the division. Each line was further subdivided into segments overseen by junior executives (e.g., menswear subdivisions included knitwear and outerwear). Junior executives, in turn, supervised selectors responsible for developing merchandise ranges and merchandisers responsible for sales estimates, production, packaging, and distribution.

The food division, though more centralized, adhered to the same basic philosophies and procedures as did textiles. Each product group within the food division had a selector and merchandiser. Merchandise teams tested new items with recipes and tasting panels. Product shelf life frequently required a shorter time span for food division operations than for textiles.

At the store level, food operations differed slightly from textiles. Store staff, responsible for determining the merchandise they carried, prepared weekly lists of stock on hand that indicated what they wanted delivered on each day of the following week. The merchandisers who controlled distribution edited these orders. After the individual store orders were submitted, a computer, programmed weekly with the production capacity and location of each supplier, generated a production plan for each supplier and geographical area. The merchandise was subsequently ordered. All food orders were transported to the stores via depots operated by independent contractors. Perishable goods were delivered daily. Each product bore a clear sell-out date, and it was the responsibility of the merchandise and store staffs to monitor the freshness of the food continually. In addition to testing all new products and resampling trail lines, M&S staff randomly selected items from stores and brought them to the laboratory for inspection.

Merchandising began with semiannual estimates for the coming season, including budgets for sale, stock, and production. Merchandisers, selectors, and merchandise executives held joint responsibility for estimates. The board of directors calculated the total estimate for the company and for each major decision. All estimates were made exclusively in pounds sterling.

Senior executives monitored sales performance personally and by means of reports. Of particular interest was the Stock Checking List Summary, which was used in both foods and textiles and circulated weekly to the directors (see Exhibit 4). Most merchandise executives believed that the basics needed monitoring while fashion items would "take care of themselves." Senior management was reluctant to accept external conditions as justification for results below plan. Generally, if department sales were unsatisfactory, internal procedures were evaluated first. Senior management constantly monitored departments when performance was smooth and eased up in the face of difficult problems. The reasoning was that good performance deteriorated easily if not continually pressured.

Store Divisional Organization

In 1974 M&S had 251 stores divided into 11 divisions, each under a corporate director with responsibility for store operations, building and equipment, transportation, packaging, and real estate. Twelve divisional superintendents, covering regional groups of stores, acted as Baker Street's field representatives and helped store managers as needed. The store managers were the senior line managers in each store and were held responsible by the board for implementing its policies.

In practice, the store manager concentrated on sales. Relieved of responsibility for profit margins and usually ignorant of individual margins, managers strove to increase volume, control store expenses, monitor turnover, eliminate "counter cloggers," and insure adequate stock in fast-moving items. The staff manageress was responsible for staff selection, training, assignment, development, and welfare. Most store managers were men, but some women had recently been promoted to that position.

The dual authority structure was designed to instill a family spirit in each store. The manager and manageress of a new store always had comparable experience in other stores and were expected to achieve a family spirit within six months.

The typical store in 1973 had a manager, an assistant manager, a staff manageress, 2 or 3 department managers, a warehouse manager, a cashier, 10 department supervisors, and 150 general staff. All managerial staff received training in company stores. By age 30, however, most staff and line managers embarked on different career paths, with staff people centralized at headquarters (see Exhibit 5).

The sales assistant occupied one of the most important positions in the company. Assigned to specific departments and attired in identical uniforms, sales assistants monitored product quality, kept stock plentiful and neat, operated the cash registers, and assisted customers. They had authority to replenish stock and to reject goods that seemed of poor quality or inappropriate for the department. However, rejection of stock seldom occurred.

A LOOK AT A STORE

A tour of a large downtown London store began in the unusually clean and tidy stock and receiving area. Merchandise was received on conveyor belts, spot-counted, and immediately put into stock. A large, spotless area, used for food stock and storage, included freezers and cold storage rooms. Unique baskets enabled stacking so that food products would not be damaged.

Staff amenities included a medical room and a nurse, with periodic visits from a physician, dentist, and chiropodist; a one-room infirmary; a hairdressing salon (charge 75¢), where women were served lunch under the dryers; a cloakroom with security lockers; shower and bathroom facilities; a staff refrigerator; a recreation room; and a staff dining room. The dining room provided lunches, coffee, and afternoon tea, and the charge for all three was 25¢ per day. The food compared favorably with that served in executive dining rooms (see Exhibits 6 and 7).

The main sales floor was arranged to reflect shopping behavior rather than production process (e.g., knitwear was separated into men's, women's, and children's). Except for area identification signs, there were no graphics or displays. Merchandise was displayed on tables and garment racks (see Exhibit 8).

The food department had a separate checkout but no barriers to the department store. All food was packaged in see-through containers. Many shelves were completely empty because M&S ordered only a one-day supply plus minimal stock for the next (see Exhibit 9). When shelf life expired, unsold goods were available to staff at half price or less.

Movement of both textiles and foods was continuously monitored by the store manager. He remarked, "By 12 noon I know the fastest-moving item in the store. It's my job to move that merchandise and make sure we get enough of it. The major problem I face is that if I can't get what I know to be the best, what will I settle for as next best?"

Finance

According to John Samuel, financial officer, M&S's financial policy aimed to provide sufficient resources for capital development, retained earnings, and dividends. The board determined the specific amounts to be committed. A pretax profit goal of 10–10½ percent and an expense level of about 12 percent together implied need for about a 25 percent gross profit margin. Only senior board members dealt with profitability, but even they regarded profit as a required residual and focused on sales volume and expenses in pounds sterling. They tried to balance food and clothing sales as related to margins and overall volume. Store-level goals were set in relation to sales and expenses, while merchandising and buying dealt with production and distribution cost and quality.

Despite growth, major percentage relationships changed little over time. For example, expenses remained at 11–12 percent of sales from 1970 to 1974. Samuel indicated that M&S's size minimized the effects of change and eliminated the threat of violent shifts.

The company made every effort to finance its continual growth internally. Although dividend payout was high, Samuel reported a "massive scaling down of proportions paid out to the shareholders in order to finance continued growth."

During the period of domestic expansion, M&S also built up exports to 159 retailers in 41 countries, who operated St. Michael shops in departments stocked exclusively with M&S merchandise. In 1974 exports rose 31 percent to $31,920,050. The company was also beginning to move directly into foreign markets. In 1972 a 50 percent joint venture was formed with People's Department Stores of Canada under the name St. Michael Shops of Canada. Major developments were also under way for France (two stores) and Belgium (one store). Although these operations required local borrowing, retained earnings remained the major source of investment funds for both Canadian and European expansion.

In recent years the company's freedom in financial matters had been increasingly circumscribed by government actions, which included (1) raising the corporate tax rate from 40 percent to 52 percent in 1974; (2) mandating, under the provisions of the Counter-Inflation Act of 1973, that the gross equivalent of ordinary dividends declared in 1973 could not exceed those of the previous year by more than 5 percent; and (3) forcing all retailers to reduce gross margins by 10 percent in the spring of 1974.

MANAGEMENT STYLE

A typical week at Baker Street began with an 8:30 A.M. meeting in the chairman's office. Generally eight or nine of the senior members met daily with the chairman, M&S's chief operational director. The members most frequently in attendance included the president, J. Edward Sieff; the vice chairmen and joint managing directors, M. Sacher and Michael Sieff; joint managing directors, Henry Lewis and Derek Rayner; and directors, R. Greenbury, W. B. Howard, and G. D. Sacher.

Upon entering the chairman's office, each member received sales and stock figures for the previous week. The chairman generally started the meeting by relating a particular incident he had observed during the previous several days. He frequently spoke for several minutes on one or two particular problems and how they related to the business. General comments were then interchanged by all present. The chairman then went around the room and asked each director if he had anything he wished to discuss, starting with the vice chairman, Michael Sacher. The following excerpts are from a meeting held on January 15, 1975.

Sir Marcus (chairman): We are not taking our markdowns fast enough or sharp enough.

Henry Lewis (joint managing director): That's related to some problems we discussed yesterday. The production cutoff date is not in adequate control. We must be able to learn from production sheets so we don't make mistakes. Production changes and cutoffs should be noted for reference next year.

Sir Marcus: If you go away from the principle, it costs you more than you gain 9 times out of 10.

Brian Howard (director): We are moving further into computers in food. From July 1975 to November 1975, stores will be converted from a daily indent (order) system to a weekly system. The computer then translates the weekly ordering into daily projections. It reduces paperwork, and by 1976 the stores probably won't be ordering at all. It's going to take a lot of training to get people to think in total terms. The one system will, however, simplify the stores' life.

J. Edward Sieff (president): I want to make a plea for self-restraint in cloth buying on price points. There's no point in buying more expensive fabrics. We are only interested in the desirability of the article. Once we see the retail price in print, it qualifies the cost price, which doesn't necessarily represent value. We should ask ourselves, "Is it better, of more value, and better quality?"

Sir Marcus: I think the president is absolutely right. It's a matter of self-restraint. Anything else, Teddy?

J. Edward Sieff: I ran across a fabric yesterday, 5-8. I think it's inferior. I hear our people saying it's lousy. It may be an achievement for technology but not for women. And ICI [major fabric supplier] is pushing it.

Sir Marcus: Are we telling them?

Michael Sacher (vice chairman and joint managing director): We have a meeting Thursday.

Sir Marcus: We must be frank with our suppliers.

J. Edward Sieff: We must be frank with ourselves.

Derek Rayner (joint managing director): I've been trying to work out priority stores for 1975. Over two thirds of the sales will come from 95 stores. We need good stock composition of basic merchandise. Can we carry both basic merchandise in all stores and specialized lines in selected stores?

Sacher: I'm concerned about two operations in the stores—training of the cashiers and methods of filling up the displays. For £45 million of goods, we handle £180 million at Marble Arch. We accept too much of this and take too many things for granted. We handle everything four times before it gets to the customer.

R. Greenbury (director): I have set up a team to look at the handling of bread and crisps [potato chips].

J. Edward Sieff: Anything to learn from Safeway or Migros [grocery chains]?

Sir Marcus: Let's ask them. Or Sainsbury. They'll tell us. No need to invent everything ourselves.

Greenbury: I've asked them.

Sir Marcus: O.K., but let's *do* something. I don't want to see the perfect solution.

On Mondays only, after the 8:30 meeting, those meeting with the chairman proceeded to a conference room for the 10 A.M. meeting of all directors and senior executives. A total of approximately 25 to 30 people gathered around a long table. The meeting was conducted similar to the 8:30 A.M. meeting. The following are excerpts of the January 30 meeting:

Sir Marcus: Henry Lewis and I visited nine of the Nottingham Manufacturing factories [the largest M&S supplier]. They are an outstanding operation, but they have failed to innovate in the design area. However, they had no criticism of our criterion in this respect. Also, they were making a line of ladies' nylons, three in a package, for 75 pence that was not making enough money for them. They asked us if we really wanted them to make lines at a substantial loss. We said certainly not, and we canceled the line.

My second point is that we brought back goods that were of appalling quality—not poor in make, but in conception. Are we sufficiently self-critical? Are our standards high enough? Do we probe enough in our eating and wearing? You must see that it applies to you—we've got to be critical.

Another point concerns customers' criticism and complaints. Ninety-four percent of them are replied to by me within a maximum of 48 hours. This procedure should apply around this table. It is a job for the senior members, not the subordinate member. "A soft answer turneth away wrath."

J. Edward Sieff: I've heard complaints about hosiery that doesn't stay up. We must look at the technicians' role. We are not calling on our technicians sufficiently. Secondly, I'd like to talk about our taste, which should be one of classic simplicity. We give too much credibility to gimmicks that we see in foreign fairs. I know the young people want the showy goods, but we must draw the balance. What are the parameters of taste?

Sir Marcus: Decent taste, reasonably up-to-date taste.

Michael Sieff (vice chairman and joint managing director): The opening of

Paris—we have very poor stock conditions. The outstanding orders aren't being filled. I want to know what's happening. Next, markdowns. The trial reports and evaluations are important. We must be cautious to avoid markdowns. Thirdly, price increases. Some of our margins have been increased to 32 or 33 percent, which makes up for the budget line of 24 percent. To talk to the stores about margin is difficult. Should we bring in margin? It may not be wise.

Sacher: Their job is to sell whatever they've got at whatever price, including the reduced items. I don't think they should be told.

Sir Marcus: I received a letter from the Wolverhampton store about our plan for extension there. As you know, we canceled plans to extend the operation. The letter was written by departmental supervisors asking for an extension of their store. It's a very well-written letter. Let me read it to you *[reads the letter]*. I think we should look into the situation again. [Sir Marcus noted in March 1975 that the supervisors' letter led to an investment of over £1 million.]

At the conclusion of the general meeting, many directors and senior executives met with their respective groups. Senior directors often joined such gatherings. At a food meeting attended by a researcher, one of the vice chairmen came in and threw a package of rhubarb crumble on the table. He scathingly commented on the poor taste and consistency of the dish. "This is the most disgusting thing I have ever had the pleasure of serving to guests. The rhubarb was unripe and overcooked—it was inedible. Also, the product is overpackaged. We should take a closer look at our packaging policies."

Elsewhere at Baker Street, a constant parade of people went in and out of offices. Standard procedure was to knock and immediately enter, without awaiting a response. The object was to project an open-door policy; often the visitor would get an answer to a question and leave. Outside each door was an "engaged" sign that could be lit from the occupant's desk to avoid being disturbed. Executives were constantly available to anyone who wanted to work with them. In each office and in the halls, was a light with four colors (much like a traffic light). Each board member and senior executive was assigned a combination of colors. These lights flashed whenever someone wanted to reach an executive who was not in his office. Those without a light combination carried pocket beepers.

Most executive offices featured two phones. One could be used for any purpose. The other was answered by an operator; the executive told the operator whom to look for, hung up, and was called back when the party was located. Thus, all executives, unless off the premises, were available to anyone who wanted to see or talk with them.

CONCERNS ABOUT THE FUTURE

The executives of M&S were figures of considerable public importance, well known in the business community. Asked about the future, the chairman spoke of his concern for the economic future of M&S and the nation.

> We believe that if we guard the standards of our goods, improve our systems, and look after both our staff and our customers, we shall continue to grow and to make profits.
>
> We need profits, after paying taxes:
>
> 1. To improve the pay and working conditions of our staff and to take care of them during retirement. The high morale and productivity of our staff owe much to these factors; most

> of them take pride in working for a successful business that is quality oriented.
>
> 2. To have funds for investment in the development of the business, which is clearly desired by our many customers.
> 3. To pay a proper dividend to our 240,000 shareholders, who include many small savers, individual pensioners, and pension funds.
>
> Marks and Spencer has, over the years, under a private enterprise system, made a significant contribution to the economic life of the country and has helped to raise the standard of living. We doubt whether we could have achieved this under any other system.

Sir Marcus was particularly upset with inept government interventions in business. When asked what these actions would mean to his basic strategy of expansion in Britain, he commented:

> First we have to be concerned with our liquidity. We will not spend our reserves. The result is, whereas we were going to spend £40 million a year to upgrade our stores, we're now going to spend £20 million. We have to preserve our position. The consequences will not be important in the short term. But as a pattern they will hurt Britain severely in three to four years' time.

A particularly clear expression of Sir Marcus's views was made in a corporate statement issued on October 8, 1974, two days before the 1974 parliamentary elections. The statement made headlines in all of Britain's major papers.

> Retailing performs a major role in the chain of production and distribution. We cooperate with whatever government is in office, but some ministers and their advisers do not seem to appreciate the significant contribution which a healthy and competitive retail industry can make in stemming the rise in the cost of living. We are not helped in this task by misguided interference.
>
> Corporation tax takes more than half our profits. The Government criticizes the private sector for its failure to invest but it omits to explain that much investment is financed out of our profits. If our profits are subject to politically motivated restrictions and massively reduced, confidence is eroded, and investment on which the maintenance of employment and the future prosperity of the country depends slows down.
>
> The remaining profit [after tax and dividends] is retained in the business to finance its future growth. Present Government policy has substantially reduced the money available for such development in the immediate future.

Michael Sacher, vice chairman, commented on some of the firm's internal issues and problems:

> What has always astounded me is how few people have learned the simple principles on which we operate. I think we have carved a market out here which is quality goods at lower prices. As long as we stick to that we'll be okay, as long as the younger people learn the principles of the business. You have to have a clear policy where you upgrade areas in which you are weak and stay out of the caviar business. The board can help here but there are so many things distracting us from being shopkeepers—bombs, the government, and so on. But we implement by generalizing from the particular. That is how you teach young people.
>
> I always try to pick out one thing and then work on it. Take frozen canneloni, it's a new line that I think will move very well. People like canneloni and it's hard to make. Someone else suggested spaghetti. The housewife can make perfectly good spaghetti with ease, why should we? It

just requires a bit of common sense. It's no good developing a slip department if everyone's wearing pants.

Researcher: Isn't it inevitable that you sell the spaghetti as well?

Michael Sacher: No, I don't think so. We don't believe in a high degree of specialization, and it has always been our practice to move selectors around the business. So much of selection is taste, feel, and common sense.

I was going to say something else, also immodest, and it's true of other senior colleagues. You have to become expert in a wide variety of activities: selecting goods, feel for merchandise, know what's coming, principles of building, and rudimentary technological questions.

I hear a lecture in Israel about tomatoes, so I know something about them. I've been shown cell sections of frozen material, so I can ask why our beans and sprouts have such lassitude. I've acquired enough garbage to ask technological questions that they can't throw out.

In the end, the decision has to be taken by management, not the experts. And you have to be humble. I just try to take a jolly good look at everything that's been here a long time in the same place. Repotting is healthy managerially if not horticulturally.

I do see problems: you can't help but lean on the strengths that you have. Take Teddy. He has an astronomic knowledge of textiles and he applies himself. His taste is not perfect, but he knows what an M&S range should be. He's done a wonderful job in his new role.

The family is a binding force. Members of the family can talk to each other in a candid way that I find extremely difficult to discover with professional managers. It happens with some, but it takes time.

Researcher: How much does great wealth have to do with it?

Michael Sacher: Well, there is something to that. We know what good taste is. We see fashion as it emerges and whether it lasts. I once suggested that we send our selectors to the Caribbean for the winter holiday to see what is being worn.

Another problem is that most of our executives have joined us straight from the university. It compels you to have a series of graded courses outside the university. Not so much for what they learn, but they can test themselves against peers. My generation had the war in which to measure themselves.

Senior members of the board agreed that the major question facing M&S concerned the proper rate of expansion in Britain, and the moves into the Common Market and Canada. Sir Marcus articulated his reasons for the moves. "First, as an opportunity for more profit. Given the deteriorating situation in Britain we think Canada can become very important for us. Second, as a chance to expand British exports. And finally, should things be really bad, it's a lifeline for us abroad."

EXHIBIT 1
FINANCIAL DATA, 1973–1974 (£000)

	Years Ended March 31	
	1974	*1973*
Profit and Loss Account		
Gross store sales	£591,570	£511,934
Export sales	13,583	10,370
Net sales	605,153	522,304
Operating profit	76,825	70,036
Taxation	39,900	24,900
Profit after taxation	36,925	45,136
Extraordinary item		
Surplus on disposal of fixed assets	2,383	176
	39,308	45,312
Dividends	19,008	21,388
Undistributed surplus	£ 20,300	£ 23,924
Earnings per share	11.4p	13.9p
Balance Sheet		
Assets		
Current assets		
Inventory	£ 31,472	£ 29,638
Cash and short-term deposits	18,460	44,612
Debtors and prepayments	10,502	8,150
Tax reserve certificates	—	4,000
Total current assets	60,434	86,400
Fixed assets		
Properties	221,895	182,710
Fixtures and equipment	19,825	15,668
Total fixed assets	241,720	198,378
Total assets	£304,364*	£284,830†
Liabilities		
Current liabilities		
Creditors and accrued charges	£ 28,055	£ 29,971
Corporation tax	28,237	23,359
Dividends (interim payable and final proposed)	12,255	21,283
Total current liabilities	68,547	74,613
Long-term liability		
Deferred taxation	18,400	13,100
Debenture stock	45,000	45,000
Total long-term liability	63,400	58,100
Net worth		
Shareholders' interest	172,417	152,117
Total liabilities	£304,364	£284,830

*Investment in subsidiary companies was £1,040; investment in associated company was £1,170.
†Investment in associated company was £52.

EXHIBIT 1 (*concluded*)
TEN-YEAR FINANCIAL STATEMENT (£000)

	Years Ended March 31									
	*1965**	*1966*	*1967*	*1968*	*1969*	*1970*	*1971**	*1972*	*1973*	*1974*
Turnover†	£208,636	£226,135	£242,954	£268,607	£299,672	£338,843	£390,915	£438,600	£522,304	£605,153
Operating profit	27,506	29,618	30,659	33,871	38,123	43,705	50,115	53,766	70,036	76,825
Profit after taxation	12,706	18,268	18,959	20,121	21,773	26,005	31,215	34,416	45,136	36,925
Corporation tax rate	nc	40%	40%	42.5%	45%	42.5%	40%	40%	40%	52%
Earnings per share	nc	5.6p	5.8p	6.2p	6.7p	8.0p	9.6p	10.6p	13.9p	11.4p‡
Dividend payments to shareholders	£ 9,258	£ 9,928	£ 9,950	£ 10,266	£ 10,609	£ 11,928	£ 13,904	£ 15,528	£ 17,826	£ 19,008
Retained profit	3,246	4,322	2,461	2,536	3,667	5,747	8,220§	9,132	23,924	17,917§
Depreciation	1,844	1,993	2,177	2,488	2,987	3,534	4,177	4,620	5,055	5,464
Ordinary share capital and reserves	105,468	109,790	112,251	114,788	118,455	123,152	127,711	136,843	150.767	171,067
Total sales area (000 square feet)	3,337	3,471	3,635	3,929	4,214	4,408	4,708	4,944	5,059	5,489

Note: nc = not comparable.
*53 weeks.
†Turnover for the year ending March 31, 1974, is shown after deduction of V.A.T. For the purpose of comparison, turnover figures for previous years have been shown after deduction of purchase tax.
‡Earnings per share are not comparable by reason of the change in basis of taxation.
§Excluding surplus on disposal of assets: 1971 = £2,393,000; 1974 = £2,383,000.
Source: Company records.

EXHIBIT 2
ORGANIZATION CHART, 1975

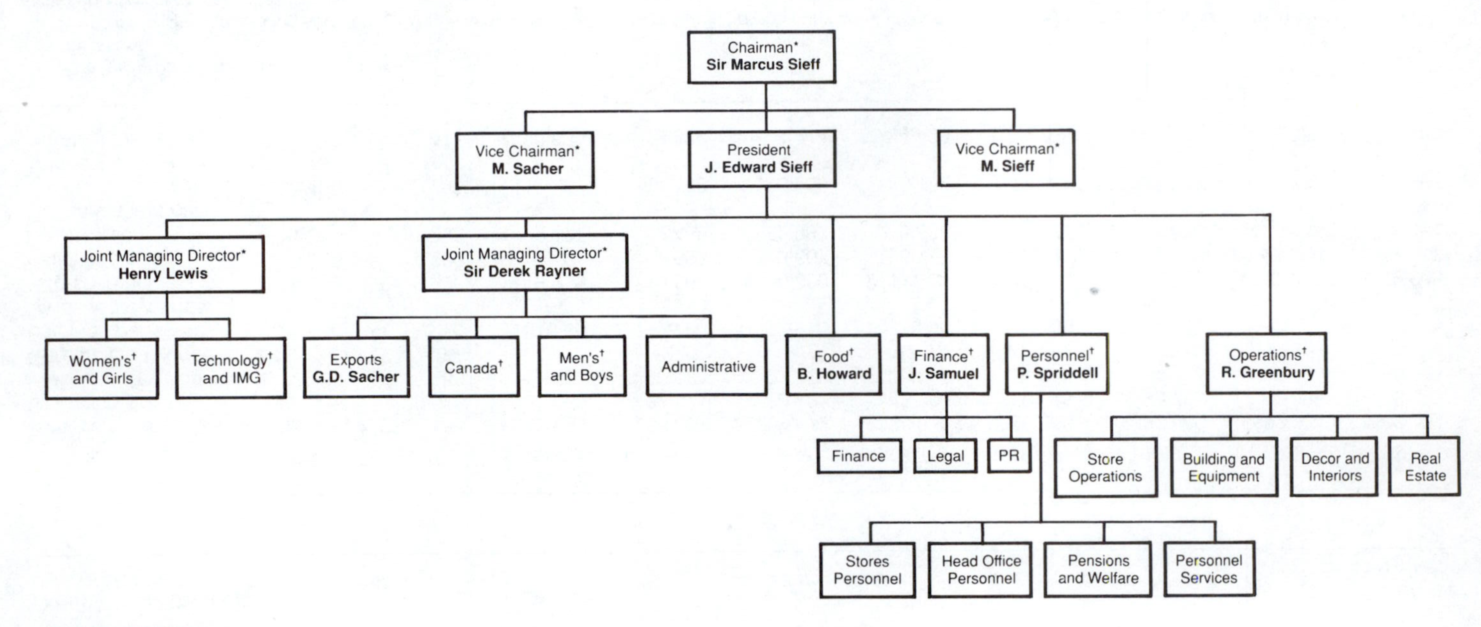

*Joint managing director.
†There were 22 directors altogether.

Source: Casewriter's notes.

EXHIBIT 3
TEXTILES DIVISION ORGANIZATION CHART WITH DETAILED ORGANIZATION FOR MENSWEAR

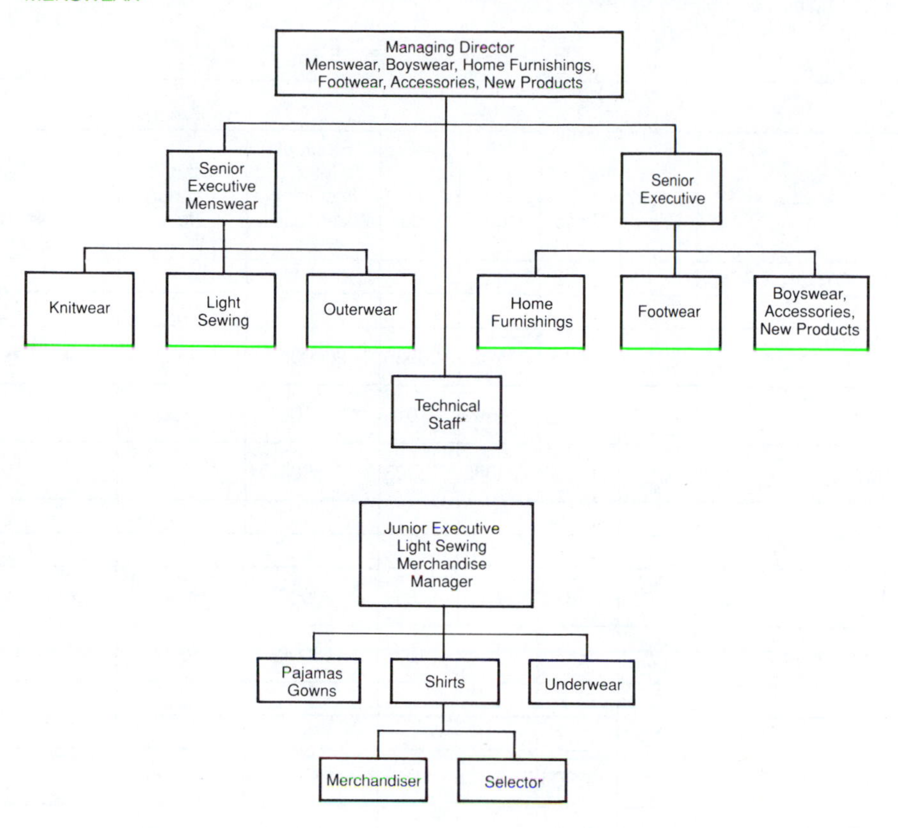

*For all individual merchandise groups.

Source: Casewriter's notes.

EXHIBIT 4
STOCK CHECKING LIST, SUMMARY

This Year FIVE Week(s) Ending DECEMBER 30, 1974
Last Year FIVE Week(s) Ending DECEMBER 31, 1973

				5 WEEKS			This Period		
	C.L. Item	Article	Selling Price £	Sales £	Stock £	On Order £	Stock at Mfrs. (Including Warehouses) £	Production Planned Next 8 Weeks	No. of Stores
		KNEE NYLON SOCKS							
	62A/B	NYLON							
	62A/B	White	22p 35p	226319	245968	38938	260000	370000	
	62C	Colours	22p 25p	22123	26529	1016	10000	75000	
	62D 64	Grey/Beige	22p 35p	15234	24685	1203	5000	70000	
		WOOL/NYLON							
	56	T.O.T.	44p 49p	41817	39758	586	20000	50000	
	63	St. Top	33p 44p	48685	55146	1386	45000	50000	
		ORLON/NYLON							
	61	Plain	30p 40p	30905	10180	420	25000	40000	
	59	Pattern	40p 49p	77388	30577	2185	5000		200
		TOTAL KNEE-HIGH SOCKS		462471	432843	45734	370000	655000	C.L.31/12/4 Reduced13/12/74
	81/82 83/84	Heavyweight Tights	ALL	148960	162994	14395	10000		
	77	Girls' One Size Tights	23p	24607	7783				140
	65/66 72	Boys' Socks	24p 45p	20112					
	65/47/48 52/55/58 68/98	Experimental & Unseasonable	ALL	42542	138793	53703	375000	290000	
		TOTAL FULL SELLING PRICE		698692	742413	113832	755000	945000	
		Reduced	ALL	28542	75303				
		GRAND TOTAL.................		727234	817716	113832	755000	945000	
		Stock Target 28th December 1974			750000		750000		
		Estimated Intake for Period £780,000							

Source: Company document.

The Chairman		Sir Derek Rayner		Mr. G. D. Sacher		Mr. A. S. Orton	
The President		Mr. M. B. Freeman		Mr. S.J. Sacher		Mr. C. V. Silver	
Mr. M. M. Sacher		Mr. L. R. Goodman		Mr. J. Salisse		Mr. T. A. Frodsham	
Mr. M. D. Sieff		Mr. R. Greenbury		Mr. D. Susman		Mr. J. Gardiner	
Mr. W. N. Lewis		Mr. J. A. Rishworth		Mr. B. J. Lynch		Mr. B. Harries	

2 WEEKS		Last Period		Last Year		5 WEEKS	
Sales £	Stock £	On Order £	Stock at Mfrs. (Including Warehouses) £	Sales £	Stock £	Selling Price £	Remarks
53764	210470	131998	320000	189116	191386	18p 29p	
8485	31076	5840	5000	36595	42063	18p 29p	
3635	41002	5367	10000	15606	55012	22p 32p	
14149	39167	19864	15000	38672	63445	35p 40p	
14829	41252	30460	45000	41315	43567	28p 37p	
8768	56510	16114	30000	60651	104163	27p 35p	
32407	92217	21707	15000	31681	37063	37p 45p	
136037	511694	231350	440000	413636	536699		
52735	178273	69730	70000	198133	98655	55p 70p	
6803	17504	6137	10000				
5622	32840	2549	20000	45595	74419	27p 45p	
2561	67240	7633	335000	18277	86555	ALL	
203758	807551	317399	875000	675601	796328		
334	2343			8931	8152	ALL	
204092	809894	317399	875000	684532	804480		

EXHIBIT 5
ORGANIZATION FOR STORE OPERATION

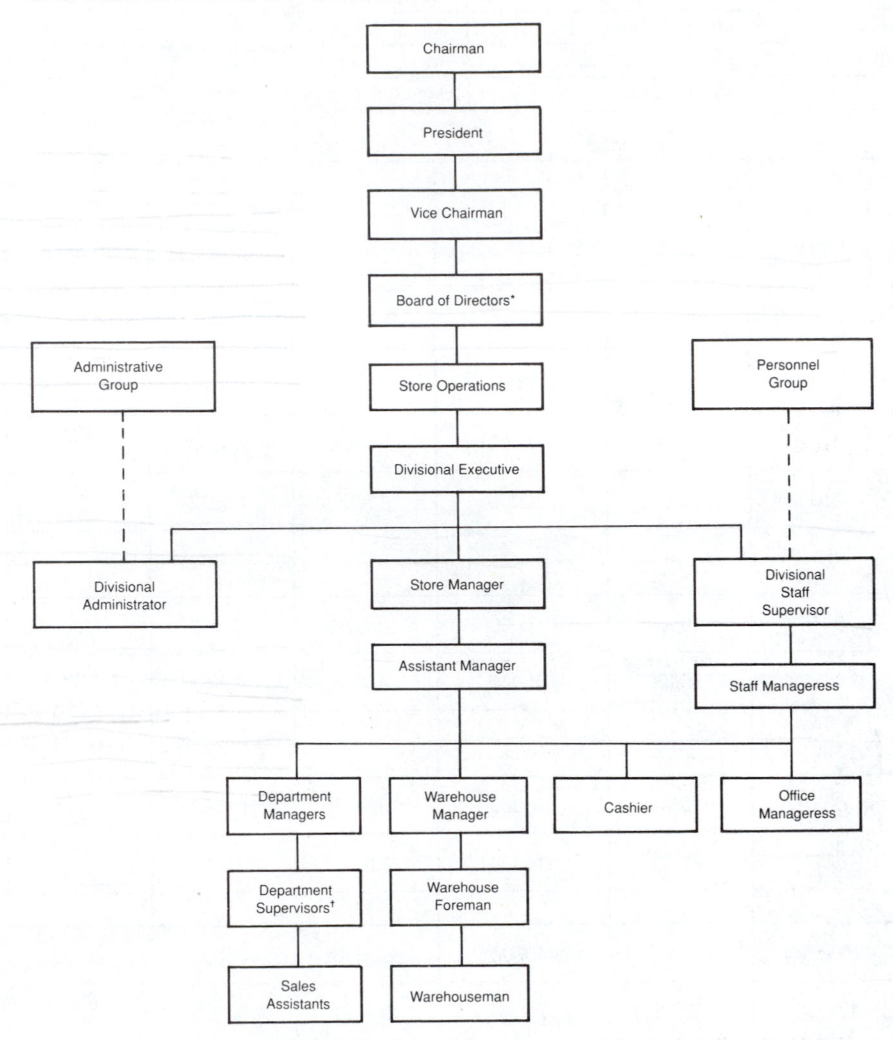

*Including managing directors.
†Present only in larger stores, but in some instances numbering 10.

EXHIBIT 6
STORE HAIRDRESSING SALON

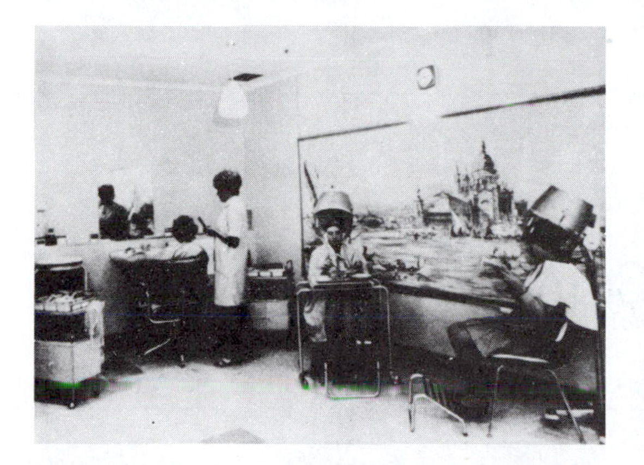

EXHIBIT 7
STORE DINING FACILITIES

EXHIBIT 8
TEXTILE AREA

EXHIBIT 9
FOOD AREA

The Lincoln Electric Company

> We're not a marketing company, we're not an R&D company, and we're not a service company. We're a manufacturing company, and I believe that we are the best manufacturing company in the world.

With these words, George E. Willis, president of The Lincoln Electric Company, described what he saw as his company's distinctive competence. For more than 30 years, Lincoln had been the world's largest manufacturer of arc welding products (Exhibit 1). In 1974, the company was believed to have manufactured more than 40 percent of the arc welding equipment and supplies sold in the United States. In addition to its welding products, Lincoln produced a line of three-phase alternating-current industrial electric motors, but these accounted for less than 10 percent of sales and profits.

Lincoln's 1974 domestic net income was $17.5 million on sales of $237 million (Exhibit 2). Perhaps more significant than a single year's results was Lincoln's record of steady growth over the preceding four decades, as shown in Exhibit 3.

During this period, after-tax return on equity had ranged between 10 and 15 percent. Lincoln's growth had been achieved without benefit of acquisition and had been financed with internally generated funds. The company's historical dividend payout policy had been to pay to the suppliers of capital a fair return each year for its use.

COMPANY HISTORY

Lincoln Electric was founded by John C. Lincoln in 1895 to manufacture electric motors and generators. James F. Lincoln, John's younger brother, joined the company in 1907. The brothers' skills and interests were complementary. John was a technical genius. During his lifetime, he was awarded more than 50 patents for inventions as diverse as an apparatus for curing meat, an electric drill, a mine-door-activating mechanism, and an electric arc lamp. James's skills were in management and administration. He began as a salesman but soon took over as general manager. The Lincoln Electric Company was undeniably built in his image.

Harvard Business School case 376–028.

In 1911, the company introduced its first arc welding machine. Both brothers were fascinated by welding, which was then in its infancy. They recognized it as an alternative use for the motor-generator sets they were already producing to recharge the batteries for electric automobiles. The success of Ford, Buick, and others indicated that the days of the electric auto might be numbered, and the brothers were anxious to find other markets for their skills and products.

John's mechanical talents gave the company a head start in welding machines which it never relinquished. He developed a portable welding machine (a significant improvement over existing stationary models) and incorporated a transformer to allow regulation of the current. As his biographer noted, "This functional industrial development gave Lincoln Electric a lead in the field that it has always maintained, although the two giants—Westinghouse and General Electric—soon entered the market."[1]

By World War II, Lincoln Electric was the leading American manufacturer of arc welding equipment. Because of the importance of welding to the war effort, the company stopped producing electric motors and devoted its full capacity to welding products. Demand continued to outpace production, and the government asked the welding equipment manufacturers to add capacity. As described by Lincoln's president, George Willis:

> Mr. Lincoln responded to the government's call by going to Washington and telling them that there was enough manufacturing capacity but it was being used inefficiently by everyone. He offered to share proprietary manufacturing methods and equipment designs with the rest of the industry. Washington took him up on it and that solved the problem. As a result of Mr. Lincoln's patriotic decision, our competitors had costs which were close to ours for a short period after the war, but we soon were outperforming them like before.

In 1955 Lincoln once again began manufacturing electric motors, and since then its position in the market had expanded steadily.

Through the years, Lincoln stock had been sold to employees and associates of the Lincoln brothers. In 1975 approximately 48 percent of employees were shareholders. About 80 percent of the outstanding stock was held by employees, the Lincoln family, and their foundations.

In its 80-year history, Lincoln had only three board chairmen: John C. Lincoln, James F. Lincoln, and William Irrgang, who became chairman in 1972.

STRATEGY

Lincoln Electric's strategy was simple and unwavering. The company's strength was in manufacturing. Management believed that Lincoln could build quality products at a lower cost than their competitors. Their strategy was to concentrate on reducing costs and passing the savings through to the customer by continuously lowering prices. Management had adhered to this policy even when products were on allocation because of shortages in productive capacity. The result had been an expansion of both market share and primary demand for arc welding equipment and supplies over the past half century. Lincoln's strategy had also encouraged the exit of several major companies (including

[1] Raymond Moley, *The American Century of John C. Lincoln* (New York: Duell, Sloan & Pearce, 1962), p. 71.

General Electric) from the industry and had caused others to seek more specialized market niches.

Management believed its incentive system and the climate it fostered were responsible in large part for the continual increase in productivity upon which this strategy depended. Under the Lincoln incentive system, employees were handsomely rewarded for their productivity, high quality, cost reduction ideas, and individual contributions to the company. Year-end bonuses averaged close to 100 percent of regular compensation, and some workers on the factory floor had earned more than $45,000 in a single year.[2]

Lincoln's strategy had remained virtually unchanged for decades. In a 1947 Harvard Business School case study on the company, James F. Lincoln described the firm's strategy as follows:

> It is the job of The Lincoln Electric Company to give its customers more and more of a better product at a lower and lower price. This will also make it possible for the company to give to the worker and the stockholder a higher and higher return.

In 1975, Chairman William Irrgang's description was remarkably similar:

> The success of The Lincoln Electric Company has been built on two basic ideas. One is producing more and more of a progressively better product at a lower and lower price for a larger and larger group of customers. The other is that an employee's earnings and promotion are in direct proportion to his individual contribution toward the company's success.[3]

Management felt it had achieved an enviable record in following this strategy faithfully and saw no need to modify it in the future. Lincoln Electric's record of increasing productivity and declining costs and prices is shown in Exhibit 4.

COMPANY PHILOSOPHY

Lincoln Electric's corporate strategy was rooted in the management philosophy of James F. Lincoln, a rugged individualist who believed that through competition and adequate incentives every person could develop to his or her fullest potential. In one of his numerous books and articles he wrote:

> Competition is the foundation of man's development. It has made the human race what it is. It is the spur that makes progress. Every nation that has eliminated it as the controlling force in its economy has disappeared, or will. We will do the same if we eliminate it by trying to give security, and for the same reason. Competition means that there will be losers as well as winners in the game. Competition will mean the disappearance of the lazy and incompetent, be they workers, industrialists, or distributors. Competition promotes progress. Competition determines who will be the leader. It is the only known way that leadership and progress can be developed if history means anything. It is a hard taskmaster. It is completely necessary for anyone, be he worker, user, distributor, or boss, if he is to grow.
>
> If some way could be found so that competition could be eliminated from life, the result would be disastrous. Any nation and any people disappear if life becomes too easy. There is no danger from a hard life as all history shows. Danger is from a life that is made soft by lack of competition.[4]

---

[2] By contrast, the median income for U.S. manufacturing employees in 1974 was less than $9,200, according to Bureau of Labor Statistics data.

[3] *Employee's Handbook* (Cleveland: The Lincoln Electric Company, 1974).

[4] James F. Lincoln, *Incentive Management* (Cleveland: The Lincoln Electric Company, 1951), p. 33.

Lincoln's faith in the individual was almost unbounded. His personal experience with the success of Lincoln Electric reinforced his faith in what could be accomplished under the proper conditions. In 1951 he wrote:

> Development in many directions is latent in every person. The difficulty has been that few recognize that fact. Fewer still will put themselves under the pressure or by chance are put under the pressure that will develop them greatly. Their latent abilities remain latent, hence useless. . . .
>
> It is of course obvious that the development of man, on which the success of incentive management depends, is a progressive process. Any results, no matter how good, that come from the application of incentive management cannot be considered final. There will always be greater growth of man under continued proper incentive. . . .
>
> Such increase of efficiency poses a very real problem to management. The profit that will result from such efficiency obviously will be enormous. The output per dollar of investment will be many times that of the usual shop which practices output limitation. The labor cost per piece will be relatively small and the overhead will be still less.
>
> The profits at competitive selling prices resulting from such efficiency will be far beyond any possible need for proper return and growth of an industry. . . .
>
> How, then, should the enormous extra profit resulting from incentive management be split? The problems that are inherent in incentive dictate the answer. If the worker does not get a proper share, he does not desire to develop himself or his skill. Incentive, therefore, would not succeed. The worker must have a reward that he feels is commensurate with his contribution.
>
> If the customer does not have a part of the saving in lower prices, he will not buy the increased output. The size of the market is a decisive factor in costs of products. Therefore, the consumer must get a proper share of the saving.
>
> Management and ownership are usually considered as a unit. This is far from a fact, but in the problem here, they can be considered together. They must get a part of the saving in larger salaries and perhaps larger dividends.
>
> There is no hard and fast rule to cover this division, other than the following. The worker (which includes management), the customer, the owner, and all those involved must be satisfied that they are properly recognized or they will not cooperate, and cooperation is essential to any and all successful applications of incentives.[5]

Additional comments by James F. Lincoln are presented in Exhibit 5.

COMPENSATION POLICIES

Compensation policies were the key element of James F. Lincoln's philosophy of "incentive management." Lincoln Electric's compensation system had three components:

- Wages based solely on piecework output for most factory jobs.
- A year-end bonus which could equal or exceed an individual's full annual regular pay.
- Guaranteed employment for all workers.

Almost all production workers at Lincoln were paid on a straight piecework plan. They had no base salary or hourly wage but were paid a set "price" for each item they produced. William Irrgang explained:

> Wherever practical, we use the piecework system. This system can be effective, and it can be destructive. The important part

[5] Ibid., pp. 7–11.

> of the system is that it is completely fair to the worker. When we set a piecework price, that price cannot be changed just because, in the management's opinion, the worker is making too much money. Whether he earns two times or three times his normal amount makes no difference. Piecework prices can only be changed when management has made a change in the method of doing that particular job and under no other conditions. If this is not carried out 100 percent, piecework cannot work.
>
> Today piecework is confined to production operations, although at one time we also used it for work done in our stenographic pool. Each typewriter was equipped with a counter that registered the number of times the typewriter keys were operated. This seemed to work all right for a time until it was noticed that one girl was earning much more than any of the others. This was looked into, and it was found that this young lady ate her lunch at her desk, using one hand for eating purposes and the other for punching the most convenient key on the typewriter as fast as she could; which simply goes to show that no matter how good a program you may have, it still needs careful supervision.[6]

A Time Study Department established piecework prices which were guaranteed by the company, until methods were changed or a new process introduced. Employees could challenge the price if they felt it was unfair. The Time Study Department would then retime the job and set a new rate. This could be higher or lower but was still open to challenge if an employee remained dissatisfied. Employees were expected to guarantee their own quality. They were not paid for defective work until it had been repaired on their own time.

Each job in the company was rated according to skill, required effort, responsibility, and so on, and a base wage rate for the job was assigned. Wage rates were comparable to those for similar jobs in the Cleveland area and were adjusted annually on the basis of Department of Labor statistics and quarterly to reflect changes in the cost of living. In this way, salaries or hourly wages were determined. For piecework jobs, the Time Study Department set piece prices so that an employee producing at a standard rate would earn the base rate for his or her job.

The second element of the compensation system was a year-end bonus, which had been paid each year since 1934. As explained in the *Employee's Handbook*, "The bonus, paid at the discretion of the company, is not a gift, but rather it is the sharing of the results of efficient operation on the basis of the contribution of each person to the success of the company for that year." In 1974 the bonus pool totaled $26 million, an average of approximately $10,700 per employee, or 90 percent of prebonus wages.

The total amount to be paid out in bonuses each year was determined by the board of directors. Lincoln's concentration on cost reduction kept costs low enough that prices could generally be set (and not upset by competition) on the basis of costs at the beginning of the year to produce a target return for stockholders and to give employees a bonus of approximately 100 percent of wages. The variance from the planned profits was usually added to (or subtracted from) the bonus pool to be distributed at year-end. Since 1945, the average bonus had varied from 78 to 129 percent of wages. In the past few years, it had been between 40 and 55 percent of

[6] William Irrgang, "The Lincoln Incentive Management Program," Lincoln Lecture Series, Arizona State University, 1972, p. 13.

pretax, prebonus profit, or as high as twice the net income after taxes.

An individual's share of the bonus pool was determined by a semiannual "merit rating" which measured individual performance compared to that of other members of the department or work group. Ratings for all employees had to average out to 100 on this relative scale. If, because of some unusual contribution, an individual deserved a rating above 110, he or she could be rewarded from a special corporate pool of bonus points, without any penalty to co-workers. Ratings above 110 were thus reviewed by a corporate committee of vice presidents who evaluated the individual's contribution. Merit ratings varied widely, from as low as 45 to as high as 160.

In determining an employee's merit rating, four factors were evaluated separately:

- Dependability.
- Quality.
- Output.
- Ideas and cooperation.

Foremen were responsible for the rating of all factory workers. They could request help from assistant foremen (dependability), the Production Control Department (output), the Inspection Department (quality), and the Methods Department (ideas and cooperation). In the office, supervisors rated their people on the same items. At least one executive reviewed all ratings. All employees were urged to discuss their ratings with their department heads if they were dissatisfied or unclear about them.

Lincoln complemented its rating and pay system with a Guaranteed Continuous Employment Plan. This plan provided security against layoffs and assured continuity of employment. Every full-time employee who had been with the company at least two years was guaranteed employment for at least 75 percent of the standard 40-hour week. In fact, the company had not had any layoffs since 1951 when initial trials for the plan were put into effect. It was formally established in 1958.

The guarantee of employment was seen by the company as an essential element in the incentive plan. Without such a guarantee, it was believed that employees would be more likely to resist improved production and efficiency for fear of losing their jobs. In accepting the guaranteed continuous employment plan, employees agreed to perform any job that was assigned as conditions required, and to work overtime during periods of high activity.

The philosophy and procedures regarding the incentive plan were the same for management and workers, except that William Irrgang and George Willis did not share in the bonus.

EMPLOYEE VIEWS

To the researchers, it appeared that employees generally liked working at Lincoln. The employee turnover rate was far below that of most other companies, and once a new employee made it through the first month or so, he rarely left for another firm (see Exhibit 6). One employee explained, "It's like trying out for a high school football team. If you make it through the first few practices, you're usually going to stay the whole season, especially after the games start."

One long-time employee who liked working at Lincoln was John "Tiny" Carrillo, an armature bander on the welding machine line, who had been with the company for 24 years. Tiny explained why:

> The thing I like here is that you're pretty much your own boss as long as you do

your job. You're responsible for your own work and you even put your stencil on every machine you work on. That way if it breaks down in the field and they have to take it back, they know who's responsible.

Before I came here, I worked at Cadillac as a welder. After two months there I had the top hourly rate. I wasn't allowed to tell anyone because there were guys who still had the starting rate after a year. But, I couldn't go any higher after two months.

I've done well. My rating is usually around 110, but I work hard, right through the smoke breaks. The only time I stop is a half hour for lunch. I make good money. I have two houses, one which I rent out, and four cars. They're all paid for. When I get my bills, I pay them the next day. That's the main thing, I don't owe anyone.

Sure, there are problems. There's sometimes a bind between the guys with low grades and guys with high ones, like in school. And there are guys who sway everything their way so they'll get the points, but they [management] have good tabs on what's going on. . . .

A lot of new guys come in and leave right away. Most of them are just mamma's boys and don't want to do the work. We had a new guy who was a produce manager at a supermarket. He worked a couple of weeks, then quit and went back to his old job.

At the end of the interview, the researcher thanked Tiny for his time. He responded by pointing out that it had cost him $7 in lost time, but that he was glad to be of assistance.

Another piece worker, Jorge Espinoza, a fine-wire operator in the Electrode Division, had been with the company for six years. He explained his feelings:

I believe in being my own man. I want to use my drive for my own gain. It's worked. I built my family a house and have an acre of land, with a low mortgage. I have a car and an old truck I play around with. The money I get is because I earn it. I don't want anything given to me.

The thing I don't like is having to depend on other people on the line and suppliers. We're getting bad steel occasionally. Our output is down as a result and my rating will suffer.

There are men who have great drive here and can push for a job. They are not leaders and never will be, but they move up. That's a problem. . . .

The first few times around, the ratings were painful for me. But now I stick near 100. You really make what you want. We just had a methods change and our base rate went from 83 to 89 coils a day. This job is tougher now and more complex. But, it's all what you want. If you want 110 coils you can get it. You just take less breaks. Today, I gambled and won. I didn't change my dies and made over a hundred coils. If I had lost, and the die plugged up, it would have cost me at least half an hour. But, today I made it.

MANAGEMENT STYLE

Lincoln's incentive scheme was reinforced by top management's attitude toward the men on the factory floor. In 1951 James Lincoln wrote:

It becomes perfectly true to anyone who will think this thing through that there is no such thing in an industrial activity as Management and Men having different functions or being two different kinds of people. Why can't we think and why don't we think that all people are Management? Can you imagine any president of any factory or machine shop who can go down and manage a turret lathe as well as the machinist can? Can you imagine any manager of any organization who can go down and manage a broom—let us get down to that—who can manage a broom as well as a sweeper can? Can you imagine

> any secretary of any company who can go down and fire a furnace and manage that boiler as well as the man who does the job? Obviously, all are Management.[7]

Lincoln's president, George Willis, stressed the equality in the company:

> We try to avoid barriers between management and workers. We're treated equally as much as possible. When I got to work this morning at 7:30, the parking lot was three-quarters full. I parked way out there like anyone else would. I don't have a special reserved spot. The same principle holds true in our cafeteria. There's no executive dining room. We eat with everyone else.[8]

Willis felt that open and frank communication between management and workers had been a critical factor in Lincoln's success, and he believed that the company's Advisory Board, consisting of elected employee representatives, had played a very important role in achieving this. Established by James F. Lincoln in 1914, the board met twice a month, providing a forum in which employees could bring issues of concern to top management's attention, question company policies, and make suggestions for their improvement. As described in the *Employee's Handbook:*

> Board service is a privilege and responsibility of importance to the entire organization. In discussions or in reaching decisions Board members must be guided by the best interests of the Company. These also serve the best interests of its workers. They should seek at all times to improve the cooperative attitude of all workers and see that all realize they have an important part in our final results.

All Advisory Board meetings were chaired by either the chairman or the president of Lincoln. Usually both were present. Issues brought up at board meetings were either resolved on the spot or assigned to an executive. After each meeting, William Irrgang or George Willis would send a memo to the executive responsible for each unanswered question, no matter how trivial, and he was expected to respond by the next meeting if possible.

Minutes of all board meetings were posted on bulletin boards in each department and members explained the board's actions to the other workers in their department. The questions raised in the minutes of a given meeting were usually answered in the next set of minutes. This procedure had not changed significantly since the first meeting in 1914, and the types of issues raised had remained much the same (see Exhibit 7).

Workers felt that the Advisory Board provided a way of getting immediate attention for their problems. It was clear, however, that management still made the final decisions.[9] A former member of the Advisory Board commented:

> There are certain areas which are brought up in the meetings which Mr. Irrgang doesn't want to get into. He's adept at steering the conversation away from

[7] James F. Lincoln, *What Makes Workers Work?* (Cleveland: The Lincoln Electric Company, 1951), pp. 3–4.

[8] The cafeteria had large rectangular and round tables. In general, factory workers gravitated toward the rectangular tables. There were no strict rules, however, and management personnel often sat with factory workers. Toward the center was a square table that seated only four. This was reserved for William Irrgang, George Willis, and their guests when they were having a working lunch.

[9] In some cases, management allowed issues to be decided by a vote of employees. Recently, for example, employees had voted down a proposal that the company give them dental benefits, recognizing that the cost of the program would come directly out of their bonuses.

> these. It's definitely not a negotiating meeting. But, generally, you really get action or an answer on why action isn't being taken.

In addition to the Advisory Board, there was a 12-member board of middle managers which met with Irrgang and Willis once a month. The topics discussed here were broader than those of the Advisory Board. The primary function of these meetings was to allow top management to get better acquainted with these individuals and to encourage cooperation between departments.

Lincoln's two top executives, Irrgang and Willis, continued the practice of James F. Lincoln in maintaining an open door to all employees. George Willis estimated that at least twice a week factory employees took advantage of this opportunity to talk with him.

Middle managers also felt that communication with Willis and Irrgang was open and direct. Often it bypassed intermediate levels of the organization. Most saw this as an advantage, but one commented:

> This company is run strictly by the two men at the top. Mr. Lincoln trained Mr. Irrgang in his image. It's very authoritarian and decisions flow top down. It never became a big company. There is very little delegated and top people are making too many small decisions. Mr. Irrgang and Mr. Willis work 80 hours a week, and no one I know in this company can say that his boss doesn't work harder than he does.

Willis saw management's concern for the worker as an essential ingredient in his company's formula for success. He knew at least 500 employees personally. In leading the researcher through the plant, he greeted workers by name and paused several times to tell anecdotes about them.

At one point, an older man yelled to Willis good-naturedly, "Where's my raise?" Willis explained that this man had worked for 40 years in a job requiring him to lift up to 20 tons of material a day. His earnings had been quite high because of his rapid work pace, but Willis had been afraid that as he was advancing in age he could injure himself working in that job. After months of Willis's urging, the worker switched to an easier but lower-paying job. He was disappointed in taking the earnings cut and even after several years let the president know whenever he saw him.

Willis pointed out another employee, whose wife had recently died, and noted that for several weeks he had been drinking heavily and reporting to work late. Willis had earlier spent about half an hour discussing the situation with him to console him and see if the company could help in any way. He explained:

> I made a definite point of talking to him on the floor of the plant, near his work station. I wanted to make sure that other employees who knew the situation could see me with him. Speaking to him had symbolic value. It is important for employees to know that the president is interested in their welfare.

Management's philosophy was also reflected in the company's physical facilities. A no-nonsense atmosphere was firmly established at the gate to the parking lot where the only mention of the company name was in a sign reading:

> $1,000 REWARD for information leading to the arrest and conviction of persons stealing from the Lincoln Electric parking lot.

There was a single entrance to the offices and plant for workers, management, and visitors. Entering, one could not avoid being struck by the company motto, in large stainless steel letters extending 30 feet across the wall:

THE ACTUAL IS LIMITED
THE POSSIBLE IS IMMENSE

A flight of stairs led down to a tunnel system for pedestrian traffic which ran under the single-story plant. At the base of the stairs was a large bronze plaque on which were inscribed the names of the 8 employees who had served more than 50 years, and the more than 350 active employees with 25 or more years of service (the Quarter Century Club).

The long tunnel leading to the offices was clean and well lit. The executive offices were located in a windowless, two-story cementblock office building which sat like a box in the center of the plant. At the base of the staircase leading up to the offices, a Lincoln automatic welding machine and portraits of J. C. Lincoln and J. F. Lincoln welcomed visitors. The handrail on the staircase was welded into place, as were the ashtrays in the tunnel.

In the center of the office building was a simple, undecorated reception room. A switchboard operator/receptionist greeted visitors between filing and phone calls. Throughout the building, decor was Spartan. The reception room was furnished with a metal coat rack, a wooden bookcase, and several plain wooden tables and chairs. All of the available reading material dealt with The Lincoln Electric Company or welding.

From the reception room, seven doors each led almost directly to the various offices and departments. Most of the departments were large open rooms with closely spaced desks. One manager explained that "Mr. Lincoln didn't believe in walls. He felt they interrupted the flow of communications and paperwork." Most of the desks and files were plain, old, and well worn, and there was little modern office equipment. Expenditures on equipment had to meet the same criteria in the office as in the plant: The Maintenance Department had to certify that the equipment replaced could not be repaired, and any equipment acquired for cost reduction had to have a one-year payback.[10] Even Xerox machines were nowhere to be found. Copying costs were tightly controlled and only certain individuals could use the Xerox copiers. Customer order forms which required eight copies were run on a duplicating machine, for example.

The private offices were small, uncarpeted, and separated by green metal partitions. The president's office was slightly larger than the others, but still retained a Spartan appearance. There was only one carpeted office. Willis explained: "That office was occupied by Mr. Lincoln until he died in 1965. For the next five years it was left vacant and now it is Mr. Irrgang's office and also the Board of Directors' and Advisory Board meeting room."

PERSONNEL

Lincoln Electric had a strict policy of filling all but entry level positions by promoting from within the company. Whenever an opening occurred, a notice was posted on the 25 bulletin boards in the plant and offices. Any interested employee could apply for an open position. Because of the company's sustained growth and policy of promoting from within, employees had substantial opportunity for advancement.

An outsider generally could join the company in one of two ways: either taking a factory job at an hourly or piece rate, or

[10] Willis explained that capital projects with paybacks of up to two years were sometimes funded when they involved a product for which demand was growing.

entering Lincoln's training programs in sales or engineering.[11] The company recruited its trainees at colleges and graduate schools, including Harvard Business School. Starting salary in 1975 for a trainee with a bachelor's degree was $5.50 an hour plus a year-end bonus at an average of 40 percent of the normal rate. Wages for trainees with either a master's degree or several years of relevant experience were 5 percent higher.

Although Lincoln's president, vice president of sales, and personnel director were all Harvard Business School graduates, the company had not hired many recent graduates. Clyde Loughridge, the personnel director, explained:

> We don't offer them fancy staff positions and we don't pretend to. Our starting pay is less than average, probably $17,000–$18,000[12] including bonus, and the work is harder than average. We start our trainees off by putting them in overalls and they spend up to seven weeks in the welding school. In a lot of ways it's like boot camp. Rather than leading them along by the hand, we like to let the self-starters show themselves.

The policy of promoting from within had rarely been violated, and then only in cases where a specialized skill was required. Loughridge commented:

> In most cases we've been able to stick to it, even where the required skills are entirely new to the company. Our employees have a lot of varied skills, and usually someone can fit the job. For example, when we recently got our first computer, we needed a programmer and systems analyst. We had twenty employees apply who had experience or training in computers. We chose two, and it really helps that they know the company and understand our business.

The company did not send its employees to outside management development programs and did not provide tuition grants for educational purposes.

Lincoln Electric had no formal organization chart and management did not feel that one was necessary. (The chart in Exhibit 9 was drawn for the purposes of this case.) As explained by one executive:

> People retire and their jobs are parceled out. We are very successful in overloading our overhead departments. We make sure this way that no unnecessary work is done and jobs which are not absolutely essential are eliminated. A disadvantage is that planning may suffer, as may outside development to keep up with your field.

Lincoln's organizational hierarchy was flat, with few levels between the bottom and the top. For example, Don Hastings, the vice president of sales, had 37 regional sales managers reporting to him. He commented:

> I have to work hard, there's no question about that. There are only four of us in the home office plus two secretaries. I could easily use three more people. I work every Saturday, at least half a day. Most of our regional men do too, and they like me to know it. You should see the switchboard light up when 37 regional managers call in at 5 minutes to 12 on Saturday.

The president and chairman kept a tight rein over personnel matters. All changes in status of employees, even at the lowest levels, had to be approved by Willis. Irr-

---

[11] Lincoln's chairman and president both advanced through the ranks in Manufacturing. Irrgang began as a pieceworker in the Armature Winding Department, and Willis began in Plant Engineering. (See Exhibit 8 for employment history of Lincoln's top management.)

[12] In 1975 the median starting salary for Harvard Business School graduates who took positions in industrial manufacturing was $19,800.

gang also had to give his approval if salaried employees were involved. Raises or promotions had to be approved in advance. An employee could be fired by his supervisor on the spot for cause, but if the grounds were questionable, the decision had to be approved afterward by either Willis or Irrgang. Usually the supervisor was supported, but there had been cases where a firing decision was reversed.

MARKETING

Welding machines and electrodes were like razors and razor blades. A Lincoln welding machine often had a useful life of 30 years or more, while electrodes (and fluxes) were consumed immediately in the welding process. The ratio of machine cost to annual consumables cost varied widely, from perhaps 7:1 for a hand welder used in a small shop to 1:5 or more for an automatic welder used in a shipyard.

Although certain competitors might meet Lincoln's costs and quality in selected products, management believed that no company could match the line overall. Another important competitive edge for Lincoln was its sales force. Al Patnik, vice president of sales development, explained:

> Most competitors operate through distributors. We have our own top field sales force.[13] We start out with engineering graduates and put them through our seven-month training program. They learn how to weld, and we teach them everything we can about equipment, metallurgy, and design. Then they spend time on the rebuild line [where machines brought in from the field are rebuilt] and even spend time in the office seeing how orders are processed. Finally, before the trainees go out into the field, they have to go into our plant and find a better way of making something. Then they make a presentation to Mr. Irrgang, just as if he were one of our customers.
>
> Our approach to the customer is to go in and learn what he is doing and show him how to do it better. For many companies our people become their experts in welding. They go in and talk to a foreman. They might say, "Let me put on a headshield and show you what I'm talking about." That's how we sell them.

George Ward, a salesman in the San Francisco office, commented:

> The competition hires graduates with business degrees (without engineering backgrounds) and that's how they get hurt. This job is getting more technical every day. . . . A customer in California who is using our equipment to weld offshore oil rigs had a problem with one of our products. I couldn't get the solution for them over the phone, so I flew in to the plant Monday morning and showed it to our engineers. Mr. Willis said to me, "Don't go back to California until this problem is solved. . . ." We use a "working together to solve your problem" approach. This, plus sticking to published prices, shows you're not interested in taking advantage of them.
>
> I had a boss who used to say: "Once we're in, Lincoln never loses a customer except on delivery." It's basically true. The orders I lost last year were because we couldn't deliver fast enough. Lincoln gets hurt when there are shortages because of our guaranteed employment. We don't hire short-term factory workers when sales take off, and other companies beat us on delivery.

The sales force was paid a salary plus bonus. Ward believed that Lincoln's sales force was the best paid and hardest

---

[13] The sales force was supplemented in some areas by distributors. Sales abroad were handled by wholly owned subsidiaries or Armco's International Division.

working in the industry. He said, "We're aggressive, and want to work and get paid for it. The sales force prides itself on working more hours than anyone else. . . . My wife wonders sometimes if you can work for Lincoln and have a family too."

MANUFACTURING

Lincoln's plant was unusual in several respects. It seemed crowded with materials and equipment, with surprisingly few workers. It was obvious that employees worked very fast and efficiently with few breaks. Even during the 10-minute smoke breaks in the morning and afternoon, employees often continued to work.

An innovative plant layout was partly responsible for the crowded appearance. Raw materials entered one side of the plant and finished goods came out the other side. There was no central stockroom for materials or work in process. Instead, everything that entered the plant was transported directly to the work station where it would be used. At a work station, a single worker or group operated in effect as a subcontractor. All required materials were piled around the station, allowing visual inventory control, and workers were paid a piece price for their production. Wherever possible, the work flow followed a straight line through the plant from the side where raw materials entered to the side where finished goods exited. Because there was no union, the company had great flexibility in deciding what could be performed at a work station. For example, foundry work and metal stamping could be carried out together by the same workers when necessary. Thus, work could flow almost directly along a line through the plant. Intermediate material handling was avoided to a great extent. The major exception arose when multiple production lines shared a large or expensive piece of machinery, and the work had to be brought to the machines.

Many of the operations in the plant were automated. Much of the manufacturing equipment was proprietary,[14] designed and built by Lincoln. In some cases, the company had modified machines built by others to run two or three times as fast as when originally delivered.

From the time a product was first conceived, close coordination was maintained between product design engineers and the Methods Department; this was seen as a key factor in reducing costs and rationalizing manufacturing. William Irrgang explained:

> After we have [an] idea . . . we start thinking about manufacturing costs, before anything leaves the Design Engineering Department. At that point, there is a complete "getting together" of manufacturing and design engineers—and plant engineers, too, if new equipment is involved.
>
> Our tooling, for instance, is going to be looked at carefully while the design of a product is still in process. Obviously, we can increase or decrease the tooling very materially by certain considerations in the design of a product, and we can go on the basis of total costs at all times. In fact, as far as total cost is concerned, we even think about such matters as shipping, warehousing, etc. All of these factors are taken into consideration when we're still at the design stage. It's very essential that this be done: otherwise, you can lock yourself out from a lot of potential economies.[15]

In 1974 Lincoln's plant had reached full capacity, operating nearly around the

---

[14] Visitors were barred from the Electrode Division unless they had a pass signed by Willis or Irrgang.

[15] "Incentive Management in Action," *Assembly Engineering,* March 1967. Reprinted by permission of the publisher. © 1967 by Hitchcock Publishing Co. All rights reserved.

clock. Land bordering its present location was unavailable and management was moving ahead with plans to build a second plant 15 miles away on the same freeway as the present plant.

Over the years, Lincoln had come to make rather than buy an increasing proportion of its components. For example, even though its unit volume of gasoline engines was only a fraction of its suppliers', Lincoln purchased engine blocks and components and assembled them rather than buying completed engines. Management was continually evaluating opportunities for backward integration and had not arbitrarily ruled out manufacturing any of Lincoln's components or raw materials.

ADMINISTRATIVE PRODUCTIVITY

Lincoln's high productivity was not limited to manufacturing. Clyde Loughridge pointed to the Personnel Department as an example: "Normally, for 2,300 employees you would need a personnel department of about 20, but we have only 6, and that includes the nurse, and our responsibilities go beyond those of the typical personnel department."

Once a year, Loughridge had to outline his objectives for the upcoming year to the president of the company, but as he explained, "I don't get a budget. There would be no point to it. I just spend as little as possible. I operate this just like my home. I don't spend on anything I don't need."

In the Traffic Department, workers also seemed very busy. There, a staff of 12 controlled the shipment of 2.5 million pounds of material a day. Their task was complex. Delivery was included in the price of their products. They thus could reduce the overall cost to the customer by mixing products in most loads and shipping the most efficient way possible to the company's 39 warehouses. Jim Biek, general traffic manager, explained how they accomplished this:

> For every order, we decide whether it would be cheaper by rail or truck. Then we consolidate orders so that over 90 percent of what goes out of here is full carload or full truckload, as compared to perhaps 50 percent for most companies. We also mix products so that we come in at the top of the weight brackets. For example, if a rate is for 20,000 to 40,000 pounds, we will mix orders to bring the weight right up to that 40,000 limit. All this is computed manually. In fact, my old boss used to say, "We run Traffic like a ma and pa grocery store."

As in the rest of Lincoln, the employees in the Traffic Department worked their way up from entry level positions. Jim Biek had become general traffic manager after nine years as a purchasing engineer. He had received an MBA degree from Northwestern after a BS in mechanical engineering from Purdue, started in the engineering training program, and then spent five years in Product Development and Methods before going to Purchasing and finally to Traffic. Lack of experience in Traffic was a disadvantage, but the policy of promoting from within also had its advantages. Biek explained:

> One of my first tasks was to go to Washington and fight to get welders reclassified as motors to qualify for a lower freight rate. With my engineering experience and knowledge of welders, I was in a better position to argue this than a straight traffic man. . . .
>
> Just about everybody in here was new to Traffic. One of my assistant traffic managers had worked on the loading platform here for 10 years before he came into the department. He had to go to night school to learn about rates, but his experience is invaluable. He knows how to load trucks and rail cars backwards and forward. Who could do a better job of consolidating

> orders than he does? He can look at an order and think of it as rows of pallets.
>
> Some day we'll outgrow this way of operating, but right now I can't imagine a computer juggling loads like some of our employees do.

Lincoln's Order Department had recently begun computerizing its operations. It was the first time a computer had been used anywhere in the company (except in engineering and research), and according to Russell Stauffer, head of the Order Department, "It was a three-year job for me to sell this to top management." The computer was expected to replace 12 or 13 employees who would gradually be moved into new jobs. There had been some resistance to the computer, Stauffer noted:

> It's like anything new. People get scared. Not all the people affected have been here for the two years required to be eligible for guaranteed employment. And even though the others are assured a job, they don't know what it will be and will have to take what's offered.

The computer was expected to produce savings of $100,000 a year, and to allow a greater degree of control. Stauffer explained:

> We're getting information out of this that we never knew before. The job here is very complex. We're sending out more than two million pounds of consumables a day. Each order might have 30 or 40 items, and each item has a bracket price arrangement based on total order size. A clerk has to remember or determine quickly whether we are out of stock on any items and calculate whether the stock-out brings the order down into another bracket. This means they have to remember the prices and items out of stock. This way of operating was okay up to about $200 million in sales, but now we've outgrown the human capability to handle the problem.

Although he had no previous experience in computers, Stauffer had full responsibility for the conversion.

> I've been here for 35 years. The first day I started, I unloaded coal cars and painted fences. Then I went to the assembly line, first on small parts, then large ones. I've been running the Order Department for 12 years. Since I've been here, we've had studies on computers every year or two and it always came out that we couldn't save money. Finally, when it looked like we'd make the switch, I took some courses at IBM. Over the last year and a half, they've totaled eight and a half weeks, which is supposed to equal a full semester of college.

To date, the conversion had gone well, but much slower than anticipated. Order pressure had been so high that many mistakes would have been catastrophic. Management thus had emphasized assuring 100 percent quality operations rather than faster conversion.

LINCOLN'S FUTURE

The 1947 Harvard Business School case study of Lincoln Electric ended with a prediction by a union leader from the Cleveland area:

> The real test of Lincoln will come when the going gets tough. The thing Lincoln holds out to the men is high earnings. They work like dogs at Lincoln, but it pays off. . . .
>
> I think [Mr. Lincoln] puts too much store by monetary incentives—but then, there's no denying he has attracted people who respond to that type of incentive. But I think that very thing is a danger Lincoln faces. If the day comes when they can't offer those big bonuses, or his people decide there's more to life than killing yourself making money, I predict the Lincoln Electric Company is in for trouble.

Lincoln's president, George Willis, joined the company the year that this comment was made. Reflecting on his 28 years with the company, Willis observed:

> The company hasn't changed very much since I've been here. It's still run pretty much like Mr. Lincoln ran it. But today's workers are different. They're more outspoken and interested in why things are being done, not just how. We have nothing to hide and never did, so we can give them the answers to their questions.

Looking forward, Willis saw no need to alter Lincoln's strategy or its policies:

> My job will continue to be to have everyone in the organization recognize that a common goal all of us can and must support is to give the customer the quality he needs, when he needs it, at the lowest cost. To do this, we have to have everyone's understanding of this goal and their effort to accomplish it. In one way or another, I have to motivate the organization to meet this goal. The basic forms of the motivation have evolved over the last 40 years. However, keeping the system honed so that everyone understands it, agrees with it, and brings out disagreements so improvements can be made or thinking changed becomes my major responsibility.
>
> If our employees did not believe that management was trustworthy, honest, and impartial, the system could not operate. We've worked out the mechanics. They are not secret. A good part of my responsibility is to make sure the mechanics are followed. This ties back to a trust and understanding between individuals at all levels of the organization.
>
> I don't see any real limits to our size. Look at a world with a present population of just under four billion now and six and a quarter billion by the year 2000. Those people aren't going to tolerate a low standard of living. So there will be a lot of construction, cars, bridges, oil and all those things that have got to be to support a population that large.
>
> My job will still be just the traditional things of assuring that we keep up with the technology and have sufficient profit to pay the suppliers of capital. Then, I have to make sure communication can be maintained adequately. That last task may be the biggest and most important part of my job in the years ahead as we grow larger and still more complex.

EXHIBIT 1
ARC WELDING

Arc welding is a group of joining processes that utilize an electric current produced by a transformer or motor generator (electric or engine powered) to fuse various metals. The temperature at the arc is approximately 10,000° Fahrenheit.

The welding circuit consists of a welding machine, ground clamp, and electrode holder. The electrode carries electricity to the metal being welded and the heat from the arc causes the base metals to join together. The electrode may or may not act as a filler metal during the process; however, nearly 60 percent of all arc welding that is done in the United States utilizes a covered electrode that acts as a very high quality filler metal.

The Lincoln Electric Company manufactured a wide variety of covered electrodes, submerged arc welding wires and fluxes, and a unique self-shielded, flux-cored electrode called Innershield. The company also manufactured welding machines, wire feeders, and other supplies that were needed for arc welding.

Lincoln Arc Welding Machines

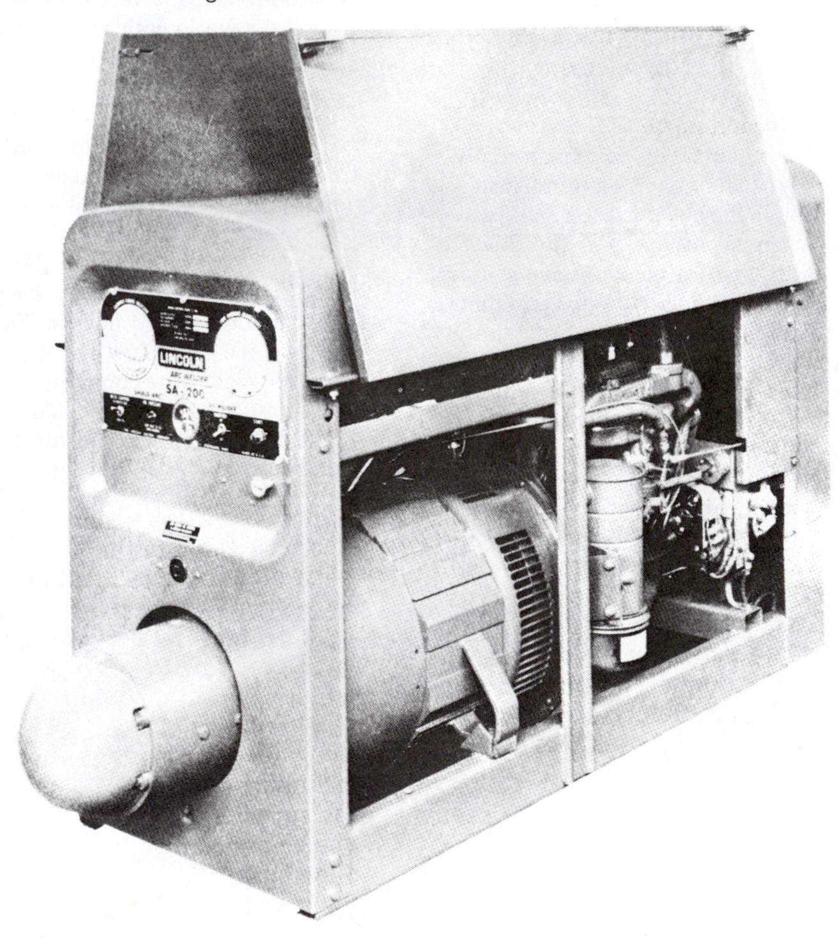

EXHIBIT 2
LINCOLN'S STATUS IN 1974

Statement of Financial Condition
(Foreign Subsidiaries Not Included)

December 31, 1974

Assets	
Current assets	
Cash and certificates of deposit	$ 5,691,120
Government securities	6,073,919
Notes and accounts receivable	29,451,161
Inventories (LIFO basis)	29,995,694
Deferred taxes and prepaid expenses	2,266,409
Total	73,478,303
Other assets	
Trustee—notes and interest receivable	1,906,871
Miscellaneous	384,572
Total	2,291,443
Intercompany	
Investment in foreign subsidiaries	4,695,610
Notes receivable	0
Total	4,695,610
Property, plant, and equipment	
Land	825,376
Buildings*	9,555,562
Machinery, tools, and equipment*	11,273,155
Total	21,654,093
Total assets	$102,119,449
Liabilities and Shareholders' Equity	
Current liabilities	
Accounts payable	$ 13,658,063
Accrued wages	1,554,225
Taxes, including income taxes	13,262,178
Dividends payable	3,373,524
Total	31,847,990
Shareholders' equity	
Common capital stock, stated value	281,127
Additional paid-in capital	3,374,570
Retained earnings	66,615,762
Total	70,271,459
Total liabilities and shareholders' equity	$102,119,449

*After depreciation.

EXHIBIT 2 (*concluded*)

Income and Retained Earnings

Year Ended December 31, 1974

Income

Net sales	$232,771,475
Interest	1,048,561
Overhead and development charges to subsidiaries	1,452,877
Dividend income	843,533
Other income	515,034
Total	236,631,480
Costs and expenses	
Cost of products sold	154,752,735
Selling, administrative, and general expenses and freight out	20,791,301
Year-end incentive bonus	24,707,297
Pension expense	2,186,932
Total	202,438,265
Income before Income Taxes	34,193,215
Provision for Income Taxes	
Federal	14,800,000
State and local	1,866,000
	16,666,000
Net Income	$ 17,527,215

EXHIBIT 3

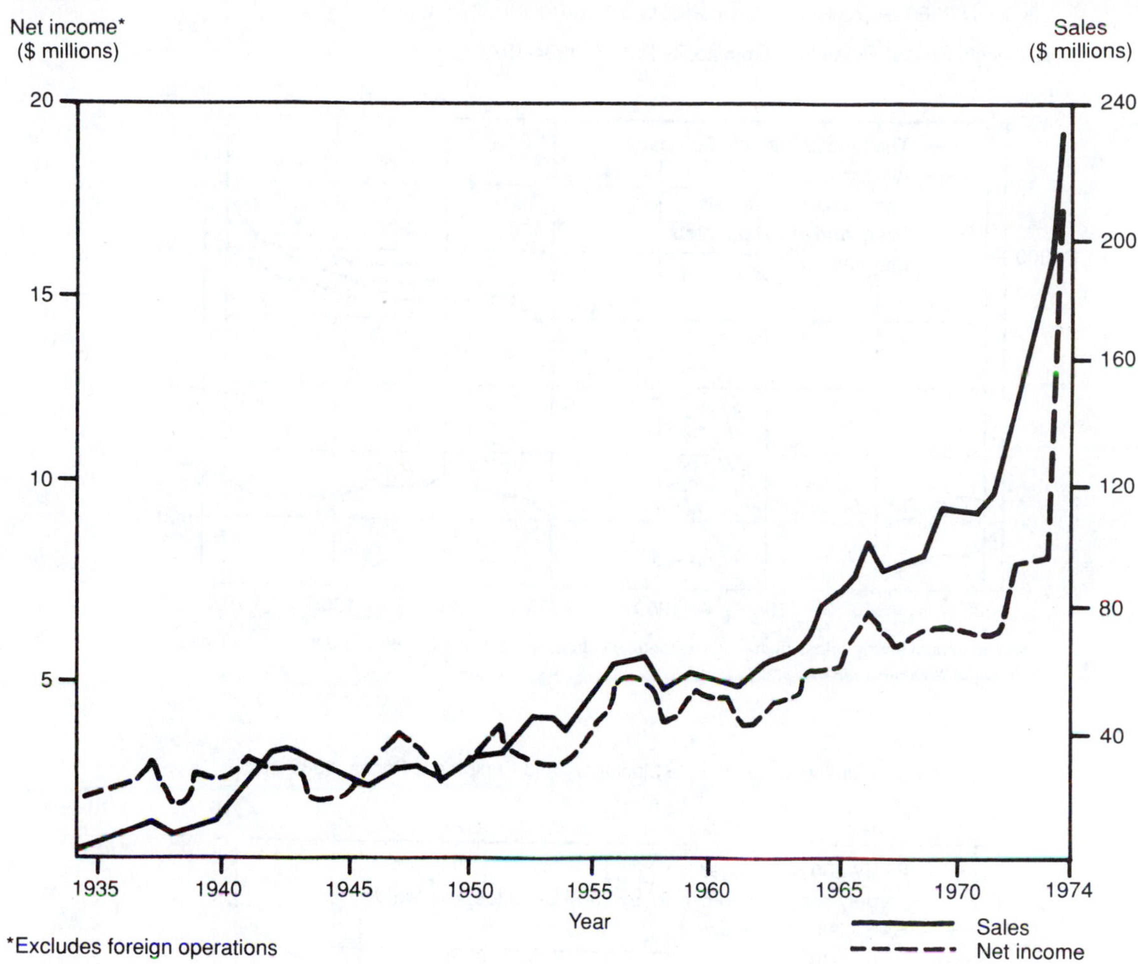

*Excludes foreign operations

EXHIBIT 4
LINCOLN ELECTRIC'S RECORD OF PRICING AND PRODUCTIVITY

A. Lincoln Prices* Relative to Commodity Prices†, 1934–1971

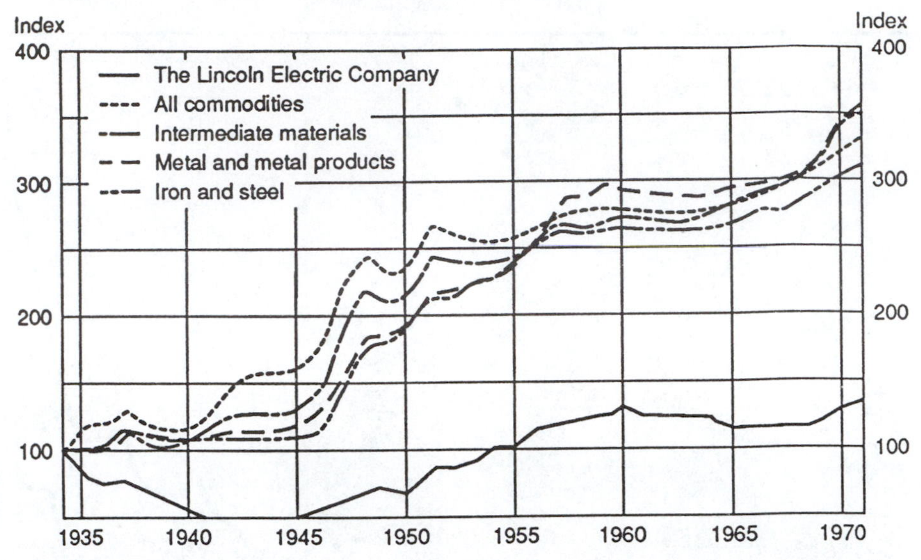

*Index of annual selling prices of 3/16-inch diameter electrode in No. 5 and No. 5P in 3,000 pound quantities
†Indexes of wholesale prices

B. Lincoln Prices‡ Relative to Wholesale Machinery and Equipment Prices, 1939–1971

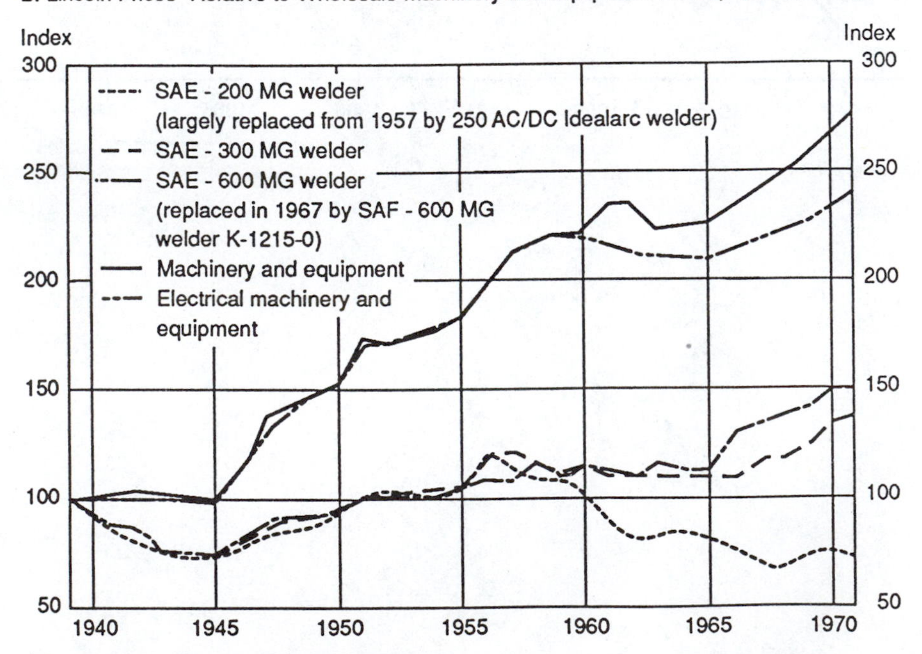

‡Average annual prices of specific Lincoln welders

EXHIBIT 4 *(concluded)*

C. Productivity of Lincoln Production Workers Relative to Workers in Manufacturing and Durable Goods Industries, 1934–1971

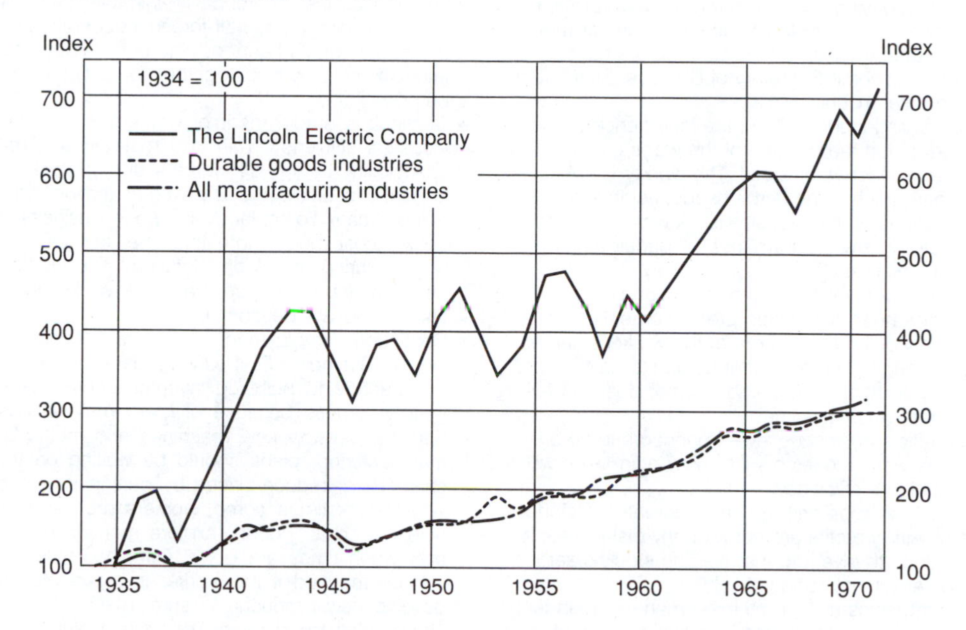

D. Lincoln Productivity Relative to Three Other Companies: Sales Value§ of Products per Employee, 1934–1971

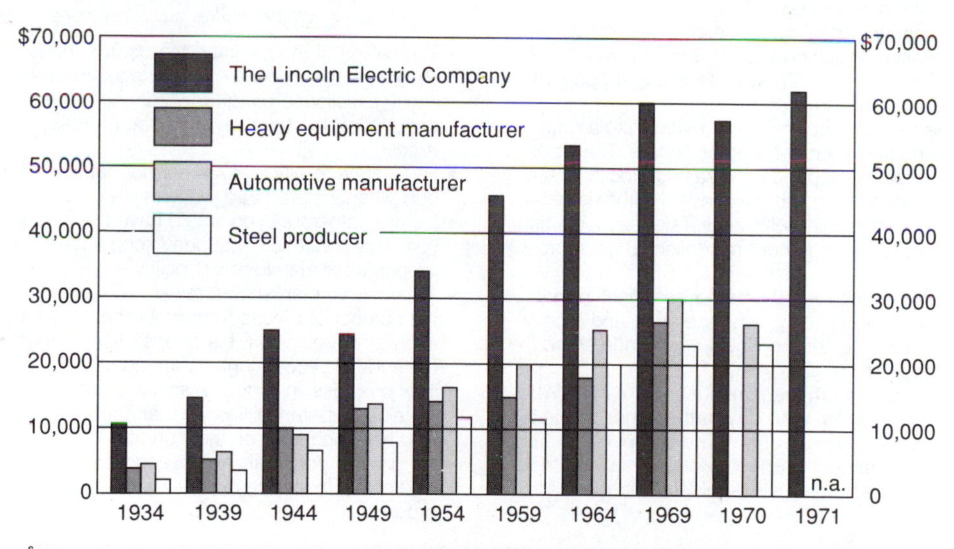

§At current prices

Source: Company records.

EXHIBIT 5
JAMES F. LINCOLN'S OBSERVATIONS ON MANAGEMENT

- Some think paying a man more money will produce cooperation. Not true. Many incentives are far more effective than money. Robert MacNamara gave up millions to become Secretary of Defense. Status is a much greater incentive.
- If those crying loudest about the inefficiencies of labor were put in the position of the wage earner, they would react as he does. The worker is not a man apart. He has the same needs, aspirations, and reactions as the industrialist. A worker will not cooperate on any program that will penalize him. Does any manager?
- The industrial manager is very conscious of his company's need of uninterrupted income. He is completely oblivious, though, to the worker's same need. Management fails—that is, profits fall off—and gets no punishment. The wage earner does not fail but is fired. Such injustice!
- Higher efficiency means fewer manhours to do a job. If the worker loses his job more quickly, he will oppose higher efficiency.
- There will never be enthusiasm for greater efficiency if the resulting profits are not properly distributed. If we continue to give it to the average stockholder, the worker will not cooperate.
- Most companies are run by hired managers, under the control of stockholders. As a result, the goal of the company has shifted from service to the customer to making larger dividends for stockholders.
- The public will not yet believe that our standard of living could be doubled immediately if labor and management would cooperate.
- The manager is dealing with expert workers far more skillful. While you can boss these experts around in the usual lofty way, their eager cooperation will not be won.
- A wage earner is no more interested than a manager in making money for other people. The worker's job doesn't depend on pleasing stockholders, so he has no interest in dividends. Neither is he interested in increasing efficiency if he may lose his job because management has failed to get more orders.
- If a manager received the same treatment in matters of income, security, advancement, and dignity as the hourly worker, he would soon understand the real problem of management.
- The first question management should ask is: What is the company trying to do? In the minds of the average worker the answer is: "The company is trying to make the largest possible profits by any method. Profits go to absentee stockholders and top management."
- There is all the difference imaginable between the grudging, distrustful, half-forced cooperation and the eager, whole-hearted, vigorous, happy cooperation of men working together for a common purpose.
- Continuous employment of workers is essential to industrial efficiency. This is a management responsibility. Laying off workers during slack times is death to efficiency. The worker thrown out is a trained man. To replace him when business picks up will cost much more than the savings of wages during the layoff. Solution? The worker must have a guarantee that if he works properly his income will be continuous.
- Continuous employment is the first step to efficiency. But how? First, during slack periods, manufacture to build up inventory; costs will usually be less because of lower material costs. Second, develop new machines and methods of manufacturing; plans should be waiting on the shelf. Third, reduce prices by getting lower costs. When slack times come, workers are eager to help cut costs. Fourth, explore markets passed over when times are good. Fifth, hours of work can be reduced if the worker is agreeable. Sixth, develop new products. In sum, management should plan for slumps. They are useful.
- The incentives that are most potent when properly offered are:

  Money in proportion to production.
  Status as a reward for achievement.
  Publicity of the worker's contributions and skill.

- The calling of the minister, the doctor, the lawyer, as well as the manager, contains incentive to excel. Excellence brings rewards, self-esteem, respect. Only the hourly worker has no reason to excel.
- Resistance to efficiency is not normal. It is present only when we are hired workers.
- Do unto others as you would have them do unto you. This is not just a Sunday school ideal, but a proper labor-management policy.
- An incentive plan should reward a man not only for the number of pieces turned out, but also for the accuracy of his work, his cooperation in improving methods of production, his attendance.
- The progress in industry so far stems from the developed potentialities of managers. Wage earners, who because of their greater numbers have far greater potential, are overlooked. Here is where the manager must look for his greatest progress.

EXHIBIT 5 (*concluded*)

- There should be an overall bonus based on the contribution each person makes to efficiency. If each person is properly rated and paid, there will not only be a fair reward to each worker but friendly and exciting competition.
- The present policy of operating industry for stockholders is unreasonable. The rewards now given to him are far too much. He gets income that should really go to the worker and the management. The usual absentee stockholder contributes nothing to efficiency. He buys a stock today and sells it tomorrow. He often doesn't even know what the company makes. Why should he be rewarded by large dividends?
- There are many forms and degrees of cooperation between the worker and the management. The worker's attitude can vary all the way from passivity to highly imaginative contributions to efficiency and progress.

Source: *Civil Engineering,* January 1973, p. 78. Reprinted by permission.

EXHIBIT 6
STABILITY OF EMPLOYMENT
A. Lincoln and Industry Labor Turnover Rates, 1958–1970

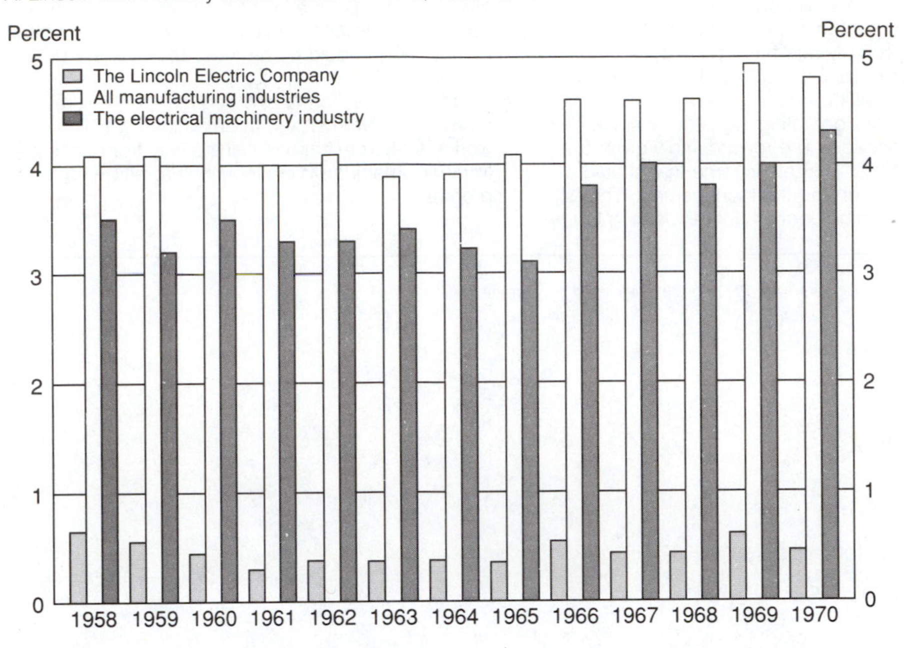

B. Employee Distribution by Years of Service, 1975

Employee's Years of Service	*Number of Employees*
Less than 1	153
1	311
2	201
3	93
4	34
5	90
6–10	545
11–20	439
21–30	274
31–40	197
41–50	27
51 or more	1
Total	2,365

EXHIBIT 7
MANAGEMENT ADVISORY BOARD MINUTES

September 26, 1944

Absent: William Dillmuth

A discussion on piecework was again taken up. There was enough detail so it was thought best to appoint a committee to study it and bring a report into the meeting when that study is complete. That committee is composed of Messrs. Gilletly, Semko, Kneen and Steingass. Messrs. Erickson and White will be called in consultation, and the group will meet next Wednesday, October 4th.

The request was made that the members be permitted to bring guests to the meetings. The request was granted. Let's make sure we don't get too many at one time.

The point was made that materials are not being brought to the operation properly and promptly. There is no doubt of this difficulty. The matter was referred to Mr. Kneen for action. It is to be noted that conditions of deliveries from our suppliers have introduced a tremendous problem which has helped to increase this difficulty.

The request was made that over-time penalty be paid with the straight time. This will be done. There are some administrative difficulties which we will discuss at the next meeting but the over-time payment will start with the first pay in October.

Beginning October 1st employees' badges will be discontinued. Please turn them in to the watchmen.

It was requested that piecework prices be put on repair work in Dept. J. This matter was referred to Mr. Kneen for action.

A request was made that a plaque showing the names of those who died in action, separate from the present plaques, be put in the lobby. This was referred to Mr. Davis for action.

The question was asked as to what method for upgrading men is used. The ability of the individual is the sole reason for his progress. It was felt this is proper.

J. F. Lincoln
President

September 23, 1974 (Excerpts)

Members absent: Tom Borkowski, Albert Sinn

Mr. Kupetz had asked about the Christmas and Thanksgiving schedules. These are being reviewed and we will have them available at the next meeting.

Mr. Howell had reported that the time clocks and the bells do not coincide. This is still being checked.

Mr. Sharpe had asked what the possibility would be to have a time clock installed in or near the Clean Room. This is being checked.

Mr. Joosten had raised the question of the pliability of the wrapping material used in the Chemical Department for wrapping slugs. The material we use at the present time is the best we can obtain at this time. . . .

Mr. Kostelac asked the question again whether the vacation arrangements could be changed, reducing the 15-year period to some shorter period. It was pointed out that at the present time, where we have radically changing conditions every day, it is not the time to go into this. We will review this matter at some later date. . . .

Mr. Martucci brought out the fact that there was considerable objection by the people involved to having to work on Saturday night to make up for holiday shutdowns. This was referred to Mr. Willis to be taken into consideration in schedule planning. . . .

Mr. Joosten reported that in the Chemical Department on the Saturday midnight shift they have a setup where individuals do not have sufficient work so that it is an uneconomical situation. This has been referred to Mr. Willis to be reviewed.

Mr. Joosten asked whether there would be some way to get chest x-rays for people who work in dusty areas. Mr. Loughridge was asked to check a schedule of where chest x-rays are available at various times. . . .

Mr. Robinson asked what the procedure is for merit raises. The procedure is that the foreman recommends the individual for a merit raise if by his performance he has shown that he merits the increase. . . .

Chairman

William Irrgang: MW
September 25, 1974

EXHIBIT 8
EMPLOYMENT HISTORY OF TOP EXECUTIVES

William Irrgang, Board Chairman

1929 Hired, Repair Department
1930 Final Inspection
1934 Inspection, Wire Department
1946 Director of factory engineering
1951 Executive vice president for manufacturing and engineering
1954 President and general manager
1972 Chairman of the board of directors

George E. Willis, President

1947 Hired, Factory Engineering
1951 Superintendent, Electrode Division
1959 Vice president
1969 Executive vice president of manufacturing and associated functions
1972 President

William Miskoe, Vice President, International

1932 Hired, Chicago sales office
1941 President of Australian plant
1969 To Cleveland as vice president, international

Edwin M. Miller, Vice President and Assistant to the President

1923 Hired, factory worker
1925 Assistant foreman
1929 Production department
1940 Assistant department head, Production Department
1952 Superintendent, Machine Division
1959 Vice president
1973 Vice president and assistant to the president

D. Neal Manross, Vice President, Machine and Motor Divisions

1941 Hired, factory worker
1942 Welding inspector
1952 General foreman, Extruding Department and assistant plant superintendent
1953 Foreman, Special Products Department, Machine Division
1956 Superintendent, Special Products Division
1959 Superintendent, Motor Manufacturing
1966 Vice president, Motor Division
1973 Vice president in charge of Motor and Machine Divisions

Albert S. Patnik, Vice President of Sales Development

1940 Hired, sales student
1940 Welder, New London, Conn.
1941 Junior salesman, Los Angeles office
1942 Salesman, Seattle office
1945 Military service
1945 Reinstated to Seattle
1951 Rural Dealer Manager, Cleveland sales office
1964 Assistant to the vice president of sales
1972 Vice president

Donald F. Hastings, Vice President and General Sales Manager

1953 Hired, sales trainee
1954 Welding engineer, Emeryville, Cal.
1959 District manager, Moline office
1970 General sales manager, Cleveland
1972 Vice president and general sales manager

EXHIBIT 9

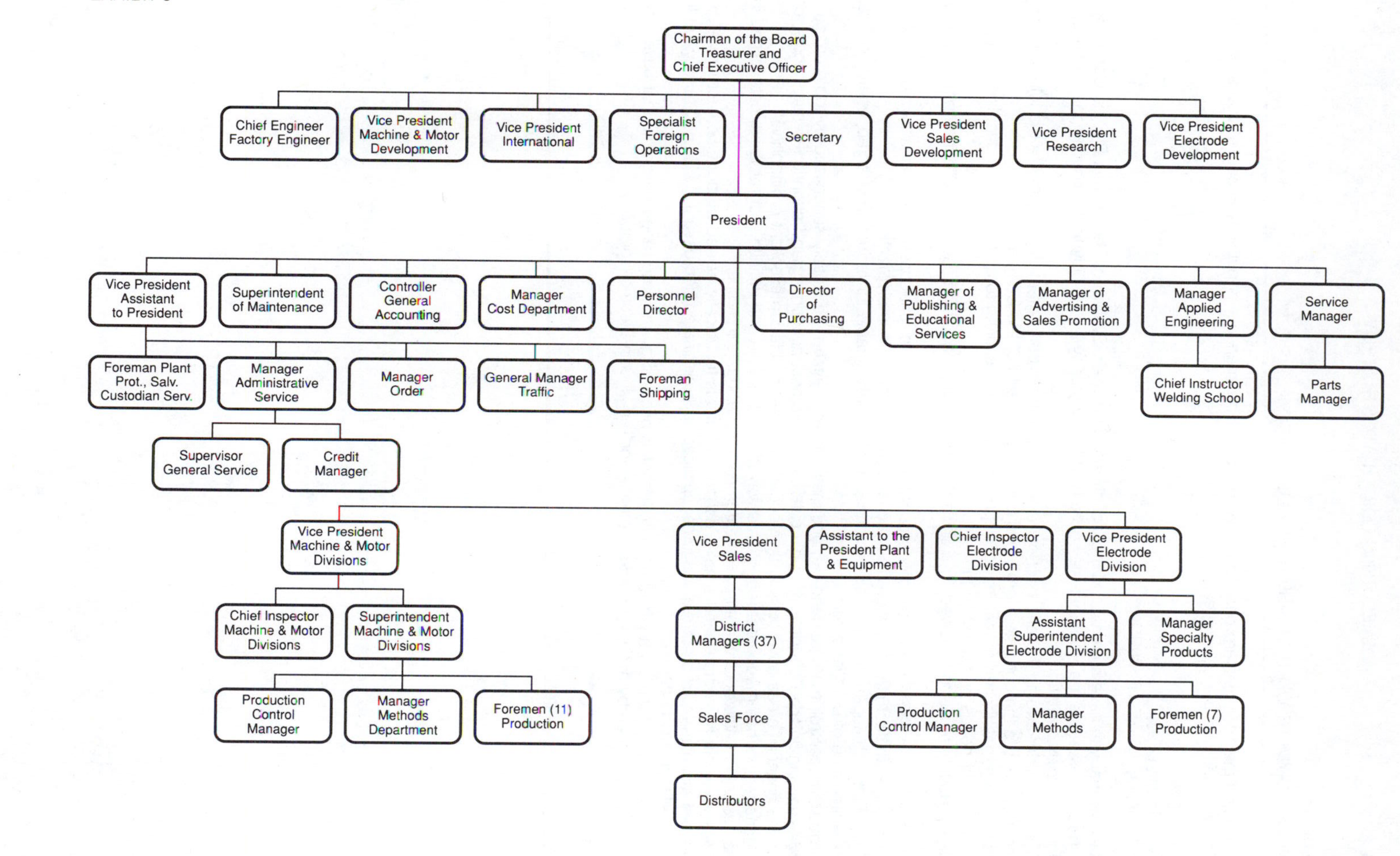

Chairman of the Board Treasurer and Chief Executive Officer
Chief Engineer Factory Engineer
Vice President Machine & Motor Development
Vice President International
Specialist Foreign Operations
Secretary
Vice President Sales Development
Vice President Research
Vice President Electrode Development
President
Vice President Assistant to President
Superintendent of Maintenance
Controller General Accounting
Manager Cost Department
Personnel Director
Director of Purchasing
Manager of Publishing & Educational Services
Manager of Advertising & Sales Promotion
Manager Applied Engineering
Service Manager
Foreman Plant Prot., Salv. Custodian Serv.
Manager Administrative Service
Manager Order
General Manager Traffic
Foreman Shipping
Chief Instructor Welding School
Parts Manager
Supervisor General Service
Credit Manager
Vice President Machine & Motor Divisions
Vice President Sales
Assistant to the President Plant & Equipment
Chief Inspector Electrode Division
Vice President Electrode Division
Chief Inspector Machine & Motor Divisions
Superintendent Machine & Motor Divisions
District Managers (37)
Assistant Superintendent Electrode Division
Manager Specialty Products
Production Control Manager
Manager Methods Department
Foremen (11) Production
Sales Force
Production Control Manager
Manager Methods
Foremen (7) Production
Distributors

EXHIBIT 10
LINCOLN COMMENT ON THE CASE

After reading the 1975 Harvard case study, Richard S. Sabo, manager of publicity & educational services, sent the following letter to the casewriter:

July 31, 1975
To: Mr. Norman Fast
Dear Mr. Fast:

I believe that you have summarized the Incentive Management System of The Lincoln Electric Company very well; however, readers may feel that the success of the Company is due only to the psychological principles included in your presentation.

Please consider adding the efforts of our executives who devote a great deal of time to the following items that are so important to the consistent profit and long range growth of the Company.

I. Management has limited research, development, and manufacturing to a standard product line designed to meet the major needs of the welding industry.

II. New products must be reviewed by manufacturing and all production costs verified before being approved by management.

III. Purchasing is challenged to not only procure materials at the lowest cost, but also to work closely with engineering and manufacturing to assure that the latest innovations are implemented.

IV. Manufacturing supervision and all personnel are held accountable for reduction of scrap, energy conservation, and maintenance of product quality.

V. Production control, material handling, and methods engineering are closely supervised by top management.

VI. Material and finished goods inventory control, accurate cost accounting and attention to sales costs, credit, and other financial areas have constantly reduced overhead and led to excellent profitability.

VII. Management has made cost reduction a way of life at Lincoln and definite programs are established in many areas, including traffic and shipping, where tremendous savings can result.

VIII. Management has established a sales department that is technically trained to reduce customer welding cost. This sales technique and other real customer services have eliminated non-essential frills and resulted in long term benefits to all concerned.

IX. Management has encouraged education, technical publishing, and long range programs that have resulted in industry growth, thereby assuring market potential for The Lincoln Electric Company.

Richard S. Sabo

bjs

Schlumberger, Ltd.: Jean Riboud Excerpts from "A Certain Poetry" by Ken Auletta

Jean Riboud

This case was excerpted from "A Certain Poetry—Parts I and II," copyright 1983, Ken Auletta, by permission of *The New Yorker* and Ken Auletta.

Harvard Business School case 384–087. Revised April 1984.

From the windows of Jean Riboud's New York office, on the 44th floor at 277 Park Avenue, one can see the buildings that house the headquarters of such corporate giants as Warner Communications, Gulf & Western, Citicorp, International Telephone and Telegraph, Colgate-Palmolive, United Brands, Bankers Trust, CBS, RCA, and International Paper. All of them are better known than Schlumberger, Ltd., the company that Riboud is chairman and chief executive officer of, but none of them can match Schlumberger's profits. In stock-market value—the number of outstanding shares multiplied by the price per share—only three companies were worth more than Schlumberger at the end of 1981. They were AT&T ($48 billion), IBM ($34 billion), and Exxon ($27 billion). Schlumberger was then worth $16 billion.

Riboud has offices in New York and Paris, and both are rather ordinary except for the art on the walls—works by Picasso, Klee, Max Ernst, Magritte, Jasper Johns, Victor Brauner, Janez Bernik. His New York office is a snug corner—16 feet by 20 feet—with beige walls. An adjoining conference room, 17 feet by 18 feet, has one couch and a round wooden table with six chairs. Riboud's office has a single telephone with just two lines, and no private bathroom; there are white blinds on the windows, and a simple beige sisal carpet on the floor. His desk is a long, rectangular teak table with chrome legs; on it are a few memorandums but no "in" or "out" box and no books. His personal New York staff consists of one secretary, Lucille Northrup, to whom he rarely dictates; memorandums and paperwork are frowned upon at Schlumberger, and when Riboud wants to send out a memorandum, he first writes in longhand. His Paris office is equally uncluttered.

Riboud is 63 years old. He is 5 feet 10 inches tall and slight of build, with wavy gray hair combed straight back. His nose is long and thin, his lips are narrow. His suits come in conservative shades, and his shirts are usually quiet solid colors. He speaks softly, sometimes almost inaudibly, in accented English, rarely gesticulates, and is an intense listener, usually inspecting his long fingers while others speak. Everything about Riboud conveys an impression of delicacy except his eyes, which are deep brown and cryptic. He arrives at work around 10 A.M., and he takes at least six weeks' vacation annually. Yet he is no figurehead; rather, he believes in delegating authority—a principle that no doubt accounts for the calm of Schlumberger's offices in New York and Paris. Schlumberger employs 75,000 people, and of that number only 197 work at the two headquarters.

* * * * *

As the chief executive of a multinational corporation—Schlumberger does business in 92 countries—Riboud has a somewhat surprising talent for avoiding publicity. He is a stranger to most other corporate executives, deliberately keeping his distance from them. He sits on no other company's board of directors.

Riboud has been the chief executive of Schlumberger for the past 18 years. Because the corporation does no mass advertising, of either the consumer or the institutional sort, because it retains no lobbyist in Washington and no public-relations agency in New York or Paris, and because it has never been involved in a public controversy, Schlumberger (pronounced "shlum-bare-zhay") remains one of the world's lesser-known major corporations. It is a high-technology company that generates the bulk of its income from the oil-field-service business—making tools that enable oil companies to find and drill for oil with great precision. The information gained and the techniques learned in oil-field services have helped the company to expand into such fields as electric, gas, and water meters; flight-test systems; transformers and semiconductors; automatic test equipment for integrated-circuit chips; electronic telephone circuits; computer-aided design and manufacturing processes; and robotics. Schlumberger is recognized on Wall Street as one of the world's best-managed multinational companies, and financial analysts can point to a number of facts to document its success. Its net income has grown by about 30 percent in each of the past 10 years up to 1981. Its earnings per share rose by more than 30 percent annually between 1971 and 1981, even though the price of oil remained stable or declined in several of those years. Its profit in 1982 totaled $1.35 billion on revenues of $6.284 billion, for a profit as a percentage of revenue of 21 percent—higher than that of any of the thousand other leading industrial companies in the world. Its return on equity in 1981 was 34 percent, while the median for the *Fortune* 500 companies was 13.8 percent. Schlumberger has relatively little long-term debt: it amounted to just $462 million at the end of 1982, or 3 percent of the company's total capitalization. And while the profits of most oil and oil-field-service companies fell sharply in 1982, Schlumberger's net income rose by 6 percent.

Science is the foundation of Schlumberger. Science is the link between the various corporate subsidiaries, for the task of most of them is collecting, measuring, and transmitting data. Science, and particularly geophysics, was at the core of the careers of Conrad and Marcel Schlumberger, the company's founders. Ever since the first oil well was drilled, in 1859, oil companies had longed for a technology that would help them find oil. Initially, prospectors had to painstakingly extract core samples and drill cuttings from rock formations, haul them slowly to the surface, ship them to a laboratory, and await a chemical analysis. This tedious, expensive process enabled the oil companies to determine whether there was oil in a given area, and even to determine its quality, but not its precise quantity, or the exact shape of the well, and it did not enable them to pinpoint where to drill. Conrad, having discovered a new geophysical principle, assigned the job of fashioning a tool and testing it to Henri Doll, who was a brilliant young engineer and also the husband of Conrad's daughter Anne. Doll's task was to chart the electric current as it encountered various kinds of rock, water, and oil. By comparing the actual current coursing through the earth with records showing the electrical resistivity of each substance, the brothers and Doll hoped to produce what amounted to the world's first X ray of an oil well.

Today, the tools are more refined, but the basic process—wireline logging, as it came to be known—is a measurement taken on just about every oil or gas well drilled in the world. And today, without benefit of a patent on its basic logging process, Schlumberger—as the original partnership was renamed in 1934—has a near-monopoly on this business, logging some 70 percent of the world's wells. In the United States alone, in 1981 the company hired 1 percent of all the engineers graduating from American colleges.

Over the years, Schlumberger's oil-field business has expanded beyond logging measurements to include a broad range of other services: drilling, testing, and completing wells; pumping; cementing. The company's Forex Neptune subsidiary, formed in the 1950s, is now the world's largest oil-drilling company. The Johnston-Macco and Flopetrol subsidiaries provide an assortment of testing and completion services after drilling has started. A subsidiary called The Analysts provides continuous detailed logs of oil wells from the moment drilling begins, in contrast to most logs, which are prepared only before drilling begins or after it ceases. The Dowell Schlumberger company, which is jointly owned by Schlumberger and Dow Chemical, offers pumping and cementing services. Together with the Wireline division, these companies make up the Oilfield Services—one of two major parts of the Schlumberger empire. The other major part is known as Measurement, Control and Components. Its subsidiaries include the world's largest manufacturer of electric, gas, and water meters; a leading manufacturer of transformers; a producer of valves and safety controls for nuclear power systems; and a manufacturer of flight-control and signal-processing systems for aerospace and military use. The Fairchild Camera & Instrument Corporation, a California-based semiconductor company that Schlumberger acquired in 1979, manufactures, among other products, integrated circuits such as microprocessors and memories; advanced bipolar microprocessors for the F-16 fighter plane; and electronic telephone circuits. Applicon, another subsidiary, is among the pioneers in computer-aided design and other efforts to automate factories.

Schlumberger has a total of 43 major subsidiaries, most of which rely on science and technology. The jewel in Schlumberger's crown is the Wireline, which in 1981 generated 45 percent of the company's $6 billion in revenues and about 70 percent of its $1.2 billion in profits. Many of Schlumberger's subsidiaries rank at or near the top of their various industries. The investment banker Felix Rohatyn, who serves on the boards of eight major corporations, including Schlumberger, and is a close friend of Riboud's, says, "By the standard of profit margins, return on investment, compound growth rate, of remaining ahead of the state of the art technically and having an efficient management structure over the last 20 years—until the recent drastic change in the energy environment—Schlumberger might well have been the single best business in the world." Rohatyn's enthusiasm is shared by independent analysts at the major Wall Street brokerage firms, and their judgment has been reflected in research reports issued by, among others, Morgan Stanley, Merrill Lynch, Paine Webber, Wertheim, L. F. Rothschild, Unterberg, Towbin. An analysis issued by Barton M. Biggs, managing director of Morgan Stanley, in January of 1982 reads, "Here is this immense, superbly—almost artistically—managed company booming along with a 35 percent compound annual growth rate in earnings and 37 percent in dividends between 1975 and 1980. . . . Our analysis of earnings variability from growth trend shows Schlumberger as having the most consistent, high-growth track of any company in the 1,400-stock universe of our dividend discount model."

Even though Schlumberger is a competitive company devoted to ever-higher profits, over the years its executives have shown a predilection for the politics of the left. Paul Schlumberger urged his sons to share the profits of their company with employees. He financed his sons only on the condition that "the interest of scientific research take precedence over financial ones." Conrad was a pacifist and a socialist until Stalin's Russia disillusioned him. Rene Seydoux, the husband of Marcel's daughter Genevieve, who ran Schlumberger's European wireline operations, and to whom Riboud reported after Marcel's death in 1953, was an ardent and active supporter of the French Socialist Party. Jean de Menil, who supervised all South American operations in the period after World War II, supported various liberal causes in the United States. Along with his wife, Dominique, a daughter of Conrad Schlumberger, de Menil became a major financial contributor to Martin Luther King, Jr., and the American civil-rights movement. And in 1981 Jean Riboud, as an intimate of President Mitterrand, supported the Socialist government's proposed nationalization of 46 enterprises.

* * * * *

Riboud is a man of contrast. He is a hugely successful capitalist, with an annual salary of $700,000 and Schlumberger stock worth about $33 million, yet he calls himself a socialist. He loves business, yet most of his friends are from the worlds of art and politics. He was born into a French banking family in Lyons, the historical birthplace of the French ruling class, yet he says that one of his principal goals in life is to battle this class. He has deep roots in France, yet he considers himself an unofficial citizen of India and of the United States. He places a premium on loyalty and sentiment, yet he is a tough businessman who has unhesitatingly fired loyal executives and has had a hand in easing out four members of the Schlumberger family. He is charming yet distant. He is a strong and independent man, yet he has a history of "more or less falling in love"—in the words of his friend the writer Francoise Giroud—with leading French politicians of the left.

Even to many of his friends, Riboud is an enigma. They do not understand his success as a capitalist—in part because he does not speak of Schlumberger to them. "Jean Riboud impersonates a businessman who is trying to hide a certain poetry," Saul Steinberg says. "He is in some sort of Sydney Greenstreet business, as far as we see it—oil, Arabia. I say, 'What's this pussycat doing as director of this company? I can see the pussycat. But where is the crocodile?' Now, no pussycat becomes officer in charge of such a company, and I tell myself that in order to be good on the highest level of anything you need mysterious sources."

Few cities dominate nations the way Lyons once dominated France. A city of over half a million people in the center of France, Lyons was synonymous with the French business establishment. The Ribouds were Roman Catholic—the right religion—and comfortable. The family lived in an apartment in Lyons until 1929, when they moved to a spacious house in the suburb of Ecully. Summers were spent 55 miles north of Lyons, at La Carelle, an estate of 1,300 acres of farmland and wooded hills, which has been in the family since 1850. Like many members of the French establishment, Camille Riboud, Jean's father, attended L'Ecole des Sciences Politiques, in Paris, where his circle of friends included Georges Boris, who became a close associate of Pierre Mendes-France; Andre Istel, a future banker; Maurice Schlumberger, who became a banking partner of Istel's; and Jean Schlumberger, who became a writer of some distinction. Maurice and Jean Schlumberger were brothers of Conrad and Marcel. Jean Riboud says, "My father was an enlightened conservative. He was really part of the establishment and wanted to be part of the establishment, and yet he wanted to be entirely independent-minded—independent of the establishment." His days were devoted to commerce. At night, he read to his children: Homer, Euripides, Baudelaire, Verlaine, Rimbaud.

Camille's wife, Helene, grew up in Lyons, and spent her summers in the nearby town of Givors, where her father's family owned a bottling factory. Helene Riboud was taught to be a devout, unquestioning

Catholic, to obey her husband, to control her emotions, and to organize a good home. She "was not a silly woman," Antoine Riboud says, but she was "ordinary"—without "the sparkle of my father." Jean Riboud offers a different memory of Helene. "She was a lively, attractive, gay woman, without the culture of my father," he says. "But she was not an ordinary person." The qualities that Jean remembers most vividly are "an extraordinary dignity and an extraordinary sense of duty." Krishna Riboud remembers her mother-in-law, who died in 1957, as a woman of "great determination and great character," but she also says that Jean has a romanticized view of his father. "He feels that all his cultural background comes from his father," she says. "All the authority he has comes from the mother. I see more of the mother in him than the father."

In 1939, at the age of 53, Camille Riboud died of a heart attack, and Jean, who was then 19, became the de facto head of the family. "Jean is exactly the portrait, the figure of my father," Antoine Riboud says. "He has the same intellectual way of thinking as my father. To all the children, he was the second father."

In 1939, after graduating from L'Ecole des Sciences Politiques, he volunteered for the Army but was rejected, because, at 19, he was too young. The next year, though, he joined the Army as a tank officer, and when Germany invaded France he was sent into battle in the Loire Valley. He was captured in June of 1940, but he escaped. In the spring of 1941, he went to the Sorbonne to study law and economics and prepare for the Civil Service. He studied and lived for two years in occupied Paris, and during this time he kept in touch with the budding Resistance movement in Lyons, attending organizational meetings and slipping back and forth between occupied France and Vichy France.

In the summer of 1943, he and a fellow student, Yves Le Portz, were urged by others in the Resistance to join the Free French Army in North Africa. To get there, they decided to take a route that had been used by, among others, Georges Schlumberger, a son of Maurice: to Perpignan, in the south, by bicycle, and from there the 25 miles or so to Spain by kayak. On a moonless August night, Riboud and Le Portz hid their bicycles at the top of a cliff, put their kayak into the water, and paddled furiously, hoping to parallel the coastline just out of sight. But a storm came up, sending water crashing into their tiny craft and shoving them out into rough seas. Frantically, they struggled back toward the shore where the water was calmer, and then they made their way south, to a point where the Pyrenees plunged straight down into the Mediterranean. They spotted a cave and, leaving their kayak outside, crawled in to sleep. They were awakened a short while later by officers from a German patrol boat, who, after one look at the detailed maps of the coast of Spain the two were carrying, arrested them. The Germans took them to be interrogated by a colonel, who first saluted their bravery and then turned them over to the Gestapo in Perpignan. After two weeks of questioning, they were taken to the city of Compiegne, north of Paris, and in September they were among 1,200 prisoners shipped by train to Buchenwald.

When Riboud and Le Portz arrived at Buchenwald, experienced prisoners gave them some advice: The Gestapo will ask if you are able to do mechanical work. Say yes. "We had no idea of mechanics at all," recalls Le Portz, who is today chairman of the European Investment Bank. But they followed the advice, and were sent to an aircraft-construction plant near Buchenwald. Prisoners who said they were ignorant of mechanics were sent on to Dachau, the extermination camp. Buchenwald was brutal—particularly the long hours working outdoors in winter without a coat. In addition to the cold, the hard labor, and the Gestapo, prisoners of war had to contend with common criminals whom the Germans had rounded up and sent to the camps. "To divide us, they mixed ordinary criminals with members of the Resistance," Le Portz says. "There were as many conflicts among inmates as between inmates and guards. Unity among the prisoners was essential."

Riboud recalls that in many of the camps "some of the Christians and the Communists became forces of order." They helped their fellow-prisoners not to lose faith, and to accept discipline and solidarity. Riboud himself soon emerged as a leader at Buchenwald. "We didn't speak German," Le Portz says. "Yet a few months after entering the camp Jean was the official German interpreter for the prisoners—and he'd read German newspapers to them. Moreover, he was a man of extraordinary humor. He tried to make life as easy as possible for other prisoners. Jean managed to establish contact with the outside world and get information to the camp. He was not a passive man."

Of his years at Buchenwald, Riboud says, "I've seen the worst and the best of human beings, to an extent that I never thought could be as bad and as good, as ominous and as perfect." The experience contributed to a lifelong conviction that, in Riboud's words, "in the presence of death there are the ones who fight and the ones who give up, the ones who survive and the ones who do not." Antoine Riboud says that Buchenwald made his brother "more liberal" and also made him "very strong, very capable of resisting anything."

* * * * *

With the war behind him, Jean assumed that a job in his father's bank awaited him. A career in banking had been Camille Riboud's wish for him, and though Jean had no ambitions along those lines he decided to fall in with his father's plan. He recalls, "I went to see the man who was the head of the bank"—his father's partner—"and he said to me, 'There is no room in the bank.'" The partner also told Riboud that he had "no gift for banking." Unsure of what he wanted to do, he went to Paris to have an interview for a job in industry, and while he was there he also went to see Andre Istel, who had been a banking partner of Maurice Schlumberger. Istel, a French Jew, had fled to the United States during the war, and now he planned to open a New York banking office, to be called Andre Istel & Company. Among Istel's clients was the oil-field-service company Schlumberger.

Two months later, in September of 1946, Riboud opened Istel's New York office, working at a salary of $200 a month. "It was another planet," he says. "Europeans had absolutely nothing. I took all my belongings to America, and I remember that they were one pair of shoes and two shirts. That's all I had—that was everything." For a year, Riboud rented a furnished room on the East Side, and then, his salary having risen, he moved into a $125-a-month apartment on Sixty-third Street between Madison and Fifth Avenues. A number of art galleries were nearby, as was the Museum of Modern Art, which he particularly enjoyed. Again, as at Buchenwald, Riboud quickly learned the language being spoken around him.

As a young man, Riboud had become accustomed to meeting his father's literary friends, and he had read the classics; he had always cared about art and about politics; and now he shared the passions and interests of his new friends in the New York literary and artistic community.

* * * * *

Riboud did well at the bank. He came to know some conservative businessmen and formed friendships with several—notably Garrard Winston, an attorney whose bloodline stretched back to the early days of the American republic. But investment banking did not inspire Riboud the way politics did. His was a generation that had been dominated from its early years by political questions: by Fascism, the Spanish Civil War, Hitler, the Second World War, the Holocaust, the United Nations, and colonialism; and now by Senator Joseph McCarthy. "We had to choose," Riboud says. He wanted the left to remain united, to remain focused on traditional enemies, to help prevent the Cold War. When Riboud thought of Communists, he thought not of a Stalin Gulag but of Buchenwald, populated in part by Communists "who had convictions and integrity," and who had saved his life.

* * * * *

The Schlumberger family had been keeping an eye on Jean Riboud. Glowing reports arrived from Andre Istel and Maurice Schlumberger. The Schlumbergers had come to know Riboud directly, because a third of the investment bank's financial-advisory business was with their company or with the family itself. Riboud was invited to family dinners, and impressed other guests with his knowledge of politics, art, and literature. One day Marcel Schlumberger arrived at the house of his niece Anne in Ridgefield, Connecticut. She recalls that he seemed depressed. Schlumberger had always been a family company, and Mr. Marcel, as he was called, usually hired its engineers himself. But the company was growing rapidly—it now had offices not only in Paris but also in New York, Ridgefield, and Houston—and Marcel worried that it was becoming too successful, too bureaucratized, and would lose its sense of intimacy and fall into the hands of men without character. Anne listened to Marcel's lament, and after a while the talk turned to Jean Riboud. "You see him now and then," he said. "What do you think of this lad?"

In "The Schlumberger Adventure," a family memoir published in the United States in January of 1983, Anne (who, divorced from Henri Doll, had become Anne Gruner Schlumberger) writes that she replied, "I think he has a heart—a feeling for humanity, I guess I want to say. That's rare enough in someone committed to high finance. If you're thinking of taking him on, I'll be surprised if he disappoints you."

"Oh, I find him *sympathique,*" Marcel said. "We'll see." He paused, then added, "I wouldn't know how to use him. Finance is not our business, and I don't believe in it."

Marcel arranged to have lunch with Riboud in Paris in July of 1950. Jean and Krishna had had a son, Christophe, that year, and had talked often of starting a new life in France. Riboud felt unfulfilled as an investment banker. He was restless in America, and was concerned that he was losing touch with France. Moreover, he had never been to India; he wanted to go there, and then settle in Paris and maybe open a bookstore. Earlier that year, he had notified Andre Istel that he planned to leave the banking business and go to India for six months. Now, when Marcel learned of these plans, he offered Riboud an undefined position with Schlumberger. "I haven't the foggiest idea what you'll do," he said at lunch. He offered to pay Riboud $500 a month—$2,500 a month less than he was then making. He proposed to send him to Houston as an assistant to his son, Pierre, but Riboud, because of his Indian-born wife, preferred not to live in the South. Still, he was intrigued by Schlumberger and by the sense of adventure that the oil business promised. He agreed to go to work for the company, but on two conditions: he must first visit India, and he must work at Schlumberger's Paris office. Marcel accepted his terms.

Upon returning to France in May of 1951 Riboud went to work at Schlumberger. He worked on finances, on merging what had become four independent Schlumberger companies into one, but mostly he listened. "For the first year, I really did nothing except listen to Marcel," he says. "Marcel used him as a gadfly," says Paul Lepercq, who is also from Lyons and was recruited by Riboud as his replacement at the New York bank; today Lepercq is the second-longest-serving member of the Schlumberger board of directors. Riboud watched Marcel—the "adapter," as Paul Schlumberger called him—spend hours asking penetrating questions, or sit through meetings without saying a word, his eyes unreadable under thick eyebrows, his expression blank. Marcel focused on personnel decisions, which, he told Riboud, were the most important decisions an executive had to make. Even though Marcel was approaching 70, he would cross the ocean to attend meetings of engineers and managers. William Gillingham, a British-born engineer who had been hired by Marcel in 1934 and had become the head of Schlumberger's oil-field-service operations, recalls saying, "Mr. Marcel, you must enjoy coming over here and hearing these technical papers," and that Marcel glared at him and said, "Mr. Gillingham, I don't come here to hear these papers. I can read them in my office. I come here to see what kind of people are running *my* company."

* * * * *

Despite his flaws, Marcel communicated to Riboud his almost religious devotion to Schlumberger. As with other corporate pioneers—Thomas J. Watson of IBM, A. P. Giannini of the Bank of America, Henry Ford—this devotion became a legend. Riboud speaks of an incident that took place in 1940, when the Germans had invaded Belgium and were poised to overwhelm France. Erle P. Halliburton, the head of the Halliburton Oil Well Cementing Company, which was Schlumberger's chief oil-field-service rival, paid a visit to Marcel. "Everybody knew that France was going to be defeated, that Paris would be totally cut off from Houston, and that Houston wouldn't survive by itself, without Paris," Riboud says. Halliburton offered to buy Schlumberger for $10 million. Marcel made no reply but slowly rose from his chair and beckoned Halliburton to follow him. They walked silently to the elevator, where Marcel thanked his visitor and said goodbye. Another executive might have hesitated, Riboud says. Why didn't Marcel? "Because there are some questions you never discuss," he says. "If somebody were to come and ask you to sell your wife, you wouldn't hesitate, would you?" Riboud draws a lesson from this tale: Marcel Schlumberger was never swayed by passing storms, because he remained anchored to a set of beliefs. "The first was: think for yourself," Riboud says. "Whatever is happening at the moment, try to think for yourself." In the summer of 1953, at the age of 69, Marcel died of heart failure.

* * * * *

Although Marcel's corporate heirs shared his sense of the company's special mission, his death robbed Schlumberger of its central authority. Feuds surfaced among the branches of the Schlumberger family. No one emerged as chief operating officer to replace Marcel. Instead, the company was divided into four fiefdoms, each ruled by a family member. The technical side of the business was the domain of Henri Doll. But Doll was a scientist, not a corporate manager; although he ranked first in seniority when Marcel died, he chose not to assume the leadership of the company.

* * * * *

Pierre Schlumberger, the only son of Marcel—and the only son of either founder—ruled the most profitable division: Schlumberger's North American wireline operations. Schlumberger came out of the war a weakened company, with its executives scattered. In 1946 Pierre set up an organization in Houston that would keep pace with the growing American oil market. Like his father, Pierre was a man of simple convictions. With his father gone, he came to believe that if Schlumberger was to grow it had to become a public company rather than remaining a family one, and that it had to make its financial operations more professional—to codify a set of rules rather than follow the whims of one man. Pierre had ambitious plans, but the other family members resisted them.

A third sector—Schlumberger's wireline operations in South America and the Middle East—was run from Houston by Jean de Menil, the husband of Conrad's daughter Dominique. For eight years after his marriage, de Menil, a Paris banker, resisted Marcel's importunings to join the company, but in 1939 he did, and became responsible for Schlumberger's financial structure. During the war de Menil successfully schemed with Marcel to free the company from potential Nazi control by shifting its base of operations from France to Trinidad. And after the war de Menil played a large part in making Schlumberger a truly international corporation by requiring that all business be conducted in English and that the dollar be the common currency, as is now customary in the oil business. Like Conrad Schlumberger, de Menil was an idealist, and lent his financial support to political and artistic movements that challenged the status quo. And, also like Conrad, he believed that Schlumberger's ability to help others find oil was a natural extension of his political beliefs. "You were bringing to human frontiers technology that helped people," says his son George de Menil, who is a professor of economics. "During the war, it contributed something crucial to the war effort. After the war, it contributed something crucial to the growth of the world economy."

Schlumberger's European operations—the fourth fiefdom—were run by Marcel's son-in-law Rene Seydoux. Like de Menil, he had intense political convictions, and he became a supporter of the French Socialist Party. During the war he was captured by the Germans and sent to a prisoner-of-war camp. After the war he returned to Schlumberger and was made head of its Paris office. Among those who worked for him following Marcel's death was Jean Riboud, who admired his gentle nature. Through Seydoux, Riboud came to know many Socialist Party leaders. Of the four family members, a person who knew them well says, "The others were stronger personalities in a sense, but Rene Seydoux was always the cement, trying to hold things together."

The cement did not adhere. For three years after Marcel Schlumberger's death, the company remained divided into four parts. Relations among the family members were amicable, professional, often affectionate. The four parts were united in their devotion to Schlumberger and its mission, but there was no central planning and coordination. Riboud and other executives disliked this arrangement and campaigned to restructure the corporation. Finally, in 1956, a new parent company, Schlumberger, Ltd., was created to unify operations. Pierre Schlumberger became president; Henri Doll was elected chairman of the board. The company was incorporated on the island of Curacao, in the Netherlands Antilles, which was then becoming one of the world's major tax havens.

In 1959, however, Pierre's wife died, and over the next 18 months Pierre stayed at home most days. When he did come to the office, he was irritable and autocratic. "Pierre was very fragile and lost his balance," observes his cousin.

The branches of the Schlumberger family disagreed about many things, but not about the value of Riboud. Everyone saw in him familiar qualities. In early May of 1965 the family asked Riboud to replace Pierre Schlumberger. Riboud says that he immediately resigned, declaring, "I will not replace Pierre, because I owe too much friendship to him. The only decent thing for me to do is to resign." The family prevailed on Pierre to resign first, and then asked Riboud to become president and chief executive officer of Schlumberger. He did so on May 13, 1965.

For 18 years Riboud has ruled Schlumberger, in the words of one company executive, "like an absolute constitutional monarch." Felix Rohatyn says, "He is the absolute, unquestioned boss in the company. His authority is as absolute as that of any chief executive I've seen." When Riboud speaks of Schlumberger, he often does so in the first person singular. Explaining, for example, Schlumberger's 1979 acquisition of the Fairchild Camera & Instrument Corporation, he says, "It seemed to *me*. . . ." Although he is not a Schlumberger, his authority within the family is comparable to that of Conrad or Marcel. "He has the unanimity of the family behind him," according to Dominique de Menil, who is now 75 and is a close friend of Riboud. Since the Schlumberger family owns about a fourth of the company's stock, the support of the family is significant. Still, because Schlumberger has generated consistently higher profits under his reign, because he has succeeded in completing the transformation of a family enterprise into a public company, because he is acclaimed on Wall Street, and because he has at times ruthlessly asserted his authority, Riboud has assured his independence.

The only overt challenge to Riboud's reign has come from Jerome Seydoux. From the time Jerome was a little boy, Marcel Schlumberger had urged his grandson to become an engineer. By the end of the 60s he had caught the attention of Riboud. In 1969 Jerome's father, Rene, retired from the board of directors, and Riboud invited Jerome to join it. He hailed the younger Seydoux as one of the brightest men of his generation, valued his advice, and took him into his counsel, as Marcel Schlumberger had done with Riboud.

In 1969 while Seydoux was vacationing in the South of France, Riboud phoned and asked to meet him on a matter of urgency. Seydoux still remembers the date of the meeting—the first day of May. Riboud offered Seydoux a job with Schlumberger. Some months later Schlumberger acquired the Compagnie des Compteurs, a French manufacturer of electric meters and other instruments, and Riboud offered Seydoux the job of president. The company had been losing money, but Riboud believed that it could become profitable. Riboud remembers telling Seydoux that if he succeeded with the new acquisition, he would have "a big future." Seydoux remembers Riboud's saying that he would become president of Schlumberger. In any case, Seydoux did succeed, transforming the company into a profitable operation that is now known as Measurement & Control–Europe. Five years later, in September of 1975, Riboud appointed Seydoux president of Schlumberger, retaining the position of chief executive officer and chairman of the board. Seydoux remained president for just 18 weeks. His memory of his tenure remains vivid. Now president of Cargeurs S.A., a Paris transportation company, Seydoux recently told a visitor to his office, "I always worked very well with Riboud. We talked easily and communicated well. Yet a few days after I became president he wasn't happy. It lasted four and one half months, but I really think it lasted only a week. Very soon after I became president, we stopped communicating."

In the opinion of people who knew him then, Seydoux began acting as if he were the chief executive—as if the family dynasty had been restored. When he moved into his new office, one of his first acts was to hang on the wall over his desk a picture of his grandfather, Marcel Schlumberger. Riboud thought that Seydoux was acting like someone who believed that his station was inherited, and not earned. Riboud's unease was intensified by complaints from executives who had been instructed to report to Seydoux. Jerome was too officious, too brusque, they protested. William Gillingham says that Jerome lacked "the human touch." Some executives were doubtless unhappy that they no longer reported directly to Riboud, and Riboud himself was unhappy, because he had discovered that at the age of 55 he did not want to step aside.

Riboud, having decided to dismiss Seydoux, carefully met with or telephoned every other member of the board—there were 16 members—and said that there was not room for two corporate heads at Schlumberger and that he planned to dismiss Seydoux. With the board's approval, he visited and won the concurrence of five of the six branches of the Schlumberger family. And then one winter morning he summoned Seydoux to his New York apartment at the Carlton House on Madison Avenue. In his soft, polite way, Riboud said that he was unhappy with the current arrangement and asked Seydoux to leave.

Riboud, as he demonstrated with Seydoux, is not timid about firing people. "Jean has less difficulty facing up to tough personnel decisions than any other executive I know. Most executives dread it," Felix Rohatyn says. Carl Buchholz, an American who started as an engineer, was once vice president of personnel and is now president of The Analysts, says, "One of my predecessors sat outside Riboud's office all day, and Riboud wouldn't talk to him. If someone was blowing hot air in my office, I'd say, 'Get the hell out of here!' If you're blowing hot air around Riboud, he'll smile and put his arm around you and walk you to the door and make you feel good—and you'll never get in there again."

A man who sulks after losing at golf or at gin rummy—something that Riboud does—is capable of holding grudges. "When something goes wrong, it's finished," says Jeanine Bourhis, Riboud's secretary in Paris for the past 13 years. "Jerome Seydoux was family. He liked Jerome very much, too. And all of a sudden—*phiff!*"

* * * * *

"Riboud handles personnel matters as if no personalities were involved," says Benno Schmidt, who is a managing partner of J. H. Whitney & Company and was a member of Schlumberger's board from 1973 to 1982. "If he considers you the wrong man, he'll remove you in five seconds. He's invariably generous as far as the personal welfare of the person is concerned, but he feels no obligation to keep people in jobs they're not doing. It's matter-of-fact." Several months after making those remarks, Schmidt himself felt the cold side of Riboud. Riboud visited Schmidt in his office on Fifth Avenue and told him that after prolonged deliberation he had decided that Schmidt and three other board members should retire. (Board members who were not also employees of the company received $24,000 annually for their services and $9,000 more if they served on the executive committee, the audit committee, or the finance committee.) Riboud did not ask whether Schmidt, a sometime golfing partner and a member of the Schlumberger executive committee, wanted to step aside. He simply told Schmidt politely that he must go.

* * * * *

Whatever personal pain Riboud feels is soothed by the conviction that loyalty to the company outweighs personal loyalties. He believes that he is simply doing his duty. "If you want to be St. Francis of Assisi, you should not head a public company," he says.

At the beginning of 1982, 70 percent of the world's active oil-drilling rigs outside the Soviet bloc were in the United States and Canada. Because of the current oil glut, the number of active drilling rigs in North America fell from 4,700 in January of 1982 to 1,990 in March of 1983, but that was still more than the 1,200 active rigs operating in the rest of the non-Communist world. The United States produces more barrels of oil daily (about 8.6 million) than Saudi Arabia (about 4.6 million). And Schlumberger's Wireline division generates 45 percent of the corporation's revenues and an estimated 70 percent of its net profits. It is therefore not surprising that this division occupies much of Riboud's time.

On a recent Friday afternoon Riboud, accompanied by Andre Misk, a former field engineer who is a vice president and the director of communications, went to Teterboro Airport in New Jersey and boarded one of six jet airplanes belonging to the company for a flight to Houston.

On Monday morning at 9 o'clock Riboud went to the office of Ian Strecker, who has been in charge of Schlumberger's wireline, engineering, and manufacturing operations in North America since the beginning of 1982. Strecker is a burly, gregarious man of 43 whose normal work outfit consists of cowboy boots, an open-necked sports shirt, and slacks. He joined Schlumberger 21 years ago in England, where he was born, and has since held 20 jobs in 18 different locations. Part of Riboud's purpose in meeting with Strecker was to get a feel for him and other employees in order to gauge, in Marcel Schlumberger's words, "what kind of people are running *my* company." One of Riboud's preoccupations is that Schlumberger will lose its drive as a company and grow complacent—a concern he had discussed on the plane to Houston. "Any business, any society has a built-in force to be conservative," he said. "The whole nature of human society is to be conservative. If you want to innovate, to change an enterprise or a society, it takes people willing to do what's not expected. The basic vision I have, and what I'm trying to do at Schlumberger, is no different from what I think should be done in French or American society." In other words, sow doubt. Rotate people. Don't measure just the profits in a given division—measure the man in charge, too, and his enthusiasm for change. Strecker's predecessor, Roy Shourd, learned at first hand just what Riboud means. Shourd headed the North American Wireline division from 1977 through 1981, and in those years its profits rose an average of 30 percent annually. But Riboud worried that Shourd was growing complacent with success, that he was surrounding himself with an inbred group of executives and becoming too clubby with the Houston oil establishment, so late in 1981 he suddenly shifted Shourd to New York and a staff job. (Typically, one year later, in another surprising move, Riboud elevated Shourd to the position of executive vice president for drilling and production services. Riboud was satisfied that Shourd's year in exile had reignited his competitive spirit.)

This visit to Houston allowed Riboud to take the measure of Strecker, whom he did not know well. Strecker's office is in a three-story, red brick building overlooking Houston's Gulf Freeway. Strecker and Riboud sat down at an oval cherrywood conference table, and then Riboud, who had arrived with no reports or notes, silently inspected his fingernails, formed his long fingers into a steeple on which he rested his chin, and began the meeting. He asked how Strecker's wife, Elaine, had adjusted to Houston, how their two sons, who had remained in school in England, were getting on, how the Streckers had enjoyed a recent visit to England. Before long, the meeting got around to specific employees. Riboud made detailed comments on them, giving not only his impression of their abilities but also his impression of how well their abilities were matched to their jobs. He emphasized that final judgments on all employees were Strecker's to make. After Riboud had finished with the personnel matters, he asked Strecker if he had been spending much time in the field—among 1,800 field engineers whom Schlumberger employed in North America.

"I feel that my biggest challenge here in the next couple of years is engineering," Strecker replied, referring to engineering research. "So I'm spending most of my time there now." He said that the next day he would join all the engineering department heads for a three-day retreat in California, at which they would evaluate priorities and challenges. Riboud suggested that the engineers might want to consider pushing the manufacturing section of Schlumberger Well Services, in Houston, which produces 60 percent of the equipment used by the Schlumberger field engineers. Even though this is more than the company's other manufacturing plant, in Clamart, France, produces, Riboud is not satisfied. He wants Schlumberger to become totally self-sufficient—to farm out less work to such companies as Grumman and International Harvester, which makes the frames for Schlumberger's trucks.

There was a long silence. Riboud sat inspecting the fingers of one hand, and finally Strecker asked if Riboud had any further questions.

"I've got a major concern about what happens to your business in the next few years," Riboud said. He then noted that Strecker's monthly report for January, which he had received in New York, revealed that North American logging operations were 11 percent below plan and that operations in completed wells—so-called cased-hole explorations—were 5 percent below plan. "The January report blames the weather," he said. "But then I read and see that the biggest decline was in log interpretation, and you can't blame the weather for that." Riboud said he was confident that the world would remain dependent on oil for at least 50 years longer, but he added that two unknowns threatened oil exploration—and thus Schlumberger revenues—in the immediate future. One was the faltering American economy. The other was a decline in the price of oil.

Even in a recession, Strecker said, independent oil drillers can earn enough to continue searching for oil as long as the price is at least $30 a barrel. He observed that after President Carter began to decontrol the price of oil in 1979, the number of oil rigs in North America climbed from 2,500 to 4,750 between 1979 and 1981. "Decontrol caused that rapid growth," Strecker said. But now, with the real price of oil declining, with the economy in recession, and with abundant, if perhaps temporary, oil surpluses, the number of rigs was back down to just under 2,500. Strecker said the natural-gas picture was totally different, with supplies plentiful but the price "probably too high."

"It's funny—the gas manufacturers are lobbying in Washington today against decontrol of all gas prices," Riboud said.

If gas should be fully decontrolled, Strecker said, gas producers would not be able to sell all their supplies in this sluggish economy, and the price should drop. (It has not yet done so.) With lower prices, gas producers would concentrate on shallow-well drilling, which was less expensive. Deep-well drilling would become prohibitively expensive, just as it was for independent oil prospectors whenever the price dipped below about $30 a barrel.

Riboud and Strecker, their session over, walked to the office of Robert Peebler, the North American Wireline's vice president of finance, to review the division's business projections for February. Surveying the expected rig counts of Schlumberger and of its competitors, Riboud seized on the figure of 90 rigs credited to competitors off the Gulf Coast. "I'm always surprised by how many offshore rigs our competitors have," he said. Peebler replied that competitors had only 10 percent of the offshore market, but this did not seem to appease Riboud; he asked Peebler to forward an analysis of the situation to his New York office. Riboud's message was clear: Only total victory counts. Schlumberger could lose its edge; competitors with more to prove could be hungrier and more aggressive. Already, Wall Street analysts who examined oil-field-service companies had reported that Dresser Industries' Atlas Oilfield Services Group, a worldwide competitor, was leading in the development of the Carbon/Oxygen log and the Spectralog—two advanced logging tools. Gearhart Industries, which was bidding for a larger share of the American market, claimed to have hired 300 graduate engineers in 1981—an increase of 100 percent over 1980. (Because of the drop-off in drilling and the recession, the number fell to 140 in 1982.) Schlumberger remains far ahead of its competitors, but to stay there, Riboud feels, it must continue to challenge its employees.

After Riboud's meeting with Peebler came a slide presentation by engineers and scientists, who talked about such things as a "neutron porosity tool," a "Gamma Spectroscopy Tool," the "radial geometric factor," and the "finite element code." The advanced technology that such arcane terminology represents is perhaps the major reason that Schlumberger stays ahead of its competitors—who concede that Schlumberger's tools are generally more advanced than theirs. And since Schlumberger spends $125 million annually on wireline research—a sum greater than the profits of any wireline competitor—its lead will be difficult to overcome. Much of the research is designed to perfect drilling and logging tools that help identify hard-to-reach oil in already drilled wells and help extract it. This residual oil is expensive to recover, and oil companies claim that as long as the price per barrel stays below $30 pursuing it is not profitable. But if the price rises above $30, and if supplies become scarce (they are now abundant), new opportunities await the oil companies and Schlumberger. An analysis made by Philip K. Meyer, a vice president with the Wall Street firm F. Eberstadt & Company, in April of 1981 explains why: "We have found in the United States roughly 450 billion barrels of original-oil-in-place of which only some 100 billion barrels have been produced to date. This means we know the location of 350 billion barrels of remaining (residual)-oil-in-place. . . . If only a third of this residual-oil-in-place were to economically respond to tertiary recovery, over 100 billion barrels would be added to U.S. reserves."

Riboud listened intently to the engineers and scientists, and when the presentation was over, he said, politely, "I have read all this. You are just preaching motherhood. Where are the problems?"

Not long after the engineering presentation, Riboud had lunch in the executive dining room with three dozen section heads, most of them in their late 20s or early 30s. A number of them said that at Schlumberger they didn't feel isolated in their offices or laboratories, as they had at other places they had worked, and that they weren't dependent on memorandums or rumors to gauge the reactions of their superiors.

"I was at Bell Labs for four years, and I don't think I ever met the vice president of research," said Dennis O'Neill, who was head of the informatics section and had been with Schlumberger for five years. "Here within six months I was making presentations to the executive vice president of the Wireline." James Hall, who had been employed by Schlumberger for 10 years, said he had had the same experience. "It's a lot more personal at Schlumberger," he said. With a Ph.D. in nuclear physics from Iowa State University and two years of advanced doctoral work at the Swiss Federal Institute of Technology in Zurich, Hall was the head of the engineering-physics section. While he was completing his studies, he worked for Mobil Oil. "You felt more isolated there, because contact with management was much less," he said of that experience. "You had contact just with your bosses. You didn't feel the direct contact with your managers you have here. It tends to build more of a team spirit when not only your boss comes to talk to you about a project but several levels of command above as well. To me, in engineering that's what the Schlumberger spirit is. The individual design engineer feels that the responsibility of the company is placed on him."

In Riboud's field visits, time is often set aside for questions from employees like Hall. During the lunch in Houston, the first question was from a young engineer-researcher, who asked for Riboud's "view of the non-wireline" part of the Schlumberger empire.

"You are an engineer," Riboud said. "Be a little more precise in your question." Riboud did not wait for the young man to rephrase the question. He apparently sensed that, like many wireline employees, the young man was concerned about Schlumberger's purchase, for $425 million, of the Fairchild Camera & Instrument Corporation—a giant semiconductor company, which lost $30 million the second year after the purchase. Now Riboud went on, "The question is really: When we have this little jewel of a wireline business, why do we bother à la Fairchild and so forth? It's really a philosophical problem. Why does the company have to grow, and in which direction? I'm not saying I'm right, but I feel two things—two dangers. One danger is of becoming a conglomerate and trying to do everything. The other danger is of just staying a wireline company. I don't think we could have maintained the profit margin we had and the motivation of our people if we'd done that. The real problem in any organization is to have new challenges, new motivations."

Lunch was followed by a session with department heads from the manufacturing division, which employed 950 people and produced $400 million worth of field equipment annually. The heads of the materials-management and purchasing sections presented Riboud with flow charts and graphs showing a steady rise in their productivity and spoke in the self-assured language of American business schools. Riboud's eyes narrowed. He listened politely but impatiently; finally he leaned forward with his elbows on the conference table and explained why the company could not measure productivity by price or sales alone. "Since we are selling equipment to ourselves, it is hard to measure," he said. There was no competition over price or product or speed of production, he said, and the charts were therefore relatively worthless.

Later that afternoon Riboud met with the 27 executives and department heads who supervise the North American Wireline division. Many of them also inquired about the acquisition of Fairchild and about Schlumberger's stock. And they asked why Schlumberger had organized a division in the Far East much like the one in Houston. Japan and the rest of the Far East, Riboud repeated, are the frontier of the 80s, as Houston was in the late 40s and 50s. There are vast reserves of oil in China. The Japanese have moved ahead of the West in consumer electronics and office automation; they are threatening to move ahead in the development of computers, semiconductors, and genetic engineering. Singapore, Hong Kong, South Korea, Taiwan, and Japan manufacture goods more cheaply and more efficiently than the West does. If Schlumberger does not feel the threat of competition in North America or the Middle East, then it will feel it from the Far East. Schlumberger has been so successful for so long, he said, that it risks losing its "intellectual humility." He added, "We have the King Kong attitude."

Riboud toured the center and then went to the company cafeteria, where he had coffee with several dozen employees. Gene Pohoriles, the general manager of this unit, was a veteran Schlumberger engineer and, like many old-timers, wore in his lapel a gold Schlumberger pin with stars that symbolize the number of years he had served the company. Pohoriles introduced Riboud to the employees and then asked the first question: Why did Schlumberger dilute the value of its stock by buying Fairchild?

"Let me be blunt about it," Riboud answered. "What people in the Wireline are asking is: Why did Riboud screw up the Schlumberger stock by purchasing Fairchild?"

"Close," Pohoriles said.

Fairchild was a necessary acquisition, Riboud told him. "I felt strongly that 20 years down the road we had to have a semiconductor capacity." Schlumberger's basic business, he went on, is information, not oil, and what the Wireline does is provide information to oil companies to help them make accurate decisions. The next generation of wireline and meter equipment, he said, will be more dependent on tiny microprocessors and semiconductors.

* * * * *

Riboud's reaction to Pohoriles—admiring his courage while excusing what Riboud thought was an ignorant question—hinted at Riboud's style of management at Schlumberger. On several occasions he has said that the company's goals should be "to strive for perfection." To this end, he searches for fighters, for independent-minded people who don't, in his words, "float like a cork." In 1974 when he appointed Carl Buchholz his vice president of personnel, it was largely because Buchholz was not afraid to speak out. Riboud recalled first seeing Buchholz at a Schlumberger management conference near Geneva. "All the people were reciting the Mass, and suddenly Buchholz said, 'You're full of it!' I said, 'This is a fellow who speaks his mind.'" The subject under discussion at the conference, Buchholz later recalled, was the development of managers. The executives in attendance rose, one after another, to congratulate themselves on their success, and finally Buchholz stood up and said that in fact the executives were not successfully developing managers at all. A debate ensued, and Riboud sided with Buchholz. Afterward, Riboud made a point of getting to know him, and not long after the conference Buchholz, who had been assistant vice president of operations for Schlumberger Well Services, in Houston, was promoted to vice president of personnel and transferred from Houston to New York, where he quickly developed a reputation as an in-house critic.

* * * * *

Of all the people who have surrounded Riboud at Schlumberger over the years, probably none has been closer than Claude Baks, who was hired by Marcel Schlumberger as an engineer in 1946 and left the company only in the fall of 1982. An enigmatic man with a blunt manner, Baks had no official duties, but he could enter any meeting uninvited and he reported only to Riboud. He was born in 1917 in Latvia. His parents were Jewish, and with the outbreak of the Second World War he joined the Free French Army, fighting in North Africa and Europe. On assignment for the company in Venezuela some years after he was hired, Baks met Krishna and Jean Riboud, who were traveling there. When he returned to Paris on holiday, he looked up the Ribouds and became close to them and their son, Christophe. Riboud, who was then general manager of Schlumberger's European operations, had a hand in getting Baks transferred from Venezuela to Paris, where he was given a staff job. Admiring Baks's independence, Riboud asked him to become his adviser. At this time, Riboud, with Henri Langlois, was raising money to finance a 12-hour film, directed by Roberto Rossellini, about the history of the world. (They raised $500,000, including $100,000 from Schlumberger.) Baks shared Riboud's interest in film, and worked closely with both Langlois and Rossellini on Riboud's behalf. Baks had no family of his own, and the Ribouds in effect became his family.

Riboud and Baks were an unlikely pair. Riboud is a man of delicate appearance and subdued manner. Baks has bushy black eyebrows, a stubbly black beard, and a bulbous nose; he is missing a few front teeth. He has a deep, raspy voice, which some find intimidating, and he is usually wearing a dirty raincoat and a baggy sports jacket and baggy pants. His office, a cubicle on the fourth floor of Schlumberger's Paris headquarters, was just two doors from Riboud's. He kept the blinds closed and would not open the windows, and visitors seldom stayed long. The walls were bare, the desk top was clear, and besides the desk the only furniture was two chairs and three metal file cabinets. Yet fellow-employees went to Baks's office to try out ideas, to get clues to Riboud's thinking, to learn something of the company's history, to ingratiate themselves with Baks.

In trying to explain the role that Baks played, Riboud has said, "His main contribution to Schlumberger has been to prevent Schlumberger from becoming an establishment." He went on, "He has never had a title in 35 years. He has never had a secretary. He has never written a letter. He has no responsibilities. Schlumberger is not a bank where everyone has to have a niche. Over the years he's had more purpose than 90 percent of the people I know. He forces people to think." What Baks helped do was keep alive, under chairman Riboud, a sort of permanent "cultural revolution" at Schlumberger.

* * * * *

"Generally, after a while people repeat themselves," observes Michel Vaillaud, who until December of 1982 was one of two Schlumberger executive vice presidents for operations, his sphere being all oil-field services. "You know what they will ask you. With him, you never feel safe. Never." Vaillaud, who is 51 years old, is a lean, regal-looking man. When he met Riboud in 1973 he was a career civil servant. He had graduated first in his class from L'Ecole Polytechnique, which Conrad Schlumberger attended and which is acknowledged to be the best scientific school in France. He then received an advanced degree from mining and petroleum schools and, entering the Civil Service, rose rapidly in the French Ministry of Industry. When Riboud and Vaillaud met, Vaillaud was the Ministry's director for oil and gas. Some weeks later, Vaillaud recalls, Riboud offered him a position at Schlumberger. Although Vaillaud's training and experience were in petroleum, Riboud asked him to move to New York and become vice president of Schlumberger's electronics division. Vaillaud spoke little English, and he felt unsure of himself in electronics, but he accepted the offer.

Two months after Vaillaud took the job, Riboud called and asked to spend the day with him in New York. Vaillaud remembers feeling that he gave inadequate answers to persistent questions from Riboud. "I came back and told my wife, 'We should pack—I'm going to be fired.' Then I heard nothing the next day, or the next." At the time, Vaillaud did not understand that his uncertain technical answers to Riboud's questions were secondary. Riboud was taking his measure as a man, not as a technocrat. Computers could give out data; Riboud was searching for character. Two years later, Vaillaud returned to France as president of the Compagnie des Compteurs. Then in 1981, when Riboud decided to divide Schlumberger into two basic parts—the Oilfield Services and Measurement, Control & Components—Vaillaud and most Schlumberger executives expected him to make Vaillaud the head of the electronics division and Roland Genin, who had been an executive vice president and manager of Drilling and Production Services, the head of the oil-field division. These appointments would have had a certain logic to them, for Vaillaud had mastered electronics and Genin had spent his career in the oil-field division, beginning in 1950 when he joined Schlumberger as a field engineer. Riboud did just the opposite: Vaillaud became the head of the oil-field division, Genin the head of the electronics division. Riboud picked the less experienced man for each job, because, he says, each would bring a "totally different view," a "fresh imagination" to his new task. Riboud had taken a similar unexpected step a year earlier when he chose Thomas Roberts, a West Point graduate who had become the vice president of finance, to be the new president of Fairchild. Roberts had asked him why, and Riboud had answered, "I like to shake the tree."

If an eagerness to shake the tree is one of Riboud's most prominent management traits, another one—allied to it—is, obviously, his preoccupation with personnel matters. As his meetings in Houston showed, he is familiar with people at many levels of the organization. Instead of closeting himself with a few top executives, he meets with large groups of employees. The vice president of personnel at Schlumberger—the job is now held by Arthur W. Alexander—reports to the president, not to an executive vice president, as is often the case at other companies. "Riboud spends more time on people and people problems, in contrast to business and business problems, than any other chief executive I've ever seen," says Benno Schmidt. "I think the thing he's most concerned with in running this vast business is coming as near as possible to having exactly the right man in the right place all the time. Most people who run a company are much more interested in business, new products, research—all that."

When it comes to evaluating individuals, Riboud can be quite blunt. Once a year he meets with each of his top executives to offer an evaluation of their performance. Carl Buchholz remembers one of his evaluations: "He said, 'Let's talk about the Buchholz problem.' He talked about my relations with other people and how I ought to improve them. He talked about what he wanted done that wasn't being done. He was quite specific."

Like his predecessors, Riboud wants people at Schlumberger to have a feeling of independence. Day-to-day decisions are left to those in the field. Riboud's job, as he sees it, is primarily to think 5, 10, 20 years ahead, and to set the basic direction of the company. On September 30, 1977, at a celebration of the 50th anniversary of Schlumberger's first log, he remarked, "I should say that the most important thing I learned from Marcel Schlumberger was to have an independent mind—to think for oneself, to analyze by oneself, not to follow fashions, not to think like everyone else, not to seek honor or decorations, not to become part of the establishment." On another occasion, he said, "When you fly through turbulence, you fasten your seat belt. The only seat belt I know in business turbulence is to determine for oneself a few convictions, a few guidelines, and stick by them."

Riboud the businessman puzzles many of his nonbusiness friends. For years, Henri Cartier-Bresson has wondered why Riboud worked in a corporation instead of plunging full time into art or politics. Cartier-Bresson—a shy man with pale blue eyes, gold-framed eyeglasses, and close-cropped white hair—recalls asking Riboud, "What are you doing there? You're not a scientist. You have no passion for making money," and that he replied, "I'm a corkscrew."

"It means he knows how a bottle must be opened—delicately and firmly," Cartier-Bresson says.

* * * * *

Riboud sees his work at Schlumberger as an extension of his political views. "Running a company is like politics," he says. "You are always balancing interests and personalities and trying to keep people motivated." On being asked how he would like to be characterized as an executive, he replied, "I would like it to be said that I'm bringing about in my professional life what I'm trying to bring about with myself—it's one and the same thing." Like Marcel and Conrad Schlumberger, the two brothers who founded the company in 1926, Riboud thinks of the company as an extension of personal values—humility, loyalty, preserving faith in an idea, serving people, being trusting, being open-minded to different cultures, being ambitious and competitive and yet mindful of tradition. The key in a corporation or in government, Riboud says, is "motivating people" and forging a consensus. "We are no longer in a society where the head of a corporation can just give orders," he says. People need to believe in something larger than themselves. To be successful, he thinks, a corporation must learn from the Japanese that "we have the responsibility that religion used to have." A good company must not be just a slave to profits; it must strive to perform a service and to beat its competitors. But more, he feels, it must measure itself against a higher standard, seeking perfection.

There is another way in which Schlumberger is an extension of Riboud's political philosophy—in its international character. Riboud says that with the possible exception of the oil company Royal Dutch/Shell, Schlumberger is "the only truly multinational company that I know of." Schlumberger has long since ceased to have a single national identity. "If I have one purpose today," Riboud says, "it is to expand the concept of merging together into one enterprise Europeans, Americans, and citizens of the Third World; to bring in Asians, Africans, and Latin Americans so they feel at home with their own culture, their own religion, and yet feel that Schlumberger is their family."

* * * * *

"I think politics is a contradiction in Riboud," says Bernard Alpaerts, who began his career with Schlumberger 30 years ago as an engineer and retired this year as executive vice president of the company's Measurement & Control operations worldwide. "Politics is far removed from the management of this company. Schlumberger is almost a company without a nation. Riboud knows very well that most of his managers don't have the same political opinions he has. And, honestly, he doesn't mind. Sometimes you don't recognize in his business decisions the political opinions he has." The investment banker Felix Rohatyn says, "Riboud is complicated. There is this mixture in the man of being the hard-headed manager of a huge company that is as intensely capitalistic as any organization I know, and at the same time being clearly involved with the Socialist government of France."

This is one of several contradictions in Riboud. He is, for example, a loyal family man—devoted to his wife, to his son and daughter-in-law and their three children, yet he has had sometimes stormy relationships with his brothers and sisters. He takes pride in being open-minded and a foe of bigotry, yet Christophe Riboud says that his father is "one of the most determined and prejudiced men I know."

* * * * *

Why is it that a company like Schlumberger succeeds? In order to answer this, one should probably first inquire into the degree of success of the company's various components. Schlumberger, according to Wall Street analysts, had a near-monopoly on the wireline business—about 70 percent of the world market. (Its nearest wireline competitor, Dresser Industries' Atlas Oilfield Services Group, has just over 10 percent.) And Schlumberger retains its near-monopoly even though it charges higher prices than its competitors. "We believe we are entitled to a certain return on investment, which we intend to maintain, and we price accordingly," says D. Euan Baird, who is 45, Scottish-born, and, like most of the company's top executives, started as a Schlumberger field engineer. A policy first established by Marcel Schlumberger remains in force today: Schlumberger charges its wireline customers twice the amount of its costs. Because Schlumberger does not sell, or even lease, its equipment, and because its equipment is the most technologically advanced, so that the company provides the best technical service, it remains the most highly regarded company in the oil-field-service industry. Of course, oil companies can afford to pay its prices. Since the cost of logging a well—the wireline process—is only 2 percent to 5 percent of the oil company's cost, wrote John C. Wellemeyer, managing director of the investment-banking firm of Morgan Stanley, in 1973, "Schlumberger should be able to increase prices as much as required to maintain its margins." Until the current oil shock, that is what it has done.

To isolate the specific reasons for Schlumberger's success, one needs to start where Conrad and Marcel Schlumberger did—with technology. Competition in the oil-field-service business hinges on technology. Marvin Gearhart, president of Gearhart Industries, an aggressive domestic competitor of Schlumberger, says, in reference to the industry and Schlumberger, "It's a high-technology business, and they've been the leader in high technology."

Helped by the Fairchild subsidiary and by a heavy investment in what is called artificial intelligence, Schlumberger may be nicely positioned for the future. In recent years, advanced technology has brought about an explosion of the well-log data that are generated at every well site. Concurrent advances in data processing have helped cope with this explosion, but an isolated field engineer cannot quickly interpret so much data, and none of Schlumberger's 44 data processing centers—which may be hundreds, or perhaps even thousands, of miles away from an oil well—can entirely replicate the skills of a trained field engineer. Consequently, a bottleneck has formed in the oil-field-service industry, with clients desperate for all possible information before they make their expensive decisions, and logging companies unable to provide a complete on-the-spot analysis of their complex logs. Enter the new world of artificial intelligence. Fairchild is at the center of a strategy to forge ahead in artificial intelligence.

Schlumberger's reliance on research and technology suggests a second reason for the company's success: Schlumberger executives are trained to think in 10-year and 20-year cycles. "The time horizon there is longer than that of any other company I know in being willing to wait for a return on their investment," says Felix Rohatyn.

Riboud points out that after the Compagnie des Compteurs was acquired in 1970 it took Schlumberger seven years to transform it into a success. "We could afford to take the seven years, because we had our basic business," he says. "If it had been 10 or 12 years, though, people would have lost faith in what we were doing." The Compagnie des Compteurs is actually one of relatively few companies that Schlumberger has acquired: 15 or so over the past 20 years—a tiny number for a company of such size and cash reserves. This is in marked contrast to the current trend among American corporations. Between 1978 and 1982, American corporations spent an estimated $258 billion to acquire other companies, many of them in unrelated fields.

Schlumberger, on the other hand, has not assumed that because it was successful in one field it could succeed in unrelated fields. This refusal to shed its basic identity is a third reason for its success. Schlumberger, Riboud says, will not engage in an unfriendly takeover of another company, believing that the hostility generated poisons the corporate atmosphere required for success.

Schlumberger's determination to stick with what it knows best contributes to a fourth reason for its success: it is relatively unburdened by debt. Unlike, say, the Du Pont company, which had long-term corporate debts of $5.7 billion in 1982, Schlumberger's long-term debt as of December 1982 was a mere $462 million; moreover, it had a readily available cash pool of $2.3 billion in short-term investments. Such a balance sheet, says Elizabeth Taylor Peek of Wertheim & Company, is "incredible for a company of that size." Interest income alone brought Schlumberger $254 million in 1982.

Schlumberger is exceptional in a fifth way: it is in good standing in the Third World. There are several reasons for Schlumberger's standing in the Third World. "You can't nationalize a spirit or brains," Riboud has said. "They could nationalize a few trucks, but what would they have? The concept from the beginning was to do everything ourselves—to manufacture the equipment and deliver the services. We never sold equipment. So how do you nationalize a service?" Schlumberger has escaped troubles of the sort that befell many oil companies in the Middle East and the United Fruit Company in Latin America, partly because it has striven to remain inconspicuous. It does not own natural resources (oil) in any nation but services those who do. It does not engage in consumer advertising, and it does not lobby governments, so it is less of a target than the well-known big corporations.

The key executives of most multinational companies tend to be of a single nationality. For example, IBM has 23 members on its board of directors, all but one of whom are Americans. Exxon has three non-Americans on its 19-member board. General Electric has only Americans on its 18-member board. This has not been the case at Schlumberger. Its board was evenly divided in 1982 between French and American nationals.

What Riboud has called "the will to win" hints at a final reason for Schlumberger's success—what employees refer to as "the Schlumberger spirit." Riboud likens the Schlumberger spirit to a religion. "It is our greatest asset, our unique strength," he says. The reason the Japanese have done so well, he told the New York Society of Security Analysts in March of 1980, is so simple and so obvious that it has been overlooked. It has less to do with their technological prowess, their productivity growth, the assistance they receive from their national government than with spirit.

"They had the same faith that the great religions had in past centuries," he said. Riboud then tried to define what makes up the Schlumberger spirit.

> (1) We are an exceptional crucible of many nations, of many cultures, of many visions. (2) We are a totally decentralized organization. . . . (3) We are a service company, at the service of our customers, having a faster response than anybody else. (4) We believe in the profit process as a challenge, as a game, as a sport. (5) We believe in a certain arrogance; the certainty that we are going to win because we are the best—arrogance only tolerable because it is coupled with a great sense of intellectual humility, the fear of being wrong, the fear of not working hard enough.

Where does this spirit come from? Surely—in part, at least—from the personalities at the top: from the Schlumberger brothers and from Jean Riboud. "Conrad and Marcel created this spirit of friendship and honesty, and Riboud kept it," says Anne Gruner Schlumberger, a daughter of Conrad Schlumberger. "Riboud is loved because he is very friendly. It is the love of people, and the interest in their life. When people left for America and Russia, Conrad escorted the engineers to the railroad station to give them advice. He knew their families, their children." The brothers communicated shared democratic values within the Schlumberger hierarchy, as Riboud does today.

The company's spirit also comes in part from the special nature of Schlumberger's business. From the start, Schlumberger has been the only wireline company to refuse to turn over raw data to clients, insisting that it alone must process these data, for it is producing a service, not a commodity. Anne Gruner Schlumberger has written that "the high quality of human relations" at the company "took its start from a 'noble' activity, in the sense that nothing produced there was mere merchandise." She goes on, "The object conceived and made there was not such as fall into an anonymous market and in their turn become anonymous. This sonde, the galvanometer, were not for sale. The tie between the man who makes and the thing made was not cut." The Schlumberger brothers stipulated at the outset that the company would not own oil wells or permit employees to buy shares in oil companies. Schlumberger was to be trusted to keep oil-company secrets, it had to be "pure." Dominique de Menil, another daughter of Conrad, who was trained as an engineer and worked closely with her father, has recalled, "You had to be totally honest, and independent of any interest." Engineers at Schlumberger sensed that they were embarking not just on a career but a calling. They were not just merchants but missionaries.

* * * * *

Summing up, Riboud said, "If we lose the drive, and fear searching for new technologies, or fear taking incredible gambles on new managers," or fear to heed the voices of "other countries and cultures, then we will become an establishment." If that happens, Schlumberger may remain powerful and profitable for the moment, but ultimately it will decline. "It's easy to be the best," Riboud has said many times. "That's not enough. The goal is to strive for perfection."

* * * * *

In sum, Riboud remains a mystery even to his friends. "He is a man who cannot be classified in any way," says Charles Gombault, the former editor of *France-Soir,* who came to know Riboud through Pierre Mendes-France. "Is he an intellectual? I don't think so. Is he a merchant? I don't think so. Is he an industrialist? It doesn't show. He is one of the few men with a strong influence over the president of France, but he will never talk about it. He never shows off. If you see La Carelle, you will understand. It's a beautiful old house with lots of antiques everywhere, extremely comfortable. But if you want to have the feeling of fortune you do not have it looking at the house. You have it looking at the ground as far as you can see. He is a man of the earth."

The Company and Its Responsibilities to Society: Relating Corporate Strategy to Ethical Values

We come at last to the fourth component of strategy formulation—the moral and social implications of what once was considered a purely economic choice. In our consideration of strategic alternatives, we have come from what strategists *might* and *can* do to what they *want* to do. We now move to what they *ought* to do—from the viewpoint of various leaders and segments of society and their standards of right and wrong.

Ethical behavior, like the exercise of preference, may be considered a product of values. To some the suggestion that an orderly and analytical process of strategy determination should include the discussion of highly controversial ethical issues, about which honest differences of opinion are common and self-deceiving rationalization endless, is repugnant.

Even when public scandal erupts over overcharges to the government by the defense industry, the egregious excesses of the savings and loan associations, and the illegal behavior in the securities industry the business community stands silent. Good reasons, including the vulnerability of all organizations to wrongdoing by subordinates under pressure, make such silence prudent. Unfortunately it suggests to the press and general public complicity in illegal, unethical, and irresponsible behavior.

THE MORAL COMPONENT OF CORPORATE STRATEGY

The emerging view in the liberal-professional leadership of our most prominent corporations is that determining future strategy must take into account—as part of its social environment—steadily rising moral and ethical standards. Reconciling the conflict in responsibility which occurs when maximum profit and social contribution appear on the same agenda adds to the complexity of strategy formulation and its already clear demands for creativity. Coming to terms with the morality of choice may be the most strenuous undertaking in strategic decision.[1]

Attention is compelled to the noneconomic consequences of corporate power and activity by a combination of forces constituting the environment of business. Most dramatic is the decline in public confidence in public and private institutions accompanying the prosecution of the Vietnam War, Watergate, and the forced resignation of a vice president and president of the United States. Distrust of business flared with the revelation by the Watergate Special Prosecutor of illegal political contributions. The Securities and Exchange Commission's probe of other illegal payments has publicized the questionable behavior of scores of well-known companies. The supposition that our respected companies are abiding by the law and professional standards of ethical conduct is no longer secure.

Discussions of the responsibility of business have usually until now taken individual personal integrity for granted or have assumed that the courts were adequate discipline to ensure compliance with the law. The obvious necessity for explicit company policy now makes it necessary for decision to be made about at least how compliance with the law can be assured. The first step is a stated policy that illegality will not be condoned and enforcement provisions will begin with corporate action rather than waiting for the law and the courts.

Since political contributions and bribery are neither illegal nor even unusual in other parts of the world, explicit policy must be made with respect to other marginal, technically legal, but in American eyes, improper kinds of payments. The Foreign Corrupt Practices Act deals with the difference between American and foreign law and custom. It includes a requirement that companies report its confidence in the adequacy of its control systems. Once embarked on this sea of uncertainty, companies are forced to include policy decisions about other corporate and personal ethical behavior.

In most reputable companies it has long been assumed that economic objectives would be pursued within the law and the bounds of ethical custom. The present-day necessity to articulate and enforce an unspoken assumption leads to detailed consideration of the ethical quality of an organization's culture and to decisions governed by noneconomic criteria. Specifying and securing ethical behavior is not easy in a large company in which responsibility is delegated through many levels of authority and

[1] See R. Edward Freeman and Daniel R. Gilbert, Jr., *Corporate Strategy and the Search for Ethics* (Englewood Cliffs, N.J.: Prentice-Hall, 1988).

degrees of autonomy. The first step is to break the custom of silence to make possible the assertion of ethical concern.[2]

The morality of personal behavior, however, is not our only concern. The dominant position of the corporation in our society, the influence it has on all citizens, its inevitable relations with local, state, and national governments make it increasingly important to consider, company by company, what its social responsibility will be. Milton Friedman, to be sure, still argues that the only social responsibility of business is to pursue profit as vigorously as possible (within the law and an undefined "ethical custom").[3] For a number of reasons, it is no longer possible to conclude that consideration of strategic alternatives should be exclusively economic and free of concern for the impact of economic activity upon society.

First, corporate executives of the caliber, integrity, intelligence, and humanity capable of coping with the problems of personal morality just cited are not happy to be tarred with the brush of bribery and corruption. They are not likely to turn their backs on other problems involving corporate behavior of the late 70s and early 80s. The recurring energy crises, the growing sensitivity to environmental damage by industrial and community operations, the protection of the consumer from intended or unwitting exploitation or deception, the extension of social justice, as exemplified by the demands of minority populations and women for opportunity and recognition, the general concern for the limits of growth and the so-called quality of life—all these cannot be ignored. The need is widely acknowledged to respond as a matter of conscience as well as a matter of law.

Second, it is increasingly clear that government regulation is not a good substitute for knowledgeable self-restraint. As expectations for the protection and well-being of the environment, of customers, and of employees grow more insistent, it is clear that if corporate power is to be regulated more by public law than by private conscience, much of our national energy will have to be spent keeping watch over corporate behavior, ferreting out problems, designing and revising detailed laws to deal with them, and enforcing these laws even as they become obsolete.

Executives assuming top-management responsibility today may be more sensitive on the average than their predecessors to the upgrading of our goals as a society and more responsive to the opportunity to relate corporate and public purposes. But if not, they can be sure that new regulation will

---

[2] For useful notes on ethical analysis in the practice of general management and an excellent bibliography of writings in the field, see John B. Matthews, Kenneth E. Goodpaster, and Laura L. Nash, *Policies and Persons: A Casebook in Business Ethics,* (New York: McGraw-Hill, 1985).

[3] The classic statement of this position, which is hardly susceptible to modernization, is still Friedman's *Capitalism and Freedom* (Chicago: University of Chicago Press, 1962). An effective counterargument appears in Robert W. Ackerman, *The Solid Challenge to Business* (Cambridge, Mass.: Harvard University Press, 1975).

force this concern upon their strategic processes. Extending the reach of strategic decision to encompass public concerns is either a voluntary response permitting latitude in choice or acquiescence to law which may involve none. New forms of regulation or effective enforcement come late to the problem without regard for feasibility or cost. The strategist can consider much earlier whether the problem is susceptible to effective and economically satisfactory solution.

CATEGORIES OF CONCERN

If you elect to admit responsiveness to society's concern about corporate power and activities to your definition of strategy, you come face to face with two major questions. What is the range of corporate involvement available to a company? What considerations should guide its choice of opportunity?

The World. The problems affecting the quality of life in the society to which the company belongs may usefully be thought of as extending through a set of densely populated spheres from the firm itself to the world community. The multinational firm, to take world society first, would find (within its economic contribution to industrialization in the developing countries) the need to measure what it takes out before it could judge its participation responsible. The willingness to undertake joint ventures rather than insist on full ownership, to share management and profits in terms not immediately related to the actual contributions of other partners, to cooperate otherwise with governments looking for alternatives to capitalism, to train nationals for skilled jobs and management positions, to reconcile different codes of ethical practices in matters of taxes and bribery—all illustrate the opportunity for combining entrepreneurship with responsibility and the terms in which strategy might be expressed. Even small firms now face the opportunity and necessity to export. In smaller ways they also must negotiate with host countries and pursue their self-interests in an environment of give-and-take.

The Nation. Within the United States, for a firm of national scope, problems susceptible to constructive attention from business occur in virtually every walk of life. To narrow a wide choice, a company would most naturally begin with the environmental consequences of its manufacturing processes or the impact of its products upon the public. Presumably a company would first put its own house in order or embark upon a long program to make it so. Then it might take interest in other problems, either through tax-deductible philanthropic contributions or through business ventures seeking economic opportunity in social need—for example, trash disposal or health care. Education, the arts, race relations, equal opportunity for women, or even such large issues as the impact upon society of technological change compete for attention. The proper role of government in providing support for American industry now under attack by foreign competitors is of immediate concern to business leaders. In beleaguered industries like textiles, they must weigh the short-term advantages of protectionism versus the long-term superiority of free trade. Through organizations like the Business Roundtable, the American Business Conference, and the National Manufacturers Association, they find themselves making recommendations to the executive branch and the Congress which must address public as well as corporate interest. Our agenda of national problems is extensive. It is not hard to find opportunities. The question, as in product-market possibilities, is which ones to choose to work on.

The Local Community. Closer to home are the problems of the communities in which the company operates. These constitute the urban manifestations of the national problems already referred to—inadequate housing, unemployment in the poverty culture, substandard medical care, and the like. The city, special focus of national decay and vulnerable to fiscal and other mismanagement, is an attractive object of social strategy because of its nearness and compactness. The near community allows the development of mutually beneficial corporate projects such as vocational training. Business cannot remain healthy in a sick community.

Industry. Moving from world to country to city takes us through the full range of social and political issues which engage the attention of corporate strategists who wish to factor social responsibility into their planning. Two other less obvious but even more relevant avenues of action would be considered—the industry or industries in which the company operates and the quality of life within the company itself. Every industry, like every profession, has problems which arise from a legacy of indifference, stresses of competition, the real or imagined impossibility of interfirm cooperation under the antitrust laws. Every industry has chronic problems of its own, such as safety, product quality, pricing, and pollution in which only cooperative action can effectively pick up where regulation leaves off or makes further regulation unnecessary.

The Company. Within the firm itself, a company has open opportunity for satisfying its aspirations to responsibility. The quality of any company's present strategy, for example, is probably always subject to improvement, as new technology and higher aspirations work together. But besides such important tangible matters as the quality of goods and services being offered to the public and the maintenance and improvement of craftsmanship, there are three other areas which in the future will become much more important than they seem now. The first of these is the review process set up to estimate the quality of top-management decision. The second is the impact upon individuals of the control systems and other organization processes installed to secure results. The third is a recognition of the role of the individual in the corporation.

Review of Management Concerns for Responsibility

The everyday pressures bearing on decisions about what to do and how to get it done make almost impossible the kind of detached self-criticism which is essential to the perpetuation of responsible freedom. The opportunity to provide for systematic review sessions becomes more explicit and self-conscious. At any rate, as a category of concern, how a management can maintain sufficient detachment to estimate without self-deception the quality of its management performance is as important as any other. The proper role of the board of directors in performing this function—long ago lost sight of—is undergoing revitalization.

The caliber and strategic usefulness of a board of directors will nonetheless remain the option of the chief executives who usually determine its function. How much they use their boards for the purposes of improving the quality of corporate strategy and planning turns, as usual, on the sincerity of their interest and their skill. Recent research has illuminated the irresponsibility of inaction in the face of problems requiring the perspective available only to properly constituted boards. This organization resource is available to general managers who recognize dormancy as waste and seek counsel in cases of conflicting responsibility. A number of large corporations, including General Motors, have established Public Responsibility Committees of the board to focus attention on social issues.

The effective provision by a board of responsible surveillance of the moral quality of a management's strategic decisions means that current stirrings of concern about conflicts of interest will soon result in the withdrawal from boards of bankers representing institutions performing services to the company, of lawyers (in some instances) representing a firm retained by the company, and other suppliers or customers, as well as more scrupulous attention to present regulations about interlocking interests. As much attention will soon be given to avoiding the possibility of imputing conflict of interest to a director as to avoiding the actual occurrence. Stronger restrictions on conflict of interest will also affect employees of the firm, including the involvement of individuals with social-action organizations attacking the firm.

Impact of Control Systems on Ethical Performance

The ethical and economic quality of an organization's performance is vitally affected by its control system, which inevitably leads people, if it is effective at all, to do what will make them look good in the terms of the system rather than what their opportunities and problems, which the system may not take cognizance of, actually require. We will examine the unintended consequences of control and measurement systems when we come to the implementation of corporate strategy; in the meantime we should note that unanticipated pressures to act irresponsibly may be applied by top management who would deplore this consequence if they knew of it. The process of promotion by which persons are moved from place to place so fast that they do not develop concern for the problems of the community in which they live or effective relationships within which to accomplish anything unintentionally weakens the participation of executives in community affairs. The tendency to measure executives in divisionalized companies on this year's profits reduces sharply their motivation to invest in social action with returns over longer times. Lifelong habits of neutrality and noninvolvement eventually deprive the community, in a subtle weakening of its human resources, of executive experience and judgment. Executive cadres are in turn deprived of real-life experience with political and social systems which they ultimately much need.

The Individual and the Corporation

The actual quality of life in a business organization turns most crucially on how much freedom is accorded to the individual. Certainly most firms consider responsibility to their members a category of concern as important as external constituencies. It is as much a matter of enlightened self-interest as of responsibility to provide conditions encouraging the convergence of the individual's aspirations with those of the corporation, to provide conditions for effective productivity, and to reward employees for extraordinary performance.

With the entry of the corporation into controversial areas comes greater interest on the part of organization members to take part in public debate. It becomes possible for individuals to make comments on social problems that could be embarrassing to the corporation. It is at best difficult to balance the freedom of individuals and the consequences of their participation in public affairs against the interests of the corporation. The difficulty is increased if the attitudes of management, which are instinctively overprotective of the corporation, are harsh and restrictive. Short-run embarrassments and limited criticism from offended groups—even perhaps a threatened boycott—may be a small price to pay for the continued productivity within the corporation of people whose interests are deep and broad enough to cause them to take stands on public issues. The degree to which an organization is efficient, productive, creative, and capable of development is dependent in large part on the maintenance of a climate in which the individual does not feel suppressed and in which a kind of freedom (analogous to that which the corporation enjoys in a free enterprise society) is permitted as a matter of course. Overregulation of the individual by corporate policy is no more appropriate internally than overregulation of the corporation by government. On the other hand, personal responsibility is as appropriate to individual liberty as corporate responsibility is to corporate freedom.

The Range of Concerns

What corporate strategists have to be concerned with, then, ranges from the most global of the problems of world society to the uses of freedom by a single person in the firm. The problems of their country, community, and industry lying between these extremes make opportunity for social contribution exactly coextensive with the range of economic opportunity before them. The problem of choice may be met in the area of responsibility in much the same way as in product-market combinations and in developing a program for growth and diversification.

The business firm, as an organic entity intricately affected by and affecting its environment, is as appropriately adaptive, our concept of corporate strategy suggests, to demands for responsible behavior as for economic service. Special satisfactions and prestige, if not economic rewards, are available for companies that are not merely adaptive but take the lead in shaping the moral and ethical environment within which their primary economic function is performed. Such firms are more persuasive than others, moreover, in convincing the public of the inherent impossibility of satisfying completely all the conflicting claims made upon business.

CHOICE OF STRATEGIC ALTERNATIVES FOR SOCIAL ACTION

The choice of avenues in which to participate will, of course, be influenced by the personal values of the managers making the decision. In the absence of powerful predispositions, the inner coherence of the corporate strategy would be extended by choosing issues most closely related to the economic strategy of the company, to the expansion of its markets, to the health of its immediate environment, and to its own industry and internal problems. The extent of appropriate involvement depends importantly on the resources available. Because the competence of the average corporation outside its economic functions is severely limited, it follows that a company should not venture into good works that are not strategically related to its present and prospective economic functions.

As in the case of personal values and individual idiosyncrasy, a company may be found making decisions erratically related to nonstrategic motives. However noble these may be, they are not made strategic and thus defensible and valid by good intentions alone. Rather than make large contributions to X University because its president is a graduate, it might better develop a pattern of educational support that blends the company's involvement in the whole educational system, its acknowledged debt for the contributions of technical or managerial education to the company, and its other contributions to its communities. What makes participation in public affairs strategic rather than improvisatory is (as we have seen in conceiving economic strategy) a definition of objectives taking all other objectives into account and a plan that reflects the company's definition of itself not only as a purveyor of goods and services but as a responsible institution in its society.

The strategically directed company then will have a strategy for support of community institutions as explicit as its economic strategy and as its decisions about the kind of organization it intends to be and the kind of people it intends to attract to its membership. It is easy and proper, when margins allow it, to make full use of tax deductibility, through contributions, from which it expects no direct return. The choice of worthy causes, however, should relate to the company's concept of itself and thus directly to its economic mission. It should enter into new social service fields with the same questions about its resources and competence that new product-market combinations inspire. In good works as in new markets, opportunity without the competence to develop it is illusory. Deliberate concentration on limited objectives is preferable to scattered short-lived enthusiasm across a community's total need.

Policy for ethical and moral personal behavior, once the level of integrity has been decided, is not complicated by a wide range of choice. The nature of the company's operations defines the areas of vulnerability—purchasing, rebates, price fixing, fee splitting, customs facilitation, bribery, dubious agents' fees, conflict of interest, theft, or falsification of records. Where problems appear or danger is sensed specific rules can be issued. As in the case of government regulation of the firm, these should not be overdetailed or mechanical, for there is no hope of anticipating the ingenuity of the willful evader. Uncompromising penalties for violations of policy intent or the rarely specified rule will do more to clarify strategy in this area than thousands of words beforehand. The complexity of elevating individual behavior is thus a matter of implementation of strategy more properly discussed in the context of organization processes such as motivation and control.

DETERMINATION OF STRATEGY

We have now before us the major determinants of strategy. The cases studied so far have required consideration of what the strategy of the firm is and what, in your judgment, it ought to be. Concerned so far with the problem of formulating a proper strategy rather than implementing it, you have become familiar with the principal aspects of formulation—namely, (1) appraisal of present and foreseeable opportunity and risk in the company's environment, (2) assessment of the firm's unique combination of present and potential corporate resources or competences, (3) determination of the noneconomic personal and organizational preferences to be satisfied, and (4) identification and acceptance of the social responsibilities of the firm. The strategic decision is one that can be reached only after all these factors have been considered and the action implications of each assessed.

In your efforts to analyze the cases, you have experienced much more of the problem of the strategist than can be described on paper. When you have relinquished your original idea as to what a company's strategy should be in favor of a more imaginative one, you have seen that the formulation process has an essential creative aspect. In your effort to differentiate your thinking about an individual firm from the conventional thinking of its industry, you have looked for new opportunities and for new applications of corporate competence. You have learned how to define a product in terms of its present and potential functions rather than of its physical properties. You have probably learned a good deal about how to assess the special competence of a firm from its past accomplishments and how to identify management's values and aspirations. You may have gained some ability to rank preferences in order of their strength—your own among others.

The problem implicit in striking a balance between the company's apparent opportunity and its evident competence and between your own personal values and concepts of responsibility and those of the company's actual management is not an easy one. The concepts we have been discussing should help you make a decision, but they will not determine your decision for you. Whenever choice is compounded of rational analysis which can have more than one outcome, of aspiration and desire which can run the whole range of human ambition, and a sense of responsibility which changes the appeal of alternatives, it cannot be reduced to quantitative approaches or to the exactness which management science can apply to narrower questions. Managers contemplating strategic decisions must be willing to make them without the guidance of decision rules, with confidence in their own judgment, which will have been seasoned by repeated analyses of similar questions. They must be aware that more than one decision is possible and that they are not seeking the single right answer. They can take encouragement from the fact that the manner in which an organization implements the chosen program can help to validate the original decision.

Some of the most difficult choices confronting a company are those which must be made among several alternatives that appear equally attractive and also equally desirable. Once the analysis of opportunity has produced an inconveniently large number of possibilities, any firm has difficulty in deciding what it wants to do and how the new activities will be related to the old.

In situations where opportunity is approximately equal and economic promise is offered by a wide range of activities, the problem of making a choice can be reduced by reference to the essential character of the company and to the kind of company the executives wish to run. The study of alternatives from this point of view will sooner or later reveal the greater attractiveness of some choices over others. Economic analysis and calculations of return on investment, though of course essential, may not crucially determine the outcome. Rather, the logjam of decision can only be broken by a frank exploration of executive aspirations regarding future development, including perhaps the president's own wishes with respect to the kind of institution he or she prefers to head, carried on as part of a free and untrammeled investigation of what human needs the organization would find satisfaction in serving. That return on investment alone will point the way ignores the values implicit in the calculations and the contribution which an enthusiastic commitment to new projects can make. The rational examination of alternatives and the determination of purpose are among the most important and most neglected of all human activities. The final decision, which should be made as deliberately as possible after a detailed consideration of the issues we have attempted to separate, is an act of will and desire as much as of intellect.

Allied Chemical Corporation (A)

In June 1976 Richard Wagner, president of the Specialty Chemicals Division at Allied Chemical, faced two difficult decisions. He had to recommend whether Allied should support passage of the Toxic Substances Control Act then pending before Congress. He also had to decide whether to implement a proposed new program, called Total Product Responsibility, in his division.

Wagner found these decisions especially difficult because of the variety of factors he had to consider, including Allied's business prospects, recent developments in the chemical industry, and the increasing public and government concern about the health, safety, and environmental effects of chemical production. Another important factor was the set of problems related to Kepone, a pesticide produced until 1974 by Allied and afterwards by an outside contractor.

ALLIED CHEMICAL

Allied Chemical was a major producer of chemicals, fibers and fabricated products, and energy. With headquarters in Morristown, New Jersey, the company operated over 150 plants, research labs, quarries, and other facilities in the United States and overseas. In 1975 Allied earned $116 million on sales of $2.3 billion. (See Exhibit 1 and Tables 1 and 2 for Allied's organization and recent financial performance.)

During the late 1960s and early 1970s, Allied had changed dramatically. One company official said Allied was run as "a loose feudal barony" in the 1960s. *Forbes* called the company "a slow-moving, low-growth, low-profit producer of basic inorganic chemicals, fertilizers, and dyestuffs."[1] Changes began in 1967 when John T. Connor resigned as Secretary of Commerce and became chairman of Allied. Over the course of several years, Connor brought in 250 new executives, pruned failing businesses, established systematic planning and tight cost control, and increased corporate supervision of the divisions. At the same time, he stressed decentralized decision making and said that innovation and flexibility were crucial to Allied's future.

Harvard Business School case 379–137.

[1] "Risk Rewarded," *Forbes*, March 15, 1977, p. 101.

TABLE 1
FINANCIAL PERFORMANCE, 1972–1975
Dollars in Millions Except per Share Data and Ratios

	1975	*1974*	*1973*	*1972*
Sales	$2,333	$2,216	$1,665	$1,501
Aftertax income	116	144	90	64
EPS	4.17	5.19	3.27	2.30
Debt/equity	0.59	0.45	0.49	0.54
Gross margin/sales	22%	23.3%	24.6%	24.3%
R&D/sales	1.51%	1.39%	1.73%	1.89%
Pollution control facilities cost	$34.4	$29.0	$28.0	$25.0

TABLE 2
LINE OF BUSINESS PERFORMANCE, 1974–1975
Dollars in Millions

	1975		*1974*	
	Sales	*Income from Operations*	*Sales*	*Income from Operations*
Energy (petroleum, nuclear, coal, and coke)	$ 581	$ 28	$ 511	$ 32
Fibers and fabricated products	504	46	484	81
Chemical (inorganic, plastics, organic, and agricultural)	1,248	144	1,221	135
Totals	$2,333	$218	$2,216	$248

Connor's most important step was an $800 million commitment to find and develop oil and gas supplies throughout the world. According to Connor, this strategy would be financed with new capital and with funds "from existing businesses that were losing, had poor prospects, or had severe environmental risks."[2] The largest investments were in Indonesian gas fields and North Sea oil fields. In Indonesia, Allied had a 35 percent interest in a joint venture with Pertamina, the Indonesian government petroleum agency. The British government had announced its intention to obtain a voluntary 51 percent participation in the North Sea oil fields, but the form that participation might take had not been determined then.

This energy investment was very risky. Finding and developing new reserves was highly competitive, technically difficult, and very costly. Changes in government regulations or tax laws, either domestic or foreign, could cut profits. And problems with weather, technology, or politics in host countries could delay the start of production. These risks seemed justified as shortages of energy and chemical feedstocks occurred during the 1970s and as the potential payoff from the investment grew. Connor stated that energy could provide as much as half of Allied's profits by the early 1980s.

[2] Ibid.

In mid-1976, however, the return on the energy investment was still small. In fact, it appeared that Allied's energy businesses, taken altogether, would just about break even in 1976. Allied's U.S. natural gas pipelines lost money because of federal price controls on interstate gas shipments. Its coal and coke business had chronic operating problems and, following a plea of no contest, the company had been fined approximately $100,000 for allegedly failing to meet the Environmental Protection Agency (EPA) air pollution requirements. Finally, obtaining government approval to operate Allied's nuclear fuel reprocessing plant could prove difficult. Company officials then hoped that 1977 would bring the first profits from North Sea oil, and they expected profits from Indonesian gas sales in 1978.

While Allied had invested heavily in energy, chemicals provided the foundation of company earnings. In 1976, for example, chemicals most likely produced 75 percent of company profits, even though they were only 50 percent of total company sales. Allied produced approximately 1,500 chemicals and sold them to all major industries. These sales were primarily to other chemical manufacturers for use in making their products. Other sales were to dealers, who sometimes resold them under their own names, and ultimately to consumers. The two best years in the history of Allied's chemical business were 1974 and 1975. Sales were expected to weaken later in 1976, however, as a result of the recession that began in 1975.

Allied's fiber and fabricated products had been a steady contributor to company profits. On average, this business accounted for one fifth of total sales and profits during the early 1970s. Allied made fibers for clothing, carpeting, and auto tires. The company was also the world's largest manufacturer of auto seat belts and shoulder harnesses.

Overall, Allied's record in the early 1970s did not compare favorably with chemical industry standards. Between 1971 and 1975, Allied's return on equity, sales growth, and return on total assets were the second lowest among the 13 major diversified U.S. chemical companies. EPS growth was exactly the average of the 13 companies. On the positive side, Allied improved its relative performance in 1974 and 1975, and its energy investment offered the prospect of major improvements in the future.

THE CHEMICAL INDUSTRY

In 1976 chemicals was one of the largest U.S. industries, with annual sales of more than $100 billion. In the 20 years after World War II, chemicals became a high-profit, glamour industry that often grew twice as fast as the GNP. From the mid-1960s to the mid-1970s, however, industry growth had slowed and financial performance dimmed. Among the reasons were higher raw material costs, increased government regulation, the slowdown in U.S. economic growth, and what many considered the maturity of major segments of the industry. Nevertheless, the industry continued to contribute $3–$5 million per year to the U.S. balance of payments.

Roughly 80,000 chemical compounds are sold in the United States and 500 to 1,000 new ones are added each year. More than 12,000 companies manufacture these chemicals, and most of these companies have sales of less than $5 million per year. The major customer for chemical products is the chemical industry itself. A typical chemical company will buy the product of one chemical company, process it, and sell its product to yet another chemical company. In most cases, a long chain of intermediate processors connects a chemical raw material with its ultimate consumer.

The industry is highly competitive. Many chemicals are commodities and compete on price. Competition comes from both natural products (such as cotton fabric) and close chemical substitutes. Chemical firms also face competition from suppliers—especially oil companies—that integrate forward, and from customers integrating backward. For a highly capital-intensive industry, chemicals have a low degree of concentration. The 10 largest chemical companies account for roughly 35 percent of industry shipments. Low concentration encourages competition by limiting oligopolistic pricing. The industry is also highly cyclical, lagging the business cycle by a few months, and vigorous price cutting usually occurs during recessions.

In the past, successful chemical companies tended to follow a basic pattern of growth. They made large investments in research and development, resulting in new products or better processes. These innovations lowered prices and took markets from other chemicals and from natural products. In turn, new markets permitted larger-scale operations, further economies, and further R&D. The R&D investments were the key to successful performance. The importance of innovation to the industry is indicated by the fact that half of all chemical products sold in 1970 were not produced commercially in the 1940s. Ammonia fertilizers, sulfa drugs, Dacron, and nylon are some of the results of chemical industry R&D.

Industry prospects were especially uncertain in 1976. The industry earned record profits in 1974 and 1975—an abrupt change from its sagging performance from 1967 to 1973. In response to these profits and to shortages in 1974, a $25 billion capital spending boom took place. This new capacity raised the specter of industrywide overcapacity and renewed price cutting. In fact, the new capacity came on line just as the economic slowdown affected chemical sales in 1976.

At the same time, costs were rising. Environmental laws and high construction costs raised the price of new plant and equipment. Companies were testing more of their products and raw materials for harmful effects, and testing costs were escalating. It was not unusual then for tests on just one substance to take several years and cost $500,000. Most important, the days of cheap and plentiful oil and natural gas had ended. Chemical companies are disproportionate users of fossil fuels because they need energy to run plants and to use as feedstock for their products. Higher energy costs meant that chemical products in general lost some of their price competitiveness against nonchemical products.

Industry executives were also concerned about an "innovation shrinkage." R&D spending in 1976 would be roughly $1.4 billion, up from $800 million 10 years before. But a higher percentage of this spending was going to modify products already on the market or into government-required health and safety research. Reduced R&D seemed to threaten future industry growth.

KEPONE

Wagner had to make his decisions at a time when Allied was in the middle of the Kepone affair. Problems related to Kepone had preoccupied Allied executives for nearly a year and seemed to be growing rather than subsiding. Kepone was a DDT-like pesticide used in ant and roach bait in the United States and as a banana pest killer abroad. It looked like fine, white dust and was toxic. Between 1966 and

1973, Allied made Kepone at its Hopewell, Virginia, plant or had Kepone made for it by outside contractors. Profits were under $600,000 a year, and Allied had no health or safety problems with its Kepone production.

In early 1973 Allied needed more capacity at Hopewell for other products, so it sought bids from companies willing to produce Kepone for Allied. This was not unusual: twice before, outside contractors had made Kepone for resale by Allied. The lowest bid by far was submitted by Life Science Products (LSP), a new company owned by two former Allied employees. Both of them had been involved in the development and manufacture of Kepone. LSP leased a former gas station near the Hopewell plant, converted it, and began making Kepone in March 1974.

For 16 months, LSP produced Kepone under conditions that might have shocked Charles Dickens, according to most accounts. Brian Kelly, a reporter for the *Washington Post,* described the plant as "an incredible mess. Dust flying through the air . . . saturating the workers' clothing, getting into their hair, even into sandwiches they munched in production areas. . . . The Kepone dust sometimes blew . . . in clouds. A gas station operator across the street said it obscured his view of the Life Science plant. . . . Two firemen in a station behind Life Science say there were times when they wondered if they could see well enough to wheel their engines out in response to a fire alarm."[3]

Two months after LSP started operations, Hopewell's sewage treatment plant broke down because Kepone allegedly killed the bacteria that digested sewage. LSP employees soon developed the "Kepone shakes"; some saw doctors provided by "informal agreement"[4] with LSP, but they were diagnosed as hypertensive. This continued until July 1975, when one worker saw a Taiwanese doctor who sent blood and urine samples to the Center for Disease Control (CDC) in Atlanta. The Kepone levels in the sample were so high that the CDC toxicologists wondered whether they had been contaminated in transit. The CDC notified the Virginia state epidemiologist.

Five days later, the epidemiologist examined several workers at LSP. He later said, "The first man I saw was a 23-year-old who was so sick, he was unable to stand due to unsteadiness, was suffering severe chest pains . . . had severe tremor, abnormal eye movements, was disoriented."[5] The next day LSP was closed by the Virginia state health authorities.

In early 1976 a federal grand jury in Richmond, Virginia, was called to consider the Kepone events. In May it indicted Allied, LSP, the two owners of LSP, four supervisors at Allied, and the City of Hopewell on a total of 1,104 counts. Most of the counts were misdemeanor charges. Hopewell was indicted for failing to report the massive Kepone discharges and for aiding and abetting LSP. Allied was also indicted for aiding and abetting LSP, for violating federal water pollution laws by dumping Kepone and non-Kepone wastes into the James River before 1974, and for conspiring to conceal the dumping. These cases would then be prosecuted by William B. Cummings, U.S. attorney for Virginia. Allied faced penalties of more than $17 million if convicted.

---

[3] Christopher D. Stone, "A Slap on the Wrist for the Kepone Mob," *Business and Society Review,* Summer 1977, p.4.

[4] Ibid., p. 5.

[5] Ibid., p. 6.

By the end of June there had been several more legal developments. Allied had publicly denied any wrongdoing. The City of Hopewell had pleaded no contest to the charges against it. Allied's attorneys favored a no contest plea on the pre-1974 dumping charges, but they were confident the company would be found innocent of the other charges. The case would not come to trial until the early fall. Allied also expected suits from the LSP workers, local fishermen, and seafood companies, as well as a large class action suit. These suits would claim damages of astronomical proportions—more than $8 billion.

The Kepone toll had been mounting week by week. The LSP workers were now out of the hospital, but more than 60 of them still reported symptoms of Kepone poisoning. (Mice fed high levels of Kepone had developed tumors that were characterized as cancerous.) The James River was closed to fishing because Kepone tends to accumulate in many species caught for seafood. The James had tens of thousands of pounds of Kepone in its bed, and sales of seafood from the Chesapeake Bay (into which the James flows) were hurt badly. A "60 Minutes" TV report on Kepone damaged Allied's image and reinforced a growing public view that chemicals equaled cancer. Finally, publicity about the Kepone incident increased the likelihood that the Toxic Substances Act would become law.

The impact of Kepone on Allied was traumatic. The company's reputation for environmental safety and responsibility seemed shattered. Settling the court cases could have a significant effect on earnings, and uncertainty about this cost would result in a qualified auditors' statement. Morale was low and hiring had become difficult. Problems also developed in Allied's dealings with federal regulatory agencies, such as the EPA and Occupational Safety and Health Administration (OSHA). These relations depended on good faith bargaining, and Allied met with increasing skepticism and even suspicion. Costly delays resulted in getting permits for new construction. Officials feared the cost of new oxime production facilities at Hopewell would rise more than $10 million because of these delays. (Oximes were organic chemicals used to produce biologically degradable pesticides.)

Allied management felt a strong sense of moral responsibility to the LSP workers, their families, and the Hopewell community. The company already funded research aimed at finding a way to eliminate Kepone from the bodies of the LSP workers. Allied also planned to establish a multimillion-dollar foundation to help with the Kepone cleanup and make grants for other environmental improvements.

Wagner found it hard to understand how the Kepone affair happened in the first place. Allied had made Kepone without any health or safety problems, and the LSP owners should have been able to do the same. Hopewell officials knew about the discharges when the sewage facility began having trouble, yet they took no action. The Virginia Air Quality Resources Board had an air-monitoring filter within a quarter of a mile of LSP, but it was not checking Kepone emissions. Virginia's Water Quality Control Board knew there was a serious problem in October 1974. The board did not use its authority to shut down the LSP plant but tried to use persuasion to get changes.

Federal agencies were also involved. In autumn 1974 the Occupational Safety and Health Administration received a letter from a former LSP employee, who claimed he was fired for refusing to work under unsafe conditions. OSHA responded by writing to the LSP owners. They, in turn, wrote back that there was no problem and OSHA accepted their assurances. The Environmental Protection Agency had sent an inspector to LSP in March 1975. The inspector was uncertain whether the EPA had jurisdiction over pesticides. His letter of inquiry to the EPA regional office in Philadelphia was unanswered in July when LSP was closed.

TOXIC SUBSTANCES CONTROL ACT

In less than a week, Wagner would report to Allied's executive committee on the Toxic Substances Control Act (TSCA). He had to recommend company support for the Act, or opposition, or continued neutrality. A neutral stand meant Allied would keep a low profile and issue public statements saying the company supported some features of the Act and opposed others.

TSCA was a new approach to government regulation of harmful chemicals. Past legislation aimed at remedial action, while TSCA aimed at prevention. Senator James B. Pearson (R., Kansas) made this distinction:

> Existing legislation simply does not provide the means by which adverse effects on human health and the environment can be ascertained and appropriate action taken before chemical substances are first manufactured and introduced into the marketplace. At present, the only remedy available under such Federal statutes as the Clean Air Act, the Federal Water Pollution Control Act, the Occupational Safety and Health Act, and the Consumer Product Safety Act, is to impose restrictions on toxic substances after they have first been manufactured.[6]

TSCA was intended to *prevent* unreasonable risks to health and the environment. It gave the Environmental Protection Agency two new powers. The EPA could compel companies to provide information on the production, composition, uses, and health effects of the chemicals they made or processed. Using this data, the EPA could then regulate the manufacture, processing, commercial distribution, use, and disposal of the chemicals.

TSCA had three key provisions. Section 4 (testing) authorized the EPA to require testing of a chemical for any of several reasons. The reasons included clarification of health effects, toxicity, and carcinogenicity. Before requiring tests, the EPA had to show that (1) the chemical could pose an unreasonable risk to health or the environment, or that human or environmental exposure to the chemical would be substantial; (2) there was insufficient data for determining the health and environmental effects of the chemical; and (3) the only way to develop this data would be by testing the chemical. The manufacturer would pay for the testing.

The most controversial provision of TSCA was section 5—premarket notification. This required a manufacturer to report its intent to produce any new chemical to the EPA 90 days before doing so. A manufacturer had to make similar notice of plans to produce a chemical for a "significant new use." These reports had to disclose the chemical's name, chemical identity and molecular structure, its proposed categories of use, the amount to be made, its manufacturing by-products, and its disposal. The manufacturer was also required to submit available data on health and environmental effects.

If the EPA found that there was not enough information to judge the health or environmental effects, it could prohibit or

[6] Library of Congress, *Legislative History of the Toxic Substances Control Act* (Washington, D.C.: Government Printing Office, 1976), p. 215.

limit the manufacture, distribution, or use of the chemical until adequate information was provided. This was the third key provision of TSCA. It gave the EPA broad new powers to regulate the operations of more than 115,000 establishments that made or processed chemicals. TSCA also directed the EPA to weigh the costs and benefits of the testing and regulations that it required under these new powers.

Wagner had to sort out a number of complicated issues to make his decision. He had to ask whether, as a citizen, he thought TSCA was in the public interest. As an Allied executive, he had to consider how support for TSCA would affect Allied's image and how the act itself would affect Allied's chemical business. This last question was especially difficult since TSCA could help business in some ways and hurt it in others. For example, TSCA might cut the chances of another Kepone incident. The costs of testing and reporting might give large chemical companies, like Allied, a competitive edge over smaller firms. But these costs would also hurt Allied's bottom line and make chemical products, particularly new ones, less competitive with natural products. Wagner had his assistant, a recent graduate of a leading eastern business school, summarize the major arguments for and against TSCA. The assistant's report is presented in the following two sections.

For TSCA

1. TSCA closes gaps in current laws. The act will require testing *before* exposure, so workers and communities will not be used as guinea pigs.
2. TSCA's cost will be low. The EPA and the General Services Administration estimate total costs to industry of $100–$200 million a year. Industry sales exceed $100 billion a year.
3. TSCA will reduce national health care costs by preventing some of the health effects of harmful chemicals. Care for cancer patients alone now costs more than $18 billion per year.
4. Under current laws, the incidence of cancer has been rising and many chemical disasters and near-disasters have occurred.
5. The act offers protection for the interests of chemical companies. When companies disagree with EPA regulations, they can file a timely lawsuit and seek a court injunction.
6. TSCA may reduce the risks of doing business in chemicals. The act may, in effect, put a "government seal of approval" on hazardous chemicals. It could also cut the risk of a company being sued because a customer used its products in a dangerous way.
7. Public support for the act will help restore Allied's image as a responsible community-minded company.
8. The act is likely to pass this year, so Allied might as well get on the bandwagon. The Senate has already passed the act and the current version lacks several features that caused House opposition in past years. Public pressure for passage is building, especially in the wake of the Kepone headlines. The membership of the Manufacturing Chemists Association, the major industry trade group, is split over the act.

Against TSCA

1. The industry is already sufficiently regulated. Twenty-seven major federal laws now cover almost every aspect of company operations. Large chem-

ical companies like Allied already deal with more than 70 government agencies.

2. Companies already do extensive testing of chemicals before marketing them. The tests sometimes cost several hundred thousand dollars and take several years. They are performed by highly trained scientists working in the most modern labs. Furthermore, companies have a strong incentive to do sufficient testing: they want to avoid the many heavy costs imposed by incidents like Kepone.
3. TSCA will be extremely costly. Dow puts the cost at $2 billion annually; the Manufacturing Chemists Association estimates $800 million to $1.3 billion. There will be less innovation because of excessive testing burdens on new chemicals. U.S. chemical exports will become more costly and less competitive, U.S. jobs will move overseas, and the testing and reporting requirements will hurt or even close many small companies. This will also affect large companies like Allied. We rely on small companies as suppliers, and Allied itself is basically a composite of 60 or 70 small specialty chemical companies.
4. The act is dangerously vague. The EPA gets very broad powers with few restrictions.
5. Reporting to the EPA under TSCA will require us to disclose trade secrets and other confidential data.
6. Supporting the act to aid our image or get on a bandwagon won't fool many people. It will be taken as a public relations move and could raise even more suspicions about Allied's motives.
7. It's not even clear there's a bandwagon. The Senate passed the act in 1972 and 1973 and the House killed it both times. Even though the EPA is lobbying hard for TSCA, the Commerce Department and the Office of Management and Budget oppose it. There is as yet no indication whether President Ford will sign or veto the act.
8. Many of the reports of chemical "disasters" have been exaggerated by the media and by environmental groups. We should not give in to pressures based on this sort of misinformation.

TOTAL PRODUCT RESPONSIBILITY

Wagner also had to decide whether to implement a new program called Total Product Responsibility (TPR). This program had been developed in 1975 by the engineering and operations services unit in the Specialty Chemicals Division. This 17-person staff unit developed policies and procedures related to health, safety, maintenance, and quality control (see Exhibit 2). TPR would use "tools of policy, procedure, control, and review" to help Allied "properly discharge its legal and moral responsibility to protect its employees, customers, the public, and the environment from harm."

TPR was first proposed in 1975 by R. L. Merrill, vice president of engineering and operations services. Merrill had come to Allied after several years with Dow Chemical and was impressed by Dow's Product Stewardship Program. According to *Business Week,* product stewardship meant Dow would assume "total responsibility for how its products affect people" and Dow's products would carry "a virtual guarantee of harmlessness."[7] Dow had 600 people involved in setting up product stewardship in 1972. They prepared environmental and safety profiles for all 1,100 of Dow's

[7] "Dow's Big Push for Product Safety," *Business Week,* April 21, 1973, p. 82.

products. Then film cassettes were made for presentations to Dow employees, customers, and distributors. In its first year, product stewardship cost $1 million.

Merrill's original proposal was not for a program as extensive as Dow's. Merrill had suggested a survey of information currently available to Allied on health and environmental effects of its products. This survey would then be followed by whatever tests were needed to supplement existing information. But during 1975 and early 1976, an expanded TPR slowly took shape around this original suggestion. If it was important to get complete health and safety information about Allied's products, it also seemed important to get similar information on raw materials, processes, and customer uses of Allied products. And, in turn, it seemed important to make sure all this information was reflected in Allied's everyday operating procedures.

The first step in implementing TPR would be for Wagner to issue a 25-page memorandum on TPR to all management personnel in his division. The memo would set out standards of operating and business practice that covered virtually every aspect of division operations. Line management would then have to make sure that operating procedures conformed to these standards. The following excerpts are from the TPR memorandum.

> *Specifications:* Specifications should exist for every raw material . . . and every finished product. . . . No specifications may be changed without the approval of the director of operations/general manager after review with operations services.
>
> *Testing:* All of the division's products will be reviewed on a priority basis, as determined by our toxicology specialists, to determine the known or suspected undesirable toxic effects which those products may have on our employees, customers, the public, and the environment.
>
> *Plant SOPs:* Standard operating procedures will be developed by plants for each product area. Procedures will be designed by engineering, technical, and operations groups to provide capability of producing uniform product quality and to insure process continuity. Use of approved procedures will be mandatory and revisions to accepted methods will require approval of pre-established authority levels.
>
> *Equipment Testing:* Testing procedures and frequencies are to be developed to insure reliability of equipment at the 95 percent confidence level to minimize the possibility of unforeseen problems arising.
>
> *Change Procedure:* Changes in R&D, product development, manufacturing, distribution, and marketing that may adversely affect the process, employees, product, customer, the public, or the environment should not be made without the approval of the director of operations, director of marketing, or research laboratory director, as appropriate, and after review with operations services.
>
> *Technical Bulletins:* Technical literature and bulletins should include all safety and environmental statements necessary to protect employees, customers, the public, and the environment. Operations services is to receive, edit, and approve all literature and bulletins to assure that all such proper statements are included.
>
> *Advertising:* Advertising copy should reflect true and accurate statements about our products. Advertising copy should be reviewed by operations services to prevent misleading statements concerning claims in the areas of environmental products' safety, health, and quality assurance.
>
> *Product End Use:* Marketing departments should make every effort to determine the end use application of each product sold. Consideration should be

given to the desirability of using the product in that application and the customer's understanding of the effect of such use on the operation. . . . A product should not be sold to a customer where it is known that the end use application is not proper.

Capability of Existing Customers: Marketing departments have the responsibility to establish the capability of our customers concerning their competency to handle our products in a manner that protects the customers' process, employees, the public, and the environment. Hazardous products should not be sold to customers whose capability is deemed inadequate. If it is determined that an application or end use of the product is improper . . . the sales of this product to that customer should be discontinued immediately.

New Customers: Hazardous products should not be sold to new customers until the capability of that customer is deemed adequate.

Outside Contractors: When outside contractors are to be used to process, reprocess, repackage, or manufacture materials for us, the review should include a determination of the toxicity and hazards of the materials to be handled, and an in-depth study of the contractor's capability to perform the work such as not to endanger the contractor's employees, the public, or the environment. . . . When a contractor is retained, it is the responsibility of the appropriate business area to arrange for periodic inspections and reviews of that contractor's operations by the operations services department.

Wagner had distributed the draft memo within the Specialty Chemicals Division and discussed the program with a variety of line and staff personnel. Reaction was mixed. Leonard Warren, director of marketing services, said:

I don't know where I come down on this. I know that chemical companies are getting burned in the newspapers and in court, and the result is more and more government people telling us how to do business. We've got to stop this, but we've also got to make money. As I read TPR, it says we're going to say "no" to some people who want to buy from us. We'll also be harassing our current customers and prospects by asking them how they use our products, who they sell to, and what their customers do with their products. Some of them are going to tell us to keep our noses out of their businesses. A lot of our products are virtually commodities and they're already hard enough to sell without the burdens of TPR paperwork, TPR costs, and the mixed signals we'll be giving to our reps.

Now I'm not completely opposed to TPR in some form. After Kepone, it will make Allied's reputation a little better. There are probably some customers that we shouldn't sell to, because they're too risky, and this program will help us get rid of them. In some cases, it might even help sales because it would be a reason for our reps to have even further contacts with customers, and more information about uses of our products could be a useful kind of market research for us.

Another hesitant view came from Joe DeStefano, a production manager at the Hopewell complex:

My first reaction is that we already do a lot of the things in the TPR memo. The difference is that our current procedures are not formalized and we don't have to get as much clearance before making changes. I can't help wondering whether TPR isn't going to make business a lot more bureaucratic. It seems to me that the government already does enough of that. Under TPR , we would have to go through operations services to do almost anything. We could end up with more paperwork,

> buck-passing, and bureaucracy. Sometimes I'm not sure what's more important: getting a good product out the door at a profit or complying with a thousand rules and restrictions.

Janet Baker, an associate corporate counsel who handled environmental cases, supported TPR:

> Allied has to do something like TPR. Kepone costs are skyrocketing and we can't afford to let another Kepone happen. TPR sends a clear message throughout the division that health and safety are top priority. We've sent the message before, but it needs vigorous emphasis. If we don't take steps to run our business as safely as possible, the government will do it for us.
>
> But there are problems. Customers and suppliers could well resent our sanctimonious attitude when we poke our noses into their businesses. Refusals to deal have to be handled unilaterally and without publicity or else we may be liable for conspiracy allegations, antitrust, trade disparagement, or libel suits.

Despite these objections and misgivings, Merrill remained enthusiastic about TPR; he argued:

> Of course TPR won't be free of problems, but it does much more good than harm. It will help our image and cut our risk of environmental and safety problems. Besides, the government is likely to require most of what's in TPR in just a few years. By starting now, Allied can learn to do business under these inevitable new conditions.
>
> It's also absolutely essential that the attitude of Allied managers and workers toward the government start to change. The government is going to be a major factor in the chemical industry for the indefinite future. We can either take an adversary approach and comply with regulations in a minimal, grudging way or we can recognize that the government is here to stay, learn to cooperate with federal agencies and, as a result, get better results in regulatory proceedings and lower our risks of future Kepones.

In making his decision, Wagner also had to consider the views of Allied's chairman and the executive committee. There was strong support among these executives for "some concrete steps" that would prevent another Kepone and change company attitudes toward government health and environmental rules. At the same time, Wagner could not ignore his division's earnings and performance. In the summer of 1976, sales were weakening as a result of the recession that began in 1975. Wagner wondered if this was the right time to divert managerial time and attention from the chemical business. He was also concerned about the possible impact of TPR on the flexibility, decentralized decision making, and innovation he had been trying to encourage in his division. He also wondered whether TPR would have kept the Kepone problem from happening in the first place.

FURTHER DEVELOPMENTS

Since 1976 was an election year, Wagner had been paying some attention to the positions candidates took on regulation in general and the chemical industry in particular. Senator Vance Hartke (D., Indiana), who then faced a serious reelection challenge, campaigned hard for greater regulation of chemicals. One of his speeches included the following remarks:

> The hazards associated with chemicals like PCB's vinyl chloride, BCME, and asbestos have all dramatically illustrated how important it is to get early

warning with respect to new chemical substances. . . .

During this (last) five-year period, there have been in excess of one million deaths in this country from cancer. Over a million infants have been born with physical or mental damage. . . . While many of the grave health risks to human beings have declined in recent years, cancer statistics have done just the opposite. In fact, the incidence of cancer was estimated in 1975 to be some 2.5 percent above the previous year. . . .

It is no accident that the hot spots for cancer in this country are in close proximity to those locations where the chemical industry is most highly concentrated.

. . . It is tragic that those who rely upon the industry for jobs have essentially become guinea pigs for discovering the adverse effects of chemical substances. It is also tragic that much of the information which has shown the cancer-producing potential of many chemicals has come from death records of employees. For example, of one million current and former American asbestos workers who still survive, fully 300,000 have been projected to die of cancer. This death rate is 50 percent higher than that of the U.S. population at large.[8]

At the same time Wagner was also aware of growing regulation. The leading presidential contenders then–Ford, Carter, and Reagan–all sounded the theme of "too much government interference." Academic studies had documented the large indirect costs of regulation and even reformers like Ralph Nader were very critical of agencies such as the FTC, which Nader said was basically a captive of the industries it regulated. Industry also joined this movement against regulation. Dow Chemical, for example, announced completion of its own "catalogue of regulatory horrors" and claimed it had spent $50 million in 1975 to meet regulations it considered excessive.[9]

---

[8] Library of Congress, *Legislative History of the Toxic Substances Act* (Washington, D.C.: Government Printing Office), p. 216.

[9] "Dow Chemical's Catalogue of Regulatory Horrors," *Business Week*, April 4, 1977, p. 50.

EXHIBIT 1
COMPANY ORGANIZATION CHART

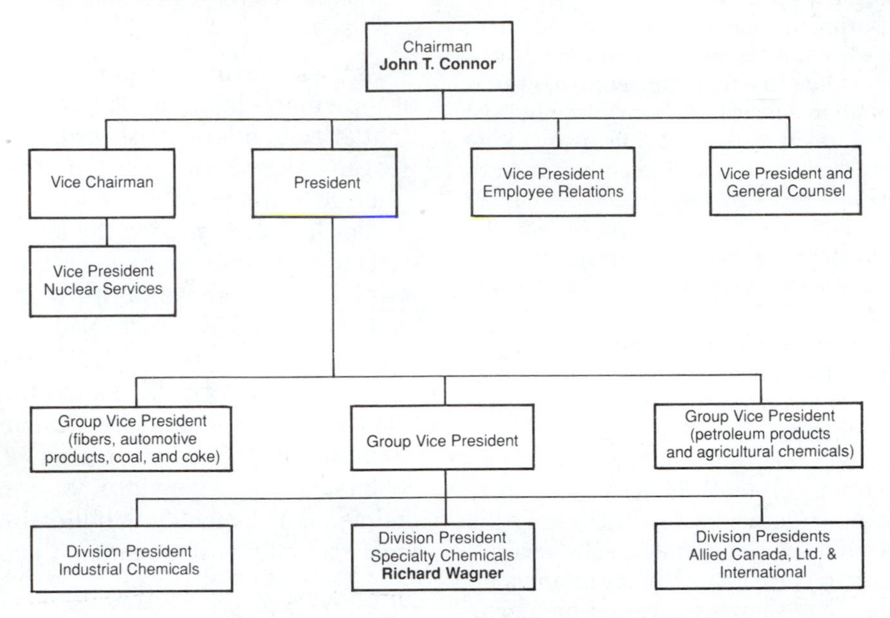

EXHIBIT 2
SPECIALTY CHEMICALS DIVISION ORGANIZATION CHART

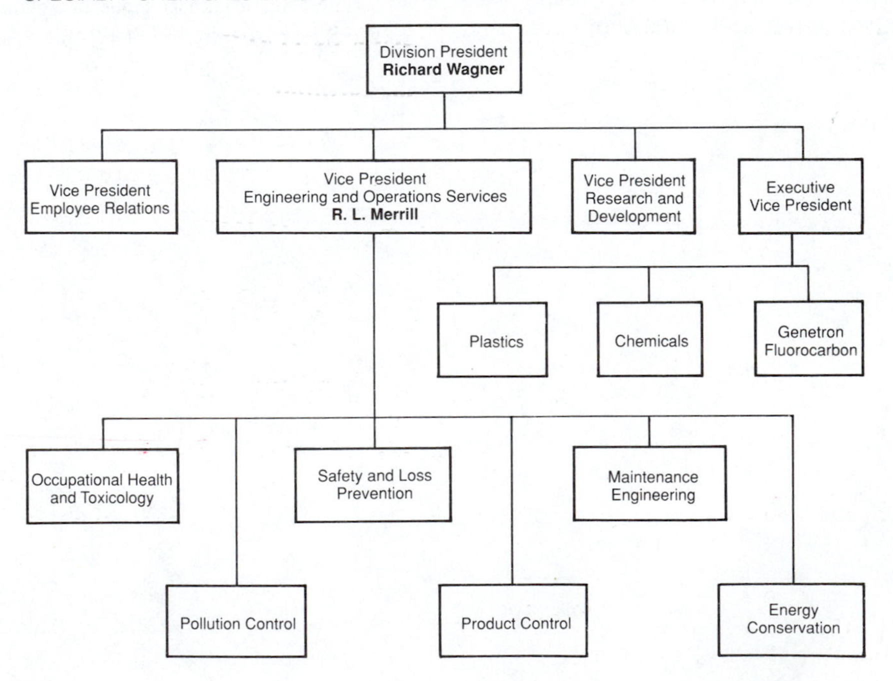

Questionable Payments Abroad: Gulf in Italy

In the aftermath of Watergate, a number of political contributions by large corporations came to light, prompting extensive enquiries by a number of government agencies including the Justice Department, Internal Revenue Service, and the Securities and Exchange Commission. In examining the extent, source, and nature of these contributions, investigators also found in several companies evidence of "questionable payments" abroad.

In this environment, the boards of many corporations began their own internal investigations, and during 1976 and 1977 over 400 "voluntary reports" relating to questionable payments abroad had been filed with the SEC.

One such report by the Special Review Committee of the Board of Directors of Gulf Oil Corporation received widespread publicity, not only for its revelation of numerous clearly illegal payments, but also because it gave some insight to some of the more common pressures and demands facing managers that are not so clearly defined.

The following incident is only one of scores documented by the special committee, but may serve to illustrate the complexity of the issues involved.

GULF IN ITALY

Background

Gulf first entered the Italian scene in the late 1940s. Drilling concessions were obtained in the Ragusa field in Sicily, and in due course Gulf found oil practically under the nose of ENI/AGIP, the Italian National Oil Company. In due course Gulf's expansion in Italy included installation or acquisition of a chain of filling stations, port and storage facilities, distribution centers, and refining capacity. Other foreign oil companies were then operating in Italy and Gulf was faced with very active competition in its effort to establish itself in the Italian market.

In these activities Gulf utilized as its Italian representative, and eventually head of operations, Nicolo Pignatelli, an Italian

Harvard Business School case 382–080.

national, who had been associated with Gulf's activities in Italy from the very start. He helped guide Gulf through numerous vicissitudes in the Italian venture including the divestment of a number of relatively unsuccessful operations as well as the successful consummation of the exchange of the Ragusa concession for a long-term Kuwait crude oil supply contract with ENI/AGIP.

Although Pignatelli enjoyed a substantial degree of independence, he maintained close association with Gulf centers of authority in London and Pittsburgh during the period of his Italian operations. In fact, he was in the habit of making rather frequent trips to Pittsburgh to acquaint the management of the progress of activities in Italy.

The audit committee's investigation acknowledged that Italy was an area where, by custom and law, political contributions by corporations were well-recognized phenomena. Prior to May 1974, corporate political contributions were, generally speaking, lawful in Italy provided the corporation's stockholders were informed.

After its investigation of Gulf's operations in Italy, the audit committee reported that there was no doubt that corporate funds of Gulf were expended in Italy by its Italian subsidiary from time to time for the purpose of inducing minor local functionaries to do, or to expedite the performance of, their normal duties or to reward them for extra services. Apparently, the giving of *omaggi*, or gifts, to lubricate the sluggish machinery of petty bureaucracy was and is an accepted way of life in Italy.[1] The practice was characterized as tipping rather than bribery and was not considered unlawful. A special "off-the-books fund" (known as the "Fondo Nero" or Black Fund) was used for this purpose, among others. However, there were other practices and events in which Gulf's management behavior was less clearly understood. One such example was provided by the events surrounding the so-called Plum Project.

Expansion of the Milan Refinery (the "Plum Project")

On January 22, 1967, Gulf obtained a license to install a refinery at Zelo Buon Persico near Milan, despite great public opposition. Numerous extremely hostile, if not vitriolic, press reports and editorials denounced Gulf and opposed its plans to construct the refinery. The opposition was expressed to be largely on ecological grounds, but there was an undercurrent of antiforeign sentiment as well. The campaign in the press against the refinery continued into 1968 and 1969, and a change in zoning requirements ultimately blocked construction at the Zelo Buon Persico site, which Gulf had already purchased.

By decree dated August 2, 1969, Gulf was granted permission to move the location of the proposed refinery to Bertonico in the Terranova Commune, also near Milan. It appears that Gulf overcame the public opposition, to some extent at least, and the refinery was constructed and went onstream in June 1972.[2] A formal opening was attended by local officials and citizens, which featured the ceremonial drinking of

[1] An example of this was the company's practice of using gas coupons as gratuities, or *omaggi*. Over $7,000 worth of gas coupons were distributed by the company in Italy during the first quarter of 1975 to various governmental functionaries and others.

[2] Of the $425,000 distributed through the "off-the-books" Fondo Nero, 11 separate payments totalling $10,800 had been made to journalists and editors for the purpose of influencing press coverage of the Milan refinery controversy.

effluent water from the refinery by Mr. Nicolo Pignatelli, Gulf's head of Italian operations; Dr. M. R. J. Wyllie, head of Gulf's Eastern Hemisphere organization; and various public officials, in an effort to dramatize its freedom from pollution. However, while the actual processing capacity was 5.8 million tons per annum, an operating permit for only 3.9 million tons was issued.

In November 1972 Gulf commenced negotiations with Mobil, looking to a transaction (ultimately referred to as the "Plum Project") under which Mobil would purchase an interest in the refinery at a price substantially higher than Gulf's cost of construction. The Mobil transaction depended upon Gulf's obtaining a license to utilize fully the actual, installed refining capacity of 5.8 million tons per annum.

Concerned with the sort of extreme opposition from the press, local communities, and various citizens and environmental groups which had plagued its efforts to build the refinery in 1968–69, Gulf felt it needed local assistance to guide it through the bureaucratic maze and to improve the public relations aspect of the application.

The decree authorizing the utilization of the full capacity of the Bertonico refinery would have to be issued jointly by the Ministry of Industry and Commerce and the Ministry of Finance after obtaining favorable opinions of an Interministerial Commission for the Testing of Plant and Equipment, made up of representatives of three ministries; an Interministerial Commission for Petroleum Affairs composed of representatives of 12 ministries; two bureaus in Milan; the regional government of Lombardy and three of its departments; and the communes of Bertonico, Terranova de' Passerini, and Turano.

Accordingly, Pignatelli enlisted the help of Mr. G. Del Bo, president of a company known as Andergip, S.A., described as a public relations and financial consulting firm with addresses in Eschen, Liechtenstein, and Lugano, Switzerland (Del Bo was also the president and principal stockholder of a company known as Carbonafta, a large petroleum jobber in Italy with which Gulf had substantial dealings, and president of the Italian Petroleum Jobbers Association). He was described by Pignatelli as "highly knowledgeable in the industry and a man of considerable influence."

On February 21, 1973, Pignatelli received a letter from Andergip, S.A., which set forth the basis on which the organization would assist Gulf in obtaining the authorization. The letter stated in full as follows (translation):

> In relation to the results of the final tests of the Bertonico Refinery, which have ascertained that it has an installed capacity of 5.8 million tons of crude per year, I wish to confirm to you on behalf of our company that we are prepared to put at the disposal of your company our organization in Italy for public relations consulting at a regional, provincial, and local level as well as our necessary technical services in the sector of urban planning and ecology, relative to the application which Gulf Italiana will submit in order to obtain the official acknowledgement of the aforementioned processing capacity of the Bertonico Refinery.
>
> The acknowledgement of said capacity is for us of relevant interest, inasmuch as the development programs of the Italian commercial activities associated with us base themselves on the availability of larger quantities of finished products in the Po Valley.
>
> For our assistance you will credit us an amount of U.S. $870,000 payable at the Bank Institute of the Swiss Confederation, after the aforementioned processing capacity will become operational.

Pignatelli described the contract as a contingency agreement and indicated that there was a "side" oral agreement that the license had to be obtained by September 30 or Andergip would bear all its expenditures. Apparently, the September 30 deadline was established because Gulf had to sign the related deal with Mobil by year-end.

In early February 1973 Pignatelli appeared in Pittsburgh before the Executive Council and made a presentation of the proposed transaction with Mobil (Plum Project). The minutes of the March 15, 1973 meeting of the Executive Council record approval "to proceed with arrangements to obtain a government permit to increase the licensed throughput of the Milan Refinery to 120,000 B/D."

In the bureaucratic proceedings relating to the Milan Refinery, all applications and formal contacts with governmental agencies were handled, according to Pignatelli, by Gulf officials. However, there was a mass of detail and "promotional" work which had to be undertaken to support the application and this, Pignatelli stated, was handled by Andergip.

In its formal application to the government for full utilization of the installed capacity, Gulf pointed out that the relocation from Zelo Buon Persico to Bertonico, due to denial of zoning authorization, had cost the company some additional $16 million over the original budgeted cost of the refinery project. Gulf also argued that expansion of production to 5.8 million tons per year would not have adverse ecological consequences or entail any local dislocation due to construction since the refinery already had that capacity. Moreover, the increased production would benefit the public as well as result in substantial economies for Gulf.

On July 4, 1973, the decree authorizing the processing of up to 5.8 million tons per year at Bertonico was issued by the appropriate ministries. Implementation of the conditions set forth in the decree concerning the installation of additional tankage involved four ministries, the regional government of Lombardy and two of its departments, the three communes referred to above, and a Consortium for the Navigation Canal Milano-Cremona-Po. The necessity of obtaining the acquiescence of all of these dispersed governmental agencies would appear to mke the implementation task a formidable one.

On July 16, 1973, an interim authority for expenditure (AFE) in the sum of $1 million was prepared and signed by Dr. Wyllie and Mr. J. J. Earnest, president and comptroller, respectively, of Gulf–Eastern Hemisphere, covering the obligation to Andergip. Under "description," the interim AFE stated:

> Preliminary Expenditures
>
> Note: This AFE will be incorporated into the final AFE for total product cost of about $28 million when finally issued.

The interim AFE was delivered for countersignature to Zane Q. Johnson, executive vice president of Gulf Oil in Pittsburgh, who returned it with a handwritten buckslip initialed by Johnson stating: "I discussed with J. Lee (president of Gulf Oil) and then advised Wyllie that he was to handle some other way." An undated memorandum for file by Mr. J. M. Turnbull, comptroller in London, stated in part:

> While Mr. Johnson did not sign AFE there were discussions between Messrs. Wyllie and Johnson on this subject and the Executive were aware that a "special" payment had to be made in order to obtain the permit.
>
> . . . in any event Mr. W. H. Meador, the Corporate Director Internal Auditing, was

> in London at the time the payment was being arranged and he was made fully aware of the transaction.

In the board's enquiry, neither Lee nor Johnson had any recollection of the transaction. However, Lee stated that his reaction would be not to sign the interim AFE, because it was not a usual or normal AFE. Lee distinguished between a "preliminary" AFE, which this was, and a "final" AFE, noting that preliminary AFEs were generally based upon concrete engineering estimates of costs, which the interim AFE in question was not, nor was it for a specific sum for a particular purpose.

On July 26, 1973, Gulf paid $868,853 to Mr. G. Del Bo, president of Andergip, and received a receipt from him. Payment was effected in the following manner. Morgan Guaranty Trust Company, London, was instructed to transfer $868,853 to Swiss Credit Bank, Chiasso, for retention pending instructions from Mr. Giartosio (administrative manager, Gulf Italy), who was to be identified by his passport. On July 26, 1973, Giartosio caused funds to be transferred to Del Bo at Swiss Credit Bank in Chiasso in exchange for appropriate receipts. These receipts were forwarded by Giartosio to Turnbull, the comptroller in London, with a buckslip stating "*Not* for Circulation in Italy." The receipt, said to have been signed by Del Bo with the left hand, stated as follows:

> This is to certify that the remittance of U.S. dollars $868,853 equivalent to Italian lire 530,000,000 attested by the attached bank receipt no. Sirenetta of 26/7/73 represents the agreed full and final settlement of all sums due in reimbursement of any expenses incurred for carrying out preliminary technical, urbanistic and ecological studies and surveys, as well as in payment of consultancy fees for public relations and administrative services rendered at national, regional and provincial levels in preparation of the application and development of information and data in support of the obtainment of the authorization, by means of debottlenecking, to process up to 5.6 million tons per year of crude oil in Gulf's Milan Refinery.

The accounting for this payment on the Gulf books was as follows: Gulf–Eastern Hemisphere charged the payment to a suspense account in July 1973. In December 1973 the charge was transferred to a fixed asset account: Milan Refinery, Italy. In May 1974 the charge was transferred back to Gulf–Eastern Hemisphere, where it was again held in a suspense account. In July 1974 the charge was transferred to Gulf Europe, a Liechtenstein corporation, where it was expensed in 1974. The records of this entry are maintained in Zurich.

Mobil ultimately paid Gulf 36.5 percent ($317,134) of this payment upon the sale to Mobil of an interest in the Milan refinery.

The committee's investigation was unable to determine what disposition was made of the $868,853. However, Pignatelli claimed that neither he nor to his knowledge any other Gulf official had any intention, understanding, or knowledge that any portion of the payment would be, or was, used for payments to political parties or government officials or in an otherwise improper manner to obtain the authorization. Nor was any part of it to be returned to Gulf for any purpose.

The board committee requested Del Bo to state in writing the general use to which the fee had been put. In response, on July 30, 1975, he wrote a letter to the chairman of the committee which stated as follows (translation):

> As you courteously requested, I am hereby reconfirming in writing what Mr. Del Bo has already declared to you verbally in the course of the meetings in London and in Rome: That is to say that

it is certain that no part of the sum turned over by GOC was directly, or indirectly, destined for political parties or political personalities or to governmental functionaries; as it is also certain that no part of that said sum was returned to dependents or organs of the Gulf Oil Company. . . .

To the extent that this will interest you, we inform you that said sums were destined approximately as follows: 50 to 55 percent to the newspaper and publication agencies specializing in the sector (Petroleum), about 35 percent to consultants and experts, and the remaining to Andergip.

We remain at your disposal for any further information and we welcome the opportunity to give you our best wishes.

Mr. Del Bo did not furnish the committee with copies of any documents constituting the "work product" of the Andergip organization or a detailed description of the work performed or the expenses incurred in obtaining the authorization. However, the committee did not feel it was in any position to demand an accounting, a lump-sum payment having been provided for, with no obligation to account for its use.

The Zeebrugge Car Ferry Disaster (A)

> It is with profound sadness that I must introduce this report with the tragic loss of the "Herald of Free Enterprise" off the Belgian coast. The Herald is a Townsend Thoresen ship and, as you know, Townsend Thoresen became part of P&O in January. At the time of writing the precise cause of the disaster is unknown. We have instituted an immediate investigation and of course both the British and Belgian governments are conducting enquiries. Whatever the outcome of these you may be assured that the safety of our ships and those who man them and travel in them is our overriding priority.

So began the somber letter by Chairman Jeffrey Sterling introducing the 1986 P&O Annual Report. The roll-on/roll-off passenger-car ferry *Herald of Free Enterprise* capsized in the approaches to the Belgian port of Zeebrugge en route to Dover in England at 7:05 P.M. local time on March 6, 1987. There was a light easterly breeze and the sea was calm. The ship had a crew of 80, and carried 459 passengers, 81 cars, 3 buses, and 47 trucks. She capsized in about 90 seconds soon after leaving the harbor, ending up on her side half-submerged in shallow water. Only a fortuitous turn to starboard in her last moments prevented her from sinking completely in deeper water.

Following the capsize a heroic search and rescue operation was mounted. At least 150 passengers and 38 members of the crew lost their lives, most inside the ship from hypothermia in the frigid water. Many others were injured. It soon became apparent to the rescuers that the *Herald of Free Enterprise* had left the port of Zeebrugge with her bow doors open. The death toll was the worst for a British vessel in peacetime since the sinking of the Titanic in 1912.

THE CROSS-CHANNEL TRANSPORT MARKET

The English Channel between England and the Continent of Europe is one of the most heavily traveled waterways in the world. In 1985 a total of 20,056,000 passengers and 3,387,200 cars, buses, trucks, and unaccompanied trailers were ferried across the channel. The most popular

 Address requests for permission to reprint to: Professor C. Boyd, College of Commerce, University of Saskatchewan, Saskatoon, Saskatchewan, Canada S7N 0W0.

crossing is the shortest one, between Dover and Calais in France, a 22-mile trip that takes 90 minutes. Exhibit 1 shows selected data on sea and air travel to and from the United Kingdom.

Fares for cross-channel travel had historically been high in comparison to other intensive ferry routes in the world, and drew criticism from British consumer groups. In the 1980s, however, prices began to decline, as shown in Exhibit 2.

The mixture of demand for channel ferry services was changing. Passenger travel had remained stable since 1982, but freight traffic was increasing. Part of this increase was due to increased trade (particularly since Britain became a member of the European Economic Community), and part was due to the technological advance represented by the introduction of roll-on/roll-off (ro-ro) ships. These ships, essentially flat pontoons covered by a superstructure, have bow and stern doors which enable vehicles to be driven on and off via adjustable ramps at the dock. The speed of ferry loading and unloading is vastly improved for a ro-ro ship, which reduces the unproductive time a ship spends in port.

For the freight shipper, ro-ro ferries also improve productivity. A tractor-trailer (or just the trailer unit) can be driven straight on and off the ferry's deck as if it were part of the road to the freight's destination. Costly intermediate transfers of cargo are eliminated, and the quantity of inventory in the distribution pipeline is reduced by speedier transportation. Exhibits 3 and 4 show data on cross-channel ro-ro freight growth.

Competition on cross-channel ferry services was influenced by the British government's July 1984 privatization of Sealink UK Ltd., previously a subsidiary of government-owned British Rail. At that time Sealink UK, its European state-owned counterparts, and Townsend Thoresen dominated the industry. Historically, channel ferry services had functioned mainly as the sea link between rail terminus points at channel ports.

Other recent developments in the industry had included the introduction of high-capacity mixed freight and passenger "jumbo" ferries; reductions in crew levels, despite the strong opposition of the maritime unions; the modernization of dockside facilities to help speed ferry turnaround time; the introduction of special freight-only ro-ro ferries; and the promotion of a wider range of fares, especially for day trippers and off-peak travel.

The Channel Tunnel poses an extreme threat to the ferry industry. After 100 years of aborted attempts to initiate a tunnel project, the French and British governments finally allowed the project to go ahead in 1986. This was bitterly opposed by the ferry operators. Eurotunnel, the Anglo-French company that will finance and manage the tunnel, plans to have the 30-mile-long dual railway tunnels underneath the channel in operation by 1993. Eurotunnel's finances of £1 billion in share capital and £5 billion in loan facilities compare with planned spending on the project of £4.9 billion.

TOWNSEND THORESEN

The following description is from the 1985 Annual Report:

> European Ferries Group plc[1] is a UK public company, with three separate classes of shares listed on the London Stock Exchange, giving a current market capitalization approaching £500 million.
>
> The origins of the Group can be traced back nearly 60 years to the time when

[1] plc is an abbreviation of public limited company.

Captain Stuart Townsend pioneered the first specialist car ferry service between Dover and Calais. Through a mixture of skilful management and acquisition the Group's Shipping Division, under the marketing name Townsend Thoresen, is now the major ferry operator in Europe, with services from Dover, Portsmouth, Felixstowe and Cairnryan to destinations in France, Belgium, Holland, and Northern Ireland.

In the 1970s the Group began diversifying, initially into Harbour Operations with the acquisition of Larne Harbour in Northern Ireland and the Felixstowe Dock & Railway Company, and then by the formation of a UK Property Division. The major asset within this UK Property Division is a 34.7 percent holding in Stockley plc, a listed property company operating in London and the southeast of England.

The Group became involved in U.S. property (real estate) in 1979 and this particular area has seen significant expansion in the intervening period, such that the Group now has an interest, both directly and through joint ventures, in substantial holdings of land in Denver, Atlanta, and Houston. The 1980s have seen further property acquisitions at La Manga Club in Spain, and, in a smaller way, in Germany.

Significant development projects have been in progress since the beginning of 1985 in our shipping and harbour divisions. Six vessels are being substantially extended ("jumboisation") and two new vessels have been ordered for delivery next year. We are also developing a major new terminal, the Trinity Container Terminal, at the Port of Felixstowe which will be completed later this year.

Exhibit 5 lists the Directors of European Ferries Group plc and the managers of Townsend Thoresen, as detailed in the 1985 report. Background financial data is given in Exhibits 6 and 7.

In 1982 the Townsend Thoresen ferry *European Gateway* capsized with the loss of six lives after a collision with a Sealink ship in the approaches to the port of Harwich. The speed of the capsize drew speculation on the lack of stability of ro-ro ferries when water enters the main vehicle deck.[2] Like the *Herald* after her, the *European Gateway* came to rest on her side half-submerged in shallow water, narrowly avoiding a deep-water sinking with heavy loss of life.

In January 1984 European Ferries purchased from the Peninsular and Oriental Steam Navigation Company (P&O) its loss-making Normandy Ferries subsidiary for £12.5m. In January 1986 P&O acquired a 50 percent interest in a firm that held shares equivalent to 16.1 percent of the voting share capital of European Ferries. Sir Jeffrey Sterling, the chairman of P&O, was invited to join the board on January 21, 1986.

On December 4, 1986 the boards of European Ferries and P&O jointly announced a recommended £340 million takeover offer for the shares of European Ferries by P&O. Geoffrey Parker, executive chairman of European Ferries, gave reasons for his firm's recent poor performance in a letter to shareholders:

> In the early part of the year our property activities in Houston were affected by the severe fall in the price of oil, upon which the economy of Houston is critically dependent. In the late spring our shipping activities were seriously affected by strike action which was not resolved for 10

---

[2] According to Lloyd's Register in London, over 30 accidents to ro-ro ferries had involved loss of life. The worst previous British accident was in 1953, when the *Princess Victoria* sank in the Irish Sea killing 134. The world's worst disaster was in 1981, when 431 died on an Indonesian ferry which caught fire and sank in the Java Sea. In roughly two thirds of the cases, the capsize took less than five minutes.

> weeks. Your Board estimates that the strikes will be responsible for some £10m in lost profits in 1986 . . . and that our U.S. activities will now make a negative contribution compared with profits before taxation of £17m in 1985.

The majority of European Ferries shareholders accepted the P&O offer by the deadline of 3 P.M. January 16, 1987. Exhibit 8 outlines P&O's recent business history.

THE CAPSIZE OF mv HERALD OF FREE ENTERPRISE

The *mv Herald of Free Enterprise,*[3] like her sister ships *Pride of Free Enterprise* and *Spirit of Free Enterprise,* was a modern ro-ro passenger/vehicle ferry designed for use on the high volume short Dover-Calais ferry route. She could accelerate rapidly to her service speed of 22 knots. She was certificated to carry a maximum total of 1,400 persons.

At 433 feet long and 7,950 gross tons, the *Herald* was of record size at her launching in 1980 and was one of the prides of the 22-ship Townsend Thoresen fleet. She had two main vehicle decks, and at Dover and Calais double-deck ramps connected to the ferry, allowing simultaneous vehicle access to both decks. At Zeebrugge there was only a single level access ramp which did not allow simultaneous deck loading, and thus ferry turnaround time was longer at this port. Also, this ramp could not quite reach the upper vehicle deck, and water ballast was pumped into tanks in the bow of the *Herald* to facilitate loading.

When the *Herald* left Zeebrugge on March 6, 1987 not all the water had been pumped out of the bow ballast tanks, causing her to be some three feet down at the bow. Mr. Stanley, the assistant bosun, was responsible for closing the bow doors. He had opened the doors on arrival at Zeebrugge, and then supervised some maintenance and cleaning activities. He was released from this work by Mr. Ayling, the bosun,[4] and went to his cabin. He fell asleep and was not awakened by the harbour station's public address call alerting crew to take their assigned positions for departure from the dock.

The bosun left the car deck at the harbour station's call to go to his assigned station. He later said "It has never been part of my duties to close the doors or make sure that anyone is there to close the doors." The Chief Officer, Mr. Leslie Sabel, stated that he remained on the car deck until he saw—or thought he saw—Mr. Stanley threading his way through the parked cars towards the door control panel. He then went to the bridge, his assigned position.

The *Herald* backed out of the berth stern first. By the time the *Herald* had swung around the bow was in darkness and the open bow doors were not obvious to the ship's Master, Captain David Lewry. As the ship increased speed, a bow wave began to build up under her prow. At 15 knots, with the bow down 2–3 feet lower than normal, water began to break over the main car deck through the open doors at the rate of 200-tons-per-minute.

In common with other ro-ro vessels, the *Herald's* main vehicle deck had no subdividing bulkheads. If water entered the deck it could flow from end to end or from side to side with ease. The flood of water through the bow doors quickly caused the

[3] mv is an abbreviation of motor vessel.

[4] The bosun (a variant spelling of the word boatswain) is responsible for ship maintenance. The rank is equivalent to sergeant; assistant bosun is equivalent to corporal.

vessel to become unstable. The *Herald* listed 30° to port almost instantaneously. Large quantities of water continued to pour in and fill the port wing of the vehicle deck, eventually causing a capsize to port. The *Herald* settled on the sea bed at slightly more than 90°, with the starboard half of her hull above water.

Under the 1894 Merchant Shipping Act, a Court of Formal Investigation of the capsize of the *Herald of Free Enterprise* was held in London between April 27 and June 12, 1987 before the Wreck Commissioner, the Hon. Mr. Justice Sheen, a respected judge. The proceedings of the court were subject to intense public scrutiny, with the tabloid press in particular concentrating on the more sensational aspects of the tragedy.

To encourage full disclosure at this Court of Investigation, the U.K. Department of Transport, which is responsible for enforcement of the various shipping acts, indicated that it did not intend to prosecute anyone responsible for the fact that the *Herald* went to sea with her bow doors open. This was a common practice for such courts of enquiry. The Court had investigative powers, the power to suspend or remove a Merchant Officer's Certificate of Competency, and the power to determine who should contribute to payment of the Investigation's costs. The Court had no other powers.

EXTRACTS FROM THE REPORT OF THE COURT OF FORMAL INVESTIGATION

mv HERALD OF FREE ENTERPRISE

The remainder of this case study consists of verbatim extracts from the Report of the Court of Formal Investigation written by the Hon. Justice Sheen, and released on July 25, 1987. Statements of opinion and interpretation of facts are his, and not the case-writer's. [Any comments or elaborations by the case-writer are shown in square brackets.]

The Manning of the *Herald* on the Zeebrugge Route

On the Dover-Calais run these ships are manned by a complement of a Master, two Chief Officers and a Second Officer. The officers are required to work 12 hours on and not less than 24 hours off. In contrast, each crew was on board for 24 hours and then had 48 hours ashore. . . . The sea passage to Zeebrugge takes 4.5 hours . . . which gives the officers more time to relax. For this reason the Company employed a Master and two deck officers [instead of three] on this run. . . .

Captain Kirby was one of five masters who took it in turn to command the *Herald*. He was the Senior Master . . . a coordinator between all the masters and officers in order to ensure uniformity in the practices operated by different crews. As three different crews served with five different sets of officers, it was essential that there should be uniformity of practice. Furthermore there were frequent changes among the officers. Captain Kirby drew attention to this in an internal memo dated November 22, 1986 addressed to Mr. M. Ridley, Chief Superintendent.

> The existing system of Deck Officer manning . . . is unsatisfactory. When *Herald* took up the Zeebrugge service our Deck Officers were reduced from 15 to 10. The surplus 5 were distributed around the fleet. On *Herald's* return to the Calais service, instead of our officers returning, we were and are being manned by officers from whatever ship is

> at refit. Due to this system, together with Trainee Master moves, *Herald* will have had a total of 30 different deck officers on the books during the period September 29, 1986 to January 5, 1987. . . .

Captain Kirby returned to this theme with a further memorandum dated January 28, 1987 which was also addressed to Mr. Ridley:

> I wish to stress again that *Herald* badly needs a *permanent* complement of good deck officers. Our problem was outlined in my memo of November 22. Since then the throughput of officers has increased even further, partly because of sickness. During the period from September 1 to January 28, 1987 a total of 36 deck officers have been attached to the ship. We have also lost two masters and gained one. To make matters worse the vessel has had an unprecedented seven changes in sailing schedule. The result has been a serious loss of continuity. Shipboard maintenance, safety gear checks, crew training, and the overall smooth running of the vessel have all suffered.

Pressure to Leave the Berth

Why could not the loading officer remain on deck until the doors were closed before going to his harbour station on the bridge? The operation could be completed in three minutes. But the officers always felt under pressure to leave after loading. . . .

The "Bridge and Navigation Procedures" guide which was issued by the Company included the following:

> Departure from Port
>
> a) O.O.W./Master should be on the Bridge approximately 15 minutes before the ship's sailing time; . . .

That order does not make it clear whether it was the duty of the O.O.W.[5] or the Master to be on the bridge 15 minutes before sailing, or whether the officer was to remain on the bridge thereafter. If the O.O.W. was the loading officer, this order created a conflict in his duties. The conflict was brought to the attention of Mr. Develin[6] by a memorandum dated August 21, 1982 from Captain Hackett, Senior Master of *Free Enterprise VIII* in which he said:

> It is impractical for the O.O.W. (either the Chief or the Second Officer) to be on the Bridge 15 minutes before sailing time. Both are fully committed to loading the ship. At sailing time, the Chief Officer stands by the bow or the stern door to see the ramp out and assure papers are on board, etc. The Second Officer proceeds to his after mooring station to assure that the propellers are clear and report to the bridge.

The order illustrates the lack of thought given by management to the organization of officers' duties. [On the Zeebrugge run there was a reduced number of officers, and the loading officer's task was more complex because of the single-level loading ramp.]

The sense of urgency to sail at the earliest possible moment was exemplified by an internal memorandum dated August 18, 1986 sent to assistant managers by Mr. D. Shipley, who was the operations manager at Zeebrugge:

> . . . put pressure on the first officer if you don't think he is moving fast enough. . . . Let's put the record straight, sailing late out of Zeebrugge isn't on. It's 15 minutes early for us.

[5] [O.O.W. stands for Officer of the Watch, who is one of the deck officers and not the Master.]

[6] [Mr. Develin joined the Company in May 1975. In 1978 he became the Chief Marine Superintendent, and in 1986 he became a Director of the Company.]

Mr. A. P. Young sought to explain away that memorandum on the basis that the language was used merely for the purpose of what he called "motivation." But it was entirely in keeping with his own thoughts at the time. . . . The Court was left in no doubt that deck officers felt that there was no time to be wasted. The Company sought to say that the disaster could have been avoided if the Chief Officer had waited on deck another three minutes. That is true. But the Company took no proper steps to ensure that the Chief Officer remained on deck until the bow doors were closed.

The Negative Reporting System

The Company has issued a set of standing orders which include the following:

> *01.09 Ready for Sea*
> Heads of Departments are to report to the Master immediately they are aware of any deficiency which is likely to cause their departments to be unready for sea in any respect at the due sailing time. In the absence of any such report the Master will assume, at the due sailing time, that the vessel is ready for sea in all respects.

That order was unsatisfactory in many respects. . . . Masters came to rely upon the absence of any report at the time of sailing as satisfying them that their ship was ready for sea in all respects. That was, of course, a very dangerous assumption.

On March 6, Captain Lewry saw the Chief Officer come to the Bridge. Captain Lewry did not ask him if the ship was all secure and the Chief Officer did not make any report. Captain Lewry was entitled to assume that the assistant bosun and the Chief Officer were qualified to perform their respective duties, but he should not have assumed they had done so. He should have insisted on a report to that effect.

In mitigation of Captain Lewry's failure to ensure that his ship was in all respects ready for sea a number of points were made on his behalf, of which the three principal ones were as follows:

1. Captain Lewry merely followed a system which was operated by all the Masters of the *Herald* and approved by the Senior Master, Captain Kirby.
2. The Court was reminded that the orders entitled "Ship's standing orders" issued by the Company make no reference, as they should have done, to opening and closing the bow and stern doors.
3. Before this disaster there had been no less than five occasions when one of the Company's ships had proceeded to sea with bow or stern doors open. Some of these incidents were known to management, who had not drawn them to the attention of other Masters. . .

The system . . . was defective. The fact that other Masters operated the same defective system does not relieve Captain Lewry of his personal responsibility for taking his ship to sea in an unsafe condition. In so doing he was seriously negligent in the discharge of his duties. That negligence was one of the causes contributing to the disaster. The Court is aware of the mental and emotional burden resulting from this disaster which has been and will be borne by Captain Lewry, but the Court would be failing in its duty if it did not suspend his Certificate of Competency.

The Management of Townsend Thoresen

. . . a full investigation into the circumstances of the disaster leads inexorably to the conclusion that the underlying or cardinal faults lay higher up in the Company. The Board of Directors did not appreciate their responsibility for the safe management of their ships. They did not apply their minds to the question: What orders should be given for the safety of our ships?

The directors did not have any proper comprehension of what their duties were. There appears to have been a lack of thought about the way in which the *Herald* ought to have been organized for the Dover-Zeebrugge run. All concerned in management, from the members of the Board of Directors down to the junior superintendents, were guilty of fault in that all must be regarded as sharing responsibility for the failure of management. From top to bottom the body corporate was infected with the disease of sloppiness. . . . It is only necessary to quote one example of how the standard of management fell short. . . . It reveals a staggering complacency.

On March 18, 1986 there was a meeting of Senior Masters with management, at which Mr. Develin was in the Chair. One of the topics raised for discussion concerned the recognition of the Chief Officer as Head of Department and the roles of the Maintenance Master and Chief Officer. Mr. Develin said, although he was still considering writing definitions of these different roles, he felt "it was more preferable not to define the roles but to allow them to evolve." That attitude was described by Mr. Owen,[7] with justification, as an abject abdication of responsibility. It demonstrates an inability or unwillingness to give clear orders. **Clear instructions are the foundation of a safe system of operation** [original emphasis].

It was the failure to give clear instructions about the duties of the Officers on the Zeebrugge run which contributed so greatly to the cause of this disaster. Mr. Clarke, [counsel] on behalf of the Company, said that it was not the responsibility of Mr. Develin to see that Company orders were properly drafted. In answer to the question, "Who was responsible?" Mr. Clarke said "Well in truth, nobody, though there ought to have been." The Board of Directors must accept a heavy responsibility for their lamentable lack of directions. Individually and collectively they lacked a sense of responsibility. This left, what Mr. Owen so aptly described as, "a vacuum at the centre."

. . . Mr. Develin [Director and Chief Superintendent] was prepared to accept that he was responsible for the safe operation of the Company's ships. Another director, Mr. Ayers, told the Court that no director was solely responsible for safety. Mr. Develin thought that before he joined the Board, the safety of ships was a collective Board responsibility.

. . . as this Investigation progressed, it became clear that shore management took very little notice of what they were told by their Masters. The Masters met only intermittently. There was one period of two and a half years during which there was no formal meeting between Management and Senior Masters. Latterly there was an improvement. But the real complaint, which appears to the Court to be fully justified, was that the "Marine Department" did not listen to the complaints or suggestions or wishes of their Masters. The Court heard of four specific areas in which the voice of the Masters fell on deaf ears ashore [each detailed in separate sections below].

[7] [Counsel for the National Union of Seamen, certain surviving crew, and the next-of-kin of deceased crew.]

Carriage of Excess Numbers of Passengers

During the course of the evidence it became apparent from the documents that there were no less than seven different Masters, each of whom found that from time to time his ship was carrying substantially in excess of the permitted number [1,400].

[The Report then details a series of memoranda between various Masters and Mr. A. P. Young, the Operations Manager, on the topic of excess passengers. These were exchanged in 1982, 1983, and 1984]. . . . But the matter became really serious in 1986. The Court heard evidence from Captain de St. Croix, who was Master of the *Pride of Free Enterprise*. On August 1, 1986 he sent a memorandum to Mr. Young. . . .

> Passenger Numbers on 15.00 D/C, 1.8.86 On the above sailing from Dover, the first passenger total given to the RO [radio operator] by the Purser was 1,228. A call from the manifest office then informed the RO to add on another 214. The RO queried this as the total then had been way over the top.
>
> After a short delay the manifest office came back with a figure of 1,014 plus an add-on of 214 making a total of 1,228.
>
> As seeds of doubt had by then been sown in my mind I decided to have a head count as they went off at Calais. The following figures were revealed . . . [detail of count omitted]
>
> | | |
> |---|---|
> | Total passengers | 1,587 |
> | Crew | 95 |
> | Total on board | 1,682 |
>
> This total is way over the life saving capacity of the vessel. The fine on the Master for this offence is £50,000 and probably confiscation of certificate. May I please know what steps the company intend to take to protect my career from mistakes of this nature.

[The report details six more memos sent to Mr. Young between August and October 1986 by various Masters complaining about overloading. In a memo sent on October 31, 1986 Mr. Develin attempted to arrange a meeting with Mr. Young to discuss the problem with a representative of the Senior Masters] . . . Mr. Young did not invite Mr. Develin to meet him to discuss the subject. Mr. Young took the view that this was not a marine matter and deliberately excluded Mr. Develin from further investigation of the problem.

. . . **The Court reluctantly concluded that Mr. Young made no proper or sincere effort to solve the problem** [original emphasis]. The Court takes a most serious view of the fact that so many of the Company's ferries were carrying an excessive number of passengers on so many occasions. . . .

. . . After it became apparent that this Court was greatly interested in the system for checking the number of passengers carried on each ship further thought was given to the matter by the Company. On May 29, 1987 Mr. Young produced a memorandum containing some ideas for improving the system of counting the number of passengers.

Door Status Warning Lights for the Bridge

On October 29, 1983 the assistant bosun of the *Pride* neglected to close both the bow and the stern doors on sailing from No. 5 berth Dover. It appears he had fallen asleep. . . . On June 28, 1985 Captain Bowers of the *Pride* wrote a sensible memorandum to Mr. Develin:

> In the hope that there might be one or two ideas worthy of consideration I am forwarding some points that have been suggested on this ship and with reference to any future new-building programme. Many of the items are mentioned because of the excessive amounts of maintenance, time, and money spent on them.
>
> 4. Mimic Panel—There is no indication on the bridge as to whether the most important watertight doors are closed or not. That is the bow and stern doors. With the very short distance between the berth and the open sea on both sides of the Channel this can be a problem if the operator is delayed or having problems in closing the doors. Indicator lights on the very excellent mimic panel could enable the bridge team to monitor the situation in such circumstances.

Mr. Develin circulated that memorandum amongst the managers for comment. It was a serious memorandum that merited serious thought and attention, and called for a serious reply. The answers which Mr. Develin received will be set out verbatim. From Mr. Alcindor, a deputy chief superintendent: "Do they need an indicator to tell them whether the deck storekeeper is awake and sober? My goodness!!" From Mr. Reynolds: "Nice but don't we already pay someone!" From Mr. Ellison: "Assume the guy who shuts the doors tells the bridge if there is a problem." From Mr. Hamilton: "Nice!" It is hardly necessary for the Court to comment that these replies display an absence of any proper sense of responsibility. Moreover the comment of Mr. Alcindor on the deck storekeeper was either ominously prescient or showed an awareness of this type of incident in the past.

If the sensible suggestion that indicator lights be installed had received, in 1985, the serious consideration which it deserved, it is at least possible that they would have been fitted in the early months of 1986 and this disaster might well have been prevented [original emphasis]. [The report details further requests for indicator lights made by two Masters in 1986, and also records their written rejection by Mr. King:]

> I cannot see the purpose or the need for the stern door to be monitored on the bridge, as the seaman in charge of closing the doors is standing by the control panel watching them close.

[The Report notes] . . . that within a matter of days after the disaster indicator lights were installed in the remaining Spirit class ships and other ships of the fleet.

Ascertaining Draughts

[Following the loss of the passenger ferry *European Gateway* in 1982, Townsend Thoresen instituted an investigation into passenger safety]. . . . As a result of that investigation, on February 10, 1983, Captain Martin sent a report to Mr. Develin. That report was seen by Mr. Ayers. It begins with the words:

> The Company and ships' Masters could be considered negligent on the following points, particularly when some are the result of "commercial interests":
>
> a. The ship's draught[8] is not read before sailing, and the draught entered into the Official Log Book is completely erroneous.
>
> b. It is not standard practice to inform the Master of his passenger figure before sailing.

[8] [The depth of a loaded vessel in the water, taken from the level of the water-line to the lowest point of the hull. Section 68(2) of the Merchant Shipping Act 1970 makes it a legal requirement for a Master to know the draught of his ship and to enter this in the official log book each time the ship puts to sea.]

c. The tonnage of cargo is not declared to the Master before sailing.
d. Full speed is maintained in dense fog.

. . . For the moment we are only concerned with the draught reading. Later in the report under the heading "recommendations" there is the statement "company to investigate installing draught recorders[9] on new tonnage." Mr. Ayers was asked if he did investigate. His answer was "somewhere in this period the answer was yes." In the light of later answers given by Mr. Ayers, that answer is not accepted by the Court.

. . . Mr. Ayers may be a competent Naval Architect, but the court formed the view that he did not carry out his managerial duties, whatever they may have been. Mr. Ayers was asked whether each director of Townsend Car Ferries was given a specific area of responsibility. His [verbatim] answer was "No; there were not written guidelines for any director." When he was asked how each director knew what his responsibilities were his [verbatim] answer was "It was more a question of duplication as a result of not knowing than missing gaps. We were a team who had grown together." The amorphous phrasing of that answer is typical of much of the evidence of Mr. Ayers. He appeared to be incapable of expressing his thoughts with clarity.

[Mr. Ayers had previously not answered another Master's request for the installation of draught recorders. The draught of the *Herald* turned out to be a critical question. Research undertaken for the Court revealed that the *Pride* and the *Spirit* each weighed about 300 tons more than previously thought. The origin of most of this excess weight was a mystery. The *Herald* was probably 300 tons overweight also. Further loading miscalculations arose from the estimates of the tonnage of freight vehicles on the ship. No weigh scales were used, as the tonnage was calculated by using drivers' declarations of vehicle weights. Experiments revealed that these were frequently false. An average ferry-load of trucks was found to weigh 13 percent more than the sum of drivers' declarations]

Captain Lewry told the Court quite frankly that no attempt had been made to read the draughts of his ship on a regular basis or indeed at all in regular service. Fictitious figures were entered in the Official Log which took no account of the trimming water ballast. . . .

The difficulties faced by the Masters are exemplified by the attitude of Mr. Develin to a memorandum dated October 24, 1983 and sent to him by Captain Martin:

> For good order I feel I should acquaint you with some problems associated with one of the Spirit class ships operating to Zeebrugge using the single deck berths. . . .
>
> 4. At full speed, or even reduced speed, the bow wave . . . comes three quarters of the way up the bow door. . . .
> 6. Ship does not respond so well when trimmed so much by the head [i.e., with water ballast in the bowl], and problems have been found when manoeuvering. . . .
> 8. As you probably appreciate we never know how much cargo we are carrying, so that a situation could arise where not only are we overloaded by 400 tons but also trimmed by the head by 4.5 feet. I have not been able to work out how that would affect our damage stability.

[9] [Such recorders enable anyone on the Bridge to determine how low in the water the ship is. Without such devices the draught markings can only be read from outside the ship.]

Mr. Develin was asked what he thought of that memorandum. His answer was: "Initially I was not happy. When I studied it further, I decided that it was an operational difficulty report and Captain Martin was acquainting me of it." Later he said: "I think if he had been unhappy with the problem he would have come in and banged my desk." When Mr. Develin was asked what he thought about the information concerning the effect of full speed he said: "I believe he was exaggerating." In subsequent answers he made it clear that he thought every complaint was an exaggeration. In reply to a further question Mr. Develin said: "If he was concerned he would not have sailed. I do not believe there is anything wrong sailing with the vessel trimmed by the head."

The Need for a High Capacity Ballast Pump

On February 28, 1984 Mr. R. C. Crone, who was a Chief Engineer, sent a memorandum to Mr. Develin. . . .

> Ballasting Spirit Class Ships on Zeebrugge Service
>
> ---
>
> Normal ballasting requirements are for Nos. 1 and 14 tanks . . . to be filled for arrival at Zeebrugge and emptied on completion of loading. . . Using one pump, the time to fill or empty the two tanks is 1 hr. 55 mins. With two pumps the time can be reduced to 1 hr. 30 mins. . . Problems associated with the operation. . . .
>
> a. Pumping time amounts to approximately half the normal passage time.
>
> b. Ship well down by the head for prolonged periods causing bad steerage and high fuel consumption.
>
> c. Continuous pressurising of tanks to overflow/vent level.
>
> d. Time consuming for staff.
>
> e. Bow doors subjected to stress not normally to be expected, certainly having its effect on door locking gear equipment.
>
> f. Dangerous complete blind operation that should not be carried out as normal service practice, i.e., no knowledge of tank capacity during operation, the tanks are pumped up until the overflow is noticed from the bridge, thereafter emptied until the pump amperage/pressure is noted to drop!
>
> Purely as a consideration realising the expense compared with possible future double ramp berths. . . . [he recommends fitting a high capacity ballast pump].

Mr. Develin . . . said that he did not agree with some of the contents. He appeared to think that the chief engineer was grossly exaggerating the problem. . . . Mr. Develin said that Mr. Crone came to his department on several occasions to press for the implementation of his recommendations but that after discussion he must have been satisfied. . . . In due course an estimate was obtained for the installation of a pump at a cost of £25,000.[10] This cost was regarded by the Company as prohibitive.

The Court's Conclusion

The Court . . . finds . . . that the capsizing of the *Herald of Free Enterprise* was partly caused or contributed to by serious negligence in the discharge of their

---

[10] [Equivalent to $45,000 at an exchange rate of US$1.80 = £1.00.]

duties by Captain David Lewry (Master), Mr. Leslie Sabel (Chief Officer) and Mr. Mark Victor Stanley (assistant bosun), and partly caused or contributed to by the fault of Townsend Car Ferries (the Owners). The Court suspends the certificate of the said Captain David Lewry for a period of one year . . . [and] suspends the certificate of the said Mr. Leslie Sabel for a period of two years.

[The Court had no power to sanction the assistant bosun, who was not a certificated officer. The final section of the Report addresses the issue of payment of costs of the enquiry. The last paragraph deals with Townsend Thoresen.][11]

There being no other way in which this Court can mark its feelings about the conduct of Townsend Car Ferries Limited other than by an order that they should pay a substantial part of the costs of this investigation, I have ordered them to pay the sum of £350,000. That seems to me to meet the justice of the case.

[11] [Townsend Thoresen had previously made some payments to the injured and to the relatives of the deceased. Note that the total level of payments received by relatives in a case of wrongful death in the United States of America is extremely high compared to the sums paid in the rest of the world. It would be a serious miscalculation to apply U.S. values, often up in the millions of dollars per victim, to this case. The actual sum that will be paid per victim of the Zeebrugge disaster is not known exactly, but would probably average £80,000 or US$144,000.]

EXHIBIT 1

SELECTED U.K. AIR AND SEA PASSENGER TRAVEL DATA, 1975–1985

By Country of Embarkation or Disembarkation, Arrivals Plus Departures

	Amounts in Thousands										
	1975	*1976*	*1977*	*1978*	*1979*	*1980*	*1981*	*1982*	*1983*	*1984*	*1985*
By sea											
Belgium	3,461	3,975	4,391	4,428	4,421	5,192	4,714	4,678	4,415	4,608	4,411
France	7,739	7,861	8,602	9,805	11,112	12,621	14,734	15,747	16,140	15,353	15,645
Holland	1,496	1,841	1,977	2,056	2,044	1,940	1,958	1,968	2,210	2,191	2,207
Totals	12,876	13,677	14,970	16,289	17,577	19,753	21,406	22,393	22,765	22,152	22,263
Note: Some traffic through these three countries is in transit to or from adjacent European countries.											
By air											
Belgium	788	850	854	874	867	809	757	748	824	942	988
France	2,740	2,901	2,904	3,026	3,102	3,070	3,105	3,193	3,275	3,537	3,746
Holland	1,634	1,835	1,934	1,994	1,959	1,903	1,813	1,843	1,808	2,014	2,227
Subtotals	5,162	5,586	5,692	5,894	5,928	5,782	5,675	5,784	5,907	6,493	6,961
FR of Germany	2,277	2,470	2,619	2,882	3,081	3,136	2,948	2,998	3,006	3,384	3,644
Switzerland	1,093	1,181	1,289	1,372	1,413	1,444	1,469	1,576	1,711	1,875	2,016
Italy	1,860	1,941	2,037	2,279	2,550	2,692	2,335	2,378	2,494	2,582	2,583
Greece	691	882	884	1,162	1,562	1,839	2,095	2,123	2,006	2,301	2,875
Portugal	309	296	399	474	591	701	849	963	1,068	1,248	1,547
Spain	5,298	4,667	4,617	5,553	5,654	5,592	6,332	7,624	8,293	9,543	7,751
All air	16,690	17,023	17,537	19,616	20,779	21,186	21,703	23,446	24,485	27,426	27,377

Source: U.K. Department of Transport Statistics Digest 1975–85.

EXHIBIT 2
FERRY FARES AT 1985 PRICES FOR SHORT SEA ROUTES ACROSS THE CHANNEL
4.5 Metre Car, Ford Cortina, Two Adults Plus Two Children, One-Way

	1975	*1980*	*1985*
Peak (most expensive single fare)	£78.21	£72.72	£81.00
Standard (cheapest published no-discount single fare)	£69.83	£55.61	£38.00

Note: £1.00 = US$1.80.
Source: Flexilink.

EXHIBIT 3

ROLL-ON/ROLL-OFF ROAD GOODS VEHICLES TO MAINLAND EUROPE, BY COUNTRY OF DISEMBARKATION, 1975–1985

Departures from U.K. Only

	Amounts in Thousands										
	1975	*1976*	*1977*	*1978*	*1979*	*1980*	*1981*	*1982*	*1983*	*1984*	*1985*
Powered vehicles											
Belgium	75.1	72.7	103.9	110.3	123.0	122.1	119.6	136.3	146.1	163.7	163.3
France	94.4	107.8	128.7	131.1	150.6	140.4	152.9	168.0	187.3	215.8	230.6
Holland	31.7	32.4	32.9	31.9	39.8	36.8	41.3	41.5	40.3	40.8	48.0
Totals	201.2	212.9	265.5	273.3	313.4	299.3	313.8	345.8	373.7	420.3	441.9
Unaccompanied trailers											
Belgium	33.6	37.1	45.8	44.6	57.5	48.2	63.5	99.1	104.4	103.6	129.9
France	25.3	28.8	35.8	43.0	56.4	53.7	63.1	58.2	61.5	59.9	65.8
Holland	72.2	81.7	69.8	94.0	103.3	97.6	110.4	128.1	140.8	146.7	145.0
Totals	131.1	147.6	151.4	181.6	217.2	199.5	237.0	285.4	306.7	310.2	340.7
Grand totals	332.3	360.5	416.9	454.9	530.6	498.8	550.8	631.2	680.4	730.5	782.6

Source: U.K. Department of Transport Statistics Digest 1975–85.

EXHIBIT 4
PORT OF DOVER FERRY TRAFFIC, 1981–1985
Arrivals and Departures

	1981	*1982*	*1983*	*1984*	*1985*
Passengers (millions)	12.46	13.82	13.95	13.86	13.78
Percent change from prior year	+12.96%	+10.94%	+0.94%	−0.67%	−0.56%
Passenger vehicles (millions)	1.65	1.78	1.74	1.73	1.72
Percent change from prior year	+11.41%	+7.42%	−1.99%	−0.69%	−0.06%
Freight vehicles (millions)	0.51	0.61	0.69	0.74	0.80
Percent change from prior year	+5.88%	+19.48%	+13.36%	+14.73%	+7.96%

Source: Port of Dover Authority.

EXHIBIT 5
EUROPEAN FERRIES GROUP plc
Directors As Listed in 1985 Annual Report

Kenneth Siddle	Chairman and Group Managing Director. *(Succeeded by Geoffrey Parker in July 1986)*
W. James Ayers	Group Technical Director.
Rodger G. Braidwood	Group Finance Director, Director of Stockley plc, Controller of Group Property interests.
John J. Briggs	Managing Director of Townsend Thoresen's Dover operations, Group Freight Director.
John W. Dick	Chairman of E F International Inc, Director of Stockley plc.
Geoffrey J. Parker	Chairman and Managing Director of Harbour Operations Division, Managing Director of Townsend Thoresen's Felixstowe and Larne Operations.
John R. Parsons	Deputy Managing Director of Townsend Thoresen's Dover operations.
William B. Pauls	Vice Chairman and Chief Executive Officer of E F International Inc.

Non Executive Directors
- Roald P. Aukner
- David J. Bradford
- Knut Dybwad
- Colin H. Fenn
- Sir Jeffrey Sterling (Alternate–Bruce D. MacPhail)

TOWNSEND THORESEN MANAGEMENT
As Listed in European Ferries Group plc 1985 Annual Report

Dover	J. J. Briggs	–Managing
	J. R. Parsons	–Deputy Managing
	A. P. Young	–Operations
Portsmouth	D. S. Donhue	–Managing
	R. N. Kirton	–Operations
Felixstowe & Larne	G. J. Parker	–Managing
	S. Livingstone	–Operations
Technical Services	W. J. Ayers	
Tourist Marketing	B. H. Thompson	

EXHIBIT 6
EUROPEAN FERRIES GROUP plc FIVE YEAR FINANCIAL RECORD
In Millions of Pounds Except Share Data

	1985	*1984*	*1983*	*1982*	*1981*
Sales revenue	403.5	309.4	322.9	292.9	277.7
Profit before taxation	48.4	44.4	45.0	30.4	26.8
Earnings per share	13.7p	14.9p	12.3p	10.5p	9.4p
Net dividend per ordinary share	4.75p	4.3p	3.8p	3.35p	3.1p
Dividend cover	2.9x	3.5x	3.2x	3.1x	3.0x
Year-end share price	139.5p	128.0p	88.5p	57.0p	74.0p
Year-end FT industrials index	1130.0	945.2	775.7	593.6	528.8
Capital expenditure	82.6	45.3	16.2	14.4	18.2
Depreciation	17.7	15.0	13.3	12.3	12.0
Tangible fixed assets	267.7	206.9	176.6	183.1	180.5
Investment in associates	118.5	73.4	79.2	62.1	30.2
Stocks	163.3	302.7	121.1	110.3	75.3
Borrowings net of cash and deposits	159.7	164.6	113.4	121.0	88.6
Shareholders funds at 31st December	327.1	302.4	254.9	225.2	207.8

Note: £1.00 = 100p = US$1.80.
Source: European Ferries Group 1985 Annual Report

EXHIBIT 7
EUROPEAN FERRIES GROUP plc DIVISION SALES AND PROFITABILITY

	Sales Revenue (£m)					*Profit before Taxation (£m)*				
	1985	*1984*	*1983*	*1982*	*1981*	*1985*	*1984*	*1983*	*1982*	*1981*
Shipping	280.1	236.4	226.7	207.7	183.0	19.0	17.5	16.6	12.8	1.9
Harbour operations	46.3	42.1	38.4	34.4	29.4	10.9	9.6	9.5	8.5	6.2
U.K. property	14.6	14.0	13.7	33.9	33.3	2.0	3.0	2.3	2.4	9.2
U.S. property	48.8	13.9	43.0	16.5	31.4	17.4	14.6	12.7	(0.9)	7.7
Spain property	13.7	3.0	1.1	—	—	(0.5)	(4.3)	(3.4)	—	—

Note: Table ignores some interest charges, other income, and exceptional items and excludes the Small Banking Division, disposed of in April 1984.
Source: European Ferries Group Annual Reports.

EXHIBIT 8
THE PENINSULAR AND ORIENTAL STEAM NAVIGATION COMPANY (P&O)

P&O was incorporated in England on December 31, 1840 in order to establish a shipping service between the United Kingdom and the Far East and to take over shipping services, established in August 1837, to Spain, Portugal, and Mediterranean ports.

Shipping routes were established throughout the Near and Far East and to Australasia and the business expanded both organically and by acquisition over the ensuing century. However, in the 1960s radical changes began to affect P&O's cargo and passenger shipping activities as a result of the introduction of cargo containerisation and the growth of intercontinental passenger air transport.

In view of the high level of capital expenditure which containerisation required, P&O and three other United Kingdom shipping companies formed OCL (Overseas Containers Limited) to take over their cargo liner trades as they were converted to container shipping. By the early 1970s P&O had phased out its scheduled passenger liner services to the Far East and Australasia, while during the same period the concept of ocean cruising was being developed as a leisure market.

As a result of the economic recession and the rapidly changing environment for both cargo and passenger shipping, P&O began to diversify its activities in the 1970s. This led to acquisition of the house building and property construction group Bovis, with its banking subsidiary TCB Limited, and to the continued development of P&O's integrated road and sea through-transport freight haulage operators, Ferrymasters Limited and Pandoro Limited, as well as the growth of its integrated subsidiary, P&O Australia, largely in materials handling, off-shore supply services, and cold storage and distribution.

Investments were also made by P&O in this period in oil and gas related activities mainly in the United States and in the North Sea, in ferry services (to Orkney and Shetland, Northern Ireland, and the Republic of Ireland, Sweden, Holland, Belgium, and France), and in liquefied petroleum gas (LPG) carriers and other bulk ships. The oil and gas related activities were subsequently sold. In January 1985 P&O sold its cross-channel ferry activity and in May 1985 P&O sold a 50 percent interest in its LPG carriers operation.

In February 1985 P&O merged with SGT, thereby bringing into the P&O Group the ownership and management of a substantial portfolio of offices, shops, and commercial properties located largely in the UK (owned by Town and Country Properties) and in the United States.

In the financial year ended December 31, 1985, profits before tax of the P&O Group were £125.6 million on sales of £1,629.3 million. At December 31, 1985, stockholders' funds amounted to £746.8 million. In May 1986 P&O acquired that proportion of OCL that it did not previously own, and in June 1986 P&O acquired Stock Conversion, a UK property company.

Reasons for the Offer

The directors of P&O believe that there is a clear commercial logic for the acquisition of European Ferries by P&O, which will undoubtedly result in improved profit potential for both companies. European Ferries will bring to P&O a range of businesses, including Townsend Thoresen, the principal European car ferry operator, and the Port of Felixstowe, the UK's leading container port. P&O's management is familiar with these businesses, which are allied to those in which P&O is already engaged both in the UK and overseas. The combination of the two groups will be a further logical step in P&O's strategy of developing its existing businesses and will increase the scope for maximizing returns to stockholders.

European Ferries' ferry services and port interests complement P&O's shipping interests and will increase P&O's participation in the continuing growth of trade within Europe. European Ferries will benefit from the addition of P&O's skills and resources in property management and development and P&O's size and financial strength will enable the problems currently being experienced in European Ferries' U.S. property portfolio to be dealt with effectively over an appropriate time scale.

Source: Various circulars sent to shareholders by P&O.

Peter Green's First Day

Peter Green came home to his wife and new baby a dejected man. What a contrast to the morning, when he had left the apartment full of enthusiasm to tackle his first customer in his new job at Scott Carpets. And what a customer! Peabody Rug was the largest carpet retailer in the area and accounted for 15 percent of the entire volume of Peter's territory. When Peabody introduced a Scott product, other retailers were quick to follow with orders. So when Bob Franklin, the owner of Peabody Rug, had called District Manager John Murphy expressing interest in "Carpet Supreme," Scott's newest commercial duty home carpet, Peter knew that a $15,000–$20,000 order was a real probability, and no small show for his first sale. And it was important to do well at the start, for John Murphy had made no bones about his scorn for the new breed of salespeople at Scott Carpet.

Murphy was of the old school. In the business since his graduation from a local high school, he had fought his way through the stiffest retail competition in the nation to be District Manager of the area at age 58. Murphy knew his textiles, and he knew his competitors' textiles. He knew his customers, and he knew how well his competitors knew his customers. Formerly, when Scott Carpet had needed to fill a sales position, it had generally raided the competition for experienced personnel, put them on a straight commission, and thereby managed to increase sales and maintain its good reputation for service at the same time. When Murphy had been promoted eight years ago to the position of District Manager, he had passed on his sales territory to Harvey Katchorian, a 60-year-old mill rep and son of an immigrant who had also spent his life in the carpet trade. Harvey had had no trouble keeping up his sales and had retired from the company the previous spring after 45 years of successful service in the industry. Peter, in turn, was to take over Harvey's accounts, and Peter knew that John Murphy was not sure that his original legacy to Harvey was being passed on to the best salesperson.

Peter was one of the new force of salespeople from Scott's Sales Management Program. In 1976 top management had created a training program to compensate for the industry's dearth of younger

Harvard Business School case 380–186.

salespeople with long-term management potential. Peter, a college graduate, had entered Scott's five-month training program immediately after college and was the first graduate of the program to be assigned to John Murphy's district. Murphy had made it known to top management from the start that he did not think the training program could compensate for on-the-job experience, and he was clearly withholding optimism about Peter's prospects as a salesperson despite Peter's fine performance during the training program.

Peter had been surprised, therefore, when Murphy volunteered to accompany him on his first week of sales "to ease your transition into the territory." As they entered the office at Peabody Rug, Murphy had even seemed friendly and said reassuringly, "I think you'll get along with Bob. He's a great guy—knows the business and has been a good friend of mine for years."

Everything went smoothly. Bob liked the new line and appeared ready to place a large order with Peter the following week, but he indicated that he would require some "help on the freight costs" before committing himself definitely. Peter was puzzled and unfamiliar with the procedure, but Murphy quickly stepped in and assured Bob that Peter would be able to work something out.

After the meeting, on their way back to Scott Carpets' district office, Peter asked Murphy about freight costs. Murphy sarcastically explained the procedure: because of its large volume, Peabody regularly "asked for a little help to cover shipping costs," and got it from all or most suppliers. Bob Franklin was simply issued a credit for defective merchandise. By claiming he had received second-quality goods, Bob was entitled to a 10–25 percent discount. The discount on defective merchandise had been calculated by the company to equal roughly the cost of shipping the 500 pound rolls back to the mill, and so it just about covered Bob's own freight costs. The practice had been going on so long that Bob demanded "freight assistance" as a matter of course before placing a large order. Obviously, the merchandise was not defective, but by making an official claim, the sales representative could set in gear the defective merchandise compensation system. Murphy reiterated, as if to a two-year-old, the importance of a Peabody account to any sales rep, and shrugged off the freight assistance as part of doing business with such an influential firm.

Peter stared at Murphy. "Basically, what you're asking me to do, Mr. Murphy, is to lie to the front office."

Murphy angrily replied, "Look, do you want to make it here or not? If you do, you ought to know you need Peabody's business. I don't know what kind of fancy thinking they taught you at college, but where I come from you don't call your boss a liar."

From the time he was a child, Peter Green had been taught not to lie or steal. He believed these principles were absolute and that one should support one's beliefs at whatever personal cost. But during college the only even remote test of his principles was his strict adherence to the honor system in taking exams.

As he reviewed the conversation with Murphy, it seemed to Peter that there was no way to avoid losing the Peabody account, which would look bad on his own record as well as Murphy's—not to mention the loss in commissions for them both. He felt badly about getting into a tiff with Murphy on his first day out in the territory, and knew Murphy would feel betrayed if one of his salespeople purposely lost a major account.

The only out he could see, aside from quitting, was to play down the whole episode. Murphy had not actually *ordered* Peter to submit a claim for damaged goods (was he covering himself legally?), so Peter could technically ignore the conversation and simply not authorize a discount. He knew very well, however, that such a course was only superficially passive, and that in Murphy's opinion he would have lost the account on purpose. As Peter sipped halfheartedly at a martini, he thought bitterly to himself, "Boy, they sure didn't prepare me for this in Management Training. And I don't even know if this kind of thing goes on in the rest of Murphy's district, let alone in Scott's 11 other districts."

BOOK TWO

IMPLEMENTING CORPORATE STRATEGY

The Implementation of Strategy: Achieving Commitment to Purpose

We now turn our attention to ideas and skills essential to the accomplishment of purpose. An idea is not complete or even completely understood until it is put into action. A unique corporate strategy is only rhetoric until it is embodied in organization activities which are actually guided by it but in turn continually reshape it. Goal-directed implementation, the essence of strategic management, is seen today as far more complex than the execution of directions implied in the classic model of the hierarchical corporation.

The determination of strategy, as we have said before, can be usefully thought of as a combination of four primarily analytical subactivities: examination of the company's environment for opportunity and risk, careful assessment of corporate strengths and weaknesses, identification and weighing of personal values built into the character of the company and its leaders, and establishment of the level of ethical and social responsibility to which it will hold itself.

The implementation of strategy may also be thought of as having essential subactivities. On the action side of corporate strategy these are primarily administrative rather than analytical in nature. Administrative action involves relationships among people, achievement and acceptance of authority, and much else, like energy or morality, that is not the product of mind alone. Implementation consists most broadly of achieving and sustaining commitment to purpose. Secondly, it is directed toward organized achievement of results through three universal structural processes: the specialization of task responsibilities, the coordination of divided responsibility, and the provision of a system of information enabling specialists and general managers alike to know what they need to know to act strategically. Each of these processes tends to develop counterstrategically by elevating its own special purposes above the needs of the total company.

Thirdly, the essential balance between individual and organization needs is sought through four familiar processes: measurement of performance, provision of incentives and rewards, establishment of constraints and controls, and recruitment and development of persons for operating and managing positions. These processes also tend to seek out their own separate purposes; they must be reined in and harnessed to corporate goals.

Finally, the role of leadership throughout the company in the accomplishment, modification, and extension of purpose in the innovative and adaptive corporation will become clear in the discussion of cases as all the more crucial as participation in strategy formulation becomes more extensive. We will come to see corporate strategy as, in part, the evolving product of commitment, vindicating and adapting to reality its initial formulation. We will see it also as the key to simplicity, economy, and superiority in the management of what would otherwise be confusing and needlessly complex affairs.

DISTORTED APPROACHES TO IMPLEMENTATION

In part, because of the neglect of implementation as integral to strategy, the concept itself has been battered by distortion over the last 20 years. False hope, oversimplification, and naïveté, as well as zest for power, have often led, for example, to the assumption that the chief executive officer conceives strategy single-mindedly, talks the board of directors into pro forma approval, announces it as fixed policy, and expects it to be promptly executed under conventional command and control procedures by subordinates. This unilateral dominance is often at least partly true in the entrepreneurial start-up stage, but when the company grows to something other than a one-person show, it becomes a political and social entity. When an established corporation is long dominated by strategic dictatorship, resistance both outspoken and covert eventually limits achievement.

That strategy formulation, under the name of strategic planning, is primarily a staff activity, assisted by consulting firms, is a related distortion made possible by ignoring the problems of implementation. The assumption that strategy is essentially a value-free appraisal and choice of economic opportunity and evaluation of results without reference to company capability, personal values, and entrenched cultural loyalties often led to strategic recommendations by staff departments and consulting firms that companies were neither able nor willing to carry out. Many planning techniques, useful in limited application, developed as quick-fix solutions to the need for better performance in competition. Goals often tended to be expressed in terms of high growth rates in sales and profits, mindlessly compounded over future years. Economic objectives were chosen more for their theoretical growth potential than from company capability to attain them. Acquisitions were pursued for the sake of growth in the 70s, just as hostile takeovers were undertaken in the 80s in pursuit of financial strategies largely unrelated to the distinctive competence to make them work. Financial strategies, in fact, following a modern finance theory divorced from the concept of corporate strategy, focus on the acquisition and divestment of assets, the extension of leverage to its limits without reference to impact on human resources, future development, and the capacity to service enormous debt should economic adversity put pressure on the company.

The catalog of strategic mismanagement made possible by ignoring the human, social, and ethical elements in the pattern of corporate purpose would make dreary reading if it were ever to be completely compiled. Even without it, poor performance in the marketplace has in due course exposed overrated techniques and fashionable shortcuts. The backlash against strategic planning occurring in the 1980s was largely justified and wholly understandable, but it has produced its own distortions. It has led to sweeping criticisms of American management and business education. Extreme incrementalism, understood as reactive improvisation, muddling through, or following one's nose, has been disinterred from the conceptual graveyard to justify avoidance of all forms of conscious planning.[1]

That organizations cannot have purposes as distinct from the special interests of individuals forming coalitions of rival aspirations is a venerable antistrategic position revived by disillusion with formal planning techniques so misapplied as to elevate quantitative analysis over qualitative appraisal of the needs of an organization viewed as a whole. Other process distortions lead to finessing strategic decision by inspiring the entire organization in folkloric simplicities like "moving close to the customer," "managing by walking around," and "fostering continuous innovation." These are attractive vacuities. What direction leadership should take, and what their substance should consist of, is missing from these prescriptions. An implicit or explicit strategy is required to encourage something to happen in the close relationship to customers, to identify what managers should have in mind when they walk around, and to suggest constructive direction and completion of innovations.

FLEXIBILITY IN PURSUIT OF PURPOSE

Intelligent implementation of the more comprehensive and substantive strategy proposed here presumes a balance between focus and flexibility, between a sense of direction and responsiveness to changing opportunities.

[1] This position is not to be confused with the purposeful incrementalism recommended in James Brian Quinn's *Strategies for Change: Logical Incrementalism* (Homewood, Ill.: Richard D. Irwin, 1980).

It is of course true that announcing very specific and restrictive objectives can close out participation. Overspecific topics can lead to centralized decision making, politicized opposition, and rigidity. Such goals should neither be adopted nor announced. Corporate strategy need not be a strait jacket. Room for variation, extension, and innovation must of course be provided. General goals, like the intention to be the leading producer in the technical product line serving a broad class of customer needs, imply product development, related innovations, and even unexpected additions that creativity may produce. In the multibusiness corporation, like General Electric, broad goals, like being first or second in every industry in which it participates, leave the full development of a more specific business strategy to achieve or maintain that position in the hands of GE's division management. Determination of even more detailed goals falls to the managers of strategic business units. The definition of special character, a common set of values, and expectations for performance does not keep IBM, Hewlett-Packard, and Xerox from being innovative.

Strategic planning is indeed a legitimate staff activity, but strategic decision is a line function. Much information gathering, competitive intelligence, and exploration of required investment, costs, and potential return can come from good staff work. The decision process is properly presided over by the executives responsible, whose judgment includes, but is not confined to, quantitative analysis. Correction to analytical distortion comes from constant reference to corporate capability and to the relevance of proposed strategic alternatives to company character and culture, either as they are or as, under leadership, they might become.

Our practitioner's theory, which you are asked to test, amend, or extend in the examination of the companies' situations described in this book, postulates conceptually that strategy formulation and implementation should be allowed to interact with each other. The formulation of strategy is not finished when implementation begins. Feedback from operations gives notice of changing environmental factors to which strategy should be adjusted. Unless it is to decline in competitiveness and performance, a business organization will change in response to the contribution of its new members, the changes in the markets and customer needs it services, and in response to success or failure in shaping its environment.

IMPLEMENTATION IN THE INNOVATIVE CORPORATION

The reciprocal relationship of strategy formulation and implementation makes middle management and employee involvement essential in both. The achievement of planned results means that goals must be known; the achievement of superior goals means they must be so wholly accepted that extraordinary effort or ingenuity, unforeseeable by distant planners, is induced. Sales or service persons often encounter in the field early clues to the need for change. In a company in which they doubt the interest of top management in responding, they may shrug their shoulders and shift their attention to other products. In a company oriented to innovation, they may report the opportunity through channels deliberately opened up to them by people prepared to listen. The development of greater individual capability and the distinctive competence of a company that is the source of competitive advantage comes from experience, the successful solving of problems, and superior service to customers.

Such a moving capability will not occur unless companies acknowledge in their behavior, if not in so many words, that their purpose is as much to maintain and develop a cooperative and creative organization and to foster effective execution as it is to lay plans and measure performance against plan. Committed team players can be involved in strategic determination by inviting their comment on the feasibility of strategic alternatives when secrecy and security are not at stake. Resistance to change, which in such discussion often produces negative response to new ideas, can be turned to constructive use by considering such objections before it is too late and attempting to achieve amendment, acceptance, and understanding beforehand rather than encounter unexpected opposition later on.

It becomes apparent that company organization structure and administrative policies and practices should permit and sustain involvement and the resultant commitment to company purposes. Being given a clearly defined job with lateral and upper limits becomes less and less attractive to present generations of educated employees and middle managers. The values they bring to a company include independence, aversion to arbitrary or unreasoned authority, and ambition to do something important enough to deserve recognition. They expect to be treated as persons capable of responsibility and judgment. They will wish to have room to experiment and explore as they carry out their assignments and reach beyond them. If a company is to profit from their spontaneous contributions, it must involve them in the strategic planning process. One of the ways to do this is to go beyond exposing new possibilities for comment by asking such middle managers for a strategy for their division, department, section, or office and to deal sympathetically with the virtues and shortcomings of the outcome.

The cases you will examine offer many opportunities for such involvement. You will have occasion to observe the everyday ways in which constructive engagement in strategic management is frustrated by what you may well conclude are archaic notions of authority, responsibility, hierarchy, status, and centralized decision making. Consider as you read "The Rose Company" how much or how little the strategy of the plant and company informs the thinking of the profit center and plant managers, respectively—or their seniors, for that matter. Do you think the structure and processes evident there reflect an appropriate strategy and the appropriate involvement by the key people who must carry it out?

The structure of the innovative organization in which we expect people to make creative contributions must clearly be dominated by relevant aspects of the corporate strategy. The way in which the structure is administered will reflect the kind of organization deemed appropriate for the nature of the contribution expected. It is becoming clear that the corporation of the 21st century will be a different kind of organization from the giant, formally controlled, and relatively centralized company of the present day. But before we examine that possibility, and before you use it in appraising and making recommendations for better performance in the cases that follow, we should pause to consider what by way of structure and process needs to be done in a conventional 1990 organization.

A reasonable profile of implementation activities goes as follows:

1. Once strategy is tentatively or finally set, the key tasks to be performed and kinds of decisions required must be identified.

2. Once the size of operations exceeds the capacity of one person, responsibility for accomplishing key tasks and making decisions must be assigned to individuals or groups. The division of labor must permit efficient performance of subtasks and must be accompanied by some hierarchical allocation of authority to assure achievement.

3. Formal provisions for the coordination of activities thus separated must be made in various ways, for example, through a hierarchy of supervision, project and committee organizations, task forces, and other ad hoc units. The prescribed activities of these formally constituted bodies are not intended to preclude spontaneous voluntary coordination.

4. Information systems adequate for coordinating divided functions (that is, for letting those performing part of the task know what they must know of the rest, and for letting those in supervisory positions know what is happening so that next steps may be taken) must be designed and installed.

5. The tasks to be performed should be arranged in a sequence comprising a program of action or a schedule of targets to be achieved at specified times. While long-range plans may be couched in relatively general terms, operating plans will often take the form of relatively detailed budgets. These can meet the need for the establishment of standards against which short-term performance can be judged.

6. Actual performance, as quantitatively reported in information systems and qualitatively estimated through observation by supervisors and judgment of customers, should be compared to budgeted performance and to standards in order to test achievement, budgeting processes, the adequacy of the standards, and the competence of individuals.

7. Individuals and groups of individuals must be recruited and assigned to essential tasks in accordance with the specialized or supervisory skills which they possess or can develop. At the same time, the assignment of tasks may well be adjusted to the nature of available skills.

8. Individual performance, evaluated both quantitatively and qualitatively, should be subjected to influences (constituting a pattern of incentives) which will help to make it effective in accomplishing organizational goals.

9. Since individual motives are complex and multiple, incentives for achievement should range from those that are universally appealing—such as adequate compensation and an organizational climate favorable to the simultaneous satisfaction of individual and organizational purposes—to specialized forms of recognition, financial or nonfinancial, designed to fit individual needs and unusual accomplishments.

10. In addition to financial and nonfinancial incentives and rewards to motivate individuals to voluntary achievement, a system of constraints, controls, and penalties must be devised to contain nonfunctional activity and to enforce standards. Controls, like incentives, are both formal and informal. Effective control requires both quantitative and nonquantitative information which must always be used together.

11. Provision for the continuing development of requisite technical and managerial skills is a high-priority requirement. The development of individuals must take place chiefly within the milieu of their assigned responsibilities. This on-the-job development should be supplemented by intermittent formal instruction and study.

12. Energetic personal leadership is necessary for continued growth and improved achievement in any organization. Leadership may be expressed in many styles, but it must be expressed in some perceptible style. This style must be natural and also consistent with the requirements imposed upon the organization by its strategy and membership.

STRUCTURE, COORDINATION, AND INFORMATION SYSTEMS

The most fundamental processes that shape any organization structure consist of dividing the work and responsibility, coordinating the divided effort, and providing, in an organization of any size, the essential information to enable people to do their part of the total job in ways that fit the whole. You will have studied elsewhere organization design and the management of information systems; we will not take up those subjects here. The implementation of corporate strategy requires that the division of responsibility facilitate the efficient performance of the key tasks identified by the strategy. The formal pattern by which tasks are identified and authority delegated should have visible relationship to corporate purpose, should fix responsibility in such a way as not to preclude teamwork, and should provide for the solution of problems as close to the point of action as possible.

In an organization governed by purpose, responsibility will usually exceed authority; the resulting ambiguity provides opportunity for initiative and clarification in terms of shared objectives rather than separate fiefdoms. The specialization of function made necessary by the growth of organization opens the door to counterstrategic departmental loyalties.

Accountants behave like accountants and engineers like engineers more than is necessary; this specialized zeal has its advantages in the performance of a specialty but can be frustrating to general managers when departmental biases and narrowness produce conflict or impede consensus in the consideration of critical issues. Functional specialists tend to interpret corporate purpose to suit themselves.

It follows, therefore, that in all organizations provision must be made to resolve differences in perspective, clarify strategy against misconceptions and special interpretations, and above all, to provide for discussion of alternatives that satisfy both departmental and organization needs. Committees, task forces, operations reviews, and planning meetings are the ordinary vehicles of common understanding. When such suborganizations are ill run, they are decried as time wasting and unproductive and make strong-willed individuals impatient. In the hands of a skilled chairman, task forces and special purpose committees can be a principal source of creativity. The more informal the distribution of authority and the more ambiguous the boundaries between functions, the more important coordinating committees can become. The innovative company of the future provides much opportunity for people to talk to each other about what new undertakings should be launched, how they should be managed, and how old undertakings can be made more successful. Such meetings become more informative than the routine information provided to the organization by its reporting system.

The design of the formal structure of an organization will reflect corporate purpose, but it is the working of the informal organization that is not only central to productive cooperation but will suggest what the formal structure should be. Landscape architects laying out sidewalks in a park or campus will wait to let people walk on the grass and then either pave the resulting paths or plant out superfluous or uancceptable routes. The entrepreneurial corporation begins in a small group of people whose understanding of what they are doing is constantly developed by close communication. What they are trying to accomplish is commanding; they have the resources to do only what most needs to be done. As such an organization grows, informality continues to dominate hierarchical distinctions, but eventually unclear separation of responsibility confuses people. The challenge becomes to clarify separate responsibilities without absolving the marketing people, for example, from knowing the strategically critical problems of production or product development.

The organization growing out of successful entrepreneurial chaos into a more structured company must somehow avoid the stultification of bureaucracy that comes from mismanaged size and complexity.[2] Incentive

---

[2] See Andrall Pearson, "Tough-Minded Ways to Get Innovation," *Harvard Business Review*, May–June 1988, pp. 99ff.

and reward systems have to be developed to introduce fairness into what was once intuitive recognition of the work of individual contributors justified by daily observation no longer possible. But rigidity need not come on stage with systems. If the latter fall into the hands of bureaucrats who are technically educated in the intricacies of the system and dedicated to its extension for its own sake, then the relation of incentives, for example, to the kind of behavior that is most relevant to successful accomplishment of purpose is lost.

What an organization is trying to accomplish can become recognized if the formalities of hierarchical organization are kept to a minimum. Assignments should never be so clear or restrictive that persons cannot contribute, within the limits of their capability, what most needs to be done. Every functional assignment should include its relevance to corporate purpose; general management perspective can be assigned to persons by evaluating their performance in teamwork terms. The conduct of inquiries into new possibilities by interdepartmental task forces, in addition to their regular duties, should be a way of life for middle managers and professional people, just as quality circles are a symbol of innovative potential on the factory floor. Independent business units, skunk works, pilot operations, high-risk experiments in which failure without penalty is possible, competitive product championing, improvisatory off-budget product development—all characterize the innovative company.

It is the assumption of the authors that you look forward to a management career in an innovative company. In any case, the large American corporation in industries undergoing massive restructuring is in the process of remaking itself.[3] The pressure for becoming slimmer, faster, more responsive, and more profitable may come more from the need for cost reduction under intense foreign competition than from voluntary aspirations to excellence. But becoming and maintaining a position as a world-class company in selected market segments is an opportunity to any entrepreneur capable of devising an innovative strategy and developing an organization to extend the strategy rather than fall into the frustrations of formality, political conflict, and other aberrations of conventional organizations.

COMMITMENT

The essence of successful implementation is commitment. Commitment comes from wanting to do something and from the satisfactions of having its importance recognized. As tasks become more difficult, wanting to contribute is not enough; greater capability is required. But most observers

[3] For important analysis of the need for restructuring, see Joseph L. Bower, *When Markets Quake* (Boston: Harvard Business School Press, 1986) and Rosabeth Kanter, *When Giants Learn to Dance* (New York: Simon & Shuster, 1989).

of established companies see a greater potential for cost reduction, product innovation, and quality enhancement than is ever fully recognized.[4] The effort to reexamine corporate capability can result in new ideas for at least minor additions to the product line or range of services, to quality, and to cost effectiveness that cumulatively support or extend market share and help bond customers to their suppliers as partners.

Strategic management is thus now being redirected toward making use of and extending organizations' strengths and the innovative resilience of committed persons continually challenged to excel competitors and to improve on past performance. It becomes part of every manager's job. How well an organization can implement purpose becomes critical. Success depends on how much the persons assigned to achieve have been involved in the process of setting the goals and how deeply they have become committed to overcoming unexpected obstacles to success. They should not be deflected from common purpose by a company's organization structure or by its measurement, compensation, incentive, and control systems.

But such systems are required. Informality cannot be absolute. Cooperation in a clearly understood common endeavor rarely occurs by chance. We will look in the next note more closely at the processes through which commitment is expected to produce results. In the meantime the cases that follow now will give you the chance to test out, challenge, or reshape for your own use the ideas expressed here. You are in the process of deciding how you will make use of the concept of strategy and its power in shaping administrative systems toward relevance and simplicity in particular companies and unique situations. Nothing will help you more than examination of the kind of real-life combinations of theory and reality that appear in the next set of cases.

If you are not going to apply to your management responsibilities a set of unrealistic textbook assumptions about how your associates should respond to your leadership, you will have to think carefully about the need in any organization for clarity of mission, commitment to purpose, and careful preparation for changes in direction. Your awareness that strategy formulation and implementation must be interdependent, simultaneous processes is fundamental to mastery of the art of management and indispensable to understanding the nature of organization.

---

[4] For a research-based account of innovative practices in the management of work, see Richard E. Walton, "From Control to Commitment in the Workplace," *Harvard Business Review*, March–April 1985, pp. 77ff, and *Up and Running: Integrating Information, Technology, and the Organization* (Boston: Harvard Business School Press, 1989).

The Adams Corporation (A)

In January 1987 the board of directors of the Adams Corporation simultaneously announced the highest sales in the company's history, the lowest aftertax profits (as a percentage of sales) in many decades, and the retirement (for personal reasons) of its long-tenured president and chief executive officer, Jerome Adams.

Founded in St. Louis in 1848, the Adams Brothers Company had long been identified as a family firm both in name and operating philosophy. Writing in a business history journal, a former family senior manager commented:

> My grandfather wanted to lead a business organization with ethical standards. He wanted to produce a quality product and a quality working climate for both employees and managers. He thought the Holy Bible and the concept of family stewardship provided him with all the guidelines needed to lead his company. A belief in the fundamental goodness of mankind, in the power of fair play, and in the importance of personal and corporate integrity were his trademarks. Those traditions exist today.

In the early 1960s two significant corporate events occurred. First, the name of the firm was changed to the Adams Corporation. Second, somewhat over 50 percent of the corporation's shares were sold by various family groups to the wider public. In 1980 all branches of the family owned or influenced less than one fifth of the outstanding shares of Adams.

The Adams Corporation was widely known and respected as a manufacturer and distributor of quality, brand-name consumer products for the American, Canadian, and European (export) markets. Adams products were processed in four regional plants located near raw material sources. (No single plant processed the full line of Adams products, but each plant processed the main items in the line.) The products were stored and distributed in a series of recently constructed or renovated distribution centers located in key cities throughout North America, and they were sold by a company sales force in thousands of retail outlets—primarily supermarkets.

In explaining the original, long-term financial success of the company, a former officer commented:

Harvard Business School case 372–263.

> Adams led the industry in the development of unique production processes that produced a quality product at a very low cost. The company has always been production-oriented and volume-oriented, and it paid off for a long time. During those decades the Adams brand was all that was needed to sell our product; we didn't do anything but a little advertising. Competition was limited, and our production efficiency and raw material sources enabled us to outpace the industry in sales and profit. Our strategy was to make a quality product, distribute it, and sell it cheap.
>
> But that has all changed in the past 20 years. Our three major competitors have outdistanced us in net profits and market aggressiveness. One of them—a first-class marketing group—has doubled sales and profits within the past five years. Our gross sales have increased to over $1 billion, but our net profits have dropped continuously during that same period. While a consumer action group just designated us as "best value," we have fallen behind in marketing techniques; for example, our packaging is just out of date.

Structurally, Adams was organized into eight major divisions. Seven of these were regional sales divisions with responsibility for distribution and sales of the company's consumer products to retail stores in their areas. Each regional sales division was further divided into organizational units at the state, county, and/or trading-area level. Each sales division was governed by a corporate price list in the selling of company products, but each had some leeway to meet the local competitive price developments. Each sales division was also assigned (by the home office) a quota of salespeople it could hire and was given the salary ranges within which these people could be employed. All salespeople were on straight salary with an expense reimbursement salary plan, which resulted in compensation under industry averages.

A small central accounting office accumulated sales and expense information for each of the several sales divisions on a quarterly basis, and it prepared the overall company financial statements. Each sales division received, without commentary, a quarterly statement showing the following information for the overall division: number of cases processed and sold, sales revenue per case, and local expenses per case.

Somewhat similar information was obtained from the manufacturing division. Manufacturing division accounting was complicated by variations in the cost of obtaining and processing the basic materials used in Adams's products. These variations—particularly in procurement—were largely beyond the control of the division. The accounting office, however, did have one rough external check on manufacturing division effectiveness: a crude market price existed for case lot goods, sold by smaller firms to some large national chains.

Once every quarter, the seven senior sales vice presidents met with general management in St. Louis. Typically, management discussion focused on divisional sales results and expense control. The company's objective of being number one—the largest selling line in its field—directed group attention to sales as compared to budget. All knew that last year's sales targets had to be exceeded, no matter what. The manufacturing division vice president sat in on these meetings to explain the product availability situation. Because of his St. Louis office location, he frequently talked with Jerome Adams about overall manufacturing operations and specifically about large procurement decisions.

The Adams Company had a trade reputation for being very conservative with its compensation program. All officers were on a straight salary program. An officer might expect a modest salary increase every two or three years; these increases tended to be in the thousand-dollar range, regardless of divisional performance or company profit position. Salaries among the seven sales divisional vice presidents ranged from $125,000 to $170,000, with the higher amounts going to more senior officers. Jerome Adams's salary of $200,000 was the highest in the company. There was no corporate bonus plan. A very limited stock option program was in operation, but the depressed price of Adams stock meant that few officers exercised their options.

The corporate climate at Adams had been of considerable pride to Jerome Adams. "We take care of our family" was his oft-repeated phrase at company banquets honoring long-service employees. "We are a team, and it is a team spirit that has built Adams into its leading position in this industry." No member of first-line, middle, or senior management could be discharged (except in cases of moral crime or dishonesty) without a personal review of his case by Mr. Adams; as a matter of fact, executive turnover at Adams was very low. Executives at all levels viewed their jobs as lifetime careers. There was no compulsory retirement plan, and some managers were still active in their mid-70s.

The operational extension of this organizational philosophy was quite evident to employees and managers. For over 75 years, a private family trust provided emergency assistance to all members of the Adams organization. Adams led its industry in the granting of educational scholarships, in medical insurance for employees and managers, and in the encouragement of its members to give corporate and personal time and effort to community problems and organizations.

Jerome noted two positive aspects of this organizational philosophy:

> We have a high percentage of long-term employees—Joe Girly, a guard at East St. Louis, completes 55 years with us this year, and every one of his brothers and sisters has worked here. And it is not uncommon for a vice president to retire with a blue pin—that means 40 years of service. We have led this industry in manufacturing process innovation, quality control, and value for low price for decades. I am proud of our accomplishments, and this pride is shown by everyone from janitors to directors.

Industry sources noted that there was no question that Adams was number one in terms of manufacturing and logistic efficiency.

In December 1986 the annual Adams management conference gathered over 80 members of Adams's senior management in St. Louis. Most expected the usual formal routines—the announcement of 1986 results and 1987 budgets, the award of the "Gold Flag" to the top processing plant and sales division for exceeding targets, and the award of service pins to executives. All expected the usual social good times. It was an opportunity to meet and drink with "old buddies."

After a series of task force meetings, the managers gathered in a banquet room—good-naturedly referred to as the "Rib Room" since a local singer, Eve, was to provide entertainment. In the usual fashion, a dais with a long, elaborately decorated head table was at the front of the room. Sitting at the center of that table was Jerome Adams. Following tradition, Adams's vice presidents, in order of seniority with the company, sat on his right. On his left sat major family shareholders, corporate staff, and a newcomer soon to be introduced.

After awarding service pins and the Gold Flags of achievement, Adams formally announced what had been corporate secrets for several months. First, a new investing group had assumed a control position on the board of Adams. Second, Price Millman would take over as president and CEO of Adams.

Introducing Millman, Adams pointed out the outstanding record of the firm's new president: "Price got his MBA in 1978, spent four years in control and marketing, and then was named as the youngest divisional president in the history of the Tenny Corporation. In the past years, he has made his division the most profitable in Tenny and the industry leader in its field. We are fortunate to have him with us. Please give him your complete support."

In a later informal meeting with the divisional vice presidents, Millman spoke about his respect for Adams's past accomplishments and the pressing need to infuse Adams with "fighting spirit" and "competitiveness." He said: "My personal and organizational philosophy are the same—the name of the game is to fight and win. I almost drowned, but I won my first swimming race at 11 years of age! That philosophy of always winning is what enabled me to build the Ajax Division into Tenny's most profitable operation. We are going to do this at Adams."

In conclusion, Millman commented: "The new owner group wants results. They have advised me to take some time to think through a new format for Adams's operations—to get a corporate design that will improve our effectiveness. Once we get that new format, gentlemen, I have but one goal—each month must be better than the past."

The Rose Company

James Pierce had recently received word of his appointment as general manager of the Jackson plant, one of the older, established units of the Rose Company. As such, Pierce would be responsible for the management and administration of all functions and personnel at the Jackson plant except sales.

Both top management and Pierce realized that there were several unique features about his new assignment. Pierce decided to assess his new situation and relationships before undertaking his assignment. He was personally acquainted with the home office executives but had met few of the Jackson personnel. This case contains some of his reflections regarding the new assignment.

The Rose Company conducted marketing activities throughout the United States and in certain foreign countries. These activities were directed from the home office by a vice president in charge of sales.

Harvard Business School case 453–002.

Manufacturing operations and certain other departments were under the supervision and control of a senior vice president as shown in Exhibit 1. For many years the company had operated a highly centralized and functional type of manufacturing organization. There was no general manager at any plant; rather, each of the departments in a plant reported on a line basis to its functional counterpart at the home office. For instance, the industrial relations manager of a particular plant reported to the vice president in charge of industrial relations at the home office, and the plant controller to the vice president–controller, and so on.

Reflecting the opinion of top management, Pierce stated that the record of the Jackson plant had not been satisfactory for several years. The Rose board had recently approved the erection of a new plant in a different part of the city and the use of new methods of production. Both lower costs of processing and reduced manpower requirements were expected at the new plant. Reduction of costs and improved quality of products were needed to maintain competitive leadership and gain some slight product advantage. The proposed combination of methods of manufacturing and mixing materials had not been tried elsewhere in the company. Some of these features would be entirely new to employees.

According to Pierce, the company's top management was beginning to question the advisability of the central control of manufacturing operations. The officers decided to test the value of decentralized operation at the Jackson plant. They apparently believed that a general management representative at Jackson was needed if the new experiment in manufacturing methods and the required rebuilding of the organization were to succeed.

Prior to the new assignment Pierce had been an accounting executive in the controller's department of the company. From independent sources the casewriter learned that Pierce had demonstrated analytical ability and general administrative capacity and that he was generally liked by people. From top management's point of view, he had an essential toughness described as an ability to get all important tasks accomplished. He was regarded by some as the company's efficiency expert. Others thought he was a perfectionist and aggressive in reaching the goals that had been set. Pierce was aware of these opinions about his personal behavior. He summarized his problems in part as follows:

> I am going into a situation involving a large number of changes. I will have a new plant, new methods, and processes, but most of all I will be dealing with a set of changed relationships. Heretofore all the heads of departments in the plant reported to their functional counterparts in the home office. Now they will report to me; I am a complete stranger, and in addition this is my first assignment in a major line job. The men will know this.
>
> When I was called into the senior vice president's office to be informed of my new assignment, he asked me to talk with each of the functional members of his staff. The vice presidents in charge of production planning, manufacturing, and industrial relations said they were going to issue all headquarters' instructions to me as plant manager, and they were going to cut off their connections with their counterparts in my plant. The other home office executives admitted their functional counterparts would report to me in line capacity. They should obey my orders and I would be responsible for their pay and promotion. But these executives proposed to follow the common practice of many companies of maintaining a dotted line or functional relationship with these men. I realize that these two different patterns of home office/plant relationships will create real administrative problems for me.

Exhibit 2 shows the organization relationships as defined in these conferences.

Project Mgm

EXHIBIT 1
OLD ORGANIZATION CHART

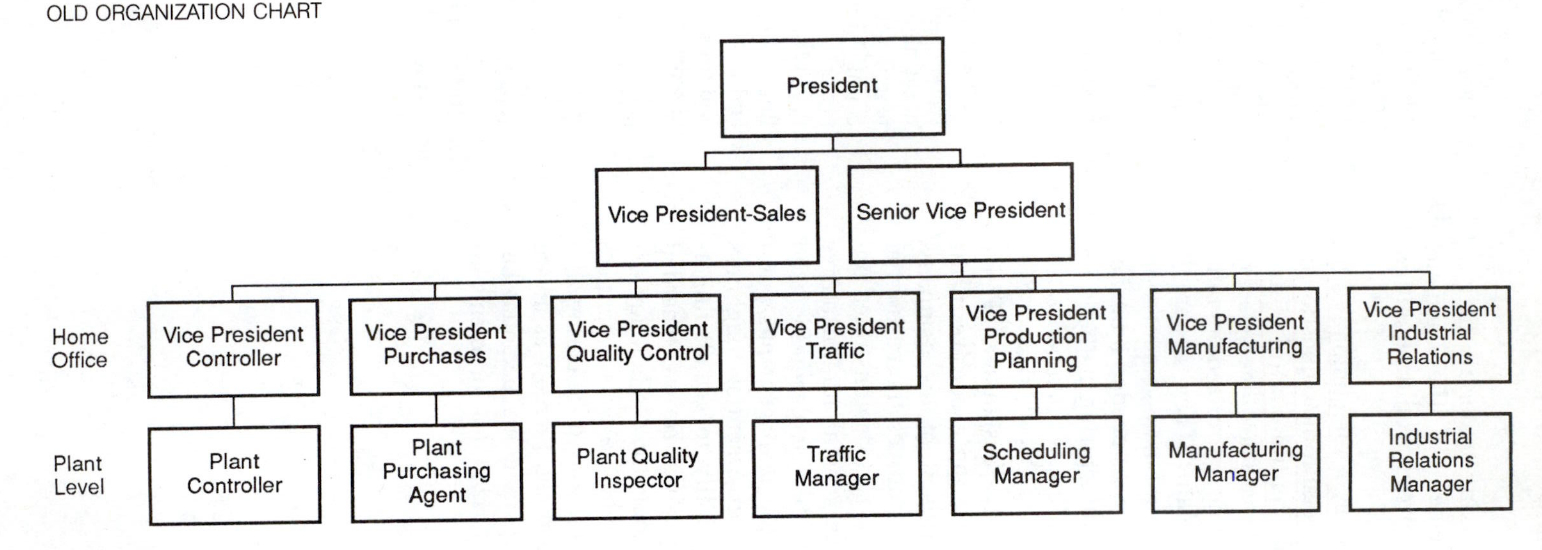

EXHIBIT 2
NEW ORGANIZATION CHART

Colgate-Palmolive, Company in Transition (A)

As Reuben Mark, currently president of the Colgate-Palmolive Company and about to be elected chief executive officer, prepared for a presentation to the members of CP's Board of Directors on May 3, 1984, he picked up a newly circulated investment analyst's report downgrading the company from a "buy" to a "hold" recommendation with the comment:

> Because of another quarter of lackluster profits, we suggest this stock only for those investors seeking a defensive posture in the event of a repeat of our recent recession.

As he read, Mark reflected on the words *lackluster* and *defensive* and the real challenge that these identified for him as the company's new CEO. He thought too of the five years of rebuilding and reestablishment of old values upon which his predecessor, Keith Crane, and he had worked so hard. He felt the success of these efforts had positioned the company once again with the strengths it had enjoyed for much of its 178-year history. Now was the time to capitalize on the strengths. The question was how.

BACKGROUND

The Colgate-Palmolive Company (CP) was one of the oldest manufacturers of consumer products in the United States, tracing its roots back to Colgate and Co. which was founded in 1806. Upon the merger in 1928 of Colgate and the Palmolive-Peet Company, a major soap producer, the foundations for the modern Colgate-Palmolive Company were laid. At the time of the acquisition, oil and perfume processing companies owned by the two firms were sold to allow them to concentrate on the production and marketing of such products as Palmolive soap, Fab washing powder, and Colgate Ribbon dental creme. In 1938 the last of the Colgate family to hold the position of president relinquished it to E. H. Little, a director and senior marketing manager.

Harvard Business School case 388–060. Revised September 1989.

The Little-Lesch Era

Mr. Little was to lead the company for 23 years. During this time primary emphasis was placed on the development of CP's international business. In 1938 the company realized 28 percent of its $99.4 million in sales and 41 percent of its $4.9 million in profits from international operations. By 1961 international sales represented 53 percent of the company's total of $604.9 million, with profits from international business making up 78 percent of the total for that year of $22.2 million. By 1961 CP was conducting business in one form or another in 85 countries. It was during this time that a global organization of philosophy was developed as well, with every senior executive expected to have extensive foreign experience.

Little's successor, George Lesch, had worked in Mexico for 15 years prior to taking responsibility for European operations. During his years as CEO (1960–1971), he adopted much the same philosophy and policies of his predecessors. He was followed by David Foster, who set out to recast the company in a different mold.

The Foster Era—A Change in Emphasis

Foster had spent his business career at Colgate, having started in the export department of the UK company. After becoming UK general manager, he had the responsibility for Europe, prior to moving to the U.S. company and then to corporate. He concluded that Colgate was a company with all of its investment in consumer businesses that he felt had limited growth potential. For that reason, in the early 1970s, he set out to diversify the company's operations. Colgate entered the health care products business in 1972 with the acquisition of the Kendall Company, a manufacturer and marketer of disposable health care products. The following year, CP acquired Helena Rubenstein, a marketer of women's cosmetics. A golf and tennis sporting goods division was begun with the acquisition in 1974 of the Ram Golf Corp. and the Bancroft Racket Co., followed by other small sport equipment companies in the United States and overseas. To promote these businesses, major sponsorship activity was initiated with women's golf and tennis tournaments.

Soon thereafter, the company acquired Riviana Foods, the largest U.S. producer and marketer of rice, sold under several brand names. Also included in the company was Hill's Pet Products, a manufacturer and marketer of specialty (dietary) pet foods sold through veterinarians, breeders, and pet stores. As part of an effort to explore alternative marketing methods, in 1978 CP acquired Princess House, Inc., a U.S. company in the business of offering crystal glassware and other "top-of-the-table" items through a party plan (in-home) sales method.

Foster's concept was that these diverse business groups would provide greater growth than Colgate could achieve in its traditional markets. A complete list of CP's acquisitions during this era is presented in Exhibit 1. Unfortunately, the anticipated growth did not occur and profitability was less than planned, putting excessive demands for profitability on the traditional businesses.

The Crane Era—Back to Basics

By 1979 when Keith Crane (who had worked across the globe for Colgate, as well as run Kendall) succeeded Foster as CEO, Colgate could claim to be a significantly diversified consumer goods company, with

30 percent of its revenues realized from products other than those in the traditional household and personal care markets. But Crane realized that the broad diversification was not working as forecast. What he inherited was a loose confederation of companies, associated with a company whose main-line general managers had seen much of the cash generated from their household and personal care products siphoned off to finance acquisitions and the operations of other businesses. And the anticipated return was nowhere in sight.

As Crane analyzed the overall business, he concluded that Colgate had become a company that was losing momentum in its traditional business. In particular, he was concerned about the quality of the company's soaps and dentrifrices, the lack of aggressive research and development activity, and the reactive nature of much of CP's marketing efforts, particularly in the United States, where it ranked poorly in many product categories, behind Procter & Gamble and Lever Brothers. He also did not like the fact that managers of the company's traditional businesses thought that they were being measured on the various ways that they were able to reduce the costs on ongoing business activity, rather than on their talent to manage their individual subsidiaries. This situation had been compounded as the size of the staff at the company's headquarters in New York had increased to track their progress, and other staff had been added to try to improve the performance of the newly acquired firms.

Crane, described by his associates as a quiet, thoughtful professional with an excellent grasp of the global business and brilliant recall, set out to get CP's management "back to basics" and put a dispirited organization back on track. Among other things, he established a pattern of visiting every one of the company's global subsidiaries at least every other year. According to one of Crane's contemporaries: "He went around the world. The people in the field couldn't wait to have him back. They knew he didn't forget, and they knew that he basically was on their side. He was the first CEO to recognize that all areas of the business were important to the whole, not just marketing. He preached the need for the total manager."

As one country manager at the time put it,

> During the Foster era, the company lived off the fat built up during the heyday of international expansion under E.H. Little and George Lesch. However, in 1979 the company was centralized and operated by putting increasing profit demands on its base businesses, especially outside the United States. I nearly quit that year. Why? Because I couldn't build the business by just delivering profits without a longer view which included investment funds. Without that outlook, the company would continue to be a mediocre performer. It was only the prospect that Crane would redirect the company against its core strength that made me decide to stay on. And that is what Crane did.

Product Health

The major rallying cry of the Crane era became "product health." One of the operating vice presidents remembered a typical meeting with a country GM at that time:

> The GMs had been rewarded for saving product costs an inch a year. Keith would ask why the formula was inferior to competition, and why it hadn't been fixed. The GM would say, "I can't fix it; it'll

> reduce profits." Keith would reply, "Put that aside. Fix it. Without a competitive product, there soon won't be any profits."

The 1982 annual report focused on this effort, emphasizing significant increases in investment in research and development, capital expenditures for new plant and equipment, product quality, advertising effectiveness, and sales "firepower," which meant improving and increasing the size of the corporation's many sales departments around the world. Nearly all of this investment was centered on household and personal care (especially dental) products. Exhibit 2 contains information showing trends in investments in product health between 1980 and 1983. These investments had produced a negative cash flow position for the company in recent years.

Global product and market informaion posed another problem. According to Reuben Mark, whom Crane named president and chief operating officer in 1982, "We couldn't make any sense out of the data we had. For a given product line, it was collected and analyzed in countries all around the world under different assumptions and with different methods."

In spite of the staff organization in New York, there was limited communication or coordination among country managers. In part, this was a legacy from an era where each country manager operated very independently. Managers of CP's most successful businesses in countries such as France, Mexico, Australia, Colombia, and the Philippines had been left to manage their businesses as they saw fit, linked only by financial reporting requirements. While this resulted in an organization able to respond to local competitive pressures, it impeded the exchange of important information about new formulas, products, advertising, manufacturing, or sales techniques that were suitable for more than one country. Further, corporate support efforts tended to be splintered by too many individual country requests, with the larger countries dominating the available resources. The result was that the company was not making use of its global strengths and knowledge to advance its business.

Business Development Groups

In 1981 Colgate decided to create Business Development Groups (BDGs) responsible for coordinating product development, manufacturing, and marketing for core product categories (oral, detergents, soaps, liquid cleaners) on a worldwide basis. Described by one manager as "the best thing as a company we ever did," the groups were officed in New York and staffed with experienced, strong general managers from CP's operating subsidiaries. Although the BDGs were organized as staff versus line, the experience level of each group, plus the corporate commitment to support them, gained them respect in the field where their suggestions received very serious attention. As one senior executive put it, "Since no one had any experience with the BDG concept, there was skepticism in the field as well as among the New York staff. In retrospect, I can't imagine how we operated without the BDGs."

The first BDG to be created was for oral products. According to the vice president selected to head it:

> I was managing Spain at the time, having come previously from the U.K. operation. The basic goal was to fix and strengthen

> the oral business on a global basis, primarily through coordinated research and development and marketing. We began comparing product quality across countries. We asked whether we were getting proper share of market and "share of voice" in our advertising. It required a lot of traveling, up to 100 days per year. I divided my time between the general manager and marketing manager in each country. On a cross-boundary product introduction, for example, the hardest person to persuade was the first guy. We didn't ever say you had to do it; but we could make cooperation sound awfully attractive. What we did insist on is that country GMs have strategies for every brand. We encouraged them to tap in to us for new ideas. And if the idea was especially good, we occasionally said, "You are going with it unless you can make a good argument for not doing it."

The BDG concept was well entrenched by the end of 1983. As a result, the company experienced an increase in situations where a product developed internally in one country could be introduced rapidly across the globe. In their report to shareholders for 1983, Crane and Mark pointed out that:

> Worldwide, the Company's market share advanced in several key categories, following the aggressive introduction of 162 new and revitalized products in 44 countries coupled with programs to increase the consumer franchise of existing brands. The development of our business was global in nature with a substantial portion of the direction and guidance being centrally driven by the Business Development Group, which manages our global category activities.

A summary of market share data for all countries in which Colgate-Palmolive sold its products is shown in Exhibit 3.

Research and Development

With the BDGs' increasing emphasis on global strategies and product development, Research and Development for household and personal products were given clear direction on development needs. Over 200 additional professionals were hired to support the global activity, and to develop the new products needed for the future. Most of these were added to the staff of the company's primary research and development facility at Piscataway, N.J.

Advertising Effectiveness

To facilitate more effective investment in advertising, and particularly to increase the creative excellence required around the world, the number of advertising agencies worldwide to which CP entrusted its advertising efforts was reduced from 13 to 3. As pointed out in the 1983 annual report, "The alignment of our major core brands with three international agencies will provide greater coordination and marketing thrust."

The Operating Committee

Keith Crane also formed an Operating Committee, composed of seven senior executives chaired by Reuben Mark, to coordinate worldwide business activities. According to one senior executive, "Keith and Reuben set about to expand these people's understanding of the business. Global business reviews were held, with all senior executives expected to attend. Over time all members of management benefited, because each gained an overall knowledge of the worldwide business and thus was more effective in their own responsibilities."

Divestiture

To refocus its efforts and free up the capital to invest in its core businesses, CP's management also began divesting some of the businesses acquired in the previous era. The first to go was Maui Divers of Hawaii Ltd. It was followed by many others, as indicated in Exhibit 1.

Control Systems

A budget was negotiated between corporate and the field. Once agreed, each subsidiary company and operating unit supplied a series of financial reports, including a breakdown of the budget by month and a substantial amount of detailed analysis, to the corporate controller's office at headquarters. After consolidation of each set of divisional data by the corporate controller's office, the resultant reports and supporting detail were then reviewed (respectively) with the three divisional operating vice presidents, each of whom controlled about one third of the world. Debates between the controller's office and divisional management often ensued, resulting in detailed and protracted discussions over the accuracy of the information, and its significance for identifying the strengths and weaknesses of the respective areas.

Performance Measurement

Although everyone had agreed upon a budget, its use as a measurement of subsequent performance was of minimal significance, since typically it was immediately superseded each year by the "latest estimate" system, a monthly submission of performance data and updated estimates from each operating unit. As a result, a general manager's remuneration and bonus, far from being related directly to performance versus his agreed budget, was often equally based on a division manager's view of how a particular GM was doing. At the time a GM's bonus amounted to only a small proportion of his salary (salaries typically ranged from $75,000 to $125,000). Stock options existed, although distribution of this benefit was also believed to be based more upon arbitrary judgment than on performance.

Strategic Planning

Prior to 1982 no real strategic plan existed, nor did the function exist.

Competition

Colgate's two principal competitors were Unilever and Procter & Gamble. While Colgate faced several sizeable local competitors in a few countries, their chief competitor was nearly always one of these two giants.

Within the United States, P&G was the dominant soap and toilet goods producer. They were regarded as aggressive, technologically strong, and a "world class" marketeer. They had a long history of successful new products and product improvements aimed at giving them a performance edge with consumers. As a result, they were the category leader in most of their key categories. P&G was a strong company financially and they consistently spent roughly 3 percent of sales on R&D and 8.5 percent on advertising.[1]

Outside the United States, Colgate's primary competitor was nearly always Unilever. In the United States, their Lever

[1] In comparison, Colgate spends 2 percent on R&D and 6.7 percent on advertising, but on a much narrower product range.

Brothers' subsidiary has historically been the second or third entry in the category behind P&G and, sometimes, Colgate. But internationally, Unilever's market position was often number one or a strong number two. Like P&G, Unilever was strong technically and an aggressive marketeer. For example, they typically spent 2 percent of sales on R&D, and 7.5 percent on advertising. They were also regarded as a truly global company, capable of adapting successfully to a wide variety of local competitive challenges. Thus, on a worldwide basis, Colgate management regarded Unilever as its chief competitive threat.

Thus, in developing its local strategies, Colgate could usually focus its efforts mainly against Unilever or P&G.

In the marketplace, however, Colgate had to take into account its key distributor customers, if they were to be successful. For they often faced a serious problem in competing for shelf space and promotional support from their retailers and wholesalers. Moreover, in most major countries, the distributive trade was growing more concentrated and, consequently, more difficult to deal with. This was a particular problem for smaller manufacturers and lower volume brands, but also for the second or third competitor in the major categories.

THE COMPANY IN 1984

In early 1984 Reuben Mark could look back on a number of accomplishments that he and Crane had accomplished. In his words:

> The BDGs were humming. Our investment in manufacturing to catch up was largely completed; we were now going further to invest in several large, new facilities. The product quality battle was being won. Our managers had their eyes once again on the core categories. Our shares were coming back from the brink of having them fall away from us.

Colgate's worldwide market shares in selected product categories for 1979 and 1984 were:

	1979	*1984*
Colgate toothpaste	29.8%	33.9%
Detergents	9.8	11.1
Hard surface cleaners	15.1	18.0

Mark believed, however, that several strategic challenges still remained. Although volume and market share growth had occurred among some products and in some markets, holes existed in the product lines themselves. In addition, product category growth between 1983 and 1988 was expected to slow to a level below that achieved between 1977 and 1983.

A chart of the organization Mark inherited in 1984 is shown in Exhibit 4.

One thing the company had not done in the eyes of a number of observers was convert strengths to profits. The latter had been relatively flat, as shown in Exhibits 5, 6, and 7.

CONVERSATIONS WITH MANAGEMENT

When Keith Crane told him confidentially in late 1983 that he was thinking about retirement, Reuben Mark initiated a series of informal conversations with his senior managers in an attempt to elicit their views about where the company should be going and how it might get there.

One country GM had offered the following:

> Somewhat to my surprise, the BDGs have worked in bringing new ideas to us. But unless you rekindle the long-held attitude among each of us that "I'm the fastest gun in my territory," we won't move fast

enough to take advantage of the opportunities and stay profitably ahead of competition.

Also, what we really need to do is increase our ability to make acquisitions at the country level in order to fill in gaps in our product offerings. For example, the UK has no presence in the household detergent market.

Another had commented:

It was hard to get through to New York for awhile. Keith changed that by coming out here a lot. But you've still got too many people in the New York office who can shut down lines of communication. What are we going to do about that? You want results, not reports.

The manager of a BDG stated:

When this function was created, we pulled some of our best people from out of our subsidiaries. I think that seriously depleted the management in several of those countries. We're going to have to think about how to fix that.

One country GM complained:

We used to be able to count on being in a country long enough, sometimes 8 to 10 years, to really understand the issues and make a significant impact. That has changed in the past few years as new positions had to be filled. How do you expect us to move every several years and do much more than learn where to shop for groceries before we're moved again? It may be great for my exposure but it isn't doing much for the management of my subisidiary.

A senior manager who previously had had responsibility for a major European subsidiary with significant manufacturing capability remarked:

We keep our eye on marketing strategy and product quality, but have not devoted enough attention to manufacturing costs. As a result, they have edged up steadily. Surely, there is a place for new techniques such as just-in-time procedures in our business. It may cost money, but it should be seen as part of our effort to build product health. Given the volume of certain products that we produce, we should be the low-cost producer. We're not.

The GM for the United States, in discussing the performance of his organization, suggested:

You know, it's difficult operating under the nose of corporate management. As a result, it's not the preferred assignment among country GMs. The U.S. company has never been run as a free-standing subsidiary. That has to change. We need to be given the tools to be the masters of our destiny, like other CP subsidiaries. And of course this is Procter & Gamble's stronghold. You can develop an inferiority complex in the United States if you don't watch out.

One senior manager in the New York office commented:

We've regained some lost ground in research and development. But that's just a beginning. We've rebuilt the core products. Now we need new products.

Another field manager said:

In the process of emphasizing cost-cutting to supply money for the late 1970s' acquisitions, and to cover profit forecast shortfalls, we beat what entrepreneurial spirit there was out of our managers. They contributed but never benefited. That doesn't develop superior managers, only defensive ones.

Importantly, though, Mark also heard managers express the opinion that politics had never played a significant role in company management. As one put it,

"Tirecutters don't stay around here long." They hoped it could be kept that way.

In one conversation, a senior manager whose experience, like most of those in the New York headquarters, had been solely with the core CP businesses, said:

> We have divested a number of the businesses that were acquired in the 70s. But those we have left still constitute a major distraction. Why don't we get rid of the lot? There is plenty of opportunity in our core businesses.

One vice president in New York commented:

> We've been able to make progress without a major change in organization. Whether this can continue or not, I'm not sure. While we've sold off companies, the closest we've come to letting anyone go in our remaining firms was an early retirement program last year. This is almost a Japanese company, in which people rarely have been terminated for reasons of poor performance. We don't even take the job of appraising performance seriously, nothing like what I experienced in the company I worked with before coming here. My experience has been that people want to be tougher appraisers but don't know how to do it. And given the geography of this company of 40,000 employees, we're going to have to supplement the "world tour" as a means of communicating. We've just started bringing in managers to our lower ranks from outside; we'll have to decide whether to accelerate the program and begin to fill more senior positions that way, too, if the company significantly changes its goals for growth.

Yet another vice president in the New York office expressed the opinion that:

> During the recent programs to rebuild the product lines, the GMs in the countries have started to develop bad habits. They're beginning to forget that the purpose of rebuilding is to strengthen our businesses in order to increase our profitability, not just stay even.

One of Mark's greatest concerns was how to reintroduce a spirit of independence and entrepreneurship that had once characterized the company's management. He envisioned the need as ranging from the contribution of new ideas of all kinds to the internal development of new products and even new businesses.

REUBEN MARK BECOMES CEO

When Keith Crane approached him to become the new CEO of Colgate, Mark echoed his thoughts:

> I was surprised by the suddenness. Keith was only 60 and I thought that he wanted to stay until at least 62. Nevertheless, it was a dream I had been holding inside for years—running my own company. Being given the opportunity to direct and lead a company like Colgate, especially since it was already on the road to recovery, and making it succeed, was something I waited for all my life. I was a little apprehensive about taking on the many essential duties that required immediate attention, yet at the same time was very excited by the challenge.

Mark was viewed as a very open, people-oriented leader and a strong motivator.[2] Outgoing by nature, Mark took delight in knowing many of the company's employees on a first-name basis. He connected with people on the plant floor as easily as he did in the boardroom.

On his plant visits he would not only address many employees individually, but would also listen and learn about their

[2] "The Man Brushing Up Colgate's Image," *Fortune*, May 11, 1987, p. 107.

jobs, their problems, and their frustrations. More important, he acknowledged each person's advice and responded personally afterwards—by letter, phone call, or card—whenever possible.

Knowing how to motivate also meant knowing when to recognize and reward good performance. Mark's "You Can Make a Difference" award was one example of his recognition of a job well done. By the same token, he did not pass out compliments for the sake of "winning" people over to his way of thinking. Instead, he opted for open discussions, inviting criticism and suggestions from his executives when disagreements arose.

Mark realized that one man could not do it all. He firmly believed that the success of Colgate was dependent not only upon his leadership ability, but also on the people who worked for and reported to him. "Mark has allowed people to take risks," stated one senior general manager. Mark knew that he needed support from people at every level who understood his goals, believed in them, and then committed themselves to making them happen. He was energetic and sensitive in his dealings with people, but direct and decisive when the circumstances warranted. Colleagues commented that: "He doesn't have an outsized ego," and "he is very much a down-to-earth individual."

Those who knew him well, both inside and outside the corporation, recognized him most for his excellent marketing mind and for an instinct that was unbeatable in the marketplace—adding to his intellectual capability and incredible memory. He had a solid financial background and an amazing talent for handling numbers.

As Reuben Mark considered his new responsibilities, he drew two important conclusions. First, he would have to be very careful to be set the right priorities in order to avoid spreading himself too thinly. Despite the company's recent progress, there were still many problems to be addressed in all aspects of the business.

Second, he felt Colgate's major strength was the quality of its managers around the world. While many industry observers felt that Colgate needed a major input of management talent to change itself into a more effective worldwide competitor, Mark disagreed. "If we can free our key managers to operate, they know what to do. They are a tremendous resource and it's my job to marshal them into action."

EXHIBIT 1
COMPANIES BOUGHT AND SOLD BY THE COLGATE-PALMOLIVE COMPANY
Between 1970 and Early 1984

Company	*Products*	*Year Bought*	*Year Sold*
Kendall Co.	Disposable health care products for consumer and hospital use	1972	–
Helena Rubenstein	Cosmetics	1973	1980
Ram Golf Corp.	Golf equipment	1974	1979
Bancroft Racket Co.	Tennis equipment	1974	1980
Charles A. Eaton Co.	Golf and tennis footwear	1976	–
Riviana Foods	Food products (rice, caviar, kosher meats, pet foods)	1976	1980 (portions)
Marisa Christina Inc.	Sport sweaters	1976	1981
Joseph Terry & Sons (U.K.)	Boxed chocolate candy	1977	1982
Respiratory Care Inc.	Health care equipment	1977	–
Maui Divers of Hawaii Ltd.	Inexpensive cosmetic jewelry	1977	1979
Leach Industries	Sport equipment for racquet ball	1977	1980
MedaSonics, Inc.	Health care equipment	1977	–
Princess House, Inc.	Glass and tableware sold via party plan sales technique	1978	–
AJD Cap Corp.	Sport caps	1978	1981
NDM Corp.	Cardiac electrode equipment	1978	–

EXHIBIT 2
TRENDS IN COMPANY INVESTMENTS IN "PRODUCT HEALTH"
Between 1979 and 1983

	1979	*1980*	*1981*	*1982*	*1983*
Sales (in millions)	$4,494	$5,130	$5,261	$4,888	$4,865
Media advertising (as percent of sales)	6.1%	5.6%	5.8%	6.5%	6.8%
R&D expenditures (as percent of sales)	0.9	0.9	1.0	1.3	1.5
Capital expenditures (as percent of sales)	3.1	2.3	2.0	2.8	3.8

EXHIBIT 3
WORLDWIDE HOUSEHOLD AND PERSONAL CARE MARKET SHARES—CATEGORY SUMMARY

Set out below is a summary of the company's international market share data for its main categories of business. This analysis covers all those markets where the corporation has a subsidiary presence and an active marketing effort. It does not, therefore, include export territories or markets assigned to licensees.

	Number of Countries			
		Brand		
Category	*Sold in*	*Leader*	*No. 2*	*50 Percent Share or More of Category*
Dentrifices	48	18	4	7
Toilet soaps	46	3	6	—
Fabric softeners	24	9	2	4
Detergents	35	3	3	1
Light duty liquids	39	9	3	3
Fine fabric detergents	16	2	—	1
All-purpose cleaners	40	3	8	2
Shampoos	36	10*	10*	1*

*Category data only.

EXHIBIT 4
ORGANIZATION CHART (1984)

Board of Directors
Chief Executive Officer & President
Special Projects
Executive Assistant to Chairman & Chief Executive Officer
Chief Financial Officer Legal-Executive Vice President
Legal Department
Financial-Controller
Treasurer
Tax & Real Estate
Investor Rel
Auditing
Human Resources Vice President

Chief of Operations Kendall & Related Hospital, Industrial & Fiber Businesses Senior-Executive Vice President
Kendall
Hospital
Industrial

Chief of Operations Worldwide Colgate & Related Companies Senior-Executive Vice President
US Company
France
Operations Executive Vice President
Riviana
Etonic
Bike
Far East Vice President
A.P. Division
Americas/Southern Hemisphere Vice President
Central America Northern
Southern
Americas Vice President
Operations Executive Vice President
Europe North Vice President
Europe South/Africa Vice President

Chief Strategic & Business Development Officer Senior-Executive Vice President
Strategic Planning
Business Development
HDD
Oral
Toilet Soap
HS Cleaners
Liquids
Toiletries
Acquisitions
MIS
New Products
New categories
Traditional and non-traditional
New ventures
Princess House
Market Research

Chief Development Officer Senior-Executive Vice President
Manufacturing/Engineering Vice President
R&D-Vice President
Packaging
Purchasing/Travel
Consumer Relations
Communications
International Business Development Vice President
Export
Special Countries

EXHIBIT 5
INDUSTRY SEGMENT DATA FROM CONTINUING OPERATIONS
In Thousands of Dollars

	1980	1981	1982	1983	1984*
Net sales:					
Household and personal care	$3,569,610	$3,639,200	$3,458,222	$3,321,340	$3,368,959
Health care and industrial	719,766	772,378	748,180	800,239	803,103
Food	653,872	658,680	492,726‡	512,209	482,114
Specialty marketing	187,216	191,106	188,867	231,010	255,781
	$5,130,464	$5,261,364	$4,887,995	$4,864,798	$4,909,957
Operating profit:					
Household and personal care	$ 290,151	$ 289,242	$ 218,560	$ 184,994	$ 190,156
Health care and industrial	83,655	86,780	81,782	96,215	63,885
Food	51,324	50,911	52,866‡	48,041	46,452
Specialty marketing	21,387	30,301	41,035	52,095	48,620
	446,517	457,234	394,243	381,345	349,113
Net unallocated expenses†	(82,689)	(62,328)	(16,516)	(30,857)	(233,719)
PBT	$ 363,828	$ 394,906	$ 377,727	$ 350,488	$ 115,394
Identifiable assets:					
Household and personal care	$1,409,697	$1,409,672	$1,265,346	$1,312,300	$1,344,758
Health care and industrial	360,896	388,345	391,605	466,541	545,592
Food	390,542	329,961	260,993‡	257,149	220,854
Specialty marketing	117,020	96,082	100,481	114,677	128,575
	2,278,155	2,224,060	2,018,425	2,150,667	2,239,779
Corporate assets	309,636	406,767	555,988	513,298	328,564
Total assets	$2,587,791	$2,630,827	$2,574,413	$2,663,965	$2,568,343
Capital expenditures:					
Household and personal care	$ 76,465	$ 66,343	$ 89,154	$ 101,859	$ 146,501
Health care and industrial	29,027	26,220	36,659	66,961	83,863
Food	9,359	9,216	8,542	8,958	7,713
Specialty marketing	2,230	5,470	4,795	4,763	5,711
	$ 117,081	$ 107,249	$ 139,150	$ 182,541	$ 243,788

*Projected.

†Net unallocated expenses include general corporate expense and income, net interest, and the 1984 provision for restructured operations.

‡Due to the divestment of certain subsidiaries, including Joseph Terry & Sons Limited in early 1982, net sales, operating profit, and identifiable assets were reduced by $83,336, $2,546, and $55,614, respectively, in the Food segment.

EXHIBIT 6
GEOGRAPHIC AREA DATA FROM CONTINUING OPERATIONS
In Thousands of Dollars

	1980	*1981*	*1982*	*1983*	*1984*
Net sales:					
United States	$1,982,665	$2,170,467	$2,029,189	$2,208,713	$2,342,678
Western Hemisphere	932,567	1,049,983	1,004,304	854,471	873,086
Europe	1,586,537	1,378,953	1,231,568	1,156,416	1,086,286
Africa and Far East	628,695	661,961	622,934	645,198	607,907
	$5,130,464	$5,261,364	$4,887,995	$4,864,798	$4,909,957
Operating profit:					
United States	$ 154,907	$ 168,124	$ 171,474	$ 198,899	$ 181,116
Western Hemisphere	106,760	124,349	89,806	78,780	95,308
Europe	94,301	81,816	71,752	46,369	25,682
Africa and Far East	90,549	82,945	61,211	57,297	47,007
	$ 446,517	$ 457,234	$ 394,243	$ 381,345	$ 349,113
Identifiable assets:					
United States	$ 920,436	$ 989,386	$ 963,595	$1,090,890	$1,252,867
Western Hemisphere	423,502	413,207	344,584	335,881	346,122
Europe	659,295	573,364	467,485	474,766	409,171
Africa and Far East	274,922	248,103	242,761	249,130	231,619
	$2,278,155	$2,224,060	$2,018,425	$2,150,667	$2,239,779

EXHIBIT 7
FINANCIAL PERFORMANCE: COLGATE VERSUS P&G AND UNILEVER

	1982	1983	1984
Colgate			
Sales	$4,888	$4,865	$4,910
Operating income	394	381	349
Operating income (%)	8.1%	7.8%	7.1%
Net income	197	198	72
Net income (%)	4.0%	4.1%	1.5%
ROE	15.0%	14.0%	11.7%
ROC	11.7%	11.2%	10.0%
Stock price			
Low	16	19	21
High	23	25	27
Earnings per share	$2.41	$2.42	$0.64
P&G*			
Sales	$11,994	$12,452	$12,946
Operating income	1,365	1,529	1,287
Operating income (%)	11.4%	12.3%	10.7%
Net income	777	866	890
Net income (%)	6.5%	7.0%	6.9%
ROE	19.4%	19.8%	18.4%
ROC	15.5%	16.1%	14.1%
Stock price			
Low	39	51	46
High	61	63	60
Earnings per share	$4.69	$5.22	$1.87
Unilever			
Sales	$21,277	$19,410	$18,760
Operating income	1,141	1,085	1,078
Operating income (%)	5.4%	5.6%	5.8%
Net income	607	559	583
Net income (%)	2.9%	2.9%	3.1%
ROE	12.9%	12.3%	13.6%
ROC	9.3%	8.8%	8.6%
Stock price			
Low	10	13	15
High	15	17	18
Earnings per share	$2.16	$1.99	$2.08

*P&G financial statistics reflect a fiscal year end June 30.
Source: Colgate, P&G, and Unilever finance departments.

Pepsi-Cola U.S. Beverages (A)

It was a late December evening in 1987. As he leaned back in his chair, Roger Enrico, president and CEO of PepsiCo Worldwide Beverages, thought again about the report on his desk. Several months ago, recognizing that regional consolidation of supermarket chains and growth in the number of Pepsi-owned bottlers were fundamentally changing the way Pepsi did business, Enrico and his top managers had decided to form a task force to investigate possible changes in the organization of Pepsi's domestic soft drink business. The task force consisted of the three divisional presidents from Pepsi USA, Pepsi Bottling Group, and the Fountain Beverage Division, along with the director of personnel (see Exhibit 1 for an organization chart). Their recommendations were contained in the report that Enrico had just finished reading for the second time.

As he thought about the report, Enrico wondered about the next day's meeting with the task force and his upcoming meeting with Wayne Calloway, chairman of PepsiCo. What course of action should he recommend? If a reorganization were necessary, which alternative was best? How would Pepsi be affected by this change? If changes were to be made, when and how should they be implemented? During the past several months, Enrico had, of course, developed some biases, but he wanted to hear the task force's presentation before he made up his mind.

PEPSICO, INC.

In 1987 PepsiCo, Inc., operated in three principal worldwide businesses: soft drinks, snack foods, and restaurants. Major soft drink brands included Pepsi, Diet Pepsi, Slice, and Mountain Dew. Frito-Lay, PepsiCo's snack food division, manufactured and marketed such well-known brands as Lay's Potato Chips, Frito's Corn Chips, and Doritos Tortilla Chips. Pepsi's restaurant chains included Pizza Hut, Taco Bell, and Kentucky Fried Chicken. For the year ended December 27, 1986, the company reported operating profits of $680 million on sales of $9.3 billion.

PepsiCo had a sharply defined corporate culture. According to an internal company document, the culture was shaped by the

Harvard Business School case 390–034.

nature of its business as well as by management design:

> Pepsi has created a results-oriented, competitive, energetic working environment that puts a premium on style and individuality; [Pepsi] has a distinctive culture, filled with stimulation, demanding of personal responsibility, and offering great reward for those able to seize opportunity. [Pepsi] is fluid, lean, open, and unbureaucratic. And the overall tone is, regardless of age, youthful.

Managers were given responsibility and autonomy early in their careers. They were encouraged to take risks. In the words of Donald Kendall, the retired CEO of PepsiCo, "If you go through your career and never make a mistake, you've never tried anything worthwhile."[1] Managers were guided by the dictum that those who rise to the challenge get promoted. Change was regarded as an opportunity to excel, not a threat. As a result, Pepsi had "the country's most sophisticated and comprehensive system for turning bright young people into strong managers."[2] Of course, there were losers as well as winners at PepsiCo. The manager who was not getting results was soon gone. According to one middle-level vice president, Pepsi would "never be nor should [it] be a warm and cuddly environment."[3]

From headquarters to the local level, informal work systems abounded at Pepsi. Things were rarely written down. Communicating by written memo was seen as a last resort, and procedural manuals were virtually nonexistent. Instead, managers were expected to use the phone and face-to-face meetings to get work done. As a result, Pepsi had a reputation for making key decisions quickly and moving ahead more aggressively than its competitors. While this approach sometimes produced mistakes others might avoid, it also gave the company a significant competitive edge in key moves such as the "Pepsi Challenge," the launch of Slice, and package innovation.

U.S. SOFT DRINKS OPERATIONS

In 1986 the soft drink side of PepsiCo contributed 39 percent of both sales and profits. U.S. operations accounted for 80 percent and 61 percent of total beverage dollar sales and profits, respectively. Presiding over this business was Roger Enrico. Reporting to Enrico for domestic operations were three separate operating divisions: Pepsi USA, Pepsi Bottling Group, and the Fountain Beverage Division. Each of these divisions had developed its own geographic and operating structures, maintained separate strategic planning, marketing, and sales departments, and used different budgeting and accounting systems. Moreover, little interaction or coordination took place among them. The result was three distinct operating cultures.

Pepsi USA

Pepsi USA had long been Pepsi's core business. Pepsi USA was designed to create a national marketing umbrella for the company's soft drinks and to sell soft drink concentrate to the Pepsi-Cola bottling network. The bottlers then carried out production, distribution, marketing, and sales at the local level (see Exhibit 2).[4]

---

[1] "Those Highflying PepsiCo Managers," *Fortune*, April 10, 1989, pp. 78–86.
[2] Ibid.
[3] Ibid.

[4] See also "The Domestic Soft Drink Industry in 1986," HBS No. 387–107.

Essentially a marketing organization, Pepsi USA was responsible for generating national marketing campaigns and helping bottlers implement these plans at the local level. The division was organized functionally, but marketing played a dominant role. Using a brand management system, a headquarters marketing staff of 112 developed broad marketing strategies and national advertising campaigns. In its field marketing offices, 86 Pepsi USA employees worked directly with bottlers to help them implement headquarters' plans and to develop local marketing plans. The field staff also provided technical assistance to the bottlers for both production and financial management. Pepsi USA's finance group was designed to manage concentrate billing and promotional allowances for the approximately 419 bottlers, both franchised and company owned, which constituted Pepsi USA's customer base. In 1986 Pepsi USA contributed $938.6 million of sales and over half the net operating profit after tax (NOPAT). (See Exhibit 3 for financial information for each of the three divisions.)

According to a senior Pepsi USA executive, the division had "the world's simplest balance sheet." Revenues were derived from the sale of concentrate to the bottling network. Costs depended primarily on how much money was spent on advertising and trade promotion. Every sale of concentrate added to profits. As a result, Pepsi USA focused its efforts on increasing the total sales volume of Pepsi products and therefore the total sales of concentrate.

Although simple in concept, Pepsi USA's objectives were difficult to execute. They required the creation of exceptional national marketing campaigns (e.g., "The Pepsi Challenge" and the widely publicized Michael Jackson campaign of 1984) as well as the management of cooperative advertising and incentives to boost bottler volume. Because franchise bottlers were independent businesspeople who *owned* the right to bottle Pepsi products in their respective territories *forever,* Pepsi USA put a high premium on its managers' negotiating skill.

Because of Pepsi USA's high visibility within the company, its position as the most profitable of the three businesses, and Pepsi's publicized success against Coke, Pepsi USA managers were proud of their division. It was Pepsi USA that had developed the company's prominent marketing campaigns and created the long-term strategic marketing direction for Pepsi-Cola. In a large, national advertising campaign like the Jackson commercials (where Michael was paid $5 million), $100,000 was considered a small commitment. Pepsi USA had big ideas, worked with big people, and counted big numbers. Moreover, many of PepsiCo's most successful leaders had come from the franchise side of the business, and Pepsi USA managers were highly sought after by executive recruiters. Pepsi USA alumni included Roger Enrico, Robert Beeby (the current president of Frito-Lay), and John Sculley, who left PepsiCo to become president of Apple Computer Inc.

Nevertheless, managers in other areas of Pepsi-Cola characterized Pepsi USA executives as "glitzy with little depth." Although managers from Pepsi USA excelled at marketing and bottler relations, they had considerably less detailed operating experience than did their counterparts in the other two U.S. beverage divisions. Because of the size of Pepsi USA's business and the tremendous profitability of concentrate sales, managers in Pepsi USA also enjoyed job levels and pay that in many cases equaled or exceeded those of their Pepsi

Bottling Group counterparts, who had significantly more operational and supervisory responsibilities. With both bonuses and performance evaluations based on the volume of concentrate sold to all bottlers, the division's managers were driven by the goal of boosting Pepsi market share and volume sales at all costs. Pepsi USA got the first pick of people and offices and employed the highest proportion of MBAs.

Pepsi Bottling Group (PBG)

PBG was the operating side of Pepsi-Cola's domestic business. It consisted of a national organization of company-owned bottling franchises. PBG bottlers bought concentrate from Pepsi USA, then bottled, sold, and distributed Pepsi products within their franchise territories. PBG had begun as a "bottler of last resort" when Pepsi found itself unable to find a competent franchisee to run one of its bottler territories. By 1975 it was a separate division of Pepsi Worldwide Beverages and grew rapidly between 1975 and 1986 (see Exhibit 4). While most of this growth had resulted from the acquisition of franchised bottlers, PBG had also increased sales and profits in its existing bottling units. By year-end 1986, if PBG had been a separate company it would have ranked 125th on the Fortune 500. And, by then, Pepsi owned and operated well over 30 percent of its entire USA bottling network.

The nature of PBG's business was fundamentally different from that of Pepsi USA, and it accounted for its managers' "grease under the fingernails" stereotype. Whereas Pepsi USA concentrated its efforts on the "big picture" of achieving high profits by increasing national sales of concentrate, PBG focused its efforts on mastering the local details of production, tactical advertising, in-store displays, pricing decisions, and managing a complex store door delivery system. On a day-to-day basis, PBG sales managers were responsible for keeping delivery trucks on the road, selling to retailers, controlling shrinkage, setting up in-store displays, and dealing with unions. As one PBG manager observed,

> You never know when you'll get to work in the morning and find that your truck drivers are on strike or that a big customer wants your advertising bid by noon. There is no time for in-depth analysis—you have to make a lot of quick decisions every day.

PBG's finance group handled the accounts of more than 10,000 retail and fountain outlet customers serviced by the company-owned bottlers. The group also managed concentrate payables and promotional allowance accounting with Pepsi USA.

Bottling was a capital-intensive business involving bottling plants, delivery trucks, and distribution warehouses. With gross margins half those of Pepsi USA, PBG counted pennies per case. It became even more cost-conscious as competition with Coca-Cola resulted in severe price competition in many of PBG's key markets. As a former PBG vice president of sales and marketing reported: "We've had no pricing increases for five years, and in many markets prices actually went down. Within that time frame, however, our profitability has actually improved, and the only way to do that is by being ruthless on costs."[5]

During its early years, PBG was organized geographically and was plagued by unprofitable operations and by ineffective "turf-minded" managers in the various

[5] "Divide and Conquer? Decentralizing the Pepsi Generation," *Beverage World,* July 1988, pp. 20–30, 88.

independent franchise bottling businesses it had been forced to purchase. According to Craig Weatherup, president of PBG, "Until the early 1980s, PBG was tagged as a second-class citizen—it had a 'loser' image. We were the afterthought to Pepsi USA and took many cheap shots from any franchise bottler who wanted to take them."

In the late 1970s, however, PBG's management structure was reorganized along functional lines and its management upgraded by transferring successful managers from Frito-Lay, hiring people from outside Pepsi, and conducting intensive training programs. By 1986 PBG had developed many strong managers, skilled at running bottling operations. PBG was considered a first-class operating company within the soft drink industry. Throughout the 1980s, for example, it had outperformed the franchised bottlers in sales and market share growth. Unfortunately, the legacy of having been a loser did not die easily. PBG had finally been successful, but many managers within PBG harbored a feeling of "not being fully appreciated."

Whereas Pepsi USA would typically hire MBAs from top schools, PBG tended to hire 250 to 300 undergraduates per year, principally from large state universities. These people filled positions in operations and distribution and began to "work their way up" in the PBG hierarchy. By 1986 PBG employed more than 15,000 people throughout its U.S. operations. A typical PBG regional manager would have 750 people reporting to him or her. Performance evaluations and bonuses were based primarily on net operating profits and a return-on-assets-employed calculation. Increased volume meant little to a local manager if he or she couldn't cover costs. As Weatherup was fond of telling his managers, "The measure that ultimately counts is PROFITS. I assure you that without NOPAT performance, the rest, in the long run, doesn't count."

Fountain Beverage Division (FBD)

While Pepsi USA and PBG focused on Pepsi sales in supermarkets, the fountain business had largely been ignored by Pepsi executives prior to 1978. Historically, Coca-Cola had dominated the fountain market and controlled both the McDonald's and Burger King accounts. In fact, Coca-Cola's fountain business was said to be six or seven times larger than Pepsi's and extremely profitable. In contrast, Pepsi's fountain business performed erratically and was an insignificant profit producer until the mid-1970s. In 1978, Pepsi created Fountain Beverages as a separate operating division in order to focus on improving fountain sales.

Fountain Beverage was responsible for the sale of all Pepsi products not sold in bottles and cans. Principal customers consisted of restaurant chains and convenience stores that mixed syrup[6] with carbonated water on-site for immediate consumption by the customer. Between 1978 and 1986, FBD was the fastest-growing division in all of PepsiCo. From virtually a "standing start," FBD sales by year-end 1986 had grown to $473 million with NOPAT of $26.8 million. National accounts included Pizza Hut, Taco Bell, and Kentucky Fried Chicken. In addition, FBD succeeded in winning the Burger King account from Coca-Cola in 1982 in addition to important parts of Hardees' and Wendy's franchisee business.

Although smaller than Pepsi USA and PBG, FBD incorporated elements of both its

---

[6] Syrup is concentrate plus a sweetener.

bigger brothers. FBD serviced two types of customers: (1) franchised and company-owned bottlers and (2) national accounts. FBD's relationship with bottlers was similar to Pepsi USA's. Bottlers handled local, smaller fountain sales and were supported by FBD with funding for advertising and trade promotions. Like PBG, which negotiated contracts directly with regional supermarket customers, Fountain Beverage handled direct customer negotiations and pricing for large, national customers.

Because of FBD's weak customer base and humble beginnings, it was essential for the division to develop sales expertise. "I like to think of our salespeople as Green Berets," stated FBD president John Cranor. "We're a smaller division and don't get the attention of Pepsi USA or PBG. Our sales force is small in number, but they're the best. They travel light and have little support staff, but they get the job done." Many of the 200 or so salespeople had come to Pepsi as "experienced hires" from the sales forces of large consumer products companies like Procter & Gamble and Johnson & Johnson. FBD's marketing department consisted primarily of transfers from other parts of Pepsi. FBD hired few people directly from undergraduate or graduate schools. Its culture was that of a small company that had to try harder to succeed in the shadow of Coke's huge fountain beverage business.

INTERACTION AMONG THE THREE U.S. SOFT DRINKS DIVISIONS

There was little coordination among these three autonomous divisions. Historically, Pepsi management had encouraged the divisions to go their separate ways in the pursuit of profits and market share. For example, PBG maintained an independent marketing department and developed its own strategic plans, which would then be implemented by the PBG bottlers. At the same time, the marketing staffs at Pepsi USA and FBD would each create separate plans for their own sales efforts. Indeed, the other two division presidents would first be exposed to the third division's plans when they were invited to sit in on each other's strategic reviews with Roger Enrico.

Because Pepsi USA's main goal was to boost concentrate sales volume, FBD's to increase the number of fountain outlets, and PBG's to maximize the net operating profit of its bottling operations, their strategic plans often contained conflicting objectives. In addition, professional rivalry, PepsiCo's winner's culture, and the independent divisional reporting structure resulted in little communication among the various marketing, sales, and finance groups within each division. Despite PepsiCo's corporate emphasis on rotating its key managers among divisions, most of the managers within U.S. beverages had spent their entire Pepsi-Cola careers within a single division.

While competition and independent thinking can be healthy, they can also produce ineffectiveness and costly redundancy of people and effort. Such problems were especially apparent in the field. For example, Pepsi USA had developed a retail marketing plan for Slice whereby in return for running an end-aisle display for four weeks a bottler would offer store managers a VCR and a cents-off coupon in their weekly newspaper supplement. Pepsi USA then presented this program to both PBG and franchised bottlers for implementation at the local level by the bottlers' sales force. At the same time, PBG's marketing department, seeking to emphasize Slice's 10 percent real fruit juice content, developed a separate Slice marketing plan. PBG's plan consisted of a point-of-purchase Slice/real fruit display for the produce section of supermarkets. Customers were offered a discount on fruit when they bought Slice.

PBG and Pepsi USA were convinced of the superiority of their own plans and the result was that the trade was offered the choice of either marketing plan. In the end, the trade preferred the Slice with fruit plan. This left Pepsi USA with a surplus of VCRs and the company with the burden of having to manage both programs. Conflict between PBG and Pepsi USA was exacerbated by the pride of ownership felt by each marketing department; each side believed its own marketing plan was superior.

Other problems arose in the coordination of local marketing issues. In Southern California, for example, Pepsi managers were unable to resolve pricing issues. Competition with Coca-Cola was particularly intense in this region, and many supermarket chains crossed both PBG and Pepsi USA territories. Due to the separation of PBG and franchised bottlers at the local level, all pricing decisions were referred through the respective chains of command to be settled at headquarters in Sommers, New York. This process could take days or even weeks. Large supermarket chains could seldom afford such delays. When preparing for a chainwide Labor Day circular, for example, a supermarket chain merchandising manager might call sales representatives from local PBG and franchised bottlers to request that Pepsi's "best deal" be the soft drink featured in this key ad piece. In many cases, the supermarket manager would demand responses in a matter of hours.

Ultimately, Roger Enrico, himself, was often called on to resolve disputes and spearhead coordination simply because no other mechanism was available. Since all three divisions reported directly to him, Enrico had to become personally involved in relatively minor issues. Although this coordination was not unduly time consuming, Roger Enrico felt there had to be a better way to bring it about.

TRENDS IN U.S. SUPERMARKET RETAILING

Historically, three major chains—A&P, Safeway, and Kroger—had dominated grocery retailing. Gradually, since the mid-1970s, the "big three" had yielded their leadership to more aggressive, flexible regional competitors. Since roughly 1980, mergers and acquisitions within the supermarket industry have resulted in fewer, larger regional retail chains. Within these regional chains, in turn, the trend was toward fewer, larger stores and centralized decision making. A typical chain, for example, could have stores in 15 different franchised bottling territories, but would demand one centralized purchasing contact. In addition, with the growth of supermarket power, Pepsi was forced to give more and bigger discounts in the quest for special promotions and crucial end-aisle displays. Price and trade promotions, not advertising, dominated battles for sales volume and took up an increasingly larger portion of systemwide costs.

COMPETITION AND COCA-COLA ENTERPRISES

As Enrico thought about the prospects for a reorganization of Pepsi's domestic soft drink business, he also reflected on the recent activities of Coca-Cola. Pepsi had not been the only soft drink concentrate producer buying parts of its franchised bottling network. Between 1979 and the fall of 1986, the Coca-Cola Company had assisted in the transfer of ownership or the financial restructuring of most of its U.S. bottler network. During this time, certain bottlers were acquired by Coke and others were resold to buyers believed to be best equipped to manage and develop those operations. Coke's stated policy was that "a stable, well-financed bottler system with long-term growth objectives is in the best interests of both the Coca-Cola Company and the bottlers of its soft drink products, whether or not the Coca-Cola Company has an ownership interest in any such bottlers."

During the summer of 1986, CCE, a wholly owned subsidiary of the Coca-Cola Company, bought out two large U.S. bottlers to become the largest Coke bottler in the world. Shortly thereafter, Coke offered 51 percent of the equity of CCE to the public. Through this public offering, Coke raised approximately $1.2 billion. Moreover, by making CCE a separate entity, Coke emphasized its belief that concentrate production/marketing and soft drink bottling are two fundamentally different businesses that need different capital structures and management systems.

The result of these changes, as well as Coke's historical evolution, meant that Coca-Cola's approach to the marketplace differed significantly from Pepsi's. Coke's company-owned bottler network was only a small part of its overall system, whereas PBG was Pepsi's dominant bottler. Coke sold its fountain syrup directly to users such as McDonald's, while Pepsi sold and delivered through its bottler network (except for sales calls on large chain restaurant operators). Exhibit 5 shows a comparison of market shares of the two companies for selected years.

CREATION OF THE TASK FORCE AND ITS ANALYSIS

Recognizing that conflict between the three divisions was (1) hurting Pepsi's ability to compete in a marketplace that increasingly put a premium on nimble reactions to local marketing issues and (2) costing the company millions of dollars in redundant general and administrative expenses, the presidents of Pepsi USA, PBG, and FBD approached Roger Enrico during the summer of 1987 with a proposal to consider a possible reorganization of Pepsi's domestic soft drink business. In response, Enrico created a task force consisting of the three division presidents, the head of Pepsi-Cola's personnel department, and an outside facilitator; its purpose was to study the idea of a reorganization and make recommendations to correct the coordination problems (see Exhibit 6 for a profile of each of the task force participants).

By October, the task force concluded that conditions warranted a reorganization of Pepsi-Cola's U.S. organization along geographic lines. Under the proposal, PBG, Pepsi USA, and FBD would be combined and subsequently divided into separate geographic units. At the local level, the jobs of field marketing, retail sales, and fountain channel management now being performed separately by managers from each of the three divisions, would be combined. Two other options were put forth: (1) the full decentralization of operating authority, or (2) a matrix organization with functional managers at the area level (see Exhibits 7 and 8).

Option 1: Full Decentralization

Under this plan, four regional presidents would report to the newly created head of domestic operations. Reporting to each regional president would be five or six area general managers who would be responsible for all of Pepsi's soft drink operations (franchise, company-owned bottlers, and fountain sales) within their respective areas. Under each of these area general managers would be functional managers in charge of retail sales, on-premises (i.e., fountain) sales, field marketing, manufacturing, distribution, finance, and personnel. Decentralization would meet the need for stronger local authority and enable the company to be more responsive to local market concerns. The area would speak with one voice in all budgeting and strategy issues, and the area general manager would have the authority to make all final decisions affecting his or her area. The general manager would have full profit-and-loss responsibility, and his or her bonus would be tied to the local area's success. Moreover, this system would provide an excellent proving ground for the type of general manager the company would need as it moved from being a concentrate and marketing organization to a fully integrated soft drink company.

On the other hand, concern arose about entrusting the organization's success to a low-level general manager. The new structure proposed to combine, into one position, elements from all three of the previous divisions. For example, under the previous system, a "retail manager" played a different role in each of the three divisions. In Pepsi USA, a retail manager worked with bottlers and, through the bottler, with the end customer. In PBG, a retail manager *was* a bottler, working directly with end customers. A retail manager in FBD dealt strictly with fountain sales. Now, within a more limited geographic area, one person would be responsible for *all* Pepsi sales through retail outlets in his or her territory. Opponents of the plan viewed this approach as too risky.

Option 2: Matrix

The other option was a matrix organization in which sales and marketing functions would be decentralized through regional presidents, while operations, finance, and human resources would remain centralized with a dotted-line report to the regional presidents (see Exhibit 8). Under this organization, each region would be again divided into five or six areas, but there would be no area general manager. Instead, a group of seven functional managers would jointly coordinate actions at the area level. This team would agree on area budget and profit targets, and each individual's bonus would be based 50 percent on individual performance and 50 percent on the area's success.

Proponents of this option emphasized that the functional expertise that had made Pepsi so successful over the past decade would be retained. The plan would, supporters claimed, help overcome the parochialism of Pepsi USA, PBG, and FBD, while forcing coordination at the local level to achieve local marketing objectives. Nevertheless, several concerns remained. Detractors of this proposal wondered if a "seven-headed general manager" would be able to make decisions in a timely fashion. Pepsi, as a company, detested committees as "dark alleys down which good ideas are led to be strangled." How would this seven-member team be able to agree on budgets, goals, and day-to-day operating decisions without a strong general manager at the area level? Would Pepsi be able to create 24 "seven-member teams" that would be both effective and efficient? Finally, would this hybrid system allow for the proper development of the new breed of general managers Pepsi would need as it continued to acquire franchise bottlers and shifted its base business?

THE DECISION

As he sipped on yet another Diet Pepsi, Enrico wondered what he would decide to recommend to Wayne Calloway after the next day's meeting. It seemed clear from the task force report that his three division presidents favored reorganization. Yet several questions remained.

Under either proposal, Enrico would have to choose a leader for the new organization. He had three managers, all highly competent and career-minded. All three had served successfully in two or three PepsiCo divisions before being promoted to their current general manager positions. If Enrico selected one of the three men to run the new organization, how would it affect the others? In Pepsi's win/lose culture, what message would his choice send to the rest of the people in Pepsi's domestic soft drink business? Would it be advisable and/or possible to find someone from outside of Pepsi to head the new organization?

Similarly, either proposal would demand a reshuffling of Pepsi's U.S. operations. This would require approximately 300 of Pepsi's 500 senior managers in the United States to develop new skills and learn new responsibilities. It would also require many executives to relocate. What impact would such a massive undertaking have both inside the company and in the marketplace?

How well would Pepsi USA, PBG, and FBD come together? Each division was fiercely proud of its independence and its ability to contribute to Pepsi's success. The task force estimated that relocations would cost about $15 million, but by consolidating the three divisions within each area, general and administrative expenses could be reduced by $20 million per year for U.S. beverage operations. He wondered how his role would change under the new organization. For example, would he have a stronger or weaker role as head of Worldwide Beverages? Would he continue to be involved in major programs like "Michael Jackson Tours?"

Assuming a reorganization was called for, which of the two options made the most sense? The fully decentralized alternative, while a radical departure from the current functional structure, seemed to be the "cleanest" alternative. There would be one person in each area who would be in charge. The matrix structure, on the other hand, offered to retain some of Pepsi's hard-won functional excellence. But it depended on cooperation among seven different area managers. Was the matrix structure a logical intermediate step away from the current organization, or was it a half-baked attempt to change that was bound to fail?

Finally, Enrico thought about the origins of the current divisional structure. FBD, for example, was created in 1978 because fountain sales were not getting the attention needed to grow the business. Would the new organization be able to keep the same degree of focus on the three essentially different parts of the soft drink business? Had the task force, in its enthusiasm for change, glossed over the other ways to eliminate some of the current problems without resorting to a radical reorganization of a $3.6 billion business?

It was very late when Enrico grabbed his coat and packed his briefcase. He knew that making the decisions to go forward with the reorganization was only part of what lay ahead. If he decided to go ahead with one of the two proposed reorganizations, how would this change be implemented? With the United States representing 80 percent of Pepsi-Cola's worldwide dollar sales, this was no small consideration. As he walked to his car, he ran through a mental list of the issues the task force would have to consider: When should a new proposal be announced to the company? How should the announcement be made? Should the switch be made incrementally, with an initial "test" area, or done all at once? How quickly should the change be made? How will the managers, suddenly placed in new jobs and new locations, react to the change? How can top management make the change as smooth as possible? How long will it take for the changes to be completed? How much "slippage" will Pepsi suffer due to the changes?

As he drove out of the parking lot, Enrico could not stop thinking about tomorrow's meeting. He had a long night ahead of him, and tomorrow promised to be an interesting and pivotal day for Pepsi, Roger Enrico, and the members of the task force.

EXHIBIT 1
PEPSI-COLA WORLDWIDE BEVERAGES ORGANIZATION, DECEMBER 1987

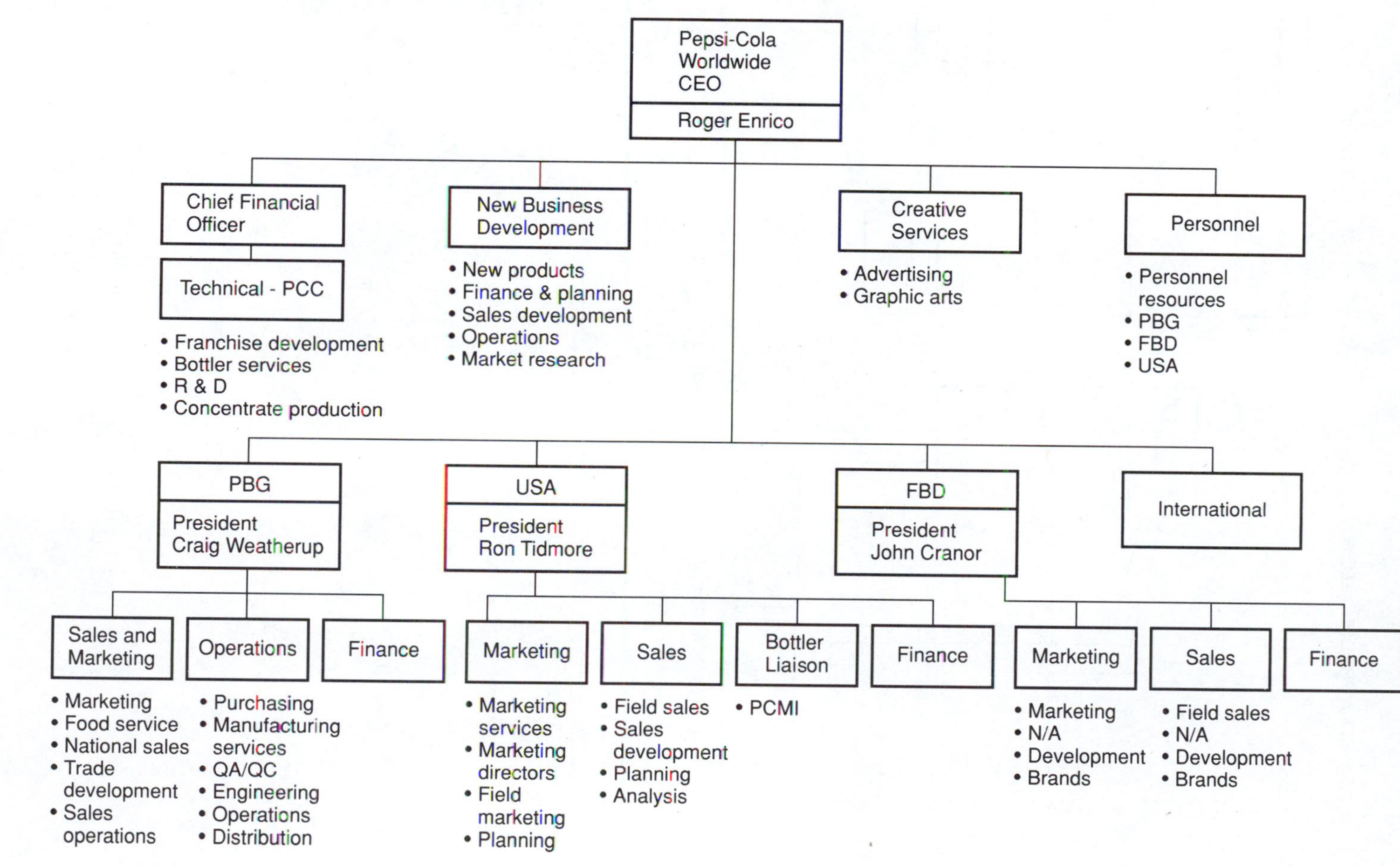

EXHIBIT 2
PEPSI-COLA PRODUCT FLOW

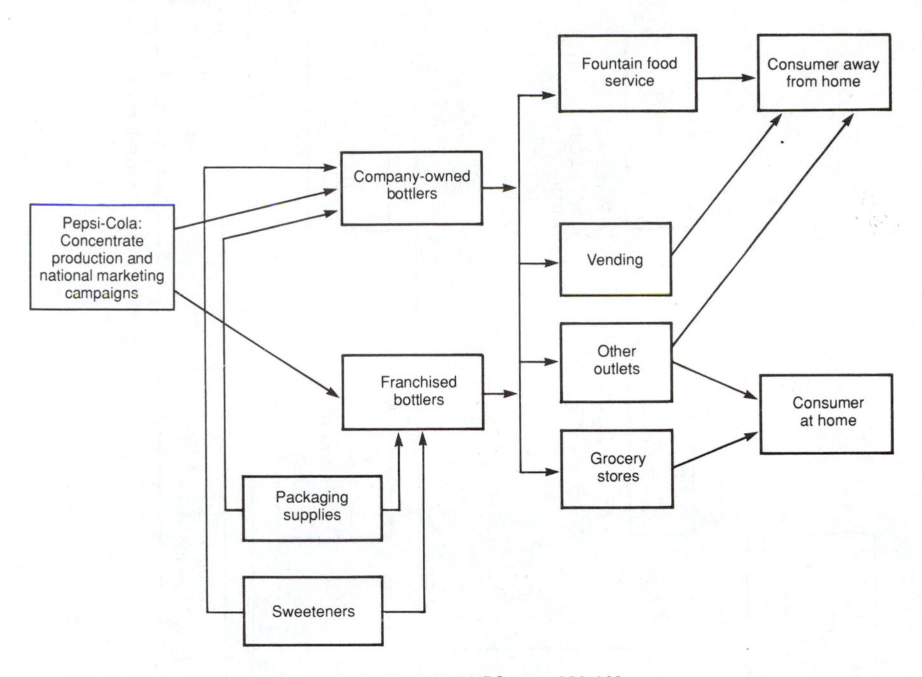

Adapted from: "The Soft Drink Industry in 1986," HBS case 389-169.

EXHIBIT 3
PEPSI-COLA DOMESTIC SOFT DRINKS FINANCIAL SUMMARY
In Thousands of Dollars

	1981	*1982*	*1983*	*1984*	*1985*	*1986**
Sales	$1,516,424	$1,487,177	$1,632,560	$1,844,560	$2,157,714	$2,757,963
NOPAT	123,713	125,509	133,843	157,278	169,721	211,277
Sales by division						
Pepsi USA						938,618
Pepsi Bottling Group						1,780,213
Fountain Beverage Division						473,440

*Division totals do not add to companywide totals due to use of different accounting methods.

1986 EMPLOYMENT DATA BY OPERATING DIVISION

Pepsi USA	
Exempt	575
Nonexempt	225
Pepsi Bottling Group	
Exempt	4,900
Nonexempt	11,100
Fountain Beverage Division	
Exempt	250
Nonexempt	75

EXHIBIT 4
COMPANY-OWNED BOTTLERS, 1975

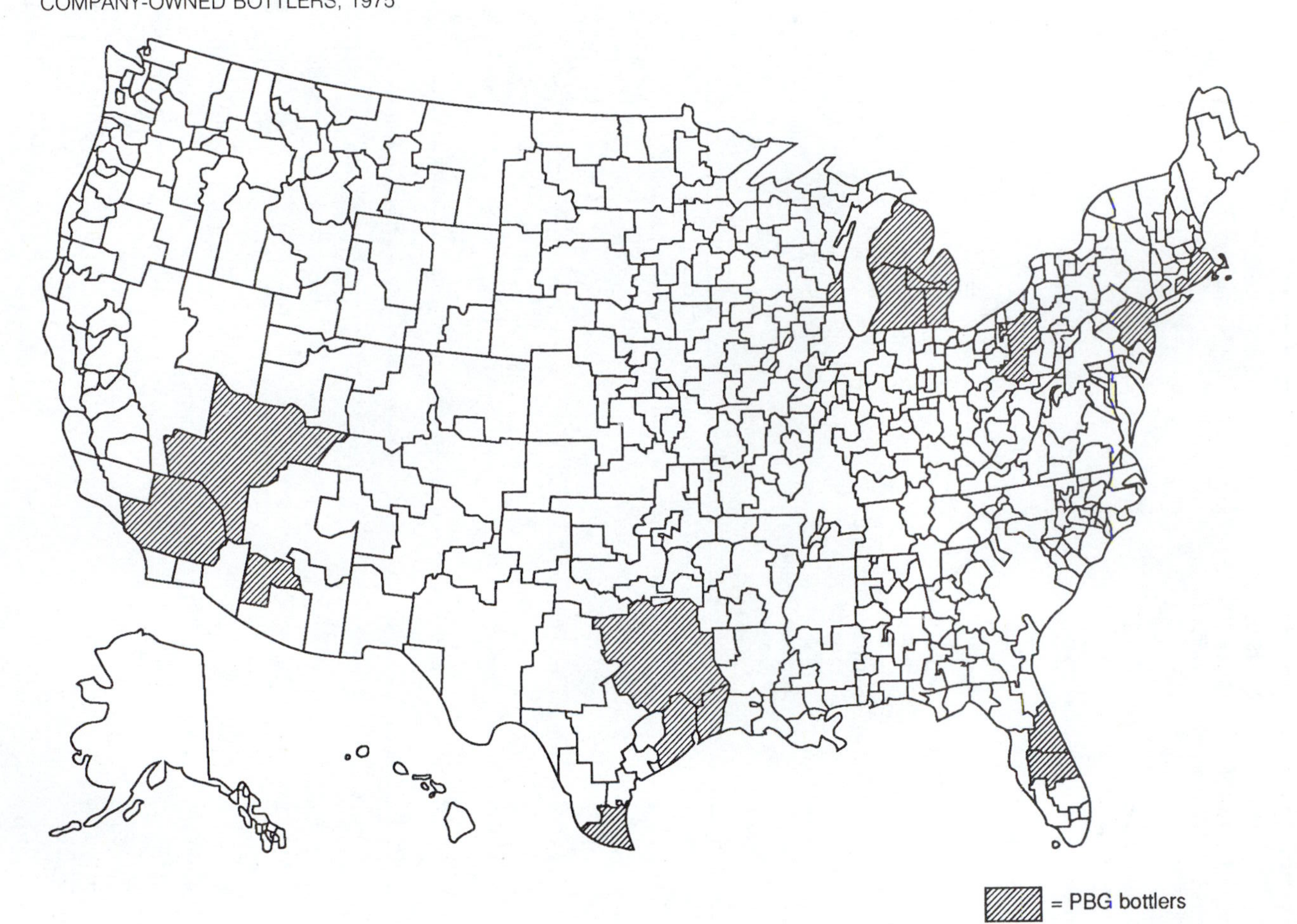

EXHIBIT 4 (*concluded*)
COMPANY-OWNED BOTTLERS, 1986

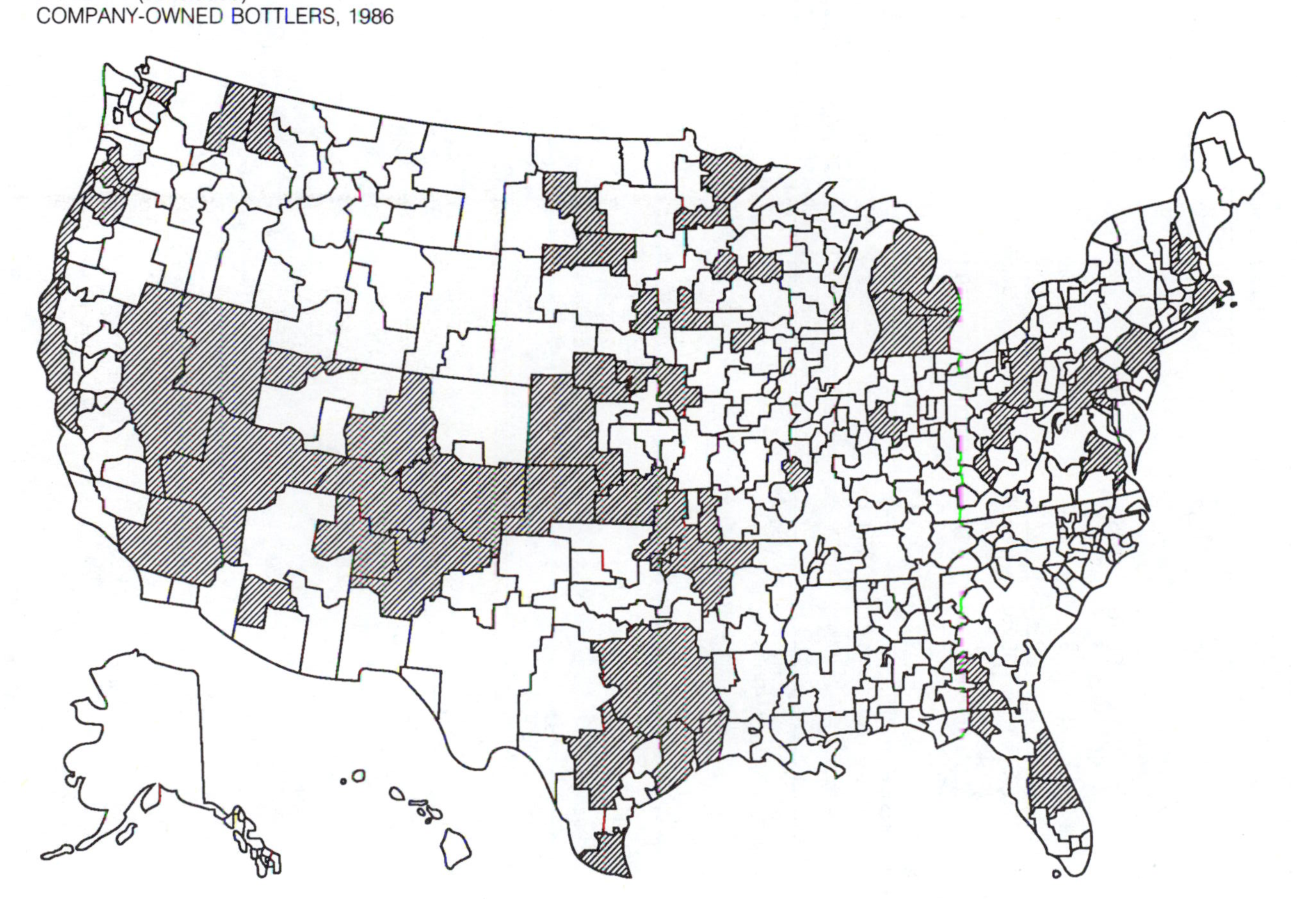

EXHIBIT 5
U.S. SOFT DRINK MARKET SHARES BY CASE VOLUME, SELECTED YEARS
All Distribution Channels

	Market Share by Volume (%)						
	1978	*1980*	*1982*	*1984*	*1985*	*1986*	*1987(E)*
Coca-Cola Company							
Classic	—	—	—	—	6.1%	19.1%	19.8%
Coca-Cola	25.8%	25.3%	24.6%	22.5%	15.0	2.4	1.7
Diet Coke	—	—	0.3	5.2	6.6	7.3	7.7
Regular and Diet Sprite	3.0	3.0	3.3	3.8	4.3	4.3	4.3
Others	6.9	7.3	6.5	6.0	6.5	6.7	6.4
Total	35.7%	35.9%	34.7%	37.5%	38.5%	39.8%	39.9%
PepsiCo, Inc.							
Pepsi-Cola	20.4%	20.4%	20.3%	19.1%	18.9%	18.6%	18.6%
Diet Pepsi	2.7	3.0	3.3	3.2	3.9	4.4	4.7
Mountain Dew	2.7	3.3	3.2	3.0	3.0	3.0	3.3
Regular and Diet Slice	—	—	—	—	1.4	2.5	2.3
Others	1.2	1.1	1.3	3.4	2.5	2.1	1.9
Total	27.0%	27.8%	28.1%	28.7%	29.7%	30.6%	30.8%

Source: Maxwell Carbonated Soft Drinks Report.

EXHIBIT 6
TASK FORCE PARTICIPANTS

Roger Enrico, President of PepsiCo Worldwide Beverages

Roger Enrico joined PepsiCo from General Mills in 1971. Since then he has held positions as vice president of marketing at Frito-Lay, area vice president/South Latin America for PepsiCo International and president of Frito-Lay/Japan for PepsiCo Foods International. Following his tours overseas, Enrico was named senior vice president of sales and marketing for PBG. He then moved to the position of executive vice president of Pepsi-Cola USA under John Sculley, and later, president of Pepsi USA. He earned a bachelor's degree in Finance from Babson College in 1977 and served three years as a supply officer in the Navy.

Ron Tidmore, President of Pepsi USA

Ron Tidmore joined PepsiCo in 1978 and held senior marketing positions at both Pepsi USA and Frito-Lay before becoming senior vice president of sales for Pepsi USA in 1982. From 1984–1986, Tidmore was president of FBD. He earned a BA and an MBA from the University of Georgia.

Craig Weatherup, President of PBG

Craig Weatherup was hired as Pepsi-Cola International's marketing director for the Far East in 1974, following seven years with General Foods in finance and brand marketing. He spent the next eight years in international operations in a variety of increasingly responsible positions, including regional vice president in Japan, and area vice president in South Latin America. In 1982 he became zone vice president with responsibility for all European and Far East markets. In late 1982 Weatherup was named senior vice president of sales and marketing at PBG. He became president of PBG in 1986. He earned a BS from Arizona State University in 1967.

John Cranor, President of FBD

Before being named president of FBD in 1986, John Cranor held a number of senior marketing positions within the PepsiCo system, including vice president of marketing for Frito-Lay, senior vice president and later president of Wilson Sporting Goods, where he supervised the sale of that company to private investors. He graduated from New College in Sarasota Florida in 1967 and earned an MBA from Harvard in 1971.

Mike Feiner, Senior Vice President of Personnel

Mike Feiner joined PepsiCo in 1975 as director of Employee Relations after spending nine years in personnel with TWA. He subsequently held the positions of corporate director of Personnel Administration and vice president of employee relations. He graduated with a BS in International Relations from Boston University in 1964 and earned an MBA from Columbia in 1966.

EXHIBIT 7
PROPOSED FULLY-DECENTRALIZED REORGANIZATION

Pepsi-Cola Co.
Worldwide Beverages
Chief Executive Officer
R. A. Enrico

Personnel
Senior
Vice President

Corporate Operations
Executive
Vice President/
Chief Financial
Officer

President

Marketing and
National Sales
Executive
Vice President

Pepsi
International
President/
Chief Executive
Officer

Personnel
Senior
Vice President

Sales/Marketing
Staff Services
Vice President

Chief
Financial
Officer

Operations
Senior
Vice President

Western
Division
President

Southern
Division
President

Eastern
Division
President

Central
Division
President

Division
Personnel

Division
Finance

Division
Operations

Division
Retail Sales

Division
On-Premise
Sales

Division
Field
Marketing

Area General
Manager (6)

Area
Personnel

Area
Finance

Area
Manufacturing

Area
Distribution to
Warehouses

Area
Retail Sales

Area
On-Premise
Sales

Area
Field
Marketing

EXHIBIT 8
PROPOSED MATRIX REORGANIZATION

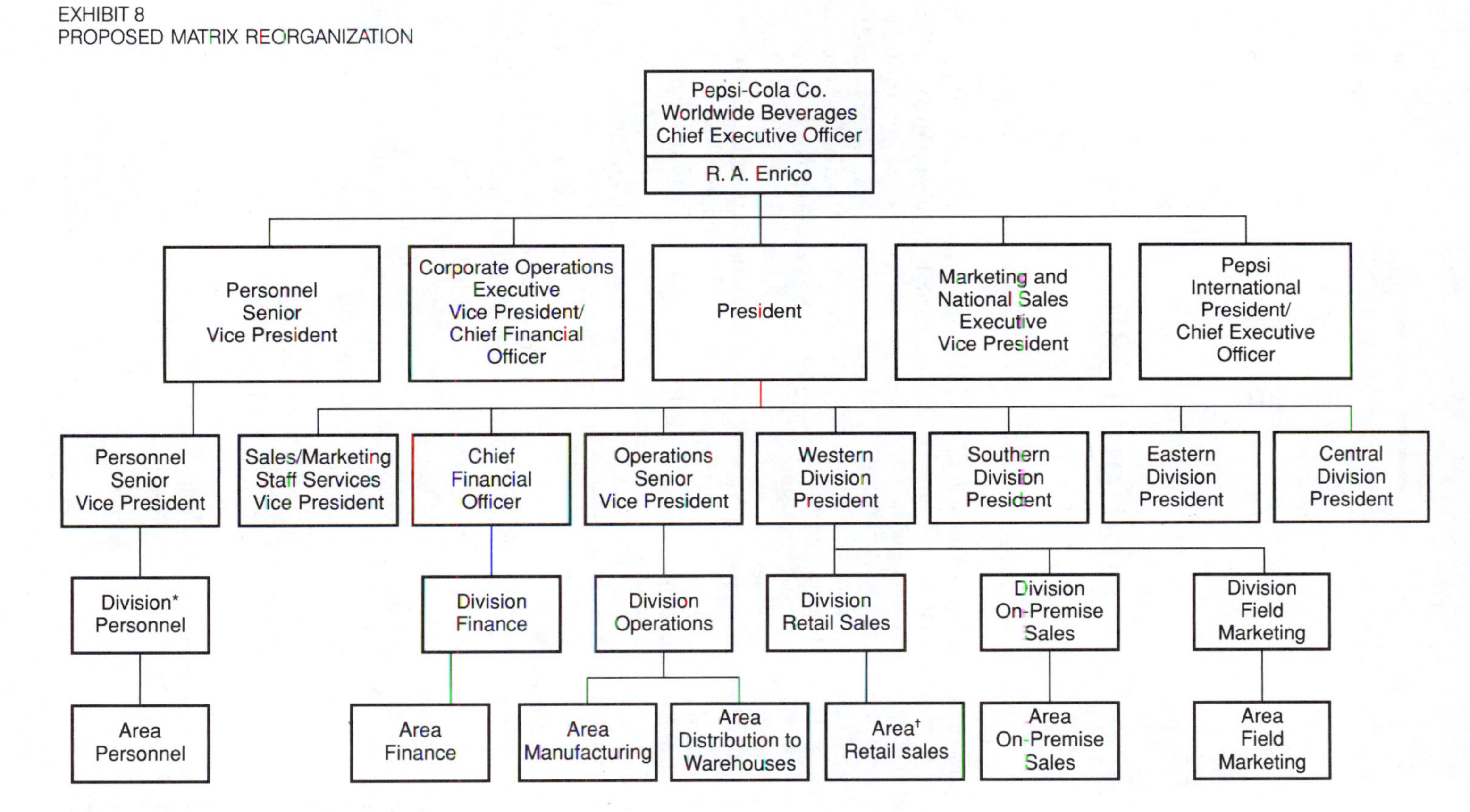

*Division level managers are located at division headquarters; area level managers are located in the field.

†Informal area team leader designate

Banc One Corporation 1989

> It is said that a bank, or any business for that matter, cannot continue to grow without making radical changes in its philosophy of doing business. Something has to give. While there is some value in that thinking, it is hardly an argument for slower growth at Banc One or for revision of a decentralized management strategy that has worked extremely well for us.[1]
>
> *John B. McCoy, 1986*
> *Then-President, Banc One Corp.*

> My role is chief personnel officer. If I get the right people in the right job, that's all I have to do.
>
> *John B. McCoy, 1989*
> *Chairman & CEO, Banc One Corp.*

John B. McCoy rose from his desk on the 16th floor of Banc One's Columbus headquarters while the video crew gathered its equipment. He had just finished taping this quarter's "Chairman's Corner" section of the company news video program. Weeks earlier, on June 29, 1989, Banc One, the largest bank holding company in Ohio and one of the U.S. banking industry's top financial performers, announced that it had beaten five other bidders to purchase 20 of MCorp's failed Texas banks. McCoy had just told employees in his taped message, "Banking is people. The uncertainty is over for the people of MCorp. The great spirit of Banc One will make a difference—we will win back customers and make it work. Our goal is to be the biggest and best bank in the state!"

McCoy knew it would be a challenge to transfer Banc One's remarkable success to its largest acquisition, especially at a time when Banc One itself was undergoing major change. With few exceptions, for two decades the company had grown by acquiring small- to medium-sized midwestern banks with good performance records in nondilutive, friendly deals. The Texas banks' assets were equal to one-half those of Banc One, they were located in the South, and they were insolvent. Banc One's past success in integrating newly acquired banks derived from its abilities to nurture an "uncommon partnership" with the new bank (called an *affiliate*) and to induce better performance from its managers.

[1] John B. McCoy, "Commentary: Small-Guy Philosophy Drives Top Performance," *Financier,* August 1988, pp. 42–44.

Harvard Business School case 390–029.

The "uncommon partnership" balanced autonomous banking decisions based on knowledge of the community at the local level with a strong set of corporate values and operating principles.

Was Banc One entering a new phase that would test McCoy's skill as a general manager and his vision as a corporate leader?

BANC ONE: SUPER-REGIONAL SUPER BANK

In March 1989, before the MCorp purchase, Banc One had 56 affiliate banks with 566 offices, 5 nonbank affiliates (i.e., subsidiaries of Banc One), 18,000 employees, and $23.7 billion in assets. Net income had increased at a compound annual growth rate of 18.39 percent since 1978 (see Exhibit 1). In 1988 Banc One was the most profitable bank holding company as measured by return on average assets among the country's 50 largest banks. Earnings per share and stock price had risen steadily over the past decade (see Exhibit 2).

Banc One was primarily a retail bank which focused on offering loans and other financial services to individual consumers and to small- and medium-sized "middle market" firms. Its branches operated as "stores" concentrating on product sales to meet income targets. McCoy liked to describe Banc One as similar to McDonald's: "Our stores have a lot in common. We're not selling chicken in one place and steaks in another. We're selling the same thing everywhere." The company sought the high-margin business in the retail and middle market loans, industry diversity, and balanced growth. In 1987 the corporation's net interest margin of 5.8 percent compared to a U.S. regional bank average of 4.41 percent. Banc One ranked among the 10 largest U.S. banks in both credit card and student lending.

In the corporate segment, Banc One confined its commercial lending to middle market customers largely in the communities in which its affiliate banks operated. Other than commercial real estate loans at 6 percent of the total loan portfolio, no standard industrial classification of loans represented over 2.5 percent of the loan portfolio. Banc One avoided energy, agriculture, and LDC loans which all had been sources of serious problems for many U.S. banks. In late 1987 and early 1988 through sales and write-offs, Banc One eliminated its small $98 million portfolio of LDC loans, thereby strengthening its loan portfolio. Banc One's significant nonbank activities included trust, leasing, and mortgage operations and extensive data processing.

Overall, Banc One's goal was to deliver superior customer service while obtaining high financial returns. Member banks prided themselves on treating customers as individuals rather than mere account numbers. One affiliate president noted, "From the customers' point of view, if you're not delivering that quality personal service they're not going to stay with you." Banc One believed that its customers saw it as an innovative, fast-paced company always on the leading edge of new products and that customers thus expected to receive from Banc One banks the best products and prices. Advertising emphasized service delivery and specific product offerings equally. Banc One invested steadily in technology R&D to develop new retail products, to improve its competitive lead time, to lower costs, and to generate fee income by providing services to other financial institutions. It used a complex and detailed central financial control system for business planning and performance measurement.

History of Innovations[2]

Banc One could trace its heritage back 121 years to when it started in Columbus, Ohio, as City National Bank. Its modern history began when John G. McCoy assumed the presidency upon his father's death in 1958. McCoy made two fundamental decisions: (1) to run "a Tiffany bank rather than a Woolworth's" and (2) to achieve that goal, "to hire the best people and then delegate; there wasn't any use of putting you in if you were the finest in the world, and then telling you how to do it." For the second decision his father offered no model; he had made every decision in the bank himself.

John G.'s guiding principle was "to provide financial services to people," whom John G. believed choose a bank "because of one word: convenience." To help implement that principle in his first year, he hired John Fisher, a young radio ad man, as head of a newly created advertising department. John G. commissioned him to "find out what the customer wants," and forbade him to learn how to open an account or make a loan. Soon in charge of marketing and public relations, Fisher created a new image for CNB with slogans like "the loaningest bank in town"; "the best all around bank all around town"; and "the good neighborhood bank," featured on a prize-winning billboard ad in 1961. In less than a decade, deposits grew from $140 million to over $400 million.

Fisher's creative vision went beyond ad pitches. Some industry observers credited him with revolutionizing banking by coupling technology with marketing. At John G.'s insistence, since the early 1960s the company had set aside approximately 3 percent of earnings each year for R&D in hopes of identifying ways that technology could improve efficiency and customer service. The company's innovations included introducing the forerunner of the automated teller machine (ATM) in 1969 and in 1972 becoming the first U.S. bank to install ATMs in every branch office. Not all of its innovations took hold. It pioneered efforts, though unsuccessfully, to build a point-of-sale credit card network in 1977 and introduce at-home banking in 1979.

CNB became the first bank to offer credit cards outside of California by introducing the City National BankAmericard (now VISA) in 1966. This innovation not only provided the bank with profits and industry visibility, but it also helped start the charge card revolution which changed spending practices in this country. The company gained additional national exposure in 1976 when Merrill Lynch picked it as the processing arm of its new Cash Management Account (CMA) venture. The CMA accounts permitted customers to use funds from their brokerage accounts via a debit card or checks provided by the bank. This path-breaking alliance helped foment the burgeoning revolution in the U.S. financial services industry.

Driven by the success of its credit cards and its partnership with Merrill Lynch, in the 1970s the company expanded its operations by selling its credit- and debit-card processing expertise to other banks, credit unions, thrifts, finance companies, and brokers. By 1989 Banc One was regarded as a data processing powerhouse.[3] It handled its own 3.2 million cards, over 3.5 million

---

[2] Portions of this section have been excerpted from the 1982 HBS case: "Banc One Corporation and the Home Information Revolution," no. 682–091, originally prepared by Dr. Karen Freeze and Professor Richard Rosenbloom.

[3] *The Wall Street Journal,* June 13, 1988, p. B1.

cards for third parties (e.g., credit unions), and supplied the check clearing and back office operations for many other banks and financial service firms. In 1989 Banc One's Future Systems Group unveiled Phase I of a new system developed in partnership with Electronic Data Systems (EDS) and Norwest, a Minneapolis bank holding company, to attempt to meet the banking industry's data processing needs for the next 20 years.

At the retail level, Banc One experimented with store concept and design. In Kingsdale, Ohio, the company introduced a full-service banking facility called a "Financial Marketplace" with supermarket hours—open 72 hours a week including Sunday afternoons. The state-of-the-art merchandising system comprised boutiques offering home financing, travel services, trust services, business loan operations, a realtor, and investment services. Colorful neon lights identified each separate service area. Interactive (touch-screen) video displays answered customer questions, and drive-in windows made for quick and easy personal service. Four companies leased boutique space: Banc One Investment Services, Banc One Travel, Nationwide Insurance Corp., and HER realtors. Leasing offered Banc One the advantage of learning how to sell products which banks by law could not provide, while creating awareness of its own investment and travel subsidiaries. It also directly challenged companies like Sears and American Express which offered a portfolio of financial services. The success of the Kingsdale store led to a second "supermarket," and both were performing well beyond expectations by 1989.

To ensure continuing innovation, Banc One established a "Greenhouse Group" under John Fisher's leadership in June 1989, to create and nurture new ideas outside of the mainstream of the organization. Initial projects included a toll-free, 24-hour-a-day telephone service; interaffiliate check cashing and deposit service; and a home banking service.

Growth through Acquisitions

Limited in growth by Ohio law to one-county branching, City National Bank merged in 1968 with a smaller bank, Farmers Savings and Trust ($55.2 million in deposits) to form a bank holding company, the First Banc Group (FBG). Another Ohio law prohibiting nonbank institutions from including the designation "Bank" in their names dictated the new spelling, "Banc." FBG began acquiring small banks around Ohio. Between 1968 and 1980 it bought 22 banks, each under $100 million in assets.

A decade old in 1977 and still growing rapidly, First Banc Group had 16 members and $1.95 billion in aggregate assets. With FBG's next decade in mind, John G. and his colleagues—including FBG's new president (and John G.'s son) John B. McCoy—began to consider the implications of federal limits on the company's growth. With the entire banking industry in upheaval as it faced challenges from other financial institutions, McCoy and others expected revisions in the law against interstate banking. Anticipating that event, FBG sought a new name unique in the country. At John Fisher's suggestion, they selected "Banc One" and registered the name in every state. The name change took place in October 1979. Thereafter, the holding company would be known as *Banc* One, and each bank as *Bank* One, followed by its location. Thus City National Bank became Bank One of Columbus.

Between 1980 and 1983 Banc One began to purchase mid-sized banks in major markets. Previous acquisitions were in rural and semi-urban county-seat-type markets. In short order, Banc One bought banks in Cleveland, Akron, Youngstown, and, in June 1983, the $1.6 billion Winters National Bank of Dayton. Winters held assets about one-third the size of those of Banc One.

In 1984 John G. McCoy retired and his son John B. became CEO in addition to his duties as president; in 1987 John B. became chairman and gave up the presidency. In the meantime, changes in state banking laws that allowed bank holding companies to bank in other states spurred a third phase of Banc One's acquisitions toward purchases of larger banks. Looking first to Indiana, Banc One made a purchase about every two weeks in the fall and winter of 1985 and gained six banks. After months of courtship, Banc One announced in May 1986 that it would purchase American Fletcher Bank of Indianapolis. Banc One increased its assets by more than a third overnight because American Fletcher held $4.5 billion in assets and was the second largest bank in Indiana. This move gave Banc One the largest market share in the state. Shortly after this, Banc One made acquisitions in Kentucky, Michigan, and Wisconsin.

Nonbank acquisitions, including a mortgage company and travel agencies, complemented Banc One's operations. Four specialty leasing companies (e.g., for photocopiers, telephone switchboards) balanced its retail strategy at the small end of the market. Nonbank holdings accounted for just 7 percent of earnings, not including the card processing business, which was considered part of the banking operation. This nonbank area, though, was seen as having the most growth potential, perhaps outpacing the rest of the business by 25–50 percent.

Integration of New Affiliates

Banc One sought successful banks run by managers with proven track records. CEO John B. McCoy commented in 1986 that "the success [of our acquisitions] will be achieved through basically two things: a local management team that knows the market and a similarity between the two organizations' [Banc One's and the acquisition's] products and services." Of the deals that never went through, 80 percent failed because of Banc One's lack of confidence in a potential acquisition's current management. With rare exception, current officers remained in place after a Banc One acquisition. McCoy recounted an often-told story that had become part of the company folklore:

> When my dad was running the bank, the head of the largest bank in Cleveland called and said, "Why don't we take us and Cincinnati and form one bank—we'd be really strong." My dad thought that was a great idea, so the guy came for breakfast to discuss putting the three banks together. As breakfast was being served, Dad asked, "So, what will I do in the new bank?" He was told, "Oh, there wouldn't be any need for you!" That was that. Our issue [when we make acquisitions] is how to use current management, not get rid of it.

Thus, assessment of people was central to acquisition decisions. For example, in the spring of 1989 during the due diligence period in Texas, a team of 20 Banc One analysts and executives from affiliate banks studied MCorp's operations. McCoy recalled:

> Our accounting guy said, "The controls aren't good, but I'm impressed by the people." Then the next guy said something similar. So we went back to focus on the people: why they're here, who the boss is, why they haven't left. When we got

> comfortable with the people, we went ahead.

McCoy expected the incumbent bank managers to operate the new affiliate profitably and soundly. Banc One put significant pressure on new affiliates to attain higher earnings. It asked each to take a look at its costs, to improve its proficiency in technology, to expand its loan-making capability, and to professionalize its banking workplace. Banc One had an exceptional track record of improving the performance of its new affiliates. The average acquisition increased its return on assets 66 percent. For example, at the time of its acquisition, Winters' (Dayton) return on assets was approximately .7 percent and net income reached $7 million. Five years later, in 1988, ROA was 1.62 percent and earnings hit $32.4 million. American Fletcher had never scored an ROA greater than 1 percent; in just three years with Banc One, its ROA stood at 1.55 percent.

To spur performance improvements Banc One assigned a "mentor bank" of comparable asset size to share information and expertise with the new bank and to help it build competence in Banc One's products, systems, and operating procedures. Typically, the mentor bank president and various staff members spent at first two or three days each month visiting the new affiliate. New member banks also sent their personnel to the mentor affiliate, and to other banks, to learn about such functions as data processing and financial controls. One affiliate president remarked:

> The operating culture gets transmitted in part by sharing information between the one with the Banc One culture and the one without. It's easy to see when you have an ROA of .6 percent and the other bank was 1.5 percent that there are [better] ways of doing things that you can learn.

Early in the assimilation of new affiliates, Banc One imposed its powerful financial control system, the Management Information Control System (MICS), as an additional tool to help the banks set and meet performance targets. The MICS tracked all balance sheet and income statement data as well as productivity and loan quality ratios (see Exhibit 3). Affiliates received an inch-thick monthly computer report that included detailed performance results.

Financial discipline was an integral value in the system, and managers placed a strong emphasis on the MICS numbers. The system recorded the yearly business plan and financial forecasts for each affiliate. While the original budget stood as a commitment to achieving a stated earnings level, actual results led to revisions in monthly targets. One affiliate manager explained:

> The MICS printout becomes an operating tool for all managers. It doesn't go into a black binder and get hidden away in some drawer. Every month we use it to update our forecasts for the rest of the year. It's the "Banc One Bible." The monthly printout is required reading for all officers and supervisors—those people who make the business forecasts.

MICS brought new affiliates a degree of financial sophistication not typically enjoyed by independent banks. In the words of one financial officer, "MICS helps an affiliate understand itself better. It tells you where you've been, who you are, and where you want to go."

McCoy also found MICS to be a powerful general management tool, because:

> Everyone is on the same financial system and accounted for the same way. In accounting class at Stanford Business School, we'd look at two banks' [income] statements and they'd be totally different;

> that left an impression on me. Our practice is to measure everyone the same way. Our other rule is that everyone has access to everyone else's numbers. Everyone can see who is the best, who is the worst. If you see you're the worst, you pick a better bank and see what's happening there. It's friendly peer competition, but not deadly competition. You're in the same company but not competing in the same market.
>
> Our commercial loan delinquency rate is 2 percent, in the top quartile in the country. Most CEOs would look at that figure and go on to other things. We start there. We list every single bank. We find that some are at 7 percent, some at 1.5 percent. We don't have to call the president with the worst number; he knows the call is coming. If I say to him, "Your loan delinquencies are bad," he would roll his eyes and say, "McCoy, you don't understand my market." He's right; I don't understand his market. But the numbers are there; it's his decision how to learn from someone else with better numbers.

Bringing new affiliates on-line with MICS did not always go without a hitch. For Banc One of Dayton (the former Winters Bank), the conversion was difficult, time-consuming, and it negatively affected customer service. One manager recalled:

> We spent a lot of time that first year fighting change. Our systems were uprooted and managers viewed that as a big loss because they had spent so much time fighting for it. Lots of turf issues arose. We fought battles from the perspective that those systems were "mine"; we really felt they were trying to take something away from us for no reason. We spent most of our energies trying to maintain what was instead of what was going to be.

Despite facing the often frustrating human dilemmas of organizational change, Banc One for the most part smoothly integrated its new acquisitions. Many affiliates gave credit for this success to one element of their new Banc One relationship: the "uncommon partnership."

The Uncommon Partnership

The First Bank Group had adopted "the uncommon partnership" as its slogan, and it became the hallmark of Banc One's relationship with its affiliate banks. McCoy's principle was, "If it involves people, we do it at the local level; if it involves paper, we centralize it." Affiliate autonomy encompassed local lending decisions, pricing based on local market conditions, personnel policies and compensation, and responses to community needs. Such autonomy was "uncommon" in banking. Most holding companies and franchisers imposed a standardized set of rules and practices on their affiliates.

The *uncommon partnership* philosophy was a strong selling point. In one case Banc One's offer to acquire a bank was $6 per share less than a competitor's, but target company directors felt that Banc One's uncommon partnership would provide more long-term value to shareholders, so they accepted the lower offer. Treasurer George Meiling explained:

> In the ideal M&A discussion, we don't even talk dollars or price until about the third meeting. We want to get all the social issues and have them understand how it is going to operate. We tell them not to listen to Columbus because we are trying to sell them on the deal. We give them our phone book and have them pick a president of an affiliate they want to talk to. And a lot of banks do it. Our best salespeople are really our presidents.

Banc One tried to bring a number of benefits to newly affiliated banks. While responsibility for traditional banking activities remained with the affiliates, the corporate office in Columbus provided (for a fee) central services including legal, new product development, and marketing. Affiliation also allowed banks to offer a broad range of products not usually offered by small independent banks, such as leasing and commercial lending. The Banc One name itself had great value in attracting customers, since the company's reputation for quality service had brought it national recognition. Affiliates gained leverage from the operational and financial resources of a much larger bank. Banc One shared its enormous product R&D experience with affiliates. Affiliates could obtain data that helped them predict which products would be most successful in their local markets. Frank McKinney, chairman of Banc One Indiana, summarized the advantages of Banc One membership this way: "It's like you have a very nice six-cylinder car that gets 18 miles per gallon, and that's the best you can do. So you ask, 'What do we have to do to get 24?' That's why we affiliated."[4] An Ohio affiliate president concluded,

> The uncommon partnership offers our customers the best of both worlds: those local [lending] decisions as well as services not generally offered by a $100 million bank. Because of the uncommon partnership, we're allowed to spend more time with our customers. For example, I don't have my staff bogged down with tracking the changes in regulations. The corporate legal staff does that. We can instead focus on serving the customers.

Work Environment

Along with the uncommon partnership, other aspects of Banc One's work environment had always been determined at the top of the company in Columbus and then diffused throughout the various affiliates. Since the Columbus bank accounted for 50 percent of total company revenue before the 1983 Winters acquisition in Dayton, the operating practices of that bank easily influenced those of the smaller affiliates. But when Dayton became 25 percent of the company, and Columbus shrank to 30 percent, John Fisher, now senior vice president, saw the need for some unifying devices.

> I concluded that if this continues, every time we do a merger we'll begin to look a lot more like the new affiliates and less like ourselves. You can just see how if we replicate the mergers, down the road there would be no surviving Banc One operating philosophy or culture. We didn't have a lot of things to give them that would make them look like us. We did have our common name and could offer shared services in data processing. We needed to develop things we could transfer to new affiliates to glue us together as a single organization.

Coincidentally, John B. McCoy had just become CEO. Fisher sensed that McCoy was searching for a platform to call his own, a way to make a distinctive mark on the company that would separate him from his father. He presented to McCoy a "white paper" in October 1984 that proposed quality as that platform. Fisher wrote:

> [Our senior staff] meetings almost invariably, and virtually exclusively, deal with the financial results. Never do they begin by asking about the customer. That's not a criticism of our emphasis on financial performance. It's only a statement of fact about our focus. Our management style is so single-minded, so inward-oriented that we have become almost totally dependent on financials. We have no other refined management tool to give direction or provide decisions for our business.

[4] Banc One Eases Fears of Wholesale Changes," *Indianapolis Star*, June 12, 1988.

To address this concern, Fisher proposed a plan that included establishing a corporate positioning theme, creating a training program for executives, and expanding intracorporate communications through a variety of vehicles.

McCoy acted on Fisher's suggestions. In 1985 Banc One selected as its positioning theme the phrase "Nine Thousand People Who Care," a statement of a goal as much as common identity. All employees were invited to Columbus to celebrate the announcement of the new slogan at a major rally televised on closed circuit around the state for employees who could not attend. By early 1989, after several acquisitions, the slogan stood at "Eighteen Thousand People Who Care."

The company song captured this theme. McCoy remembered once attending an IBM function with Fisher and hearing its company song. "I said, 'We'd never sing a song in our company.' John Fisher said, 'We will, and I'll have tears in your eyes.' A year later, we had a song." Banc One's broadcast advertising included the song, and employees sang it at various celebrations and company events. In the spring of 1988, McCoy challenged employees to form groups and record their performance of the company song; the winning performers would star in a "music video" produced for company-wide broadcast. Other songs played a part in the Banc One culture as well, as special company events would inspire employees to write a set of lyrics for the occasion. For example, a group of managers sang its own version of "Leaving on a Jet Plane" to Senior Vice President Bill Boardman while he was in the middle of negotiating the Texas acquisition (see Exhibit 4).

One of the most prominent and successful vehicles for transmitting Banc One's values and operating standards was Bank One College. The college was an internal training program originally designed to give senior managers experience working together and to be a catalyst for collaboration and idea exchange among affiliates. The college took participants from their geographically dispersed locations and immersed them in two weeks of intense day and evening experiences. Top executives, including McCoy and Fisher, presented the corporation's operating philosophy and plans. Other classes and presentations honed the managers' problem-solving skills. The college used role-playing and "Outward Bound"–type team building activities to develop trust, sharing, unity, and cooperation.

College director Beth Luchsinger commented, "Our challenge is to continue fostering innovation while sustaining growth. We use the college as a vehicle to achieve that." While the college's emphasis was always on sharing information and promoting learning between affiliates, conversations with McCoy before each session produced an agenda of specific discussion themes based on current Banc One issues.

Although the semiannual program had a long waiting list of participants, some potential candidates were skeptical about the college. A few considered it a form of brainwashing and refused to attend. On each of these occasions, McCoy contacted these executives and urged them to attend and then report their evaluation back to him. Three presidents resigned shortly after their two-week experience. Luchsinger reported that each had realized over the course of the college that "this was not the company they wanted to work for. They didn't buy into the philosophy or the way of operating here."

One important by-product of the college was the expanded network of relationships formed by the participants. Annual reunions of all the graduates helped maintain these ties. Most who had attended the college praised this consequence of their experience. "It was a fantastic experience," extolled one college alum. "I have 24 great friends now that I'm in touch with all the time. I go to reunions, and the network of relationships just grows and grows, which means more and more information is available. You can't get too much information in this business—it just changes too quickly."

Information-sharing and idea-exchange were central to Banc One's operating philosophy. Management stressed face-to-face meetings, preferring personal interactions to electronic communications. One Banc One executive, who had spent most of his career with IBM, remarked, "The informality of the organization is unique in banks. I was surprised by the willingness to question procedures. That shows a commitment by the organization to encourage people to think and express their ideas." The annual corporatewide Presidents' Council meetings brought together all the bank presidents to discuss current issues with corporatewide relevance. In addition, the state holding companies held similar Presidents' Council meetings frequently throughout the year. McCoy and other top corporate executives attended these meetings when invited and participated in open discussion forums. One president remarked, "McCoy doesn't have a problem with dissent. He encourages it. People are not shrinking violets in this company."

Many affiliate officers reported calling their peers to inquire about how another achieved a particularly good performance or solved a problem. Karen Horn, CEO of Bank One, Cleveland, a highly experienced bank executive who came to Banc One from the presidency of the Federal Reserve Bank of Cleveland, saw value in this peer exchange:

> When we are dealing with an issue, there are 59 other folks out there that are vaguely in the same business we are that might have good ideas about it. There are also some people in Columbus who might have good ideas about it, and they may be more or less forceful, depending on the situation, in trying to get their ideas implemented. The openness and interchange between the affiliates is one of the enormous strengths of Banc One.

Communication to employees was frequent and detailed. The monthly company newsletter, *The Wire,* reported the latest events, internal organizational changes, promotions, work anniversaries, and assorted items of employee interest. Beginning in 1986, Banc One broadcast systemwide a 30-minute, network news-style video magazine, *The Quarterly Report.* Local affiliates taped professional quality reports, and senior managers appeared to answer questions about the past quarter's results and current company issues.

The corporatewide quality program was another unifying force. Bill Bennett, chairman of Bank One, Dayton, had developed a formal quality program in response to lapses in quality caused by merging data systems shortly after its acquisition. His hands-on approach included walking around the various banks' facilities, monitoring quality and encouraging employees to focus on improving customer service. The success of the program in Dayton led to a systemwide, participative quality program under John Fisher's leadership. Included were competitive rankings of affiliates' performance on quality ratings and annual Chairman's Awards for quality leaders. In 1988 some 488 quality teams were addressing issues ranging from the process of sending out a customer statement to the design of a proposed new account.

Awards were abundant. The Chairman's Award was given annually at the Corporate Quality Awards banquet. "We Care" awards were presented regularly to employees to recognize individual or group contributions to superior customer service; for example, two administrative assistants received "We Care" awards for volunteering to work until 2 A.M. to draw up a crucial buy/sell agreement by the deadline. In 1988, 210 employees earned this recognition. The most coveted award was the "Blue One" award, given to the banks scoring highest on profitability, credit quality, reserves and liquidity, and productivity. Names and photos of award recipients regularly appeared in *The Wire* (see Exhibit 5).

Other celebrations regularly took place. One particularly enthusiastic event welcomed the new Wisconsin affiliates in 1988. June 13 was declared "Name Change Day," the day when the acquired banks would be called Bank One. The day began with a pancake breakfast served by top executives to all Wisconsin employees. Each employee received a Bank One bag filled with "welcome aboard" gifts, including a T-shirt, cap, and balloons. CEO McCoy and other officials spoke at a rally later in the morning. The employee band played the "Bank One" song and, reading off mimeographed pages, everyone sang along and was officially initiated onto the Banc One team.

One of the more controversial aspects of Banc One's culture was its Code of Ethics. Banc One defined ethics as its accountability and responsibility to its depositors and shareholders. When a new bank joined Banc One, each of its employees received a copy of the Code of Ethics that she/he must sign, attesting knowledge of, and agreement with, its contents. The code provided guidelines for behavior regarding conflict of interest, personal conduct, and financial affairs (see Exhibit 6). These latter, personal issues raised concerns about violations of privacy and discomfort at the corporation's seeming imposition of a strict morality. Roman Gerber, corporate general counsel, remarked: "To be very frank, our code probably goes a bit further than some corporate codes go in trying to dictate or guide conduct."

The code also had strict disclosure requirements for officers and directors regarding personal financial obligations. Gerber reported, "This perhaps more than any other piece of the Code of Ethics has been resisted." Some affiliates believed that such disclosure went beyond what an employer was entitled to know. This component of the code was optional for the individual banks. Gerber commented that "rather than just jamming it down their throats, we would rather have them come to understand and come to accept it over time."

Leadership

McCoy described his role and activities this way:

> Besides chief personnel officer, my other job is Goodwill Ambassador. There are times I feel I'm running for office. On the first day in Texas I tried to walk around as many floors as I could, let people see who we are. We had dinners for all the officers; I talked about our philosophy.

McCoy held informal weekly staff meetings (no minutes); in 1989 they included Fisher, Don McWhorter (Chairman of Services Corp.), John Westman (CFO), Bill Boardman (SVP Acquisitions), and Gerber. Others were invited to discuss particular issues. He also held a monthly policy committee meeting that added the state company heads to the staff meeting group to examine events and results across the company. In addition to chairing meetings of the board of directors, McCoy attended the state Presidents' Council meetings when invited. But he noted that, "When things are running well, I don't have to go to a lot of meetings. Because of the strengths of our forecasts and financial systems, we don't do a lot of reviews—only if there is a problem." In fact, McCoy joked, "No one wants to take my phone calls, because they know that I only get called with bad news."

McCoy relied on Fisher as a confidant and sounding board for a variety of business decisions. He regarded Fisher as the company's "idea man" and believed that Fisher's successful efforts over the years to make Banc One a marketing-driven company were the reason that human resource and quality programs often emanated from the Marketing area.

> He's a unique individual. He's always coming at you with ideas. John is a good observer of what's going on in the company. He's at the point in his career where he has nothing to lose if he says, "That guy in Dayton is in trouble," or, "There's a problem in Cleveland." I can talk to him. He'll say, "That's dumb. That's right."

Fisher attributed his influence to McCoy's vision and interest in innovations and fresh thought. "The thing that has helped make us unique is the creative flame he has helped nurture," he explained.

Most press accounts as well as investment analyst reports described Banc One as a superior company with talented and dynamic managers. McCoy personally selected people for the top corporate slots including the state holding-company presidents, though he discussed candidates with his key managers individually. Each holding company chose its local bank presidents and officers, though there had not been too many selection decisions due to the usual retention of existing management after acquisitions. According to McCoy, successful managers at Banc One affiliates were entrepreneurial in their outlook toward opportunities, willing to share information and decision-making power with their peers and subordinates, and open to new ideas; they were good at turnarounds but also able to sustain growth by avoiding major mistakes.

McCoy set a high common standard for managerial performance. According to Fisher he used "a velvet glove" to motivate the affiliates. McCoy tried to create a work environment that reflected his belief that people are good, bright, and want to do the right things but don't always know what they are. "The affiliates have a sharing relationship," McCoy remarked. "It's not, 'Hey, you dumb guy.' I'd much rather have a friendly company than an unfriendly one."

Affiliate officers were evaluated on budgeted versus actual earnings (adjusted for events outside of affiliate control) and on ROA. Their bonuses varied as a percentage of total compensation, but were between 10 and 50 percent. To earn 100 percent of the bonus, managers had to meet their budget targets and earn a 1.4 percent ROA. There were payoff curves for other combinations of these two variables. Several senior managers acknowledged that while the monetary bonus played a distinct motivational role, it was not the most important factor. According to one affiliate president, friendly competition among the affiliates was the greatest incentive:

> No one wants to be on the bottom of the lists. Lots of [senior] people could have moved to different organizations and made more money. But once you get the Banc One spirit in your blood you can't leave it. You want to win the Blue One award, the Chairman's Award.

Banc One held onto its best managers. One officer reported that while many of his peers frequently received calls from executive search firms, none had been stolen away by other companies. Low turnover meant high retention of experience and knowledge and maintenance of the extensive networks of relationships among the various affiliates. But high standards meant that jobs were not sinecures. In the case of one affiliate bank president with 20 years' service whose job grew too big for him to handle, McCoy reported:

> I told him I'm convinced he can't do [the job], that I've given him a chance for the past year and I must make a change. I said he has two choices: we can get him an outplacement counselor to help him get an outside job or he can become the president of a smaller bank. He chose to take the outside job. It was announced in the company that he simply wanted that job. There was no embarrassment, no cutting him off at the knees. That's the style I want. If everyone feels the hammer is coming right at him, it's harder to get good performance. Of course, if someone breaks the law, they're out the next minute; that's happened.

McCoy believed that leaders came from every level in the company. One effort to emphasize this philosophy proved unworkable. McCoy tried to do away with the proliferation of officer titles at Banc One. Remarked McCoy, "We do a lot of team projects here. There was a junior analyst on the due diligence team in Texas, a great contributor. He was treated as an equal, not as a gofer. If we get a lot of good people on a team it doesn't matter what their titles are." Focus groups conducted with employees below the officer level agreed with the elimination of titles. Senior managers, however, resisted this change, and McCoy did not force the issue.

Organizational Dilemmas of Growth

In 1987, in response to the complexities of multistate and nonbanking operations, Banc One organized its affiliates into a state holding-company structure, with corporate headquarters and staff offices in Columbus (see Exhibit 7). In January 1989, Banc One Ohio had 26 affiliates including banks in Ohio, Michigan, and Kentucky; Banc One Indiana, 11 affiliates; and Banc One Wisconsin, 19 affiliates. The state holding-company structure allowed for future growth since it could be duplicated as new states were added; it encouraged development of local management talent; and it helped successfully integrate new affiliates.

Sandwiched between the centralized and decentralized features of the Banc One system were some "centralized, shared responsibilities": those activities with which central subsidiaries or offices assisted the local banks and holding companies by providing expertise, policy guidelines, and resources for particular products and services. For example, the corporate marketing department assisted affiliates in product development and promotion, and Banc One Services Corporation supplied the data processing/item processing services for all units. In addition, Banc One corporate offices in Columbus in conjunction with the state holding companies and affiliates performed financial analyses and forecasting. Mortgages, investment banking, insurance, and leasing were all shared with central nonbank subsidiaries. To add structure and some direction to these "centralized, shared responsibilities," Banc One created the Services Corporation in January 1988, to handle operations functions for all the affiliate banks. These functions included data and credit card processing as well as software and system development to support new products. A year later, in a move that further centralized some operations, the Services Corporation was restructured into five major groups to separate the data processing for information services from that for financial services.

For some affiliates, however, the existence of a more centralized Services organization created tension regarding locus of control. A particularly sore spot was the price affiliates were charged for central services. Mike Elvir, executive vice president of the Services Corporation, commented:

> This is a source of major irritation. They don't want us to be a profit center. They think it is unfair and makes it hard for them to compete. [The issue of pricing] is raised within the first 20 minutes of almost all dialogues I have with people. Currently our price is based on a market-based price; it is 90 percent of the composite price found. But affiliates still argue. They go out and find one supplier who will give it to them for less. They forget that same one supplier will not give them all the services they need at such a low price. A lot of energy is wasted on this issue as affiliates try to prove us wrong. McCoy believes the organization gains a lot by letting affiliates feel they can challenge our pricing. But McCoy and his minions put such a large pressure on increasing margins that the affiliates will never be happy with what we do. This is the cost we pay for the uncommon partnership—as aggravating as it is, I agree with it. The benefits gained from their operating like independent business people outweighs what we lose.

Elvir identified a second trouble spot Banc One had with its affiliates: meeting the needs of diverse entities.

> Regional banks all want autonomy but all require operational support. What is good for one bank is not good for another—a $4.5 million bank in Indiana does not want the same thing as a $700 million bank in Wisconsin. The decisions made are meant to satisfy the majority. Systems need to be common.

This lack of similar needs extended throughout the corporation and raised some crucial questions. Some managers continued to express the concerns voiced by John Fisher in 1983 at the time of the Winters acquisition. How could Banc One maintain a single set of practices and values when the organization's "culture" continued to be diluted with new affiliates, each bringing its own systems, styles, and needs? Craig Kelley, vice president–director affiliate marketing commented:

> We have created a monster. We have commonality in name, and we share a slogan and a corporate logo. But there are no common operating procedures—not even in how to open an account. For example, there is no common check-cashing system. We have a great franchise system, but customers are not guaranteed that they can cash a check at various Bank One locations—it is up to the whim of local management.
>
> How can we maintain the sense of affiliate self-ownership and impose some commonality, some sense of sameness? So much is driven down to the bank level that there is not a feeling of family; there is not the sense of being a part of something larger. We must put the uncommon partnership aside and say who we are.

Moves away from local autonomy were particularly prominent in two other areas: product line and procurement. In the summer of 1988 Banc One announced a corporatewide uniform product line. After months of discussions involving participants from every Banc One affiliate, the corporate product uniformity committee reduced the number of financial products offered from 63 to 10. New guidelines standardized features, marketing approaches, and product terms and conditions. These changes would make pricing decisions easier, simplify marketing tasks, and streamline operations. For example, uniform products were expected to help solve the marketing problem of creating ads for affiliates that each had its own way of packaging and selling identical and/or similar services.

At the same time, Banc One extended to the entire organization a central office materials procurement program developed at Banc One, Wisconsin. Savings opportunities were estimated at around $5 million annually. Banc One hoped to use its leverage as a $24 billion company to obtain better prices than any individual local unit. McCoy respected the desire of local banks to buy from local suppliers with whom they had long-established relationships, so initially the program was optional. He hoped, however, that the participating banks' bottom-line results would provide incentives for others to join. On this point, one Michigan affiliate president acknowledged that he supported the move to centralized purchasing with one caveat: The group must serve him at least as well, if not better, than his in-house operations had. "I have the authority," he said assuredly, "to find my own suppliers if I'm not happy with the job Columbus is doing."

Some affiliate managers saw the movement toward increased centralization and standardization as part of a systematic plan to take away the power of local banks. A few were unconcerned—as long as Banc One continued to leave the banking functions of making loans and accepting deposits to local officials. Nevertheless, managers in Columbus, including John Fisher, saw corporate unity as the paramount concern. Commented Fisher:

> We're here saying, "Hey, McCoy, the way to do this baby is to have more central programs. If you don't have central programs, then there is nothing here to help you steer." Yet, the other folks out in the field are saying, "You don't need that. We can do all that stuff out here. We don't need corporate ads. We don't need uniform products." McCoy is caught and his two ears are hearing different voices. One group calls for centralization and another wants more autonomy.

THE FUTURE CHALLENGE

In February 1989, *Financial World* magazine named Banc One one of 30 great companies for the 1990s, calling it "the cream of a pack of excellent super-regionals" and noting its "highly innovative products and services" and its skill at "digesting new technology and smaller banks." Despite such accolades, concern at the company over limited future growth of its existing customer base and pressure to maintain its record of superior financial performance had led to conservative actions, such as selling credit card receivables to investors and limiting consumer credit lines, and had intensified Banc One's willingness to make a major acquisition.

In June 1989, Banc One agreed to purchase MCorp's 20 banks for $375–510 million, depending on the banks' financial results, to be paid over five years. The banks' 65 branch offices across the state made up the Deposit Insurance Bridge Bank, which with $13.1 billion in assets was the third largest Texas bank. The FDIC offered an incentive by agreeing to indemnify all the Bridge Bank's identified and classified nonperforming loans, reducing the asset value of the acquisition by essentially cleaning the balance sheet and leaving only the good assets; it was the third costliest bailout in FDIC history. The biggest risk in entering Texas was the future uncertainty of the state's economy. The depressed oil and gas industry had hit the state hard. Even if the depression had bottomed out, any further weakness could hurt the bank's financial performance.

The Bridge Bank purchase was Banc One's first acquisition outside of the Midwest; it involved a large bank, not a small- or medium-sized one. Not only was Bridge Bank unsuccessful and unprofitable, but it was insolvent as well. Unlike all other Banc One acquisitions, Bridge Bank had little strength in the retail or middle market segments. Nor did Bridge Bank lease small ticket items or have a mortgage department. Its focus, and what had led to its downfall, was the commercial lending sector. McCoy commented that there was a major clash of cultures involved not because of Texas and Ohio styles but because of loan size: "Ours are $1 million loans, theirs are $50 million."

Banc One named its Chairman McCoy as chairman of Banc One Texas. Thomas Hoaglin, chairman and CEO of Bank One, Dayton, was named president and CEO of the new Texas entity. Under Hoaglin's leadership, Dayton was Banc One's top financial performer in 1988, and the bank won a special quality service award that year. While Banc One also planned to name several more senior executives, McCoy told *The Wall Street Journal,* "We found what appeared to us to be good management at the grassroots level, and that's one of the main things that kept our interest in the organization. . . .Believe me, those of us from Columbus don't know much about Texas, so we're going to rely on Texans to run our Texas bank."[5] At the time of purchase, the Bridge Bank had its central headquarters in Dallas directing all major decisions. Banc One was considering changing the organization to a state holding-company–type structure along the lines of the rest of Banc One: separate banks, each with a president and the autonomy to make lending decisions, reporting to a Banc One, Texas, headquarters.

Banc One received approval for the purchase on June 29, 1989. McCoy described the days following:

> We were told the Friday before the 4th of July we could go ahead. We sent 80 people selected by the Marketing department [down to Texas] on the 4th. On the 5th and 6th of July there were Banc One people in every office. We held training sessions with videos, we gave [our new employees] videos to take home, we had dinners. We told them how we operate. We sent people from Wisconsin and Indiana who told them, "We didn't believe it two years ago either, but this is how we operate."

As McCoy thought about the future, he told a visitor,

> The reason we are in Texas is we think there are really good people [in those banks]. We are buying a $10 billion bank with very capable people. They will question us hard about why we do things the way we do. It will just mean lots and lots of trips for them to our other banks. Success will not happen by my telling them why, but by their going to Indianapolis or Akron and seeing how those banks got their results.

But would Banc One's traditional methods for upgrading people and improving performance work fast enough and effectively enough in the new environment, especially in light of other challenges to the "uncommon partnership?" Should McCoy be considering any new ways for Banc One to meet the challenges ahead?

[5] *The Wall Street Journal,* June 29, 1989, p. A6; June 30, 1989, p. A3.

EXHIBIT 1
SELECTED FINANCIAL DATA, 1978–1988

Income and Expenses
In Millions of Dollars

Year	Total Income	Net Interest Income	Non Interest Income	Non Interest Expense	Income before Securities Transactions	Net Income
1988	$2,734.5	$1,142.0	$452.3	$902.6	$332.9	$340.2
1987	2,384.8	1,092.6	346.8	838.6	227.7	231.5
1986	2,260.6	1,005.2	306.8	757.7	216.0	236.5
1985	2,096.8	869.6	274.1	648.7	198.5	204.5
1984	1,889.2	715.8	227.7	552.3	161.4	162.7
1983	1,457.4	545.8	182.6	454.3	129.2	128.2
1982	1,355.7	460.1	142.3	380.6	101.5	96.6
1981	1,133.3	365.2	107.5	305.8	75.1	73.8
1980	883.9	332.8	87.6	259.0	73.4	73.2
1979	735.0	319.4	70.5	233.3	70.2	69.7
1978	586.4	283.9	60.8	202.6	62.4	62.9
Annual Growth:						
1988/87	14.67%	4.52%	30.42%	7.63%	46.20%	46.95%
Compound Growth:						
5 Years	13.41	15.91	19.89	14.72	20.84	21.55
10 Years	16.65	14.93	22.22	16.11	18.23	18.39

Balance Sheet
In Millions of Dollars

	Yearly Average Balances			*Year-End Balances*		
Year	Total Assets	Common Equity	Earning Assets	Loans and Leases	Deposits	Primary Capital
1988	$23,484	$1,906	$21,054	$17,325	$19,502	$2,278
1987	21,854	1,650	19,479	15,629	18,176	2,028
1986	20,244	1,437	17,961	14,028	16,741	1,741
1985	17,662	1,223	15,485	12,399	15,480	1,537
1984	15,217	1,008	13,351	10,498	13,348	1,218
1983	12,689	830	11,122	8,346	11,510	1,017
1982	10,783	701	9,300	6,265	8,866	832
1981	8,887	572	7,566	5,371	7,463	683
1980	8,024	523	6,852	4,761	6,602	610
1979	7,410	477	6,354	4,635	6,242	549
1978	6,713	431	5,769	4,057	5,643	494
Annual Growth:						
1988/87	7.46%	15.52%	8.09%	10.85%	7.30%	12.33%
Compound Growth:						
5 Years	13.10	18.09	13.61	15.73	11.12	17.50
10 Years	13.34	16.03	13.82	15.62	13.20	16.52

EXHIBIT 1 (*continued*)

Consolidated Condensed Balance Sheet
In Thousands of Dollars

	December 31, 1988	December 31, 1987
Assets:		
Cash and equivalents	$ 2,191,511	$ 2,172,607
Securities (market value approximates $4,556,300 and $4,417,600 at December 31, 1988 and 1987)	4,624,612	4,453,264
Loans and leases		
Commercial, financial, and agricultural	6,992,281	6,337,308
Real estate, construction	765,504	729,408
Real estate, mortgage	2,802,756	2,434,652
Consumer, net	5,450,426	4,858,713
Tax exempt	635,796	726,050
Leases, net	678,024	542,850
Total loans and leases	17,324,787	15,628,981
Reserve for possible loan and lease losses	237,342	216,547
Net loans and leases	17,087,445	15,412,434
Other assets	1,370,086	1,114,978
Total assets	$25,273,654	$23,153,283
Liabilities:		
Deposits		
Non-interest bearing	$ 3,363,214	$ 3,487,548
Interest bearing	16,138,542	14,688,528
Total deposits	19,501,756	18,176,076
Short-term borrowings	2,745,559	2,335,800
Long-term borrowings	378,874	327,710
Other liabilities	606,634	511,064
Total liabilities	23,232,823	21,350,650
Preferred stock	25,454	26,353
Common stockholders' equity	2,015,377	1,776,280
Total liabilities, preferred stock, and common stockholders' equity	$25,273,654	$23,153,283

EXHIBIT 1 (*concluded*)

Consolidated Condensed Statement of Income
In Thousands of Dollars Except per Share Amounts

	1988	*1987*	*1986*
Interest Income:			
Interest and fees on loans and leases	$1,875,841	$1,651,697	$1,514,010
Interest and dividends on securities	367,831	344,225	332,644
Other interest income	27,806	38,691	73,762
Total interest income	2,271,478	2,034,613	1,920,416
Interest expense:			
Interest on deposits	1,013,102	873,128	920,497
Other borrowings	197,923	184,233	168,885
Total interest expense	1,211,025	1,057,361	1,089,382
Net interest income	1,060,453	977,252	831,034
Provision for loan and lease losses	183,422	206,974	146,746
Net interest income after provision for loan and lease losses	877,031	770,278	684,288
Other income	463,070	350,149	340,145
Other expenses	902,557	838,619	757,742
Income before income taxes	437,544	281,808	266,691
Income tax provision	97,356	50,312	30,160
Net income	$ 340,188	$ 231,496	$ 236,531
Per common share information (amounts reflect the 10% stock dividend effective February 19, 1988)			
Net income per common share	$ 2.61	$ 1.82	$ 1.92
Weighted average common shares outstanding (000)	129,410	125,123	119,307

Source: Banc One Corporation 1988 Annual Report.

EXHIBIT 2
EARNINGS PER SHARE AND STOCK PRICE, 1978–1988
Data per Common Share

	Net income					
Year	Pooled	As Originally Reported	Income before Securities Transactions	Cash Dividends	Book Value	Stock Price
1988	$2.61	$2.61	$2.57	$.92	$15.59	$22.25
1987	1.82	1.98	1.82	.82	13.91	21.82
1986	1.92	1.94	1.81	.75	12.88	20.80
1985	1.74	1.83	1.75	.63	11.58	21.28
1984	1.48	1.58	1.53	.54	10.12	14.12
1983	1.29	1.41	1.35	.47	9.45	12.90
1982	1.10	1.21	1.17	.40	8.84	12.86
1981	.99	1.10	1.02	.36	8.40	7.89
1980	1.01	.94	1.01	.33	8.06	6.58
1979	.96	.86	.97	.30	7.44	5.05
1978	.88	.75	.87	.25	6.73	4.83
Annual Growth:						
1988/87	43.41%	31.82%	41.21%	12.20%	12.08%	1.97%
Compound Growth:						
5 years	15.14	13.11	13.74	14.38	10.53	11.52
10 years	11.48	13.28	11.44	13.92	8.76	16.50

COMMON STOCK DATA
As Originally Reported

Year	*Average Shares Outstanding (000)*	*Common Shares Traded (000)*	*Common Shareholders*	*Stock Splits and Dividends*	*Total Market Capital (in millions)*	*Year-End Price/ Earnings*
1988	129,410	42,347	43,892	10%	$2,876	8.5x
1987	105,009	38,297	37,693		2,360	11.0
1986	100,238	21,457	36,855	10%	2,082	10.7
1985	68,254	8,270	24,748	3:2	1,491	11.6
1984	64,673	4,116	24,998	10%	929	8.9
1983	57,031	5,361	21,529	3:2	802	9.1
1982	47,785	2,919	12,974	3:2/10%	655	10.6
1981	34,988	1,466	10,564		301	7.2
1980	34,119	764	8,833	10%	222	7.0
1979	34,245	557	8,709		173	5.9
1978	34,245	535	8,535	10%	165	6.4

Source: Banc One Corporation 1988 Annual Report.

EXHIBIT 3
MANAGEMENT INFORMATION CONTROL SYSTEM (MICS)
"Major Highlights" Summary Data Sheet, February 1989

	FEB ACTUAL	B/(W) PR FCST	B/(W) BGT	FCST F-Y-F	B/(W) FR FCST	B/(W) BGT	PYR 4TH QTR	1ST QTR	2ND QTR	3RD QTR	4TH QTR
					EARNINGS ANALYSIS						
LOAN INT											
LOAN FEES											
INV INC											
INT EXP											
NIM											
PROVISION											
NET FUNDS FNCT											
SERVICE CHGS											
NON-INT INC											
NON-INT EXP											
PRETAX NET											
NET TAX											
NOE											
NET SEC											
NET INCOME											
INCOME											
LOAN YIELD %											
INV YIELD %											
E/A YIELD %											
OVERALL RATE											
NIM %											
FUNDS FNCT %											
ROA %											
ROE %											
LOAN QUALITY											
RES RATIO EOM %											
CHG-OFFS/LOANS %											
NPL/LOANS %											
BALANCE SHEET											
LOAN GROWTH %											
DEPOSIT GROWTH %											
LOAN/DEPOSIT %											
LG LIAB DEP %											
EQUITY/ASSETS %											
PRODUCTIVITY											
FTE/MM ASSETS											
DEP'S/OFFICE											
N-I EXP/ASSETS %											
N-I EXP/NOE %											
N-I EXP/REV %											

EXHIBIT 4
SONGS

Bank One Song
(Advertising Campaign Since 1985)

In our hometown we're proud to be
The finest bankers there.
And one by one we do our best
It's how we show we care.
So when you cross the heartland states
You'll find us standing strong.
With all of us behind each one
You'll hear us sing this song. . .

We are Eighteen Thousand People
Who Care
BANK ONE,
Yes, we're Eighteen Thousand People
Who Care about our customers.
Eighteen Thousand People Who Care
How well we serve.
We're a company,
A winning team
Of Eighteen Thousand People Who Care.

Leaving On a Jet Plane
(Banc One version, Spring 1989)

All my bags are packed, I'm ready to go.
I'm standing here on the 16th floor,
I hate to return again without a deal.
But the dawn is breakin', it's early morn,
The plane is waitin', I'm ready to board.
I'm Texas bound and so
It's a hell of a steal.

There's no solution to dilution.
MBank's pain is Banc One's gain . . .
Their customer will never be the same.
I'm leaving on a jet plane,
Don't know when I'll be back again.
Oh John, I love to go.

EXHIBIT 5
EXCERPTS FROM *THE WIRE*, JULY 1989

We Care Awards

BANK ONE, FREMONT employees **Wendi Jay, Ann King** and **Mary Ann Woessner** assisted in the capture and arrest of a suspected felon to earn their We Care Awards.

In April, a local business contacted the bank and reported two stolen payroll checks. Later that morning a customer asked Wendi to cash a payroll check at the drive-through window.

Wendi recognized the check as one that was stolen and contacted her supervisor, Ann. Ann had the bank's security officer call the police and made note of which direction the customer went after leaving the bank. Meanwhile, Mary Ann, a commercial note teller, got a complete description of the car and its license number and turned this information over to the authorities. The police officer on the scene contacted a police cruiser in the area, and the suspect was apprehended.

We Care Recipients

ANTIGO
Diane Molle, Executive Secretary
Ethel Wenek, Bookkeeper
Sue Zupon, Bookkeeper

CRAWFORDSVILLE
Vicki Lutes, Cashier
Sandy Porter, Loan Clerk

DAYTON
Dan Johnson, Auditor
Carol Chester, Retail Banking Administration Specialist

DOVER
Wanda Prysi, Bookkeeping Clerk
Cheryl Morgan, Assistant Branch Manager

FREMONT
Wendi Jay, Teller
Ann King, Teller Supervisor
Mary Ann Woessner, Commercial Note Teller

INDIANAPOLIS
Peggy Jennings, Cash Management Specialist

LAFAYETTE
Cheryl Myers, Customer Service Representative
Elizabeth Derringer, Merchant Representative

LIMA
Brent Gibson, Branch Manager
Donna Martello, Assistant Branch Manager

SIDNEY
Mary Putnam, Teller

STURGIS
Lou Ann James, Teller
Susan Osmun, Teller

YOUNGSTOWN
Alice Bovo, Mortgage Loan Closer
Obadiah Hall, Credit Processor
Kevin Lamar, Vault Supervisor

SERVICES CORPORATION
Audrey Martin, Authorizations Supervisor
David Kocak, Authorizations Supervisor
Doug Kirby, Proof Operator
William Tredick, Clerk

New Code of Ethics to Be Distributed

A new BANC ONE CORPORATION Code of Ethics soon will be distributed to all BANK ONE employees.

The brochure has been rewritten to answer questions that have been raised about BANK ONE policies and to better explain certain legal provisions in those policies. The new edition is also written in a more understandable language style.

Because of the importance of the message in the Code of Ethics, all employees will be required to sign a statement acknowledging that they have received the brochure. The statement will be kept in each employee's personnel file.

EXHIBIT 6
EXCERPTS FROM *BANC ONE CODE OF ETHICS*

I. *Introduction*

BANC ONE's success is directly related to customer and investor trust and confidence. We must recognize that our first duty to our customers and to our stockholders is to act in all matters in the manner that merits public trust and confidence. Basic to this obligation is the requirement that every director, officer, and employee conduct their business affairs in strict compliance with all applicable laws and regulations.

For this reason, this Code of Ethics is issued as standards for all directors, officers, and employees of BANC ONE. Just as the policies in this Code are not all-inclusive, these policies must be followed in conjunction with good judgment and basic principles of sound banking.

II. *Conflict of Interest*

The basic policy of BANC ONE is that no director, officer, or employee should have any position of interest (either financial or otherwise), make or receive any payment, or engage in any activity which conflicts, or might reasonably conflict, with the proper performance of his or her duties and responsibilities to BANC ONE. . . . Each director, officer, and employee must manage his or her personal and business affairs so as to avoid situations that might lead to conflict, or even the appearance of a conflict. . . .

III. *Personal Conduct and Financial Affairs*

A. Personal Conduct. Directors, officers, and employees of BANC ONE are expected to conduct their personal and financial affairs on a sound moral, ethical, and legal basis. They are expected to conduct their personal as well as their financial affairs in a manner which (1) is consistent with, and does not violate, basic moral or ethical standards within the community and (2) recognizes and respects the personal property rights of others. They are also expected to comply with applicable personnel policies of their BANC ONE employer, including those set forth in company personnel manuals, relating to the use, possession, or sale of alcoholic beverages or illegal drugs, to personal appearance, to conduct in the performance of their employment, and to dealing with personnel, customers, and suppliers.

(1) Financial Affairs. Directors, officers, and employees shall maintain their personal financial affairs in a manner which is prudent. Officers are required to complete and to submit at least annually to their CEO a questionnaire relative to their compliance with various provisions of the Code of Ethics and legal requirements applicable to them as BANC ONE officers. . . .

EXHIBIT 7
BANC ONE STATE HOLDING-COMPANY STRUCTURE, JUNE 1989

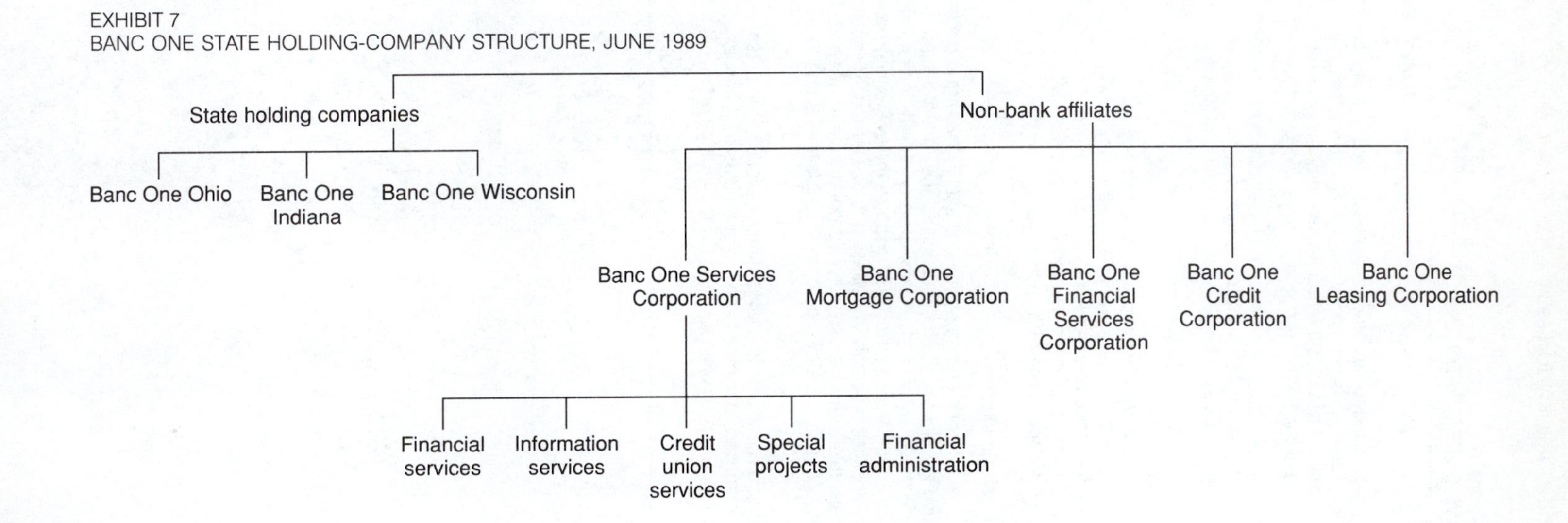

EXHIBIT 7 (*concluded*)
BANC ONE CORPORATE ORGANIZATION, JUNE 1989
Pre-Texas

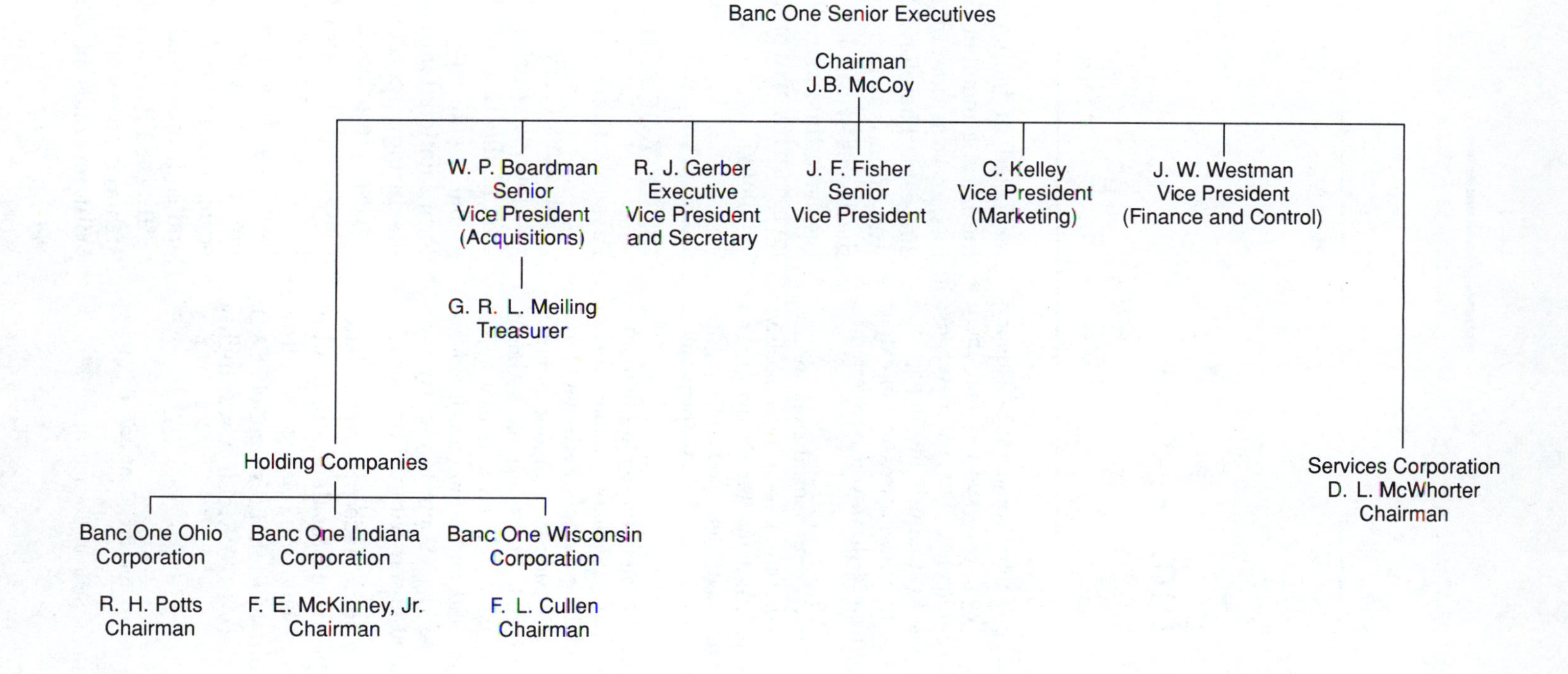

PC&D, Inc.

> When we promoted you to the presidency five years ago, we expected that there would be changes, but we never expected you to diminish the importance of the old line businesses to the extent that you have. I think you have erred in doing so. . . .
>
> The new entrepreneurial subs are certainly dynamic and have brought positive press to the company. But, by investing all new resources in them, you are jeopardizing the health of the company as a whole. . . .
>
> My division's reputation has been built over the past 50 years on the superior quality of its products and sales force. But, as the leadership of our products begins to erode, my salesmen are beginning to leave. Without resources, I cannot stop this trend, and, as much as it saddens me to say so, I am losing my own motivation to stay with the company.

These were some excerpts from a letter that the senior vice president and head of the Machinery Division, George McElroy, 58, sent to John Martell, president of PC&D, Inc., in February 1976. McElroy was highly respected in both the company and the industry, a member of the board of directors, and a senior officer of the company for 20 years. Therefore, Martell knew that it was important to respond and to resolve the issues with McElroy successfully. At the same time Martell had no intention of giving up his own prerogatives to direct the company.

HISTORY OF PC&D, INC.

Payson & Clark Co.

Payson & Clark, the forerunner of PC&D, was founded during the merger movement around the turn of the century. Four regional machinery companies merged to form a national industrial machinery manufacturing corporation named after the two largest enterprises in the merger, Payson & Clark. With the growth of industry across the country at the time, the demand for heavy machinery also grew rapidly. The new company benefited from economies of scale, both in production and distribution, and so it prospered.

By 1965 Payson & Clark Co. was an old, stable company still producing machinery. With revenues of $300 million and net

Harvard Business School case 380–072.

aftertax profits of $6 million, it was still the largest firm in the industry (see Exhibits 1 and 2 for additional financial information). The company offered the most complete line of heavy industrial equipment in the industry, with its different configurations of standard and custom models filling a large, encyclopedic sales manual. The consistently high quality and unusual breadth of the product line had made attracting high-caliber salespeople relatively easy. These people were highly knowledgeable in the applications of the product line and saw themselves as consultants to their industrial customers.

Although Payson & Clark was the leader in quality and breadth of its product line, it was not the leader in innovations. Rather, it left expensive R&D to others, copying products after they were widely accepted. It could afford to follow others primarily because the industry itself was slow moving. In 1965 the business was essentially the same as when the company was founded. Its growth depended on the general growth of U.S. industry, efficiencies in purchasing raw materials, and the scale and automation of production. Indeed, the company's major innovation came in the early 1950s with the introduction of plastics in some of its models.

In 1965 the company was still structured as it had been in the 1920s, with a standard functional organization and highly centralized chain of command. Its top executives were old-time managers, the average age being 55. Many had spent their entire careers with the firm and could remember the days when old Mr. Payson had kept tight reins on the company in the 1930s and 1940s. Harold C. Payson IV, aged 53 in 1965, was president of the company from the late 1940s and the president and chairman since 1955. Although the company was publicly held, the Payson family still owned a considerable amount of its stock.

In the early 1960s Mr. Payson began to consider succession. He wanted to leave the company in good condition not only for his own personal pride but for the betterment of his heirs. From discussions with his investment bankers and friends in the business world, Mr. Payson had recognized that an association with a high-technology, high-growth industry would strengthen Payson & Clark's image. One way in which Mr. Payson sought to implement this suggestion was to use some of the excess capital thrown off by the machinery business to enter into joint ventures with young, new companies developing high-technology, innovative products. Several such investments were made in the early 1960s, including one with the Datronics Company in 1962.

Datronics Company

In 1965 the Datronics Company was 10 years old with revenues of $50 million (see Exhibits 3 and 4 for additional financial information). The company had started as an engineering firm subsisting on government research grants and contracts. As a by-product of the government projects, the company also developed several types of sophisticated electronic equipment with wide industrial applications. The company concentrated its efforts on R&D, however, subcontracted production, and bought marketing services for its commercial products. The lack of control over marketing and production and the lost profits passed to the marketers and subcontractors displeased the company's young president, John Martell. In his opinion, the company's growth was limited until the right product emerged to justify becoming a full manufacturing and marketing company.

Following Payson & Clark's investment in 1962, Datronic's engineers developed an existing new product toward the end of 1964 that promised to sell extremely well due to its increased capacity and lower cost. Martell saw the promise of the new product as the waited-for opportunity to expand the company. It was clear, however, that a major influx of capital was needed to bring the product to the market, build a sales force, and begin volume production. Therefore, Martell began a search for external capital that included a presentation to the joint venture partner, Payson & Clark, which already owned 20 percent of Datronic's stock.

Meanwhile, Mr. Payson had been following the activities of Datronics closely and was quite aware of the growth potential of the company before Martell's visit. Further, Mr. Payson recognized that Datronics, once its manufacturing operations started, would have a continual need for new capital. If Payson & Clark invested once, it would not be long until another request for resources came from Datronics. With these factors in mind, Mr. Payson decided that the most beneficial arrangement for both parties would be for his company to acquire Datronics. Martell agreed to this offer and negotiations for a friendly takeover were consummated. Payson & Clark acquired Datronics for $42 million in November 1965, with Martell himself receiving $8.4 million in cash, notes, and securities. The acquisition provided an opportunity for Payson & Clark to update its image. Patterning itself after other successful growth companies of the time, it changed its name to PC&D, Inc., to denote the beginning of a new era in the company.

PC&D, 1965–1970

After the acquisition, Mr. Payson restructured the company with the help of consultants, setting up a divisional organization. The old Payson & Clark Co. now became the Machinery Division headed by George McElroy, formerly vice president of manufacturing. The Datronics Co. became the Electronics Division headed by Martell.

Electronics Division

At the time of the acquisition the Datronics Co. consisted of several scientific labs, some test equipment, 10 professional engineers, an administrative staff, and Martell. An electrical engineer by training, Martell was a man in his mid-30s. He was energetic and a risk taker by nature, and even as a child in Iowa could not imagine working for someone else all his life. After college at M.I.T., he worked for 8 years at a large scientific equipment company in the Boston area. Initially, he was hired for the research group, but he was more attracted to the company's management positions. He transferred first to the corporate planning office and then became a division plant manager. With his technical competence and management experience, it was not surprising that he was approached by several of the more innovative of the company's research engineers to invest in and head up a new, independent R&D company. Martell bought in for 25 percent of the founding stock and thus began the Datronics Company.

During his term as president of Datronics, Martell was highly regarded by the small group of employees. Although he had a respectable command of the technology, he left the research to the engineers, devoting his time to developing sources of challenging and lucrative contracts.

After the acquisition by the Payson & Clark Co., Martell retained full control of the operations of his old organization, which became the Electronics Division. He hired an experienced industrial marketer from a large technical firm to set up the marketing operations and a friend from his old employer to head up the production operations. As expected, the demand for the division's new product was very high. Five years later in 1970, the division was a successful growing enterprise, having expanded into other electronics fields. It had 700 employees; marketing offices established or opening throughout the United States, Europe, and Japan; plants at three different sites; and revenues of over $160 million. The business press reported these activities very favorably, giving much credit to Martell's leadership.

Machinery Division

Meanwhile, the Machinery Division continued to be the stalwart of the industry it had always been, retaining its structure and activities of the earlier time. George McElroy, division manager and senior vice president, was considered the division's mainstay. He had joined the company in the early 1950s and was primarily responsible for the plastics innovations of that time. Advisor and confidant of Mr. Payson, McElroy was thought by his subordinates to be next in line for the presidency.

Mr. Payson limited his involvement in the company's internal affairs to reviewing budgets and year-end results, while spending most of his time with community activities and lobbying in Washington. He felt justified in this hands-off policy because of the quality of both his division vice presidents, McElroy and Martell. PC&D's performance further supported Mr. Payson's approach. Revenues climbed to $530 million, and profits after tax to $14 million by 1970. The solid 26 multiple of its stock price reflected the confidence in PC&D's prospects (see Exhibits 5 and 6).

The compensation schemes reflected the extent to which Mr. Payson allowed the division managers to be autonomous. McElroy's compensation was 90 percent salary, with a 10 percent bonus based on ROI. Martell received two thirds of his pay as a bonus based on growth in revenues. Compensation policies within each division were entirely at the discretion of either Martell or McElroy. In general, Martell made much greater use of incentive compensation than McElroy.

Change at PC&D, 1970

Toward the end of 1970 Mr. Payson decided that it was time to limit his involvement to that of chairman of the board and to name a new president of PC&D. He supported the appointment of McElroy as the next president. McElroy was the next senior officer in the company and, after years of working with Mr. Payson, held many of the same views on the traditional values of PC&D. Mr. Payson agreed with the school of thought, however, that chief executives should not choose their own successors. He, therefore, established a search committee, consisting of three outside members of the board of directors (see box for a list of board members), and a thorough job was done. The committee interviewed several candidates within PC&D, including Martell and McElroy, and outside candidates were also considered. The committee utilized executive search firms and consultants to identify candidates and carefully compared external and internal prospects. The result was the nomination of Martell. Although his relative youth was a surprise to some, the search committee's report explained the thinking behind the choice: "During the past five years PC&D has experienced an exciting and profitable period of growth and diversification. But it is essential that the company not become complacent. One of our major criteria in choosing a new president was to find a person with the energy and vision to continue PC&D's growth and expansion." The Board unanimously approved the selection of Martell as president and CEO.

Board of Directors, 1970

Harold Payson IV, president, PC&D
George McElroy, senior vice president, Machinery Division, PC&D
John Martell, vice president, Electronics Division, PC&D
Carl Northrup, treasurer, PC&D
David S. Curtis, partner, Barth & Gimbel, Wall Street brokerage firm
Elizabeth B. Payne, partner, Payne, Bartley & Springer, Washington law firm
Charles F. Sprague, president, Forrest Products, Inc., a large manufacturing firm
Gardner L. Stacy III, dean, business school, State University
James Hoffman, vice president, Baltimore Analysts Association, an international firm

Martell began his new position with the board's mandate in mind. He planned to continue the diversification of PC&D into high-growth industries. He expected to follow both an acquisition mode and a start-up mode, using the excess funds from the Machinery Division and PC&D's rising stock to finance the growth. For start-ups, Martell planned to use joint ventures supporting newer companies, much as the old Payson & Clark Co. had supported his venture in its early days.

Martell brought to his position a very definite management style. He was a strong believer in the benefits derving from an opportunistic, entrepreneurial spirit, and he wanted to inject PC&D with this kind of energy. He was concerned, however, that the people with this kind of spirit would not be attracted to work with PC&D because of the stigma, real or imagined, of working for a large company. Martell commented:

> It was my experience that there are two worlds of people, some of whom are very secure and comfortable and satisfied in their career pursuits in large institutionalized companies, and others of whom are, I think, wild ducks, and who are interested in perhaps greater challenges that small companies present in terms of the necessity to succeed or die.
>
> In many work environments, the constraints placed upon the individual by the nature of the institution are such as to sometimes make people uncomfortable.
>
> The decision-making process is long and involved, sometimes not known, in the sense that the people who act upon decisions are not in close proximity to those who benefit or suffer from the effects of those decisions.
>
> The formalization of the decision-making process is frequently an irritant, and for people who are unusually energetic and demanding, in the sense of desiring, themselves, to take action and to have their actions complemented by the actions of other people upon whom they are dependent, I would characterize these people as perhaps being wild ducks rather than tame ducks. In that sense, I wanted more wild ducks in our company.

Martell himself credited the success of the Electronics Division to Mr. Payson's willingness to turn the reins completely over to him. The secret, Martell thought, was in spotting the right person with both ability and integrity. Corporate headquarters' role should be to provide resources in terms of both money and expertise as needed, to set timetables, to provide measurement points and incentive, and then to keep its hands off.

Although the board's directives were clear to Martell, the specifics for implementation were not. Not only were the larger questions of which way to diversify or how to encourage innovation unanswered, but questions of how to plan and whom to involve were also left unclear. Martell was not given the luxury of time to resolve these issues. Within the first week in his new position, three professionals from the Electronics Division called on Martell. Bert Rogers and Elaine Patterson were the key engineers from the research department and Thomas Grennan was head of marketing, western region. They had been working on some ideas for a new product (not competing with any of PC&D's existing lines), and they were ready to leave the company to start their own business to develop and market it. Indeed, they had already had a prospectus prepared for their new venture with the hope that either Martell, personally, or PC&D might be able to provide some venture capital. The president particularly liked these three and admired their willingness to take such personal risks with a product as yet unresearched as to market or design. With his energy and can-do aggressive style, Grennan reminded Martell of himself just a few years ago when he left to start the Datronics Company.

Martell liked the product and saw the idea as a possible route for continuing PC&D's diversification and growth, but there was a problem. It was clear from the presentation of the three, that much of their motivation came from the desire to start their own company and, through their equity interest, reap the high rewards of their efforts if successful. Martell did not fault this motivation, for it had been his route as well. He could not expect PC&D's managers to take large personal risks if there was no potential for a large payoff. Further, a fair offer to the group, if in salary, required more than PC&D could afford or could justify to the older divisions. Martell told Rogers, Patterson, and Grennan that he was very interested and asked if he could review the prospectus overnight and get back to them the next day. That night he devised a plan with a major feature called the Entrepreneurial Subsidiary. Martell presented this proposal to Grennan, Rogers, and Patterson the next day. They readily accepted it, and thus a pattern began for most of PC&D's diversification over the next five years.

THE ENTREPRENEURIAL SUBSIDIARY

Martell's plan, of which he was particularly proud, worked as follows. When a proposal for a new product area was made to the PC&D corporate office, a new subsidiary would be incorporated—the entrepreneurial subsidiary. The initiators of the idea would leave their old division or company and become officers and employees of the new subsidiary. In the above example, the new subsidiary would be the Pro Instrument Corporation with Grennan as president and Rogers and Patterson as vice presidents.

The new subsidiary would issue stock in its name, $1 par value, 80 percent of which would be bought by PC&D and 20 percent by the entrepreneurs involved—engineers and other key officers. This initial capitalization, plus sizable direct loans from PC&D, provided the funds for the research and development of the new product up to its commercialization. In the case of Pro Instruments, Patterson and Rogers hired 10 other researchers, while Grennan hired a market researcher and a finance-accounting person. These 15 people invested $50,000 together and PC&D invested another $200,000.

Two kinds of agreements were signed between the two parties. The first was a research contract between the parent company and the subsidiary, setting time schedules for the research, defining requirements for a commercializable product, outlining budgets, and otherwise stipulating obligations on both sides. In general, the subsidiary was responsible for the R&D and production and testing of a set number of prototypes of a new product, while the parent company would market and produce the product on an international scale. Pro Instruments' agreement stipulated two phases, one lasting 18 months to produce a prototype, and another lasting 6 months to test the product in the field and produce a marketing plan. Detailed budget and personnel needs were outlined, providing for a $900,000 working capital loan from PC&D during the first phase and $425,000 during the second.

Although PC&D had proprietary rights on the product and all revenues received from marketing it, the agreement often included an incentive kicker for the key engineers in the form of additional stock to be issued if the finished product produced certain specified amounts of revenue by given dates. This was the case for Pro Instruments: 5,000 shares in year 1, to be issued if net profits were over $250,000; 20,000 shares in year 2 if profits were over $1 million; and 10,000 in year 3 if profits were over $3 million.

The second agreement specified the financial obligations and terms for merger. Once the terms of the research contract were met, PC&D, with board approval, had the option for a stated period of time (usually four years) to merge the subsidiary through a one-for-one exchange of PC&D stock for the stock of the subsidiary, which would then be dissolved. To protect the interests of entrepreneurs, PC&D was required to vote on merger of the subsidiary within 60 days if it met certain criteria. For Pro Instruments, the criteria were (1) the product earned cumulative profits of $500,000 and (2) if the earnings of PC&D and the subsidiary were consolidated, dilution of PC&D's EPS would not have occurred over three consecutive quarters. If PC&D did not choose to merge during the 60 days, then the subsidiary had a right to buy out PC&D's interest.

Since PC&D's stock was selling for $103 in 1970 and subsidiary stock was bought for $1/share, the exchange of stock represented a tremendous potential return. Depending on the value of PC&D's stock at the time of merger, the net worth of the entrepreneurs who originally invested in the subsidiary multiplied overnight. Indeed, as subsidiaries were merged in ensuing years, typical gains ranged from 100 to 200 times the original investments in the entrepreneurial subsidiary. For example, PC&D exercised its option to merge Pro Instruments when its product was brought to market in 1972. Grennan, who had bought 6,000 shares of Pro Instruments stock, found his 6,000 shares of PC&D valued at $936,000 (PC&D common selling for $156 on the New York Stock Exchange at the time). By the end of 1974, Pro Instruments' new product had earned $50 million in revenue and $4.8 million in profits, thus qualifying the original entrepreneurs for stock bonuses. Grennan received another 4,200 shares valued at $684,600. Thus, in four years, he had earned about $1.6 million on a $6,000 investment.

By setting up entrepreneurial subsidiaries like Pro Instruments, Martell had several expectations. In the process of setting up a subsidiary with the dynamics of a small, independent group, Martell hoped to create the loyalty, cohesion, and informal structure conducive to successful R&D efforts. The subsidiary would have a separate location and its own officers who decided structure and operating policies. Further, it provided the opportunity to buy into and reap the benefits of ownership in the equity of a company. Martell spoke:

> I think the concept of the entrepreneurial subsidiaries was the outgrowth of the insight that in many industrial corporations the system of rewards is perhaps inverted from what many people think it should be; that the hierarchy of the institution commends itself to those people who are capable of managing other people's efforts, and those people at lower echelons who are unusually creative and who, as a result of their creativity and innovation and daring in the technical sense or perhaps in a marketing sense, are unusually responsible for the accomplishments of the business, are very frequently forgotten about in the larger rewards of the enterprise.
>
> I, on the other hand, recognized that such persons are frequently, perhaps by training, inclination or otherwise, not capable of marshalling the financial resources or organizing the manufacturing and marketing efforts required to exploit their creativity. Without the kind of assistance that PC&D was capable of lending to them—an assured marketing capability was often a key concern—they are wary of undertaking new ventures.

Further, it was Martell's opinion that the organizational and incentive structure of the entrepreneurial subsidiary would attract the best engineers from older, more secure firms to PC&D—the so-called wild ducks.

More important, Martell hoped to encourage the timely development of new products with minimal initial investment by PC&D. If Pro Instruments, for example, did not meet its timetable with the original money invested, its officers would have to approach PC&D for new money just as if they were an outside company. PC&D would then have multiple opportunities to review and consider the investment. If the entrepreneurial subsidiary failed or could not get more money from the parent, PC&D was under no obligation to keep the company alive or to rehire its employees. If loans were involved, PC&D could act as any other creditor. Martell observed: "The benefit of PC&D shareholders was in the rapid expansion of PC&D's products, the size of the company, the ability of the company to compete in the marketplace in a way which PC&D, dependent upon only internal development projects, could never have achieved, or could have achieved only at much greater costs and over a longer period of years."

Martell believed that the stock incentives would properly reward the genius of creative engineers for the service performed, however, without having to pay high salaries over a long potentially unproductive period after the initial product was developed. Employees did not have to be rehired, nor were they obligated to continue employment, even if the subsidiary was merged. Those who were rehired would be paid at the normal salary levels of comparable people at PC&D. Martell's reasoning here centered on the following points:

> There were two criteria for establishing an entrepreneurial subsidiary. The first criterion was that the R&D objectives of the subsidiary could not be reached except under the aegis of the subsidiary, because it involved people who were not involved in PC&D's main lines of business.

> The other criterion was that considerable career risk must exist for the people who would leave their established positions within the management structure of PC&D to undertake the entrepreneurial venture of the new subsidiary. Also, the people, in some part, had to be new talent who came from outside PC&D. When I refer to career risk, I mean for example that if a director of engineering at PC&D left his or her post to join an entrepreneurial subsidiary, a new director of engineering would be appointed, and given the lack of success of the entrepreneurial subsidiary, there would in effect be no position of director of engineering to which the person could return. Moreover, it is probable that we would not want the individual to return.

The stock incentive also motivated the engineers to produce without having to commit any resources of the parent company for the future, since the corporation was not required to merge the subsidiary or to produce and market the new product. The incentive kicker, moreover, would insure quality. A product that was rushed through development would be more likely to have problems and not reach revenue goals.

Another advantage of the entrepreneurial subsidiary was its effect on decision making. Without the need to go through the entire corporate hierarchy, decisions would be made closer to the operating level. This would enhance the quality of decisions because managers performed best, according to Martell, when given objectives and resources from top managers but were left with operating decisions unfettered.

Finally, Martell expected that the entrepreneurial subsidiary would be the training and proving ground of PC&D's future top managers. By providing the means for these executives to gain great personal wealth, Martell expected to gain their loyalty and continued efforts for both himself and PC&D.

PC&D, 1970–1975

During the first five years of Martell's presidency, PC&D's growth was quite impressive. With revenues topping the billion dollar mark in 1975, growth had averaged about 15 percent in revenues and 35 percent in profits after tax during the five years (see Exhibits 7 and 8 for financials). Such growth had been achieved, to a large extent, from new products developed in entrepreneurial subsidiaries. In 1975 sales of $179.2 million and profit before taxes and interest of $22.1 million came from these new products.[1] All together, 11 entrepreneurial subsidiaries had been organized during the 1970–1975 time frame. Of these, 4 had successfully developed products and had been merged into PC&D—1 in 1972, 1 in 1973, and 2 in 1974. The other 7 were younger and their work was still in process; to date, none had failed.

Most subsidiaries grew out of needs of the Electronics Division or Pro Instruments. Competitors in the electronics equipment industry were beginning to integrate backward, thus lowering costs by producing their own semiconductors. The need to remain cost competitive caused PC&D to establish entrepreneurial subsidiaries to develop specialized components, including semiconductors, assuming that these could be both used by PC&D and sold in outside markets. In the process of selling semiconductors to outside customers,

[1] Of PC&D's total assets in 1975, approximately 40 percent was devoted to the Machinery Division, 35 percent to the traditional Electronics Division, and 25 percent to the entrepreneurial subsidiaries.

ideas for new products using PC&D components were stimulated, and new subsidiaries were formed to develop these equipment products. The cost of merging the two types of subsidiaries—components or equipment—however, differed. Equipment subsidiaries were cheaper because they could share the already existent sales force of the Electronics Division; many parts could be standard ones already utilized in other products; and the processes were similar to other Electronics products. But with semiconductors, new plant, new sales channels, new manufacturing processes, and new skills at all levels had to be built. Although Martell thought the move into semiconductors promised a large cash flow in the future in a booming industry, some in the company were concerned that the cash drain was not the best use of scarce cash resources.

When Martell first became president, he made few changes in PC&D's organization structure. McElroy continued as vice president of the Machinery Division and retained control over that division's structure and policies. Martell himself retained his responsibilities as manager of the Electronics Division. This he did reluctantly and with all intentions of finding a new executive for the job; however, the unexpected nature of his promotion left Martell without a ready candidate.

As the subsidiaries were merged, beginning with Pro Instruments in 1972, questions of organization began to rise. In typical fashion, Martell wanted to pass involvement in these decisions down to the appropriate managers. There was also no question that Pro Instruments' president, Grennan, had proven himself with the new subsidiary. Therefore, in 1972 Martell appointed Grennan to division vice president, Electronics, based on Grennan's superlative performance. Further, because the products were complementary, all of the subsidiaries merged during this period were placed in the Electronics Division. Moreover, in recognition of the increased number of products, Grennan reorganized the Electronics Division. He appointed his Pro Instruments colleague, Bert Rogers, to be director of research, which was organized by product area. Manufacturing, also organized by product, reflected the development by subsidiary as well. Marketing, on the other hand, was organized by region as it had been previously. Until they were merged, however, subsidiary presidents reported directly to Martell for resolution of problems that arose (see Exhibit 9 for a 1975 organization chart).

By 1975 the Electronics Division's enlarged marketing and production departments employed 4,000 people with production plants in three different locations. Electronics then had sales of $561.4 million as compared to Machinery's $440.6 million.

Although successful development projects from subsidiaries had been largely responsible for the sales growth at PC&D, this result had not come without costs. First, the subsidiaries required funds—$60 million by the end of 1975. Some of these funds came from retained earnings, but much was new money raised in the form of long-term debt. Further, stock issued to capitalize subsidiaries and pay bonuses to entrepreneurs had a diluting effect on PC&D's shares. If all subsidiaries were merged and successful, the number of new shares could be significant. Although raising such a sizable amount of new funds was not particularly difficult for a company as large as PC&D, the needs arising from the subsidiaries left little new money for the core businesses of PC&D. The Machinery Division, for example, had not had their development budget increased at all during the 5 years ending 1975.

Further Concerns

Despite PC&D's successes, Martell was not without worries—several problems had appeared in both the Electronics and Machinery Divisions. In Electronics, personnel and products originating in subsidiaries now equalled or surpassed those from the original division. It had been part of the strategy of the entrepreneurial subsidiaries to use them as devices to attract talent from other firms. A key researcher hired from outside was encouraged to hire, in turn, the best of his or her former colleagues. Thus, the loyalty and friendships between key entrepreneurs and their staffs were often strong and long-standing. As the entrepreneurial subsidiaries were merged, their personnel tended to retain this loyalty to the president or key officers of the old subsidiary rather than transferring it to PC&D. Thus, several warring spheres of influence were developing in the division, particularly in the research department and between research and other departments. Martell was concerned that such influences and warring would lead to poor decisions and much wasted energy in this division.

Turnover in Electronics was also increasing. This was of particular concern to Martell for it was those talented engineers that the entrepreneurial subsidiaries were meant to attract who were beginning to leave. For example, Elaine Patterson, formerly of Pro Instruments, left during 1975 to start her own company, taking 20 research engineers with her. The source of the turnover was unclear but possible factors included distaste for the kind of warring atmosphere mentioned above and the inability to be a part of a large corporate R&D department with its demand for budgets and reports.

For many employees, however, the sudden absence of monetary incentives changed the climate drastically. This lack of incentive, coupled with the discovery that the most challenging projects were taken on by newly formed subsidiaries, which favored hiring outside expertise, caused dissatisfaction. For Martell, such turnover was of greatest concern in the long run, for the inability to create a strong central R&D department in Electronics created a continuing need for more entrepreneurial subsidiaries. These subsidiaries were still too new an idea for Martell to want to risk his entire future R&D program on their successes. Further, most of the new products were in highly competitive areas. Without continuing upgrades these products would soon become obsolete. A strong central R&D department was needed for follow-up development of products started by subsidiaries.

Finally, Martell was concerned by indications of serious operating problems in the Electronics Division. This was particularly disturbing since Martell had placed complete faith in Grennan's managerial ability. The most recent cost report, for example, indicated that the division's marketing, G&A, and engineering expenses were way out of line. Further, the marketing and production departments reported problems in several products originating in the subsidiaries. One product, with expected obsolescence of four years, now showed a six-year break-even just to cover the engineering and production costs. Another product, completing its first year on the market, had been forecasted by the subsidiary to achieve $20 million in sales in its first two years. During the first six months, however, losses had been incurred because of customer returns. A report on the causes of the returns showed a predominance of product failures. The chances for break-even on this product looked bleak. While none of these problems had affected operating results to date, Martell was especially concerned that these operating problems would have a negative impact on 1976 first-quarter earnings.

Martell had not confronted Grennan with these operating problems. He wanted to see how the division itself was attacking these issues through its long-range plan. Martell had requested Grennan to prepare a long-range plan (five years) as well as the usual one-year operating plan. The product of this effort had just arrived (February 1976) and Martell had not had a chance to study it. Its 100-page bulk loomed on Martell's desk. Quick perusal had indicated four pages of prose scattered through the plan, and dozens of charts, graphs, and tables of numbers, every one of which manifested an upward trend. (The report's table of contents is reproduced as Table 1.)

In an attempt to get employee feedback on all of these problems, Martell contracted an outside consulting firm to carry out confidential interviews with personnel in the Electronics Division. The interviews found middle managers quite concerned over the confusion in the division, which was causing a loss of morale there. The consultant's report cited concrete problems, including lost equipment, missed billings, and confusion in the plant. Typical comments from lower-level personnel included the following:

> Either upper management is not being informed of problems or they don't know how to solve them.
>
> Morale is very poor, job security is nil.
>
> There is little emphasis on production efficiencies.

TABLE 1
TABLE OF CONTENTS FOR ELECTRONICS DIVISION, 1976 OPERATING PLAN AND 1977–1980 LONG-RANGE OUTLOOK

SECTION	PAGE NO.
I. EXECUTIVE SUMMARY	1
Division Strategy	2
Organization	4
II. MARKETING	5
Marketing Objectives	6
Organization	7
Product Assumptions/ Descriptions	8
Consolidated Product Forecast	23
Resources:	
1) Manpower	28
2) Expense	29
New Product Content and Sales Plan	30
III. ENGINEERING	31
Engineering Objectives	32
Organizations	33
Company Product Plans:	
1) Pro I	34
2) Entrepreneurial Subsidiary #2	39
3) Entrepreneurial Subsidiary #3	43
4) Entrepreneurial Subsidiary #4	48
5) General Electronics	50
Resources:	
1) Manpower	53
2) Expense	54
3) Capital	55
IV. MANUFACTURING	56
Manufacturing Objectives	57
Organization	58
1976 Operating Plan	61
1977–1980 Long-Range Outlook	66
Facilities Plan	71
V. ENGINEERING SUPPORT	77
Support Objectives	78
Organization	79
Resources	80
VI. FUTURE ENTREPRENEURIAL SUBSIDIARIES ORIGINATING IN ELECTRONICS DIVISION	81
Strategy	82
Objectives	84
Program Resource Summary	85
Manufacturing Shipments	86

TABLE 1 *(concluded)*

Scrap is unaccounted for.

Market forecasts are grossly inaccurate.

Production schedules have a definite saw-tooth pattern. There is very little good planning.

There are no systematic controls.

These were not the sort of comments Martell expected from the division responsible for the major portion of PC&D's future growth. His concern was not so much the problems themselves, but what was being done about them. His preferred policy was to stay out of day-to-day operating problems. He wondered how long it was prudent to allow such problems to continue without some intervention on his part.

Meanwhile, the Machinery Division had its own problems. The last major construction of new plant had been in the early 1950s. Since that time, McElroy had upgraded production methods, which succeeded in checking rising costs. Since 1965, however, resources for such improvements had not been increased, and with inflation in the 1970s less and less could be done on a marginal basis. McElroy believed that capacity was sufficient for the short term, but that it was impossible to remain state of the art.[2] Indeed, the Machinery Division's products were beginning to fall behind the new developments of competitors, and the costs of Machinery's products were beginning to inch up. As the production line aged, quality control reported an increasing percentage of defective goods. In contrast to the situation in Machinery, the rather extensive investment in new plant for the production of semiconductors did not sit too well with McElroy, who was concerned with the lack of flexibility that could result from backward integrating. He thought component needs should be farmed out to the cheapest bidder from the numerous small component firms. Martell was concerned with how long he could keep McElroy satisfied without a major investment in Machinery and how long he could count on the cash flow from Machinery for other users.

Turnover, a problem never before experienced in the Machinery Division, had also appeared. Here, however, it was the salespeople who were leaving. Martell worried about this trend, for the sales force was the division's strength. According to the head of marketing, the salespeople considered themselves the best in the industry, and they did not wish to sell products that were not the best. They saw Machinery's products as no longer the best in quality nor state of the art. Further, they did not

[2] McElroy suspected that the Machinery Division would require an investment of $100–$125 million over two or three years to revitalize the product line and plant and equipment. McElroy believed that in the long term the return on this investment would match the division's historic ROI.

wish to work for a company where they felt unimportant. Whether true or not, the sales force appeared less aggressive than it had in previous times.

Martell was not overly surprised, therefore, when he received McElroy's letter, nor was he certain that some of McElroy's anger concerning the Electronics Division was not justified. Martell knew he had to do something about McElroy, as well as Grennan and the Electronics Division. He also had to decide whether entrepreneurial subsidiaries should continue to be part of PC&D's research and development strategy. Finally, all of Martell's decisions concerning the divisions and subsidiaries needed to be consistent with a strategy that would continue PC&D's growth.

EXHIBIT 1

PAYSON & CLARK CO. INCOME STATEMENTS, 1956–1965
In Millions of Dollars Except per Share Data

	1956	*1957*	*1958*	*1959*	*1960*	*1961*	*1962*	*1963*	*1964*	*1965*
Sales	$177.6	$190.7	$205.0	$220.5	$237.2	$247.9	$259.1	$273.3	$288.1	$302.7
Cost of goods sold	136.1	145.8	157.6	171.0	184.4	192.4	202.1	218.7	230.8	243.6
Gross profit	41.5	44.9	47.4	49.5	52.8	55.5	57.0	54.6	57.3	59.1
Expenses										
Depreciation	5.0	5.0	5.0	4.0	4.0	4.0	4.0	4.0	3.5	3.5
Marketing and G&A	18.2	19.7	20.5	22.2	25.6	27.5	28.4	28.0	30.0	33.3
Engineering and product development	8.1	8.6	9.9	10.1	10.6	11.0	11.4	8.8	9.2	7.1
Total expenses	31.3	33.3	35.4	36.3	40.2	42.5	43.8	40.8	42.7	43.9
Profit before interest and taxes	10.2	11.6	12.0	13.2	12.6	13.0	13.2	13.8	14.6	15.2
Interest	3.0	4.0	4.0	4.0	3.0	3.0	3.0	3.0	3.0	3.0
Profit before taxes	7.2	7.6	8.0	9.2	9.6	10.0	10.2	10.8	11.6	12.2
Taxes	3.6	3.8	4.0	4.6	4.8	5.0	5.1	5.4	5.8	6.1
Profit after taxes	$ 3.6	$ 3.8	$ 4.0	$ 4.6	$ 4.8	$ 5.0	$ 5.1	$ 5.4	$ 5.8	$ 6.1
Earnings per share	$1.29	$1.36	$1.44	$1.65	$1.72	$1.80	$1.83	$1.94	$2.08	$2.19
Average stock price	$18	$22	$19	$30	$29	$29	$27	$31	$35	$33

EXHIBIT 2

PAYSON & CLARK CO. BALANCE SHEETS, 1956–1965
In Millions of Dollars

	1956	1957	1958	1959	1960	1961	1962	1963	1964	1965
Assets										
Current assets										
Cash and securities	$ 6	$ 7	$ 3	$ 1	$ 2	$ 2	$ 2	$ 1	$ 1	$ 1
Accounts receivable	33	36	38	39	41	43	45	47	51	55
Inventories	56	61	64	66	69	74	78	82	88	91
Total current assets	95	103	105	106	112	119	125	130	140	147
Plant and equipment	65	60	60	61	63	67	65	65	64	65
Investments in joint ventures							5	10	11	14
Total assets	$160	$163	$165	$167	$175	$186	$195	$205	$215	$226
Liabilities and Net Worth										
Current liabilities										
Accounts payable	$ 31	$ 33	$ 36	$ 38	$ 46	$ 54	$ 62	$ 65	$ 70	$ 75
Accrued liabilities	7	9	10	11	13	17	22	25	31	36
Long-term debt due	6	6	6	6	6	6	6	6	6	6
Total current liabilities	44	48	52	55	65	77	86	96	107	117
Long-term debt	52	47	41	35	29	23	18	12	6	–
Total liabilities	96	95	93	90	94	100	104	118	113	117
Common stock	27	27	27	27	27	27	27	27	27	27
Retained earnings	37	41	45	50	54	59	64	70	75	82
Total liabilities and net worth	$160	$163	$165	$167	$175	$186	$195	$205	$215	$226

EXHIBIT 3

DATRONICS COMPANY INCOME STATEMENTS, 1956–1965
In Millions of Dollars Except per Share Data

	1956	*1957*	*1958*	*1959*	*1960*	*1961*	*1962*	*1963*	*1964*	*1965*
Contracts	$ 1.2	$6.4	$8.2	$7.5	$ 8.0	$ 7.9	$ 6.0	$ 4.3	$ 3.4	$ 2.4
Sales			.2	2.1	4.4	8.1	14.3	22.5	34.2	48.1
Revenues	1.2	6.4	8.4	9.6	12.4	16.0	20.3	26.8	37.6	50.5
Cost of goods sold	1.0	4.5	6.0	6.9	8.9	11.5	14.7	19.6	27.8	37.9
Gross profits	0.2	1.9	2.4	2.7	3.5	4.5	5.6	7.2	9.8	12.6
Expenses	0.5	0.6	0.7	.7	.7	.7	.9	.9	1.0	1.1
R&D		0.7	0.8	1.0	1.2	1.5	2.2	3.0	4.0	5.1
Profit before tax	(0.3)	0.6	0.9	1.0	1.6	2.3	2.5	3.3	4.8	6.4
Tax	(0.15)	0.2	0.4	0.5	0.8	1.1	1.2	1.6	2.4	3.2
Net profit	($ 0.15)	$0.4	$0.5	$0.5	$ 0.8	$ 1.2	$ 1.3	$ 1.7	$ 2.4	$ 3.2
Earnings per share	($ 1.50)	$4	$5	$5	$ 8	$12	$10.40	$13.60	$19.20	$25.60

EXHIBIT 4

DATRONICS COMPANY BALANCE SHEETS, 1956–1965
In Millions of Dollars

	1956	1957	1958	1959	1960	1961	1962	1963	1964	1965
Assets										
Current assets										
Cash	$ 0.05	$0.10	$0.10	$0.40	$0.20	$ 0.60	$ 0.60	$ 0.65	$ 1.56	$ 0.70
Inventories	0.20	2.60	2.70	3.70	5.20	6.20	6.80	10.15	15.22	20.10
Accounts receivable		0.30	0.50	1.00	2.00	2.20	3.00	4.00	5.12	6.00
Total current assets	0.25	3.00	3.30	5.10	7.30	9.00	10.40	14.85	21.90	26.80
Plant and equipment	0.50	1.00	1.20	1.40	2.00	3.10	5.10	7.50	8.50	9.00
Total assets	$ 0.75	$4.00	$5.50	$6.50	$9.30	$12.10	$15.50	$22.35	$30.40	$35.80
Liabilities and Net Worth										
Liabilities										
Accounts payable	0.10	2.15	2.20	2.60	3.65	4.75	5.50	8.78	12.10	14.25
Accrued liabilities	0.10	1.00	1.05	1.25	1.65	2.25	1.70	2.77	3.80	3.85
	0.20	3.15	3.25	3.85	5.30	7.00	7.20	11.55	15.90	18.10
Notes payable	0.60	0.50	1.40	1.30	1.85	1.75	2.50	2.20	3.50	3.50
Total liabilities	0.80	3.65	4.65	5.15	7.15	8.75	9.70	13.75	19.45	21.60
Additional paid-in capital	—	—	—	—	—	—	1.125	2.225	2.225	2.225
Common stock ($1 par)	0.10	0.10	0.10	0.10	0.10	0.10	0.125	0.125	0.125	0.125
Retained earnings	(0.15)	0.25	0.75	1.25	2.05	3.25	4.55	6.25	8.65	11.85
Total liabilities and net worth	$ 0.75	$4.00	$5.50	$6.50	$9.30	$12.10	$15.50	$22.35	$30.40	$35.80

EXHIBIT 5

PC&D, INC. INCOME STATEMENT, 1966–1970
In Millions of Dollars Except per Share Data

	1966	1967	1968	1969	1970
Sales					
Machinery	$315.1	$327.5	$340.2	$354.1	$368.2
Electronics	66.1	84.7	106.7	132.3	161.4
Total sales	381.2	412.2	446.9	486.4	529.6
Cost of goods sold					
Machinery	251.7	264.3	271.8	284.7	297.9
Electronics	49.6	63.0	79.6	96.8	118.5
Total cost of goods sold	301.3	327.3	351.4	381.5	416.4
Gross margin	79.9	84.9	95.5	104.9	113.2
Expenses					
Marketing G&A expense	46.1	48.3	50.3	51.6	53.1
Product development – machinery	6.9	4.6	4.7	4.1	4.5
R&D – electronics	4.2	5.3	10.3	17.8	27.3
Total expense	52.2	58.2	65.3	73.5	84.9
Profit before interest and taxes	24.7	26.7	30.2	31.4	28.3
Interest	3.0	3.0	0.2	0.2	0.2
Profit before taxes	21.7	23.7	30.0	31.2	28.1
Taxes	10.8	11.8	15.0	15.6	14.0
Net profit	$ 10.9	$ 11.9	$ 15.0	$ 15.6	$ 14.1
Earnings per share	$3.63	$3.97	$5.00	$5.20	$4.70
Average stock price	$94	$111	$145	$146	$103

EXHIBIT 6

PC&D, INC. BALANCE SHEETS, 1966–1970
In Millions of Dollars

	1966	1967	1968	1969	1970
Assets					
Current assets					
Cash and securities	$ 2	$ 5	$ 9	$ 7	$ 11
Accounts receivable	67	71	77	87	101
Inventories	118	128	145	166	180
Total current assets	187	214	231	260	292
Plant and equipment	83	95	97	108	120
Investments in joint ventures	10	11	12	12	10
Goodwill	6	6	5	5	5
Total assets	$286	$320	$345	$385	$427
Liabilities and Net Worth					
Current liabilities					
Accounts payable	90	96	103	111	127
Accrued liabilities	31	33	31	32	35
Long-term debt due	1	1	1	2	3
Total current liabilities	122	130	135	145	165
Long-term debt	16	30	35	49	57
Total liabilities	138	160	170	194	222
Common stock and paid-in capital	55	55	55	55	55
Retained earnings	93	105	120	136	150
Total liabilities and net worth	$286	$320	$345	$385	$427

EXHIBIT 7

PC&D, INC. INCOME STATEMENTS, 1971–1975
In Millions of Dollars Except per Share Data

	1971	*1972*	*1973*	*1974*	*1975*
Sales					
Machinery	$382.9	$397.8	$412.5	$426.9	$ 440.6
Electronics*	193.6	235.6	300.1	397.4	561.4
Total sales	576.5	633.4	712.6	824.3	1,002.0
Cost of goods sold					
Machinery	311.3	322.6	338.2	350.9	359.1
Electronics	145.2	174.3	216.1	282.2	421.1
Total cost of goods sold	456.5	496.9	554.3	633.1	780.2
Gross margin	120.0	136.5	158.3	191.2	221.8
Expenses					
Marketing G&A expense	54.7	56.3	59.1	63.3	67.7
Development—machinery	5.0	5.1	5.2	5.2	5.3
R&D—electronics	28.4	29.5	30.7	31.9	33.5
Total expenses	88.1	90.9	95.0	100.4	106.5
Profit and taxes before interest	31.9	45.6	63.3	90.8	115.3
Interest	0.2	3.0	3.0	7.0	11.0
Profit before taxes	31.7	42.6	60.3	83.8	104.3
Taxes	15.8	21.3	30.1	41.9	52.1
Net profit	$ 15.9	$ 21.3	$ 30.2	$ 41.9	$ 52.2
Earnings per share	$5.30	$6.45†	$8.39	$10.47	$13.05
Average stock price	$106	$156	$158	$163	$238

*Sales figures for Electronics included both sales by the original division plus sales of new subsidiaries after they are merged. Thus in 1975, the $561.4 million in sales for Electronics included $179.2 from products developed in subs. Profit before interest and taxes from new products was $22.1 million.

†Number of shares increased in 1972 by .3 million from the merger of Pro Instruments. They increased in 1973 by .3 million from the merger of Sub #2, and again by .4 million in 1974 from the merger of Subs #3 and #4. Thus in 1974 there was a total of 4 million shares outstanding. In late 1973, there was a secondary offering of 1 million shares.

EXHIBIT 8

PC&D, INC. BALANCE SHEETS, 1971–1975
In Millions of Dollars

	1971	*1972*	*1973*	*1974*	*1975*
Assets					
Current assets					
Cash and securities	$ 10	$ 5	$ 2	$ 2	$ 3
Accounts receivable	117	131	155	171	213
Inventories	200	223	270	327	401
Total current assets	327	505	586	706	882
Plant and equipment	122	124	125	178	232
Investments in joint ventures	10	8	10	9	6
Investments in subsidiaries	5	10	21	16	25
Goodwill	4	4	3	3	2
Total assets	$468	$505	$586	$706	$882
Liabilities and Net Worth					
Current liabilities					
Accounts payable	$151	$160	$179	$193	$243
Accrued liabilities	37	41	46	51	65
Long-term debt due	4	4	4	6	7
Total current liabilities	192	205	229	250	315
Long-term debt	55	58	84	138	193
Total liabilities	247	263	313	388	508
Common stock and paid-in capital	55	55	56	57	57
Retained earnings	166	187	217	261	317
Total liabilities and net worth	$468	$505	$586	$706	$882

EXHIBIT 9
ORGANIZATION CHART, 1975

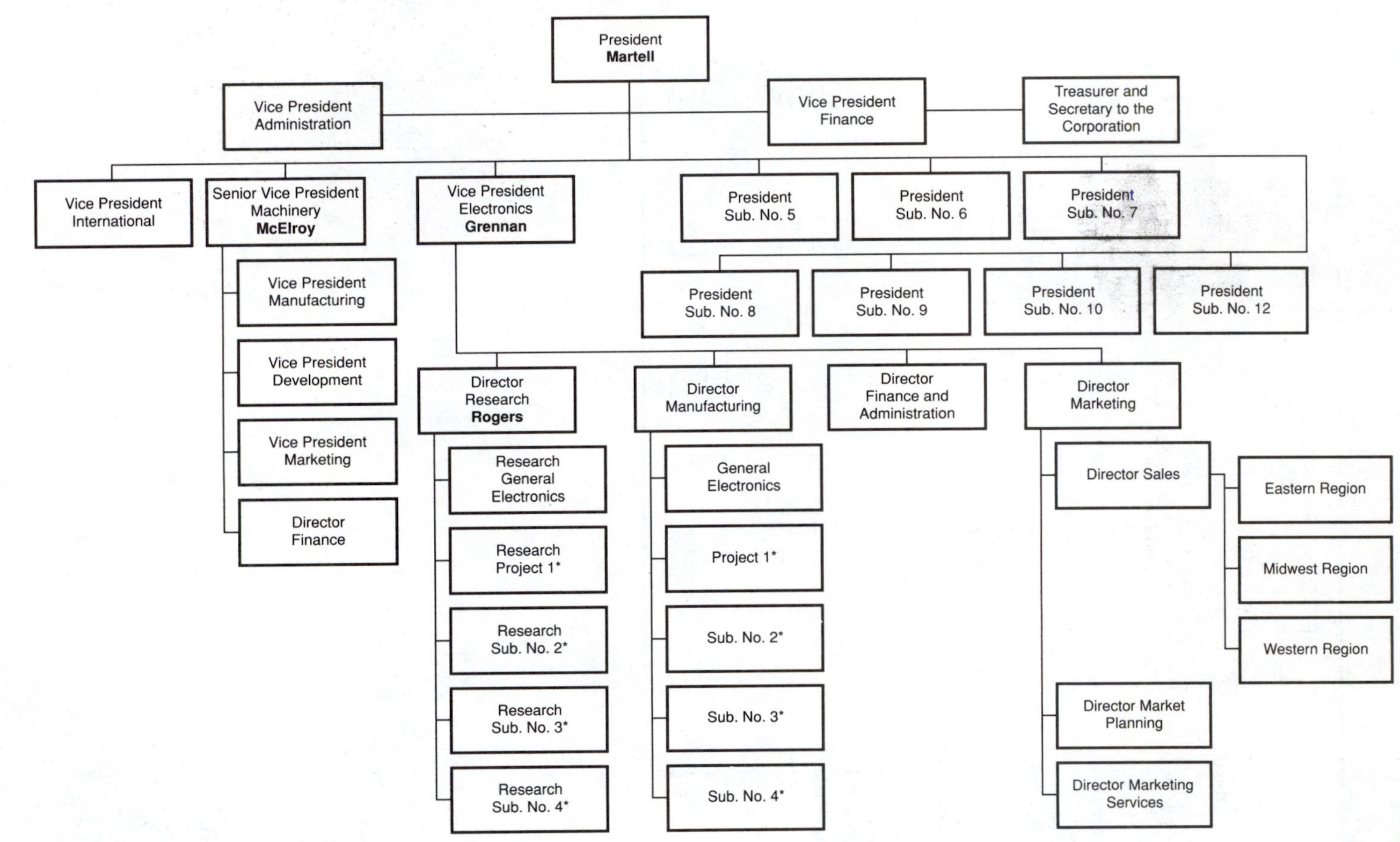

*References to subsidiaries indicates origin of personnel and product.

Cleveland Twist Drill (A)

"Run a tight ship and manage for cash."

This was the seemingly uncomplicated mandate given by Acme-Cleveland's CEO Chuck Ames to Jim Bartlett when Bartlett assumed the presidency of Cleveland Twist Drill (CTD) – a subsidiary of Acme-Cleveland Corporation – in August 1981.

The economy, however, had been souring; sales and profitability were declining considerably. Rather than fine-tuning a sound business, Jim Bartlett soon found himself overhauling CTD's entire organization and strategy. He realized that his immediate priorities were to make CTD competitive in labor costs and to rationalize a product line that had proliferated to over 16,000 products.

His approach to these goals, however, had somewhat disoriented the old-line management, who found it difficult to accept the dramatic change in the character and direction of this 107-year-old company. Consequently, Bartlett brought in a new team and replaced virtually all of the inherited department heads, many of whom had devoted their entire careers to the company.

Although Bartlett felt he had been able to formulate the main elements of a turnaround, he knew some major unresolved problems still stood in the way of achieving his objectives. To address the issue of labor costs, Bartlett had to decide whether he should (1) request from the Acme-Cleveland board $17 million to build new manufacturing facilities in lower-cost locations or (2) attempt to win concessions from the existing work force in Cleveland. Even if Bartlett got the relocation funds, he was unsure how he should handle the prospect of major work force reductions in Cleveland. In addition, Bartlett faced a host of other problems in consolidating CTD's operations and changing its strategy: How could the unwieldy product line be rationalized? How could he maintain morale and a sense of purpose during a period of retrenchment? How could he turn a manufacturing-driven company into a marketing-driven one?

INDUSTRY BACKGROUND

In 1981 Cleveland Twist Drill was the second-largest U.S. manufacturer of cutting

---

Harvard Business School case 384–083.

tools. The high-speed drills, reamers, taps, dies, gauges, end mills, saws, cutters, and other products of this approximately $1 billion industry were used primarily in metalworking, where they were expendable "razor blades" in machining and metal removal (see Exhibit 1).

The cutting tool industry was mature, with little prospect of long-term real growth. In fact, unit demand had declined approximately 1 to 2 percent per year during the 1970s. Three major trends were evident:

1. Conglomerate acquisition of privately owned firms.
2. A change in product demand.
3. Increasing foreign competition.

Industry Undergoes Changes in Ownership

Until the late 1960s all of the firms in the expendable cutting tool industry were privately owned. Between 1965 and 1970, however, most were acquired by conglomerates such as Litton, TRW, and Bendix. During this period, Cleveland Twist Drill merged with National Acme, a machine tool manufacturer, to form Acme-Cleveland and reduce the probability of being acquired by a much larger company. Since more than half of Acme-Cleveland's top management came from Cleveland Twist Drill, the latter was able to remain relatively unchanged. But CTD's competitors changed rapidly from family-owned and family-managed concerns to publicly owned and professionally managed firms.

In the early 1970s United Greenfield, a TRW subsidiary and CTD's largest competitor, built a major new facility in Augusta, Georgia. CTD did not build its first southern plant until almost nine years later, and even then the new plant's output was an insignificant percentage of the company's total production.

Change in Product Demand

New materials, technologies, and methods were steadily reducing demand for the industry's bread-and-butter product, high-speed steel drills. Titanium nitride coatings and carbide solid and tipped tools, while priced higher than steel, had a significantly longer-wear life. Lasers were being used increasingly as a cutting medium, and a shift from fastening to bonding of metal parts eliminated the need for drills.

Also affecting demand was a trend from specialty to commodity products in much of the market. Traditionally, cutting tool manufacturers had established close working relationships with the manufacturing and engineering departments of their customers. This enabled them to demonstrate the technical superiority of their products and qualified them to bid on high-quality jobs that commanded a price premium. The entry of new competitors and the centralization of purchasing in many large companies increased the importance of price in the buying decision. This, together with a shrinkage of perceived quality differentiation between top-line manufacturers like CTD and the new entrants, had divided the market place into a large commodity-like segment and a small high-quality segment. In the commodity segment, service was less valued, and many manufacturers sold directly to the end users through their sales force.[1]

[1] In 1981 approximately 60 percent of cutting tools were sold through industrial distributors and 40 percent by company sales forces.

Increased Competition

In the mid-1970s CTD's major end-user customers, such as Boeing, began informing CTD of the availability of high-quality tools at a lower price from Canada, Japan, and Yugoslavia. CTD management felt that this competition was in the lower price quality end of the market and hence not a significant threat. Competition continued to increase, however, as Japanese and Western European manufacturers increased their shares of the American market. In addition, automated equipment for producing cutting tools eliminated many key skills normally required in manufacturing a quality product, thus opening the door for competition from Third World and Eastern bloc countries. Also, small, "short-line" specialists based in the United States were gaining ground against major competitors like CTD.

COMPANY BACKGROUND

Cleveland Twist Drill was founded in 1876 by Jacob Dolson Cox in partnership with C. C. Newton. Although neither of Cox's two sons followed in his father's footsteps, the business continued to grow under family ownership. CTD's growth paralleled the growth of industrial distributors, and it was through its distributor network that CTD became the dominant force in the industry. Bert Finlay, vice president for sales and marketing who had joined the company in 1956, recalled:

> From 1930 to 1950 CTD concentrated on building market share and distribution channels. When I came aboard in 1956, CTD had control of the marketplace and maintained that position right up to the Vietnam War. The distributors having the CTD line had virtual entrée to any other line (of complementary products).

In 1968 Arthur Armstrong, Cox's son-in-law and CTD's chief executive, engineered a merger with the slightly larger National Acme. As stated in their first combined annual report:

> The result is a major resource for production systems, know-how, tools, and automated machines which increase efficiency and reduce costs. Virtually every product manufactured by industry, from surgical needles to automobiles to spacecraft, requires products such as we design, produce, and market throughout the free world.

The new company grew rapidly, from combined sales of $109 million in 1968 to $405 million by 1980. Profits increased more slowly, from $9 million to $16 million. (See Exhibit 2 for financial highlights.) Some old-timers saw this merger as a turning point for CTD. According to one:

> This was the beginning of the decline. There really was no synergy in the two businesses getting together. National Acme was the sick company which never got well. The top management of the merged company tried to bail out National Acme's business by using CTD's resources. As a result they did not pay enough attention, or allocate enough resources, to keep CTD in the forefront. As business boomed, we could not make our delivery commitments. Though the product quality was good, Manufacturing was not responsive to the needs of the customer; Product and Applications Engineering and Sales would want to respond to the customers' needs, and Manufacturing would not, and therein lay the conflict.

Enter Jim Bartlett

After graduating from the Harvard Business School in 1961, Jim Bartlett joined McKinsey & Co. in New York City. Two years later he was selected to move to Cleveland, where McKinsey was opening a new office. The partner in charge was Chuck Ames.

After five years with McKinsey, Jim went into the venture capital business, first with Laird & Co., and then with a group of partners. Their business was essentially one of acquiring privately held companies ranging from $2 million to $30 million in revenues. Jim's group increased the companies' profitability, installed professional management, and then sold them at a gain. In his 15-year involvement in venture capital, Jim and his partners actively invested in and managed roughly 20 privately held manufacturing businesses. Not only did they achieve a solid return on their investment, but Jim found this work challenging and satisfying. A minority investor and participant in some of Jim's ventures was Chuck Ames, his old boss and mentor from McKinsey.

In 1972 Ames left McKinsey to become president and chief operating officer of Reliance Electric Company. In 1976 he was made chief executive officer. During his tenure, Reliance's sales rose from $339 million in 1972 to $1.34 billion in 1979, net earnings rose from $13.6 million to $67.9 million, and ROE went from 11 to 22 percent. In 1979 Reliance was acquired by Exxon for $1.2 billion. Chuck Ames resigned a year after the acquisition was completed.

For over 10 years Arthur Armstrong, the chief executive officer of Acme-Cleveland, had been a member of the board of directors at Reliance. By 1980 Armstrong and his key associate and successor, Paul Cooper, decided to reach out to Chuck Ames to lead Acme-Cleveland through the coming difficult period. Ames, having served on the board of Acme-Cleveland, was familiar with the situation facing the firm.

Shortly after he became president in January 1981, Ames called Jim Bartlett and offered him the presidency of his Cleveland Twist Drill division. "I need management," Chuck said to Jim, but Jim Bartlett was not interested. His venture capital firm had just bought another company, which he was in the process of guiding through the transition to professional management. Despite Jim's initial lack of interest, Chuck continued to pursue him. Finally in March 1981, Jim agreed to join Acme-Cleveland as president of Cleveland Twist Drill. But he could not start until August because he had to wind up his affairs and help find some professional management for the company he was running.

Between March and August, Bartlett had several discussions with Chuck Ames about CTD's history, present status, and mission. According to Jim, Ames's perception was that CTD was a very solid business that merely needed a good general manager who could set an explicit long-term strategy. Ames and the rest of Acme's board considered CTD as "solid as the Bank of England . . . number one in the industry . . . a flagship company . . . with unassailable strength."

JIM BARTLETT'S FIRST NINE MONTHS

Strategic Planning at CTD

When Bartlett arrived, CTD was in the midst of preparing its 1982 budget and sales forecasts. He decided to involve himself in the process right away and asked to see management's strategic plans. Bartlett described what he found:

> For at least three years prior to my arrival, the strategic planning process had consisted primarily of the top management of

> the division getting together at a hotel and committing to some broad goals which did not change much from year to year, except for increased sales and profit projections. Their strategy could best be captured by the opening statement of the five-year, long-range plan developed in 1978: "In 1983 CTD will be the same as it is today, but different. The essential difference will be REAL GROWTH in sales and profits, as compared with 1978." The opening sentence of the 1980 five-year, long-range plan was exactly the same: "In 1985 CTD will be the same as it is today, but different. The essential difference will be REAL GROWTH in sales and profits, as compared with 1980 results."

This real growth in sales was projected as shown in Table 1. Profit growth was projected at 6 percent of sales in the 1978 plan and was raised to 6.5 percent in the 1980 plan. As for the actual strategies to achieve these projections, Bartlett said:

> This was merely an exercise where the outside consultant who had been brought in would ask the managers everything they would like to do during the next five years. As a result, the major strategies for the last three years were generalizations that did not amount to much. Their key strategy statments were (1) to achieve increased productivity in manufacturing and throughout all division operations; (2) to achieve conversion from purchased to manufactured for major items now resold; (3) to provide management depth and skilled employees required to achieve the division's long-range growth goals; (4) to be more responsive to the physical, emotional, and social needs of employees and to the needs of our communities; and (5) to expand international market participation.
>
> Upon learning this, I immediately came to the conclusion that planning would have to change because we needed to develop much more relevant strategies. Besides, Chuck Ames had already suspended these kinds of long-range planning efforts and asked the divisions to focus on their short-term results. In a memo to the division heads, Chuck had written, "I would suggest that the operating division heads begin to think through the strategy they will employ to raise the return on sales of their division to 7 percent on a continuing basis. And that all of us think in terms of the strategy required to achieve, on a continuing basis, returns of 7 percent on sales, 22 percent on equity, and 14 percent growth rate in earnings per share."

Bartlett indicated how the 1982 plans were completed:

> When I arrived, CTD was about to complete fiscal 1981. At that time we expected the sales volume for the year to come in at about $120 million, and the people there had viewed the results for the year as being pretty good. Like most others at that time, the people in the division had assumed that the economy would rebound in 1982, and so the forecast of $140 million for 1982 seemed pretty reasonable to me.

TABLE 1
CTD'S PROJECTED REAL GROWTH IN SALES AND PROFITS
In Millions

	1978	*1979*	*1980*	*1981*	*1982*	*1983*
1978 Plan	$92	$103	$114	$126	$146	$160
1980 Plan	—	—	$126	$133	$156	$183

Within six months into the fiscal year Bartlett realized that not only would he not achieve his forecast but he would be hard-pressed to even do as well as the last year. He felt the plan relied too heavily on assumptions about economic recovery, which did not happen. Bartlett believed, however, that this downturn was a double-edged sword. He explained:

> The bad edge of the sword was that the decline in sales had caused considerable profit pressures on the business. The good or opportunity edge of the sword was that these results produced a climate that made it easier to institute strategic changes, which otherwise would have been much more difficult to get people to accept.

Manufacturing

Because CTD was basically a manufacturing company, the next task Bartlett set for himself was to learn about its manufacturing capabilities and vulnerabilities. CTD's facilities comprised 10 acres of manufacturing floor space, including 19 buildings. The main plant, a 5-story, 500,000-square-foot building on top of which sat CTD's headquarters, was located on East 49th Street, just one block from Lake Erie, in a heavily industrialized section of Cleveland. The Cleveland plant complex accounted for 75 percent of domestic production.[2] Another 15 percent was produced in Mansfield, Massachusetts; the remaining 10 percent was produced in Cranston, Rhode Island, and Cynthiana, Kentucky. There were also three foreign plants, but they were of only minor importance.

CTD had traditionally organized its manufacturing operations by process. Grinding was done in one area, testing in another, milling in another, and finishing in yet another. Many of the processes were not even in the same building. One department did nothing but move goods in process from one floor to another, from one building to another, and even between plants in Cleveland, Cynthiana, and Cranston. One result of this practice and the plant layout was that CTD had more indirect than direct labor costs.

When Jim Bartlett arrived, he got involved in the manufacturing budget right away and targeted a $5 million reduction in manufacturing wages. He asked the manager of industrial relations, Gordon Streit, for ideas on how to achieve this. Streit, who was 57 years old and had spent his entire career at CTD, seemed to be confused by this approach and was at a loss for suggestions. According to Bartlett, Streit made some suggestions like "maybe we should cut salaries by 10 percent across the board." Bartlett, finding such responses totally inadequate, fired Streit during his first week at CTD. Needless to say, Streit was shocked and asked Bartlett, "How can you do this to me? No one has ever told me I was not doing my job well."

Streit was the first among Bartlett's inherited, nine-member top management team to be dismissed. Bartlett commented: "Firing Gordon was an unpleasant and difficult thing to do, and I sensed that most of the employees felt I was shooting from the hip. But I couldn't tolerate a key executive who could not give me any good ideas on the major problems we faced. Of course, we made

[2] In total, CTD had 524,000 square feet of manufacturing space in Cleveland; 65,000 square feet in Mansfield; 49,000 square feet in Cranston; and 145,000 square feet in Cynthiana. The number of hourly employees at these locations was approximately 530, 100, 50, and 90, respectively.

a generous severance arrangement with Gordon."[3]

Streit was replaced by Jack Sims from the corporate industrial relations staff at Acme-Cleveland. Bartlett asked Sims to investigate how CTD's wages compared with those of competitors. By contacting the Metal Cutting Tool Institute (the industry trade association), Sims was able to develop a comparison between CTD's wages (excluding benefits) and the industry averages (see Table 2). When benefits were included, the gap between CTD and its competitors widened to $4.50 per hour in the Cleveland area.

In addition, CTD's productivity and quality were compared with competitors' levels. These studies showed that productivity varied little throughout the industry and that CTD's quality ran somewhat higher. From these studies, Bartlett concluded that CTD was at a competitive disadvantage and that significant changes in manufacturing strategy would be required:

> When I started at CTD, I thought the company was in reasonably good shape and that I would be addressing the longer-term issue of substitute products. Instead, within the first month or two, I realized that the company faced a very serious and dangerous cost situation that had to be corrected. And with our industry actually decreasing in size and with very tough competition, I concluded that our survival was at stake.

Bartlett then met with the head of manufacturing, Sam Colt—42 years old and described as articulate, soft-spoken, well liked by the rank and file, and a hard worker. Colt had started as a trainee at CTD, had worked his way up, and was considered the number one candidate to succeed to the top position (so Bartlett had been informed upon joining the company). All the manufacturing plants reported to Colt. As a hands-on manager, he knew the production output for every plant on a shift-by-shift and product-by-product basis.

According to Bartlett, when he and Colt started discussing manufacturing strategy, Colt wanted to talk only about operating data. Bartlett had to steer the conversation around to CTD's comparative cost position in order to impress on Colt that CTD was not cost competitive in its present facilities and would always have trouble catching up with competitors that had more efficient facilities.

In October 1981, Bartlett asked Colt to begin work on a change in CTD's manufacturing strategy. In a four-page memo a month later, Bartlett spelled out specifically what he was looking for. The memo began this way:

> The presentation for preliminary five-year plans by each product group is now scheduled for February 25, 1982. These plans will have a major influence on the direction CTD will take in the location and very nature of its manufacturing base. However, as we discussed earlier, there are a number of questions that must be addressed, the answers to which will have a major impact on how we should reposition our manufacturing base. Your responsibility in preparing for the late February meeting is to develop the clearest possible answers to these questions.

There followed a series of questions (see Exhibit 3) listed under four headings: (1) East 49th Street Dispersion; (2) Plant Network Design; (3) Organization and Staffing;

[3] Streit was given one year's salary as severance pay, was allowed to begin to collect retirement benefits as if he were 65, and was offered the services of an outplacement company at CTD's expense.

TABLE 2
COMPARATIVE WAGE ANALYSIS: INDUSTRY VERSUS CTD

Industry Average		*CTD Average*	
United States (excluding CTD)	$7.51	Mansfield, Mass.	$ 9.89
New York, New England, Mid-Atlantic	7.15	Cranston, R.I.	7.32
Chicago and West	7.55	Cynthiana, Ky.	7.65
Cleveland and Detroit (excluding CTD)	8.30	Cleveland	10.67

and (4) Capital Investment. This memo was never answered to Bartlett's satisfaction, and in February 1982 Sam Colt was fired. Bartlett commented:

> This was a very difficult decision because Sam was so well liked and because he really was just a product of the corporate culture he had grown up in. When I called my first staff meeting, for example, Sam and his people got up to leave when the marketing people arrived. Cross-functional discussion just wasn't part of the culture. Despite all my sympathy and efforts, I realized that it would be impossible to achieve what we had to without someone else in Sam's position.

Sam Colt was replaced by Pete Manzoni, former vice president of manufacturing for Bailey Controls, a division of Babcock & Wilcox. Manzoni explained how he came to join CTD:

> I have always played the stock market, and my investment philosophy is to buy shares in companies where there is some major change or chance for change going on. In about half of the situations, I am able to win big, and in the other half I hope to break even by getting out in time. Thus, when Chuck Ames joined Acme-Cleveland, knowing of his track record at Reliance, I bought a large block of shares in Acme-Cleveland. A year later, when Acme's stock had gone down, and having read in the local papers about management changes at Acme and CTD, I wrote a letter to Ames stating that all he had done was fire a lot of people and changed around positions, but the business meanwhile had continued to go downhill. As a result of this letter, Ames contacted me, and soon I was talking to Jim Bartlett about joining CTD, which I did on March 1, 1982.

After about a month on the job, Manzoni, with Bartlett, began formulating a manufacturing strategy for CTD.

Labor Relations

Only the Cleveland and Mansfield plants were unionized, though with different unions and separate labor agreements. Management's relationship with the workers in Cleveland was not only conflict-free but benevolent and harmonious. While the Mansfield workers were represented by the United Steel Workers union, the Cleveland plant had its own house union.[4] The company's relationship with this union was quite good and rather informal. Until 1969 there was not even a written labor contract. Instead, verbal agreements and clarifying memos were used. All through the 1960s and 1970s, as CTD prospered, it shared its gains generously with its workers. The company was one of the first to provide dental insurance and unlimited

[4] A house union is an independent union organized solely within a specific company and has no affiliation with international unions.

medical coverage. A provision in its contract for a cost of living allowance (COLA) was without a cap to enable the workers to recover fully increases in the consumer price index (CPI); moreover, the company had agreed in 1972 to an 8 percent minimum annual COLA, which in 1980 turned out to be slightly higher than the increase in the CPI. CTD also had a long tradition of providing piece-rate incentives for increased productivity, ranging frm 25 to 40 percent of base salary.

There had never been a layoff in the company's history. During the 1974–1975 recession the salaried employees took a 10 percent cut, but the hourly workers kept working full time and built up inventory that was used later when business picked up. Morale was high, and management and the workers were close; not only the plant manager, but also the president, spent considerable time on the shop floor and knew people by their first names.

Management's benevolence toward its workers included not only financial rewards, but also psychological and social benefits. In the 1970s, CTD had a bowling league with about 40 teams, two golf leagues, and a softball league. There were also an annual sports awards banquet, a big Christmas dinner, and a Christmas party for the children: the personnel department kept track of all the employees' children's ages and sexes to ensure that they received the appropriate presents. A club for retirees offered medical checkups, social events, and other benefits.

Other employee-assistance programs listed in the company's 1978 and 1980 long-range plans were alcohol- and drug-abuse counseling, physical fitness courses, CPR and first aid classes, preretirement counseling, financial planning and tax return preparation at company expense, legal referrals, and marital, family, and personal counseling. Social activities included photography and radio classes, picnics, open houses, and family activities. To serve the community there were plans for trial job interviews for high school students, summer jobs at CTD for local teachers, economics courses for employees and students, and encouragement for employees to serve on local community agencies and educational boards.

But all was not a bed of roses. Roy Martin, 38, newly promoted Cleveland plant manager and a 20-year veteran, provided a perspective on CTD's culture and the changes Jim Bartlett had made:

> Even before Jim came, things had started to change. In the recession of 1975, they cut out the Christmas party for the kids. Also for the banquet, instead of the shrimp cocktail and steaks, we had a spaghetti dinner in the basement. There were also some management layoffs and a 10 percent salary cut. Basically these were the easy things. The tough things had not been done and the tough questions were, do we really need all these levels of management, and do we even need all these managers?
>
> I was one of the last of the manufacturing guys left, and I suddenly went from a Young Turk to the last of the good old boys. This put me in a peculiar position. I was Sam Colt's lieutenant and when Sam was fired by Bartlett this was a real blow culturally to the organization because Sam was well liked. Conceptually I did not have a problem with what Jim wanted to get done and so in a way I had one foot in either camp; one camp wanted to continue as before and not make too many changes, while the other camp wanted to do things differently and change the business practices. So the new team basically wanted to make all the changes, and the old people were in a way divided.

> What hurts us the most is the COLA provision, which was negotiated in 1972, that went out of control. The incentive program was out of control too. Previously it was about 25 percent of the base; now 10 years later it is 42 percent of the base, and the problem is that everyone expects to get it, so it is no longer a real incentive. When people don't get the incentives that they have come to expect, we get grievances that our standards are too tight.

Having collected comparative wage data, management was in a quandary on how to proceed because contract negotiations were not due until November 1983. Some of the senior management wanted to seek immediate wage and work rule concessions from the union bargaining committee (the most important work rule change would be a reduction in the over 500 job classifications, which seriously reduced plant flexibility). There was, however, legitimate concern that the rank and file would resist even if the union leadership went along because they had never been told there were any real problems. The workers' perception of the company and their part in it was that they produced the best-quality goods and as a result CTD was the leader in the industry. Other members of senior management felt CTD should communicate the grim realities directly to the workers.

Against this backdrop Pete Manzoni, with Bartlett's concurrence, began informal discussions with the union bargaining committee in the middle of March. The committee was headed by Greg Thompson, who had recently been reelected president of the house union. Thompson was a decent, understanding sort of person who was sympathetic to CTD's problems. So far not much had been accomplished by these talks. According to Manzoni:

> Thompson's reaction to our proposals has been one of absolute shock, followed by disbelief and anger. His reaction has been something like this: "You guys are new here, and you don't know what's going on. We have been here for 25 years and we have never been treated like this by past management. They never told us there was any big wage- or benefit-differential problem. I don't know where you got your numbers from, but they can't be right. Besides, our productivity and quality are much higher than our competition's, so the numbers are not even comparable."

Bartlett soon realized that they had placed Thompson in a terrible bind:

> Thompson is a very intelligent, sensitive man who is well respected by his union members. He is a real statesman. He has calmed many management-labor problems and relationships in the past. Now we're telling him to convince his rank and file that a major concession has to be made before the contract expires.

Marketing and Sales

CTD's traditional market objectives were to serve as broad a market as possible and to maintain the highest product quality. To achieve these goals, CTD supplied a very large distributor network with a product line that included about 16,000 standard products and many specials. It also had on its own payroll 70 highly trained service representatives who worked directly with end users to solve problems with the existing products and to design new ones for special applications.

Largely because of the sales reps' work, CTD had established a reputation for superior quality. In recent years, however, other manufacturers had improved the quality of their products considerably, and CTD had not sufficiently kept abreast of technological advances to maintain its position. It became increasingly difficult for CTD to obtain a price premium for its products, and top management began questioning the wisdom of an annual outlay of approximately $5 million to maintain a specialized service force.

Drills accounted for 40 percent of CTD's product. Four other important product groups each accounted for between 10 and 13 percent of the total: (1) reamers; (2) taps, dies, and gauges; (3) end mills and aircraft specials; and (4) assembled threading tools (ATT).

Three other categories—Nobur, saws and cutters, and miscellaneous tools—accounted for the remaining 10 percent. (See Exhibit 4 for market segment analysis and six-year market share trends.)

Before Jim Bartlett arrived, P&L responsibility at Acme-Cleveland rested primarily with the president of each division or subsidiary. Both Chuck Ames and Bartlett believed, however, that product managers should also have profit responsibility (see Exhibit 5). Accordingly, Bartlett, shortly after his arrival, appointed three product managers who would have P&L responsibility for major segments of the business: one for drills and reamers; one for end mills, taps, dies, gauges, and Nobur; and one for ATT, saws, and cutters. Before, the product manager position had reported to the vice president for sales and was basically a staff position (Exhibit 6); now the product managers would report directly to the president (Exhibit 7).

Although the product managers had P&L responsibility, they had no product-line P&Ls with which to manage. As Jack Massey, the vice president of finance, put it:

> There are big problems in getting product-line profitability data. When I got here I started looking at the financial systems and there was no way to do a good analytical job. The people in the financial department were just bookkeepers. There were no proper information systems. All we had was a P&L and balance sheet—one for the United States, one for Canada, one for Mexico, one for Germany, and one total consolidated. There were no other operating reports to identify profitability, inventory turnover, variance analysis, or efficiency. All they were used to doing was looking at inventory cycles. Also, there was no way to identify opportunities or problems. We thought we would have product-line performance in place within six months. Now it seems it's going to take us two years. The problem is that people don't report against the routings; they just produce pieces and get paid, and there are no cost standards. Also, with business going down, we can't afford to allocate the resources to develop the information we need.

Besides the problem of establishing profitability figures, the product managers also found themselves spending more time responding to short-term pressures. One said:

> As demand began to fall, more and more of our time is being spent in forecasting sales figures and renegotiating production targets with manufacturing. Also, pricing issues have become quite important in the face of declining demand. There was, for example, pressure to lower prices so as to keep up demand. However, analysis showed that each 10 percent cut in prices would require 20 percent more sales to make up the lower level of profit. In light of declining overall demand, such a sales increase would have been most unlikely.

The product managers did not have an easy time dealing with the sales organization, either. The vice president for sales, Bert Finlay, had been with CTD for over 20 years and was described as "a very bright, energetic guy, though he was not on board with the new concept." Over time, the product managers hired product specialists to help them with their jobs. When they tried to fill these positions from the field sales and service organization, they encountered considerable opposition from Finlay, who resisted the development of the product-manager organization at the expense of field sales.

The product managers also faced a difficult task in developing strategies for growth markets. In addition to finding a very broad product line that was almost unmanageable, they found their competitors firmly entrenched in the commodity segment of the drill market (see Table 3). At the high-quality end of the market, in spite of a strong engineering and R&D department, CTD found itself far behind in seeking growth opportunities outside high-speed tools. As one of the product managers summed it up:

> The market perception of CTD is one of a high-cost producer resting on past successes, with little growth or technological drive. Though our premier product line—Cleforge—is still well respected in the industry, it is too high priced for the price-conscious buyers.
>
> Our lower-priced line—Celine—with which we can be price competitive, is not broad enough. We consistently have trouble putting together complete packages in this line. We really have no choice here. The commodity segment is now more than half the market and growing. We must have a complete, price-competitive line.

BARTLETT'S OPTIONS

In the past nine months, Jim Bartlett had dramatically changed the organizational structure of CTD and put new people in most of the key management positions. The administrative staff had also been cut back, and there had been significant volume-related layoffs in manufacturing. Even before Bartlett took over, Chuck Ames had begun restructuring and cutting back the entire Acme-Cleveland organization, and CTD had received a taste of the new management style when 75 management positions had been pared away.

Jack Sims, vice president of personnel, described how there had been opportunities to do away with entire departments:

> Since June 1981, 341 salaried people have been let go, for an annual savings of $10.6 million. For example, there was the wage standards department with 15 people who spent all their time administering the incentive system and writing job descriptions. This department was cut to one person. There was a customer service department with 70 people; these people did nothing but order processing and order entry. That responsibility has now been put into the hands of the sales offices, and the customer service department has been cut to 10 or 12 people. They also had 17 people in the personnel department administering all sorts of pro-

TABLE 3
1982 ESTIMATED SALES OF HIGH-SPEED STEEL DRILL COMMODITY SEGMENT
In Millions

CTD	*Company A*	*Company B*	*Company C*	*Company D*	*Company E*	*Others*
$4	$40	$20	$15	$15	$10	$25.5

> grams. That has now been cut to 5 people. And the company also employed its own cafeteria workers, paying them a wage rate of $10 per hour and $5 per hour in benefits; in addition, the cafeteria operation was being subsidized by $300,000 a year. All of these workers were let go, and a food service company was hired to run the cafeteria.

Sims continued:

> I am thoroughly convinced that we are doing the right thing here. We should have addressed these issues many years ago. Of our salaried people, about one half of them were in shock when we started to make the changes, but the other half felt that it was about time. I think that the greatest risk of what we are doing is that we may be doing too much too soon. There is just a lot of change all at once.

While Bartlett was pondering the pros and cons of the various options, he knew he had to act fast because of CTD's poor performance. For the first six months of fiscal 1982, sales were already 10 percent below the previous year and 15 percent below budget. While earnings were slightly above the previous year, they were considerably below budget. More disturbing was that the trend in both sales and earnings had been deteriorating.

Jim Bartlett realized that many of CTD's problems were rooted in the sharp decline in demand caused by the recession, but he also felt that the recession only highlighted CTD's underlying weaknesses. As Bartlett looked back, he realized he had got into more than he had bargained for. The industry had matured. CTD's sales were on the decline, and he had a major problem with the union on wages and benefits.

By early April 1982, Bartlett felt he knew what had to be done. First, he had to improve CTD's competitive cost position dramatically in its core markets, while maintaining service and delivery. Achieving a competitive cost position was essential for CTD to compete effectively in the large and growing commodity segment and maintain its position in the high-quality segment. As he wondered how he could pull this off, three possibilities kept churning in his mind:

1. He could step up the pace and pressure of negotiations with the union bargaining committee and hope for an early breakthrough.
2. He could bypass the bargaining committee and appeal directly to union employees.
3. He could immediately seek board approval for the necessary funds to proceed with plans to transfer work to other locations without involving the union leadership or its members.

None of these alternatives was particularly attractive. Whether Greg Thompson could persuade his union members to accept something as traumatic as wage concessions was an open question. For Thompson to endorse or recommend pay and benefit givebacks might seem tantamount to selling out to the new management.

Going directly to the rank and file might have been feasible a couple of years earlier, when there was still a very strong family feeling. But recently, because of the firings and forced retirements of many of the managers who had spent their entire careers with the company, and because many of the company's beneficences, like Christmas dinner and other social activities, had already been cut out, the production employees were already wary.

Requesting board approval for funds to transfer work at this stage also concerned Bartlett. He had a mandate to "manage for cash." To request $15 million to $20 million—when Acme-Cleveland was considering several acquisitions—might be viewed as contradicting that mandate. Because Acme-Cleveland was having a bad year, all capital requests were given very close scrutiny. And because most of the board had strong ties to Cleveland, a major move out of Cleveland might not be looked on favorably. Finally, although CTD had begun limited production at its Cynthiana, Kentucky, plant in early 1979, Bartlett wondered how responsible it would be to his employees and the community in Cleveland to launch a full-scale "southern strategy" before at least exploring all possible alternatives to gain wage and benefit concessions.

Complicating these alternatives were the facts that the current contract wasn't due to expire for 18 months and that it would take one to two years to bring any new facilities to competitive levels of productivity. Bartlett featured a three-year delay in achieving a competitive cost position if he waited to negotiate a new contract and then was unable to gain the necessary concessions.

Bartlett's second major objective was to maintain CTD's position in the marketplace because its sales and customer order backlog were dropping precipitously. What the company needed here were sound product-line strategies. But this component still perplexed him because CTD had no financial analysis or history on the profitability of its product lines.

The third major element of Bartlett's program was to move CTD into established growth markets. To accomplish this, CTD needed to develop a capability in new technologies, such as titanium nitride coatings, powdered metallurgy, and ceramics, rather than continue its investments in high-speed steel.

Thus, as shown in Exhibit 8, Bartlett felt he had conceived the main aspects of his strategy. What he needed to establish now was how the key elements of each aspect would be realized.

EXHIBIT 1
PRODUCTS MANUFACTURED BY THE CLEVELAND TWIST DRILL CO.

EXHIBIT 2
ACME-CLEVELAND'S FINANCIAL PERFORMANCE, 1973–1981

	1981	*1980*	*1979*	*1978*
I. Financial Highlights				
Summary of operations				
Net sales	$400,743,537	$405,235,999	$344,460,395	$289,509,329
Cost of products sold	318,721,315	301,847,698	246,286,255	210,201,261
Interest expense less interest income	6,942,653	6,651,559	3,592,141	4,328,008
Earnings before taxes	18,145,346	27,931,887	35,832,636	24,971,294
Income taxes	7,214,000	10,949,000	16,357,000	11,813,000
Net earnings	10,931,346	16,982,887	19,475,636	13,158,294
Net earnings to net sales	2.7%	4.2%	5.7%	4.5%
Earnings per common share	2.41	3.96	4.34	2.96
Dividends per common share	1.40	1.35	1.15	.80
Other financial information				
Current assets	168,751,234	182,884,833	156,791,868	132,945,224
Current liabilities	70,964,020	71,953,727	59,461,457	39,394,887
Working capital	97,787,214	110,931,106	97,330,411	93,550,337
Property, plant, and equipment—net	75,596,288	75,120,585	56,196,074	47,716,898
Capital expenditures	16,299,044	26,097,516	14,732,829	9,005,924
Depreciation	8,042,833	6,370,516	5,340,020	5,032,188
Long-term obligations	53,082,173	70,534,284	49,737,582	47,017,089
Total assets	252,437,417	263,712,017	219,574,767	184,463,445
Redeemable preferred shares	162,874	162,874	-0-	62,215
Shareholders' equity	121,668,098	116,330,248	107,079,591	93,964,096
Shareholders' equity per common share	$27.15	$26.37	$23.81	$21.10
II. Expendable Products Segment* (in thousands)				
Total sales	$148,360	$148,045	$144,521	$115,207
Operating profit	14,188	10,795	21,665	17,092
Identifiable assets	86,444	95,071	72,741	69,135
Depreciation	3,845	3,347	2,940	2,799
Capital expenditures	$7,321	$13,338	$8,113	$3,947

Note: Fiscal years ended September 30.
*This includes products other than those manufactured by Cleveland Twist Drill.

1977	*1976*	*1975*	*1974*	*1973*
$218,191,699	$194,088,642	$231,489,665	$169,442,363	$127,850,966
160,159,308	143,008,384	170,670,207	126,022,710	90,417,166
4,756,829	4,756,829	6,569,948	3,102,128	672,111
8,753,201	5,389,716	12,771,499	10,493,880	12,563,828
3,915,000	2,478,000	5,816,000	4,785,000	5,876,000
4,838,201	2,911,716	6,955,499	5,708,880	6,687,828
2.2%	1.5%	3.0%	3.4%	5.2%
1.08	.65	1.56	1.43	1.74
5.25	.50	6.25	1.00	.82
123,794,140	100,570,415	129,570,415	133,731,029	72,362,351
41,166,527	26,264,216	46,884,880	47,980,021	27,206,073
82,627,613	74,306,199	82,685,535	85,751,008	45,156,278
44,352,655	44,259,575	47,054,224	43,890,446	31,169,157
4,608,876	8,528,286	8,235,977	5,968,552	5,023,718
4,817,117	4,925,867	4,757,590	3,706,216	3,234,652
42,195,043	38,849,752	45,153,231	51,075,644	9,679,581
171,071,286	150,001,052	178,141,229	179,894,704	105,258,535
62,215	62,125	62,215	62,215	-0-
84,255,799	81,800,056	81,160,550	77,028,520	66,855,616
$18.92	$18.37	$18.22	$17.28	$17.42
$97,277	$89,854	$91,416	$94,620	$80,653
$11,895	$10,516	$7,155	$10,901	$11,325

EXHIBIT 3
EXCERPTS FROM JIM BARTLETT'S MEMO (11/13/81) TO SAM COLT ON MANUFACTURING STRATEGY

I. East 49th Street Dispersion

- What are the common manufacturing operations at East 49th Street to *all* the products manufactured there? How many hourly persons function in relevant departments and what are the costs associated today?
- What skills are required by hourly operators in these departments? What is the age and seniority profile of these persons performing these operations today? Which of these skills will disappear via attrition over the next five years that are not being replaced through training?
- Through matrix analysis, where does each major product group produced at East 49th Street depart from a list of operations common to all? Which of these product groups, by virtue of their separate (or separable) manufacturing process, lend themselves to relatively easy exit?
- Of those products that are readily separable from a process viewpoint, which represent the highest content of critical manual skills? Which represent a high "automation cost" if duplicated elsewhere?

II. Plant Network Design

- How many plants should we have? What is the optimum size of a plant?
- How many different product lines should be produced in each plant? To what extent can we continue to do early-stage operations on a tool class in one plant to support the production of other plants?

III. Organization and Staffing

- What should the organization be for each of our plants presently on line, including East 49th Street?
- What management resources are available to us in developing the necessary details to execute a major series of manufacturing moves (plant start-ups, line relocations, etc.)? What must be done to shore up these resources in time to have knowledgeable people making decisions and carrying out the required actions?
- What services, support, or direction will manufacturing require from outside its own organization?

IV. Capital Investment

- What are the major elements of our existing in-place capital structure for manufacturing? Which of these elements (heat treating, centerless grinding, NC equipment, broaching, etc.) will require major overhaul or substantial capacity upgrading during the next five years?
- Again using matrix analysis, where do we have duplication of facilities or equipment today? What additional duplication (or capacity) is already programmed through our present Cranston and Cynthiana moves?
- Are there major segments of capital equipment capability missing in our present plants that impair our competitive ability? What investments might we make to add to our productivity today?

EXHIBIT 4
MARKET SEGMENT AND MARKET SHARE TRENDS

A. Market Segment Analysis

Segment	*Mix*	*Market Share*	*Competitive Market Share*	
Drills and reamers	52%	14%	Company A	15%
			Company B	13
Taps and dies	13	9	Company B	15
			Company C	
End mills and aircraft specials	11	10	Company D	20
			Company B	20
			Company E	10
			Company F	10
ATT (assembled threading tools)	10	33	Company B	35
			Company G	20
Saws and cutters	4		(over 100 domestic manufacturers)	
Other/miscellaneous	10			
	100%			

B. Six-Year Market Share

	1981	*1980*	*1979*	*1978*	*1977*	*1976*
Drills	21.4%	21.2%	22.3%	22.9%	21.3%	21.6%
Reamers	21.5	21.5	22.2	23.0	21.8	22.8
End mills	10.9	11.6	10.3	10.7	10.5	10.8
Taps and dies	10.7	11.7	10.7	10.0	10.0	9.9

Note: Some figures have been disguised. Key relationships have been preserved.

EXHIBIT 5
BARTLETT'S MEMO ON PRODUCT MANAGEMENT CONCEPT

Date: March 31, 1982
Office:
Office:

To: Field Selling Organization
From: J. T. Bartlett
Subject: Role of the Product Manager in Our Business

Even though we have done considerable communicating about the role of the product manager in our business, I think we have a way to go in making this concept work to produce solid benefits. I am therefore writing to underscore some fundamental points about the product management function and how it should work in CTD's business.

The first and most important point you should understand is our product managers' function as general managers. They have profit and loss responsibility for major segments of our business. Whenever there is a problem in the field, whenever a customer is not being served, whenever we are missing a promised delivery date, whenever a competitor is introducing a product or launching a new initiative in pricing or promotion, the product managers should know. When you are not receiving the kind of support you need from the managers of manufacturing, engineering, or customer service, you should immediately contact your area manager who in turn will call the appropriate product manager. If your area manager is not available and the situation is urgent, you should reach Bert Finlay or one of the product managers directly. Let me stress that this does not mean that the product managers are a "dumping ground" for minor complaints and petty gripes. On the contrary, we expect you to handle that level of customer dissatisfaction.

However, if we are about to miss a major opportunity because of our inability to respond in a timely manner, the product manager should know. Only by communication at this level will it be possible for the product managers to be effective.

Secondly, it is impossible for our product managers to function unless they are aware of our competitors' moves and your thoughts on how we should serve our customers or markets better. I never cease to be impressed when I'm with you to hear your ideas and market intelligence. These ideas, particularly those coming from your knowledge of competitors, are invaluable input for our tactical planning as well as our long-term strategic thinking. We need to hear as much as we can from the field about these activities. Without a keen sense of competition, we are surely going to hit endless foul balls in our marketing direction. Hence, everything you know relating to our competition must be communicated to the product managers. A written format for this information will be forthcoming.

EXHIBIT 6
ORGANIZATION CHART AS OF JANUARY 1981

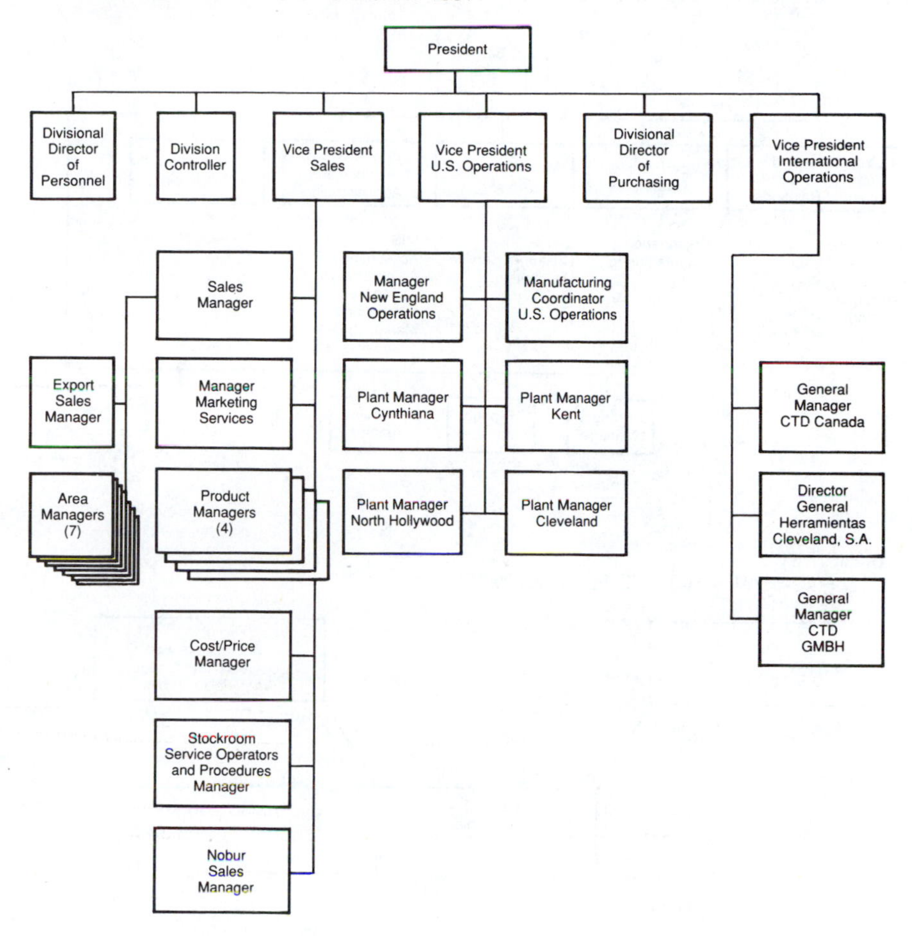

EXHIBIT 7
ORGANIZATION CHART AS OF APRIL 1982

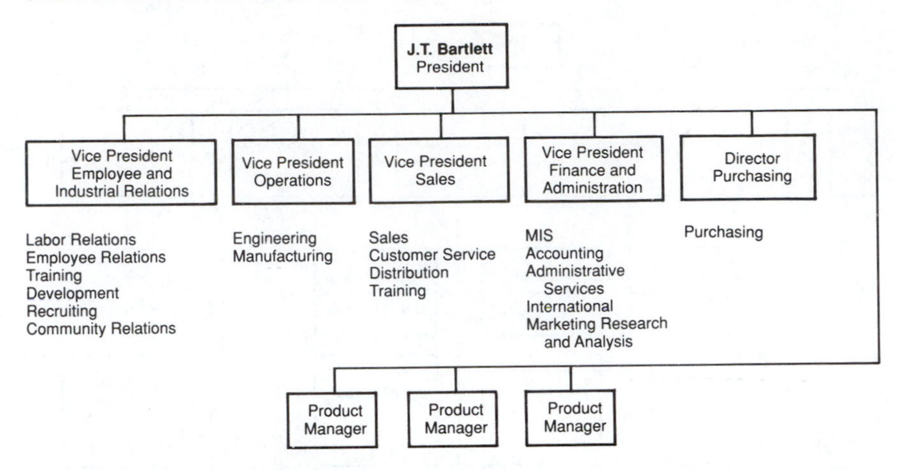

EXHIBIT 8
CTD FIVE-YEAR STRATEGIC PLAN SUMMARY

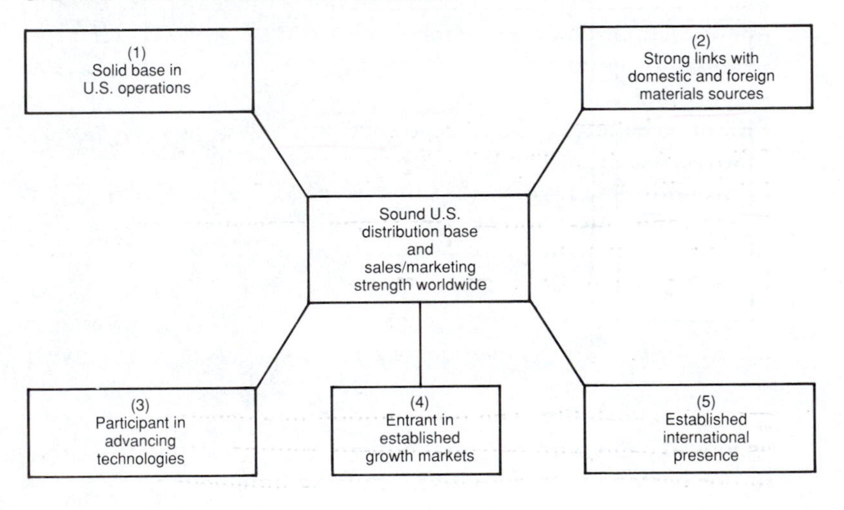

The Implementation of Strategy: From Commitment to Results

Our study of strategy has brought us to the prescription that the way work and responsibility are divided, the choice of means for directing specialized attention to interdepartmental issues, and the design of information systems should not be allowed to divert attention from strategic goals. Structure should follow strategy, but structure once sufficiently well established to influence behavior and decision will then tend to arrange that strategy also follows structure. The latter tendency can go too far. Making flexibility and informality values of high rank, turning frequently to temporary ad hoc teams and task forces, involving specialists and interdepartmental inquiries—all help prevent organization structure from dominating and routinizing behavior. The effort to avoid the rigidity that limits the innovative capacity of static organizations means, for example, that job descriptions should never be regarded as anything more than a snapshot of the current status of a job designed to grow in responsibility as its performer grows in capability. The presumption in a developing organization is that as jobs expand with personal growth, routine activities can be delegated to junior persons with activities requiring judgment and decision performed by fewer people at senior level. The route to lean organizations is through expansion of responsibility, with higher levels of compensation rewarding the efforts of fewer people.

But deliberately checking the counterstrategic influence of bureaucratization will not in itself ensure that people assigned to different tasks in different locations will spontaneously choose the best course toward even those goals to which in principle they are all committed. They will not automatically seek out the new skills they need as what they must accomplish becomes more complex. The innovative corporation is bent, to be sure, on preserving creativity, initiative, and the individual autonomy that make original contribution possible. But even such an organization, one more typical of the 1990s than the 1970s, will need a set of administrative systems that will attempt equitable evaluation of performance, effective stimulus and reward for achievement, reasonable discipline and enforcement of policy, and the development of management, technical specialists, and producers at all levels.

The first purpose of such systems is to focus individual energy on organizational goals in such a way that individual goals are not needlessly thwarted. Another function of such systems is to acquaint new members of the organization, before they are qualified to be autonomous contributors to innovation, with the ways things are done currently, the kind of organization they have joined, and the standards by which they will be judged. A less attractive but necessary purpose is to constrain behavior that is irrelevant or destructive. Commitment to purpose will prosper if it is rewarded but founder if it is taken for granted or ignored.

As you have probably observed, the processes we will look at have been studied and developed by specialists of several kinds. We will not attempt to summarize the state of the separate arts involved in influencing organizational behavior. We are concerned first with the limited but important ways in which the specialized bodies of knowledge can be put to use in the implementation of a given strategy rather than in the homogenization of organized activity. We will be suspicious of formality, rigidity, and uniformity but remain mindful that policy in the management of human resources is necessary for fairness and equitable opportunity for growth and advancement, for the protection of individuals against eccentric or biased management behavior, and for the defense of corporate strategy against willful opportunists pursuing their own purposes.

ESTABLISHMENT OF STANDARDS AND MEASUREMENT OF PERFORMANCE

In any organization the overall corporate strategy must be translated into more or less detailed plans that permit comparison of actual to predicted performance. Whether standards are being set at exactly the proper level is never demonstrable. Commitment to attainment comes from negotiation to strike the balance between unreasonable expectations and unchallenged potential. The establishment of a plan will usually include improvement in performance over previous levels, but problems in the marketplace may make plans unattainable. Evidence that plans may not be achieved by the time predicted should be the occasion for inquiry into the problem rather than immediate conclusion that performance is defective. The insecurity that shortfall produces in a manager aware of measurement and the counterstrategic action that such anxiety can produce commonly jeopardize achievement.

The most urgent duty of any manager is to see that properly planned results are indeed accomplished. The pressure of this duty may lead to exaggerated respect for specific measures and the short-run results they quantify and thus to ultimate misevaluation of performance. Ready recourse to alibis and refusal to admit the validity of changed circumstances as excuses are equally inappropriate. So is too quick a tendency to pass judgment rather than to take stock of the problem and to find new ways to deal with it. The problems of measurement cluster about the fallacy of the single criterion. When any single measure like return on investment, for example, is used to determine the compensation, promotion, or reassignment of a manager, the resultant behavior will often lead to unplanned and undesired outcomes. No single measure can encompass the total contribution of an individual either to immediate and longer term results or to the efforts of others. The sensitivity of individuals to evaluation leads them to produce the performance that will measure up in terms of the criterion rather than in terms of more important purposes. Since managers respond to the measures management actually takes to reward performance, mere verbal exhortations to behave in the manner required by long-range strategy carry no weight and cannot be relied upon to preclude undesirable actions encouraged by a poorly designed measurement and reward system.

Faith in the efficacy of a standard measure like return on investment can reach extreme proportions, especially among managers to whom the idea of strategy is apparently unfamiliar. Instances in which performance is measured in terms of just one figure or ratio are so numerous as to suggest that the pursuit of quantification and measurement as such has overshadowed the real goal of management evaluation. If we return to our original hypothesis that profit and return on investment are terms that can be usefully employed to denote the results to be sought by business, but are too general to characterize its distinctive mission or purpose, then we must say that *short-term profitability is not by itself an adequate measure of managerial performance.* Return on investment, when used alone, is another dangerous criterion since it can lead businesspeople to postpone needed product research or the modernization of facilities in the interest of keeping down the investment on the basis of which their performance is measured. Certainly we must conclude that evaluation of performance must not be focused exclusively upon the criterion of short-run profitability or any other single standard which may cause managers to act contrary to the long-range interests of the company as a whole.

Need for Multiple Criteria

As you discuss the cases that follow, you will be concerned with developing more adequate criteria. Our concern for strategy naturally leads us to suggest that the management evaluation system which plays so great a part in influencing management performance must employ a number of criteria, some of which are subjective and thus difficult to quantify. It is easy to argue that subjective judgments are unfair. But use of a harmful or irrelevant criterion just because it lends itself to quantification is a poor exchange for alleged objectivity.

If multiple criteria are to be used, it is not enough for top management simply to announce that short-term profitability and return on investment are only two measures among many—including responsibility to society—by which executives are going to be judged. To give subordinates freedom to exercise judgment and simultaneously to demand profitability produces an enormous pressure which cannot be effectively controlled by endless talk about tying rewards to factors other than profit.

The tragic predicament of people who, though upright in other ways, engage in bribery, "questionable payments," price fixing, and subtler forms of corruption, and of their superiors who are often unaware of these practices, should dramatize one serious flaw of the profit center form of organization. Characteristically management expects this format to solve the problems of evaluation by decentralizing freedom of decision to subordinates so long as profit objectives are met. Decentralization seems sometimes to serve as a cloak for nonsupervision, except for the control implicit in the superficial measure of profitability. It would appear to preclude accurate evaluation, and the use of multiple criteria may indeed make a full measure of decentralization inappropriate.

Effective Evaluation of Performance

To delegate authority to profit centers and to base evaluation upon proper performance must not mean that the profit center's strategic decisions are left unsupervised. *Even under decentralization, top management must remain familiar with divisional substrategy, with the fortunes—good and bad—that attend implementation, and with the problems involved in attempting to achieve budgeted performance.* The true function of measurement is to increase perceptions of the problems limiting achievement. If individuals see where they stand in meeting schedules, they may be led to inquire why they are not somewhere else. If this kind of question is not asked, the answer is not proffered. An effective system of evaluation must include information which will allow top management to understand the problems faced by subordinates in achieving the results for which they are held responsible. And certainly if evaluation is to be comprehensive enough to avoid the distortions cited thus far, immediate results will not be the only object of evaluation. The effectiveness with which problems are handled along the way will be evaluated, even though this judgment, like most of the important decisions of management, must remain subjective.

The process of formulating and implementing strategy, which is supervised directly by the chief executive in a single-unit company, can be shared widely in a multiunit company. It can be the theme of the information exchanged between organization levels. Preoccupation with final results need not be so exclusive as to prevent top management from working with divisional management in establishing objectives and policies or in formulating plans to meet objectives. Such joint endeavor helps to ensure that divisional performance will not be evaluated without full knowledge of the problems encountered in implementation.

When the diversified company becomes so large that this process is impracticable, then new means must be devised. *Implicit in accurate evaluation is familiarity with performance on a basis other than through accounting figures.*

A shared interest in the problems to be overcome in successfully implementing departmental and individual strategies makes possible a kind of communication, an accuracy of evaluation, and a constructive influence on behavior that cannot be approached by application of a single criterion. For one manager as for a whole company, the quality of objective and of subsequent attempts to overcome obstacles posed by circumstance and by competition is the most important aspect of a manager's performance to be evaluated.

INCENTIVES AND MOTIVATION

Of the varieties of incentives available to influence behavior toward the attainment of results, monetary compensation is the most conspicuous and important. Whatever the necessity for and the difficulties of performance evaluation, the effort to encourage and reward takes precedence over the effort to deter and restrain.

Unfortunately for the analyst of executive performance, it is harder to describe for executives than for operators at the machine what they do and how they spend their time. The terminology of job descriptions is full of phrases like "has responsibility for," "maintains relationships with," and "supervises the operation of." The activities of planning, problem solving, and directing or administering are virtually invisible. And the activities of recruiting, training, and developing subordinates are hardly more concretely identifiable.

In any case it is fallacious to assume that quality of performance is the only basis for the compensation of executives. Many other factors must be taken into account. The job itself has certain characteristics that help to determine the pay schedules. These include complexity of the work, the general education required, and the knowledge or technical training needed. Compensation also reflects the responsibility of job incumbents for people and property, the nature and number of decisions they must make, and the effect of their activities and decisions upon profits.

In addition to reflecting the quality of performance and the nature of the job, an executive's compensation must also have some logical relationship to rewards paid to others in the same organization.

Furthermore, in a compensation system, factors pertaining to the individual are almost as important as those pertaining to performance, the job, or the structure of the organization. People's age and length of service, the state of their health, some notion of their future potential, some idea of their material needs, and some insight into their views about all of these should influence either the amount of total pay or the distribution of total pay among base salary, bonuses, stock options, and other incentive measures.

Besides the many factors already listed, still another set of influences—this time coming from the environment—ordinarily affects the level of executive compensation. Included here are regional differences in the cost of living, the increments allowed for overseas assignment, the market price of given qualifications and experience, the level of local taxation, the desire for tax avoidance or delay, and the effect of high business salaries on other professions.

Just as multiple criteria are appropriate for the evaluation of performance, so many considerations must be taken into account in the compensation of executives. The company which says it pays only for results does not know what it is doing.

Role of Incentive Pay

In addition to the problem of deciding what factors to reward, there is the equally complex issue of deciding what forms compensation should take. We would emphasize that financial rewards are especially important in business, and no matter how great the enthusiasm of people for their work, attention to the level of executive salary is an important ingredient in the achievement of strategy. Even after the desired standard of living is attained, money is still an effective incentive. Businesspeople used to the struggle for profit find satisfaction in their own growing net worth.

There is no question about the desirability of paying high salaries for work of great value. But in addition, profit-sharing, executive bonuses, stock options, performance shares, stock purchase plans, deferred compensation contracts, pensions, insurance, savings plans, and other fringe benefits have multiplied enormously. Regarded as incentives to reward *individual* performance, many of these devices encounter two immediate objections. First, how compatible are the assumptions back of such rewards with the aspirations of the businessperson to be viewed as a professional? The student who begins to think of business as a profession will wonder what kind of executive will perform better with a profit-sharing bonus than with an equivalent salary. We may ask whether doctors should be paid according to the longevity of their patients and whether surgeons would try harder if given a bonus when their patients survived an operation. Second, how feasible is it to distinguish any one individual's contribution to the total accomplishment of the company? And even if contribution could be distinguished and correctly measured, what about the implications of the fact that the funds available for added incentive payments are a function of total rather than of individual performance? In view of these considerations, it can at least be argued that incentives for individual performance reflect dubious assumptions.

If, then, incentives are ruled out as an inappropriate or impractical means of rewarding individual effort, should they be cast out altogether? We believe not. There is certainly merit in giving stock options or performance shares to the group of executives most responsible for strategy decisions, if the purpose is to assure reward for attention to the middle and longer run future. There is some rationale for giving the same group current or even deferred bonuses, the amount of which is tied to annual profit, if the purpose is to motivate better cost control. Certainly, too, incentive payments to the key executive group must be condoned where needed to attract and hold the scarce managerial talent without which any strategy will suffer.

In any case, as you examine the effort made by companies to provide adequate rewards, to stimulate effective executive performance, and to inspire commitment to organizational purposes, you will wish to look closely at the relation between the incentive offered and the kind of performance needed. This observation holds as true, of course, for nonmonetary as it does for financial rewards.

Nonmonetary Incentives

The area of nonmonetary incentive systems is even more difficult to traverse quickly than that of financial objectives. Executives, as human as other employees, are as much affected as anyone else by pride in accomplishment, the climate for free expression, pleasure in able and honest associates, and satisfaction in work worth doing.

The climate most commonly extolled by managers is one in which they have freedom to experiment and apply their own ideas without unnecessary constraints. Given clear objectives and a broad consensus, then latitude can be safely granted to executives to choose their own course—so long as they do not conceal the problems they encounter. In other words, executives can be presumed to respond to the conditions likely to encourage the goal-oriented behavior expected of them.

We may not always know the influence exerted by evaluation, compensation, and promotion, but if we keep purpose clear and incentive systems simple, we may keep unintended distractions to a minimum. Above all we should be able to see the relevance to desired outcomes of the rewards offered. The harder it is to relate achievement to motives, the more cautious we should be in proposing an incentives program.

CONSTRAINTS AND CONTROL

Like the system of incentives, the system of restraints and controls should be designed with the requirements of strategy in mind, rather than the niceties of complex techniques and procedures. It is the function of penalties and controls to enforce rather than to encourage—to inhibit strategically undesirable behavior rather than to create new patterns. Motivation is a complex of both positive and negative influences. Working in conjunction, these induce desired performance and inhibit undesirable behavior.

The need for controls—even at the executive level—is rooted in the central facts of organization itself. The inevitable consequence of divided activity is the emergence of substrategies, which are at least slightly deflected from the true course by the needs of individuals and the concepts and procedures of specialized groups, each with its own quasi-professional precepts and ideals. We must have controls, therefore, even in healthy and competent organizations manned by people of goodwill who are aware of organization purpose.

Formal Control

Like other aspects of organizational structure and processes, controls may be both formal and informal, that is, both prescribed and emergent. Both types are needed, and both are important. It is, however, in the nature of things that management is more likely to give explicit attention to the formal controls that it has itself prescribed than to the informal controls emergent within particular groups or subgroups.

Formal and informal controls differ in nature as well as in their genesis. The former have to do with quantifiable data, the latter with subjective values and behavior. Formal control derives from accounting; it reflects the conventions and assumptions of that discipline and implies the prior importance of what can be quantified over what cannot. Its influence arises from the responsiveness of individuals—if subject to supervision and appraisal—to information that reveals variances between what is recorded as being expected of them and what is recorded as being achieved. If the information depicts variances from strategically desirable behavior, then it tends to direct attention toward strategic goals and to support goal-oriented policy. But if, as is more often the case, the information simply focuses on those short-run results which the state of the art can measure, then it directs effort toward performance which, if not undesirable, is at least biased toward short-run objectives.[1]

To emphasize the probable shortcomings of formal or quantifiable controls is not to assert that they have no value. Numbers do influence behavior—especially when pressures are applied to subordinates by superiors contemplating the same numbers. Numbers are essential in complex organizations since personal acquaintance with what is being accomplished and personal surveillance over it by an owner-

[1] See H. Thomas Johnson and Robert S. Kaplan, *Relevance Lost: The Rise and Fall of Management Accounting*, (Boston: Harvard Business School Press, 1987).

manager is no longer possible. As we have seen, the performance of individuals and subunits cannot be left to chance, even when acceptance and understanding of policy have been indicated and adequate competence and judgment are assured. Whether for surveillance from above or for self-control and self-guidance, numbers have a meaningful role to play, and well-selected numbers have a very meaningful role. We in no way mean to diminish the importance of figures but only to emphasize that numerical measurement must be supplemented by informal or social controls.

Integrating Formal and Social Control

Just as the idea of formal control is derived from accounting, the idea of informal control is derived from the inquiries of the behavioral sciences into the nature of organizational behavior. In all functioning groups, norms develop to which individuals are responsive if not obedient. These norms constitute the accepted way of doing things; they define the limits of proper behavior and the type of action that will meet with approval from the group. In view of the way they operate, the control we have in mind is better described as *social* rather than *informal*. It is embedded in activities, interactions, and sentiments characterizing group behavior. Sentiments take the form of likes and dislikes among people and evaluative judgments exercised upon each other. Negative sentiments, of great importance to their objects, may be activated by individual departure from a norm; such sentiments can either constitute a punishment in themselves or can lead to some other form of punishment.

The shortcomings of formal control based on quantitative measurements of performance can be largely obviated by designing and implementing a system in which formal and social controls are integrated. For example, meetings of groups of managers to discuss control reports can facilitate inquiry into the significance of problems lying behind variances, can widen the range of solutions considered, and can bring pressure to bear from peers as well as from superiors. All these features can in turn contribute to finding a new course of action which addresses the problem rather than the figures.

Enforcing Ethical Standards

One of the most vexing problems in attempting to establish a functional system of formal and social controls lies in the area of ethical standards. In difficult competitive situations, the pressure for results can lead individuals into illegal and unethical practices. Instead of countering this tendency, group norms may encourage yielding to these pressures. For example, knowing that others were doing the same thing undoubtedly influenced highly competitive branch managers, rewarded for profit, in a national brokerage firm to systematically overdraft their bank accounts to secure, in effect, interest-free loans of funds to invest. Recurring violations of price-fixing regulations, in industries beset by overcapacity and aggressive competition, are sometimes responses to pressures to meet sales and profit expectations of a distant home office.

When top management refuses to condone pursuit of company goals by unethical methods, it must resort to penalties like dismissal that are severe enough to dramatize its opposition. If a division sales manager, who is caught having arranged call-girl attentions for an important customer, against both the standards of expected behavior and the policy of the company, is not penalized at all, or only mildly because of the volume of his sales and the profit he generates, ethical standards will not long be of great importance. If he is fired, then his successor is likely to think twice about the means he employs to achieve the organizational purposes that are assigned to him. When, as has happened, a regional vice president of a large insurance firm is fired for misappropriating $250,000 of expense money but is retained as a consultant because he controls several millions of revenue, mixed signals are given which may confuse the communication but call attention to the dilemmas of enforcement.

But there are limits to the effectiveness of punishment, in companies as well as in families and in society. If violations are not detected, the fear of punishment tends to weaken. A system of inspection is therefore implicit in formal control. But besides its expense and complexity, such policing of behavior has the drawback of adversely affecting the attitudes of people toward their organizations. Their commitment to creative accomplishment is likely to be shaken, especially if they are the kinds of persons who are not likely to cut corners in the performance of their duties. To undermine the motivation of the ethically inclined is a high price to pay for detection of the weak. It is the special task of the internal audit function and the audit committee of the corporate board of directors not only to make investigation more effective but to minimize its negative police-state connotations and distortions.

The student of general management is thus confronted by a dilemma: if an organization is sufficiently decentralized to permit individuals to develop new solutions to problems and new avenues to corporate achievement, then the opportunity for wrongdoing cannot be eliminated. This being so, a system of controls must be supplemented by a selective system of executive recruitment and training. No system of control, no program of rewards and penalties, no procedures of measuring and evaluating performance can take the place of the individual who has a clear idea of right and wrong, a consistent personal policy, and the strength to stand the gaff when results suffer because he or she stands firm. His or her development is greatly assisted by the systems that permit the application of qualitative criteria and avoid the oversimplification of numerical measures. It is always the way systems are administered that determines their ultimate usefulness and impact.

RECRUITMENT AND DEVELOPMENT OF MANAGEMENT

Organizational behavior consistent with the accomplishment of purpose is the product of interacting *systems* of measures, motives, standards, incentives, rewards, penalties, and controls. Put another way, behavior is the outcome of *processes* of measurement, evaluation, motivation, and control. These systems and processes affect and shape the development of all individuals, most crucially those in management positions. Management development is therefore an ongoing process in all organizations, whether planned or not. As you examine cases which permit a wide-angled view of organizational activities, it is appropriate to inquire into the need to plan this development, rather than to let it occur as it will.

The supply of men and women who, of their own volition, can or will arrange for their own development is smaller than required. Advances in technology, the internationalization of markets, the progress of research on information processing, and above all, the unexplored territory into which the innovative corporation will repeatedly venture make it absurd to suppose that persons can learn all they will need to know from what they are currently doing. In particular, the activities of the general manager differ so much in kind from those of other management that special preparation for the top job should be considered. In addition to assignment to a planned succession of jobs in different areas, this may include attendance at university programs of executive education, custom-tailored opportunity to study business-government relationships, or membership on the board of another company or a public service organization.

Strategy can be our guide to (1) the skills which will be required to perform the critical tasks; (2) the number of persons with specific skill, age, and experience characteristics who will be required in the light of planned growth and predicted attrition; and (3) the number of new individuals of requisite potential who must be recruited to ensure the availability, at the appropriate time, of skills that require years to develop.

No matter what the outcome of these calculations, it can safely be said that every organization must actively recruit new talent if it aims to maintain its position and to grow. These recruits should have adequate ability not only for filling the junior positions to which they are initially called but also for learning the management skills needed to advance to higher positions. Like planning of all kinds, recruiting must be done well ahead of the actual need. The choice of new members of an organization may be the most crucial function of management development and the most telling test of judgment.

The labor force requirements imposed by commitment to a strategy of growth mean quite simply that men and women overqualified for conventional beginning assignments must be sought out and carefully cultivated thereafter. Individuals who respond well to the opportunities devised for them should be assigned to establish organization positions and given responsibility as fast as capacity to absorb it is indicated. To promote rapidly is not the point so much as to maintain the initial momentum and to provide work to highly qualified individuals that is both essential and challenging. The innovative company will find challenge for rapidly developing competence; it cannot remain innovative without doing so.

Continuing Education

The rise of professional business education and the development of advanced management programs make formal training available to men and women not only at the beginning of their careers but also at appropriate intervals thereafter. Short courses for executives are almost always stimulating and often of permanent value. But management development as such is predominantly an organizational process which must be supported, not thwarted, by the incentive and control systems to which we have already alluded. Distribution of rewards and penalties will effectively determine how much attention executives will give to the training of their subordinates. No amount of lip service will take the place of action in establishing effective management development as an important management activity. To evaluate managers in part on their effort and effectiveness in bringing along their juniors requires subjective measures and a time span longer than one fiscal year. These limitations do not seriously impede judgment, especially when both strategy and the urgency of its implications for manpower development are clearly known.

In designing on-the-job training, a focus on strategy makes possible a substantial economy of effort in that management development and management evaluation can be carried on together. The evaluation of performance can be simultaneously administered as an instrument of development. For example, any manager could use a conference with his superiors not only to discuss variances from budgeted departmental performance but also to discover how far his or her suggested solutions are appropriate or inappropriate and why. In all such cases discussion of objectives proposed, problems encountered, and results obtained provides opportunities for inquiry, for instruction and counsel, and for learning what needs to be done and at what level of effectiveness.

Besides providing an ideal opportunity for learning, concentration on objectives permits delegation to juniors of choice of means and other decision-making responsibilities otherwise hard to come by. Throughout the top levels of the corporation, if senior management is spending adequate time on the surveillance of the environment and on the study of strategic alternatives, then the responsibility for day-to-day operations must necessarily be delegated. Since juniors cannot learn how to bear responsibility without having it, this necessity is of itself conducive to learning. If, within limits, responsibility for the choice of means to obtain objectives is also delegated, opportunity is presented for innovation, experimentation, and creative approaches to problem solving. Where ends rather than means are the object of attention and agreement exists on what ends are and should be, means may be allowed to vary at the discretion of the developing junior manager. The clearer the company's goals, the smaller the emphasis that must be placed on uniformity and the greater the opportunity for initiative. Freedom to make mistakes and achieve success is more productive in developing executive skills than practice in following detailed how-to-do-it instructions designed by superiors or staff specialists. Commitment to purpose rather than to procedures appears to energize initiative.

Management Development and Corporate Purpose

A stress on purpose rather than on procedures suggests that organizational climate, though intangible, is more important to individual growth than the mechanisms of personnel administration. The development of each individual in the direction best suited both to his or her own powers and to organizational needs is most likely to take place in the company where everybody is encouraged to work at the height of his or her ability and is rewarded for doing so. Such a company must have a clear idea of what it is and what it intends to become. With this idea sufficiently institutionalized so that organization members grow committed to it, the effort required for achievement will be forthcoming without elaborate incentives and coercive controls. Purpose, especially if considered worth accomplishing, is the most powerful incentive to accomplishment. If goals are not set high enough, they must be reset—as high as developing creativity and accelerating momentum suggest.

In short, from the point of view of general management, management development is not a combination of staff activities and formal training designed to provide neophytes with a common body of knowledge or to produce a generalized good manager. Rather, development is inextricably linked to organizational purpose, which shapes to its own requirements the kind, rate, and amount of development which takes place. It is a process by which men and women are professionally equipped to be—as far as possible in advance of the need—what the evolving strategy of the firm requires them to be, at the required level of excellence.

Chief executives will have a special interest of their own in the process of management development. For standards of performance, measures for accurate evaluation, incentives, and controls will have a lower priority in their eyes than a committed organization, manned by people who know what they are supposed to do and committed to the overall ends to which their particular activities contribute.

* * * * *

In examining the cases that follow and in reflecting on the companies already examined, try to identify the strategy of the company and the structure of relationships established to implement it. What pattern of possible incentives encouraging appropriate behavior can be identified? Do they converge on desired outcomes? What restraints and controls discouraging inappropriate behavior are in force? What changes in measurement, incentive, and control systems would you recommend to facilitate achievement of goals? If your analysis of the company's situation suggests that strategy and structure should be changed, such recommendations should, of course, precede your suggested plans for effective implementation.

Basic Industries

In May 1966 Pete Adams, plant manager of Basic Industries' Chicago plant, was worried about the new facilities proposal for Toranium. His division, Metal Products, was asking for $1 million to build facilities that would be at full capacity in less than a year and a half, if forecast sales were realized. Yet the divisional vice president for production seemed more interested in where the new facility was to go than in how big it should be. Adams wondered how his salary and performance review would look in 1968 with the new facility short of capacity.

METAL PRODUCTS DIVISION

Basic Industries engaged in a number of activities ranging from shipbuilding to the manufacture of electronic components. The corporation was organized into five autonomous divisions (see Exhibit 1), which in 1965 had sales totaling $500 million. Of the five, the Metal Products Division was the most profitable. In 1965, this division realized an aftertax income of $16 million on sales of $110 million and an investment of $63.7 million.

Metal Products had not always held this position of profit leadership within the company. In fact, in the early 1950s Basic's top management had considered dropping the division. At that time, the division's market share was declining owing to high costs, depressed prices, and a lack of manufacturing facilities.

A change in divisional management resulted in a market improvement. Between 1960 and 1965, for example, the division's sales grew at 8 percent a year and profits grew at 20 percent a year. The division's ROI rose from 12 to 25 percent over the same period.

Ronald Brewer, president of Metal Products Division since 1955, explained how this growth had been achieved.

> Planning goes on in many places in the Metal Products Division, but we do go through a formal planning process to establish goals. We establish very specific goals for products and departments in every phase of the business. This formal and detailed planning is worked out on a yearly basis. We start at the end of the

Harvard Business School case 313–121.

second quarter to begin to plan for the following year.

We plan on the basis of our expectations as to the market. If it's not there, we live a little harder. We cut back to assure ourselves of a good cash flow. Our record has been good, but it might not always be. Some of our products are 30 years old. We've just invested $5 million, which is a lot of money for our division, in expanding capacity for a 25-year-old product. But we're making money out of it and it's growing.

Along with detailed planning for the year to come, we ask for plans for years three and four. Our goal is to make sure that we can satisfy demand.

Any time we approach 85 percent of capacity at one of our plants, our engineers get busy. They will give the plant manager the information as to what he needs in the way of new equipment. The plant manager will then fit the engineer's recommendation into his expansion plans. The plant manager's plan then goes to our control manager. The marketing people then add their forecasts, and by that time we have built up the new facilities proposal.

On the other hand, the marketing people may have spearheaded the project. Sometimes they alert the plant manager to a rapid growth in his product, and he goes to the engineers. In this division, everyone is marketing-minded. . . . We measure plants, and they measure their departments against plan. For example, we have a rule of thumb that a plant must meet its cost reduction goals. So if one idea doesn't work out, a plant must find another one to get costs to the planned level. We make damned sure that we make our goals as a division. Our objective is to have the best product in the market at the lowest cost. It's a simple concept, but the simpler the concept, the better it's understood.

Well, on the basis of his performance against plan, a man is looked at by his superior at least once a year, maybe more. We take a pretty hard-nosed position with a guy. We tell him what we think his potential is, where he is going to go, what he is going to be able to do. We have run guys up *and* down the ladder. In this division, it's performance and fact that count. We have no formal incentive plan, but we do recognize performance with salary increases and with promotions.

You know, we have divisions in this company which are volume happy. We here are profit conscious—we had to be to survive. What I'd like to see is interest allocated on a pro rata basis according to total investment. I grant you that this would hurt some of the other divisions more than us, but I think that treating interest as a corporate expense, as we do, changes your marketing philosophy and your pricing philosophy.

For example, most new facilities proposals are wrong with respect to their estimates of market size—volume attainable at a given price—and timing. You can second-guess a forecast, though, in several ways and hedge to protect yourself. There is a feeling at Basic Industries that there is a stigma attached to coming back for more money. That means that if you propose a project at the bare minimum requirement and then come back for more, some people feel that you've done something wrong. Generally, this leads to an overestimate of the amount of capital required. It turns out that if you have the money you do spend it, so that this stigma leads to overspending on capital projects. We at Metal Products are trying to correct this. First, we screen projects closely. We go over them with a fine-toothed comb. Second, internally, we set a goal to spend less than we ask for where there is a contingency.

Also, when a project comes in at an estimated 50 percent return, we cut the estimate down. Everyone does. The figure might go out at 30 percent. But this practice works the other way too. For example, in 1958 Bill Mason [Metal Products' vice president of production] and I worked like hell to get a project through; although it looked like 8 percent on paper, we knew that we could get the costs way down once it got going, so we put it through at 12 percent. We're making double that on it today. We haven't had a capital request rejected by the finance committee in eight years [see Exhibit 1].

Of course, every once in a while we shoot some craps, but not too often. We are committed to a specific growth rate in net income and ROI. Therefore, we are selective in what we do and how we spend our money. It's seldom that we spend $500,000 to develop something until we know it's got real market potential. You just don't send 100 samples out and then forecast a flood of orders. New products grow slowly. It takes six or seven years. And, given that it takes this long, it doesn't take a lot of capital to develop and test out new ideas. Before you really invest, you've done your homework. Over the years we've done a good job in our new products, getting away from the aircraft industry. In 1945, 70 percent of our business was based on aircraft. Today it's 40 percent. The way we do things protects us. We have to have a very strong sense of the technical idea and the scope of the market before we invest heavily.

Metal Products Division's main business was producing a variety of basic and rare nonferrous metals and alloys such as nickel, nickel-beryllium, and titanium in a myriad of sizes and shapes for electrical, mechanical, and structural uses in industry. One of the division's major strengths was its leadership in high-performance material technology, thanks to patents and a great deal of proprietary experience. Metal Products had a substantial technological lead on the competition.

TORANIUM

In the late 1950s Metal Products decided to follow its technological knowledge and proprietary production skills into the high-performance materials market. One of Metal Products' most promising new materials was Toranium, for which Jim Roberts was product manager.

Roberts was 33 years old and had a Ph.D. in chemical engineering. Prior to becoming a product manager, he had worked in one of Metal Products' research labs. Roberts explained some of Toranium's history:

> Developing Toranium was a trial-and-error process. The lab knew that the properties of the class of high-performance materials to which Toranium belonged were unusually flexible and therefore felt such materials had to be useful. So it was an act of faith that led R&D to experiment with different combinations of these materials. They had no particular application in mind.
>
> In 1957 we developed the first usable Toranium. Our next problem was finding applications for it. It cost $50 a pound. However, since a chemist in the lab thought we could make it for less, we began to look for applications.
>
> In 1962 I entered the picture. I discovered it was an aerospace business. When the characteristics of our material were announced to the aerospace people, they committed themselves to it. Our competitors were asleep. They weren't going to the customer. I went out and called on the customers and developed sales.
>
> In 1963 we decided to shift the pilot plant from the lab and give it to the production people at Akron. We decided that we simply were not getting a good production-oriented consideration of the process problems. The people at Akron cut the costs by two thirds, and the price stayed the same.

In 1963 I also chose to shut off R&D on Toranium because it couldn't help in the marketplace. We had to learn more in the marketplace before we could use and direct R&D.

I ought to mention that, under the management system used by Mr. Samuels [vice president of R&D], the product manager—along with R&D and production—shares in the responsibility for monitoring and directing an R&D program. This arrangement is part of an attempt to keep everyone market oriented.

From 1962 to 1965, sales of Toranium increased from $250,000 a year to $1 million a year just by seeking them, and in 1965 we put R&D back in.

This material can't miss. It has a great combination of properties: excellent machinability, thermal shock resistance, and heat insulation. Moreover, it is an excellent electrical conductor. We can sell all that we can produce. Customers are coming to us with their needs. They have found that Toranium's properties and our technical capacities are superior to anything or anyone in the market.

Moreover, pricing has not been a factor in the development of markets to date. In fact, sales have been generated by the introduction of improved grades of Toranium at premium prices. Presently, General Electric represents our only competition, but we expect that Union Carbide will be in the marketplace with competitive materials during the next few years. However, I don't expect anyone to be significantly competitive before 1968. Anyway, competition might actually help a little bit in expanding the market and stimulating the customers, as well as in educating our own R&D [people].

Now, if one assumes that no other corporation will offer significant competition to Toranium until 1968, the only real uncertainty in our forecasts for Toranium is related to Metal Products' technical and marketing abilities. R&D must develop the applications it is currently working on, and production will have to make them efficiently.

This production area can be a real headache. For example, R&D developed a Toranium part for one of our fighter bombers. However, two out of three castings cracked. On the other hand, we've got the best skills in the industry with respect to high-pressure casting. If we can't do it, no one can.

The final uncertainty is new demand. I've got to bring in new applications, but that shouldn't be a problem. You know, I've placed Toranium samples with over 17 major customers. Can you imagine what will happen if even two or three of them pay off? As far as I'm concerned, if the forecasts for Toranium are inaccurate, they're underestimates of future sales.

NEW FACILITIES PROPOSAL

Sam Courtney, district works manager (to whom the plant managers of the Chicago, Akron, and Indianapolis plants reported), explained the origin of the new Toranium facilities proposal:

> The product manager makes a forecast once a year, and when it comes time to make major decisions, he makes long-range forecasts. In January 1965 we were at 35 percent of the Toranium pilot-plant capacity. At that time we said, "We have to know beyond 1966; we need a long-range forecast. Volume is beginning to move up."
>
> The production control manager usually collects the forecasts. Each year it is his responsibility to see where we are approaching 85 or 90 percent of capacity. When that is the case in some product line, he warns the production vice president. However, in this instance, Toranium was a transition product, and Akron [where the pilot plant was located] picked up the problem and told the

> manager of product forecasting that we were in trouble.

The long-range forecast that Courtney requested arrived at his office early in March 1965 and clearly indicated a need for new capacity. Moreover, Roberts's 1966 regular forecast, which was sent to production in October 1965, was 28 percent higher than the March long-range projection. It called for additional capacity by October 1966.

Courtney's first response was to request a new long-range forecast. He also authorized the Akron plant to order certain equipment on which there would be a long lead time. The district works manager explained, "It is obvious we are going to need additional capacity in a hurry, and the unique properties of Toranium require special, made-to-order equipment. We can't lose sales. Producing Toranium is like coining money."

At the same time, Courtney began discussions on the problem with Bill Mason, vice president of production for Metal Products. They decided that the Akron plant was probably the wrong location in which to expand the Toranium business. Courtney commented, "There are 20 products being produced at Akron, and that plant cannot possibly give Toranium the kind of attention it deserves. The business is a new one, and it needs to be cared for like a young child. They won't do that in a plant with many important, large-volume products. We have decided over a period of years that Akron is too complex, and this seems like a good time to do something about it."

The two locations proposed as new sites for the Toranium facilities were Pittsburgh and Chicago. Each was a one-product plant that "could use product diversification." While Pittsburgh seemed to be favored initially, Mason and Courtney were concerned that the Toranium would be contaminated if it came in contact with the rather dirty products produced at Pittsburgh. Therefore, Courtney asked engineering to make studies of both locations.

The results of these initial studies were inconclusive. The Pittsburgh plant felt that the problem of contamination was not severe, and the economic differential between the locations was not substantial.

After the initial studies were completed, Roberts's new long-range forecast arrived. Table 1 compares this forecast with Roberts's previous ones.

In response to this accelerating market situation, Courtney and Mason asked Adams, plant manager at Chicago, to make a "full-fledged study of the three locations" (Akron, Pittsburgh, and Chicago). At the same time, Mason told Brewer, president of Metal Products:

> We're now about 90 percent certain that Chicago will be the choice. Associated

TABLE 1
ACTUAL AND PROJECTED SALES
In Millions of Dollars

Date of Forecast	*1965*	*1966*	*1967*	*1968*	*1969*	*1970*	*1971*
Projected Sales							
March 1964	1.08	1.3	—	—	2.2	—	—
March 1965	1.17	1.4	1.6	—	—	2.8	—
March 1966	—	1.8	2.5	3.4	—	—	5.6
Actual Sales	1.0	—	—	—	—	—	—

with the newness of the material is a rapidly changing technology. The Metal Products R&D center at Evanston is only 10 minutes away. Another important factor is Adams. Titanium honeycomb at Chicago was in real trouble. We couldn't even cover our direct costs. Adams turned it around by giving it careful attention. That's the kind of job Toranium needs.

Peter Adams was 35 years old. He had worked for Basic since he graduated from college with a B.S. in engineering. After spending a year in the corporate college training program, Adams was assigned to the Metal Products Division. There he worked as an assistant to the midwestern district manager for production. Before becoming Chicago plant manager in 1963, Adams had been the assistant manager at the same plant for two years.

In working through the financial data on the Toranium project, Adams chose to compare the three sites with respect to internal rates of return (see Table 2). He made this comparison for the case where capacity was expanded to meet forecast sales for 1967 ($2.5 million), the case where capacity was expanded to meet forecast sales for 1971 ($5.6 million), and the case where capacity was expanded from $2.5 to $5.6 million.

While the economics favored Akron, Adams was aware that Mason favored Chicago. This feeling resulted from conversations with Courtney about the Toranium project. Courtney pointed out the importance of quality, service to customers, liaison with R&D, and production flexibility to a new product like Toranium. Furthermore, Courtney expressed the view that Chicago looked good in these respects, despite its cost disadvantage. He also suggested that a proposal asking for enough capacity to meet 1967 forecast demand would have the best prospects for divisional acceptance.

By the end of April 1966, Adams's work had progressed far enough to permit preparation of a draft of a new facilities proposal recommending a Chicago facility. Except for the marketing story he obtained from Roberts, he had written the entire text. On May 3 Adams brought the completed draft to New York for a discussion with Mason and Courtney. The meeting, which was quite informal, began with Adams reading his draft proposal aloud to the group. Mason and Courtney commented on the draft as he went along. Some of the more substantial comments are included in the following excerpts from the meeting.

TABLE 2
COMPARISON OF SITES AND INTERNAL RATES OF RETURN
In Thousands of Dollars

	Chicago	*Pittsburgh*	*Akron*
1. Incremental capital investment for capacity through 1967	$ 980	$1,092	$ 675
Internal rate of return	34%	37%	45%
2. Incremental capital investment for capacity through 1971	$1,342	$1,412	$1,272
Internal rate of return	52%	54%	55%
3. Incremental capital investment to raise capacity from $2.5 to $5.6 million	$ 710	$ 735	$ 740
Internal rate of return	45%	47%	46%

MEETING ON THE DRAFT PROPOSAL

Adams: We expect that production inefficiencies and quality problems will be encountered upon start-up of the new facility in Chicago. In order to prevent these problems from interfering with the growth of Toranium, the new facilities for producing Toranium powder, pressing ingots, and casting finished products will be installed in Chicago and operated until normal production efficiency is attained. At that time, existing Akron equipment will be transferred to the Chicago location. Assuming early approval of the project, Chicago will be in production in the first quarter of 1967, and joint Akron and Chicago operations will continue through September 1967. The Akron equipment will be transferred in October and November 1967, and Chicago will be in full operation in December 1967.

Mason: Wait a minute! You're not in production until the first quarter of 1967, and the forecasts say we are going to be short in 1966!

Adams: There is a problem in machinery order lag.

Mason: Have you ordered a press?

Adams: Yes, and we'll be moving by October.

Mason: Well, then, say you'll be in business in the last quarter of 1966. Look, Pete, this document has to be approved by Brewer and then the finance committee. If Chicago's our choice, we've got to *sell* Chicago. Let's put our best foot forward!

The problem is to make it clear that, on economics alone, we would go to Akron . . . but you have to bring out the flaw in the economics: that managing 20 product lines, especially when you've got fancy products, just isn't possible.

Courtney: And you have a better building.

Mason: All of this should be in a table in the text. It ought to cover incremental cost, incremental investment, incremental expense, incremental ROI, and the building space.

And Sam's right. Akron is a poor building; it's a warehouse. Pittsburgh is better for something like high-pressure materials. But out in Chicago you've got a multistory building with more than enough space that is perfect for this sort of project.

Courtney: Pete, are we getting this compact enough for you?

Mason: Hey, why don't we put some sexy-looking graphs in the thing? I don't know, but maybe we could plot incremental investment versus incremental return for each location. See what you can do, Pete.

Courtney: Yes, that's a good idea.

Mason: Now, Pete, one other thing. You'll have to include discounted cash flow on the other two locations. Some of those guys [division and corporate top management] are going to look at just the numbers. You'll show them they're not too different.

Mason: [*A bit later in the discussion*] The biggest discussion will be, "Why the hell move to Chicago?"

Courtney: You know, Pete, you should discuss the labor content in the product.

Mason: Good. We have to weave in the idea that it's a product with a low labor content and explain that this means the high Chicago labor cost will not hurt us.

Adams: One last item: Shouldn't we be asking for more capacity? Two and one-half million dollars only carries us through 1967.

Mason: Pete, we certainly wouldn't do this for one of our established products.

Where our main business is involved, we build capacity in five- and ten-year chunks. But we have to treat Toranium a little differently. The problem here is to take a position in the market. Competition isn't going to clobber us if we don't have the capacity to satisfy everyone. If the market develops, we can move quickly.

After the meeting, Courtney explained that he and Mason had been disappointed with Adams's draft and were trying to help him improve it without really "clobbering" him. "Adams's draft was weak. His numbers were incomplete and his argument sloppy. I've asked him to meet with Bob Lincoln [assistant controller for Metal Products] to discuss the proposal."

The result of Adams's five meetings with Lincoln was three more drafts of the Toranium proposal. The numerical exhibits were revised for greater clarity and the text was revised to lessen the number of technical terms.

Adams, however, was still very much concerned with the appropriate size of the new facility. "Mason is only interested in justifying the location of the new facility!" Adams exclaimed. "We plan to sell $5.6 million worth of Toranium in 1971, yet we're asking for only $2.5 million worth of capacity. It's crazy! But, you know, I think Mason doesn't really care what capacity we propose. He just wants 'sexy-looking graphs.' That's OK for him, because I'm the one who's going to get it in the neck, in 1968. So far as I can see, Brewer has built his reputation by bringing this division from chronic undercapacity to a full-capacity, high ROI position."

The next step in the Toranium facilities proposal was a formal presentation to the top management of Metal Products on June 2, 1966. There were two capital projects on the agenda. Brewer began the meeting by announcing that its purpose was to "discuss the proposals and decide if they were any good." He turned the meeting over to Mason, who in turn asked Adams to "take over and direct the meeting."

Adams began reading the draft proposal, after first asking for comments. He had gotten halfway down the first page when Brewer interrupted.

Brewer: Let me stop you right here. You have told them [*the proposal was aimed at Basic Industries' financial committee*] the name, and you have told them how much money you want, but you haven't told them what the name means, and you haven't told them what the products are.

At this point a discussion began as to what the name of the project was going to be. The meeting then continued with Adams reading and people occasionally making comments on his English and on the text.

Brewer: Look, let's get this straight. What we are doing in this proposal is trying to tell them what it is we are spending their money on. That's what they want to know. Tell me about the electronic applications in that table you have there. I have to be able to explain them to the finance committee. I understand "steel" and "aerospace" but I don't understand "electronic applications" and I don't understand "electronic industry." I need some more specific words.

Samuels: [*Vice President of R&D*] Let me ask you a question which someone in the finance committee might ask. It's a nasty one. You forecast here that the industry sales in 1971 are going to be about $7 million, or maybe a little less. You think we are going to have 75 or 85 percent of this business. You also think we are going to get competition from GE and others. Do you think companies of that stature are going to be satisfied with sharing $1.5 million of the business? Don't you think that we may lose some of our market share?

This question was answered by Roberts and pursued by a few others. Essentially Roberts argued that the proprietary technology of the Metal Products Division was going to be strong enough to defend its market share.

Brewer: Let me tell you about an item which is much discussed in the finance committee. They are concerned—and basically this involved other divisions—with underestimating the cost of investment projects. I think, in fact, that there was a request for additional funds on a project recently which was as large as our entire annual capital budget [$7.9 million in 1965]. Second of all, as a result of the capital expenditure cutback, there was a tendency—and again it has been in other divisions—to cut back on or delay facilities. Now, it's not really just the capital expenditure cutback that is the reason for their behavior. If they had been doing their planning, they should have been thinking about these expenditures five or six years ago, not two years ago. But they didn't do the estimates, or their estimates weren't correct, and now they are sold out on a lot of items and are buying products from other people and reselling them and not making any money. It's affecting the corporate earnings, so the environment in the finance committee today is very much (1) "Tell us how much you want, and tell us *all* that you want," and (2) "Give us a goddamned good return." Now I don't want us to get *sloppy,* but, Bill, if you need something, ask for it. And then make Pete meet his numbers.

Adams: Well, on this one, as I think you may know, the machinery is already on order, and we are sure that our market estimates are correct.

Brewer: Yes, I know that. I just mean that if you want something, then plan it right and tell them what you are going to need so you don't come back asking for more money six months later.

Brewer: I am going to need some words on competition. I am also going to need some words on why we are ready so soon on this project. We are asking for money now, and we say we are going to be in operation in the fourth quarter.

Samuels: Foresight [*followed by some general laughter*].

Mason: Well, it's really quite understandable. This began last October, when we thought we were going to expand at Akron. At that time, it was obvious that we needed capacity, so we ordered some machines. Then, as the thing developed, it was clear that there would be some other things we needed, and because of the timing lag we had to order them.

Brewer: OK, now another thing. Numerical control is hot as a firecracker in the finance committee. I am not saying that we should have it on this project, but you should be aware that the corporation is thinking a lot about it.

Brewer: [*Much later in the discussion*] There are really three reasons for moving. Why not state them? (1) You want to free up some space at Akron, which you need. (2) There are 20 products at Akron, and Toranium can't get the attention it needs. (3) You can get operating efficiencies if you move.

> If you set it out, you can cut out all of this "crap." You know, it would do you people some good if you read a facilities proposal on something you didn't know beforehand. [The finance committee reviewed about 190 capital requests in 1965.] You really have to think about the guy who doesn't know what you're talking about. I read a proposal yesterday that was absolutely ridiculous. It had pounds per hour and tons per year and tons per month and tons per day and—except for the simplest numbers, which were in a table—all the rest were spread out through the story.

The meeting continued for several hours, taking up other agenda items.

Adams indicated that he was disappointed with the meeting. Brewer seemed to him to be preoccupied with "words," and the topic of additional capacity never really came up. The only encouraging sign was Brewer's statement, "Tell us all that you want." But it seemed that all Mason "wanted" was $2.5 million worth of capacity.

Adams saw three possibilities open to him. First, he could ask for additional capacity. This alternative meant that Adams would have to speak with Courtney and Mason, and, as Chicago plant manager, he viewed the prospect of such a conversation with mixed feelings. In the past his relations with Courtney and Mason had been excellent. He had been able to deal with these men on an informal and relaxed level. However, the experience of drafting the Toranium proposal left Adams a little uneasy. Courtney and Mason had been quite critical of his draft and had made him meet with Bob Lincoln to revise it. What would be their reaction if he were to request a reconsideration of the proposal at this late date? Moreover, what new data or arguments could he offer in support of a request for additional capacity?

On the other hand, Adams saw a formal request for additional capacity as a way of getting his feelings formally on record. Even if his superiors refused his request, he would be in a better position with respect to the 1968 performance review. However, Adams wondered how his performance review would go if he formally requested and received additional capacity and then the market did not develop as forecast.

As his second alternative, Adams believed he could ask that the new facilities proposal specify that Metal Products would be needing more money for Toranium facilities in the future. This alternative did not pose the same problems as the first with respect to Courtney and Mason. Adams felt that saying more funds might be needed would be acceptable to Courtney and Mason, whereas asking for more might not be. However, the alternative introduced a new problem. Brewer had been quite explicit on insisting that the division ask for all that was needed, so that it would not have to come back and ask for more in six months. To admit a possible need for additional funds, therefore, might jeopardize the entire project.

In spite of this drawback, Adams felt that this alternative was the best one available. It was a compromise between his point of view and Mason's. And, if top management felt that the future of Toranium was too uncertain, then why not ask for contingent funds? This would get Adams off the hook and still not actually increase Metal Products' real investment.

As his third alternative, Adams decided he could drop the issue and hope to be transferred or promoted before 1968.

EXHIBIT 1
ORGANIZATION CHART

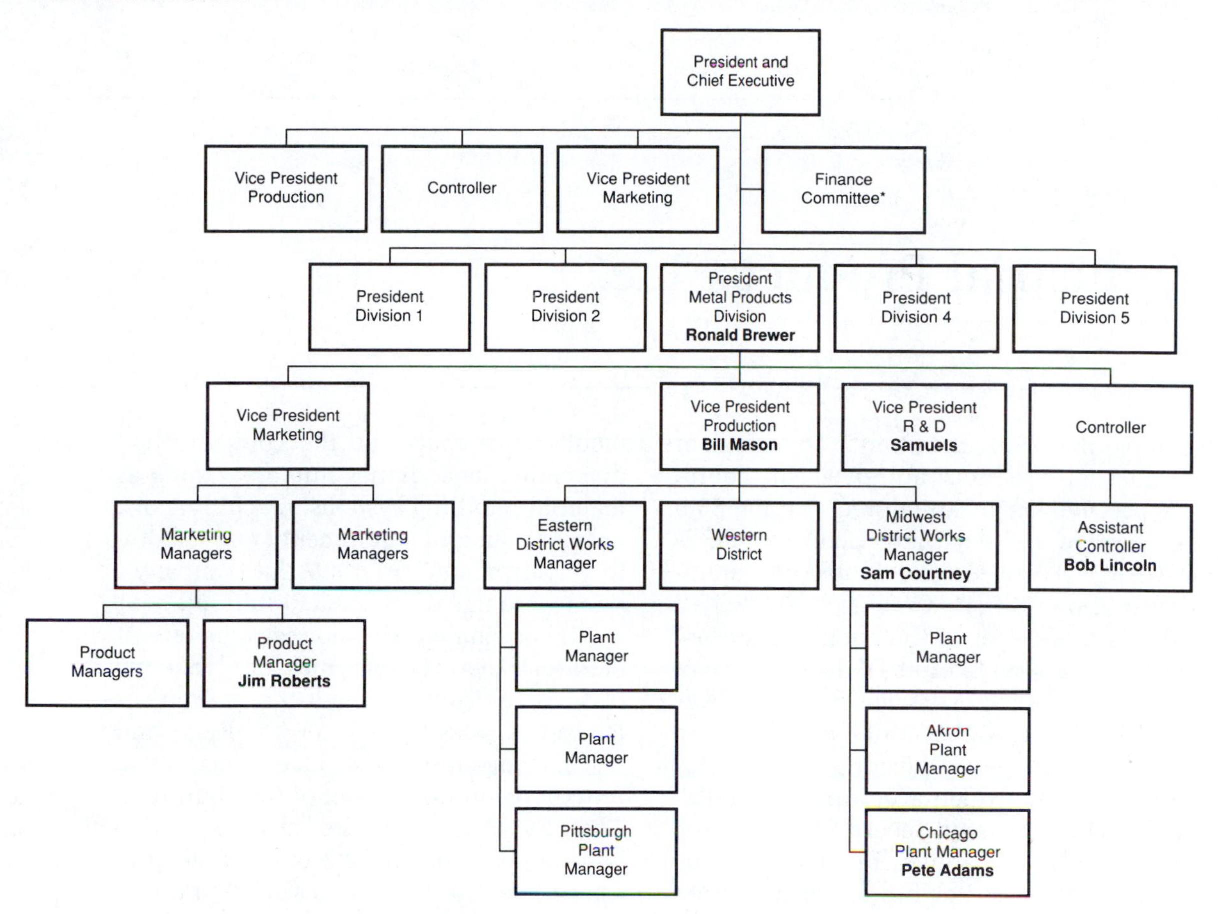

*Chairman, president of Basic; members included divisional presidents and corporate vice presidents.

Source: Casewriter's notes.

Industrial Products, Inc.

On April 5, 1967, the finance committee of Industrial Products approved its Equipment Division's capital request for $5.8 million to build a new plant for FIREGUARD, a line of fire protection equipment. However, in October 1967 Robert Kendall, manager of the chemical process department (see Exhibit 1), the department in which FIREGUARD was produced, was considering the possibility of killing the expansion project. Divisional pressure for improved departmental earnings and FIREGUARD's continued record of substantial operating losses argued for not using the appropriated capital funds. On the other hand, Kendall was well aware that many people in his department were committed to growing this business and would be quite upset if the project were killed. Kendall had to make his decision in the following context.

EQUIPMENT DIVISION

Industrial Products was founded in 1949 as a producer of refrigeration equipment. Since that time the company had diversified its activities into areas such as material-handling systems, machine tools, heavy industrial equipment, and laboratory instruments. In 1966 the company's sales were in excess of $350 million.

The Equipment Division was the largest of Industrial's divisions, measured in terms of sales revenue. In 1966, the Equipment Division's sales were $135.4 million, and its net income before taxes was $31.2 million on an investment of $96.5 million. The division's new fire protection line contributed sales of $2.2 million but produced a net loss before taxes of $1.1 million in 1966. However, with forecast potential sales in excess of $30 million per year and forecast net income before taxes in excess of $6.0 million per year, FIREGUARD was considered one of the most promising new products in the Equipment Division.

FIREGUARD

In its continuing work on refrigerants, the Equipment Division's refrigeration department had developed a number of new plastic materials that exhibited superior fire extinguishing properties. At the same time, the division already produced some

Harvard Business School case 369–019.

of the kinds of equipment needed to extinguish fires. Because both the equipment and materials required were readily available in existing businesses, experimental and then commercial sales soon followed. The brand name under which the division developed this business was FIREGUARD.

Division management was highly optimistic concerning FIREGUARD's commercial prospects. Whereas all automatic fire extinguishing equipment required extensive piping to create a system, FIREGUARD was able to operate with a number of physically independent modules. Thus, the size of a FIREGUARD system depended principally on the number of module units in the area to be protected.

The source of FIREGUARD's advantage lay in the chemical process used to extinguish fires. The Equipment Division's scientists had discovered a relatively inexpensive chemical substance they called NO-OX that expanded with explosive speed when exposed to air, reacting with the oxygen to free a heavy inert gas. The fire extinction properties of the gas were immediately recognized as superb.

The attack on the fire protection and extinguishing market called for early sales of single module equipment to the "traditional" market for portable extinguishers (local governments, schools, fire departments, industrial plants, commercial offices). Sales of automatic fire protection systems to the same users would follow. Finally, the strategy called for expanding primary demand by eventually introducing automatic residential systems. The automatic systems market was entered for the first time during 1966. The following list shows sales of the portable units from 1961 to 1966.

	Number of Units
1961	400
1962	820
1963	1,450
1964	1,985
1965	3,775
1966	4,362

The FIREGUARD business was the responsibility of Robert Kendall, manager of the Equipment Division's chemical process department (see the organization chart, Exhibit 1). The department manufactured and sold equipment for chemical manufacturing processes. In 1960 the division's general manager, Lon Fischer, had become concerned with the quality of performance in the manufacturing and construction of chemical process equipment while it was part of the general refrigeration area and had reorganized the activity in a new department—chemical processes—so that "the chemical phase of the business could get separate attention." Because FIREGUARD was a "chemical" business, it was moved into the chemical process department at the time of its formation.[1]

The Equipment Division's assessment of the market was described by George Kramer, product manager for FIREGUARD:

> When we went into FIREGUARD we thought we knew a great deal about the fire protection business. However, we discovered that we knew very little and our customers knew less. They couldn't have cared less about the product. They were protected because they had to be, according to the law or the insurance company.

[1] The NO-OX business remained in the refrigeration department. The chemical process department purchased the chemical from the refrigeration department at a negotiated market price.

> So we have had to study the job for the customer. The result has been that we have had a big learning and education program.

Commenting on Kramer's description, Kendall observed:

> We got into the FIREGUARD business because we knew how to build some equipment and we had superior extinguishing materials. In fact, we know how to build the containers very well. We make them at our Akron, Ohio, factory. But we're still learning how to put together the support equipment.
>
> The difficulty in engineering has been to learn the requirements of different applications. We are marketing a system, not equipment, and not extinguishing material. Thus, most of our learning has to be in the field in a sequence of trial-and-error steps.
>
> Out of the first 300 units, we had to take back 100 over time. Now it's 200 out of 3,000. The engineers are still worried: they can explain what happens after the fact, but the problem of responding in a controlled way to undesired fires or explosions is still there.
>
> The other aspect of FIREGUARD planning has been market definition. It has been going on for five or six years as we have tried to move from fire departments to industrial plants, to office building systems, to homeowners. Each area is a different problem in the field. Different costs can be cut, different customers have to be educated, and in some instances different parts of our division have to be educated.
>
> For example, we have had an endless series of arguments with our automatic systems design group, trying to define what fire protection was. When we finally got it settled, we found that we needed a larger container unit.
>
> However, the decision to build a larger container posed an important facility problem for us. We knew we were going to have to expand, because FIREGUARD was already using 250,000 out of 750,000 production man-hours available at Akron. The forecasts indicated that by 1970 FIREGUARD would require 650,000 man-hours. And our other lines were growing.
>
> Add to this the problem of the large containers, and it's clear we needed a new facility. We really weren't up to handling them in the existing facility. Therefore, I asked Steve Matthews, facilities planner for FIREGUARD, to study the Akron plant and make recommendations.

Steve Matthews's career at Industrial Products had begun at Akron. He left the company only to rejoin it later to work on a task force that introduced a new data processing system to the Cleveland facility. His performance on that job led to his assignment in February 1966 to head a team put together to study the organization and operation of the Equipment Division's activities at their Cleveland and Akron locations. This assignment was later expanded to cover an in-depth study of the FIREGUARD facilities at Akron. Matthews commented on his approach to the study:

> My problem was to get a feel for each of Akron's businesses out of marketing. I wanted a definition of the way we did business in each of these markets. It was not easy. For example, in FIREGUARD, George Kramer's forecast was the greatest problem. It was absurdly conservative. I needed to know everything about the business, the way it was going to grow, the role of the parts business, the nature of customer service, and exactly how the business was going to be run so we could design a facility that would meet these needs.
>
> We started the study on the assumption that the business would expand at Akron because it appeared economic to do so. It seemed that the question of relocation costs, the problem of building a new building, and the location of the market indicated that we stay at Akron.

> So we were evaluating existing facilities in the light of the markets of 1970 and beyond. If our product managers didn't give us the forecast, we interpolated as best we could. We wanted to build a facility that would enable us to do business the right way in 1970.

Matthews had found that the major elements of his problems were the following:

1. Akron was poorly run, the data available were poor, and the manpower available to gather data was not always adequate.
2. Problems at Akron resulted from the way in which the relationship between engineering and production was organized, an issue outside the scope of the study.
3. Many of the study group's findings reflected unfavorably on Akron management and therefore raised political problems.
4. The group came to feel that the need was for a "mass production" type of activity although Akron was typically "job shop" oriented. As a result, the facility being planned looked as if it would be a radical departure from existing facilities in terms of both physical design and the mode of operation.

In fact, by November 1966, when Matthews was to meet with Kendall for a final review of the FIREGUARD project, he was ready to recommend a new plant in the Carolinas.[2] It was Matthews's judgment that it would be easier to implement the critical nonfacility[3] part of the FIREGUARD expansion project in the new location. He explained to Kendall that "failure to undertake and effectively implement nonfacility programs would negate the effects of the proposed physical facility plan."

The last part of the meeting with Kendall, held November 15, concerned the size of the capital investment and its timing. An excerpt from the conversation follows:

Matthews: I may be wrapping it up too soon, but we strongly recommend going to South Carolina. The existing manufacturing facilities are theoretically adequate to meet the FIREGUARD market demands through 1969. But, practically, we believe that conditions demand the acceleration of this project. Expanding production to meet 1967 and 1968 forecasts plus inventory buildup in anticipation of moving the production lines will be very difficult to achieve under the existing conditions. The new factory will be needed as soon as it can be constructed. We prefer to schedule the physical construction program to fit into the program for an orderly transfer of personnel, equipment, and procedures. Systems and procedures are to be completely worked out before this move is made. Our schedule calls for completion of the plant in the late fall of 1968, assuming that authorization to proceed is obtained in the first quarter of 1967.

Kendall: There is no way we can invest incrementally?

Matthews: I don't really think so.

Kendall: What are we going to do when they won't give us $5.8 million?

---

[2] While Matthews formally reported to the Akron plant manager, he kept in close contact with Kendall throughout the FIREGUARD study. The Akron plant manager attended many of these meetings and was aware of Matthews's assessment of the Akron facility and its management. However, since the demand for Akron's other products was growing and their production caused fewer problems than FIREGUARD's, the Akron plant manager was not upset at the prospect of losing FIREGUARD.

[3] Accounting and information systems, inventory and production control systems, and material handling systems.

Matthews: You either bet on a business or you don't. You either believe the forecasts or you don't.

Kendall: What if you believe half a forecast?

Matthews: You couldn't build half a plant. You save some, but not a lot. What's a half? What forecast are you going to hang your hat on?

Kendall: Half, I'll commit myself for half but I want to be able to make the whole thing. Can't you build one plant for 1971 and then another just like it for 1975? Or what about some added subcontracting? Why can't we do more subcontracting, since our manufacturing process isn't that unique?

Matthews: As for two plants, you put machines in for the product and you don't need more than one, even for peak volume. As for subcontracting, our make-or-buy analysis shows that if we realize forecast sales, we can improve our return by manufacturing some parts that we now subcontract.

Kendall: Well, yes, but if we really don't have a proprietary position in terms of knowledge and so on, why can't we subcontract our expansion in this area?

Matthews: The trouble with subcontracting is that you never make your delivery promises. It's just impossible to get yourself organized so that you can produce the kind of customer service you need.

Bob, I know your problem. You're thinking about our original estimate of $1.9 million back in June. The original facility was just a factory. This is also a warehouse and a service center. And given the nonfacility expenditures for systems, the investment per unit of capacity is the same as the original proposal.

Kendall had accepted Matthews's argument and arranged to have the FIREGUARD project presented to a meeting of the Equipment Division's executive committee on December 16.[4] Matthews began the meeting by describing the basic strategic assumptions of the FIREGUARD business as "a business selling hardware at a profit, based on warehousing, service, and parts." He noted that, at the rate the business was growing, by 1969 they would be handling five million parts. That meant, he argued, that FIREGUARD was a large-volume, production-oriented operation rather than the traditional job-shop kind of business typical of Akron.

The meeting included the following exchange:

Briggs (general manager): The rumor mill had it that the new facility at Akron was going to cost only $2 million. Why is it that your proposal is so expensive?

Kendall: The original facility the people were talking about was simply a plant for the large containers. This is a much larger operation with many more products.

Matthews: The original facility was just a factory. Not only are there more products, but this is a warehouse and service center.

A substantial discussion of labor costs and related problems led to the question of systems:

Hughes (manager engineering): What about systems? Do you have any allowance for the cost of all these systems you are installing?

---

[4] The divisional executive committee consisted of the division's general manager, the assistant general manager, department managers, and top functional managers.

Matthews: You have $175,000 project costs and $185,000 engineering, and that ought to cover it.

Hughes: That's not enough. How many programmers do you have?

Matthews: Five, I think.

Hughes: I think that is low. We had 10 programmers at East St. Louis [an earlier project] if I am not mistaken.

Golden (assistant general manager): How many accountants do you have?

Matthews looked the figure up in his backup notebook. He explained that the nature of the FIREGUARD operation was such that it would produce for a full warehouse rather than on the basis of meeting customer demand. Therefore, the demand on accounting was different from traditional equipment businesses:

Golden: I think traditionally we have had our overrun on systems and accounting.

Matthews: I think I understand your point, Bill, and we will do our best to take care of it.

After this discussion, Matthews presented the project summary shown in Exhibit 2.

On April 5, 1967, Briggs presented the FIREGUARD project to the corporate finance committee. While questions of subcontracting, poor current performance, and future ROI were raised, the general feeling of the group was that the project was a good one and the business very promising. Therefore, after a short discussion, the project was approved.

SECOND THOUGHTS

Kendall was still uneasy about the FIREGUARD project. Matthews argued that the future market for these products was large and lucrative. Yet the earnings record of FIREGUARD since its inception in 1961 had been poor. Moreoever, as sales for the product grew, so did the losses (see Exhibit 3).

Kendall's concern was intensified when the review of his department's 1968 business plan was conducted in October 1967.[5] Divisional executives had expressed concern with the department's recent earnings record shown in Exhibit 4. Moreover, Kendall was well aware that the corporation had specifically asked about the FIREGUARD business the previous fall. Since corporate requests for detailed information on an individual business were quite unusual, Kendall knew that FIREGUARD was in the limelight and that most likely there was pressure on the division officers to see that the business's performance improved.

In an effort to secure some guidance in this matter, Kendall asked Mike Richards, corporate director of planning, to discuss FIREGUARD with him. While Richards reflected corporate thinking, he did not represent it. Therefore, the meeting between Kendall and Richards was in the nature of "informal advice" rather than "formal corporate review." The October 27 meeting began with Kendall expressing his concerns to Richards:

---

[5] The Equipment Division's business plan attempted to answer the questions "What will happen to our products next year and the year after that?" and "What do we plan to do about it?" Departmental plans were reviewed each fall by the division. (Performance against current plan was reviewed quarterly.) This plan review was a formal meeting in which departmental managers made presentations of their business plan to divisional officers. Officers were free to make comments and often did.

Plans were typically concerned with market size, market share, product volume, product price, and profit. Return on investment was sometimes used as a tool to measure the quality of a "business," but the business plans did not include specific investment planning. At most, a crude forecast of "capital requirement" was included.

Kendall: Mike, Briggs is putting pressure on me to raise the department's profits. But if FIREGUARD goes ahead with the approved expansion, earnings are not going to get much better. On the other hand, Matthews has some convincing arguments for FIREGUARD's market potential. To tell the truth, I'm perplexed.

Richards: Well, from my point of view, FIREGUARD doesn't fit with the rest of our products. We make machine tools, material handling systems, and refrigeration equipment. We enjoy a close relationship with our customers so that we can understand and help solve their technical problems. On the other hand, FIREGUARD is a mass-produced, standard-design product. Moreover, compared to our existing product line, FIREGUARD is mass marketed. That means problems of distribution and service that we haven't faced before.

Kendall: OK, but FIREGUARD's got a fantastic future potential. Its sales in 1975 could easily exceed the total department's sales today.

Richards: Look, I'm not arguing that you drop FIREGUARD completely. I'm merely saying that you don't really know how to market or produce the product very well. If I were you, I would be inclined to concentrate on improving FIREGUARD's profits and then grow the business after you've learned how to run it profitably.

Kendall: That's easier said than done. We've already asked for and received approval for a new plant. The division will not be too pleased if I now say that FIREGUARD should not be expanded for awhile. Moreover, I'm sure Matthews will hit the roof.

Richards: Mike, you asked for my opinion and I've given it to you. I think it's better to retrench now rather than sacrifice current earnings to a project that has yet to make a profit.

Following his conversation with Richards, Kendall decided to speak with Matthews about the FIREGUARD project. Kendall began the meeting by explaining his concern over FIREGUARD's past and current performance and expressing pessimism about its future performance. To support this view, Kendall used many of Richards's arguments. Matthews responded quickly:

Matthews: First, it seems to me that the issue is closed, since the corporation approved our request for capital funds. Moreover, I think their decision was a wise one. It takes money to build the marketing and systems capabilities we need to take advantage of the FIREGUARD opportunity. If we don't spend money today, we'll surely fail in the years to come.

Anyway, we've carefully timed our expenditures for capital and noncapital items so that we can cut back if the assumed market doesn't develop. For example, by December we will have ordered about $1.1 million in equipment and spent about $160,000 on noncapital items. Yet, since the penalty for canceling the equipment order is only $290,000, our total exposure as of the beginning of 1968 will be $450,000. [Cancellation of equipment was not allowed after January 1, 1968.] Moreover, while the entire capital budget of $5.8 million will be irrevocably committed by the end of 1968, we will have spent only $650,000 of our $1.1 million noncapital budget by that time. In fact, we wouldn't spend our entire noncapital budget until September 1969.

Also, even if FIREGUARD doesn't make it, you've always got a new plant, even though most of the machinery is specially designed for the FIREGUARD product line. [The plant represented 70 percent of the capital budget.]

But this isn't going to happen. FIREGUARD has an enormous business potential. Moreover, the division will make as much on the NO-OX as it does on the equipment. But we both know that FIREGUARD is a new kind of product for the Equipment Division. It depends on the sales and servicing of hardware. This, coupled with distribution, are major factors to cope with. It's just going to take time and money to develop the capabilities we need.

Kendall: But we haven't done very well in the six years we've been trying, to date.

Matthews: That's because we've been producing at Akron. Our new plant in South Carolina will solve many of our problems. Bob, it takes time to develop a new business. The payoff doesn't come right away.

Kendall: Steve, that all sounds very good but have you looked at Kramer's monthly reports for the first seven months of this year? [See Exhibit 5] After six years it still sounds as if we just began.

Matthews: Even a great business can do poorly if it's mismanaged. We haven't been coordinating design with production. We haven't had a production line suitable for high-volume manufacturing. We haven't had adequate part standardization. We haven't put nearly enough money into developing the needed management and production control systems. Bob, I could go on like this for 10 minutes, but you know these problems as well as I do. How do you expect to make money given this situation? And you certainly can't blame Kramer for a manufacturing problem.

Kendall: You've got a point, but then where the hell does Kramer get his forecasts? Doesn't he take the production constraint into consideration?

Matthews: OK, you've got a point. However, I don't think that should influence your view of the future of FIREGUARD. A lot of people here have spent a lot of time on this project.[6] We have finally got it out from under Akron and have the resources to make it. I don't see how you can even consider changing it at this late date.

---

[6] While Matthews and about a dozen other employees had spent over a year and a half on the project, the possibility of moving the operation to South Carolina had been kept highly confidential because of its potential impact on the Akron work force. Thus, in addition to the people planning the facility, only the top division and corporate officers were aware of the decision to move the FIREGUARD production operation.

Moreover, while the construction of the new plant had not begun by the time of the Matthews-Kendall meeting, some equipment had been ordered and options had been taken on a piece of land. The cost of canceling the equipment order and the land option would be $105,000. Moreover, $114,500 had already been spent for noncapital items.

EXHIBIT 1
EQUIPMENT DIVISION—PARTIAL ORGANIZATION CHART, MARCH 1966

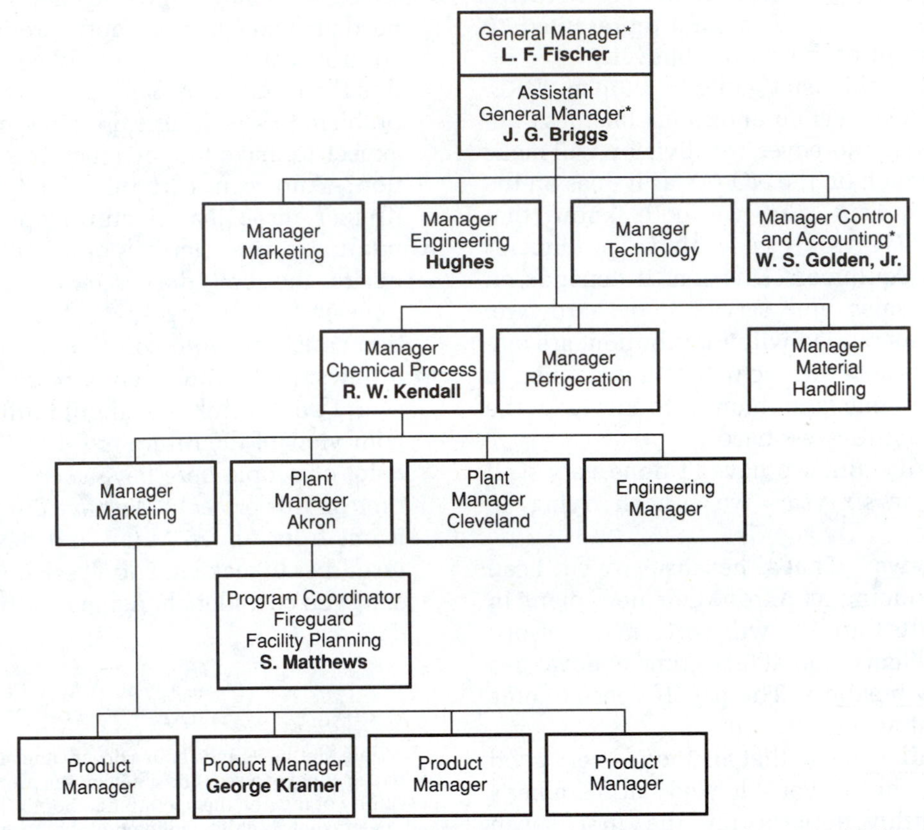

*After Fischer's promotion to a corporate officer position in July 1966, Briggs was made division general manager and Golden was made assistant general manager.

EXHIBIT 2
SUMMARY OF FIREGUARD LONG-RANGE FORECAST, 1967–1970, 1975
In Millions of Dollars

	1967	*1968*	*1969*	*1970*	*1975*
Sales	3.6	9.0	17.7	24.5	41.5
Net income before taxes	(1.1)*	(0.4)*	0.8*	3.9	7.5
ROI	—	—	7.4	26.0	32.0
Fixed investment	1.0†	1.2†	4.3†	6.9†	8.0‡
Working capital	2.5	4.7	6.5	8.1	15.5
Total investment	3.5	5.9	10.8	15.0	23.5

*Included $1.1 million for noncapital items associated with the move: costs of transfers, layoffs, training, equipment moving, and project management.

†Would provide space to satisfy forecast sales through 1975 and equipment to satisfy forecast sales through 1970.

‡$1.1 million additional equipment would be needed to satisfy 1975 forecast sales.

EXHIBIT 3
PROJECTED AND ACTUAL SALES FOR FIREGUARD
In Millions of Dollars

Date of Forecast	*1964*	*1965*	*1966*	*1967*	*1968*
Projected Sales					
September 1964	1.1	2.5	4.3		13.3
July 1965		2.2	4.2	8.1	
July 1966			3.4	4.8	9.2
April 1967				3.6	

	1961	*1962*	*1963*	*1964*	*1965*	*1966*
Actual sales and earnings						
Sales	0.20	0.41	0.73	1.0	1.9	2.2
Net income before taxes						
Actual	(0.05)	(0.15)	(0.38)	(0.45)	(0.8)	(1.1)
Plan					(0.3)	0.1

EXHIBIT 4
CHEMICAL PROCESS DEPARTMENT SALES AND INCOME, 1960–1966
In Millions of Dollars

	1960	*1961*	*1962*	*1963*	*1964*	*1965*	*1966*
Sales	12.4	13.4	15.1	16.2	17.8	20.4	23.2
Net income before taxes	(0.50)	0.04	0.75	1.72	2.3	3.0	3.1

EXHIBIT 5
PRODUCT MANAGER'S COMMENTS ON THE MONTHLY PROGRESS REPORTS FOR FIREGUARD

January 1967: Equipment sales are 49 percent of plan because of large factory backlog ($790,000 on January 31, 1966, from $439,000 on December 31, 1965).

February 1967: Total equipment shipments are only 46 percent of plan. While Akron backlog has risen $500,000 this year, part of this is the customary seasonal buildup. It appears we may well be 20 percent below plan.

March 1967: Total shipments continue to lag with year-to-date sales at 50 percent of plan, up only 4 percent from February. We continue to have new equipment production difficulties, as represented by a backlog of orders at Akron of $850,000. Backlog as a result of shipments withheld due to production difficulties is $450,000, leaving sales to date substantially below plan as reflected by the latest yearly forecast.

April 1967: Sales continue to lag due to a continuing sales failure to penetrate the commercial market. Automatic systems sales have been delayed due to a lack of production of the new sensing device. Year-to-date total sales have improved 7 percent from March due to heavy overseas shipments. This foreign business is accomplished at significantly lower margins, accounting for the continuing higher manufacturing cost versus sales.

May 1967: Sales continue to lag as reported in April with only slight improvement (0.4 percent). Equipment backlog is $725,000, about $300,000 above normal for sales to date. All costs to date are in line with the latest forecast except for development, where there will be an overrun of $120,000 for 160 percent of plan due to automatic systems problems.

June 1967: The above-listed low sales have been reflected in our 1968 business plan. Our entry into the industrial systems market has been set back at least one year for lack of satisfactory sensing equipment and is reflected in our 1968 business plan by a 94 percent reduction in plan sales in this area.

July 1967: The high manufacturing costs were due to accounting errors at Akron. One group of costs was cleared prior to sales clearing. Another group was cleared to cost of product when it should have been transferred to an inventory account. When these are corrected in August, the net effect will be to increase our August gross margin by about $75,000.

Kentucky Fried Chicken (Japan) Limited

In January 1983 Dick Mayer leaned back in his chair and gazed absentmindedly at the Norman Rockwell portrait of Colonel Sanders on his office wall. Mayer, a veteran Kentucky Fried Chicken (KFC) executive, had recently been promoted from vice chairman and head of the company's U.S. operations to chairman and chief executive officer, and for the past few weeks had been focusing his attention on the challenges facing him in Kentucky Fried Chicken-International (KFC-I). As he talked to KFC-I managers about their problems, opportunities, and challenges, he was exposed to a wide range of opinion on what was needed to continue KFC's growth and profitability overseas.

At one end of the spectrum was Loy Weston, president of KFC's highly successful joint venture in Japan. Weston's view was that in recent years headquarters staff interference in local national operations was increasingly compromising the spirit of entrepreneurship that had built the overseas business. In Louisville, however, Mayer heard a different story. For example, Gary Buhrow, vice president of strategic planning, felt that the lack of effective planning and control in the early years of KFC-I had led to suboptimal financial performance, inconsistent strategies, and stalled expansion into new markets. He emphasized that the recent efforts by headquarters staff were aimed at supporting the overseas subsidiaries and bringing to them the very considerable resources and experience of the parent company.

THE BEGINNINGS

Harland Sanders was born in Henryville, Indiana, in 1890, the son of a farmhand. A sixth-grade dropout, he occasionally worked as a cook. In his late 40s, he developed a recipe for chicken based on a pressure cooking method and a secret seasoning mix of 11 herbs and spices. When Sanders' gas station, restaurant, and motel were bypassed by the new interstate highway system in 1956, he decided to try to franchise his chicken recipe. With his

Harvard Business School case 387–043. Revised September 1987.

white suit, goatee, string tie, and benign charm, he sold some 700 franchises in less than nine years. In allocating franchising rights for KFC, Sanders was generous to his friends and relatives. His management style was to rely on the basic goodness of the people around him and trust his franchisees to play fair. There were no management systems or strategic controls.

Industry Growth and Development

Colonel Sanders became a pioneer in one of the fastest-growing industries of the postwar era. Many of the practices he initiated were quickly imitated by others, and within a few years, several "rules of the game" came to be accepted in the U.S. fast food industry.

One of the first norms to be established was expansion through franchising. The high capital cost of opening new stores, together with the need to expand rapidly to stake out the territory, quickly forced companies toward this option. Franchising also allowed companies to capture operating economies, particularly in advertising and raw materials purchasing. As franchises matured, chain managements often became interested in buying them back or opening their own stores. This not only gave them better understanding and control of operations, it also allowed franchising fees to be supplemented by profits.

At the store level, the importance of scale economies was also quickly recognized. Because each restaurant outlet had high fixed costs and small returns on unit sales, traffic volume was crucial. This made location a key success factor, and decisions on which region, town, neighborhood, or even side of the street, could mean the difference between success and failure.

Within the industry, companies soon learned that effective store management was also a key factor in profitability. Because margins were small and the opportunities for waste, shrinkage, and inefficiency were many, it took a special kind of individual to keep a fast food outlet operating smoothly and profitably. In addition to ensuring short-term profits, store managers were also responsible for building local public relations, maintaining employee morale, developing customer goodwill, keeping tabs on competing chains, and so on. And yet the salaries paid to these entrepreneurial individuals were relatively low for the 60–80 hours a week they devoted to their work. Most were attracted to the company-owned outlets by the prospects for promotion into regional and divisional positions.

As the industry developed, the importance of the chain's overall market image also became increasingly clear. The need for a focused theme or product line was acknowledged to be critical, as was the importance of the consistency and reliability of the product throughout the chain. Successful new product innovations were difficult, and management was always conscious of the risk of confusing the chain's image if it deviated too far from its basic menu and core theme.

Acquisition and Growth: The Late 1960s

By 1964 the 700 KFC outlets were grossing over $37 million a year and the Colonel, now in his mid-70s, had begun to mutter that the "damned business is beginning to run right over me." The time seemed ripe for a change of ownership. When a 29-year-old Kentucky lawyer, John Y. Brown, and a 60-year-old financier, Jack Massey, offered Sanders $2 million, a lifetime salary, and a position in charge of quality control in the business, the Colonel accepted.

Under Brown and Massey, growth exploded. During the next five years, KFC's revenue grew 96 percent a year (from $7 million to $200 million). In 1970 the company was building 1,000 stores a year in the United States. Brown recognized that the key to continued growth was to find, motivate, and retain hard-working and entrepreneurial managers and franchisees. His philosophy was that everyone involved with a KFC operation had a right to expect to become wealthy.

But with the rapid growth, problems soon cropped up. KFC headquarters experienced high turnover in its management ranks, with a number of senior executives leaving in quick succession to become franchisees for KFC's new ventures. If he was to keep these key people, Brown had to find new challenges and promotion opportunities within the company.

About this time, Brown became fascinated with the apparently boundless opportunities for KFC to expand overseas. The rapid economic growth and trend toward two-income families that had fueled the growth of the fast food industry in the 1950s and 1960s were appearing in the late 1960s in other countries. Despite warnings from some who felt that food tastes differed widely from one country to the next, and that the whole concept of fast food was a cultural phenomenon that could not be transported outside the United States, Brown was convinced there was an opportunity. Besides, he felt he would be able to keep some of his entrepreneurial executives challenged by sending them to start new KFC ventures abroad. One executive later described Brown's international expansion strategy in these terms: "He just threw some mud against the map on the wall and hoped some of it would stick."

The country managers were like Roman governors sent to govern distant provinces with nothing more than an exhortation to maintain Rome's imperial power and reputation. Few had any operating expertise, they were offered little staff support, and the only attention paid to operations was Colonel Sanders' personal efforts to maintain the quality of his original product. Each country manager was on his own to make a success of his venture, and most had to learn the business from scratch.

CHANGES IN THE EARLY 1970s

KFC (Japan): Getting Started

It was against this background that Mitsubishi approached KFC with a proposal to start a joint venture in Japan. The giant Japanese trading company had a large poultry operation and wanted to develop the demand for chicken in its home country. Finding a perfect fit with his priorities, Brown was quick to seize the opportunity. The only problem was, he had nobody in the company equal to such a challenging assignment. But he thought he knew a good candidate—an IBM salesman named Loy Weston.

During the Korean War, Weston had been stationed in Japan and became intrigued with Japanese culture. After the war, he joined IBM's sales department and studied law at night. While at IBM, he started a dozen entrepreneurial ventures in his spare time, including airplane leasing, coffee machine sales, and sandpaper wholesaling. In the 60s he was based in Lexington, Kentucky, as a member of IBM's new-product sales group. It was then he met John Y. Brown.

After the Mitsubishi contact in 1969, Brown called Weston and asked if he would go to Japan and start a new company. Weston agreed, and soon the two men were discussing how to make the venture work. Brown's directions to Weston were simple. He asked him not to franchise until he had proven the fast food concept with company-owned stores. Brown's dictum was: "Build a store and make it work; then build another and another." Weston was to receive $200,000 as start-up capital and an annual salary of $40,000. He was promised an expense account after the company had been successfully established. His training consisted of two weeks cooking chicken at a KFC restaurant in Detroit.

Heading east to Japan, Weston decided to stop over in Greece. In Athens, he met the president of Dai Nippon, an Osaka-based printing firm. When the Japanese manager learned that Weston was going to start a new company that would require a lot of printing, he offered to telex to his office and have someone meet Loy. That individual was Shin Ohkawara, a Dai Nippon sales representative.

Weston thought he recognized some real potential in this young salesman and decided to cultivate a friendship with a view to persuading him to join KFC. He asked Ohkawara to take him to different restaurants so he could learn more about the Japanese food industry. This gave Loy an opportunity to scout the market and at the same time to get to know the young Japanese better. Weston used these occasions to impress Ohkawara with the grand plans he had for the new company, playing up the Mitsubishi connection to emphasize KFC's strength and commitment. After about six months, Shin Ohkawara agreed to join KFC.

Despite the fact that no formal joint venture agreement had been signed between Mitsubishi and KFC in the six months following his arrival in Japan, Weston had gone ahead with the test marketing of KFC products in a local department store, although without a Japanese partner such an operation was strictly illegal. He found that Japanese disliked the mashed potatoes in the KFC standard menu and that the coleslaw was too sweet for local palates. On the spot Weston decided to substitute french fries for the prescribed mashed potatoes, and reduced the coleslaw sugar content from the company-set standard. "These were no-brainers. The idea of getting clearance from the United States didn't even occur to me." The first real KFC store was in the American Park in the EXPO–70 in Osaka. KFC Corp. sent the equipment from Louisville, and the store was erected in just two weeks.

The joint venture agreement was finally signed on July 4, 1970. To build on the exposure gained at EXPO–70, two more stores were opened in Osaka. Sites were chosen where land was relatively cheap and where new shopping centers were opening up. In keeping with U.S. practice, stores were large, free-standing structures with 4,400 square feet of floor space. Shin Ohkawara, who managed one of the stores, recalled the early days: "The stores were exact replicas of the U.S. take-out stores. Although the distinctive architecture was a big plus in the United States, nobody in Japan recognized what we were selling, and sales were very poor. The U.S. manual said that we could not keep the food more than two hours after cooking. So we threw out more chicken than we sold."

The new venture was soon in trouble. Losses mounted, and the company had exhausted the $400,000 put up by the joint venture partners. Weston needed to borrow more. Meanwhile he also had to recruit people to run the existing stores. Both he and Ohkawara were putting in 15-hour days and they knew they could not do that indefinitely. The latest threat was the appearance of McDonald's in Tokyo. With all its problems, it appeared KFC–J was heading for an early demise, and Weston wondered how he could turn the operation around.

U.S. Operations: Emerging Problems

By late 1970 KFC faced a changed environment in the United States. The economy went into a recession and the company's revenues and profits began to plateau. Meanwhile, its new diversification ventures, like fish and chips and roast beef, were failing to meet expectations. KFC's stock price fell from a peak of $58 to $18, leading many of those who had hoped to get rich to quit the company. As the management exodus continued, Brown saw an opportunity to install a more professional team to build the systems necessary to gain control.

Competition in fast food in the United States was becoming more intense, and an industry shakeout began. KFC managers started hearing field reports about poor product quality and customer service in their stores. So concerned were they about the emerging economic, competitive, and operating problems in the United States, that they tended to leave the foreign operations to fend for themselves. Amid all this came a rift in the echelons of top management, and in mid-1971, Brown and Massey sold KFC in an exchange of stock valued at more than $275 million to Heublein, Inc., a packaged goods company that had developed strong brand franchises such as Smirnoff Vodka in the United States and many other countries.

To fit into the Heublein organization, which was structured along domestic and international lines, KFC's small international staff was merged with Heublein's international group in Farmington, Connecticut, and a manager from Heublein's international operations was brought in to serve as the vice president of KFC-International. A small staff was assigned exclusively to KFC-I to serve as a link between the overseas subsidiaries and Heublein headquarters. (See Exhibit 1A.)

Despite efforts to establish more control over the subsidiaries, headquarters management found KFC-I's independent-minded subsidiary managers uncooperative. Reports often came too late or with too little information. Sometimes they were not sent at all. Although visits from corporate headquarters to the subsidiaries became more frequent, they were usually limited to general exchanges of views about the way the subsidiaries were functioning. In the end, each country manager was left with responsibility for expanding within his territory, using funds generated from his existing operations.

LURCHING TOWARD THE MID-1970s

KFC (Japan): Shaky Beginnings

In the early 1970s KFC-J was struggling to get on its feet. After heavy losses in Osaka and a not-so-propitious start in Kobe, the company was operating on a shoestring. In early 1972 Weston went to the United States to make a pitch to the new parent company for additional financing. To his surprise, Heublein agreed to increase their share of KFC-J's equity by $400,000. With matching funds from Mitsubishi, and bank guarantees from both parents, he now received a warmer welcome when he applied for additional debt. Now all he had to do was to make the stores work.

As he continued to wrestle with the start-up challenges, Weston was struck by what he described as a "simple but profound insight." He began thinking of KFC-Japan not as a fast food company but as a firm in the fashion industry. "Recognizing that we were selling to young, trendy Japanese who wanted to emulate American habits helped us develop a totally new strategic vision. It also led to lots of changes. First, it meant we had to focus on Tokyo since this was the center of fashion and the source of new trends in Japan. Then we began to focus all marketing efforts on our target group—upscale young couples and children."

These decisions resulted in further changes in product and market strategy. To build volume, stores were located not in suburban shopping centers but near key stations on the commuter lines. High rents and limited space forced them to reduce the standard store size to less than half the area specified in the KFC operations manual. This meant kitchens and equipment had to be totally redesigned. To build volume Loy and his team also decided to add fried fish and smoked chicken products—two favorite foods of the Japanese—to the menu. They also adjusted prices to compete with a typical take-out Japanese pork dish called *katsudon.* Advertising increasingly deviated from KFC themes, and to accommodate smaller Japanese appetites, "mini-barrels" with 12 rather than the U.S. standard of 21 chicken pieces were introduced. All these decisions, Loy Weston proudly acclaimed, were made locally, without consulting corporate headquarters.

By the end of 1972 the company had opened 14 new stores, most of them in Tokyo. In 1973, 50 more were added. Weston was optimistic that 1974 would be the year KFC-J would turn its first profit. Then the oil crisis hit the Japanese economy, and continuing losses forced a refinancing and a slowdown in store expansion. Loy felt he was starting all over again.

U.S. Operations: Facing Difficulties

Meanwhile KFC's domestic operations were in turmoil. Many former franchisees who had become corporate executives under Brown either left on their own or were fired. KFC's sales stagnated. There was widespread discontent among the franchisees, some of whom felt the new owners did not understand the chicken business and were not providing the leadership expected from a franchisor. There was even talk of a class action suit against Heublein among the more disgruntled franchisees. Company stores floundered and began underperforming the franchised operations, further convincing franchisees that the company did not know its own business. Even founder Colonel Sanders was reported to be unhappy, telling a group of journalists that the "chain's gravy was beginning to acquire the look and taste of wallpaper paste." Such disarray was a boon for competitors. The emerging Churches franchise and a number of regional chains began to cut deeply into KFC's dominance of the market.

Not only had growth stopped but by 1976 KFC's sales actually showed a four-year decline of 8 percent. Store-level profits were declining 26 percent annually. As Dick Mayer was to recount later: "Quality, service, and cleanliness [in the company-owned stores] were just terrible. . . . Product ratings were inconsistent, standards were almost nonexistent, service time was highly variable, employees were often surly, and the buildings were dirty and run down." In this period, Heublein was not keen on committing funds to what appeared to be a lost cause. Except for sending a few cost-cutting experts to help ease the cash flow problems, management did little to deal with the developing crisis.

The prevailing attitude seemed to be that they were in a competitive segment of a saturated industry, and better opportunities lay in diversification.

THE LATE 1970s: NEW DIRECTIONS

KFC–I: Changes in Management

In late 1975 Michael Miles was appointed vice president of international operations for Heublein. At the time, he had had no international experience. Miles had a journalism degree from Northwestern, and before joining KFC in 1971 had spent 10 years with the Leo Burnett advertising agency where he had been responsible for the Colonel Sanders account. In 1972 he was named a Heublein vice president and became the head of the Grocery Products Division, which marketed the Grey Poupon, Ortega, and A.1. Steak Sauce brands. In that capacity, he initiated and completed the first strategic plan for the company. Strategic planning was to become his credo.

As vice president of the international group, Miles was responsible for all of Heublein's international operations, which was primarily its offshore KFC stores and its non-U.S. liquor business. He quickly decided that the collection of largely autonomous KFC subsidiaries would require most of his attention. The performance of many of them left much to be desired. The few operating standards that had been communicated were poorly controlled. Even the basic menu varied widely—South Africa offering hamburgers, Australia serving roast chicken, Japan with its fish, and Brazil with a full-scale wide-choice menu. Some, like KFC-J, had yet to achieve breakeven, and other more established operations had begun to show declining profits. Many cited market saturation and more competitive environments as the reason for these poor results. Miles approached the international operations with a firm conviction that overseas subsidiaries needed more support and control from corporate headquarters, and that a good strategic planning system was the basic starting point. (See Exhibit 1B for organizational impact of changes.)

Recognizing that he was in unfamiliar territory, however, Miles moved with deliberation. He saw planning essentially as an approach to foster a thought process among the country managers. He wanted those individuals who knew how to run the business to make the plans and implement them. Despite immense resistance from the subsidiaries, he persisted in his efforts, and the subsidiaries gradually began adopting his strategic planning approach.

Miles also offered to help the subsidiaries develop new marketing skills. Through periodic seminars he introduced them to market research and new techniques in television advertising that would enhance brand awareness. After about two years, most of the subsidiaries had learned to use these tools and were beginning to apply them routinely.

KFC (Japan): Maturing Operations

In recalling Miles's efforts to introduce planning systems, Loy Weston was blunt:

> One fine morning, he rolled out this nine-page planning document. Headquarters wanted all kinds of data—environment conditions, strengths and weaknesses of our operation, objectives for the next five years, projections, action plans, and so on. It was useless for our needs. It was the same thing with marketing. They said we should be more professional. They asked us to hire a market research company to do a consumer survey. We paid a lot of

> money for that, and what did it show? That people bought our chicken because it tasted good. Fascinating!

Shin Ohkawara was a little less blunt, but also appeared somewhat skeptical:

> It was ironic. Here we had built our business from scratch with no assistance from the United States and were finally approaching break-even. In contrast to the situation in the States, our stores were known for their quality, service, and cleanliness, and we had a highly motivated team. Yet the people from the United States were trying to teach us how to manage. They even sent over an American controller so their monthly reports would be filled in correctly.
>
> But we learned to live with it. The strategic planning exercises actually helped us by forcing us to project and to quantify uncertainty for the first time. Of course, we adapted it to Japanese practices. Our Presidents Review is a handwritten document that comes up from all sections and is collated into two 3-inch-thick books. We go through this process the first month of the year—not six months ahead as required by the U.S. planning cycle, and obviously not in their prescribed format.
>
> We also learned how to manage our relationships with headquarters better. We learned the rules of the game, like "never show a big jump" and "manage sales and profit to show consistent growth."

In 1976 KFC-J reported its first profit, a modest 14 million yen. Miles offered warm congratulations all around.

THE EARLY 1980s: REORGANIZATION

Headquarters Changes: U.S. Turnaround

During the latter half of the 1970s, KFC's domestic operations continued to slide to the point that the problems could no longer be ignored. In early 1977 Mike Miles was given the company's most challenging assignment: to find out what was wrong with the U.S. business, which accounted for two thirds of KFC's worldwide sales, and fix it. Miles asked Dick Mayer, who was Heublein's vice president for marketing and planning in the Grocery Products Group, to come to KFC's Louisville headquarters to help with this Herculean task. Mayer worked with Miles and played a major role in developing a turnaround strategy for KFC.

Just as he had done in International, Miles's first act as president of Kentucky Fried Chicken was to introduce a strategic planning process. His analysis identified that the company had lost touch with its customers and was being outflanked by aggressive new competitors such as Churches. The centerpiece of Miles's turnaround program was what he called a "back-to-basics" program. It stressed quality, service, and cleanliness (QSC) inspections by headquarters-directed mystery shoppers, training programs, strict management control systems, five-year rolling plans, a revamped advertising approach, investments to improve the visual image of stores, and effective franchise relationships.

By 1979 these various programs were beginning to show results. Average sales per store turned around and began increasing at a better than 10 percent per annum rate. Store-level profits rebounded even more dramatically, bringing them close to the levels of industry leader, McDonald's.

In July 1981, with his reputation greatly enhanced, Mike Miles was named senior vice president responsible for all Heublein's food products in the United States and internationally. Immediately, his attention returned to KFC's foreign subsidiaries where he saw great opportunity to benefit from the techniques just applied so successfully in turning around the U.S. operations.

Soon after taking charge of KFC-I, Miles made three important organizational changes. First, he decided that the international operations could learn more from the U.S. experience if the KFC-I headquarters were moved back to Louisville with the rest of KFC. Second, he hired as the new president of KFC-I, a professional manager with extensive experience in consumer products marketing (with Procter & Gamble) and general management (with the Swift Group of Esmark Corporation). Third, he expanded the staff expertise at KFC-I headquarters to reinforce the planning, service, and control functions he felt were required (Exhibit 2).

Bob Hiatt, the new president of KFC-I, outlined his broad objectives:

> When I came here in September 1981, the strategic planning mode was well on its way, but the subsidiaries' independent heritage was still clearly evident. Our objective was to convince them that better strategic plans meant better bottom-line results. In operating terms, you could say our aim was and is to achieve consistency and control worldwide. We want consistency of products and facilities, and we need to control the production and marketing approaches if we are to maintain that consistency.

Gary Buhrow, vice president of strategic planning for KFC-I, discussed the changes in his area of responsibility.

> Up to 1981 planning in international had really been a perfunctory exercise. Miles wanted me to make it a more integrated, ongoing activity. To ensure consistency, we developed a standard format to be used by all subsidiaries, we adopted a five-year rolling plan process, and we implemented a more formal staged review procedure [Exhibit 3]. As might be expected, the country managers were not overjoyed.

Donald Lee was the financial vice president at KFC-I. Earlier he had been the international controller and had also served at Heublein headquarters in the finance area. He said:

> The number of reports we require has multiplied over the years [Exhibit 4]. But we don't apply our requirements rigidly. KFC-Japan is a good example. They balked when we introduced the new capital expenditure approval procedure for new store openings, and argued that they had traditionally been making such investment decisions without headquarters approval. They also said that Mitsubishi did not require prior approval. So we agreed to give them a blanket approval for capital expenditures in the beginning of the year. The problem is that by making such exceptions you weaken the whole system, leaving yourself open for other subsidiaries to demand similar treatment.
>
> In general, we tend to treat the folks in Japan with kid gloves. Loy claims that staff interference will only stifle him. But Loy and Shin cannot take this autonomy business too far. They must realize they are part of a company with lots of opportunities and needs. We need procedures like the capital expenditure approval so we can make sensible choices among competing demands. In Tokyo, they think that we should take a long-term view and ignore short-term losses. But the reality is we are an American public company and Wall Street will start screaming if the quarterly earnings dip.

In addition to the strategic and financial systems, a new set of controls was introduced at this time. The international operations group was established to transfer to KFC's overseas companies some of the database management systems that had been so helpful in turning around its U.S. business.

Gary Masterton, a key manager in the international operations group explained:

> Our objectives are simple—to increase efficiency and ensure standards on a worldwide basis. The product is sacred, and we must do all we can to ensure its quality and consistency. The sooner we get back to basics—eliminating the ribs in England and the fish in Japan—the sooner we can get control and squeeze out cost savings. And if the U.S. operations were able to use our database system to help drive up per store sales by 60 percent and to double store level margins in less than six years, we'd be crazy not to try to learn from them in our overseas units.

The new operations control systems asked for store level information on numbers of chickens, customer traffic, ticket average, menu mix, and speed of service. The availability of comparable data on a worldwide basis, as well as some expert input (such as time and motion studies to establish labor efficiencies), allowed management to set standards, measure performance, and reward store managers. Efficiency targets, QSC ratings, and performance bonus levels were introduced, and reports on trends at the store level were produced.

The subsidiaries' reaction to the new database operations system varied. For example, New Zealand adopted it with enthusiasm, but in Australia there was a lot of resistance. But there had been a disturbing deterioration in quality, service, and cleanliness in the Australian outlets in recent years, and the Louisville operations group used the resulting decline in sales and profits as the opportunity to step in and implement the back-to-basics program and the supporting database system. Japan also questioned its need to adopt the new systems and programs and challenged headquarters' ideas. Louisville management emphasized it was trying not to be too dogmatic and was willing to adapt the system to their special needs. "We don't ram it down their throats, but we do want the system operating universally," said Masterton. "Those that accept it find it can be a very useful system they can apply locally, and not just data sent back to headquarters for control. We want this to be one of *their* management tools."

KFC (Japan) Reaction

The new management direction and systems of 1981 did not sit well with Loy Weston:

> We are slowly being reduced to the role of order-takers. In the first year after Miles came back, we had 22 man-weeks of visitors from the corporate headquarters. Quality control audits, computer people, planners, operations guys, and so on. They questioned everything from our store designs to the smoked chicken, yogurt, and fish on our menu. They gave us hurdle rates for real estate, and operating instructions straight from the American manuals.
>
> They acted as if they had all the answers and we knew nothing. Just because they had introduced crispy chicken in the United States, they thought we should too. I knew it wouldn't work. But I agreed to a test market. It bombed. They didn't like our TV commercials so they made one for us that was so inappropriate we never aired it. Finally, I had to remind them they couldn't do this. We are a joint venture, not a wholly owned subsidiary.

Shin Ohkawara sounded philosophical:

> I guess it is all inevitable as we change from a venture-oriented to a professionally managed company. They want us to follow their ideas. OK, we will give them a try. But we kept thinking there were lots of ways they could also learn from us. For

instance, we felt that our 12-piece "mini-barrel" could be a big success elsewhere. And our small store layouts, with their flexible kitchen design, might be very suitable for U.S. shopping malls. We were even experimenting with chicken nuggets in 1981 until we were told to stop.

What worries me, though, is this constant pressure from the United States for improved margins. (Incidentally, Mitsubishi has never asked us for more profit.) People at headquarters want to know why we have not raised prices for 4 years now, and only twice in the last 12 years. By pricing our products just 20 percent above supermarket fresh chicken prices, we have expanded demand tremendously. If we use the U.S. pricing formula we will just invite competition.

New Challenges

Just as its new international programs were shaping up, KFC entered an important new chapter in its history. Attracted by Heublein's solid sales growth and strong profit performance, R.J. Reynolds (RJR) acquired the company in October 1982 as part of its continuing strategy of diversifying away from tobacco products (Exhibit 5 shows overall Heublein performance by business). Soon thereafter, Mike Miles was offered the opportunity to become president of Dart and Kraft and was succeeded as chairman and chief executive of KFC by Richard Mayer.

Mayer, an MBA from Rutgers, had begun his career at General Foods. He joined Heublein in 1973 as director of business development, and subsequently became vice president of strategic planning and marketing at the time Miles was trying to get the company to take a more sophisticated approach to such matters. As the driving force behind KFC's more professional management approach, Mayer held strong convictions about the value of strategic planning:

> Strategic planning pervades everything we do at KFC. It has brought great and effective change to our business and the way we market. But it clearly reduced marketing's ability to "do its own thing." As more people knew precisely what was going on, there was less tap dancing and more accountability in the marketing function. For example, all menu and pricing proposals required exhaustive marketing analysis. Proposals were reviewed by top management and evaluated by how they would help meet long-term strategic goals, not quarter-to-quarter earnings spikes. . . .
>
> Our best marketing people have become even better after exposure to the planning process. They quickly saw the logic and applied this tool to improve the business . . . and their careers. Our weaker performers—the "tap dancers" who never saw the light—are now tap dancing on someone else's stage.

As he reviewed the international operations, Dick Mayer focused a good deal of time on KFC-Japan. Not only was it one of KFC-I's largest, fastest-growing, and highest potential units, but in many ways it reflected the challenges that faced the company's entire international operations. Four issues seemed of particular importance in Japan, and indeed for KFC-I.

The most fundamental issue concerned the appropriate level of performance expectations for the overseas units (Exhibit 6 shows KFC-J's growth record). For example, although KFC-Japan expected to open its 400th store by the end of 1983, on a per-capita basis this represented less than one-quarter the level of penetration in the United States. And penetration levels in other countries were even lower. Mayer felt it was important for management to resist the temptation to regard the more established overseas units as mature. KFC-I had to maintain its drive for aggressive growth. But what did he need to do to ensure that such growth would continue?

The second challenge related to the overall issue of headquarters control of international operations. Mayer was aware of resistance to the administrative operational controls and systems and considered how hard he should push for their implementation. For example, how could headquarters turn a blind eye to the fact that some overseas units were force-fitting their numbers to meet hurdle rates, submitting approval forms after decisions had been implemented, and writing management reports to appease headquarters rather than provide proper analysis? Should they be willing to accept operational variations like the Japanese company's continued resistance to suggestions that it give up its obsession with menu expansion and devote more attention to improving the basics of its operations? At headquarters, managers claimed there was proven evidence that menu diversity affected the bottom line and hurt quality, but Japan rejected both notions.

A third important issue Mayer identified was the continuing problem of how to expand into new countries. Six countries (Japan, Australia, South Africa, New Zealand, United Kingdom, and Germany) accounted for over 95 percent of overseas earnings, and over the past decade numerous attempts to expand into a variety of new countries had met with very limited success (see Exhibit 7). A diversity of opinion existed on how the company should proceed. Gary Buhrow, vice president–strategic planning, felt the company had to move away from the highly opportunistic and people-dependent approach of the past:

> The world is more complicated than it was 15 years ago. We have to pay more attention to political risks, currency risks, and legal issues. And we need more sophisticated measures of market potential. We have begun to develop a capability at headquarters, a systematic analysis and comparison of new market risks and opportunities. This has helped us prepare a list of priority international market opportunities for KFC. In addition, when managers make market entry proposals and present details of their entry strategy, we have much more data against which to evaluate it and to set financial and operational expectations.

Loy Weston, on the other hand, felt that the string of failures and below-expectation performances in new markets could be tied directly to the deviation from John Y. Brown's mud-on-the-map approach of selecting entrepreneurs, giving them the challenge, and leaving them alone. He explained:

> Expansion into new markets requires a combination of sensitivity and entrepreneurial spark that is found in a different kind of person from your normal breed of corporate officer. When you find the right person—someone with energy, vision, imagination, and above all, willingness to take quick and unorthodox decisions—you have to leave him alone. You can't succeed if there are constant audits, visits, and forms to fill in for headquarters.
>
> Hong Kong is a perfect example of what not to do. They sent an insensitive and patronizing Australian who saw himself as a high-powered corporate executive. He breezed in, hired a secretary, bought a Mercedes, and immediately began driving around to inspect potential sites. There was no effort to understand local tastes or customs. He paid exorbitant prices for the sites, entered a joint venture with, of all parties, a U.K.-based conglomerate, and set up standard stores with standard

> menus. When stores opened, he was not close to the operations and wasn't even aware that the fish-meal-fed chicken he was buying had a strong unpleasant taste. It was a total disaster.

Dick Mayer had an open mind on the issue. But he was concerned that KFC had such limited positions in Korea, Taiwan, Thailand, and Hong Kong—four of the highest priority countries identified by the new market potential analysis. He learned that these countries were the responsibility of Loy Weston, who, four years earlier, had been named vice president for the North Pacific. Shin Ohkawara had succeeded Weston as president and chief executive in Japan, leaving Loy free to concentrate entirely on new market entries, but progress was slow. Mayer wondered if he should leave Weston alone, or whether he should authorize more headquarters involvement at this stage?

The question raised the whole issue of the appropriate management skills required to manage the company's overseas operations, and this topic represented the fourth item on Mayer's list of challenges. In considering the matter, he theorized that there were three stages in country management evolution:

> In the entrepreneurial stage there is not much room for managerial orientation. Loy Weston is a real go-getter. But he is an organizational nightmare who gets great joy in pricking the balloons of bureaucracy. At the second stage, we see the development of local baronies as managers use their local knowledge in developing operating skills to build their autonomy. The third stage is marked by the appearance of professional management who respond to planning, measurement, and business development ideas. Only this group can build for the long term.
>
> Unfortunately, there is a widespread belief that professional managers cannot be venturesome or entrepreneurial. But a fast food operation is inherently an entrepreneurial venture, and the country manager has to deal with the franchisees, who are generally entrepreneurs themselves. If you want to succeed in this business, you can't be a pin-stripe type. So by a kind of natural selection, the right types of managers rise to the top. I believe our professional managers can be the source of the entrepreneurial expansion we are looking for.

EXHIBIT 1

A. KFC INTERNATIONAL, ORGANIZATION STRUCTURE, 1972–73

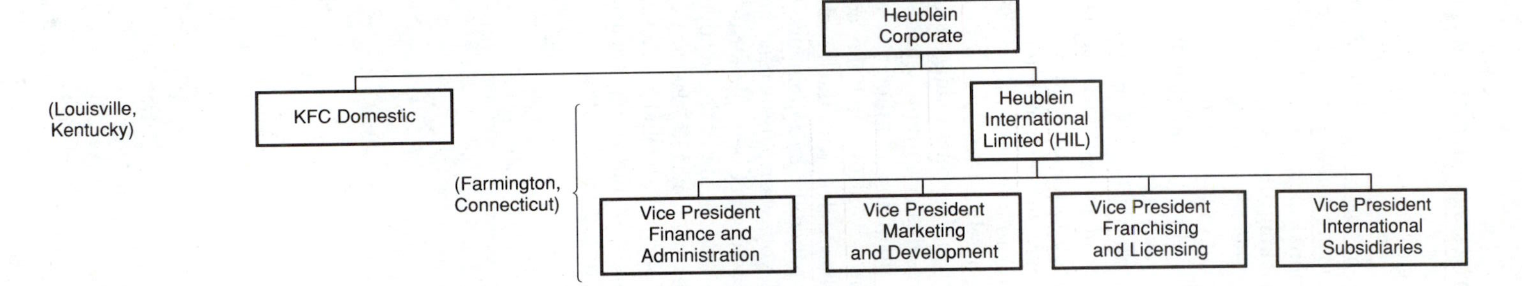

HIL headquarters staff—approximately 20 people. Responsible for KFC and Heublein overseas beverage sales. All overseas operations reported to the vice president International subsidiaries.

B. KFC INTERNATIONAL, ORGANIZATION STRUCTURE, 1975–76

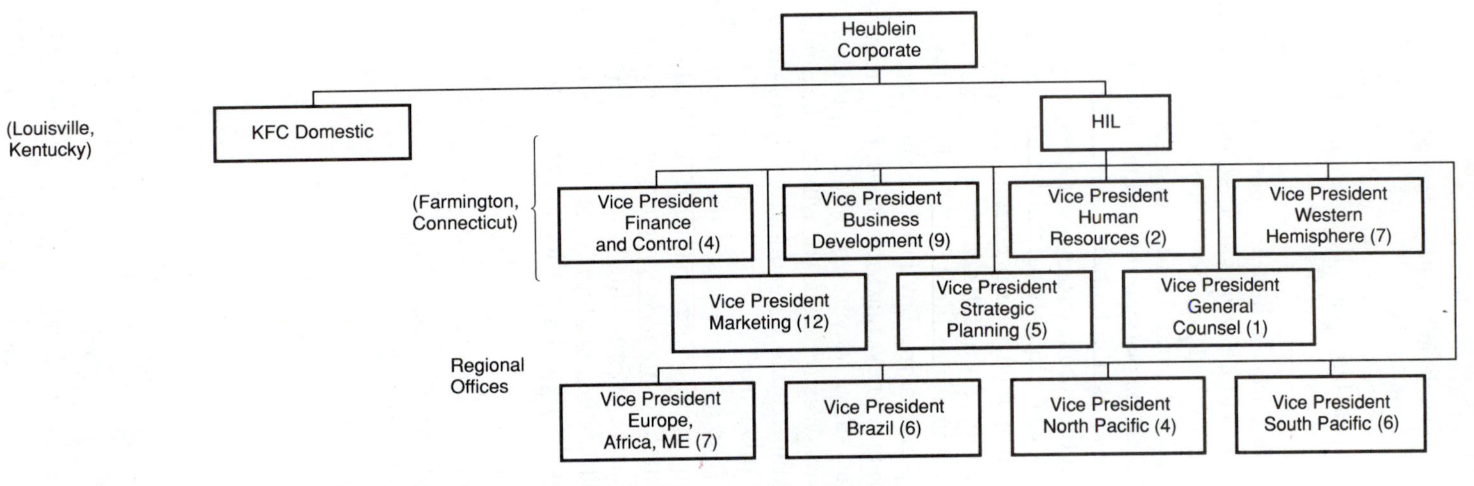

Number of direct reports. HIL headquarters staff—approximately 100. Responsible for KFC and beverage.

EXHIBIT 2
KFC INTERNATIONAL ORGANIZATION, 1981

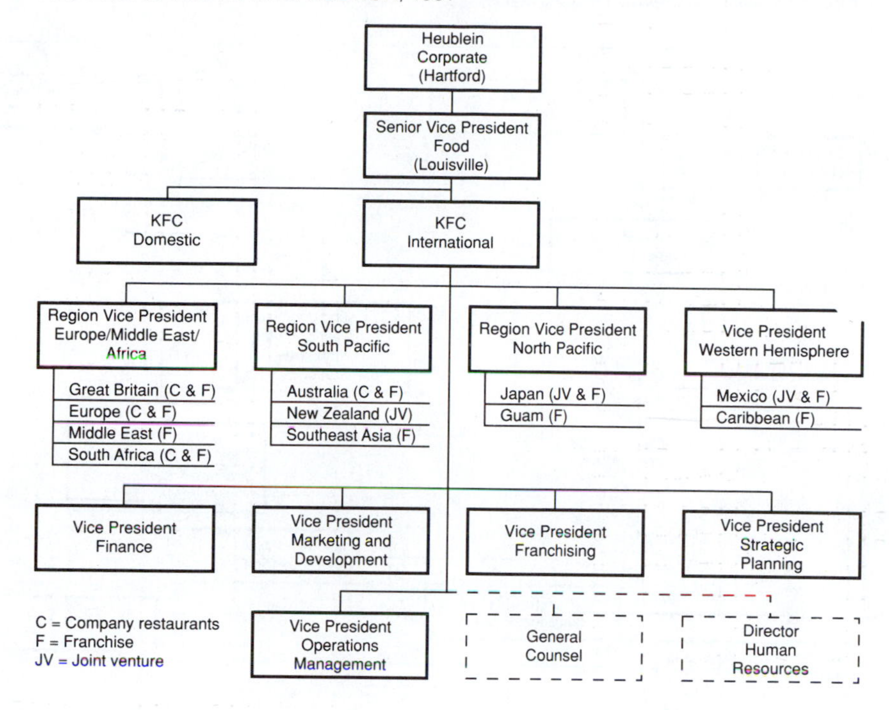

EXHIBIT 3
KFC–I PLANNING CYCLE OF CALENDAR

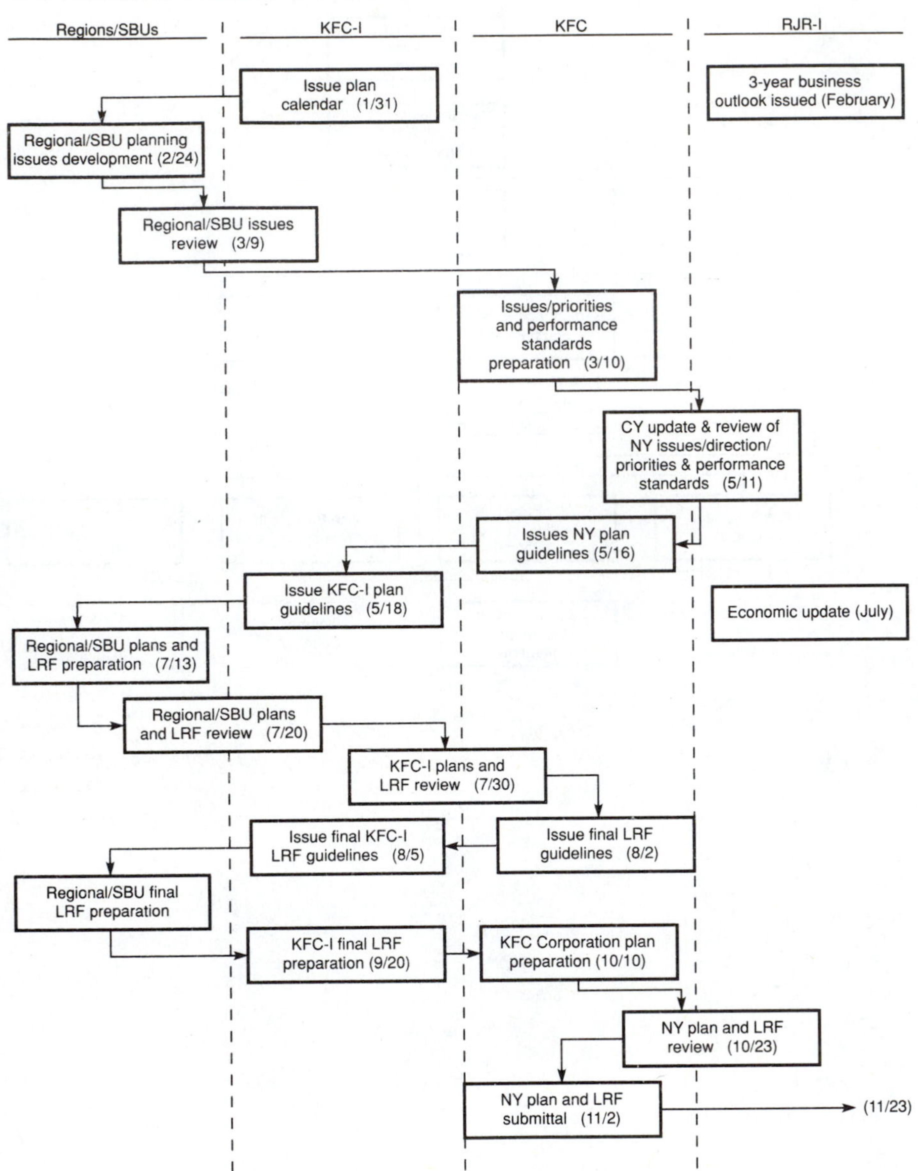

Note: LRF = Long Range Forecast; LY = Last Year; CY = Current Year; NY = Next Year.

EXHIBIT 4
LIST OF REPORTING SCHEDULES IN THE MONTHLY FINANCIAL PACKAGE

1. Statement of Earnings—Local Currency: Current month
1A. Statement of Earnings—Local Currency: Year-to-date
2. Statement of Earnings—U.S. $
3. Full Year Forecast—Local Currency
4. Current Forecast—U.S. $: Full year
4A. Current Forecast—U.S. $: Quarter by month
5. Balance Sheet
6. Balance Sheet Variance Analysis
7. Other Earnings Data
8. Personnel Status Report
8A. Equivalent Employee Analysis
9. Capital Expenditure Status Report
10. Intercompany Transactions—Statement of Earnings
11. Store Closing Report—Reserve Reconciliation
11A. Store Closing Report—Explanation
12. Risks and Opportunities
13. Receivables Management Report
14. Intercompany Account Reconciliation
14A. Intercompany Charges/Payments

Source: KFC–International.

EXHIBIT 5
SUMMARY FINANCIAL DATA OF HEUBLEIN, INC.

The company operated worldwide principally in four business segments: production and marketing of distilled spirits and prepared cocktails (Spirits); production and/or marketing of wines and brandies (Wines); production and sale of specialty food products (Grocery); and operating and franchising principally Kentucky Fried Chicken restaurants (Restaurants). The business segment information for each of the five years ended June 30 is presented below (in thousands):

	1982	*1981*	*1980*	*1979*	*1978*
Revenues:					
Spirits	$ 877,041	$ 876,546	$ 883,419	$ 819,563	$ 742,575
Wines	387,130	378,497	386,938	368,972	324,794
Grocery	173,545	153,552	131,511	114,193	118,160
Restaurants	699,687	641,526	520,011	466,346	434,583
Consolidated	$2,137,403	$2,050,121	$1,921,879	$1,769,074	$1,620,112
Operating profit:					
Spirits	$ 114,696	$ 107,078	$ 93,341	$ 87,599	$ 73,105
Wines	25,965	26,551	32,655	29,422	28,895
Grocery	26,447	21,545	17,904	17,989	17,949
Restaurants	84,087	69,126	51,302	34,966	26,711
Consolidated	251,195	224,300	195,202	169,976	146,660
Interest expense	33,214	28,581	25,361	23,106	25,041
Corporate and miscellaneous—net	20,251	27,683	22,933	15,851	12,319
Income before income taxes	$ 197,730	$ 168,036	$ 146,908	$ 131,019	$ 109,300
Identifiable assets:					
Spirits	$ 312,322	$ 318,695	$ 320,379	$ 300,605	$ 272,257
Wines	310,984	318,137	308,445	281,969	221,748
Grocery	58,389	61,601	63,219	66,696	61,170
Restaurants	353,882	316,519	276,682	242,266	227,659
Corporate	140,531	107,900	80,067	80,382	100,412
Consolidated	$1,176,108	$1,122,852	$1,048,792	$ 971,918	$ 883,246

Source: Form 10-K reports.

EXHIBIT 6
KFC-JAPAN PERFORMANCE CHARTS, 1978–1982

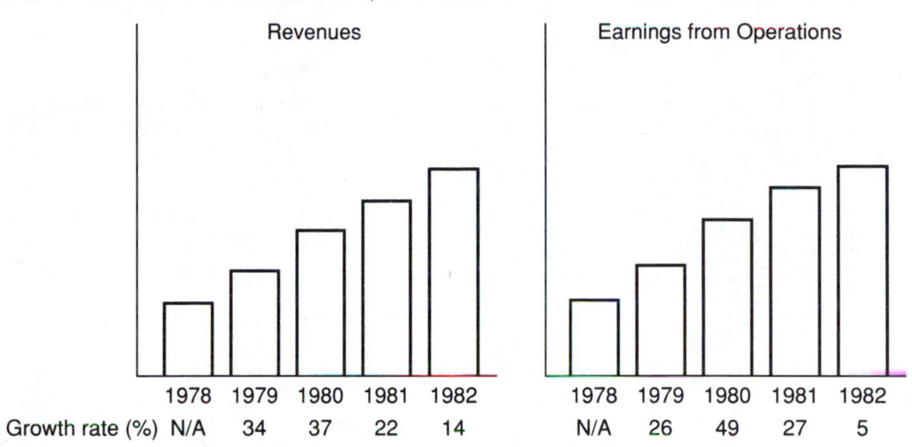

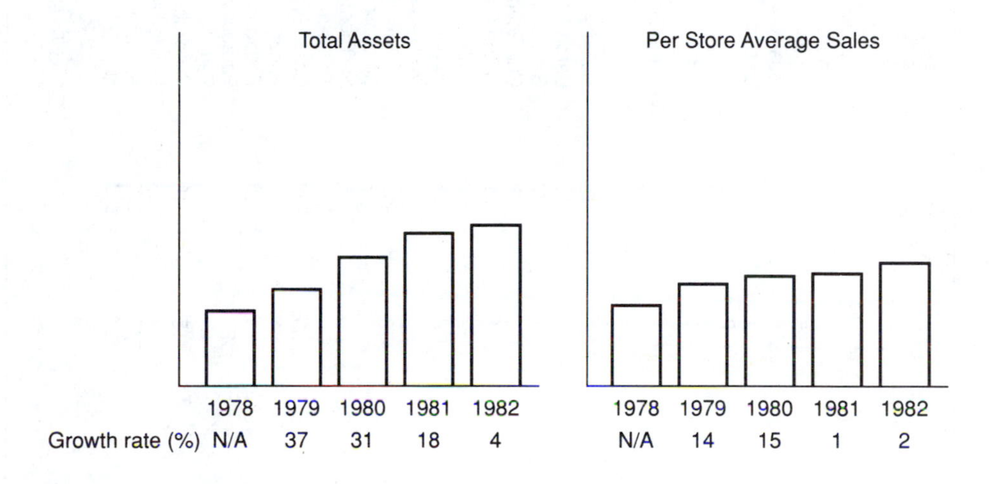

EXHIBIT 7
KFC SUBSIDIARIES ABROAD IN 1983

Country	Number of Stores		
	Company	Franchise	Total
Europe, Middle East, and Africa			
South Africa	48	95	143
Great Britain	61	308	369
Germany	3	11	14
Holland	5	2	7
Spain	4	6	10
Denmark	—	3	3
Iceland	—	1	1
Sweden	—	1	1
Switzerland	—	1	1
Kuwait	—	15	15
U.A.E.	—	10	10
Saudi Arabia	—	7	7
Bahrain	—	2	2
Qatar	—	1	1
Lebanon	—	2	2
Yemen	—	2	2
Egypt	—	6	6
	121	473	594
South Pacific			
Australia	157	69	226
Fiji	—	1	1
Indonesia	—	20	20
Malaysia	—	27	27
New Zealand	42	—	42
Philippines	—	15	15
Singapore	—	23	23
	199	155	354
North Pacific			
Japan	149	270	419
Guam	—	3	3
Saipan	—	1	1
	149	274	423
Western Hemisphere			
Argentina	—	1	1
Aruba	—	1	1
Bahamas	—	11	11
Barbados	—	3	3
Bermuda	—	1	1
Cuaracao	—	3	3
Grand Cayman	—	1	1
Haiti	—	3	3
Jamaica	—	10	10
Martinique	—	1	1
St. Maarten	—	1	1
St. Croix	—	3	3
St. Thomas	—	3	3
Trinidad	—	8	8
Costa Rica	—	4	4
Panama	—	7	7
Ecuador	—	5	5
Paraguay	—	1	1
Peru	—	4	4
Venezuela	—	1	1
Puerto Rico	26	—	26
Mexico	38	18	56
	64	90	154
Grand Total	533	992	1,525

Source: KFC International.

Honda Motor Company and Honda of America

In its 43-year history the Honda Motor Company had developed from a small, struggling enterprise selling surplus war engines in Japan into a $24 billion corporation producing cars, motorcycles, and power equipment in 77 plants in 40 countries. By 1989, Honda was the world's largest engine producer, the world's 11th largest automobile producer, and the 4th largest automobile producer in the United States. As a low-cost producer, it was second only to Toyota, and its quality had outrated that of Mercedes for three years running.

The basis of Honda's success was its expertise in developing and manufacturing products which incorporated its high-performance internal-combustion-engine technology. Honda institutionalized its commitment to innovation, along with the management philosophies and styles of its founders, Soichiro Honda and Takeo Fujisawa, into "The Honda Way." These policies guided the company's success and were expected to lead it through its growth in the future. But as Honda expanded its organization overseas, many wondered whether this growth would threaten the Honda Way of doing business.

Harvard Business School case 390–111.

THE HISTORY OF SOICHIRO HONDA AND THE HONDA MOTOR COMPANY

Soichiro Honda's love of mechanics and engineering began in his childhood, when he worked repairing bicycles for his father. After graduating from the eighth grade and serving a six-year apprenticeship at an automobile repair shop, Honda developed a successful business building piston rings for engines.

During the post–World War II rebuilding of Japan, the bicycle was the principle means of transportation around the country. With a personal investment of $3,200, Mr. Honda purchased 500 small surplus war engines to provide auxiliary power for bicycles. In 1946 the Honda Motor Company was formed to compete with 247 other Japanese participants in this loosely defined motorcycle industry.

In late 1949 a friend urged Honda to take a partner, Takeo Fujisawa, who was then running a merchant steel business in Tokyo. Like Honda, Fujisawa had begun working after finishing middle school. After a brief conversation, the two men agreed to work together. Fujisawa concentrated on finance and marketing, while Honda devoted his time and energy to technology.

Throughout the 1950s, Soichiro Honda built and raced high-performance, special-purpose motorcycles. Realizing the importance of creating, manufacturing, and selling superior products, Fujisawa convinced Honda to adapt this technology for commercial motorcycles. With the success of these machines—especially the Honda 50cc Supercub, with an automatic clutch, three-speed transmission, automatic starter, and safe and attractive look—the company skyrocketed into first place among Japanese motorcycle manufacturers, selling 285,000 units by the end of 1959.

Despite the success of the motorcycle business, Mr. Honda had always dreamt of manufacturing automobiles. In the mid-1960s, MITI planned to prevent additional Japanese companies from entering the automotive industry. Honda needed to produce a car by 1963 simply to qualify the firm as a producer; and in 1962, Honda introduced its first minicar. Described by critics as an enclosed golf cart, the vehicle proved a disaster.

As with motorcycles, Honda again turned to racing as an impetus for technological development. Following a tour on the Grand Prix Formula 1 circuit, it concentrated on applying its accumulated knowledge of race cars to passenger vehicles.

In 1967 Honda launched the N360 minicar. The car was well received in Japan, and sales grew rapidly. In 1971 the company announced the development of the water-cooled, compound, vortex-controlled, combustion (CVCC) automobile engine—more fuel efficient and "cleaner" in exhaust emission than all existing engines. This technology was incorporated into the Honda Civic 1200 which was marketed in 1972. The Accord and Prelude models followed in 1976 and 1978. In 1986 Honda became the first Japanese car company to launch a luxury car division, with its Acura models.

THE HONDA WAY

From the beginning, Honda's success was attributed to a philosophy of seeking the toughest challenges and applying creativity, innovation, and imagination to solve them. The management team of Fujisawa and Honda played a critical role in developing this philosophy. One Honda executive said of Fujisawa:

> He was an enthusiastic man who had a dream to help build an organization that was different from others in Japan, or anywhere else. He wanted to create a firm that had the spirit of a small- or medium-sized company, an organization with individuals who could maintain their own vitality, an organization that could utilize the full resources of its people.

Unique among companies at the time, Honda committed itself in 1956 to an international viewpoint and to supplying highly efficient products at reasonable prices worldwide. Dedication to this principle led it to build an enormous business outside Japan, especially in the United States. As Mr. Honda explained his internationalization philosophy:

> In my company, we have sometimes sacrificed short-range profits in an effort

> to contribute to and achieve harmony with our society. As an example, I would like to point out that Honda's motorcycles, cars, and parts are manufactured and assembled around the world. If we were seeking nothing but profits, it would be easier for us to export finished products alone. We have thought that if we want to be well received in the countries where we do business, it is imperative that we contribute to those countries' economic and industrial development and create employment opportunities.

Honda adopted an explicit corporate charter in 1956 (see Exhibit 1). This philosophy focused on three areas: technology, quality, and cost; innovation; and values.

TECHNOLOGY, QUALITY, AND COST

In the early 1950s, Honda toured a number of motorcycle manufacturing plants worldwide. Impressed by the advanced machine tools that he saw, he invested $1.5 billion between 1952 and 1954 to import this technology. He ran the machines at 100 to 150 to 200 percent of rated capacity until they failed. Then he modified them until, by reverse engineering, he made his own line of production equipment capable of tolerances and volume higher than any others in the world.

Honda Engineering, a wholly owned subsidiary, was responsible for all of Honda's proprietary manufacturing machinery, which in 1989, constituted approximately 60 percent of the firm's machine tooling. This production technology allowed Honda to build cars better, cheaper, and faster than its competitors (see Exhibit 2). For example, Honda was able to build its high-end Accord for $1,500 less than either General Motors or Ford could build their comparable Oldsmobile Cutlass or Ford Topaz.

In addition, Honda's product development cycle averaged two and one half years compared with four years for the best American car company and three years for the best Japanese company. Honda could launch its second-generation vehicles while competitors were just launching their first.

Honda believed that the quality of its products was critical to its success. It focused on teaching quality as a satisfying way of life. It asked each associate, or employee, to take individual responsibility for product. The quality goal for each associate was: Accept no bad parts, make no bad parts, and approve no bad parts.

To ensure it received no bad parts, Honda insisted on quality products from its vendors. Explained Shoichiro Irimajiri, former president of Honda of America and managing director of Honda, "When we look for suppliers, we seek companies that believe in the same things we do; because they are not selling their products merely to Honda, they are selling their products to our customers, through Honda."[1]

When Honda considered contracting with a vendor, it went through an extensive process of review, conducting formal interviews, inspecting vendors' plants, and reviewing cleanliness and quality standards. Honda sent its vendors monthly reports on its quality performance as well as suggestions for improvement. Because of its reputation for quality, it had become a source of pride within the industry to be known as a Honda supplier.[2]

---

[1] Robert L. Shook, *Honda: An American Success Story* (New York: Prentice Hall Press), p. 173.

[2] Ibid., p. 117.

INNOVATION AT HONDA

Mr. Honda talked about the importance of technological leadership in these terms:

> On one side, we have the customer, who is always changing. And on the other side, technology is changing. To survive in the automobile industry, we must change before our competitors do. It is the auto maker who makes the fastest changes that wins."[3]

To emphasize the importance of technology development, Honda spun off its R&D organization in 1957 as a wholly owned company. This arrangement enabled R&D to work on long-term projects without the hindrance of marketing and manufacturing demands for short-term profits. Honda committed about 5 percent of total sales—and 18 percent of its work force—to R&D (compared with 4 percent committed by all U.S. car manufacturers).

In addition, Honda established a tradition of drawing its CEOs from the R&D subsidiary. By making it explicit that the president of the R&D subsidiary would become heir to the entire enterprise, those aspiring to this position were groomed to think in terms broader than R&D's interests.

Honda employees were encouraged to aim for the highest efficiency possible. Instead of expecting a 3 percent improvement in productivity, Honda pushed its organization to aim for 30 percent improvement. This dedication is evident in a story Irimajiri told about the 1984 Honda Accord:

> In 1984 the Honda Accord was our best-selling automobile. In January 1985, it was named by *Car and Driver,* for the third consecutive year, as one of the 10 best cars sold in America. They said, "There is nothing wrong with the Honda Accord. Nothing."
>
> Yet, in September 1985, we made a full model change of the Accord. We changed everything. Why would we do that to a car that had nothing wrong with it? The answer is that we believed we could make it better. And in 1986 and 1987, *Car and Driver* again named the new Honda Accord as one of the 10 best cars sold in America.
>
> It is tough, but our experience has taught us to believe that no matter how good a product we have made, we can make it better.

The Development of the City Car and the SED Process

Product development at Honda followed a process called "SED." Sales (S) conceived of the image for a new product through discussions with customers; research and development (D) created the specific design based on the sales image; and production and engineering (E) found a way to build the design. None of these groups worked alone. The creation of the image, the design, and the production process took place simultaneously; and with the division of labor unclear, associates were encouraged to invade one another's areas. There was constant feedback and communication among all three groups.

Design teams were orchestrated in such a fashion so as not only to generate initiatives but also to weave conflicting views and various disciplines together. The principal ingredients of this process were (1) framing project goals in a dramatic way that challenged engineers; (2) creating the right blend of personalities and expertise—including people from unorthodox disciplines who were unfamiliar with the core technology so as to force the group to look at the problem differently; (3) using paral-

[3] Ibid., p. 193.

lel project teams and engendering competition between them; and (4) terminating nonproductive projects in such a way as to avoid participants losing face.

The aim was to manage development opportunities more systematically by integrating the knowledge and wisdom of ordinary people instead of relying on a "hero" like founder Soichiro Honda.

An example of this process at work was the development of the City car. Faced with the need for a small, inexpensive breakthrough car for the Japanese market in 1978, Honda's top management formed the design team to create a new product. The group had very little industry experience, and the average age of the team members was 27.

The overall assignment from headquarters was stated in very general and ambiguous terms on one sheet of paper: "Create something different from the existing concept." The group first attempted to develop a "mini Civic." Recalled team leader Mr. Watanabe: "No matter how we refined development plans of this kind, they were rejected again and again. We were told to start all over from the very beginning. We didn't know what to do, so we were finally persuaded to try it."[4]

Eventually, the team began to question the fundamentals of its designs, to reject convention, and to design a new car completely from scratch. The result was the Honda City, which became a top-selling automobile in Japan. A special engine, suspension, and radial tire were developed exclusively for the new car, and 90 patents were applied for during the project. As one team member commented:

> I feel, however illogical it sounds, that the success of this project owes a lot to the very wide gap between the ideal and the actual. We could not achieve the ideal goal by incremental improvement of the actual. Revolutionary reformation was necessary, and in order to achieve this, new technologies and concepts were generated one after another.

A Honda executive explained the rationale for this process:

> We take the chance of giving young people basic goals and responsibilities and then letting them go by themselves. In other words, we put them upstairs, remove the ladders, and say "You have to figure out a way to get down." Then we set fire to the first floor. I think human beings display their greatest creativity under these circumstances.

After completion of a project, participants were assigned to other projects so that the knowledge they had acquired could be disseminated throughout the organization. An engineer commented:

> I think it's pretty difficult to articulate really meaningful know-how in text, figures, or other measurable forms. The best way to transfer it is through human interaction.[5] Although Honda promoted breakthroughs, it also recognized the value of incremental improvement. Mr. Honda used to say: "In a race competing for a split second, one tire length on the finish line will decide whether you are a winner or a loser. If you understand that, you cannot disregard even the smallest improvement."

Mr. Irimajiri added:

> So many times the highest efficiency is achieved by a series of improvements,

[4] Ikujiro Nonaka, "Toward Middle-Up-Down Management: Accelerating Information Creation," *Sloan Management Review,* Spring 1988, p. 10.

[5] Ibid., p. 11.

> each of which seems very small. We are now making major improvements in efficiency not from any single big change, but rather from thousands of improvements made by our associates.

THE HONDA VALUES

In its early days, Honda was considered a maverick company. Its employees were college dropouts or rejects from the traditional, established companies. Honda was a young organization as well. The average age of its board members was 52, and the average age of its employees was 31.

Part of Honda's uniqueness was reflected in a commitment to its employees, in whom, Fujisawa believed, was the enduring source of Honda's success. The Honda Way emphasized respect for the individual. No rigid hierarchy existed; all employees were referred to as associates. All employees wore the same white uniform and green cap and ate in the same cafeteria. There were no reserved spaces in the parking lot and no private offices.

Involving Employees in Decision Making

A basic philosophy of Honda Motor Company was that everybody had the equal right to work and the equal right to think. Everyone was encouraged to come up with ideas. Commented Mr. Honda:

> There is a limit to what can be thought out by big shots sitting at their desks. Where 100 people think, there are 100 powers; if 1,000 people think, there are 1,000 powers.[6]

[6] Jon Alston, *The American Samurai* (New York: De Gruyter, 1989), p. 34.

The idea that everyone was involved as equals was not simply an employee involvement scheme. It was fundamental to how Honda worked. Employees went to work assuming that they would be expected to increase performance each day.

The company resisted tight home-office controls over its faraway plants and divisions. Instead, management was decentralized, and responsibilities were delegated to those in charge of day-to-day operations. Problems were solved by the people at each plant, with small groups and divisions operating as small independent businesses.

To eliminate the fear of making mistakes, associates were encouraged to discuss their problems and apply their creativity to solving them. Said Mr. Honda of risk taking:

> Only through failure can precious experience be gained. But be sure to always learn from your mistakes. Failure by itself is not necessarily failure. We learn that we failed because we took a certain route, and this is how we now know what route we then must take to succeed.

Employees were involved and their ideas were solicited and acted upon in a number of different ways. To improve quality and communication among associates, Honda introduced the NH quality circle. These groups of 5 to 10 associates voluntarily assembled to work on problems and create solutions in a variety of areas such as quality, safety, communication, and work environment.

Another process was called *waigaya,* a phonetic term for the noise Japanese made when they argued. In waigaya sessions, rank was disregarded and subordinates were permitted to speak candidly, disagree, question, and challenge. Sessions could be initiated by managers and associates alike. Explained President Kume:

> If you don't make the daily effort, people tend to agree with executives. I tell people that if the president says a crow is white, they have to argue that the crow is really black. If juniors don't rebel against their seniors, that means there is no progress.

In fact, when Kiyoshi Kawashima, Kume's predecessor, resigned as president of Honda, he said, "I decided to step down because the employees began agreeing with me 70 percent of the time."

Employee Training

A further aspect of the Honda Way derived from Fujisawa's management style. He rarely issued orders or gave directions, but would instead ask probing, Socratic questions, forcing employees to think independently. As the company expanded, Fujisawa felt the next generation of managers needed to learn his ability to question in a penetrating manner. In the 1950s he learned of a method developed by the Kepner Tregoe firm in Princeton, New Jersey, which taught how to think systematically and get to the root cause of problems. The methodology, licensed and taught to all managerial-level employees, was later termed "The Honda Rational Thinking Process." It taught that if you ask the right questions, the correct answers follow; and it became second nature to the way plant managers thought.

Honda also stressed the importance of cross-training. Associates rotated among jobs, which prevented the boredom of tedious tasks and increased knowledge of the overall production process so that if a particular process became obsolete, the associate would not. Employees were also encouraged to attend lectures and lab courses to upgrade their technical skills.

Annually, each Honda manager had to exchange jobs with a counterpart in another function for a two-week period. In addition, all R&D staff members had to spend three months a year attending dealer shows and automotive conventions around the world to indoctrinate themselves with a marketing outlook. In Japan, all engineering and manufacturing managers were required to spend six months working at a dealership to develop a clear understanding of customer needs. And all top officers visited dealerships constantly and looked for feedback from those closest to the Honda customer.

The Role of Management

The role of management was not viewed as setting goals and ensuring they were met. MBOs (Management by Objectives) were seen as inhibitors to learning because they strove for results largely *within* the existing system. According to one plant manager:

> At Honda, we believe that 85 percent of our problems stem from systems deficiencies. If the system is 85 percent of the problem, MBOs distract us from improving the system and thus subtly confine our efforts to optimizing that which is suboptimal.

Managers were encouraged to spend a great deal of their time on the factory floor becoming involved in what was going on. Mr. Honda, who believed that managers should demonstrate good leadership by performing the most undesirable jobs at least once, was known to sweep floors, empty ashtrays, and pick up paper towels off the rest room floors. He explained:

> It is wrong for executives to act like feudal lords and not know what is going on

> below them. What is most important in the process of democratization is for the upper people to come down. And that is where the sense of equality is found.[7]

Executive Offices

Fujisawa was a firm believer in management by walking around. As president, he found himself spending more and more time talking with subordinates, asking questions, and working alongside them. To encourage this behavior among his senior executives, he made sure there were always fewer desks and offices available than executives. Top executives were thus forced to be out on the factory floor and be involved in on-the-spot problem solving and decision making.

Honda's top 40 directors and managing directors were housed in a single open area with only six individual desks and five large circular conference tables. Forty chairs were arranged around the tables to encourage executives to work alongside one another and to enable all managers to keep in touch with what was going on throughout the company. Each person had one file drawer, and there were only 11 secretaries.

This executive workroom was located on the 10th floor of a 16-floor building. According to the company president, the rationale was: "When you are on the 10th floor, it is easier to go up and down because you never have far to travel."

The Triad Organization

As mentioned previously, Honda spun off its R&D and engineering businesses and left Honda Manufacturing with responsibility for sales, marketing, and administration. Through transfer pricing, Engineering and R&D negotiated contracts for projects with Honda Manufacturing and sold their services on a time-and-materials basis. This process of haggling over what ideas to fund and for how much was termed "the Persian market."

Each of these three subsidiaries viewed the organization and pushed and pulled it from a different perspective. This created constructive tension within the Honda organization. The focus on continual change and improvement led one executive to comment: "There's a hunger for change here. We've become conditioned to the challenges it creates. So many people here need this kind of excitement; it's part of the Honda culture."

HONDA OF AMERICA MANUFACTURING INC.

Success in Japan fueled Mr. Honda's appetite for new and different challenges and set the stage for entry into the U.S. market.

In 1958 Honda began exporting its larger motorcycles to the United States. A few began to sell—then disaster struck. Honda machines were leaking oil and encountering clutch failure. As it turned out, people drove motorcycles in the United States much farther and much faster than in Japan. Honda was forced to airfreight the bikes back to Japan to redesign them.

Until then, Honda had not tried to sell its small, but popular, Supercub bikes. Although they were a large success in Japan, they did not seem to fit the U.S. market, where everything was bigger and more luxurious. Honda was hesitant to promote the 50cc bikes, fearing they might harm its image in a heavily "macho" market. But when the larger bikes began breaking down, they had no choice.

[7] Alston, *American Samurai,* p. 123.

In 1963 the company introduced its "You Meet the Nicest People on a Honda" campaign, aimed at everyday Americans, a largely untapped segment of the marketplace. The campaign boosted U.S. sales. By 1964 nearly one of every two motorcycles sold in the United States was a Honda.

In 1969 Honda began shipping cars to the United States. They were sold in "Big Three" dealerships with foreign car departments and in a select number of Honda motorcycle dealerships. By 1975 Honda was selling 10,000 Civics a month.

The following year, Honda introduced its Accord, which was immediately named *Motor Trend* magazine's "Import Car of the Year." The Accord continued to be a popular model in the United States, and by 1989 it had been chosen by *Car and Driver* magazine as one of the 10 best cars sold in America for seven consecutive years.

Relying on Honda philosophy to manufacture products in the markets where they were sold, Honda became the first Japanese company to establish a production facility for motorcycles in the United States. Production began in 1979 with 64 associates in a 258,000-square-foot factory outside Marysville, Ohio. The initial investment of $35 million was followed by the construction of a 1-million-square-foot automobile manufacturing facility at a cost of $250 million. Production of the 1983 model Accord began in November 1982. A 700,000-square-foot expansion of the automobile plant was completed, at a cost of $240 million, to provide a second production line. A separate $30 million engine plant was completed in 1984.

By 1986 North America was the largest single market and home of the largest production base outside of Japan. In 1988 North American sales accounted for 45 percent of Honda's total sales—a larger percentage than Honda's domestic Japanese business: 36 percent of total sales. By 1989 more than 60 percent of the Hondas sold in America were being produced in Ohio. Company performance was strong (see Exhibit 3), and Honda slowly began to gain market share in the United States (see Exhibit 4).

Americanizing Honda

From its inception, Shoichiro Irimajiri, then president of HAM (Honda of America), was concerned about developing an organization that would be a hybrid of Japanese and American management practices:

> I have been concerned with how to make both Japanese and American employees work together toward common goals. For this, neither a Japanese way nor an American way will do.
>
> In solving this problem, I used the way of thinking at Honda as a base. I discussed the Honda way of thinking with my Japanese colleagues, put it into our own words, translated it into English, and relayed it to key American managers. After many rounds of discussions, they then set down their own interpretations—"it must mean this"—in English.
>
> There were further discussions: "No, that's not quite right. . . ." Each week we explained the documents to a different group of American managers so as to share the basic principles with them.
>
> But even today, almost every day, views of Japanese managers and American managers differ on some point or other, and I tell them both to pull hard on the rope.

HAM's five-tiered management structure was composed of the president, vice president, department heads, managers, and coordinators. Both the president and vice president were Japanese. Of the 11 department heads, 3 were American. Mr. Irimajiri explained the role of the Japanese managers:

> If the Japanese have the upper hand and all we have on the other side are yes men, highly motivated Americans will quit. At the present stage, Japanese control is a good thing, but it may prove to be harmful in the long run. On the other hand, if Americans have control, I think that HAM will wind up on the same road as the Big Three auto makers. We have a policy of giving Americans increasing control while phasing ourselves out. Once our American associates have begun to truly understand The Honda Way, it will remain here even after all the Japanese are gone.

Recruiting

Beyond developing a management philosophy that would work in America, Honda concentrated on selecting the right personnel by interviewing HAM applicants extensively. The first interview generally lasted an hour, and good candidates were interviewed twice more, often by two or three top managers. Although HAM did not have a lifetime employment policy, it did seek associates for long-term employment. One of the objectives of the extensive interviewing process was to determine how well people would do as HAM associates.[8] Explained one manager:

> We try to be candid with everyone so there won't be any surprises later on. If somebody doesn't feel comfortable with our work environment, open-office concept, uniforms, or lack of perks, then they probably won't fit in at HAM.

Chino, managing director, explained:

> We hired nonexperienced workers because we thought that if we hired experienced workers they might have some bad habits. We thought it better to train them fresh. We sent key personnel to Japanese factories to learn how to make cars and how to maintain quality. They came back and trained their colleagues.

The number of associates at HAM totaled 4,700, with 180 of them Japanese expatriates. The absentee rate hovered at about 2 percent.

Introduction of Honda-isms

As in Honda Manufacturing in Japan, there were no reserved parking spaces, executive dining rooms, or private offices at HAM. All employees referred to one another as associates, including the executive vice presidents; and they all wore white jumpsuits with first names stitched above the pocket.

Commented Mr. Iwamoto on the uniforms:

> In America, if you want to persuade most people of something, you have to use logical reasoning. We had to use the reasoning that it [the uniform] was to prevent scratching their product and that they are safer in the uniform than in their personal clothing.

The issue of morning exercises also engendered debate among the HAM management group. Some believed employees would interpret it as too "Japanese." However, conducting brief limbering-up exercises before each shift was believed to help reduce stiffness and would decrease injuries. Therefore an affirmative decision was reached.[9]

Training

Each associate received on-the-job training, which concentrated on demonstrations, followed by trainees copying what

---

[8] Shook, *Honda: An American Success*, pp. 168–69.

[9] Ibid., p. 47.

they had watched their managers do. New workers were encouraged to ask questions and were always given a reason why, not simply ordered to do something. Onda, assistant manager for purchasing, had these comments:

> In order to transplant the Honda Way, it is essential to personally show how to do things in detail. For example, if we have a problem with defective parts from a supplier, it is important that the purchasing supervisor actually go to the assembly line to find out what is wrong and then rush out to the supplier's plant. Not only the words, but demonstrating the action is required. If someone sees you do this, he will come to do it himself.

Then administration manager Iwamoto added:

> To a Japanese, the golden rule of "the four S's"—seiri, seiton, seiso, and seiketsu [arrangement, order, cleaning, and neatness] — is taken for granted, but over here you must show workers in a logical way how neatness and cleanliness is related to the quality of their products. This is much more difficult than we had anticipated.

On teaching employees the value of quality, Al Kinzer, a vice president at HAM, commented:

> When it comes to quality, we never compromise. *Never.* There is only one standard that is acceptable, and it never varies. It's so easy to let people off the hook in the heat of the day when you're being pushed. So you always must remember that no product, under any circumstances, ever goes out the door if quality is compromised. You can't say, "Okay, shipping must go out today. Just this one time we'll slacken our standards and let the car go out the door." Once you do, you've taught your people that a double standard exists. You've violated the rules on what your real objective is, and you've lost it. And once it's lost, you can never get it back.[10]

Honda paid a great deal of attention to external benchmarks. Shoichiro Irimajiri used to assemble the top 30 plant managers every third Thursday evening of the month to personally disassemble a competitor's part—a carburetor or a shock absorption system. The plant manager would compare its inner workings with Honda's counterpart, evaluate the strengths and weaknesses of the alternative designs, and send suggestions for improving the Honda part to Honda R&D in Japan.

Technology at HAM

In the Honda plant, the company produced long runs of nearly identical cars, which was far more efficient than offering the hundreds of features that domestic car producers did. The shop floor equipment was new and sophisticated. From where welding began until the finished product drove off the assembly line, the car was moved entirely by hooks and conveyors; no human handlers were needed. The stamping machines that bent steel sheets into side panels, hoods, and trunk lids could change stamping dies in less than 10 minutes. With stamping, welding, painting, plastic injection molding, and assembly all under one roof, when a problem occurred, the associate who identified it just walked over to the relevant department to solve it.[11]

HAM also made use of a Tech Line, a group of skilled technicians who were on call to analyze any problem that a dealership mechanic could not solve. All solutions were stored in a computer for future

[10] Ibid., p. 116.
[11] Ibid., p. 121.

reference. The Tech Line also provided quick feedback about problems in newly released models. Said one executive: "If we spot a trend, the information is relayed within hours to the factory to make the necessary corrections."[12]

Production and technology were as quick and flexible as in Japan, with HAM performing two major production changes. The 1986 Accord was a different car than the 1985 model, and this changeover was effected in a single night. At the time the last 1985 Accord was being driven off the assembly line, the completely new 1986 model was starting down the line. In addition, the 1987 and 1988 Civic models were completely different, and the changeover, too, occurred without any disruption to the assembly line.

The Honda Research of America (HRA) design center was established in 1977. Its employees designed, researched, and tested Hondas and competitors' models. They also participated in joint design projects on such cars as the 1983 Civic CRX and the 1984 Quint Integra.

HAM began doing some of its own engineering by developing Honda Engineering of America (EGA), whose task was to develop better manufacturing methods. EGA had a staff of 110 in 1988 and planned to increase it to 200 by 1990. HAM believed that special technology development was an asset that helped keep the organization unique.

Core parts for Honda cars, such as engines and transmissions, were imported from Japan; tires, steel, batteries, and glass were purchased locally. The local content for 1988 models was 60 percent. Fearing U.S. government retaliation and in an effort to increase its local parts content, Honda constructed an engine manufacturing plant in Anna, Ohio, in 1984. In addition, it formed two joint ventures with its Japanese suppliers to produce parts in the United States.

Empowering Employees at HAM

As in Japan, Honda of America focused on involving its employees in the decision making that would affect their jobs. For example, in developing the Integra car in the Acura division, designers in Los Angeles worked with their counterparts in Japan. Honda's American sales staff road tested the vehicle and then conferred with the designers on what changes needed to be made.

When a U.S. design team became stalemated over a trunk design project, its members spent an afternoon in a Disneyland parking lot observing what people put into and removed from their car trunks and what kind of motion was involved.

Initiatives were encouraged in manufacturing, too. Associates formed voluntary groups to develop more efficient production techniques. More than 1,400 employees are involved in such groups and could earn free cars and trips to Japan for new ideas that would make the company more efficient.

HAM operated a company suggestion program in which associates were given the opportunity to change anything about their job to improve their work. Associates would write their proposed ideas on a single-page suggestion form and submit it to their department manager for review. A response would be given within 48 hours, and associates would see quick results. Of all the suggestions submitted, 59 percent were implemented.[13]

[12] Ibid., pp. 81–82.

[13] Ibid., pp. 136–37.

Impressions of the American Work Force at HAM

Teaching and training American workers the Honda Way of business proved to be an exhausting and time-consuming task for Japanese managers. A number of them commented on the differences they saw between Japanese employees and their American counterparts. Explained Irimajiri:

> It seems that in an American organization, you must always be motivating your employees from the top. Because Japanese plants generally have a solid bureaucratic organization, even if top management shifts its attention to matters other than day-to-day operations, you can be sure that all will go well with very little deviation. But in this country, you cannot be assured that things will go well without your total involvement. Unless you keep giving impetus incessantly, you can't avoid a feeling that things could come to a standstill.

Onda, assistant manager for purchasing, made these comments:

> Americans can do precisely what they set out to do, but they are not accustomed to organizing their jobs among themselves or to paying attention to what their neighboring co-workers are doing. If paired with a Japanese one-on-one and if the exchange of guidance and information is satisfactory, they come around. Workers fresh from school have an easier time picking up the Honda Way.

Commented Planning Manager Nakayama:

> It can be said that the quality that U.S. workers lack most is that of doing extra work beyond what they have been told to do. They are quick to learn their jobs and to reach the fighting ability that is expected, but they seem to lack the will to move a step further. But they are gradually getting to understand the Honda Way, and American managers are already appearing who seem prepared to shoulder the future of HAM.

American Unions and the Equal Employment Opportunity Commission

In April 1982, several months before HAM began producing automobiles, three boilermen joined the United Auto Workers (UAW) Union. The company agreed to recognize them as a bargaining unit, but stressed that this approval did not mean that all workers at the Ohio plant would be represented by the UAW.

In October 1985 the UAW demanded that President Irimajiri approve the UAW as the representative unit of all HAM employees. A UAW charge: Can you keep up with the pace when you get older? had considerable appeal for many workers. One worker commented:

> Honda has an operational tactic of routinely keeping workers in a state of overwork. If you refuse to work on Saturday, it will be recorded and taken into account in your evaluation.

Another worker countered:

> We have the best pay and allowances in this region. There's no fear of losing our jobs. Everyone is treated equally. I doubt a union can get us better conditions.

The company conducted an opinion poll on whether or not it would be appropriate to give automatic approval to the UAW. Ninety-eight percent of the employees responded, and of those, 75 percent replied that they were opposed to automatic approval. The UAW filed a lawsuit with the NLRB, claiming that HAM had resorted to unfair labor practices in conducting a survey of employees' opinions and in allowing a faction of employees to conduct an antiunion campaign.

On January 31, 1986, the NLRB rejected the UAW's suit against HAM, the UAW withdrew its demand for a vote, and the problem of organizing a union at HAM was settled for the moment.

Honda's problems with its labor practices were not over. In June 1987 HAM accepted a recommendation of the U.S. Equal Employment Opportunity Commission (EEOC) and paid approximately $457,000 each to more than 85 people over 40 years of age who had applied and been rejected for assembly-line and welding work in 1984 and 1985. EEOC concluded that because there was a disproportionately small number of workers over 40 among those newly hired in 1984 and 1985, there had been discriminatory treatment of those applicants over 40.

Masai Miyamoto, manager of International Human Resource Management of Honda Motor Company, commented:

> We never anticipated that problems with discrimination by race, sex, or—least of all—age would ever be encountered. I think that the spirit of "looking out for the underdog" in American society is wonderful. The reaction of almost everyone was to regard the compensation as a sort of tuition for doing business in the United States, a valuable lesson learned.

Again, in March 1988, EEOC ordered HAM to pay a $6 million settlement to 370 blacks and women who had been systematically discriminated against when they applied for jobs at Honda.

NEW DEVELOPMENTS AT HAM

New Competition in the Luxury Car Segment

In 1986 Honda entered the luxury automobile market with its Acura line. Acura was sold through a separate sales and dealership network. Tom Elliott, senior vice president of Automobile Operations, explained the rationale for the second line:

> When you think about cars in the class of a Mercedes or a BMW, the name Honda doesn't spring to mind because we've created an image that our products stand for lower-priced fuel economy, a good value for your money, and quality.
>
> Honda owners know that we make the Acura. We have customers who bought the Civic in the mid-1970s. Many of these same customers became Accord owners. Now we have something to offer them as they get older and become more affluent.[14]

The Acura was chosen by J.D. Power and Associates as first in its Customer Satisfaction Index in 1988. That made it three years in a row that Honda/Acura held that distinction.

In 1989 Toyota and Nissan entered the luxury car segment with the Lexus and Infiniti models, respectively. Both of these cars were priced comparably to Acura and about $10,000 less than BMW or Mercedes. The market's reaction to these new cars was very favorable. As a result, Toyota prepared to double Lexus output to 100,000 cars a year.[15]

A New Organizational Structure in North America

In March 1987, Honda established Honda North America to be the headquarters of its 11 subsidiaries in the United States, Canada, and Mexico; to chart American strategy; and to augment decision making and coordination of Honda's production and sales activities in North America. A member of Honda's top management explained:

---

[14] Ibid., p. 70.

[15] "Infiniti and Lexus: Characters in a German Nightmare," *Business Week*, October 9, 1989, p. 64.

> Executives of the 11 companies had to wait for [confirmation] from headquarters in Japan on any strategic decisions they made. Because sales in the United States and Canada account for such a large percentage of our total sales, we had to have a way for operations in North America to be carried out quickly.

> It is not enough that our U.S. operations attain capabilities that compare to our operations in Japan. With all of these efforts, we will develop our U.S. operations to the point that it will be a self-reliant, integrated motor vehicle company capable of competing in the world marketplace.

Expansion Plans for HAM

In 1987 Honda set a new goal. It wanted to see HAM accepted as an American company. Toward this end, it adopted a five-part U.S. strategy:

1. Export 70,000 cars per year, built in Ohio, to Japan and other countries by 1991.
2. Increase U.S. R&D activities, including further commitments to plan an important role in designing, engineering, and testing cars in the United States for sale in America, as well as expanding U.S. parts sourcing efforts. Increase R&D personnel from the current 180 to 500 by 1991.
3. Increase domestic content from 60 percent to 75 percent by 1991.
4. Expand Honda's production engineering in the United States, including new model development. Increase the number of engineering office personnel from 50 to 200 by 1991.
5. Construct a second U.S. auto plant with a production capacity of 150,000 automobiles per year and employing 1,800 associates at a cost of $380 million, with production beginning in August 1989. Invest $450 million to increase engine production and begin the production of transmissions, suspensions, assemblies, and brakes.

In his speech announcing these plans, Kume said:

PERPETUATING THE HONDA WAY[16]

The reaction to these plans was mixed. Demand for Japanese cars in the United States continued to be strong. Japanese car manufacturers planned to increase production by 41 percent in the fourth quarter of 1989 while American car producers were announcing an 18 percent decrease in output.[17] A year-end survey showed that the Honda Accord had surpassed the Ford Escort as the best-selling car in America in 1989. And in December 1989, both Honda and Toyota sold more cars in the United States than Chrysler, which had never happened before.

But the enormous cost of Honda's aggressive expansion caused long-term debt to jump 47 percent in 1988. Earnings in the first half of 1989 plunged 42 percent as well. Increasing capacity by 50 percent was a risk. If Honda did not meet its sales targets, it would suffer the kind of excess manufacturing capacity that had badly depressed the earnings of the Big Three.

"During the past two to three years, the speed of decision making has dropped because of size," complained Irimajiri, in 1989 a senior managing director of Honda. "We have to change direction."

---

[16] "Aggressive Expansion at Honda Is Straining Both Staff and Finances," *The Wall Street Journal*, October 9, 1989, p. 1.

[17] "Shaking Up Detroit," *Business Week*, August 14, 1989, p. 75.

As a result, Honda eliminated its dress code and introduced flexible work hours at Tokyo headquarters. It also announced plans for a joint-venture factory with Rover Group of Britain to bolster its weak position in Europe. This joint venture would be Honda's first-ever manufacturing alliance.

The questions on many minds were: Had Honda stretched itself too thin? Could the Honda Way continue to maintain the company or was it making the company too slow and inflexible?

EXHIBIT 1
HONDA CORPORATE PHILOSOPHY

HONDA
HONDA MOTOR CO., LTD.
Company Principle
"Maintaining an international viewpoint, we are dedicated to supplying products of the highest efficiency yet at a reasonable price for worldwide customer satisfaction."

Management Policy

- Proceed always with ambition and youthfulness.
- Respect sound theory, develop fresh ideas, and make the most effective use of time.
- Enjoy your work, and always brighten your working atmosphere.
- Strive constantly for a harmonious flow of work.
- Be ever mindful of the value of research and endeavor.

Operating Priorities
In all areas of manufacturing operations, Honda of America Manufacturing, Inc. observes the following priorities:

1. Safety
2. Quality
3. Production

Operating Principles

Quality in All Jobs
Learn, Think, Analyze, Evaluate, and Improve

Reliable Products
On Time, with Excellence and Consistency

Better Communication
Listen, Ask, and Speak Up

1988 SLOGAN
"Quality for the world from our hands and minds."

EXHIBIT 2
QUALITY AND PRODUCTIVITY COMPARISON OF MAJOR AUTOMOBILE PLANTS, 1986

	Productivity (hours per unit)	*Quality (defects per 100 units)*	*Automation Level (0: none)*	
Nummi, California	19	69	63	Organization
Honda, Ohio	19	72	77	Commitment
Nissan, Tennessee	25	70	89	Commitment
GM, Massachusetts	34	116	7	Compliance
GM, Michigan	34	137	100	Compliance

Source: Adapted from Krafcik, 1987.

EXHIBIT 3 HONDA'S BALANCE SHEETS 1980–1989 In Millions of Dollars

	March 1989	March 1988	February 1987	February 1986	February 1985	February 1984	February 1983	February 1982	February 1981	February 1980
Assets										
Cash and equivalents	$ 1,873.469	$ 1,053.162	$ 880.948	$ 658.610	$ 539.480	$ 458.192	$ 334.014	$ 407.743	$ 466.557	$ 535.200
Net receivables	3,046.310	1,384.873	888.516	700.786	509.123	675.154	796.317	642.709	539.362	423.980
Inventories	3,599.832	3,248.237	2,814.424	2,442.574	1,589.863	1,951.685	1,782.125	1,794.770	1,640.071	1,155.572
Other current assets	1,095.234	1,880.057	1,051.993	860.100	515.995	565.494	383.481	306.304	287.686	258.348
Total current assets	9,614.847	7,566.328	5,635.878	4,662.070	3,154.461	3,650.525	3,295.936	3,151.528	2,933.675	2,373.097
Gross plant, property, and equipment	12,404.125	10,720.683	8,103.179	6,211.429	3,632.367	3,545.100	3,098.643	2,493.907	2,359.476	1,627.504
Accumulated depreciation	5,842.800	5,133.558	3,607.646	2,668.345	1,626.386	1,521.724	1,233.475	1,031.198	984.519	674.628
Net plant, property, and equipment	6,561.324	5,587.125	4,495.535	3,543.085	2,005.981	2,023.376	1,865.168	1,462.709	1,374.957	952.876
Investments at equity	362.636	844.279	543.529	723.146	595.255	200.162	162.048	129.114	130.862	114.740
Other investments	527.114	358.133	309.092	280.293	189.100	210.428	202.493	181.080	186.743	117.448
Deferred charges	0.000	101.129	91.026	70.551	28.869	29.222	32.592	21.725	21.405	14.824
Other current assets	240.508	0.000	0.000	0.000	0.000	0.000	0.000	0.000	0.000	0.000
Total assets	$17,306.402	$14,457.003	$11,075.000	$9,279.144	$5,973.632	$6,113.707	$5,558.230	$4,946.144	$4,647.640	$3,572.986
Liabilities										
Long-term debt due in one year	$ 418.000	$ 128.782	$ 78.065	$ 58.239	$ 57.368	$ 111.956	$ 75.758	$ 70.637	$ 70.495	$ 103.508
Notes payable	2,279.870	848.815	686.569	453.470	414.303	635.397	899.029	869.084	776.710	0.000
Accounts payable	2,947.401	3,534.888	2,527.360	2,253.413	1,250.372	1,288.37	1,239.491	1,194.756	1,100.491	1,760.256
Taxes payable	227.311	273.877	248.131	83.401	90.885	145.080	124.091	132.650	225.752	163.708
Accrued expenses	1,581.652	1,340.105	828.163	681.030	451.054	439.436	362.531	367.827	332.114	239.744
Other current liabilities	480.386	380.546	262.725	178.959	121.098	128.516	114.501	102.907	108.662	79.016
Total current liabilities	7,934.617	6,507.011	4,631.011	3,708.512	2,385.080	2,748.760	2,815.400	2,737.861	2,614.224	2,346.232
Long-term debt	2,284.635	1,372.634	1,324.085	1,180.188	700.925	848.702	676.422	564.844	393.562	317.428
Deferred taxes	257.947	238.804	182.712	158.305	66.121	51.229	33.761	24.219	23.248	1.248
Other liabilities	0.000	23.166	15.922	14.594	15.440	13.511	12.508	10.101	10.895	6.744
Equity										
Common stock	521.924	512.827	377.804	308.950	210.376	210.110	164.894	155.726	174.971	124.280
Capital surplus	1,180.227	1,075.113	834.412	646.840	426.984	449.345	426.252	310.557	343.524	208.440
Retained earnings	5,127.074	4,727.441	1,709.117	3,261.763	2,168.741	1,792.056	1,429.005	1,142.848	1,087.219	568.616
Common equity	6,829.222	6,315.382	4,921.332	4,217.542	2,806.101	2,451.512	2,020.149	1,609.131	1,605.714	901.336
Total equity	6,829.222	6,315.378	4,921.332	4,217.550	2,806.101	2,451.511	2,020.151	1,609.131	1,605.714	901.336
Total liabilities and equity	$17,306.402	$14,457.003	$1,1075.000	$9,279.144	$5,973.632	$6,113.707	$5,558.230	$4,946.144	$4,647.640	$3,572.986

EXHIBIT 3 (*concluded*)
HONDA'S INCOME STATEMENTS, 1980–1989
In Millions of Dollars

	March 1989	*March 1988*	*February 1987*	*February 1986*	*February 1985*	*February 1984*	*February 1983*	*February 1982*	*February 1981*	*February 1980*
Sales	$26,433.707	$27,240.305	$18,747.004	$16,115.003	$10,222.300	$10,166.000	$9,375.652	$7,945.390	$7,980.015	$5,230.980
Cost of goods sold	18,282.305	18,971.105	12,725.703	10,060.000	6,354.292	6,333.621	5,979.664	5,169.300	5,024.117	3,288.377
Gross profit	8,151.402	8,269.199	6,021.301	6,055.003	3,868.008	3,832.379	3,395.988	2,776.090	2,955.898	1,942.603
Selling, general, and administrative expense	5,818.269	5,889.449	4,190.964	3,803.195	2,378.509	2,452.437	2,302.010	1,901.466	1,948.109	1,294.608
Operating income before depreciation	2,333.133	2,379.750	1,830.336	2,251.809	1,489.499	1,379.942	1,093.979	874.624	1,007.790	647.995
Depreciation, depletion, and amortization	991.780	1,071.938	721.562	559.584	337.880	371.741	284.944	219.667	177.252	132.140
Operating profit	1,341.353	1,307.812	1,108.774	1,692.225	1,151.619	1,008.201	809.035	654.957	830.538	515.855
Interest expense	185.962	187.313	160.340	171.958	163.288	191.868	219.937	190.793	169.086	120.688
Non-operating income/expense	192.024	435.310	162.386	171.066	57.626	58.089	43.654	72.067	186.439	−151.412
Pretax income	1,347.410	1,555.799	1,110.837	1,691.331	1,045.990	874.383	632.752	536.232	847.891	243.760
Total income taxes	610.296	684.968	563.850	879.911	550.681	465.082	329.031	259.055	407.048	132.712
Net income	$ 737.114	$ 870.831	$ 546.987	$ 811.421	$ 495.309	$ 409.301	$ 303.721	$ 277.177	$ 440.843	$ 111.048
Earnings per share (primary)—including extra items and discontinued operations	1.492	1.730	1.118	1.652	1.070	0.892	0.714	0.684	1.102	0.298
Dividends per share	0.197	0.199	0.157	0.128	0.093	0.098	0.072	0.076	0.082	0.067
Average exchange rate (yen: $)	128	143	169	239	243	237	251	226	220	229
Average total employment	71,200	65,500	63,000	59,000	50.609	51,355	46,238	42,415	38,481	33,405

EXHIBIT 4
HONDA, U.S. MARKET SHARE

Manufacturer	*1988*	*1987*	*1986*	*1985*	*1984*	*1983*	*1982*	*1981*	*1980*
General Motors	35.9	36.3	41.0	42.5	44.3	44.2	44.1	44.5	46.0
Ford	21.5	20.1	18.2	18.9	19.1	17.1	16.9	16.6	17.3
Chrysler	11.2	10.7	11.4	11.3	10.4	10.4	9.9	9.8	8.8
Honda	7.2	7.2	6.1	5.0	4.9	4.4	4.6	4.3	4.2
Toyota	6.5	6.1	5.5	5.6	5.4	6.0	6.6	6.7	6.5
Nissan (Datsun)	4.8	5.6	4.8	5.2	4.7	5.7	5.9	5.5	5.8

Source: Ward's Automotive Yearbook (1980–1988).

Transformation at Ford*

In 1980 the world's second-largest automaker and the United States's sixth-largest corporation recorded the worst financial performance in its 78 years of existence. Ford Motor Company amassed a loss of $1.54 billion—the second-highest loss in U.S. industrial history. Ford went on to lose over $3 billion from 1980 through 1982. Unit sales of autos dropped in virtually all markets. The company's U.S. market car-share eroded from over 23 percent in 1978 to a low of 16.6 percent in 1981.

But by 1986 Ford's profits exceeded those of General Motors (GM) for the first time since the 1920s. And in 1987 Ford posted auto industry record profits of $4.6 billion and improved on that by $700 million in 1988. Ford's return on sales was 5.7 percent in 1988; its return on stockholders' equity was an outstanding 26.5 percent.[1]

"If you sat down and wrote a fairy tale about Ford's future for the 1980s, everything would have come true by 1989," said a Ford executive in the fall of 1989.

A BRIEF HISTORY OF FORD

Founded in 1903 by Henry Ford, the corporation started with a capitalization of $28,000, a dozen employees, and a 250 × 50 foot plant. Ford was dedicated to constructing a "car for the great multitude." In 1908 Ford introduced the four-cylinder Model T in two types, priced at $825 and $850. It quickly became the mainstay of the booming American market for new cars, enjoying a 50 percent or higher market share in the years before World War I.

To satisfy an enormous demand, Ford developed innovative production methods, refining the mass-production concepts first introduced by Ransom Olds. Ford also pioneered in labor relations, instituting the eight-hour day in 1913 and offering an unprecedented daily wage of $5.

Model T production peaked at over 1.8 million units per year in 1923 when Ford captured 50.4 percent of the domestic market. Later in the 1920s, Ford encountered

*It draws heavily on Malcolm Salter's note entitled "Ford Motor Company—1987"; Richard T. Pascale, *Managing on the Edge* (New York: Simon and Schuster, 1990); and Ford Motor Company (A).

[1] "Fortune 500," *Fortune*, April 24, 1989, p. 354.

Harvard Business School case 390–083.

stiffer competition from GM's broader, more customized model line. Model T sales fell consistently despite regular price reductions and increases in the number of dealers. Ford shut down its operations for nine months in 1927 to retool for a Model T replacement, the Model A. During the changeover, Chevrolet assumed market leadership, a position it rarely relinquished.

When Henry Ford II assumed leadership in 1945, the company was in serious decline. Market share was sliding, cash reserves were low, and the organization was heavily politicized. He sought to reverse Ford's fortunes by adopting a simplified version of GM's finance-oriented management system. He fired hundreds of executives and brought in dozens of newcomers; in November 1945 he hired the "Whiz Kids," a group of 10 Air Force officers.

The "Whiz Kids" quickly reshaped Ford's operations, investing over $1 billion in new plant and automation, decentralizing management along profit-center lines, instituting an accounting system, liberalizing labor practices, and recruiting new executives. In 1954 Ford moved past Chrysler, regaining second place in domestic sales with 30 percent of the market.

Ford proliferated and upgraded models throughout the 1960s. It scored notable successes in cultivating segments ill-served by GM: the four-seat Thunderbird, the compact Falcon, the sporty Mustang, and the luxurious Mercury Cougar. But overall Ford lost ground; throughout the 1960s, Ford trailed GM by an average of 25 market-share points.

In the 1970s, growth in imports and the oil embargo in 1973 threatened the Big Three. GM reacted to the fall-off in demand and the switch to small cars by downsizing its cars and investing $300 million in new small-car capacity. But Ford intended to double its subcompact production to 2 million units.

As small-car inventories climbed and import penetration increased, domestic manufacturers responded with lower prices and extensive rebate plans. But within a year the market again shifted; sales rose and consumers returned to larger cars. In response, Ford decided that larger models would be lightened, made more economical, and restyled to preserve interior dimensions.

Observers wondered how Ford's product line would fare against increasing competition. A number of product liability suits with their associated negative publicity and consumers' growing concerns about quality also presented a challenge to Ford. As a result, market performance slid.

STRATEGY FOR THE 1980s

During this period of large losses and deteriorating market share, Ford executives devised a strategy to reverse their fortunes:

- Emphasize quality and review new-product planning and design.
- Keep investing in new products and processes.
- Pay more attention to costs and efficiency.
- Make employee relations a source of competitive advantage.[2]

Ford continued to invest in new designs while losing billions of dollars; and it focused most of its resources in the automotive business while GM began to diversify.

Quality Enhancements and New Designs. The quality of Ford's cars and trucks fueled its resurgence. Quality

[2] Malcolm Salter, "Ford Motor Company–1987," p. 1.

improvements increased from 2 to 3 percent a year to better than 40 percent over three years. Although past quality improvements had been engineered into the product and muscled through by management, fully 80 percent of Ford's improvements in quality and productivity from 1981 to 1989 were attributed to contributions from human beings—not automation. Harold Poling, Ford's vice chairman, said that by 1988 quality was up 65 percent over 1980.[3]

Ford set up a computer network between international design offices so that designs and modifications could be evaluated instantly at all headquarters. In designing the Taurus and Sable lines, Ford created a team of 100 employees who designed the new line concurrently rather than in the traditional sequential manner.

The results of the new approach to design were indisputable. *Motor Trend* magazine awarded their "Car of the Year" award to the Ford Taurus in 1986, to Ford's Thunderbird Turbo Coupe in 1987, and to its Thunderbird Super Coupe in 1989.

Keeping Up Capital Expenditures.[4] Automobile manufacturing is capital-intensive: Retooling an engine or transmission line can cost $150–$500 million. A new vehicle line can require as much as $4 billion and five years from concept to production. By keeping capital expenditure levels high in the early 1980s, Ford signaled that it was not pursuing a cautious strategy of retrenchment. In 1980–81 Ford's capital expenditures were more than five times greater than funds generated by the company's operations.

Ford generated the needed cash in several ways. Management reduced working capital by improving productivity and inventory turns. Short-term debt was added to the balance sheet, and the company showed a net year-end increase in long-term debt for the first time since 1975. By 1982 Ford's ratio of debt to equity had risen to 75 percent from only 20 percent in 1979. While this leveraging lowered the company's bond rating, it also signaled that Ford had an aggressive strategy to regain market share and profitability.

Capital expenditures for facilities in 1988 totaled over $3.1 billion. Including Special Tooling, total capital expenditures reached $4.7 billion. In the 1990s, Ford planned to invest even greater amounts, including $900 million to enlarge Ford's Ohio truck plant for a minivan project with Nissan, $208 million for a new automatic transmission at the Livonia, Michigan, transmission plant, and $200 million for modernizing the Dearborn assembly plant.

At the end of 1988, Ford still had $3 billion of debt on its balance sheet but also had $9 billion in cash and marketable securities in its automotive business. Looking at the automotive segment only, the debt-to-equity ratio was about 14 percent. (See Exhibits 6–9 for details of Ford's capital expenditures and capital structure.)

Lowering Costs. Much of Ford's success was due to its cost-cutting. Decline in production volume hit the company hard. Capacity utilization was substantially reduced from 1978 to 1980, particularly in standard car and light truck facilities. Between 1978 and 1986 Ford closed eight plants in North America (15 were closed worldwide), reduced the North American

[3] "Productivity Transcends New Plants: Harold A. Poling, Vice Chairman Ford Motor Company," *Ward's Auto World*, December 1988, p. 45.

[4] Except for the material on 1988 and 1989 capital expenditures, this section came directly from Salter's 1987 note.

hourly work force by 45 percent, lowered its break-even volume by 40 percent, and increased productivity 6 percent per year.[5]

As a hedge against downturns, Ford kept plant capacity low and squeezed out all of the productivity possible from existing plants. As then President Donald Petersen explained, "The total investment in a truly new product in our business is becoming extraordinarily high." By revamping existing assembly plants rather than building new, Ford hoped to save 30 to 50 percent of the potential cost. While some analysts saw this move as defensive, others were impressed that Ford resisted temptation to expand long-term capacity in the face of the popularity of its new models.

Ford traditionally purchased about half its components from companies in North America. The local content of Ford's American products usually exceeded 95 percent. But cost-price pressures turned management's attention to the option of tapping foreign sources of materials and parts. Overseas suppliers offered lower costs and often high quality, added capacity, and experience with new technologies. To enhance control over suppliers, vendor ranks were reduced from 7,000 to 3,000, and the survivors had to meet much more stringent quality and delivery standards.

Implementing Employee Involvement Programs. Another important development at Ford was the adoption of the Employee Involvement (EI)/Participative Management programs in the late 1970s and early 1980s. The urgency of Ford's situation in the early 1980s combined with a commitment of cash to the program gave the initiative teeth. The unions embraced the program; by 1989 it was in place in nearly all Ford plants.[6]

EI was credited with much of the quality improvement that had catapulted Ford from last to first place in quality among the Big Three. It was also regarded as an important factor in improving productivity. Ford squeezed out 400,000 more cars in 1988 than its plants' rated capacity. Both the 1982 and 1984 labor agreements established standards of behavior for Ford management. Because the language of these agreements was left open to interpretation, the success of the relationship between management and workers depended on good-faith cooperation.

THE RESULTS

Financial. By any measure, the results of Ford's changes were dramatically positive. Ford's revenues for 1988 topped $92 billion with profits of $5.3 billion. These numbers compare with $79 billion and $4.6 billion in 1987. In 1988 the company earned $10.96 per share and traded at about 5 times earnings. Ford paid $2.30 in dividends in 1988 and reported an after-tax return on stockholders' equity of 26.5 percent. (See Exhibits 1, 2, 4, and 5 for financial results.)

Market Share. Ford's U.S. market share rose from a low of 16.6 percent in 1981 to over 21.5 percent in 1988. While this increase was impressive, more so was the change in relationship with GM. In 1981 GM's U.S. market share was 44.5 percent, nearly three times that of Ford. But in 1987, Ford's Escort and Taurus were the best-selling cars in the United States and by 1988, Ford trailed GM by only 14.4 market

[5] Beverly Geber, "The Resurrection of Ford," *Training*, April 1989, p. 24.

[6] Geber, "The Resurrection of Ford."

share points.[7] (See Exhibit 12 for market share data.)

In European sales, Ford consistently led GM in share. In 1988 Ford had 11.3 percent of the market compared to GM's 10.5 percent. Ford ranked fourth overall in Europe with 1.5 million vehicles registered.[8] Ford's worldwide share of the market made it the second-largest automaker in the world behind GM.[9] (See Exhibit 13 for worldwide regional market shares.)

Productivity. In 1988 productivity increased 7 percent over 1987.[10] Ford also managed its inventory better, thus decreasing the need for working capital and reducing both repair work and scrap.

Ford reduced its U.S. work force from 244,000 workers in 1979 to 161,000 in 1982. The trend was reversed by modest expansion to 185,500 workers by 1988. Over the same period, the worldwide work force was steadily reduced from 495,000 in 1979 to 358,000 in 1988.

Over this period productivity showed steady increases. In 1979, Ford sold 5.8 million vehicles worldwide or about 11.7 per worker; by 1988 it sold over 6.5 million cars and trucks—over 18.2 per worker. It earned $2,400 per employee in 1979 and over six times that much ($14,800 per worker) in 1988.

Becoming Global. Finally, in line with the overall industry, Ford became a more global company in the 1980s. Joint ventures and programs with Mazda took advantage of Japanese production and design. Ford had manufacturing operations in 15 countries. Ford wanted to acquire a luxury, import division to complement its existing products and made a $2.5 billion bid for 100 percent of Jaguar in the fourth quarter of 1989. It beat out General Motors, which had also been interested in some type of alliance with the British luxury-car manufacturer. Some analysts claimed that Ford offered too much for Jaguar. At the time of the acquisition, Ford had just ended its import into the United States of the Merkur Scorpio, a $28,000 luxury sedan built in West Germany. Ford had begun negotiations with Saab-Scania, a Swedish luxury-automobile producer, but negotiations ended with Saab in late October 1989. (See Exhibits 10, 11, and 13 for international data for Ford.)

The Analysts Agree. "In short," Paine Webber's automotive analysts wrote in 1989 about Ford, "almost everything in the world was right." Paine Webber listed many of the reasons for Ford's turnaround discussed above as well as the high value of the yen and stable labor relations globally. *Chilton's Automotive Industries'* "Report Card" gave Ford an overall grade of "A" in 1989. This positive evaluation stemmed from improving quality as measured by J.D. Power's Customer Satisfaction Index, high profit per unit ($1,014 earnings per vehicle) and return on sales (5.7 percent), improving market share in the face of stiffer competition and GM's loss of share, and more efficient operations as measured by productivity and inventory turns.

THE TRANSFORMATION PROCESS

Ford's dramatic improvement in performance confirmed the success of its strategic initiatives; however, left unanswered were difficult questions about the transformation process itself. For example:

---

[7] "1989 Market Data Book Issue," *Automotive News*, May 31, 1989, p. 40.

[8] Ibid., p. 25.

[9] Alex Taylor III, "Who's Ahead in the World Auto War," *Fortune*, November 9, 1987, p. 76.

[10] John McElroy, "1989 Industry Report Card," *Chilton's Automotive Industries* (April 1989), p. 51.

1. How did one of the most autocratic and politicized companies in America shift to a participative style of management and pull it off with such seeming ease? Ford made major strides without reorganizing, dismissing "old-style" executives, or hiring new executives.
2. In the midst of a $3.3 billion loss between 1980 and 1982, how did top management make a decision to spend $3 billion on a risky new Taurus/Sable design? Were they prudent or lucky?
3. The most likely sponsors of Ford's most ambitious change efforts were antagonists. The Human Resources chief viewed novel programs as unproven and possibly injurious to the preservation of management's rights. The Labor Relations head and his UAW counterpart did not openly support the early EI experiments. How were they able to achieve the cooperation necessary to implement EI?
4. Ford won employees' commitment to "involvement and cooperation with management" even while it was eliminating 45 percent of hourly jobs and many salaried positions. How did Ford elicit cooperation instead of cynicism and sabotage?

Ford's transformation process involved a confluence of initiatives undertaken at every level of the organization from line workers to middle managers to senior executives. The following sections describe how the programs developed and were implemented within each level of the company. (See Exhibit 14 for a map of Ford's change initiatives.)

The catalyst for the organizational and structural changes that reshaped Ford was a crisis mentality that one executive vice president described in this way.

> You can never underestimate how scared we were in 1980–81. We *really* believed Ford could die. From top executives through middle management and down to the hourly employees, a lot of people got religion. It enabled us to deal with the turf, the egos, and the "not invented here" attitudes that were killing us. This shared sense of impending disaster was so deeply etched that we did not lose intensity in 1984 when things began to look better.

The view that there was no master plan was widely held by Ford management. One Ford executive commented:

> The remarkable occurrence at Ford was that, coincidently, a set of independent initiatives flowed together and became mutually reinforcing. Ford succeeded despite missteps. There were turf wars, resource constraints, "personalities," and serious political obstacles. Some of these represented formidable barriers.

Another observer commented:

> After it happened, even the participants asked: "How did it start?" Ours was certainly not a top-down effort. The first real change happened in the plants. Top management's widespread support of the EI program (as with its predecessors) came after the plant-sponsored EI programs produced significant results in quality. The point here isn't to disparage or to discredit top management. Rather, I believe that the most profound and lasting change occurs when the rank and file want it so badly that *they* take the initiative and manage upward.

EMPLOYEE INVOLVEMENT: CHANGE AT THE GRASS ROOTS LEVEL

A stimulus for reexamining old assumptions occurred in the late 1970s and early 1980s when various task forces visited Japan. Chrysler and GM had also made such journeys to the Far East. Whereas Chrysler focused exclusively on stark economics (closing plants, accelerating outsourcing, laying off employees, and reducing the break-even point by 50 percent) and GM sought to sidestep the Japanese onslaught through automation and technology, Ford's managers—and the UAW officials who accompanied them—came to believe that the secret to Japanese success was *people and organizations.* Companies in Japan seemed to thrive "on a wave of ideas—accumulated drop by drop." The Ford executives visiting Japan were struck by the Japanese methods of motivating and then harvesting tiny improvements in a thousand places. Ford did not have the financial resources or unlimited faith in the "technological silver bullet," so instead it began to focus on the painstaking task of fixing the organization.

Ernie Savoie, regarded as one of the architects of EI, recounts its beginning:

> In 1978 I went to Japan. The clear lesson was that if you involve the hourly worker, he'll willingly contribute far more than management could imagine. But I had no idea how to execute this at Ford. We had a built-in assumption that no program like this could ever justify giving hourly workers paid time off to discuss what they did and how they did it. We called a conference of plant managers in late 1978. Sixty came . . . four volunteered to try EI. There was not much enthusiasm. In two of these plants the local unions said, "Sounds okay; it might help job security." The other two locals said, "We'll go along but if it fails it won't be our fault."

Lo and behold, in the next six months these four pilot plants started their efforts and the results were pretty good. Next, EI got an important supporter in Philip Caldwell (former CEO of Ford Motor Company). One former staff member recounted the occasion:

> Caldwell heard favorable things about involving employees. In 1979 he issued a policy memo (the 21st in Ford's entire history) encouraging EI. It was a paper "event"—a sanctioning document at best. Insofar as EI was concerned, Caldwell was pretty much invisible. But the policy memo got managers to open their minds a little bit, and it gave our pilot experiments a better chance.

The program got another boost from some personnel changes. The UAW official in charge of EI retired and was replaced by Don Ephlin, a progressive thinker with firsthand experience of GM's successes in worker participation at Tarrytown. Coincidentally, Henry Ford II had grown restive with his labor relations chief, who later retired. For the first time in Ford's history, the company went outside to fill the job. Pete Pestillo, hired from Goodrich, was a champion of worker participation. Ephlin and Pestillo got along well together and became an effective team. Savoie continued:

> EI started to gain momentum. Suddenly senior executives began to take it seriously and wanted to manage it. One executive wanted a PERT chart so we could roll it out *nationally* within six months. Fortunately the union's leadership killed this idea. "No way," they said, "you're over-systematizing it; you're taking away local initiative." Another ill-advised thrust was to establish *mandatory* teams of workers and let the supervisors run everything. Again the union leadership said, "Far better to have 8 volunteers who want to be there than 20 who don't. Let the workers run it. Don't impose the old hierarchy on them if you want them to behave differently."

> No sooner did we head off these perils than the well-intended Finance organization, anxious over Poling's $3 million investment in EI training, wanted to impose measurements to track results. They proposed we count the number of suggestions, the savings realized, etc. Our plant managers helped us kill this one. "Look," they said, "by comparing EI teams, ranking plants, etc., you'll destroy the program. You'll have to be content with anecdotal and descriptive evidence."

Poling took the lead role in repositioning North American Automotive Operations (NAAO) on a solid footing. Given the losses of 1980, controlling costs commanded immediate attention. But one of the paradoxes of Ford was that top management was tightening some controls while relaxing others. Historically, the rigidity and regimentation were nowhere more apparent than on the assembly lines, the arena where the Japanese had demonstrated great success by permitting employees to exercise initiative.

An important factor contributing to EI's success at Ford was agreement that management would not dictate which projects employees worked on. Management was convinced that employees needed to be educated and trained to exploit EI's full potential. In 1982 Ford funded a development and training program; it contributed five cents to it for each blue-collar hour worked. These resources, later increased, could be spent only with UAW concurrence; Ford could not redirect or reclaim the funds if there was a stalemate. These restrictions prevented Ford from abandoning the program if times got tough.

As EI got under way, the trickle of new ideas grew into a stream of initiatives. Thousands of proposals began to overload Ford's creaky organizational machinery.

As a further mechanism to involve its employees, Ford negotiated a profit-sharing program as part of its contract in 1982. Caldwell and Petersen played a major role in this initiative, which reflected the new philosophy of seeking ways to tie all employees to a common purpose. In 1987 Ford paid $636 million in profit sharing—the largest payout in U.S. corporate history—with the average hourly employee (in the United States) receiving a check for over $3,700. No one disputed that the profit-sharing program contributed directly to Ford's earlier cited improvements in productivity.

In 1983 Ephlin moved on to a new assignment at General Motors. His successor regarded EI as "mostly a local matter." Notwithstanding this loss of a champion within the UAW, rank and file support of EI was strong enough to maintain the program's momentum.

THE MANAGEMENT CHANGE TASK FORCE

There were important initiatives undertaken within the middle management ranks as well. Professional employees, seeing their jobs also at risk in the competitive environment, began to clamor for "white collar" EI. Said one observer, "Working at Ford in the early 1980s was like participating in a social revolution. There was a tremendous upwelling of initiative from the ranks. Somehow we channeled it constructively."

One of the organizational entities to feel the impact of these events was Ford's Diversified Products Operations. DPO was a $15 billion miniconglomerate that supplied everything from windshields and wiper blades to castings and compressors. DPO was given an ultimatum: "Either meet Japanese standards of quality and cost or we'll close you down. Period." The imminent crisis broke through age-old union/management antagonisms. EI was seen by many as *the last chance* and it took root rapidly.

DPO's executive vice president, Tom Page, championed these changes. Feeling that organizational barriers were stifling the energy and initiative flowing from EI, he sponsored a series of executive workshops, one for each of his 10 business units. The open identification of problems and later improvements in productivity flowing from these five-day sessions were remarkable.

During one 10-month period, 10 such workshops were held, each attended by the top 100 to 120 people of the respective business units. In each instance, rival functions within the businesses confronted one another and identified the operational problems that prevented them from working together. Stated one executive: "The roll-out of workshops on this massive scale generated tremendous momentum and built a critical mass for change." Page decided to run a special session for his own staff. The 10 division executive committees were invited, as was Petersen, to examine the *systemwide* obstacles facing all the business units within DPO.

Page knew he could achieve only a limited degree of reform before running headlong into the barrier of Ford's corporatewide controls. His solution was to create a Management Change Task Force whose mission ostensibly was to improve DPO's performance. The Management Change Task Force surveyed well-run companies and identified ideas that could work at Ford. A task force member recalled:

> We used our report on well-run companies to get people thinking about Ford. We did it by simply presenting a systematic picture of successful organizations. We didn't say anything negative about Ford but left it to the listeners to draw their own conclusions about where we needed to improve.

To help disseminate the task force's ideas outside of DPO, Petersen arranged for the task force to present its conclusions to the top five executives, including Poling. One participant recalled:

> I remember the presentation. I had eight words out of my mouth when Red (Poling) said: "You're telling me Dana (the corporation) is soft on accountability?" My answer: "No, in fact there is tighter accountability at Dana and many of these companies than we experience at Ford. But there is a better balance." He asked lots of tough questions but we did well. When we were finished, each of these top executives invited us to present to his management team. Before it was over, we had given 100 presentations cascading through automotive operations in the United States, Europe, Latin America, and the Pacific Rim.

DPO's Management Change Task Force was one example of Ford's efforts to address the problems of overcontrol. By 1985–86, the efforts had resulted in higher sign-off limits, decentralization of staff functions, and a variety of corporate changes consistent with the initiatives being taken at the plant level. It generated pressures for a common set of values, a revised performance appraisal, and a reward system more consistent with the way the organization needed to operate.

CREATING A BALANCE OF CONTROL

The achievements of the Management Change Task Force were indicative of Ford's efforts to balance control mechanisms throughout its management ranks. This meant counteracting the dominance of Ford's Finance Department. The Finance Department had dominated Ford's culture since the time of the "Whiz Kids." It had historically derived its strength from recruiting the best people available, usually MBAs. It took care of its own, shepherded by a legendary figure, Ed Lundy, who, until his retirement from management in 1979, personally interviewed every new Finance staff recruit and oversaw their development by means of rigorous rotations through finance positions throughout the world. One observer remarked, "Finance overshadowed the other functions in the Ford power structure, not so much because of its overt status but as a result of the pervasive nature of its influence."

First, the implicit value system emphasized "measurables" and volume. Second, Finance was at the top of the pyramid of approval. Initiatives at Ford were handled sequentially. A particular department would request resources, and the proposal would work its way upward for approval. Finance, armed with the best and most balanced analysis, always held the trump card. Commented one executive: "They didn't win through blatant power plays. They just outmaneuvered the line by doing better homework."

Not surprisingly, the line lost faith in their convictions. An excessively financial focus sometimes led to suboptimal decisions. For example, a plant manager seeking to hold a factorywide meeting to communicate details of a major assembly line reconfiguration would be prevented from doing so because the session translated into $100,000 in "lost" wages (i.e., workers would be paid while being briefed instead of working on the line).

Management's challenge in the 1980s was to sustain Finance's strengths while strengthening Engineering, Manufacturing, and Design. This was addressed through three major efforts: (1) maintaining competence in Finance but decentralizing and redelegating some of its activities to the line; (2) upgrading the product disciplines through investments in new tools, such as computerized workstations, and giving these functions a greater voice in policy matters; and (3) reducing the Finance staff and shifting their role from policing to servicing the line. In Europe alone Finance decreased its staff by 40 percent over two years and the central finance staff had a similar reduction.

Allan Gilmour, a close ally of Petersen and the new CFO, made a variety of adjustments to ease the burden of controls. He agreed, for example, to allow each operating unit the option to close the books quarterly rather than monthly. This permitted the company to devote more time and energy to daily business.

The reorientation of Finance made Ford's control systems less formidable. As line managers were given a greater role in their financial destiny, their sense of ownership increased. One executive commented:

> Ford had a good budget system but it was taken too literally. People didn't make intelligent decisions; they just kept within

budget. Petersen began experimenting when he ran DPO in 1975. We had budgets, of course, but he kept saying, "Don't treat them as inflexible." After a while we began to believe him. That philosophy has caught on today. Good decisions are expected to be driven by their merits—not the budget. To be sure, Poling holds people accountable. But top management has made it clear through the review process that, while your goals and budget are damn important, making good decisions is always your ultimate objective.

BALANCE AT THE TOP

Ford also sought balance among its senior executives. Ford's executives had different managerial strengths. Caldwell and Poling were known as outstanding organizational managers. They had a strong command of business fundamentals and emphasized control through discipline and accountability. Others (such as Petersen, Page, Veraldi, Pestillo, and the UAW's Ephlin) had styles best suited to managing change. These managers were transformational leaders who energized people and created an environment that permitted new and unforeseen possibilities to emerge. Petersen noted: "Red Poling and I had different styles and different expertise. I supported the cultural change experiments getting underway in DPO. His role was to zero in on reestablishing Ford's mastery of the business fundamentals within NAAO."

There was also a great deal of mutual respect. Petersen conveyed his esteem for Poling with the following comment:

> Red reinstated control—I *really* mean discipline—when he took over NAAO. His approach was to say, "You decide when your deadline's going to be, the timetable of your programs, the quality you're going to achieve, and then we'll hold you accountable."

Petersen seemed an improbable change agent for a turnaround of this magnitude. Commented one industry observer:

> Picture the opposite of Henry Ford II, Lee Iacocca, and a host of other egotistical and dominating managers who have played significant leadership roles at Ford, and you get the man who could be Detroit's first Japanese-style executive. He lives and breathes participative management, taking to heart suggestions from vice presidents and assembly line workers. Most remarkably, he subordinates his ego to the needs of the company. Says Petersen: "I want you to remember one thing. The credit here goes to our team, not me." So low is his profile that even after becoming chairman in 1985, the company proxy statement misspelled his name.

The Petersen-Poling team appeared to be a constructive synthesis of opposites. But they did engage in strenuous debates over such key issues as whether to delegate their line of compact cars to their Japanese partner, Mazda, and whether to build additional capacity. The issue of capacity was especially vexatious because Ford was sacrificing up to two percentage points in market share by virtue of being unable to meet demand. Yet it also feared a capacity glut in the decade ahead. The "miracle" at Ford was that this contention was channeled to Ford's benefit—not its detriment.

CONTENTION AND CHIMNEYS

The issue of contention was particularly evident among Ford's divisions. Ford executives worked hard to soothe relations among the divisions. Before Petersen's tenure, Ford had divided itself like Italian city-states, each at war with the others. Conflict was pronounced. Hostility was often present in the plants and on the assembly line. One plant engineer recalled: "The games we played were amazing. We'd sabotage the others' projects. We'd freeze the other side out of discussions, swear, blow up, ignore people, or simply not show up at meetings."

Within its major operational divisions—North American Automotive Operations (NAAO), International Automotive, and Diversified Products—Ford was vertically organized by function. The vertical organizations had become so parochial and self-contained that they were referred to as "chimneys" of power. Each function had its own goals and perspectives and each tended to view the others as part of any problem rather than as part of its solution.

Petersen recalled:

> At the topmost levels confrontation was mostly avoided. You dealt *only* with issues that the "Statements of Authorities and Responsibilities" said were yours. You learned real fast to stay inside your limits.
>
> When I was head of the truck division, I went to the company product planning sessions for the first time. You quickly got the message that you shouldn't even dream of saying anything out loud about cars, even though I'd spent virtually my entire career working on product development in the automotive line. But once assigned to the truck division, I lost all credibility as a source. This same phenomenon held true when I went from product planning to marketing. I lost all credibility as a source of good ideas for products when I was wearing the marketing hat.
>
> There was little or no interaction and no problem solving. The stylists would say, "If you guys were half-decent engineers, you could make it like we designed it," and the engineers would say, "If you guys were half-decent industrial designers, you'd be able to design something that could be built." The only way to get a new idea in place was to be able to point out that some competitor was already doing it. Built on a series of negative concepts and negative thinking, it was an atmosphere in which rationality had a hell of a time flowering.
>
> What's more, the financial rewards were geared to results in managing your own chimney: if a guy in engine development came up with a way to make a lighter engine, or one that was more fuel efficient, there was little incentive to consult with manufacturing so they could prepare themselves for different assembly parameters. So the car would come together and the pieces wouldn't fit.
>
> Top management knew this was a problem, but there were historical barriers in the way. An entire layer of people at the chimney tops—the equivalent of divisional presidents—had come up through their respective chimneys and had enormous loyalty to their former colleagues. It was civil war at the top. The question was never, "Are we winning against the Japanese?" but rather, "Are we winning against each other?" You had to reach your objectives, even if they were in conflict with the other chimneys or in conflict with the broader objectives of the company.

The outcome of such extreme forms of contention management was revealed in the final product. One example was Ford's attempt to make the European-designed Escort a world car. It sought to build a vehicle with common parts that could be assembled in different global locations for a variety of local markets. What happened, *in fact,* was that each geographical region *re*designed the car. In the United States only six of the Escort's 5,000 parts remained in common with their European counterparts. And one of these six was the radiator cap.

The task of breaking into these vertical structures, each a self-contained unit, and developing an ability to work across them horizontally became known as chimney breaking. The purpose of chimney breaking wasn't to destroy functional disciplines but to achieve better working relationships between them.

In executive workshops DPO executives engaged in a novel contention management exercise. Each functional discipline was asked to identify the positive and negative impacts of the other functional departments on its ability to fulfill its role. They were written on Post-its, affectionately termed "valentines." At the conclusion of the exercise, participants circulated and delivered their valentines to one another. Next, each function was asked to analyze its feedback, identify patterns, and share publicly what it had heard and how it intended to proceed to respond to perceived problems.

The designer and lead facilitator of the exercise explained: "The valentines exercise got people to own up to what they were doing to each other. The ah-ha was the realization that no one was working toward a common goal but toward narrow functional goals."

The inroads toward more constructive conflict management within DPO were paralleled by a variety of efforts elsewhere within Ford. Petersen engaged in team building with his top executives. Petersen and Poling also completed personal-style profiles, and an outside consultant coached them on improving their working relationship.

Petersen made it clear that he valued cooperation. One senior Ford executive said: "Petersen identifies people who can motivate others and favors good team players. He reinforced these values through the simple expedient of promoting certain individuals and not others. The word spread fast."

THE BLUE RIBBON COMMITTEE

One early promoter of chimney breaking was Stuart Frey, vice president of Engineering. He had a challenge: The new head of NAAO, Poling, wanted costs reduced and design and engineering to run more efficiently.

Frey asked all 12,000 salaried employees under his command: "What do we need to do to make engineering efficient and effective?" The responses revealed some very clear patterns: Ford needed faster, higher-quality communications and more decentralized decision making. Frey established a Blue Ribbon Committee to address these concerns.

Created in early 1980, it wrestled with its assignment of delays in communications and downsizing the engineering ranks for six months. Then it decided to enlarge its membership from beyond the engineering functions to include Design, Manufacturing, and Truck Operations. It also invited in a facilitator. Reconstituted as a truly cross-functional group, it took two years from its inception to recommend (1) a reduction from five to three layers within the engineering hierarchy, and (2) identification of over 200 middle managers whose positions could be eliminated. But there was a hitch. The committeee stipulated that none of the redundant individuals should be laid off and that if their jobs were downgraded, they should be protected at their current compensation and benefits levels for four years. (Attractive early-retirement packages were proposed to encourage individuals to leave voluntarily.) While top management ultimately accepted these recommendations, many at the periphery viewed this endeavor with skepticism as having consumed a lot of executive time with underwhelming results. Poling himself chided the committee for taking too long. Yet curiously, this endeavor did not become an object of derision and scorn. To the contrary, it was regarded as a valiant first try from which others could learn. The Blue Ribbon Committee reconstituted itself, learned from its mistakes, and spearheaded some of Ford's most ambitious change initiatives in later years.

Commented one observer:

> What *was* revolutionary about the Blue Ribbon Committee was that the chimney heads of the two arch-enemy functions chose to meet every Thursday evening from 5 to 7 P.M. for two years! Recall that this was a time of crisis; everyone was working long hours under great stress. Imagine the impatience and frustration these senior executives experienced as they struggled to find a way out of the box. Here was the real revolution in the sincerity and persistence of managers who recognized that *they* needed to change if Ford was going to change. This is the rarest, yet most essential, ingredient in successful change: top executives who are willing to suffer and change themselves.

The problem-solving example set by the Blue Ribbon Committee had a cascading effect throughout NAAO. By 1985 there were more than 100 cross-functional chimney-breaking efforts under way. Most noteworthy, the subordinates of the Blue Ribbon Committee members created the Ad Hoc and Engineering and Manufacturing Interface Committees. Its members had held the most deep-seated prejudices toward one another. Early meetings were

punctuated with temper tantrums and other efforts to disrupt the process. They worked on the basic operational problems and in two years halved Ford's product-development cycle from seven to three-and-a-half years.

Ford's success in breaking down functional walls was supported by a great deal of senior management involvement. Poling kept the pressure on and constantly asked how things were going. He also sent reports to people outside of NAAO and borrowed ideas from other parts of the company. Once seniors set the example, subordinates revealed their capacity to do the same.

EXECUTIVE EDUCATION

Another powerful vehicle for creating a strong new culture was Ford's innovative approach to Executive Development. "Outwardly it looks like many corporate education centers," says Nancy Badore, "but at Ford it is recognized as an agent of change. We challenge our executives more fully than almost any place you're going to see." Petersen's and Poling's commitment to executive education was evidenced by the time they invested in it: alternately, the last half-day of each of the week-long sessions.

Each of Ford's 2,000 senior managers attended one of the Development Center's workshops. It took two years for the cycle to repeat itself. They came in groups of 50—a heterogeneous cross section of Ford's divisions around the world. Badore noted:

> The crucial dimension in these get-togethers is that we treat the same issues that the chairman and president are grappling with. Participants are expected to add real value by working on these problems, arguing, and listening to different points of view from different functions, levels, and markets around the world. As

> the nature of the problem requires, we bring in experts and offer specialized briefings. Then the participants present their reactions and recommendations to Petersen and Poling. Both sides challenge each other with their most serious questions and concerns. It's very intense stuff.

Getting Ford executives to speak frankly in front of Petersen and Poling was the biggest challenge. Executives who normally assumed a low profile were called upon. A young manager from the Tractor Division recounted: "At first I suspected it had to be some kind of trap. I thought, 'What? Am I going to commit political suicide by telling bad news to the boss?' But they really do want you to say what you think, even if it's critical."

Participants learned to set their disciplinary biases aside and look at an issue from a larger perspective, beginning to grasp how the pieces of a complex issue fit together. Above all, they left informed on major policy questions that were apt to affect the company in the future. Indeed, participants were sought-after couriers of "the latest scoop" when they returned home.

EXAMPLES OF FORD'S CHANGING CULTURE

Team Taurus. A centerpiece in Ford's efforts to establish appropriate levels of autonomy was Team Taurus. This highly visible, bet-your-company project required a strong mission and identity to succeed. (See Exhibit 15 for the Team Taurus principles.)

The challenge: Could Ford build a car with some of the imports' features, quality, and styling flair? Would Ford's traditional buyers agree with its new approach? The company had never designed, engineered, or manufactured a car that could compete with the imports. "We recognized that the learning curve was going to be steep and scary," recalled one Ford engineer. "We were gambling on our ability first to *produce* and then *persuade* our traditional purchaser to buy a very different car. It's the sort of move you make when you have little left to lose."

The moment of truth occurred in April 1981. Planning had earlier projected gasoline prices of $3.40 per gallon for the late 1980s, but by spring 1981 fuel price projections were converging on $1.50 per gallon. Did the revised projections point toward the feasibility of a larger car? Henry Ford II, historically an advocate of bigger vehicles, stepped forward to champion this proposal. Discarding a whole year's work, the team increased Taurus's wheelbase, increased capacity from five to six passengers, widened its tread, and shifted from a four-cylinder engine to a V-6. Ford was agile enough to make this shift and still meet Taurus's targeted introduction deadline. Stated Lew Veraldi, the executive with overall responsibility for Taurus:

> All members of Team Taurus knew the reason for changing the architecture of this car. They all rallied around the change and gave it their full support. Had the team not been in place to do things simultaneously instead of sequentially, this decision would have delayed the car at least 18 months.

Taurus was not just the prototype for Ford's new styling; it was also in the vanguard of transforming the firm's organizational culture. Team Taurus gave an equal voice to all its members, shielded itself from interference by the functional disciplines, and established norms within the team that fostered listening and problem solving and punished territorial rights. Team Taurus evolved a "soft" kind of technology for giving operational integrity to cross-functional teams.

Team Taurus used a concept called "Best in Class." This system called for the analysis of 400 separate features of 50 mid-sized cars from around the world. After establishing which car had the best of each feature, Team Taurus set out to do better. Employee input and suggestions were solicited; all told, 500 employee suggestions were incorporated into the final design.

Taurus's gains, while significant, offered no guarantee that creative styling and flexible opportunism would become a part of Ford's institutional fabric. Petersen knew all too well that Ford had hit home runs in the past with the Mustang and Thunderbird, only to lapse back into stagnancy. He began searching for ways to prevent this.

Concept-to-Customer, a project to streamline the entire work flow of automotive development, was one significant outgrowth of this concern. It reflected Petersen's desire to institutionalize continuous learning. Industry success required predicting consumer trends and shaping input into winning product concepts. If Ford concentrated on being the *best* at this process, it would offer more marketable products and bring them to market more quickly. In the years since Taurus was introduced, Ford demonstrated a persistent dedication to both of these areas. The company in 1989 surveyed 2.5 million customers and regularly invited owners to meet engineers and dealers to discuss quality problems.[11]

Quality as the Tie-Breaker. Poling embraced quality as a top priority. Without it, he believed Ford's vehicles could never withstand the Japanese onslaught. As a former Finance "insider," he could champion quality and strengthen the product functions yet never be seen as a threat to the finance organization. He was one of them. An industrial relations manager in Body and Assembly Operations commented:

> There is no question that Red Poling has a tremendous commitment to the financial end of the business. But quality is the king now. It took time. By the mid-80s people started to think it might be real. Gradually, the audits and media attention forced people to acknowledge that quality was the tie-breaker. It takes something measurable and concrete like quality to hold finance in check.

Poling made quality safe by setting concrete quality targets and by delaying the launch of new products when quality was not up to snuff. Employees knew he was serious when in 1983 he delayed the launch of an entire car line because, after a test drive, he didn't think the automatic transmission shifted smoothly enough.

Ford Values. By 1984 Ford was experiencing change on many fronts. Employees began to demand that management take a stand on what it all meant and, in particular, to make explicit the values implied by the many programs and projects. Petersen convened a team of Ford's top 20 executives to draft a response. The result was a simply worded statement of Ford's mission, values, and guiding principles (see Exhibit 16).

TRANSFORMATION: NEVER COMPLETE

Ford regards its "transformation" as highly suspect and monitors itself scrupulously. When it went from worst to best in

[11] "King Customer," *Business Week,* March 12, 1990, p. 90.

U.S. vehicle quality, it might have celebrated its triumph and shifted into cruise control. Ford officials boast that quality has improved 70 percent between 1980 and 1989. When corrective design changes (made once a car is in production) dropped from $135 million to $35 million per introduction, there was cause for elation. Yet a noteworthy trait of Ford's management philosophy today is that "good" is never good enough. Although proud of its achievements, Ford management openly discusses its many shortfalls. For example, quality was the best among the Big Three, but Japanese quality was better.

Petersen believed that Ford was at year 9 of a 20-year change process. As his tenure neared its close, "learning" was added to Ford's list of values. "There is little to be complacent about," he said. "We have to purge from our minds the notion that there is an end point, a point where we will reach the best quality at lowest cost or best products for our customers." Petersen constantly stressed the serious overcapacity the industry would face by 1990. The only way to compete was to be obsessively vigilant, self-disciplined, and lean. Ford strove to spark this vigilance through its use of outward-looking surveys of customers, external benchmarks, and careful monitoring of competition. As one senior executive put it: "MBOs are not helpful. We do not want static objectives. We want a process that is obsessed with constantly improving things.

"In the last analysis," this executive continued, "Ford's continued ability to learn and adapt depends on our philosophy of management. There has been a radical change in the company's thinking regarding the managers' role. They are viewed today as change agents and facilitators, not just experts and controllers. If we can internalize this mindset as a way of life at Ford, we may indeed have reason to hope that we can continue to revitalize ourselves."

Ernie Savoie presented this view:

> Survival in the 1990s requires ongoing transformation. That's why the deeply ingrained value of continuous learning is so important. We survived changes of UAW leadership and a change in top management when Caldwell and Henry Ford II left. If we can hold course through one more leadership rotation, I'll feel confident that we've really got this process sufficiently embedded.

THE SITUATION IN 1989

Skeptics of Ford's success during the 1980s attributed it to the recovery of the U.S. economy and the auto industry in particular. In 1980, U.S. dealers sold 11.5 million new cars and trucks; by 1988, sales had increased to 15.8 million units.[12] Sales declined in 1989 to 14.9 million cars and trucks; beginning in mid-year, most domestic and foreign manufacturers launched substantial incentive programs to reduce an unexpectedly large inventory of 1989 models prior to the introduction of 1990 models.

The *National Journal* predicted in 1989 that for the early part of the 1990s the Big Three would be able to build more cars each year than they were expected to be able to sell domestically. Besides this overcapacity, they also faced stronger international competition and downward pressure on prices. A particular problem cited by the *National Journal* was the emergence of the "transplant," car or truck plants located in the United States that were wholly or partly owned by Japanese manufacturers.[13] In

---

[12] *1989 Ward's Automotive Yearbook,* p. 19.

[13] Bruce Stokes, "AutoGlut," *National Journal,* September 23, 1989, p. 2311.

fact, while U.S. automakers planned to decrease production 10.4 percent in the fourth quarter of 1989, output of Japanese transplants was projected to increase by 42 percent.[14]

Ford faced a problem even if these pessimistic forecasts did not come true: living up to the success of the 1980s. The Paine Webber automotive analysts wrote in 1989, "Ford is going to have a difficult time improving upon its own spectacular record, at least for the next few years."

Nevertheless, Ford's U.S. car market share in 1989 was 22.3 percent, the highest in a decade, and Ford was the only Big Three company to increase its share of the total vehicle market in the 1980s. The Ford Escort was the best-selling car in the 1989 model year for the fourth year in a row, and the Ford F-Series pickup was North America's best-selling vehicle. In late 1989, Ford's all-new Lincoln Town Car received *Motor Trend* magazine's "Car of the Year" award.

Ford's net income in 1989 was $3.8 billion including a charge to net income of $424 million resulting from the sale of its Rouge Steel subsidiary. Although the U.S. market weakened during the second half of 1989, earnings were the third highest in Ford's history. Capital spending in 1989 was $6.8 billion including special tools, compared to $4.8 billion in 1988.

Ford altered its strategy in this period with several significant acquisitions and divestitures. Ford acquired the British luxury carmaker, Jaguar, for $2.5 billion. Ford also acquired The Associates, the third largest finance company in the United States, and Meritor Credit Corporation, a home equity and manufactured home lender. Ford strategy calls for its Financial Services Group to provide 30 percent of Ford's earnings and help to balance the more cyclical results of Ford's automotive business. In December 1989, Ford sold Rouge Steel.

Major personnel changes were made in the boardroom of Ford in late 1989. In November 1989, Don Petersen announced his intention to retire earlier than expected. Red Poling, a year older than Petersen, was elected to succeed him and agreed to stay beyond the normal retirement age. When asked why he had decided to retire earlier than expected, Petersen replied, "I have been chief executive officer or chief operating officer for 10 years, and I think it is time for me to make a change in my life." Philip Benton, who had been head of Ford's worldwide automotive operations, was elected president.

In a press release announcing the 1989 financial results, Petersen and Poling stated: "We have serious challenges in the coming decade that will demand continuous improvement in the quality of our products, in the efficiency of our organization, and in the skills of our work force. We believe our 1989 accomplishments and our future plans provide a solid base for the future of Ford."

APPENDIX

SELECTED COMPETITOR STRATEGY SUMMARIES[15]

General Motors

Though it seems almost a contradiction in terms, GM attempted to stage a turnaround in the late 1980s. GM was the

[14] *The Wall Street Journal,* October 17, 1989, p. 1.

[15] This section was revised from Salter's 1987 analysis.

largest industrial company in the United States in 1989 and had dominated the worldwide automotive industry for over 50 years. Yet in the second half of the 1980s, GM began losing market share to Ford and Japanese imports and was surpassed in profitability by Ford in 1986 for the first time since the Model T. So GM took a lesson from Ford and began reducing capacity and driving costs down to improve profitability.

Following its time-honored tradition, GM planned to continue to produce a full line of automobiles from the Cadillac to the Chevrolet. In an attempt to regain market share it also spent heavily on design and manufacturing improvements. Between 1980 and 1988, GM had capital expenditures of $67 billion for an average of about $7.5 billion per year (Exhibit 6).

Another significant addition for GM was the creation of a new division: Saturn. Saturn was created to manufacture a new car that was cost- and quality-competitive with Japanese imports. GM also owned equity in several Asian manufacturers. GM's joint venture with Toyota, the NUMMI plant in Fremont, California, became a showcase for new manufacturing and human resource management methods.

GM expanded its technological capability by acquiring Electronic Data Systems and Hughes Aircraft.

Chrysler

Since the early 1970s, Chrysler pursued a series of "fix or fold" strategies that led to domestic contraction, disintegration, and international outsourcing. Chrysler traded jobs for a run on corporate survival. In 1979 Chrysler nearly went bankrupt but was salvaged by a combination of government bailouts and new management. Chrysler's goals were to retain a minimum 10 percent share of the U.S. auto market and to keep investment low.

To keep investment low, Chrysler used the same platform, the K car, to spin off an entire family of cars.[16] In 1988 Chrysler finally began making changes in the design of its cars and was achieving some technological advances for 1990s models.

Spearheaded by Iacocca, Chrysler's charismatic CEO, an aggressive sales campaign kept the dealer network intact throughout the troubled times of the late 1970s and early 1980s. Chrysler's improved vehicle warranties helped its share grow to 11.3 percent of the U.S. market by 1985 (Exhibit 12).

In 1987 Chrysler bought AMC from Renault. In the deal, Chrysler got a new midsize car, four plants, the Jeep (selling at 250,000 units per year in 1987), and 1,400 more dealers.[17] Chrysler's relationship with Mitsubishi was important; Chrysler owned a 15 percent stake in the Japanese automaker and imported from it some 140,000 cars and trucks in addition to engines and other components.

Toyota

Overseas business was vital to Toyota which sold, during the late 1980s, just under half of its production abroad with very few offshore manufacturing facilities. To make sure its automobiles could meet the diverse consumer demands of the countries to which it exported, Toyota sent teams overseas to collect data on driving habits and styling preferences.

---

[16] Wendy Zellner, "Chrysler's Next Generation," *Business Week*, December 19, 1988, p. 52.

[17] Jerry Flint, "The 'Hail Mary' Acquisition," *Forbes*, January 11, 1988, p. 78.

Toyota was slower than other Japanese automakers to move operations abroad. Some sources attributed this reluctance to the top management of the company who, by 1989, were nearing retirement and were not as prone as younger managers to get involved in the globalization sweeping the industry. Several top managers were preparing to retire in 1989 and 1990, and analysts predicted that their replacements would move Toyota toward more overseas manufacture and assembly.

Toyota was reported to have the lowest break-even point among the Japanese auto manufacturers. It also had financial stability because of its ties to large Japanese banks. Some industry analysts compared Toyota to McDonald's both because of its low-cost production and its large volume of sales. In 1989 Toyota was the third-largest auto manufacturer in the world after GM and Ford.

In 1989 Toyota introduced a new line of automobiles under the name Lexus. Like Honda's Acura, these cars were to be sold through a separate and exclusive dealer network. Lexus was developed to compete with Mercedes and other luxury nameplates but was expected to be priced at around $35,000, some $30,000 less than the comparable Mercedes.[18]

Honda

What began as a small motorcycle company in the mid-1940s grew to become Japan's largest company founded after WWII and the 11th-biggest automaker in the world. This remarkable growth was the result of a two-pronged strategy stressing technological innovation and sophisticated styling. As early as 1967, Honda introduced front-wheel-drive technology, which the company continued to refine as a means of gaining a competitive edge in the quest for increased market share.

Honda focused on stylish appearance even when the company produced automobiles for the low end of the market. As Honda began moving upscale, it challenged German luxury cars with the introduction of its Acura line. Acuras were sold by an exclusive dealership network and were priced above Honda's nameplate but well below the German automobiles with which they competed. As noted in the Toyota description, the introduction of Honda's upscale line inspired Toyota to produce its Lexus line of luxury automobiles. Nissan also introduced a line of luxury sedans called Infiniti. Other Japanese manufacturers were rumored to be planning similar introductions in the early 1990s.

Honda had less than a 10 percent share of its home market while exports accounted for roughly 65 percent of its Japanese production. Nearly 60 percent of its sales worldwide were in North America, a higher percentage than any other major Japanese automaker.

Honda pursued a strategy of localization of production, by 1989 building plants in 35 countries with the aim of manufacturing in large markets in which their products were sold. In the United States, Honda's assembly capacity in Marysville, Ohio, reached 300,000 units in 1987. An engine plant and a plastics plant were finished in 1987, and a second automobile plant was scheduled to begin production by the end of 1989.

Honda received high marks from consumers and analysts alike. Its Acura line was rated the highest for three years in a row by J.D. Power's survey of

[18] Alex Taylor III, "Here Come Japan's New Luxury Cars," *Fortune,* August 14, 1989, p. 62.

customer satisfaction (CSI 1987–1989). The Honda line was rated third, behind Acura and Mercedes, by the same survey in 1989.

Renault

Nationalized after World War II to be the showcase of state-owned enterprises, Renault was described by the *Economist* as a "ward of the state." After losing $1 billion in 1984, the chairman was fired and replaced by a son of Greek immigrants, educated at MIT, named Raymond H. Levy. Levy produced about $1.5 billion in profits in 1988 even though the French company lost share in Europe.

An interesting problem for Renault was the sometimes conflicting goals of profitability and full employment. Levy laid off 30,000 workers, though, and instilled something of a profit culture. Other enhancing measures included closing plants, selling AMC to Chrysler, and reducing debt (some by getting the government to forgive debt).

Renault had 14.6 percent share of the European market in 1982, but the share had slipped to 10 percent by 1989. With the coming changes in the European community in 1992, the Japanese manufacturers had begun building plants in Europe. The quota that would be set for their share of the market was projected to be around 10 percent, higher than the current 3 percent allowed by France and the even lower share allowed by Spain and Italy. Because Renault was particularly strong in those southern European countries and weaker in the rest of Europe, the increasing Japanese quota provided a significant threat.

In 1989 Levy was considering signing deals with other automakers to help drive production costs down. But Renault's options for these joint ventures would perhaps be restricted to some extent because of its status as a state-owned company. Levy claimed that despite the fact that the company was owned completely by the state, he had nearly complete control over the operations of the company.

After achieving profitability in 1987, Renault's next goal was to improve the qualtity of the product. By the end of the 1980s, competitors were acclaiming Renault's improvements in qualty design and production.[19]

Volkswagen

Engineering was the key to the competitive strategy at Volkswagen (VW). The parent company ran on the concept of affordable technology. Audi, the company's luxury nameplate, emphasized performance engineering.

Even though VW faced one of the highest costs of labor of all European auto manufacturers, it had mixed success with overseas operations. It was the first overseas company to build a plant in the United States in what became a rash of "transplants" from Japanese automakers. But the mediocre results from its overseas operations left the company slow to expand worldwide.

Like many European auto manufacturers, VW rarely changed its design. While that custom worked for the higher-priced Mercedes and BMW, some analysts thought it wouldn't work for VW.[20]

A combination of the rise of Japanese auto manufacturers and exchange-rate

---

[19] Stewart Toy, "Is Renault's New Engine Built for the Long Haul?" *Business Week*, August 21, 1989, p. 38.

[20] Jerry Flint, "Can Volkswagen Stop Its U.S. Decline?" *Forbes*, April 3, 1989, p. 64.

problems reduced its sales in the United States and elsewhere. In the 1960s, VW sold about 600,000 automobiles per year in the United States, most of them Beetles. Since then its sales declined to under 170,000 by 1989. In that same year, it still led in the European market and was the sixth-largest automaker in the world.

The challenge for VW in 1989 was the battle against Japanese imports, which were beginning to gain share in Europe and had some 40 percent share in some unprotected markets. In the United States, it faced the same problem of competing with Japanese imports with the additional exchange-rate disadvantage against domestic manufacturers.[21]

[21] Ibid.

EXHIBIT 1
BALANCE SHEET (1978–1988)

	Dec. 88*	Dec. 87	Dec. 86	Dec. 85	Dec. 84
Assets					
Cash and equivalents	14,770.003	10,097.000	8,553.085	5,903.765	5,943.167
Net receivables	95,686.625	4,401.597	3,487.799	2,851.899	2,526.100
Inventories	6,638.199	6,321.296	5,792.585	4,601.871	4,115.167
Other current assets	1,793.800	1,161.600	624.500	656.600	746.200
Total current assets	118,888.627	21,981.504	18,458.004	14,014.101	13,330.601
Gross plant, property, and equipment	31,667.605	28,600.906	26,387.703	24,305.801	21,126.500
Accumulated depreciation	15,675.402	14,567.402	13,187.101	11,884.500	10,577.500
Net plant, property, and equipment	15,992.203	14,033.503	13,200.601	12,421.300	10,549.000
Investments at equity	2,102.699	7,573.898	5,088.386	4,176.371	2,832.099
Other investments	1,010.500	0.000	0.000	0.000	0.000
Intangibles	0.000	0.000	0.000	0.000	0.000
Other current assets	5,372.496	1,366.800	1,185.900	991.600	773.700
Total assets	143,366.000	44,955.711	37,933.008	31,603.508	27,485.508
Liabilities					
Long-term debt due in one year	5,736.695	79.400	73.900	318.000	651.300
Notes payable	32,098.809	1,803.299	1,230.100	956.600	696.700
Accounts payable	28,902.605	6,564.000	5,752.285	4,751.871	4,433.496
Taxes payable	1,065.300	647.600	737.500	446.600	509.700
Accrued expenses	6,856.199	6,075.000	5,285.687	4,478.667	3,919.499
Other current liabilities	2,374.699	2,624.099	2,546.099	1,825.600	1,757.000
Total current liabilities	77,034.307	17,793.402	15,625.503	12,777.300	11,967.601
Long-term debt	32,112.809	1,751.899	2,137.099	2,157.200	2,110.899
Deferred taxes	3,933.099	2,354.699	1,328.100	1,214.000	1,000.900
Minority interest	164.100	136.500	105.700	114.400	137.900
Other liabilities	8,593.199	4,426.496	3,877.000	3,071.899	2,430.499
Equity					
Common stock	490.800	507.500	536.800	372.200	372.200
Capital surplus	586.700	595.100	605.500	754.300	580.100
Retained earnings	20,451.504	17,390.102	13,717.101	11,142.000	8,885.371
Common equity	21,529.004	18,492.703	14,859.503	12,268.500	9,837.667
Total equity	21,529.000	18,492.699	14,859.398	12,268.496	9,837.667
Total liabilities and equity	143,366.000	44,955.711	37,933.008	31,603.508	27,485.508

*Finance subsidiary consolidated in 1988.

Dec. 83	Dec. 82	Dec. 81	Dec. 80	Dec. 79	Dec. 78
3,152.101	1,555.400	2,100.000	2,587.200	2,192.600	3,799.000
2,767.600	2,376.500	2,595.800	2,998.100	2,723.700	2,105.600
4,111.687	4,123.292	4,642.878	5,129.593	5,891.894	5,647.199
787.700	743.700	838.200	844.100	763.100	818.800
10,819.000	8,798.894	10,176.800	11,559.000	11,571.300	12,370.601
19,920.891	19,683.094	18,805.766	18,017.992	16,442.496	14,043.093
10,119.000	9,546.894	8,959.382	7,992.191	7,215.496	6,624.597
9,801.890	10,136.199	9,846.382	10,025.800	9,227.000	7,418.496
2,582.701	2,413.400	2,348.200	2,142.200	2,041.800	1,721.099
0.000	0.000	0.000	0.000	0.000	0.000
0.000	0.000	0.000	0.000	279.000	279.200
665.200	613.100	649.900	620.500	405.500	312.000
23,868.805	21,961.605	23,021.305	24,347.605	23,524.605	22,101.406
109.200	315.900	128.700	83.800	213.300	255.500
832.800	1,949.101	2,049.000	2,321.800	977.100	610.100
4,097.585	3,117.501	2,800.200	3,370.600	3,425.600	3,395.099
362.100	383.000	208.900	234.600	424.000	486.200
3,764.701	3,656.400	3,663.701	3,711.301	3,186.101	3,528.800
1,149.500	1,002.100	1,089.800	1,349.900	1,036.900	1,002.300
10,315.800	10,424.000	9,940.281	11,072.000	9,263.000	9,278.000
2,712.901	2,353.301	2,709.701	2,058.800	1,274.600	1,144.500
1,103.200	1,054.100	1,004.800	1,069.000	1,046.200	763.300
137.200	130.100	148.200	135.900	145.300	151.700
2,054.400	1,922.699	1,856.200	1,444.400	1,374.800	1,077.600
366.000	241.200	241.200	241.200	241.000	239.900
465.400	522.400	526.100	526.900	524.300	492.700
6,713.886	5,313.890	6,594.878	7,799.394	9,655.398	8,953.695
7,545.289	6,077.496	7,362.179	8,567.496	10,420.703	9,686.296
7,545.285	6,077.488	7,362.175	8,567.492	10,420.695	9,686.292
23,868.805	21,961.605	23,021.305	24,347.605	23,524.605	22,101.406

EXHIBIT 2
INCOME STATEMENT (1980–1988)

	Dec. 88*	Dec. 87	Dec. 86	Dec. 85	Dec. 84
Sales	92,445.625	71,643.375	62,715.719	52,774.313	52,366.313
Cost of goods sold	75,205.813	58,993.418	52,577.516	45,126.613	44,092.211
Gross profit	17,239.813	12,649.957	10,138.203	7,647.699	8,274.102
Selling, general, and administrative expense	—	3,281.400	3,122.099	2,525.200	2,544.099
Operating income before depreciation	17,239.813	9,368.554	7,016.101	5,122.496	5,730.000
Depreciation, depletion, and amortization	3,792.299	3,167.400	2,959.600	2,392.800	2,307.800
Operating profit	13,447.511	6,201.152	4,056.502	2,729.696	3,422.200
Interest expense	6,138.000	440.600	482.900	446.600	536.000
Non-operating income/expense	1,033.000	1,619.400	1,495.700	1,347.200	1,396.600
Pretax income	8,342.496	7,380.000	5,069.285	3,630.299	4,282.789
Total income taxes	2,998.699	2,726.000	1,774.200	1,103.100	1,328.900
Minority interest	43.600	28.800	10.000	11.800	47.100
Income before extraordinary items and discontinued operations	5,300.199	4,625.199	3,285.099	2,515.400	2,906.800
Net income	5,300.199	4,625.199	3,285.099	2,515.400	2,906.800
Available for common	5,300.199	4,625.199	3,285.099	2,515.400	2,906.800
savings due to common					
Adjusted available for common	5,300.199	4,625.199	3,285.099	2,515.400	2,906.800
Earnings per share (primary) excluding extra items and discontinued operations	10.960	9.050	6.160	4.543	5.263
Earnings per share (primary) including extra items and discontinued operations	10.960	9.050	6.160	4.543	5.263
Earnings per share (fully diluted) excluding extra items and discontinued operations	10.800	8.920	6.055	4.407	4.973
Earnings per share (fully diluted) including extra items and discontinued operations	10.800	8.920	6.055	4.407	4.973
Dividends per share	2.300	1.575	1.109	0.800	0.667

*Finance subsidiary consolidated in 1988.
NA means not available.

Dec. 83	Dec. 82	Dec. 81	Dec. 80	Dec. 79	Dec. 78
44,454.613	37,067.211	38,247.008	37,085.508	43,513.711	42,784.109
37,959.109	33,094.008	35,281.109	35,463.809	39,290.512	37,451.309
6,495.504	3,973.203	2,965.898	1,621.699	4,223.199	5,332.801
2,399.701	2,300.400	2,042.301	1,930.699	1,701.800	1,490.600
4,095.803	1,672.803	923.598	−309.000	2,521.399	3,842.201
2,292.101	2,156.400	2,179.400	1,969.301	1,604.400	1,313.700
1,803.703	−483.597	−1,255.802	−2,278.301	917.000	2,528.501
567.200	745.500	674.700	432.500	246.800	194.800
929.800	821.200	792.400	730.100	839.200	615.000
2,166.301	−407.900	−1,138.100	1,980.700	1,509.400	2,778.699
270.200	256.600	−68.300	−435.400	330.100	1,175.000
29.200	−6.700	−6.700	−2.000	10.000	14.800
1,866.899	−657.800	−1,060.100	−1,543.300	1,169.300	1,588.900
1,866.899	−657.800	−1,060.100	−1,543.300	1,169.300	1,588.900
1,866.899	−657.800	−1,060.100	−1,543.300	1,169.300	1,588.900
1,866.899	−657.800	−1,060.100	−1,543.300	1,169.300	1,588.900
3.430	−1.213	−1.958	−2.851	2.167	2.967
3.430	−1.213	−1.958	−2.851	2.167	2.967
3.213	NA	NA	−2.629	2.033	2.760
3.213	NA	NA	−2.629	2.033	2.760
0.167	0.000	0.267	0.578	0.867	0.778

EXHIBIT 3
U.S. LIGHT VEHICLE RETAIL SALES 1975–1988
(Units in Millions of Vehicles)

	1975	1976	1977	1978	1979	1980	1981
Cars	8.6	10.1	11.2	11.3	10.6	9.0	8.5
Trucks	2.5	3.2	3.6	4.1	3.5	2.5	2.3
Total	11.1	13.3	14.8	15.4	14.1	11.5	10.8
	1982	*1983*	*1984*	*1985*	*1986*	*1987*	*1988*
Cars	8.0	9.2	10.4	11.0	11.5	10.3	10.6
Trucks	2.6	3.1	4.1	4.7	4.8	4.9	5.1
Total	10.6	12.3	14.5	15.7	16.3	15.2	15.7

Source: *1989 Wards' Automotive Yearbook.*

EXHIBIT 4
BIG THREE SALES 1980–1988*
($ Billions)

	1980	*1981*	*1982*	*1983*	*1984*	*1985*	*1986*	*1987*	*1988*
GM	57.7	62.7	60.0	74.6	83.9	93.4	102.8	101.8	110.2
Ford	37.1	38.2	37.1	44.5	52.5	52.9	62.9	71.8	82.2
Chrysler	8.6	10.0	10.1	13.3	19.6	21.3	22.6	26.3	31.9

*Revenue members do not include finance subsidiary amounts.
Source: Annual reports.

EXHIBIT 5
BIG THREE FINANCIAL RESULTS 1987–1988

	Sales			*Net Income*		
	1987	*1988*	*Increase*	*1987*	*1988*	*Increase*
GM	114.9	123.6	7.6%	3.6	4.9	36.1%
Ford	79.9	92.5	15.8	4.6	5.3	15.2
Chrysler	29.3	35.5	21.2	1.3	1.1	−15.4
Total	224.1	251.6	12.3	9.5	11.3	18.9

Note: Includes all subsidiaries.
Source: Annual reports.

EXHIBIT 6
BIG THREE CAPITAL EXPENDITURES 1980–1988
($ Billions)

	GM	*Ford*	*Chrysler*	*Total*
1980	7.7	2.8	0.8	11.3
1981	9.7	2.3	0.4	12.4
1982	6.2	3.0	0.3	9.5
1983	4.0	2.3	1.0	7.3
1984	6.0	3.5	1.2	10.6
1985	9.2	3.8	1.5	14.5
1986	11.7	3.5	2.0	17.2
1987	7.1	3.7	2.0	12.8
1988	5.5	4.7	1.6	11.8
1980s cumulative	67.1	29.6	10.8	107.5

Source: Annual reports.

EXHIBIT 7 CAPITAL SPENDING PER UNIT SOLD

	GM	*Ford*	*Chrysler*
Cumulative capital expenditure 1980–1988 ($B)	67.1	29.6	10.8
Average annual capital expenditure 1980–1988 ($B)	7.5	3.3	1.2
Vehicles sold 1988 (000)	8,108	6,441	2,567
Average annual capital expenditure 1980–1988 ($)	920	512	467
Cumulative capital expenditures ($)	8,276	4,596	4,207

Source: Annual reports.

EXHIBIT 8
CAPITAL EXPENDITURES TO CASH GENERATED FROM OPERATIONS "BIG THREE" 1980–1989

	GM			*Ford*			*Chrysler*		
	Capital Expenditures	*Cash**	*Ratio†*	*Capital Expenditures*	*Cash**	*Ratio†*	*Capital Expenditures*	*Cash**	*Ratio†*
1980	7.7	3.5	2.2	2.8	0.5	5.6	0.8	−0.5	−1.6
1981	9.7	4.8	2.0	2.3	1.6	1.4	0.4	0.3	1.3
1982	6.2	5.6	1.1	3.0	2.6	1.2	0.3	0.9	0.3
1983	4.0	9.5	0.4	2.3	5.0	0.5	1.0	2.1	0.5
1984	6.0	8.2	0.7	3.5	6.7	0.5	1.2	3.3	0.4
1985	9.2	9.7	0.9	3.8	5.4	0.7	1.5	3.0	0.5
1986	11.7	9.0	1.3	3.5	7.6	0.5	2.0	2.5	0.8
1987	7.1	9.8	0.7	3.7	8.3	0.4	2.0	2.7	0.7
1988	5.5	11.1	0.5	4.7	8.3	0.6	1.6	3.5	0.5

* Cash flow = cash generated from operations.
† Ratio = capital expenditures to cash generated from operations.
Source: Figures from automotive business only (excludes finance subsidiaries).

EXHIBIT 9 DEBT* TO EQUITY: "BIG THREE" 1980–1988

	GM	*Ford*	*Chrysler*
1980	20%	52%	560%
1981	31	65	300
1982	31	75	230
1983	21	48	114
1984	23	36	24
1985	18	28	64
1986	22	23	47
1987	20	31	55
1988	17	14	51

* (Long-term debt + current portion of long-term debt + short-term debt)/total capital excludes finance subsidiaries.
Source: Annual reports

EXHIBIT 10
FORD INTERNATIONAL PRODUCTION OPERATIONS

Location	*Type of Operation*
Canada	Manufacturing and assembly
Mexico	Manufacturing and assembly
Brazil	Joint venture
Venezuela	Manufacturing and assembly
Argentina	Joint venture
Japan	Minority ownership
Australia	Manufacturing and assembly
Spain	Manufacturing and assembly
Portugal	Manufacturing
France	Manufacturing
Belgium	Manufacturing and assembly
United Kingdom	Manufacturing and assembly
West Germany	Manufacturing and assembly
Taiwan	Manufacturing and assembly
Korea	Minority ownership

Source: Company records.

EXHIBIT 11
WORLD VEHICLE PRODUCTION OF LEADING AUTOMAKERS IN 1988

Company	*Vehicles* Produced*	*Percent of Total*
General Motors	7,497,063	16.3
Ford	5,882,267	12.8
Toyota	3,729,719	8.1
Nissan	2,658,255	5.8
Peugeot-Citroen	2,511,502	5.5
Volkswagen	2,475,347	5.4
Chrysler	2,187,706	4.8
Renault	2,053,444	4.5
Fiat	1,880,408	4.1
VAZ (USSR)	1,604,740	3.5
Honda	1,580,872	3.4
Mitsubishi	1,321,169	2.7
Suzuki	867,860	1.9
Daimler-Benz	822,649	1.8
Total world production	45,914,276	

*Includes cars, trucks, and commercial vehicles.
Source: Motor Vehicle Manufacturers' Association (MVMA), *Motor Vehicle Facts and Figures 1989*.

EXHIBIT 12
U.S. CAR MARKET SHARE 1980–1988

	1980	*1981*	*1982*	*1983*	*1984*	*1985*	*1986*	*1987*	*1988*
General Motors	45.9%	44.5%	44.1%	44.2%	44.3%	42.5%	41.0%	36.3%	35.9%
Ford	17.2	16.6	16.9	17.1	19.1	18.8	18.2	20.1	21.5
Chrysler	8.8	9.9	10.0	10.4	10.4	11.3	11.4	10.7	11.2
Imports	28.2	29.1	29.1	28.4	26.2	27.4	29.5	33.0	31.3

EXHIBIT 13
FORD REGIONAL MARKET SHARES 1986–1988

	1986	*1987*	*1988*
Europe	11.8%	12.1%	11.4%
Latin America	16.1	14.6	16.1
Asia-Pacific and others	4.5	4.8	5.0
Total outside United States and Canada	10.0	10.1	9.7

Source: Ford annual reports.

EXHIBIT 14
ROAD MAP OF FORD'S MAJOR CHANGE INITIATIVES (1980–1988)

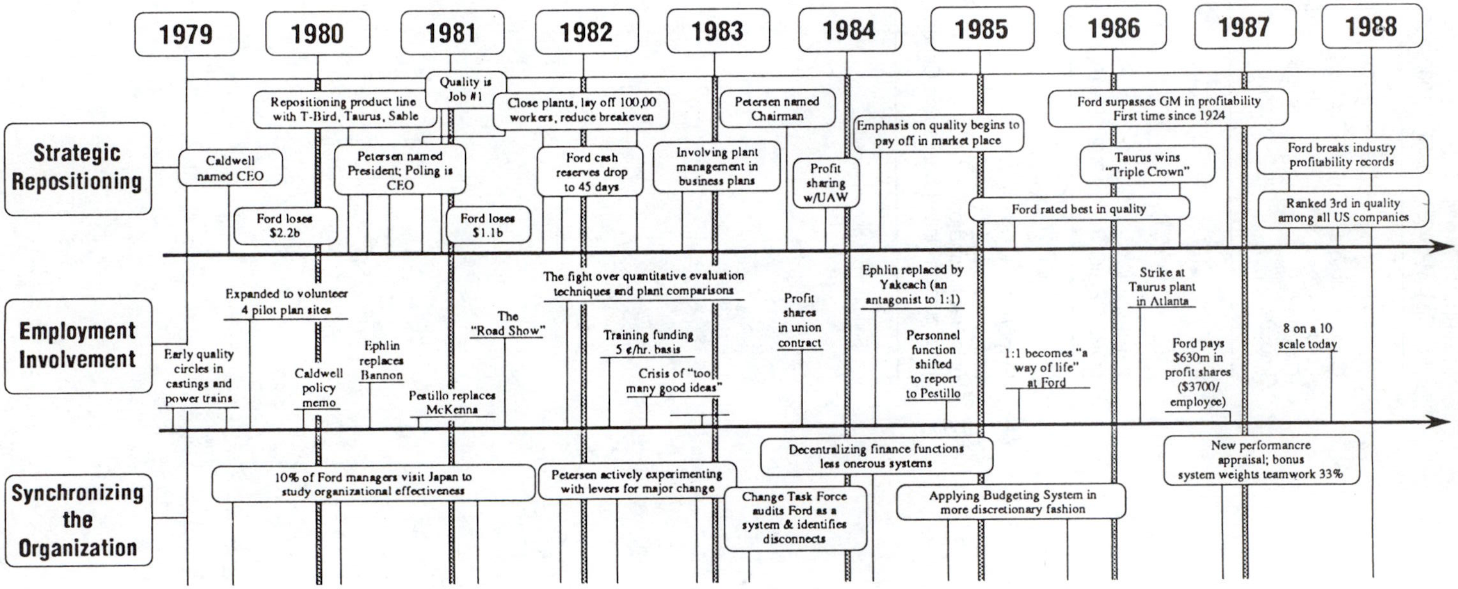

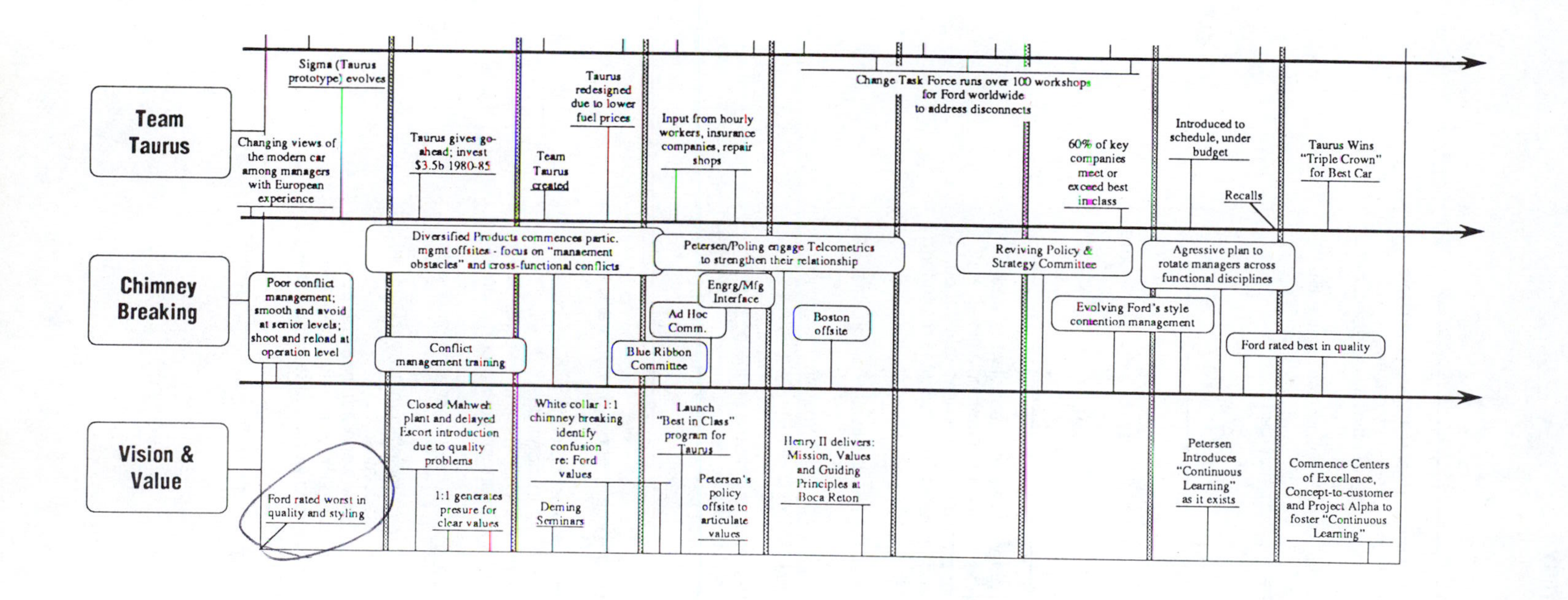

Team Taurus
Chimney Breaking
Vision & Value
Sigma (Taurus prototype) evolves
Changing views of the modern car among managers with European experience
Taurus gives go-ahead; invest $3.5b 1980-85
Team Taurus created
Taurus redesigned due to lower fuel prices
Input from hourly workers, insurance companies, repair shops
Change Task Force runs over 100 workshops for Ford worldwide to address disconnects
60% of key companies meet or exceed best inclass
Introduced to schedule, under budget
Recalls
Taurus Wins "Triple Crown" for Best Car
Poor conflict management; smooth and avoid at senior levels; shoot and reload at operation level
Diversified Products commences partic. mgmt offsites - focus on "manaement obstacles" and cross-functional conflicts
Conflict management training
Petersen/Poling engage Telcometrics to strengthen their relationship
Engrg/Mfg Interface
Ad Hoc Comm.
Blue Ribbon Committee
Boston offsite
Reviving Policy & Strategy Committee
Evolving Ford's style contention management
Agressive plan to rotate managers across functional disciplines
Ford rated best in quality
Ford rated worst in quality and styling
Closed Mahweh plant and delayed Escort introduction due to quality problems
1:1 generates presure for clear values
White collar 1:1 chimney breaking identify confusion re: Ford values
Deming Seminars
Launch "Best in Class" program for Taurus
Petersen's policy offsite to articulate values
Henry II delivers: Mission, Values and Guiding Principles at Boca Reton
Petersen Introduces "Continuous Learning" as it exists
Commence Centers of Excellence, Concept-to-customer and Project Alpha to foster "Continuous Learning"

EXHIBIT 15
TEAM TAURUS PRINCIPLES

1. Clear-cut, nonconflicting goals and measurements for the program and its team members.
2. Companywide recognition and prestige associated with membership on the team.
3. Empowerment of the team and its members, by top management, to officially represent the interests of their respective vertical organizations.
4. Acceptance of the customer, instead of the most powerful vertical organization, as the tie-breaker.
5. Core development team members report directly to the program manager.
6. Continuity of key team members.
7. Joint responsibility for team success.

EXHIBIT 16
FORD'S VISION AND VALUES

MISSION Ford Motor Company is a worldwide leader in automotive and automotive-related products and services as well as in newer industries such as aerospace, communications, and financial services. Our mission is to improve continually our products and services to meet our customers' needs, allowing us to prosper as a business and to provide a reasonable return for our stockholders, the owners of our business.

VALUES How we accomplish our mission is as important as the mission itself. Fundamental to success for the Company are these basic values:

People Our people are the source of our strength. They provide our corporate intelligence and determine our reputation and vitality. Involvement and teamwork are our core human values.

Products Our products are the end result of our efforts, and they should be the best in serving customers worldwide. As our products are viewed, so are we viewed.

Profits Profits are the ultimate measure of how efficiently we provide customers with the best products for their needs. Profits are required to survive and grow.

GUIDING PRINCIPLES

Quality comes first. To achieve customer satisfaction, the quality of our products and services must be our number one priority.

Customers are the focus of everything we do. Our work must be done with our customers in mind, providing better products and services than our competition.

Continuous improvement is essential to our success. We must strive for excellence in everything we do: our products, in their safety and value—and in our services, our human relations, our competitiveness, and our profitability.

Employee involvement is our way of life. We are a team. We must treat each other with trust and respect.

Dealers and suppliers are our partners. The Company must maintain mutually beneficial relationships with dealers, suppliers, and our other business associates.

Integrity is never compromised. The conduct of our Company worldwide must be pursued in a manner that is socially responsible and commands respect for its integrity and for its positive contribution to society. Our doors are open to men and women alike without discrimination and without regard to ethnic origin or personal beliefs.

General Electric Strategic Position—1981

On December 21, 1980, the General Electric Company announced that John F. Welch, Jr., 45, would become chairman and chief executive officer effective April 1, 1981. Welch had spent 20 years in GE's operating organization—first in the plastics business, later in consumer products, and then as vice chairman. He would be replacing the retiring Reginald H. Jones, a man described by some as a "legend." Indeed, *The Wall Street Journal* reported that GE had "decided to replace a legend with a live wire."

The company that Jack Welch would be leading was the 10th largest industrial corporation in the United States and the only firm among *Fortune's* 10 largest that could be characterized as diversified. Its financial performance was solid—AAA bond rating, 19.5 percent return on equity, and $2.2 billion in cash and marketable securities. In addition, GE's management systems and in particular its strategic planning system were most highly regarded; the following comments were typical:

> Probably no single company has made such a singular contribution to the arts and wiles, the viewpoints and the techniques of large-scale corporate management as GE. . . . Today the technique uppermost in the minds of GE top management is planning—a preoccupation in which GE is again an acknowledged master and innovator among corporate giants.
>
> *Management Today*, August 1978

> Shortly after I took this job, I visited some people at the Defense Department because I had heard that they had just finished an exhaustive survey of industrial planning systems. They told me I was probably inheriting the world's most effective strategic planning system and that Number Two was pretty far behind.
>
> Daniel J. Fink, Senior V.P.,
> Corporate Planning and Development,
> General Electric

When Japanese managers come to visit us, they don't ask to see our research

---

Harvard Business School case 381–174.

> centers or manufacturing facilities. All they want to know about is our management system.
>
> A General Electric executive

GE's excellent performance and reputation were no guarantee of future success. Jack Welch would be challenged to meet the company's long-term objective of increasing earnings per share 25 percent faster than the growth in GNP in the face of tougher foreign competition and a continued slowdown in the growth of GE's traditional businesses. To meet this challenge, he would have to decide how to stimulate and promote growth and what role GE's famed planning system would play in the years ahead.

ORIGINS OF STRATEGIC PLANNING

As the decade of the 1960s was nearing a close, a number of circumstances came together which led to a major reexamination of the way General Electric was being managed. One of the more salient of these was the company's profitless growth (see Exhibit 1 for financial information). While sales in 1968 of $8.4 billion were 91 percent higher than in 1960, net income had increased only 63 percent and return on total assets had fallen from 7.4 percent to 6.2 percent. This lackluster profit performance came at the same time that three major ventures—commercial jet engines, mainframe computers, and nuclear power systems—were demanding more and more of the company's financial resources. Pressure on corporate management was mounting: GE's "sacred Triple A bond rating" was in jeopardy.

Improving this financial situation was no easy task. In 1968 GE was widely diversified, competing in 23 of the 26 two-digit SIC industry categories, and was decentralized into 10 groups, 46 divisions, and over 190 departments. Indeed, diversification and decentralization had been the major strategic and organizational thrusts of GE's two prior CEOs—Ralph Cordiner, 1950 to 1963, and Fred Borch, 1963 to 1972. Under decentralization, GE's departments became organizational building blocks, each with its own product-market scope and its own marketing, finance, engineering, manufacturing, and employee-relations functions. One GE executive noted:

> In the 1950s Cordiner led a massive decentralization of the company. This was absolutely necessary. GE had been highly centralized in the 1930s and 1940s. Cordiner broke the company down into departments that, as he used to say, "were a size that a man could get his arms around." And what the company would say after giving a man his department was, "Here take this $50 million department and grow it into $125 million." Then the department would be split into two departments, like an amoeba.

In addition to decentralization, Cordiner pushed for expansion of GE's business and product lines. With growth and diversity, however, came problems of control:

> The case for Cordiner lies in his improvement of GE's numerators and in his creation of a truly remarkable "can-do" organization. He was the champion of volume and diversity and of make rather than buy. He built a company unmatched in American business history in the capacity to pursue those objectives. In the sense of home grown know-how, GE *could* do almost anything; and, in the sense of in-house capacity, GE could do a lot of a lot of things, simultaneously.
>
> But the very expansiveness and evangelism that were Cordiner's strengths were flawed by permissiveness and lack of

proportion. "We can do it" too often became "we should do it." For example, massive investments with long payback periods were undertaken simultaneously in nuclear power, aerospace, and computers, with a blithe self-confidence in GE's ability to "do-it-ourselves." A sort of "marketing macropia" persisted in which previously constrained market segmentations and product definitions were escalated beyond experience or prudence.[1]

As Fred Borch faced the challenges of leading General Electric in the mid-1960s, internal studies of the company's problems began to proliferate. One such study set out to give management a tool for evaluating business plans by delineating the key factors associated with profitable results.[2] Another study undertaken by GE's Growth Council tried to determine how the company would properly position itself to meet its long-time goals of growing faster than the GNP. Despite these and other staff studies, however, profitless growth continued.

Reg Jones assessed the company's situation at the time:

> Our performance reflected poor planning and a poor understanding of the businesses. A major reason for this weakness was the way we were organized. Under the existing structure with functional staff units at the corporate level, business plans only received functional reviews. They were not given a *business* evaluation.
>
> True, we had a corporate planning department, but they were more concerned with econometric models and environmental forecasting than with hard-headed business plan evaluation. Fortunately, Fred Borch was able to recognize the problem.

In 1969 Borch commissioned McKinsey & Co. to study the effectiveness of GE's corporate staff and of the planning done at the operating level. He commented on McKinsey's study:

> They were totally amazed at how the company ran as well as it did with the planning that was being done or not being done at various operating levels. But they saw some tremendous opportunities for moving the company ahead if we devoted the necessary competence and time to facing up to these, as they saw it, very critical problems.
>
> In their report, they made two specific recommendations. One was that we recognize that our departments were not really businesses. We had been saying that they were the basic building blocks of the company for many years, but they weren't. They were fractionated and they were parts of larger businesses. The thrust of the recommendation was that we reorganize the company from an operation standpoint and create what they call Strategic Business Units—the terminology stolen from a study we made back in 1957. They gave certain criteria for these and in brief what this amounted to were reasonably self-sufficient businesses that did not meet head-on with other strategic business units in making the major management decisions necessary.[3] They also recommended as part of this that the 33 or

[1] James P. Baughman, "Problems and Performance of the Role of Chief Executive in the General Electric Company, 1892–1974," mimeographed discussion paper, July 15, 1974.

[2] This approach eventually led to the PIMS model that has been made available to industry at large by the Strategic Planning Institute.

[3] The general characteristics of an SBU were defined as follows: a unique set of competitors, a unique business mission, a competitor in external markets (as opposed to internal supplier), the ability to accomplish integrated strategic planning, and the ability to "call the shots" on the variables crucial to the success of the business.

35 or 40 strategic business units report directly to the CEO regardless of the size of the business or the present level in the organization.

Their second recommendation was that we face up to the fact that we were never going to get the longer-range work done necessary to progress the company through the 70s, unless we made a radical change in our staff components. The thrust of their recommendation was to separate out the ongoing work necessary to keep General Electric going from the work required to posture the company for the future.

INTRODUCTION OF STRATEGIC PLANNING

In reporting the results of the McKinsey study to GE's management in May 1970, Fred Borch noted: "We decided that their recommendations on both the operating front and the staff front conceptually were very sound. They hit right at the nut of the problem, but the implementation that they recommended just wouldn't fly as far as General Electric was concerned. We accepted about 100 percent of their conceptual contribution and virtually none of their implementation recommendations."

To develop an approach for implementing the McKinsey recommendations in a way suitable for GE, Borch had set up a task force headed by Group Vice President W. D. Dance. This group spent two intensive months preparing alternatives and recommendations for consideration by the corporate executive office.

As a result of these efforts, a decision was made to restructure GE's corporate staff into two parts. The existing staff units, which provided ongoing services to the CEO[4] and to the operating units, were grouped as the corporate administrative staff reporting to a senior vice president. The administrative staff would deal with functional, operational matters. As a counterpart, a corporate executive staff was created to help the CEO plan the future of the company. It comprised four staff components—finance, strategic planning, technology, and legal and governance—each headed by a senior vice president.

Establishing Strategic Business Units

The task force anticipated several problems in implementing McKinsey's recommendation to create strategic business units reporting directly to the CEO. One problem had to do with GE's existing line reporting structure of groups, divisions, and departments. McKinsey's proposal had been to abandon GE's current organizational structure and to reorganize on the basis of SBUs. The task force was concerned that such a change might seriously jeopardize the successful functioning of GE's operational control system. To avoid this risk, management decided to superimpose the SBU structure on the existing line reporting structure. For ongoing operations, managers would report according to the group-division-department structure. However, only units designated SBUs would prepare strategic plans.

As shown in Figure 1, a group, division, or department could be designated an SBU. This overlay of a strategic planning struc-

[4] The CEO here refers to the corporate executive office, which included the chairman and chief executive officer and the vice chairmen. GE usually had two or three vice chairmen.

FIGURE 1
SBU OVERLAY ON EXISTING ORGANIZATION

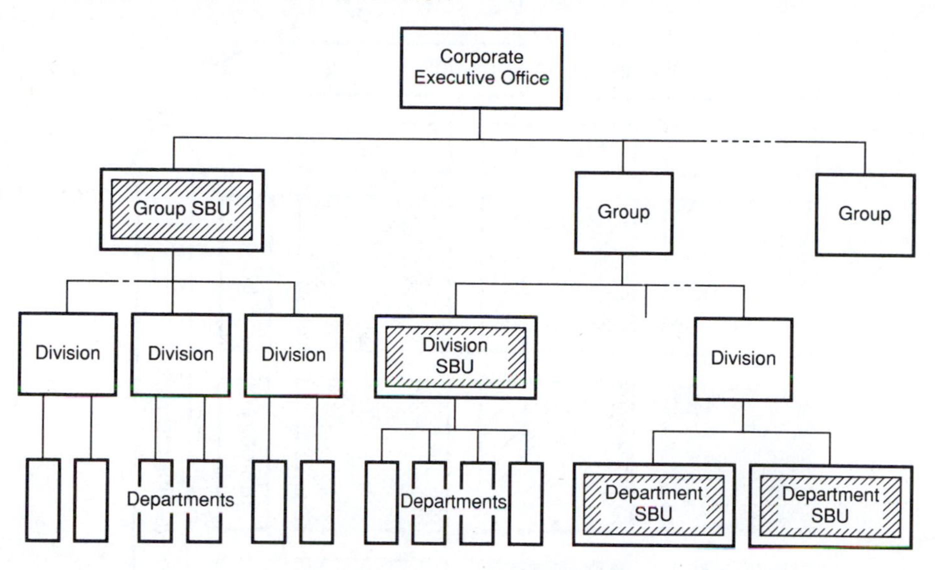

ture on the operating structure resulted in a variety of reporting relationships. When a department was named an SBU, for example, the department manager would report directly to the CEO for planning purposes, but to a division manager for operating purposes. GE managers expressed the opinion that this approach provided the company with the best of both worlds – tight operational control on a comprehensive basis and planning at the relevant levels. One manager commented:

> In theory, the intervening layers of management were supposed to be transparent for planning purposes and opaque for control purposes. In practice, they were translucent for both. Even though the department or division SBU managers were to report directly to the CEO for planning, they would normally review their plans with the group executive. In a sense, we loosened the SBU structure to allow personal influence and power to shape the important strategic decisions.

The designation of SBUs posed a second problem for the task force. According to GE executives, about 80 percent of the SBU designations could be readily agreed upon. The remaining 20 percent required considerable judgment whether the appropriate SBU level was the department, division, or group. In these cases Fred Borch would make the final judgment, often based on his "comfort index" with the business and with the manager running the business. Not until the end of 1972 were all of the SBU designations completed. Of the 43 SBUs, 4 were groups, 21 were divisions, and 18 were departments. Two other problems on the task force's agenda concerned the kind of information to be contained in an SBU plan and the numbers and kinds of people to staff the planning effort.

Defining a Business Plan

Even with the reduction in the number of business plans from 190 departments to 43 SBUs, the CEO faced a formidable task

FIGURE 2
INVESTMENT PRIORITY SCREEN

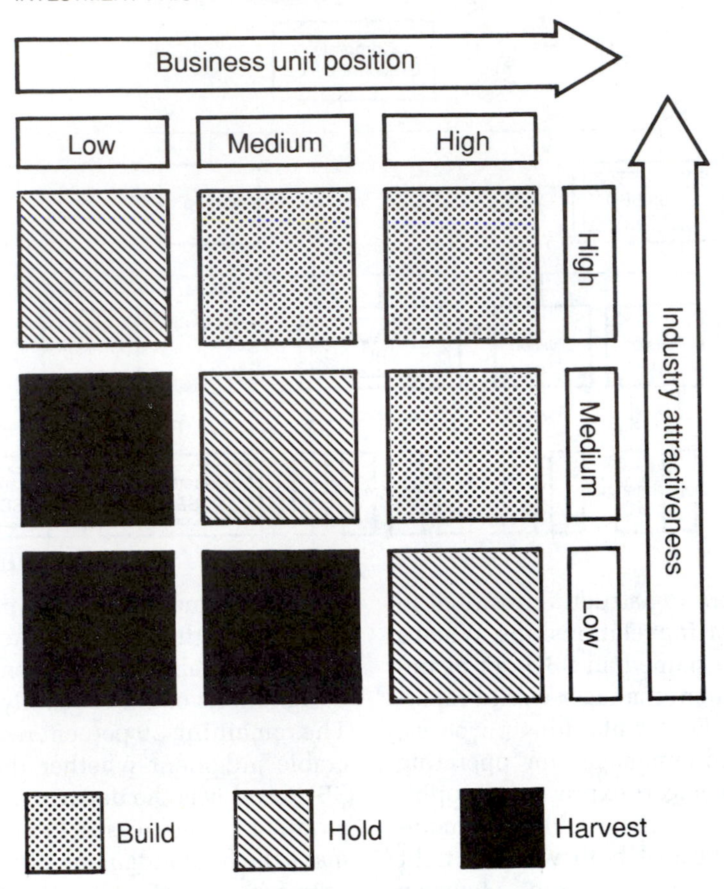

of review. One GE manager noted that "Borch had a sense that he wasn't looking for lots of data on each business unit, but really wanted 15 terribly important and significant pages of data and analysis."

To deal with this problem, three of the group vice presidents were asked to work with three different consulting companies (Arthur D. Little, Boston Consulting Group, and McKinsey & Co.) to find a way to compress all of the strategic planning data into as effective a presentation as possible. For example, GE's collaborative effort with McKinsey led to the development of the 9-block summary of business and investment strategy shown in Figure 2.[5] One GE executive commented that "the 9-block summary had tremendous appeal to us not only because it compressed a lot of data, but also because it contained enough subjective evaluation to appeal to the thinking of GE management."

The only instructions for the SBU manager on the content of a business plan were

[5] See Exhibit 2 for a description of GE's 1980 criteria for assessing industry attractiveness and business position.

a listing of the topics to be covered. Over time, new topics were added and some were deleted. But the corporate office never specified how each topic should be treated. The following list contains the topics specified for the 1973 SBU plans:

1. Identification and formulation of environmental assumptions of strategic importance.
2. Identification and in-depth analysis of competitors, including assumptions about their probable strategies.
3. Analysis of the SBU's own resources.
4. Development and evaluation of strategy alternatives.
5. Preparation of the SBU strategic plan, including estimates of capital spending for the next five years.
6. Preparation of the SBU operating plan, which detailed the next year of the SBU strategic plan.

Reg Jones, who became GE's chairman and chief executive officer in December 1972, added a proviso on how the plans were to be presented:

> At our general management conference in January 1973, I stirred up quite a few members of that audience when I said that I expected every SBU manager to be able to stand before a peer group and, without benefit of visual aids, give a clear and concise statement of his strategic plan. And that every manager reporting to him should fully understand that statement and be able to explain it to his troops. I meant it. When that happens, then you can say that planning has become a way of life.

Staffing the Planning Effort

With the new SBU planning approach in place, the question remained of how to staff the effort. Here, two important actions were taken. First, each SBU manager was required to hire an SBU strategic planner. Because of the limited number of experienced strategic planners in the company at that time, many of the people filling these posts were hired from outside the company, an unusual practice for GE.[6]

Second, both the SBU general managers and strategic planners were required to attend special strategic planning seminars set up at GE's Management Development Center in Crotonville, New York. Each department and division general manager (over 240 in number) was also given a metal suitcase with a slide and tape show to present to subordinates after taking the course.

ACCEPTANCE OF PLANNING: 1972–1977

In the 1950s and 1960s, a characteristic of GE was the belief that the company could succeed in all of the businesses in which it competed. A frequently voiced reaction to strategic planning and particularly to the 9-block analysis, on the other hand, was that it legitimized exiting from certain businesses. According to *Fortune*, "GE stopped making vacuum cleaners, fans, phonographs, heart pacemakers, an industrial X-ray system, and numerous other products that failed to deliver the returns Jones demanded." During Jones's entire tenure as CEO, a total of 73 product lines were exited.

GE's successful exit from the mainframe computer business in May 1970

[6] Over time, many of the SBUs developed planning staffs and the planning positions were filled internally. By 1980 there were approximately 200 senior level planners in GE. About half of these were career planners, while the others rotated through the position as part of their career development.

TABLE 1
GE'S BUSINESS MIX (Percent)

	Sales		Earnings	
	1970	*1977*	*1970*	*1977*
Consumer products and services	22.8	23.5	29.6	29.6
Power systems	21.5	18.0	26.5	6.9
Industrial components and systems	23.1	20.6	28.4	17.6
Technical systems and materials	28.5	23.1	9.1	22.7
Natural resources	0.0	5.4	0.0	18.0
International	15.9	14.3	20.1	6.5
Corporate eliminations	(11.8)	(4.9)	(13.7)	(1.3)

Source: General Electric 10-K reports for 1970 (recast for organizational changes) and 1977.

also played a pivotal role in legitimizing divestitures; as one manager commented:

> While the sale of GE's computer business actually preceded the adoption of strategic planning, somehow people began to connect the two. From then on it became fashionable to prune businesses. And Jones's subsequent promotion gave even more credibility to those managers who were willing to face up to the fact that certain businesses had to be exited.
>
> The planning system was just another tool which enabled a manager to face up to certain inevitabilities. Prior to this, we had really operated with a "floating J curve." In other words, businesses would forecast two or three years of flat or declining profitability, but then all of the numbers would point upwards. What Jones was able to do with the computer business and what strategic planning revealed was that the floating J curve was a fantasy.

Impact on the Business Mix

As shown in Table 1, one impact of strategic planning was a shift in GE's mix of businesses. Reg Jones commented:

> Another source of confidence for us is the continued development of a strategic planning system that provides a strong discipline for differentiating the allocation of resources—that is, investing most heavily in areas of business that we identify as offering the greatest leverage for earnings growth, while minimizing our investments in sectors we see as growing more slowly or remaining static. [1973 annual report]
>
> Comparing the company today with the General Electric of only a few years ago shows that, in selectively allocating our resources to the growth opportunities identified through strategic planning, we have developed decidedly different sources of earnings and a different mix of businesses, whose potentials for profitable growth exceed those of our historic product lines. [1976 annual report]

As Table 1 illustrates, a major contributor to the shift in GE's business mix was the acquisition in 1976 of Utah International, a billion dollar mining company with substantial holdings of metallurgical coal.[7]

[7] General Electric's 1976 annual report related a pooling-of-interest exchange of 41 million shares of GE common stock for all outstanding shares of Utah International, effective December 20, 1976. Utah International's 1976 earnings were $181 million and sales were $1,001 million. The company's principal operations included the mining of coking coal, steam coal, uranium, iron ore, and copper. By far the most important contribution to 1976 earnings came from Australian coking coal supplied under long-term contracts to Japanese and European steel producers.

Many saw in Utah a potential hedge against inflation and numerous opportunities for synergy with GE's other businesses. While not denying these benefits, *Fortune* reported:

> Jones wanted to make a lasting imprint on his corporation by providing a new source of earnings growth and creating what he likes to call "the new GE." Utah provided him with a means to make that concept credible. When the opportunity arose, he relied not on his hallowed planning staff, but rather seized the chance to personally lead his company into its biggest move in many years. As Jones himself now acknowledges: "Nothing in our strategic planning said that we should acquire Utah International."[8]

Internal developments also contributed to the shift in business mix, as described by one of GE's senior executives: "Much of the recent growth has come from the internal development of businesses brand new to GE. For example, engineered materials didn't even exist as a business in 1960. It was just a bunch of research projects. Now, it will have sales of $2 billion, it will make $200 million net, with a ROI of 18 percent, and it will have plants all over the world. The company's experiences with aircraft engines, information services, and several other businesses have been much the same."

Impact on Management Systems

By 1977 the impact of strategic planning was being felt by GE's other management systems. For example, manpower evaluation and selection had been keyed to the strategic plans. A manager in the executive manpower department noted: "The strategic plans gave us, for the first time, a means by which we could evaluate if a manager really delivered on what he said he would do. All we have to do is check the previous plans. This also helps when there are job changes. We can now determine what current problems are caused by earlier mistakes, so the wrong person doesn't get blamed."

In the area of incentive compensation, performance screens were developed that separated financial and nonfinancial objectives for the business. This was intended to provide greater emphasis on longer-term considerations, and it did to some extent, but as one manager noted, "It's a great theory, but in a crunch it's the financial results that matter."

In terms of GE's organization structure, only one major change was apparent. This was the dissolution of the corporate executive staff and the return to a number of separate functional staff components. Reg Jones explained: "The corporate executive staff was originally set up with two major objectives: to straighten out the venture messes and to devise a planning system to prevent those troubles in the future. By 1974 the venture problems were solved, and we had a planning staff that was managing the new strategic planning process. By 1975 we dissolved the [corporate executive] staff."

Assessment of Strategic Planning

By 1977 strategic planning had won widespread management support for a variety of reasons. GE executives commented as follows:

> In the views of some managers, there was more planning being done in the mid-1960s than today. There was lots of futurism, scenario writing, contingency

[8] "General Electric's Very Personal Merger," *Fortune*, August 1977.

> planning, and model building. But those efforts were not related to the problems of our ongoing businesses as in the SBU analysis.
>
> Not specifying the precise format of a strategic plan turned out to be very useful. For one thing, it enabled the SBUs to avoid spending time on issues that weren't important to them. More important, it provided room for some creativity and originality in the writing of the plans.
>
> Since strategic planning was implemented, our real growth businesses have been funded, even when we were cash short in 1974 and 1975. The key is for the guy who is running a growth business that requires resources to gain the confidence of the people at the top of the organization. Strategic planning can help to get that confidence.

An internal audit of strategic planning, completed in December 1974, reported that "the overwhelming feeling is that strategic planning has become ingrained in General Electric: 80 percent felt there would be no slippage and 16 percent only minor slippage if corporate requirements for SP [strategic planning] were removed."

Not surprisingly, complaints of shortcomings in GE's strategic planning were also voiced. Some of the complaints reported in the audit had to do with the excessive effort devoted to cosmetics and upward merchandising of strategic plans. Another set of complaints had to do with a perceived ineffective review of SBU plans. The audit reported, "One issue is clear: the operations managers feel that corporate-level reviewers do not understand their businesses well enough to be competent reviewers."

The earlier review of strategic plans at the division and group levels was also considered by many managers as ineffective. The reason for this failing was attributed to the fact that managers at these levels typically "were really participants in generating the plans and thus were not objective reviewers." At the CEO level, on the other hand, the review of all 43 SBU strategic plans was requiring an inordinate amount of time and effort.

Pressures for current earnings were also cited as undermining the strategic planning process. One executive, quoted in the audit, commented: "Strategic planning process won't work in General Electric, at least not in the context in which we are trying to make it work. The company needs to project an attractive financial and cash-flow image. The pressure to provide a steady profit growth and a sustained P/E ratio results in short-term demands on operations which disrupt long-term programs."

A Single General Electric and Value Added

The problem corporate management had in evaluating 43 SBU strategic plans was coupled with a growing concern about a lack of integration and cohesiveness among the many business initiatives under way. By the mid-1970s, SBU planning, while helping to strengthen GE's competitive positions and to improve profits, was also leading to a balkanization of the company. GE appeared to be moving in the direction of becoming a holding company.

The development ran directly counter to a basic GE management tenet. As early as 1973 Jones addressed management about the need to work "with the grain" rather than against it in reshaping the company. Prominent among the "abiding characteristics of General Electric," according to Jones, was "a strong preference for a single General Electric identity, despite our broad diversification." The world-famous GE monogram symbolized this core identity.

Coupled with the concept of a single GE identity was the notion of "value added."

The recurrent attacks on big business, aimed at dismantling U.S. industry giants in the interest of increased competition, posed a serious potential threat to GE. As one senior GE executive explained: "The whole has got to be significantly greater than the sum of its parts. We have nothing to defend (against increasing external pressures to break up or, at a minimum, harass very large companies) unless we have a very effective, productive corporate level." Given top management's strong preference for a cohesive General Electric, SBU strategic planning, good as it was, was not adequate for GE's needs. Something more was needed.

INTEGRATING STRATEGIC PLANNING: 1977–1980

At the general management conference in January 1977, Reg Jones announced his intention "to revise GE's strategic planning system and to establish a 'sector' organization structure as the pivotal concept for the redesign effort." The proposed changes aimed to improve the strategic planning review process and to develop a cohesive plan for GE as a single, integrated entity.

Improving the Strategic Planning Review Process

In Jones's mind, corporate review of SBU plans suffered from overload. He explained:

> Right from the start of SBU planning in 1972, the vice chairmen and I tried to review each plan in great detail. This effort took untold hours and placed a tremendous burden on the corporate executive office. After awhile I began to realize that no matter how hard we would work, we could not achieve the necessary in-depth understanding of the 40-odd SBU plans. Somehow, the review burden had to be carried on more shoulders.

Creating the sector structure was Jones's way of spreading the review load. The sector was defined as a new level of management which represented a macrobusiness or industry area.[9] The sector executive would serve as the GE spokesperson for that industry and would be responsible for providing management direction to the member SBUs and for integrating the SBU strategies into a sector strategic plan. The sector strategic plan would focus heavily on development opportunities transcending SBU lines but still within the scope of the sector. The corporate executive office would thereafter focus its review on the strategic plans of the six sectors.

Below the sector, the SBU continued to be the basic business entity. To permit greater competitiveness (and visibility) for important strategic businesses within certain SBUs, however, GE introduced the concept of business segments. For example, the Audio Department became a business segment within the Housewares and Audio SBU because it was a unique business that could operate more effectively within the SBU than on its own.

The new organizational line structure is depicted in Figure 3. The dual organization in use since 1971 – SBUs for planning; group, divisions, and departments for operations – was supplemented by the sector-SBU structure. The earlier designations of group, division, and department were retained to indicate the relative size of an SBU.

[9] Robert Frederick, the executive who had been assigned the tasks of introducing the sector structure and making it work, explained the new nomenclature: "We picked the word *sector* because no one knew what it meant. In that way there would be no preconceived notions of what the sectors would do."

FIGURE 3
SECTOR-SBU STRUCTURE

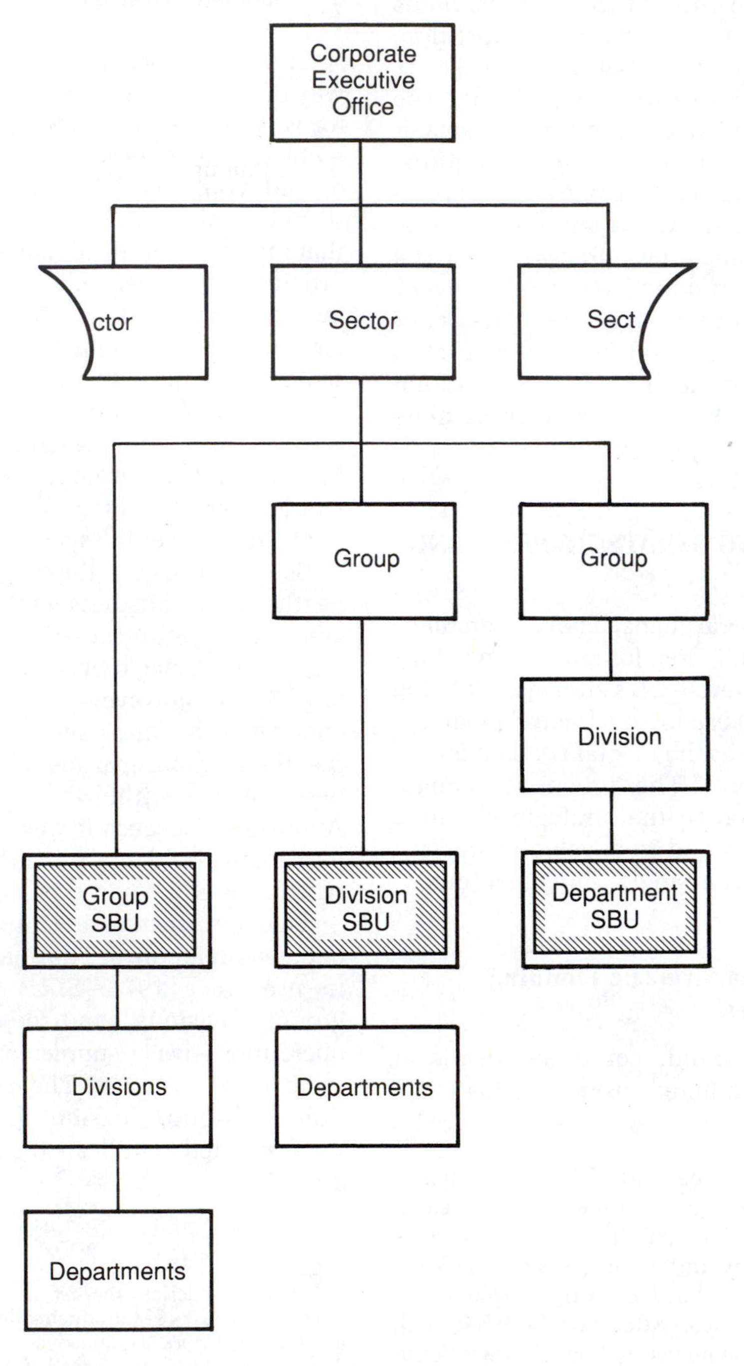

Along with improved review, the new sector structure was also seen as clarifying the responsibilities for business development in GE. According to a senior corporate strategic planning staff executive: "Conceptually, SBUs are expected to develop new business opportunities by extending into contiguous product-market areas. Sectors are expected to develop new SBUs by diversifying within their macroindustry scopes. And corporate is expected to develop new sectors by diversifying into unserved macroindustries."

Improving strategy review and business development were two visible reasons for the new sector structure. (The organization chart in Exhibit 3 shows the new sector structure and management assignments.) Jones also had a private reason for this organizational change:

> I had a personal road map of the future and knew when I wanted to retire. Time was moving on, and I could see a need to put the key candidates for my job under a spotlight for the board to view. The sector executive positions would provide the visibility.
>
> The men were assigned to sectors with businesses different from their past experience. I did this not only to broaden these individuals but also to leaven the businesses by introducing new bosses who had different perspectives. For example, major appliances had long been run by managers who had grown up in the business. I put Welch, whose previous experience had been with high-technology plastics, in charge to see if he could introduce new approaches.

Strategic Integration and Corporate Challenges

Along with improving strategic review, Jones saw a need to develop a cohesive plan for GE as a single, integrated entity. His concern reflected two problems that appeared to be growing in parallel with SBU planning itself:

> Over the years, we were discovering serious discontinuities among the SBU plans. At the operating level, we were suffering unnecessary costs from duplication and from uncoordinated actions.
>
> At the strategic level, we seemed to be moving in all directions with no sense of focus on what I saw as major opportunities and threats for the 1980s. For example, I saw a need to push forward on the international front, a need to move from our electromechanical technology to electronics, and a need to respond to the problems of productivity. We needed a way to challenge our managers to respond to these pressing issues in an integrated fashion.

To provide corporate direction and impetus on such issues, GE introduced the concept of corporate planning challenges. As shown in Figure 4, the planning challenges set the stage for the annual strategic planning cycle. Each year the CEO would issue a number of specific challenges that had to be addressed in the strategic plans of the SBUs and the sectors. For example, a 1980 corporate challenge called for SBUs and sectors to plan for a productivity improvement appropriate for their industry to counter worldwide competitive threats. The productivity target for GE as a whole was set for 6 percent.

The selection of challenges was seen by Jones as a vital function of the chief executive officer:

> It's the job of the CEO to look ahead. Planning can be helpful, but it is really our job to look at the decade ahead. You look at the environment and couple that with your knowledge of the operations. You begin to see gaps that are beyond the plans. You have studies made to examine the possible shortcomings.

FIGURE 4
ANNUAL PLANNING CYCLE

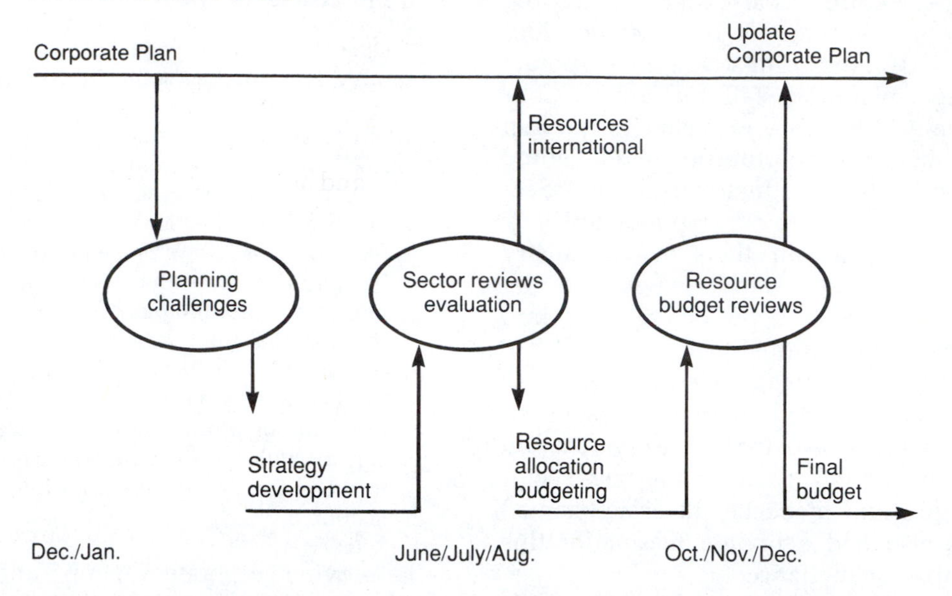

For example, as a defrocked bookkeeper, I have always had a concern about technology. In 1976, I commissioned a companywide study of our strengths, weaknesses, and needs in technology. The findings—16 volumes of them—triggered a technological renaissance in GE. We stepped up our R&D budgets, built up our electronic capabilities, and reoriented our recruiting and training activities. Now every SBU has a firm technological strategy integrated with its business strategy.

In addition to the CEO as a source of challenges, the restructured management system included two new approaches for generating planning challenges. One element aimed at fostering GE's international activities, the other at integrating GE's planning for critical resources.

International Sector. To increase the importance and the visibility of international operations in GE, Jones set it up as a sector. It was, however, to play a special role among sectors. In addition to preparing a sector plan for GE's overseas affiliates, the international sector was also given responsibility for fostering and integrating international business for General Electric as a whole.

A subsequent effort to integrate electric iron manufacturing on a worldwide basis illustrates one of the roles that the international sector was intended to play. The SBU responsible for irons had developed a newly designed iron which it planned for production in a single small country. At international sector urging, the SBU reconsidered and ultimately decided on rationalized multicountry production in three countries, including two larger countries with international sector affiliates. This approach improved cost and market share potentials in affiliate countries as well as cost effectiveness on a total GE system basis. This intervention led to an internal joint venture for irons between the international sector and the SBU to share risks and rewards on a worldwide basis.

Resource Planning. Corporate management's concerns with GE's handling of critical resources were to be dealt with through another companywide integrating mechanism. For this purpose, senior corporate staff executives were given responsibility "for an objective assessment of key resources and the identification of issues impacting the company's strategic strengths." These assessments of financial resources, human resources, technology resources, and production resources would lead to planning challenges to the sectors and SBUs wherever practices needed to be improved.

Planning for human resources illustrated how this approach was to work. The vice president in charge of this planning described two of the issues he had subsequently raised for management consideration:

> One of the major human resources issues GE has had to face had to do with the potential impact of transferring work and jobs to overseas locations. This practice has important implications for the company, for the employees, and for the communities involved which had to be thought through beforehand. Another important issue had to do with GE's image as it relates to recruiting college graduates. In the next few years GE has to hire some 2,800 scientists and engineers, competing with some glamorous firms for the good people.

Implementing the New Structure

In characteristic fashion, GE management recognized the need to allow time for the new structure to take root. As the initiating report stated: "The objective of integrated levels of planning is just that—an objective. It may take two or three cycles to accomplish."

True to this schedule, Jones made the following assessment three years later: "The sector approach has turned out to be very successful. It even exceeded my expectations. Now I can look at six planning books and understand them well enough to ask the right questions. I could not do that before. The sectors also gave the board and me an excellent means for deciding on my successor. By 1979 the competition had been narrowed down to Burlingame, Hood, and Welch, and these men were moved up to vice chairman positions." (Exhibit 4 contains biographical data on Jones, Welch, Burlingame, and Hood.)

Jones was also pleased with the progress GE had made in responding to a number of corporate challenges. He pointed with particular pride to the "technological renaissance" that had been launched at GE:

> These past few years, we have pressed hard the challenge to change the company's basic technology from electromechanical to electronics. Today we have a true companywide effort to apply the new microelectronics and the related information-based technologies to every possible product, service, and process in GE.
>
> The proposed purchase of Calma, a leading producer of interactive graphics equipment, and the acquisition of Intersil, a maker of advanced microelectronic chips, give evidence to this commitment.[10] Perhaps our commitment to

---

[10] According to GE's 1980 annual report, Intersil was acquired for $235 million. The Calma acquisition was cleared by the Federal Trade Commission in early 1981. The purchase agreement called for an initial payment of $100 million and additional payments of up to $70 million with the exact amount determined by Calma's sales over the next four years.

broad-based innovation is best expressed by our rising investment in research and development. Since 1977 we have increased GE-funded R&D expenditures 85 percent to $760 million. Total R&D, including external funding, reached $1.6 billion in 1980.

GE IN 1980: A CALL FOR GROWTH

In a presentation to the financial community at the Hotel Pierre in New York City on December 11, 1979, Jones pointed to how GE was "positioned to achieve the objective of sustained earnings growth, faster than the growth of the U.S. economy, in the 1980s." He added: "General Electric is embarked on a course of large-scale innovation, productivity improvement, and business development for the 1980s, and we have built up the financial resources to bring that bold and entrepreneurial strategy to a successful conclusion."

Challenging Static Forecasts

This public promise of rapid growth carried major implications for strategic planning. At the annual general management conference at Belleair held a month later, Daniel Fink, the newly appointed senior vice president for corporate planning and development (development had been added to stress the growth objective), questioned the adequacy of the existing strategic plans to meet Jones's growth challenge. He began by reviewing the recent and projected changes in business mix. The relative earnings figures are summarized in Table 2. (See Exhibits 5 and 6 for more detailed financial statements.) Armed with these figures, Fink then argued:

TABLE 2
GE'S BUSINESS MIX (Percent)

	1968	*1979*	*1984*	*Projected Change*
Electrical equipment	80	47	44	−3
Materials	6	27	27	0
Services	10	16	19	+3
Transportation	4	10	10	0
International	16	40	43	+3

> Our implied strategy seems to be one of slowing, or even halting, the aggressive and successful diversification of the past decade. The vision of GE in 1984 that we get from the long-range forecasts is very much like GE in 1979—same product mix, same international mix, same strategy of leveraging earnings over sales growth.
>
> How can that be? And—more important—do you believe it? Do you believe we'll really have the same product mix in view of even the most obvious technological changes we can see ahead? Do you really think that international mix will hold, despite the faster growth of many world markets? And that we can have the same strategy of leveraging earnings over sales, just as if that last tenth of a point was as easy to achieve as the first?
>
> It's that contradiction of a steady-state GE and a rapidly changing world that gives us, I think, the key strategic issue as we enter the 80s. How do we attain the vision now to reject that static forecast and then take the strategic actions that will move us forward in the 80s, just as we did in the 70s?

Fink next disputed the basis on which the existing strategic plans had projected growth:

> Back in '68 we earned 4½ percent on sales, by '74 it was 5 percent, 6 percent in '78, and the LRFs [long-range forecasts] say 7 percent in 1984, but it doesn't follow that just because the company went from 5 to 6 percent in the 70s, it will easily move up to 7 percent in the 80s.

> There are several reasons for caution. First, most of our SBUs, urged on by last year's business development challenge, carry the expense burden of major investment plans. And finally, we'll be twice as dependent on productivity, rather than price, for inflation recovery. So, under these circumstances, we certainly must consider the 7 percent at risk.
>
> Just suppose we hold our ROS at the current 6 percent level. The difference in '84 would be almost $400 million of net income and widening each year. To compensate for that shortfall, we would have to add something like $6–$7 billion of sales. That's another sector.
>
> These are big increments. They aren't going to be achieved by simple extensions of our current businesses. They do demand a period of unprecedented business development in the 1980s. Unprecedented business development. Consider what that has to mean to a company that has already made the largest acquisition in U.S. business history; that has produced more patentable inventions than any other company in the world; and that already is the largest diversified corporation on the *Fortune* 500 list.

Realigning GE's Resources

The first step to generating unprecedented business growth in the 1980s was to select the target areas with the greatest potential for GE. In-depth corporate planning staff analysis led to the definition of six broad business areas. These areas, called *arenas*, were identified as follows:

- Energy.
- Communication, information, and sensing.
- Energy applications–productivity.
- Materials and resources.
- Transportation and propulsion.
- Pervasive services (nonproduct-related services such as financial, distribution, and construction).

A common characteristic of the arenas was that they cut across sector organizational lines. Fink described the dilemma and indicated a need for new approaches:

> How are we going to tackle these new opportunities which cut across organization lines? Sometimes the solution is to reorganize and collect those synergistic businesses under single management. But there are too many opportunities out there. We'd have to reorganize every three days just to keep up with them.
>
> How many times have you heard customers, or even competitors, say, "If you guys could only get your act together!" Well, we're going to have to get our act together if we're to tackle some of these new opportunities. We're going to have to develop coventuring techniques, motivation and measurement techniques that have thus far eluded us. It won't come easy; it's nontraditional. It's not traditional for those of us who learned to manage at the John Wayne school of rugged individualism.

To get GE's "act together," the CEO issued explicit arena-related challenges to launch the 1981 planning cycle. Each challenge listed the specific sectors and corporate staff units to be involved and designated the sector responsible to lead the effort. One of the specific challenges related to the energy applications–productivity arena, for example, was to develop a strategic business plan to exploit the growing opportunities associated with factory automation and robotics. The industrial products and components sector, which was already heavily involved with factory automation, was given lead responsibility for this factory of the future challenge. Support roles were assigned to the information and communications systems group (a unit in the technical systems and materials sector) because of its experience with mobile communications, and to the corporate production and operating services staff unit because of its responsibility for improving productivity within GE itself.

Just how this cross-organizational business development would function still had to be worked out. Jones clearly viewed this approach as preliminary and evolving: "I don't want operating managers worrying about arenas for a while. At this point in time, arenas are for our use at the corporate level. They help to give us another view of the company." The provisional nature of the arena approach was also indicated in the following comment by a senior executive: "The success or failure of the arena concept will depend to a great extent on how hard corporate management pushes it."

The Next Steps

The General Electric Jack Welch was preparing to lead in 1981 was in the midst of actively probing a panoply of new technology businesses. Lively discussions were being held in offices throughout the company on what GE should do about the factory of the future, the office of the future, the house of the future, the electric car, synthetic fuel, and the like. The list of opportunities seemed endless. Clearly, GE would have to make some hard choices. In this connection, Welch was reported to have said: "My biggest challenge will be to put enough money on the right gambles and to put no money on the wrong ones. But I don't want to sprinkle money over everything."[11]

What kind of management system would he need to meet this challenge? Jack Welch had used SBU and sector planning to build businesses and later had a hand in shaping GE's approach to strategic management. He laid to rest any idea of dismantling the apparatus in place: "GE was a well-run company before anyone ever heard of John Welch. Most of the corporate revolutions you hear about are when a guy moves from company X to company Y and tips it upside down. Sometimes it works and sometimes it doesn't. That won't happen here."

Despite this commitment, Welch was inheriting a management system undergoing major changes. Crossroad choices would have to be made here as well. The 1981 management audit indicated numerous important management system issues for attention:

- Can the sectors as presently defined accommodate the size and diversity of company operations in 1985? In 1990? Alternatives?
- The 1981 corporate strategy was developed through an arena segmentation which is deliberately different from the GE sector segmentation. Is this useful to the CEO in developing a vision for the company? Will it be a workable approach that leads to truly integrated strategies?
- Is there a better way than our international integration process to determine and pursue company international objectives?

How these management system issues were handled would be influenced by the broad substantive issues GE faced. While opinions differed as to priorities, senior managers agreed on several key challenges. Reg Jones put dealing with inflation at the top of his list. Increasing productivity and

[11] *Business Week*, March 16, 1981.

increasing international business were also high on his and everyone else's list of major issues. For many senior executives, increasing entrepreneurship and new ventures in GE were also a major challenge in view of the company's ambitious growth goals.

The list of issues – both those having to do with substance and those having to do with management systems – was long, far too long for all to be dealt with in depth. Management would have to be selective in choosing areas for attention. One executive neatly summed up his views of the situation with the comment: "GE is going to be a very exciting company these next few years. You can just feel the electricity in the air."

EXHIBIT 1
TEN-YEAR STATISTICAL SUMMARY, 1961–1970
In Milliions of Dollars Except per Share Amounts

	1970	1969	1968	1967	1966	1965	1964	1963	1962	1961
Sales of products and services	$ 8,726.7	$ 8,448.0	$ 8,381.6	$ 7,741.2	$ 7,177.3	$ 6,213.6	$ 5,319.2	$ 5,177.0	$ 4,986.1	$ 4,666.6
Net earnings	$ 328.5	$ 278.0	$ 357.1	$ 361.4	$ 338.9	$ 355.1	$ 219.6	$ 272.2	$ 256.5	$ 238.4
Earnings per common share	$ 3.63	$ 3.07	$ 3.95	$ 4.01	$ 3.75	$ 3.93	$ 2.44	$ 3.05	$ 2.89	$ 2.70
Earnings as a percentage of sales	3.8%	3.3%	4.3%	4.7%	4.7%	5.7%	4.1%	5.3%	5.1%	5.1%
Earned on share owners' equity	12.6%	11.0%	14.8%	15.9%	15.7%	17.5%	11.5%	14.9%	15.0%	14.8%
Cash dividends declared	$ 235.4	$ 235.2	$ 234.8	$ 234.2	$ 234.6	$ 216.7	$ 197.7	$ 183.1	$ 177.5	$ 176.4
Dividends declared per common share	$ 2.60	$ 2.60	$ 2.60	$ 2.60	$ 2.60	$ 2.40	$ 2.20	$ 2.05	$ 2.00	$ 2.00
Market price range per share	94½–60¼	98¼–74⅛	100⅜–80¼	115⅞–82½	120–80	120¼–91	93⅝–78¾	87½–71¾	78½–54¼	80¾–60½
Current assets	$ 3,334.8	$ 3,287.8	$ 3,311.1	$ 3,207.6	$ 3,013.0	$ 2,842.4	$ 2,543.8	$ 2,321.0	$ 2,024.6	$ 1,859.7
Current liabilities	$ 2,650.3	$ 2,366.7	$ 2,104.3	$ 1,977.4	$ 1,883.2	$ 1,566.8	$ 1,338.9	$ 1,181.9	$ 1,168.7	$ 1,086.6
Total assets	$ 6,309.9	$ 6,007.5	$ 5,743.8	$ 5,347.2	$ 4,851.7	$ 4,300.4	$ 3,856.0	$ 3,502.5	$ 3,349.9	$ 3,143.4
Total share owners' equity	$ 2,665.1	$ 2,540.0	$ 2,493.4	$ 2,342.2	$ 2,211.7	$ 2,107.0	$ 1,944.2	$ 1,889.2	$ 1,764.3	$ 1,654.6
Plant and equipment additions	$ 581.4	$ 530.6	$ 514.7	$ 561.7	$ 484.9	$ 332.9	$ 237.7	$ 149.2	$ 173.2	$ 179.7
Depreciation	$ 334.7	$ 351.3	$ 300.1	$ 280.4	$ 233.6	$ 188.4	$ 170.3	$ 149.4	$ 146.0	$ 131.6
Total taxes and renegotiation	$ 309.4	$ 313.2	$ 390.5	$ 390.1	$ 409.1	$ 403.8	$ 277.3	$ 331.4	$ 298.7	$ 289.9
Provision for income taxes	$ 220.6	$ 231.5	$ 312.3	$ 320.5	$ 347.4	$ 352.2	$ 233.8	$ 286.7	$ 254.0	$ 248.9
Employees—average worldwide	396,583	410,126	395,691	384,864	375,852	332,991	308,233	297,726	290,682	279,547
Gross national product (current $ billions)	$ 982	$ 936	$ 869	$ 796	$ 753	$ 688	$ 636	$ 595	$ 564	$ 523

Source: General Electric annual reports; *Business Statistics,* U.S. Department of Commerce, p. 245, for GNP.

EXHIBIT 2
GE'S 1980 CRITERIA FOR INVESTMENT PRIORITY SCREEN

Criterion	*Measure*	*Criterion*	*Measure*
Industry Attractiveness		Business Position	
1. Market size	• 3-year average served industry market dollars	1. Market position	• 3-year average market share (total market) • 3-year average international market share • 2-year average relative market share (SBU/"Big Three" competitors)
2. Market growth	• 10-year constant dollar average annual market growth rate		
3. Industry profitability	[Box] 3-year average ROS, SBU, and "Big Three" competitors • Nominal • Inflation adjusted		
		2. Competitive position	Superior, equal, or inferior to competition in 1980: • Product quality • Technological leadership • Manufacturing/cost leadership • Distribution/marketing leadership
4. Cyclicality	• Average annual percent variation of sales from trend		
5. Inflation recovery	• 5-year average ratio of combined selling price and productivity change to change in cost due to inflation	3. Relative profitability	[Box] 3-year SBU's ROS, less average ROS, "Big Three" competitors • Nominal • Inflation adjusted
6. Importance of non-U.S. markets	• 10-year average ratio of international to total market		

Note: Boxes indicate measure used for the first time in 1980.

EXHIBIT 3
ORGANIZATION CHART, JUNE 1, 1978

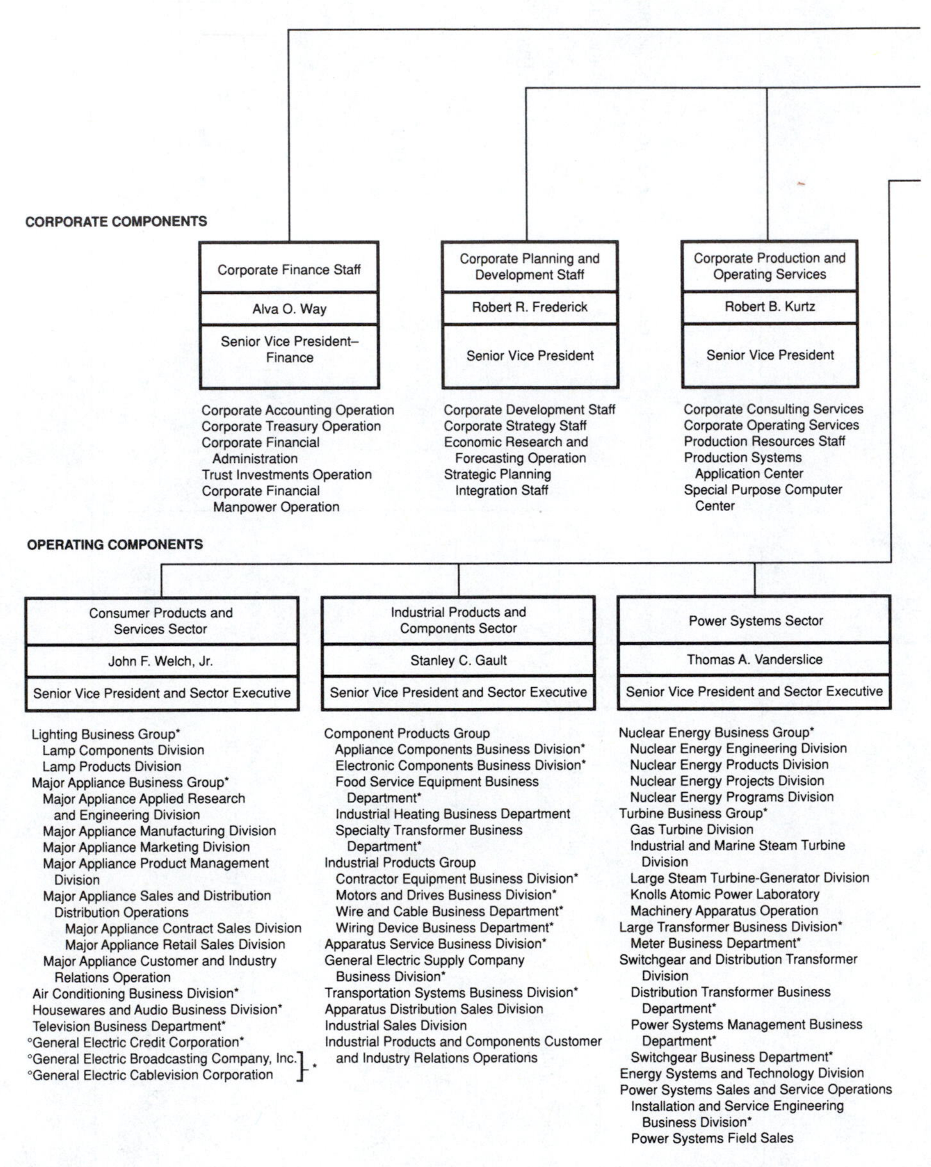

° - Affiliate
* - Strategic Business Unit

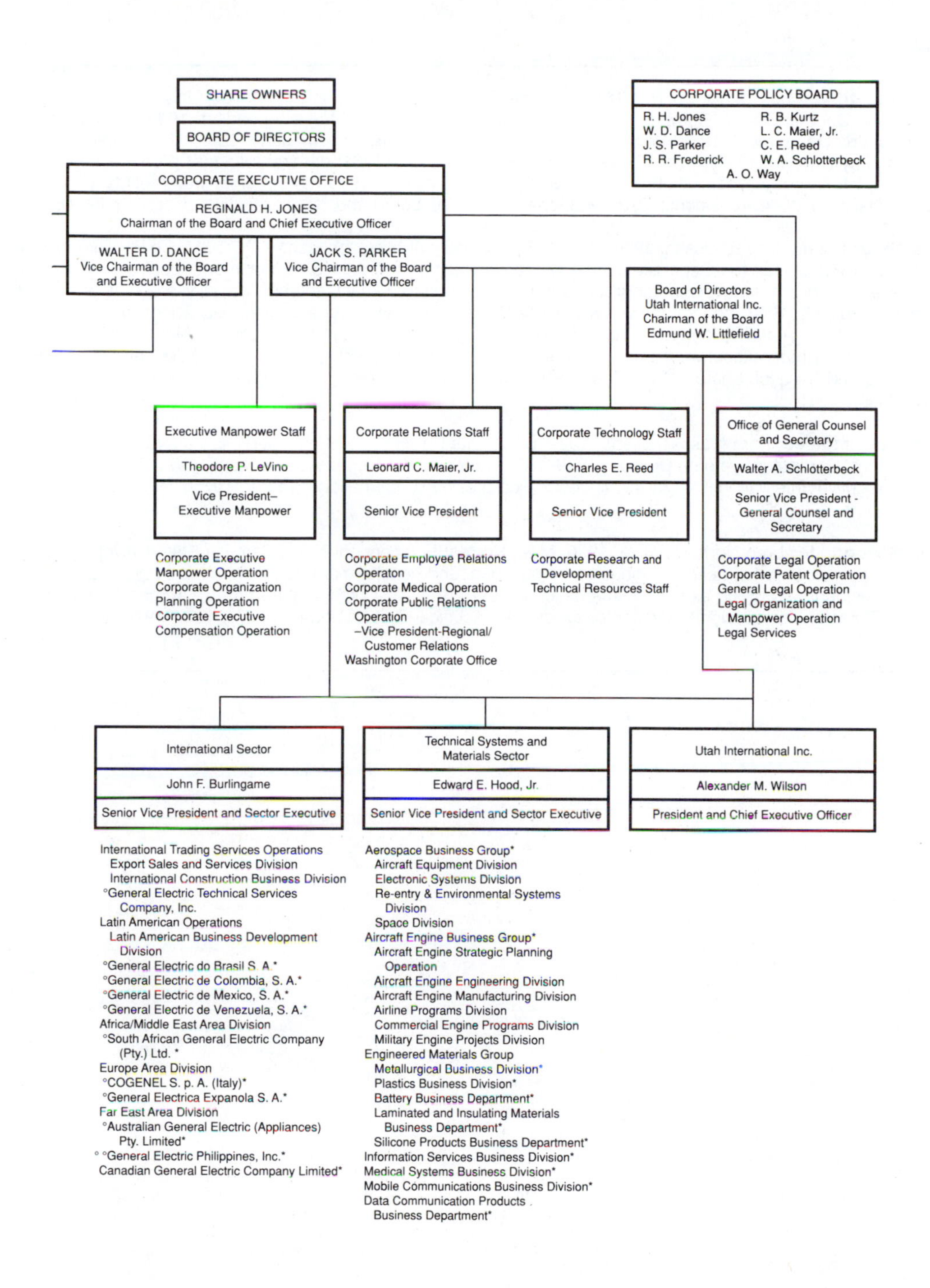
SHARE OWNERS
BOARD OF DIRECTORS
CORPORATE EXECUTIVE OFFICE
REGINALD H. JONES
Chairman of the Board and Chief Executive Officer
WALTER D. DANCE
Vice Chairman of the Board and Executive Officer
JACK S. PARKER
Vice Chairman of the Board and Executive Officer
CORPORATE POLICY BOARD
R. H. Jones
W. D. Dance
J. S. Parker
R. R. Frederick
R. B. Kurtz
L. C. Maier, Jr.
C. E. Reed
W. A. Schlotterbeck
A. O. Way
Board of Directors Utah International Inc. Chairman of the Board Edmund W. Littlefield
Executive Manpower Staff
Theodore P. LeVino
Vice President–Executive Manpower
Corporate Executive Manpower Operation
Corporate Organization Planning Operation
Corporate Executive Compensation Operation
Corporate Relations Staff
Leonard C. Maier, Jr.
Senior Vice President
Corporate Employee Relations Operaton
Corporate Medical Operation
Corporate Public Relations Operation
–Vice President-Regional/Customer Relations
Washington Corporate Office
Corporate Technology Staff
Charles E. Reed
Senior Vice President
Corporate Research and Development
Technical Resources Staff
Office of General Counsel and Secretary
Walter A. Schlotterbeck
Senior Vice President - General Counsel and Secretary
Corporate Legal Operation
Corporate Patent Operation
General Legal Operation
Legal Organization and Manpower Operation
Legal Services
International Sector
John F. Burlingame
Senior Vice President and Sector Executive
International Trading Services Operations
Export Sales and Services Division
International Construction Business Division
°General Electric Technical Services Company, Inc.
Latin American Operations
Latin American Business Development Division
°General Electric do Brasil S. A.*
°General Electric de Colombia, S. A.*
°General Electric de Mexico, S. A.*
°General Electric de Venezuela, S. A.*
Africa/Middle East Area Division
°South African General Electric Company (Pty.) Ltd. *
Europe Area Division
°COGENEL S. p. A. (Italy)*
°General Electrica Expanola S. A.*
Far East Area Division
°Australian General Electric (Appliances) Pty. Limited*
° °General Electric Philippines, Inc.*
Canadian General Electric Company Limited*
Technical Systems and Materials Sector
Edward E. Hood, Jr.
Senior Vice President and Sector Executive
Aerospace Business Group*
Aircraft Equipment Division
Electronic Systems Division
Re-entry & Environmental Systems Division
Space Division
Aircraft Engine Business Group*
Aircraft Engine Strategic Planning Operation
Aircraft Engine Engineering Division
Aircraft Engine Manufacturing Division
Airline Programs Division
Commercial Engine Programs Division
Military Engine Projects Division
Engineered Materials Group
Metallurgical Business Division*
Plastics Business Division*
Battery Business Department*
Laminated and Insulating Materials Business Department*
Silicone Products Business Department*
Information Services Business Division*
Medical Systems Business Division*
Mobile Communications Business Division*
Data Communication Products Business Department*
Utah International Inc.
Alexander M. Wilson
President and Chief Executive Officer

EXHIBIT 4
BIOGRAPHICAL DATA

Reginald Harold Jones: born Stoke-on-Trent, Staffordshire, England, 1917. B.S. in Economics, University of Pennsylvania, 1939. Joined the General Electric Company in 1939 as a business trainee and traveling auditor, 1939–1950; assistant to controller, Apparatus Department, 1950–1956; general manager, Air Conditioning Division, 1956–1958; general manager, Supply Company Division, 1958–1961; vice president, General Electric, 1961; general manager, Construction Industries Division, 1964–1967; group executive, 1967–1968; vice president finance, 1968–1970; senior vice president, 1970–1972; vice chairman, 1972; president, 1972-1973; chairman of the board and chief executive officer, 1973–1981.

John F. Welch, Jr.: born Massachusetts, 1935. B.S.Ch.E., University of Massachusetts, 1957; M.S.Ch.E., University of Illinois, 1958; Ph.D., 1960. Joined the General Electric Company in 1960 as a process development specialist for chemical development operations; process development group leader, 1962; manager–manufacturing polymer products and chemical development operations, 1963; general manager, Plastics Department, 1968; general manager, Chemical Division, then Chemical and Metallurgical Division, 1971; vice president and general manager, Chemical and Metallurgical Division, 1972; vice president and group executive, Components and Materials Group, 1973; senior vice president and executive, Consumer Products and Services Sector, 1977; vice chairman and executive officer, 1979; chairman of the board and chief executive officer, 1981.

John Francis Burlingame: born Massachusetts, 1922. B.S., Tufts University, 1942. Joined GE in 1946; vice president and general manager, Computer Systems Division, 1969–1971; vice president–employee relations, 1971–73; vice president and group executive, International, 1973–1977; senior vice president, International sector, 1977–1979; vice chairman, 1979–.

Edward Exum Hood, Jr.: born North Carolina, 1930. M.S., Nuclear Engineering, North Carolina State University, 1953. Joined GE in 1957 as a powerplant design engineer; vice president and general manager, Commercial Engine Division, 1968–1972; vice president and group executive, International, 1972–1973; vice president and group executive, Power Generation, 1973–1977; senior vice president and sector executive, Technical System and Materials, 1977–1979; vice chairman 1979–.

EXHIBIT 5 TEN-YEAR STATISTICAL SUMMARY, 1971–1980 (In Millions of Dollars Except per Share Amounts)

	1980	*1979*	*1978*	*1977*	*1976*	*1975*	*1974*	*1973*	*1972*	*1971 (2-for-1 stock split)*
Summary of operations										
Sales of products and services to customers	$24,959	$22,461	$19,654	$17,519	$15,697	$14,105	$13,918	$11,945	$10,474	$9,557
Operating margin	2,243	2,130	1,958	1,698	1,528	1,187	1,171	1,070	877	772
Earnings before income taxes and minority interest	$2,493	$2,391	$2,153	$1,889	$1,627	$1,174	$1,181	$1,130	$963	$847
Taxes	958	953	894	773	668	460	458	457	385	333
Net earnings	$1,514	$1,409	$1,230	$1,088	$931	$688	$705	$661	$573	$510
Earnings per common share	$6.65	$6.20	$5.39	$4.79	$4.12	$3.07	$3.16	$2.97	$2.57	$2.30
Dividends declared per common share	$2.95	$2.75	$2.50	$2.10	$1.70	$1.60	$1.60	$1.50	$1.40	$1.38
Earnings as a percentage of sales	6.1%	6.3%	6.3%	6.2%	5.9%	4.9%	5.1%	5.5%	5.5%	5.3%
Earned on average share owners' equity	19.5%	20.2%	19.6%	19.4%	18.9%	15.7%	17.8%	18.4%	17.5%	17.2%
Dividends	$670	$624	$570	$477	$333	$293	$291	$273	$255	$250
Market price range per share	63–44	55⅛–45	57⅝–43⅝	57¼–47⅜	59¼–46	52⅞–32⅜	65–30	75⅞–55	73–58¼	66½–46½
Price/earnings ratio range	9–7	9–7	11–8	12–10	14–11	17–10	19–9	24–17	25–20	26–18
Current assets	$9,883	$9,384	$8,755	$7,865	$6,685	$5,750	$5,334	$4,597	$4,057	$3,700
Current liabilities	7,592	6,872	6,175	5,417	4,605	4,163	4,032	3,588	2,921	2,894
Share owners' equity	8,200	7,362	6,587	5,943	5,253	4,617	4,172	3,774	3,420	3,106
Total capital invested	10,447	9,332	8,692	8,131	7,305	6,628	6,317	5,679	5,118	4,754
Earned on average total capital invested	17.3%	17.6%	16.3%	15.8%	15.1%	12.5%	13.4%	13.7%	12.7%	12.3%
Total assets	$18,511	$16,644	$15,036	$13,697	$12,050	$10,741	$10,220	$9,089	$8,051	$7,472
Property, plant, and equipment additions	$1,948	$1,262	$1,055	$823	$740	$588	$813	$735	$501	$711
Employees—average worldwide	402,000	405,000	401,000	384,000	380,000	380,000	409,000	392,000	373,000	366,000
Gross national product (current $ billions)	$2,626	$2,414	$2,128	$1,900	$1,702	$1,529	$1,413	$1,307	$1,171	$1,063
Common stock performance: General Electric common share price	$44–63									$47–67
Dow Jones Industrial Index	759–1000									798–950
Standard & Poor's Industrial Index	111–161									99–116

Source: General Electric annual report, 1980; U.S. Department of Commerce for GNP; Moody's.

EXHIBIT 6
FINANCIAL STATEMENTS, 1979 AND 1980
In Millions of Dollars

Balance Sheets

	1980	1979
Assets		
Cash	$1,601	$1,904
Marketable securities	600	672
Current receivables	4,339	3,647
Inventories	3,343	3,161
Current assets	9,883	9,384
Property, plant, and equipment	5,780	4,613
Investments	1,820	1,691
Other assets	1,028	956
Total assets	$18,511	$16,644
Liabilities and Equity		
Short-term borrowings	$1,093	$871
Accounts payable	1,671	1,477
Progress collections and price adjustments accrued	2,084	1,957
Dividends payable	170	159
Taxes accrued	628	655
Other costs and expenses accrued	1,947	1,753
Current liabilities	7,592	6,872
Long-term borrowings	1,000	947
Other liabilities	1,565	1,311
Total liabilities	$10,157	$9,130
Minority interest in equity of consolidated affiliates	154	152
Common stock	579	579
Amounts received for stock in excess of par value	659	656
Retained earnings	7,151	6,307
	$8,389	$7,542
Deduct common stock held in treasury	(189)	(190)
Total share owners' equity	8,200	7,362
Total liabilities and equity	$18,511	$16,644

Income Statements

	1980	1979
Sales		
Sales of products and services to customers	$24,959	$22,461
Operating costs		
Cost of goods sold	17,751	15,991
Selling, general, and administrative expense	4,258	3,716
Depreciation, depletion, and amortization	707	624
Operating costs	$22,716	$20,331
Operating margin	2,243	2,130
Other income	564	519
Interest and other financial charges	(314)	(258)
Earnings		
Earnings before income taxes and Minority interest	2,493	2,391
Provision for income taxes	(958)	(953)
Minority interest in earnings of consolidated affiliates	(21)	(29)
Net earnings applicable to common stock	$1,514	$1,409
Earnings per common share (in dollars)	$6.65	$6.20
Dividends declared per common share (in dollars)	$2.95	$2.75
Operating margin as a percentage of sales	9.0%	9.5%
Net earnings as a percentage of sales	6.1%	6.3%

General Electric, 1984

When Jack Welch took office in April 1981 as the new chairman and chief executive officer of General Electric, he described his vision for the company he was going to lead:

> A decade from now I would like General Electric to be perceived as a unique, high-spirited, entrepreneurial enterprise . . . a company known around the world for its unmatched level of excellence. I want General Electric to be the most profitable, highly diversified company on earth, with world-quality leadership in every one of its product lines.

By 1984 Welch had regrouped sectors, invested heavily in both new and core businesses, divested from other GE businesses, changed the company's approach to planning, and cut back staff. According to the 1984 annual report:

> Across your company, a strategy has been formulated, with clear focus on our key businesses and where they're going. The resources are in place to get them there. And most important, an atmosphere, a culture, is being created where concepts like agility, excellence, and entrepreneurship—the real stuff of world competitiveness—are coming to life.

The results were impressive. Profits rose from $1.5 billion in 1980, the year before Welch became CEO, to $2.3 billion in 1984. The increase in earnings, credited to improved operating margins, had occurred despite only slight increases in sales over the same period. Increased profits had also gone hand in hand with increased investment in future growth. Funds for research and development programs in 1984 reached a record $2.3 billion, over 8 percent of sales. (Exhibits 1-A, 1-B, and 1-C contain a financial summary.)

GE often made the news, and a favorite pastime of the business press was to evaluate Welch's actions and plans. One article concluded with Welch admitting that he was "only at the 15 percent mark of what he intends to do."[1] He did not elaborate on the specifics of the 85 percent that remained to be accomplished. Regardless of the future

Harvard Business School case 385–315. Revised May 1989.

[1] "General Electric—Going with the Winners," *Forbes*, March 26, 1984, p. 106.

direction he would take, virtually everyone agreed that GE had changed during Welch's first four years.

THE EARLY MONTHS

When Welch took office, he proclaimed that anything and everything was open to question. For example, what would the role of sectors be? How would strategic planning change? Would acquisitions play a greater or lesser role than in the past compared with internal development? Would the corporate staff play a greater or lesser role in transforming GE? Different answers to these questions would vie for attention and support, with Welch as the final arbiter.

He began by traveling throughout the $28 billion GE territory, meeting people, looking at operations, and asking questions. He returned to corporate headquarters in Fairfield, Connecticut, with a firmer idea of how he would proceed.

Several months later, in early August, Welch announced a restructuring of GE's organization, which had been in place since 1977. Two new sectors were created to implement the firm's commitment to grow its microelectronics and other technology-related businesses and to develop opportunities in its financial and information service businesses. The two sectors were called Technical Systems and Services and Materials. (See Exhibit 2 for the entire organizational structure.)

Technical Systems combined all of GE's business units that made intensive use of microelectronics, such as industrial electronics, advanced microelectronics, medical systems, mobile communications, and aerospace. As such, the sector contained nearly all activities that were critically involved in GE's Factory-of-the-Future strategy.

Services and Materials combined some of GE's fastest-growing businesses, including GE Credit Corp. (GECC), whose recent earnings had been growing 18 percent annually; GE Information Services Co. (GEISCO), whose sales had been increasing 24 percent annually over the past 10 years; and the Engineering Materials Group, which had been growing at 20 percent annually. Besides pursuing growth, the sector was to seek opportunities for integrating GE's credit and information services offerings and operations.

This change in the sector structure accompanied a new approach to planning. Strategic planning reviews under Welch significantly departed from earlier practice in two respects. First, top management dealt directly with the strategic business units (SBUs) and not with the sectors. Replacing the larger meetings held in the past, Welch involved only the SBU manager and the responsible vice chairman in the review. Second, he directed the review around key issues for each business and not around comprehensive strategic documentation or planning concepts. For example, one issue that repeatedly surfaced in these early reviews was what each SBU would be doing to benefit GE in 1990.

Welch disclosed some of the reasons for these changes in a classroom discussion at the Harvard Business School on April 27, 1981:[2]

> One of the things that's happened is with our planning system. It was dynamite when we first put it in. The thinking was fresh; the form was little—the format got no points—it was idea-oriented. Then we hired a head of planning, and he hired two

[2] "General Electric Co.: Jack Welch and Standley Hoch" 5-182-024. Transcript for videotape HBS no. 9-882-004.

vice presidents, and then he hired a planner, and then the books got thicker, and the printing got more sophisticated, and the covers got harder, and the drawings got better. The meetings kept getting larger with as many as 16 to 18 people involved. Nobody can say anything with that many people around.

So one of the things that we have put into place is a way to achieve more candor, more constructive conflict. So we've gone to what we're going to call CEO[3] meetings, where the three of us will have meetings with SBU managers, one on three, two on three, in a small room.

Welch did not believe, at the time, that one could describe an overall strategy for a company like GE. He said:

> Everyone likes to ask me what's the strategy for General Electric. Well, how can you have a strategy for a company that in the last five months has committed a billion and a half dollars in Montgomery, Alabama, for plastics plants; has made five acquisitions of software companies; has put $300 million into Erie, Pennsylvania, to expand a locomotive operation; has built a microelectronics center in North Carolina; and has opened a new copper-exploration venture in Chile with Getty. There is no neat bow one can put on this.
>
> But one can set an objective, one central theme to run through every bone of that company, every corner of it, every person in it, and that is—look at where you are in '82, where you'll be in '85, and probably, more importantly, where you'll be in '90. The issue facing every one of the people who manage our business is, can you be number one or number two in the game you're going to play, in the war you're going to wage, in the skirmish you're going to be in? Can you clearly go to war, go to the skirmish, with good equipment, good arms, good troops, with anything else you want to use as a metaphor? Can you play in that arena as a number one or number two player?[4]

For Welch, being number one or number two meant stressing quality and excellence. He made the following comments to GE managers early in his tenure:

> To me quality and excellence mean being better than the best. This achievement requires an introspective assessment of everything we are, do, say, or make, and an honest inquiry, "Are we better than the best?" If we aren't, we should ask ourselves, "What will it take?" then quantify the energy and resources required to get there. If the economics, the environment, or our abilities determine that we can't get there, we must take the same spirited action to disengage ourselves from that which we can't make better than the best.

BECOMING NUMBER ONE OR NUMBER TWO

During his first four years, Welch pursued his plan for being "better than the best" by building businesses through acquisition and internal development and by exiting businesses that could not meet the test of being number one or number two. Within this broad spectrum of efforts to reallocate GE's resources, Welch primarily concerned himself with building those areas designated for growth, specifically microelectronics and financial/information services. These businesses would most change GE's configuration.

---

[3] Corporate Executive Office: Chairman Welch, Vice Chairman J. Burlingame, and Vice Chairman E. Hood.

[4] Transcript no. 5-383-002, "General Electric: Jack Welch Transcript," comments to a class of Harvard Business School students, December 4, 1981.

Building Growth Businesses

Factory automation was targeted for development. Estimating the world market for automation at $30 billion by the early 1990s, GE announced in 1981 that it would spend $500 million to become a "world supermarket of automation."

James A. Baker, the sector executive of Technical Systems and the oft-quoted spokesperson for the company's move toward automation, referred to the concept as the Factory of the Future. Baker warned industry leaders that they would have to "automate, emigrate, or evaporate." He spoke of the need for automation and the part GE would play:

> Automation is the last best hope for American industry and must be pursued no matter what the cost. The choice is biting the bullet or biting the dust. . . . There are few options left. And what we're telling you is that we can do it better than anyone else.[5]

Calma and Intersil, acquired several months before Welch took office, filled in some of the gaps in GE's high-technology capabilities. Calma was the world's fourth-largest manufacturer of CAD (computer-aided design) systems and produced CAM (computer-aided manufacturing) systems as well. CAD/CAM systems, able to cut production time in half, would provide the operating mechanisms for the Factory of the Future. Calma, growing at a rate of 40 percent annually, was purchased for $100 million down and $70 million to be paid later from earnings.

Intersil, one of the world's major manufacturers of integrated circuits, cost $235 million. The acquisition was GE's second entry into the integrated circuit industry. Twenty years earlier, GE had been one of the first manufacturers of integrated circuits but had exited the business after selling its mainframe computer business in 1970. Intersil provided state-of-the-art semiconductor technologies for GE and non-GE products and systems.

The highly touted success of Japanese manufacturing seemed to assure major growth for factory automation in the Western world. Notwithstanding this favorable outlook, GE continued to look for a breakthrough in the field. Its 1983 annual report stated that the large development expenses (associated with its drive for world leadership in automation), coupled with flat sales in industrial electronics (because of the slow economic recovery), had caused losses of nearly $40 million during the year. In 1984 a similar loss was reported on "modestly improved revenues."

Another area that GE had targeted for high-technology growth was medical systems. GE was the number one manufacturer of diagnostic imaging equipment worldwide. In the early 1970s, GE turned its lackluster X-ray business around by putting an advanced CAT (computer-assisted tomography) scanner on the market, which soon had worldwide market share approaching 70 percent. In the early 1980s, GE developed a Nuclear Magnetic Resonance (NMR or MR) imaging device that used a powerful magnet to produce cross-sectional photos of the body's tissue, painlessly, without X rays or surgery. An MR machine pinpointed areas missed by a CAT scan, since it could "see" through solid mass.

An indication of GE's competitive strength in the field was given in the following account about Johnson & Johnson's Technicare Corp. "In MR scanners, for instance, GE's Welch makes no bones about his willingness to spend whatever it takes to be the leader. Technicare president, Joseph G. Teague, however,

[5] *Stock Market Magazine,* April/May 1982.

says: 'We don't have it as a realistic strategy to be number one,' in the United States in several years. Matching GE's expenditures dollar for dollar, he adds, could be "frivolous and very expensive.'"[6]

Besides the MR scanner, the Medical Systems Division was developing a lower-cost, simpler version of its CAT scanner. Total funds invested in both projects topped $100 million.

GE carried the supermarket concept over to its information services, with the goal of becoming a "supermarket of software services." GEISCO (GE Information Services Co.) launched a program to acquire computer software companies to strengthen its business portfolio in five target areas: banking, manufacturing, financial services, management reporting, and energy. Total funds for acquisitions and investments in key service businesses amounted to $650 million in 1983.

Building Core Businesses

Despite all the investments in the more glamorous growth businesses, GE did not ignore its older, core businesses where special opportunities could be found. In practice, many of these opportunities were connected to GE's high-technology thrust into the Factory of the Future. As one sector executive noted, "We never appreciated just how profitable a 2 percent growth business could be when automated."

In a speech in 1982 to the Association of Iron and Steel Engineeers on the topic of revamping basic industry, James Baker advised his audience, "Go back to your mills. Look at the operation as if you were preparing to serve a growth market and ask yourself if its yield . . . and particularly its quality . . . is what it should be."

GE itself took Baker's advice, automating many of its older plants to keep them number one or number two. A $300 million project to automate the firm's 70-year-old locomotive facilities in Erie, Pennsylvania, was the largest such investment in GE's history.

Between 1980 and 1983, the company spent close to $500 million modernizing its major appliance group. A $38.6 million investment set up a CIM (computer-integrated manufacturing) system in the dishwasher plant, automating production from order to delivery. The showcase factory was to be a model for other appliance operations, such as the refrigerator plant, which was scheduled to be gutted and refitted for robot assembly at a cost of $100 million. Another $135 million was slated to expand and automate the production of a new rotary compressor for use in GE refrigerators and small air conditioners. Similar investments were planned for the next four years amounting to $800 million.

The locomotive and dishwasher units were named by *Fortune* as being among America's 10 best-managed, most efficient factories. The article reported on the automation of the locomotive plant, "The payoff has already been impressive: automation has saved the huge Erie works from extinction and propelled GE into the front ranks of the world's locomotive manufacturers."[7]

In some instances, business development was more than investments in plant and equipment, it was a shift in the manufacturing base. For example, the decision to consolidate GE's lamp operations and invest $250 million to modernize

[6] "Changing a Corporate Culture," *Business Week*, May 14, 1984, p. 132.

[7] "America's Best-Managed Factories," *Fortune*, May 28, 1984, pp. 20–21.

production closed 10 plants in five states and reduced the work force by 1,400 employees.

Exiting Businesses

While GE was building businesses, it was also examining those businesses that could not meet the challenge of being number one or number two. If the analysis showed top management that additional investments could not promote a good return and competitive success, the decision was made to divest. As a result, GE sold off 118 businesses from 1981 through 1983, for more than $3.5 billion.

One of the most newsworthy divestitures was the sale of Utah International, an Australian coal property that had been a sector by itself, for $2.4 billion. The sale was announced in October 1983 and was finalized in April 1984. *Forbes* commented on the sale, "Utah International was a highly profitable property producing coking coal, but GE saw no future in it. Vice Chairman John Burlingame, one of Welch's former rivals for the top job, handled the negotiations with the Australians and says, "There are better places that we would rather put our money and effort. The more so since Utah's main market, coking coal for steel, is depressed and in surplus capacity." GE kept just one part of Utah, Ladd Petroleum, as insurance for GE's plastics needs."[8]

The press also took note at the end of 1983 when GE sold its housewares division to Black & Decker for $300 million in cash and notes. The division, which produced small appliances, such as irons and toaster ovens, had been part of GE since the early 1900s. GE explained that the divestiture allowed the consumer sector to concentrate its resources in the major appliance line. Even though GE had the dominant market share in small appliances, its profits were still below company averages.

In 1982 GE also began exiting from one of its more recent business entries, nuclear plant construction. The company accepted no new plant orders, agreeing to fulfill a backlog of orders stretching into the 1990s. Because of earlier commitments, it would remain in the nuclear fuel business and the nuclear plant servicing business after the backlog was fulfilled.

Other divestitures included the sale of all but one of GE's broadcasting outfits, spurred by the success of competitors. Vulnerability to housing cycles was the factor in the sale of the residential central air-conditioning business to the Trane Company for $150 million in cash and 15 percent of Trane stock. However, GE decided to remain in the small air conditioner business (units for windows and walls) because of its strong competitive position.

THE THREE-CIRCLE CONCEPT

As GE built and exited businesses, Welch grappled with the problem of finding a concise way to talk about GE to managers and outsiders. He wanted a concept that would have strategic meaning for GE as well as providing a simple description of what the company *was* as well as what it *was not.*

As Welch and corporate management looked at potential acquisitions and divestitures in 1983, a notion of major business configuration began to emerge. The result was a conceptualization of the company competing in three areas.

In the three-circle concept, as it came to be called, all businesses were divided into (1) core, (2) high-technology, or (3)

---

[8] "General Electric—Going with the Winners," *Forbes,* March 26, 1984, p. 98.

FIGURE 1
THE THREE-CIRCLE CONCEPT

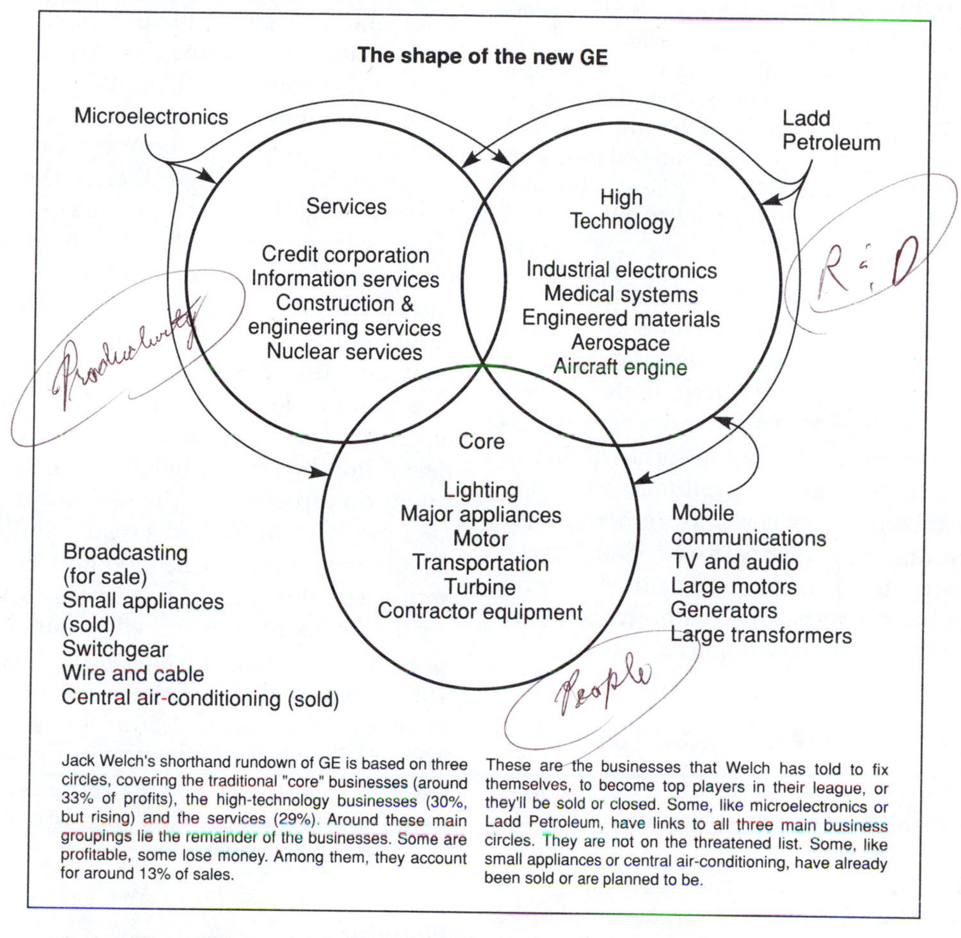

Source: "General Electric—Going with the Winners," *Forbes*, March 26, 1984, p. 106. Reprinted by permission of *Forbes* magazine, © 1984, Forbes, Inc.

service areas. *Only* businesses that dominated their markets would be placed in one circle or another. Fifteen businesses qualified (see Figure 1). Those outside these circles—the businesses that did not meet the criteria of being number one or number two—either had to come up with a strategy to get in a circle or be divested.

Investment planning became aligned with the three-circle concept. Welch announced the strategies in the 1983 annual report. The six core businesses focused on "reinvestment in productivity and quality," while the five high-tech businesses made certain that they stayed "on the leading edge through a combination of synergistic acquisitions and substantial investments in R&D." In the key service businesses, the strategy was to "grow these opportunities by adding outstanding people, who often can create new ventures all by themselves, and by making contiguous acquisitions."

Welch said of the three-circle concept:

> We have our hands on a simple, understandable strategy for where we are, where we are not, where we can't find a solution, and where we have to disengage. We have to get used to the idea that disengaging does not mean bad people or bad management—it's a bad situation, and we can't tie up good resources, good dollars, chasing it.

In GE's thinking, the three circles were interrelated. The core businesses needed advanced process technology and strong service offerings to improve their competitiveness. High-tech companies served customers who were looking for solutions to problems as well as products, so that a linkage with services was important for maintaining a competitive edge in the industry. In turn, service businesses could not remain competitive without the benefits of the latest technology.

THE CHANGING GE ORGANIZATION

Besides the evolution of GE's strategy, structural and administrative changes occurred under Welch's chairmanship. Destaffing received considerable press coverage. Other important areas of change were planning, organization structure, and incentives.

Destaffing

When Jack Welch took office, the U.S. economy was in its deepest decline since the Great Depression. Besides the external pressure, Welch came to the chairman's office with the sense that GE's bureaucracy and the levels of organization and staff had grown too large. As a result, he emphasized what became known as destaffing. From 1980 to 1984, the total work force was reduced from 402,000 to 330,000. Of this total, about 37 percent could be attributed to cutbacks in businesses experiencing lower sales volume. The remaining reductions represented a conscious effort to reduce staff and levels of organization.

These efforts earned Welch the nickname of "Neutron Jack" in the press, an allusion to the neutron bomb, which wiped out people while leaving the buildings intact. Although Welch believed the label to be exaggerated, he was convinced that a company the size of GE needed to stay "lean and agile" to be competitive. Welch acknowledged that becoming lean required destaffing, but he stated that GE had no intention of becoming "mean" in the process. He felt that GE had a responsibility to people who were not needed and that any action should "pass the fairness test that we'd like to be treated with ourselves." *Crain's Cleveland Business* of July 11, 1983, conceded that GE had used a "humane ax" in laying off 1,500 Ohio workers. The article pointed to the firm's offers of job counseling and placement alternatives and its efforts to explain "the inescapable necessity of it all."

Planning

As already noted, two changes Welch made in the planning process were to reinstate direct SBU reviews and to focus the reviews around key issues. Welch also advocated less reliance on staff. The planning staff of 200 in 1980 had been cut in half by 1984. The purpose was to have "general managers talking to general managers about strategy, rather than planners talking to planners."

Welch therefore dropped the requirement that every business have a strategy approved each year. A stable business with an approved strategy in place would only have to be reviewed every two to three years. A business in a dynamic environment with changing strategies would be under continuous review.

Mike Carpenter, GE's recently hired vice president of corporate planning, having spent the previous decade as a vice president of the Boston Consulting Group, explained these changes:

> I've tried to separate strategy and planning. Strategy is thinking through the basics of a business; planning is developing programs to support those strategies. I've been trying to put more emphasis on strategies and less on formal planning. Most of my staff is spending its time looking for acquisitions. When we do get involved in SBU strategies, it's as a member of the team working to develop viable, competitive strategies for the business. We spend little staff time consolidating or comparing plan books.
>
> Many of the changes in planning were begun before I joined the company. The objectives of the changes are to debureaucratize the process, focus the process on strategy, make it an ongoing process which is responsive to the time-frame needs of the business, make it the general manager's process, not the planner's process, and make it selective. This has implied some significant changes for the role of my organization. The most important being that we are no longer the corporate policeman, and our relationship with the SBUs is cooperative, not adversarial.

Organization Structure

When Welch became chairman in 1981, GE was administered by six sector organizations reporting to the Corporate Executive Office. By 1984 the sectors had been reduced to four and several major businesses reported directly to the CEO. As shown in Exhibit 2B, medical systems, financial services, and plastics were among the businesses reporting to the CEO. A senior executive commented, "No one is quite sure what the role of the sectors will be in the future. My hunch is that they will slowly disappear and eventually the 15 major businesses that fall within the three circles will all report directly to the Corporate Executive Office."

In mid-1984, John Burlingame, one of the vice chairmen, announced his planned retirement at the end of the year. Larry Bossidy, formerly sector executive for Services and Materials and the individual most often associated with the growth and success of the General Electric Credit Corporation, was promoted to vice chairman and a member of the CEO.

Welch considered choosing good people to be his most important job. Accordingly, he extended and increased his role in both the selection and review of key managers.

Incentives

Welch sought to institute new incentives to recognize employees for their individual contributions. For example, Corporate Executive Office (CEO) Awards were given to individuals who made special one-time contributions to a business venture, project, disposition, acquisition, and so forth.

Special Stock Option Awards were developed to help build long-term identification with the company for new people, to retain key individuals in an acquired company, to reward a long-term contribution made by individuals not eligible for regular stock-option grants, and to induce individuals to either take or stay in an unusually difficult or high-risk position.

Other incentives included restricted stock and special bonuses for meeting sales and income objectives in key positions in critical new businesses.

WELCH'S PHILOSOPHY

As the strategic moves and changes to organization and management processes occurred during the four years of his chairmanship, Welch was forming a management philosophy. Over time, Welch had coalesced his thinking around 10 key company values, which he described at a corporate officers meeting in the fall of 1983. Being number one or number two headed the list, followed by becoming and staying lean and agile. The remaining eight fell into three categories: how to get to the top, how to behave as a company to stay there, and how to fund the process.

Getting to the Top: Ownership, Stewardship, and Entrepreneurship

Welch believed that one of the keys to GE's success was a sense of pride in the company, such as that exhibited at several plants where employees wore T-shirts reading "GE is ME." He called this ownership. He tried to encourage ownership behavior by giving greater powers of delegation, by raising capital appropriations levels, and by holding fewer and faster reviews. His aim was to drive the ability to act further down in the organization.

> If we can think of ownership as just saying more "Grab it! Run with it! Take responsibility. Make the decision. Give the management awards. Make the sales plans. Do the things you want to do to run your business faster every day," we've got something.

Stewardship, which had been a popular word at GE for 20 years, was the responsibility that accompanied ownership. It was not only an obligation toward GE's assets (i.e., people, buildings, balance sheets) but it was also working at capacity to further the company's competitive success. Welch said:

> Stewardship is an obligation. It's not some noblesse oblige attitude where people can work at 45 to 50 percent of capacity or believe they have lifetime employment. Stewardship is working at 100 to 150 percent. Stewardship in the end is what your jobs are all about. It's your challenge: to take the assets you have, drive them to newer and better heights through excellence, through taking charge, and make this enterprise better in 1990 than it is today.

Entrepreneurship was the kindling with which Welch wanted to start the fires of the other values leading to competitive success. To attain ownership and stewardship, he advocated that managers create and maintain an entrepreneurial environment and a sense of entrepreneurial responsibility. Because the risks and rewards were not the same for entrepreneurship in a $30 billion enterprise as they were in a small company, he conceded that the term might be a misnomer. The concept, nonetheless, was essential to allow new ideas to surface and to create new ventures for the company.

How to Behave: Excellence, Quality, Reality and Candor, and Communications

Having a company ethic dedicated to ownership, stewardship, and entrepreneurship could get GE to the first spot in a tough, competitive world, according to Welch, but other values would keep it there.

Excellence, like ownership, was a behavior at the individual level. Welch suggested the best way to measure excellence was the "mirror test":

> This is the one, whether you're putting on makeup or shaving, where only you know whether or not the excellence is there—is absolutely at the heart of your everyday activity. You can't be at this level at all times, but you've got to keep driving yourself. Are you setting the standards of excellence? Are you demanding the very best of yourself?

Quality was accomplished by the individual excellence of every GE employee. Product quality had always epitomized GE's policy, but Welch wanted to push that value beyond the product to instill a commitment to quality as a pervasive way of life, to have an all-embracing concept that included products, services, fulfillment of citizen responsibilities, and communication to the outside world.

Excellence and quality could not be realized if there was no atmosphere allowing reality and candor. The early move to have one or two SBU managers meet with the CEO was made to foster a willingness to share problems and develop trust in the corporate hierarchy. Welch believed that, at every level, each employee should have enough trust in his or her boss to seek a joint solution to a problem and should have enough self-confidence and belief in the company to approach that process with reality and candor. Trust was critical to the concepts of quality and excellence.

Besides the internal dialogue necessary for successful operations, Welch felt that communicating GE's strengths and values to the outside world was central to implementing GE's philosophy. Understanding, embracing, and being able to articulate to the financial and shareholder communities what GE was doing was essential to successfully remaining number one or number two. To understand and communicate GE's philosophy, Welch said, "You've got to embrace it, feel it, believe it. If you don't, you come back and recheck it and understand what we're doing. Without that group in Louisville or that group in Cleveland, everybody embracing what we're going to do, we haven't got a prayer."

Funding: The Investment Philosophy

The values that focused on getting to the top and staying there were necessary but insufficient without the financial support to bring them to fruition. The 10th value of Welch's management philosophy dealt with how to pay for competitive success.

Welch believed that all investments should be directed only to the markets that GE *could* dominate. Those markets that did not fit the long-term growth strategy would be abandoned. He set 15 percent as the overall annual growth rate, with the admonition that short-term investment decisions should not be made simply to meet the growth rate at the expense of long-term issues.

REACTIONS

In a company as large and diverse as GE, reactions to Welch's first four years as CEO were bound to be varied. The following sample of comments from GE managers gives some idea of the range of impressions and judgments to be found in the GE organization:

> There was a lot of resentment to the destaffing in my department and Welch was feared. But personally, I welcomed it. I knew we had deadwood, and I was happy that we were being forced to face up to it.
>
> All the words sound great—entrepreneurship, ownership, risk taking—but at my level [subsection manager] it's making budget that still counts.
>
> During the first two years, I didn't see much change. But then we got a new general manager who is right out of Welch's mold. Our business is now a different place—much more spirited, self-critical, and energetic.
>
> I don't see much change. My business has been in the fast-moving part of the company, and we've been managed this way for years. I think that some of the older parts of the company may be feeling some change, but for me it's been a continuation of the way things have always been and the way they should be.
>
> Welch has succeeded in keeping us from becoming complacent and is focusing our attention on worldwide competitors. That's an important accomplishment in a big company where we tend to become complacent and focus on our own organizations and promotions.
>
> Many of the changes [in planning] have been excellent. But we are relying almost totally on people. That's fine until some of those people make big mistakes. Then we may miss not having those systematic plans.
>
> The key issue for me is what happens if you take a risk and fail. Welch is trying hard to convince us that it's OK as at Halarc.[9] But I wonder. The people who get rewarded in a failure are those who recommend getting out, not those who recommended getting in.

ISSUES

Among the many issues faced by GE management since Welch had become CEO in 1981, two had garnered extensive publicity. One issue addressed the huge funds GE had accumulated for investment. The other issue involved Welch's desire to increase the level of risk taking and entrepreneurship within the company.

The $5 Billion War Chest

At the end of 1983 GE had $2.5 billion in cash and securities. With the sale of Utah International, that amount rose to over $5 billion, prompting questions about whether or not GE would join the current trend toward major acquisitions. Welch responded in the 1983 annual report: "The question has been raised: What will we do with the money? The short answer is: It's not going to burn a hole in our pocket."

In 1983 GE had used a database of 6,000 potential candidates to identify potential acquisition candidates. The business development staff conducted an in-depth analysis of more than 100 large candidates within this group, identifying only four as strategically and financially attractive.

---

[9] See the *Appendix* for a description of the Halarc venture.

Guidelines for analysis had been laid out by corporate planner Mike Carpenter. The most important criterion was that ownership by GE should increase shareholder value by causing the acquired company's growth rate or profitability (or both) to increase over what it otherwise would have been. He pointed out that the acquisition would have to create enough value to pay the acquisition premium, noting that premiums had increased to 50 percent from 20 percent in 1970. "Acquisitions take place in a marketplace like any other [business deal]," he said. "It's tough making good acquisitions when you have to pay a 50 percent premium."

To emphasize this point, Carpenter described how he and his staff had ruled out several large ($1 billion to $8 billion) high-technology candidates as overpriced. According to their analyses, the share-price premiums needed to complete these acquisitions placed in doubt GE's ability to earn an attractive return on its investment.

Although Carpenter stressed that the highest return would come from those acquisitions that built on the strategic strengths of GE's existing businesses, he advised against limiting thinking to a certain size of possible acquisitions or to those that would fit neatly into the current GE boundary lines. He said, "We can acquire businesses bigger than our existing ones. We can acquire businesses that cut across group or sector boundaries. We can acquire particular businesses from large companies. We can acquire companies where only specific pieces are of interest to us."

In the spring of 1984 GE Credit Corp. announced the purchase of Employers Reinsurance Corp. for $1.08 billion, expanding GE's financial services activities. Carpenter explained the thinking behind the acquisition and how the opportunity arose:

> We have analyzed many financial services businesses in the last year or so and reinsurance has consistently come near the top of the list in terms of growth, return on investment, and competitive defensibility. It's a business GE knows through its Puritan Insurance Company [a subsidiary of GECC], although we have been a small player in the past. In looking at the largest 250 financial services companies and screening them for business attractiveness and company performance (in terms of return on investment and growth), ERC was identified as a member of an elite group of top-performing financial services companies. ERC is the number two or three reinsurer in the United States and has grown more rapidly and earned higher returns—a 24 percent return on equity in reinsurance—than the leader, General Re. Nevertheless, we're buying the company at the same multiple (1.9 times book value) that General Re shares sell for in the stock market at what we believe is at, or close to, the bottom of the reinsurance cycle.
>
> Interestingly, the original idea for the ERC acquisition came from Puritan Insurance. At an early stage in the game, my organization got involved, tried to help them evaluate the acquisition, and framed the issues that needed to be addressed before raising it with the CEO. But I think it is important to note that one of our smaller, farther-flung entities was the prime mover in the largest acquisition GE has made in recent years.
>
> ERC became available when its parent, Getty Oil, was acquired by Texaco, which wanted to concentrate on historic businesses in the oil and gas industry. We negotiated with Texaco to buy ERC at a price we thought was fair.

Despite the ERC acquisition and numerous smaller acquisitions (GE had acquired over 50 businesses since 1981), how GE would spend its considerable cash reserves remained unclear.

Internal Growth

Closely related to the problem of investing GE's cash reserves was the issue of encouraging internal growth, new business development, and entrepreneurship within the company. Welch stressed these developments and attempted to foster them in several ways: encouraging investments in growth businesses; reinforcing the organizational values of entrepreneurship, ownership, and stewardship; and changing compensation practices.

Besides these efforts, Welch emphasized new business ventures within the corporation. Although these ventures were not funded at the corporate level, the ventures focused attention on between 60 to 80 new business development efforts and their managers. Indeed, Welch often commented on the importance of ventures in developing managers:

> The ventures are far less important than the product of the processes, which are the people. By having high visibility on these people—each having their own P&L statement, their own game, competing against the world—we get a chance to look at how they perform. They can blow it and they lose a little money, it doesn't matter. We get a feel for who they are and what they can manage. We get far more out of the people end of ventures than we do out of the earnings end.

GE intentionally publicized venture activities to encourage managers to propose their own ventures. For example, a recent issue of the *GE Monogram*, the company magazine, highlighted three particular ventures (see the *Appendix*). Nevertheless, Welch was probably correct in stating that GE got less out of the earnings end of ventures than the people end. For on the earnings side, ventures not only faced the problems inherent in any start-up business but also had the added problems of being part of a big company and dealing with existing organizational boundaries. For example, the company's cogeneration venture had dealings with five GE businesses and nine departments. Finally, even if a venture was successful, there remained the problem of size. As one executive noted, "We have a problem with ventures because of our need to think big. At GE unless you can create a $150 million business it's not going to affect things much. We can create lots of small businesses. The problem is in creating the $150 million departments, and even more important, creating the groups and sectors of the future."

Financial Systems

Although some of the problems in creating internal business development only pertained to ventures, many managers indicated that GE's financial systems had a more pervasive negative effect on entrepreneurship. As one manager noted, "More than ever before, we are being told to innovate and invest for the long haul. But our financial system tells us to make our quarterly and annual projections. At times, the profit pressure is intense."

Traditionally, GE's financial systems had centered around the annual budget for each operating unit. The preparation of these budgets, leading to a set of figures by December, began in July and involved extensive negotiation between the operating units, the intervening layers of management, and the corporate office. An operating unit's budgeted net income, the bottom line, had generally come to be regarded as a commitment that each general manager would meet "at all costs." Dennis Dammerman, GE's chief financial officer, described some of the problems that the company experienced with this approach to budgeting:

> The stress on making your numbers had some unfortunate consequences for us. First, because it was so important to meet your budgeted commitments, there was a lot of gaming going on on the part of the operating managers to get a low enough target. Then, once the budgets were set, some operating managers would resort to dysfunctional actions when necessary to meet their targets. For example, if a business experienced a downturn in demand, important development programs might be halted. This behavior obviously flies in the face of our efforts to make this a more entrepreneurial company.
>
> Jack Welch was also dissatisfied with a budgeting system which locked us into a set of figures prepared 18 months in advance of their use. This practice didn't enable us to respond to new opportunities that arose in the interim.

To address these problems, two changes were introduced into GE's budgeting process. First, the controller's office prepared a set of financial objectives for each operating unit. These targets were based on an analysis of economic forecasts and of ongoing programs and commitments at each of the operating units. Although the operating units were free to suggest revisions to the proposed target, the intent was to reduce the amount of game playing and bargaining over targets and to establish targets that more realistically reflected each unit's prospects.

Second, relabeling budgets as operating plans in 1984 contributed further to realistic target setting. Operating managers would now be free to propose a revision of the figures at any time that business conditions or the competitive situation changed significantly from the original assumptions. This change was intended to provide operating management with a more flexible structure under which he or she could respond to new opportunities or unexpected setbacks. Performance evaluation was made against the revised targets. The new approach also served to bring new developments to top management's attention.

Dammerman commented on these changes:

> The changes we have made in our financial system reflect Welch's desires to have GE responsive to changes in the environment and to new opportunities, and to have important resource allocation trade-offs surface to the top of the organization.
>
> Overall, I would rate the underlying concepts of our new approach to be quite good. Our execution to date, however, has left a lot to be desired. One undesirable result has been the inclination of our operating units to call in changes without adequate documentation. And, as you might expect, we are more likely to receive calls from businesses in trouble than from those experiencing better-than-planned-for results. When the troubled businesses submit new operating plans, they often call for lower revenues, unchanged expense levels, and lower net income. Under the old system

there was no question that people would respond to the lower sales forecast by cutting costs in order to meet net income. We seem to have lost some of the commitment to fixing problems that we used to have from our general managers.

Despite these problems, we are committed to making the concept of operating plans work, because we are convinced that it is consistent with developing a more responsive and entrepreneurial climate within the company.

EXHIBIT 1-A
FIVE-YEAR STATISTICAL SUMMARY, 1980–1984
In Millions of Dollars Except per Share Amounts

	1984	*1983*	*1982*	*1981*	*1980*
Sales of products and services to customers	$ 27,947	$ 26,797	$ 26,500	$ 27,240	$ 24,959
Operating margin	2,845	2,549	2,405	2,447	2,243
Operating margin as a percentage of sales	10.2%	9.5%	9.1%	9.0%	9.0%
Earnings before business restructurings, income taxes, and minority interest	$ 3,501	$ 3,063	$ 2,753	$ 2,660	$ 2,493
Net earnings	2,280	2,024	1,817	1,652	1,514
Net earnings as a percentage of sales	8.2%	7.6%	6.9%	6.1%	6.1%
Net earnings on average share owners' equity	19.1%	18.9%	18.8%	19.1%	19.5%
Net earnings per share	$ 5.03	$ 4.45	$ 4.00	$ 3.63	$ 3.33
Dividends declared per share	2.05	1.875	1.675	1.575	1.475
Total assets	24,730	23,288	21,615	20,942	18,511
Property, plant, and equipment additions	$ 2,488	$ 1,721	$ 1,608	$ 2,025	$ 1,948
Average employment					
Worldwide	330,000	340,000	367,000	404,000	402,000
United States	241,000	245,000	261,000	289,000	285,000
Gross national product (current $ billions)	$ 3,661	$ 3,305	$ 3,073	$ 2,938	$ 2,626
Common stock performance					
GE common share price	$59⅜–48¼	$58⅞–45⅜	$50–27½	$35–25⅝	$31½–22
Dow Jones Industrial Average	1287–1087	1287–1027	1070–777	1024–824	1000–759
Standard & Poor's Industrial Index	170–147	173–138	143–102	138–113	140–98

Source: General Electric annual report, 1984; U.S. Department of Commerce for GNP; Moody's.

EXHIBIT 1–B
INDUSTRY AND GEOGRAPHIC SEGMENT INFORMATION (In Millions of Dollars)

	Total Revenues					*Net Earnings*					*Assets*			*Plant, Property, and Equipment Additions*			*Depreciation, Depletion, and Amortization*		
	1984	*1983*	*1982*	*1981*	*1980*	*1984*	*1983*	*1982*	*1981*	*1980*	*1984*	*1983*	*1982*	*1984*	*1983*	*1982*	*1984*	*1983*	*1982*
Consumer products	$ 3,858	$ 3,741	$ 3,943	$ 4,202	$ 3,998	$ 228	$ 163	$ 146	$ 225	$ 241	$ 2,382	$ 2,297	$ 1,997	$ 283	$ 235	$ 180	$ 143	$ 120	$124
Major appliances	3,650	3,078	2,751	3,132	3,012	223	156	79	82	104	1,370	1,030	1,101	111	80	78	75	68	73
Industrial systems	4,274	4,228	4,705	5,364	4,907	73	84	148	212	218	2,670	2,569	2,478	264	228	251	151	158	139
Power systems	6,010	5,878	6,093	6,015	5,703	486	439	384	242	223	3,689	3,242	3,574	243	252	228	179	173	185
Aircraft engines	3,835	3,495	3,140	2,950	2,660	251	196	161	149	141	3,317	2,523	2,174	356	218	140	136	129	93
Materials	2,241	2,060	1,791	2,050	1,877	262	182	148	189	170	2,362	2,030	1,682	425	231	243	149	147	120
Technical products and services	4,803	3,825	3,546	3,005	2,424	232	210	218	144	99	2,778	2,052	1,698	340	216	198	166	124	106
Financial services*	448	397	286	239	193	336	285	203	145	126	2,312	1,929	1,634	—	—	—	—	—	—
Natural resources	609	1,579	1,575	1,722	1,374	117	301	218	284	224	946	2,558	2,565	347	162	237	67	122	114
Corporate items and eliminations	(792)	(598)	(638)	(825)	(625)	72	8	12	(20	(32)	2,904	3,058	2,712	119	99	53	34	43	30
Total	$28,936	$27,683	$27,192	$27,854	$25,523	$2,280	$2,024	$1,717	$1,652	$1,514	$24,730	$23,288	$21,615	$2,488	$1,721	$1,608	$1,100	$1,084	$984
Outside the United States	$ 7,703	$ 9,148	$ 9,412	$10,190	$ 9,597	$ 419	$ 668	$ 680	$ 574	$ 639									

*Note 4 of 1984 and 1982 annual reports explain GE's income from financial services and other sources as follows:

Other Income ($ millions)	*1984*	*1983*	*1982*	*1981*	*1980*
GECC	$329	$271	$205	$129	$115
Marketable securities and bank deposits	323	239	239	230	229
Royalty and technical assets	83	58	60	59	52
Customer financing	75	69	58	80	72
Other items	179	247	130	116	95
Total	$989	$884	$692	$614	$563

EXHIBIT 1–C
FINANCIAL CONDITION
In Millions of Dollars

	As of December 31	
	1984	1983
Assets		
Cash	$ 1,859	$ 1,828
Marketable securities	514	677
Current receivables	5,509	5,249
Inventories	3,670	3,158
Current assets	11,552	10,912
Property, plant, and equipment net	7,690	7,697
Investments	3,717	2,945
Other assets	1,771	1,734
Total assets	$24,730	$23,288
Liabilities and Equity		
Short-term borrowings	$ 1,047	$ 1,016
Accounts payable	1,931	1,993
Progress collections and price adjustments accrued	2,403	2,551
Dividends payable	250	228
Taxes accrued	673	685
Other costs and expenses accrued	2,303	2,215
Current liabilities	8,607	8,688
Long-term borrowings	753	915
Other liabilities	2,668	2,247
Total liabilities	12,028	11,850
Minority interest in equity of consolidated affiliates	129	168
Common stock	579	579
Other capital	640	657
Retained earnings	11,667	10,317
Less common stock held in treasury	(313)	(283)
Total share owners' equity	12,573	11,270
Total liabilities and equity	$24,730	$23,288

EXHIBIT 2A
GE'S ORGANIZATION CHART, SEPTEMBER 1981

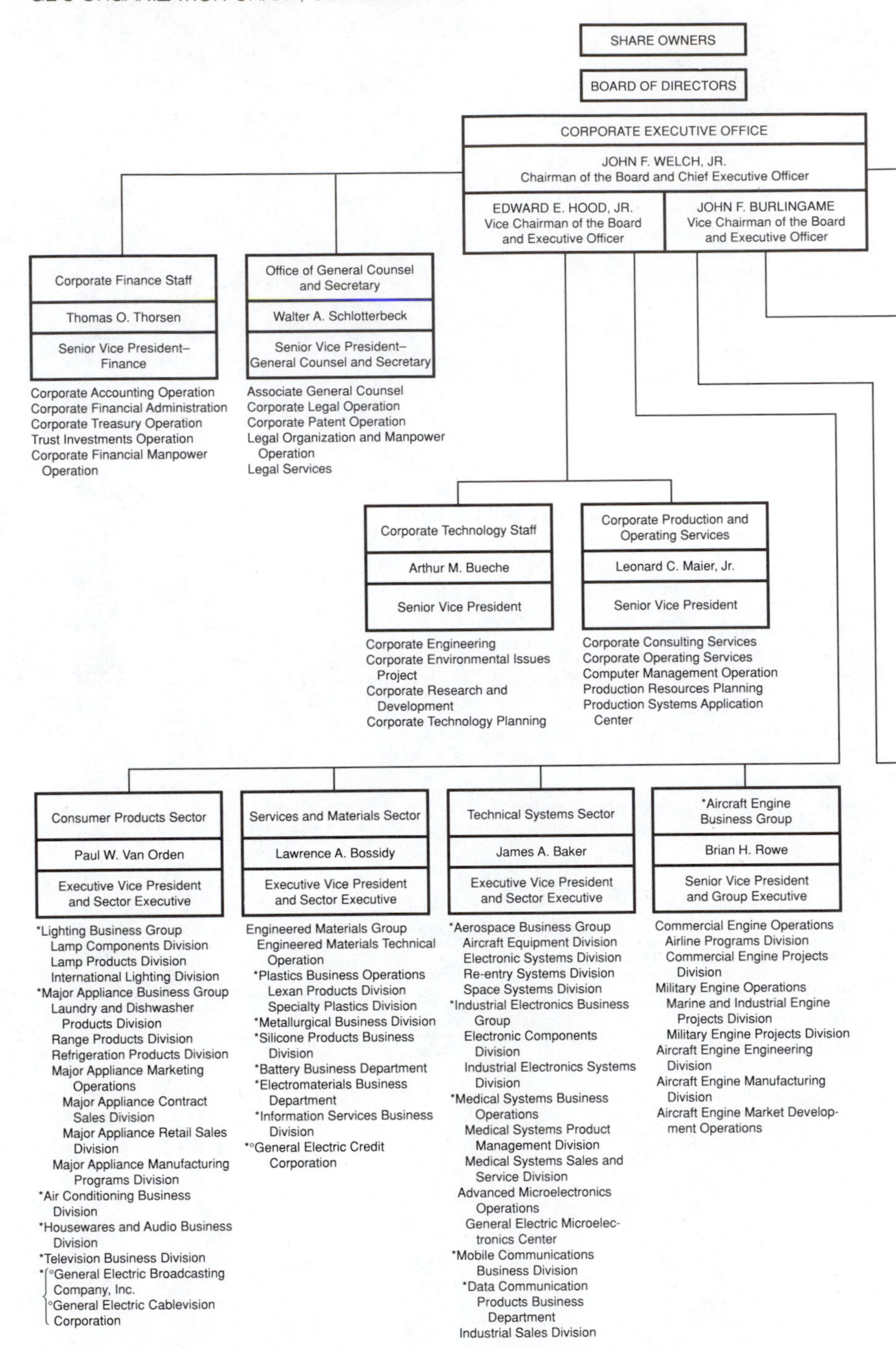

*Strategic Business Unit (Total = 38)
°Affiliate

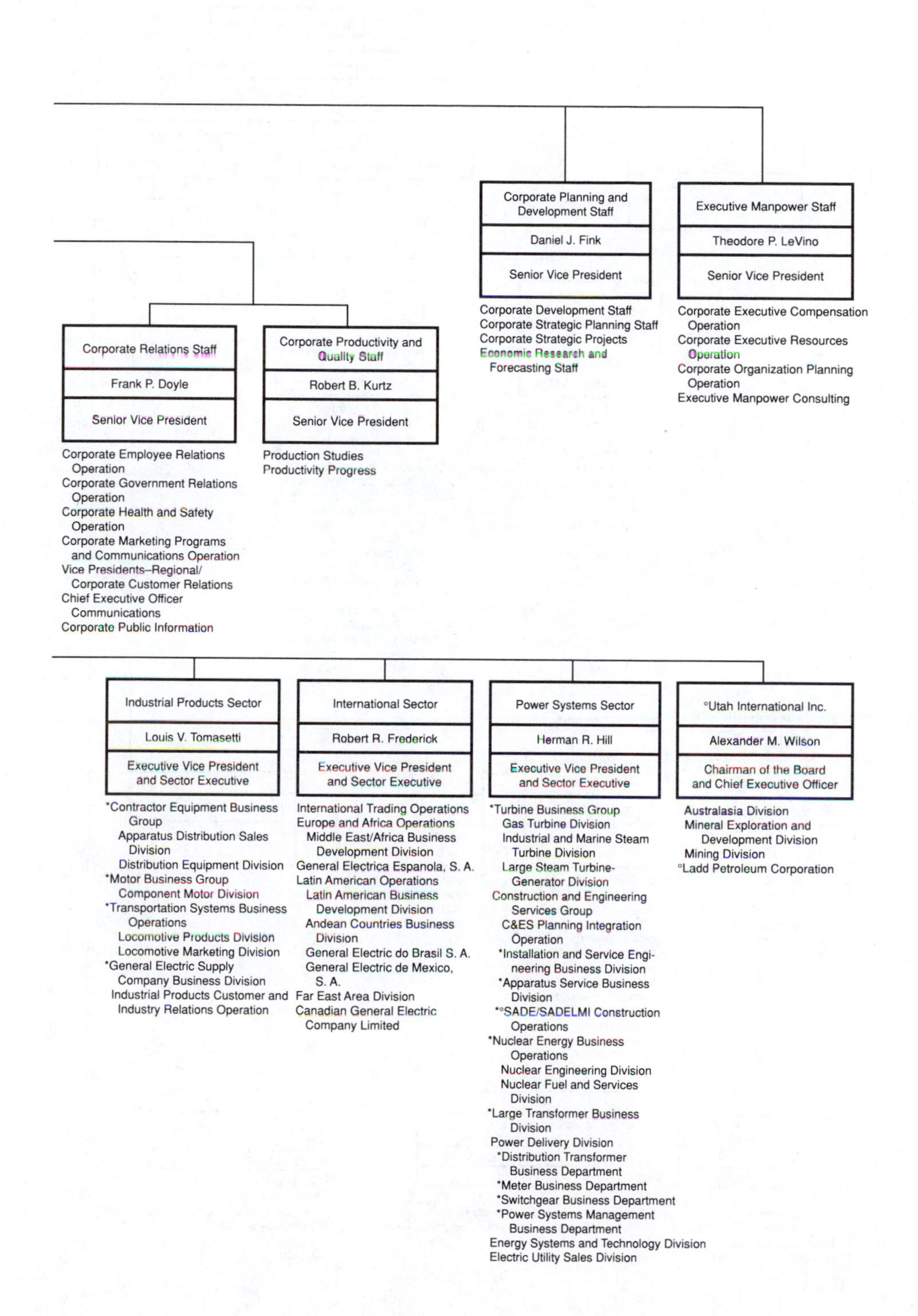
Corporate Planning and Development Staff
Daniel J. Fink
Senior Vice President
Corporate Development Staff
Corporate Strategic Planning Staff
Corporate Strategic Projects
Economic Research and Forecasting Staff
Executive Manpower Staff
Theodore P. LeVino
Senior Vice President
Corporate Executive Compensation Operation
Corporate Executive Resources Operation
Corporate Organization Planning Operation
Executive Manpower Consulting
Corporate Relations Staff
Frank P. Doyle
Senior Vice President
Corporate Employee Relations Operation
Corporate Government Relations Operation
Corporate Health and Safety Operation
Corporate Marketing Programs and Communications Operation
Vice Presidents–Regional/ Corporate Customer Relations
Chief Executive Officer Communications
Corporate Public Information
Corporate Productivity and Quality Staff
Robert B. Kurtz
Senior Vice President
Production Studies
Productivity Progress
Industrial Products Sector
Louis V. Tomasetti
Executive Vice President and Sector Executive
*Contractor Equipment Business Group
Apparatus Distribution Sales Division
Distribution Equipment Division
*Motor Business Group
Component Motor Division
*Transportation Systems Business Operations
Locomotive Products Division
Locomotive Marketing Division
*General Electric Supply Company Business Division
Industrial Products Customer and Industry Relations Operation
International Sector
Robert R. Frederick
Executive Vice President and Sector Executive
International Trading Operations
Europe and Africa Operations
Middle East/Africa Business Development Division
General Electrica Espanola, S. A.
Latin American Operations
Latin American Business Development Division
Andean Countries Business Division
General Electric do Brasil S. A.
General Electric de Mexico, S. A.
Far East Area Division
Canadian General Electric Company Limited
Power Systems Sector
Herman R. Hill
Executive Vice President and Sector Executive
*Turbine Business Group
Gas Turbine Division
Industrial and Marine Steam Turbine Division
Large Steam Turbine-Generator Division
Construction and Engineering Services Group
C&ES Planning Integration Operation
*Installation and Service Engineering Business Division
*Apparatus Service Business Division
*°SADE/SADELMI Construction Operations
*Nuclear Energy Business Operations
Nuclear Engineering Division
Nuclear Fuel and Services Division
*Large Transformer Business Division
Power Delivery Division
*Distribution Transformer Business Department
*Meter Business Department
*Switchgear Business Department
*Power Systems Management Business Department
Energy Systems and Technology Division
Electric Utility Sales Division
°Utah International Inc.
Alexander M. Wilson
Chairman of the Board and Chief Executive Officer
Australasia Division
Mineral Exploration and Development Division
Mining Division
°Ladd Petroleum Corporation

EXHIBIT 2B
GE'S ORGANIZATION CHART, 1984

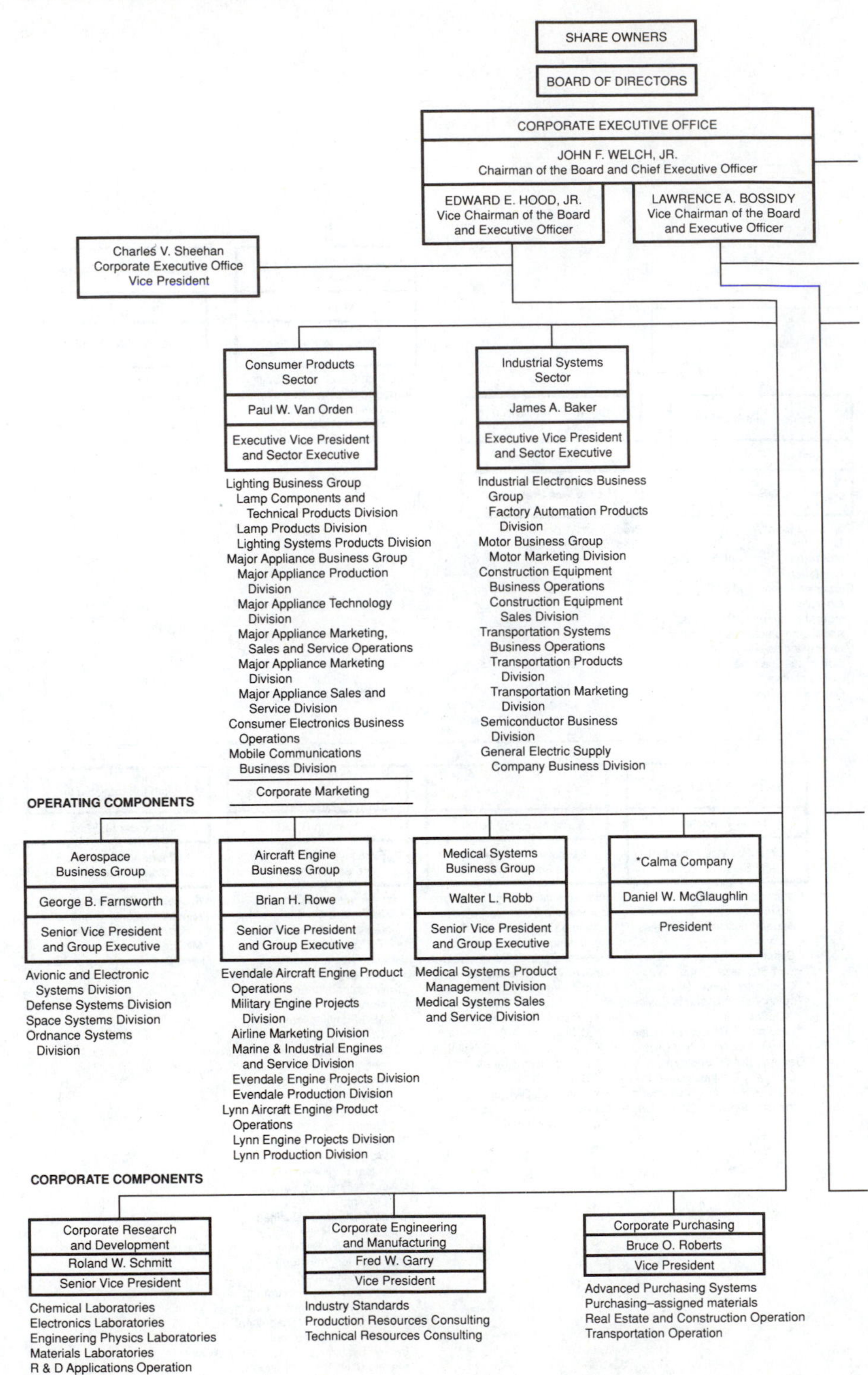

*Affiliate

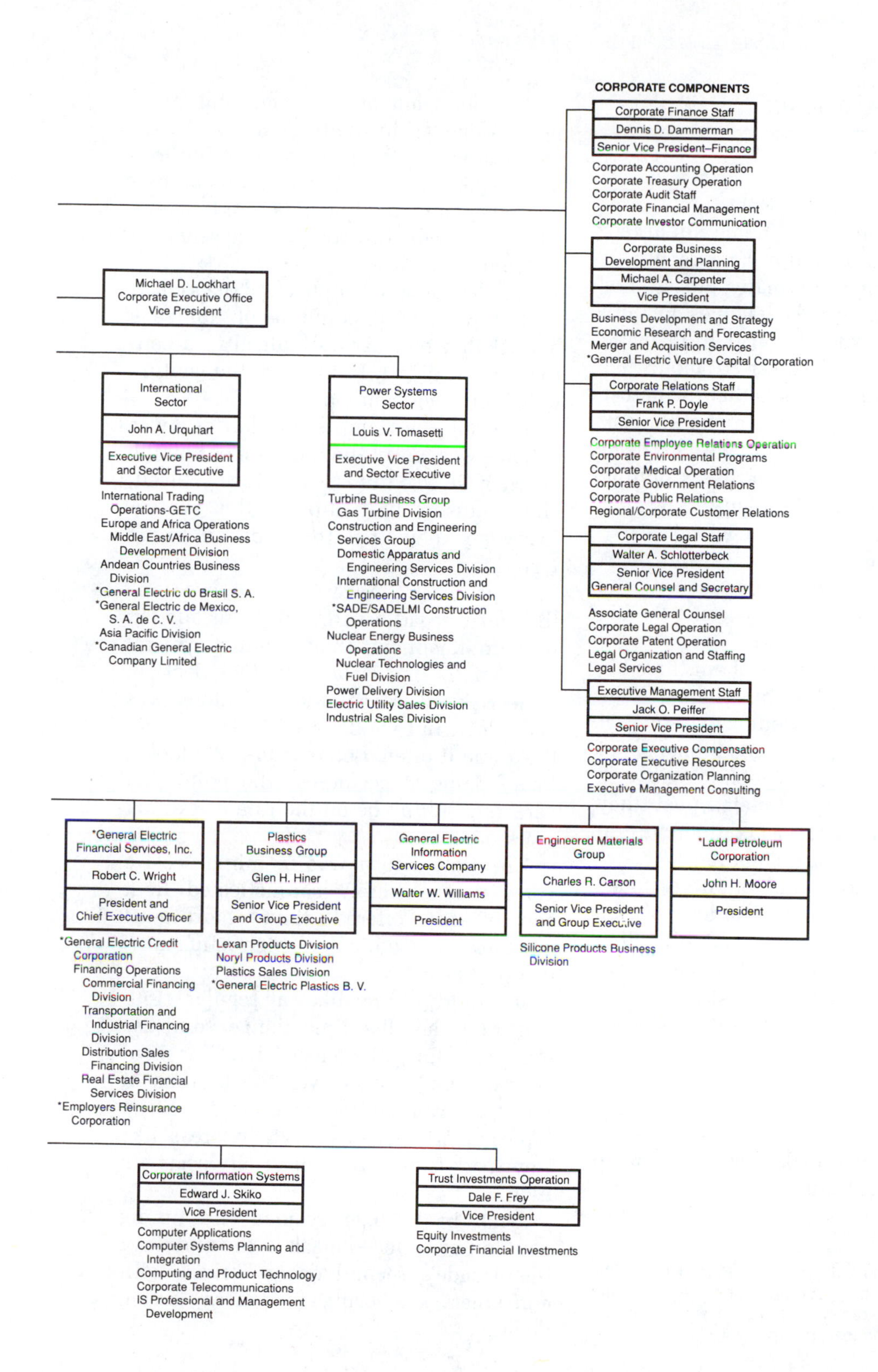
CORPORATE COMPONENTS
Corporate Finance Staff
Dennis D. Dammerman
Senior Vice President–Finance
Corporate Accounting Operation
Corporate Treasury Operation
Corporate Audit Staff
Corporate Financial Management
Corporate Investor Communication
Corporate Business Development and Planning
Michael A. Carpenter
Vice President
Business Development and Strategy
Economic Research and Forecasting
Merger and Acquisition Services
*General Electric Venture Capital Corporation
Corporate Relations Staff
Frank P. Doyle
Senior Vice President
Corporate Employee Relations Operation
Corporate Environmental Programs
Corporate Medical Operation
Corporate Government Relations
Corporate Public Relations
Regional/Corporate Customer Relations
Corporate Legal Staff
Walter A. Schlotterbeck
Senior Vice President
General Counsel and Secretary
Associate General Counsel
Corporate Legal Operation
Corporate Patent Operation
Legal Organization and Staffing
Legal Services
Executive Management Staff
Jack O. Peiffer
Senior Vice President
Corporate Executive Compensation
Corporate Executive Resources
Corporate Organization Planning
Executive Management Consulting
Michael D. Lockhart
Corporate Executive Office
Vice President
International Sector
John A. Urquhart
Executive Vice President and Sector Executive
International Trading Operations-GETC
Europe and Africa Operations
Middle East/Africa Business Development Division
Andean Countries Business Division
*General Electric do Brasil S. A.
*General Electric de Mexico, S. A. de C. V.
Asia Pacific Division
*Canadian General Electric Company Limited
Power Systems Sector
Louis V. Tomasetti
Executive Vice President and Sector Executive
Turbine Business Group
Gas Turbine Division
Construction and Engineering Services Group
Domestic Apparatus and Engineering Services Division
International Construction and Engineering Services Division
*SADE/SADELMI Construction Operations
Nuclear Energy Business Operations
Nuclear Technologies and Fuel Division
Power Delivery Division
Electric Utility Sales Division
Industrial Sales Division
*General Electric Financial Services, Inc.
Robert C. Wright
President and Chief Executive Officer
*General Electric Credit Corporation
Financing Operations
Commercial Financing Division
Transportation and Industrial Financing Division
Distribution Sales Financing Division
Real Estate Financial Services Division
*Employers Reinsurance Corporation
Plastics Business Group
Glen H. Hiner
Senior Vice President and Group Executive
Lexan Products Division
Noryl Products Division
Plastics Sales Division
*General Electric Plastics B. V.
General Electric Information Services Company
Walter W. Williams
President
Engineered Materials Group
Charles R. Carson
Senior Vice President and Group Executive
Silicone Products Business Division
*Ladd Petroleum Corporation
John H. Moore
President
Corporate Information Systems
Edward J. Skiko
Vice President
Computer Applications
Computer Systems Planning and Integration
Computing and Product Technology
Corporate Telecommunications
IS Professional and Management Development
Trust Investments Operation
Dale F. Frey
Vice President
Equity Investments
Corporate Financial Investments

APPENDIX

TAKING A SWING

Aaron. Ruth. Mays. Robinson. Killebrew. Mantle. The top six home run hitters in baseball history. Hall of Famers all.

But fame comes in many guises. For these baseball immortals, it comes not only in slugging records but also from being among the leaders in career strikeouts.

One reason, of course, is that the fiercer the swing a batter takes, the higher the risk of walking back to the dugout with his head down rather than circling the bases, doffing his cap, and collecting applause. The cautious hitters, the bunters, may not strike out as often, but their names and faces don't show up on bronze plaques with the same frequency as those who take the big swing.

What follows are stories about three big swings taken by GE entrepreneurs.[1] One missed. The others connected—and it looks like they have a good chance of clearing the fences. Their technologies and markets are totally unrelated, yet they share one thing: an almost countercultural view of the risk/reward equation.

If GE is to continue to put distance between itself and the bunters of the business world, it *must* take the big swing with increasing frequency. That may mean some strikeouts along the way. But the prospects of hitting a home run make the risks worthwhile.

Halarc

In 1979 General Electric decided to reinvent the light bulb.

A small team of engineers and planners assembled in the back shops of GE's Lamp Products Division to bring life to a bold decision—skip the traditional low-volume commercial market, and take a $10 light bulb directly to price-sensitive consumers.

The design was complex, the risks clear.

If it worked, it could revolutionize a market that had hardly budged in a century. But it didn't. In the end, the venture failed, but the team won.

The halide arc lamp—or Halarc as it was called—was one of the hottest ideas on the board of GE's ventures game since . . . well, since Edison first flipped the switch. Everyone knew that the odds on losing were high.

"This wasn't a case where everyone thought we had a sure thing," recalls Dr. Richard Kashnow, then product general manager for the Halarc Product Section. "The risk/reward equation all along was very clear. But we believed in Halarc and the value it offered consumers. We took a lot of pains to get across the point that careers wouldn't be on the line if it didn't work out."

The Halarc idea was to miniaturize a version of a highly sophisticated light source that offered three hard-to-get advantages: good color, high efficiency, compact size.

It could shine like a regular 150-watt bulb, last five times longer, and use only one-third the electricity. For consumers, the savings over the lifetime of the bulb were attractive—about $40 in typical markets, up to $75 in areas like New York City, where electricity costs are high.

Back in 1979 it seemed the timing couldn't be better—smack in the middle of the decade's second energy crisis, with consumers clamoring for energy-saving devices.

---

[1]Only one of the stories is reproduced here. The other two dealt with cogeneration and programmable controllers. Reproduced with permission from the *General Electric Monogram*, Spring 1984.

As in most ventures, the team struggled through months of design failures and breakthroughs. A miniature electronic power supply had to be designed so that the whole unit could be screwed into a regular incandescent socket.

The technology of the lamp design only permitted it to operate in base-down positions, such as in table lamps. A more versatile design, planned for the second phase of development, proved to be more difficult than anticipated. So the marketing plan was altered.

Finally, after two years of technical and market-niche modifications, Halarc went into a 10-month marketing test study in two cities—Des Moines, where it sold for roughly $10, and Salt Lake City, where it carried an eye-popping price tag of about $15.

Consumers balked. While they liked the product, they didn't like the price tag.

Part of the problem was that the onetime frantic interest in energy efficiency and long-term value had dimmed. By 1981, in the heat of recession, consumers had shifted away from energy savings and demanded bargains. It was lights out for Halarc.

But that's only half the story. Halarc is now a living legend for GE's risk takers. Because looking over the shoulder of the Halarc team was every other ventures group throughout the company, watching to see if General Electric was willing to make good on its promise to reward those who try as well as those who win.

"We wanted to make sure that all the people involved in Halarc—who had really done a good job and made a lot of progress—didn't get their careers disrupted because of the way it worked out in the marketplace," says Kashnow, now general manager of the Quartz and Chemical Products Department. "We took a lot of care not only to communicate that but to make sure that they had appropriate career opportunities when it was over."

The bargain held up. When the decision was made in the summer of 1983 to put Halarc on the back burner, the section held award parties, dinners, and ceremonies for the group.

Top management—from the CEO to the sector executive, group executive, and division manager—got the message through to those who devoted years of their careers to Halarc that their work was appreciated.

Additional attention was given to team members to make sure that appropriate job assignments were waiting for them. It was not hard. Since the team had attracted a lot of the best in the business, they were in demand.

"Only certain people are attracted to risk taking," Kashnow explains. "We've got to preserve the kind of culture that allows people to take those risks."

Far from collecting dust on museum shelves, Halarc opened new frontiers in state-of-the-art technology for the industrial market, where buyers are more accustomed to high initial costs and lifecycle paybacks. And, as the technology matures, Halarc may find its way back into the consumer market at a lower price.

For risk managers and players, Halarc offered another reminder—to recognize risk up front, manage it properly, and not get caught off guard when the project does not work out.

Even though the big swing never connected, it left its mark.

It got the message through to people about the company's concern for individuals, about a culture that encourages people to try again, and about the commitment of management to share the risks.

CONCLUSION

In Retrospect: Strategic Management and Corporate Governance

Many of the cases in this book have given you an opportunity to observe the range, unity, and interrelation of the concepts and subconcepts essential to the conscious formulation and implementation of a strategy governing the planned development of a total organization. The idea and its components have now been quite carefully and separately explored. It becomes appropriate at this point, as you reflect on the cases you have studied, to return to the view of corporate strategy not as a concept complete and still but as an organizational process forever in motion, never ending. The merger of the process and substantive content of the concept of strategy takes us to the principal problems of corporate governance and the responsibilities of the board of directors.

STRATEGY AS A PROCESS

For the purposes of analysis, as you have already noted, we have presented strategy formulation as being reasonably complete before implementation begins, as if it made sense to know where we are going before we start. Yet we know that we often move without knowing where we will end; the determination of purpose is in reality in dynamic interrelation with implementation. Implementation is itself a complex process including many subprocesses of thought and organization which introduce into prior resolution tentativeness and doubt and lead us to change direction.

That strategy formulation is itself a *process of organization,* rather than the masterly conception of a single mind, must finally become clear. We introduced you to it when we were considering organization design. Many facts of life conspire to complicate the simple notion that persons or organizations should decide what they can, want, and should do and then do it. The sheer difficulty of recognizing and reconciling uncertain environmental opportunity, unclear corporate capabilities and limited resources, submerged personal values, and emerging aspirations to social responsibility suggests that at least in complicated organizations strategy must be an organizational achievement and may often be unfinished. Important as leadership is, the range of strategic alternatives which must be considered in a decentralized or diversified company exceeds what one person can conceive of. As technology develops, chief executives cannot usually maintain their own technical knowledge at the level necessary for accurate personal critical discriminations. As a firm extends its activities internationally, the senior person in the company cannot learn in detail the cultural and geographical conditions which require local adaptation of both ends and means.

As in all administrative processes managing the process becomes a function distinct from performing it. The principal strategists of technically or otherwise complex organizations therefore manage a strategic decision-making process rather than make strategic decisions. When they "make" a decision approving proposals originating from appraisals of need and opportunity made by others, they are ratifying decisions emerging from lower echelons in which the earliest and most junior participants may have played importantly decisive roles.[1] The structure of the organization, as observed earlier, may predetermine the nature of subsequent changes in strategy. In this sense strategy formulation is an activity widely shared in the hierarchy of management, rather than being concentrated at its highest levels.

Participation in strategy formulation, as we have observed before, may begin with the market manager who sees a new product opportunity or the analyst who first arranges the assumptions that make possible a 30 percent return on investment in a new venture. (A return-on-investment hurdle may in itself contribute to a distortion of strategy by becoming an illusory goal rather than an achieved result.) Because of the response to reward and punishment systems considered earlier, the strategic alternatives generated in autonomous corporate units may be the product of competition for limited resources or of divisional empire building.

The strategy process, with its evolutionary, structural, analytical, and emotional components, encounters then the real-life challenges for which conscious professional management has been devised. Opportunism remains the principal counterforce; it need not be put down, for it can be turned to use. In the course of an established strategy, changing only

---

[1] See Joseph L. Bower, *Managing the Resource Allocation Process* (Boston: Division of Research, Harvard Business School, 1970).

imperceptibly in response to changing capabilities and changing market environments, sudden opportunity or major tactical decision may intrude to distract attention from distant goals to immediate gain. Thus the opportunity for a computer firm to merge with a large finance company may seem too good to pass up, but the strategy of the company will change with the acquisition or its ability to implement its strategy will be affected. A strategy may suddenly be rationalized to mean something very different from what was originally intended because of the opportunism which at the beginning of this book we declared the conceptual enemy of strategy. The necessity to accommodate unexpected opportunity in the course of continuous strategic decision is a crucial aspect of process. Accepting or refusing specific opportunity will strengthen or weaken the capability of an organization and thus alter what is probably the most crucial determinant of strategy in an organization with already developed market power.

MANAGING THE PROCESS

It is clear then that the strategic process should not be left untended.[2] Study of the cases and ideas of this book usually leads to acceptance of the need for a continuous process of strategic decision as the basis for management action. This process extends from the origin of a discrete decision to its successful completion and incorporation into subsequent decisions. With this need established in an organization the next step is to initiate the process and secure the participation first of those in senior management positions and then of those in intermediate and junior positions. The simplest way for the chief executive of a company to begin is to put corporate objectives on the agenda of appropriate meetings of functional staff, management, or directors.

Consider, for example, a large, long-established, diversified, and increasingly unprofitable company. Its principal division was fully integrated from ownership of sources of raw materials to delivery of manufactured products to the consumer. Its president, after a day's discussion of the concept of strategy, asked his seven vice presidents, who had worked together for years, to submit to him a one-page statement expressing each officer's concept of the company's business, a summary statement of its strategy. He had in mind to go on from there, as users of this book have done in handling these cases. After identifying the strategy deducible from the company's established operations and taking advantage of their participation in resource allocation decisions, the vice presidents would be asked to evaluate apparent current strategy and make suggestions for its change and improvement. This first effort to establish a conscious process of strategic decision came to a sudden halt when the president found that it took weeks

[2] See Richard G. Hamermesh, *Making Strategy Work* (New York: John Wiley & Sons, 1986).

to get the statements submitted and that, once collected, they read like descriptions of seven different companies.

When discussion of current strategy resumed, a number of key issues emerged from a study of a central question—why once so successful a company was seeing its margins shrink and its profits decline. The communication of similar issues to those assigned responsibility to deal with the function they affect was an obvious next step. The soundness of the company's recent diversification was assigned as a question to the division managers concerned. They found themselves asked to present a strategy for a scheduled achievement of adequate return or of orderly divestment. The alternative uses of the company's enormous resources of raw material were examined for the first time. The record of the research and development department, venerable in the industry for former achievements, was suddenly seen to be of little consequence in the competition that had grown up to take away market share. Decisions long since postponed or ignored began to seem urgent. Two divisions were discontinued, and expectations of improved performance began to alert the attention of division and functional managers throughout the organization to strategic issues.

Getting people who know the business to identify issues needing resolution, communicating these issues to all the managers affected, and programming action leading to resolution usually leads to the articulation of a strategy to which annual operating plans—otherwise merely numerical extrapolations of hope applied to past experience—can be successively related. It is not our purpose here, however, to present a master design for formal planning systems. This is a specialty of its own, which like all such other specialties, needs to be related to corporate strategy but not allowed to smother it.

When formal plans are prepared and submitted as the program to which performance is compared as a basis for evaluation, managers in intermediate position are necessarily involved in initiating projects within a concept of strategy rather than proceeding ad hoc from situation to situation. Senior managers can be guided in their approval of investment decisions by a pattern more rational than their hunches, their instinct for risk, and their faith in the track record of those making proposals, important as all these are. They have a key question to ask: What impact upon present and projected strategy will this decision make?

Sustaining the strategic process requires monitoring resource allocation with awareness of its strategic—as well as operational—consequences and its social and political, as well as financial, characteristics. Seeing to it that the process works right means that the roles of the middle-level general manager be known and appropriately supported.

Middle-level general managers occupy a role quite different from that of the senior general manager, relevant as is their experience as preparation for later advancement. With strategic language and summary corporate goals coming to them from their superiors and the language and problems of everyday operations coming to them from their subordinates, they have the responsibility of translating the operational proposals, improvisations, and piecemeal solutions of their subordinates into the strategic pattern suggested to them by their superiors.

Faced with the need to make reconciliation between short-term and long-term considerations, they must examine proposals and supervise operations with an eye to their effect on long-term development. As they transform general strategic directions into operating plans and programs, they are required to practice the overview of the general manager under the usual circumstance that their responsibility for balanced attention to short- and long-term needs and for bringing diverse everyday activities within the stream of evolving strategy far outruns their authority to require either change in strategy or to alter radically the product line of their division.

General managers at middle level, certainly in a crucial position to implement strategy in such a way as to advance it rather than depart from it, need to be protected against such distractions as performance evaluation systems overemphasizing short-term performance. They need to be supported continually in their duty of securing results which run beyond their authority to order certain outcomes. They need to learn how to interpret the signals they get as proposals they submit for top-management approval are accepted or turned down. Their superiors will be dependent upon their judgment as their proposals for new investment come in and will often be guided more by past performance or the desire to give them greater responsibility than by the detailed content of their proposals. Their seniors will do well then to realize the complexity of their juniors' positions and the necessity of the juniors being equal to the exigencies of making tactical reality subject to strategic guidance and to directing observation of operations toward appropriate amendment of strategy.

Developing the accuracy of strategic decision in a multiproduct, technically complex company requires ultimately direct attention to organization climate and individual development. The judgment required is to conduct operations against a demanding operating plan and to plan simultaneously for a changing future, to negotiate with superiors and subordinates the level of expected performance, and to see, in short, the strategic implications of what is happening in the company and in its environment. The capacity of the general manager, outlined early in this book, must be consciously cultivated as part of the process of managing strategy if the firm is to mature in its capacity to conduct its business and be able to recognize in time the changes in strategy it must effect.

Executive development, viewed from the perspective of the general manager, is essentially the nurturing of the generalist capabilities referred to throughout the text portions of this book. The management of the process of strategic decision must be concerned principally with continuous surveillance of the environment and development of the internal capabilities and distinctive competence of the company. The breadth of vision and the quality of judgment brought to the application of corporate capability to environmental opportunity are crucial. The senior managers who keep their organization involved continuously in appraising its performance against its goals, appraising its goals against the company's concept of its place in industry and in society, and debating openly and often the continued validity of its strategy will find corporate attention to strategic questions gradually proving effective in letting the organization know what it is, what its activities are about, where it is going, and why its existence and growth are worth the best contributions of its members.

The chief executive of a company has as his or her highest function the management of a continuous process of strategic decision in which a succession of corporate objectives of ever-increasing appropriateness provides the means of economic contribution, the necessary commensurate return, and the opportunity for the men and women of the organization to live and develop through productive and rewarding careers.

THE STRATEGIC FUNCTION OF THE BOARD OF DIRECTORS

If the highest function of the chief executive is the management of the future-oriented purposeful development of the enterprise, then it is necessarily the responsibility of the board of directors to see that this job is adequately done. Although in the common conception of corporate governance the board is ultimately responsible, its outside directors cannot themselves customarily originate the strategy they must approve. The chief recourse of directors ratifying strategy in highly complex situations is not to substitute their judgment for that of management but to see that the proposals presented to them have been properly prepared and can be defended as strategically consistent and superior to available alternatives. If they are flawed they are usually withdrawn for revision by management. Although the board is usually unable to originate strategy, its detachment from operations equips it to analyze developing strategic decisions with fresh objectivity and breadth of experience. It can be free of the management myopia sometimes produced by operations in places where keeping things going obscures the direction they are taking.

The cases comprising this book give you at least a partial opportunity to visualize the role and function of the board. Under pressure from the public, the Securities and Exchange Commission, and indirectly by the U.S. Senate's Subcommittee on Shareholders' Rights, the board of directors is undergoing revitalization as the only available source of legitimacy for corporate power and assurance of corporate responsibility, given the archaism of corporation law and the dispersed ownership of the large public corporation.

The consensus developing in the current revival of board effectiveness is that working boards will not only actively support, advise, and assist management but also will monitor and evaluate management's performance in the attainment of planned objectives. Boards nowadays are expected to exhibit in decision behavior their responsibility (while representing the economic interest of the shareholders) for the legality, integrity, and ethical quality of the corporation's activities and financial reporting and their sensitivity to the interests of segments of society legitimately concerned about corporate performance.

For our purposes here the central function of a working board is to review the management's formulation and implementation of strategy and to exercise final authority in ratifying with good reason management's adherence to established objectives and policy or in contributing constructively to management's recommendation for change.

It is now widely recognized that boards should be diversely composed, should consist largely of outside directors, and should structure themselves to make their monitoring functions practicable. All firms registered on the New York Stock Exchange, for example, must have audit committees as a condition of membership. Their functions are to recommend to the board and then to shareholders the choice of external auditors, to ensure to the extent possible that the company's control personnel are generating and reporting accurate and complete data fairly representing the financial performance of the company, and to ascertain that internal auditors are examining in detail those situations in which the company is vulnerable to fraud or improper behavior.

Despite the assumptions of some regulatory agency personnel, it is of course not possible for outside directors to detect fraud or identify questionable payments with their own eyes when well-intentioned and competent management auditors have not been able to do so. Their contribution is to inquire into the quality of intention, competence, and process, to observe the capability and command of information of those reporting to the committee, and to raise questions prompted by experience not available in the company. When necessary they recommend to the board replacement of controllers or change of auditors.

Executive compensation committees are expected to oversee the incentive salary programs of the companies and to set the compensation of the most senior managers, evaluating their performance in the course of that activity. A trend is developing toward the establishment of nominating committees to consider executive succession, board composition and performance and to make recommendations to the board of new members. The flow of information to these committees is supposed to economize the time and inform the judgment of the independent directors and to enable them to appraise the caliber of the company's management. The possibility of overwhelming outsiders with information is always imminent. Information useable by the board cannot usually be siphoned off the management information systems. Organization and selection to serve the special functions of the board are required.

In view of the difficulty entailed in enabling independent directors to pass judgment on strategic decisions, it is interesting to note that among the development of other committees (like public responsibility and legal affairs) strategy committees of the board are coming into wider use. It appears likely that as boards become aware of the need to relate approval of specific investment decisions to the purposes of the company, they may wish to focus the attention of some of the directors upon strategic questions now presented without prior detailed consideration to the full board.

Like members of the audit and compensation committees, board members assigned to give additional time to the evaluation of total strategy become famililar not necessarily with the detailed debates shaping specific strategic alternatives but with how the strategic process is managed in the company. You may wish to consider the extent to which familiarity with the strategy of the company and the ability to relate financial performance to it would affect the evaluation by the board of the chief executive officer's performance and to what extent it is available otherwise.

In most boards, at the moment, it is assumed that the independent directors will support the chief executive until it is necessary to remove him. Removal ordinarily comes late after disaster has struck or after early strategic mistakes have produced repeated irretrievable losses. The go/no-go dilemma, which does not apply in any other superior-subordinate relationship in the corporation, could be replaced by discussion and debate at board level of strategic questions presented to the board by the chief executive officer. When interim remediable dissatisfaction with the quality of this discussion appeared, advice to the chief executive officer could be offered in time for it to do some good. Chief executives' longevity is extended in some situations by their securing the participation of the board in crucial strategic decisions. When one of these fails after such participation, responsibility is shared by the board and the chief executive rather than borne by the latter alone. Routine ratification, without real discussion, does not secure the commitment of directors to any major decision. The attainment of proper participation is sometimes complicated by insecurity, unwillingness to share power, and lack of skill in board management on the part of chief executive officers.

The problem of securing competent outside director preparation and participation is compounded by the relationship resulting from the simple fact that independent directors have ordinarily owed their board membership to the chairman or chief executive officer they are supposed to evaluate. The active participation of nominating committees has increased the independence of boards, especially when the chief executive officers participating in the selection process have wanted such a result.

The management of effective boards of directors is a proper research topic in Business Policy and is indeed being studied. The power of strategy as a simplifying concept enabling independent directors to *know* the business (in a sense) without being *in* the business will one day be more widely tested at board level. If strategic management can be made less intuitive and more explicit, it will be possible for management directors and chief executive officers to identify existing strategy, evaluate it against the criteria we suggested at the beginning of this book, consider alternatives for improvement in the presence of the board, and make recommendations to a board equipped to make an intelligent critical response in strategic terms—that is, relating specific proposals to corporate strategy. It is the hope of the authors of this book that your practice in identification, evaluation, and recommendation of strategy in analysis of these cases has introduced you to the possibilities of effectiveness in your own future participation in strategic management at whatever level. The ability to sense the pattern of process in the welter of operations is essential not only as an economizing analytical concept for outside directors but to junior executives who do not want to get lost among the trees and thickets through which they move.

Strategic management comes to its culmination in the chairmanship of effective boards. For the moment, the Securities and Exchange Commission, the Department of Justice, and the Federal Trade Commission appear to prefer the restructured and revitalized board of directors as the route to a kind of corporate governance sufficiently responsible to meet current concerns about autonomous management power. Most defenders of our mixed economic system prefer this approach to the introduction of new regulation. Voluntary adaptation to public expectations allows the special circumstances of each industry and company situation to be taken into account; regulation does not. On the other hand doing nothing remains a possible though unsatisfactory response to the call for voluntary action.

The mastery of the concept of strategy makes easier the kind of discussion in board rooms that helps managements make better decisions. It performs this function by reducing the world of detail to be considered to those central aspects of external environment and internal resources that affect the company and bear on the definition of its business. The special skill involved in perceiving and communicating the strategic significance of a business decision may be of the highest importance in engaging independent directors in the exercise of their assumed responsibility and in establishing active and effective boards as normal adjuncts to competent professional management. Such a development may reduce the likelihood that corporate governance be judged sufficiently irresponsible that radical legislative checks are imposed upon corporate freedom and initiative.

Millipore Corporation (A)

SUMMER/FALL 1985

It was July 10, 1985, at the Bedford, Massachusetts, headquarters of the Millipore Corporation, a medium-sized firm (1984 worldwide sales of $332 million) engaged in the development, manufacture, and marketing of products used for the analysis and purification of fluids in critical applications. Fresh from a two-week vacation, chief financial officer John Gilmartin was called into a meeting with Millipore president John (Jack) Mulvany. He emerged with a new title: president of the Millipore Products Division (MPD). The new head of Millipore's largest operating division had these comments on his assignment:

> The whole change took me by surprise. I had just finished telling Jack about my vacation, when he announced that Fred Hildebrandt, the president of MPD, would be leaving and that I was the board's choice for the job. Jack said that things just didn't feel right in MPD. MPD was supposed to be growing at 15–20 percent worldwide but had stalled at 10–12 percent. Jack's feeling was that innovation had been made secondary, that job descriptions and cost controls and procedures all were inhibiting the development of new products and applications and markets. So the mandate was to get the top line moving, and one piece of that was putting together a more market-focused, innovative, entrepreneurial setting. I didn't get any specifics from Jack and had no crisp four-point plan going into the job, although with six years in the company, I came with some strong suspicions. I felt a strong need to make an impact, to say someone's in charge and we'll be going in a different direction . . . though I didn't know what that direction would be.

MILLIPORE AND THE BUSINESS OF SEPARATIONS TECHNOLOGY

Corporate History[1]

Millipore was founded in 1954 when chemist Jack Bush licensed a technology

Harvard Business School case 487–023. Revised November 1987.

[1] This section draws from Donald K. Clifford, Jr. and Richard F. Cavanaugh, *The Winning Performance: How America's High-Growth Midsize Companies Succeed* (New York: Bantam Books, 1985).

that had originated in Germany for microporous plastic membranes, based on a hunch that there was a market for it. By varying the number of pores per square centimeter of the membrane, Millipore could filter just about any size of microscopic particle from just about any fluid. The challenge was to identify the most economical and high-potential applications. The key to success proved to be a customer-oriented strategy and a series of creative niche entries. Jack Bush, joined in the early 1960s by a Harvard MBA named Dee d'Arbeloff, traveled around the country talking to potential customers who provided a steady stream of ideas for high value-added applications. Over the years, the most important applications proved to be these: the purification of drugs by pharmaceutical manufacturers; the removal of defect-causing contaminants from integrated circuit-process fluids by microelectronics producers; the protection of patients from the complications of intravenous therapy by health care practitioners; the clarification of wine by the beverage industry; the bacteriological monitoring of drinking water supplies by public health agencies; gene harvesting by bioresearchers; and the purification of water for a wide range of industrial, research, and medical uses. For each application, Millipore custom-tailored a membrane-based solution to the customer's problem, creating niches for continued growth.

From 1960 to 1979, Millipore was one of the hottest high-tech stars. From a specialized filter manufacturer with scarcely more than $1 million in sales, it grew to a multinational corporation with sales of almost $195 million and operating profits of more than $35 million. The financial community came to rely on Millipore's predictable 20 percent-plus earnings growth, and the company's pride in this outstanding performance was evident in its high-energy, fast-paced work environment. Then came a modest decline in profits in 1980, followed by a steep drop in 1981. Millipore's difficulties could be traced to a number of external factors: deep recession in its key markets, international currency dislocations, and intensified competition. Some observers, however, pointed to four *internal* problem sources: (1) "indigestion" from acquisitions of technologically related businesses, which were acquired in pursuit of d'Arbeloff's vision of Millipore as a broad-based separations company; (2) confusion and bureaucracy resulting from organizational experiments with dividing MPD into smaller divisions and adopting a formal matrix structure; (3) a shift at the operating level from emphasis on long-term, value-related goals, such as quality, innovation, and customer service, to emphasis on short-term financial goals; and (4) weak internal monitoring systems and financial controls.

In response to these problems, a dozen of Millipore's top managers met off-site in the fall of 1981 for a review of the company's values, objectives, and general direction. The result was a decision "to bite the bullet" and to take a series of action steps that included: reduction of expenses and staffing levels; sale of a division and use of proceeds to reduce long-term debt; reintegration of the Millipore Products Division; committee review and companywide reaffirmation of Millipore's core values; and control system improvements that involved the "cleaning up" of Millipore's balance sheet by chief financial officer John Gilmartin. Following these 1981 decisions, three years of steady improvements in operating profits culminated in a near-record performance in 1984, which also saw sales grow 14 percent. (See Exhibit 1 for financial details.)

Millipore's $332 million in sales made it a world leader in the field of high value-added separations technology. In 1984 the worldwide market was estimated at approximately $2 billion and was expected to grow 15 to 20 percent over the next five years. Millipore's product lineup (2,000 major products and systems backed up by 8,000 accessories, supplies, and consumables) encompassed three technologies that collectively addressed over 80 percent of the total separations market: membranes, ion exchange, and high-performance liquid chromatography.[2] Millipore's broad technology base was believed to provide a competitive advantage in meeting a wide range of customer needs. Pharmaceutical, chemical, and food industry customers were Millipore's traditional stronghold and still accounted for more than half of total sales in 1984. Microelectronics and biotechnology were considered future growth markets. Millipore products were distributed in 60 countries, with foreign sales accounting for 47 percent of total revenues in 1984.

In 1985, Millipore employees were working toward four long-term objectives: (1) 15 percent annual average revenue growth, (2) 10 percent return on sales, (3) creation of new and attractive niches in the field of high value-added separations, and (4) improvement of present applications. Jack Mulvany discussed Millipore's business strategy at a May 1985 meeting of the firm's shareholders. Mulvany described the application life cycle and the differing criteria for success in the early market development phase and in the subsequent competitive phase. (See Exhibit 2 for a follow-up interview published in the employee newsletter.) Mulvany closed on an upbeat note, predicting $1 billion in sales by the turn of the decade.

Just one month later, Millipore's mood was dampened by the death of Dee d'Arbeloff after a courageous seven-month battle with cancer. Although clearly a designated successor,[3] Mulvany stepped into the role of chairman of the board aware of the fact that some outsiders questioned whether Millipore could sustain its momentum without d'Arbeloff, a man described as a prototypical entrepreneur and the architect of Millipore's growth.

Millipore Products Division

In 1983 the Millipore Products Division (MPD) was reassembled from smaller divisional units (i.e., business units each with its own marketing, sales, and research and development responsibilities), which had been in place for approximately five years. In 1984 MPD, which had worldwide profit and loss responsibility for Millipore's membrane and ion exchange product lines, contributed approximately $30 million in operating profits on sales of $169 million. (See Exhibit 3 for MPD income statements.) The MPD mission statement read as follows:

---

[2] Although 30 companies sold products similar to Millipore's, no single competitor offered as broad a line. In 1984 Millipore's chief competitors were Pall and Gelman in membranes and Perkin Elmer, Varian, and Pharmacia in high-performance liquid chromatography. Also, Japanese manufacturers employing low-cost supplier strategies were a growing force in both of these technology segments.

[3] Mulvany, who held degrees in chemistry and physics, was hired by d'Arbeloff in 1966 as a sales manager for Millipore's British subsidiary and subsequently became its managing director. In 1970 he joined the marketing department at corporate headquarters. He was elected president, chief operating officer, and a director in 1980, and succeeded d'Arbeloff to the chief executive post in February 1984.

> Millipore Products Division (MPD) is a worldwide leader in the applications of membrane-based products for the analysis and purification of fluids. MPD will enhance its market leadership position through exploiting new membrane-based opportunities. MPD will continue to focus on high value-added products for membrane purification products in the pharmaceutical, electronics, and beverage markets, and on discovering new opportunities in other markets. MPD will pursue market needs for water purification by applying both membrane and ion exchange technology, and will continue to exploit existing and new opportunities in laboratory and health care applications.

MPD's core technology was the removal of particles from liquids and gases via filtration through membranes, which were thin plastic sheets with millions of pores per square centimeter. The company's first product was a simple filter disk used with a holder. Over the years, MPD had broadened its membrane technology to include three types of increasingly fine filtration materials—microporous, ultrafiltration, and reverse osmosis—which were packaged in convenient forms and tailored to specific applications. In 1985 MPD offered a variety of materials designed to suit the size of the particle to be filtered and the chemical properties of the fluid of interest. It also offered a number of configurations, including pleated cartridges, spiral-bound cartridges, and stacked disks. Membrane-filtration systems ranged from simple disposable plastic devices (for which the only hardware needed was a stainless steel housing), to sophisticated capital equipment.

Millipore had acquired the Continental Water Conditioning Corporation and its ion exchange technology in 1979 to enable the company to better meet its customers' needs for high-purity water. The new product line consisted of ion exchange cartridges, which used a chemical process to remove salts from water. The customer could use the ion exchange cartridges for several days or weeks and then have them picked up and "regenerated" at local service centers. In addition to these local service centers, the acquisition included nationwide service centers from which Millipore's other traditional water products could be distributed and serviced.

In 1985 MPD offered more than 2,000 individual products (see Exhibit 4 for sampling) to research scientists, production and quality control engineers, and physicians. Most products were stock items ordered by mail or telephone from the MPD catalog. Traditionally, consumable products with unit prices of under $100 represented the bulk of MPD's business; the rest was accounted for by capital equipment ranging in price from $20 for a cartridge housing to $86,000 for an industrial scale water system assembled from standard modules and accessories.[4] MPD management further grouped products into four broad application categories: (1) laboratory products, used in thousands of analytical and quality control applications by a highly fragmented customer base; (2) industrial products, used to clean or sterilize manufacturing process fluids by pharmaceutical, chemical, beverage, and electronics companies;[5] (3) water systems,

---

[4] Company observers noted that consumable sales had eroded from an optimal level of 80 percent of total revenues to under 65 percent in 1985.

[5] Millipore was unique in offering both laboratory and manufacturing scale filtration systems. At a process development scale-up facility in Bedford, MPD engineers helped customers move the processing of pharmaceutical and other products from the research laboratory into full-scale production.

used in a wide range of customer settings, and (4) OEM (original equipment manufacturer) medical devices, used as intravenous therapy filters by health care practitioners who purchased them from Millipore's customers, the hospital supply companies. (See Exhibit 5 for MPD sales by product category.)

MPD ORGANIZATION AND OPERATIONS

Hildebrandt Era

Frederic (Fred) Hildebrandt began his three-year tenure as MPD president in 1982, following Millipore's worst year of performance. He held an engineering degree and had 20 years of work experience, including his most recent position as a divisional general manager at Foxboro Analytical Instruments. At Millipore, Hildebrandt had broad discretion in operating matters and full responsibility for MPD's worldwide business. Described as polite but distant, Hildebrandt brought to MPD a professional management style and an efficiency-oriented approach that clashed sharply with the division's freewheeling culture. Although his success in instituting much-needed cost controls was widely acknowledged, Hildebrandt also drew criticism. In the words of a product manager:

> Fred was very strong on discipline: systems, structures, controls, organizational charts. He was a drastic change for a loose company where people were used to being independent and free to make decisions on new initiatives. It was apparent here in the trenches that people were losing their desire to do new things, that market creativity was being stifled. There was too much structure and control, and this affected morale.

According to a second marketing employee:

> Hildebrandt brought how Foxboro did things and tried to impose that on Millipore. His smokestack approach of leveraging the cost side and building systems makes sense in a predictable environment where you're being incremental. But it appeared inappropriate in a situation where new ideas are always coming up, where you need to be entrepreneurial and opportunistic. If we want to keep our customers on the leading edge of technology, we have to keep pace with the rate of change. Fred was lauded for bringing discipline but at what cost? He did controls *instead* of innovation, but we need both. You don't need rules and procedures for that. You need a common understanding of goals, good communication, teamwork, and an atmosphere where opinions are valued. Hildebrandt's personal style was radically different from past senior managers'. For example, he built a wall around his office area and put in executive parking places. The end result was that people got turned off and either left or kept their head[s] down.

When Hildebrandt arrived at MPD, he found it organized into four divisions described as "fiefdoms fighting over customers." The four profit centers were: (1) the industrial processing division, which marketed high-volume filtration systems to pharmaceutical, electronics, and beverage manufacturers; (2) the analytical products division, which served a wide variety of laboratory customers; (3) the medical products division, which sold devices used in the administration of intravenous solutions; (4) the water systems division, which provided laboratory, medical, and industrial customers with water purification products capable of treating volumes of water ranging from 25 to 200,000 gallons per day. Noting that MPD's decentralized structure had resulted in considerable duplication of staff functions, Hildebrandt consolidated the four divisions and reorganized along functional lines. One MPD manager had these comments on the reorganization: "The rationale for the original move to smaller, market-focused divisions was that we weren't responsive enough to customer needs. Fred, though, saw a need to be more efficient and leaner. The new functional organization accomplished those objectives but also made communication among ourselves and with our customers more difficult."

In 1985 the MPD employee roster included about 2,000 persons, of whom 40 percent were professionals and 21 percent were located outside the United States. As division president, Hildebrandt reported to Jack Mulvany and supervised the heads of eight functional units: human resources, finance and administration, research and development, operations, North American sales, marketing, Europe, and Japan. (See Exhibit 6 for a partial organization chart.) Descriptions of these functional units follow.

Human Resources

Vice president of MPD human resources Wayne Kennedy described his role as follows: "I'm on the payroll to be proactive, to be a midwife to the organization, to make sure things are happening." His 15-person staff, which included a central services group and representatives assigned to specific functional areas, was responsible for U.S. personnel administration.

Finance and Administration

Financial support for MPD's worldwide business was provided by an 80-person group divided into three broad areas of responsibility—accounting, operations finance, and sales and marketing analysis—all of which reported to the division controller.

Research and Development

To maintain its traditional role as a leader in membrane separations technology, MPD supported a sizable internal research and development (R&D) organization and had also entered into some joint venture agreements. When Hildebrandt centralized the function, Leon Mir was assigned to the position of R&D vice president. Mir subsequently divided his organization into three activity-based sections: (1) research, which worked primarily to extend or enhance existing membrane technology and to develop new membrane materials; (2) applications engineering, which included four application-focused teams—water, life science, industrial/medical, and analytical laboratories—charged with finding new uses for existing and evolving technology; and (3) product development, which responded to new application needs by designing new configurations for MPD membranes and also developed hardware and accessories to incorporate membrane filters, modules, and devices into total separation systems. By 1985 Mir's Bedford-based organization had grown to 126 persons, was highly regarded, and attracted top research talent.

Although Millipore had broadened its membrane technology base over the years, microporous membranes remained, in 1985, the backbone of its business. The evolution of MPD's microporous technology and product line was described as follows, by one R&D manager:

> For the first 20 years of our existence, we essentially lived off the original technology on which Jack Bush founded the company. By the 1970s, we were encountering strong competition worldwide. In

that time frame, the Pall Corporation, always a worthy competitor, began offering a pleated membrane cartridge made out of a special nylon formulation, which had substantial competitive advantages. As we began to feel the impact in the market, we realized that we needed additional technological strengths. The edict from Dee d'Arbeloff was: "Develop a new membrane and products based on it." This sparked a major undertaking which, by the early 1980s, had resulted in the introduction of Millipore's Dura Pore R product line. This product line is based on a polyvinyl fluoride membrane. When initially commercialized, product costs were high and profits low, but process improvements over the past few years have helped margins. Today, the Dura Pore R product line is a large success in the marketplace and an important contributor to MPD's sales and profits.

Traditionally, Millipore's product strategy was to offer a broad line of high-quality, differentiated products. MPD's ability to be the first to identify and respond to customer needs for membrane filtration remained an important competitive strength. Leon Mir offered these comments on new-product activity at MPD:

> If you develop a good membrane, which requires a fair amount of art as well as science, it can have a lifetime of 50 years. A new membrane material can take four to five years to develop but you'll get products out of it along the way. Currently, we put an R&D person in charge of each new product project, which typically takes about two years to complete. It would be good to get marketing people involved, but their turnover is too high. Fred Hildebrandt wasn't deeply involved in the operations of research and development, and had limited impact on the choice of new products. In the fall of 1984, the senior marketing people and I decided we needed to plan to execute the new long-range plan, so we started a new product committee that meets three or four times a year to discuss resource allocation issues.

In the early 1980s, senior management had begun to voice concern over a perceived slowdown in MPD's flood of new products, which historically generated about one third of annual revenues. The problem was blamed on poor hand-offs in the product delivery process. Hildebrandt's solution was the addition of a pilot plant, which was credited with reducing product delays and improving efficiency. (See Exhibit 7 for a description of the six-step new-product delivery process.) In 1985, however, MPD's failure to field enough new products to meet growth targets remained an issue. Some managers pointed to a lack of clear accountability for individual new-product projects. Other managers were more concerned by the fact that considerable effort was being expended on projects with questionable market potential. The then head of MPD product development explained:

> Millipore is the only place I've ever worked where there legitimately are too many opportunities. The issue is the dollar value of opportunities and whether we're doing the right thing strategically. We had delegated resource allocation for product development to marketing managers with a myopic view. The real decisions were made at lunchtime negotiations where the product manager who got along with the development people was the one whose stuff got done. I tried to break up this network by putting in forms that asked things like: "What will the product do? How many units will you sell?" But that smacked of bureaucracy and didn't work. The problem was that no one "owned" the new-product process. Department heads tried to work it out and make trade-offs, but it was hard to resolve conflicts.

Operations

Hildebrandt focused considerable attention on the operations area, where staff generally was supportive of his cost-control efforts. In the summer of 1985, vice president of operations Edward Lary oversaw a 1,200-person organization divided into seven broad responsibility areas:

1. Manufacturing. MPD conducted manufacturing operations in five locations: Bedford, Massachusetts, which served primarily as a pilot plant for new membranes and products; Jaffrey, New Hampshire, which specialized in industrial process products; Ceidra, Puerto Rico, which produced high-volume products, including membranes, and was an automated plant; Molsheim, France, which fabricated U.S.-developed membranes into filtration products tailored to Common Market customer needs; and Japan, which did custom work for the Pacific Basin and was a small facility.

2. Engineering. A staff of mechanical and industrial engineers based in Bedford addressed manufacturing issues for all MPD plants from a current product-technology standpoint and also worked with R&D on new-product development.

3. Quality Control. The MPD quality control group was responsible for production quality control and for regulatory affairs. It also managed the Acquisition of Customer Experience (ACE) programs, which involved reviewing and reporting all customer complaints and suggestions.

4. Safety. Safety personnel monitored and worked to improve MPD safety standards and performance.

5. Distribution. The distribution group was responsible for the warehouses in San Francisco and Bedford. They performed production scheduling, inventory control, and order-processing functions. The order-processing staff quoted discounts, took telephone orders from customers for processing into MIS for shipment, and provided some minimal technical advice on customer applications.

6. Service Deionization (SDI). SDI branches in 20 U.S. locations provided customers with on-site water purification. These service facilities included regeneration plants, where ion exchange cartridges were chemically treated for reuse; trucks for transportation of cartridges to and from customer sites; and service technicians for customer calls regarding problems such as equipment failure.

7. Facilities. Located in a wooded commercial park setting bought in 1960, Millipore's Bedford complex had grown to include five interconnected buildings housing both corporate and MPD divisional headquarters plus a membrane products pilot plant (see Exhibit 8 for floor plans). In 1985 space constraints were forcing the issue of another expansion.

North American Sales

MPD's 122-person North American sales organization consisted of the U.S. field sales force; Canadian subsidiary personnel; and a Bedford-based sales administration and technical service group, whose duties included responding by telephone to customers' application questions and technical problems. In 1984 Thomas Gilmore was hired as vice president of North American sales, bringing a background that included degrees in engineering and business administration, three years in the U.S. Navy, and nine years of marketing experience. One fellow MPD manager offered this assessment of Gilmore: "He was bright and very professional but had no sales experience. Also, he was from outside the industry and so lacked the relevant technology base."

In 1985 U.S. field sales responsibility was divided between Eastern and Western area managers. Each of these managers supervised four regional managers who in turn oversaw 8 to 12 application specialists who were responsible for selling all MPD products to all customer markets in their assigned geographic territories.[6] New field sales hires participated in a standardized training program at Bedford headquarters and then received in-field supervision from their regional managers. Field sales activities included servicing existing accounts, developing selected new market opportunities, and following leads generated by promotion pieces, trade shows, referrals, or telephone inquiries. The 1985 compensation system, designed to attract and keep qualified specialists, offered such employees total earnings of $50,000 to $60,000, including a base salary of $30,000, plus commissions linked to achievement of sales quotas. Wayne Kennedy explained that compensation had become a major issue:

> Compensation was an issue because no one was making a nickel. The application specialists were very unhappy. Actually, it was the fault of the targeting system rather than the compensation system. The bottoms-up sales forecast for 1985 fell considerably short of the sales growth objectives targeted by senior management. Gilmore's solution was to divide the difference equally among his application specialists, so everyone's quota was raised by the same percentage regardless of geographic opportunities. This change in targets met with a lot of resentment and resistance. By mid-year, the problems had been complicated by the fact that overall business was down to slumps first in electronics and then in pharmaceutical and lab markets; targets then became a cause celebre. Gilmore and I were unable to convince Hildebrandt that the problem was sufficiently acute to justify special adjustment in the incentive program.

Many MPD managers felt that the U.S. selling effort had been hurt by the 1982 switch from four divisional sales forces specialized by application area to a single (and smaller) sales organization that expected salespeople to cope with a broad range of customer needs. Sales force morale dropped, and many Ph.D.-trained application specialists left to be replaced by less technically expert "salespeople." By 1985, concern about sales-force competence had grown: "Our goal is to match Millipore technology with customer needs, yet our sales reps have a poor understanding of how our products work and what our customers' applications needs are." Struggling to cope with customers' very technical questions, field representatives frequently turned to MPD marketing managers for help.

Marketing

The demands of "firefighting" for the U.S. sales force left MPD marketers with little time for their assigned responsibilities: worldwide strategy formulation, new-product planning, and new-market development. Hildebrandt had tried to address the problem by dividing the marketing function into nuts-and-bolts product management and real marketing management. Marketing managers tended to be highly resistant to Hildebrandt's insistence

[6] In 1985 the average sales territory encompassed 50 customer accounts. Twenty percent of field representatives were dedicated to specific major accounts (e.g., Texas Instruments, Pfizer, IBM).

that they focus on internal cost issues rather than on external growth opportunities. Morale sagged as the marketing department came under a barrage of criticism. International subsidiaries felt estranged; U.S. sales needed more support; new-product development wasn't being integrated with market needs; R&D efforts weren't being commercialized. Furthermore, as turnover increased, the age and experience of marketing staff dropped.

In partial response, Hildebrandt reinstituted the position of marketing vice president in 1985. Paul White, who was recruited from the Foxboro Company for the job of "pulling together marketing" and who held degrees in chemical engineering and business administration, had 20 years of work experience. In his new position, White directly supervised the heads of product management and marketing management. The 69-person product management group included promotion managers, who prepared sales literature; product managers, who were assigned to specific product lines; field service engineers, who were responsible for the installation and maintenance of capital equipment; and a product trainer, who educated sales hires on product positioning, applications, and other technical details. The small marketing management group included a market development manager charged with identifying new market opportunities, and managers for two specific customer markets—electronics and pharmaceuticals.

Europe

The general manager of MPD's European operations supervised a 167-person staff consisting of 65 sales representatives, a financial support group, and a marketing group that focused on the wine/beverage industry. Geoffrey Woodard, former director of marketing for MPD Europe, offered these observations six months into his new assignment at division headquarters in Bedford:

> There's much less customer responsiveness in Bedford relative to the subsidiaries, where the attitude that the priority is to serve the customer's needs permeates the organization. Maybe that's because of the size of the U.S. organization compared to the subsidiary, where everyone knows everyone. In the United States, there are more systems and less freedom. For example, Millipore has standard housings for membranes. In a subsidiary, if a customer wants different specs, a guy in a garage shop fixes it up in 15 minutes. A big part of Europe's success is because it will give the customer what he wants. In the United States, there's a big long process, fussing with engineers, formal specs, and so on. As a result, there's no risk taking here. For example, a product manager recently requested a test market for a new product that involved low quantities and no capital investment. A test market makes sense in a case where $400 million in tooling is required but not in this case. We need judgment. People ask: "Do you have any product failures?" I say: "We don't have enough." We should take risks. We have to in order to get the big wins. We must create an organization that tolerates failure. Everyone will make some mistakes.

Japan

Japanese subsidiary operations encompassed sales and administrative staff plus a small manufacturing facility geared to Pacific Basin market needs. The efforts of general manager Takahashi's 146-person organization were supplemented by extensive use of third-party distributors.

SUMMER OF 1985

Business Trends

Midway through 1985 concern was mounting over MPD's lackluster business results. Worldwide sales had been reforecasted to amount to only $177 million in 1985, an increase of less than 5 percent from the preceding year and well below the original budget of $191 million. Regional business analyses showed healthy growth projections from Europe (+16 percent) and Japan (+10 percent) but a disturbing 6 percent decline in U.S. sales. Mulvany's frustration with MPD management's failure to resolve U.S. business problems peaked at a late June meeting. Wayne Kennedy related the following account of the meeting:

> The background to the meeting was that Jack Mulvany was deeply concerned because he thought the average application specialist was spread too thin to understand or to cover all our markets. In addition, application specialists calling on large process customers weren't calling on the laboratory researcher at the front end. Jack believed that you needed to make the investment and get into the lab and felt MPD wasn't addressing the problem. As the result of discussions between Jack and Fred, a meeting was arranged with Jack, Fred, and Fred's staff. At this meeting, for which no agenda had been distributed, Jack's initial question was, "What are you doing about declining U.S. sales?" The response was silence. No one was prepared. Jack was asking good questions about sales, but getting few answers. Jack got frustrated and finally said, "It's clear to me you're unprepared for this problem," and walked out. Jack's loss of faith in Fred's ability to solve the sales growth problem, combined with Fred's lack of support from other senior managers and outside directors, eventually led to agreement that it would be in everybody's best interest for Fred to pursue other career opportunities.

Leadership Transition

At 4:30 P.M. on July 17, 1985, Fred Hildebrandt called together MPD department heads and informed them that he would be leaving Millipore due to irreconcilable differences in management philosophy between Jack Mulvany and himself. At department staff meetings early the next morning, MPD employees were informed that John Gilmartin would be assuming the position of president. Gilmartin, whose background included an MBA from Harvard plus 12 years of finance and general management experience at Pfizer, had joined Millipore as corporate controller in 1979 and had subsequently been promoted to senior vice president and chief financial officer. Shortly after these department staff meetings, the leadership change was publicly announced. The reaction was widespread surprise, as explained by corporate communications officer John Glass:

> Externally, no one realized anything was wrong with Fred. The financial community had just finished a few years of getting used to Fred and had come to like and respect him, so they were very surprised. The Gilmartin choice also raised some eyebrows. Shareholders were saying, "What? You're always telling us how important our customers and markets are, and now you put a finance guy in charge?" Security analysts knew John in his CFO role and liked the guy but also were skeptical so I had them come in and talk to him. They asked, "How is it you have any business running a division?" He said, "Good question. Give me some time." Basically, he recognized their concerns

as legitimate and went on to say he would take the time to learn and showed he had already done some learning by picking a few examples and digging in and describing technology and markets. He said that obviously the company had done many things right, so he wouldn't be tearing up plans but rather would reassess the current plan and put his mark on portions of it. Internally, too, there were questions about putting the CFO in charge of the family jewels. People on the board, especially Jack Bush, were sensitive to the fact that the MPD president's role involved more than managing the company's largest division and core business. It meant being custodian of the home office site, keeper of the faith, guardian of the corporate culture.

GILMARTIN'S FIRST STEPS

Getting Acquainted

John Gilmartin offered this account of his first days in the role of MPD president:

> The first thing I did was to knock down walls, literally. Senior management had walled itself in, and the walls had become symbols of the attitude "This used to be a fun place to work. Now, I do what I'm told." I also pulled up the executive parking place signs. These were symbolic moves intended to break down structure and show people we're all in this together. I wanted people to open up. My first staff meeting was indicative of just how tense things had become around here. The meeting started with a capital spending request, which I approved. Then an old-time engineering guy put up a slide of an improved mold for a petrie dish. Everyone said: "Not yet. It's not worked out yet." It turns out that all the forms hadn't been filled out. Yet here it was July with no staff meeting scheduled for six weeks, so we would have lost time just because all the functional groups weren't signed off on it. I said, "Wait. What do you think? Do it. Place the order with the supplier and do the paper later." In the cafeteria at lunch, some manufacturing guys came up and said, "You really came through. We made a test, put up a proposal that was half-baked but clearly right. You really are going to change things. Word will go out." This was part of an interesting process of the organization—watching, testing, probing. At this point, I was still working on culture and attitudes and didn't see a clear direction yet.

Gilmartin eagerly launched into the task of learning about MPD, taking the high-visibility approach of informal visits to various departments, frequent attendance at meetings, and "just walking the halls." The normal budget cycle, which confirmed the urgency of the U.S. sales slump and provided evidence of a shrinking new-product flow, provided a natural forum for discussion of broad business issues with the marketing group. When Gilmartin turned to product and market managers, he discovered that they were spending most of their time on U.S. sales-support activities. The results of Gilmartin's observations were three budget themes for 1986—customer focus, invest in sales and marketing, and new-product planning—in addition to some important steps toward addressing organizational problems.

Focus on Sales

Gilmartin moved quickly to address U.S. business problems, turning to field personnel for answers:

> I went to a sales meeting in July and found most applications specialists getting up and saying they were going to come in well below target. I was probing and finally a regional manager said, "Look,

this budget was given to me. I never thought it was right. Is it OK for me to tell you that?" I took them out to dinner and said, "I can't run this business without openness. Open up. Let's share our problems and go forward." The story was that, by midyear, applications specialists knew they had no chance of making bonus. Actually, they knew that going into the year, because quotas were all out of whack, but a second quarter downturn in the electronics industry clinched it. Essentially, they had given up. The problem was clear from talking with applications specialists, who also were asking what I was going to do about it.

Sales Crisis Management. Recognizing that the vice president of sales had lost all credibility with the field organization, Gilmartin replaced him with Henry (Hank) Clemente. Clemente, whose background included a degree in biochemistry and work experience as an analytical chemist, had joined Millipore in 1977 and had subsequently served in a number of sales and marketing positions domestically and abroad. Clemente described his first steps as head of MPD's North American sales group as follows, "I started by meeting with area and regional managers, 95 percent of whom I already knew. For three 12-hour days we focused on two questions: What are the problems? How do we solve them? Basically, the problems were people problems, motivational problems. The overriding complaint was that the organization was not sensitive to their needs in the field."

Over the second half of 1985, Gilmartin authorized approximately $1.5 million in incremental funding for three major initiatives: (1) a new bonus program that maintained established quotas but stepped up dollar incentives, (2) the addition of 12 sales representatives as part of Clemente's plan to reduce territory size and to specialize the field force by customer markets (which plan included creating a separate sales group for water systems products), and (3) a "Sales Action Millipore" system to replace a previously eliminated lead-qualifying program. Observers noted a dramatic improvement in morale under Clemente's leadership: "Clemente was a tough cookie and tolerated no sniveling. He commanded a lot of respect from the sales force and gave them someone to follow. Within three months, the sales force's attitude had turned 100 percent."

Clemente also identified some serious structural problems with the U.S. selling organization:

> We had lots of people trying to help us, but the U.S. structure was getting in the way of our ability to respond to customer needs. For example, water systems are sold by my application specialists but serviced by engineers who report to operations, which causes huge delays when a customer with a service problem calls the rep who sold him the unit. As another example, one of our biggest semiconductor customers was asking for just-in-time inventory, a new thing for us. I called our California distribution center to say: "Let's experiment with $10,000 in inventory." Distribution, however, reports to purchasing, who began asking questions. Seven meetings and three months later, we got the go-ahead.

U.S. Sales Subsidiary. Although there was broad consensus at MPD on the need to make the U.S. sales group more self-sufficient, the "U.S. Sales Subsidiary" concept was actually born of Gilmartin's efforts to address space problems at Bedford headquarters. Gilmartin explained his thinking this way:

> We had outgrown our Bedford office space and so were considering leasing an adjacent building. The first idea was to split off the administrative group. But the more I thought of sales and the differences between our foreign and domestic selling operations, the more I thought that maybe we should physically separate the U.S. sales group from corporate headquarters in order to cut the amount of bureaucracy and make it easier to focus externally. The idea generated huge enthusiasm, and we put together a task force under Wayne Kennedy to design a sales organization that would bring together all our customer activity under Clemente's direction.

The 16-person U.S. Sales Subsidiary task force, which included functional representatives from every MPD department, had a clear objective: "To provide for a more customer-responsive integrated selling team in the U.S. market similar to the organization that exists in MPD's foreign subsidiaries." Subcommittees were formed to address the question of which pre- and post-sales functions to add to the U.S. selling organization, to determine staffing requirements, and to delineate organizational interdependencies. Separate subcommittees simultaneously looked at space requirements, communications, MIS support needs, and financial requirements. The task force's final report recommended that the new organization include three major functions: field marketing, field sales, and sales support. The report also provided a financial schedule detailing incremental costs of $1.2 million over 1986 budget plans and presented an implementation timetable with a May 1986 target date for the move to new facilities. At an early December presentation to MPD and corporate management, the report met with overwhelming approval and the observation that the divisional marketing group would benefit significantly from the shifting of its current sales support duties to the new field marketing function. (See Exhibit 9 for U.S. Sales Subsidiary organization chart.)

Product Planning

Gilmartin believed that new products and innovation required involvement of the top officers of the organization. His early efforts to "come up to speed on technology" were noted with approval by R&D staff, who also commented on the difference in comparison with his predecessor's more distant role. Mir welcomed the greater top-management involvement as "helpful interference" that would help build companywide consensus and commitment to R&D efforts. By the end of 1985, company observers were seeing an improvement in MPD's new-product flow: "Gilmartin went through all the R&D projects and dusted some off. So, it's not that he started a bunch of new initiatives. He just went back and said, 'That one in the corner looks good. Go for it.'"

Headquarters Reorganization

Over his first few months, Gilmartin struggled with the question of how to address problems in MPD's functional organization:

> When I got here, I found a strongly entrenched functional organization structure. People were doing a good job within their functional definitions, but there was a compartmental mentality. Coordination at lower levels probably was better than at middle or upper largely for survival reasons: they had to ship *something.* The problem was that in the absence of upper level involvement, lower levels were mak-

ing almost all policy decisions. Another problem was that in all of the interface issues, customer needs got lost. We had got too caught up in managing ourselves versus managing the customer.

I didn't want to be one of those funny stories about reorganizations, but I talked with Jack Mulvany, and he agreed we needed a fast switch from a functional to a divisional structure. The challenge was *how* to do it. I really wrestled with that because I knew we could lose a lot if it was done the wrong way. It was tremendously threatening to people, because they were married to their functions. Mulvany favored fully integrated divisions but I wasn't so sure, partly because there was still a sour taste from the small integrated divisions adopted in the late 1970s.

CURRENT SITUATION

Early in the fall of 1985, Gilmartin announced that he intended to restructure MPD marketing with the objective of creating small units focused on the customer. The announcement, which prompted the marketing vice president's resignation, marked the beginning of a three-month organizational design effort led by Gilmartin:

In September I signaled that we would be going to some sort of divisional structure. I said I would take several weeks, talk to all affected, listen to all opinions, and then make a decision. I saw a long line of people and probably made and unmade five or six organizations in the process. Part of the task was deciding how many divisions to create and which markets to focus on, but the fundamental dilemma was which functions to attach and which to keep separate. The research piece was the hardest because there were benefits to keeping R&D centralized under Mir, but our problems with new product delivery seemed to argue for having R&D report directly to the divisions. I also had to think about who would head the new divisions. I wanted people who would think and act like general managers, but we didn't have any; one of the problems of a functional organization is that it breeds functional people. On the other hand, newcomers in high positions have such a high mortality rate here that I didn't want to bring in an outsider.

EXHIBIT 1
MILLIPORE 10-YEAR SUMMARY OF OPERATIONS
In Thousands, Except per Share and Employee Data

	1984	1983	1982	1981	1980	1979	1978	1977	1976	1975
Net sales	$332,102	$292,464	$271,835	$255,803	$234,363	$194,615	$158,013	$118,456	$88,636	$70,752
Cost of sales	153,463	133,433	126,635	125,914	100,036	79,770	62,110	46,280	34,806	28,848
Gross profit	178,639	159,031	145,200	129,889	134,327	114,845	95,903	72,176	53,830	41,904
Selling, general, and administrative expenses	118,756	108,746	105,328	97,817	89,283	67,629	54,023	38,952	28,615	20,514
Research and development expenses	24,603	21,824	17,724	13,886	13,686	11,573	8,961	6,600	5,309	4,581
Operating income	35,280	28,461	22,148	18,186	31,358	35,643	32,919	26,624	19,906	16,809
Income before income taxes	36,289	28,235	22,880	13,740	27,834	33,372	31,864	26,226	19,852	16,462
Net income	30,493*	20,664	33,318	10,928	18,763	21,848	18,747	15,139	11,310	8,572
Net income per common share	2.21*	1.52	2.46	.81	1.40	1.67	1.45	1.18	.88	.70
Cash dividends declared per share	.43	.39	.35	.31	.27	.23	.19	.15	.11	.09
Average shares outstanding	13,776†	13,635	13,546	13,526	13,406	13,104	12,931	12,876	12,839	12,278
Financial Data										
Working capital	121,075	107,102	96,166	96,037	95,691	80,829	64,255	46,940	40,231	33,406
Total assets	300,714	275,199	256,802	252,319	239,204	183,828	148,270	108,262	85,284	68,203
Shareholders' equity	214,199	192,796	177,754	152,155	142,759	122,462	98,067	79,018	65,284	53,072
Number of employees at year-end	4,215	4,070	4,001	3,860	3,959	3,441	3,240	2,665	2,270	1,673

*Includes $4 million ($0.29 per share) nonrecurring DISC benefit.

†Distribution of ownership: 60 percent in hands of institutions (including Dow, the sole corporate owner, which owned over 9 percent) with balance owned by individuals and families. Only 2 percent was held by Millipore officers or directors.

Source: Millipore Corporation Annual Report.

EXHIBIT 2
MULVANY INTERVIEW EXCERPTS
Jack Mulvany: On Millipore's Strengths, Strategies, and Culture

Editor's note: At last month's annual shareholders meeting in Milford, Massachusetts, Millipore's President Jack Mulvany evaluated the company's success and talked about the directions he sees Millipore taking in the next few years. He touched on the growth of Millipore's markets, the company's ability to compete, and its business strategies. The interview below is a follow-up to that presentation; in his remarks here Mulvany elaborates on Millipore's strategies and directions, and discusses how the company will remain competitive and achieve its goal of an annual 15 percent growth rate. He also talks about Millipore's culture, and offers some personal insights about his role as CEO.

Milliscope: *In your remarks at the shareholders meeting you talked about there being a shift from defining Millipore in terms of technologies to defining the company in terms of "high value-added applications." Could you elaborate on this concept, and explain how it is different from what the company has done in the past?*

Jack Mulvany: It's important to understand that Millipore's strength is discovering new customer problems we can solve with our technological capabilities, and then providing the customer *solutions* to those problems. The term "applications" is a good word to describe what really drives us. There must be a continuous interaction between technology and the marketplace—you make those two things work for you to end up with a new product and application.

This concept is not different from what we've *done* in the past; it's different from how we've *talked* about ourselves in the past. What we've been doing for 30 years is discovering applications and using our technology to develop new products to serve those applications. But we've tended to talk about ourselves in technology terms as a chromatography company or a membrane company. We're really an applications-driven company.

Milliscope: *Isn't this focus on future needs and applications somewhat in conflict with what you described as the need for price and performance competition, and the need for efficiency?*

Mulvany: Yes, it would seem to be in conflict—unless you consider what I call the "applications life cycle." There are really two very different phases to an application: the market development phase, and the competitive phase.

During the market development phase, a customer has a problem and doesn't know how to resolve it, so we come in with our solution and educate the customer. The education is an example of our "value added." At some point, as the customer begins to get educated, and the application is becoming widely used, a phase of rapid growth occurs. The customer says "I know what I want, because I have the application knowledge, and now I'm going to look for the best buy." That's when the competition frequently moves in.

If we develop the applications and aren't positioned to compete effectively, then we'll lose the major return. We must have a mindset that recognizes there are times in every application when we have to be competitive. And during the development phase we need to prepare for the competitive phase, so that when it comes, we can win.

Milliscope: *So is Millipore's primary goal to be a low-cost producer, rather than a differentiated supplier?*

Mulvany: This applications life cycle pulls the concepts together and says we've got to be *both.* You can't say Millipore is always going to be differentiated and never be a low-cost producer, and you can't say we're going to be only a low-cost producer—because we'll never develop the new businesses that way. We've got to be a player for all seasons, if you will. There are times when we should educate and price accordingly, and there are times when we must be the most efficient producer and effectively compete. Both are legitimate; they're just different stages of the application life cycle.

Milliscope: *What does Millipore need to do to become a "low-cost producer," when that is appropriate?*

Mulvany: Actually, I prefer the term "most efficient producer" rather than "low-cost producer," which can be misinterpreted to mean low quality or minimal capability. The first thing we have to do, as I mentioned, is *recognize* that there is a competitive phase, and be innovative in thinking about designs that can be efficiently produced. Once into the competitive phase, we need to optimize manufacturing: What really ought to be the performance capability of this product? Have we designed it for efficient production? Are we making it in the right location? What can we do about uniformity between products so we maximize the use of common equipment and components, etc.?

EXHIBIT 2 (*concluded*)

Milliscope: *You issued two challenges in your talk: to give top priority to maintaining the ability to compete, and to remain committed to growth of at least 15 percent per year. How can Millipore meet these challenges?*

Mulvany: We're participating in markets with technologies that have inherent and sustainable growth. We have to continue to discover new applications for our technologies—and push our technologies to new levels of capability. We've also got to maintain our market share during that competitive cycle. We've got to be efficient, and be the best competitor in our industry. I think these challenges involve everyone in the company.

Milliscope: *What are the biggest obstacles to Millipore achieving that kind of growth?*

Mulvany: I don't think there are any big obstacles. The biggest challenges for us are maintaining an entrepreneurial, innovative environment, and not letting complacency or bureaucracy get in the way. We need to recognize that even though we're winners, we must work hard to keep our values and intensity alive.

Milliscope: *In describing Millipore's environment and the effort to keep this intensity alive, you talked about penalizing bureaucracy and rewarding risk. How would you define bureaucracy, and risk?*

Mulvany: One example of bureaucracy is people putting in systems, procedures, and hurdles in business that are a function of minimizing risk and protecting themselves. It's the mentality that says cover yourself, and don't second-guess. We need to have an environment that climbs above that kind of thinking. I'd like everyone to ask themselves what they would do if it was their business, and they didn't have anyone looking over their shoulders. We all need to focus on the important things, and if something doesn't make sense, question it and escalate it.

Milliscope: *Isn't there a fine line, though, between fostering that kind of entrepreneurialism and maintaining a certain needed structure in a company that's growing as fast as Millipore?*

Mulvany: Yes, we've got to have certain systems and procedures; we don't want chaos. But we want to avoid *unproductive* behavior. It's hard to gain experience unless we attempt new hurdles, some of which we won't make the first time around. But it's far better to make attempts that don't always work out, than to avoid making attempts because we are afraid to fail.

Milliscope: *You've been CEO for a little more than a year now; what has it been like for you? What have been your biggest challenges?*

Mulvany: I'd been with the company nearly 20 years, so it wasn't like walking into a brand new job. But I think the biggest challenge for me has been shifting from dealing with operational issues to thinking about the company's long term, about how our goals and strategies are going to get us through the 1990s. I guess most people regard me as an operational type of person, but we've got a sound management team here, and I've been able to unhook myself from the operational level and really start thinking about how we leverage our capabilities, whether we're in the right markets, how to add to our technology base, and how we're going to meet our growth targets.

Milliscope: *What is the most fun part of your job?*

Mulvany: I think the most enjoyable part of my job is recognizing other people's successes. It really feels good to be in a position where you can say to an individual or a group, "That was a task well done. Thanks." I also really enjoy the challenges of the long term market and technology issues. I like walking around the R&D labs and talking to people who deal with customers, finding out what's going on. That's exciting.

Milliscope: *What are your personal goals for the company?*

Mulvany: I want to see us be an even more successful company than we have been. I want us to feel good about what we do. And as we grow I want us to keep the openness and the candidness you can have in a smaller environment. You know, Millipore is a super company, and I hope that we all will remain as proud of Millipore as we have been in the past.

Source: *Milliscope,* **June 1985.**

EXHIBIT 3
MPD INCOME STATEMENTS
Dollars in Thousands

	1983 (Actual)	1984 (Actual)	1985 Budget	1985 Projected
Sales	$153,245	$169,240	$191,420	$176,730
Cost of sales	77,357	85,716	96,104	86,589
Gross margin	75,888	83,524	95,316	90,141
Selling, marketing, and service expenses	35,059	30,062	32,762	32,347
General and administrative expenses	9,608	9,432	8,955	8,707
Research and development expenses	12,606	13,894	14,794	13,923
Corporate contribution	$ 18,615	$ 30,136	$ 38,805	$ 35,164

Source: Millipore Corporation.

EXHIBIT 4
SAMPLING OF MPD PRODUCTS

Source: Millipore Corporation.

EXHIBIT 5
MPD 1985 PRODUCT LINE SALES BY QUARTER (PROJECTED)
Dollars in Thousands

*Product Center**	*Application*	*Worldwide*					*United States Only*				
		First Quarter	*Second Quarter*	*Third Quarter*	*Fourth Quarter*	*Total*	*First Quarter*	*Second Quarter*	*Third Quarter*	*Fourth Quarter*	*Total*
1. Chemical & electronics	Industrial process (chemicals/ semiconductors)	$ 5,175	$ 5,001	$ 4,243	$ 4,032	$ 18,450	$ 2,421	$ 2,228	$ 2,110	$ 1,725	$ 8,484
2. Biological Filtration/ Clarification	Industrial process (pharmaceutical/ food & beverage)	7,842	7,893	7,479	8,208	31,422	3,976	3,613	3,616	3,669	14,874
3. Tangential Filters		585	611	354	487	2,037	524	293	76	131	1,024
4. Fabricated Filters	Laboratory research and analysis	5,673	5,923	5,221	5,898	22,715	2,302	2,379	2,216	2,288	9,185
5. Analytical Filters	(industrial/medical/ government)	11,920	11,932	10,955	11,479	46,286	5,951	6,031	5,699	5,576	23,257
6. Water Systems	Water purification (all markets)	9,945	10,294	10,099	11,215	41,553	6,785	7,310	7,030	7,234	28,359
7. Medical	Intravenous filters (OEM)	2,708	2,590	2,155	2,702	10,155	2,681	2,500	2,161	2,633	9,975
8. Miscellaneous		1,125	951	752	1,284	4,112	31	−30	16	150	167
Total		$44,972	$45,195	$41,258	$45,305	$176,730	$24,671	$24,324	$22,924	$23,406	$95,325

*Each product center included about a dozen major product lines tailored to a particular customer application.
Source: Millipore Corporation.

EXHIBIT 6
MPD PARTIAL ORGANIZATION CHART – JUNE 1985

President
Hildebrandt

Japan
Takahashi
Plant
Administration
Sales

Europe
Massot
Sales
Marketing
Finance

North American Sales
Gilmore
Sales Administration/Technical Service
Area Manager-East
Regional Managers
Applications Specialists
Area Manager-West
Regional Managers
Applications Specialists
Area Manager-Canada

Marketing
White
Marketing Management
Jacoby
- Electronics
- Pharmaceuticals
- Market development

Product Management
Woodard
- Field service
- Promotion managers
- Technical service
- Product managers
- Product trainer

Research and Development
Mir
Research
- Separations
- Membranes
- Biochemistry

Product Development
- Product design
- Medical/Laboratory products
- Industrial products
- Systems
- Safety/Efficacy test

Applications Engineering
- Water
- Life science
- Industrial/Medical
- Analytical lab

Operations
Lary
Facilities
Engineering
Quality Control
Distribution
- San Francisco warehouse
- Bedford warehouse
- Inventory control
- Production scheduling
- Order processing

Service De-ionization
- Northeast
- Midwest
- Southwest

Safety
Manufacturing
- Bedford, MA
- Jaffrey, NH
- Ceidra, PR
- Molsheim, France
- Japan

Finance and Administration
Open
- Accounting
- Operations finance
- Sales and marketing analysis

Human Resources
Kennedy
- Central services
- Functional reps

Source: Millipore Corporation.

EXHIBIT 7
MPD NEW-PRODUCT DELIVERY PROCESS

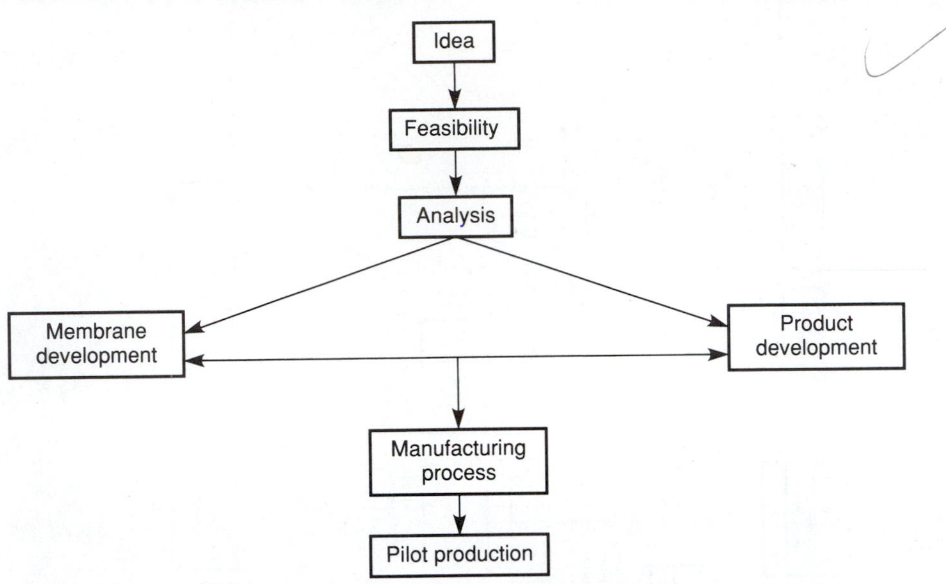

MPD's new product development process was described as follows by one R&D manager:

The process starts with an *idea*, which may come from a laboratory person who sees an interesting and potentially useful new membrane property or from a marketing person who has identified a customer need and asks R&D to see if it can be satisfied. Next, R&D must confirm the *feasibility* of the product idea. If successful, we move to the *analysis* stage, where a decision must be made on whether or not to proceed with full-scale production and commercialization, based on our assessment of the product's market potential and the investment required to develop and launch it. If the project is "a go," we proceed along two paths that actually form an interactive loop: *membrane development* where the basic membrane and a scale-up plan are developed; and *product development* where engineers take the membrane and create a laboratory prototype of the final product. Next, a *manufacturing process* must be designed, followed by *pilot production* to debug the process and develop routines for full scale production.

EXHIBIT 8
MILLIPORE'S BEDFORD FACILITIES
Summer 1985

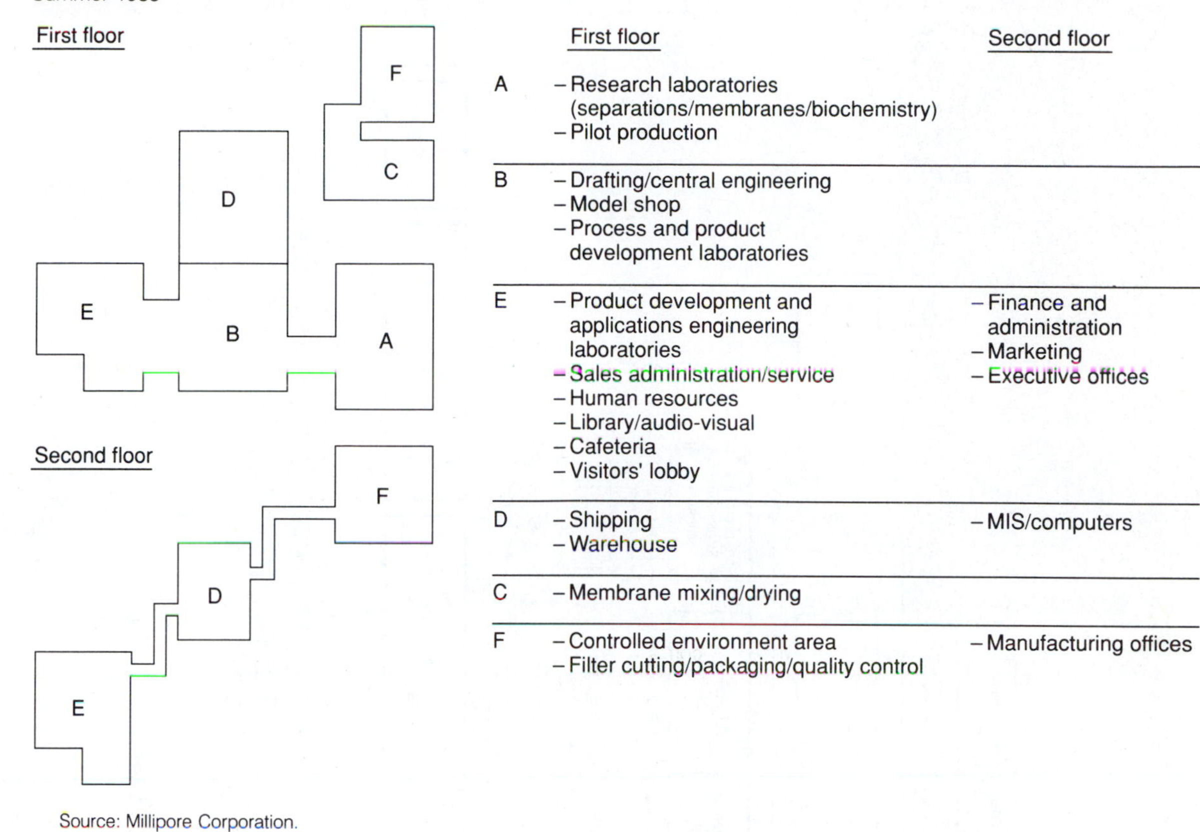

	First floor	Second floor
A	– Research laboratories (separations/membranes/biochemistry) – Pilot production	
B	– Drafting/central engineering – Model shop – Process and product development laboratories	
E	– Product development and applications engineering laboratories – Sales administration/service – Human resources – Library/audio-visual – Cafeteria – Visitors' lobby	– Finance and administration – Marketing – Executive offices
D	– Shipping – Warehouse	– MIS/computers
C	– Membrane mixing/drying	
F	– Controlled environment area – Filter cutting/packaging/quality control	– Manufacturing offices

Source: Millipore Corporation.

EXHIBIT 9
U.S. SALES SUBSIDIARY ORGANIZATION CHART

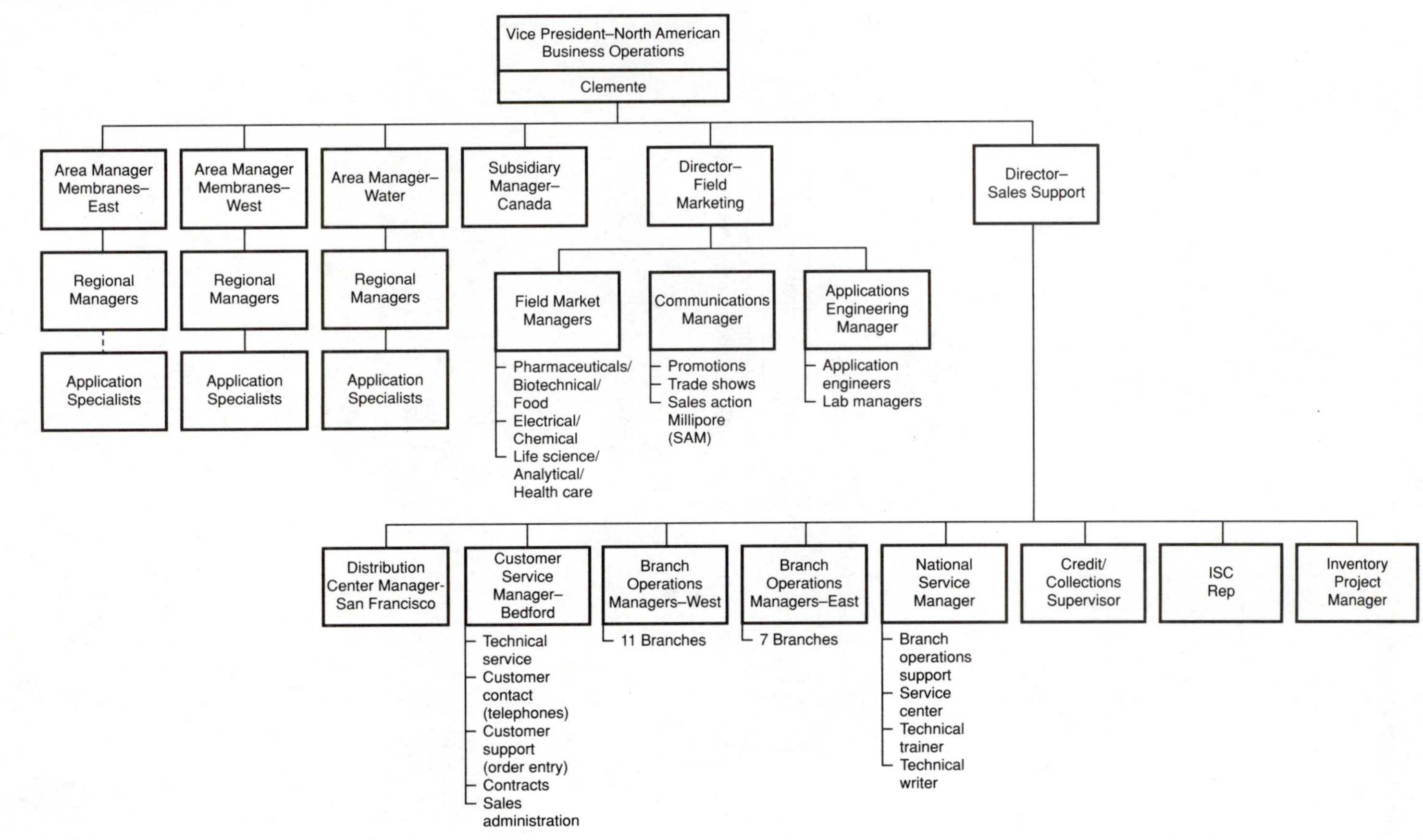

Source: Millipore Corporation (U.S. Sales Subsidiary Task Force Report–December 1985).

Index of Cases